PEARSON

Saundra K. Ciccarelli • J. Noland White

Psychology
An Exploration

Third Custom Edition for Missouri State University

Taken from:
Psychology: An Exploration, Third Edition
by Saundra K. Ciccarelli and J. Noland White

Cover art by Erin K. Snider, Missouri State University Student.

Taken from:

Psychology: An Exploration, Third Edition
by Saundra K. Ciccarelli and J. Noland White
Copyright © 2007 by Pearson Education, Inc.
New York, New York 10013

Pearson Learning Solutions, 501 Boylston Street, Suite 900, Boston, MA 02116
A Pearson Education Company
www.pearsoned.com

Printed in the United States of America

4 16

000200010271961681

TG

ISBN 10: 1-323-10933-1
ISBN 13: 978-1-323-10933-5

Welcome! The students and faculty of the Psychology Department are glad to have you join our course this semester. In and beyond the classroom, our focus is student learning and development–informed and energized by the university's Public Affairs Mission. Realizing that we could employ technology, space, and ourselves more effectively, we worked to redesign PSY 121 from the ground up several years ago. The result is a course that has universities around the country taking notice.

To prepare yourself for this course, you will want to familiarize yourself with the Psychology Department's people and programs, read about all the resources for psychology students and tips from past successful students, and appreciate the context provided by the university's Public Affairs Mission. Our course and the successful outcomes of prior students, have been published in various ways. We are including a brief case study published by Pearson Education in this text so you can see for yourself the improvements in learning that have occurred as a result of our course design.

MISSOURI STATE UNIVERSITY'S DEPARTMENT OF PSYCHOLOGY

Housed in the College of Health and Human Services, the department features undergraduate majors in psychology and gerontology, minors in psychology and gerontology, a graduate certificate program in forensic child psychology, a master's degree in applied behavior analysis, and a master's degree program with tracks in experimental, clinical, and industrial/organizational psychology. The department's Learning Diagnostic Clinic provides services and support to help students with Learning Disabilities (or those otherwise qualified) achieve success. The department also provides vibrant academic clubs–the Psychology Club and the Gerontology Club. Regardless of your particular major, memberships are available to all students. Students striving for excellence may be eligible for induction into the department's chapter of Psi Chi, the International Honor Society in Psychology.

The Psychology Department features dozens of faculty members working together to serve students, the university, their professions, and the larger community. Each chapter of your textbook will highlight a particular subfield of psychology, and we have faculty members in our department who specialize in each of these areas. If you find a particular chapter interesting, consider contacting faculty members in that subfield to discuss your ideas and learn more. As a student in PSY 121, you will have opportunities to learn about research through participation. Many students, while participating in research studies, start to think about working alongside faculty members on future research projects.

Help is available for those seeking to find their place in the department. The Psychology Advisement Center in Hill Hall provides information about the department's programs and assists students with setting and achieving educational and career-related goals.

The Psychology Major

The psychology major is recognized to be among the best preparations for professional success and civic engagement. More than ninety thousand students nationwide graduate each year with a degree in psychology. Fewer than half of those students go on to graduate school and eventually work in a field of psychology; most students use their knowledge and skills in psychology to launch any of a variety of careers.

If you become interested in psychology through your experience in PSY 121, you have several great options. Many students choose to take additional psychology courses as electives–significantly enriching the experience in their chosen major. Some students choose to major in psychology, and others choose to pursue a minor program in psychology.

The Gerontology Major

Gerontology is the scientific study of aging and developmental processes, offering insight into the perceptions and realities of our older adult population. Gerontology, a multidisciplinary field, prepares students to work in the community as professional gerontologists. Currently, one of six Americans is 65 years of age or older, and the number is expected to grow during the next three decades. There is and will continue to be a need for professionals to work with the growing population of older adults in our society.

Given the "graying of America," many jobs related to gerontology are available in the following areas: administration, social services, recreation and leisure, advocacy, retirement planning, elder law, or business. Graduates of the program are currently working at offices on aging overseeing regional services to elders; hospitals running programs that provide services to older adults; independent living facilities as administrators and directors of social services; parks and recreation departments developing specialized activities in the community; assisted living facilities as assistant administrators and activity coordinators; long-term care facilities as administrators, coordinators, and ombudsmen monitoring quality of care; and in businesses as sales personnel for independent housing communities, home health care, and tourism.

The Bachelor of Science in Gerontology is offered as a comprehensive major (no minor is required). The multidisciplinary curriculum avails students to academic training with an applied focus, including a full-semester practicum placement in the field. Upon graduation, some students treat the program as a terminal degree and immediately apply their skills in a career, while other gerontology students want to pursue graduate degrees in a variety of disciplines. A minor in gerontology is available for students wishing to develop aging expertise as they pursue a major in another discipline.

The Dual Major

The gerontology program is housed within the Psychology Department, resulting in a unique option–the dual major in psychology and gerontology. With careful planning, students can complete the dual major in the 125 credit hours required for graduation.

The dual major potentially increases career options, and many students enjoy being able to fully explore two complementary majors. Anyone who pursues the gerontology major or the dual major in psychology and gerontology receives personalized advisement by accessible faculty who are invested in understanding the student's career goals and supporting progress toward those goals.

The Master of Science in Applied Behavior Analysis

The Master of Science in Applied Behavior Analysis at Missouri State University trains students in: the theoretical and philosophical foundations of Applied Behavior Analysis (ABA). Coursework covers research on basic and applied problems; and applied techniques that can be utilized in a variety of settings, including work with institutionalized populations and developmentally disabled individuals. Students may choose to specialize in organizational behavior management, clinical and behavioral medicine, developmental, or older adults. A unique feature of the program is its partnership with the Department of Counseling, Leadership, and Special Education. This allows students to gain valuable experience with disabled populations and Autism-spectrum disorders. ABA is a scientific approach to behavior, and as such, strives to establish evidence-based practices for treatment and education. This approach is consistent with a scientist-practitioner model of graduate training. The purpose of the program is to train students in behavior analysis through a balanced combination of in-class coursework and practical experience in community settings.

The Master of Science in Psychology

After completing a college degree, many students want to gain specialized education in psychology. The Master of Science in Psychology at Missouri State includes challenging courses, engaging research experiences, and hands-on internships. Admission is competitive, with successful applicants having achieved at a high level as undergraduate students. The program includes three tracks that represent major subdivisions: experimental, clinical, and industrial/organizational psychology. Some graduate students in the program have the opportunity to support the department's undergraduate programs through teaching and advising.

The Graduate Certificate Program in Forensic Child Psychology

When graduate students want to add to their curriculum or professionals seek training without a full degree program, then a certificate program may fit their needs. The Psychology Department offers a graduate certificate in Forensic Child Psychology. The program addresses the role of psychology in legal settings–for example, helping students understand factors that influence the reliability and validity of child interviews in criminal cases. This Missouri State program is one of the first of its kind.

RESOURCES FOR PSYCHOLOGY STUDENTS

We have learned a lot of things over the last few years, most of which came from students just like you. We are thankful to the thousands of students and hundreds of *Undergraduate Learning Assistants* who have helped us figure out how best to teach and deliver content. Take a look at the case study in the pages ahead, but here are a few things you should know:

- Students who successfully complete their MyPsychLab study plan prior to attending class perform much better on exams! You may not know what a correlation is yet, but if you do, we have found the correlation between MyPsychLab posttest score and exam score to be .65—this means, the better students do on their homework, the better grade they get on exams.

- Students in this course are learning more than double what they were in the traditional course that existed prior to Fall 2012.

There are many resources available to you in this course. Every member of the course staff is dedicated to student success, and we know that students who succeed are likely to take advantage of the many opportunities for assistance in the course. Please take a moment to review the following list of course resources.

1) Blackboard Course Site. Think of Blackboard as your "virtual classroom." This is where you will find the following:

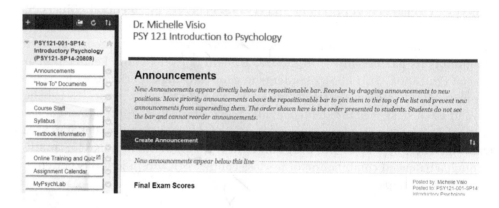

- Details of all weekly assignments
- Grades
- Tutorial videos and/or handouts on how to complete assigned tasks (such as registering for MyPsychLab, completing research requirements, registering your clicker)
- Link to MyPsychLab (you will always access MPL via Blackboard)

2) MyPsychLab. If Blackboard is your "virtual classroom" then MyPsychLab is your "virtual lab." MyPsychLab contains the following:

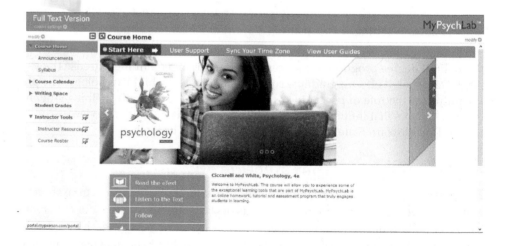

- E-book
- MyPsychLab study plan
- MPL media assignments

- Extra credit assignments
- All supplemental materials (including chapter exams, study guides, dynamic study modules, and flashcards)

3) Bear CLAW. The Bear CLAW is Missouri State University's Center for Learning and Writing located on the first floor of the Meyer Library. There is an area within the Bear CLAW that is devoted to students in PSY 121 and is staffed by Undergraduate Learning Assistants 25–30 hours a week. The Bear CLAW schedule can be found on your Blackboard course site. You do not need an appointment to receive individual assistance with course materials or technology questions. Simply check the schedule and walk in at your convenience to receive assistance with any course-related questions or concerns.

4) Study Sessions. In an effort to help prepare you for exams, you will be required to attend a one-hour-long study session during the two weeks prior to each unit exam. Study sessions will be led by the Undergraduate Learning Assistants and supervised by the Senior Learning Assistant and faculty member. Since there are four unit exams, you are required to attend four study sessions.

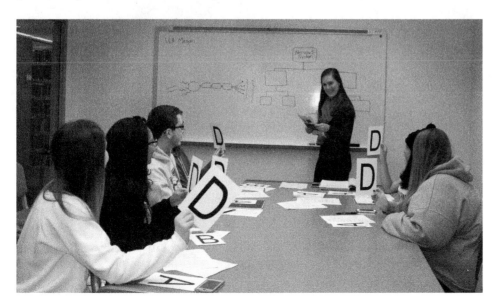

5) Course Staff. While large classes can certainly be intimidating, your PSY 121 course staff is dedicated to making sure each individual student receives the assistance and support necessary for success in the course. There are three levels of staff for your course.

- *Course Instructor*: Your course instructor will be the person leading your class during the seated portion of the course and will be in charge of all other aspects of the course. Your instructor has office hours posted in the syllabus and on your Blackboard course site. Please consider taking advantage of your instructor's office hours to discuss your progress in the course, questions/concerns, or even your own interest in the field of psychology.

- *Senior Learning Assistant (SLA)*: Your SLA is either a graduate student in the department of psychology or an adjunct faculty member. You will see your SLA in your seated class, but much of the SLAs work is behind the scenes helping to assist students, grading assignments, and helping manage the online portions of the course. Your SLA has weekly office hours and his/her email address can be found on the course Blackboard site.

- *Undergraduate Learning Assistants (ULAs)*: You will have 5-6 ULAs assisting in your course. The ULAs will be assigned to a smaller group of students and you will have lots of contact with your own ULA. In addition, study sessions will be led by ULAs from every section of PSY 121. Email addresses for your ULA can be found on your course Blackboard site. Please don't hesitate to email your ULA if you need assistance.

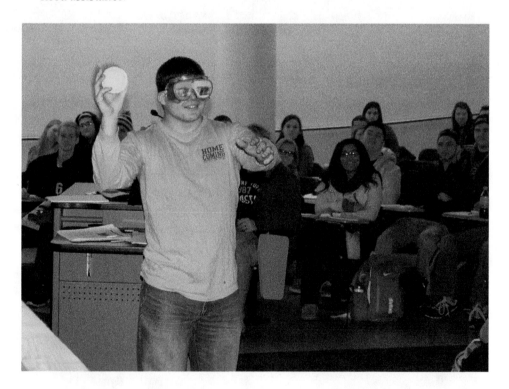

Tips from 'A' Students

We asked our most successful students at the end of the semester to tell us their "tips" for succeeding in this class. They provided some excellent advice. Take some time to read through these suggestions and see how they can help you.

Reading/Using the Textbook

"I read (not skimmed) the textbook chapter for every MyPsychLab assignment, and I walked away from the assignment actually knowing the material."

"Every week I outlined the entire chapter assigned. That way I could use it to help me on the post-test and always had a study guide for when the tests came. Writing it down helped put it in my brain, then all I had to do was read the 3 outlined chapters before the test for review."

"When studying for tests, doing the "End of Chapter" quizzes in the book was a really accurate representation of how well you knew the material in the chapter. If you did well on those, you will probably do well on the test."

MyPsychLab Study Plan

"Overall the biggest contributor to my A was MyPsychLab activities."

"Take the post-test over and over until you get 100%: The 25 questions are different every time, so retaking the test until I got a perfect score gave me the opportunity to see a lot of different questions."

"For me, when I did the pretest, I would see what I knew and didn't know and took the test without any help. I would take the study materials seriously and that would help a lot. When I took the post-test, I read over the chapter and key terms and looked up every question in the book."

"I always made sure to set a specific time each week to get my Pre-test, post-test, and media assignment all done at one time. I also made sure I would get 100% on all of those because those were easy points!"

Time Management

"I would say one of the best things someone can do to succeed in PSY 121 is to not procrastinate. I started reviewing test material a week before the actual exam. I would have to say the worst thing someone can do is cram the material in a one day span."

"I made sure to do all my psych lab stuff in a timely manner, allowing myself plenty of time to do it before it was due."

MyPsychLab Student Resources

"My favorite resource (and also number one tip!) throughout this course was the "Study Guide" in MyPsychLab."

"I went through the online flash cards in the study plan and I took the practice exams multiple times."

"I used the flash cards and speed drill on MyPsychLab."

Attendance/Note Taking

"Attend class every day. By attending class, you fully understand the little things in this class, as in the questions about psych lab, study sessions, and research participation. In addition when a movie day is on, go to the movie. It gives you a visual to different concepts to help you remember."

"Attend class! The lectures were very helpful in reviewing and understanding the material learned through MPL the previous week."

"Attend every lecture–the demonstrations and examples given are very helpful."

Study Sessions

"The study sessions also really helped. There's so much information in the text that it's necessary to make it more organized and clear, which is helped with the study sessions!"

"Make sure you are going to a study session that will give you enough time to really understand the material. Don't wait until right before the exam to go."

Extra Credit

"Make sure to take advantage of the extra credit."

"I made sure to take advantage of the extra credit! That helped tremendously."

Seeking Help

"Go to the psych person in the Bear Claw for questions and to get explanations for things you don't understand."

"I think my greatest piece of advice for someone to succeed in your class is don't be afraid to ask for help. I think a lot of the topics in psychology can seem overwhelming but the ULAs usually have good tips and tricks for learning and remembering the information! I hope this helps!"

Attitude

"I retained more of the information starting my work with a positive attitude and being open to what I was about to read and learn."

"Take the class seriously. It's only hard if you make it hard!"

Other Helpful Tips

"Check your email frequently."

"I really enjoyed taking this class. At first I was a little worried about how much is on-line, but it makes the class roll much smoother. In a couple of weeks, I had a routine and stuck with it through the end."

"Find other people who are in your class and have little study sessions with them a few days before the test. This gives you some time to explain concepts to other people and also learn the material by just talking through the chapter with each other."

"Predict what kinds of questions are going to be on the test and make sure to study those concepts thoroughly."

THE PUBLIC AFFAIRS MISSION AS A CONTEXT FOR PSY 121

Missouri State University provides outstanding educational opportunities in the context of a unique public affairs mission. This mission presents a profound challenge and confers a tremendous advantage for Missouri State students. As you review the three pillars of the mission you share, consider how those pillars will guide your learning in PSY 121 and how your learning in PSY 121 will empower you to fulfill the mission.

Our Public Affairs Mission[1]

Ethical Leadership is striving for excellence and integrity as one continually develops ethical and moral reasoning while contributing to the common good. Ethical leaders have the courage to live by their principles in all parts of their personal and professional lives. Students will articulate their value systems, act ethically within the context of a democratic society, and demonstrate engaged and principled leadership.

---

[1]Excerpted with permission of the Board of Governors of Missouri State University, owner of copyrighted material.

Cultural Competence begins with cultural self-awareness and expands to knowledge of, respect for, and skills to engage with those of other cultures. Culturally-competent individuals respect multiple perspectives and are able to successfully negotiate cross-cultural differences. Students will recognize and respect multiple perspectives and cultures.

Community Engagement is recognizing needs in the communities to which one belongs, then contributing knowledge and working with the community to meet those needs. Community engagement requires extending beyond one's self for the betterment of the community–a process that fosters greater awareness and personal growth. Students will recognize the importance of contributing their knowledge and experiences to their own community and the broader society. Students will also recognize the importance of scientific principles in the generation of sound public policy.

MyPsychLab	CASE STUDY

School Name   Missouri State University, Springfield, MO

Course Name   Introductory Psychology

Course Format   Flipped, Hybrid

Key Results   With MyPsychLab, student learning gains increased over the past three years from 32 percent to an average of 76 percent, as measured by a comparison of pre- and post-test scores. In addition, the university's per-student costs were reduced by 10 percent.

Submitted by

Danae L. Hudson, Brooke L. Whisenhunt, Carol F. Shoptaugh, Ann D. Rost, Rachel N. Fondren-Happel, and Christie Cathey

Course materials

Psychology, Ciccarelli and White; MyPsychLab

About the Course

From 2010 to 2013, the governor of Missouri and Missouri's public four-year institutions established a major course redesign initiative. The institutions partnered with the National Center for Academic Transformation (NCAT), utilizing the successful models and lessons learned from NCAT's course redesign programs. Our Introductory Psychology course, which serves over 2,500 students each year, was selected as Missouri State University's representative in this initiative and was one of the first to go through this redesign process.

Challenges and Goals

Despite being a popular course, Introductory Psychology had delivered less-than-satisfactory learning outcomes for many students. The course, before redesign, was lecture-based and typically taught by approximately 65 percent full-time faculty and 35 percent adjunct instructors. While there were common general education goals across all sections, each instructor was responsible for the choice of content and delivery of course material. This produced significant variability in what material was covered from section to section and led to "course drift" and inconsistent outcomes.

The goals we identified included improving student learning, reducing course drift, incorporating best practices teaching strategies, increasing course completion rates, and reducing institutional costs. Five full-time faculty members worked together as a team throughout the planning, pilot, and implementation of the course redesign. All sections were redesigned using the same syllabus, textbook, online course materials, and staffing plan.

Implementation

The redesign included significant changes to the staffing structure. The traditional course had one instructor per section. The redesigned course utilizes seven staff members per section including one full-time instructor, one Senior Learning Assistant (a graduate assistant or adjunct instructor), and five Undergraduate Learning Assistants. So, although the redesigned course seats 300 students per section compared to 153 in the traditional course, the ratio of staff to students decreased from 1:153 to 1:43.

To improve learning outcomes, we transformed the traditional course into a blended or hybrid course with a flipped classroom. In this model, students read their text and complete the MyPsychLab chapter study plan and media assignments prior to class, allowing for more active learning during class time.

Assessments

48 percent	Unit exams (four)
18 percent	MyPsychLab chapter study plan and media assignments
16 percent	Comprehensive final exam
7.5 percent	Participation
6 percent	Study session attendance
3 percent	Research participation
1.5 percent	Introduction letter + online training and quiz

Results and Data

Student learning gains have more than doubled, as measured by increases in a comprehensive pre- to post-test before redesign vs. after redesign with MyPsychLab (Figure 1). Further, more students are achieving overall course grades of A or B with MyPsychLab compared to previous semesters without MyPsychLab (Figure 2), indicating that many more students are now demonstrating mastery of the material. Additionally, despite having an already relatively inexpensive traditional course at $73

"Because students are reading the textbook and actively engaging with the material in MyPsychLab outside of class, they've started coming to class better prepared and more willing to participate in class discussions."

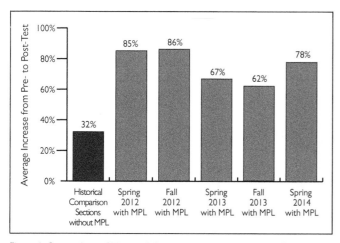

Figure 1. Comparison of historical department means without MyPsychLab ($n = 2079$) to redesign means with MyPsychLab (Spring 2012, $n = 102$; Fall 2012, $n = 1202$; Spring 2013, $n = 602$; Fall 2013, $n = 1368$; Spring 2014, $n = 785$) on 30-item comprehensive Pre- and Post-Test Exams.

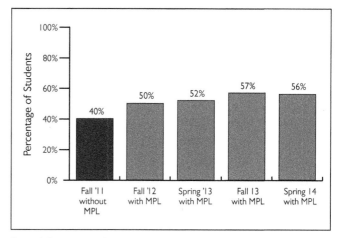

Figure 2. Percentage of students achieving overall course grades of A or B without MyPsychLab (Fall 2011, $n = 302$) vs. with MyPsychLab (Fall 2012, $n = 1340$; Spring 2013, $n = 693$; Fall 2013, $n = 1450$; Spring 2014, $n = 847$).

per student, the combination of increasing section size and more efficiently assigning instructors and learning assistants brought the cost down to $66 per student—a 10 percent reduction in instructional costs. The implementation of MyPsychLab played a major role in producing these improved results.

The Student Experience

One of the challenges we faced before the redesign was the inability to identify and proactively reach out to struggling students early in the semester. In the redesigned course, early intervention teaching strategies, were introduced. The combination of frequent online assignments in MyPsychLab, used formatively to identify students' areas of weakness, and a staffing structure that allowed for more frequent and personalized monitoring of student progress, resulted in clear gains in learning.

Because students read the text and actively engage with the material in MyPsychLab outside of class, they come to class better prepared to participate in discussions. As a result, we now focus on more difficult concepts (based on students' performance on MyPsychLab assignments) and incorporate more active learning strategies (e.g., use of clickers, classroom demonstrations, online activities) into the seated class period. The students report they find these methods more engaging, and data indicates they are achieving greater mastery of the course content.

Conclusion

After three years, and through the use of a number of quantifiable measures, we have clear evidence of the efficacy of our redesigned course. Further, we've accomplished the majority of our initial goals. Reducing the number of students who receive a grade of D or F, or who withdraw from the course, proved to be the most challenging goal; however, data from the past two semesters shows substantial reductions. Overall, we created an innovative class utilizing many best practices in teaching. We developed a course that reduced course drift, was implemented at a lower cost than its traditional counterpart, and—most important—resulted in greater student learning. Looking forward, we plan further research in an effort to better understand the impact MyPsychLab is having on specific groups, including low-income and first generation students.

References

Hudson, D. L., Hudson, A. L., Whisenhunt, B. L., Shoptaugh, C. F., Rost, A., & Fondren-Happel, R. N. (2014) Redesigning a large enrollment course: The impact on academic performance, course completion and student perceptions in introductory psychology. Psychology Learning and Teaching 13 (2),107-119. http://dx.doi.org/10.2304/plat.2014.13.2.107

Drab-Hudson, D. L., Whisenhunt, B. L., Shoptaugh, C. F., Newman, M. C., Rost, A. & Fondren-Happe, R. N. (2012)Transforming Introductory Psychology: a systematic approach to course redesign. Psychology Learning and Teaching 11 (2), 146-157. http://dx.doi.org/10.2304/plat.2012.11.2.14

Brief Contents

Contents

learner-centered approach

Curiosity and Dialogue

Our goal is to awaken students' curiosity and energize their desire to learn by having them read and engage with the material. We are delighted with the feedback from students and instructors who tell us this approach is working, and we are pleased with this edition to extend that experience in a new format, REVEL™.

Fully digital and highly engaging, REVEL offers an immersive learning experience designed for the way today's students read, think, and learn. Enlivening course content with media interactives and assessments, REVEL empowers educators to increase engagement with the course, and to better connect with students. **pearsonhighered.com/revel**

Chapter 5
Learning

Yoshiko's first-grade teacher started a reading contest. For every book read, a child would get a gold star on the reading chart, and at the end of one month the child with the most stars would get a prize. Yoshiko went to the library and checked out several books each week. At the end of the month, Yoshiko had the most gold stars and got to stand in front of her classmates to receive her prize. Would it be candy? A toy? She was so excited! Imagine her surprise and mild disappointment when the big prize turned out to be another book! Disappointing prize aside, Yoshiko's teacher had made use of a key technique of learning called *reinforcement*. Reinforcement is anything that, when following a response, increases the likelihood that the response will occur again. The reinforcers of gold stars and a prize caused Yoshiko's reading to increase.

How have you used reinforcement to modify your own behavior or the behavior of others?

164

Chapter opening Student Voice Videos
Chapters now open with videos in which psychology students share personal stories about how the chapter theme directly applies to their lives.

Success Center
At the start of each chapter students can access an interactive timeline of the history of psychology and study tip videos. Eight **Videos**, based on the *Psychology in Action* introductory chapter, provide practical advice on study methods, time management, reading the text, taking notes during lectures, preparing for exams, paper writing, improving memory, and becoming a critical thinker.

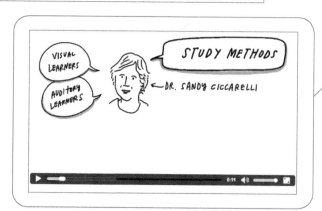

Success Center
Interactive Timeline
👁 Watch the Video
Study Methods
Managing Time
Reading the Text
Lecture Notes
Exam Prep
Paper Writing
Improve Memory
Critical Thinking

Embedded Interactive Content

Interactive content has been fully incorporated into all aspects of the text, allowing students a more direct way to access and engage with the material.

Watch **Videos** of topics as they are explained.

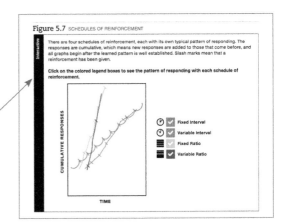

Interactive Figures walk students through some of the more complex processes in psychology. **Interactive Tables** offer students the ability to evaluate their knowledge of key topics.

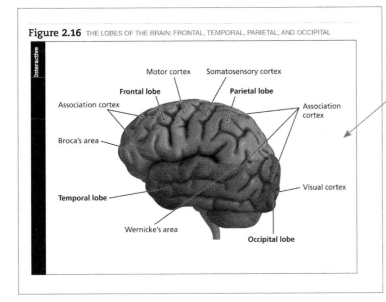

Interactive versions of brain-based figures allow students to rotate the brain 360 degrees and isolate regions.

Simulate **experiments** and answer **surveys** right from the narrative.

Reinforce connections across topics with **Interactive Concept Maps.**

Take **Practice Quizzes** as you read.

Critical Thinking Journal Prompts allow students to write short critical thinking based journal entries about the chapter content.

Teaching and Learning Package

INTEGRATION AND FEEDBACK

It is increasingly true today that as valuable as a good textbook is, it is still only one element of a comprehensive learning package. The teaching and learning package that accompanies *Psychology: An Exploration*, 3e, is the most comprehensive and integrated on the market. We have made every effort to provide high-quality instructor resources that will save you preparation time and will enhance the time you spend in the classroom.

MyPsychLab

MyPsychLab is an online homework, tutorial, and assessment program that truly engages students in learning. It helps students better prepare for class, quizzes, and exams—resulting in better performance in the course—and provides educators with a dynamic set of tools for gauging individual and class progress. MyPsychLab comes from Pearson, your partner in providing the best digital learning experience.

NEW! DYNAMIC STUDY MODULES Not every student learns the same way and at the same rate. And now, thanks to advances in adaptive learning technology, you no longer have to teach as if they do. The Dynamic Study Modules in MyPsychLab continuously assess student performance and activity in real time, and, using data and analytics, personalize content to reinforce concepts that target each student's strengths and weaknesses.

WRITING SPACE Better writers make great learners—who perform better in their courses. To help you develop and assess concept mastery and critical thinking through writing, we created the Writing Space in MyPsychLab. It's a single place to create, track, and grade writing assignments, provide writing resources, and exchange meaningful, personalized feedback with students, quickly and easily, including auto-scoring for practice writing prompts. Plus, Writing Space has integrated access to Turnitin, the global leader in plagiarism prevention.

MyPsychLab VIDEO SERIES Current, comprehensive, and cutting edge, the six video segments for every chapter (approximately five minutes each) take the viewer from the research laboratory to inside the brain to out on the street for real-world applications.

To learn more about MyPsychLab visit **mypsychlab.com**.

Presentation and Teaching Resources

The Instructor's Resource Center (**www.pearsonhighered.com/irc**) provides information on the following supplements and downloadable files:

Instructor's DVD (ISBN 0-133-94026-8): Bringing all of the third edition's instructor resources together in one place, the Instructor's DVD offers Interactive PowerPoints, standard Lecture PowerPoints, and Classroom Response System PowerPoints, along with the Test Bank, and the Instructor's Resource Manual to help instructors customize their classroom experience.

- **Interactive PowerPoint Slides** bring the Ciccarelli/White design into the classroom, drawing students into the lecture and providing appealing interactive activities, visuals, and videos. The slides are built around the text's learning objectives and offer many direct links to interactive exercises, simulations, and activities.
- **Standard Lecture PowerPoint Slides** have lecture notes, photos, and figures.
- **Learning Catalytics** is a "bring your own device" student engagement, assessment, and classroom intelligence system. It allows instructors to engage students in class with real-time diagnostics. Students can use any modern, web-enabled device (smartphone, tablet, or laptop) to access it.
- **Classroom Response System (CRS) PowerPoint Slides** allow you to integrate clicker technology into your classroom.
- **Peer Instruction Clicker Activities** offered as a PowerPoint presentation for introductory psychology courses is also available on the Instructor's DVD.

Instructor's Resource Manual, prepared by Alan Swinkels, St. Edwards University, offers detailed chapter lecture outlines, chapter summaries, learning objectives, activities, exercises, assignments, handouts, and demonstrations for in-class use, as well as useful guidelines for integrating the many Pearson media resources into your classroom and syllabus.

The **Test Item File (ISBN 0-133-93027-0)** prepared by Jason Spiegelman, The Community College of Baltimore County, contains over 1,800 questions categorized by learning objective and question type (factual, conceptual, or applied). Rationales for each correct answer and the key distracter in the multiple-choice questions help instructors evaluate questions and provide more feedback to students.

Pearson MyTest (ISBN 0-133-94025-X), a powerful assessment generation program, helps instructors easily create and print quizzes and exams. Questions and tests can be authored online, allowing instructors ultimate flexibility! For more information, go to **www.PearsonMyTest.com**.

APA ASSESSMENT BANK

Available within MyPsychLab, a unique bank of assessment items allows instructors to assess student progress against the American Psychological Association's Learning Goals and Outcomes.

ACCESSING ALL RESOURCES

For a list of all student resources available with Ciccarelli/White, *Psychology: An Exploration*, 3e, go to **www.mypearsonstore.com**, enter the text ISBN 0-133-93446-2, and check out the "Everything That Goes with It" section under the photo of the book cover.
For access to all instructor resources for Ciccarelli/White, *Psychology: An Exploration*, 3e, simply go to **http://pearsonhighered.com/irc**.
For technical support for any of your Pearson products, you and your students can contact **http://247.pearsoned.com**.

Learning Outcomes and Assessment

LEARNING OBJECTIVES

Based on APA recommendations, each chapter is structured around detailed learning objectives. All of the instructor and student resources are also organized around these objectives, making the text and resources a fully integrated system of study. The flexibility of these resources allows instructors to choose which learning objectives are important in their courses as well as which content they want their students to focus on.

∨ Learning Objectives

5.1   Discuss the meaning of the term *learning*.

5.2   Describe and explain the origins of classical conditioning and its important elements.

5.3   Define conditioned emotional responses, and explain conditioned taste aversions.

5.4   Describe the theory of operant conditioning and how it differs from classical conditioning, and explain the contributions of Thorndike and Skinner.

5.5   Differentiate between primary and secondary reinforcers and the processes of positive and negative reinforcement.

5.6   Distinguish among the schedules of reinforcement.

5.7   Compare and contrast punishment with reinforcement, and list some of the problems associated with using punishment.

5.8   Describe the role of operant stimuli in controlling behavior as well as other concepts that can enhance or limit operant conditioning.

5.9   Describe how operant conditioning is used to change animal and human behavior, and identify some limitations to its use.

5.10   Define and explain the concept of latent learning.

5.11   Explain the concept of insight learning.

5.12   Explain the concept of learned helplessness.

5.13   Describe the process of observational learning.

5.14   List the four elements of observational learning.

5.15   Provide and describe an example of conditioning in the real world.

GOALS AND STANDARDS

In recent years many psychology departments have been focusing on core competencies and how methods of assessment can better enhance students' learning. In response, the American Psychological Association (APA) established recommended goals for the undergraduate psychology major beginning in 2008 with a set of ten goals, and revised again in 2013 with a new set of five goals. Specific learning outcomes were established for each of the goals and suggestions were made on how best to tie assessment practices to these goals. In writing this text, we have used the APA goals and assessment recommendations as guidelines for structuring content and integrating the teaching and homework materials. For details on the APA learning goals and assessment guidelines, please see **www.apa.org/**.

Knowledge Base

Students should demonstrate fundamental knowledge and comprehension of the major concepts, theoretical perspectives, historical trends, and empirical findings to discuss how psychological principles apply to behavioral phenomena. Foundation students should demonstrate breadth in their knowledge and applications of psychological ideas to simple problems; baccalaureate students should show depth in their knowledge and application of psychological concepts and frameworks to problems of greater complexity.

1.1 Describe key concepts, principles, and overarching themes in psychology

Ch 1: 1.1, 1.2, 1.3, 1.4, 1.6

Ch 2: 2.1, 2.2, 2.3, 2.4, 2.5, 2.6, 2.7, 2.8, 2.9, 2.10, 2.11, 2.12, 2.13, 2.14, 2.15

Ch 3: 3.1, 3.2, 3.3, 3.4, 3.5, 3.6, 3.7, 3.8, 3.9, 3.10. 3.11, 3.12, 3.13, 3.14

Ch 4: 4.1, 4.2, 4.3, 4.4, 4.5, 4.6, 4.7, 4.8, 4.9, 4.10, 4.11

Ch 5: 5.1, 5.2, 5.3, 5.4, 5.5, 5.6, 5.7, 5.8, 5.9, 5.10, 5.11, 5.12, 5.13, 5.14

Ch 6: 6.1, 6.2, 6.3, 6.4, 6.6, 6.7, 6.8, 6.9, 6.10

Ch 7: 7.1, 7.2, 7.5, 7.6, 7.7, 7.8, 7.9

Ch 8: 8.2, 8.3, 8.4, 8.5, 8.6, 8.7, 8.8, 8.9, 8.10, 8.11, 8.12, 8.13, 8.14, 8.15, 8.16, 8.17, 8.18

Ch 9: 9.1, 9.2, 9.3, 9.4, 9.5, 9.6, 9.7, 9.8, 9.9, 9.10, 9.11, 9.12

Ch 10: 10.1, 10.2, 10.3, 10.4, 10.5, 10.6, 10.7, 10.8, 10.10, 10.11, 10.12, 10.13, 10.14, 10.15

Ch 11: 11.1, 11.2, 11.3, 11.4, 11.5, 11.6, 11.8, 11.9, 11.12, 11.13

Ch 12: 12.1, 12.2, 12.3, 12.4, 12.5, 12.6, 12.7, 12.8, 12.9, 12.10, 12.11, 12.12, 12.13, 12.14, 12.15, 12.16

Ch 13: 13.1, 13.2, 13.3, 13.4, 13.5, 13.6, 13.8, 13.9, 13.10, 13.11, 13.12

Appendix A: A.1, A.2, A.3, A.4, A.5, A.6

Appendix B: B.1, B.8

1.2 Develop a working knowledge of psychology's content domains

Ch 1: 1.1, 1.2, 1.3, 1.4

Ch 5: 5.4

Ch 8: 8.2

Ch 9: 9.1

Ch 11: 11.1, 11.2, 11.3

Ch 12: 12.2, 12.10

Ch 13: 13.2, 13.4

1.3 Describe applications of psychology

Ch 1: 1.1, 1.3, 1.4, 1.5, 1.6, 1.7, 1.12

Ch 2: 2.1, 2.3, 2.4, 2.5, 2.6, 2.7, 2.8, 2.9, 2.10, 2.11, 2.12, 2.13, 2.14, 2.15

Ch 3: 3.1, 3.2, 3.3, 3.4, 3.5, 3.6, 3.7, 3.8, 3.9, 3.10. 3.11, 3.12, 3.13, 3.14, 3.15

Ch 4: 4.2, 4.4, 4.5, 4.6, 4.8, 4.9, 4.10, 4.11, 4.12

Ch 5: 5.2, 5.3, 5.4, 5.7, 5.8, 5.9, 5.15

Ch 6: 6.2, 6.4, 6.5, 6.7, 6.9, 6.10, 6.11, 6.14

Ch 7: 7.1, 7.2, 7.3, 7.4, 7.6, 7.7, 7.8, 7.10, 7.11, 7.12

Ch 8: 8.3, 8.8, 8.9, 8.10, 8.12, 8.13, 8.14, 8.15, 8.17, 8.18

Ch 9: 9.3, 9.5, 9.6, 9.7, 9.8, 9.9, 9,.11, 9.12, 9.13

Ch 10: 10.1, 10.2, 10.3, 10.4, 10.5, 10.6, 10.7, 10.8, 10.9, 10.10, 10.11, 10.12, 10.13, 10.14, 10.15

Ch 11: 11.1, 11.3, 11.5, 11.7, 11.9, 11.10, 11.11, 11.12, 11.13, 11.14, 11.15, 11.16

Ch 12: 12.1, 12.3, 12.7, 12.8, 12.11, 12.12, 12.15, 12.17, 12.18

Ch 13: 13.1, 13.2, 13.3, 13.4, 13.5, 13.7, 13.8, 13.11, 13.12

Appendix A: A.1

Appendix B: B.8

APA LEARNING OBJECTIVES	CICCARELLI/WHITE TEXT LEARNING OBJECTIVES

2 Scientific Inquiry and Critical Thinking

The skills in this domain involve the development of scientific reasoning and problem solving, including effective research methods. Foundation students should learn basic skills and concepts in interpreting behavior, studying research, and applying research design principles to drawing conclusions about behavior; baccalaureate students should focus on theory use as well as designing and executing research plans.

2.1	Use scientific reasoning to interpret psychological phenomena	**Ch 1:** 1.6, 1.7, 1.8, 1.9, 1.10 **Ch 2:** 2.9 **Ch 3:** 3.15 **Ch 8:** 8.1 **Ch 11:** 11.10, 11.14, 11.15 **Appendix A:** A.1, A.3, A.4
2.2	Demonstrate psychology information literacy	**Ch 1:** 1.6 **Ch 8:** 8.1 **Appendix A:** A.5, A.6
2.3	Engage in innovative and integrative thinking and problem solving	**Intro:** PIA.1, PIA.2, PIA.3, PIA.4, PIA.5, PIA.6, PIA.7 **Ch 1:** 1.6, 1.7, 1.8, 1.9, 1.10, 1.12 **Ch 7:** 7.2, 7.3, 7.4, 7.12 **Ch 11:** 11.10 **Ch 13:** 13.8, 13.12
2.4	Interpret, design, and conduct basic psychological research	**Ch 1:** 1.6, 1.7, 1.8, 1.9, 1.10 **Ch 8:** 8.4 **Ch 11:** 11.10 **Ch 13:** 13.9 **Appendix A:** A.1, A.3, A.4, A.5, A.6
2.5	Incorporate sociocultural factors in scientific inquiry	**Ch 1**: 1.6, 1.7, 1.10 **Ch 7:** 7.6, 7.10 **Ch 8:** 8.18

3 Ethical and Social Responsibility in a Diverse World

The skills in this domain involve the development of ethically and socially responsible behaviors for professional and personal settings. Foundation students should become familiar with the formal regulations that govern professional ethics in psychology and begin to embrace the values that will contribute to positive outcomes in work settings and in society. Baccalaureate students should have more direct opportunities to demonstrate adherence to professional values that will help them optimize their contributions.

3.1	Apply ethical standards to psychological science and practice.	**Ch 1:** 1.11
3.2	Build and enhance interpersonal relationships.	**Ch 10:** 10.1, 10.2, 10.3, 10.4, 10.5, 10.6, 10.7, 10.9, 10.10, 10.11, 10.12, 10.14, 10.15 **Ch 11:** 11.13
3.3	Adopt values that build community at local, national, and global levels.	**Ch 10:** 10.1, 10.2, 10.3, 10.4, 10.5, 10.6, 10.7, 10.9, 10.14, 10.15

APA LEARNING OBJECTIVES   CICCARELLI/WHITE TEXT LEARNING OBJECTIVES

Communication

Students should demonstrate competence in written, oral, and interpersonal communication skills. Foundation students should be able to write a cogent scientific argument, present information using a scientific approach, engage in discussion of psychological concepts, explain the ideas of others, and express their own ideas with clarity. Baccalaureate students should produce a research study or other psychological project, explain scientific results, and present information to a professional audience. They should also develop flexible interpersonal approaches that optimize information exchange and relationship development.

4.1	Demonstrate effective writing for different purposes	**Intro:** PIA.6
4.2	Exhibit effective presentation skills for different purposes	**Ch 10:** 10.2, 10.3, 10.4
4.3	Interact effectively with others	**Ch 10:** 10.2, 10.4, 10.5, 10.6, 10.7, 10.9, 10.11, 10.14, 10.15

Professional Development

The skills in this domain refer to abilities that sharpen student readiness for post-baccalaureate employment, graduate school, or professional school. The emphasis in the domain involves application of psychology-specific content and skills, effective self-reflection, project management skills, teamwork skills, and career preparation. These skills can be developed and refined both in traditional academic settings and extracurricular involvement. In addition, career professionals can be enlisted to support occupational planning and pursuit.

5.1	Apply psychological content and skills to career goals	**Appendix B:** B.1, B.2, B.3, B.4, B.5, B.6, B.7, B.9
5.2	Exhibit self-efficacy and self-regulation	**Appendix B:** B.6, B.7, B.9
5.3	Refine project-management skills	**Appendix B:** B.7, B.9
5.4	Enhance teamwork capacity	**Appendix B:** B.7, B.9
5.5	Develop meaningful professional direction for life after graduation	Ch 1: 1.5 **Appendix B:** B.1, B.2, B.3, B.4, B.5, B.6, B.7, B.9

Acknowledgments

I have to thank my husband, Joe Ciccarelli, for his love and support while I spent many long hours writing this textbook. My children, Al and Liz, also put up with my odd working hours and frequent trips and deserve my thanks as well.

There are so many people to thank for their support! Erin Mitchell, Amber Mackey, Dickson Musslewhite, Sarah Henrich, Reena Dalal, Sharon Geary, Linda Behrens, Sherry Lewis, and Lindsay Bethoney of the editorial team supported and advised me—thank you all so much. Special thanks to Kate Stewart and Lindsey Prudhomme Gill for a fantastic sales and marketing campaign.

The design is the collaborative work of Blair Brown and Kathryn Foot. The great student videos were the efforts of Debbie Coniglio, Stephanie Ruland, Joshua Paul Johnson, and Paul Sauline—marvelous work. Thanks also to Tom Scalzo and Pam Weldin for their work on the mountain of media. A big, heartfelt thank you to Crystal McCarthy, Sherry Lewis and Kate Cebik, supplement managers, and my supplement authors Alan Swinkels, Alisa Diop, Heather Hussey, John Gambon, Holly Schofield, and Jason Spiegelman; and to Rocky Buckley for his careful review. You are fantastic!

We are grateful to all of the instructors and students who have contributed to the development of this text and package over the last four editions. Please see *http://www.pearsonhighered.com/product?ISBN=0133851990* for a complete list of those who have reviewed content, participated in focus groups, evaluated learning tools, appeared in videos, and offered their feedback and assistance in numerous other ways. We thank you.

Special thanks to Julie Swasey, our new development editor, who fits us like a glove and made the whole process of editing this edition so much easier. We love you, Julie!

And, of course, I can't forget Noland White, my coauthor, pal, and Grand High Expert. His expertise in neuropsychology and clinical psychology is a valuable resource, and his revisions of half of the chapters and all of the chapter maps have once again made this edition a real standout. Thank you from the bottom of my heart, buddy!

Sandy Ciccarelli
Gulf Coast State College
Panama City, Florida
sandy243@comcast.net

I would like to personally thank:

My wife and best friend, Leah, and our wonderful children, Sierra, Alexis, and Landon, thank you for your love and patience. I would not be able to do any of this without you;

My lead author and collaborator, Sandy Ciccarelli, for making all of this possible—and for your friendship, support, assistance, advice, and continuing to be the most amazing mentor and writing partner I could ever hope to work with!

My students, for your inspiration, encouragement, and for all of the things you continue to teach me;

The student and faculty users and reviewers of this text, for your support and ever-helpful comments and suggestions;

My friends and colleagues in the Department of Psychological Science at Georgia College, for your encouragement, frequent discussions, and feedback, with special thanks to Lee Gillis, John Lindsay, Walt Isaac, and Greg Jarvie for your individual input and support along the way;

Julie Swasey and Erin Mitchell, for your guidance, creativity, collaboration, and for being so awesome!

Jessica Mosher and Leah Jewell, for being there in the beginning and for all that you have done;

Amber Mackey, Stephen Frail, Amber Chow, Brandy Dawson, Craig Campanella, Nicole Kunzmann, Paul Deluca, Beth Stoner, and all of the other Pearson and associated staff, for your contributions and for continuing to make this such a great experience!

Noland White
Georgia College
Milledgeville, Georgia
noland.white@gcsu.edu

About the Authors

SAUNDRA K. CICCARELLI is a Professor Emeritus of Psychology at Gulf Coast State College in Panama City, Florida. She received her Ph.D. in Developmental Psychology from George Peabody College of Vanderbilt University, Nashville, Tennessee. She is a member of the American Psychological Association and the Association for Psychological Science. Originally interested in a career as a researcher in the development of language and intelligence in developmentally delayed children and adolescents, Dr. Ciccarelli had publications in the *American Journal of Mental Deficiency* while still at Peabody. However, she discovered a love of teaching early on in her career. This led her to the position at Gulf Coast State College, where she taught Introductory Psychology and Human Development for over 30 years. Her students loved her enthusiasm for the field of psychology and the many anecdotes and examples she used to bring psychology to life for them. Before writing this text, Dr. Ciccarelli authored numerous ancillary materials for several introductory psychology and human development texts.

J. NOLAND WHITE is a Professor of Psychology at Georgia College, Georgia's Public Liberal Arts University, located in Milledgeville. He received his A.A. in Psychology from Macon State College, and both his B.S. and M.S. in Psychology from Georgia College. After receiving his Ph.D. in Counseling Psychology from the University of Tennessee, he joined the faculty of Georgia College in 2001. He is a licensed psychologist and has worked primarily with adolescents and adults, in a variety of clinical and community settings. On campus, he teaches Introductory Psychology, Psychology of Adjustment, Behavioral Neuroscience, Advanced Behavioral Neuroscience, Senior Seminar, and a section of Advanced Research Methods focusing on psychophysiology. He has an active lab and, with his students, is investigating the psychophysiological characteristics and neuropsychological performance of adults with and without ADHD. Outside of the lab, Dr. White is engaged in collaborative research examining the effectiveness of incorporating various technologies in and out of the college classroom to facilitate student learning. He also serves as a mentor for other faculty wanting to expand their use of technology with their classes. In April 2008 he was a recipient of the Georgia College Excellence in Teaching Award.

Psychology in Action

Secrets for Surviving College and Improving Your Grades

Pamela was struggling in her psychology class. She would read the text assignments, but nothing seemed to "stick," no matter how many times she read it. She understood nearly all of what was said in class but found it hard to listen and take notes. There was so much content to learn, how should she focus her efforts? Her grades were mediocre Cs. Feeling depressed and overwhelmed, she went to the instructor to ask for advice.

Her professor suggested that Pamela go to the college's counseling center to learn about alternate ways to study. The center's guidance counselor suggested recording the lectures so that Pamela would be able to listen without having to worry about taking notes. The counselor suggested Pamela try reciting what she has just read aloud—a text reading technique called the "SQ3R" method. After following the suggestions, all of Pamela's grades have improved to As.

Based on what you know now, what advice would you share with a student just starting out in college?

Video

00:00 / 02:28

Why study how to study?

Pamela's story is not uncommon. Many students find that they need to study in different ways, and also to use the old "listen and write notes" technique. This chapter will detail some helpful study tips as well as provide you with some good information you can use to improve your reading, writing, and memory skills.

∨	Learning Objectives

PIA.1   Identify some different methods of studying.

PIA.2   Describe some strategies for time management.

PIA.3   Describe how to go about reading a textbook so that you get the most out of your reading efforts.

PIA.4   Identify some of the best methods for taking notes in class and while reading the text.

PIA.5   Describe how you should approach studying for exams, and explain why different kinds of test questions require different study approaches.

PIA.6   List and describe the key steps in writing papers for college.

PIA.7   Explain how using mnemonics can help you improve your memory for facts and concepts.

Success Center

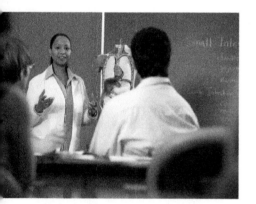

Teachers often use multiple methods to present a point, but trying to cover all learning methods in one lecture would not be practical.

Some students find it helpful to hear the content in addition to reading it. This is especially true when learning a new language. This woman is listening to an audio recording from her textbook as she follows along and looks at the figures and photos.

Study Skills

Many students entering college have developed a system of taking notes, reading the textbook, and reviewing for exams that may have worked pretty well in the past; but what worked in grade school and high school may not work in college, where the expectations from teachers are higher and the workload is far greater. Students should know seven things in order to do their absolute best in any college course:

1. How to identify which study methods work best for them and for different kinds of materials.

2. How to manage their time and avoid procrastination.

3. How to read a textbook and take notes that are understandable and memorable the *first* time.

4. How to listen and take useful notes during lectures.

5. How to study efficiently for exams.

6. How to write good term papers.

7. How to improve their memory for facts and concepts.

This introduction presents various techniques and information aimed at maximizing knowledge and skills in each of these seven areas. In addition, brief videos are available on each of these topics from the "Success Center" section located at the start of every chapter.

 💬 I want to make better grades, but sometimes it seems that no matter how hard I study, the test questions turn out to be hard and confusing and I end up not doing very well. Is there some trick to getting good grades?

Many students would probably say that their grades are not what they want them to be. They may make the effort, but they still don't seem to be able to achieve the higher grades that they wish they could earn. A big part of the problem is that despite many different educational experiences, students are rarely taught how to study.

STUDY METHODS: DIFFERENT STROKES FOR DIFFERENT FOLKS

PIA.1 Identify some different methods of studying.

Most college students, at one point or another in their educational experiences, have probably run into the concept of a *learning style*, but what exactly is it? In general, a learning style is the particular way in which a person takes in, or absorbs, information (Barsch, 1996; Dunn et al., 1989, 2001; Felder & Spurlin, 2005).

We learn many different kinds of things during our lives, and one method of learning probably isn't going to work for everyone. Some people seem to learn better if they can read about a topic or put it into their own words (verbal learners). Others may find that looking at charts, diagrams, and figures help them more (visual learners). There are those who learn better if they can hear the information (auditory learners), and there are even people who use the motion of their own bodies to help them remember key information (action learners). While instructors would have a practical nightmare if they tried to teach to every individual student's particular learning style, students who are aware of their own style can use it to change the way they study. Furthermore, no real evidence exists to show that tailoring the presentation of information to different learning styles has any effect on a student's ability to learn the information (Pashler et al., 2009). So instead of focusing on different learning styles, this *Psychology in Action* introduction will focus on different *study methods*. Take the opportunity to try them out and find which methods work best for you. **Table PIA.1** lists just some of the ways in which you

Table PIA.1 Multiple Study Methods			
Verbal Methods	**Visual Methods**	**Auditory Methods**	**Action Methods**
Use flash cards to identify main points or key terms.	Make flash cards with pictures or diagrams to aid recall of key concepts.	Join or form a study group or find a study partner so that you can discuss concepts and ideas.	Sit near the front of the classroom and take notes by jotting down key terms and making pictures or charts to help you remember what you are hearing.
Write out or recite key information in whole sentences or phrases in your own words.	Make charts and diagrams and sum up information in tables.	While studying, speak out loud or into a digital recorder that you can play back later.	While studying, walk back and forth as you read out loud.
When looking at diagrams, write out a description.	Draw out a concept map for main ideas.	Make speeches.	Study with a friend.
Use "sticky" notes to remind yourself of key terms and information, and put them in the notebook or text or on a mirror that you use frequently.	Use different colors of highlighter for different sections of information in text or notes.	Record the lectures (with permission). Take notes on the lecture sparingly, using the recording to fill in parts that you might have missed.	While exercising, listen to recordings you have made of important information.
Practice spelling words or repeating facts to be remembered.	Visualize charts, diagrams, and figures.	Read notes or text material into a digital recorder or get study materials recorded and play back while exercising or doing chores.	Write out key concepts on a large board or poster.
Rewrite things from memory.	Trace letters and words to remember key facts.	When learning something new, state or explain the information in your own words out loud or to a study partner.	Make flash cards, using different colors and diagrams, and lay them out on a large surface. Practice putting them in order.
	Redraw things from memory.	Use musical rhythms as memory aids, or put information to a rhyme or a tune.	Make a three-dimensional model.
			Spend extra time in the lab.
			Go to off-campus areas such as a museum or historical site to gain information.

can study. All of the methods listed in this table are good for students who wish to improve both their understanding of a subject and their grades on tests. See if you can think of some other ways in which you might prefer to practice the various study methods.

WHEN AND WHERE DO YOU FIT IN TIME TO STUDY?

PIA.2 Describe some strategies for time management.

One of the biggest failings of college students (and many others) is managing the time for all the tasks involved. Procrastination, the tendency to put off tasks until some later time that often does not arrive, is the enemy of time management. There are some strategies to defeating procrastination (The College Board, 2011):

- Make a map of your long-term goals. If you are starting here, what are the paths you need to take to get to your ultimate goal?

- Get a calendar and write down class times, work times, social engagements, everything!

- Before you go to bed, plan your next day, starting with when you get up and prioritizing your tasks for that day. Mark tasks off as you do them.

- Go to bed. Getting enough sleep is a necessary step in managing your tasks. Eating right and walking or stretching between tasks is a good idea, too.

- If you have big tasks, break them down into smaller, more manageable pieces. How do you eat an elephant? One bite at a time.

- Do small tasks, like answering emails or writing the first paragraph of a paper, in those bits of time you might otherwise dismiss: riding the bus to school or work, waiting in a doctor's office, and so on.

- Build in some play time—all work and no play pretty much ensures that you will fail at keeping your schedule. Use play time as a reward for getting tasks done.

- If your schedule falls apart, don't panic—just start again the next day. Even the best time managers have days when things don't go as planned.

Another problem that often interferes with time management is the enduring myth that we can effectively multitask. In today's world of technological interconnectedness, people tend to believe that they can learn to do more than one task at a time. The fact, however, is that the human mind is not meant to multitask and trying to do so not only can lead to car wrecks and other disasters, but also may result in changes in how individuals process different types of information, and not for the better. One study challenged college students to perform experiments that involved task switching, selective attention, and working memory (Ophir et al., 2009). The expectation was that students who were experienced at multitasking would outperform those who were not, but the results were just the opposite: the "chronic multitaskers" failed miserably at all three tasks. The results seemed to indicate that frequent multitaskers use their brains less effectively, even when focusing on a single task.

Another study found that people who think they are good at multitasking are actually not (Sanbonmatsu et al., 2013), while still another study indicates that video gamers, who often feel that their success at gaming is training them to be good multitaskers in other areas of life such as texting or talking while driving, are just as unsuccessful at multitasking as nongamers (Donohue et al., 2012). In short, it's better to focus on one task and only one task for a short period of time before moving on to another than to try to do two things at once.

Concept Map L.O. PIA.1, PIA.2

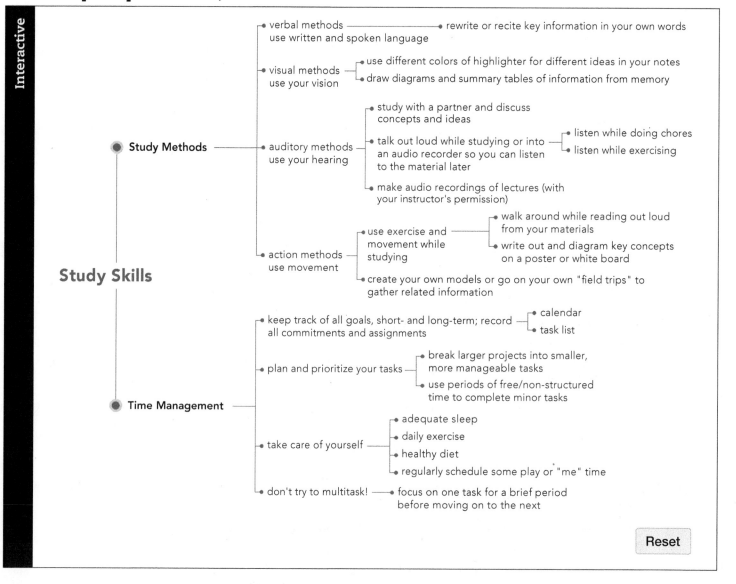

Practice Quiz   How much do you remember? ANSWERS AVAILABLE IN ANSWER KEY.

Pick the best answer.

1. Which of the following is *not* a question that students should ask themselves in order to maximize their studying effectiveness?
   a. How can I most effectively highlight while I am reading my textbook?
   b. How should I improve my memory for facts and concepts?
   c. How can I best manage my time and avoid procrastination?
   d. How can I write good term papers?

2. Gilbert has been advised by a learning expert to study using techniques like using flashcards, writing out important points in his own words and then reciting them, using sticky notes to emphasize important points, and creating descriptions of figures and images. Gilbert's tutor is recommending the use of _____ study methods.
   a. auditory
   b. action
   c. visual
   d. verbal

3. Which of the following is a suggestion to help you with time management skills?
   a. When you have a big project to complete, try to complete it all at once rather than breaking it down into smaller pieces so that you don't put it off until later.
   b. Try to focus only on short-term goals, since looking at long-term goals can be defeating and upsetting.
   c. Build in some play time, using it as a reward for getting tasks done.
   d. If your schedule falls apart, make sure to panic immediately!

4. What does the research show in regards to multitasking?
   a. Chronic multitaskers have developed strategies that allow them to use their brains more effectively.
   b. Chronic multitasking may be related to less effective ways of processing different types of information.
   c. Multitasking is effective, but only if you limit the number of tasks to 5 or fewer.
   d. Video gamers are better at multitasking in all areas of life.

Mastering the Course Content

It would be nice if there were a magical way to get the content of a college course into your head, but the sad fact is that you must work at learning. The two things you must do above all else: Read the textbook and attend the class lectures. The following sections give you some good tips for getting the most out of both necessary evils.

READING TEXTBOOKS: TEXTBOOKS ARE NOT MEATLOAF

PIA.3 Describe how to go about reading a textbook so that you get the most out of your reading efforts.

No matter what the study method, students must read the textbook to be successful in the course. (While that might seem obvious to some, many students today seem to think that just taking notes on lectures or slide presentations will be enough.) This section deals with how to read textbooks for understanding rather than just to "get through" the material.

Students make two common mistakes about reading a textbook. The first mistake is simple: Many students don't bother to read the textbook *before* going to the lecture that will cover that material. Trying to get anything out of a lecture without having read the material first is like trying to find a new, unfamiliar place without using a GPS or any kind of directions. It's easy to get lost. This is especially true because of the assumption that most instructors make when planning their lectures: They take for granted that the students have already read the assignment. The instructors then use the lecture to go into detail about the information the students supposedly got from the reading. If the students have not done the reading, the instructor's lecture isn't going to make a whole lot of sense.

The second mistake that most students make when reading textbook material is to try to read it the same way they would read a novel: They start at the first page and read continuously. With a novel, it's easy to do this because the plot is usually interesting and people want to know what happens next, so they keep reading. It isn't necessary to remember every little detail—all they need to remember are the main plot points. One could say that a novel is like meatloaf—some meaty parts with lots of filler. Meatloaf can be eaten quickly, without even chewing for very long.

Before reading any chapter in a text, survey the chapter by reading the outline and the section headings.

With a textbook, the material may be interesting but not in the same way that a novel is interesting. A textbook is a big, thick steak—all meat, no filler. Just as a steak has to be chewed to be enjoyed and to be useful to the body, textbook material has to be "chewed" with the mind. You have to read slowly, paying attention to every morsel of meaning.

So how do you do that? Probably one of the best-known reading methods is called SQ3R, first used by F. P. Robinson in a 1946 book called *Effective Study*. The letters S-Q-R-R-R stand for:

SURVEY   Look at the chapter you've been assigned to read. Read the outline, learning objectives, or other opening materials. Then scan through the chapter and read the headings of sections, and look at tables and figures. Quickly read through the chapter summary if one is provided.

It might sound like it takes too much time to do this, but you should just be skimming at this point—a couple of minutes is all it should take. Why do this at all? Surveying the chapter, or "previewing" it, as some experts call it, helps you form a framework in your head around which you can organize the information in the chapter when you read it in detail. Organization is one of the main ways to improve your memory for information. (L) (I) (N) K to Learning Objective 6.5.

QUESTION   After previewing the chapter, read the heading for the first section. *Just* the first section! Try to think of a question based on this heading that the section should answer as you read. For example, in Chapter One there's a section titled "Pavlov, Watson, and the Dawn of Behaviorism." You could ask yourself, "What did Pavlov and Watson do for psychology?" or "What is behaviorism?" In this text, a list of learning objectives for the key concepts in the chapter is presented in the form of questions that can be used with the SQ3R method. There are also student questions that can serve the same purpose. Now when you read the section, you aren't *just* reading—you're reading to *find an answer*. That makes the material much easier to remember later on.

READ   Now read the section, looking for the answers to your questions. As you read, take notes by making an outline of the main points and terms in the section. This is another area where some students make a big mistake. They assume that using a highlighter to mark words and phrases is as good as writing notes. One of the author's former students conducted research on the difference between highlighting and note taking, and her findings were clear: Students who wrote their own notes during the reading of a text or while listening to a lecture scored significantly higher on their exam grades than students who merely used a highlighter on the text (Boyd & Peeler, 2004). Highlighting requires no real mental effort (no "chewing," in other words), but writing the words down yourself requires you to read the words in depth and to understand them. When we study memory, you'll learn more about the value of processing information in depth. (L) (I) (N) K to Learning Objective 6.1.

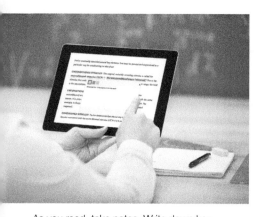

As you read, take notes. Write down key terms and try to summarize the main points of each paragraph and section in the chapter. These notes will be useful when you later review the chapter material.

RECITE   It may sound silly, but reciting out loud what you can remember from the section you've just read is another good way to process the information more deeply and completely. How many times have you thought you understood something, only to find that when you tried to explain it to someone, you didn't understand it at all? Recitation forces you to put the information in your own words—just as writing it in notes does. Writing it down accesses your visual memory; saying it out loud gives you an auditory memory for the same information. If you have ever learned something well by teaching it to someone else, you already know the value of recitation. If you feel self-conscious about talking to yourself, talk into a digital recorder—and it's a great way to review later.

Now repeat the Question, Read, and Recite instructions for each section, taking a few minutes' break after every two or three sections. Why take a break? There's a process that has to take place in your brain when you are trying to form a permanent memory for information, and that process takes a little time. When you take a break every 10 to 20 minutes, you are giving your brain the time to accomplish this process. A break will help you avoid a common problem in reading texts—finding yourself reading the same sentence over and over again because your brain is too overloaded from trying to remember what you just read.

RECALL/REVIEW   Finally, you've finished reading the entire chapter. If you've used the guidelines listed previously, you'll only have to read the chapter as thoroughly this one time, instead of having to read it over and over throughout the semester and just before exams. Once you've read the chapter, take a few minutes to try to remember as much of what you learned as you can. A good way to do this is to take any practice quizzes that might be available, either in your text or that come with other resources, WITHOUT looking back at the text or your notes. Many publishers have Web sites for their textbooks that have practice quizzes available. For this text, we offer both practice quizzes within the text, and online quizzes and study materials. If there are no quizzes, read the chapter summary in detail, making sure that you understand everything in it. If there's anything that's confusing, go back to that section in the chapter and read again until you understand it.

Some educators and researchers now add a fourth R: *Reflect*. To reflect means to try to think critically about what you have read by trying to tie the concepts into what you already know, thinking about how you can use the information in your own life, and deciding which of the topics you've covered interests you enough to look for more information on that topic (Richardson & Morgan, 1997). For example, if you have learned about the genetic basis for depression, you might better understand why that disorder seems to run in your best friend's family. Ⓛ Ⓘ Ⓝ Ⓚ to Learning Objective 12.10.

Reading textbooks in this way means that, when it comes time for the final exam, all you will have to do is carefully review your notes to be ready for the exam—you won't have to read the entire textbook all over again. What a time-saver! Recent research suggests that the most important steps in this method are the three R's: Read, Recite, and Review. In two experiments with college students, researchers found that when compared with other study methods such as rereading and note-taking study strategies, the 3R strategy produced superior recall of the material (McDaniel et al., 2009).

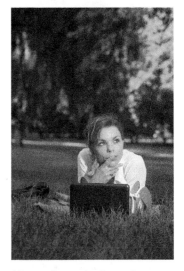

After reading a chapter section, take time to reflect on what the information means and how it might relate to real-world situations.

GETTING THE MOST OUT OF LECTURES

PIA.4 Identify some of the best methods for taking notes in class and while reading the text.

As mentioned earlier, mastering course content means you have to attend the lectures. Even if lectures are online, you have to read or watch them. But just attending or reading or watching is not enough; you have to process the information just as you have to process the text material. Furthermore, writing out lecture notes by hand has been found to be more beneficial than taking notes on a laptop (Mueller & Oppenheimer, 2014). To get the most out of lectures, you need to take notes on the content, and taking notes involves quite a bit more than just writing down the words the instructor says or printing out the PowerPoint slides.

One very important fact you must remember: PowerPoint slides are not meant to be notes at all; they are merely talking points that help the instructor follow a particular sequence in lecturing. Typically, the instructor will have more to say about each point on the slide, and that is the information students should be listening to and writing down. In Table PIA.1, the suggestion to use highlighters of different colors is not meant to replace taking notes but instead to supplement the notes you do take.

How should you take notes? As stated earlier, you should try to take notes while reading the chapter (*before* attending the lecture) by writing down the main points

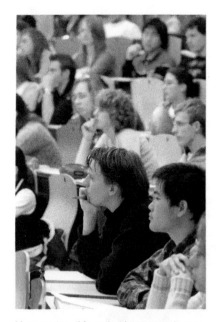

Here are two things that instructors love to see: attentive looks and note taking during the lecture. And for the student who learns better just listening, a small digital recorder (used with permission) can help for later review of the lecture. How should these students have prepared before coming to this class?

and the vocabulary terms *in your own words* as much as possible. This forces you to think about what you are reading. The more you think about it, the more likely it is that the concepts will become a part of your permanent memory. (L)(I)(N)K to Learning Objective 6.5.

Taking notes while listening to the lecture is a slightly different procedure. First, you should have your notes from your earlier reading in front of you, and it helps to leave plenty of space between lines to add notes from the lecture. A major mistake made by many students is to come to the lecture without having read the material first. This is an EXTREMELY BAD IDEA. If you come to the lecture totally unprepared, you will have no idea what is important enough to write down and what is just the instructor's asides and commentary. Reading the material first gives you a good idea of exactly what is important in the lecture and reduces the amount of notes you must take.

There is an art to really listening to someone, too, often called *active listening*. Active listeners make eye contact with the speaker and sit facing the speaker in a place where they can easily hear and see the speaker. Active listeners focus on what is being said rather than how the speaker looks or sounds (not always an easy task) and ask questions when they do not understand something or need a clarification. Asking questions during a lecture is a good way to stay engaged in actively processing the speaker's message.

If you are like Pamela in the introduction, ask your instructor if you can bring a digital recorder to class to record the lecture. You will then be able to listen during the class and use the recording to take notes from later. Some students may prefer to jot down diagrams, charts, and other visual aids along with their written notes. When you have good notes taken while reading the text and from the lectures, you will also have ready-made study aids for preparing to take exams. The next section deals with the best ways to study for exams.

WRITING PROMPT

What are some reasons why not relying on the instructor's PowerPoints might be beneficial in committing information to memory?

▶ | The response entered here will be saved to your notes and may be collected by your instructor if he/she requires it.

[Submit]

Concept Map L.O. PIA.3, PIA.4

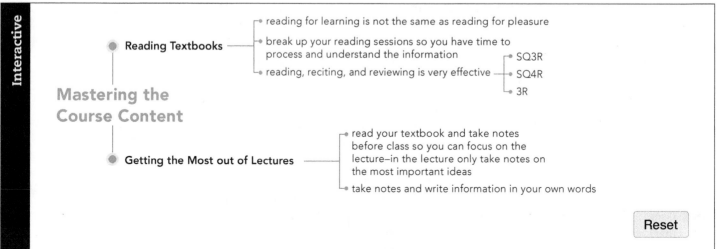

Interactive

Mastering the Course Content

- **Reading Textbooks** ─┬─ reading for learning is not the same as reading for pleasure
  - break up your reading sessions so you have time to process and understand the information
  - reading, reciting, and reviewing is very effective ──┬─ SQ3R
    - SQ4R
    - 3R

- **Getting the Most out of Lectures** ──┬─ read your textbook and take notes before class so you can focus on the lecture—in the lecture only take notes on the most important ideas
  - take notes and write information in your own words

[Reset]

Practice Quiz   How much do you remember? ANSWERS AVAILABLE IN ANSWER KEY.

Pick the best answer.

1. What does the "S" in SQ3R stand for?
   a. survey
   b. study
   c. synthesize
   d. stand

2. Candice has surveyed the material, developed questions to consider, and begun reading the material to find the answers to her questions. What should she do next?
   a. Recite out loud what she can remember from the section she just read.
   b. Re-read the material a second time.
   c. Review the material from the chapter that she has read.
   d. Retain the material by committing it to memory.

3. To maximize success, which method of note-taking should Juan use?
   a. He should highlight the text rather than writing his own notes.
   b. He should write down every word from the PowerPoint slides used in class.
   c. He should take notes in his own words as much as possible.
   d. He should make sure that his notes contain the exact words used by his instructor.

4. Avery maintains eye contact when listening to her instructors. She also places herself so that she can see and hear the instructors. Additionally, she works to listen to the content of the lecture instead of focusing on how they look or what they are wearing. Avery would be described as a(n)
   a. accomplished student.
   b. passive listener.
   c. social listener.
   d. active listener.

Demonstrating Your Knowledge: Tests and Papers

Inevitably, the time will come when your instructor wants some hard evidence that you have truly learned at least some of the material to which you have been exposed. Tests and paper writing are two common ways in which this evidence is gathered.

STUDYING FOR EXAMS: CRAMMING IS NOT AN OPTION

PIA.5 Describe how you should approach studying for exams, and explain why different kinds of test questions require different study approaches.

There is a right way to study for a test, believe it or not. Here are some good things to remember when preparing for an exam, whether it's a quiz, a unit test, a midterm, or a final (Carter et al., 2002; Reynolds, 2002):

Could this be you? The scattered materials, the frantic phone call to a friend or professor, the tense and worried facial expression are all hallmarks of that hallowed yet useless student tradition, cramming. Don't let this happen to you.

- **Timing is everything.** One of the worst things that students can do is to wait until the last minute to study for an exam. Remember the analogy about "chewing" the steak? (Just as a steak has to be chewed to be enjoyed and to be useful to the body, textbook material has to be "chewed" with the mind.) The same concept applies to preparing for an exam: You have to give yourself enough time. If you've read your text material and taken good notes as discussed in the previous sections, you'll be able to save a lot of time in studying for the exam, but you still need to give yourself ample time to go over all of those notes. The time management tips given earlier in this chapter will help you prioritize your studying.

- **Find out as much as you can about the type of test and the material it will cover.** The type of test can affect the way in which you want to study the material. An objective test, for example, such as multiple-choice or true/false, is usually fairly close to the text material, so you'll want to be very familiar with the wording of concepts and definitions in the text, although this is not a suggestion to memorize a lot of material.

   These kinds of tests can include one of three types of questions:

- **Factual:** Questions that ask you to remember a specific fact from the text material. For example, "Who built the first psychological laboratory?" requires that you recognize a person's name. (The answer is Wilhelm Wundt.)

- **Applied:** Questions that ask you to use, or apply, information presented in the text. For example, consider the following question:

  Ever since she was scared by a dog as a young child, Angelica has been afraid of all dogs. The fact that she is not only afraid of the original dog but all types of dogs is an example of

  a. stimulus generalization.
  b. stimulus discrimination.
  c. spontaneous recovery.
  d. shaping.

  This question requires you to take a concept (in this case, generalization) and apply it to a real-world example.

- **Conceptual:** Questions that demand that you think about the ideas or concepts presented in the text and demonstrate that you understand them by answering questions like the following: "Freud is to _____ as Watson is to _____." (The answers could vary, but a good set would be "the unconscious" and "observable behavior.")

Notice that although memorizing facts might help on the first type of question, it isn't going to help at all on the last two. Memorization doesn't always help on factual questions either, because the questions are sometimes worded quite differently from the text. It is far better to understand the information rather than be able to "spit it back" without understanding it. "Spitting it back" is memorization; understanding it is true learning. **LINK** to Learning Objective 6.1. There are different levels of analysis for information you are trying to learn, and the higher the level of analysis, the more likely you are to remember (Anderson et al., 2001; Bloom, 1956). *Factual questions* are the lowest level of analysis: knowledge. *Applied questions* are a higher level and are often preferred by instructors for that reason—it's hard to successfully apply information if you don't really understand it. *Conceptual questions* are a kind of analysis, a level higher than either of the other two. Not only do you have to understand the concept, you have to understand it well enough to compare and contrast it with other concepts. They might be harder questions to answer, but in the long run, you will get more "bang for your buck" in terms of true learning.

Subjective tests, such as essay tests and short-answer exams, require that you not only are able to recall and understand the information from the course but also that you are able to organize it in your own words. To study for a subjective test means that you need to be familiar with the material *and* that you need to be able to write it down. Make outlines of your notes. Rewrite both reading and lecture notes, and make flash cards, charts, and drawings. Practice putting the flash cards in order. Talk out loud or study with someone else and discuss the possible questions that could be on an essay test. You may find that only a few of these methods work best for you, but the more ways in which you try to study, the better you will be able to retrieve the information when you need it. It may sound like a big investment of your time, but most students vastly underestimate how long it takes to study—and fail to recognize that many of these techniques are doable when first reading the textbook assignment and preparing for the classroom lecture. DON'T CRAM!

You might also look at old tests (if the instructor has made them available) to see what kinds of questions are usually asked. If this is not possible, make sure that you pay close attention to the kinds of questions asked on the first exam so that you will know how to prepare for future tests. Write out your own test questions as if you were the instructor. Not only does this force you to think about the material the way it will appear on the test, it also provides a great review tool. Other helpful advice:

- **Use SQ3R.** You can use the same method that you used to read the text material to go over your notes. Skim through your notes, try to think of possible test questions, recite the main ideas and definitions of terms, either out loud, into a digital recorder, or to a friend or study group. Review by summarizing sections of material or by making an outline or flash cards that you can use in studying important concepts.

- **Use the concept maps if provided.** When surveying the chapter, make sure you look over any concept maps. (In this text, they are provided at the end of each major section of the chapters, just before the practice quizzes). A **concept map** is a visual organization of the key concepts, terms, and definitions that are found in each section and is an excellent way to "see" how various concepts are linked together (Carnot et al., 2001; Novak, 1995; Wu et al., 2004). They are also a great way to review the chapter once you have finished reading it, just to check for understanding—if the concept maps don't make sense, then you've missed something and need to go back over the relevant section. You can also make your own concept maps as you take notes on the chapter.

- **Take advantage of all the publisher's test materials.** Practice does help, and most textbooks come with a study guide or a Web site (such as **www. mypsychlab.com** for this text). Those materials should have practice quizzes available—take them. The more types of quiz questions you try to answer, the more successful you will be at interpreting the questions on the actual exam. You'll also get a very good idea of the areas that you need to go back and review again. And remember, retrieval practice, or actually testing your recall through tests or quizzes, is a great way to improve long-term learning (Karpicke, 2012; Karpicke & Blunt, 2011), even when just thinking about the information or rehearsing it over in your mind (Smith et al., 2013)! Retrieval practice works better than simply re-studying or rereading. The key is testing your retrieval of information, not your recognition of information.

Many students studying for exams ignore one of the most valuable resources to which they have access: the instructor. Most instructors are happy to answer questions or schedule time for students who are having difficulty understanding the material.

- **Make use of the resources.** If you find that you are having difficulty with certain concepts, go to the instructor well in advance of the exam for help. (This is another good reason to manage your study time so that you aren't trying to do everything in a few hours the night before the exam.) There are help centers on most college and university campuses with people who can help you learn to study, organize your notes, or tutor you in the subject area.

- **Don't forget your physical needs.** Studies have shown that not getting enough sleep is bad for memory and learning processes (Stickgold et al., 2001; Vecsey et al., 2009). Try to stop studying an hour or so before going to bed at a reasonable time to give your body time to relax and unwind. Get a full night's sleep if possible. Do not take sleep-inducing medications or drink alcohol, as these substances prevent normal stages of sleep, including the stage that seems to be the most useful for memory and learning (Davis et al., 2003). Do eat breakfast; hunger is harmful to memory and mental performance. A breakfast heavy on protein and light on carbohydrates is the best for concentration and recall (Benton & Parker, 1998; Dani et al., 2005; Pollitt & Matthews, 1998; Stubbs et al., 1996).

Holding your eyes open is not going to help you study when you are this tired. Sleep has been shown to improve memory and performance on tests, so get a good night's sleep before every exam.

WRITING PROMPT

Many elementary and secondary school programs now offer breakfast to their students. What foods would benefit these children the most and why?

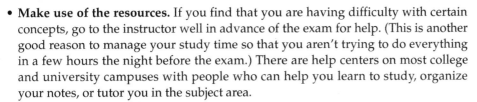

▶ | The response entered here will be saved to your notes and may be collected by your instructor if he/she requires it.

Submit

- **Use your test time wisely.** When taking the test, don't allow yourself to get stuck on one question that you can't seem to answer. If an answer isn't clear, skip that question and go on to others. After finishing all of the questions that you can answer easily, go back to the ones you have skipped and try to answer them again. This accomplishes several things: You get to experience success in answering the questions that you can answer, which makes you feel more confident and relaxed; other questions on the test might act as memory cues for the exact information you need for one of those questions you skipped; and once you are more relaxed, you may find that the answers to those seemingly impossible questions are now clear because anxiety is no longer blocking them. This is a way of reducing stress by dealing directly with the problem, one of many ways of dealing effectively with stress. ⓛⓘⓝⓚ to Learning Objective 9.5.

The next section gives some helpful information about another form of assessment: the term paper.

WRITING PAPERS: PLANNING MAKES PERFECT

PIA.6 List and describe the key steps in writing papers for college.

Several steps are involved in writing a paper, whether it is a short paper or a long one. You should begin all of these steps well in advance of the due date for the paper (not the night before):

Instructors are a good source of suggestions for paper topics—they know the kind of information they want to be reading and grading in the wee hours of the night.

1. **Choose a topic.** The first step is to choose a topic for your paper. In some cases, the instructor may have a list of acceptable subjects, which makes your job easier. If that is not the case, don't be afraid to go to your instructor during office hours and talk about some possible topics. Try to choose a topic that interests you, one that you would like to learn more about. The most common mistake students make is to choose subject matter that is too broad. For example, the topic "autism" could fill a book. A narrower focus might discuss a single form of autism in detail. Again, your instructor can help you narrow down your topic choices.

2. **Do the research.** Find as many sources as you can that have information about your topic. Don't limit yourself to encyclopedias or textbooks. Go to your school library and ask the librarian to point you in the direction of some good scientific journals that would have useful information on the subject. Be very careful about using the Internet to do research: Not everything on the Internet is correct or written by true experts—avoid other students' papers and "encyclopedia" Web sites that can be written and updated by darn near anyone.

3. **Take notes.** While reading about your topic, take careful notes to remember key points and write down the reference that will go along with the reading. References for psychology papers are usually going to be in APA (American Psychological Association) style, which can be found at **www.apastyle.org** and in MyPsychLab. Remember, taking notes helps you avoid **plagiarism**, the copying of someone else's ideas or exact words (or a close imitation of the words) and presenting them as your own. Note taking also helps you avoid using too many direct quotes—papers are supposed to be in *your* words, not someone else's, even if you give them credit.

4. **Decide on the thesis.** The thesis is the central message of your paper—the message you want to communicate to your audience—which may be your instructor, your classmates, or both, depending on the nature of the assignment. Some papers are persuasive, which means the author is trying to convince the reader of a particular point of view, such as "Autism is not caused by immunizations." Some papers are informative, providing information about a topic to an audience that may have no prior knowledge, such as "Several forms of autism have been identified."

5. **Write an outline.** Using your notes from all your readings, create an outline of your paper—a kind of "road map" of how the paper will go. Start with an introduction (e.g., a brief definition and discussion of what autism is). Then decide what the body of the paper should be. If your paper is about a specific type of autism, for example, your outline might include sections about the possible causes of that type. The last section of your outline should be some kind of conclusion. For example, you might have recommendations about how parents of a child with autism can best help that child to develop as fully as possible.

6. **Write a first draft.** Write your paper using the outline and your notes as guides. If using APA style, place citations with all of your statements and assertions. Failure to use citations (which point to the particular reference work from which your information came) is also a common mistake that many students make. It is very important that you avoid plagiarism, as discussed in step 3. When you use a source, you are supposed to explain

the information that you are using in your own words *and* cite the source, as in the following example:

In one study comparing both identical and fraternal twins, researchers found that stressful life events of the kind listed in the SRRS were excellent predictors of the onset of episodes of major depression (Kendler & Prescott, 1999).

Your paper's reference section would have the following citation: Kendler, K. S., & Prescott, C. A. (1999). A population-based twin study of lifetime major depression in men and women. *Archives of General Psychiatry*, 56(1): 39–44. [Author's note: The number in front of the parentheses is the volume of the journal, the one inside is the issue number, and the last numbers are the page numbers of that article.]

7. **Let it sit.** Take a few days (if you have been good about starting the paper on time) to let the paper sit without reading it. Then go back over and mark places that don't sound right and need more explanation, a citation, or any other changes. This is much easier to do after a few days away from the paper; the need to reword will be more obvious.

8. **Write the revised draft.** Some people do more than one draft, while others do only a first draft and a final. In any case, revise the draft carefully, making sure to check your citations—and your spelling!

In earlier times, people actually had to write or type their first, second, and sometimes third drafts on real paper. The advent of computers with word-processing programs that allow simple editing and revision have no doubt saved a lot of trees from the paper mill. This also means there is no good excuse for failing to write a first draft and proofreading one's work.

Before we end this introduction, here are some excellent books and Web resources available for help in maximizing your studying:

Carter, C., Bishop, J., & Kravits, S. (2011). *Keys to effective learning: Study skills and habits for success* (6th ed.) Upper Saddle River, NJ: Prentice Hall.

Carter, C., Bishop, J., Kravits, S., & Block, J. (2009). *Keys to success: Building analytical, creative, and practical skills* (6th ed.). Upper Saddle River, NJ: Prentice Hall.

Sellers, D., Dochen, C. W., & Hodges, R. W. (2011). *Academic transformation: The road to college success* (2nd ed.) Upper Saddle River, NJ: Prentice Hall.

A good source created by Joe Landsberger is the Web site Study Guides and Strategies, available at www.studygs.net.

A good resource for the background behind concept maps and how to use them is at cmap.ihmc.us/Publications/ResearchPapers/TheoryCmaps/TheoryUnderlyingConceptMaps.htm.

MyPsychLab contains study materials, practice quizzes, and resources for doing research and writing papers.

Concept Map L.O. PIA.5, PIA.6

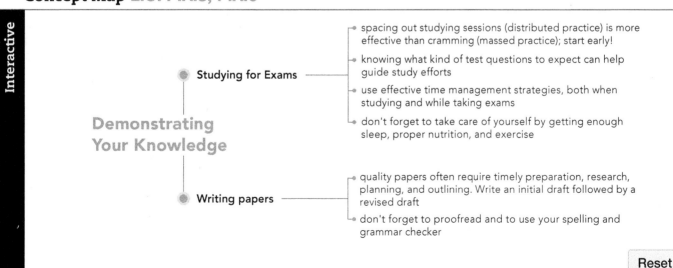

Interactive

Demonstrating Your Knowledge

Studying for Exams
- spacing out studying sessions (distributed practice) is more effective than cramming (massed practice); start early!
- knowing what kind of test questions to expect can help guide study efforts
- use effective time management strategies, both when studying and while taking exams
- don't forget to take care of yourself by getting enough sleep, proper nutrition, and exercise

Writing papers
- quality papers often require timely preparation, research, planning, and outlining. Write an initial draft followed by a revised draft
- don't forget to proofread and to use your spelling and grammar checker

Reset

Practice Quiz   How much do you remember? ANSWERS AVAILABLE IN ANSWER KEY.

Pick the best answer.

1. Which category is the following question an example of? *True or False: Psychology is the study of behavior and mental processes.*

a. factual question

b. conceptual question

c. applied question

d. critical question

2. Which questions are the highest level of analysis and often considered the hardest to answer on a test?

a. factual   **c.** conceptual

b. applied   **d.** true/false

3. Tom is studying for his first psychology exam. What should he do to ensure he remembers all that he has studied?

a. Wait until just before the scheduled exam, so that the information will be fresh in his mind.

b. Study all night long before the exam—he can sleep after the test.

c. Memorize as much of the information as possible.

d. Begin studying many days in advance so as to give his brain time to commit the material to memory and repeatedly testing his retrieval of information.

4. What is the value of retrieval practice?

a. It helps to increase long-term learning.

b. It allows students more opportunities to study.

c. It assists only in preparing for essay-based exams.

d. No research exists to prove that retrieval practice is effective

5. Simply spitting information back out on a test is likely more indicative of _____, while truly understanding information is more indicative of actual _____.

a. memorization; learning   **c.** behavior; action

b. learning; memorization   **d.** a process; a gift

6. Tamika has developed and researched a topic for her paper. She has taken notes as she read about the topic, and has developed a strong thesis for her paper. What should she do next?

a. Begin writing a rough draft.

b. Begin writing as if her first draft will be her final draft.

c. Develop an outline as a road map to help her stay on track when writing her paper.

d. Let everything sit for a couple of days before beginning her rough draft.

Applying Psychology to Everyday Life
Strategies for Improving Your Memory

PIA.7 Explain how using mnemonics can help you improve your memory for facts and concepts.

Everyone needs a little memory help now and then. Even memory experts use strategies to help them perform their unusual feats of remembering. These strategies may be unique to that individual, but there are many memory "tricks" that are quite simple and available for anyone to learn and use. A memory trick or strategy to help people remember is called a **mnemonic**, from the Greek word for memory. Here are a few of the more popular mnemonics, some of which may sound familiar:

- **Linking.** Make a list in which items to be remembered are linked in some way. If trying to remember a list of the planets in the solar system, for example, a person could string the names of the planets together like this: *Mercury* was the messenger god, who carried lots of love notes to *Venus*, the beautiful goddess who sprang from the *Earth's* sea. She was married to *Mars*, her brother, which didn't please her father *Jupiter* or his father *Saturn*, and his uncle *Uranus* complained to the sea god, *Neptune*. That sounds like a lot, but once linked in this way, the names of the planets are easy to recall in proper order.

- **The peg-word method.** In this method, it is necessary to first memorize a series of "peg" words, numbered words that can be used as keys for remembering items associated with them. A typical series of peg words is:

  One is a bun

  Two is a shoe

  Three is a tree

  Four is a door

  Five is a hive

Six is bricks

Seven is heaven

Eight is a gate

Nine is a line

Ten is a hen

To use this method, each item to be remembered is associated with a peg word and made into an image. For instance, if you are trying to remember the parts of the nervous system, you might picture the brain stuck inside a bun, the spinal cord growing out of a shoe or with shoes hanging off of it, and the peripheral nerves as the branches of a tree.

- **The method of loci (LOW-kee or LOW-si).** In this method, the person pictures a very familiar room or series of rooms in a house or other building. Each point of the speech is then made into an image and "placed" mentally in the room at certain locations. For example, if the first point was about military spending, the image might be a soldier standing in the doorway of the house throwing money out into the street. Each point would have its place, and all the person would need to do to retrieve the memories would be to take a "mental walk" around the house.

- **Verbal/rhythmic organization.** How do you spell relief? If, when spelling a word with an *ie* or an *ei* in it, you resort to the old rhyme "I before E except after C, or when sounded as A as in neighbor or weigh," you have made use of a verbal/rhythmic organization mnemonic. "Thirty days hath September, April, June, and November . . ." is another example of this technique. Setting information into a rhyme aids memory because it uses verbal cues, rhyming words, and the rhythm of the poem itself to aid retrieval. Sometimes this method is accomplished through making a sentence by using the first letters of each word to be remembered and making them into new words that form a sentence. The colors of the rainbow are ROY G BIV (red, orange, yellow, green, blue, indigo, and violet). The notes on the musical staff are "Every Good Boy Does Fine." There are countless examples of this technique.

- **Put it to music (a version of the rhythmic method).** Some people have had success with making up little songs, using familiar tunes, to remember specific information. The best example of this is the alphabet song.

This *Psychology in Action* introduction has covered several different ways to help you get more out of your psychology class as well as all of your other college course work. If you follow the advice given in this chapter for reading, taking notes, studying, writing papers, and improving your memory, you will find that making good grades will be easier than ever before and that you will actually remember a great deal of what you've studied long after the last final exam is over.

Questions for Further Discussion

1. The use of images appears to help form better memories. How might imagery be linked to the earliest kinds of memories we have?

2. What are some mnemonics that you or people you know have used? Which method do you think those personal mnemonics represent?

Psychology in Action Summary

Study Skills

PIA.1 Identify some different methods of studying.

- While students may have preferred methods of learning, research has shown that using multiple methods to study is probably more useful than trying to learn in any one particular style.

PIA.2 Describe some strategies for time management.

- Making a calendar of prioritized tasks, breaking tasks down into smaller ones, and avoiding multitasking are some ways to improve time management.

Mastering Course Content

PIA.3 Describe how to go about reading a textbook so that you get the most out of your reading efforts.

- Textbooks must be read in a different way from novels or popular books.
- The SQ3R method is an excellent way to approach reading a textbook: survey, question, read, recite, review.

PIA.4 Identify some of the best methods for taking notes in class and while reading the text.

- Notes should be in your own words and written or typed, not highlighted in the text or on handouts.
- When taking notes from a lecture, you should be prepared by having the notes from your reading in front of you; writing out lecture notes by hand is recommended and some people may benefit from recording the lecture and taking notes afterward.

Demonstrating Your Knowledge: Tests and Papers

PIA.5 Describe how you should approach studying for exams, and explain why different kinds of test questions require different study approaches.

- Don't wait until the last minute to study.
- Find out about the types of questions on the exam.
- Use concept maps, the SQ3R method, and the publisher's practice-test materials.
- Engage in retrieval practice; test your recall, not just recognition, of content often.
- Get plenty of sleep and eat breakfast, preferably something with protein.

PIA.6 List and describe the key steps in writing papers for college.

- Key steps in writing a research paper are to choose a topic, read about the topic, take notes on your reading, decide upon the central message of your paper, write an outline, complete a first draft, and allow the paper to sit for a few days before going back and writing the final draft.

Applying Psychology to Everyday Life: Strategies for Improving Your Memory

PIA.7 Explain how using mnemonics can help you improve your memory for facts and concepts.

- There are memory strategies called mnemonics, including methods that use imagery, rhymes, linking, and even music to improve memory.

Test Yourself   ANSWERS AVAILABLE IN ANSWER KEY.

Pick the best answer.

1. A(n) _____ learner learns most effectively by using the motion of their body to remember key information.
   a. action
   b. SQ3R
   c. test yourself
   d. concept maps

2. Scientists have developed a fourth "R" in the SQ3R sequence. What is it?
   a. recite
   b. re-read
   c. retain
   d. reflect

3. What learning aid gives the student the ability to more effectively read and remember material?
   a. MyPsychLab
   b. content maps
   c. SQ3R
   d. practice quizzes

4. What type of question requires that you understand the material so well that you are able to compare and contrast it to other material as well?
   a. factual
   b. applied
   c. conceptual
   d. true/false

5. Joaquin is rewriting his notes and making note cards to help him thoroughly understand the material. He even talks aloud to himself as if he were lecturing to an imaginary class. Such a level of preparation is best for what type of test?
   a. subjective test
   b. objective test
   c. true/false test
   d. practice test

6. Which resource is considered one of the most valuable yet least used by students?
   a. MyPsychLab
   b. PowerPoints
   c. the instructor
   d. lecture notes

7. Your mom wants you to eat some breakfast before going off to your first psychology exam. What will you tell her?
   a. No thanks. A big meal will probably put me to sleep.
   b. Sounds good. Can I have some cereal and toast?
   c. All I want is some coffee. Caffeine will help me do my best!
   d. Thank you. Just some ham and eggs and maybe a small slice of bread.

8. Tabitha is stuck on a question while taking her psychology exam. What should she do?
   a. Stay on that question until she can figure out what the answer is.
   b. Go on to the other questions. Maybe she can find a clue to the one she skipped.
   c. Take a guess as to the correct answer. She probably will get it correct anyways.
   d. Review the questions she already has answered to find a clue there.

9. What is one of the most common mistakes students make when choosing a topic for a research paper?
   a. The topic is too broad.
   b. The topic is too narrow.
   c. The topic is unclear.
   d. The topic has no research to support it.

10. Keela has finished a draft of her research paper almost two weeks before the date it is due. What should she do now?
   a. Let it sit for a few days before reviewing it.
   b. Complete the final draft immediately while the material is still fresh in her head.
   c. Hand in her rough draft as if it were the final draft. Most students tend to make their paper worse when they revise it.
   d. Keela needs to start again, since papers finished early tend not to be well written.

Chapter 1
The Science of Psychology

Most people think of psychology as the study of weird people and odd behavior. But in reality, psychology is much, much more: the study of how each of us thinks, feels, and acts in our everyday life. You may not realize it, but you use psychology every day: when you correct a child's behavior, teach a pet a new trick, get a salesperson to give you what you want, or fall victim to a telemarketer's come-on. It's psychology in action when you talk with your significant other (or a friend or relative) when he or she is feeling down. Psychology is involved in both the tragedy of a person who commits an act of violence or terrorism for no apparent reason and in our reaction to that horrifying act. From everyday actions and interactions to the rarer triumphs and tragedies of life, psychology is all around us.

How would you define psychology? What do you hope to learn about psychology, yourself, and others after taking this course?

Video

00:00 / 02:28

Why study psychology?

Psychology not only helps you understand why other people do the things they do, it also helps you better understand yourself and your reactions to other people. Psychology can help you understand how your brain and body are connected, how to improve your learning abilities and memory, and how to deal with the stresses of life, both ordinary and extraordinary. In studying psychology, an understanding of the methods psychologists use is important because research can be flawed, and knowing how research should be done can bring those flaws to light. Finally, psychology and its research methods promote critical thinking, which can be used to evaluate not just research but also claims of all kinds, including those of advertisers and politicians.

Learning Objectives

1.1 Define psychology as a field of study, and identify psychology's four primary goals.

1.2 Identify some of the early pioneers in psychology, and differentiate between structuralism and functionalism.

1.3 Describe the basic ideas and important people behind the early approaches known as Gestalt, psychoanalysis, and behaviorism.

1.4 Summarize the seven modern perspectives, and identify the important contributions of Skinner, Maslow, and Rogers.

1.5 Differentiate between a psychologist and a psychiatrist, and describe the other types of professionals who work in the various areas of psychology.

1.6 Explain why psychology is considered a science, and identify the steps of the scientific method.

1.7 Describe some methods used to describe behavior and summarize the main advantages and drawbacks of each.

1.8 Explain the correlational technique and describe its usefulness to researchers.

1.9 Identify the steps involved in designing an experiment.

1.10 Identify two common sources of problems in an experiment, and list some ways to control for these effects.

1.11 Identify ethical concerns that can occur when conducting research with people and animals.

1.12 Summarize the basic principles of critical thinking, and explain how it is useful in everyday life.

What Is Psychology?

1.1 Define psychology as a field of study, and identify psychology's four primary goals.

Some people believe psychology is just the study of people and what motivates their behavior. Psychologists do study people, but they study animals as well. To better understand what motivates behavior, psychologists study not only what people and animals do but also what happens in their bodies and in their brains as they do it. Before examining the field of psychology, complete the survey *What Do You Know About Psychology?* to understand more about your own preconceived notions of people and human behavior.

Survey   WHAT DO YOU KNOW ABOUT PSYCHOLOGY?

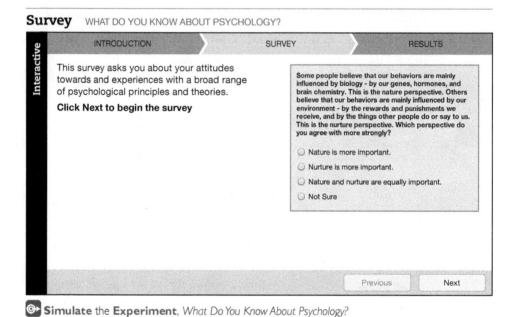

Simulate the Experiment, *What Do You Know About Psychology?*

Psychology is the scientific study of behavior and mental processes. *Behavior* includes all of our outward or overt actions and reactions, such as talking, facial expressions, and movement. The term *mental processes* refers to all the internal, covert (hidden) activity of our minds, such as thinking, feeling, and remembering. Why "scientific"? To study behavior and mental processes in both animals and humans, researchers have to observe them. Whenever a human being is observing anyone or anything, there's always a possibility the observer will see only what he or she expects to see. Psychologists don't want to let these possible biases* cause them to make faulty observations. They want to be as precise as possible and measure as carefully as they can, so they use the scientific method to study psychology.

Every science has the common goal of learning how things work. The goals specifically aimed at uncovering the mysteries of human and animal behavior are description, explanation, prediction, and control.

- **Description: What Is Happening?** The first step in understanding anything is to describe it. *Description* involves observing a behavior and noting everything about it: what is happening, where it happens, to whom it happens, and under what circumstances it seems to happen.

    For example, a psychologist might wonder why so many computer scientists seem to be male. She makes further observations and notes that many "non-techies" stereotypically perceive the life and environment of a computer scientist as

---

*biases: personal judgments based on beliefs rather than facts.

one in which someone lives and breathes at the computer and surrounds himself with computer games, junk food, and science-fiction gadgets—characteristics that add up to a very masculine ambiance.

That's what *seems* to be happening. The psychologist's observations are a starting place for the next goal: Why do females seem to avoid going into this environment?

- **Explanation: Why Is It Happening?** Based on her observations, the psychologist might try to come up with a tentative explanation, such as "women feel they do not belong in such stereotypically masculine surroundings." In other words, she is trying to understand or find an *explanation* for the lower proportion of women in this field. Finding explanations for behavior is a very important step in the process of forming theories of behavior. A *theory* is a general explanation of a set of observations or facts. The goal of description provides the observations, and the goal of explanation helps to build the theory.

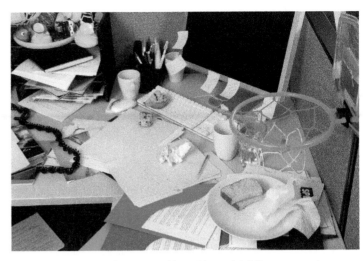

Is this an environment that you would want to work in? Some researchers have wondered if your answer might be influenced by your gender.

The following example comes from a real experiment conducted by psychologist Sapna Cheryan and colleagues (Cheryan et al., 2009). Professor Cheryan (who teaches psychology at the University of Washington in Seattle) set up four experiments with more than 250 female and male student participants who were not studying computer science. In the first experiment, students came into a small classroom that had one of two sets of objects: either Star Trek® posters, video-game boxes, and Coke™ cans; or nature posters, art, a dictionary, and coffee mugs (among other things). Told to ignore the objects because they were sharing the room with another class, the students spent several minutes in the classroom. While still sitting in the classroom, they were asked to fill out a questionnaire asking about their attitude toward computer science. Although the attitudes of male students were not different between the two environments, women exposed to the stereotypically masculine setup were less interested in computer science than those who were exposed to the nonstereotypical environment. The three other similar experiments yielded the same results.

- **Prediction: When Will It Happen Again?** Determining what will happen in the future is making a *prediction*. In the Cheryan et al. study, the prediction is clear: If we want more women to go into computer science, we must do something to change either the environment or the perception of the environment typically associated with this field. This is the purpose of the last of the four goals of psychology: changing or modifying behavior.

- **Control: How Can It Be Changed?** The focus of *control*, or the modification of some behavior, is to change a behavior from an undesirable one (such as women avoiding a certain academic major) to a desirable one (such as more equality in career choices).

Professor Cheryan suggests that changing the image of computer science may help increase the number of women choosing to go into this field. Not all psychological investigations will try to meet all four of these goals. In some cases, the main focus might be on description and prediction, as it would be for a personality theorist who wants to know what people are like (description) and what they might do in certain situations (prediction). Some psychologists are interested in both description and explanation, as is the case with experimental psychologists who design research to find explanations for observed (described) behavior. Therapists may be more interested in controlling or influencing behavior and mental processes, although the other three goals would be important in achieving this objective.

Although these goals have not really changed over the years since psychology's beginnings, the methods of achieving them certainly have changed. In the next section, we'll take a look at the early pioneers in psychology.

Concept Map L.O. 1.1

Interactive

● it has methods for studying phenomena

● it has four primary goals ———
  → describe
  → explain
  → predict
  → control

What Is Psychology?
(it is the scientific study of behavior and mental processes)

Reset

Practice Quiz   How much do you remember? ANSWERS AVAILABLE IN ANSWER KEY.

Pick the best answer.

1. In the definition of psychology, *mental processes* means
   a. internal, covert processes.
   b. unconscious processes.
   c. outward or overt actions and reactions.
   d. only human behavior.

2. Dr. Baker designs an experiment for studying lab rats' reaction to energy drinks in relation to problem solving. Dr. Baker is most interested in the goal of
   a. description.
   b. explanation.
   c. prediction.
   d. control.

3. Results of the study by Cheryan et al. (2009) suggest that changes must occur to the perception of the computer science field. This illustrates the goal of
   a. description.   c. prediction.
   b. explanation.   d. control.

4. James is conducting research that he hopes will give psychotherapists more information about how to prevent their clients from attempting suicide. In the long run he hopes that a significant reduction in suicidal behavior among those with mental illnesses will be the result. The primary goal of James's research is
   a. description.   c. prediction.
   b. explanation.   d. control.

Psychology Then: The History of Psychology

  ● How long has psychology been around?

Psychology is a relatively new field in the realm of the sciences; it is only about 130 years old. It's not that no one thought about what makes people tick before then; on the contrary, many philosophers,* medical doctors, and physiologists* thought about little else. Famous philosophers such as Plato, Aristotle, and Descartes wrote about the relationship of the soul (or mind) and the body (Durrant, 1993; Everson, 1995; Jackson, 2001; Kenny, 1968, 1994). Medical doctors and physiologists wondered about the physical connection between the body and the brain. For example, physician Hermann von Helmholtz (von Helmholtz, 1852, 1863) performed groundbreaking experiments in visual and auditory perception. ⓁⒾⓃⓀ to Learning Objectives 3.4 and 3.6.

IN THE BEGINNING: WUNDT, TITCHENER, AND JAMES

1.2 **Identify some of the early pioneers in psychology, and differentiate between structuralism and functionalism.**

The efforts to understand human behavior actually began in several different places around the world, and the people who were psychology's pioneers came from very different backgrounds. Eventually these varied ideas were recognized as the beginnings of a new field of inquiry, psychology.

German physiologist Wilhelm Wundt.

———————————

*philosophers: people who seek wisdom and knowledge through thinking and discussion.
*physiologists: scientists who study the physical workings of the body and its systems.

It really all started to come together in a laboratory in Leipzig, Germany, in 1879. It was here that Wilhelm Wundt (VILL-helm Voont, 1832–1920), a physiologist, attempted to apply scientific principles to the study of the human mind. In his laboratory, students from around the world were taught to study the structure of the human mind. Wundt believed that consciousness, the state of being aware of external events, could be broken down into thoughts, experiences, emotions, and other basic elements. In order to inspect these nonphysical elements, students had to learn to think objectively about their own thoughts—after all, they could hardly read someone else's mind. Wundt called this process **objective introspection**, the process of objectively examining and measuring one's own thoughts and mental activities (Rieber & Robinson, 2001). For example, Wundt might place an object, such as a rock, into a student's hand and have the student tell him everything that he was feeling as a result of having the rock in his hand—all the sensations stimulated by the rock. (Objectivity* was—and is—important because scientists need to remain unbiased. Observations need to be clear and precise, but unaffected by the individual observer's beliefs and values.)

This was really the first attempt by anyone to bring objectivity and measurement to the concept of psychology. This attention to objectivity, together with the establishment of the first true experimental laboratory in psychology, is why Wundt is known as the "father of psychology."

TITCHENER AND STRUCTURALISM IN AMERICA One of Wundt's students was Edward Titchener (1867–1927), an Englishman who eventually took Wundt's ideas to Cornell University in Ithaca, New York. Titchener expanded on Wundt's original ideas, calling his new viewpoint **structuralism** because the focus of study was the structure of the mind. He believed that every experience could be broken down into its individual emotions and sensations (Brennan, 2002). Although Titchener agreed with Wundt that consciousness could be broken down into its basic elements, Titchener also believed that objective introspection could be used on thoughts as well as on physical sensations. For example, Titchener might have asked his students to introspect about things that are blue rather than actually giving them a blue object and asking for reactions to it. Such an exercise might have led to something like the following: "What is blue? There are blue things, like the sky or a bird's feathers. Blue is cool and restful, blue is calm," and so on.

In 1894, one of Titchener's students at Cornell University became famous for becoming the first woman to receive a Ph.D. in psychology (Goodman, 1980; Guthrie, 2004). Her name was Margaret F. Washburn, and she was Titchener's only graduate student for that year. In 1908 she published a book on animal behavior that was considered an important work in that era of psychology, *The Animal Mind* (Washburn, 1908).

Structuralism was a dominant force in the early days of psychology, but it eventually died out in the early 1900s, as the structuralists were busily fighting among themselves over just which key elements of experience were the most important. A competing view arose not long after Wundt's laboratory was established, shortly before structuralism came to America.

WILLIAM JAMES AND FUNCTIONALISM Harvard University was the first school in America to offer classes in psychology in the late 1870s. These classes were taught by one of Harvard's most illustrious instructors, William James (1842–1910). James began teaching anatomy and physiology, but as his interest in psychology developed, he began teaching psychology almost exclusively (Brennan, 2002). His comprehensive textbook on the subject, *Principles of Psychology*, is so brilliantly written that copies are still in print (James, 1890, 2002).

Unlike Wundt and Titchener, James was more interested in the importance of consciousness to everyday life rather than just the analysis of it. He believed that the scientific

Structuralists would be interested in all of the memories and sensations this woman is experiencing as she smells the rose.

---

*objectivity: expressing or dealing with facts or conditions as they really are without allowing the influence of personal feelings, prejudices, or interpretations.

Mary Whiton Calkins, despite being denied a Ph.D. degree by Harvard because she was a woman, became the first female president of the American Psychological Association and had a successful career as a professor and researcher.

Francis Cecil Sumner, the first African American to receive a Ph.D. in psychology, went on to chair the psychology department at Howard University and is considered by many to be the father of African American psychology.

study of consciousness itself was not yet possible. Conscious ideas are constantly flowing in an ever-changing stream, and once you start thinking about what you were just thinking about, what you were thinking about is no longer what you *were* thinking about, it's what you *are* thinking about, and . . . excuse me, I'm a little dizzy. I think you get the picture, anyway.

Instead, James focused on how the mind allows people to *function* in the real world—how people work, play, and adapt to their surroundings. He called this viewpoint **functionalism**. (James was heavily influenced by Charles Darwin's ideas about *natural selection*, in which physical traits that help an animal adapt to its environment and survive are passed on to its offspring, becoming part of the animal's traits.) If physical traits could aid in survival, why couldn't behavioral traits do the same? Animals and people whose behavior helped them to survive would pass those traits on to their offspring, perhaps by teaching or even by some mechanism of heredity.* (Remember that this was early in the days of trying to understand how heredity worked.) For example, a behavior such as avoiding the eyes of others in an elevator can be seen as a way of protecting one's personal space—a kind of territorial protection that may have its roots in the primitive need to protect one's home and source of food and water from intruders (Manusov & Patterson, 2006) or as a way of avoiding what might seem like a challenge to another person (Brown et al., 2005; Jehn et al., 1999).

One of James's early students was Mary Whiton Calkins, who completed every course and requirement for earning a Ph.D. but was denied that degree by Harvard University because she was a woman. Calkins eventually established a psychological laboratory at Wellesley College. Her work was some of the earliest research in the area of human memory and the psychology of the self. In 1905, she became the first female president of the American Psychological Association (Furumoto, 1979, 1991; Zedler, 1995). Unlike Washburn, Calkins never earned the elusive Ph.D. degree despite a successful career as a professor and researcher (Guthrie, 2004).

Women were not the only minority to make contributions in the early days of psychology. In 1920 Francis Cecil Sumner became the first African American to earn a Ph.D. in psychology at Clark University. He eventually became the chair of the psychology department at Howard University and is assumed by many to be the father of African American psychology (Guthrie, 2004). Kenneth and Mamie Clark worked to show the negative effects of school segregation on African American children (Lal, 2002). Hispanic psychologist Jorge Sanchez conducted research in the area of intelligence testing, focusing on the cultural biases in such tests (Tevis, 1994). While psychology recently has seen an increase in the contributions of all minorities, the percentages are still small when compared to the population at large. For a summary of the contributions of African Americans to the early days of psychology, see the following feature, *Issues in Psychology: Psychology's African American Roots*.

 Is functionalism still an important point of view in psychology?

In the new field of psychology, functionalism offered an alternative viewpoint to the structuralists. But like so many of psychology's early ideas, it is no longer a major perspective. Instead, one can find elements of functionalism in the modern fields of *educational psychology* (studying the application of psychological concepts to education) and *industrial/organizational psychology* (studying the application of psychological concepts to businesses, organizations, and industry), as well as other areas in psychology. (L)(I)(N)(K) to Learning Objectives B.6 and B.7. Functionalism also played a part in the development of one of the more modern perspectives, evolutionary psychology, discussed later in this chapter.

---

*heredity: the transmission of traits and characteristics from parent to offspring through the actions of genes.

Issues in Psychology

Psychology's African American Roots

Even the Rat Was White is a book written by the late Dr. Robert V. Guthrie in 1976 and recently republished (Guthrie, 2004). It is a summary of the history of African Americans in the field of psychology. The contributions of African American psychologists to early psychology have often been ignored in textbooks. Dr. Guthrie includes in his text a detailed listing of the important African American psychologists and their contributions to the relatively new field of psychology. The following is a brief summary of just a few of the achievements of these often neglected scholars.

- Dr. Charles Henry Thompson (1896–1980) was the first African American to receive a doctorate in educational psychology (University of Chicago, 1925). For 30 years he was the editor of the *Journal of Negro Education*.
- Dr. Albert Sidney Beckham (1897–1964) received his Ph.D. in psychology in 1930 from New York University. In the 1930s he was senior assistant psychologist at the National Committee for Mental Hygiene at the Illinois Institute for Juvenile Research; he also counseled many black youths in his role as the psychologist at DuSable High School in Chicago. He had many publications of his research in the areas of intelligence and social concerns of the African American youth of his time.
- Dr. Robert Prentiss Daniel (1902–1968) earned his Ph.D. in educational psychology from Columbia University in 1932. At one time the director of the Division of Educational Psychology and Philosophy at Virginia Union University, he became president of Shaw University in North Carolina and finally the president of Virginia State College.
- Dr. Inez Beverly Prosser (1897–1934) earned her Ph.D. in educational psychology from the University of Cincinnati in 1933 and was the first African American woman to earn this degree. Her promising teaching career met a tragic end when she died in an automobile accident only one year after earning her doctorate.
- Dr. Howard Hale Long (1888–1948) received his Ed.D. in educational psychology from Harvard University in 1933. After teaching psychology and doing research in educational psychology for many years, Dr. Long became dean of administration at Wilberforce State College in Ohio.
- Dr. Ruth Howard (1900–1997) is known as the first African American woman to earn a Ph.D. in psychology (not educational psychology) in 1934 from the University of Minnesota. She served with her husband, Dr. Albert Beckham, as codirector for the Center for Psychological Services and also maintained a private practice in clinical psychology.

These African American pioneers in the field of psychology represent only a fraction of all those who made important contributions to psychology's early days.

Questions for Further Discussion

1. What kind of challenges might African American women have faced in the early days of psychology?

2. Are there people or areas of study in psychology today that you think might face similar challenges?

THREE INFLUENTIAL APPROACHES

1.3 **Describe the basic ideas and important people behind the early approaches known as Gestalt, psychoanalysis, and behaviorism.**

While the structuralists and functionalists argued with each other and among themselves, other psychologists were looking at psychology in several other ways.

Figure 1.1   A Gestalt Perception

The eye tends to "fill in" the blanks here and see both of these figures as circles rather than as a series of dots or a broken line.

GESTALT PSYCHOLOGY: THE WHOLE IS GREATER THAN THE SUM OF ITS PARTS   Max Wertheimer (VERT-hi-mer), like James, objected to the structuralist point of view but for different reasons. Wertheimer felt that psychological events such as perceiving* and sensing* could not be broken down into any smaller elements and still be properly understood. As a melody is made up of individual notes that can only be understood if the notes are in the correct relationship to one another, so perception can only be understood as a whole, entire event. Hence, the familiar slogan, "The whole is greater than the sum of its parts." Wertheimer and others believed that people naturally seek out patterns ("wholes") in the sensory information available to them. See **Figure 1.1** for an example of Gestalt perceptual patterns.

Wertheimer and others devoted their efforts to studying sensation and perception in this new perspective called **Gestalt psychology**. *Gestalt* (Gesh-TALT) is a German word meaning "an organized whole" or "configuration," which fit well with the focus on studying whole patterns rather than small pieces of them. Today, Gestalt ideas are part of the study of *cognitive psychology*, a field focusing not only on perception but also on learning, memory, thought processes, and problem solving; the basic Gestalt principles of perception are still taught within this newer field (Ash, 1998; Kohler, 1992; Wertheimer, 1982). Ⓛ Ⓘ Ⓝ Ⓚ to Learning Objective 3.12. The Gestalt approach has also been an influential concept in psychological therapy, becoming the basis for a major therapeutic technique called *Gestalt therapy*. Ⓛ Ⓘ Ⓝ Ⓚ to Learning Objective 13.3.

SIGMUND FREUD'S THEORY OF PSYCHOANALYSIS   It should be clear by now that psychology didn't start in one place and at one particular time. People of several different viewpoints were trying to promote their own perspective on the study of the human mind and behavior in different places all over the world. Up to now, this chapter has focused on the physiologists and philosophers who became interested in psychology, with a focus on understanding consciousness but little else. The medical profession took a whole different approach to psychology.

 💬 What about Freud? Everybody talks about him when they talk about psychology. Are his ideas still in use?

Sigmund Freud had become a noted physician in Austria while the structuralists were arguing, the functionalists were specializing, and the Gestaltists were looking at the big picture. He was a medical doctor—a neurologist, someone who specializes in disorders of the nervous system—and he and his colleagues had long sought a way to understand the patients who were coming to them for help.

Freud's patients suffered from nervous disorders for which he and other doctors could find no physical cause. Therefore, it was thought, the cause must be in the mind, and that is where Freud began to explore. He proposed that there is an *unconscious* (unaware) mind into which we push, or *repress*, all of our threatening urges and desires. He believed that these repressed urges, in trying to surface, created the nervous disorders in his patients (Freud et al., 1990). Ⓛ Ⓘ Ⓝ Ⓚ to Learning Objective 11.2.

Freud stressed the importance of early childhood experiences, believing that personality was formed in the first six years of life; if there were significant problems, those problems must have begun in the early years.

Some of his well-known followers were Alfred Adler, Carl Jung, and his own daughter, Anna Freud. Anna Freud began what became known as the ego movement in psychology that produced one of the most famous psychologists in the study of personality development, Erik Erikson. Ⓛ Ⓘ Ⓝ Ⓚ to Learning Objective 8.9.

---

*perceiving: becoming aware of something through the senses.
*sensing: seeing, hearing, feeling, tasting, or smelling something.

Freud's ideas are still influential today, although in a somewhat modified form. He had a number of followers in addition to those already named. Many of them became famous by altering his theory to fit their own viewpoint, but his basic ideas are still discussed and debated today. ⓛⓘⓝ︎к to Learning Objective 11.3.

Although some might think that Sigmund Freud was the first person to deal with people suffering from various mental disorders, the truth is that mental illness has a fairly long (and not very pretty) history. ⓛⓘⓝ︎к to Learning Objective 12.1.

Freudian **psychoanalysis**, the theory and therapy based on Freud's ideas, has been the basis of much modern *psychotherapy*—a process in which a trained psychological professional helps a person gain insights into and change his or her behavior. But another major and competing viewpoint has actually been more influential in the field of psychology as a whole.

PAVLOV, WATSON, AND THE DAWN OF BEHAVIORISM Ivan Pavlov, like Freud, was not a psychologist. He was a Russian physiologist who, working with dogs, had shown that a reflex (an involuntary reaction) such as salivation, which is normally produced by actually having food in one's mouth, could be caused to occur in response to a totally new and formerly unrelated stimulus,* such as the sound of a ticking metronome. He would turn on the metronome, give the dogs food, and they would salivate. After several repetitions, the dogs would salivate to the sound of the metronome *before* the food was presented—a learned (or "conditioned") reflexive response (Klein & Mowrer, 1989). This process was called *conditioning*. ⓛⓘⓝ︎к to Learning Objective 5.2.

In the early 1900s, psychologist John B. Watson had tired of the arguing among the structuralists; he challenged the functionalist viewpoint, as well as psychoanalysis, with his own "science of behavior," or **behaviorism** (Watson, 1924). Watson wanted to bring psychology back to a focus on scientific inquiry, and he felt that the only way to do that was to ignore the whole "consciousness" issue and focus only on *observable behavior*—something that could be directly seen and measured. He had read of Pavlov's work and thought that conditioning could form the basis of his new perspective of behaviorism.

Watson was certainly aware of Freud's work and his views on unconscious repression. Freud believed that all behavior stems from unconscious motivation, whereas Watson believed that all behavior is learned. Freud had stated that a *phobia*, an irrational fear, is really a symptom of an underlying, repressed conflict and cannot be "cured" without years of psychoanalysis to uncover and understand the repressed material.

Watson believed that phobias are learned through the process of conditioning and set out to prove it. Along with his colleague Rosalie Rayner, he took a baby, known as "Little Albert," and taught him to fear a white rat by making a loud, scary noise every time the infant saw the rat, until finally just seeing the rat caused the infant to cry and become fearful (Watson & Rayner, 1920). Even though "Little Albert" was not afraid of the rat at the start, the experiment worked very well—in fact, "Little Albert" became afraid of other fuzzy things, including a rabbit, a dog, and a sealskin coat.

💬 This sounds really bizarre—what does scaring a baby have to do with the science of psychology?

Watson wanted to prove that all behavior was a result of a stimulus–response relationship such as that described by Pavlov. Because Freud and his ideas about unconscious motivation were becoming a dominant force, Watson felt the need to show the world that a much simpler explanation could be found. Although scaring a baby sounds

Mary Cover Jones, one of the early pioneers of behavior therapy, earned her master's degree under the supervision of John Watson. Her long and distinguished career also included the publication in 1952 of the first educational television course in child development (Rutherford, 2000).

---

*stimulus: anything that causes an organism to have a reaction or response.

a little cruel, he felt that the advancement of the science of behavior was worth the baby's relatively brief discomfort.

One of Watson's students was Mary Cover Jones, who completed her master's degree in 1920 under Watson's supervision (Rutherford, 2000). She duplicated the "Little Albert" study with another child, "Little Peter," successfully conditioning Peter to be afraid of a white rabbit (Jones, 1924). She then began a process of *counterconditioning*, in which Peter was exposed to the white rabbit from a distance while eating a food that he really liked. The pleasure of the food outweighed the fear of the far-away rabbit. Day by day, the situation was repeated with the rabbit being brought closer each time, until Peter was no longer afraid of the rabbit. Jones went on to become one of the early pioneers of behavior therapy. Behaviorism is a major perspective in psychology today. It has also influenced the development of other perspectives, such as *cognitive psychology*.

Concept Map L.O. 1.2, 1.3

Interactive

A relatively new science that formally began in 1879 when Wilhelm Wundt ("father of psychology") established the first psychological laboratory in Leipzig, Germany

- studied nonphysical structure (i.e., thought, experiences, emotions, etc.) of the human mind
- used objective introspection to study processes that were the result of physical sensations
- first attempt to bring objectivity and measurement to psychology

was a student of Wundt's

Structuralism
founded by Edward Titchener

- expanded Wundt's original ideas; believed every experience could be broken down into individual emotions and sensations
- applied introspection method to thoughts as well as physical sensations

Functionalism
founded by William James

- influenced by Darwin's ideas about natural selection—focused on how the mind allows people to function in the real world
- interested in how behavioral traits could aid in survival
- influenced development of evolutionary psychology
- has elements in educational psychology and industrial/organizational psychology

Psychology Then: The History of Psychology
(has roots in several disciplines, including philosophy, medicine, and physiology, and has developed through several perspectives)

Gestalt psychology
founded by Max Wertheimer

did not believe that psychological events could be broken down into smaller elements; could only be understood as a whole, entire event; has influenced field of cognitive psychology and a form of psychological therapy, Gestalt therapy

Psychoanalysis
ideas put forth by Sigmund Freud

stressed importance of early life experiences, the role of the unconscious, and development through stages

Behaviorism
associated with work of John B. Watson, who was greatly influenced by Ivan Pavlov's work in conditioning/learning

wanted to bring focus back on scientific inquiry and believed only way to do so was to focus on observable behavior and ignore "consciousness" issue; early work examined phobias

Reset

Practice Quiz How much do you remember? ANSWERS ON PAGE AK-1.

Pick the best answer.

1. Which of the following early psychologists would have been most likely to agree with the statement, "The study of the mind should focus on how it functions in everyday life"?

   a. Wilhelm Wundt

   b. William James

   c. John Watson

   d. Sigmund Freud

2. Who was the first woman to complete the coursework for a doctorate at Harvard University?

   a. Mary Whiton Calkins

   b. Mary Cover Jones

   c. Margaret Washburn

   d. Ruth Howard

3. The early perspective of _____ was developed by a neurologist, and emphasized the importance of both the unconscious and early childhood experiences.

   a. psychoanalysis

   b. Gestalt psychology

   c. functionalism

   d. structuralism

4. Which early perspective tried to return to a focus on scientific inquiry by ignoring the study of consciousness?

   a. behaviorism

   b. functionalism

   c. psychoanalysis

   d. Gestalt

Psychology Now: Where We Are Today

Even in the twenty-first century, there isn't one single perspective that is used to explain all human behavior and mental processes. There are actually seven modern perspectives.

MODERN PERSPECTIVES

1.4 Summarize the seven modern perspectives, and identify the important contributions of Skinner, Maslow, and Rogers.

Two of psychology's modern perspectives are updated versions of psychoanalysis and behaviorism, while the others focus on people's goals, thought processes, social and cultural factors, biology, and genetics.

PSYCHODYNAMIC PERSPECTIVE Psychoanalysis has become the more modern **psychodynamic perspective**. While the focus still includes the unconscious mind and its influence over conscious behavior and on early childhood experiences, there is less emphasis on sex and sexual motivations and more emphasis on the development of a sense of self, social and interpersonal relationships, and the discovery of other motivations behind a person's behavior. Ⓛ Ⓘ Ⓝ Ⓚ to Learning Objective 13.2. Some modern psychodynamic practitioners have even begun to recommend that the link between neurobiology (the study of the brain and nervous system) and psychodynamic concepts should be more fully explored (Glucksman, 2006).

BEHAVIORAL PERSPECTIVE The behaviorism perspective also remains very influential. When its primary supporter, John B. Watson, moved on to greener pastures in the world of advertising, B. F. Skinner became the new leader of the field.

Skinner not only continued research in classical conditioning, but he also developed a theory of how voluntary behavior is learned called *operant conditioning* (Skinner, 1938). In this theory, behavioral responses that are followed by pleasurable consequences are strengthened, or *reinforced*. For example, a child who cries and is rewarded by getting his mother's attention will cry again in the future. Skinner's work is discussed in much greater depth in Chapter Five. Ⓛ Ⓘ Ⓝ Ⓚ to Learning Objective 5.4. In addition to the psychodynamic and behavioral perspectives, five newer perspectives have developed within the last 50 years.

HUMANISTIC PERSPECTIVE Often called the "third force" in psychology, humanism was really a reaction to both psychoanalytic theory and behaviorism. If you were a

Behaviorist B. F. Skinner puts a rat through its paces. What challenges might arise from applying information gained from studies with animals to human behavior?

psychologist in the early to mid-1900s, you were either a psychoanalyst or a behaviorist—there weren't any other major viewpoints to rival those two.

In contrast to the psychoanalytic focus on sexual development and behaviorism's emphasis on external forces in guiding personality development, some professionals began to develop a perspective that would allow them to focus on people's ability to direct their own lives. Humanists held the view that people have *free will*, the freedom to choose their own destiny, and that they strive for *self-actualization*, the achievement of one's full potential.

Two of the earliest and most famous founders of this view were Abraham Maslow (1908–1970) and Carl Rogers (1902–1987). Today, humanism exists as a form of psychotherapy aimed at self-understanding and self-improvement. **LINK** to Learning Objective 13.3.

COGNITIVE PERSPECTIVE   Cognitive psychology, which focuses on how people think, remember, store, and use information, became a major force in the field in the 1960s. It wasn't a new idea, as the Gestalt psychologists had themselves supported the study of mental processes of learning. The development of computers (which just happened to make ideal models of human thinking), the work of Piaget with children, Chomsky's analysis of Skinner's views of language, and discoveries in biological psychology all stimulated an interest in studying the processes of thought. The **cognitive perspective** with its focus on memory, intelligence, perception, thought processes, problem solving, language, and learning has become a major force in psychology. **LINK** to Chapter Seven: Cognition.

Within the cognitive perspective, the relatively new field of **cognitive neuroscience** includes the study of the physical workings of the brain and nervous system when engaged in memory, thinking, and other cognitive processes. Cognitive neuroscientists use tools for imaging the structure and activity of the living brain, such as magnetic resonance imaging (MRI), functional magnetic resonance imaging (fMRI), and positron emission tomography (PET). **LINK** to Learning Objective 2.9. The continually developing field of brain imaging is important in the study of cognitive processes.

SOCIOCULTURAL PERSPECTIVE   Another modern perspective in psychology is the **sociocultural perspective**, which actually combines two areas of study: *social psychology*, which is the study of groups, social roles, and rules of social actions and relationships; and *cultural psychology*, which is the study of cultural norms,* values, and expectations. These two areas are related in that both are about the effect that people have on one another, either individually or in a larger group such as a culture (Peplau & Taylor, 1997). **LINK** to Chapter Ten: Social Psychology. Think about it: Don't you behave differently around your family members than you do around your friends? Would you act differently in another country than you do in your native land? Russian psychologist Lev Vygotsky (1978) also used sociocultural concepts in forming his sociocultural theory of children's cognitive development. **LINK** to Learning Objective 8.7.

The sociocultural perspective is important because it reminds people that the way they and others behave (or even think) is influenced not only by whether they are alone, with friends, in a crowd, or part of a group but also by the social norms, fads, class differences, and ethnic identity concerns of the particular culture in which they live. *Cross-cultural research* also fits within this perspective. In cross-cultural research, the contrasts and comparisons of a behavior or issue are studied in at least two or more cultures. This type of research can help illustrate the different influences of environment (culture and training) when compared to the influence of heredity (genetics, or the influence of genes on behavior).

———————————

*norms: standards or expected behavior.

For example, in a classic study covered in Chapter Ten, researchers Darley and Latané (1968) found that the presence of other people actually *lessened* the chances that a person in trouble would receive help. ⓛⓘⓝⓚ to Learning Objective 10.14. The phenomenon is called the "bystander effect," and it is believed to be the result of *diffusion of responsibility*, which is the tendency to feel that someone else is responsible for taking action when others are present. But would this effect appear in other cultures? Shorey (2001), in his discussion of the brutal beating death of a Somali prisoner in a Canadian military facility while bystanders looked on without acting, suggests that it just might. But is Canadian culture too similar to our own to lead us to this conclusion? Would another culture very different from Western culture show the same effect? This is exactly the kind of question that the sociocultural perspective asks and attempts to answer, using cross-cultural research.

BIOPSYCHOLOGICAL PERSPECTIVE   *Biopsychology*, or the study of the biological bases of behavior and mental processes, isn't really as new a perspective as one might think. Also known as physiological psychology, biological psychology, psychobiology, and behavioral neuroscience, biopsychology is part of the larger field of *neuroscience*: the study of the physical structure, function, and development of the nervous system. Also, the previously discussed field of cognitive neuroscience often overlaps with biopsychology and the sociocultural perspective.

In the **biopsychological perspective**, human and animal behavior is seen as a direct result of events in the body. Hormones, heredity, brain chemicals, tumors, and diseases are some of the biological causes of behavior and mental events. ⓛⓘⓝⓚ to Chapter Two: The Biological Perspective. Some of the topics researched by biopsychologists include sleep, emotions, aggression, sexual behavior, and learning and memory—as well as disorders. While disorders may have multiple causes (family issues, stress, or trauma, for example), research in biopsychology points clearly to biological factors as one of those causes.

For example, evidence continues to mount for a genetic cause for *schizophrenia*, a mental disorder involving delusions (false beliefs), hallucinations (false sensory impressions), and extremely distorted thinking (Brzustowicz et al., 2004; Maziade et al., 1997; Pogue-Geile & Yokley, 2010). ⓛⓘⓝⓚ to Learning Objective 12.15. Other research suggests that human sexual orientation may be related to the developing baby's exposure in the womb to testosterone (G. Brown et al., 2002) as well as the birth order of male children (Puts et al., 2006). The birth order study suggests that the more older brothers a male child has, the more likely he is to have a homosexual orientation. Still another example of research in this field is a study finding a possible link between the tendency to lose one's train of thought in later adulthood—staring into space, unexplained excessive daytime sleepiness, and disorganized thinking, for example—and the development of Alzheimer's disease (Escandon et al., 2010). ⓛⓘⓝⓚ to Learning Objective 6.14.

EVOLUTIONARY PERSPECTIVE   The **evolutionary perspective** focuses on the biological bases for universal mental characteristics that all humans share. It seeks to explain general mental strategies and traits, such as why we lie, how attractiveness influences mate selection, why fear of snakes is so common, or why people universally like music and dancing. This approach may also overlap with biopsychology.

In this perspective, the mind is seen as a set of information-processing machines, designed by the same process of natural selection that Darwin (1859) first theorized, allowing human beings to solve the problems faced in the early days of human evolution— the problems of the early hunters and gatherers. The video *The Evolutionary Perspective* provides an overview of how evolutionary psychologists explain various behaviors and mental processes.

These scans highlight gray matter loss in the brains of individuals with very early-onset, adolescent schizophrenia over a five-year period, highlighting one focus of the biological perspective.

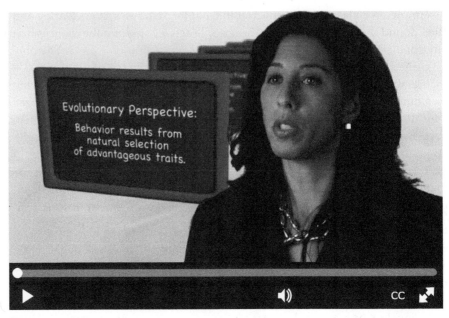

👁 **Watch** the **Video**, *The Evolutionary Perspective.*

💬 That explains why people don't like bitter stuff, such as the white part of an orange peel, but that's really a physical thing. How would the evolutionary perspective help us understand something psychological like relationships?

Relationships between men and women are one of the many areas in which evolutionary psychologists conduct research. For example, in one study researchers surveyed young adults about their relationships with the opposite sex, asking the participants how likely they would be to forgive either a sexual infidelity or an emotional one (Shackelford et al., 2002). Evolutionary theory would predict that men would find it more difficult to forgive a woman who had sex with someone else than a woman who was only emotionally involved with someone because the man wants to be sure that the children the woman bears are his (Geary, 2000, 2012). Why put all that effort into providing for children who could be another man's offspring? Women, on the other hand, should find it harder to forgive an emotional infidelity, as they are always sure that their children are their own, but (in evolutionary terms, mind you) they need the emotional loyalty of the men to provide for those children (Buss et al., 1992; Daly et al., 1982; Edlund et al., 2006). The results of the study support the prediction: Men find it harder to forgive a partner's sexual straying and are more likely to break up with the woman than if the infidelity is purely emotional; for women, the opposite results were found. Other research concerning mating has found that women seem to use a man's kissing ability to determine his worthiness as a potential mate (Hughes et al., 2007; Walter, 2008).

You may have realized as you read through the various perspectives that no one perspective has all the answers. Some perspectives are more scientific (e.g., behavioral and cognitive) while others are based more in thinking about human behavior (e.g., psychodynamic and humanistic). Some, like sociocultural, biopsychological, and evolutionary perspectives, are related to each other. Psychologists will often take an *eclectic* perspective—one that uses the "bits and pieces" of several perspectives that seem to best fit a particular situation.

Psychologists with an evolutionary perspective would be interested in how this couple selected each other as partners.

Dr. Mike Clayton
Missouri State Psychology Department
The Applied Behavior Analysis Program at MSU

Dr. Carol Shoptaugh
Missouri State Psychology Department
Industrial/Organizational Psychology Program at MSU

Do you believe that violence is a part of human nature? Is violent behavior something that can someday be removed from human behavior or, at the very least, controlled? Think about this question from each of the perspectives discussed in this chapter.

▶ The response entered here will be saved to your notes and may be collected by your instructor if he/she requires it.

Submit

PSYCHOLOGICAL PROFESSIONALS AND AREAS OF SPECIALIZATION

1.5 **Differentiate between a psychologist and a psychiatrist, and describe the other types of professionals who work in the various areas of psychology.**

Psychology is a large field, and the many professionals working within it have different training, different focuses, and perhaps different goals from the typical psychologist.

A **psychologist** has no medical training but has a doctorate degree. Psychologists undergo intense academic training, learning about many different areas of psychology before choosing a specialization. Because the focus of their careers can vary so widely, psychologists work in many different vocational* settings as described in the video *What Do Psychologists Do?*. **Figure 1.2a** on the next page shows the types of settings in which psychologists work. Remember, not all psychologists are trained to do counseling! Psychologists in the counseling specialization must also be licensed to practice in their states.

Rachel Happel, M.S.
Missouri State Psychology Department
Forensic Child Psychology Certificate at MSU

Dr. Wayne Mitchell
Missouri State Psychology Department
The Experimental Psychology Program at MSU

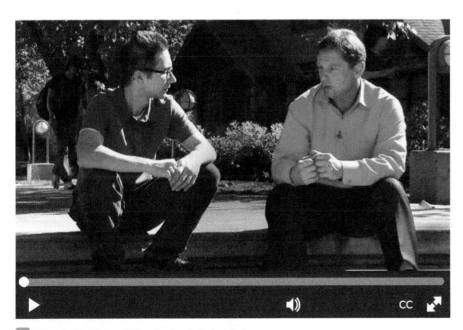

👁 **Watch** the **Video**, *What Do Psychologists Do?*

Dr. Bradley Fisher
Missouri State Psychology Department
Gerontology and Psychology Dual Major

In contrast, a **psychiatrist** has a medical degree and is a physician who specializes in the diagnosis and treatment (including the prescription of medications) of psychological disorders. A **psychiatric social worker** is trained in the area of social work and

---

*vocational: having to do with a job or career.

Dr. Dave Lutz
Missouri State Psychology Department
The Clinical Psychology Program at MSU

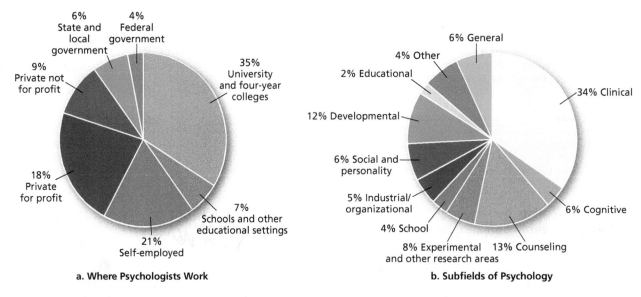

a. Where Psychologists Work

b. Subfields of Psychology

Figure 1.2 Work Settings and Subfields of Psychology

(a) There are many different work settings for psychologists. Although not obvious from the chart, many psychologists work in more than one setting. For example, a clinical psychologist may work in a hospital setting as well as teach at a university or college (Tsapogas et al., 2006). (b) This pie chart shows the specialty areas of psychologists who recently received their doctorates (Hoffer et al., 2007).

usually possesses a master's degree in that discipline. These professionals focus more on the environmental conditions that can have an impact on mental disorders, such as poverty, overcrowding, stress, and drug abuse.

💬 You said not all psychologists do counseling. But I thought that was all that psychologists do—what else is there?

Although many psychologists do participate in delivering therapy to people who need help, there is a nearly equal number of psychologists who do other tasks: researching, teaching, designing equipment and workplaces, and developing educational methods, for example. Also, not every psychologist is interested in the same area of human—or animal—behavior and most psychologists work in several different areas of interest, as shown in **Figure 1.2b**, "Subfields of Psychology."

Those psychologists who do research have two types of research to consider: basic research versus applied research. **Basic research** is research for the sake of gaining scientific knowledge. For example, a researcher might want to know how many "things" a person can hold in memory at any one time. The other form of research is **applied research**, which is research aimed at answering real-world, practical problems. An applied researcher might take the information from the basic researcher's memory study and use it to develop a new study method for students. Some of the subfields in Figure 1.2b tend to do more basic research, such as experimental and cognitive psychologists, while others may focus more on applied research, such as educational, school, and industrial/organizational psychologists.

There are many other areas of specialization: Psychology can also be used in fields such as health, sports performance, legal issues, business concerns, and even in the design of equipment, tools, and furniture. For a more detailed look at some of these areas in which psychological principles can be applied and a listing of careers that can benefit from a degree in psychology, see Ⓛ Ⓘ Ⓝ Ⓚ to Appendix B: Applied Psychology and Psychology Careers.

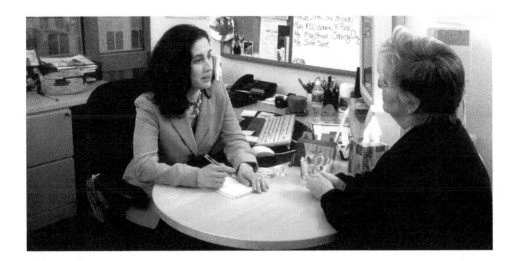

Psychiatric social workers help many kinds and ages of people. The woman on the right might be going through a divorce, dealing with the loss of a spouse, or even recovering from drug abuse.

Concept Map L.O. 1.4, 1.5

Interactive

Psychodynamic
based on Freud's theory — focuses on the role of the unconscious mind and its influence on conscious behavior, early childhood experiences, development of sense of self, and other motivations

Behavioral — focuses on how behavioral responses are learned through classical or operant conditioning
based on early work
of Watson and later B. F. Skinner

Humanistic — focuses on human potential, free will, and possibility of self-actualization
two pioneers are Carl Rogers
and Abraham Maslow

Cognitive — focuses on memory, intelligence, perception, thought processes, problem solving, language, and learning
has roots in
Gestalt psychology

Psychology Now: Modern Perspectives

(no one single perspective is used to explain all human behavior and processes)

Sociocultural — focuses on the behavior of individuals as the result of the presence (real or imagined) of other individuals, as part of groups, or as part of a larger culture

Biopsychological — focuses on influences of hormones, brain structures and chemicals, disease, etc.; human and animal behavior is seen as a direct result of events in the body

Evolutionary — focuses on the biological bases for universal mental characteristics, such as why we lie, how attractiveness influences mate selection, the universality of fear, and why we enjoy things like music and dance

Psychological Professionals and Areas of Specialization

(people working in the field of psychology have a variety of training experiences and different focuses)

psychologist

- has a doctorate degree (Ph.D., Psy.D., or Ed.D.) and works with either humans or animals in a variety of settings based on the area of specialization

- must be licensed to practice independently; typically does not prescribe medications but can go through specialized training to do so in a few states

psychiatrist

- medical doctor who specializes in diagnosis and treatment of psychological disorders; can prescribe medication

psychiatric social worker

- has training in area of social work (M.S.W.) and often has a professional license to practice (L.C.S.W.)

Reset

Practice Quiz   How much do you remember?   ANSWERS ON PAGE AK-1.

Pick the best answer.

1. Which of the following perspectives focuses on the biological bases of universal mental characteristics?

   a. humanistic   **c.** psychodynamic

   b. behaviorial   **d.** evolutionary

2. Which perspective offers the best explanation for schizophrenia?

   a. psychodynamic   **c.** biopsychological

   b. behaviorial   **d.** humanistic

3. Which perspective would a researcher be taking if she were studying a client's early childhood experiences and his resulting development of self?

   a. psychodynamic   **c.** behaviorial

   b. cognitive   **d.** evolutionary

4. Which of the following professionals in psychology has no medical training but has a doctoral degree?

   a. psychiatrist

   b. psychiatric nurse

   c. psychiatric social worker

   d. psychologist

5. If Dr. Swasey is like most psychologists, where does she probably work?

   a. university/college

   b. self-employed

   c. federal government

   d. state or local government

Scientific Research

Have you ever tried to guess what people do for a living based only on their appearance? People's guesses sometimes reveal the biases that they may have about certain physical appearances: Men with long hair are musicians, people wearing suits are executives, and so on. Psychology is about trying to determine facts and reduce uncertainty and bias.

THE SCIENTIFIC METHOD

1.6 **Explain why psychology is considered a science, and identify the steps of the scientific method.**

In psychology, researchers want to see only what is really there, not what their biases might want them to see. The way to do that is by using the **scientific method**, a system for reducing bias and error in the measurement of data. The scientific method is a way to accomplish the goals of psychology as discussed earlier: description, explanation, prediction, and control.

    The first step in any investigation is to have a question to investigate, right? So the first step in the scientific method is this:

1. **Perceiving the Question:** You notice something interesting happening in your surroundings for which you would like to have an explanation. An example might be that you've noticed that your children seem to get a little more aggressive with each other after watching a particularly violent children's cartoon program on Saturday morning. You wonder if the violence in the cartoon could be creating the aggressive behavior in your children. This step is derived from the goal of description: What is happening here?

      Once you have a question, you want an answer. The next logical step is to form a tentative* answer or explanation for the behavior you have seen. This tentative explanation is known as a **hypothesis**.

2. **Forming a Hypothesis:** Based on your initial observations about what's going on in your surroundings, you form an educated guess about the explanation for your observations, putting it into the form of a statement that can be tested in some way. Going back to the previous example, you might say, "Children who watch violent cartoons will become more aggressive." (Forming a hypothesis based on observations is related to the goals of *description* and *explanation*.)

The scientific method can be used to determine if children who watch violence on television are more likely to be aggressive than those who do not.

*tentative: something that is not fully worked out or completed as yet.

The next step is testing the hypothesis. People have a tendency to notice only things that agree with their view of the world, a kind of selective perception called *confirmation bias*. **L I N K** to Learning Objective 7.3. For example, if a person is convinced that all men with long hair smoke cigarettes, that person will tend to notice only those long-haired men who are smoking and ignore all the long-haired men who don't smoke. The scientific method is designed to overcome the tendency to look at only the information that confirms people's biases by forcing them to actively seek out information that might *contradict* their biases (or hypotheses). So when you test your hypothesis, you are trying to determine if the factor you suspect has an effect and that the results are not due to luck or chance. That's why psychologists keep doing research over and over—to get more evidence that hypotheses are "supported."

3. **Testing the Hypothesis:** The method you use to test your hypothesis will depend on exactly what kind of answer you think you might get. You might make more detailed observations or do a survey in which you ask questions of a large number of people, or you might design an experiment in which you would deliberately change one thing to see if it causes changes in the behavior you are observing. In the example, the best method would probably be an experiment in which you select a group of children, show half of them a cartoon with violence and half of them a cartoon with no violence, and then find some way of measuring aggressive behavior in the two groups.

   What do you do with the results of your testing? Of course, testing the hypothesis is all about the goal of understanding behavior, which leads to the next step.

4. **Drawing Conclusions:** Once you know the results of your hypothesis testing, you will find that either your hypothesis was supported—which means that your little experiment worked, or your measurements supported your initial observations—or it wasn't supported, which means that you need to go back to square one and think of another possible explanation for what you have observed. (Could it be that Saturday mornings make children a little more aggressive? Or Saturday breakfasts?)

   The results of any method of hypothesis testing won't be just the raw numbers or measurements. Any data that come from your testing procedure will be analyzed with some kind of statistical method that helps to organize and refine the data. **L I N K** to Appendix A: Statistics. Drawing conclusions can be related to the goal of *prediction*: If your hypothesis is supported, you can make educated guesses about future similar scenarios.

5. **Reporting Your Results:** You have come to some conclusion about your investigation's success or failure, and you want to let other researchers know what you have found.

  Why tell anyone what happened if it failed?

   Just because one experiment or other study did not find support for the hypothesis does not necessarily mean that the hypothesis is incorrect. Your study might have been poorly designed, or there might have been factors not under your control that interfered with the study. But other researchers are asking the same kinds of questions that you might have asked. They need to know what has already been found out about the answers to those questions so that they can continue investigating and adding more knowledge about the answers to those questions. Even if your own investigation didn't go as planned, that tells other researchers what *not* to do in the future. So the final step in any scientific investigation is reporting the results.

   At this point, you would want to write up exactly what you did, why you did it, how you did it, and what you found. If others can **replicate** your research (meaning, do exactly the same study over again and get the same results), it gives much more support to your findings. This allows others to predict behavior based on your findings and to use the results of those findings to modify or *control* behavior, the last goal in psychology.

This might be a good place to make a distinction between questions that can be scientifically or empirically studied and those that cannot. For example, "What is the meaning of life?" is not a question that can be studied using the scientific or empirical method. Empirical questions are those that can be tested through direct observation or experience. For example, "Has life ever existed on Mars?" is a question that scientists are trying to answer through measurements, experimentation, soil samples, and other methods. Eventually they will be able to say with some degree of confidence that life could have existed or could not have existed. That is an empirical question because it can be supported or disproved by gathering real evidence. The meaning of life, however, is a question of belief for each person. One does not need proof to *believe*, but scientists need proof (in the form of objectively gathered evidence) to *know*. Questions that involve beliefs and values are best left to philosophy and religion.

In psychology, researchers try to find the answers to empirical questions. They can use a variety of research methods depending on the scientific question to be answered as seen in the video *Research Methods*.

👁 **Watch** the **Video**, *Research Methods.*

DESCRIPTIVE METHODS

1.7 **Describe some methods used to describe behavior and summarize the main advantages and drawbacks of each.**

There are a number of different ways to investigate the answers to research questions, and which one researchers use depends on the kind of question they want to answer. If they want to simply gather information about what has happened or what is happening, they would want a method that gives them a detailed description.

NATURALISTIC OBSERVATION Sometimes all researchers need to know is what is happening to a group of animals or people. The best way to look at the behavior of animals or people is to watch them behave in their normal environment. That's why animal

This researcher is studying the behavior of a group of meerkats. Is this naturalistic observation? Why or why not?

researchers go to where the animals live and watch them eat, play, mate, and sleep in their own natural surroundings. With people, researchers might want to observe them in their workplaces, homes, or on playgrounds. For example, if someone wanted to know how adolescents behave with members of the opposite sex in a social setting, that researcher might go to the mall on a weekend night.

What is the advantage of naturalistic observation? It allows researchers to get a realistic picture of how behavior occurs because they are actually watching that behavior. In a more artificial setting, like a laboratory, they might get behavior that is contrived or artificial rather than genuine. Of course, precautions must be taken. An observer should have a checklist of well-defined and specific behavior to record, perhaps using a special handheld computer to log each piece of data. In many cases, animals or people who know they are being watched will not behave normally anyway, in a process called the **observer effect**, so often the observer needs to remain hidden from view. When researching humans, this is often a difficult thing to do. In the mall setting with the teenagers, a researcher might find that pretending to read a book is a good disguise, especially if one wears glasses to hide the movement of the eyes. Then the researchers would be able to look up at what goes on between the teens without them knowing that they were being watched. In other cases, researchers might use one-way mirrors, or they might actually become participants in a group, a technique called **participant observation**.

The researcher in the foreground is watching the children through a one-way mirror to get a description of their behavior. Observations such as these are just one of many ways that psychologists have of investigating behavior. Why is it important for the researcher to be behind a one-way mirror?

Are there disadvantages? Unfortunately, yes. One of the disadvantages of naturalistic observation is the possibility of **observer bias**. That happens when the person doing the observing has a particular opinion about what he or she is going to see or expects to see. If that is the case, sometimes that person sees only those actions that support that expectation and ignores actions that don't fit. For example, if you think girls initiate flirting, you might not see the boys who initiate flirting. One way to avoid observer bias is to use *blind observers*: people who do not know what the research question is and, therefore, have no preconceived notions about what they "should" see. It's also a good idea to have more than one observer so that the various observations can be compared.

Another disadvantage is that each naturalistic setting is unique and unlike any other. Observations that are made at one time in one setting may not hold true for another time, even if the setting is similar, because the conditions are not going to be exactly the same time after time—researchers don't have that kind of control over the natural world. For example, famed gorilla researcher Dian Fossey had to battle poachers who set traps for the animals in the area of her observations (Mowat, 1988). The presence and activities of the poachers affected the normal behavior of the gorillas she was trying to observe.

LABORATORY OBSERVATION Sometimes observing behavior in animals or people is simply not practical in a natural setting. For example, a researcher might want to observe the reactions of infants to a mirror image of themselves and record the reactions with a camera mounted behind the one-way mirror. That kind of equipment might be difficult to set up in a natural setting. In a laboratory observation, the researcher would bring the infant to the equipment, controlling the number of infants and their ages as well as everything else that goes on in the laboratory.

As mentioned previously, laboratory settings have the disadvantage of being an artificial situation that might result in artificial behavior—both animals and people often react differently in the laboratory than they would in the real world. The main advantage of this method is the degree of control that it gives to the observer.

Both naturalistic and laboratory observations can lead to the formation of hypotheses that can later be tested.

Phineas Gage survived a steel tamping rod going through his head after some explosive powder went off unexpectedly. The steel tamping rod entered above the left side of his mouth, passed through his left frontal lobe, and exited through the top of his skull.

CASE STUDIES Another descriptive technique is called the **case study**, in which one individual is studied in great detail. In a case study, researchers try to learn everything they can about that individual. For example, Sigmund Freud based his entire theory of psychoanalysis on numerous case studies of his patients in which he gathered information about their childhoods and relationships with others from the very beginning of their lives to the present. (L)(I)(N)(K) to Learning Objective 11.2.

The advantage of the case study is the tremendous amount of detail it provides. It may also be the only way to get certain kinds of information. One famous case study is that of Phineas Gage, who had a large metal rod driven through his head and survived, but experienced major personality and behavioral changes during the time immediately following the accident (Damasio et al., 1994; Ratiu et al., 2004; Van Horn et al., 2012). Researchers couldn't study such a case with naturalistic observation, and of course an experiment is out of the question—you wouldn't get many volunteers for brain damage. Case studies are also good ways to study rare conditions such as multiple personality (now called *dissociative identity disorder*). (L)(I)(N)(K) to Learning Objective 12.7.

The disadvantage of the case study is that researchers can't really apply the results to other similar people. In other words, they can't assume that a person having the same kind of experiences as the person in their case study would turn out just like the subject of the case study. People are unique and have too many complicating factors in their lives to be that predictable. So what researchers find in one case won't necessarily apply or generalize to other cases. Another weakness of this method is that case studies are a form of detailed observation and are vulnerable to bias on the part of the person conducting the case study, just as observer bias can occur in naturalistic or laboratory observation.

SURVEYS Sometimes psychologists want to know very personal things—such as what people do in their sexual relationships, for example. The only way to find out about very private (covert) behavior is to ask questions.

In the survey method, researchers will ask a series of questions about the topic they are studying. Surveys can be conducted in person in the form of interviews or on the telephone, the Internet, or with a questionnaire. The questions in interviews or on the telephone can vary, but usually the questions in a survey are all the same for everyone answering the survey. In this way, researchers can ask lots of questions and survey

Experiment PARTICIPATING IN A RESEARCH SURVEY

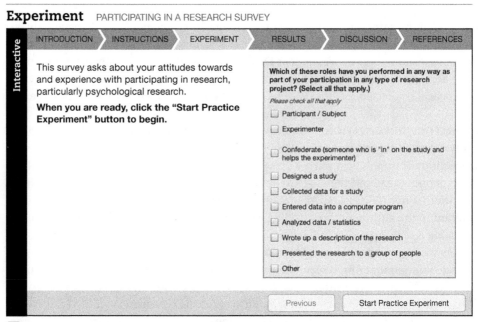

Simulate the **Experiment**, *Participating in a Research Survey*.

literally hundreds of people. To gain a better understanding of what it is like to complete a survey, try your hand at *Participating in a Research Survey.*

That is the big advantage of surveys, aside from their ability to elicit private information. Researchers can obtain a tremendous amount of data on a very large group of people. Of course, there are disadvantages. For one thing researchers have to be very careful about the group of people they survey. If they want to find out what college freshmen think about politics, for example, they can't really ask every single college freshman in the entire United States. But they can select a **representative sample** from that group. They can randomly* select a certain number of college freshmen from several different colleges across the United States, for example. Why randomly? Because the sample has to be *representative* of the **population**, which is the entire group in which the researcher is interested. If researchers selected only freshmen from Ivy League schools, for example, they would certainly get different opinions on politics than they might get from small community colleges. But if they take a lot of colleges and select their *participants* (people who are part of the study) randomly, they will be more certain of getting answers that a broad selection of college students would typically give.

That brings up the other major disadvantage of the survey technique: People don't always give researchers accurate answers. People tend to misremember things, distort the truth, and may lie outright—even if the survey is an anonymous* questionnaire. Remembering is not always a very accurate process, especially when people think that an honest answer might make them come off sounding undesirable or socially inappropriate. Other people deliberately give what they think is the more socially correct answer rather than their true opinion in order not to offend anyone; this process is called *courtesy bias.* Researchers must therefore take their survey results with a big grain of salt.*

Both the wording of survey questions and the order in which they appear on the survey can affect the outcome. It is difficult to word questions so that everyone who reads them will understand them in exactly the same way. For example, questions can be phrased in such a way that the desired answer becomes obvious (often resulting in courtesy bias–type answers). For example, "Do you agree that the new procedures for registering for classes are too complicated?" is obviously looking for a confirmation, while "What is your opinion of the new procedures for registering for classes?" is much more open to differing responses. Even the order of questions in a survey matters: A question about how much should be spent on public safety might have a very different answer at the beginning of a survey than after a long list of questions about crimes and criminal activity.

"Next question: I believe that life is a constant striving for balance, requiring frequent tradeoffs between morality and necessity, within a cyclic pattern of joy and sadness, forging a trail of bittersweet memories until one slips, inevitably, into the jaws of death. Agree or disagree?"

CORRELATIONS: FINDING RELATIONSHIPS

1.8 Explain the correlational technique and describe its usefulness to researchers.

The methods discussed so far only provide descriptions of behavior. Actually, only two methods give researchers more than just a description of what has happened: correlations and experiments. Correlation is a statistical technique, a particular way of organizing numerical information so that it is easier to look for patterns in the information. This method will be discussed here rather than in the statistics appendix found at the back of this text because correlation, like the experiment, is about finding relationships.

---

*randomly: in this sense, selected so that each member of the group has an equal chance of being chosen.

*anonymous: not named or identified.

*big grain of salt: a phrase meaning to be skeptical; to doubt the truth or accuracy of something.

In fact, the data from the descriptive methods just discussed are often analyzed using the correlational technique.

A **correlation** is a measure of the relationship between two or more variables. A *variable* is anything that can change or vary—scores on a test, temperature in a room, gender, and so on. For example, researchers might be curious to know whether or not cigarette smoking is connected to life expectancy—the number of years a person can be expected to live. Obviously, the scientists can't hang around people who smoke and wait to see when those people die. The only way (short of performing a really unethical and lengthy experiment) to find out if smoking behavior and life expectancy are related to each other is to use the medical records of people who have already died. (For privacy's sake, personal information such as names and social security numbers would be removed, with only facts such as age, gender, and weight available to researchers.) Researchers would look for two facts from each record: the number of cigarettes the person smoked per day and the age of the person at death.

Now the researcher has two sets of numbers for each person in the study that go into a mathematical formula, to produce a number called the **correlation coefficient**. The correlation coefficient represents two things: the direction of the relationship and its strength. (L)(I)(N)(K) to Learning Objective A.6

 💬 Direction? How can a mathematical relationship have a direction?

Whenever researchers talk about two variables being related to each other, what they really mean is that knowing the value of one variable allows them to predict the value of the other variable. For example, if researchers find that smoking and life expectancy are indeed related, they should be able to predict how long someone might live if they know how many cigarettes a person smokes in a day. But which way does that prediction work? If a person smokes a lot of cigarettes, does that mean that he or she will live a longer life or a shorter one? Does life expectancy go up or down as smoking increases? That's what is meant by the *direction* of the relationship.

In terms of the correlation coefficient (represented by the small letter r), the number researchers get from the formula will either be a positive number or a negative number. If positive, the two variables increase in the same direction—as one goes up, the other goes up; as one decreases, the other also decreases. If negative, the two variables have an inverse* relationship. As one increases, the other decreases. If researchers find that the more cigarettes a person smoked, the younger that person was when he or she died, that would mean that the correlation between the two variables is negative. (As smoking goes up, life expectancy goes down—an inverse relationship.)

The strength of the relationship between the variables will be determined by the actual number itself. That number will always range between +1.00 and −1.00. The reason that it cannot be greater than +1.00 or less than −1.00 has to do with the formula and an imaginary line on a graph around which the data points gather, a graph called a scatterplot (see **Figure 1.3**). If the relationship is a strong one, the number will be closer to +1.00 or to −1.00. A correlation of +.89, for example, would be a very strong, positive correlation. That might represent the relationship between scores on the SAT and an IQ test, for example. A correlation of −.89 would be equally strong but negative. That would be more

---

*inverse: opposite in order.

Figure 1.3 FIVE SCATTERPLOTS

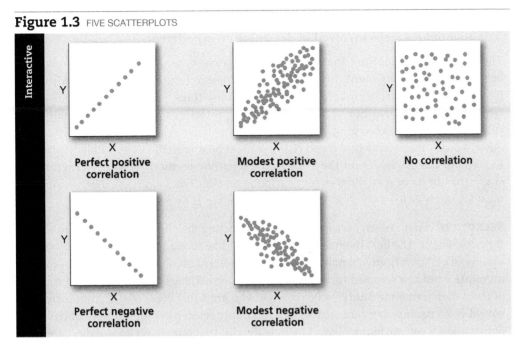

These scatterplots show direction and strength of correlation. It should be noted that perfect correlations, whether positive or negative, rarely occur in the real world.

like the correlation researchers would probably find between smoking cigarettes and the age at which a person dies.

Notice that the closer the number is to zero, the weaker the relationship becomes. Researchers would probably find that the correlation coefficient for the relationship between people's weight and the number of freckles they have is pretty close to zero, for example.

 💬 Go back to the cigarette example—if we found that the correlation between cigarette smoking and life expectancy was high, does that mean that smoking causes your life expectancy to be shortened?

Not exactly. The biggest error that people make concerning correlation is to assume that it means one variable is the cause of the other. Remember that *correlation does not prove causation*. Although adverse health effects from cigarette smoking account for approximately 438,000 deaths each year in the United States alone, correlation by itself cannot be used to prove causation (Centers for Disease Control and Prevention, 2009b). Just because two variables are related to each other, researchers cannot assume that one of them causes the other one to occur. Both variables could be related to some other variable that is the cause of both. For example, cigarette smoking and life expectancy might be linked only because people who smoke may be less likely to take care of their health by eating right and exercising, whereas people who don't smoke may tend to eat healthier foods and exercise more than smokers do.

To sum up, a correlation will tell researchers whether there is a relationship between the variables, how strong the relationship is, and in what direction the relationship goes. If researchers know the value of one variable, they can predict the value of the other. If they know someone's IQ score, for example, they can predict what score that person should get on the SAT—not the exact score, just a reasonable estimate. Also, even though correlation does not prove causation, it can provide a starting point for examining causal relationships with another type of study, the experiment.

1.9 **Identify the steps involved in designing an experiment.**

The only research method that will allow researchers to determine the cause of a behavior is the **experiment**. In an experiment, researchers deliberately manipulate (change in some purposeful way) the variable they think is causing some behavior while holding all the other variables that might interfere with the experiment's results constant and unchanging. That way, if they get changes in behavior (an effect, in other words), they know that those changes must be due to the manipulated variable. Remember the discussion of the steps in the scientific method? It focused on how to study the effects of watching violent cartoons on children's aggressive behavior. The most logical way to study that particular relationship is by an experiment.

SELECTION   First, researchers might start by selecting the children they want to use in the experiment. The best method to do that would be to make a random selection of a sample of children from a certain population as determined by the researchers—just as a sample would be selected for a survey. Ideally, researchers would decide on the age of child they wanted to study—say, children who are 3 to 4 years old. Then researchers would go to various day care centers and randomly select a certain number of children of that age. Of course, that wouldn't include the children who don't go to a day care center. Another way to get a sample in this age range might be to ask several pediatricians to send out letters to parents of children of that age and then randomly select the sample from those children whose parents responded positively.

THE VARIABLES   Another important step is to decide on the variable the researchers want to manipulate (which would be the one they think causes changes in behavior) and the variable they want to measure to see if there are any changes (this would be the effect on behavior of the manipulation). Often the decision on the variables in the experiment comes before selection of the participants or subjects.

In the example of aggression and children's cartoons, the variable that researchers think causes changes in aggressive behavior is the violence in the cartoons. Researchers would want to manipulate that variable in some way, and in order to do that they have to define the term *violent cartoon*. They would have to find or create a cartoon that contains violence. Then they would show that cartoon to the participants and try to measure their aggressive behavior afterward. In measuring the aggressive behavior, the researchers would have to define exactly what they mean by "aggressive behavior" so that it can be measured. This definition is called an **operational definition** because it specifically names the operations (steps or procedures) that the experimenter must use to control or measure the variables in the experiment. An operational definition of aggressive behavior might be a checklist of very specific actions such as hitting and pushing that

The act of hitting each other with toy swords could be part of an operational definition of aggressive behavior.

an observer can mark off as the children do the items on the list. If the observers were just told to look for "aggressive behavior," the researchers would probably get half a dozen or more different interpretations of what aggressive behavior is.

The name for the variable that is manipulated in any experiment is the **independent variable** because it is *independent* of anything the participants do. The participants in the study do not get to choose or vary the independent variable, and their behavior does not affect this variable at all. In the preceding example, the independent variable would be the presence or absence of violence in the cartoons.

The participants' response to the manipulation of the independent variable *is* a dependent relationship, so the response of the participants that is measured is known as the **dependent variable**. Their behavior, if the hypothesis is correct, should *depend* on whether or not they were exposed to the independent variable, and in the example, the dependent variable would be the measure of aggressive behavior in the children. The dependent variable is always the thing (response of subjects or result of some action) that is measured to see just how the independent variable may have affected it.

THE GROUPS

 💬 If researchers do all of this and find that the children's behavior is aggressive, can they say that the aggressive behavior was caused by the violence in the cartoon?

No, what has been described so far is not enough. The researchers may find that the children who watch the violent cartoon are aggressive, but how would they know if their aggressive behavior was caused by the cartoon or was just the natural aggressive level of those particular children or the result of the particular time of day they were observed? Those sorts of *confounding variables* (variables that interfere with each other and their possible effects on some other variable of interest) are the kind researchers have to control for in some way. For example, if most children in this experiment just happened to be from a fairly aggressive family background, any effects the violent cartoon in the experiment might have had on the children's behavior could be confused (confounded) with the possible effects of the family background. The researchers wouldn't know if the children were being aggressive because they watched the cartoon or because they liked to play aggressively anyway.

The best way to control for confounding variables is to have two groups of participants: those who watch the violent cartoon, and those who watch a nonviolent cartoon for the same length of time. Then the researchers would measure the aggressive behavior in both groups. If the aggressive behavior is significantly greater in the group that watched the violent cartoon (statistically speaking), then researchers can say that in this experiment, violent cartoon watching caused greater aggressive behavior.

The group that is exposed to the independent variable (the violent cartoon in the example) is called the **experimental group**, because it is the group that receives the experimental manipulation. The other group that gets either no treatment or some kind of treatment that should have no effect (like the group that watches the nonviolent cartoon in the example) is called the **control group** because it is used to *control* for the possibility that other factors might be causing the effect that is being examined. If researchers were to find that the group that watched the violent cartoon and the group that watched the nonviolent cartoon were equally aggressive, they would have to assume that the violent content did not influence their behavior at all.

THE IMPORTANCE OF RANDOMIZATION   As mentioned previously, random selection is the best way to choose the participants for any study. Participants must then be assigned to either the experimental group or the control group. Not surprisingly, **random assignment** of participants to one or the other condition is the best way to ensure control over other interfering, or *extraneous*, variables. Random assignment means that each participant has an equal chance of being assigned to each condition. If researchers simply looked at the children and put all of the children from one day care center or one pediatrician's recommendations into the experimental group and the same for the control group, they would run the risk of biasing their research. Some day care centers may have more naturally aggressive children, for example, or some pediatricians may have a particular client base in which the children are very passive. So researchers want to take the entire participant group and assign each person randomly to one or the other of the groups in the study. Sometimes this process is as simple as picking names out of a hat.

To see how these pieces all fit together to form an experiment, watch the video *A Sample Experiment.*

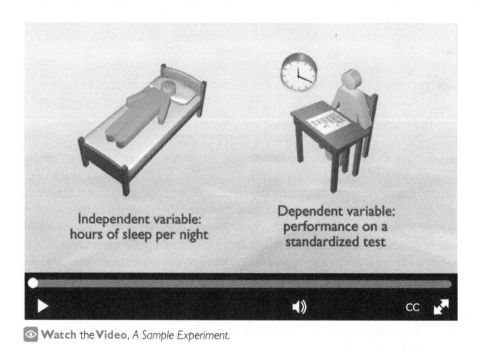

Independent variable: hours of sleep per night

Dependent variable: performance on a standardized test

👁 **Watch** the **Video**, *A Sample Experiment.*

EXPERIMENTAL HAZARDS AND CONTROLLING FOR EFFECTS

1.10 **Identify two common sources of problems in an experiment, and list some ways to control for these effects.**

A few other problems might arise in any experiment, even with the use of control groups and random assignment. These problems are especially likely when studying people instead of animals, because people are often influenced by their own thoughts or biases about what's going on in an experiment.

THE PLACEBO EFFECT AND THE EXPERIMENTER EFFECT   Let's say there is a new drug that is supposed to improve memory in people who are in the very early stages of Alzheimer's disease (a form of mental deterioration that occurs in some people as they grow old). ⓛ ⓘ ⓝ ⓚ to Learning Objective 6.14. Researchers wanting to test the drug to see if it really is effective in helping to improve memory would get a sample of people who are in the early stages of the disease, divide them into two groups, give one group the drug, and then test for improvement. They would probably have to do a test of memory both before and after the administration of the drug to be able to measure improvement.

 💬 Let me see if I've got this straight. The group that gets the drug would be the experimental group, and the one that doesn't is the control group, right?

Right, and getting or not getting the drug is the independent variable, whereas the measure of memory improvement is the dependent variable. But there's still a problem with doing it this way. What if the researchers do find that the drug group had greater memory improvement than the group that received nothing? Can they really say that the drug itself caused the improvement? Or is it possible that the participants who received the drug *knew* that they were supposed to improve in memory and, therefore, made a major effort to do so? The improvement may have had more

to do with participants' *belief* in the drug than the drug itself, a phenomenon*
known as the **placebo effect**: The expectations and biases of the participants
in a study can influence their behavior. In medical research, the control group
is often given a harmless substitute for the real drug, such as a sugar pill or
an injection of salt water, and this substitute (which has no medical effect)
is called the *placebo*. If there is a placebo effect, the control group will show
changes in the dependent variable even though the participants in that group
received only a placebo.

Another way that expectations about the outcome of the experiment can
influence the results, even when the participants are animals rather than people,
is called the **experimenter effect**. It has to do with the expectations of the experimenter, not the participants. As discussed earlier in the section about naturalistic
observations, sometimes observers are biased—they see what they expect to see. Observer
bias can also happen in an experiment. When the researcher is measuring the dependent
variable, it's possible that he or she could give the participants clues about how they are
supposed to respond—with body language, tone of voice, or even eye contact. Although
not deliberate, it does happen. It could go something like this in the example: You, the
Alzheimer's patient, are in the experimenter's office to take your second memory test
after trying the drug. The experimenter seems to pay a lot of attention to you and to every
answer that you give in the test, so you get the feeling that you are supposed to have improved a lot. So you try harder, and any improvement you show may be caused only by
your own increased effort, not by the drug. That's the experimenter effect: The behavior of
the experimenter caused the participant to change his or her response pattern.

This elderly woman has Alzheimer's
disease, which causes a severe loss of
recent memory. If she were given a new
drug in the very early stages of her disease,
in the attempt to improve her memory,
the researcher could not be certain that
any improvement shown was caused
by the drug rather than by the elderly
woman's belief that the drug would work.
The expectations of any person in an
experimental study can affect the outcome
of the study, a phenomenon known as the
placebo effect.

CONTROLLING FOR EFFECTS: SINGLE-BLIND AND DOUBLE-BLIND STUDIES Fortunately, there are ways to control for these effects. The classic way to control for the placebo effect is to give the control group an actual placebo—some kind of treatment that
doesn't affect behavior at all. In the drug experiment, the placebo would have to be some
kind of pill or solution that looks like and is administered just like the actual drug. The
participants in both the experimental and the control groups would not know whether
they got the real drug or the placebo. That way, if their expectations have any effect at
all on the outcome of the experiment, the experimenter will be able to tell by looking at
the results for the control group and comparing them to the results of the experimental
group. Even if the control group improves a little, the drug group should improve significantly more if the drug is working. This is called a **single-blind study** because the
participants are "blind" to the treatment they receive.

For a long time, that was the only type of experiment researchers did in psychology. But researchers Robert Rosenthal and Lenore Jacobson reported in their 1968
book, *Pygmalion in the Classroom*, that when teachers were told that some students
had a high potential for success and others a low potential, the students showed significant gains or decreases in their performance on standardized tests depending on
which "potential" they were supposed to have (Rosenthal & Jacobson, 1968). Actually, the students had been selected randomly and randomly assigned to one of the
two groups, "high" or "low." Their performances on the tests were affected by the
attitudes of the teachers concerning their potential. This study and similar studies
after it highlighted the need to have the experimenter as well as the participants in
research be "blind." So in a **double-blind study** neither the participants nor the person or persons measuring the dependent variable know who got what. That's why
everything in a double-blind experiment gets coded in some way, so that only after
all the measurements have been taken can anyone determine who was in the experimental group and who was in the control group.

---

*phenomenon: an observable fact or event.

1.11 Identify ethical concerns that can occur when conducting research with people and animals.

 ● The study that Dr. Watson did with "Little Albert" and the white rat seems pretty cruel when you think about it. Do researchers today do that kind of study?

Actually, as psychology began to grow and more research with people was being done, psychologists began to realize that some protections had to be put in place. No one wanted to be thought of as a "mad scientist," and if studies were permitted that could actually harm people, the field of psychology might die out pretty quickly. Ⓛ Ⓘ Ⓝ Ⓚ to Learning Objectives 5.3 and 10.3. Scientists in other areas of research were also realizing that ethical treatment of the participants in studies had to be ensured in some way. Ethical treatment, of course, means that people who volunteer for a study will be able to expect that no physical or psychological harm should come to them. The video *Ethical Guidelines for Research* explains how researchers in the field of psychology draw the line between what is ethical and what is not and explains some of the safeguards in place today.

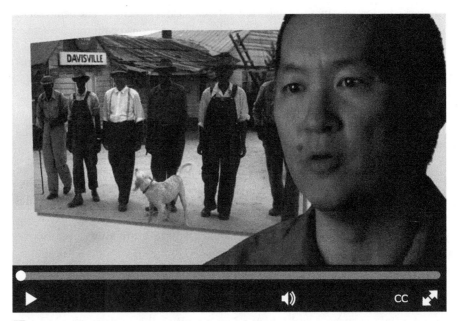

⊙ **Watch** the **Video**, *Ethical Guidelines for Research.*

Universities and colleges (where most psychological research is carried out) usually have *institutional review boards*, groups of psychologists or other professionals who look over each proposed research study and judge it according to its safety and consideration for the participants in the study. These review boards look at all aspects of the proposed research, from the written materials that explain the research to the potential subjects to the equipment that may be used in the study itself.

THE GUIDELINES FOR DOING RESEARCH WITH PEOPLE   Quite a few ethical concerns arise when dealing with human subjects in an experiment or other type of study. Here is a list of the most common ethical guidelines:

1. **Rights and well-being of participants must be weighed against the study's value to science.** In other words, people come first, research second.

2. **Participants must be allowed to make an informed decision about participation.** This means that researchers have to explain the study to the people they want to include before they do anything to them or with them—even children—and it has to be in terms that the participants can understand. If researchers are using infants or children, their parents have to be informed and give their consent. This is known as *informed consent*. Even in single- or double-blind studies, it is necessary to tell the participants that they may be members of either the experimental or the control group—they just won't find out which group they were actually in until after the experiment is concluded.

3. **Deception must be justified.** In some cases, it is necessary to deceive the participants because the study wouldn't work any other way. However, the participants have to be told after the study exactly why the deception was important. This is called *debriefing*.

4. **Participants may withdraw from the study at any time.** The participants must be allowed to drop out for any reason. For example, sometimes people get bored with the study, decide they don't have the time, or don't like what they have to do. Children participating in studies often decide to stop "playing" (play is a common part of studies of children). Researchers have to let them go, even if it means having to get more participants.

5. **Participants must be protected from risks or told explicitly of risks.** For example, if researchers are using any kind of electrical equipment, care must be taken to ensure that no participant will experience a physical shock from faulty electrical equipment.

6. **Investigators must debrief participants, telling the true nature of the study and expectations of results.** This is important in all types of studies but particularly in those involving a deception.

7. **Data must remain confidential.** Freud recognized the importance of confidentiality, referring to his patients in his books and articles with false names. Likewise, psychologists and other researchers today tend to report only group results rather than results for a single individual so that no one could possibly be recognized.

8. **If for any reason a study results in undesirable consequences for the participant, the researcher is responsible for detecting and removing, or correcting, these consequences.** Sometimes people react in unexpected ways to the manipulations in an experiment, despite the researcher's best efforts to prevent any negative impact on participants. If this happens, the researcher must find some way of helping the participant overcome that impact (American Psychological Association, 2002).

"He says he wants a lawyer."

WRITING PROMPT

You are testing a new drug to treat a serious, often fatal medical condition. Before your experiment is over, it becomes obvious that the drug is working so well that the people in the experimental group are going to recover completely. Should you stop the experiment to give the drug to the people in the control group?

▶ | The response entered here will be saved to your notes and may be collected by your instructor if he/she requires it.

    Submit

ANIMAL RESEARCH Psychologists also study animals to find out about behavior, often drawing comparisons between what the animals do and what people might do under similar conditions.

💬 But why not just study people in the first place?

Some research questions are extremely important but difficult or impossible to answer by using human participants. Animals live shorter lives, so looking at long-term effects becomes much easier. Animals are also easier to control—the scientist can control diet, living arrangements, and even genetic relatedness. The white laboratory rat has become a recognized species different from ordinary rats, bred with its own kind for many decades until each white rat is essentially a little genetic "twin" of all the others. Animals also engage in much simpler behavior than humans do, making it easier to see the effects of manipulations. But the biggest reason that researchers use animals in some research is that animals can be used in ways that researchers could never use people. For example, it took a long time for scientists to prove that the tars and other harmful substances in tobacco cause cancer because they had to do correlational studies with people and experiments only with animals. There's the catch—researchers can do many things to animals that they can't do to people. That might seem cruel at first, but when you think that without animal research there would be no vaccines for deadly diseases, no insulin treatments for diabetics, no transplants, and so on, then the value of the research and its benefits to humankind far outweigh the hazards to which the research animals are exposed. Still, some animal rights activists disagree with this point of view.

There are also ethical considerations when dealing with animals in research, just as there are with humans. With animals, though, the focus is on avoiding exposing them to any *unnecessary* pain or suffering. So if surgery is part of the study, it is done under anesthesia. If the research animal must die in order for the effects of some drug or other treatment to be examined in necropsy (autopsy performed on an animal), the death must be accomplished humanely. Animals are used in only about 7 percent of all psychological studies (Committee on Animal Research and Ethics, 2004).

Concept Map L.O. 1.6, 1.7, 1.8, 1.9, 1.10, 1.11

Interactive

scientific method
- perceiving the question about some empirical event for which you would like an explanation; can be derived from the goal of description: What is happening here?
- forming a hypothesis, a tentative explanation about an event
- testing the hypothesis by collecting data, analyzing results
- drawing conclusions about investigation's success or failure to explain event
- reporting your results: share exactly what, why, and how you did it, which provides means for replication

Psychology: The Scientific Methodology
(psychology uses the scientific method to try to determine facts and reduce uncertainty)

descriptive data collection methods
- **naturalistic observation:** observe people or animals in natural environment ◄----
- **laboratory observation:** observe people or animals in laboratory setting ◄----
- **case studies:** individual is studied in greater detail, researchers try to learn everything they can about the individual
- **surveys:** ask questions about topic researchers are studying via telephone, Internet, or a questionnaire

> can lead to formation of hypotheses that can later be tested

Correlations
- is a measure of relationship between two or more variables (anything that can change or vary)
- produces a value called the *correlation coefficient* that represents both direction and strength of relationship
- does not prove causation—variables can be related but you can not assume that one of them causes the other to occur

Experiments
(the only research method that will allow researchers to determine the cause of a behavior by deliberately manipulating some variable and measuring changes in the variable of interest)

- **operational definition** specifically names the steps or procedures used to control or measure the variable in the experiment
  - independent variable is the variable that is manipulated, it is independent of anything participants do
  - dependent variable is the measure used to evaluate the manipulation of the independent variable

- **groups**
  - **experimental:** gets the independent variable or experimental manipulation
  - **control:** receives no treatment or treatment that should not have an effect
    - random assignment to conditions is the best way to assure control over extraneous variables or confounding variables, variables that interfere with each other, and/or on the variable of interest

- **hazards**
  - **placebo effect:** beliefs or expectations about a study can influence their behavior
  - **experimenter effect:** experimenter's biases can affect or influence participants' behavior
    - can be controlled through single-blind (participant "blind" to treatment/condition) and double-blind studies where the experimenter measuring the dependent variable does not know the treatment/condition associated with the data

guidelines for research with humans
- rights and well-being of participants must be weighed against the study's value to science
- participants must be allowed to make an informed decision about participating (informed consent)
- deception must be justified
- participants may withdraw from the study at any time
- participants must be protected from risks or told explicitly of risks
- investigator must debrief participants, telling the true nature of the study and expectations of results
- data must remain confidential

Ethics of Psychological Research
(psychological scientists have a primary goal of protecting the health and welfare of their animal or human participants)

research with animals
- any animal research is also covered by ethical considerations; primary focus is on avoiding any unnecessary pain or suffering
- why use animals?
  - some research questions are important but can be difficult or dangerous to answer with human participants
  - animals are easier to control
  - animals have shorter lives; easier to study long-term effects

Reset

Practice Quiz   How much do you remember?   ANSWERS ON PAGE AK-1.

Pick the best answer.

1. In the scientific method, the final step is
   a. reporting your results.
   b. perceiving a question.
   c. drawing conclusions.
   d. testing the hypothesis.

2. Which of the following is an example of observer bias?
   a. You ask your fellow students to be participants in a study of adult memory.
   b. You ask people from your church to participate in a study of family values.
   c. You develop an opinion of what you expect to see in an experiment.
   d. You allow a student to quit an experiment simply because he or she is bored.

3. The main advantage of a survey is that
   a. only a small number of subjects need to be accessed.
   b. a large amount of data can be gathered.
   c. the chance of experimenter error is removed.
   d. subjects will not know if they are part of a control or experimental group.

4. Which of the following would indicate the weakest relationship and thus be close to complete randomness?
   a. +1.04
   b. −0.89
   c. +0.01
   d. −0.98

5. In an experiment to examine the effects of sleep deprivation on completion of a puzzle, one group is allowed to sleep eight hours while another group is made to stay awake. In this experiment, the control group is
   a. the group that gets to sleep.
   b. the group that remains awake.
   c. the puzzle.
   d. the difference in time for each group to complete the puzzle.

6. In a _____ study, the participants do not know if they are part of the control group or the experimental group. Only the experimenter knows who is in each group.
   a. placebo
   b. single-blind
   c. double-blind
   d. triple-blind

7. What is the first guideline for doing research with people?
   a. Participants have to give informed consent.
   b. Deception cannot be used in any studies with human beings.
   c. The rights and well-being of the participants must come first.
   d. Data must remain confidential.

Applying Psychology to Everyday Life
Thinking Critically about Critical Thinking

1.12 **Summarize the basic principles of critical thinking, and explain how it is useful in everyday life.**

💬 What good is all this focus on science and research going to do for me? I live in the real world, not a laboratory.

The real world is full of opportunities for scientific thinking. Think about all the commercials on television for miracle weight loss, hair restoration, or herbal remedies for arthritis, depression, and a whole host of physical and mental problems. Wouldn't it be nice to know how many of these claims people should believe? Wouldn't you like to know how to evaluate statements like these and possibly save yourself some time, effort, and money? That's exactly the kind of "real-world" problem critical thinking can help sort out.

According to Beyer (1995), **critical thinking** means making reasoned judgments. The word *reasoned* means that people's judgments should be logical and well thought out. Critical thinking also includes the ability to ask and seek answers for critical questions at the right time (Browne & Keeley, 2009). (A relevant example of a critical question might be, "Is someone paying you to do this research, and is this a conflict of interest?" or "Do you have any good evidence for your assertions, or are you just giving your opinion?")

While the word *critical* is often viewed as meaning "negative," that is not the use of this term here. Instead, it's more related to the word *criteria*,* as in thinking that meets certain

*criteria: standards on which a judgment or decision may be based.

high criteria or standards (Nosich, 2008). People should remember four basic criteria for critical thinking when they are faced with statements about the world around them (Browne & Keeley, 2009; Gill, 1991; Shore, 1990):

1. **There are very few "truths" that do not need to be subjected to testing.** Although people may accept religious beliefs and personal values on faith, everything else in life needs to have supporting evidence. Questions that can be investigated empirically should be examined using established scientific methods. One shouldn't accept anything at face value but should always ask, "How do you know that? What is the evidence? Can you be more specific in your terms?" (These are more examples of those important questions to ask when thinking critically.) For example, many people still believe that astrology, the study of the supposed influence of the stars and planets on the birth of an infant, can be used to make predictions about that infant's personality and life events as he or she grows. But scientific investigations have shown us, time after time, that astrology is without any basis in truth or scientific fact (Ben-Shakhar et al., 1986; Bunge, 1984; Dean et al., 1992; Dean & Kelly, 2000; Hines, 2003; Kelly, 1980; Wiseman, 2007).

2. **All evidence is not equal in quality.** One of the most important, often overlooked steps in critical thinking is evaluating how evidence is gathered before deciding that it provides good support for some idea. For example, there are poorly done experiments, incorrect assumptions based on correlations rather than experiments, studies that cannot be replicated, and studies in which there is either no control group or no attempt made to control for placebo effects or experimenter effects. There are also studies that have been deliberately manipulated to produce the findings that the researcher (or whoever is paying the researcher) would prefer. For example, the results of a study on the effectiveness of a particular drug would be immediately suspect if the researcher is being paid by the company making the drug. As a critical thinker you should be aware that the wilder the claim, the better the evidence should be: For example, I have not yet seen any evidence that convinces me of alien visitations or abductions!

3. **Just because someone is considered to be an authority or to have a lot of expertise does not make everything that person claims automatically true.** One should always ask to see the evidence rather than just take some expert's word for anything. How good is the evidence? Are there other alternative explanations? Is the alternative explanation simpler? If there are two explanations for some phenomenon and both account for the phenomenon equally well, the *simplest* explanation is *more often* the best one—a rule of thumb known as *the law of parsimony*). For example, let's look at crop circles, those geometric patterns of flattened crop stalks that have at times been discovered in farmers' fields. Two possible explanations for crop circles exist: Either they are made by aliens in space ships—as is the claim by many alleged experts—or they are made by human beings as a hoax*. Which explanation is simpler? Obviously, the hoax rationalization is the simplest, and it turned out to be correct for the crop circles that appeared in England in the late 1970s and 1980s. David Bower and Doug Chorley, two British men, confessed to creating the crop circles as a prank, thought up in a barroom and meant to make fun of people who believe in alien visitations (Nickell, 1995; M. Ridley, 2002; Schnabel, 1994).

4. **Critical thinking requires an open mind.** Although it is good to be a little skeptical, people should not close their minds to things that are truly possible. At the same time, it's good for people to have open minds but not so open that they are gullible* and apt to believe anything. Critical thinking requires a delicate balance between skepticism and willingness to consider possibilities—even possibilities that contradict previous

Many people believe that crop circles are created by alien visitors, despite clear evidence that crop circles are hoaxes created by ordinary people.

*hoax: something intended to fool people, a trick or lie.
*gullible: easily fooled or cheated.

judgments or beliefs. For example, scientists have yet to find any convincing evidence that there was once life on Mars. That doesn't mean that scientists totally dismiss the idea, just that there is no convincing evidence *yet*. I don't believe that there are Martians on Mars, but if I were shown convincing evidence, I would have to be willing to change my thinking—as difficult as that might be.

Questions for Further Discussion

1. How might critical thinking be applied to the issue of global climate change?
2. Why do you think some people (even very smart people) sometimes avoid thinking critically about issues such as politics, the existence of ESP, or the supernatural?

Chapter Summary

What Is Psychology?

1.1 Define psychology as a field of study, and identify psychology's four primary goals.

- Psychology is the scientific study of behavior and mental processes.
- The four goals of psychology are description, explanation, prediction, and control.

Psychology Then: The History of Psychology

1.2 Identify some of the early pioneers in psychology, and differentiate between structuralism and functionalism.

- In 1879 psychology began as a science of its own in Germany with the establishment of Wundt's psychology laboratory. He developed the technique of objective introspection.
- Titchener, a student of Wundt, brought psychology in the form of structuralism to America. Structuralism died out in the early twentieth century. Margaret F. Washburn, Titchener's student, was the first woman to receive a Ph.D. in psychology in 1894 and published *The Animal Mind*.
- William James proposed a countering point of view called functionalism, which stressed the way the mind allows us to adapt.
- Many of psychology's early pioneers were minorities such as the African Americans who, despite prejudice and racism, made important contributions to the study of human and animal behavior.
- Functionalism influenced the modern fields of educational psychology, evolutionary psychology, and industrial/organizational psychology.

1.3 Describe the basic ideas and important people behind the early approaches known as Gestalt, psychoanalysis, and behaviorism.

- Wertheimer and others studied sensation and perception, calling the new perspective Gestalt (an organized whole) psychology.

- Freud proposed that the unconscious mind controls much of our conscious behavior in his theory of psychoanalysis.
- Watson proposed a science of behavior called behaviorism, which focused only on the study of observable stimuli and responses.
- Watson and Rayner demonstrated that a phobia could be learned by conditioning a baby to be afraid of a white rat.
- Mary Cover Jones, one of Watson's more famous students in behaviorism and child development, later demonstrated that a learned phobia could be counterconditioned.

Psychology Now: Where We Are Today

1.4 Summarize the seven modern perspectives, and identify the important contributions of Skinner, Maslow, and Rogers.

- Modern Freudians such as Anna Freud, Jung, and Adler changed the emphasis in Freud's original theory into a kind of neo-Freudianism.
- Skinner's operant conditioning of voluntary behavior became a major force in the twentieth century. He introduced the concept of reinforcement to behaviorism.
- Humanism, which focuses on free will and the human potential for growth, was developed by Maslow and Rogers, among others, as a reaction to the deterministic nature of behaviorism and psychoanalysis.
- Cognitive psychology is the study of learning, memory, language, and problem solving, and includes the field of cognitive neuroscience.
- Biopsychology emerged as the study of the biological bases of behavior, such as hormones, heredity, chemicals in the nervous system, structural defects in the brain, and the effects of physical diseases.
- The principles of evolution and the knowledge we currently have about evolution are used in this perspective to look at the way the mind works and why it works as it does. Behavior is seen as having an adaptive or survival value.

1.5 **Differentiate between a psychologist and a psychiatrist, and describe the other types of professionals who work in the various areas of psychology.**

- Psychologists have academic degrees and can do counseling, teaching, and research and may specialize in any one of a large number of areas within psychology.
- There are many different areas of specialization in psychology, including clinical, counseling, developmental, social, and personality as areas of work or study.
- Psychiatrists are medical doctors who provide diagnosis and therapy for persons with mental disorders.
- Psychiatric social workers are social workers with special training in the influences of the environment on mental illness.

Scientific Research

1.6 **Explain why psychology is considered a science, and identify the steps of the scientific method.**

- The scientific method is a way to determine facts and control the possibilities of error and bias when observing behavior. The five steps are perceiving the question, forming a hypothesis, testing the hypothesis, drawing conclusions, and reporting the results.

1.7 **Describe some methods used to describe behavior, and summarize the main advantages and drawbacks of each.**

- Naturalistic observations involve watching animals or people in their natural environments but have the disadvantage of lack of control.
- Laboratory observations involve watching animals or people in an artificial but controlled situation, such as a laboratory.
- Case studies are detailed investigations of one subject, whereas surveys involve asking standardized questions of large groups of people that represent a sample of the population of interest.
- Information gained from case studies cannot be applied to other cases. People responding to surveys may not always tell the truth or remember information correctly.

1.8 **Explain the correlational technique and describe its usefulness to reasearchers.**

- Correlation is a statistical technique that allows researchers to discover and predict relationships between variables of interest.
- Positive correlations exist when increases in one variable are matched by increases in the other variable, whereas negative correlations exist when increases in one variable are matched by decreases in the other variable.
- Correlations cannot be used to prove cause-and-effect relationships.

1.9 **Identify the steps involved in designing an experiment.**

- Experiments are tightly controlled manipulations of variables that allow researchers to determine cause-and-effect relationships.
- The independent variable in an experiment is the variable that is deliberately manipulated by the experimenter to see if related changes occur in the behavior or responses of the participants and is given to the experimental group.
- The dependent variable in an experiment is the measured behavior or responses of the participants.
- The control group receives either a placebo treatment or nothing.
- Random assignment of participants to experimental groups helps to control for individual differences both within and between the groups that might otherwise interfere with the experiment's outcome.

1.10 **Identify two common sources of problems in an experiment, and list some ways to control for these effects.**

- Experiments in which the subjects do not know if they are in the experimental or control groups are single-blind studies, whereas experiments in which neither the experimenters nor the subjects know this information are called double-blind studies.

1.11 **Identify ethical concerns that can occur when conducting research with people and animals.**

- Ethical guidelines for doing research with human beings include the protection of rights and well-being of participants, informed consent, justification when deception is used, the right of participants to withdraw at any time, protection of participants from physical or psychological harm, confidentiality, and debriefing of participants at the end of the study. Researchers are also responsible for correcting any undesirable consequences that may result from the study.
- Animals in psychological research make useful models because they are easier to control than humans, they have simpler behavior, and they can be used in ways that are not permissible with humans.

Applying Psychology to Everyday Life: Thinking Critically About Critical Thinking

1.12 **Summarize the basic principles of critical thinking, and explain how it is useful in everyday life.**

- Critical thinking is the ability to make reasoned judgments. The four basic criteria of critical thinking are that there are few concepts that do not need to be tested, evidence can vary in quality, claims by experts and authorities do not automatically make something true, and keeping an open mind is important.

Test Yourself ANSWERS ON PAGE AK-1

Pick the best answer.

1. In the definition of psychology, the term *behavior* means
   a. internal, covert processes.
   b. outward behavior.
   c. overt actions and reactions.
   d. only animal behavior.

2. A psychologist is interested in finding out why married couples seemingly begin to look like each other after several years of marriage. This psychologist is most interested in the goal of
   a. description.   **c.** prediction.
   b. explanation.   **d.** control.

3. Who is considered to be the father of African American psychology?
   a. Charles Henry Thompson
   b. Robert V. Guthrie
   c. Francis Cecil Sumner
   d. Howard Hale Long

4. Sigmund Freud's psychoanalysis focused on
   a. observable behavior.
   b. Gestalt perceptions.
   c. introspection.
   d. early childhood experiences.

5. Which psychologist dared to ignore the whole consciousness issue and return to a study of scientific inquiry by focusing on observable behavior?
   a. Ivan Pavlov
   b. John Watson
   c. Sigmund Freud
   d. William James

6. Which perspective is often referred to as the "third force" in psychology and focuses on a person's freedom of choice in determining their behavior?
   a. biopsychological perspective
   b. behaviorism
   c. cognitive psychology
   d. humanism

7. Which perspective best explains the bystander effect whereby individuals will be less likely to help someone in need because of the presence of others close by?
   a. psychoanalysis
   b. behaviorism
   c. cognitive psychology
   d. sociocultural

8. If Dr. Byers uses an eclectic approach in her clinical treatment of children, what is she doing?
   a. She is relying primarily on one psychological perspective to treat all her patients.
   b. She is using medications with all her patients, especially those suffering from depression.
   c. She relies heavily on the Freudian psychodynamic perspective to help children who show abnormal behavior.
   d. She is using a combination of perspectives to treat different clients.

9. Dr. Colton identifies himself with the largest subfield of psychology. What kind of psychologist is he?
   a. counseling   **c.** school
   b. clinical   **d.** experimental

10. Micah has recently been diagnosed with a psychological disorder that is best addressed initially with medication. He would likely benefit the most by first seeing a _____.
   a. psychiatrist.
   b. psychoanalyst.
   c. psychiatric social worker.
   d. psychologist.

11. Which step in the scientific method is derived from the goal of description?
   a. reporting your results   **c.** drawing conclusions
   b. perceiving a question   **d.** forming a hypothesis

12. Brianne has made a prediction about the behavior the lab rats in her study will demonstrate. Next, she runs the rats through a maze to see if they behave as predicted. Which step in the scientific method is Brianne currently focusing on?
   a. testing a hypothesis
   b. perceiving the question
   c. drawing conclusions
   d. reporting her results

13. The famous study of Phineas Gage, who survived when a metal rod pierced his skull, is an example of a
   a. laboratory experiment.
   b. correlation.
   c. case study.
   d. survey.

14. A researcher finds that as her subjects increased the number of hours they spent exercising, the overall weight of her subjects decreased. This would be an example of a _____ correlation.
   a. positive
   b. negative
   c. zero
   d. causal

15. A researcher wants to study the effects of texting on driving. Students in Group A drive a car in a computer game and see how many virtual accidents they have. Students in Group B are asked to drive the same virtual car but they must respond to and send at least three texts. The number of virtual accidents is measured for each group. What is the independent variable?
   a. the virtual car
   b. texting
   c. the number of virtual accidents
   d. the group assignment

16. A researcher asks an assistant to conduct a study on her behalf. She specifically tells her assistant to only share the results anonymously and not include the students' names along with their scores. Such an experiment would be considered a
   a. double-blind experiment.
   b. single-blind experiment.
   c. correlational study.
   d. laboratory observation.

17. Double-blind studies control for
   a. the placebo effect.
   b. the experimenter effect.
   c. the placebo effect and the experimenter effect.
   d. extrinsic motivation.

18. Tillie is going to volunteer to be a participant in a research study for the very first time. She arrives 20 minutes before her scheduled participation time so that she can complete paperwork. Part of the paperwork tells her about the project in very simple, straightforward language. She is provided with this description because all research participants must

  a. give informed consent before participating.

  b. provide a waiver of confidentiality regarding their participation in the study.

  c. provide documentation that they are psychologically competent to participate in research.

  d. agree to receive some level of pain or discomfort in a research study.

19. Dr. Calvin needs just one more participant to complete her experiment. Lisa, a student of Dr. Calvin, has almost completed the experiment when she announces she wants to quit because the experiment is boring. What options does Dr. Calvin have?

  a. Dr. Calvin can require that Lisa finish because students don't have the same rights to quit an experiment as the general public does.

  b. Dr. Calvin can require that Lisa finish because boredom is not an acceptable excuse for quitting.

  c. Dr. Calvin can make Lisa stay since she is a student of hers and she requires students to take part in her experiments.

  d. Dr. Calvin must let Lisa go and find another participant.

20. A famous golfer advertises a new golf bracelet that helps minimize fatigue while playing. If Bethany decides to order the bracelet because she believes that such a well-known personality should know if it works or not, she has made an error in which of the following?

  a. Few "truths" do not need to be tested.

  b. All evidence is not equal in quality.

  c. Authority or expertise does not make the claims of the authority or expert true.

  d. Critical thinking requires an open mind.

Chapter 2
The Biological Perspective

The Ironman® competition consists of a 2.4-mile swim, a 112-mile bike ride, and a 26.2-mile run. Dick Hoyt pulls his son Rick in a boat that is attached to a bungee cord, then he peddles Rick on a special two-seater bicycle, and finally he pushes Rick across the finish line in a customized running chair.

Why the unusual approach? Rick was born with spastic quadriplegia and cerebral palsy as the result of anoxia during birth. Unable to walk or talk, Rick learned to communicate by tapping his head against a head piece on his wheelchair when specific letters of the alphabet were highlighted on a specially designed computer screen. He eventually graduated from Boston University with a degree in special education.

Current research to help individuals with brain injuries or neurological conditions has moved far beyond the computer that assisted Rick. Some of the most promising areas are in brain–computer interfaces (BCI) that use the brain's electrical activity to communicate with others. It is possible that in the future, brain activity will enable individuals to control such assistive devices as prosthetic limbs or wheelchairs.

What do you see as the brain's role in our behavior? How much do you think your behavior is influenced by hormones and chemicals in the nervous system?

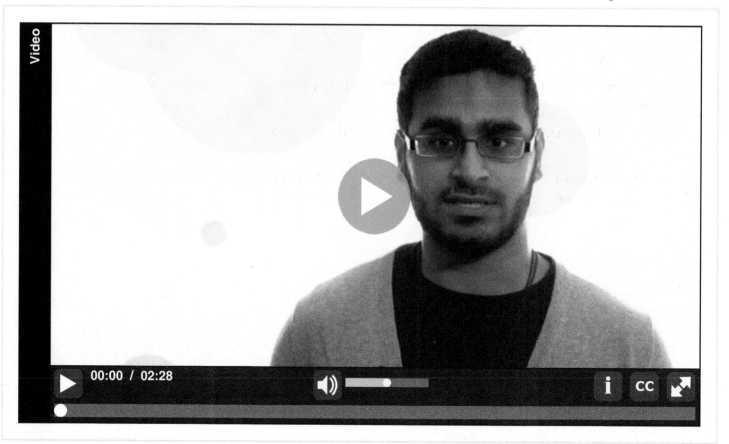

Video

00:00 / 02:28

Why study the nervous system and the glands?

How could we possibly understand any of our behavior, thoughts, or actions without knowing something about the incredible organs that allow us to act, think, and react? If we can understand how the brain, the nerves, and the glands interact to control feelings, thoughts, and behavior, we can begin to truly understand the complex organism called a human being.

Learning Objectives

2.1 Identify the parts of a neuron and describe the function of each.

2.2 Describe the action potential.

2.3 Describe how neurons use neurotransmitters to communicate with each other and with the body.

2.4 Explain how the brain and spinal cord interact, describe some misconceptions about the brain, and explain neuroplasticity.

2.5 Describe the role of the somatic and autonomic nervous systems

2.6 Explain how the hormones released by glands interact with the nervous system and affect behavior.

2.7 Describe how the autonomic nervous system and body are impacted by stress.

2.8 Describe how lesioning studies and brain stimulation are used to study the brain.

2.9 Describe how neuroimaging techniques can provide information about the brain's structure and function.

2.10 Identify the different structures of the bottom part of the brain, and describe the function of each.

2.11 Identify structures of the brain involved in emotion, learning, memory, and motivation.

2.12 Identify the parts of the cortex that process the different senses and those that control movement of the body.

2.13 Identify the parts of the cortex that are responsible for higher forms of thought, such as language.

2.14 Explain how some brain functions differ between the left and right hemispheres.

2.15 Identify some potential causes of attention-deficit/hyperactivity disorder.

Neurons and Nerves: Building the Network

This chapter will explore a complex system of cells, organs, and chemicals that work together to produce behavior, thoughts, and actions. The first part of this complex arrangement is the **nervous system**, a network of cells that carries information to and from all parts of the body. The field of **neuroscience** is a branch of the life sciences that deals with the structure and functioning of the brain and the neurons, nerves, and nervous tissue that form the nervous system. **Biological psychology**, or **behavioral neuroscience**, is the branch of neuroscience that focuses on the biological bases of psychological processes, behavior, and learning, and it is the primary area associated with the biological perspective in psychology.

STRUCTURE OF THE NEURON: THE NERVOUS SYSTEM'S BUILDING BLOCK

2.1 **Identify the parts of a neuron and describe the function of each.**

In 1887, Santiago Ramón y Cajal, a doctor studying slides of brain tissue, first theorized that the nervous system was made up of individual cells (Ramón y Cajal, translation, 1995). Although the entire body is composed of cells, each type of cell has a special purpose and function and, therefore, a special structure. For example, skin cells are flat, but muscle cells are long and stretchy. Most cells have three things in common: a nucleus, a cell body, and a cell membrane holding it all together. The **neuron** is the specialized cell in the nervous system that receives and sends messages within that system. Neurons are one of the messengers of the body, and that means that they have a very special structure, which we will explore in **Video Figure 2.1:** *The Structure of the Neuron*.

The parts of the neuron that receive messages from other cells are called the **dendrites**. The name *dendrite* means "tree-like," or "branch," and this structure does indeed look like the branches of a tree. The dendrites are attached to the cell body, or **soma**, which is the part of the cell that contains the nucleus and keeps the entire cell alive and functioning. The **axon** (from the Greek for "axis") is a fiber attached to the soma, and its job is to carry messages out to other cells. The end of the axon branches out into several

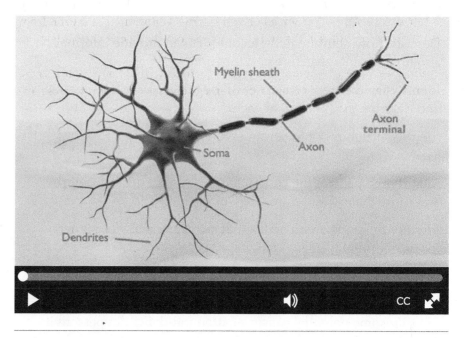

Video Figure 2.1   *The Structure of the Neuron.*

shorter fibers that have swellings or little knobs on the ends called **axon terminals** (may also be called *presynaptic terminals*, *terminal buttons*, or *synaptic knobs*), which are responsible for communicating with other nerve cells.

Neurons make up a large part of the brain but they are not the only cells that affect our thinking, learning, memory, perception, and all of the other facets of life that make us who we are. The other primary cells are called glia, or **glial cells**, which serve a variety of functions. Some glia serves as a structure on which the neurons develop and work and that hold the neurons in place. For example, during early brain development, radial glial cells (extending from inner to outer areas like the spokes of a wheel) help guide migrating neurons to form the outer layers of the brain. Other glia are involved in getting nutrients to the neurons, cleaning up the remains of neurons that have died, communicating with neurons and other glial cells, and providing insulation for neurons. Glial cells affect both the functioning and structure of neurons and specific types also have properties similar to stem cells, which allow them to develop into new neurons, both during prenatal development and in adult mammals (Bullock et al., 2005; Kriegstein & Alvarez-Buylla, 2009). Glial cells are also being investigated for their possible role in a variety of psychiatric disorders, including major depressive disorder and schizophrenia. It appears in some areas of the brain, major depressive disorder is characterized by lower numbers of specific glial cells whereas in schizophrenia, parts of the brain have a greater number (Blank & Prinz, 2013). **L I N K** to Learning Objectives 12.10 and 12.15. Recent findings also implicate glial cells in learning and behavior, both by affecting synaptic connectivity during development, and in mice transplanted with human glial cells, faster learning across a variety of learning and memory tasks (Han et al., 2013; Ji et al., 2013).

Two special types of glial cells, called *oligodendrocytes* and *Schwann cells*, generate a layer of fatty substances called **myelin**. Oligodendrocytes produce myelin in the brain and spinal cord (the central nervous system); Schwann cells produce myelin in the neurons of the body (the peripheral nervous system). Myelin wraps around the shaft of the axons, forming an insulating and protective sheath. Bundles of myelin-coated axons travel together as "cables" in the central nervous system called *tracts*, and in the peripheral nervous system bundles of axons are called **nerves**. Myelin from Schwann cells has a unique feature that can serve as a tunnel through which damaged nerve fibers can reconnect and repair themselves. That's why a severed toe might actually regain some function and feeling if sewn back on in time. Unfortunately, myelin from oligodendrocytes covering axons in the brain and spinal cord does not have this feature, and these axons are more likely to be permanently damaged.

The myelin sheath is a very important part of the neuron. It not only insulates the neuron, but it also offers a little protection from damage and speeds up the neural message traveling down the axon. Sections of myelin bump up next to each other on the axon, similar to the way sausages are linked together. The places where the myelin seems to bump are actually small spaces on the axon called nodes, which are not covered in myelin. Myelinated and unmyelinated sections of axons have slightly different electrical properties. There are also far more ion channels at each node. Both of these features affect the speed at which the electrical signal is conducted down the axon. When the electrical impulse that is the neural message travels down an axon coated with myelin, the electrical impulse is regenerated at each node and appears to "jump" or skip rapidly from node to node down the axon (Koester & Siegelbaum, 2013; Schwartz et al., 2013). That makes the message go much faster down the coated axon than it would down an uncoated axon of a neuron in the brain. In the disease called *multiple sclerosis* (MS), the myelin sheath is destroyed (possibly by the individual's own immune system), which leads to diminished or complete loss of neural functioning in those damaged cells. Early symptoms of MS may include fatigue, changes in vision, balance problems, and numbness, tingling, or muscle weakness in the arms or legs.

This electron micrograph shows a stem cell in the process of becoming a neuron.

Exactly how does this "electrical message" work inside the cell?

GENERATING THE MESSAGE WITHIN THE NEURON—THE NEURAL IMPULSE

2.2 Describe the action potential.

A neuron that's at rest—not currently firing a neural impulse or message—is actually electrically charged. The inside of the cell is really a semiliquid (jelly-like) solution in which there are charged particles, or *ions*. A semiliquid solution also surrounds the outside of the cell and contains ions, too. Although both positive and negative ions are located inside and outside of the cell, the relative charge of ions inside the cell is mostly negative, and the relative charge of ions outside the cell is mostly positive due to both **diffusion**, the process of ions moving from areas of high concentration to areas of low concentration, and *electrostatic pressure*, the relative balance of electrical charges when the ions are at rest. The cell membrane itself is *semipermeable*. This means some substances that are outside the cell can enter through tiny protein openings, or *channels*, in the membrane, while other substances in the cell can go outside. Many of these channels are gated—they open or close based on the electrical potential of the membrane—more about that in a minute. Inside the cell is a concentration of both smaller positively charged potassium ions and larger negatively charged protein ions. The negatively charged protein ions, however, are so big that they can't get out, which leaves the inside of the cell primarily negative when at rest. Outside the cell are lots of positively charged sodium ions and negatively charged chloride ions, but they are unable to enter the cell membrane when the cell is at rest because the ion channels that would allow them in are closed. But because the outside sodium ions are positive and the inside ions are negative, and because opposite electrical charges attract each other, the sodium ions will cluster around the membrane. This difference in charges creates an electrical potential.

Think of the ions inside the cell as a baseball game inside a stadium (the cell walls). The sodium ions outside the cell are all the fans in the area, and they want to get inside to see the game. When the cell is resting (the electrical potential is in a state called the **resting potential**, because the cell is at rest), the fans are stuck outside. The sodium ions cannot enter when the cell is at rest, because even though the cell membrane has all these channels, the *particular* channels for the sodium ions aren't open yet. But when the cell receives a strong enough stimulation from another cell (meaning that the dendrites are activated), the cell membrane opens up those *particular* channels, one after the other, all down its surface, allowing the sodium ions (the "fans") to rush into the cell. That causes the inside of the cell to become mostly positive and the outside of the cell to become mostly negative, because many of the positive sodium ions are now inside the cell—at the point where the first ion channel opened. This electrical charge reversal will start at the part of the axon closest to the soma, the *axon hillock,* and then proceed down the axon in a kind of chain reaction. (Picture a long hallway with many doors in which the first door opens, then the second, and so on all the way down the hall.) This electrical charge reversal is known as the **action potential** because the electrical potential is now in action rather than at rest. Each action potential sequence takes about one-thousandth of a second (See **Figure 2.2**.) Now the action potential is traveling down the axon. When it gets to the end of the axon, something else happens: The message will get transmitted to another cell (that step will be discussed momentarily). Meanwhile, what is happening to the parts of the cell that the action potential has already left behind? How does the cell get the "fans" back outside? Remember, the action potential means that the cell is now positive inside and negative outside at the point where the channel opened. Several things happen to return the cell to its resting state. First, the sodium ion channels close immediately after the action potential has passed, allowing no more "fans" (sodium ions) to enter. The cell membrane also literally pumps the positive sodium ions back outside

The Neuron at Rest
During the resting potential, the neuron is negatively charged inside and positively charged outside.

Axon

Negatively charged inner cell membrane

Nerve cell body   Positive sodium ion   Synaptic knob

Nerve impulse →

Movement of sodium ions

The Neural Impulse
The action potential occurs when positive sodium ions enter into the cell, causing a reversal of the electrical charge from negative to positive.

Sodium ions, along with potassium ions, move outside membrane

Sodium ions enter next segment of axon

The Neural Impulse Continues
As the action potential moves down the axon toward the axon terminals, the cell areas behind the action potential return to their resting state of a negative charge as the positive sodium ions are pumped to the outside of the cell, and the positive potassium ions rapidly leave.

Figure 2.2   The Neural Impulse Action Potential

In the graph, voltage readings are shown at a given place on the neuron over a period of 20 or 30 milliseconds (thousandths of a second). At first the cell is resting; it then reaches threshold and an action potential is triggered. After a brief hyperpolarization period, the cell returns to its resting potential.

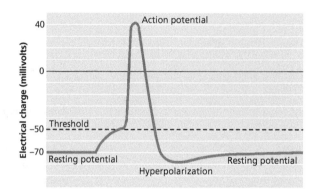

the cell, kicking the "fans" out until the next action potential opens the ion channels again. This pumping process is a little slow, so another type of ion gets into the act. Small, positively charged potassium ions inside the neuron move rapidly out of the cell after the action potential passes, helping to more quickly restore the inside of the cell to a negative charge. Now the cell becomes negative inside and positive outside, and the neuron is capable of "firing off" another message. Once the sodium pumps finish pumping out the sodium ions, the neuron can be said to have returned to its full resting potential, poised and ready to do it all again.

To sum all that up, when the cell is stimulated, the first ion channel opens and the electrical charge *at that ion channel* is reversed. Then the next ion channel opens and *that* charge is reversed, but in the meantime the *first* ion channel has been closed and the charge is returning to what it was when it was at rest. The action potential is the *sequence* of ion channels opening all down the length of the cell.

> 💬 So if the stimulus that originally causes the neuron to fire is very strong, will the neuron fire more strongly than it would if the stimulus were weak?

Neurons actually have a threshold for firing, and all it takes is a stimulus that is just strong enough to get past that threshold to make the neuron fire. Here's a simple version of how this works: Each neuron is receiving many signals from other neurons. Some of these signals are meant to cause the neuron to fire, whereas others are meant to prevent the neuron from firing. The neuron constantly adds together the effects of the "fire" messages and subtracts the "don't fire" messages, and if the "fire" messages are great enough, the threshold is reached and the neuron fires. When a neuron does fire, it does so in an **all-or-none** fashion. Neurons are either firing at full strength or not firing at all—there's no such thing as "partial" firing of a neuron. It would be like turning on a light switch—it's either on or it's off.

So what's the difference between strong stimulation and weak stimulation? A strong message will cause the neuron to fire repeatedly (as if someone flicked the light switch on and off as quickly as possible), and it will also cause more neurons to fire (as if there were a lot of lights going on and off instead of just one).

💬 Now that we know how the message travels within the axon of the cell, what is that "something else" that happens when the action potential reaches the end of the axon?

NEUROTRANSMISSION

2.3 Describe how neurons use neurotransmitters to communicate with each other and with the body.

Once a neural signal reaches the axon terminals of a neuron, several events take place to allow neurons to communicate with each other. These events are dependent upon key structures within a neuron and on the surface of adjacent neurons.

SENDING THE MESSAGE TO OTHER CELLS: THE SYNAPSE Figure 2.3 shows an axon terminal enlarged to giant scale. Notice that the presynaptic terminal is not empty. It has a number of little sac-like structures in it called synaptic vesicles. The word *vesicle* is Latin and means a "little blister" or "fluid-filled sac."

Inside the synaptic vesicles are chemicals suspended in fluid, which are molecules of substances called **neurotransmitters**. The name is simple enough—they are inside a neuron and they are going to transmit a message. (Neurons have traditionally been viewed as containing a single type of neurotransmitter, but it is now accepted that neurons may release more than one neurotransmitter. For simplicity and unless otherwise specified, our discussion throughout the text will assume a single, predominant neurotransmitter is being released.) Next to the synaptic knob is the dendrite of another neuron (see Figure 2.3). Between them is a fluid-filled space called the **synapse (synaptic gap)**. Instead of an electrical charge, the vesicles at the end of the axon (also called the presynaptic membrane) contain the molecules of neurotransmitters, and the surface of the dendrite next to the axon (the postsynaptic membrane) contains ion channels that have **receptor sites**, proteins that allow only particular molecules of a certain shape to fit into it, just as only a particular key will fit into a keyhole.

How do the neurotransmitters get across the gap? Recall the action potential making its way down the axon after the neuron has been stimulated. When that action potential, or electrical charge, reaches the synaptic vesicles, the synaptic vesicles release their neurotransmitters into the synaptic gap. The molecules then float across the synapse and many of them fit themselves into the receptor sites, opening the ion channels and allowing sodium to rush in, activating the next cell. It is this very activation that stimulates, or releases, the action potential in that cell. It is important to understand that the "next cell" may be a neuron, but it may also be a cell on a muscle or a gland. Muscles and glands have special cells with receptor sites on them, just like on the dendrite of a neuron.

So far, we've been talking about the synapse as if neurotransmitters always cause the next cell to fire its action potential (or, in the case of a muscle or gland, to contract or start secreting its chemicals). But the neurons must have a way to be turned *off* as well as on. Otherwise, when a person burns a finger, the pain signals from those neurons would not stop until the burn was completely healed. Muscles are told

Figure 2.3 The Synapse

The nerve impulse reaches the axon terminal, triggering the release of neurotransmitters from the synaptic vesicles. The molecules of neurotransmitter cross the synaptic gap to fit into the receptor sites that fit the shape of the molecule, opening the ion channel and allowing sodium ions to rush in.

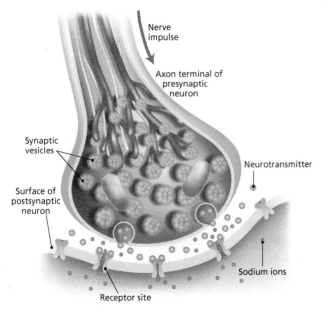

Nerve impulse

Axon terminal of presynaptic neuron

Synaptic vesicles

Surface of postsynaptic neuron

Neurotransmitter

Sodium ions

Receptor site

to contract or relax, and glands are told to secrete or stop secreting their chemicals. The neurotransmitters found at various synapses around the nervous system can either turn cells on (called an *excitatory* effect) or turn cells off (called an *inhibitory* effect), depending on exactly what synapse is being affected. Although some people refer to neurotransmitters that turn cells on as *excitatory* neurotransmitters and the ones that turn cells off as *inhibitory* neurotransmitters, it's really more correct to refer to **excitatory synapses** and **inhibitory synapses**. In other words, it's not the neurotransmitter itself that is excitatory or inhibitory, but rather it is the effect of that neurotransmitter that is either excitatory or inhibitory at the receptor sites of a particular synapse.

NEUROTRANSMITTERS: MESSENGERS OF THE NETWORK   The first neurotransmitter to be identified was named *acetylcholine* (ACh). It is found at the synapses between neurons and muscle cells. Acetylcholine serves to stimulate the skeletal muscles to contract but actually slows contractions in the heart muscle. If acetylcholine receptor sites on the muscle cells are blocked in some way, then the acetylcholine can't get to the site and the muscle will be incapable of contracting—paralyzed, in other words. This is exactly what happens when *curare*, a drug used by South American Indians on their blow darts, gets into the nervous system. Curare's molecules are just similar enough to fit into the receptor site without actually stimulating the cell, making curare an **antagonist** (a chemical substance that blocks or reduces the effects of a neurotransmitter) for ACh.

This electron micrograph shows a motor neuron making contact with muscle fibers.

What would happen if the neurons released too much ACh? The bite of a black widow spider does just that. Its venom stimulates the release of excessive amounts of ACh and causes convulsions and possible death. Black widow spider venom is an **agonist** (a chemical substance that mimics or enhances the effects of a neurotransmitter) for ACh.

ACh also plays a key role in memory, arousal, and attention. For example, ACh is found in the hippocampus, an area of the brain that is responsible for forming new memories, and low levels of ACh have been associated with Alzheimer's disease, the most common type of dementia. (L I N K) to Learning Objective 6.14. We will focus more on agonists and antagonists later in the chapter.

The venom of the black widow spider causes a flood of acetylcholine to be released into the body's muscle system, causing convulsions.

Since the discovery of ACh, many other neurotransmitters have been identified. These substances have a variety of roles ranging from general excitatory and inhibitory effects to influencing eating, sleeping, movement, and consciousness. Others influence cognition, memory, and mood. Refer to **Table 2.1** on the next page for an overview of various neurotransmitters and their functions.

A group of substances known as *neuropeptides* can serve as neurotransmitters, hormones, or influence the action of other neurotransmitters (Schwartz & Javitch, 2013). You may have heard of the set of neuropeptides called *endorphins*—pain-controlling chemicals in the body. When a person is hurt, a neurotransmitter that signals pain is released. When the brain gets this message, it triggers the release of endorphins. The endorphins bind to receptors that open the ion channels on the axon. This causes the cell to be unable to fire its pain signal and the pain sensations eventually lessen. For example, you might bump your elbow and experience a lot of pain at first, but the pain will quickly subside to a much lower level. Athletes may injure themselves during an event and yet not feel the pain until after the competition is over, when the endorphin levels go down.

The name *endorphin* comes from the term *endogenous morphine*. (*Endogenous* means "native to the area"—in this case, native to the body.) Scientists studying the nervous system found receptor sites that fit morphine molecules perfectly and decided that there must be a natural substance in the body that has the same effect as morphine. Endorphins are the reason that heroin and the other drugs derived from opium are so addictive—when people take morphine or heroin, their bodies neglect to produce endorphins. When the drug wears off, they are left with no protection against pain at all, and *everything* hurts.

Table 2.1 Neurotransmitters and Their Functions	
Neurotransmitters	**Functions**
Acetylcholine (ACh)	Excitatory or inhibitory; involved in arousal, attention, memory, and controls muscle contractions
Norepinephrine (NE)	Mainly excitatory; involved in arousal and mood
Dopamine (DA)	Excitatory or inhibitory; involved in control of movement and sensations of pleasure
Serotonin (5-HT)	Excitatory or inhibitory; involved in sleep, mood, anxiety, and appetite
Gamma-aminobutyric acid (GABA)	Major inhibitory neurotransmitter; involved in sleep and inhibits movement.
Glutamate	Major excitatory neurotransmitter; involved in learning, memory formation, nervous system development, and synaptic plasticity
Endorphins	Inhibitory neural regulators; involved in pain relief

This pain is why most people want more heroin, creating an addictive cycle of abuse. **L I N K** to Learning Objective 4.11.

> 💬 If the neurotransmitters are out there in the synaptic gap and in the receptor sites, what happens to them when they aren't needed anymore?

CLEANING UP THE SYNAPSE: REUPTAKE AND ENZYMES The neurotransmitters have to get out of the receptor sites before the next stimulation can occur. Some just drift away through the process of diffusion, but most will end up back in the synaptic vesicles in a process called **reuptake**. (Think of a little suction tube, sucking the chemicals back into the presynaptic neuron, to be repackaged into the vesicles.) In this way the synapse is cleared for the next release of neurotransmitters. Some drugs, like cocaine, affect the nervous system by blocking the reuptake process, as shown in **Video Figure 2.4: Neurotransmitters: Reuptake.**

There is one neurotransmitter that is not taken back into the vesicles, however. Because ACh is responsible for muscle activity, and muscle activity needs to happen rapidly and continue happening, it's not possible to wait around for the "sucking up" process to occur. Instead, an enzyme* specifically designed to break apart ACh clears the synaptic gap very quickly (a process called **enzymatic degradation**). There are enzymes that break down other neurotransmitters as well.

> 💬 I think I understand the synapse and neurotransmitters now, but how do I relate that to the real world?

Knowing how and why drugs affect us can help us understand why a physician might prescribe a particular drug or why certain drugs are dangerous and should be avoided. Because the chemical molecules of various drugs, if similar enough in shape to the neurotransmitters, can fit into the receptor sites on the receiving neurons just like the neurotransmitters do, drugs can act as agonists or antagonists. Drugs acting as agonists, for example, can mimic or enhance the effects of neurotransmitters on the receptor sites of the next cell. This can result in an increase or decrease in the activity of the receiving cell, depending on what the effect of the original neurotransmitter (excitatory

---

*enzyme: a complex protein that is manufactured by cells.

Axon terminal of presynaptic neuron

Dopamine is removed from the synapse by reuptake sites.

Cocaine acts by blocking dopamine reuptake sites, allowing dopamine to remain active in the synapse longer.

Dopamine molecules in synapse

Dendrite of postsynaptic neuron

Video Figure 2.4 *Neurotransmitters: Reuptake*

or inhibitory) was going to be. So if the original neurotransmitter was excitatory, the effect of the agonist will be to increase that excitation. If it was inhibitory, the effect of the agonist will be to increase that inhibition. Another deciding factor is the nervous system location of the neurons that use a specific neurotransmitter.

For example, some antianxiety medications, such as diazepam (Valium®), are classified as benzodiazepines (Ⓛ Ⓘ Ⓝ Ⓚ to Learning Objective 13.10) and are agonists for GABA, the primary inhibitory neurotransmitter in the brain. Areas of the brain that you will learn about later that play a role in controlling anxiety, agitation, and fear include the amygdala, orbitofrontal cortex, and the insula (LeDoux & Damasio, 2013; Zilles & Amunts, 2012). By increasing the inhibitory (calming) action of GABA, the benzodiazepines directly calm these specific brain areas (Julien et al., 2011; Preston et al., 2008).

Other drugs act as antagonists, blocking or reducing a cell's response to the action of other chemicals or neurotransmitters. Although an antagonist might sound like it has only an inhibitory effect, it is important to remember that if the neurotransmitter that the antagonist affects is inhibitory itself, the result will actually be an *increase* in the activity of the cell that would normally have been inhibited; the antagonist *blocks* the inhibitory effect.

Lastly, some drugs yield their agonistic or antagonistic effects by impacting the amount of neurotransmitter in the synapse. They do so by interfering with the regular reuptake or enzymatic degradation process. Remember that the neurotransmitter serotonin helps regulate and adjust people's moods, but in some people the normal process of adjustment is not working properly. Some of the drugs used to treat depression are called SSRIs (selective serotonin reuptake inhibitors). SSRIs block the reuptake of serotonin, leaving more serotonin available in the synapse to bind with receptor sites. Over several weeks, the individual's mood improves. Although the reason for this improvement is not as simple as once believed (i.e., low levels of serotonin = low levels of mood) or fully understood, SSRIs are effective for depression, anxiety, and obsessive-compulsive disorder (Hyman & Cohen, 2013; Julien et al., 2011; Stahl, 2013).

This section covered the neuron and how neurons communicate. The next section looks at the bigger picture—the nervous system itself.

Concept Map L.O. 2.1, 2.2, 2.3

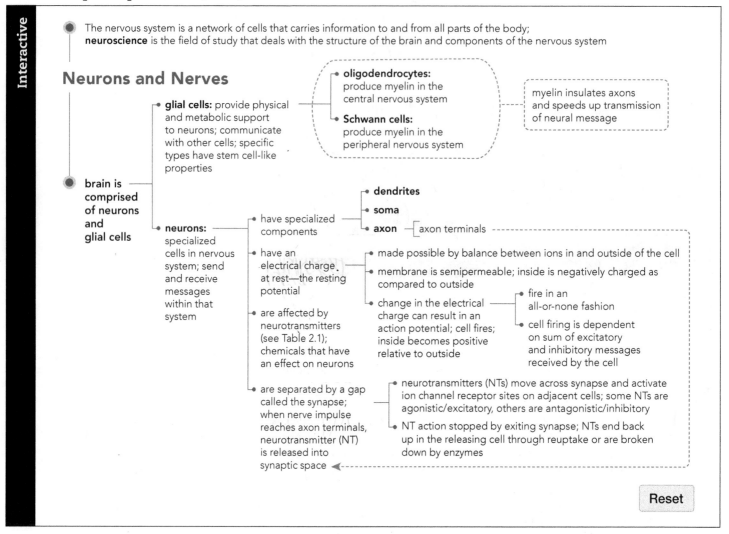

Interactive

The nervous system is a network of cells that carries information to and from all parts of the body; **neuroscience** is the field of study that deals with the structure of the brain and components of the nervous system

Neurons and Nerves

glial cells: provide physical and metabolic support to neurons; communicate with other cells; specific types have stem cell-like properties

oligodendrocytes: produce myelin in the central nervous system

Schwann cells: produce myelin in the peripheral nervous system

myelin insulates axons and speeds up transmission of neural message

brain is comprised of neurons and glial cells

neurons: specialized cells in nervous system; send and receive messages within that system

have specialized components
- **dendrites**
- **soma**
- **axon** — axon terminals

have an electrical charge at rest—the resting potential
- made possible by balance between ions in and outside of the cell
- membrane is semipermeable; inside is negatively charged as compared to outside
- change in the electrical charge can result in an action potential; cell fires; inside becomes positive relative to outside
  - fire in an all-or-none fashion
  - cell firing is dependent on sum of excitatory and inhibitory messages received by the cell

are affected by neurotransmitters (see Table 2.1); chemicals that have an effect on neurons

are separated by a gap called the synapse; when nerve impulse reaches axon terminals, neurotransmitter (NT) is released into synaptic space
- neurotransmitters (NTs) move across synapse and activate ion channel receptor sites on adjacent cells; some NTs are agonistic/excitatory, others are antagonistic/inhibitory
- NT action stopped by exiting synapse; NTs end back up in the releasing cell through reuptake or are broken down by enzymes

Reset

Practice Quiz   How much do you remember? ANSWERS ON PAGE AK-1.

Pick the best answer.

1. Which part of the neuron carries messages to other cells?
  a. axon   **c.** soma
  b. dendrite   **d.** myelin

2. Which one of the following is NOT a function of glial cells?
  a. getting nutrients to the neurons
  b. generating action potentials
  c. cleaning up the remains of dead neurons
  d. providing insulation

3. When a neuron's resting potential is occurring, the neuron is _____ charged on the inside.
  a. positively
  b. negatively
  c. both positively and negatively
  d. neutrally

4. Neurotransmitters must pass from an axon terminal to the next dendrite by crossing a fluid-filled space called the
  a. synaptic gap.   **c.** neuron.
  b. reuptake inhibitor.   **d.** glial cell.

5. The venom of a black widow spider acts like a(n) _____ by mimicking the effects of acetylcholine.
  a. agonist   **c.** protagonist
  b. antagonist   **d.** glial cell

6. Which of the following is associated with pain relief?
  a. acetylcholine
  b. glutamate
  c. serotonin
  d. endorphins

An Overview of the Nervous System

Now that we have looked at the cells that make up the nervous system and ways in which they process and communicate information, take a look at **Figure 2.5**. This figure shows the organization of the various parts of the nervous system and will help in understanding how all the different parts work together in controlling the way people and animals think, act, and feel.

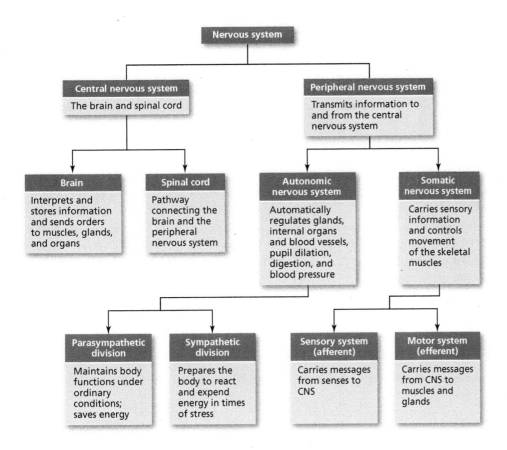

Figure 2.5 An Overview of the Nervous System

THE CENTRAL NERVOUS SYSTEM—THE "CENTRAL PROCESSING UNIT"

2.4 Explain how the brain and spinal cord interact, describe some misconceptions about the brain, and explain neuroplasticity.

The **central nervous system (CNS)** is composed of the brain and the spinal cord. Both the brain and the spinal cord are composed of neurons and glial cells that control the life-sustaining functions of the body as well as all thought, emotion, and behavior.

THE BRAIN   The brain is the core of the nervous system, the part that makes sense of the information received from the senses, makes decisions, and sends commands out to the muscles and the rest of the body. Later parts of this chapter will cover the brain in more detail, but for now, you should know the brain is organized into different regions, each with primary functions. While the neurons in each of the different areas work in much the same way, it is the groups of cells and the connections between them and other parts of the brain or components of the nervous system, and our experiences, that influence the various functions found in specific brain areas (Amaral & Strick, 2013; Heimer, 1995; Squire & Kandel, 2009).

THE SPINAL CORD   The **spinal cord** is a long bundle of neurons that serves two vital functions for the nervous system. Look at the cross-sectional view of the spinal cord in **Figure 2.6** on the next page. Notice that it seems to be divided into two areas, a lighter outer section and a darker inner section. If it were a real spinal cord, the outer section would appear to be white

The look on this young woman's face clearly indicates that she has experienced pain in her finger. Pain is a warning signal that something is wrong—in this case that touching the thorns on the stem of the rose was a bad idea. What might be some of the problems encountered by a person who could feel no pain at all?

and the inner section would seem gray. That's because the outer section is composed mainly of myelinated axons and nerves, which appear white, whereas the inner section is mainly composed of cell bodies of neurons, which appear gray. The purpose of the outer section is to carry messages from the body up to the brain and from the brain down to the body. It is simply a message "pipeline."

The inside section, which is made up of cell bodies separated by glial cells, is actually a primitive sort of "brain." This part of the spinal cord is responsible for certain reflexes—very fast, lifesaving reflexes. To understand how the spinal cord reflexes work, it is important to know there are three basic types of neurons: **afferent (sensory) neurons** that carry messages from the senses to the spinal cord, **efferent (motor) neurons** that carry messages from the spinal cord to the muscles and glands, and **interneurons** that connect the afferent neurons to the motor neurons (and make up the inside of the spinal cord and much of the brain itself). (See Figure 2.6.) Touch a flame or a hot stove with your finger, for example, and an afferent neuron will send the pain message up to the spinal column where it enters into the central area of the spinal cord. The interneuron in that central area will then receive the message and send out a response along an efferent neuron, causing your finger to pull back. This all happens very quickly. If the pain message had to go all the way up to the brain before a response could be made, the response time would be greatly increased and more damage would be done to your finger. So having this kind of **reflex arc** controlled by the spinal cord alone allows for very fast response times. (A good way to avoid mixing up the terms *afferent* and *efferent* is to remember "a̲fferent neurons a̲ccess the spinal cord, e̲fferent neurons e̲xit.") The pain message does eventually get to the brain, where other motor responses may be triggered, like saying "Ouch!" and putting the finger in your mouth.

Figure 2.6 THE SPINAL CORD REFLEX

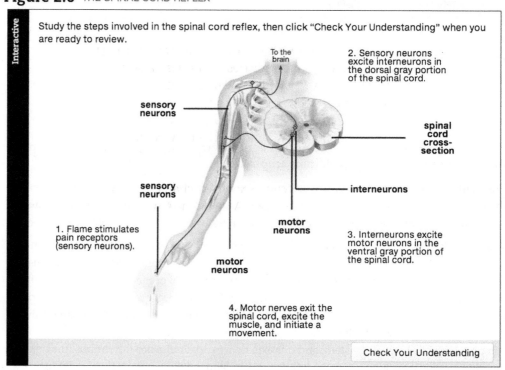

The pain from the burning heat of the candle flame stimulates the afferent nerve fibers, which carry the message up to the interneurons in the middle of the spinal cord. The interneurons then send a message out by means of the efferent nerve fibers, causing the hand to jerk away from the flame.

Psychology in the News

Fact or Fiction: Focus on the Brain, but Check Your Sources!

As stressed in Chapter One, critical thinking is a valuable skill and one that is very useful in the study of psychology. One of the basic points highlighted was that not all evidence is equal in quality. (L) (I) (N) K to Learning Objective 1.12. Have you ever heard a claim about the brain that you were not sure was true?

Whether you get your news from blogs or from Web sites, listen to podcasts, or watch the local or national news on your television, computer, or smartphone, you have probably read, heard, or seen a segment that addresses some aspect of the human brain. Some recent and not-so-recent brain-related news items have included the following:

"Older brains can't make new cells."

"Listening to classical music makes you smarter—also known as the *Mozart Effect.*"

"Autism is caused by childhood vaccinations."

"People only use 10 percent of their brain."

Items adapted from Neuromyths, BrainFacts.org, Society for Neuroscience. Available at http://www.brainfacts.org/neuromyths/

Do any of the above headlines look familiar? Given the inherent interest in many of these topics and the number of people who reportedly "know" these facts, they have often been considered the truth. But in fact, all of the above items have been found to be *false* or have not been supported by conclusive scientific evidence. So how do you go about evaluating brain-related news the next time it flashes across the headlines or shows up on your news feed?

Think back to the research methods and discussed in Chapter One. (L) (I) (N) K to Learning Objectives 1.6–1.11. Did the news item provide details about the actual study? If it did, what were the data collection methods used in the study? Do the methods used support the reported findings? Was a representative sample used? Did the researchers conduct an experiment or did the news item confuse correlation with causation?

Some of the best sources are the original research studies, assuming the researchers collected data in an unbiased manner and followed established research methods. Findings that are published in peer-reviewed journals (where research is reviewed by other experts in that area) are especially helpful, as are edited books with contributions by experts in the associated field. The challenge for students early in their psychological studies is that it is not so easy to fully understand the methods, statistics, or terminology used in the studies.

For students, aside from your textbooks and professors, other good resources are the educational materials provided by professional organizations. For psychology in general, the American Psychological Association (APA) and the Association for Psychological Science (APS) are two great sources of information. In addition to various peer-reviewed journals and other educational publications, they both have informative Web sites.

For information more specifically related to the brain and neuroscience, one of the best sources of research and educational material is the Society for Neuroscience (SfN). The four misconceptions mentioned earlier are based on eight myths about the brain that are covered in one of their educational Web sites, *Neuromyths*, and can be viewed on their Web site, http://www.brainfacts.org/neuromyths/

So the next time you see a news item about the brain, check your sources and remain mindful that some sources are certainly more helpful than others.

Useful Web sites:

American Psychological Association (APA)—www.apa.org

Association for Psychological Science (APS)—www.psychologicalscience.org

Society for Neuroscience (SfN)—www.sfn.org

BrainFacts.org—www.brainfacts.org

💬 If the spinal cord is such an important link between the body and the brain, what happens if it is damaged?

DAMAGE TO THE CENTRAL NERVOUS SYSTEM   Damage to the central nervous system was once thought to be permanent. Neurons in the brain and spinal cord were not seen as capable of repairing themselves. When people recovered from a stroke, for example, it was assumed that it was primarily due to healthy brain cells taking over the functions of the damaged ones. Scientists have known for a while now that some forms of central nervous system damage can be repaired by the body's systems, and in recent years great strides have been made in repairing spinal cord damage. The brain actually exhibits a great deal of **neuroplasticity**, the ability to constantly change both the structure and function of many cells in the brain in response to experience and even trauma (Neville & Bavelier, 2000; Rossini et al., 2007; Sanders et al., 2008).

The brain can change itself quite a bit by adapting neurons to serve new functions when old neurons die or are damaged. Dendrites grow and new synapses are formed in at least some areas of the brain, as people learn new things throughout life (Sanes & Jessell, 2013a, 2013b). Researchers are also examining the effects of implanting Schwann cells from the peripheral nervous system to the central nervous system to aid in treating spinal cord injuries (Deng et al., 2013).

Another avenue of research has involved scientists investigating the possibility of transplanting **stem cells** to repair damaged or diseased brain tissue. Stem cells can become any cell in the body and may offer promise for addressing diseases such as Parkinson's and Alzheimer's, or the repair of damaged spinal cords or brain tissue.

💬 Okay, that takes care of the central nervous system, except for the detail on the brain. How does the central nervous system communicate with the rest of the body?

THE PERIPHERAL NERVOUS SYSTEM—NERVES ON THE EDGE

2.5 Describe the role of the somatic and autonomic nervous systems.

The term *peripheral* refers to things that are not in the center or that are on the edges of the center. The **peripheral nervous system** or **PNS** (see **Figure 2.7** and also refer back to Figure 2.5) is made up of all the nerves and neurons that are not contained in the brain and spinal cord. It is this system that allows the brain and spinal cord to communicate with the sensory systems and enables the brain and spinal cord to control the muscles and glands of the body. The PNS can be divided into two major systems: the **somatic nervous system**, which consists of nerves that control the voluntary muscles of the body, and the **autonomic nervous system (ANS)**, which consists of nerves that control the involuntary muscles, organs, and glands.

THE SOMATIC NERVOUS SYSTEM   One of the parts of a neuron is the soma, or cell body (remember that the word *soma* means "body"). The somatic nervous system is made up of the **sensory pathway**, which is all the nerves carrying messages from the senses to the

Brain (CNS)

Spinal cord (CNS)

Nerves (PNS)

Figure 2.7   The Peripheral Nervous System

central nervous system (those nerves containing afferent neurons), and the **motor pathway**, which is all the nerves carrying messages from the central nervous system to the voluntary, or skeletal,* muscles of the body—muscles that allow people to move their bodies (those nerves composed of efferent neurons). When people are walking, raising their hands in class, smelling a flower, or directing their gaze toward the person they are talking to or to look at a pretty picture, they are using the somatic nervous system. (As seen in the discussion of spinal cord reflexes, although these muscles are called the voluntary muscles, they can move involuntarily when a reflex response occurs. They are called "voluntary" because they *can* be moved at will but are not limited to only that kind of movement.)

Involuntary* muscles, such as the heart, stomach, and intestines, together with glands such as the adrenal glands and the pancreas are all controlled by clumps of neurons located on or near the spinal column. (The words *on* or *near* are used quite deliberately here. The neurons *inside* the spinal column are part of the central nervous system, not the peripheral nervous system.) These large groups of neurons near the spinal column make up the *autonomic nervous system*.

THE AUTONOMIC NERVOUS SYSTEM   The word *autonomic* suggests that the functions of this system are more or less automatic, which is basically correct. Whereas the somatic division of the peripheral nervous system controls the senses and voluntary muscles, the autonomic division controls everything else in the body—organs, glands, and involuntary muscles. The autonomic nervous system is divided into two systems, the *sympathetic division*, and the *parasympathetic division*. (See **Figure 2.8** on the next page).

THE SYMPATHETIC DIVISION   The **sympathetic division** is usually called the "fight-or-flight system" because it allows people and animals to deal with all kinds of stressful events. (L)(I)(N)(K) to Learning Objective 2.7. Emotions during these events might be anger (hence, the term *fight*) or fear (that's the "flight" part, obviously) or even extreme joy or excitement. Yes, even joy can be stressful. The sympathetic division's job is to get the body ready to deal with the stress. Many of us have experienced a fight-or-flight moment at least once in our lives. We will look more closely at how the body responds to stress later in the chapter but for now, participate in the survey *Do You Fly or Fight?* to learn more about how your body responds in certain situations.

These young soccer players are using their senses and voluntary muscles controlled by the somatic division of the peripheral nervous system. What part of the autonomic nervous system are these girls also using at this time?

Survey   DO YOU FLY OR FIGHT?

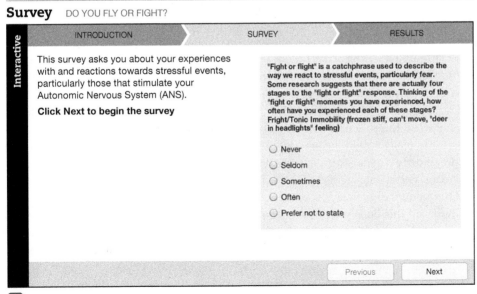

INTRODUCTION	SURVEY	RESULTS

This survey asks you about your experiences with and reactions towards stressful events, particularly those that stimulate your Autonomic Nervous System (ANS).

Click Next to begin the survey

"Fight or flight" is a catchphrase used to describe the way we react to stressful events, particularly fear. Some research suggests that there are actually four stages to the "fight or flight" response. Thinking of the "fight or flight" moments you have experienced, how often have you experienced each of these stages? Fright/Tonic Immobility (frozen stiff, can't move, "deer in headlights" feeling)

○ Never
○ Seldom
○ Sometimes
○ Often
○ Prefer not to state

Previous   Next

Simulate the **Experiment,** *Do You Fly or Fight?*

*skeletal: having to do with the bones of the body, or skeleton.
*involuntary: not under deliberate control.

Figure 2.8 Functions of the Parasympathetic and Sympathetic Divisions of the Nervous System

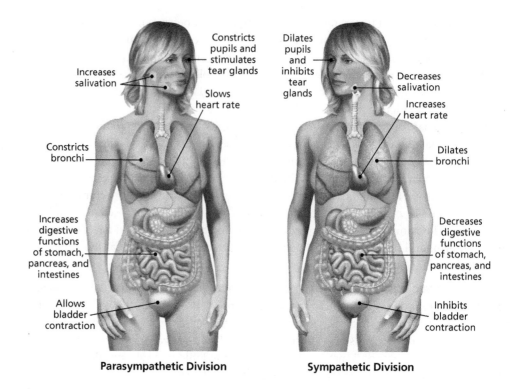

Increases salivation

Constricts pupils and stimulates tear glands

Slows heart rate

Constricts bronchi

Increases digestive functions of stomach, pancreas, and intestines

Allows bladder contraction

Parasympathetic Division

Dilates pupils and inhibits tear glands

Decreases salivation

Increases heart rate

Dilates bronchi

Decreases digestive functions of stomach, pancreas, and intestines

Inhibits bladder contraction

Sympathetic Division

What are the specific ways in which this division readies the body to react? (See Figure 2.8.) The pupils seem to get bigger, perhaps to let in more light and, therefore, more information. The heart starts pumping faster and harder, drawing blood away from nonessential organs such as the skin (so at first the person may turn pale) and sometimes even the brain itself (so the person might actually faint). Blood needs lots of oxygen before it goes to the muscles, so the lungs work overtime, too (so the person may begin to breathe faster). One set of glands in particular receives special instructions. The adrenal glands will be stimulated to release certain stress-related chemicals (members of a class of chemicals released by glands called *hormones*) into the bloodstream. These stress hormones will travel to all parts of the body, but they will only affect certain target organs. Just as a neurotransmitter fits into a receptor site on a cell, the molecules of the stress hormones fit into receptor sites at the various target organs—notably, the heart, muscles, and lungs. This further stimulates these organs to work harder. But not every organ or system will be stimulated by the activation of the sympathetic division. Digestion of food and excretion* of waste are not necessary functions when dealing with stressful situations, so these systems tend to be "shut down" or inhibited. Saliva, which is part of digestion, dries right up (ever try whistling when you're scared?). Food that was in the stomach sits there like a lump. Usually, the urge to go to the bathroom will be suppressed, but if the person is really scared the bladder or bowels may actually empty (this is why people who die under extreme stress, such as hanging or electrocution, will release their urine and waste). The sympathetic division is also going to demand that the body burn a tremendous amount of fuel, or blood sugar.

Now, all this bodily arousal is going on during a stressful situation. If the stress ends, the activity of the sympathetic division will be replaced by the activation of the parasympathetic division. If the stress goes on too long or is too intense, the person might actually collapse (as a deer might do when being chased by another animal). This collapse occurs because the parasympathetic division overresponds in its inhibition of the sympathetic activity. The heart slows, blood vessels open up, blood pressure in the brain drops, and fainting can result.

---

*excretion: in this sense, the act of eliminating waste products from the body.

THE PARASYMPATHETIC DIVISION   If the sympathetic division can be called the fight-or-flight system, the **parasympathetic division** might be called the "eat-drink-and-rest" system. The neurons of this division are located at the top and bottom of the spinal column on either side of the sympathetic division neurons (*para* means "beyond" or "next to" and in this sense refers to the neurons located on either side of the sympathetic division neurons).

In looking at Figure 2.8, it might seem as if the parasympathetic division does pretty much the opposite of the sympathetic division, but it's a little more complex than that. The parasympathetic division's job is to restore the body to normal functioning after a stressful situation ends. It slows the heart and breathing, constricts the pupils, and reactivates digestion and excretion. Signals to the adrenal glands stop because the parasympathetic division isn't connected to the adrenal glands. In a sense, the parasympathetic division allows the body to put back all the energy it burned—which is why people are often very hungry *after* the stress is all over.

The parasympathetic division does more than just react to the activity of the sympathetic division. It is the parasympathetic division that is responsible for most of the ordinary, day-to-day bodily functioning, such as regular heartbeat and normal breathing and digestion. People spend the greater part of their 24-hour day eating, sleeping, digesting, and excreting. So it is the parasympathetic division that is normally active. At any given moment, then, one or the other of these divisions, sympathetic or parasympathetic, will determine whether people are aroused or relaxed.

Concept Map L.O. 2.4, 2.5

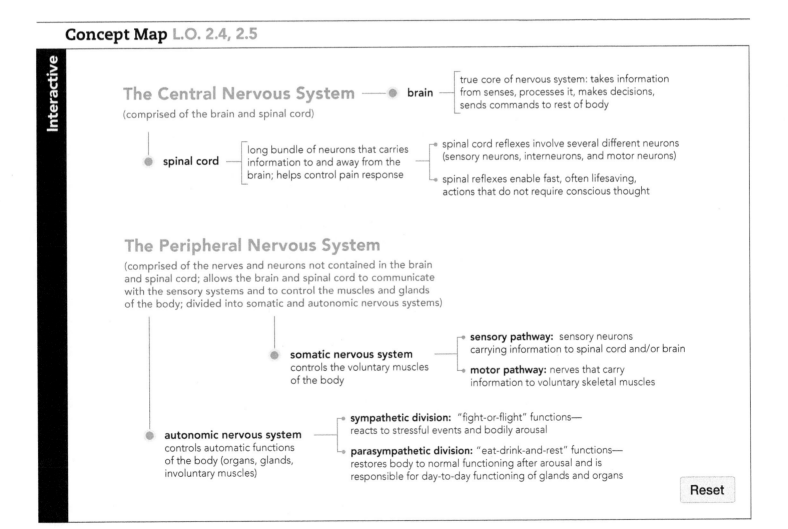

Practice Quiz   How much do you remember?   ANSWERS ON PAGE AK–1.

Pick the best answer.

1. If you touch a hot stove, your spinal cord can prompt you to withdraw your hand without having to send the message all the way to the brain. This is due to what scientists call

   a. the reflex arc.

   b. neuroplasticity.

   c. the parasympathetic nervous system.

   d. the sympathetic nervous system.

2. What is the process whereby the structure and function of brain cells change in response to trauma, damage, or even learning?

   a. shallow lesioning   **c.** cell regeneration

   b. deep lesioning   **d.** neuroplasticity

3. The neurons of the sensory pathway contain

   a. efferent neurons.

   b. afferent neurons.

   c. both efferent and afferent neurons.

   d. voluntary muscle fibers.

4. Yvonne's ability to reach for and pick up her book is largely due to the functions of the _____ pathway of the _____ nervous system.

   a. sensory; somatic

   b. motor; somatic

   c. autonomic; peripheral

   d. parasympathetic; autonomic

5. Which of the following would be active if you have just had an automobile accident?

   a. sympathetic division

   b. parasympathetic division

   c. somatic division

   d. motor division

 💬 How do the glands fit into all of this? Aren't there more glands than just the adrenal glands? How do they affect our behavior?

Distant Connections: The Endocrine Glands

Earlier we addressed the subject of neurons and the neurotransmitters and how they release into the synapse to communicate with postsynaptic neurons. This type of chemical communication is fairly specific, primarily affecting neurons in the immediate vicinity of the originating neuron, and also very fast (almost immediate). Other structures also use chemical communication but do so at a different rate and act in a more far-reaching manner. For example, glands are organs in the body that secrete chemicals.

GLANDS AND HORMONES

2.6 **Explain how the hormones released by glands interact with the nervous system and affect behavior.**

Some glands, such as salivary glands and sweat glands, secrete their chemicals directly onto the body's tissues through tiny tubes, or ducts. This kind of gland affects the functioning of the body but doesn't really affect behavior. Other glands, called **endocrine glands**, have no ducts and secrete their chemicals directly into the bloodstream. (See **Figure 2.9**.) The chemicals secreted by this type of gland are called **hormones**. As mentioned earlier in the chapter when talking about the sympathetic division of the autonomic nervous system, these hormones flow into the bloodstream, which carries them to their target organs. The molecules of these hormones then fit into receptor sites on those organs to fulfill their function, affecting behavior as they do so. As compared to synaptic communication, endocrine communication is generally slower due to the time it takes hormones to travel to target organs; the behaviors and responses they affect may not occur until hours, weeks, or years later.

    The hormones affect behavior and emotions by stimulating muscles, organs, or other glands of the body. Some theories of emotion state that the surge in certain hormones actually triggers the emotional reaction (Izard, 1988; Zajonc, 1980, 1984).

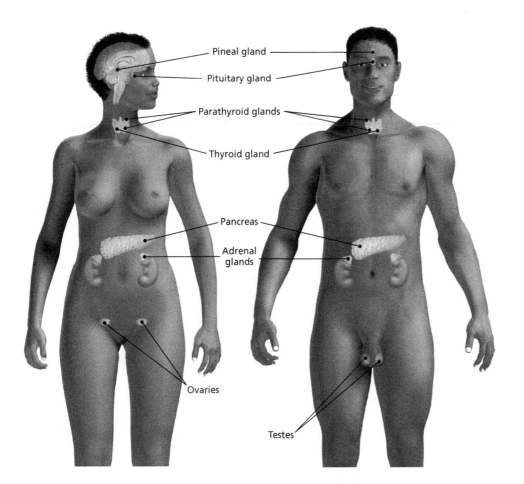

Pineal gland

Pituitary gland

Parathyroid glands

Thyroid gland

Pancreas

Adrenal glands

Ovaries

Testes

Figure 2.9 The Endocrine Glands

The endocrine glands secrete hormones directly into the bloodstream, which carries them to organs in the body, such as the heart, pancreas, and sex organs.

Ⓛⓘⓝⓚ to Learning Objective 9.11. Some of the hormones produced by endocrine glands also influence the activity of the brain, producing excitatory or inhibitory effects (Schwartz & Javitch, 2013).

THE PITUITARY, MASTER OF THE HORMONAL UNIVERSE The **pituitary gland** is located in the brain itself, just below the hypothalamus. The hypothalamus controls the glandular system by influencing the pituitary. That is because the pituitary gland is the *master gland*, the one that controls or influences all of the other endocrine glands. One part of the pituitary controls things associated with pregnancy, through the hormone **oxytocin**, such as production of milk for nursing infants and the onset of labor, as well as the levels of salt and water in the body, through the hormone *vasopressin*. Another part of the pituitary secretes several hormones that influence the activity of the other glands. Most notable of these hormones is a *growth hormone* that controls and regulates the increase in size as children grow from infancy to adulthood.

As the master gland, the pituitary forms a very important part of a feedback system, one that includes the hypothalamus and the organs targeted by the various hormones. The balance of hormones in the entire endocrine system is maintained by feedback from each of these "players" to the others.

THE PINEAL GLAND The **pineal gland** is also located in the brain, near the back, directly above the brain stem. It plays an important role in several biological rhythms. The pineal gland secretes a hormone called melatonin, which helps track day length (and seasons). In some animals, this hormone influences seasonal behaviors such as breeding and molting. In humans, melatonin levels are more influential in regulating the sleep–wake cycle. Ⓛⓘⓝⓚ to Learning Objective 4.3.

THE THYROID GLAND The **thyroid gland** is located inside the neck and secretes hormones that regulate growth and metabolism. One of these, a hormone called thyroxin,

When the pancreas does not secrete enough insulin, the result is diabetes. Many diabetic people must give themselves insulin shots to supply enough of the hormone.

regulates metabolism (controlling how fast the body burns its available energy). As related to growth, the thyroid plays a crucial role in body and brain development.

PANCREAS The **pancreas** controls the level of blood sugar in the body by secreting *insulin* and *glucagons*. If the pancreas secretes too little insulin, it results in *diabetes*. If it secretes too much insulin, it results in *hypoglycemia*, or low blood sugar, which causes a person to feel hungry all the time and often become overweight as a result.

THE GONADS The **gonads** are the sex glands, including the **ovaries** in the female and the **testes** in the male. They secrete hormones that regulate sexual behavior and reproduction. They do not control all sexual behavior, though. In a very real sense, the brain itself is the master of the sexual system—human sexual behavior is not only controlled by instincts and the actions of the glands as in the animal world but also by psychological factors such as attractiveness.

THE ADRENAL GLANDS Everyone has two **adrenal glands**, one on top of each kidney. The origin of the name is simple enough; *renal* comes from a Latin word meaning "kidney" and *ad* is Latin for "to," so *adrenal* means "to or on the kidney." Each adrenal gland is actually divided into two sections, the *adrenal medulla* and the *adrenal cortex*. It is the adrenal medulla that releases epinephrine and norepinephrine when people are under stress and that aids in sympathetic arousal.

The adrenal cortex produces over 30 different hormones called *corticoids* (also called steroids) that regulate salt intake and help initiate* and control stress reactions; it also provides a source of sex hormones in addition to those provided by the gonads. One of the most important of these adrenal hormones is *cortisol*, released when the body experiences stress, both physical stress (such as illness, surgery, or extreme heat or cold) and psychological stress (such as an emotional upset). **LINK** to Learning Objective 9.5. Cortisol is important in the release of glucose into the bloodstream during stress, providing energy for the brain itself, and in the release of fatty acids from the fat cells that provide the muscles with energy.

Overall, the interactions between the sympathetic and parasympathetic systems provide an important framework in how we respond to both internal and external events or challenges. Next we will look at how they work together to protect us, or if activated for too long, can lead to some undesirable effects.

HORMONES AND STRESS

2.7 Describe how the autonomic nervous system and body are impacted by stress.

The sympathetic and parasympathetic systems, and various hormones, figure prominently in our body's physiological reactions to stress.

THE GENERAL ADAPTATION SYNDROME Endocrinologist Hans Selye was the founder of the field of research concerning stress and its effects on the human body. He studied the sequence of physiological reactions that the body goes through when adapting to a stressor. This sequence (see **Figure 2.10**) is called the **general adaptation syndrome (GAS)** and consists of three stages (Selye, 1956).

- **Alarm:** When the body first reacts to a stressor, the sympathetic nervous system is activated. The adrenal glands release hormones that increase heart rate, blood pressure, and the supply of blood sugar, resulting in a burst of energy. Reactions such as fever, nausea, and headache are common.

- **Resistance:** As the stress continues, the body settles into sympathetic division activity, continuing to release the stress hormones that help the body fight off, or resist, the stressor. The early symptoms of alarm lessen and the person or animal may actually feel better. This stage will continue until the stressor ends or the organism has used up

---

*initiate: begin or start.

all of its resources. Researchers have found that one of the hormones released under stress, noradrenaline (norepinephrine), actually seems to affect the brain's processing of pain, so that when under stress a person may experience a kind of analgesia (insensitivity to pain) if, for example, the person hits an arm or a shin (Delaney et al., 2007).

- **Exhaustion:** When the body's resources are gone, exhaustion occurs. Exhaustion can lead to the formation of stress-related diseases (e.g., high blood pressure or a weakened immune system) or the death of the organism if outside help is unavailable (Stein-Behrens et al., 1994). When the stressor ends, the parasympathetic division activates and the body attempts to replenish its resources.

Alarm and resistance are stages that people experience many times throughout life, allowing people to adapt to life's demands (Selye, 1976). It is the prolonged secretion of the stress hormones during the exhaustion stage that can lead to the most harmful effects of stress. It was this aspect of Selye's work that convinced other researchers of the connection between stress and certain *diseases of adaptation* as Selye termed them, such as high blood pressure.

IMMUNE SYSTEM AND STRESS As Selye first discovered, the **immune system** (the system of cells, organs, and chemicals in the body that responds to attacks on the body from diseases and injuries) is affected by stress. The field of **psychoneuroimmunology** concerns the study of the effects of psychological factors such as stress, emotions, thinking, learning, and behavior on the immune system (Ader, 2003; Cohen & Herbert, 1996; Kiecolt-Glaser, 2009; Kiecolt-Glaser et al., 1995, 1996, 2002). Researchers in this field have found that stress triggers the same response in the immune system that infection triggers (Maier & Watkins, 1998). Certain enzymes and other chemicals (including antibodies) are created by immune cells when the immune cells, or white blood cells, encounter an infection in the body. The white blood cells surround the bacteria or other infectious material and release the chemicals and enzymes into the bloodstream. From there, these chemicals activate receptor sites on the *vagus nerve*, the longest nerve that connects the body to the brain. It is the activation of these receptor sites that signals the brain that the body is sick, causing the brain to respond by further activation of the immune system.

Stress activates this same system but starts in the brain rather than in the bloodstream. The same chemical changes that occur in the brain when it has been alerted by the vagus nerve to infection in the body occurred in laboratory animals when they were kept isolated from other animals or given electric shocks (Maier & Watkins, 1998). This has the effect of "priming" the immune system, allowing it to more successfully resist the effects of the stress, as in Selye's resistance stage of the GAS.

Hormones also play a part in helping the immune system fight the effects of stress. Researchers (Morgan et al., 2009) have found that a hormone called dehydroepiandrosterone (DHEA), known to provide antistress benefits in animals, also aids humans in stress toleration—perhaps by regulating the effects of stress on the hippocampus (part of the limbic system). ⓁⒾⓃⓀ to Learning Objective 2.11.

💬 So stress actually increases the activity of the immune system? But then how does stress end up causing those diseases, like high blood pressure?

The positive effects of stress on the immune system only seem to work when the stress is not a continual, chronic condition. As stress continues, the body's resources begin to fail in the exhaustion phase of the general adaptation to stress (Kiecolt-Glaser et al., 1987, 1995, 1996; Prigerson et al., 1997). In one study, college students who were

Figure 2.10 General Adaptation Syndrome

In the alarm stage, resistance drops at first as the sympathetic system quickly activates. But resistance then rapidly increases as the body mobilizes its defense systems. In the resistance stage, the body is working at a much increased level of resistance, using resources until the stress ends or the resources run out. In the exhaustion stage, the body is no longer able to resist as resources have been depleted, and at this point disease and even death are possible.

undergoing a stressful series of exams were compared to a group of similar students relaxing during a time of no classes and no exams (Deinzer et al., 2000). The exam group tested significantly lower for immune system chemicals that help fight off disease than did the relaxing control group, even as long as 14 days after the exams were over. The suppression of immune system functioning by stress apparently can continue even after the stress itself is over.

One reason that the early stress reaction is helpful but prolonged stress is not might be that the stress reaction, in evolutionary terms, is really only "designed" for a short-term response, such as running from a predator (Sapolsky, 2004). That level of intense bodily and hormonal activity isn't really meant to go on and on, as it does for human beings in the modern, stress-filled life we now know. Humans experience the stress reaction over prolonged periods of times and in situations that are not necessarily life-threatening, leading to a breakdown in the immune system.

HEART DISEASE   Of course, anything that can weaken the immune system can have a negative effect on other bodily systems. Stress has been shown to put people at a higher risk of **coronary heart disease (CHD)**, the buildup of a waxy substance called plaque in the arteries of the heart. This relationship is at least in part because the liver, which is not activated while the sympathetic nervous system is aroused, does not have a chance to clear the fat and cholesterol from the bloodstream, leading to clogged arteries and eventually the possibility of heart attacks or strokes. In one study, middle-aged men were questioned about stress, diet, and lifestyle factors and were examined for biological risk factors for heart disease: obesity, high blood sugar, high triglycerides (a type of fatty acid found in the blood), and low levels of HDL or "good" cholesterol. (See **Figure 2.11**) Stress and the production of stress hormones were found to be strongly linked to all four biological risk factors: The more stress the men were exposed to in their work environment and home life, the more likely they were to exhibit these risk factors (Brunner et al., 2002).

Other studies have produced similar findings. One study looked at the heart health of people who suffered acute stress reactions after the 9/11 terrorist attacks and found a 53 percent increase in heart ailments over the 3 years following the attacks (Holman et al., 2008), whereas another large-scale study found that work stress is highly associated with an increased risk of coronary heart disease due to negative effects of stress on the autonomic nervous system and glandular activity (Chandola et al., 2008). Recent studies have shown a clear relationship between stress in the workplace and an increased risk of coronary heart disease as well as depression, sleep disturbances, and unhealthy habits such as a lack of physical activity—none of which are good for coronary health (Emeny et al., 2012, 2013). Prolonged stress is simply not good for the heart.

CANCER   Cancer is not one disease but rather a collection of diseases that can affect any part of the body. Unlike normal cells, which divide and reproduce according to genetic instructions and stop dividing according to those same instructions, cancer cells divide

Figure 2.11   Stress and CHD

The blue box on the left represents various sources of stress (Type A personality refers to someone who is ambitious, always working, and usually hostile). In addition to the physical reactions that accompany the stress reaction, an individual under stress may be more likely to engage in unhealthy behavior such as overeating, drinking alcohol or taking other kinds of drugs, avoiding exercise, and acting out in anger or frustration. This kind of behavior also contributes to an increased risk of coronary heart disease.

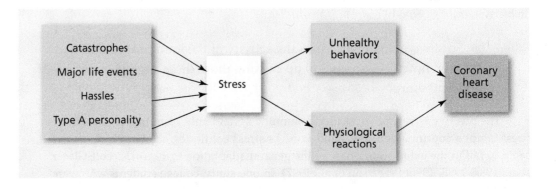

without stopping. The resulting tumors affect the normal functioning of the organs and systems they invade, causing them to fail, eventually killing the organism.

Although stress itself cannot directly give a person cancer, stress can have a suppressing effect on the immune system, making the unchecked growth of cancer more likely. In particular, an immune-system cell called a **natural killer (NK) cell** has as its main functions the suppression of viruses and the destruction of tumor cells (Herberman & Ortaldo, 1981). Stress has been shown to depress the release of natural killer cells, making it more difficult for the body's systems to fight cancerous growths (Zorilla et al., 2001). The hormone adrenaline is released under stress and has been found to interfere with a protein that normally would suppress the growth of cancer cells (Sastry et al., 2007). In other research, stress has been linked to the release of hormones such as adrenaline and noradrenaline that, over time, can cause mistakes (such as damage to the telomeres, structures at the ends of chromosomes that control the number of times a cell can reproduce) in the instructions given by the genes to the cells of the body. As these mistakes "pile up" over the years, cells can begin to grow out of control, causing the growth of tumors and possibly cancer (Kiecolt-Glaser et al., 2002).

Stress may impact the effectiveness of cancer treatments as well. In one study of mice implanted with human prostate cancer cells, treatment with a drug to destroy the cancer cells and prevent growth of tumors was effective when the mice were kept calm and stress-free, but failed miserably when the mice were stressed (Hassan et al., 2013).

One possible bit of positive news: Unlike the research linking stress at work to heart disease and diabetes, one study has found that work-related stress does not appear to be linked to developing cancer of the colon, lungs, breasts, or prostate (Heikkila et al., 2013). While 5 percent of over 100,000 participants in the 12 years over which the study took place developed some form of cancer, there was no association between job-related stress and risk of cancer.

OTHER HEALTH ISSUES   Heart disease and cancer are not the only diseases affected by stress. As indicated earlier, weight problems may also become associated with stress. One chronic illness sometimes associated with excessive weight gain is *diabetes*, specifically **Type 2 diabetes** (Type 1 diabetes is associated with failure of the pancreas to secrete enough insulin, necessitating medication, and is usually diagnosed before the age of 40). Type 2 diabetes is associated with excessive weight gain and occurs when pancreas insulin levels become less efficient as the body size increases. Type 2 diabetes can respond favorably to proper diet, exercise, and weight loss, but may also require medication. Typically, it is associated with older adults, but with the rise in obesity among children, more cases of Type 2 diabetes in children are now occurring.

Research has continued to link high levels of stress with increased risk of diabetes. A 35-year study in Sweden monitored the health and stress factors of 7,500 men who began the study with no history of diabetes or coronary heart disease (Novak et al., 2013). Those men who reported experiencing permanent stress, related to home life and/or work life, had a 45 percent higher chance of developing diabetes compared to men who reported no stress or only periodic stress. Another study found that high levels of stress in the workplace can accurately predict who will develop diabetes, particularly in those people who had low levels of social support (Toker et al., 2012).

Studies have shown that children in families experiencing ongoing stress are more likely to develop fevers with illness than are other children (Wyman et al., 2007). (Oddly enough, this same study showed that in children, stress actually seems to improve the function of their natural killer cells, just the opposite effect that is seen in adults.) A review of research and scientific literature (Cohen et al., 2007) found stress to be a contributing factor in a variety of human diseases and disorders, including heart disease, depression, and HIV/AIDS. Another longitudinal study's findings suggest that experiencing work-related stress in middle age may increase an individual's chances of developing both physical and mental disabilities in old age (Kulmala et al., 2013).

Concept Map L.O. 2.6, 2.7

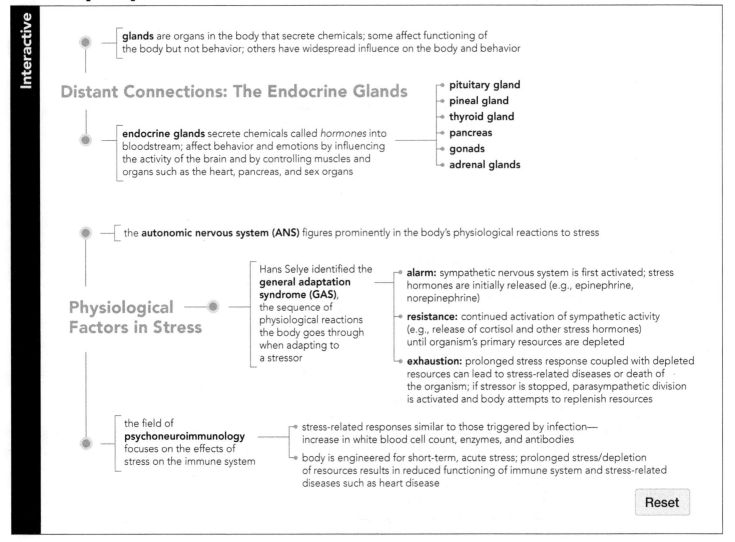

Distant Connections: The Endocrine Glands

glands are organs in the body that secrete chemicals; some affect functioning of the body but not behavior; others have widespread influence on the body and behavior

endocrine glands secrete chemicals called *hormones* into bloodstream; affect behavior and emotions by influencing the activity of the brain and by controlling muscles and organs such as the heart, pancreas, and sex organs

- pituitary gland
- pineal gland
- thyroid gland
- pancreas
- gonads
- adrenal glands

the **autonomic nervous system (ANS)** figures prominently in the body's physiological reactions to stress

Physiological Factors in Stress

Hans Selye identified the **general adaptation syndrome (GAS)**, the sequence of physiological reactions the body goes through when adapting to a stressor

- **alarm:** sympathetic nervous system is first activated; stress hormones are initially released (e.g., epinephrine, norepinephrine)
- **resistance:** continued activation of sympathetic activity (e.g., release of cortisol and other stress hormones) until organism's primary resources are depleted
- **exhaustion:** prolonged stress response coupled with depleted resources can lead to stress-related diseases or death of the organism; if stressor is stopped, parasympathetic division is activated and body attempts to replenish resources

the field of **psychoneuroimmunology** focuses on the effects of stress on the immune system

- stress-related responses similar to those triggered by infection—increase in white blood cell count, enzymes, and antibodies
- body is engineered for short-term, acute stress; prolonged stress/depletion of resources results in reduced functioning of immune system and stress-related diseases such as heart disease

Reset

Practice Quiz How much do you remember? ANSWERS ON PAGE AK–1.

Pick the best answer.

1. Andrew has always been thin. In fact, he often seems to be able to eat whatever he wants without gaining weight. The doctor told his parents that Andrew's _____ gland is the cause of his fast metabolism.

- **a.** pituitary
- **b.** adrenal
- **c.** thyroid
- **d.** pancreas

2. Your friend Melissa has suffered from diabetes for her entire life. She regularly tests her blood to make sure her sugar levels are not too high or low. Which gland in her endocrine system is responsible for regulating her blood sugar?

- **a.** pancreas
- **b.** thyroid
- **c.** pituitary
- **d.** adrenal

3. Of the following, which is **NOT** one of the stages of the general adaptation syndrome?

- **a.** resistance
- **b.** exhaustion
- **c.** compensation
- **d.** alarm

4. Part of the human immune system is the presence of _____ cells, whose primary function is to suppress viruses and destroy tumor cells

- **a.** leukotriene
- **b.** histamine
- **c.** natural killer (NK)
- **d.** blastocyst

Looking Inside the Living Brain

Scientists can't be sure what brain tissue really looks like when it's inside the skull of a living person—nor can they be certain that it looks identical to that of a brain sitting on a dissecting table. How can scientists find out if the brain is intact, if parts are missing or damaged, or what the various parts of the brain do?

METHODS FOR STUDYING SPECIFIC REGIONS OF THE BRAIN

2.8 **Describe how lesioning studies and brain stimulation are used to study the brain.**

Researchers are able to learn about the brain through accidental damage, or through intentional manipulation of brain tissue. When appropriate, such manipulation can be accomplished through *lesioning* or *stimulation* methods.

LESIONING STUDIES   One way to get some idea of the functions that various areas of the brain control is to study animals or people with damage in those areas. In animals, that may mean researchers will deliberately damage a part of the brain, after which, they test the animal to see what has happened to its abilities. In such an experiment, once the test animal is anesthetized and given medication for pain, a thin wire, which is insulated everywhere but at its tip, is surgically inserted into the brain. An electrical current strong enough to kill off the target neurons is sent through the tip of the wire. This procedure is called **lesioning**.

It should be obvious that researchers cannot destroy areas of brains in living human beings. One method they can use is to study and test people who already have brain damage. However, this is not an ideal way to study the brain. No two case studies of humans are likely to present damage in exactly the same area of the brain, nor would the cases involve exactly the same amount of damage.

BRAIN STIMULATION   In contrast to lesioning, a less harmful way to study the brain is to temporarily disrupt or enhance the normal functioning of specific brain areas through electrical stimulation, and then study the resulting changes in behavior or cognition. The procedure of stimulating a specific area of the brain is much the same as in lesioning, but the much milder current in this research does no damage to the neurons. It does cause the neurons to react as if they had received a message. This is called *electrical stimulation of the brain*, or *ESB*. It has become an important technique in psychology, as its use in animals (and in humans under very special circumstances such as testing before surgery to address seizure disorders) has informed us in many areas of investigation, including new directions for therapy.

Dr. Carly Yadon
Missouri State Psychology Department
Brain and Behavior Lab

INVASIVE TECHNIQUES: STIMULATING FROM THE INSIDE   A specific type of ESB called *deep brain stimulation (DBS)* has been shown to be very helpful in some disorders in humans. In this procedure, neurosurgeons place electrodes in specific deep-brain areas and then route the electrode wires to a pacemaker-like device called an impulse generator that is surgically implanted under the collarbone. The impulse generator then sends impulses to the implanted electrodes, stimulating the specific brain areas of interest. Deep brain stimulation has been widely used as a treatment for Parkinson's disease and may play an important role in the treatment of seizure disorder, chronic pain, and possibly some psychiatric disorders (Fisher et al., 2010; Rabins et al., 2009; Weaver et al., 2009) among other areas. Techniques such as DBS are typically used only after all other less intrusive treatments have been shown to be ineffective or whose side effects have been deemed undesirable. For example, DBS is being investigated for the treatment of anorexia nervosa in individuals where other treatments have not been effective (Lipsman et al., 2013).

NONINVASIVE TECHNIQUE: STIMULATING FROM THE OUTSIDE   There are also noninvasive techniques for stimulating the brain that contribute to research and our knowledge of the brain in a variety of areas. In *transcranial magnetic stimulation* (TMS), magnetic pulses are applied to the cortex using special copper wire coils that are positioned over the head.

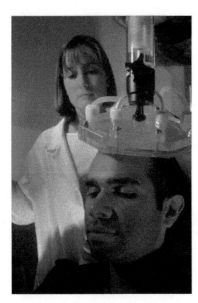

A doctor at the National Institute of Mental Health in Bethesda, Maryland, uses an electromagnet as part of an experimental treatment for depression. This treatment, called repetitive transcranial magnetic stimulation (rTMS), excites neurons in the brain, triggering activity.

The resulting magnetic fields stimulate neurons in the targeted area of the cortex. Longer lasting stimulation results when the pulses are administered in a repetitive fashion, and is referred to as *repetitive TMS* (rTMS). Another procedure, called *transcranial direct current stimulation* (tDCS), uses scalp electrodes to pass very low amplitude direct current to the brain to change the excitability of cortical neurons directly below the electrodes. Both rTMS and tDCS are being evaluated as research tools in studies of cognition such as memory retrieval and decision making (Boggio et al., 2010; Boggio, Fregni et al., 2009) and as possible treatment options for a variety of psychological disorders including post-traumatic stress disorder (PTSD) and depression, and physical disorders due to suffering a stroke (Boggio, Rocha et al., 2009; Nitsche et al., 2009; Williams et al., 2010).

Bear in mind that stimulating the cortex may facilitate specific functions or behaviors but impair others. For example, if someone is counting from 1 to 20 and the brain is stimulated in the correct location of the motor cortex, the person's speech would be disrupted, but perhaps stimulating in other areas of the frontal lobe may assist the person in attending to the counting task. Furthermore, the brain has widespread connections, so stimulation in one area is likely to affect other areas. In one recent study, inhibitory stimulation of the left prefrontal cortex resulted in reduced blood oxygenation on both the left and right sides of the prefrontal cortex (Tupak et al., 2013).

Note: tDCS is NOT the same as electroconvulsive therapy, which uses much higher levels of current through the entire brain, resulting in a grand mal seizure and changes in the brain chemistry associated with depression. **LINK** to Learning Objective 13.11.

NEUROIMAGING TECHNIQUES

2.9 Describe how neuroimaging techniques can provide information about the brain's structure and function.

All of these methods of stimulation yield important information about the brain, thinking, and behavior, but they do not allow us to see what is going on with the brain as a whole. Instead, various neuroimaging techniques can do this, either by directly imaging the brain's structure (the different parts) or its function (how the parts work). These methods also vary in their degree of spatial resolution (ability to see fine detail) and temporal resolution (ability to time lock a recorded event.)

MAPPING STRUCTURE   Historically, scientists and researchers would have to wait until someone died to examine the structure of their brain. Thankfully that is no longer the case. Scientists have several ways to study the parts of the human brain without causing harm to the person.

COMPUTED TOMOGRAPHY (CT)   One way to examine the brain of a living person is to take a series of X-rays of the brain, aided by a computer. This is accomplished during a **CT scan** (**computed tomography** involves mapping "slices" of the brain by computer). CT scans can show stroke damage, tumors, injuries, and abnormal brain structure. (See **Figure 2.12a**) A CT scan is often the structural imaging method of choice when there is metal in the body (e.g., a bullet or surgical clips) and useful for imaging possible skull fractures. (See **Figure 2.12b**.)

MAGNETIC RESONANCE IMAGING (MRI)   As useful as a CT scan can be for imaging the skull, it doesn't show very small details within the brain. The relatively newer technique of **magnetic resonance imaging, or MRI**, provides much more detail (see **Figure 2.12c** and **2.12d**), even allowing doctors to see the effects of very small strokes. The person getting an MRI scan is placed inside a machine that generates a powerful magnetic field to align hydrogen atoms in the brain tissues (these normally spin in a random fashion); then radio pulses are used to make the atoms spin at a particular frequency and direction. The time it takes for the atoms to return to their normal spin allows a computer to create a three-dimensional image of the brain and display "slices" of that image on a screen.

Figure 2.12   Mapping Brain Structure

Fig 2.12a CT scan from a 5-year-old girl with a head injury and skull fracture, depicting the brain and swelling associated with the injury; Fig 2.12b Same CT scan highlighting the skull fracture (indicated by the red arrow). Contrast the brain detail of Fig 2.12a with the MRI scan in Fig 2.12c (different, adult individual). Note the scans are in the horizontal plane, separating the brain into upper and lower portions. Fig 2.12d. Different type of MRI image from an older adult, with cortical cell loss (atrophy) and white matter changes. Notice the enlarged ventricles, and widening of the grooves (sulci) in the outer cortex as compared to 2.12c. Figs 2.12a, b, c, and d images created with OsiriX software; CT and MRI data courtesy of N. White.

Using MRI as a basis, researchers have developed several techniques that allow us to study other aspects of the brain. *MRI spectroscopy* allows researchers to estimate the concentration of specific chemicals and neurotransmitters in the brain. Another fascinating technique is called *DTI,* or *diffusion tensor imaging.* The brain has two distinct color regions, *gray matter,* the outer areas consisting largely of neurons with unmyelinated axons, and *white matter,* the fiber tracts consisting of myelinated axons (the myelin is responsible for the lighter color). DTI uses MRI technology to provide a way to measure connectivity in the brain by imaging these white matter tracts. DTI has been used to investigate many disorders and conditions, including multiple sclerosis, dementia, and schizophrenia (Assaf & Pasternak, 2008; Catani & Thiebaut de Schotten, 2012; Ulmer et al., 2006; Voineskos et al., 2010).

MAPPING FUNCTION   As important as imaging brain structure is, it is sometimes important to know how different brain areas function. And just as scientists and researchers have various options for examining the physical parts of the brain, there are also different options for studying brain function.

THE ELECTROENCEPHALOGRAM (EEG)   A fairly harmless way to study the activity of the living brain is to record the electrical activity of the cortex just below the skull using a device called an **electroencephalograph**. The first **electroencephalogram (EEG)** recording in humans was accomplished in 1924 by Hans Berger (Niedermeyer, 2005). Recording the EEG involves using small metal-disk or sponge-like electrodes placed directly on the scalp, and a special solution to help conduct the electrical signals from the cortex just below. These electrodes are connected to an amplifier and then to a computer to view the information. The resulting electrical output forms waves that indicate many things, such as stages of sleep, seizures, and even the presence of tumors. The EEG can also be used to help determine which areas of the brain are active during various mental tasks that involve memory and attention. EEG activity can be classified according to appearance and frequency, and different waves are associated with different brain activity. For example, *alpha waves* in the back of the brain are one indication of relaxed wakefulness (seen in bottom two lines in **Figure 2.13a** on the next page). EEG waveforms are covered in more detail in Chapter Four. ⓛ ⓘ ⓝ ⓚ to Learning Objective 4.4.

Another common EEG-based technique focuses on *event-related potentials,* or *ERPs.* In ERP studies, multiple presentations of a stimulus are measured during an EEG and then averaged to remove variations in the ongoing brain activity that is normally recorded during the EEG. The result is a measurement of the response of the brain related to the stimulus event itself, or an event-related potential. ERPs allow the study of different stages of cognitive processing. For example, one recent study has investigated differences in brain processing associated with the recognition of facial expression of emotion in individuals with and without schizophrenia (Lee et al., 2010); in other studies ERPs are being studied as a possible method of lie detection (Hu et al., 2013; Rosenfeld et al., 2008). This modality is also being used as part of brain–computer interfaces (BCIs) to assist people like Rick from the chapter opener better communicate and interact with others and the world around them.

POSITRON EMISSION TOMOGRAPHY (PET)   The functional neuroimaging methods discussed so far rely on the electrical activity of the brain. Other techniques make use of other indicators of brain activity, including energy consumption or changes in blood oxygen levels (if areas of the brain are active, they are likely using fuel and oxygen). In **positron emission tomography (PET)**, the person is injected with a radioactive glucose (a kind of sugar). The computer detects the activity of the brain cells by looking at which cells are using up the radioactive glucose and projecting the image of that activity onto a monitor. The computer uses colors to indicate different levels of brain activity, with lighter colors often indicating greater activity. (See **Figure 2.13b**.) With this method, researchers can actually have the person perform different tasks while the computer shows what his or her brain is doing during the task. A related technique is **single photon emission computed tomography (SPECT)**, which measures brain blood flow and uses more easily obtainable radioactive tracers than those used for PET (Bremmer, 2005).

FUNCTIONAL MRI (FMRI)   Although traditional MRI scans only show structure, there is a technique called **functional MRI (fMRI)** in which the computer tracks changes in the oxygen levels of the blood (see **Figure 2.13c**). By superimposing this picture of where the oxygen goes in the brain over the picture of the brain's structure, researchers can identify what areas of the brain are active. By combining such images taken over a period of time, a sort of "movie" of the brain's functioning can be made (Lin et al., 2007). Functional MRIs can give more detail, tend to be clearer than PET scans, and are an incredibly useful tool for research into the workings of the brain. For example, fMRI has been used to demonstrate that older adults with a genetic risk for Alzheimer's disease show greater activation in brain areas associated with semantic knowledge and word retrieval when compared to older adults without that genetic risk. This finding may one day help clinicians and researchers identify individuals at risk for Alzheimer's much earlier in the disease process (Wierenga et al., 2010). There is also exciting research suggesting individuals can use fMRI to learn how to regulate their own brain processes. Individuals with schizophrenia were able to use real-time fMRI (rtfMRI) to learn how to control a portion of their brain that assists in recognition of facial emotions, which is a common deficit in schizophrenia (Ruiz et al., 2013).

Figure 2.13   Mapping Brain Function

Various methods for mapping brain function. An EEG record is shown in Figure 2.13a, a PET scan image in Figure 2.13b, and an image from an fMRI study in Figure 2.13c. Data for Figure 2.13a courtesy of N. White.

a.

b.

c.

Concept Map L.O. 2.8, 2.9

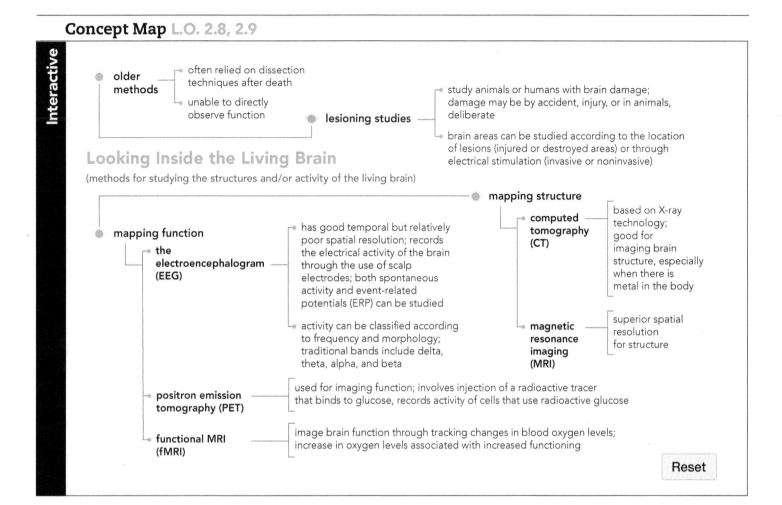

Practice Quiz How much do you remember? ANSWERS ON PAGE AK–1.

Pick the best answer.

1. Which of the following techniques involves passing a mild current through the brain to activate certain structures without damaging them, and has become an important technique in psychology?

a. electroconvulsive tomography (ECT)

b. magnetic resonance imaging (MRI)

c. deep brain lesioning

d. electrical stimulation of the brain (ESB)

2. Which of the following techniques analyzes blood oxygen levels to examine the functioning of the brain?

a. EEG

b. CT

c. fMRI

d. PET

3. Dr. Roll is conducting a research study. She wants to measure the connectivity in the research participants' brains by imaging their white matter. Which of the following methods will she use?

a. diffusion tensor imaging (DTI)

b. MRI spectroscopy

c. functional magnetic resonance imaging (fMRI)

d. computed tomography (CT)

4. If you were suffering from neurological problems and your neurologist wanted to have a study done of your brain and its electrical functioning, which of the following techniques would involve placing metal or sponge-like electrodes directly onto your scalp?

a. PTI

b. EEG

c. PET

d. DTI

🗨 Okay, now I understand a little more about how we look inside the brain. What exactly IS inside the brain?

From the Bottom Up: The Structures of the Brain

Now it's time to look at the various structures of the brain, starting from the bottom and working up to the top. This text won't be discussing every single part of the brain; only the parts interesting to psychologists as explorers of human behavior will be covered. Many parts of the brain also overlap in their functions, but a full understanding of the brain is not truly possible within one chapter of an introductory psychology text.

THE HINDBRAIN

2.10 **Identify the different structures of the bottom part of the brain, and describe the function of each.**

The brain can be divided into three main divisions early in our development that later subdivide into smaller divisions. The three primary divisions are the forebrain, the midbrain, and the hindbrain. The forebrain includes the cortex, basal ganglia, and the limbic system. The midbrain is important for both sensory and motor functions. The hindbrain includes the medulla, pons, and cerebellum.

MEDULLA   The **medulla** is located at the top of the spinal column. In **Figure 2.14**, it is the first "swelling" at the top of the spinal cord, just at the very bottom of the brain. This is the part of the brain that a person would least want to have damaged, as it controls life-sustaining functions such as heartbeat, breathing, and swallowing. It is in the medulla that the sensory nerves coming from the left and right sides of the body cross over, so that sensory information from the left side of the body goes to the right side of the brain and vice versa.

Figure 2.14 MAJOR STRUCTURES OF THE HUMAN BRAIN

*for illustration purposes, the right hemisphere is transparent in this image

PONS   The **pons** is the larger "swelling" just above the medulla. This term means "bridge," and the pons is indeed the bridge between the lower parts of the brain and the upper sections. As in the medulla, there is a crossover of nerves, but in this case it is the motor nerves carrying messages from the brain to the body. This allows the pons to coordinate the movements of the left and right sides of the body. (It will be useful to remember these nerve crossovers when reading about the functions of the left and right sides of the brain in a later part of this chapter.) The pons also influences sleep, dreaming, and arousal. The role that the pons plays in sleep and dreams will be discussed in more detail in Chapter Four. **(L)(I)(N)(K)** to Learning Objective 4.6.

THE RETICULAR FORMATION   The **reticular formation (RF)** is an area of neurons running through the middle of the medulla and the pons and slightly beyond. These neurons are responsible for people's ability to selectively attend to certain kinds of information in their surroundings. Basically, the RF allows people to ignore constant, unchanging information (such as the noise of an air conditioner) and become alert to changes in information (for example, if the air conditioner stopped, most people would notice immediately).

The reticular formation is also the part of the brain that helps keep people alert and aroused. One part of the RF is called the *reticular activating system (RAS)*, and it stimulates the upper part of the brain, keeping people awake and alert. When a person is driving along and someone suddenly pulls out in front of the vehicle, it is the RAS that brings the driver to full attention. It is also the system that lets a mother hear her baby cry in the night, even though she might sleep through other noises.

Studies have shown that when the RF of rats is electrically stimulated while they are sleeping, they immediately awaken. If the RF is destroyed (by deep lesioning, for example), they fall into a sleeplike coma from which they never awaken (Moruzzi & Magoun, 1949; Steriade & McCarley, 1990). The RF is also implicated in comas in humans (Plum & Posner, 1985).

CEREBELLUM   At the base of the skull, behind the pons and below the main part of the brain, is a structure that looks like a small brain. (See Figure 2.14) The **cerebellum** (meaning "little brain") is the part of the lower brain that controls all involuntary, rapid, fine motor movement. People can sit upright because the cerebellum controls all the little muscles needed to keep them from falling out of their chair. It also coordinates voluntary movements that have to happen in rapid succession, such as walking, skating, gymnastics, dancing, playing a musical instrument, and even the movements of speech. Learned reflexes, skills, and habits are also stored here, which allows them to become more or less automatic. Because of the cerebellum, people don't have to consciously think about their posture, muscle tone, and balance.

💬 So if your cerebellum is damaged, you might be very uncoordinated?

Yes. In fact, in a disease called *spinocerebellar degeneration* the first symptoms are tremors, an unsteady walk, slurred speech, dizziness, and muscle weakness. The person suffering from this disease will eventually be unable to walk, stand, or even get a spoon to his or her own mouth (Schöls et al., 1998). These symptoms are similar to what one might see in a person who is suffering from alcohol intoxication.

Just like we are starting to better understand the various roles of glial cells, researchers and scientists are still working to better understand other functions of the cerebellum. Research suggests the cerebellum is involved in much more than motor control and may be involved with a variety of higher functions, with parts of the cerebellum activated during sensorimotor tasks and other parts involved in cognitive or emotional tasks (Stoodley & Schmahmann, 2009).

This pitcher must count on his cerebellum to help him balance and coordinate the many fine motor commands that allow him to pitch the baseball accurately and swiftly. What other kinds of professions depend heavily on the activity of the cerebellum?

STRUCTURES UNDER THE CORTEX: THE LIMBIC SYSTEM

2.11 **Identify structures of the brain that are involved in emotion, learning, memory, and motivation.**

The forebrain includes the two cerebral hemispheres of the brain, including the cortex, which is discussed in detail later in this chapter, and a number of important structures located under the cortex in each hemisphere. These subcortical structures (the prefix *sub* means "under" or "below") play a part in our thinking and behavior. While there are subcortical structures that influence motor control and the learning of motor skills, the *basal ganglia*, and white matter fiber pathways that connect the cortex to other parts of the brain and spinal cord, we will focus on the subcortical structures that have been collectively referred to as the *limbic system*. (See **Figure 2.15**.)

The **limbic system** (the word *limbic* means "marginal" and these structures are found in the inner margin of the upper brain) includes the thalamus, hypothalamus, hippocampus, amygdala, and the cingulate cortex. In general, the limbic system is involved in emotions, motivation, and learning.

THALAMUS   The **thalamus** ("inner chamber") is in some ways similar to a triage* nurse. This somewhat round structure in the center of the brain acts as a kind of relay station for incoming sensory information. Like a nurse, the thalamus might perform some processing of that sensory information before sending it on to the part of the cortex that deals with that kind of sensation—hearing, sight, touch, or taste. Damage to the thalamus might result in the loss or partial loss of any or all of those sensations.

The sense of smell is unique in that signals from the neurons in the sinus cavity go directly into special parts of the brain called **olfactory bulbs**, just under the front part of the brain. Smell is the only sense that does not have to first pass through the thalamus.

HYPOTHALAMUS   A very small but extremely powerful part of the brain is located just below and in front of the thalamus (see Figure 2.15). The **hypothalamus** ("below the inner chamber") regulates body temperature, thirst, hunger, sleeping and waking, sexual activity, and emotions. It sits right above the pituitary gland. The hypothalamus controls the pituitary, so the ultimate regulation of hormones lies with the hypothalamus.

Figure 2.15 THE LIMBIC SYSTEM

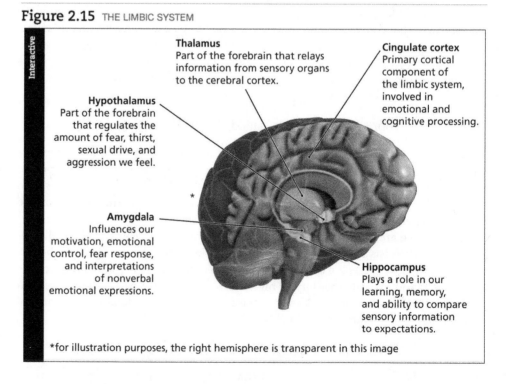

Thalamus
Part of the forebrain that relays information from sensory organs to the cerebral cortex.

Cingulate cortex
Primary cortical component of the limbic system, involved in emotional and cognitive processing.

Hypothalamus
Part of the forebrain that regulates the amount of fear, thirst, sexual drive, and aggression we feel.

Amygdala
Influences our motivation, emotional control, fear response, and interpretations of nonverbal emotional expressions.

Hippocampus
Plays a role in our learning, memory, and ability to compare sensory information to expectations.

*for illustration purposes, the right hemisphere is transparent in this image

---

*triage: a process for sorting injured people into groups based on their need for, or likely benefit from, immediate medical treatment.

HIPPOCAMPUS   Like many structures in the brain, the **hippocampus** was named based on its appearance. Hippocampus is the Greek word for "seahorse" and it was given to this brain structure because the first scientists who dissected the brain thought it looked like a seahorse. The hippocampus is located within the medial temporal lobe on each side of the brain (medial means "toward the middle"). Research has shown that the hippocampus is instrumental in forming long-term (permanent) declarative memories that are then stored elsewhere in the brain (Squire & Kandel, 2009). **L I N K** to Learning Objective 6.12. As mentioned earlier, ACh, the neurotransmitter involved in muscle control, is also involved in the memory function of the hippocampus. People who have Alzheimer's disease, for example, have much lower levels of ACh in that structure than is normal, and the drugs given to these people boost the levels of ACh.

AMYGDALA   The **amygdala** ("almond") is another area of the brain named for its shape and appearance. It is located near the hippocampus. The amygdala is involved in fear responses and memory of fear. Information from the senses goes to the amygdala before the upper part of the brain is even involved, so that people can respond to danger very quickly, sometimes before they are consciously aware of what is happening. In 1939 researchers found that monkeys with large amounts of their temporal lobes removed—including the amygdala—were completely unafraid of snakes and humans, both of which are normally fear-provoking stimuli (Klüver & Bucy, 1939. This effect came to be known as the *Klüver-Bucy syndrome.* Rats that have damaged amygdala structures will also show no fear when placed next to a cat (Maren & Fanselow, 1996). Case studies of humans with damage to the amygdala also show a link to decreased fear response (Adophs et al., 2005). Although the amygdala plays a vital role in forming emotional memories, it is still unclear if the memories are stored in the amygdala (Squire & Kandel, 2009).

CINGULATE CORTEX   The cingulate cortex is the limbic structure that is actually found in the cortex. It is found right above the corpus callosum in the frontal and parietal lobes and plays an important role in both emotional and cognitive processing. The cingulate cortex can be divided into up to four regions that play different roles in processing emotional, cognitive, and autonomic information (Vogt & Palomero-Gallagher, 2012). It has been shown to be active during a variety of cognitive tasks such as selective attention, written word recognition, and working memory (Cabeza & Nyberg, 2000) and has been implicated in a variety of psychological and mental disorders, including attention-deficit/hyperactivity disorder (Bush et al., 1999; Bush et al., 2008), schizophrenia, major depressive disorder, and bipolar disorder (Fornito et al., 2009; Maletic et al., 2007). The next section further explores the cortex and its functions.

THE CORTEX

2.12 **Identify the parts of the cortex that process the different senses and those that control movement of the body.**

As stated earlier, the **cortex** ("rind" or outer covering) is the outermost part of the brain, which is the part of the brain most people picture when they think of what the brain looks like. It is made up of tightly packed neurons and actually is only about one-tenth of an inch thick on average (Fischl et al., 2001; MacDonald et al., 2000; Zilles, 1990). The cortex has a very recognizable surface anatomy because it is full of wrinkles.

 Why is the cortex so wrinkled?

The wrinkling of the cortex allows a much larger area of cortical cells to exist in the small space inside the skull. If the cortex were to be taken out, ironed flat, and measured, it would be about 2 to 3 square feet. (The owner of the cortex would also be dead, but that's fairly obvious, right?) As the brain develops before birth, it forms a smooth outer covering on all the other brain structures. This will be the cortex, which will get more and

This young woman's thirst is regulated by her hypothalamus.

From top to bottom, a rat brain, sheep brain, and human brain (not to scale!). Note the differences in the amount of corticalization, or wrinkling, of the cortex between these three brains. Greater amounts of corticalization are associated with increases in size and complexity.

more wrinkled as the brain increases in size and complexity. This increase in wrinkling is called "corticalization."

CEREBRAL HEMISPHERES   The brain is divided into two sections called the **cerebral hemispheres**, which are connected by a thick, tough band of neural fibers (axons) called the **corpus callosum** (literally meaning "hard bodies," as calluses on the feet are hard). (Refer back to Figure 2.15.) The corpus callosum allows the left and right hemispheres to communicate with each other. Each hemisphere can be roughly divided into four sections or lobes by looking at the deeper wrinkles, or fissures, in its surface. The lobes are named for the skull bones that cover them (see **Figure 2.16**).

Another organizational feature of the cortex is that for specific regions, each hemisphere is responsible for the opposite side of the body, either for control, or for receiving information. For example, the motor cortex controls the muscles on the opposite side of the body. If we are writing with our right hand, the motor cortex in the left hemisphere is responsible for controlling those movements. This feature, referred to as *contralateral organization*, plays a role in information coming from many of the sense organs to the brain, and in the motor commands originating in the brain going to the rest of the body.

Information from our body can also be transmitted to both sides of the brain, or *bilaterally* (as in hearing and vision), or to only one side of the brain, or *ipsilaterally* (as in taste and olfaction). These aspects are also important in the study of *brain lateralization*, which we will come back to later in the chapter. Why do we have this arrangement for some functions and not for others? No one really knows, but at least for some information, it assists with identifying where information from the environment is coming from. For auditory information from the ears, having sensory information projected to both hemispheres allows us to localize sounds by comparing the slightly different information coming from each ear.

OCCIPITAL LOBES   At the base of the cortex, toward the back of the brain is an area called the **occipital lobe**. This area processes visual information from the eyes in the *primary visual cortex*. The *visual association cortex*, also in this lobe, is the part of the brain that helps identify and make sense of the visual information from the eyes. The famed neurologist Oliver Sacks once had a patient who had a tumor in his right occipital lobe area. He could still see objects perfectly well and even describe them in physical terms,

Figure 2.16 THE LOBES OF THE BRAIN: FRONTAL, TEMPORAL, PARIETAL, AND OCCIPITAL

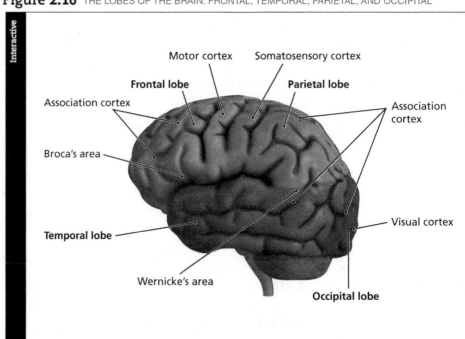

but he could not identify them by sight alone. For example, Sacks once gave him a rose to look at. The man turned it around and around and began to describe it as a "red inflorescence" of some type with a green tubular projection. Only when he held it under his nose (stimulating the sense of smell) did he recognize it as a rose (Sacks, 1990). Each area of the cortex has these association areas that help people make sense of sensory information.

PARIETAL LOBES   The **parietal lobes** are at the top and back of the brain, just under the parietal bone in the skull. This area contains the **somatosensory cortex**, an area of neurons (see **Figure 2.17**) at the front of the parietal lobes on either side of the brain. This area processes information from the skin and internal body receptors for touch, temperature, and body position. The somatosensory cortex is laid out in a rather interesting way—the cells at the top of the brain receive information from the bottom of the body, and as one moves down the area, the signals come from higher and higher in the body. It's almost as if a little upside-down person were laid out along this area of cells.

TEMPORAL LOBES   The beginning of the **temporal lobes** are found just behind the temples of the head. These lobes contain the *primary auditory cortex* and the *auditory association area.* Also found in the left temporal lobe is an area that in most people is particularly involved with language. We have already discussed some of the medial structures of the temporal lobe, the amygdala and hippocampus, that are involved in aspects of learning and memory. There are also parts of the temporal lobe that help us process visual information.

FRONTAL LOBES   These lobes are at the front of the brain, hence, the name **frontal lobes**. (It doesn't often get this easy in psychology; feel free to take a moment to appreciate it.) Here are found all the higher mental functions of the brain—planning, personality, memory storage, complex decision making, and (again in the left hemisphere in most people) areas devoted to language. The frontal lobe also helps in controlling emotions by means of its connection to the limbic system. The most forward part of the frontal lobes is called the prefrontal cortex. The middle area toward the center (medial prefrontal cortex) and bottom surface above the eyes (orbitofrontal prefrontal cortex—right above the orbits of the eye) have strong connections to the limbic system. Phineas Gage, who was mentioned in Chapter One, suffered damage to his left frontal lobe. He lacked emotional control because of the damage to his prefrontal cortex and the connections with limbic system structures. Overall, he had connections damaged from the left frontal cortex to many other parts of the brain (Ratiu et al., 2004; Van Horn et al., 2012). People with damage to the frontal lobe may also experience problems with performing mental or motor tasks, such as getting stuck on one step in a process or on one wrong answer in a test and repeating it over and over again, or making the same movement over and over, a phenomena called *perseveration* (Asp & Tranel, 2013; Luria, 1965; Goel & Grafman, 1995).

The frontal lobes also contain the **motor cortex**, a band of neurons located at the back of each lobe. (See Figure 2.17.) These cells control the movements of the body's voluntary muscles by sending commands out to the somatic division of the peripheral nervous system. The motor cortex is laid out just like the somatosensory cortex, which is right next door in the parietal lobes.

This area of the brain has been the focus of a great deal of recent research, specifically as related to the role of a special type of neuron. These neurons are called **mirror neurons**, which fire when an animal performs an action—but they also fire when an animal observes that same action being performed by another. Previous brain-imaging studies in humans

This boxer must rely on his parietal lobes to sense where his body is in relation to the floor of the ring and the other boxer, his occipital lobes to see his target, and his frontal lobes to guide his hand and arm into the punch.

Figure 2.17   The Motor and Somatosensory Cortex

The motor cortex in the frontal lobe controls the voluntary muscles of the body. Cells at the top of the motor cortex control muscles at the bottom of the body, whereas cells at the bottom of the motor cortex control muscles at the top of the body. Body parts are drawn larger or smaller according to the number of cortical cells devoted to that body part. For example, the hand has many small muscles and requires a larger area of cortical cells to control it. The somatosensory cortex, located in the parietal lobe just behind the motor cortex, is organized in much the same manner and receives information about the sense of touch and body position.

As this boy imitates the motions his father goes through while shaving, certain areas of his brain are more active than others, areas that control the motions of shaving. But even if the boy were only *watching* his father, those same neural areas would be active—the neurons in the boy's brain would *mirror* the actions of the father he is observing.

suggested that we, too, have mirror neurons in this area of the brain (Buccino et al., 2001; Buccino et al., 2004; Iacoboni et al., 1999). However, recent single-cell and multicell recordings in humans have demonstrated that neurons with mirroring functions are found not only in motor regions but also in parts of the brain involved in vision and memory. This suggests that such neurons provide much more information than previously thought about our own actions as compared to the actions of others (Mukamel et al., 2010). These findings may have particular relevance for better understanding or treating specific clinical conditions that are believed to involve a faulty mirror system in the brain such as autism (Oberman & Ramachandran, 2007; Rizzolatti et al., 2009). (L)(I)(N)K to Learning Objective 8.8.

WRITING PROMPT

Phineas Gage reportedly experienced profound personality and behavioral changes during the time period immediately following an accident where a tamping rod was driven through his frontal lobe. Discuss the extent to which the nature of his injuries and subsequent behavior change were the result of biological changes, or if they could have been due to other, possibly "social" causes.

▶   The response entered here will be saved to your notes and may be collected by your instructor if he/she requires it.

Submit

💬 You've mentioned association cortex a few times. Do the other lobes of the brain contain association cortex as well?

THE ASSOCIATION AREAS OF THE CORTEX

2.13 Identify the parts of the cortex that are responsible for higher forms of thought, such as language.

Association areas are made up of neurons in the cortex that are devoted to making connections between the sensory information coming into the brain and stored memories, images, and knowledge. In other words, association areas help people make sense of the incoming sensory input. Although the association areas in the occipital and temporal lobes have already been mentioned, much of the brain's association cortex is in the frontal lobes. Furthermore, some special association areas are worth talking about in more detail.

BROCA'S AREA   In the left frontal lobe of most people is an area of the brain devoted to the production of speech. (In a small portion of the population, this area is in the right frontal lobe.) More specifically, this area allows a person to speak smoothly and fluently. It is called *Broca's area* after nineteenth-century neurologist Paul Broca, who first provided widely-accepted clinical evidence that deficits in fluent and articulate speech result from damage to this area (Finger, 1994). Damage to Broca's area causes a person to be unable to get words out in a smooth, connected fashion. People with this condition may know exactly what they want to say and understand what they hear others say, but they cannot control the actual production of their own words. Speech is halting and words are often mispronounced, such as saying "cot" instead of "clock" or "non" instead of "nine." Some words may be left out entirely, such as "the" or "for." This is called **Broca's aphasia**. *Aphasia* refers to an inability to use or understand either written or spoken language (Goodglass et al., 2001). (Stuttering is a somewhat different problem in getting words *started*, rather than mispronouncing them or leaving them out, but may also be related to Broca's area.)

WERNICKE'S AREA   In the left temporal lobe (again, in most people) is an area called *Wernicke's area*, named after the physiologist and Broca's contemporary, Carl Wernicke, who first studied problems arising from damage in this location. This area of the brain appears to be involved in understanding the meaning of words (Goodglass et al., 2001). A person with **Wernicke's aphasia** would be able to speak fluently and pronounce words correctly, but the words would be the wrong ones entirely. For example, Elsie suffered a stroke to the temporal lobe, damaging this area of the brain. In the emergency room the nurse tried to take her blood pressure, and when the cuff inflated, Elsie said, "Oh, that's so Saturday hard." Elsie *thought* she was making sense. She also had trouble understanding what the people around her were saying to her.

SPATIAL NEGLECT   A condition that can sometimes occur following a stroke is **spatial neglect**, or unilateral neglect, in which a person with damage to the right parietal and occipital lobes of the cortex will ignore everything in the left visual field. Unilateral refers to one side of the body, and this type of brain damage most often only affects attention to objects in the left visual field. Damage to areas of the frontal and temporal lobes may also play a part along with the parietal damage. Spatial neglect can affect the left hemisphere, but this condition occurs less frequently and in a much milder form than right-hemisphere neglect (Corbetta et al., 2005; Heilman et al., 1993; Springer & Deutsch, 1998).

Dr. V. S. Ramachandran reported an interesting case of spatial neglect in his book, *Phantoms in the Brain* (Ramachandran & Blakeslee, 1998). A woman who was typically neat and conscientious about her appearance was discovered by her son on a visit to look messy and totally odd. Her hair was uncombed on the left side. Her green shawl was hanging neatly over her right shoulder but hanging onto the floor on the left. Her lipstick was neatly applied to the right side of her lips, and *only to the right side—the left side of her face was completely bare of makeup!* Yet her eyeliner, mascara, and rouge were all neatly applied to the right side of her face. This woman had suffered a stroke that left her with unilateral spatial neglect.

As this woman brushes the right side of her hair, is she really "seeing" the left side? If she has spatial neglect, the answer is "no." While her eyes work just fine, her damaged right hemisphere refuses to notice the left side of her visual field.

THE CEREBRAL HEMISPHERES: ARE YOU IN YOUR RIGHT MIND?

2.14 **Explain how some brain functions differ between the left and right hemispheres.**

Most people tend to think of the two cerebral hemispheres as identical twins. Both sides have the same four lobes and are arranged in much the same way. But language seems to be confined to the left hemisphere in about 90 percent of the population (Toga & Thompson, 2003). What other special tasks do the two halves of the **cerebrum** (the upper part of the brain consisting of the two hemispheres and the structures connecting them) engage in, and how do researchers know about such functions? Participate in the experiment *Hemispheric Specialization* to test the language abilities of the two hemispheres.

Experiment   HEMISPHERIC SPECIALIZATION

Interactive

| INTRODUCTION | INSTRUCTIONS | EXPERIMENT | RESULTS | DISCUSSION | REFERENCES |

This experiment tests the language abilities of the two hemispheres of the brain. By exposing the two hemispheres to a language test we can determine if the left hemisphere is dominant in language function.

When you are ready, click the "Start Practice Experiment" button to begin.

Left visual field   Right visual field

Retina   Retina

Optic chiasm

Left hemisphere   Right hemisphere

Corpus callosum

Previous   Start Practice Experiment

Simulate the **Experiment**, *Hemispheric Specialization.*

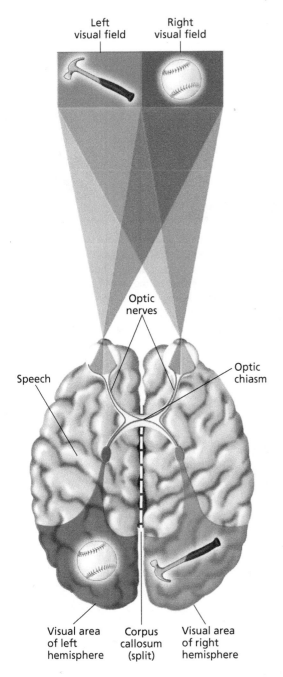

Figure 2.18   The Split-Brain Experiment

Roger Sperry created this experiment to demonstrate the specialization of the left and right hemispheres of the brain.

SPLIT-BRAIN RESEARCH   Roger Sperry was a pioneer in the field of hemisphere specialization. He won a Nobel Prize for his work in demonstrating that the left and right hemispheres of the brain specialize in different activities and functions (Sperry, 1968). In looking for a way to cure epilepsy (severe muscle spasms or seizures resulting from brain damage), Sperry cut through the corpus callosum, the thick band of neural fibers that joins the two hemispheres. In early research with animals, this technique worked and seemed to have no side effects. The first people to have this procedure done also experienced relief from their severe epileptic symptoms, but testing found that (in a sense) they now had two brains in one body.

The special testing involves sending messages to only one side of the brain, which is now possible because the connecting tissue, the corpus callosum, has been cut. **Figure 2.18** shows what happens with a typical split-brain patient.

In a split-brain patient, if a picture of a ball is flashed to the right side of the screen, the image of the ball will be sent to the left occipital lobe. The person will be able to say that he or she sees a ball. If a picture of a hammer is flashed to the left side of the screen, the person will not be able to *verbally* identify the object or be able to state with any certainty that something was seen. But if the *left hand* (controlled by the right hemisphere) is used, the person can point to the hammer he or she "didn't see." The right occipital lobe clearly saw the hammer, but the person could not *verbalize* that fact (Sperry, 1968). By conducting studies such as these, researchers have found that the left hemisphere specializes in language, speech, handwriting, calculation (math), sense of time and rhythm (which is mathematical in nature), and basically any kind of thought requiring analysis. The right hemisphere appears to specialize in more global (widespread) processing involving perception, visualization, spatial perception, recognition of patterns, faces, emotions, melodies, and expression of emotions. It also comprehends simple language but does not produce speech. (See **Table 2.2.**)

In general, the left hemisphere processes information in a sequence and is good at breaking things down into smaller parts, or performing analysis (Springer & Deutsch, 1998). The right hemisphere, by contrast, processes information all at once and simultaneously, a more global or holistic* style of processing. Remember the discussion in Chapter One of the early days of psychology, the structuralists, and the Gestalt psychologists? One could almost say that the left hemisphere of the brain is a structuralist who wants to break everything down into its smallest parts, and the right side of the brain is a Gestaltist, who wants to study only the whole.

💬 So there really are left-brained and right-brained people?

Actually, unless one is a split-brain patient, the two sides of the brain are always working together as an integrated whole. For example, the right side might recognize someone's face, while the left side struggles to recall the person's name. People aren't really left- or right-brained; they are "whole-brained." Michael Gazzaniga was one of Roger Sperry's students and collaborators and is a long-time researcher in the area of brain asymmetry and cognitive neuroscience. Gazzaniga's continuing work in brain lateralization has led to insights of the integrated mind, and he continues to work in related areas including human consciousness, perception, and neuroethics (Gazzaniga, 2006, 2009).

*holistic: relating to or concerned with complete systems or wholes.

Table 2.2 Specialization of the Two Hemispheres

Left Hemisphere	Right Hemisphere
Controls the right hand	Controls the left hand
Spoken language	Nonverbal
Written language	Visual-spatial perception
Mathematical calculations	Music and artistic processing
Logical thought processes	Emotional thought and recognition
Analysis of detail	Processing of the whole
Reading	Pattern recognition
	Facial recognition

HANDEDNESS   The separate functions of the left and right sides of the brain are often confused with handedness, or the tendency to use one hand for most fine motor skills. While most right-handed people also have their left hemisphere in control of their other fine motor skills, such as speech, a few right-handers actually have their language functions in the right hemisphere, in spite of the dominance of the left hemisphere for controlling the right hand. Among left-handed people, there are also many who, although right-brain dominant, still have their language functions on the left side of the brain. Why? Unfortunately, there are far too many theories of why we use one hand rather than the other to cover in this text.

Concept Map L.O. 2.10, 2.11, 2.12, 2.13, 2.14

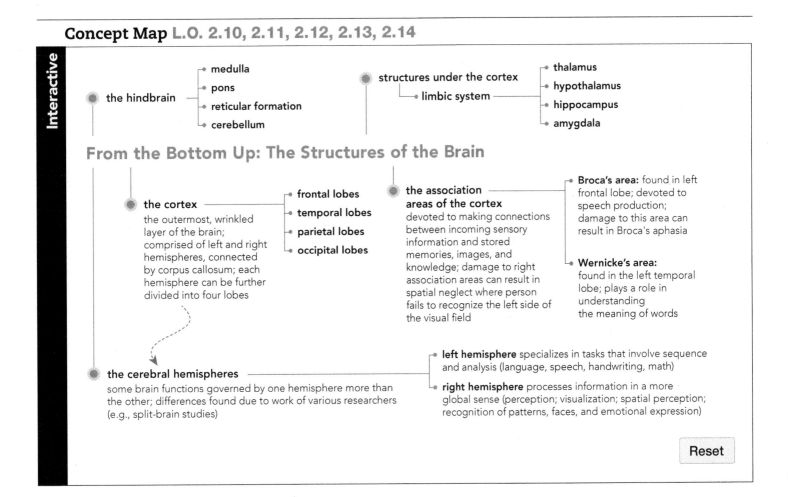

Practice Quiz   How much do you remember?   ANSWERS ON PAGE AK–1.

Pick the best answer.

1. If you were to develop a rare condition in which you were not able to remember to be afraid of certain situations, animals, or events, which part of the brain would most likely be damaged?

   a. cingulate cortex   **c.** thalamus

   b. hypothalamus   **d.** amygdala

2. If your roommate has a problem paying attention, it may be due to damage to this part of the limbic system.

   a. hippocampus   **c.** cerebellum

   b. hypothalamus   **d.** cingulate cortex

3. What part of the brain can sometimes be referred to as the "rind" or outer covering?

   a. thalamus   **c.** corpus callosum

   b. medulla   **d.** cortex

4. The ability to detect changes in temperature, pressure, and body position is due in part to the functions of the _____ lobe.

   a. frontal   **c.** temporal

   b. parietal   **d.** corpus

5. You have a dream in which you wake up to find that people around you are using words that make no sense. What's more, your friends don't seem to understand you when you speak. At one point in your dream, your mom tells you that you almost forgot your tree limb today. When you give her a puzzled look, she holds up your lunchbox and repeats, "You know, your tree limb." Your predicament in your dream is most like which of the following disorders?

   a. Wernicke's aphasia

   b. Broca's aphasia

   c. apraxia

   d. spatial neglect

6. Which part of the brain tends to process information globally?

   a. left hemisphere

   b. right hemisphere

   c. corpus callosum

   d. cerebellum

Applying Psychology to Everyday Life
Paying Attention to the Causes of Attention-Deficit/Hyperactivity Disorder

2.15 **Identify some potential causes of attention-deficit/hyperactivity disorder.**

Attention-deficit/hyperactivity disorder (ADHD) is a developmental disorder involving behavioral and cognitive aspects of inattention, impulsivity, and hyperactivity. Previously referred to as attention deficit disorder (ADD), there are currently three diagnostic categories for this disorder in the *Diagnostic and Statistical Manual of Mental Disorders (DSM-5)*. These include ADHD predominantly hyperactive/impulsive presentation, ADHD predominantly inattentive presentation, and ADHD combined presentation (American Psychiatric Association, 2013). Although ADHD is most commonly diagnosed in children, the disorder tends to persist into adolescence and adulthood. Inattention and impulsivity are often reported in adults, whereas symptoms of hyperactivity tend to decline with age. The ADHD-related problems in adults can range from strained relations with family, friends, or a significant other to problems with substance abuse, traffic accidents, or job stability (Barkley et al., 2008). A recent longitudinal study found a group of males diagnosed with ADHD in childhood were more likely to have issues across a variety of domains when followed up with as adults. At a mean age of 41, the men with ADHD had significantly worse educational, occupational, economic, and social outcomes and more divorces than non-ADHD comparisons (Klein et al., 2012).

There are not only ongoing issues from the disorder itself, but also with the medications used to treat it. In the United States there is a growing concern over the misuse of prescription drugs on college campuses, for example, by students without ADHD in the attempt to improve their attention or concentration when studying. And for some students, the most common source of the medication is a friend with a prescription (Garnier-Dykstra et al., 2012). Furthermore, an ongoing increase in the number of ADHD diagnoses and prescriptions for stimulant medications appears to coincide with the use of ADHD medications as "neuroenhancers" in otherwise healthy children and adolescents, and has prompted the American Academy of Neurology to publish a position paper against such practices (Graf et al., 2013).

The brain areas involved in the behavioral and cognitive characteristics of ADHD are typically divided into those responsible for regulating attention and cognitive control and those responsible for alertness and motivation (Nigg, 2010). The cortical and subcortical brain areas involved, and found to be smaller in neuroimaging studies of ADHD, are the prefrontal cortex (primarily on the right side), basal ganglia (subcortical structures involved in response control), cerebellum, and corpus callosum (Nigg, 2006).

Since ADHD involves a variety of behaviors and cognitive aspects, research has often looked for specific markers that may lead to the actual causes of the disorder. These markers may be biological, cognitive, or behavioral measures (Nigg, 2010). To assess individual markers, researchers may combine neuroimaging and electrophysiological studies of individuals with ADHD while at rest or while they perform specific cognitive tasks (like various tests of attention). Some studies use EEG or ERPs (Clarke et al., 2007; Loo et al., 2009; Missonnier et al., 2013; van der Stelt et al., 2010; White et al., 2005) whereas others use MRI, fMRI, or PET (Bush et al., 2008; Volkow et al., 2007).

Much of the research over the past 10 years has focused on the cognitive markers for ADHD, such as attention problems, that may or may not be combined with neuroimaging. More recent research suggests that some aspects of attention are actually normal in individuals with ADHD. The aspect of attention with which individuals with ADHD do have problems is vigilance (being able to "watch out" for something important). Another cognitive area that appears to be impaired is being able to effectively control one's own cognitive processes such as staying on task, maintaining effort, or engaging in self-control (Nigg, 2010).

These findings have prompted researchers to reexamine the causes of ADHD and have highlighted the likelihood of more than one cause and more than one brain route to ADHD. Current research is looking at a variety of areas including environmental factors such as low-level lead exposure, genetic influences, the role of heredity and familial factors, and personality factors (Nigg, 2010). Furthermore, causes for the prevalence of ADHD continue to be examined, with variables ranging from the impact of sleep, circadian rhythms, and environmental light exposure (Arns et al., 2013) to the manner in which ADHD symptoms are characterized and diagnosed. While some of these areas of investigation are not completely new and have been examined before, but the possibility of multiple causes and interactions between these causes has not been studied as closely as it is at present in ADHD research.

Questions for Further Discussion

1. How might a psychology professional help parents or teachers understand the neuroimaging techniques and brain areas associated with ADHD?
2. If a college student has ADHD, what aspects of his or her school or personal life might be impacted by problems with vigilance or cognitive control?
3. What kinds of problems may arise in individuals taking ADHD medications when they do not have the actual symptoms of the disorder?

Chapter Summary

Neurons and Nerves: Building the Network

2.1 Identify the parts of a neuron and describe the function of each.

- The nervous system is a complex network of cells that carries information to and from all parts of the body.
- The brain is made up of two types of cells, neurons and glial cells.
- Neurons have four primary components: dendrites that receive input, a soma or cell body, axons that carry the neural message to other cells, and axon terminals that are the site of neurotransmitter release.
- Glial cells separate, support, and insulate neurons, and influence thinking, memory, and other forms of cognition.
- Myelin insulates and protects the axons of neurons that travel in the body. These axons bundle together in "cables" called nerves. Myelin also speeds up the neural message.

2.2 Describe the action potential.

- A neuron contains charged particles called ions. When at rest, the neuron is negatively charged on the inside and positively charged on the outside. When stimulated, this reverses the charge by allowing positive sodium ions to enter the cell. This is the action potential.
- Neurons fire in an all-or-nothing manner. It is the speed and number of neurons firing that tell researchers the strength of the stimulus.

2.3 Describe how neurons use neurotransmitters to communicate with each other and with the body.

- Synaptic vesicles in the end of the axon terminal release neurotransmitter chemicals into the synapse, or gap, between one cell and the next. The neurotransmitter molecules fit into receptor sites on the next cell, stimulating or inhibiting that cell's firing. Neurotransmitters may be either excitatory or inhibitory.
- The first known neurotransmitter was acetylcholine (ACh). It stimulates muscles, helps in memory formation, and plays a role in arousal and attention.
- GABA is the major inhibitory neurotransmitter; high amounts of GABA are released when drinking alcohol.
- Serotonin is associated with sleep, mood, and appetite.
- Dopamine is associated with Parkinson's disease and schizophrenia.
- Endorphins are neural regulators that control our pain response.
- Most neurotransmitters are taken back into the synaptic vesicles in a process called reuptake.
- ACh is cleared out of the synapse by enzymes that break up the molecules.

An Overview of the Nervous System

2.4 Explain how the brain and spinal cord interact, describe some misconceptions about the brain, and explain neuroplasticity.

- The central nervous system consists of the brain and the spinal cord.
- The spinal cord serves two functions. The outer part of the cord transmits messages to and from the brain, whereas the inner part controls lifesaving reflexes such as the pain response.
- Spinal cord reflexes involve afferent neurons, interneurons, and efferent neurons, forming a simple reflex arc.
- The peripheral nervous system is all the neurons and nerves that are not part of the brain and spinal cord and that extend throughout the body.
- There are two systems within the peripheral nervous system, the somatic nervous system, and the autonomic nervous system.
- Some common misconceptions about the brain are that older brains can't make new cells and that people use only 10 percent of their brain. It is important to use critical thinking skills to evaluate news stories about the brain.
- Neuroplasticity refers to the brain's ability to modify its structure and function as the result of experience or injury; researchers are examining ways to capitalize on this feature to assist individuals with brain injury or disease.

2.5 Describe the role of the somatic and autonomic nervous systems.

- The somatic nervous system contains the sensory pathway, or neurons carrying messages to the central nervous system, and the motor pathway, or neurons carrying messages from the central nervous system to the voluntary muscles.
- The autonomic nervous system consists of the parasympathetic division and the sympathetic division. The sympathetic division is our fight-or-flight system, reacting to stress, whereas the parasympathetic division is our eat-drink-and-rest system that restores and maintains normal day-to-day functioning of the organs.

Distant Connections: The Endocrine Glands

2.6 Explain how the hormones released by glands interact with the nervous system and affect behavior.

- Endocrine glands secrete chemicals called hormones directly into the bloodstream, influencing the activity of the muscles and organs.
- The pituitary gland is found in the brain just below the hypothalamus. Among its many functions, it helps us conserve water and controls oxytocin, a hormone involved in the onset of labor and lactation. The pituitary also regulates growth hormone and influences the activity of the other glands.

- The pineal gland is also located in the brain. It secretes melatonin, a hormone that regulates the sleep–wake cycle, in response to changes in light.
- The thyroid gland is located inside the neck. It controls metabolism (the burning of energy) by secreting thyroxin.
- The pancreas controls the level of sugar in the blood by secreting insulin and glucagons. Too much insulin produces hypoglycemia, whereas too little causes diabetes.
- The gonads are the ovaries in women and testes in men. They secrete hormones to regulate sexual growth, activity, and reproduction.
- The adrenal glands, one on top of each kidney, control the stress reaction through the adrenal medulla's secretion of epinephrine and norepinephrine. The adrenal cortex secretes over 30 different corticoids (hormones), controlling salt intake, stress, and sexual development.

Hormones and Stress

2.7 **Describe how the autonomic nervous system and body are impacted by stress**

- The general adaptation syndrome is the body's reaction to stress and includes three stages: alarm, resistance, and exhaustion.
- Stress causes the immune system to react as though an illness or invading organism has been detected, increasing the functioning of the immune system.
- As the stress continues or increases, the immune system can begin to fail.

Looking Inside the Living Brain

2.8 **Describe how lesioning studies and brain stimulation are used to study the brain.**

- We can study the brain by using lesioning techniques to destroy certain areas of the brain in laboratory animals or by electrically stimulating those areas (ESB).
- We can use case studies of human brain damage to learn about the brain's functions but cannot easily generalize from one case to another.
- rTMS and tDCS are noninvasive methods for stimulating the brain.

2.9 **Describe how neuroimaging techniques can provide information about the brain's structure and function**

- Different neuroimaging methods allow scientists to investigate the structure or the function of the living brain.
- The electroencephalograph allows researchers to look at the electroencephalogram (EEG), or electrical activity of the surface of the brain, through the use of electrodes placed on the scalp that are then amplified and viewed using a computer. ERPs allow researchers to look at the timing and progression of cognitive processes.
- CT scans are computer-aided X-rays of the brain and show the skull and brain structure.

- MRI scans use a magnetic field, radio pulses, and a computer to give researchers an even more detailed look at the structure of the brain.
- fMRI allows researchers to look at the activity of the brain over a time period.
- PET scans use a radioactive sugar injected into the bloodstream to track the activity of brain cells, which is enhanced and color-coded by a computer. SPECT allows for the imaging of brain blood flow.

From the Bottom Up: The Structures of the Brain

2.10 **Identify the different structures of the bottom part of the brain, and describe the function of each.**

- The medulla is at the very bottom of the brain and at the top of the spinal column. It controls life-sustaining functions such as breathing and swallowing. The nerves from each side of the body also cross over in this structure to opposite sides.
- The pons is above the medulla and acts as a bridge between the lower part of the brain and the upper part. It influences sleep, dreaming, arousal, and coordination of movement on the left and right sides of the body.
- The reticular formation runs through the medulla and the pons and controls our general level of attention and arousal.
- The cerebellum is found at the base and back of the brain and coordinates fine, rapid motor movement, learned reflexes, posture, and muscle tone. It may also be involved in some cognitive and emotional functions.

2.11 **Identify structures of the brain that are involved in emotion, learning, memory, and motivation.**

- The limbic system consists of the thalamus, hypothalamus, hippocampus, and amygdala.
- The thalamus is the relay station that sends sensory information to the proper areas of the cortex.
- The hypothalamus controls hunger, thirst, sexual behavior, sleeping and waking, and emotions. It also controls the pituitary gland.
- The hippocampus is the part of the brain responsible for the formation of long-term declarative memories.
- The amygdala controls our fear responses and memory of fearful stimuli.

2.12 **Identify the parts of the cortex that process the different senses and those that control movement of the body.**

- The cortex is the outer covering of the cerebrum and consists of a tightly packed layer of neurons about one tenth of an inch in thickness. Its wrinkles, or corticalization, allow for greater cortical area and are associated with greater brain complexity.
- The cortex is divided into two cerebral hemispheres connected by a thick band of neural fibers called the corpus callosum.

- The occipital lobes at the back and base of each hemisphere process vision and contain the primary visual cortex.
- The parietal lobes at the top and back of the cortex contain the somatosensory area, which processes our sense of touch, temperature, and body position.
- The temporal lobes contain the primary auditory area and are also involved in understanding language.
- The frontal lobes contain the motor cortex, which controls the voluntary muscles, and are also where all the higher mental functions occur, such as planning, language, and complex decision making.

2.13 Identify the parts of the cortex that are responsible for higher forms of thought, such as language.

- Association areas of the cortex are found in all the lobes but particularly in the frontal lobes. These areas help people make sense of the information they receive from primary sensory areas and the lower areas of the brain.
- A region called Broca's area in the left frontal lobe is responsible for producing fluent, understandable speech. If damaged, the person has Broca's aphasia, in which words will be halting and pronounced incorrectly.
- An area called Wernicke's area in the left temporal lobe is responsible for the understanding of language. If damaged, the person has Wernicke's aphasia, in which speech is fluent but nonsensical. The wrong words are used.

2.14 Explain how some brain functions differ between the left and right hemispheres.

- Studies with split-brain patients, in which the corpus callosum has been severed to correct epilepsy, reveal that the left side of the brain seems to control language, writing, logical thought, analysis, and mathematical abilities. The left side also processes information sequentially.
- The right side of the brain processes information globally and controls emotional expression, spatial perception, and recognition of faces, patterns, melodies, and emotions. Information presented only to the left hemisphere can be verbalized, but information only sent to the right cannot.

Applying Psychology to Everyday Life: Paying Attention to the Causes of Attention-Deficit/Hyperactivity Disorder

2.15 Identify some potential causes of attention-deficit/hyperactivity disorder.

- ADHD is often diagnosed in children but may persist into adulthood. Multiple causes are possible including genetic, environmental, and several differences in brain structure and function.

Test Yourself   ANSWERS ON PAGE AK–1.

Pick the best answer

1. In the structure of the neuron, the _____ receives messages from other cells.
   a. axon
   b. dendrite
   c. soma
   d. myelin

2. Oligodendrocytes and Schwann cells generate a fatty substance known as
   a. glial.
   b. soma.
   c. myelin.
   d. neurilemma.

3. Which of the following may surround a neuron's axon, as well as help to speed along electrical impulses?
   a. synaptic knobs
   b. receptor sites
   c. myelin sheath
   d. neuromodulators

4. When a neuron is in the resting state, the neuron is negatively charged on the _____ and positively charged on the _____.
   a. inside; outside
   b. outside; inside
   c. top; bottom
   d. bottom; top

5. Which neurotransmitter stimulates muscle cells to contract but slows contractions in the heart?
   a. acetylcholine (ACh)
   b. GABA
   c. serotonin
   d. endorphin

6. Heroin mimics the actions of endorphins, inhibiting pain signals and creating a "high" feeling. Heroin is an example of a(n):
   a. protagonist.
   b. antagonist.
   c. agonist.
   d. glial cell.

7. Involuntary muscles are controlled by the _____ nervous system.
   a. somatic
   b. autonomic
   c. sympathetic
   d. parasympathetic

8. As you take notes, your heart beats at a normal rate. Your breathing is normal and your stomach slowly digests your earlier meal. What division of the peripheral nervous system is currently in action?
   a. sympathetic
   b. parasympathetic
   c. autonomic
   d. somatic

9. Robert has had difficulty sleeping for the past 6 months and his body seemingly no longer differentiates between night and day. His doctor believes the problem lies with Robert's endocrine system. What gland will Robert's physician focus on?

   a. pituitary

   b. adrenal

   c. thyroid

   d. pineal

10. Which gland(s) is/are known to influence all other glands within the endocrine system?

   a. pineal gland

   b. pituitary gland

   c. thyroid gland

   d. adrenal glands

11. In which of Selye's stages is death a possible outcome?

   a. alarm

   b. resistance

   c. reaction

   d. exhaustion

12. Bailey is a subject in a study on memory and problem solving. The researcher is applying magnetic pulses to her brain through copper wire coils positioned directly above her scalp. Bailey's study would best be described as a(n)

   a. invasive stimulation technique.

   b. noninvasive stimulation technique.

   c. EEG technique.

   d. PET technique.

13. Maria often sleeps soundly and rarely awakens to any outside noise. However, the cries of Maria's baby can awaken her immediately. What part of the brain is responsible for this reaction?

   a. medulla

   b. pons

   c. reticular formation

   d. cerebellum

14. Alexis and Theresa are synchronized swimmers for their college swim team. They often work long hours to ensure the movements in their routine are perfectly timed. What part of their brains must Alexis and Theresa rely most upon?

   a. medulla

   b. pons

   c. reticular formation

   d. cerebellum

15. Your psychology professor refers to this as the great sensory relay station of the brain. What part is he or she referring to?

   a. thalamus

   b. hypothalamus

   c. hippocampus

   d. amygdala

16. Which part of the brain is involved in the creation of memories and is often linked to Alzheimer's disease?

   a. hippocampus

   b. thalamus

   c. hypothalamus

   d. amygdala

17. Jessica has suffered a severe blow to the back of her head when she was thrown from her horse. Subsequently, her occipital lobe has been injured. Which of her senses has the highest chance of being affected?

   a. hearing

   b. touch

   c. taste and smell

   d. vision

18. Jaime's grandfather recently suffered a stroke and has had difficulty with language production ever since. Most likely, he has experienced damage to the _____ area of his brain.

   a. right rear

   b. left frontal

   c. left rear

   d. right frontal

19. Felicia is recovering from a brain injury. She is able to speak fluently but often uses incorrect words in a sentence. In one instance at a friend's birthday party, she said, "I would like something to drink. Can I have some battery?" Felicia's problem is known as

   a. spatial neglect.

   b. visual agnosia.

   c. Broca's aphasia.

   d. Wernicke's aphasia.

20. Although the brain works largely as a whole, which of the following is not a correct pairing of hemisphere and function?

   a. left; control of right-handed motor functions

   b. right; control of right-handed motor functions

   c. right; recognition of faces

   d. left; reading

Chapter 3
Sensation and Perception

Taria Camerino is a pastry chef who experiences music, colors, shapes, and emotions as taste; Jamie Smith is a sommelier, or wine steward, who experiences smells as colors and shapes; and James Wannerton is an information technology consultant who experiences sounds, words, and colors as tastes and textures (Carlsen, 2013, March 18). All three of these individuals have a condition known as **synesthesia**, which literally means "joined sensation." Recent studies suggest roughly 2%–4% of the population may experience some form of synesthesia. While the causes of synesthesia are still being investigated, it appears in some forms that signals that come from the sensory organs, such as the eyes or the ears, go to places in the brain where they weren't originally meant to be or are processed differently. Overall, there is increased communication between sensory regions that results in synesthetes experiencing the world differently than others.

Which of your sensory abilities do you rely on most during a typical day? Are certain senses more important than others depending on the social context or setting?

Video

00:00 / 02:28

Why study sensation and perception?

Without sensations to tell us what is outside our own mental world, we would live entirely in our own minds, separate from one another and unable to find food or any other basics that sustain life. Sensations are the mind's window to the world that exists around us. Without perception, we would be unable to understand what all those sensations mean—perception is the process of interpreting the sensations we experience so that we can act upon them.

Learning Objectives

3.1 Define sensation, and explain sensory thresholds.

3.2 Explain why some sensory information is ignored.

3.3 Explain the nature of light, and describe how light travels through the various parts of the eye.

3.4 Describe the major theories about how we see color, and explain color blindness.

3.5 Explain the nature of sound, and describe how it travels through the various parts of the ear.

3.6 Summarize the three theories of how the brain processes information about pitch.

3.7 Explain why some people are unable to hear, and describe ways their hearing may be improved.

3.8 Describe how the sense of taste works, and identify the five basic tastes.

3.9 Describe how the sense of smell works.

3.10 Describe how we experience the sensations of touch, pressure, temperature, and pain.

3.11 Describe the senses that tell us about balance and the position and movement of our bodies.

3.12 Describe how perceptual constancies and the Gestalt principles account for common perceptual experiences.

3.13 Explain how we perceive depth using both monocular and binocular cues.

3.14 Describe some common visual illusions, and summarize factors that can influence and alter perception.

3.15 Describe how the neuroscientific study of magic can help to explain visual and cognitive illusions.

The ABCs of Sensation

 How do we get information from the outside world into our brains?

Information about the world has to have a way to get into the brain, where it can be used to determine actions and responses. The way into the brain is through the sensory organs and the process of sensation.

WHAT IS SENSATION?

3.1 Define sensation, and explain sensory thresholds.

Sensation occurs when special receptors in the sense organs—the eyes, ears, nose, skin, and taste buds—are activated, allowing various forms of outside stimuli to become neural signals in the brain. This process of converting outside stimuli, such as light, into neural activity is called **transduction**. Before examining sensory receptors more closely, watch the video *How We Sense the World*.

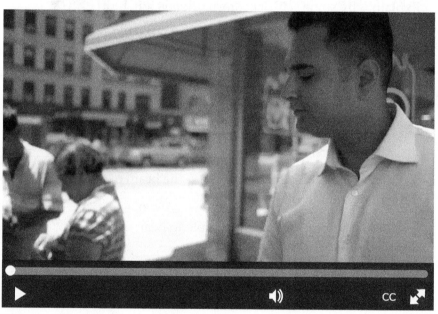

 Watch the **Video**, *How We Sense the World.*

SENSORY RECEPTORS   The *sensory receptors* are specialized forms of neurons, the cells that make up the nervous system. Instead of receiving neurotransmitters from other cells, these receptor cells are stimulated by different kinds of energy—for example, the receptors in the eyes are stimulated by light, whereas the receptors in the ears are activated by vibrations. Touch receptors are stimulated by pressure or temperature, and the receptors for taste and smell are triggered by chemical substances. Each receptor type transduces the physical information into electrical information in different ways, which then either depolarizes or hyperpolarizes the cell, causing it to fire more or to fire less based on the timing and intensity of information it is detecting from the environment (Gardner & Johnson, 2013).

SENSORY THRESHOLDS   Ernst Weber (1795–1878) did studies trying to determine the smallest difference between two weights that could be detected. His research led to the formulation known as Weber's law of **just noticeable differences** (**jnd**, or the **difference threshold**). A jnd is the smallest difference between two stimuli that is detectable 50 percent of the time, and Weber's law simply means that whatever the difference between stimuli might be, it is always a *constant*. If to notice a difference in the amount of sugar a person would need to add to a cup of coffee that is already sweetened with 5 teaspoons is 1 teaspoon, then the percentage of change needed to detect a just noticeable difference is one-fifth, or 20 percent. So if the coffee has 10 teaspoons of sugar in it, the person would have to add another 20 percent, or 2 teaspoons, to be able to taste the difference half of the time. Most people would not typically drink a cup of coffee with 10 teaspoons of sugar in it, let alone 12 teaspoons, but you get the point. To see a visual example of this, participate in the experiment *Weber's Law* and discover the amount of change needed to detect a just noticeable difference between two circles of light.

Experiment   WEBER'S LAW

| INTRODUCTION | INSTRUCTIONS | EXPERIMENT | RESULTS | DISCUSSION | REFERENCES |

In this experiment, you will be presented a series of boxes containing two circles of light. In each presentation, the circles will either be the same brightness or color saturation or they will vary in brightness or color saturation. Your task is to decide if the two circles appear to have the same brightness or different brightness.

When you are ready, click the "Start Practice Experiment" button to begin.

Previous   Start Practice Experiment

Simulate the **Experiment**, *Weber's Law.*

Gustav Fechner (1801–1887) expanded on Weber's work by studying something he called the **absolute threshold** (Fechner, 1860). An absolute threshold is the lowest level of stimulation that a person can consciously detect 50 percent of the time the stimulation is present. (Remember, the jnd is detecting a difference *between two* stimuli.) For example, assuming a very quiet room and normal hearing, how far away can someone sit and you might still hear the tick of their analog watch on half of the trials? For some examples of absolute thresholds for various senses, see **Table 3.1**.

💬 I've heard about people being influenced by stuff in movies and on television, things that are just below the level of conscious awareness. Is that true?

Stimuli that are below the level of conscious awareness are called *subliminal stimuli.* (The word *limin* means "threshold," so *sublimin* means "below the threshold.") These

Table 3.1	Examples of Absolute Thresholds
Sense	**Threshold**
Sight	A candle flame at 30 miles on a clear, dark night
Hearing	The tick of a watch 20 feet away in a quiet room
Smell	One drop of perfume diffused throughout a three-room apartment
Taste	1 teaspoon of sugar in 2 gallons of water
Touch	A bee's wing falling on the cheek from 1 centimeter above

stimuli are just strong enough to activate the sensory receptors but not strong enough for people to be consciously aware of them. Many people believe that these stimuli act upon the unconscious mind, influencing behavior in a process called *subliminal perception*.

Researchers have gathered scientific evidence that subliminal perception does not work in advertising (Bargh et al., 1996; Broyles, 2006; Moore, 1988; Pratkanis & Greenwald, 1988; Trappey, 1996; Vokey & Read, 1985). This is not to say that subliminal perception does not exist—there is a growing body of evidence that we process some stimuli without conscious awareness, especially stimuli that are fearful or threatening (LeDoux & Phelps, 2008; Öhman, 2008). In this effort, researchers have used *event-related potentials* (ERPs) and functional magnetic resonance imaging (fMRI) to verify the existence of subliminal perception and associated learning in the laboratory (Babiloni et al., 2010; Bernat et al., 2001; Fazel-Rezai & Peters, 2005; Sabatini et al., 2009). ⓁⒾⓃⓀ to Learning Objective 2.9. These studies use stimuli that are detectable by our sensory systems but below the level of full conscious perception. Participants are not aware or conscious that they have been exposed to the stimuli due to masking or manipulation of attention. Furthermore, the stimuli typically influence automatic reactions (such as an increase in facial tension) rather than direct voluntary behaviors (such as going to buy something suggested by advertising).

HABITUATION AND SENSORY ADAPTATION

3.2 Explain why some sensory information is ignored.

Some of the lower centers of the brain filter sensory stimulation and "ignore" or prevent conscious attention to stimuli that do not change. The brain is primarily interested in changes in information. That's why people don't really "hear" the noise of the air conditioner unless it suddenly cuts off, or the noise made in some classrooms, unless it gets very quiet or someone else directs their attention toward it. Although they actually are *hearing* it, they aren't paying attention to it. This is called **habituation**, and it is the way the brain deals with unchanging information from the environment. ⓁⒾⓃⓀ to Learning Objective 2.10.

💬 Sometimes I can smell the odor of the garbage can in the kitchen when I first come home, but after a while the smell seems to go away—is this also habituation?

Although different from habituation, **sensory adaptation** is another process by which constant, unchanging information from the sensory receptors is effectively ignored. In habituation, the sensory receptors are still responding to stimulation but the lower centers of the brain are not sending the signals from those receptors to the cortex. The process of sensory adaptation differs because the receptor cells *themselves* become less responsive to an unchanging stimulus—garbage odors included—and the receptors no longer send signals to the brain.

For example, when you eat, the food that you put in your mouth tastes strong at first, but as you keep eating the same thing, the taste does fade somewhat, doesn't it? Generally speaking, all of our senses are subject to sensory adaptation.

You might think, then, that if you stare at something long enough, it would also disappear, but the eyes are a little different. Even though the sensory receptors in the back of the eyes adapt to and become less responsive to a constant visual stimulus, under ordinary circumstances the eyes are never entirely still. There's a constant movement of the eyes, tiny little vibrations called "microsaccades" or "saccadic movements" that people don't consciously notice. These movements keep the eyes from adapting to what they see. (That's a good thing, because otherwise many students would no doubt go blind from staring off into space.)

This young woman does not feel the piercings on her ear and nose because sensory adaptation allows her to ignore a constant, unchanging stimulation from the metal rings. What else is she wearing that would cause sensory adaptation?

Concept Map L.O. 3.1, 3.2

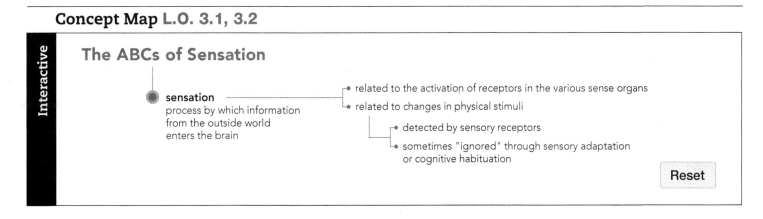

Interactive

The ABCs of Sensation

sensation ———————————
process by which information
from the outside world
enters the brain

- related to the activation of receptors in the various sense organs
- related to changes in physical stimuli
  - detected by sensory receptors
  - sometimes "ignored" through sensory adaptation or cognitive habituation

Reset

Practice Quiz   How much do you remember? ANSWERS ON PAGE AK–1.

Pick the best answer.

1. _____ involves the detection of physical stimuli from our environment and is made possible by the activation of specific receptor cells.
   a. Perception
   b. Sublimination
   c. Adaptation
   d. Sensation

2. The lowest level of stimulation that a person can consciously detect 50 percent of the time the stimulation is present is called
   a. absolute threshold.
   b. just noticeable difference.
   c. sensation.
   d. sensory adaptation.

3. After being in class for a while, _____ is a likely explanation for not hearing the sound of the lights buzzing above you until someone says something about it.
   a. accommodation
   b. adaptation
   c. sublimation
   d. habituation

4. You are drinking a strong cup of coffee that is particularly bitter. After a while, the coffee doesn't taste as strong as it did when you first tasted it. What has happened?
   a. sensory adaptation
   b. subliminal perception
   c. habituation
   d. perceptual defense

The Science of Seeing

💬 I've heard that light is waves, but I've also heard that light is made of particles—which is it?

Light is a complicated phenomenon. Although scientists have long argued over the nature of light, they finally have agreed that light has the properties of both waves and particles. The following section gives a brief history of how scientists have tried to "shed light" on the mystery of light.

LIGHT AND THE EYE

3.3 **Explain the nature of light, and describe how light travels through the various parts of the eye.**

It was Albert Einstein who first proposed that light is actually tiny "packets" of waves. These "wave packets" are called *photons* and have specific wavelengths associated with them (Lehnert, 2007; van der Merwe & Garuccio, 1994).

LIGHT   When people experience the physical properties of light, they are not really aware of its dual, wavelike and particle-like, nature. With regard to its psychological properties, there are three aspects to our perception of light: *brightness, color,* and *saturation.*

Brightness is determined by the amplitude of the wave—how high or how low the wave actually is. The higher the wave, the brighter the light appears to be. Low waves are dimmer. *Color,* or hue, is largely determined by the length of the wave. Short wavelengths (measured in nanometers) are found at the blue end of the *visible spectrum* (the portion of the whole spectrum of light that is visible to the human eye), whereas longer wavelengths are found at the red end. To examine how both brightness and color are related to wave-like properties, watch the video *The Visible Spectrum.*

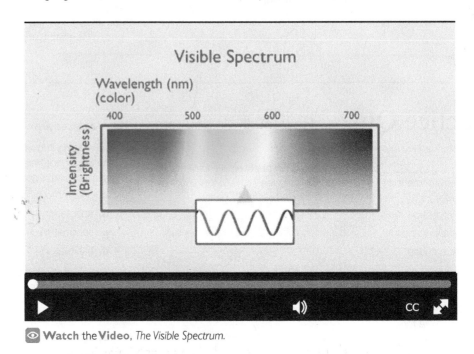

👁 **Watch** the **Video**, *The Visible Spectrum.*

Saturation refers to the purity of the color people perceive: A highly saturated red, for example, would contain only red wavelengths, whereas a less saturated red might contain a mixture of wavelengths. For example, when a child is using the red paint from a set of poster paints, the paint on the paper will look like a pure red, but if the child mixes in some white paint, the paint will look pink. The hue is still red, but it will be less of a saturated red because of the presence of white wavelengths. Mixing in black or gray would also lessen the saturation. (Note that when combining different colors, light behaves differently than pigments or paint. We will look at this distinction when we examine perception of color.)

THE STRUCTURE OF THE EYE The best way to talk about how the eye processes light is to talk about what happens to an image being viewed as the photons of light from that image travel through the eye. Refer to **Figure 3.1** to follow the path of the image.

Light enters the eye directly from a source (such as the sun) or indirectly by reflecting off of an object. To see clearly, a single point of light from a source or reflected from an object must travel through the structures of the eye and end up on the retina as a single point. Light bends as it passes through substances of different densities, through a process known as refraction. For example, have you ever looked at a drinking straw in a glass of water through the side of the glass? It appears that the straw bends, or is broken, at the surface of the water. That optical illusion is due to the refraction of light. The structures of the eye play a vital role in both collecting and focusing of light so we can see clearly.

The surface of the eye is covered in a clear membrane called the *cornea.* The cornea not only protects the eye but also is the structure that focuses most of the light coming into the eye. The cornea has a fixed curvature, like a camera that has no option to adjust the focus. However, this curvature can be changed somewhat through vision-improving

This photo illustrates an optical illusion caused by the refraction of light. The straw is not really broken although it appears that way.

Figure 3.1 STRUCTURE OF THE EYE

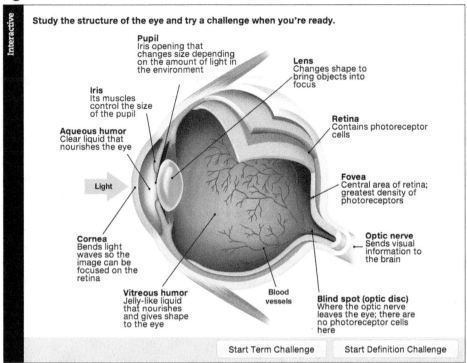

Study the structure of the eye and try a challenge when you're ready.

Pupil
Iris opening that changes size depending on the amount of light in the environment

Lens
Changes shape to bring objects into focus

Iris
Its muscles control the size of the pupil

Retina
Contains photoreceptor cells

Aqueous humor
Clear liquid that nourishes the eye

Fovea
Central area of retina; greatest density of photoreceptors

Light

Cornea
Bends light waves so the image can be focused on the retina

Optic nerve
Sends visual information to the brain

Vitreous humor
Jelly-like liquid that nourishes and gives shape to the eye

Blood vessels

Blind spot (optic disc)
Where the optic nerve leaves the eye; there are no photoreceptor cells here

Start Term Challenge   Start Definition Challenge

Light enters the eye through the cornea and pupil. The iris controls the size of the pupil. From the pupil, light passes through the lens to the retina, where it is transformed into nerve impulses. The nerve impulses travel to the brain along the optic nerve.

techniques that change the shape of the cornea. For example, ophthalmologists, physicians who specialize in medical and surgical treatment of eye problems, can use both *photoreactive keratectomy (PRK)* and *laser-assisted in situ keratomileusis (LASIK)* procedures to remove small portions of the cornea, changing its curvature, and thus the focus in the eye.

The next visual layer is a clear, watery fluid called the *aqueous humor*. This fluid is continually replenished and supplies nourishment to the eye. The light from the visual image then enters the interior of the eye through a hole, called the *pupil*, in a round muscle called the *iris* (the colored part of the eye). The iris can change the size of the pupil, letting more or less light into the eye. That also helps focus the image; people try to do the same thing by squinting.

Behind the iris, suspended by muscles, is another clear structure called the *lens*. The flexible lens finishes the focusing process begun by the cornea. In a process called **visual accommodation**, the lens changes its shape from thick to thin, enabling it to focus on objects that are close or far away. The variation in thickness allows the lens to project a sharp image on the retina. People lose this ability as the lens hardens through aging (a disorder called *presbyopia*). Although people try to compensate* for their inability to focus on things that are close to them, eventually they usually need bifocals because their arms just aren't long enough anymore. In nearsightedness, or *myopia*, visual accommodation may occur but the shape of the eye causes the focal point to fall short of the retina. In farsightedness, or *hyperopia*, the focus point is behind the retina (see **Figure 3.2** on the next page). Glasses, contacts, or corrective surgery like LASIK or PRK can correct these issues.

Once past the lens, light passes through a large, open space filled with a clear, jelly-like fluid called the *vitreous humor*. This fluid, like the aqueous humor, also nourishes the eye and gives it shape.

———————————
*compensate: to correct for an error or defect.

Figure 3.2   Nearsightedness and Farsightedness

(a) Nearsighted eye   (b) Farsighted eye

The final stop for light within the eye is the *retina*, a light-sensitive area at the back of the eye containing three layers: ganglion cells, bipolar cells, and the **rods** and **cones**, special receptor cells (*photoreceptors*) that respond to the various wavelengths of light. While the retina is responsible for absorbing and processing light information, the rods and the cones are the business end of the retina—the part that actually receives the photons of light and turns them into neural signals for the brain, sending them first to the *bipolar cells* (a type of interneuron; called bipolar or "two-ended" because they have a single dendrite at one end and a single axon on the other; Ⓛ Ⓘ Ⓝ Ⓚ to Learning Objective 2.4) and then to the retinal *ganglion cells* whose axons form the optic nerve. Watch the video, *Rods and Cones*, for more detail on how they work.

👁 **Watch** the **Video**, *Rods and Cones*.

The rods and cones are responsible for different aspects of vision. While located all over the retina, cones are more concentrated at its very center where there are no rods (an area called the fovea). Some cones have a private line to the optic nerve (one bipolar cell for each cone). This means cones are the receptors with the greatest visual acuity, or ability, to see fine detail. Cones require a lot more light to function than rods do and work best in bright light. Cones are also sensitive to different wavelengths of light, so they are responsible for color vision.

Rods are found all over the retina except the fovea but are concentrated in the periphery and responsible for peripheral vision. They are sensitive to changes in brightness but only a narrow band of wavelengths, so they see in black and white and shades of gray. Many rods connect to a single bipolar cell. If only one rod in a region of the retina is stimulated, the brain perceives the whole region as stimulated. But because the brain doesn't know exactly what part of the region is actually sending the message, visual acuity is quite low. That's why in low levels of light, such as twilight or a dimly lit room, things tend to be less clear and grayish.

Figure 3.3 The Blind Spot Demonstration.

Hold the image in front of you. Close your right eye and stare at the picture of the dog with your left eye. Slowly bring the image closer to your face. The picture of the cat will disappear at some point because the light from the picture of the cat is falling on your blind spot. If this does not seem to work for you, trying moving the image more slowly.

The eyes don't adapt to constant stimuli under normal circumstances because of saccadic movements. But if people stare with one eye at one spot long enough, objects that slowly cross their visual field may at one point disappear briefly because there is a "hole" in the retina—the place where all the axons of those ganglion cells leave the retina to become the optic nerve, the optic disk. There are no rods or cones here, so this is referred to as the blind spot. You can demonstrate the **blind spot** for yourself by following the directions in **Figure 3.3**.

HOW THE EYE WORKS You may want to first look at **Figure 3.4** for a moment before reading this section. Light entering the eyes can be separated into the left and right visual fields. Light from the right visual field falls on the left side of each eye's retina; light from the left visual field falls on the right side of each retina. Light travels in a straight line through the cornea and lens, resulting in the image projected on the retina actually being upside down and reversed from left to right as compared to the visual fields. Thank goodness our brains can compensate for this!

The retina can be divided into halves. The halves toward the temples of the head are the temporal retinas and the halves toward the center, or nose, are called the nasal retinas. Look at Figure 3.4 again. The axons from the temporal halves of each retina project

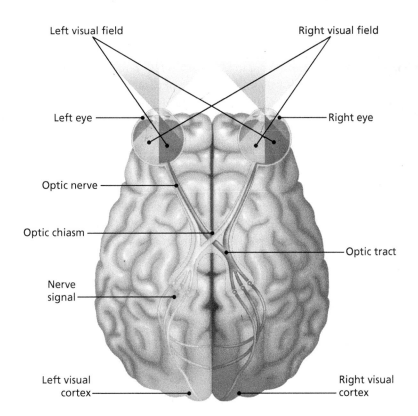

Figure 3.4 Crossing of the Optic Nerve

Light falling on the left side of each eye's retina (from the right visual field, shown in yellow) will stimulate a neural message that will travel along the optic nerve to the thalamus, and then on to the visual cortex in the occipital lobe of the left hemisphere. Notice that the message from the temporal half of the left retina goes to the left occipital lobe, while the message from the nasal half of the right retina crosses over to the left hemisphere (the optic chiasm is the point of crossover). The optic nerve tissue from both eyes joins together to form the left optic tract before going on to the lateral geniculate nucleus (LGN) of the thalamus and the left occipital lobe. For the left visual field (shown in blue), the messages from both right sides of the retinas will travel along the right optic tract to the right visual cortex in the same manner.

While this deer may seem to see relatively well at night, the oncoming headlights of a car will briefly blind it. It may only take a few seconds for light adaptation to occur, but until it does, the deer is unable to fully see, so it does not move.

to the visual cortex on the same side of the brain while the axons from the nasal halves cross over to the visual cortex on the opposite side of the brain. The optic chiasm is the point of crossover.

Because rods work well in low levels of light, they are also the cells that allow the eyes to adapt to low light. **Dark adaptation** occurs as the eye recovers its ability to see when going from a brightly lit state to a dark state. (The light-sensitive pigments that allow us to see are able to regenerate or "recharge" in the dark.) The brighter the light was, the longer it takes the rods to adapt to the new lower levels of light (Bartlett, 1965). When going from a darkened room to one that is brightly lit, the opposite process occurs. The cones have to adapt to the increased level of light, and they accomplish this **light adaptation** much more quickly than the rods adapt to darkness—it takes a few seconds at most (Hood, 1998).

PERCEPTION OF COLOR

3.4 **Describe the major theories about how we see color, and explain color blindness.**

💬 Earlier you said the cones are used in color vision. There are so many colors in the world—are there cones that detect each color? Or do all cones detect all colors?

Although experts in the visual system have been studying color and its nature for many years, at this point in time there is an ongoing theoretical discussion about the role the cones play in the sensation of color.

TRICHROMATIC THEORY   Two theories about how people see colors were originally proposed in the 1800s. The first is called the **trichromatic ("three colors") theory**. First proposed by Thomas Young in 1802 and later modified by Hermann von Helmholtz in 1852, this theory proposed three types of cones: red cones, blue cones, and green cones, one for each of the three primary colors of light.

Most people probably think that the primary colors are red, yellow, and blue, but these are the primary colors when talking about *painting*—not when talking about *light*. Paints *reflect* light, and the way reflected light mixes is different from the way direct light mixes. For example, if an artist were to blend red, yellow, and blue paints together, the result would be a mess—a black mess. The mixing of paint (reflected light) is subtractive, removing more light as you mix in more colors. As all of the colors are mixed, more light waves are absorbed and we see black. But if the artist were to blend a red, green, and blue light together by focusing lights of those three colors on one common spot, the result would be white, not black. The mixing of direct light is additive, resulting in lighter colors, more light, and when mixing red, blue, and green, we see white, the reflection of the entire visual spectrum.

In the trichromatic theory, different shades of colors correspond to different amounts of light received by each of these three types of cones. These cones then fire their message to the brain's vision centers. It is the combination of cones and the rate at which they are firing that determine the color that will be seen. For example, if the red and green cones are firing in response to a stimulus at fast enough rates, the color the person sees is yellow. If the red and blue cones are firing fast enough, the result is magenta. If the blue and green cones are firing fast enough, a kind of cyan color (blue-green) appears.

Paul K. Brown and George Wald (1964) identified three types of cones in the retina, each sensitive to a range of wavelengths, measured in nanometers (nm), and a peak sensitivity that roughly corresponds to three different colors (although hues/colors can vary depending on brightness and saturation). The peak wavelength of light the cones seem to be most sensitive to turns out to be just a little different from Young and von Helmholtz's original three corresponding colors: Short-wavelength cones detect what we see

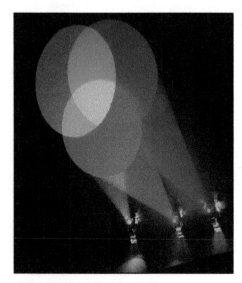

In trichromatic theory, the three types of cones combine to form different colors much as these three colored lights combine.

as blue-violet (about 420 nm), medium-wavelength cones detect what we see as green (about 530 nm), and long-wavelength cones detect what we see as green-yellow (about 560 nm). Interestingly, none of the cones identified by Brown and Wald have a peak sensitivity to light where most of us see red (around 630 nm). Keep in mind, though, each cone responds to light across a range of wavelengths, not just its wavelength of peak sensitivity. Depending on the intensity of the light, both the medium and long wavelength cones respond to light that appears red.

OPPONENT-PROCESS THEORY The trichromatic theory would, at first glance, seem to be more than adequate to explain how people perceive color. But there's an interesting phenomenon that this theory cannot explain. If a person stares at a picture of the American flag for a little while—say, a minute—and then looks away to a blank white wall or sheet of paper, that person will see an afterimage of the flag. **Afterimages** occur when a visual sensation persists for a brief time even after the original stimulus is removed. The person would also notice rather quickly that the colors of the flag in the afterimage are all wrong—green for red, black for white, and yellow for blue. If you follow the directions for **Figure 3.5**, in which the flag is yellow, green, and black, you should see a flag with the usual red, white, and blue.

 Hey, now the afterimage of the flag has normal colors! Why does this happen?

The phenomenon of the color afterimage is explained by the second theory of color perception, called the **opponent-process theory** (De Valois & De Valois, 1993; Hurvich & Jameson, 1957), based on an idea first suggested by Edwald Hering in 1874 (Finger, 1994). In opponent-process theory, there are four primary colors: red, green, blue, and yellow. The colors are arranged in pairs, with each member of the pair as opponents. Red is paired with its opponent green, and blue is paired with its opponent yellow. If one member of a pair is strongly stimulated, the other member is inhibited and cannot be working—so there are no reddish-greens or bluish-yellows.

So how can this kind of pairing cause a color afterimage? From the level of the bipolar and ganglion cells in the retina, all the way through the thalamus, and on to the visual cortical areas in the brain, some neurons (or groups of neurons) are stimulated by light from one part of the visual spectrum and inhibited by light from a different part of the spectrum. For example, let's say we have a red–green ganglion cell in the retina whose baseline activity is rather weak when we expose it to white light. However, the cell's activity is increased by red light, so we experience the color red. If we stimulate the cell with red light for a long enough period of time, the cell becomes fatigued. If we then swap out the red light with white light, the fatigued cell responds even less than the original baseline. Now we experience the color green because green is associated with a decrease in the responsiveness of this cell.

So which theory is the right one? Both theories play a part in color vision. Trichromatic theory can explain what is happening with the raw stimuli, the actual detection of various wavelengths of light. Opponent-process theory can explain afterimages and other aspects of visual perception that occur after the initial detection of light from our environment. In addition to the retinal bipolar and ganglion cells, opponent-process cells are contained inside the thalamus in an area called the lateral geniculate nucleus (LGN). The LGN is part of the pathway that visual information takes to the occipital lobe. It is when the cones in the retina send signals through the retinal bipolar and ganglion cells

Figure 3.5 Color Afterimage
Stare at the white dot in the center of this oddly colored flag for about 30 seconds. Now look at a white piece of paper or a white wall. Notice that the colors are now the normal, expected colors of the American flag. They are also the primary colors that are opposites of the colors in the picture and provide evidence for the opponent-process theory of color vision.

that we see the red versus green pairings and blue versus yellow pairings. Together with the retinal cells, the cells in the LGN appear to be the ones responsible for opponent-processing of color vision and the afterimage effect.

💬 So which theory accounts for color blindness? I've heard that there are two kinds of color blindness: when you can't tell red from green and when you can't tell blue from yellow.

COLOR BLINDNESS From the mention of red-green and yellow-blue color blindness, one might think that the opponent-process theory explains this problem. But in reality "color blindness" is caused by defective cones in the retina of the eye and as a more general term, *color-deficient vision* is more accurate, as most people with "color blindness" have two types of cones working and can see many colors.

There are really three kinds of color-deficient vision. In a very rare type, *monochrome color blindness*, people either have no cones or have cones that are not working at all. Essentially, if they have cones, they only have one type and, therefore, everything looks the same to the brain—shades of gray. The other types of color-deficient vision, or *dichromatic vision*, are caused by the same kind of problem—having one type of cone that does not work properly. So instead of experiencing the world with normal vision based on combinations of three cones or colors, trichromatic vision, individuals with dichromatic vision experience the world with essentially combinations of two cones or colors. Red-green color deficiency is due to the lack of functioning red or green cones. In both of these, the individual confuses reds and greens, seeing the world primarily in blues, yellows, and shades of gray. A lack of functioning blue cones is much less common and causes blue-yellow color deficiency. These individuals see the world primarily in reds, greens, and shades of gray. To get an idea of what a test for color-deficient vision is like, look at **Figure 3.6**.

 💬 Why are most of the people with color-deficient vision men?

Color-deficient vision involving one set of cones is inherited in a pattern known as *sex-linked inheritance*. The gene for color-deficient vision is *recessive*. To inherit a recessive trait, you normally need two of the genes, one from each parent. Ⓛ Ⓘ Ⓝ K to Learning Objective 8.3. But the gene for color-deficient vision is attached to a particular chromosome (a package of genes) that helps to determine the sex of a person. Men have one X chromosome and one smaller Y chromosome (named for their shapes), whereas women have two X chromosomes. The smaller Y has fewer genes than the larger X, and one of the genes missing is the one that would suppress the gene for color-deficient vision. For a woman to have color-deficient vision, she must inherit two recessive genes,

Figure 3.6 Ishihara Color Test Example

Two facsimiles of the Ishihara Color Test. In the circle on the left, the number 8 should be easier to see for those with normal color vision, and on the right, the number 96. In both circles, individuals with color-deficient vision will have difficulty identifying the numbers or may see nothing but a circle of dots.

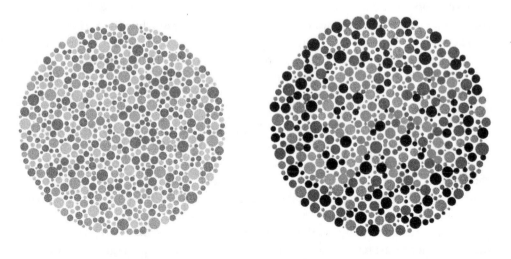

one from each parent, but a man only needs to inherit *one* recessive gene—the one passed on to him on his mother's X chromosome. His odds are greater; therefore, more males than females have color-deficient vision.

Concept Map L.O. 3.3, 3.4

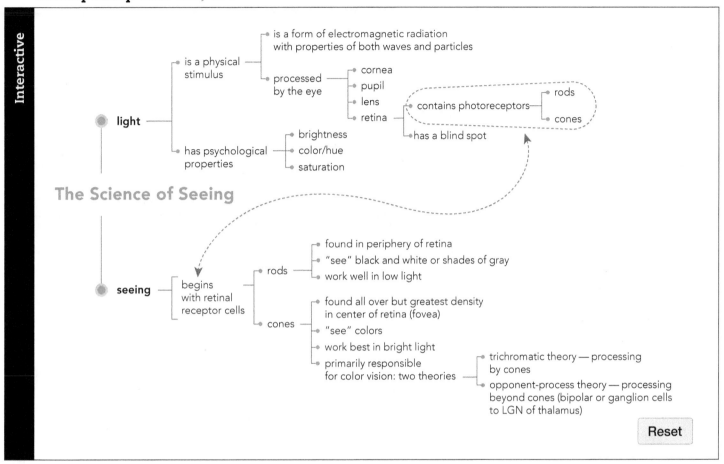

Practice Quiz How much do you remember? ANSWERS ON PAGE AK-1.

Pick the best answer.

1. Which of the following is largely determined by the length of a light wave?

   a. color

   b. brightness

   c. saturation

   d. duration

2. Aside from the lens, damage to the _____ can affect the eye's ability to focus light.

   a. iris

   b. cornea

   c. pupil

   d. retina

3. In farsightedness, also known as _____, the focal point is _____ the retina.

   a. presbyopia; above

   b. myopia; below

   c. hyperopia; behind

   d. presbyopia; in front of

4. Colleen stares at a fixed spot in her bedroom using only one eye. After a while, what might happen to her vision?

   a. Any object that slowly crosses her visual field may at one point disappear.

   b. Any object that she focuses on will begin to rotate, first clockwise, then counterclockwise.

   c. Objects will become more focused the longer she looks at them.

   d. Objects will become more distorted the longer she looks at them.

5. What are the three primary colors as proposed by the trichromatic theory?

   a. red, yellow, blue

   b. red, green, blue

   c. white, black, brown

   d. white, black, red

6. Which of the following best explains afterimages?

   a. trichromatic theory

   b. opponent-process theory

   c. color-deficient vision

   d. monochrome color blindness

The Hearing Sense: Can You Hear Me Now?

💬 If light works like waves, then do sound waves have similar properties?

The properties of sound are indeed similar to those of light, as both senses rely on waves. But the similarity ends there, as the physical properties of sound are different from those of light.

SOUND WAVES AND THE EAR

3.5 **Explain the nature of sound, and describe how it travels through the various parts of the ear.**

Sound waves do not come in little packets the way light comes in photons. Sound waves are simply the vibrations of the molecules of air that surround us. Sound waves do have the same properties of light waves though—wavelength, amplitude, and *purity*. Wavelengths are interpreted by the brain as the frequency or *pitch* (high, medium, or low). Amplitude is interpreted as *volume*, how soft or loud a sound is. (See **Figure 3.7**.) Finally, what would correspond to saturation or purity in light is called *timbre* in sound, a richness in the tone of the sound. And just as people rarely see pure colors in the world around us, they also seldom hear pure sounds. The everyday noises that surround people do not allow them to hear many pure tones.

Just as a person's vision is limited by the visible spectrum of light, a person is also limited in the range of frequencies he or she can hear. Frequency is measured in cycles (waves) per second, or **hertz (Hz)**. Human limits are between 20 and 20,000 Hz, with the most sensitivity from about 2000 to 4000 Hz, very important for conversational speech. (In comparison, dogs can hear between 50 and 60,000 Hz, and dolphins can hear up to 200,000 Hz.) To hear the higher and lower frequencies of a piece of music on their iPod® or iPhone®, for example, a person would need to increase the amplitude or volume—which explains why some people like to "crank it up."

"And only you can hear this whistle?"

THE STRUCTURE OF THE EAR: FOLLOW THE VIBES   The ear is a series of structures, each of which plays a part in the sense of hearing, as shown in **Figure 3.8** on page 104.

THE OUTER EAR   The **pinna** is the visible, external part of the ear that serves as a kind of concentrator, funneling* the sound waves from the outside into the structure of the ear. The pinna is also the entrance to the **auditory canal** (or ear canal), the short tunnel that runs down to the *tympanic membrane*, or eardrum. When sound waves hit the eardrum, they cause three tiny bones in the middle ear to vibrate.

THE MIDDLE EAR: HAMMER, ANVIL, AND STIRRUP   The three tiny bones in the middle ear are known as the hammer (*malleus*), anvil (*incus*), and stirrup (*stapes*), each name stemming from the shape of the respective bone. Collectively they are referred to as the ossicles, and they are the smallest bones in the human body. The vibration of these three bones amplifies the vibrations from the eardrum. The stirrup, the last bone in the chain, causes a membrane covering the opening of the inner ear to vibrate.

---

*funneling: moving to a focal point.

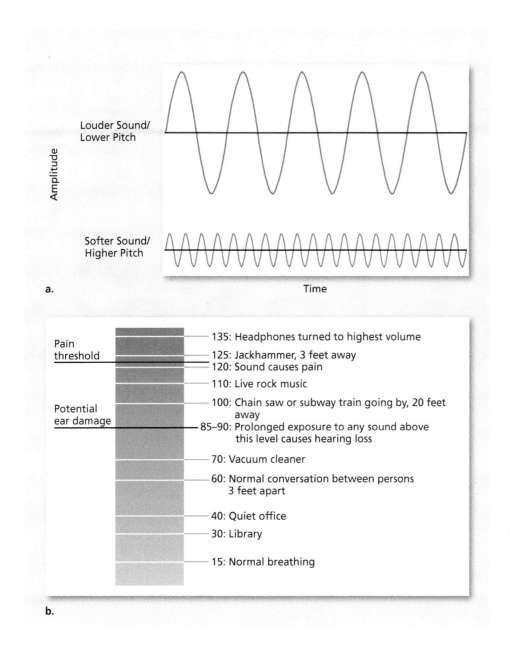

Figure 3.7   Sound Waves and Decibels

(a) Two sound waves. The higher the wave, the louder the sound; the lower the wave, the softer the sound. If the waves are close together in time (high frequency), the pitch will be perceived as a high pitch. Waves that are farther apart (low frequency) will be perceived as having a lower pitch.
(b) Decibels of various stimuli. A *decibel* is a unit of measure for loudness. Psychologists study the effects that noise has on stress, learning, performance, aggression, and psychological and physical well-being.

THE INNER EAR   This membrane is called the *oval window,* and its vibrations set off another chain reaction within the inner ear. The inner ear is a snail-shaped structure called the **cochlea,** which is filled with fluid. When the oval window vibrates, it causes the fluid in the cochlea to vibrate. This fluid surrounds a membrane running through the middle of the cochlea called the *basilar membrane.*

The basilar membrane is the resting place of the *organ of Corti,* which contains the receptor cells for the sense of hearing. When the basilar membrane vibrates, it vibrates the organ of Corti, causing it to brush against a membrane above it. On the organ of Corti are special cells called *hair cells,* which are the receptors for sound. When these auditory receptors or hair cells are bent up against the other membrane, it causes them to send a neural message through the **auditory nerve** (which contains the axons of all the receptor neurons) and into the brain, where after passing through the thalamus, the auditory cortex will interpret the sounds (the transformation of the vibrations of sound into neural messages is transduction). The louder the sound in the outside world, the stronger the vibrations that stimulate more of those hair cells—which the brain interprets as loudness.

Figure 3.8 The Structure of the Ear

(a) This drawing shows the entire ear, beginning with the outer ear (pinna, ear canal, and eardrum). The vestibular organ includes the semicircular canals and the otolith organs (inside the round structures just above the cochlea). (b) The middle ear. Sound waves entering through the ear canal cause the eardrum to vibrate, which causes each of the three bones of the middle ear to vibrate, amplifying the sound. The stirrup rests on the oval window, which transmits its vibration to the fluid in the inner ear. (c) The inner ear. Large spaces are filled with fluid (shown in purple) that vibrates as the oval window vibrates. A thin membrane suspended in this fluid is called the basilar membrane, which contains the organ of Corti, the structure composed of the hairlike cells that send signals via the auditory nerve to the thalamus, which then relays information to the auditory cortex. (d) A close-up view of the basilar membrane (in dark pink) with the hair cells of the organ of Corti (in lighter pink). Notice the axons (small green lines) leaving the hair cells to form the auditory nerve.

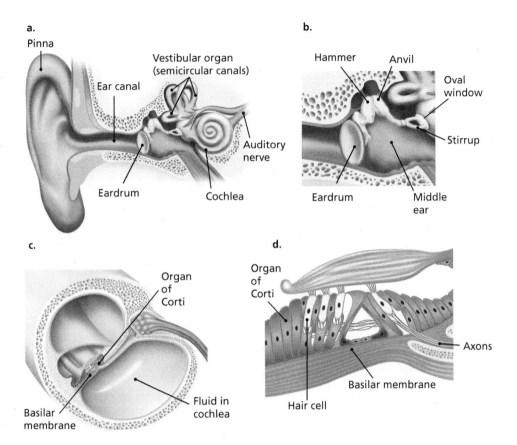

💬 I think I have it straight—but all of that just explains how soft and loud sounds get to the brain from the outside. How do we hear different kinds of sounds, like high pitches and low pitches?

PERCEIVING PITCH

3.6 Summarize the three theories of how the brain processes information about pitch.

Pitch refers to how high or low a sound is. For example, the bass beats in the music pounding through the wall of your apartment from the neighbors next door are low pitch, whereas the scream of a 2-year-old child is a very high pitch. *Very* high. There are three primary theories about how the brain receives information about pitch.

The oldest of the three theories, **place theory**, is based on an idea proposed in 1863 by Hermann von Helmholtz and elaborated on and modified by Georg von Békésy, beginning with experiments first published in 1928 (Békésy, 1960). In this theory, the pitch a person hears depends on where the hair cells that are stimulated are located on the organ of Corti. For example, if the person is hearing a high-pitched sound, all of the hair cells near the oval window will be stimulated, but if the sound is low pitched, all of the hair cells that are stimulated will be located farther away on the organ of Corti.

Frequency theory, developed by Ernest Rutherford in 1886, states that pitch is related to how fast the basilar membrane vibrates. The faster this membrane vibrates, the higher the pitch; the slower it vibrates, the lower the pitch. (In this theory, all of the auditory neurons would be firing at the same time.)

So which of these first two theories is right? It turns out that both are right—up to a point. For place theory to be correct, the basilar membrane has to vibrate unevenly—which it does when the frequency of the sound is *above* 1000 Hz. For the frequency theory to be correct, the neurons associated with the hair cells would have to fire as fast as the basilar membrane vibrates. This only works up to 1000 Hz, because neurons don't appear to fire at exactly the same time and rate when frequencies are faster than 1000 times per second. Not to mention the maximum firing rate for neurons is approximately 1000 times per second due to the refractory period.

The frequency theory works for low pitches, and place theory works for moderate to high pitches. Is there another explanation? Yes, and it is a third theory, developed by Ernest Wever and Charles Bray, called the **volley principle** (Wever, 1949; Wever & Bray, 1930), which appears to account for pitches from about 400 Hz up to about 4000. In this explanation, groups of auditory neurons take turns firing in a process called *volleying*. If a person hears a tone of about 3000 Hz, it means that three groups of neurons have taken turns sending the message to the brain—the first group for the first 1000 Hz, the second group for the next 1000 Hz, and so on.

TYPES OF HEARING IMPAIRMENTS

3.7 **Explain why some people are unable to hear, and describe ways their hearing may be improved.**

Hearing impairment is the term used to refer to difficulties in hearing. A person can be partially hearing impaired or totally hearing impaired, and the treatment for hearing loss will vary according to the reason for the impairment.

Conduction hearing impairment, or conductive hearing loss, refers to problems with the mechanics of the outer or middle ear and means that sound vibrations cannot be passed from the eardrum to the cochlea. The cause might be a damaged eardrum or damage to the bones of the middle ear (usually from an infection). In this kind of impairment the causes can often be treated, for example, hearing aids may be of some use in restoring hearing.

In *nerve hearing impairment*, or sensorineural hearing loss, the problem lies either in the inner ear or in the auditory pathways and cortical areas of the brain. This is the most common type of permanent hearing loss. Normal aging causes loss of hair cells in the cochlea, and exposure to loud noises can damage hair cells. *Tinnitus* is a fancy word for an extremely annoying ringing in one's ears, and it can also be caused by infections or loud noises—including loud music in headphones. Prolonged exposure to loud noises further leads to permanent damage and hearing loss, so you might want to turn down that stereo or personal music player!

Because the damage is to the nerves or the brain, nerve hearing impairment cannot typically be helped with ordinary hearing aids, which are basically sound amplifiers, or the hearing aids are not enough. A technique for restoring some hearing to those with irreversible nerve hearing impairment makes use of an electronic device called a *cochlear implant*. This device sends signals from a microphone worn behind the ear to a sound processor worn on the belt or in a pocket, which then translates those signals into electrical stimuli that are sent to a series of electrodes implanted directly into the cochlea, allowing transduction to take place and stimulating the auditory nerve. (See **Figure 3.9** on the next page.) The brain then processes the electrode information as sound.

This child is able to hear with the help of a cochlear implant. Hearing spoken language during the early years of a child's life helps in the development of the child's own speech.

WRITING PROMPT

How might someone who has had total hearing loss from birth react to being able to hear?

▶ The response entered here will be saved to your notes and may be collected by your instructor if he/she requires it.

 Submit

Figure 3.9 COCHLEAR IMPLANT

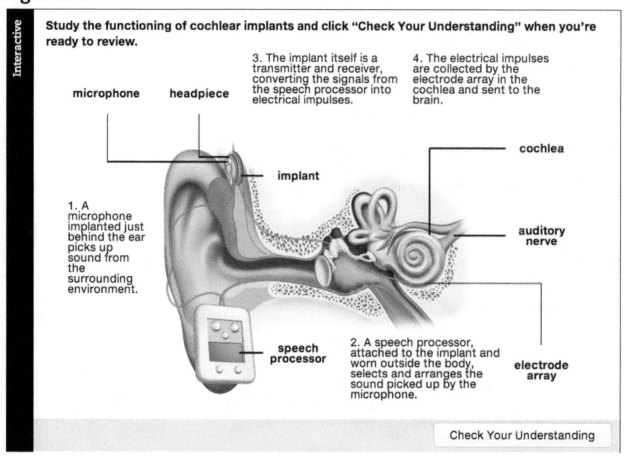

Interactive

Study the functioning of cochlear implants and click "Check Your Understanding" when you're ready to review.

microphone   headpiece

3. The implant itself is a transmitter and receiver, converting the signals from the speech processor into electrical impulses.

4. The electrical impulses are collected by the electrode array in the cochlea and sent to the brain.

implant

cochlea

1. A microphone implanted just behind the ear picks up sound from the surrounding environment.

auditory nerve

speech processor

2. A speech processor, attached to the implant and worn outside the body, selects and arranges the sound picked up by the microphone.

electrode array

Check Your Understanding

Concept Map L.O. 3.5, 3.6, 3.7

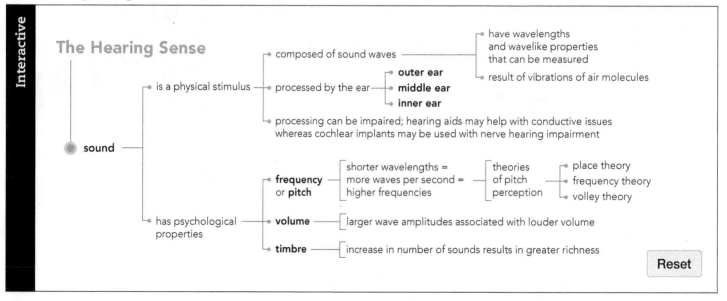

Interactive

The Hearing Sense

sound

- is a physical stimulus
  - composed of sound waves
    - have wavelengths and wavelike properties that can be measured
    - result of vibrations of air molecules
  - processed by the ear
    - **outer ear**
    - **middle ear**
    - **inner ear**
  - processing can be impaired; hearing aids may help with conductive issues whereas cochlear implants may be used with nerve hearing impairment
- has psychological properties
  - **frequency** or **pitch**
    - shorter wavelengths = more waves per second = higher frequencies
    - theories of pitch perception
      - place theory
      - frequency theory
      - volley theory
  - **volume** — larger wave amplitudes associated with louder volume
  - **timbre** — increase in number of sounds results in greater richness

Reset

Practice Quiz   How much do you remember? ANSWERS ON PAGE AK–1.

Pick the best answer.

1. The part of the ear that can be seen is also called the
   a. pinna.
   b. oval window.
   c. organ of Corti.
   d. cochlea.

2. The oval window is found in what part of the ear?
   a. outer ear
   b. middle ear
   c. inner ear
   d. The oval window is not a structure of the ear.

3. Which theory cannot adequately account for pitches above 1000 hz?
   a. place
   b. frequency
   c. volley
   d. adaptive

4. Ethan has suffered minor damage to the bones in his left middle ear. What treatment, if any, might help to restore his hearing?
   a. a hearing aid
   b. a cochlear implant
   c. both a hearing aid and a cochlear implant
   d. Such damage is permanent and cannot be remedied.

5. Which is considered the most common type of permanent hearing loss?
   a. psychological hearing loss
   b. conductive hearing loss
   c. frequency-based hearing loss
   d. sensorineural hearing loss

Chemical Senses: It Tastes Good and Smells Even Better

The sense of taste (taste in food, not taste in clothing or friends) and the sense of smell are very closely related. Have you ever noticed that when your nose is all stopped up, your sense of taste is affected, too? That's because the sense of taste is really a combination of taste and smell. Without the input from the nose, there are actually only four, and possibly five, kinds of taste sensors in the mouth.

GUSTATION: HOW WE TASTE THE WORLD

3.8 Describe how the sense of taste works, and identify the five basic tastes.

Our food preferences, or aversions, start to form very early in life, very early! Taste is one of our earliest developed senses. Research suggests developing babies are exposed to substances the mother inhales or digests and these impart flavor to the amniotic fluid, which the baby also ingests. Along with exposure to different flavors early in life after we are born, these experiences may affect food choices and nutritional status, that is, picking certain foods over others, for a long time to come (Beauchamp & Mennella, 2011; Mennella & Trabulsi, 2012).

TASTE BUDS *Taste buds* is the common name for the taste receptor cells, special kinds of neurons found in the mouth that are responsible for the sense of taste, or **gustation**. Most taste buds are located on the tongue, but there are a few on the roof of the mouth, the cheeks, and under the tongue, and in the throat as well. How sensitive people are to various tastes depends on how many taste buds they have; some people have only around 500, whereas others have 20 times that number. The latter are called "super-tasters" and need far less seasoning in their food than those with fewer taste buds (Bartoshuk, 1993).

 💬 So taste buds are those little bumps I can see when I look closely at my tongue?

No, those "bumps" are called *papillae,* and the taste buds line the walls of these papillae. Each taste bud has about 20 receptors that are very similar to the receptor sites on receiving neurons at the synapse. Ⓛ Ⓘ Ⓝ Ⓚ to Learning Objective 2.3. In fact, the

Microphotograph of the surface of the tongue, showing two different sizes of papillae. The taste buds are located under the surface of the larger red papillae, whereas the smaller and more numerous papillae form a touch-sensitive rough surface that helps in chewing and moving food around the mouth.

receptors on taste buds work exactly like receptor sites on neurons—they receive molecules of various substances that fit into the receptor like a key into a lock. Taste is often called a chemical sense because it works with the molecules of foods people eat in the same way the neural receptors work with neurotransmitters. When the molecules (dissolved in saliva) fit into the receptors, a signal is fired to the brain, which then interprets the taste sensation. The video *Taste Buds* describes this process in more detail.

👁 **Watch** the **Video**, *Taste Buds.*

💬 What happens to the taste buds when I burn my tongue? Do they repair themselves? I know when I have burned my tongue, I can't taste much for a while, but the taste comes back.

In general, the taste receptors get such a workout that they have to be replaced every 10 to 14 days (McLaughlin & Margolskee, 1994). And when the tongue is burned, the damaged cells no longer work. As time goes on, those cells get replaced and the taste sense comes back.

THE FIVE BASIC TASTES   In 1916 a German psychologist named Hans Henning proposed that there are four primary tastes: sweet, sour, salty, and bitter. Lindemann (1996) supported the idea that there is a fifth kind of taste receptor that detects a pleasant "brothy" taste associated with foods like chicken soup, tuna, kelp, cheese, and soy products, among others. Lindemann proposed that this fifth taste be called *umami*, a Japanese word first coined in 1908 by Dr. Kikunae Ikeda of Tokyo Imperial University to describe the taste. Dr. Ikeda had succeeded in isolating the substance in kelp that generated the sensation of umami—glutamate (Beyreuther et al., 2007). **LINK** to Learning Objective 2.3. Glutamate exists not only in the foods listed earlier but is also present in human breast milk and is the reason that the seasoning MSG—monosodium *glutamate*—adds a pleasant flavor to foods.

Although researchers used to believe that certain tastes were located on certain places on the tongue, it is now known that all of the taste sensations are processed all over the tongue (Bartoshuk, 1993). The taste information is sent to the gustatory cortex, found in the front part of the *insula* and the *frontal operculum*. (See **Figure 3.10**.) These areas

Figure 3.10   Gustatory Cortex

The gustatory cortex is found in the anterior insula and frontal operculum. The insula is an area of cortex covered by folds of overlying cortex, and each fold is an operculum. In the coronal section of a human brain above, the gustatory cortex is found in the regions colored a light red.

are involved in the conscious perception of taste whereas the texture, or "mouth-feel," of foods is processed in the somatosensory cortex of the parietal lobe (Buck & Bargmann, 2013; Pritchard, 2012; Shepherd, 2012). The five taste sensations work together, along with the sense of smell and the texture, temperature, and "heat" of foods, to produce thousands of taste sensations, which are further affected by our culture, personal expectations, and past learning experiences. For example, boiled peanuts are not an uncommon snack in parts of the southern United States, but the idea of a warm, soft and mushy, slightly salty peanut may not be appealing in other parts of the country. The cortical taste areas also project to parts of the limbic system, which helps explain why tastes can be used for both positive and negative reinforcement (Pritchard, 2012). **L I N K** to Learning Objective 5.5.

Just as individuals and groups can vary on their food preferences, they can also vary on level of perceived sweetness. For example, obese individuals have been found to experience less sweetness than individuals who are not obese; foods that are both sweet and high in fat tend to be especially attractive to individuals who are obese (Bartoshuk et al., 2006). Such differences (as well as genetic variations like the supertasters) complicate direct comparison of food preferences. One possible solution is to have individuals rate taste in terms of an unrelated "standard" sensory experience of known intensity, such as the brightness of a light or the loudness of a sound or preference in terms of all pleasurable experiences, and not just taste (Bartoshuk et al., 2005; Snyder & Bartoshuk, 2009).

Turning our attention back to how things taste for us as individuals, have you ever noticed that when you have a cold, food tastes very bland? Everything becomes bland or muted because you can taste only sweet, salty, bitter, sour, and umami—and because your nose is stuffed up with a cold, you don't get all the enhanced variations of those tastes that come from the sense of smell.

THE SENSE OF SCENTS: OLFACTION

3.9 Describe how the sense of smell works.

Like the sense of taste, the sense of smell is a chemical sense. The ability to smell odors is called **olfaction**, or the **olfactory sense.**

The outer part of the nose serves the same purpose for odors that the pinna and ear canal serve for sounds: Both are merely ways to collect the sensory information and get it to the part of the body that will translate it into neural signals.

The part of the olfactory system that transduces odors—turns odors into signals the brain can understand—is located at the top of the nasal passages. This area of olfactory receptor cells is only about an inch square in each cavity, yet contains about 10 million olfactory receptors. (See **Figure 3.11** on the next page.)

OLFACTORY RECEPTOR CELLS   The *olfactory receptor cells* each have about a half dozen to a dozen little "hairs," called *cilia*, that project into the cavity. Like taste buds, there are receptor sites on these hair cells that send signals to the brain when stimulated by the molecules of substances that are in the air moving past them.

 💬 Wait a minute—you mean that when I can smell something like a skunk, there are little particles of skunk odor *in* my nose?

Yes. When a person is sniffing something, the sniffing serves to move molecules of whatever the person is trying to smell into the nose and into the nasal cavities. That's okay when it's the smell of baking bread, apple pie, flowers, and the like, but when it's skunk, rotten eggs, dead animals—well, try not to think about it too much.

Olfactory receptors are like taste buds in another way, too. Olfactory receptors also have to be replaced as they naturally die off, about every 5 to 8 weeks. Unlike the taste buds, there are many more than five types of olfactory receptors—in fact, there are at least 1,000 of them.

a.

Olfactory bulb

Cilia of olfactory receptor cell

Olfactory epithelium

b.

Olfactory bulb

Nerve fiber

Supporting cell

Receptor cell

Cilia

Figure 3.11   The Olfactory Receptors

(a) A cross section of the nose and mouth. This drawing shows the nerve fibers inside the nasal cavity that carry information about smell directly to the olfactory bulb just under the frontal lobe of the brain (shown in green). (b) A diagram of the cells in the nose that process smell. The olfactory bulb is on top. Notice the cilia, tiny hairlike cells that project into the nasal cavity. These are the receptors for the sense of smell.

Signals from the olfactory receptors in the nasal cavity do not follow the same path as the signals from all the other senses. Vision, hearing, taste, and touch all pass through the thalamus and then on to the area of the cortex that processes that particular sensory information. But the sense of smell has its own special place in the brain—the olfactory bulbs, which are actually part of the brain.

THE OLFACTORY BULBS   The **olfactory bulbs** are located right on top of the sinus cavity on each side of the brain directly beneath the frontal lobes. (Refer back to Figure 3.11.) The olfactory receptors send their neural signals directly up to these bulbs, bypassing the thalamus, the relay center for all other sensory information. The olfactory information is then sent from the olfactory bulbs to higher cortical areas, including the primary olfactory cortex (the *piriform cortex*), the orbitofrontal cortex, and the amygdala (remember from Chapter Two that the orbitofrontal cortex and amygdala play important roles in emotion). Ⓛ Ⓘ Ⓝ Ⓚ to Learning Objectives 2.11 and 2.12.

Concept Map L.O. 3.8, 3.9

Interactive

Chemical Senses

smell/olfaction
- called a chemical sense because substance molecules are suspended in the air, carried to the nasal cavity, and fit into receptor sites
- nose serves as a collection device
- unique in that signals do not first travel to the thalamus before going to the brain

taste/gustation
- made possible largely through the role of taste buds (taste receptor cells)
- five basic tastes (receptor types)
  - sweet
  - sour
  - salty
  - bitter
  - umami
- called a chemical sense because food molecules dissolve in saliva, which then fits into receptor sites

Reset

Practice Quiz   How much do you remember?   ANSWERS ON PAGE AK–1.

Pick the best answer.

1. Taste is often called a _____ sense because it works with the molecules of foods that people eat.

   a. physical   **c.** chemical

   b. psychological   **d.** electrical

2. Research has found that taste information is sent to the

   a. pons and medulla.

   b. suprachiasmatic nucleus.

   c. cerebellum and parietal lobe.

   d. insula and frontal operculum.

3. How often are olfactory receptors replaced by new olfactory receptors?

   a. every 12–24 hours   **c.** every 30 days

   b. every 2–3 days   **d.** every 5–8 weeks

4. Olfactory receptors project directly to the _____, and are unique in that signals do not first connect to the thalamus.

   a. occipital lobe   **c.** hypothalamus

   b. olfactory bulbs   **d.** gustatory cortex

Somesthetic Senses: What the Body Knows

So far, this chapter has covered vision, hearing, taste, and smell. That leaves touch. What is thought of as the sense of touch is really several sensations, originating in several different places in—and on—the body. It's really more accurate to refer to these as the body senses, or **somesthetic senses**. The first part of that word, *soma*, means "body," as mentioned in Chapter Two. The second part, *esthetic*, means "feeling," hence the name. We will discuss each of the three somesthetic sense systems.

PERCEPTION OF TOUCH, PRESSURE, TEMPERATURE, AND PAIN

3.10 **Describe how we experience the sensations of touch, pressure, temperature, and pain.**

Here's a good trivia question: What organ of the body is about 20 square feet in size? The answer is the skin. Skin is an organ. Its purposes include more than simply keeping bodily fluids in and germs out; skin also receives and transmits information from the outside world to the central nervous system (specifically, to the somatosensory cortex). **LINK** to Learning Objective 2.12. Information about light touch, deeper pressure, hot, cold, and even pain is collected by special receptors in the skin's layers known as the **skin senses**.

TYPES OF SENSORY RECEPTORS IN THE SKIN There are about half a dozen different receptors in the layers of the skin. (See **Figure 3.12** on the next page.) Some of them will respond to only one kind of sensation. For example, the *Pacinian corpuscles* are just beneath the skin and respond to changes in pressure. There are nerve endings that wrap around the ends of the hair follicles, a fact people may be well aware of when they tweeze their eyebrows, or when someone pulls their hair. These nerve endings are sensitive to both pain and touch. There are *free nerve endings* just beneath the uppermost layer of the skin that respond to changes in temperature and to pressure—and to pain.

 💬 How exactly does pain work? Why is it that sometimes I feel pain deep inside? Are there pain receptors there, too?

Yes, there are pain nerve fibers in the internal organs as well as receptors for pressure. How else would people have a stomachache or intestinal* pain—or get that full feeling of pressure when they've eaten too much or their bladder is full?

Her sense of touch is allowing this girl with visual impairment to "read" a Braille book with her fingers. The fingertips are extremely sensitive to fine differences in texture, allowing her to distinguish between small dots representing the different letters of the alphabet.

*intestinal: having to do with the tubes in the body that digest food and process waste material.

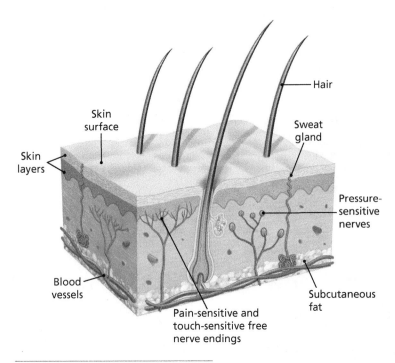

Figure 3.12 Cross Section of the Skin and Its Receptors

The skin is composed of several types of cells that process pain, pressure, and temperature. Some of these cells are wrapped around the ends of the hairs on the skin and are sensitive to touch on the hair itself, whereas others are located near the surface, and still others just under the top layer of tissue.

There are actually different types of pain. There are receptors that detect pain (and pressure) in the organs, a type of pain called *visceral pain*. Pain sensations in the skin, muscles, tendons, and joints are carried on large nerve fibers and are called *somatic pain*. Somatic pain is the body's warning system that something is being, or is about to be, damaged and tends to be sharp and fast. Another type of somatic pain is carried on small nerve fibers and is slower and more of a general ache. This somatic pain acts as a kind of reminder system, keeping people from further injury by reminding them that the body has already been damaged. For example, if you hit your thumb with a hammer, the immediate pain sensation is of the first kind—sharp, fast, and bright. But later the bruised tissue simply aches, letting you know to take it easy on that thumb.

PAIN DISORDERS People may not like pain, but its function as a warning system is vitally important. There are people who are born without the ability to feel pain, rare conditions called *congenital analgesia* and *congenital insensitivity to pain with anhidrosis (CIPA)*. Children with these disorders cannot feel pain when they cut or scrape themselves, leading to an increased risk of infection when the cut goes untreated (Mogil, 1999). They fear nothing—which can be a horrifying trial for the parents and teachers of such a child. These disorders affect the neural pathways that carry pain, heat, and cold sensations. (Those with CIPA have an additional disruption in the body's heat–cold sensing perspiration system [anhidrosis], so that the person is unable to cool off the body by sweating.)

A condition called *phantom limb pain* occurs when a person who has had an arm or leg removed sometimes "feels" pain in the missing limb (Nikolajsen & Jensen, 2001; Woodhouse, 2005). As many as 50 to 80 percent of people who have had amputations experience various sensations: burning, shooting pains, or pins-and-needles sensations where the amputated limb used to be. Once believed to be a psychological problem, some now believe that it is caused by the traumatic injury to the nerves during amputation (Ephraim et al., 2005).

WRITING PROMPT

What kinds of changes in your life would you have to make if you suddenly could not feel pain?

▶ The response entered here will be saved to your notes and may be collected by your instructor if he/she requires it.

Submit

Dr. Ann Rost

Missouri State Psychology Department

Pain Perception Research

PAIN: GATE-CONTROL THEORY One explanation for how the sensation of pain works is called *gate-control theory*, first proposed by Ronald Melzack and Patrick Wall (1965) and later refined and expanded (Melzack & Wall, 1996). In this theory, the pain signals must pass through a "gate" located in the spinal cord. The activity of the gate can be closed by nonpain signals coming into the spinal cord from the body and by signals coming from the brain. The gate is not a physical structure but instead represents the relative balance in neural activity of cells in the spinal cord that receive information from the body and then send information to the brain. Additional research has revealed that the activity of relay centers in the brain can also be influenced and the exact locations and mechanisms are still being investigated. The video *Gate-Control Theory of Pain* provides a simulation of how pain signals travel along the spinal cord.

 Watch the **Video**, *Gate-Control Theory of Pain.*

Stimulation of the pain receptor cells releases a neuromodulator called *substance P* (for "pain," naturally). Substance P released into the spinal cord activates other neurons that send their messages through spinal gates (opened by the pain signal). From the spinal cord, the message goes to the brain, activating cells in the thalamus, somatosensory cortex, areas of the frontal lobes, and the limbic system. The brain then interprets the pain information and sends signals that either open the spinal gates farther, causing a greater experience of pain, or close them, dampening the pain. Of course, this decision by the brain is influenced by the psychological aspects of the pain-causing stimulus. Anxiety, fear, and helplessness intensify pain, whereas laughter, distraction, and a sense of control can diminish it. (This is why people might bruise themselves and not know it if they were concentrating on something else.) Pain can also be affected by competing signals from other skin senses, which is why rubbing a sore spot can reduce the feeling of pain.

Those same psychological aspects can also influence the release of the *endorphins*, the body's natural version of morphine. Ⓛ Ⓘ Ⓝ Ⓚ to Learning Objective 2.3. Endorphins can inhibit the transmission of pain signals in the brain, and in the spinal cord they can inhibit the release of substance P.

💬 I've always heard that women are able to stand more pain than men. Is that true?

On the contrary, research has shown that women apparently feel pain more intensely than do men, and they also report pain more often than men do (Chesterton et al., 2003; Faucett et al., 1994; Norrbrink Budh et al., 2003). Men have been shown to cope better with many kinds of pain, possibly because men are often found to have a stronger belief than women that they can (or should) control their pain by their own efforts (Jackson et al., 2002).

Congenital insensitivity to pain with anhidrosis (CIPA) is a rare genetic disorder that makes 5-year-old Ashlyn unable to feel pain. She must be examined carefully for scrapes and cuts after recess at school because she cannot feel when she hurts herself, putting her at risk for infection. What are some of the problems that Ashlyn and her parents may face as she grows older?

THE KINESTHETIC AND VESTIBULAR SENSES

3.11 Describe the senses that tell us about balance and the position and movement of our bodies.

In addition to the skin senses just covered, there are two other somesthetic senses. The **kinesthetic sense** (having to do with the location of body parts in relation to each other), and the **vestibular sense** (having to do with movement and body position).

THE KINESTHETIC SENSE Special receptors located in the muscles, tendons, and joints are part of the body's sense of movement and position in space—the movement and location of the arms, legs, and so forth in relation to one another. This sense is called *kinesthesia*, from the Greek words *kinein* ("to move") and *aesthesis* ("sensation"). When you close your eyes and raise your hand above your head, you know where your hand is because these special receptors, called proprioceptors, tell you about joint movement or the muscles stretching or contracting.

If you have ever gotten sick from traveling in a moving vehicle, you might be tempted to blame these proprioceptors. Actually, it's not the proprioceptors in the body that make people get sick. The culprits are special structures in the ear that tell us about the position of the body in relation to the ground and movement of the head that make up the *vestibular sense*—the sense of balance.

THE VESTIBULAR SENSE The name of this particular sense comes from a Latin word that means "entrance" or "chamber." The structures for this sense are located in the innermost chamber of the ear. There are two kinds of vestibular organs, the otolith organs and the semicircular canals.

The *otolith organs* are tiny sacs found just above the cochlea. These sacs contain a gelatin-like fluid within which tiny crystals are suspended (much like pieces of fruit in a bowl of Jell-O®). The head moves and the crystals cause the fluid to vibrate, setting off some tiny hairlike receptors on the inner surface of the sac, telling the person that he or she is moving forward, backward, sideways, or up and down. (It's pretty much the way the cochlea works but with movement being the stimulus instead of sound vibrations.)

The *semicircular canals* are three somewhat circular tubes that are also filled with fluid that will stimulate hairlike receptors when rotated. Having three tubes allows one to be located in each of the three planes of motion. Remember learning in geometry class about the *x*-, *y*-, and *z*-axes? Those are the three planes through which the body can rotate, and when it does, it sets off the receptors in these canals. When you spin around and then stop, the fluid in the horizontal canal is still rotating and will make you feel dizzy because your body is telling you that you are still moving, but your eyes are telling you that you have stopped.

This disagreement between what the eyes say and what the body says is pretty much what causes *motion sickness*, the tendency to get nauseated when in a moving vehicle, especially one with an irregular movement. Normally, the vestibular sense coordinates with the other senses. But for some people, the information from the eyes may conflict a little too much with the vestibular organs, and dizziness, nausea, and disorientation are the result. This explanation of motion sickness is known as **sensory conflict theory** (Oman, 1990; Reason & Brand, 1975). The dizziness is the most likely cause of the nausea. Many poisons make a person dizzy, and the most evolutionarily adaptive thing to do is to expel the poison. Even without any poison in a case of motion sickness, the nausea occurs anyway (Treisman, 1977).

One way some people overcome motion sickness is to focus on a distant point or object. This provides visual information to the person about how he or she is moving, bringing the sensory input into agreement with the visual input. This is also how ballerinas and ice skaters manage not to get sick when turning rapidly and repeatedly—they focus their eyes at least once on some fixed object every so many turns.

This tightrope-walking violinist is performing an amazing feat of coordination and muscular control. He must not only use his vestibular organs to help maintain his balance but also his kinesthetic sense to be aware of exactly where each foot is in relation to the rope.

Concept Map L.O. 3.10, 3.11

Interactive

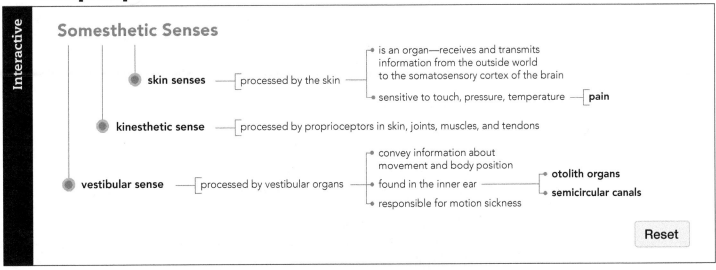

Somesthetic Senses

skin senses — processed by the skin — is an organ—receives and transmits information from the outside world to the somatosensory cortex of the brain

— sensitive to touch, pressure, temperature — **pain**

kinesthetic sense — processed by proprioceptors in skin, joints, muscles, and tendons

vestibular sense — processed by vestibular organs — convey information about movement and body position

— found in the inner ear — **otolith organs** / **semicircular canals**

— responsible for motion sickness

Reset

Practice Quiz   How much do you remember? ANSWERS ON PAGE AK–1.

Pick the best answer.

1. _____ are tactile receptors that are located just beneath the skin and respond to changes in pressure.
   - **a.** Oligodendrocytes
   - **b.** Free nerve endings
   - **c.** Tactile interneurons
   - **d.** Pacinian corpuscles

2. Juan suffers from a rare genetic condition that leaves him unable to experience pain and at the same time unable to perspire to cool down his body. This condition is called _____
   - **a.** Crohn's disease
   - **b.** CIPA
   - **c.** protanopia
   - **d.** tinnitus

3. In gate-control theory, substance P
   - **a.** opens the spinal gates for pain.
   - **b.** closes the spinal gates for pain.
   - **c.** is unrelated to pain.
   - **d.** is similar in function to endorphins.

4. Special receptors located in the muscles, tendons, and joints are part of the body's sense of movement and position in space (i.e., the movement and location of the arms, legs, and so forth in relation to one another). This sense is called _____.
   - **a.** proprioception
   - **b.** kinesthesia
   - **c.** the vestibular sense
   - **d.** gustation

5. Motion sickness often results from conflicting signals sent from the _____ and from the _____.
   - **a.** eyes; vestibular organs
   - **b.** brain; internal organs
   - **c.** conscious; unconscious
   - **d.** extremities; brain

The ABCs of Perception

Perception is the method by which the brain takes all the sensations people experience at any given moment and allows them to be interpreted in some meaningful fashion. Perception has some individuality to it. For example, two people might be looking at a cloud and while one thinks it's shaped like a horse, the other thinks it's more like a cow. They both *see* the same cloud, but they *perceive* that cloud differently.

HOW WE ORGANIZE OUR PERCEPTIONS

3.12 Describe how perceptual constancies and the Gestalt principles account for common perceptual experiences.

As individual as perception might be, some similarities exist in how people perceive the world around them. As such, there are some circumstances during which stimuli are seemingly automatically perceived in almost the same way by various individuals.

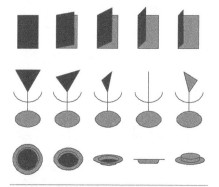

Figure 3.13 Shape Constancy

Three examples of shape constancy are shown here. The opening door is actually many different shapes, yet we still see it as basically a rectangular door. We do the same thing with a triangle and a circle—and, although when we look at them from different angles they cast differently shaped images on our retina, we experience them as a triangle and a circle because of shape constancy.

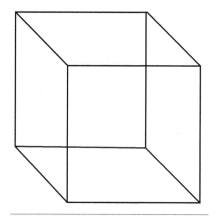

Figure 3.14 The Necker Cube

This is an example of a reversible figure. It can also be described as an ambiguous figure, since it is not clear which pattern should predominate.

THE CONSTANCIES: SIZE, SHAPE, AND BRIGHTNESS One form of perceptual constancy* is **size constancy**, the tendency to interpret an object as always being the same size, regardless of its distance from the viewer (or the size of the image it casts on the retina). So if an object that is normally perceived to be about 6 feet tall appears very small on the retina, it will be interpreted as being very far away.

Another perceptual constancy is the tendency to interpret the shape of an object as constant, even when it changes on the retina. This **shape constancy** is why a person still perceives a coin as a circle even if it is held at an angle that makes it appear to be an oval on the retina. Dinner plates on a table are also seen as round, even though from the angle of viewing they are oval. (See **Figure 3.13**.)

A third form of perceptual constancy is **brightness constancy**, the tendency to perceive the apparent brightness of an object as the same even when the light conditions change. If a person is wearing black pants and a white shirt, for example, in broad daylight the shirt will appear to be much brighter than the pants. But if the sun is covered by thick clouds, even though the pants and shirt have less light to reflect than previously, the shirt will still appear to be just as much brighter than the pants as before—because the different amount of light reflected from each piece of clothing is still the same difference as before (Zeki, 2001).

THE GESTALT PRINCIPLES Remember the discussion of the Gestalt theorists in Chapter One? Their original focus on human perception can still be seen in certain basic principles today, including the basic principles of the Gestalt tendency to group objects and perceive whole shapes.

FIGURE–GROUND RELATIONSHIPS Take a look at the drawing of the cube in **Figure 3.14**. Which face of the cube is in the front? Look again—do the planes and corners of the cube seem to shift as you look at it?

This is called the "Necker cube." It has been around officially since 1832, when Louis Albert Necker, a Swiss scientist who was studying the structure of crystals, first drew it in his published papers. The problem with this cube is that there are conflicting sets of depth cues, so the viewer is never really sure which plane or edge is in the back and which is in the front—the visual presentation of the cube seems to keep reversing its planes and edges.

A similar illusion can be seen in **Figure 3.15**. In this picture, the viewer can switch perception back and forth from two faces looking at each other to the outline of a goblet in the middle. Which is the figure in front and which is the background?

Figure–ground relationships refer to the tendency to perceive objects or figures as existing on a background. People seem to have a preference for picking out figures from backgrounds even as early as birth. The illusions in Figures 3.14 and 3.15 are **reversible figures**, in which the figure and the ground seem to switch back and forth.

PROXIMITY Another very simple rule of perception is the tendency to perceive objects that are close to one another as part of the same grouping, a principle called **proximity**, or "nearness." (See **Figure 3.16**.)

SIMILARITY **Similarity** refers to the tendency to perceive things that look similar as being part of the same group. When members of a sports team wear uniforms that are all the same color, it allows people viewing the game to perceive them as one group even when they are scattered around the field or court.

CLOSURE **Closure** is the tendency to complete figures that are incomplete. A talented artist can give the impression of an entire face with just a few cleverly placed strokes of the pen or brush—the viewers fill in the details.

---

*constancy: something that remains the same, the property of remaining stable and unchanging.

CONTINUITY   The principle of **continuity** is easier to see than it is to explain in words. It refers to the tendency to perceive things as simply as possible with a continuous pattern rather than with a complex, broken-up pattern. Look at Figure 3.16 for an example of continuity. Isn't it much easier to see the figure on the left as two wavy lines crossing each other than as the little sections in the diagrams to the right?

CONTIGUITY   **Contiguity** isn't shown in Figure 3.16 because it involves not just nearness in space but nearness in time also. Basically, contiguity is the tendency to perceive two things that happen close together in time as being related. Usually the first event that occurs is seen as causing the second event. Ventriloquists* make vocalizations without appearing to move their own mouths but move their dummy's mouth instead. The tendency to believe that the dummy is doing the talking is due largely to contiguity.

There is one other principle of perceptual grouping that was not one of the original principles. It was added to the list (and can be seen at the bottom of Figure 3.16) by Stephen Palmer (Palmer, 1992). In *common region*, the tendency is to perceive objects that are in a common area or region as being in a group. In Figure 3.16, people could perceive the stars as one group and the circles as another on the basis of similarity. But the colored backgrounds so visibly define common regions that people instead perceive three groups—one of which has both stars and circles in it.

Figure 3.15   Figure–Ground Illusion

What do you see when you look at this picture? Is it a wine goblet? Or two faces looking at each other? This is an example in which the figure and the ground seem to "switch" each time you look at the picture.

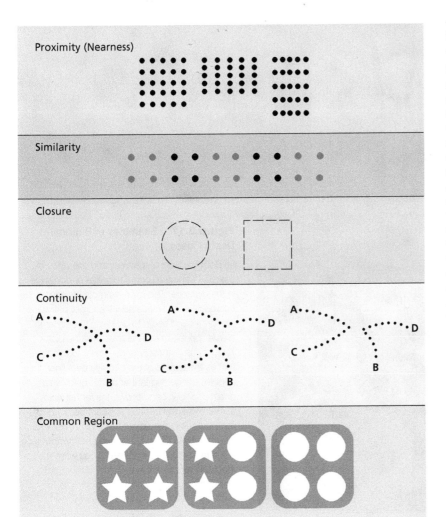

Figure 3.16   Gestalt Principles of Grouping

The Gestalt principles of grouping are shown here. These are the human tendency to organize isolated stimuli into groups on the basis of five characteristics: proximity, similarity, closure, continuity, and common region.

Proximity: The dots on the left can be seen as horizontal or vertical rows—neither organization dominates. But just by changing the proximity of certain dots, as in the other two examples, we experience the dots as vertical columns (middle) or horizontal rows (right).

Similarity: The similarity of color here makes you perceive these dots as forming black squares and color squares rather than two rows of black and colored dots.

Closure: Even though the lines are broken, we still see these figures as a circle and a square—an example of how we tend to "close" or "fill in" missing parts from what we know of the whole.

Continuity: Because of continuity, we are much more likely to see the figure on the left as being made up of two lines, A to B and C to D, than we are to see it as a figure made up of lines A to D and C to B or A to C and B to D.

Common Region: Similarity would suggest that people see two groups, stars and circles. But the colored backgrounds define a visible common region, and the tendency is to perceive three different groups.

*ventriloquist: an entertainer who, through the use of misdirection and skill, makes other objects, such as a dummy, appear to talk.

3.13 **Explain how we perceive depth using both monocular and binocular cues.**

The capability to see the world in three dimensions is called **depth perception**. It's a handy ability because without it you would have a hard time judging how far away objects are. How early in life do humans develop depth perception? It seems to develop very early in infancy, if it is not actually present at birth. People who have had sight restored have almost no ability to perceive depth if they were blind from birth. Depth perception, like the constancies, seems to be present in infants at a very young age. Ⓛ Ⓘ Ⓝ K to Learning Objective 8.6.

Various cues exist for perceiving depth in the world. Some require the use of only one eye (**monocular cues**), and some are a result of the slightly different visual patterns that exist when the visual fields* of both eyes are used (**binocular cues**).

MONOCULAR CUES Monocular cues are often referred to as **pictorial depth cues** because artists can use these cues to give the illusion of depth to paintings and drawings. Examples of these cues are discussed next and can be seen in **Figure 3.17**.

1. **Linear perspective:** When looking down a long interstate highway, the two sides of the highway appear to merge together in the distance. This tendency for lines that

Figure 3.17 Examples of Pictorial Depth Cues

(a) Both the lines of the trees and the sides of the road appear to come together or converge in the distance. This is an example of *linear perspective*. (b) Notice how the larger pebbles in the foreground seem to give way to smaller and smaller pebbles near the middle of the picture. *Texture gradient* causes the viewer to assume that as the texture of the pebbles gets finer, the pebbles are getting farther away. (c) In *aerial* or *atmospheric perspective*, the farther away something is the hazier it appears because of fine particles in the air between the viewer and the object. Notice that the road and farmhouse in the foreground are in sharp focus while the mountain ranges are hazy and indistinct. (d) The depth cue of *relative size* appears in this photograph. Notice that the flowers in the distance appear much smaller than those in the foreground. Relative size causes smaller objects to be perceived as farther away from the viewer.

*visual field: the entire area of space visible at a given instant without moving the eyes.

are actually parallel to *seem* to converge[*] on each other is called **linear perspective**. It works in pictures because people assume that in the picture, as in real life, the converging lines indicate that the "ends" of the lines are a great distance away from where the people are as they view them.

2. **Relative size:** The principle of size constancy is at work in **relative size**, when objects that people expect to be of a certain size appear to be small and are, therefore, assumed to be much farther away. Movie makers use this principle to make their small models seem gigantic but off in the distance.

3. **Overlap:** If one object seems to be blocking another object, people assume that the blocked object is behind the first one and, therefore, farther away. This cue is also known as **interposition**.

4. **Aerial (atmospheric) perspective:** The farther away an object is, the hazier the object will appear to be due to tiny particles of dust, dirt, and other pollutants in the air, a perceptual cue called **aerial (atmospheric) perspective**. This is why distant mountains often look fuzzy, and buildings far in the distance are blurrier than those that are close.

5. **Texture gradient:** If there are any large expanses of pebbles, rocks, or patterned roads (such as a cobblestone street) nearby, go take a look at them one day. The pebbles or bricks that are close to you are very distinctly textured, but as you look farther off into the distance, their texture becomes smaller and finer. **Texture gradient** is another trick used by artists to give the illusion of depth in a painting.

6. **Motion parallax:** The next time you're in a car, notice how the objects outside the car window seem to zip by very fast when they are close to the car, and objects in the distance, such as mountains, seem to move more slowly. This discrepancy in motion of near and far objects is called **motion parallax**.

7. **Accommodation:** A monocular cue that is not one of the pictorial cues, **accommodation** makes use of something that happens inside the eye. The lens of the human eye is flexible and held in place by a series of muscles. The discussion of the eye earlier in this chapter mentioned the process of visual accommodation as the tendency of the lens to change its shape, or thickness, in response to objects near or far away. The brain can use this information about accommodation as a cue for distance. Accommodation is also called a "muscular cue."

BINOCULAR CUES   As the name suggests, these cues require the use of two eyes.

1. **Convergence:** Another muscular cue, **convergence**, refers to the rotation of the two eyes in their sockets to focus on a single object. If the object is close, the convergence is pretty great (almost as great as crossing the eyes). If the object is far, the convergence is much less. Hold your finger up in front of your nose, and then move it away and back again. That feeling you get in the muscles of your eyes is convergence. (See the left side of **Figure 3.18** on the next page.)

2. **Binocular disparity: Binocular disparity** is a scientific way of saying that because the eyes are a few inches apart, they don't see exactly the same image. The brain interprets the images on the retina to determine distance from the eyes. If the two images are very different, the object must be pretty close. If they are almost identical, the object is far enough away to make the retinal disparity very small. You can demonstrate this cue for yourself by holding an object in front of your nose. Close one eye, note where the object is, and then open that eye and close the other. There should be quite a difference in views. But if you do the same thing with an object that is across the room, the image doesn't seem to "jump" or move nearly as much, if at all. (See Figure 3.18, right.)

In spite of all the cues for perception that exist, even the most sophisticated perceiver can still fail to perceive the world as it actually is, as the next section demonstrates.

_____

[*]converge: come together.

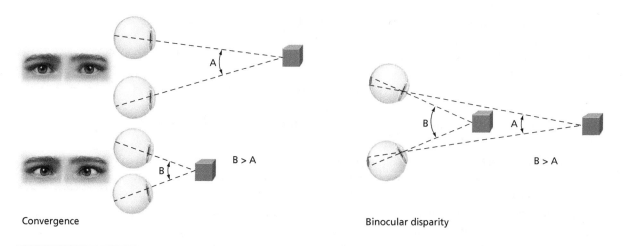

Convergence

Binocular disparity

Figure 3.18 Binocular Cues to Depth Perception

(left) Convergence is a depth cue that involves the muscles of the eyes. When objects are far away, the eye muscles are more relaxed; when objects are close, the eye muscles move together, or converge. (right) Binocular disparity. Because your eyes are separated by several centimeters, each eye sees a slightly different image of the object in front of you. In A, the object is far enough away that the difference is small. In B, while the object is closer, there is a greater difference between what each eye sees. The brain interprets this difference as the distance of the object.

PERCEPTUAL ILLUSIONS

3.14 Describe some common visual illusions, and summarize factors that can influence and alter perception.

💬 You've mentioned the word *illusion* several times. Exactly what are illusions, and why is it so easy to be fooled by them?

An *illusion* is a perception that does not correspond to reality: People *think* they see something when the reality is quite different. Another way of thinking of illusions is as visual stimuli that "fool" the eye. (Illusions are not hallucinations: An illusion is a distorted perception of something that is really there, but a hallucination originates in the brain, not in reality.)

Research involving illusions can be very useful for both psychologists and neuroscientists. These studies often provide valuable information about how the sensory receptors and sense organs work and how humans interpret sensory input.

Sometimes illusions are based on early sensory processes, subsequent processing, or higher-level assumptions made by the brain's visual system (Eagleman, 2001; Macknik et al., 2008).

We've already discussed one visual illusion, color afterimages, which are due to opponent-processes in the retina or lateral geniculate nucleus (LGN) of the thalamus after light information has been detected by the rods and cones. Another postdetection, but still rather early, process has been offered for yet another illusion.

THE HERMANN GRID Look at the matrix of squares in **Figure 3.19**. Notice anything interesting as you look at different parts of the figure, particularly at the intersections of the white lines? You probably see gray blobs or diamonds that fade away or disappear completely when you try to look directly at them. This is the Hermann grid.

Figure 3.19 The Hermann Grid

Look at this matrix of squares. Do you notice anything interesting at the white intersections? What happens if you focus your vision directly on one of the intersections?

One explanation for this illusion is attributed to the responses of neurons in the primary visual cortex that respond best to bars of light of a specific orientation (Schiller & Carvey, 2005). Such neurons are called "simple cells" and were first discovered by David Hubel and Torsten Wiesel (Hubel & Wiesel, 1959). They also discovered other cells including "complex cells," which respond to orientation and movement, and "end-stopped cells," which respond best to corners, curvature, or sudden edges. Collectively these cells have been referred to as *feature detectors* because they respond to specific features of a stimulus. Hubel and Wiesel were later awarded the Nobel Prize for extensive work in the visual system. Other research into the Hermann grid illusion has documented that straight edges are necessary for this illusion to occur, as the illusion disappears when the edges of the grid lines are slightly curved, and further suggests that the illusion may be due to a unique function of how our visual system processes information (Geier et al., 2008).

MÜLLER–LYER ILLUSION   One of the most famous visual illusions is the **Müller–Lyer illusion**. The distortion happens when the viewer tries to determine if the two lines are exactly the same length. They are identical, but one line looks longer than the other. (It's always the line with the angles on the end facing outward.) You can try to determine the length of the lines yourself in the experiment *Müller–Lyer Illusion*.

Experiment   MÜLLER-LYER ILLUSION

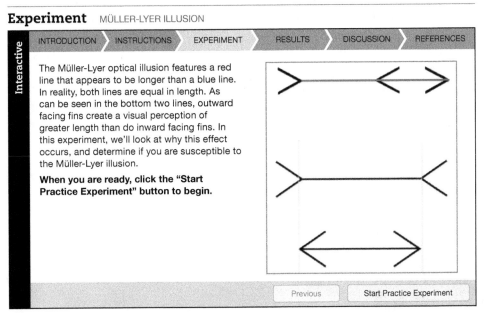

Simulate the **Experiment**, *Müller-Lyer Illusion*.

Why is this illusion so powerful? The explanation is that most people live in a world with lots of buildings. Buildings have corners. When a person is outside a building, the corner of the building is close to that person, while the walls seem to be moving away (like the line with the angles facing inward). When the person is inside a building, the corner of the room seems to move away from the viewer while the walls are coming closer (like the line with the angles facing outward). In their minds, people "pull" the inward-facing angles toward them like the outside corners of a building, and they make the outward-facing angles "stretch" away from them like the inside corners of the room (Enns & Coren, 1995; Gregory, 1990).

Marshall Segall and colleagues (Segall et al., 1966) found that people in Western cultures, having carpentered buildings with lots of straight lines and corners (Segall and colleagues refer to this as a "carpentered world"), are far more susceptible to this illusion than people from non-Western cultures (having round huts with few corners—an "uncarpentered world"). Richard Gregory (1990) found that Zulus, for example, rarely see this illusion. They live in round huts arranged in circles, use curved tools and toys, and experience few straight lines and corners in their world.

The moon illusion. When this moon is high in the night sky, it will still be the same size to the eye as it is now. Nevertheless, it is perceived to be much larger when on the horizon. In the sky, there are no objects for comparison, but on the horizon, objects such as this tree are seen as being in front of a very large moon.

THE MOON ILLUSION   Another common illusion is the *moon illusion*, in which the moon on the horizon* appears to be much larger than the moon in the sky (Plug & Ross, 1994). One explanation for this is that the moon high in the sky is all alone, with no cues for depth surrounding it. But on the horizon, the moon appears behind trees and houses, cues for depth that make the horizon seem very far away. The moon is seen as being behind these objects and, therefore, farther away from the viewer. Because people know that objects that are farther away from them and yet still appear large are very large indeed, they "magnify" the moon in their minds—a misapplication of the principle of size constancy. This explanation of the moon illusion is called the *apparent distance hypothesis*. This explanation goes back to the second century A.D., first written about by the Greek–Egyptian astronomer Ptolemy and later further developed by an eleventh-century Arab astronomer, Al-Hazan (Ross & Ross, 1976).

ILLUSIONS OF MOTION   Sometimes people perceive an object as moving when it is actually still. One example of this phenomenon takes place as part of a famous experiment in conformity called the *autokinetic* effect. In this effect, a small, stationary light in a darkened room will appear to move or drift because there are no surrounding cues to indicate that the light is *not* moving. Another is the *stroboscopic motion* seen in motion pictures, in which a rapid series of still pictures will seem to be in motion. Many a student has discovered that drawing little figures on the edges of a notebook and then flipping the pages quickly will also produce this same illusion of movement.

Another movement illusion related to stroboscopic motion is the *phi phenomenon*, in which lights turned on in sequence appear to move. For example, if a light is turned on in a darkened room and then turned off, and then another light a short distance away is flashed on and off, it will appear to be one light moving across that distance. This principle is used to suggest motion in many theater marquee signs—flashing arrows indicating direction that have a series of lights going on and off in a sequence, and even in strings of decorative lighting, such as the "chasing" lights seen on houses at holiday times.

What about seeing motion in static images? There are several examples, both classic and modern, of illusory movement or apparent motion being perceived in a static image. The debate about the causes for such illusions, whether they begin in the eyes or the brain, has been going on for at least 200 years (Troncoso et al., 2008).

Look at **Figure 3.20**. What do you see?

Figure 3.20   "Rotating Snakes"

Notice anything as you move your eyes over this image? The image is not moving; seeing the "snakes" rotate is due at least in part to movements of your eyes.

Created by and courtesy of Dr. Akiyoshi Kitaoka, Ritsumeikan University.

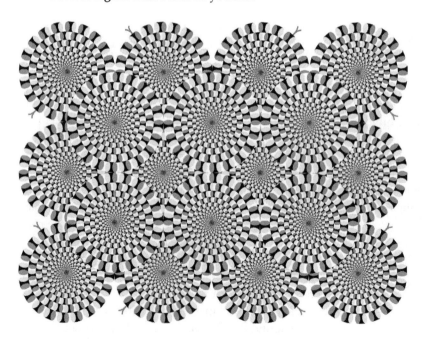

*horizon: the place where the earth apparently meets the sky.

The "rotating snakes" illusion is one of many motion-illusion images designed by Dr. Akiyoshi Kitaoka. There have been a variety of explanations offered for this type of motion illusion, ranging from factors that depend on the image's luminance and/or the color arrangement, or possibly slight differences in the time it takes the brain to process this information. When fMRI and equipment used to track eye movements were used to investigate participants' perception of the illusion, researchers found that there was an increase in brain activity in a visual area sensitive to motion. However, this activity was greatest when accompanied by guided eye movements, suggesting eye movements play a significant role in the perception of the illusion (Kuriki et al., 2008).

Eye movements have also been found to be a primary cause for the illusory motion seen in images based on a 1981 painting by Isia Levant, *Enigma*. Look at the center of **Figure 3.21**: notice anything within the green rings? Many people will see the rings start to "sparkle" or the rings rotating. Why does this occur? By using special eye-tracking equipment that allowed them to record even the smallest of eye movements, researchers found that tiny eye movements called *microsaccades*, discussed earlier in the chapter, are directly linked to the perception of motion in *Enigma* and are at least one possible cause of the illusion (Troncoso et al., 2008).

These two studies highlight some of the advances researchers have made in examining questions related to visual perception. For more information about the study of visual illusions as used in magic, and the study of such illusions from a neuroscientific perspective, see the Applying Psychology section at the end of the chapter.

OTHER FACTORS THAT INFLUENCE PERCEPTION Human perception of the world is obviously influenced by things such as culture and misinterpretations of cues. Following are other factors that cause people to alter their perceptions.

People often misunderstand what is said to them because they were expecting to hear something else. People's tendency to perceive things a certain way because their previous experiences or expectations influence them is called **perceptual set or perceptual expectancy**. Although expectancies can be useful in interpreting certain stimuli, they can also lead people down the wrong path. Participate in the experiment *Ambiguous Figures* to see how perceptual set influences how you identify various ambiguous figures.

Figure 3.21   "Reinterpretation of Enigma"

As in Figure 3.20, the motion you see in this static image is because of movements of your eyes, this time due more to tiny movements called *microsaccades*.

Created by and courtesy of Jorge Otero-Millan, Martinez-Conde Laboratory, Barrow Neurological Institute.

Experiment AMBIGUOUS FIGURES

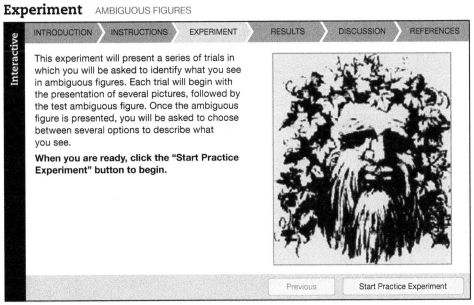

| INTRODUCTION | INSTRUCTIONS | EXPERIMENT | RESULTS | DISCUSSION | REFERENCES |

This experiment will present a series of trials in which you will be asked to identify what you see in ambiguous figures. Each trial will begin with the presentation of several pictures, followed by the test ambiguous figure. Once the ambiguous figure is presented, you will be asked to choose between several options to describe what you see.

When you are ready, click the "Start Practice Experiment" button to begin.

Previous   Start Practice Experiment

Simulate the **Experiment**, *Ambiguous Figures*.

The Ames Room illusion. This illusion is influenced by our past experiences and expectancies. The viewer perceives the room as a rectangle, but in reality it is a trapezoid with angled walls and floor.

The way in which people *interpret* what they perceive can also influence their perception. For example, people can try to understand what they perceive by fusing information they already have (as is the case of perceptual expectancy). But if there is no existing information that relates to the new information, they can look at each feature of what they perceive and try to put it all together into one whole.

Anyone who has ever worked on a jigsaw puzzle knows that it's a lot easier to put it together if there is a picture of the finished puzzle to refer to as a guide. It also helps to have worked the puzzle before—people who have done that already know what it's going to look like when it's finished. In the field of perception, this is known as **top-down processing**—the use of preexisting knowledge to organize individual features into a unified whole. This is also a form of perceptual expectancy.

If the puzzle is one the person has never worked before or if that person has lost the top of the box with the picture on it, he or she would have to start with a small section, put it together, and keep building up the sections until the recognizable picture appears. This analysis of smaller features and building up to a complete perception is called **bottom-up processing** (Cave & Kim, 1999). In this case, there is no expectancy to help organize the perception, making bottom-up processing more difficult in some respects. Fortunately, the two types of processing are often used together in perceiving the surrounding world.

Would people of different cultures perceive objects differently because of different expectancies? Some research suggests that this is true. For example, take a look at **Figure 3.22**. This figure is often called the "devil's trident." Europeans and North Americans insist on making this figure three dimensional, so they have trouble looking at it—the figure is impossible if it is perceived in three dimensions. But people in less technologically oriented cultures have little difficulty with seeing or even reproducing this figure, because they see it as a two-dimensional drawing, quite literally a collection of lines and circles rather than a solid object (Deregowski, 1969). By contrast, if you give Europeans and North Americans the task of reproducing a drawing of an upside-down face, their drawings tend to be more accurate because the upside-down face has become a "collection of lines and circles." That is, they draw what they actually see in terms of light and shadow rather than what they "think" is there three dimensionally.

Figure 3.22   The Devil's Trident

At first glance, this seems to be an ordinary three-pronged figure. But a closer look reveals that the three prongs cannot be real as drawn. Follow the lines of the top prong to see what goes wrong.

Concept Map L.O. 3.12, 3.13, 3.14

Interactive

The ABCs of Perception

perception —

— method by which the sensations experienced at any given moment are interpreted and organized in some meaningful fashion — has a subjective nature; no two people perceive the world in the exact same way

— may have unique features depending on sensory modality — e.g., vision — **depth perception** — ability to perceive the world in three dimensions / made possible by differential information from the eyes

— may not always be based on an accurate interpretation of the stimulus — **perceptual illusions** — an illusion is a perception that does not correspond to physical reality / can be caused by default mode of sensory or brain processing and perceptual sets or expectancies

Reset

Practice Quiz   How much do you remember? ANSWERS ON PAGE AK–1.

Pick the best answer.

1. When opening a door, the actual image on your retina changes drastically but you still perceive the door as a rectangle. This is an example of

a. size constancy.

b. shape constancy.

c. color constancy.

d. brightness constancy.

2. Hunters who wear camouflage so that they can blend in with their surroundings are relying on which principle of perception?

a. shape constancy

b. expectancy

c. figure–ground relationships

d. depth perception

3. What monocular depth cue best explains why railroad tracks appear to come together in the distance?

a. convergence

b. linear perspective

c. overlap

d. texture gradient

4. Elijah likes to play a game where he holds a pencil in front of his nose, and moves it away from his face and back toward his face. While the pencil moves farther and nearer, he keeps focusing on it with his eyes, and his sister giggles as his eyes appear to "cross" as the pencil gets closer to his nose. Elijah doesn't realize that this tendency of the eyes to move closer to each other when an object gets nearer to him is an important binocular depth cue called _____.

a. convergence

b. linear perspective

c. overlap

d. texture gradient

5. The Müller-Lyer illusion occurs more frequently in

a. children than adults.

b. men than women.

c. people living in a Western culture.

d. individuals living in poverty.

6. Jason's uncle claimed to have seen a black panther in the trees beside the highway although no one else saw it. Knowing that his uncle has been looking for a black panther for years, Jason attributes his uncle's "sighting" to

a. perceptual set.

b. perceptual defense.

c. bottom-up processing.

d. cognitive convergence.

7. The first time Megan had to install a ceiling fan in her new home, it took a long time. But later when she helped install a ceiling fan in her best friend's home, she completed the job very quickly. Her improved speed and skill can partially be attributed to

a. bottom-up processing.

b. top-down processing.

c. perceptual expectancy.

d. perceptual set.

Applying Psychology to Everyday Life

Beyond "Smoke and Mirrors"—The Psychological Science and Neuroscience of Magic

3.15 **Describe how the neuroscientific study of magic can help to explain visual and cognitive illusions.**

Many people enjoy watching magic acts in person or on television. Perhaps you have been amazed by a Mindfreak® performed by Criss Angel or the performance and edgy antics of Penn & Teller. If you are one of those people, you likely witnessed a performance that included many various illusions. And like many of us, you probably wondered at some point in the performance, "How did they do that?!" Did you think the tricks were due to some type of special device (such as a fake thumb tip for hiding a scarf), or perhaps they were accomplished with "smoke and mirrors," or maybe the magician distracted the audience with one movement while actually doing something else to pull off the illusion? Magicians use many techniques to take advantage of, or manipulate, our actual level of awareness of what is happening right in front of us or perhaps to manipulate our attention.

Though magic is not a new topic of interest in psychology, there has been renewed interest in recent years, especially in the neuroscientific study of magic. This view suggests that researchers can work alongside magicians so we may be able to gain a better understanding of various cognitive and perceptual processes by not only examining the sensory or physical mechanics behind magic tricks, or even the psychological

Penn & Teller have performed together for over 30 years and have joined neuroscientists in the effort to gain insights into the brain mechanisms behind magical illusions.

explanations, but to look further by examining what is happening in the brain (Macknik & Martinez-Conde, 2009).

Dr. Stephen L. Macknik and Dr. Susanna Martinez-Conde of the Barrow Neurological Institute are two neuroscientists who have teamed up with professional magicians to study their techniques and tricks in the effort to better understand the brain mechanisms underlying the illusions and how that information can be used by researchers in the laboratory. They have identified several types of illusions that can be used alone or in combination with others to serve as a basis for various magic tricks; two of these are visual illusions and cognitive illusions (Macknik et al., 2008).

As discussed earlier in the chapter, visual illusions occur when our individual perception does not match a physical stimulus. These illusions are caused by organizational or processing biases in the brain. Furthermore, our brain activity from the perception does not directly match the brain activity associated with the physical stimulus (Macknik et al., 2008). One example Dr. Macknik and Dr. Martinez-Conde point out is similar to a trick you may have performed yourself in grade school. Did you ever take a pencil or pen, grasp it in the middle, and then shake or wiggle it up and down? If you did it correctly, the pen or pencil would appear to bend or be made of rubber. Magicians use this illusion when they "bend" solid objects, such as spoons. So what is the brain explanation? We have special neurons in the visual cortex that are sensitive to both motion and edges called *end-stopped neurons*. These neurons respond differently if an object is bouncing or moving up and down quickly, causing us to perceive a solid spoon or pencil as if it is bending.

Another effect or trick that is based on the functioning of our visual system is when a magician makes an object disappear, such as a ball vanishing into the air or perhaps the outfit of an assistant changing suddenly. By showing the audience the target object, such as the ball or outfit, and then removing it very quickly from the visual field, the *persistence of vision* effect will make it appear that the object is still there. This is due to a response in vision neurons called the after-discharge, which will create an afterimage that lasts for up to 100 milliseconds after a stimulus is removed (Macknik et al., 2008). Again, you may have performed a similar trick if you have ever taken a lit sparkler or flashlight and twirled it around quickly to make a trail of light in the dark.

Questions for Further Discussion

1. The examples highlighted in this discussion are based on visual illusions; can you think of a magic trick or performance that may have been based on an illusion in a different sensory modality?

2. Of the neuroimaging methods covered in Chapter Two, which methods might be best for examining the brain activity of someone who is watching a magic performance? Why?

Chapter Summary

The ABCs of Sensation

3.1 Define sensation, and explain sensory thresholds.

- Sensation is the activation of receptors located in the eyes, ears, skin, nasal cavities, and tongue.
- Sensory receptors are specialized forms of neurons that are activated by different stimuli such as light and sound.
- A just noticeable difference is the point at which a stimulus is detectable half the time it is present.

- Weber's law of just noticeable differences states that the just noticeable difference between two stimuli is always a constant.
- Absolute thresholds are the smallest amount of energy needed for conscious detection of a stimulus at least half the time it is present.
- Subliminal stimuli are stimuli presented just below the level of conscious awareness and subliminal perception has been demonstrated in the laboratory. It has not been shown to be effective in advertising.

3.2 Explain why some sensory information is ignored.

- Habituation occurs when the brain ignores a constant stimulus.
- Sensory adaptation occurs when the sensory receptors stop responding to a constant stimulus.

The Science of Seeing

3.3 Explain the nature of light, and describe how light travels through the various parts of the eye.

- Brightness corresponds to the amplitude of light waves, whereas color corresponds to the length of the light waves.
- Saturation is the psychological interpretation of wavelengths that are all the same (highly saturated) or varying (less saturated).
- Light enters the eye and is focused through the cornea, passes through the aqueous humor, and then through the hole in the iris muscle called the pupil.
- The lens also focuses the light on the retina, where it passes through ganglion and bipolar cells to stimulate the rods and cones.

3.4 Describe the major theories about how we see color, and explain color blindness.

- Rods detect changes in brightness but do not see color and function best in low levels of light. They are found everywhere in the retina except the center, or fovea.
- Cones are sensitive to colors and work best in bright light. They are responsible for the sharpness of visual information and are found in the fovea.
- Trichromatic theory of color perception assumes three types of cones: red, green, and blue. All colors would be perceived as various combinations of these three.
- Opponent-process theory of color perception assumes four primary colors of red, green, blue, and yellow. Colors are arranged in pairs, and when one member of a pair is activated, the other is not.
- Color blindness is a total lack of color perception, whereas color-deficient vision refers to color perception that is limited primarily to yellows and blues, or reds and greens only.

The Hearing Sense: Can You Hear Me Now?

3.5 Explain the nature of sound, and describe how it travels through the various parts of the ear.

- Sound has three aspects: pitch (frequency), loudness, and timbre (purity).
- Sound enters the ear through the visible outer structure, or pinna, and travels to the eardrum and then to the small bones of the middle ear.
- The bone called the stirrup rests on the oval window, causing the cochlea and basilar membrane to vibrate with sound.
- The organ of Corti on the basilar membrane contains the auditory receptors, which send signals to the brain about sound qualities as they vibrate.

3.6 Summarize the three theories of how the brain processes information about pitch.

- Place theory states that the location of the hair cells on the organ of Corti correspond to different pitches of sound. This can explain pitch above 1000 Hz.
- Frequency theory states that the speed with which the basilar membrane vibrates corresponds to different pitches of sound. This can explain pitch below 1000 Hz.
- The volley principle states that neurons take turns firing for sounds above 400 Hz and below 4000 Hz.

3.7 Explain why some people are unable to hear, and describe ways their hearing may be improved.

- Conduction hearing impairment is caused by damage to the outer or middle ear structures, whereas nerve hearing impairment is caused by damage to the inner ear or auditory pathways in the brain.
- Hearing aids may be used for those with conductive hearing impairment, while cochlear implants may restore some hearing to those with nerve hearing impairment.

Chemical Senses: It Tastes Good and Smells Even Better

3.8 Describe how the sense of taste works, and identify the five basic tastes.

- Gustation is the sense of taste. Taste buds in the tongue receive molecules of substances, which fit into receptor sites.
- The five basic types of taste are sweet, sour, salty, bitter, and umami (brothy).

3.9 Describe how the sense of smell works.

- Olfaction is the sense of smell. The olfactory receptors in the upper part of the nasal passages receive molecules of substances and create neural signals that then go to the olfactory bulbs under the frontal lobes.
- Both gustation and olfaction are chemical senses. Gustation involves detection of chemicals dissolved in saliva whereas olfaction involves detection of chemicals suspended in the air.

Somesthetic Senses: What the Body Knows

3.10 Describe how we experience the sensations of touch, pressure, temperature, and pain.

- The somesthetic senses include the skin senses and the vestibular senses.
- Pacinian corpuscles respond to pressure, certain nerve endings around hair follicles respond to pain and pressure, and free nerve endings respond to pain, pressure, and temperature.
- The gate-control theory of pain states that when receptors sensitive to pain are stimulated, a neurotransmitter called substance P is released into the spinal cord, activating other pain receptors by opening "gates" in the spinal column and sending the message to the brain.

3.11 **Describe the senses that tell us about balance and the position and movement of our bodies.**

- The kinesthetic senses allow the brain to know the position and movement of the body through the activity of special receptors responsive to movement of the joints and limbs.

- The vestibular sense also contributes to the body's sense of spatial orientation and movement through the activity of the otolith organs (up-and-down movement) and the semicircular canals (movement through arcs).

- Motion sickness is explained by sensory conflict theory, in which information from the eyes conflicts with information from the vestibular sense, causing nausea.

The ABCs of Perception

3.12 **Describe how perceptual constancies and the Gestalt principles account for common perceptual experiences.**

- Perception is the interpretation and organization of sensations.

- Size constancy is the tendency to perceive objects as always being the same size, no matter how close or far away they are.

- Shape constancy is the tendency to perceive objects as remaining the same shape even when the shape of the object changes on the retina of the eye.

- Brightness constancy is the tendency to perceive objects at a certain level of brightness, even when the light changes.

- The Gestalt psychologists developed several principles of perception that involve interpreting patterns in visual stimuli. The principles are figure–ground relationships, closure, similarity, continuity, contiguity, and common region.

3.13 **Explain how we perceive depth using both monocular and binocular cues.**

- Depth perception is the ability to see in three dimensions.

- Monocular cues for depth perception include linear perspective, relative size, overlap, aerial (atmospheric) perspective, texture gradient, motion parallax, and accommodation.

- Binocular cues for depth perception include convergence and binocular overlap.

3.14 **Describe some common visual illusions, and summarize factors that can influence and alter perception**

- Illusions are perceptions that do not correspond to reality or are distortions of visual stimuli.

- Perceptual set or expectancy refers to the tendency to perceive objects and situations in a particular way because of prior experiences.

- Top-down processing involves the use of preexisting knowledge to organize individual features into a unified whole.

- Bottom-up processing involves the analysis of smaller features, building up to a complete perception.

Applying Psychology to Everyday Life: Beyond "Smoke and Mirrors"—The Psychological Science and Neuroscience of Magic

3.15 **Describe how the neuroscientific study of magic can help to explain visual and cognitive illusions.**

- Magicians take advantage of some well-known properties of our visual system to accomplish a variety of magic tricks.

- By collaborating with magicians, psychologists and neuroscientists can learn more about magic and the brain processes responsible for our perception of magic tricks.

Test Yourself ANSWERS ON PAGE AK-1.

Pick the best answer.

1. In making a large pot of chili for a family reunion, you find that you have to add 1 onion to your pot of chili that already has 5 onions mixed in it to notice a difference. According to Weber's Law, how many onions would you have to add to notice a difference if you are making twice as much chili with 10 onions?
   a. 1   **c.** 4
   b. 2   **d.** 5

2. Stimuli that fall below the threshold of conscious awareness are called _____ stimuli.
   a. encoded
   b. automatic
   c. preconscious
   d. subliminal

3. You detect the strong smell of cedar when you enter a furniture store. However, after a short while in the store, you no longer can detect the smell. This process is known as
   a. sensory adaptation.
   b. habituation.
   c. perceptual constancy.
   d. accommodation.

4. Which of the following terms refers to the amplitude of a light wave such as how high or low the wave is?
   a. color
   b. brightness
   c. pitch
   d. hue

5. When an ophthalmologist surgically corrects a patient's vision through LASIK or PRK, the doctor is making adjustments to the patient's
   a. cornea.
   b. lens.
   c. retina.
   d. iris.

6. What part of the eye hardens as we age, thus causing many to suffer from presbyopia?
   a. rods
   b. cones
   c. lens
   d. vitreous humor

7. A deer's inability to quickly respond to the headlights of an approaching car is due to what sensory phenomenon?
a. dark adaptation
b. light adaptation
c. afterimage
d. opponent-process theory

8. The hammer, the anvil, and the stirrup are part of the
a. outer ear.
b. middle ear.
c. inner ear.
d. cochlea.

9. John has played his music loudly for years. Now, in his 20s, he finds he has a continuous ringing in both of his ears. What would John probably be diagnosed with?
a. Tinnitus, which is a nerve-based disorder that has no permanent cure.
b. Conduction-based hearing impairment; however, hearing aids may be able to help.
c. Damage to the pinna, which can be corrected with surgery.
d. Regardless of the disorder, John will ultimately require a cochlear implant.

10. Studies show that taste preference can typically begin
a. before a baby is born.
b. in the first 3–6 months after birth.
c. by age 1.
d. during preschool.

11. Jude is suffering from a severe cold. His nose has been stopped up for several days. What effect, if any, might his cold have on his sense of taste?
a. His sense of taste will be increased since he isn't receiving additional sensory input from his smell.
b. His sense of taste will be dulled since taste and smell often work together.
c. His sense of taste will get better but not until 48 hours after he loses his sense of smell.
d. His sense of taste will be no better or worse since the senses of taste and smell are completely separate.

12. If a child suffers from congenital analgesia, why must he or she be careful when playing outside?
a. The child often cannot hear sounds unless he or she is within 3 feet of the source.
b. The child cannot feel pain and can suffer injuries without even knowing it.
c. The child lacks the ability to react to a dangerous situation.
d. The child's sense of smell does not work properly.

13. If Tabitha closes her eyes when she rides in her parent's car, she can still tell that the car is moving. This is due to the movement of tiny crystals in the
a. outer ear.
b. cochlea.
c. otolith organs.
d. middle ear.

14. A child may sometimes play by quickly turning around in a circle. When the child stops, he or she often feels like his or her head is still spinning. What is responsible for this sensation?
a. fluid still rotating in the semicircular canals
b. proprioceptors
c. compression of the otolith organs
d. disruption of the otolith crystals

15. Little Karla is with her mother at the docks waiting for her daddy to return from his naval deployment. While the boat is still a ways out, her mother says, "There is daddy's boat." Karla is confused. She cannot understand how her dad can be on a boat that is so small that she can hold up her thumb and the boat disappears. It's safe to assume that Karla does not yet understand
a. size constancy.
b. shape constancy.
c. brightness constancy.
d. color constancy.

16.
XX XX XX   XXXXX
XX XX XX   XXXXX
XX XX XX   XXXXX

In viewing the items above, seeing three columns of Xs on the left versus three rows of Xs on the right can be explained by the Gestalt principle of _____.
a. closure
b. similarity
c. proximity
d. contiguity

17. From past experience, you know that commercial jets typically fly around 500 miles per hour at a height of 30,000 feet. However, as you watch one fly high overhead, it seems to slowly pass by. What monocular depth cue best explains this?
a. motion parallax
b. linear perspective
c. overlap
d. texture gradient

18. The Müller–Lyer illusion is influenced greatly by one's
a. age.
b. gender.
c. level of intellect.
d. culture.

19. Allison opened her new jigsaw puzzle but soon realized that she had the same puzzle when she was a child. With her past experience to rely upon, Allison will probably use _____ to help her reassemble the puzzle.
a. bottom-up processing
b. top-down processing
c. perceptual expectancy
d. perceptual set

20. Kip enjoys playing with sparklers on the 4th of July. He always loves watching a friend run with a sparkler and the momentary trail of light that seems to be left behind. Which aspect of our visual system best explains this trail of light?
a. lateral inhibition
b. microsaccades of the eyes
c. persistence of vision
d. achromatopsia

Chapter 4
Consciousness

California police departments are cracking down on texting and talking on cell phones while driving, using a video game–like simulator to teach college students just how dangerous trying to do two such demanding mental processes at once can be. AT&T has a safety campaign in which public service announcements recount the disastrous, and often fatal, consequences of texting while driving—both sending texts and receiving them. A majority of states now ban all cell phone use by new drivers and text messaging for all drivers. Why? Because contrary to common belief, we cannot truly multitask, and both driving and talking or texting on a phone are thought processes that make heavy demands on our conscious awareness.

What are some ways in which you multitask throughout the day? How does multitasking impact your awareness or affect the quality of your work, if at all?

Why study consciousness?

In a very real sense, to understand consciousness is to understand what it means to be who we are. Waking, sleeping, dreaming, daydreaming, and other forms of conscious awareness make up the better part of the human experience. Lack of sleep may increase the likelihood of diabetes, interfere with the onset of puberty changes, decrease memory for learning, and increase weight gain. Drug use can affect consciousness as well, and not always to our benefit. Clearly, an understanding of the workings of the conscious mind is important to both our mental and our physical well-being.

Learning Objectives

4.1   Define what it means to be conscious.

4.2   Describe the different levels of consciousness.

4.3   Explain the need for sleep and the biological processes involved in sleep.

4.4   Describe the different stages of sleep and explain the importance of REM sleep.

4.5   Describe and differentiate among the various sleep disorders.

4.6   Summarize the theories of why people dream and describe the gender and cultural differences of dream content.

4.7   Define hypnosis and explain the process by which hypnosis is accomplished.

4.8   Describe two major theories of why hypnosis works.

4.9   Define meditation and explain some of its benefits.

4.10   Define the term psychoactive drug, and distinguish between physical and psychological dependence upon drugs.

4.11   Describe the effects of stimulants, depressants, and hallucinogens on consciousness and summarize the dangers associated with taking them.

4.12   Describe how the workings of our consciousness can explain "supernatural" visitations.

What Is Consciousness?

💬 What exactly is meant by the term *consciousness*? I've heard it a lot, but I'm not sure that I know everything it means.

Consciousness is one of those terms that most people think they understand until someone asks them to define it. Various sorts of scientists, psychologists, neuroscientists, philosophers, and even computer scientists (who have been trying to develop an artificial intelligence for some time now), have tried to define consciousness, and so there are several definitions—one for nearly every field in which consciousness is studied.

DEFINITION OF CONSCIOUSNESS

4.1 Define what it means to be conscious.

Although early psychologist William James spoke of a "stream of consciousness" in which ideas, sensations, and thoughts flow from one into another (James, 1890), philosopher Daniel Dennett asserts that there is no single stream of consciousness but rather multiple "channels," each of which is handling its own tasks (Dennett, 1991). All of these channels operate in parallel, in a kind of chaos of consciousness. People must somehow organize all this conscious experience, and their particular social groups and culture influence that organization.

Do animals experience consciousness in the same way as people? That is a question too complex to answer fully here, but many researchers into animal behavior, language, and cognition have some reason to propose that a kind of consciousness exists in at least some animals, although its organization would naturally not be the same as human consciousness (Block, 2005; Browne, 2004; Hurley & Nudds, 2006; Koch & Mormann, 2010). In their chapter on neurobiology and consciousness, Dr. Christof Koch and Dr. Florian Mormann (Koch & Mormann, 2010, p. 1225) state that "there is little reason to doubt that other mammals share conscious feelings . . . with humans." Chapter Seven in this text includes a discussion of animal language that touches on some of these issues. **Ⓛ Ⓘ Ⓝ Ⓚ** to Learning Objective 7.11.

 💬 So where does that leave us in the search for a working definition of consciousness?

For our purposes, a more useful definition of consciousness might be the following: **Consciousness** is your awareness of everything that is going on around you and inside your own head at any given moment, which you use to organize your behavior (Farthing, 1992), including your thoughts, sensations, and feelings. In a cognitive neuroscience view, consciousness is generated by a set of action potentials in the communication among neurons just sufficient to produce a specific perception, memory, or experience in our awareness (Crick & Koch, 1990, 2003; Koch & Mormann, 2010). In other words, your eyes see a dog, the neurons along the optic pathway to the occipital lobe's visual cortex are activated, and the visual association cortex is activated to identify the external stimulus as a "dog." Bam!—consciousness! **Ⓛ Ⓘ Ⓝ Ⓚ** to Learning Objective 2.12.

ALTERED STATES OF CONSCIOUSNESS

4.2 Describe the different levels of consciousness.

Much of people's time awake is spent in a state called **waking consciousness** in which their thoughts, feelings, and sensations are clear and organized, and they feel alert. But there are many times in daily activities and in life when people experience states of consciousness that differ from this organized waking state. These variations are called "altered states of consciousness."

An **altered state of consciousness** occurs when a shift takes place in the quality or pattern of your mental activity. Thoughts may become fuzzy and disorganized and

The driver of this car has several competing demands on his attention: working his cell phone, listening to the passenger read to him, and driving his car. If he manages to get himself and his passenger safely to their destination—and by multitasking while driving he is certainly endangering both of their lives and others as well—it's possible that he won't even remember the trip; he may be driving in an altered state of consciousness.

you may feel less alert, or your thoughts may take bizarre turns, as they so often do in dreams. Sometimes being in an altered state may mean being in a state of *increased* alertness, as when you are under the influence of a stimulant. You may also divide your conscious awareness, as when you drive to work or school and then wonder how you got there—one level of conscious awareness was driving, while the other was thinking about the day ahead, perhaps. This altered state of divided consciousness can be a dangerous thing, as many people who try to drive and talk on a cell phone at the same time have discovered. Driving and carrying on a phone conversation are both processes that should demand focused attention, and it is simply not possible to do both at once in a safe and efficient manner. Studies have shown that driving while talking on a cell phone, even a hands-free phone, puts a person at the same degree of risk as driving under the influence of alcohol (Alm & Nilsson, 1995; Briem & Hedman, 1995; Strayer & Drews, 2007; Strayer & Johnston, 2001; Strayer et al., 2006). Texting while driving is more than risky—it can be murderous (Eastern Virginia Medical School, 2009; Wang et al., 2012). Ⓛ Ⓘ Ⓝ Ⓚ to Learning Objective PIA.2. Complete the survey *What Altered States Have You Experienced?* to discover more about your own encounters with various states of consciousness.

Survey   WHAT ALTERED STATES HAVE YOU EXPERIENCED?

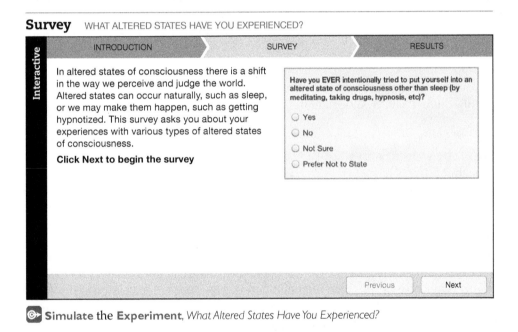

Simulate the Experiment, *What Altered States Have You Experienced?*

There are many forms of altered states of consciousness, such as being under the influence of certain drugs, daydreaming, being hypnotized, or achieving a meditative state. But the most common altered state people experience is the one they spend about a third of their lives in on a nightly basis—sleep.

Concept Map L.O. 4.1, 4.2

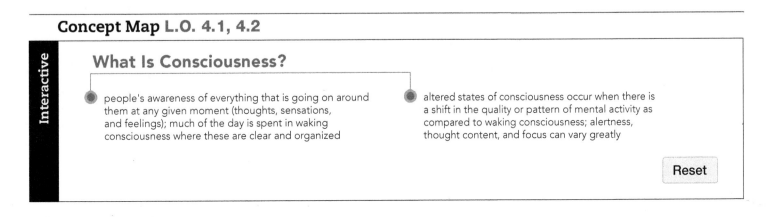

Practice Quiz How much do you remember? ANSWERS ON PAGE AK-1.

Pick the best answer.

1. Which early psychologist referred to a "stream of consciousness," in which ideas, sensations, and thoughts flow from one into another?
   a. Aaron T. Beck
   b. Fritz Perls
   c. Wilhelm Wundt
   d. William James

2. _____ refers to your awareness of everything going on around you and inside you at any given moment in time.
   a. Consciousness
   b. Memory
   c. The unconscious
   d. Personality

3. Dawn woke up about an hour ago. She took a shower, got dressed, combed her hair, and is now sitting at her kitchen table eating a light breakfast, drinking a cup of coffee, and reading her newspaper. She is alert, oriented, and clearly aware of everything going on around her. Dawn is currently experiencing a state of
   a. heightened awareness.
   c. waking consciousness.
   b. altered consciousness.
   d. meditation.

4. A change in the quality or pattern of mental activity, such as increased alertness or divided consciousness, is called a(n)
   a. waking consciousness.
   b. altered state of consciousness.
   c. transient state of consciousness.
   d. hallucination.

Sleep

Have you ever wondered why people have to sleep? They could get so much more work done if they didn't have to sleep, and they would have more time to play and do creative things.

THE BIOLOGY OF SLEEP

4.3 Explain the need for sleep and the biological processes involved in sleep.

Sleep was once referred to as "the gentle tyrant" (Webb, 1992). People can try to stay awake, and sometimes they may go for a while without sleep, but eventually they *must* sleep. One reason for this fact is that sleep is one of the human body's *biological rhythms*, that is, natural cycles of activity that the body must go through. Some biological rhythms are monthly, like the cycle of a woman's menstruation, whereas others are far shorter—the beat of the heart is a biological rhythm. But many biological rhythms take place on a daily basis, like the rise and fall of blood pressure and body temperature or the production of certain body chemicals (Moore-Ede et al., 1982). The most obvious of these is the sleep–wake cycle (Baehr et al., 2000).

THE RHYTHMS OF LIFE: CIRCADIAN RHYTHMS The sleep–wake cycle is a **circadian rhythm**. The term actually comes from two Latin words, *circa* ("about") and *diem* ("day"). So a circadian rhythm is a cycle that takes "about a day" to complete.

For most people, this means that they will experience several hours of sleep at least once during every 24-hour period. The sleep–wake cycle is ultimately controlled by the brain, specifically by an area within the *hypothalamus*, the tiny section of the brain that influences the glandular system. **L I N K** to Learning Objective 2.11. Ever heard of melatonin? A lot of people were buying supplements of *melatonin* (a hormone normally secreted by the pineal gland) several years ago, hoping to sleep better and perhaps even slow the effects of aging (Folkard et al., 1993; Herxheimer & Petrie, 2001; Young, 1996). The release of melatonin is influenced by a structure deep within the hypothalamus in an area called the *suprachiasmatic* (SOO-prah-ki-AS-ma-tik) *nucleus*, or SCN, the internal clock that tells people when to wake up and when to fall asleep (Quintero et al., 2003; Yamaguchi et al., 2003; Zisapel, 2001). Sleep researcher Dr. Jerry Siegel explains the function of the SCN in the video, *Sleep and the SCN.*

Sleep, according to Webb (1992), is the "gentle tyrant." As this picture shows, when the urge to sleep comes upon a person, it can be very difficult to resist—no matter where that person is at the time. Can you think of a time or place when you fell asleep without meaning to do so? Why do you think it happened?

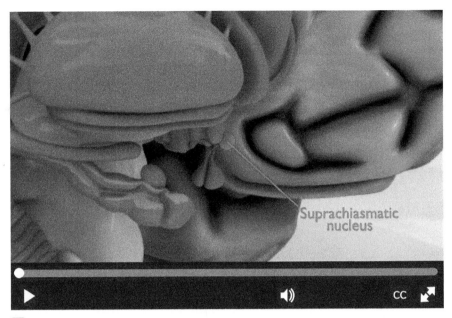

👁 **Watch** the **Video**, *Sleep and the SCN.*

The suprachiasmatic nucleus is sensitive to changes in light. As daylight fades, the SCN tells the pineal gland (located in the base of the brain) to secrete melatonin (Bonda-renko, 2004; Delagrange & Guardiola-Lemaitre, 1997). As melatonin accumulates, a person will feel sleepy. As the light coming into the eyes increases (as it does in the morning), the SCN tells the pineal gland to stop secreting melatonin, allowing the body to awaken.

HOW MUCH SLEEP DO PEOPLE NEED?   How much sleep is enough sleep? The answer varies from person to person depending on age and possibly inherited sleep needs (Feroah et al., 2004), but most young adults need about 7 to 9 hours of sleep each 24-hour period in order to function well. (See **Figure 4.1**.) Some people are short sleepers, needing

Figure 4.1 SLEEP PATTERNS OF INFANTS AND ADULTS

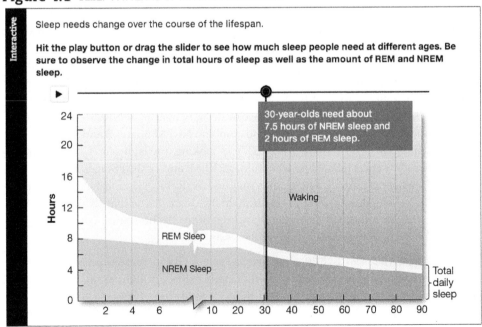

Infants need far more sleep than older children and adults. Both REM sleep and NREM sleep decrease dramatically in the first 10 years of life, with the greatest decrease in REM sleep. Nearly 50 percent of an infant's sleep is REM, compared to only about 20 percent for a normal, healthy adult (Roffwarg et al., 1966).

Contrary to popular belief, sleep deprivation often affects younger people more than it does older people, who need less sleep. Does this young man look well rested and able to successfully complete the task of brushing his teeth?

Dr. Carol Shoptaugh

Missouri State Psychology Department

Effects of Shiftwork

only 4 or 5 hours, whereas others are long sleepers and require more than 9 hours of sleep (McCann & Stewin, 1988). As we age, we seem to sleep less during each night until the average length of sleep approaches only 6 hours.

Sleep deprivation, or loss of sleep, is a serious problem, which many people have without realizing it. Students, for example, may stay up all night to study for an important test the next day. In doing so, they will lose more information than they gain, as a good night's sleep is important for memory and the ability to think well (Gillen-O'Neal et al., 2012). ⓛ ⓘ ⓝ ⓚ to Learning Objective PIA.5. Even a few nights of poor sleep have serious consequences for mental and physical functioning (Van Dongen et al., 2003; Jackson et al., 2013).

THE STAGES OF SLEEP

4.4 **Describe the different stages of sleep and explain the importance of REM sleep.**

 💬 So are there different kinds of sleep? Do you go from being awake to being asleep and dreaming—is it instant?

There are actually two kinds of sleep: **REM (rapid eye movement) sleep** and **non-REM (NREM) sleep**. REM sleep is a relatively active type of sleep when most of a person's dreaming takes place, whereas non-REM sleep is a much deeper, more restful kind of sleep. In REM sleep, the voluntary muscles are inhibited, meaning that the person in REM sleep moves very little, whereas in non-REM sleep the person's body is free to move around (including kicking one's bed partner!). There are also several different stages of sleep that people go through each night in which REM sleep and non-REM sleep occur. A machine called an electroencephalograph allows scientists to record the brain-wave activity as a person passes through the various stages of sleep and to determine what type of sleep the person has entered (Aserinsky & Kleitman, 1953). See **Figure 4.2**, and **Figure 4.3** on page 138 for a look at what happens in each stage of sleep.

A person who is wide awake and mentally active will show a brain-wave pattern on the electroencephalogram (EEG) called **beta waves**. Beta waves are very small and very fast. As the person relaxes and gets drowsy, slightly larger and slower **alpha waves** appear. The alpha waves are eventually replaced by even slower and larger **theta waves**. In the deepest stages of sleep, the largest and slowest waves appear, called **delta waves**.

Much of existing sleep research is based on terminology describing sleep stages that dates back to the 1960s (Carskadon & Dement, 2011; Rechtschaffen & Kales, 1968). This terminology describes four stages (NREM) in addition to REM and wakefulness. The American Academy of Sleep Medicine (AASM) has published updated guidelines for the recording and scoring of sleep activity, which includes changes in some of the terminology. The new guidelines use R in place of REM, N instead of NREM, and W instead of wakefulness. The AASM guidelines also combine NREM Stages 3 and 4 into a single stage, now indicated by N3 (Iber et al., 2007). In looking at past research, you might encounter the sleep stages labeled as wakefulness, REM, and NREM Stages 1–4 (or simply Stages 1–4), whereas more recent studies may use W, R, N1, N2, and N3. As the area of sleep research is still in a period of transition, in the descriptions that follow, we will use the new AASM terminology as primary and the older Rechtschaffen and Kales (1968) sleep manual terminology noted in parentheses as "R&K."

N1 (R&K STAGE 1): LIGHT SLEEP As theta wave activity increases and alpha wave activity fades away, people are said to be entering N1 sleep, or light sleep. Several rather interesting things can happen in this non-REM stage of sleep. If people are awakened at this point, they will probably not believe that they were actually asleep. They may also experience vivid visual events called *hypnogogic images* or *hallucinations* (Mavromatis, 1987; Mavromatis & Richardson, 1984). (The Greek word *hypnos* means "sleep.") Some researchers believe that peoples' experiences of ghostly visits, alien abductions, and near-death experiences may be most easily explained by these hallucinations (Moody

Figure 4.2 BRAIN ACTIVITY DURING SLEEP

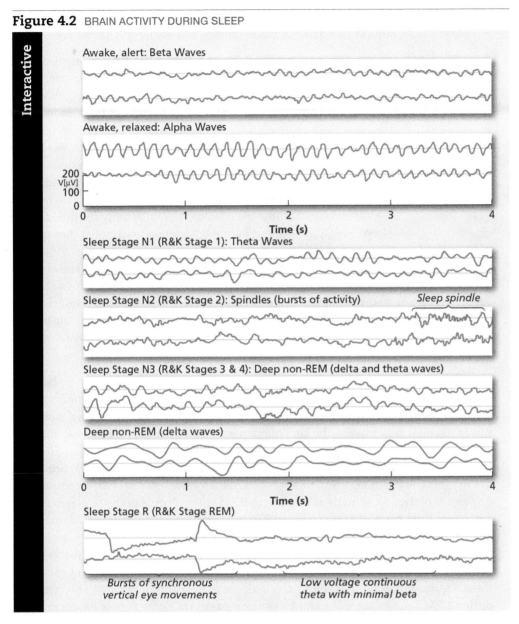

The EEG reflects brain activity during both waking and sleep. This activity varies according to level of alertness while awake (top two segments) and the stage of sleep. Stage N3 of sleep is characterized by the presence of delta activity, which is much slower and accounts for the larger, slower waves on these graphs. REM has activity that resembles alert wakefulness but has relatively no muscle activity except rapid eye movement. EEG data and images in this figure are courtesy of Dr. Leslie Sherlin.

& Perry, 1993). For more about hypnogogic experiences and the role they may play in "hauntings," see the Applying Psychology section at the end of this chapter.

A much more common occurrence is called the *hypnic jerk* (Mahowald & Schenck, 1996; Oswald, 1959). Have you ever been drifting off to sleep when your knees, legs, or sometimes your whole body gives a big "jerk"? Although experts have no solid proof of why this occurs, many believe that it has something to do with the possibility that our ancestors slept in trees: The relaxation of the muscles as one drifts into sleep causes a "falling" sensation, at which point the body jerks awake to prevent the "fall" from the hypothetical tree (Coolidge, 2006; Sagan, 1977).

N2 (R&K STAGE 2): SLEEP SPINDLES As people drift further into sleep, the body temperature continues to drop. Heart rate slows, breathing becomes more shallow and irregular, and the EEG will show the first signs of *sleep spindles*, brief bursts of activity lasting only a

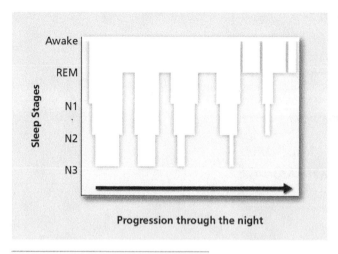

Figure 4.3 A Typical Night's Sleep

The graph shows the typical progression through the night of Stages N1–N2 and REM sleep. The REM periods occur about every 90 minutes throughout the night (based on Dement, 1974).

second or two. Theta waves still predominate in this stage, but if people are awakened during this stage, they will be aware of having been asleep.

N3 (R&K STAGES 3 AND 4): DELTA WAVES ROLL IN In the third stage of sleep, the slowest and largest waves make their appearance. These waves are called delta waves. These waves increase during this stage from about 20 percent to more than 50 percent of total brain activity. Now the person is in the deepest stage of sleep, often referred to as slow-wave sleep (SWS) or simply deep sleep (Carskadon & Dement, 2011). It is during this stage that growth hormones (often abbreviated as GH) are released from the pituitary gland and reach their peak. The body is at its lowest level of functioning. Eventually, the delta waves become the dominant brain activity for this stage of sleep. See Figure 4.2 and Figure 4.3 to show movement through the sleep stages throughout one night.

Children spend more time in deep sleep so that their bodies will grow and are even harder to wake up during this stage than are adults. The fact that children do sleep so deeply may explain why certain sleep disorders are more common in childhood. Indeed, many sleep disorders are more common in boys than in girls because boys sleep more deeply than do girls due to high levels of the male hormone testosterone (Miyatake et al., 1980; Thiedke, 2001).

R (R&K REM) After spending some time in N3, the sleeping person will go back up through N2 and then into a stage in which body temperature increases to near-waking levels, the eyes move rapidly under the eyelids, the heart beats much faster, and brain waves resemble beta waves—the kind of brain activity that usually signals wakefulness. The person is still asleep but in the stage known as rapid eye movement sleep (REM).

When a person in REM sleep is awakened, he or she almost always reports being in a dream state (Shafton, 1995). REM sleep is, therefore, associated with dreaming, and 90 percent of dreams actually take place in REM sleep. People do have dreams in the other non-REM (or NREM) stages, but REM dreams tend to be more vivid, more detailed, longer, and more bizarre than the dreams of NREM sleep. NREM dreams tend to be more like thoughts about daily occurrences and far shorter than REM dreams (Foulkes & Schmidt, 1983; Takeuchi et al., 2003). Fortunately, the body is unable to act upon these dreams under normal conditions because the voluntary muscles are paralyzed during REM sleep, a condition known as **sleep paralysis**. Some people have a rare disorder in which the brain mechanisms that normally inhibit the voluntary muscles fail, allowing the person to thrash around and even get up and act out nightmares. This disorder is called **REM behavior disorder**, which is a fairly serious condition (Shafton, 1995). Usually seen in men over age 60, it can happen in younger men and in women.

WHAT IS THE PURPOSE OF REM SLEEP? Why two kinds of sleep? REM sleep seems to serve a different purpose than does NREM, or deep sleep. After a very physically demanding day, people tend to spend more time in NREM deep sleep than is usual as the body recovers. But an emotionally stressful day leads to increased time in REM sleep (Horne & Staff, 1983). Perhaps the dreams people have in REM sleep are a way of dealing with the stresses and tensions of the day, whereas physical activity would demand more time for recovery of the body in NREM sleep. Also, if deprived of REM sleep (as would occur with the use of sleeping pills or other depressant drugs), a person will experience greatly increased amounts of REM sleep the next night, a phenomenon called **REM rebound** (Vogel, 1975, 1993).

An early study of REM sleep deprivation (Dement, 1960) seemed to suggest that people deprived of REM sleep would become paranoid, seemingly mentally ill from lack of this one stage of sleep. This is called the *REM myth* because later studies failed to reliably produce the same results (Dement et al., 1969).

REM sleep in early infancy differs from adult REM sleep in a couple of ways: Babies spend nearly 50 percent of their sleep in REM as compared to adults' 20 percent, the brain-wave patterns on EEG recordings are not exactly the same in infant REM when compared to adult REM recordings, and infants can and do move around quite a bit during REM sleep (Carskadon & Dement, 2005; Davis et al., 2004; Sheldon, 2002; Tucker et al., 2006). These differences can be explained: When infants are engaged in REM sleep, they are not dreaming but rather forming new connections between neurons (Carskadon & Dement, 2005; Davis et al., 2004; Sheldon, 2002).

The infant brain is highly plastic, and much of brain growth and development takes place during REM sleep. (L I N K) to Learning Objective 2.4. As the infant's brain nears its adult size by age 5 or 6, the proportion of REM sleep has also decreased to a more adultlike ratio of REM to non-REM. For infants, to sleep is to grow synapses.

While this infant is sleeping, her REM sleep (occurring about half of the time she is asleep) allows her brain to make new neural connections.

SLEEP DISORDERS

4.5 **Describe and differentiate among the various sleep disorders.**

What happens when sleep goes wrong? Nightmares, sleepwalking, and being unable to sleep well are all examples of sleep disorders.

NIGHTMARES   **Nightmares** are bad dreams that take place during REM sleep, and some nightmares can be utterly terrifying. Children tend to have more nightmares than adults do because they spend more of their sleep in the REM state, as discussed earlier. As they age, they have fewer nightmares because they have less opportunity to have them. But some people still suffer from nightmares as adults.

NIGHT TERRORS   **Night terrors** are a rare disorder, although one that is more likely in children and also likely to disappear as the child grows older (Garland & Smith, 1991). A night terror is essentially a state of panic experienced while in deep non-REM sleep (distinguishing them from nightmares occurring in REM sleep). People may sit up, scream, run around the room, or flail at some unseen attacker. It is not uncommon for people to feel unable to breathe as well. Considering that people suffering a night terror episode are in a deep stage of sleep and breathing shallowly, one can understand why breathing would seem difficult when they are suddenly active. Most people do not remember what happened during a night terror episode, although a few people can remember vividly the images and terror they experienced.

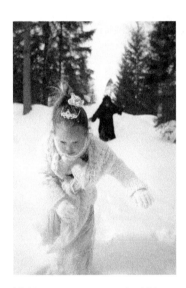

Nightmares are common in children and often involve being chased by a monster or similar frightening creature or being lost in a strange place like this young boy.

SLEEPWALKING   True **sleepwalking, or somnambulism**, occurs in about 20 percent of the population and is at least partially due to heredity (Abe et al., 1984; Kales et al., 1980). It typically occurs during N3 deep sleep, is much more common in childhood, and also occurs more frequently in boys than in girls. Although the old movies portray sleepwalkers as zombie-like and with arms outstretched, in reality a sleepwalker may do nothing more than sit up in bed. But other sleepwalking episodes may involve walking around the house, looking in the refrigerator or even eating, and getting into the car. Most sleepwalkers do not recall their nightly activities the next morning. This lack of memory is typical of most sleepwalking episodes.

Many people with this disorder grow out of their sleepwalking by the time they become adolescents. Many parents have found that preventing sleep loss makes sleepwalking a rare occurrence. This is most likely due to the deeper N3 sleep becoming even deeper during sleep loss, which would make fully waking even more difficult (Pilon et al., 2008; Zadra et al., 2008, 2013). The only real precaution that the families of people who sleepwalk should take is to clear their floors of obstacles and to put not-easy-to-reach locks on the doors. And although it is not dangerous to wake sleepwalkers, they may seem confused or disoriented and strike out at others before awakening.

"Wait! Don't! It can be dangerous to wake them."
©The New Yorker Collection J. Dator from cartoonbank.com.
All Rights Reserved.

INSOMNIA Most people think that **insomnia** is the inability to sleep. Although that is the literal meaning of the term, in reality insomnia is the inability to get to sleep, stay asleep, or get a good quality of sleep (Kryger et al., 1999).

People can take several steps to help them sleep (Kupfer & Reynolds, 1997; National Sleep Foundation, 2009):

1. Go to bed only when you are sleepy. Rather than trying too hard to go to sleep, after 20 minutes of lying there, get up and do something like reading or other light activity (avoid watching TV or being in front of a computer screen) until you feel sleepy, and then go back to bed.

2. Don't do anything in your bed but sleep. Your bed should be a cue for sleeping, not for studying or watching television. Using the bed as a cue for sleeping is a kind of learning called *classical conditioning*, or the pairing of cues and automatic responses. **L I N K** to Learning Objective 5.2.

3. Don't try too hard to get to sleep, and especially do not look at the clock and calculate how much sleep you aren't getting. That just increases the tension and makes it harder to sleep.

4. Keep to a regular schedule. Go to bed at the same time and get up at the same time, even on days that you don't have to go to work or class.

In addition to these four steps, the video *Insomnia* describes some of the main causes and treatment options for this disorder and cautions against the use of sleeping pills.

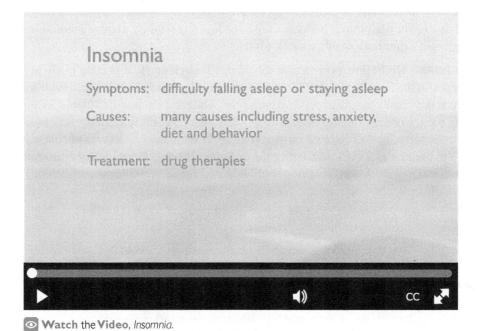

👁 **Watch** the **Video**, *Insomnia*.

If none of these steps seems to be working, there are sleep clinics and sleep experts who can help people with insomnia. The American Academy of Sleep Medicine has an excellent Web site at **www.aasmnet.org** that provides links to locate sleep clinics in many areas.

SLEEP APNEA Snoring is fairly common, occurring when the breathing passages (nose and throat) get blocked. Most people snore only when they have a cold or some other occasional problem, but some people snore every night and quite loudly. It is this type of snoring that is often associated with a condition called **sleep apnea**, in which the person stops breathing for nearly 10 seconds or more. When breathing stops, there will be a sudden silence, followed shortly by a gasping sound as the person struggles to get air into the lungs. Many people do not wake up while this is happening, but they do not get a good, restful night's sleep because of the apnea.

Apnea is a serious problem. According to the National Institutes of Health (2011), from 5 to 25 percent of adults in the United States suffer from apnea (it is difficult to

Table 4.1 Sleep Disorders	
Name of Disorder	**Primary Symptoms**
Somnambulism	Sitting, walking, or performing complex behavior while asleep
Night terrors	Extreme fear, agitation, screaming while asleep
Restless leg syndrome	Uncomfortable sensations in legs causing movement and loss of sleep
Nocturnal leg cramps	Painful cramps in calf or foot muscles
Hypersomnia	Excessive daytime sleepiness
Circadian rhythm disorders	Disturbances of the sleep–wake cycle such as jet lag and shift work
Enuresis	Urinating while asleep in bed

be precise, as many people are unaware that they have apnea). Not only does it disturb nightly sleep, making the person excessively sleepy in the daytime, but also it can cause heart problems (Flemons, 2002). If a person suspects the presence of apnea, a visit to a physician is the first step in identifying the disorder and deciding on a treatment. With mild apnea, treatment may be a device worn on the nose at night to open the nostrils and prevent blockage. Obesity is a primary cause of apnea, especially in men, so another solution might be to lose excess weight. There are also sprays that are supposed to shrink the tissues lining the throat (much as a nasal decongestant spray shrinks the tissues of the nasal passages). Some people sleep with a device that delivers a continuous stream of air under mild pressure, called a *continuous positive airway pressure (CPAP) device*. Others undergo a simple surgery in which the *uvula* (the little flap that hangs down at the back of the throat) and some of the soft tissues surrounding it are removed.

Some very young infants also experience a kind of apnea due to immaturity of the brain stem. These infants are typically placed on monitors that sound an alarm when breathing stops, allowing caregivers to help the infant begin breathing again. Although sleep apnea in infants is often associated with sudden infant death syndrome, or SIDS, it is not necessarily caused by it: Many infants who die of SIDS were never diagnosed with sleep apnea (Blackmon et al., 2003).

NARCOLEPSY A disorder affecting one in every 2,000 persons, **narcolepsy** is a kind of "sleep seizure." In narcolepsy, the person may slip suddenly into REM sleep during the day (especially when the person experiences strong emotions). Another symptom is excessive daytime sleepiness that results in the person falling asleep throughout the day at inappropriate times and in inappropriate places (Overeem et al., 2001). These sleep attacks may occur many times and without warning, making the operation of a car or other machinery very dangerous for the *narcoleptic* (person who suffers from narcolepsy). The sudden REM attacks are especially dangerous because of the symptom of *cataplexy*, or a sudden loss of muscle tone. This sleep paralysis may cause injuries if the person is standing when the attack occurs. The same hypnogogic images that may accompany N1 (R&K Stage 1) sleep may also occur in the narcoleptic person. **Table 4.1** has a more detailed list of known sleep disorders.

"On your application it says you have narcolepsy. What is that?"

DREAMS

4.6 **Summarize the theories of why people dream and describe the gender and cultural differences of dream content.**

Dreams have long been a source of curiosity. People of ancient times tried to find meaning in dreams. Some viewed dreams as prophecy, some as messages from the spirits. But the real inquiry into the process of dreaming began with the publication of Freud's *The Interpretation of Dreams* (1900).

FREUD'S INTERPRETATION: DREAMS AS WISH FULFILLMENT Sigmund Freud (1856–1939) believed that the problems of his patients stemmed from conflicts and events that had been buried in their unconscious minds since childhood. One of the ways Freud devised to get at these early memories was to examine the dreams of his patients, believing that conflicts, events, and desires of the past would be represented in symbolic* form in the dreams. Freud believed dreams to be a kind of wish fulfillment for his patients. ⓛ ⓘ ⓝ ⓚ to Learning Objective 11.2.

While many current professionals are no longer as fond of Freud's dream analysis as they once were, there are still some people who insist that dreams have symbolic meaning. For example, dreaming about being naked in a public place is very common, and most dream analyzers interpret that to mean feeling open and exposed, an expression of childhood innocence, or even a desire for sex. Exactly how the dream is interpreted depends on the other features of the dream and what is happening in the person's waking life.

The development of techniques for looking at the structure and activity of the brain (ⓛ ⓘ ⓝ ⓚ to Learning Objectives 2.8 and 2.9) has led to an explanation of why people dream that is more scientific and concrete than that of Freud.

THE ACTIVATION-SYNTHESIS HYPOTHESIS Using brain-imaging techniques such as a PET scan (ⓛ ⓘ ⓝ ⓚ to Learning Objective 2.9), researchers have found evidence that dreams are products of activity in the pons (Hobson, 1988; Hobson & McCarley, 1977; Hobson et al., 2000). This lower area inhibits the neurotransmitters that would allow movement of the voluntary muscles while sending random signals to the areas of the cortex that interpret vision, hearing, and so on (see **Figure 4.4**).

When signals from the pons bombard* the cortex during waking consciousness, the association areas of the cortex interpret those signals as seeing, hearing, and so on.

Figure 4.4 THE BRAIN AND ACTIVATION-SYNTHESIS THEORY

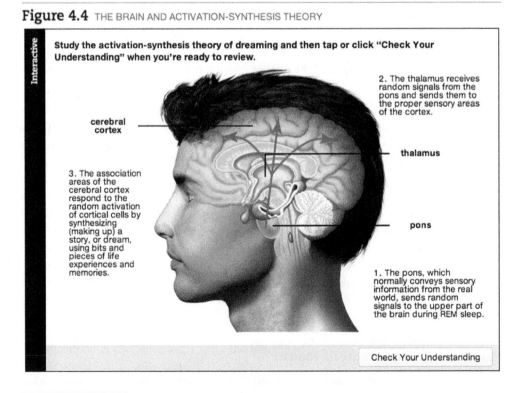

Study the activation-synthesis theory of dreaming and then tap or click "Check Your Understanding" when you're ready to review.

2. The thalamus receives random signals from the pons and sends them to the proper sensory areas of the cortex.

cerebral cortex

thalamus

3. The association areas of the cerebral cortex respond to the random activation of cortical cells by synthesizing (making up) a story, or dream, using bits and pieces of life experiences and memories.

pons

1. The pons, which normally conveys sensory information from the real world, sends random signals to the upper part of the brain during REM sleep.

Check Your Understanding

*symbolic: having the quality of representing something other than itself.
*bombard: to attack or press.

Because those signals come from the real world, this process results in an experience of reality. But when people are asleep, the signals from the brain stem are random and not necessarily attached to actual external stimuli, yet the brain must somehow interpret these random signals. It *synthesizes* (puts together) an explanation of the cortex's activation from memories and other stored information.

In this theory, called the **activation-synthesis hypothesis**, a dream is merely another kind of thinking that occurs when people sleep, as the higher centers of the cortex create a "story" to explain the cortical activation coming from the brain stem during REM. It is less realistic because it comes not from the outside world of reality but from within people's memories and experiences of the past. The frontal lobes, which people normally use in daytime thinking, are more or less shut down during dreaming, which may also account for the unrealistic and often bizarre nature of dreams (Macquet & Franck, 1996).

> 💬 My dreams can be really weird, but sometimes they seem pretty ordinary or even seem to mean something. Can dreams be more meaningful?

There are dream experts who suggest that dreams may have more meaning than Hobson and McCarley originally theorized. A survey questioning subjects about their dream content, for example, concluded that much of the content of dreams is meaningful, consistent over time, and fits in with past or present emotional concerns rather than being bizarre, meaningless, and random (Domhoff, 1996, 2005).

Hobson and colleagues have reworked the activation-synthesis hypothesis to reflect concerns about dream meaning, calling it the **activation-information-mode model**, or **AIM** (Hobson et al., 2000). In this newer version, information that is accessed during waking hours can have an influence on the synthesis of dreams. In other words, when the brain is "making up" a dream to explain its own activation, it uses meaningful bits and pieces of the person's experiences from the previous day or the last few days rather than just random items from memory.

WRITING PROMPT

Have you ever had a dream that seemed to predict the future? Can you think of logical explanations for such a dream?

▶ The response entered here will be saved to your notes and may be collected by your instructor if he/she requires it.

Submit

WHAT DO PEOPLE DREAM ABOUT?   Most dreams reflect the events that occur in everyday life (Hall, 1966). People run, jump, talk, and do all of the actions that they do in normal daily life. There are gender differences in the content of dreams, although whether those differences are caused by hormonal or genetic influences, sociocultural influences, or a combination of influences remains to be seen. In his book *Finding Meaning in Dreams*, Dr. William Domhoff (1996) concluded that across many cultures, men more often dream of other males whereas women tend to dream about males and females equally. Men across various cultures also tend to have more physical aggression in their dreams than do women, and women are more often the victims of such aggression in their own dreams. Domhoff also concluded that where there are differences in the content of dreams across cultures, the differences make sense in light of the culture's "personality." For example, American culture is considered fairly aggressive when compared to the culture of the

Netherlands, and the aggressive content of the dreams in both cultures reflects this difference: There were lower levels of aggression in the dreams of those from the Netherlands when compared to the Americans' dream content.

Girls and women tend to dream about people they know, personal appearance concerns, and issues related to family and home. Boys and men tend to have more male characters in their dreams, which are also typically in outdoor or unfamiliar settings and may involve weapons, tools, cars, and roads. Men also report more sexual dreams, usually with unknown and attractive partners (Domhoff, 1996; Domhoff & Schneider, 2008; Foulkes, 1982; Van de Castle, 1994). Take the survey *Are Dreams Meaningful?* to discover more about your own experiences and attitudes toward dreams.

Survey ARE DREAMS MEANINGFUL?

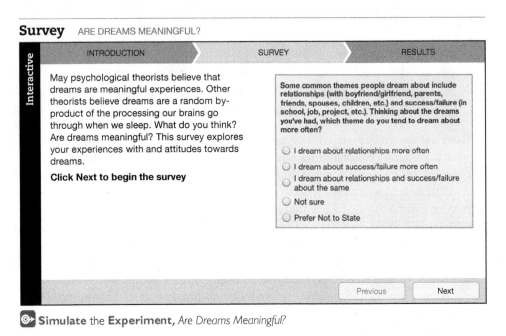

May psychological theorists believe that dreams are meaningful experiences. Other theorists believe dreams are a random by-product of the processing our brains go through when we sleep. What do you think? Are dreams meaningful? This survey explores your experiences with and attitudes towards dreams.

Click Next to begin the survey

Some common themes people dream about include relationships (with boyfriend/girlfriend, parents, friends, spouses, children, etc.) and success/failure (in school, job, project, etc.). Thinking about the dreams you've had, which theme do you tend to dream about more often?

○ I dream about relationships more often
○ I dream about success/failure more often
○ I dream about relationships and success/failure about the same
○ Not sure
○ Prefer Not to State

Previous | Next

Simulate the **Experiment,** *Are Dreams Meaningful?*

Concept Map L.O. 4.3, 4.4, 4.5, 4.6

consist of both REM (rapid eye movement) and non-REM stages; REM is relatively active whereas non-REM is much deeper and restful; stages defined by level of brain activity as measured by the EEG (beta, alpha, theta, delta waves); sleep cycle is made up of various stages repeated 4–5 times a night

N1 (R&K Stage 1): while awake, primarily beta activity, more alpha as one relaxes, onset of sleep in N1 is associated with alpha being replaced by theta

N2 (R&K Stage 2): EEG sleep spindles appear; theta activity is predominant; body temperature continues to drop, heart rate and breathing slow

N3 (R&K Stages 3 and 4): deepest stage of sleep; delta activity makes up 20% to more than 50% of EEG activity; body is at lowest level of functioning and people are hard to awaken; sleep disorders such as sleepwalking and night terrors occur in this stage

R (R&K REM): dreaming occurs, including nightmares; eyes move rapidly under the eyelids and EEG indicates presence of beta, but body is typically still, due to sleep paralysis; REM behavior disorder occurs when body is not still or acts out dreams, usually seen in men over age 60

SCN is sensitive to light—influences pineal gland's secretion of melatonin (↑ melatonin = ↑ sleepiness)

hypothalamus contains the suprachiasmatic nucleus (SCN)

light through eyes relayed to SCN; SCN signals pineal gland to stop producing melatonin (↓ melatonin = ↑ alertness / ↓ sleepiness)

SCN also influences body temperature (↓ temperature = ↑ sleepiness)

Sleep

(sleep is one of the body's daily [circadian] biological rhythms; sleep–wake cycle controlled by the brain including the hypothalamus and the neurotransmitter serotonin)

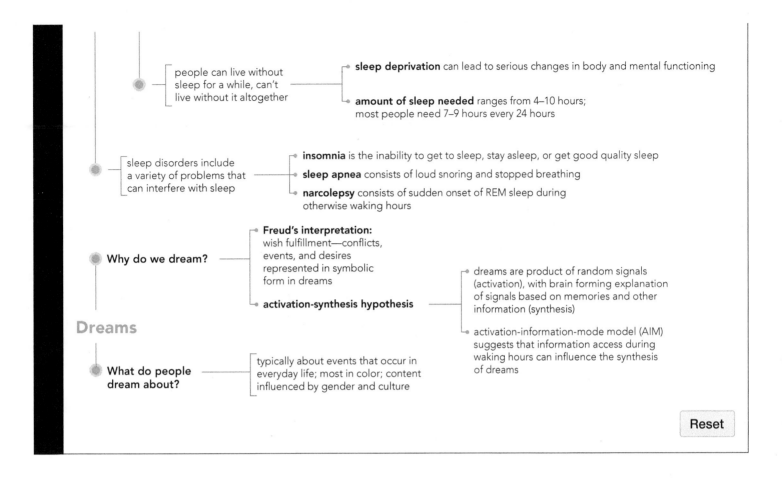

people can live without sleep for a while, can't live without it altogether

sleep deprivation can lead to serious changes in body and mental functioning

amount of sleep needed ranges from 4–10 hours; most people need 7–9 hours every 24 hours

sleep disorders include a variety of problems that can interfere with sleep

insomnia is the inability to get to sleep, stay asleep, or get good quality sleep

sleep apnea consists of loud snoring and stopped breathing

narcolepsy consists of sudden onset of REM sleep during otherwise waking hours

Why do we dream?

Freud's interpretation: wish fulfillment—conflicts, events, and desires represented in symbolic form in dreams

activation-synthesis hypothesis

dreams are product of random signals (activation), with brain forming explanation of signals based on memories and other information (synthesis)

activation-information-mode model (AIM) suggests that information access during waking hours can influence the synthesis of dreams

Dreams

What do people dream about?

typically about events that occur in everyday life; most in color; content influenced by gender and culture

Reset

Practice Quiz   How much do you remember? ANSWERS ON PAGE AK-1.

Pick the best answer.

1. The sleep–wake cycle typically follows a 24-hour cycle and is regulated by the _____.
- **a.** cerebellum
- **b.** frontal lobe
- **c.** pituitary gland
- **d.** suprachiasmatic nucleus

2. The pineal gland receives instructions from the _____ to release _____.
- **a.** thalamus; dopamine
- **b.** occipital lobe; serotonin
- **c.** suprachiasmatic nucleus; melatonin
- **d.** spinal cord; acetylcholine

3. In which stage(s) of sleep do people typically experience hypnogogic images?
- **a.** N1 (R&K Stage 1)
- **b.** N2 (R&K Stage 2)
- **c.** N3 (R&K Stages 3 and 4)
- **d.** REM

4. A person who relies heavily on sleeping pills or alcohol to sleep might experience _____ the following night.
- **a.** sleep apnea
- **b.** night terrors
- **c.** REM rebound
- **d.** REM behavior disorder

5. The last thing Marguerite remembers is going to bed last night. She has recently awoken and found herself sitting in the back seat of her car, which is parked in the garage. She is worried because she doesn't exactly know how she got there. Based on this information, it would appear that Marguerite suffers from:
- **a.** sleep apnea
- **b.** night terrors
- **c.** narcolepsy
- **d.** somnambulism

6. If you find yourself lying in bed unable to sleep for more than 20 minutes, what should you do?
- **a.** Start watching television or read so as to help you fall off to sleep.
- **b.** Brew some tea to help relax you.
- **c.** Get out of bed and find some light activity to do (e.g., reading a book).
- **d.** Lie in bed until you fall asleep, even if it takes several hours.

7. Michael finds that most of his dreams are little more than random images that seemingly have been put into a strange storyline. Which theory of dreams best explains this?
- **a.** Freudian dream theory
- **b.** dreams for survival theory
- **c.** activation-synthesis hypothesis
- **d.** Hall's dreams as reflections of everyday life

Other Altered States: Hypnosis and Meditation

Like sleep, *hypnosis* and *meditation* are other examples of altered states of consciousness. Although a lot of misunderstandings exist about hypnosis, it can be a useful tool when properly managed.

HOW HYPNOSIS WORKS

4.7 **Define hypnosis and explain the process by which hypnosis is accomplished.**

Hypnosis is a state of consciousness in which a person is especially susceptible to suggestion. There are four key steps in inducing hypnosis (Druckman & Bjork, 1994):

1. The hypnotist tells the person to focus on what is being said.
2. The person is told to relax and feel tired.
3. The hypnotist tells the person to "let go" and accept suggestions easily.
4. The person is told to use vivid imagination.

The real key to hypnosis seems to be a heightened state of suggestibility.* People can be hypnotized when active and alert, but only if they are willing to be hypnotized. Only 80 percent of all people can be hypnotized, and only 40 percent are good hypnotic subjects. The ability to be hypnotized may lie in the way the brain functions. Using brain-scanning techniques, researchers found that two areas in the brains of highly hypnotizable people, areas associated with decision-making and attention, seem to be more active and connected when compared to people who cannot be hypnotized (Hoeft et al., 2012).

💬 Is it true that people can be hypnotized into doing things that they would never do under normal conditions?

Although the popular view is that the hypnotized person is acting involuntarily, the fact is that the hypnotist may only be a guide into a more relaxed state, while the subject actually hypnotizes himself or herself (Kirsch & Lynn, 1995). People cannot be hypnotized against their will. The tendency to act as though their behavior is automatic and out of their control is called the *basic suggestion effect* (Kihlstrom, 1985); it gives people an excuse to do things they might not otherwise do because the burden of responsibility for their actions falls on the hypnotist.

For a more detailed discussion of the problems in using hypnosis for memory retrieval, watch the video, *Hypnosis and Therapy.* **LINK** to Learning Objective 6.9.

In general, hypnosis is a handy way to help people relax and to control pain. These subjective experiences are very much under people's mental influence. Actual physical behavior is harder to change, and that is why hypnosis is not as effective at changing eating habits or helping people to stop smoking (Druckman & Bjork, 1994). Hypnosis is sometimes used in psychological therapy to help people cope with anxiety or deal with cravings for food or drugs. For a concise look at what hypnosis can and cannot do, see **Table 4.2**.

THEORIES OF HYPNOSIS

4.8 **Describe two major theories of why hypnosis works.**

There are two views of why hypnosis works. One emphasizes the role of **dissociation**, or a splitting of conscious awareness, whereas the other involves a kind of social role-playing.

---

*suggestibility: being readily influenced.

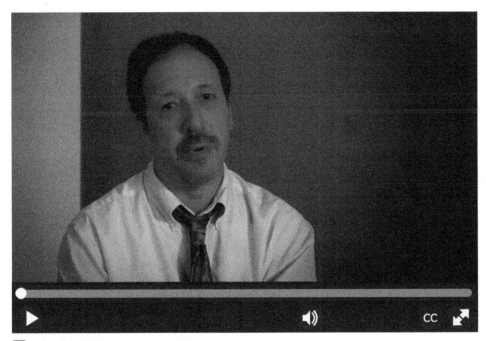

👁 **Watch** the **Video**, *Hypnosis and Therapy.*

HYPNOSIS AS DISSOCIATION: THE HIDDEN OBSERVER   Ernest Hilgard (1991; Hilgard & Hilgard, 1994) believed that hypnosis worked only on the immediate conscious mind of a person, while a part of that person's mind (a "hidden observer") remained aware of all that was going on. It's the same kind of dissociation that takes place when people drive somewhere familiar and then wonder how they got there. Hilgard believes that there is a hidden part of the mind that is very much aware of the hypnotic subject's activities and sensations, even though the "hypnotized" part of the mind is blissfully unaware of these same things.

In one study (Miller & Bowers, 1993), subjects were hypnotized and told to put their arms in ice water, although they were instructed to feel no pain. There had to be pain—most people can't even get an ice cube out of the freezer without *some* pain—but subjects reported no pain at all. The subjects who were successful at denying the pain also reported that they imagined being at the beach or in some other place that allowed them to dissociate* from the pain.

Table 4.2   Facts About Hypnosis

Hypnosis Can:	Hypnosis Cannot:
Create amnesia for whatever happens during the hypnotic session, at least for a brief time (Bowers & Woody, 1996).	Give people superhuman strength. (People may use their full strength under hypnosis, but it is no more than they had before hypnosis.)
Relieve pain by allowing a person to remove conscious attention from the pain (Holroyd, 1996).	Reliably enhance memory. (There's an increased risk of false-memory retrieval because of the suggestible state hypnosis creates.)
Alter sensory perceptions. (Smell, hearing, vision, time sense, and the ability to see visual illusions can all be affected by hypnosis.)	Regress people back to childhood. (Although people may act like children, they do and say things children would not.)
Help people relax in situations that normally would cause them stress, such as flying on an airplane (Muhlberger et al., 2001).	Regress people to some "past life." There is no scientific evidence for past-life regression (Lilienfeld et al., 2004).

---

*dissociate: break a connection with something.

HYPNOSIS AS SOCIAL ROLE-PLAYING: THE SOCIAL-COGNITIVE EXPLANATION   The other theory of why hypnosis works began with an experiment in which participants who were *not* hypnotized were instructed to behave as if they were (Sarbin & Coe, 1972). These participants had no trouble copying many actions previously thought to require a hypnotic state, such as being rigidly suspended between two chairs. The researchers also found that participants who were not familiar with hypnosis, and had no idea what the "role" of a hypnotic subject was supposed to be, could not be hypnotized.

Stage hypnotists often make use of people's willingness to believe that something ordinary is extraordinary. This woman was hypnotized and suspended between two chairs after the person supporting her middle stepped away. The hypnotist led the audience to believe that she could not do this unless hypnotized, but in reality anyone can do this while fully conscious.

Add to those findings the later findings that expectancies of the hypnotized person play a big part in how the person responds and what the person does under hypnosis (Kirsch, 2000). The **social-cognitive theory of hypnosis** assumes that people who are hypnotized are not in an altered state but are merely playing the role expected of them in the situation. They might believe that they are hypnotized, but in fact it is all a very good performance, so good that even the "participants" are unaware that they are role-playing. Social roles are very powerful influences on behavior, as anyone who has ever worn a uniform can understand—the uniform stands for a particular role that becomes very easy to play (Zimbardo, 1970; Zimbardo et al., 2000). **LINK** to Learning Objective 10.13.

Hypnosis is one way to relax, but there are simpler ways to reduce tension and stress. See the following *Psychology in the News* section for information about another relaxation technique: meditation.

Psychology in the News
The Benefits of Meditation

4.9   Define meditation and explain some of its benefits.

Meditation is a series of mental exercises meant to refocus attention and achieve a trancelike state of consciousness. **LINK** to Learning Objective 4.1. Meditation can produce a state of relaxation that can aid in coping with the physiological reactions to a stressful situation. When properly meditating, brain waves change to include more theta and alpha waves (indicating deep relaxation) but little to no delta waves, which would indicate deep sleep (Lagopoulos et al., 2009). Meditation also lowers blood pressure and increases the amounts of melatonin secreted at night (the hormone that helps induce sleep) (Benson, 1975; Benson et al., 1974a, 1974b).

👁 **Watch** the **Video**, *Meditation.*

Some research even suggests that practicing meditation may lead to permanent changes in the brain, as described in the video, *Meditation*.

Researchers recently examined 47 clinical trials of the effects of meditation on psychological stress and physical health (Goyal et al., 2014). They found that meditation did improve levels of anxiety, depression, and pain to a moderate degree and also improved the subjective experience of stress and quality of life related to mental health, although to a lesser degree. Other research has shown that meditation is a good way to relax and lower blood pressure in adolescents and adults, men and women, and both Whites and African Americans (Barnes et al., 1997; Rainforth et al., 2007; Schneider et al., 1995; Wenneberg et al., 1997).

Some studies suggest that meditation can reduce the levels of chronic pain (Brown & Jones, 2010; Kabat-Zinn et al., 1986); reduce the symptoms of anxiety, depression, and hostility (Kabat-Zinn et al., 1985); reduce the risk of heart disease (Schneider et al., 2010); and reduce stress levels in cancer patients (Speca et al., 2000). Reducing stress levels in cancer patients through meditation will increase the likelihood of recovery and reduce the incidence of recurrence.

Meditation is not a miracle cure, nor is it superior to other methods of relaxation such as reading a good book or taking a warm bath. Even simply resting for the same amount of time as one might meditate can be just as relaxing. The advantage of meditation is that people can do it almost anywhere, even in the classroom just before a big test. (It would be a little difficult to take a warm bath then.)

Questions for Further Discussion

1. What might be some other advantages of meditation over other ways of relaxing?

2. Is it difficult to take meditation seriously because of its portrayal in movies and television? Why or why not?

Concept Map L.O. 4.7, 4.8, 4.9

Interactive

Other Altered States: Hypnosis and Meditation

Hypnosis (state of consciousness during which person is more susceptible to suggestion)
- can be assessed by scale of hypnotic susceptibility
- induction typically involves relaxed focus and "permission" to "let go"; person being hypnotized is in control—cannot be hypnotized against your will
- can be used in therapy—help people deal with pain, anxiety, or cravings (e.g., food, drug)
- **Theories**
  - dissociation - one part of mind is aware of actions/activities taking place while the "hypnotized" part is not
  - social-cognitive theory suggests that we assume roles based on expectations for a given situation

Meditation (series of mental exercises meant to refocus attention and achieve a trancelike state of consciousness)
- associated with changes in brain activity that can be measured through EEG and other modalities
- helps to promote relaxation, calm anxiety, improve sleep, reduce chronic pain, and lower blood pressure

Reset

Practice Quiz   How much do you remember?   ANSWERS ON PAGE AK-1

Pick the best answer.

1. The primary key to hypnosis is finding someone who
  a. accepts suggestions easily.
  b. has a vivid imagination.
  c. is already very tired.
  d. is easily distracted.

2. Some researchers have suggested that hypnosis may work due to an individual's personal expectations about what being hypnotized is supposed to be like, and the individual's ability to play a particular role in the given social situation. Which theory of hypnosis best accounts for these possible explanations for an individual's behavior while hypnotized?
  a. dissociative theory
  b. expectancy theory
  c. social-cognitive theory
  d. biological theory

3. Your friend tells you she is seeing a therapist who wishes to use hypnosis as part of her therapy. However, your friend is concerned that she might be hypnotized without knowing it. What might you tell her?
  a. Be careful. Hypnotists are in control of you while hypnotized.
  b. Not to worry. Hypnotists can only control their patient's behavior about 40 percent of the time.
  c. That you actually hypnotize yourself and you cannot be hypnotized against your will.
  d. Don't worry. Hypnosis is just an illusion and doesn't really work.

4. What is the role of a hypnotist during a hypnotic therapy session?
  a. They are in complete control.
  b. They are partially in control.
  c. They create the illusion that the patient is in control.
  d. They are little more than a guide.

5. Which of the following is the primary advantage of meditation as a relaxation technique?
  a. It is superior to other techniques, such as reading a book or taking a bath, in helping people to relax.
  b. It can help someone achieve a full state of dissociation.
  c. People can do it almost anywhere, even in a classroom just before a big test.
  d. It requires only very low doses of medication to perform.

Psychoactive Drugs

Whereas some people seek altered states of consciousness in sleep, daydreaming, meditation, or even hypnosis, others try to take a shortcut and use drugs. Although many such drugs have practical purposes (sedation during surgery, control of pain, or controlling anxiety, for example), there are often dangers in using these drugs.

4.10 **Define the term psychoactive drug, and distinguish between physical and psychological dependence upon drugs.**

The term **psychoactive drugs** refers to chemical substances that alter thinking, perception, memory, or some combination of those abilities. When taken for pleasure, to get "high," or to dull psychological pain, or when taken without the supervision of a qualified medical professional, these drugs can pose serious risks to one's health and may even cause death. One danger of such drugs is their potential to create either a physical or psychological dependence, both of which can lead to a lifelong pattern of abuse as well as the risk of taking increasingly larger doses, leading to one of the clearest dangers of dependence: a drug overdose. Drug overdoses do not happen only with illegal drugs; even certain additives in so-called natural supplements can have a deadly effect.

PHYSICAL DEPENDENCE Drugs that people can become physically dependent on cause the user's body to crave the drug (Abadinsky, 1989; Fleming & Barry, 1992; Pratt, 1991). After using the drug for some period of time, the body becomes unable to function normally without the drug and the person is said to be dependent or addicted, a condition commonly called **physical dependence**.

One sign of physical dependence is the development of a **drug tolerance** (Pratt, 1991). As the person continues to use the drug, larger and larger doses of the drug are needed to achieve the same initial effects of the drug.

Another sign of a physical dependence is that the user experiences symptoms of **withdrawal** when deprived of the drug. Depending on the drug, these symptoms can range from headaches, nausea, and irritability to severe pain, cramping, shaking, and dangerously elevated blood pressure. These physical sensations occur because the body is trying to adjust to the absence of the drug. Many users will take more of the drug to alleviate the symptoms of withdrawal, which makes the entire situation worse. This is actually an example of *negative reinforcement*, the tendency to continue a behavior that leads to the removal of or escape from unpleasant circumstances or sensations. Negative reinforcement is a very powerful motivating factor, and scores of drug-dependent users exist as living proof of that power. **LINK** to Learning Objective 5.5.

The "high" of drug use often takes place in certain surroundings, with certain other people, and perhaps even using certain objects, such as the tiny spoons used by cocaine addicts. These people, settings, and objects can become cues that are associated with the drug high. When the cues are present, it may be even harder to resist using the drug because the body and mind have become conditioned, or trained, to associate drug use with the cues. This is a form of *classical conditioning*. **LINK** to Learning Objective 5.2. The mechanisms of dependence are not just a product of learning—the brain itself plays an important part. Drugs that can lead to dependence cause the release of dopamine in a part of the brain called the mesolimbic pathway, a neural track that begins in the midbrain area (just above the pons); connects to limbic system structures, including the amygdala and the hippocampus; and continues to the middle of the prefrontal cortex (Hnasko et al., 2010; Schmitt & Reith, 2010). **LINK** to Learning Objective 2.11. When a drug enters the body, it goes quickly to this area, known as the brain's "reward pathway," causing a release of dopamine and intense pleasure. The brain tries to adapt to this large amount of dopamine by decreasing the number of synaptic receptors for dopamine. The next time the user takes the drug, he or she needs more of it to get the same pleasure response because of the reduced number of receptors—drug tolerance has developed (Koob & Le Moal, 2005; Laviolette et al., 2008; Salamone & Correa, 2012).

💬 But not all drugs produce physical dependence, right? For example, some people say that you can't get physically dependent on marijuana. If that's true, why is it so hard for some people to quit smoking pot?

PSYCHOLOGICAL DEPENDENCE   Not all drugs cause physical dependence; some cause **psychological dependence**, or the belief that the drug is needed to continue a feeling of emotional or psychological well-being, which is a very powerful factor in continued drug use. The body may not need or crave the drug, and people may not experience the symptoms of physical withdrawal or tolerance, but they will continue to use the drug because they *think* they need it. In this case, it is the rewarding properties of using the drug that cause a dependency to develop. This is an example of *positive reinforcement*, or the tendency of a behavior to strengthen when followed by pleasurable consequences. ⓛⓘⓃⓚ to Learning Objective 5.5. Negative reinforcement is also at work here, as taking the drug will lower levels of anxiety.

Although not all drugs produce physical dependence, *any* drug can become a focus of psychological dependence. Indeed, because there is no withdrawal to go through or to recover from, psychological dependencies can last forever. Some people who gave up smoking marijuana decades ago still say that the craving returns every now and then (Roffman et al., 1988).

One of the dangers of psychoactive drugs is that they may lead to physical or psychological dependence

CATEGORIES OF DRUGS

4.11 **Describe the effects of stimulants, depressants, and hallucinogens on consciousness and summarize the dangers associated with taking them.**

The effect of a particular drug depends on the category to which it belongs and the particular neurotransmitter the drug affects. ⓛⓘⓃⓚ to Learning Objective 2.3. In this chapter we will describe several of the major drug categories, including **stimulants** (drugs that increase the functioning of the nervous system), **depressants** (drugs that decrease the functioning of the nervous system), and **hallucinogenics** (drugs that alter perceptions and may cause hallucinations).

STIMULANTS: UP, UP, AND AWAY   Stimulants are a class of drugs that cause either the sympathetic division or the central nervous system (or both) to increase levels of functioning, at least temporarily. In simple terms, stimulants "speed up" the nervous system—the heart may beat faster or the brain may work faster, for example. Many of these drugs are called "uppers" for this reason.

AMPHETAMINES   **Amphetamines** are stimulants that are synthesized (made) in laboratories rather than being found in nature. Among the amphetamines are drugs like Benzedrine, Methedrine, and Dexedrine. A related compound, *methamphetamine*, is sometimes used to treat attention-deficit/hyperactivity disorder or narcolepsy. "Crystal meth" is a crystalline form that can be smoked and is used by recreational drug users, people who do not need drugs but instead use them to gain some form of pleasure.

Like other stimulants, amphetamines cause the sympathetic nervous system to go into overdrive. ⓛⓘⓃⓚ to Learning Objective 2.5. Some truck drivers use amphetamines to stay awake while driving long hours. Stimulants won't give people any extra energy, but they will cause people to burn up whatever energy reserves they do have. They also depress the appetite, which is another function of the sympathetic division. Many doctors used to prescribe these drugs as diet pills. Today they are only used on a short-term basis and under strict medical supervision. Diet pills sold over the counter usually contain another relatively mild stimulant, caffeine.

When the energy reserves are exhausted or the drug wears off, a "crash" is inevitable, and the tendency is to take more pills to get back "up." The person taking these pills finds that it takes more and more pills to get the same stimulant effect (drug tolerance). Nausea, vomiting, high blood pressure, and strokes are possible, as is a state called "amphetamine psychosis." This condition causes addicts to become delusional (losing contact with what is real) and paranoid. They think people are out to "get" them. Violence is a likely outcome, both against the self and others (Kratofil et al., 1996; Paparelli et al., 2011).

COCAINE Unlike amphetamines, **cocaine** is a natural drug found in coca plant leaves. It produces feelings of euphoria (a feeling of great happiness), energy, power, and pleasure. It also deadens pain and suppresses the appetite.

Far from being illegal, cocaine was once used in many health drinks and medications, such as this toothache medicine used in the late 1800s. Many patent medicines contained small traces of cocaine, including the now famous Coca-Cola™, once marketed as a nerve tonic.

Cocaine is a highly dangerous drug, not just for its addictive properties. Some people have convulsions and may even die when using cocaine for the first time (Lacayo, 1995). It can have devastating effects on the children born to mothers who use cocaine and has been associated with increased risk of learning disabilities, delayed language development, and an inability to cope adequately with stress, among other symptoms (Cone-Wesson, 2005; Eiden et al., 2009; Kable et al., 2008; Morrow et al., 2006). Laboratory animals have been known to press a lever to give themselves cocaine rather than eating or drinking, even to the point of starvation and death (Iwamoto & Martin, 1988; Ward et al., 1996).

Although cocaine users do not go through the same kind of physical withdrawal symptoms that users of heroin, alcohol, and other physically addictive drugs go through, users will experience a severe mood swing into depression (the "crash"), followed by extreme tiredness, nervousness, an inability to feel pleasure, and paranoia. The brain is the part of the body that develops the craving for cocaine because of chemical changes caused by the drug (Hurley, 1989; Schmitt & Reith, 2010). Ⓛ Ⓘ Ⓝ Ⓚ to Learning Objective 2.3.

As addictive as cocaine is, there is one other stimulant that is usually described as even more addictive. Most experts in addiction seem to agree that nicotine produces addiction in 99 percent of the people who use it (Benowitz, 1988; Centers for Disease Control and Prevention [CDC], 1992; Franklin, 1990; Henningfield et al., 1991; Hilts, 1998; Perrine, 1997).

 💬 Hasn't nicotine just been the victim of a lot of bad press? After all, it's legal, unlike cocaine and heroin.

NICOTINE Every year, more than 440,000 people in the United States die from illnesses related to smoking. That's more people than those who die from accidents in motor vehicles; alcohol, cocaine, heroin, and other drug abuse; AIDS; suicide; and homicide *combined* (CDC, 2008; U.S. Department of Health and Human Services, 2010).

Nicotine is a relatively mild but nevertheless toxic stimulant, producing a slight "rush" or sense of arousal as it raises blood pressure and accelerates the heart, as well as providing a rush of sugar into the bloodstream by stimulating the release of adrenalin in addition to raising dopamine levels in the brain's reward pathway (Kovacs et al., 2010; Rezvani & Levin, 2001). As is the case with many stimulants, it also has a relaxing effect on most people and seems to reduce stress (Pormerleau & Pormerleau, 1994).

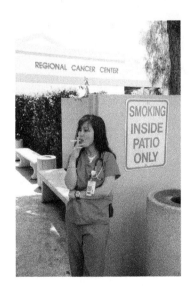

Nicotine is highly addictive, and many smokers will go to great lengths to be able to smoke—including smoking right next to the "No Smoking" sign.

Why is it so difficult to quit using tobacco products? Aside from the powerfully addictive nature of nicotine, the physical withdrawal symptoms can be as bad as those resulting from alcohol, cocaine, or heroin abuse (Epping-Jordan et al., 1998). People don't think about nicotine as being as bad as cocaine or heroin because nicotine is legal and easily obtainable, but in terms of its addictive power, it is *more powerful* than heroin or alcohol (CDC, 2010; Henningfield et al., 1990).

Sleep deprivation causes this man to struggle to wake up. Caffeine can help with alertness but may worsen his sleep deprivation when he tries to get a decent night's sleep tonight.

Actor Heath Ledger died on January 22, 2008, from an accidental drug interaction. Six different types of depressant drugs were found in his system. He was 28.

CAFFEINE   There is one stimulant that almost everyone uses, with many using it every day. This, of course, is **caffeine**, the stimulant found in coffee, tea, most sodas, chocolate, and even many over-the-counter drugs. Caffeine is another natural substance, like cocaine and nicotine, and is found in coffee beans, tea leaves, cocoa nuts, and at least 60 other types of plants (Braun, 1996). It is a mild stimulant, helps maintain alertness, and can increase the effectiveness of some pain relievers such as aspirin. Caffeine is often added to pain relievers for that reason and is the key ingredient in medications meant to keep people awake.

Contrary to popular belief, coffee does not help induce sobriety. All one would get is a wide-awake drunk. Coffee is fairly acidic, too, and acids are not what the stomach of a person with a hangover needs.

DEPRESSANTS: DOWN IN THE VALLEY   Another class of psychoactive drugs is *depressants,* drugs that slow the central nervous system.

MAJOR AND MINOR TRANQUILIZERS   Commonly known as the *major tranquilizers* (drugs that have a strong depressant effect) or sleeping pills, **barbiturates** are drugs that have a sedative (sleep-inducing) effect. Overdoses can lead to death as breathing and heart action are stopped.

The *minor tranquilizers* (drugs having a relatively mild depressant effect) include the **benzodiazepines**. These drugs are used to lower anxiety and reduce stress. Some of the most common are Valium, Xanax, Halcion, Ativan, and Librium.

Both major and minor tranquilizers can be addictive, and large doses can be dangerous, as can an interaction with alcohol or other drugs (Olin, 1993).

Rohypnol is a benzodiazepine tranquilizer that has become famous as the "date rape" drug. Unsuspecting victims drink something that has been doctored with this drug, which causes them to be unaware of their actions, although still able to respond to directions or commands. Rape or some other form of sexual assault can then be carried out without fear that the victim will remember it or be able to report it (Armstrong, 1997; Gable, 2004).

ALCOHOL   The most commonly used and abused depressant is **alcohol**, the chemical resulting from fermentation or distillation of various kinds of vegetable matter. Aside from the obvious health risks to the liver, brain, and heart, alcohol is associated with loss of work time, loss of a job, and loss of economic stability.

Alcohol indirectly stimulates the release of a neurotransmitter called GABA, the brain's major depressant (Brick, 2003; Santhakumar et al., 2007). GABA slows down or stops neural activity. As more GABA is released, the brain's functioning actually becomes more and more inhibited, depressed, or slowed down. The areas of the brain that are first affected by alcohol are unfortunately the areas that control social inhibitions, so alcohol (due to its simulation of GABA) has the effect of

Although many young adults see drinking as a rite of passage into adulthood, few may understand the dangers of "binge" drinking, or drinking four to five drinks within a limited amount of time. Inhibitions are lowered and poor decisions may be made, such as driving while intoxicated. Binge drinking, a popular activity on some college campuses, can also lead to alcoholism.

depressing the inhibitions. As the effects continue, motor skills, reaction time, and speech are all affected.

Anywhere from 10 to 20 million people in the United States suffer from alcoholism. Many people are alcoholics but deny the fact. Many college students and even older adults engage in binge drinking (drinking four or five drinks within a limited amount of time, such as at "happy hour"). Binge drinking quickly leads to being drunk, and drunkenness is a major sign of alcoholism. Some other danger signs are feeling guilty about drinking, drinking in the morning, drinking to recover from drinking, drinking alone, being sensitive about how much one drinks when others mention it, drinking so much that one does and says things one later regrets, drinking enough to have blackouts or memory loss, drinking too fast, lying about drinking, and drinking enough to pass out.

The dangers of abusing alcohol cannot be stressed enough. According to the Centers for Disease Control and Prevention (CDC, 2011), the number of alcohol-induced deaths in 2010 was 25,692. This figure does *not* include deaths due to accidents and homicides that may be related to abuse of alcohol—only those deaths that are caused by the body's inability to handle the alcohol. Of these deaths, 15,990 were attributed to liver disease caused by alcoholism. The National Institute on Alcoholism and Alcohol Abuse (National Institute on Alcoholism and Alcohol Abuse [NIAAA], 2007) has statistics from 2001 to 2002 showing that the rate of psychiatric disorders, including alcohol and other drug abuse as well as depression and anxiety disorders, increases from about 2.5 percent for a light drinker to 13.2 percent for a moderate drinker and around 17.1 percent for a heavy drinker. Alcohol was involved in nearly 22.5 percent of the fatal traffic crashes for drivers under 21 years old and 24.8 percent of the fatal crashes for those over 21 (NIAAA, 2007).

If you are concerned about your own drinking or are worried about a friend or loved one, there is a free and very simple online assessment at this site on the Internet: **www.alcoholscreening.org**.

NARCOTICS: I FEEL YOUR PAIN   **Narcotics** are a type of depressant that suppress the sensation of pain by binding to and stimulating the nervous system's natural receptor sites for endorphins, the neurotransmitters that naturally deaden pain sensations (Olin, 1993). Because they also slow down the action of the nervous system, drug interactions with alcohol and other depressants are possible—and deadly. All narcotics are a derivative of a particular plant-based substance—opium.

Opium, made from the opium poppy, has pain-relieving and euphoria-inducing properties that have been known for at least 2,000 years. Highly addictive, it mimics the effects of endorphins, the nervous system's natural painkillers. The nervous system slows or stops its production of endorphins. When the drug wears off, there is no protection against any kind of pain, causing the severe symptoms of withdrawal associated with these drugs. It was not until 1803 that opium was developed for use as a medication by a German physician. The new form—morphine—was hailed as "God's own medicine" (Hodgson, 2001).

Morphine was created by dissolving opium in an acid and then neutralizing the acid with ammonia. Morphine was thought to be a wonder drug, although its addictive qualities soon became a major concern to physicians and their patients. Morphine is still used today to control severe pain, but in carefully controlled doses and for very short periods of time.

Ironically, **heroin** was first hailed as the new wonder drug—a derivative of morphine that did not have many of the disagreeable side effects of morphine. The theory was that heroin was a purer form of the drug, and that the impurities in morphine were the substances creating the harmful side effects. It did not take long, however, for doctors and others to realize that heroin was even more powerfully addictive than morphine or opium. Although usage as a medicine ceased, it is still used by many people.

Drugs such as *methadone, buprenorphine,* and *naltrexone* may be used to control withdrawal symptoms and help treat opiate addictions (Kahan & Sutton, 1998; Kakko et al., 2003; Ward et al., 1999). Eventually, as the addicted person is weaned from these drugs, the natural endorphin system starts to function more normally.

HALLUCINOGENS: HIGHER AND HIGHER   Hallucinogens actually cause the brain to alter its interpretation of sensations (Olin, 1993) and can produce sensory distortions very similar to *synesthesia* (Ⓛ Ⓘ Ⓝ Ⓚ) to Chapter Three: Sensation and Perception), in which sensations cross over each other—colors have sound, sounds have smells, and so on. False sensory perceptions, called *hallucinations,* are often experienced, especially with the more powerful hallucinogens. There are two basic types of hallucinogens—those that are created in a laboratory and those that are from natural sources. Before we begin our discussion of hallucinogens, take the survey *What Drugs Have You Used?* to discover more about your experiences and attitudes toward these drugs.

Survey   WHAT DRUGS HAVE YOU USED?

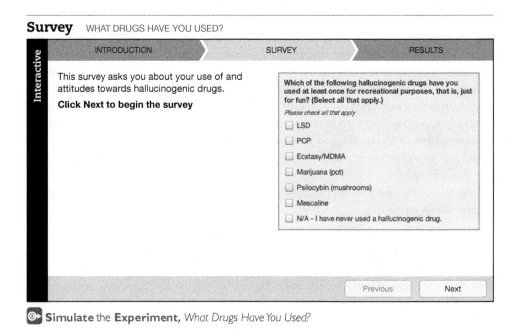

Simulate the Experiment, *What Drugs Have You Used?*

MANUFACTURED HIGHS   There are several drugs that were developed in the laboratory instead of being found in nature. Perhaps because these drugs are manufactured, they are often more potent than drugs found in the natural world.

LSD, or **lysergic acid diethylamide**, is synthesized from a grain fungus called *ergot*. Ergot fungus commonly grows on rye grain but can be found on other grains as well. First manufactured in 1938, LSD is one of the most potent, or powerful, hallucinogens (Johnston et al., 2007; Lee & Shlain, 1986). It takes only a very tiny drop of LSD to achieve a "high."

People who take LSD usually do so to get that high feeling. Some people feel that LSD helps them expand their consciousness or awareness of the world around them. Colors seem more intense, sounds more beautiful, and so on. But the experience is not always a pleasant one, just as dreams are not always filled with positive emotions. "Bad trips" are quite common, and there is no way to control what kind of "trip" the brain is going to decide to take.

One of the greater dangers in using LSD is the effect it has on a person's ability to perceive reality. Real dangers and hazards in the world may go unnoticed by a person "lost" in an LSD fantasy, and people under the influence of this drug may make poor decisions, such as trying to drive while high.

Another synthesized drug was found to be so dangerous that it remains useful only in veterinary medicine as a tranquilizer. The drug is **PCP** (which stands for *phenyl cyclo-hexyl piperidine*, a name which is often contracted as *phencyclidine*) and can have many different effects. Depending on the dosage, it can be a hallucinogen, stimulant, depressant, or an analgesic (painkilling) drug. As with LSD, users of PCP can experience hallucinations, distorted sensations, and very unpleasant effects. PCP can also lead to acts of violence against others or suicide (Brecher 1988; Cami et al., 2000; Johnston et al., 2007). Users may even physically injure themselves unintentionally because PCP causes them to feel no warning signal of pain.

The last synthetic drug we will address here is technically an amphetamine, but it is capable of producing hallucinations as well. In fact, both **MDMA** (a "designer drug" known on the streets as **Ecstasy** or simply **X**) and PCP are now classified as **stimulatory hallucinogenics**, drugs that produce a mixture of psychomotor stimulant and hallucinogenic effects (National Institute on Drug Abuse, 2006; Shuglin, 1986). Although many users of MDMA believe that it is relatively harmless, the fact is that it—like many other substances—can be deadly when misused. MDMA causes the release of large amounts of serotonin and also blocks the reuptake of this neurotransmitter (Hall & Henry, 2006; Liechti & Vollenweider, 2001; Montgomery & Fisk, 2008). The user feels euphoria, energized, and may feel increased emotional warmth toward others. But there is some evidence that MDMA may damage the serotonin receptors, which could lead to depression. Other negative effects include severe dehydration and raised body temperature, which can lead to excessive intake of liquids—with possible fatal results (Leccese et al., 2000).

NONMANUFACTURED HIGH: MARIJUANA   One of the best known and most commonly abused of the hallucinogenic drugs, **marijuana** (also called "pot" or "weed") comes from the leaves and flowers of the hemp plant called *Cannabis sativa*. (*Hashish* is the concentrated substance made by scraping the resin from these leaves, and both marijuana and hashish contain *cannabinoids*.) The most psychoactive cannabinoid, and the active ingredient in marijuana, is *tetrahydrocannabinol* (THC). Marijuana is best known for its ability to produce a feeling of well-being, mild intoxication, and mild sensory distortions or hallucinations.

The effects of marijuana are relatively mild compared to the other hallucinogens. In fact, an inexperienced user who doesn't know what to expect upon smoking that first marijuana cigarette may feel nothing at all. Most people do report a feeling of mild euphoria and relaxation, along with an altered time sense and mild visual distortions. Higher doses can lead to hallucinations, delusions, and the all-too-common paranoia. Most studies of marijuana's effects have concluded that while marijuana can create a powerful psychological dependency, it does not produce physical dependency or physical withdrawal symptoms. However, after alcohol and nicotine, cannabis dependence is the most common form of drug dependence in the United States, Canada, and Australia (Hall & Degenhardt, 2009).

Even at mild doses, it is not safe to operate heavy machinery or drive a car while under the influence of marijuana because it negatively affects reaction time and perception of surroundings; the drug reduces a person's ability to make the split-second decisions that driving a car or other equipment requires. Information processing in general, attention, and memory are all likely to be impaired in a person who has used marijuana.

Although no one has ever been known to die from an overdose of marijuana, smoking it is not a healthy habit. Research linking marijuana smoking and lung cancer is not definitive due to the fact that many studies have not been able to control

Many of these young people enjoying themselves at a rave may be using MDMA, or Ecstasy. The dehydrating effect of the drug, together with the intense dancing and physical activity at raves like this one, can have a deadly effect on the user.

This woman is preparing a cannabis (marijuana) cigarette. Cannabis is reported to relieve pain in cases of multiple sclerosis and chronic pain from nerve damage. Such use is controversial as cannabis is classified as an illegal drug in some countries.

for confounding variables, such as cigarette smoking, alcohol use, or other risk factors (Hall & Degenhardt, 2009). (L)(I)(N)K to Learning Objective 1.10. Aside from those previously mentioned, probable adverse effects from chronic nonmedical marijuana use also include increased risk of motor vehicle crashes, chronic bronchitis or other lung problems, and cardiovascular disease. In adolescents who are regular users, psychosocial development, educational attainment, and mental health can be negatively impacted (Hall & Degenhardt, 2009). With regard to the possible mental health problems, there especially appears to be an increased risk for psychotic symptoms and disorders later in life for adolescents who are regular and heavier users (Hall & Degenhardt, 2009; Moore et al., 2007).

WRITING PROMPT

Compare the dangers of marijuana use to nicotine or alcohol—in your opinion, which is the "lesser evil?"

> ▶   The response entered here will be saved to your notes and may be
>   collected by your instructor if he/she requires it.

Submit

Table 4.3 summarizes the various types of drugs, their common names, and their effects on human behavior.

Table 4.3	How Drugs Affect Consciousness		
Drug Classification	**Common Name**	**Main Effect**	**Adverse Effects**
Stimulants		Stimulation, excitement	
Amphetamines	Methamphetamine, speed, Ritalin, Dexedrine		Risk of addiction, stroke, fatal heart problems, psychosis
Cocaine	Cocaine, crack		Risk of addiction, stroke, fatal heart problems, psychosis
Nicotine	Tobacco		Addiction, cancer
Caffeine	Coffee, tea		Addiction, high blood pressure
Depressants		Relaxation	
Barbiturates (major tranquilizers)	Nembutal, Seconal		Addiction, brain damage, death
Benzodiazepines (minor tranquilizers)	Valium, Xanax, Halcion, Ativan, Rohypnol		Lower risk of overdose and addiction when taken alone
Alcohol	Beer, wine, spirits		Alcoholism, health problems, depression, increased risk of accidents, death
Narcotics	Opium, morphine, heroin	Euphoria	Addiction, death
Hallucinogens	LSD, PCP, MDMA (Ecstasy), marijuana	Distorted consciousness, altered perception	Possible permanent memory problems, bad "trips," suicide, overdose, and death

Concept Map LO. 4.10, 4.11

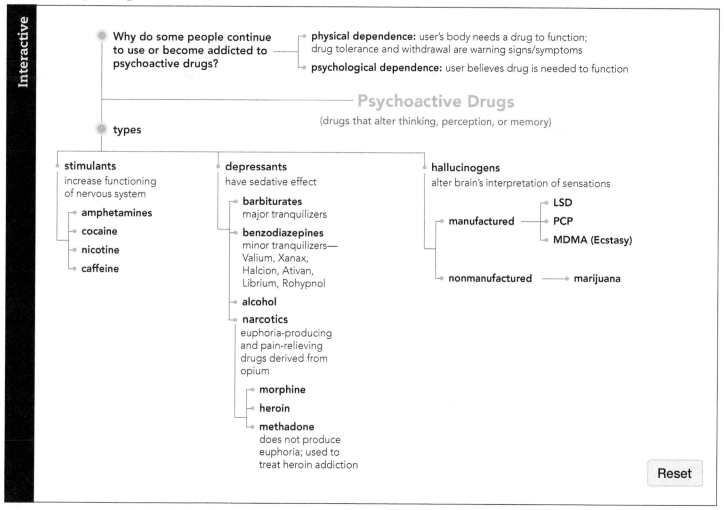

Interactive

Why do some people continue to use or become addicted to psychoactive drugs?

physical dependence: user's body needs a drug to function; drug tolerance and withdrawal are warning signs/symptoms

psychological dependence: user believes drug is needed to function

Psychoactive Drugs
(drugs that alter thinking, perception, or memory)

types

stimulants
increase functioning of nervous system

- **amphetamines**
- **cocaine**
- **nicotine**
- **caffeine**

depressants
have sedative effect

- **barbiturates**
  major tranquilizers
- **benzodiazepines**
  minor tranquilizers—
  Valium, Xanax,
  Halcion, Ativan,
  Librium, Rohypnol
- **alcohol**
- **narcotics**
  euphoria-producing
  and pain-relieving
  drugs derived from
  opium
  - **morphine**
  - **heroin**
  - **methadone**
    does not produce
    euphoria; used to
    treat heroin addiction

hallucinogens
alter brain's interpretation of sensations

manufactured
- LSD
- PCP
- MDMA (Ecstasy)

nonmanufactured — marijuana

Reset

Practice Quiz How much do you remember? ANSWERS ON PAGE AK-1.

Pick the best answer.

1. As consequences to stopping drug use, headaches, nausea, shaking, and elevated blood pressure are all signs of
  a. withdrawal.
  b. overdose.
  c. psychological dependency.
  d. amphetamine toxicity.

2. What drug's physical withdrawal symptoms include severe mood swings (crash), paranoia, extreme fatigue, and an inability to feel pleasure?
  a. heroin
  b. caffeine
  c. alcohol
  d. cocaine

3. Which of the following statements about nicotine are true?
  a. In terms of addictive power, nicotine is more powerful than heroin or alcohol.
  b. Nicotine can slow the heart and therefore create a sense of relaxation.
  c. Overall, the number of Americans smoking is on the increase.
  d. Overall, the number of women and teenagers smoking is on the decrease.

4. _____ is a tranquilizer that is also known as the "date rape" drug.
  a. Halcion
  b. Librium
  c. Rohypnol
  d. Xanax

5. Typically, narcotics have the ability to
  a. cause intense hallucinations.
  b. suppress the sensation of pain.
  c. stimulate the user.
  d. cause deep levels of depression.

6. Most studies of marijuana's effects have found that
  a. it creates a powerful psychological dependency.
  b. it creates a strong physical dependency.
  c. it produces intense withdrawal symptoms.
  d. it is easy to overdose on the substance.

Individuals sometimes awaken with the very real feeling that they have been visited by aliens, or a ghost, demon, or even an angel. The more logical explanation is that they have been startled awake from either a hypnogogic or hypnopompic hallucination experienced at some point as they were sleeping.

Applying Psychology to Everyday Life
Thinking Critically about Ghosts, Aliens, and Other Things That Go Bump in the Night

4.12 **Describe how the workings of our consciousness can explain "supernatural" visitations.**

Down through the ages, people have been visited by ghosts, spirits, and other sorts of mystical or mysterious visitors—or so they have believed. In more modern times, ghostly visitations have often given way to aliens, who may perform some sort of medical examination or who may abduct the person, only to return them to their beds. And it is to their beds that they are usually returned, and such visitations typically are experienced when the person is in bed. Is there a simpler explanation for these experiences?

As mentioned earlier in this chapter, a type of hallucination can occur just as a person is entering N1 (R&K Stage 1) sleep, called a *hypnogogic hallucination* (Ohayon et al., 1996; Siegel & West, 1975). If you remember that people in N1, when awakened, will deny having been asleep, a simple explanation for so-called supernatural visitations does present itself. Hypnogogic hallucinations are not dreamlike in nature. Instead, they feel very real to the person experiencing them (who does not think he or she is asleep, remember). Most common are the auditory hallucinations, in which a person might hear a voice calling out the person's name, not all that unusual and probably not remembered most of the time.

Imagine for a moment, though, that your hypnogogic hallucination is that of some person whom you know to be dead or ill, or a strange and frightening image, perhaps with equally strange and frightening sound effects. That you will remember, especially since you are likely to wake up right after *and be completely convinced that you were awake at the time of the hallucination*. Combine this experience with the natural tendency many people have to want to believe that there is life after death or that there are other sentient life forms visiting our planet, and *voilà!*—a ghost/spirit/alien has appeared.

Sometimes people have a similar experience in the middle of the night. They awaken to find that they are paralyzed and that something—ghost, demon, alien—is standing over them and perhaps doing strange things to their helpless bodies. When a hallucination happens just as a person is in the between-state of being in REM sleep (in which the voluntary muscles are paralyzed) and not yet fully awake, it is called a *hypnopompic hallucination* and is once again a much simpler explanation of visits by aliens or spirits during the night than any supernatural explanation. Such visitations are not as rare as you might think, but once again, it is only the spectacular, frightening, or unusual ones that will be remembered (Cheyne, 2003; Greeley, 1987; Ohayon et al., 1996).

Questions for Further Discussion

1. Have you ever had one of these experiences? Can you now understand how that experience might have been one that you would remember?

2. Talk to friends or family about their similar experiences, looking for the simpler explanation.

Chapter Summary

What Is Consciousness?

4.1 Define what it means to be conscious.

- Consciousness is a person's awareness of everything that is going on at any given moment. Most waking hours are spent in waking consciousness.

4.2 Describe the different levels of consciousness.

- Altered states of consciousness are shifts in the quality or pattern of mental activity, such as waking consciousness and altered states of consciousness.

Sleep

4.3 Explain the need for sleep and the biological processes involved in sleep.

- The sleep–wake cycle is a circadian rhythm that occurs over a 24-hour period and is controlled by the activity of the hypothalamus and glandular system.
- The average amount of sleep needed by most young adults is about 7 to 9 hours within each 24-hour period.

4.4 Describe the different stages of sleep and explain the importance of REM sleep.

- N1 (R&K Stage 1) sleep is light sleep.
- N2 (R&K Stage 2) sleep is indicated by the presence of sleep spindles, bursts of activity on the EEG.
- N3 (R&K Stages 3 and 4) is highlighted by the first appearance of delta waves, the slowest and largest waves, and the body is at its lowest level of functioning.
- REM sleep occurs four or five times a night, replacing N1 after a full cycle through N1–N3 and then ascending back to lighter stages of sleep. It is accompanied by paralysis of the voluntary muscles but rapid movement of the eyes.

4.5 Describe and differentiate among the various sleep disorders.

- Nightmares are bad or unpleasant dreams that occur during REM sleep.
- Night terrors are attacks of extreme fear that the victim has while sound asleep.
- Sleepwalking occurs in N3 (R&K Stages 3 and 4) sleep
- Insomnia is an inability to get to sleep, stay asleep, or get enough sleep.
- Sleep apnea occurs when a person stops breathing for 10 seconds or more.
- Narcolepsy is a genetic disorder in which the person suddenly and without warning collapses into REM sleep.

4.6 Summarize the theories of why people dream and describe the gender and cultural differences of dream content.

- Freud believed dreams to be a form of wish fulfillment.

- Without outside sensory information to explain the activation of the brain cells in the cortex by the pons area, the association areas of the cortex synthesize a story, or dream, to explain that activation in the activation-synthesis hypothesis.
- A revision of activation-synthesis theory, the activation-information-mode model (AIM) states that information experienced during waking hours can influence the synthesis of dreams.

Other Altered States: Hypnosis and Meditation

4.7 Define hypnosis and explain the process by which hypnosis is accomplished.

- Hypnosis is a state of consciousness in which a person is especially susceptible to suggestion.

4.8 Describe two major theories of why hypnosis works.

- Dissociative theory states that a person under hypnosis is in a state of dissociation, in which one part of consciousness is hypnotized and susceptible to suggestion, while another part is aware of everything that occurs.
- Social-cognitive theory states that the hypnotized subject is merely playing a social role—that of the hypnotized person.

4.9 Define meditation and explain some of its benefits.

- Meditation can produce a state of relaxation and reduce the physical reactions common to stressful situations.

Psychoactive Drugs

4.10 Define the term psychoactive drug, and distinguish between physical and psychological dependence upon drugs.

- Drugs that are physically addictive cause the user's body to crave the drug. When deprived of the drug, the user will go through physical withdrawal.
- Drug tolerance occurs as the user's body becomes conditioned to the level of the drug. After a time, the user must take more and more of the drug to get the same effect.
- In psychological dependence, the user believes that he or she needs the drug to function well and maintain a sense of well-being. Any drug can produce psychological dependence.

4.11 Describe the effects of stimulants, depressants, and hallucinogens on consciousness and summarize the dangers associated with taking them.

- Stimulants are drugs that increase the activity of the nervous system, particularly the sympathetic division and the central nervous system. Stimulants include amphetamines, cocaine, nicotine, and caffeine. They help people stay awake and reduce appetite but are physically addictive.

- Depressants, which slow down the nervous system, include the major tranquilizers or barbiturates, the minor tranquilizers or benzodiazepines, alcohol, and narcotics such as opium, morphine, and heroin. Alcohol is the most commonly used and abused depressant.

- Hallucinogens are stimulants that alter the brain's interpretation of sensations, creating hallucinations. Three synthetically created hallucinogens are LSD, PCP, and MDMA.

- Marijuana is a mild hallucinogen, producing a mild euphoria and feelings of relaxation in its users. Larger doses can lead to hallucinations and paranoia. It contains substances that may be carcinogenic and impairs learning and memory.

Applying Psychology to Everyday Life: Thinking Critically about Ghosts, Aliens, and Other Things That Go Bump in the Night

4.12 Describe how the workings of our consciousness can explain "supernatural" visitations.

- Vivid, realistic hallucinations that occur in N1 (R&K Stage 1) sleep are called hypnogogic hallucinations and are often misinterpreted as ghosts or other supernatural visitations.

- Similar hallucinations that occur when awakening from REM sleep are called hypnopompic hallucinations.

Test Yourself   ANSWERS ON PAGE AK–1.

Pick the best answer.

1. Jane is aware that she is sitting in her psychology class and it is almost lunchtime. She is also aware of how tired she is since staying up late to watch a movie. Thus, if Jane is aware of what is going on around her and what is going on within her, then it is safe to say that she is in a(n)
   a. state of waking consciousness.
   b. altered state of consciousness.
   c. unconscious state.
   d. preconscious state.

2. What part of the brain is influential in determining when to sleep?
   a. hippocampus
   b. hypothalamus
   c. thalamus
   d. frontal lobe

3. As the sun begins to set, Winston finds himself becoming more and more sleepy. What structure is sensitive to light and influences when to go to sleep and when to awaken?
   a. corpus callosum
   b. occipital lobe
   c. thalamus
   d. suprachiasmatic nucleus

4. Carlos is pulling an all-nighter in preparation for his big psychology test tomorrow. According to the research, what is the result on Carlos's memory when he deprives himself of sleep the night prior to his exam?
   a. Carlos will retain information from staying up all night, but only if his test is early in the morning.
   b. The ability to retain information can be influenced by the presence of sunlight. Thus, if the sun is shining, Carlos will remember more than if it is a cloudy day.
   c. Carlos will actually remember less if he deprives himself of sleep the night before.
   d. Carlos's memory will not be affected in any way assuming he stays awake for only one all-night study session.

5. In REM sleep
   a. voluntary muscles are inhibited.
   b. the body sleeps deeply.
   c. brain wave activity is very slow.
   d. people are rarely dreaming.

6. Hypnogogic images are experienced in _____ sleep.
   a. N1 (R&K Stage 1)
   b. N2 (R&K Stage 2)
   c. N3 (R&K Stages 3 and 4)
   d. REM

7. Which of the following is a characteristic of N3, or slow-wave sleep?
   a. people are seldom aware they were asleep if awakened.
   b. people typically experience hypnic jerks of the muscles.
   c. it is the deepest level of sleep.
   d. it is when the majority of our dreams occur.

8. In which stage of sleep do sleep spindles occur?
   a. N1 (R&K Stage 1)
   b. N2 (R&K Stage 2)
   c. hypnagogic sleep
   d. REM

9. Josef has had a very demanding day. Though his work is not physically challenging, it tends to mentally drain him. What type of sleep will Josef probably require more of?
   a. N1 (R&K Stage 1)
   b. N2 (R&K Stage 2)
   c. N3 (R&K Stages 3 and 4)
   d. REM sleep

10. Your doctor has told you that your youngest son suffers from somnambulism. What is another name for somnambulism?
    a. insomnia
    b. sleepwalking
    c. sleep apnea
    d. narcolepsy

11. Sleep disorders are often more common in childhood, most likely because children
    a. sleep very deeply and spend more time in deep sleep.
    b. are so easily awakened in the deep sleep stage.
    c. spend less time in REM sleep than adults.
    d. need less sleep than adults.

12. Gerald has difficulty falling off to sleep. Harley can fall off to sleep easily but often wakes up early. Dale typically sleeps for 10 hours. All three are tired and not rested upon rising. Who seems to be experiencing insomnia?
    a. Gerald
    b. Harley
    c. Dale
    d. All three suffer from insomnia.

13. Bill suddenly and without warning slips into REM sleep during the day. He often falls to the ground and is difficult to awaken. Bill may have a condition called
  a. sleep apnea.
  b. insomnia.
  c. narcolepsy.
  d. epilepsy.

14. Some infants experience a kind of sleep apnea that is due to:
  a. an ongoing obstruction of their airway.
  b. an underdeveloped brain stem.
  c. swelling of the tissue that lines their nasopharynx and oropharynx.
  d. pediatric obesity.

15. When Tawny is asked to write down her dreams as a class assignment, she is embarrassed by the fact that her dreams often seem very bizarre and unrealistic. What theory best explains her dreams?
  a. activation-synthesis
  b. dreams-for-survival
  c. sociocultural theory
  d. Freudian

16. Anthony's therapist is using hypnosis to help him recall the night he was supposedly abducted by aliens. Danny's therapist is using hypnosis to help him prepare for the pain of dental surgery since Danny is allergic to the dentist's painkillers. Patrick's therapist is using hypnosis to help him quit drinking and smoking. Which client has the highest chance for success?
  a. Anthony
  b. Danny
  c. Patrick
  d. All three can benefit from hypnosis since each technique is proven effective.

17. Bobby agreed to be hypnotized during a comedy routine. While hypnotized, he stood on his chair and crowed like a rooster. Later, when his friends asked why he did this, Bobby defended his behavior by saying that he had to do those things because he was hypnotized and "that is how hypnotized people act." What theory best explains his behavior?
  a. the social-cognitive explanation of hypnosis
  b. the hidden observer theory of hypnosis
  c. the biological theory of hypnosis
  d. the behavioral theory of hypnosis

18. Which of the following is NOT one of the effects of meditation?
  a. reduction of levels of chronic pain
  b. reduction of anxiety
  c. reduction of the need for sleep
  d. lowering of blood pressure

19. Jackie has found that when she tries to quit drinking, she gets headaches, has night sweats, and shakes uncontrollably. Such a reaction is an example of
  a. psychological dependence.
  b. overdose.
  c. withdrawal.
  d. learned behavior.

20. What is the most commonly used and abused depressant?
  a. alcohol
  b. Prozac
  c. tranquilizers
  d. caffeine

Chapter 5
Learning

Yoshiko's first-grade teacher started a reading contest. For every book read, a child would get a gold star on the reading chart, and at the end of one month the child with the most stars would get a prize. Yoshiko went to the library and checked out several books each week. At the end of the month, Yoshiko had the most gold stars and got to stand in front of her classmates to receive her prize. Would it be candy? A toy? She was so excited! Imagine her surprise and mild disappointment when the big prize turned out to be another book! Disappointing prize aside, Yoshiko's teacher had made use of a key technique of learning called *reinforcement*. Reinforcement is anything that, when following a response, increases the likelihood that the response will occur again. The reinforcers of gold stars and a prize caused Yoshiko's reading to increase.

How have you used reinforcement to modify your own behavior or the behavior of others?

Video

00:00 / 02:28

Why study learning?

If we had not been able to learn, we would have died out as a species long ago. Learning is the process that allows us to adapt to the changing conditions of the world around us. We can alter our actions until we find the behavior that leads us to survival and rewards, and we can eliminate actions that have been unsuccessful in the past. Without learning, there would be no buildings, no agriculture, no lifesaving medicines, and no human civilization.

Learning Objectives

5.1   Discuss the meaning of the term *learning*.

5.2   Describe and explain the origins of classical conditioning and its important elements.

5.3   Define conditioned emotional responses, and explain conditioned taste aversions.

5.4   Describe the theory of operant conditioning and how it differs from classical conditioning, and explain the contributions of Thorndike and Skinner.

5.5   Differentiate between primary and secondary reinforcers and the processes of positive and negative reinforcement.

5.6   Distinguish among the schedules of reinforcement.

5.7   Compare and contrast punishment with reinforcement, and list some of the problems associated with using punishment.

5.8   Describe the role of operant stimuli in controlling behavior as well as other concepts that can enhance or limit operant conditioning.

5.9   Describe how operant conditioning is used to change animal and human behavior, and identify some limitations to its use.

5.10   Define and explain the concept of latent learning.

5.11   Explain the concept of insight learning.

5.12   Explain the concept of learned helplessness.

5.13   Describe the process of observational learning.

5.14   List the four elements of observational learning.

5.15   Provide and describe an example of conditioning in the real world.

Definition of Learning

5.1 Discuss the meaning of the term *learning.*

The term *learning* is one of those concepts whose meaning is crystal clear until one has to put it into actual words. "Learning is when you learn something." "Learning is learning how to do something." A more useful definition is as follows: **Learning** is any relatively permanent change in behavior brought about by experience or practice.

What does "relatively permanent" mean? And how does experience change what we do?

The "relatively permanent" part of the definition refers to the fact that when people learn anything, some part of their brain is physically changed to record what they've learned. This is actually a process of memory, for without the ability to remember what happens, people cannot learn anything. Although there is no conclusive proof as yet, research suggests strongly that once people learn something, it is always present somewhere in memory (Barsalou, 1992; Smolen et al., 2008). They may be unable to "get" to it, but it's there. **LINK** to Learning Objective 6.5.

As for the inclusion of experience or practice, think about the last time you did something that caused you a lot of pain. Did you do it again? You didn't want to experience that pain again, so you changed your behavior to avoid the painful consequence.* This is how children learn not to touch hot stoves. In contrast, if a person does something resulting in a very pleasurable experience, that person is more likely to do that same thing again. This is another change in behavior and is explained by the law of effect, a topic we will discuss later in this chapter.

the neighborhood. Jerry Van Amerongen

An instantaneous learning experience.

Not all change is accomplished through learning. Changes like an increase in height or the size of the brain are another kind of change controlled by a genetic blueprint. This kind of change is called *maturation* and is due to biology, not experience. For example, children learn to walk *when* they do because their nervous systems, muscle strength, and sense of balance have reached the point where walking is possible for them—all factors controlled by maturation, not by how much practice those children have had in trying to walk. No amount of experience or practice will help that child walk before maturation makes it possible—in spite of what some eager parents might wish.

Concept Map L.O. 1.1

Interactive

Definition of Learning

(any relatively permanent change in behavior brought about by experience or practice)

- "relatively permanent" aspect of learning refers to learning being associated with physical changes in the brain

- although physical changes may be present we may not always be able to "get" to the information

Reset

---

*consequence: an end result of some action.

Practice Quiz   How much do you remember? ANSWERS ON PAGE AK-1.

Pick the best answer.

1. Learning can best be described as
  a. a relatively permanent change in behavior.
  b. a permanent change in behavior.
  c. due primarily to unconscious motives.
  d. momentary changes that require biological changes from within.

2. Which of the following statements regarding learning is **not** true?
  a. Learning can be the result of experience.
  b. Learning, once established in the brain, is a permanent change that cannot be undone, but can only be altered.
  c. Learning can be the result of practice.
  d. The brain physically changes when a person undergoes learning.

3. Which of the following statements on the relationship between learning and memory is true?
  a. One need not learn a piece of information in order to remember it.
  b. Memory can exist independent of learning, and learning can exist independent of memory.
  c. Once a person learns something, it is always present somewhere in memory.
  d. Memory skills develop far earlier in life than learning skills, and there is evidence that we actually have memories from as far back as the moment we are conceived.

4. Changes in our lives that result from heredity rather than our personal experiences are called _____.
  a. development
  b. learning
  c. typographic changes
  d. maturation

It Makes Your Mouth Water: Classical Conditioning

In the early 1900s, research scientists were unhappy with psychology's focus on mental activity. **L I N K** to Learning Objective 1.3. Many were looking for a way to bring some kind of objectivity and scientific research to the field. It was a Russian *physiologist* (a person who studies the workings of the body) named Ivan Pavlov (1849–1936) who pioneered the empirical study of the basic principles of a particular kind of learning (Pavlov, 1906, 1926).

PAVLOV AND THE SALIVATING DOGS

5.2 **Describe and explain the origins of classical conditioning and its important elements.**

Studying the digestive system in his dogs, Pavlov had built a device that would accurately measure the amount of saliva produced by the dogs when they were fed a measured amount of food. Normally, when food is placed in the mouth of any animal, the salivary glands automatically start releasing saliva to help with chewing and digestion. This is a normal **reflex**—an unlearned, involuntary* response that is not under personal control or choice—one of many that occur in both animals and humans. The food causes the particular reaction of salivation. A *stimulus* can be defined as any object, event, or experience that causes a *response*, the reaction of an organism. In the case of Pavlov's dogs, the food is the stimulus and salivation is the response.

Pavlov soon discovered that his dogs began salivating when they weren't supposed to be salivating. Some dogs would start salivating when they saw the lab assistant bringing their food, others when they heard the clatter of the food bowl from the kitchen, and still others when it was the time of day they were usually fed. Pavlov spent the rest of his career studying what eventually he termed **classical conditioning**, learning to elicit*

---

*involuntary: not under personal control or choice.
*elicit: to draw forth.

Dr. Ivan Pavlov and students working in his laboratory. Pavlov, a Russian physiologist, was the first to study and write about the basic principles of classical conditioning.

an involuntary, reflex-like response to a stimulus other than the original, natural stimulus that normally produces it.

Pavlov eventually identified several key elements that must be present and experienced in a particular way for conditioning to take place.

UNCONDITIONED STIMULUS   The original, naturally occurring stimulus mentioned in the preceding paragraph is called the **unconditioned stimulus (UCS)**. The term *unconditioned* means "unlearned" or "naturally occurring." This is the stimulus that ordinarily leads to the involuntary response. In the case of Pavlov's dogs, the food is the unconditioned stimulus.

UNCONDITIONED RESPONSE   The automatic and involuntary response to the unconditioned stimulus is called the **unconditioned response (UCR)** for much the same reason. It is unlearned and occurs because of genetic "wiring" in the nervous system. For example, in Pavlov's experiment, the salivation to that food is the UCR (unconditioned response).

CONDITIONED STIMULUS   Pavlov determined that almost any kind of stimulus could become associated with the unconditioned stimulus (UCS) if it is paired with the UCS often enough. In his original study, for example, the sight of the food dish itself became a stimulus for salivation *before* the food was given to the dogs. Every time they got food (to which they automatically salivated), they saw the dish. At this point, the dish was called a **neutral stimulus (NS)** because it had no effect on salivation. After being paired with the food so many times, the dish came to produce the same salivation response, although a somewhat weaker one, as did the food itself. When a previously neutral stimulus, through repeated pairing with the unconditioned stimulus, begins to cause the same kind of involuntary response, learning has occurred. The neutral stimulus can now be called a **conditioned stimulus (CS)**. (*Unconditioned* means "unlearned," and *conditioned* means "learned.")

CONDITIONED RESPONSE   The response that is given to the CS (conditioned stimulus) is not usually quite as strong as the original unconditioned response (UCR), but it is essentially the same response. However, because it comes as a response to the conditioned stimulus (CS), it is called the **conditioned response (CR)**.

PUTTING IT ALL TOGETHER: PAVLOV'S CANINE CLASSIC, OR TICK TOCK, TICK TOCK
Pavlov did a classic experiment in which he paired the ticking sound of a metronome (a simple device that produces a rhythmic ticking sound) with the presentation of food to see if the dogs would eventually salivate at the sound of the metronome (Pavlov, 1927). Since the metronome's ticking did not normally produce salivation, it was a neutral stimulus (NS) before any conditioning took place. The repeated pairing of a NS and the UCS (unconditioned stimulus) is usually called *acquisition*, because the organism is in the process of acquiring learning. **Figure 5.1** is a chart of how each element of the conditioning relationship worked in Pavlov's experiment.

Notice that the responses, CR (conditioned response) and UCR (unconditioned response), are the same—salivation. They simply differ in what they are the response *to*. An *unconditioned* stimulus (UCS) is always followed by an *unconditioned* response (UCR), and a *conditioned* stimulus (CS) is always followed by a *conditioned* response (CR).

Is this rocket science? No, not really. Classical conditioning is actually one of the simplest forms of learning. It's so simple that it happens to people all the time without them even being aware of it. Does your mouth water when you merely *see* an advertisement for your favorite food on television? Does your stomach get upset every time you hear the high-pitched whine of the dentist's drill? These are both examples of classical conditioning.

After all the dog stories, the salivation to the TV ad probably needs no explanation, but what about the dentist's drill? Over the course of many visits, the body comes to associate that sound (CS) with the anxiety or fear (UCR) the person has felt while receiving a painful dental treatment (UCS), and so the sound produces a feeling of anxiety (CR) whether that person is in the chair or just in the outer waiting area.

Figure 5.1 CLASSICAL CONDITIONING

Before Conditioning

Neutral Stimulus
(NS) Metronome

No Salivation

During Conditioning

Neutral Stimulus
(NS) Metronome

Unconditioned Stimulus
(UCS) Food

Unconditioned Response
(UCR) Salivation

After Conditioning

Conditioned Stimulus
(CS) Metronome

Conditioned Response
(CR) Salivation

Before conditioning takes place, the sound of the metronome does not cause salivation and is a neutral stimulus, or NS. During conditioning, the sound of the metronome occurs just before the presentation of the food, the UCS. The food causes salivation, the UCR. When conditioning has occurred after several pairings of the metronome with the food, the metronome will begin to elicit a salivation response from the dog without any food. This is learning, and the sound of the metronome is now a CS and the salivation to the bell is the CR.

Although classical conditioning happens quite easily, there are a few basic principles that Pavlov and other researchers discovered (although we will see that there are a few exceptions to some of these principles):

1. The CS must come *before* the UCS. If Pavlov started the metronome just after he gave the dogs the food, they did not become conditioned (Rescorla, 1988).

2. The CS and UCS must come very close together in time—ideally, no more than 5 seconds apart. When Pavlov tried to stretch the time between the potential CS and the UCS to several minutes, no association or link between the two was made. Too much could happen in the longer interval of time to interfere with conditioning (Pavlov, 1926; Wasserman & Miller, 1997). Recent studies have found that the interstimulus interval (ISI, or the time between the CS and UCS) can vary depending on the nature of the conditioning task and even the organism being conditioned. In these studies, shorter ISIs (less than 500 milleseconds) have been found to be ideal for conditioning (Polewan et al., 2006).

3. The neutral stimulus must be paired with the UCS several times, often many times, before conditioning can take place (Pavlov, 1926).

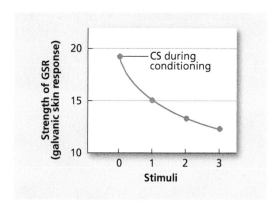

Figure 5.2 Strength of the Generalized Response

An example of stimulus generalization. The UCS was an electric shock and the UCR was the galvanic skin response (GSR), a measure associated with anxiety. The subjects had been conditioned originally to a CS tone (0) of a given frequency. When tested with the original tone, and with tones 1, 2, and 3 of differing frequencies, a clear generalization effect appeared. The closer the frequency of the test tone to the frequency of tone 0, the greater was the magnitude of the galvanic skin response to the tone (Hovland, 1937).

4. The CS is usually some stimulus that is distinctive* or stands out from other competing stimuli. The ticking was a sound that was not normally present in the laboratory and, therefore, distinct (Pavlov, 1926; Rescorla, 1988).

STIMULUS GENERALIZATION AND DISCRIMINATION Pavlov did find that similar sounds would produce the same conditioned response from his dogs. He and other researchers found that the strength of the response to the similar sounds was not as strong as to the original one, but the more similar the other sound was to the original sound (be it a metronome or any other kind of sound), the more similar the strength of the response was as well (Siegel, 1969). (See **Figure 5.2**.) The tendency to respond to a stimulus that is only similar to the original conditioned stimulus is called **stimulus generalization**. For example, a person who reacts with anxiety to the sound of a dentist's drill might react with some slight anxiety to a similar-sounding machine, such as an electric coffee grinder. Of course, Pavlov did not give the dogs any food after the similar ticking sound. It didn't take long for the dogs to stop responding (generalizing) to the "fake" ticking sounds altogether. Because only the real CS was followed with food, they learned to tell the difference, or *discriminate*, between the "fake" ticking and the CS ticking, a process called **stimulus discrimination**. Stimulus discrimination occurs when an organism learns to respond to different stimuli in different ways. For example, although the sound of the coffee grinder might produce a little anxiety in the dental-drill-hating person, after a few uses that sound will no longer produce anxiety because it isn't associated with dental pain.

EXTINCTION AND SPONTANEOUS RECOVERY What would have happened if Pavlov had stopped giving the dogs food after the real CS? Pavlov did just that, and the dogs gradually stopped salivating to the sound of the ticking. When the metronome's ticking (CS or conditioned stimulus) was repeatedly presented in the absence of the UCS (unconditioned stimulus or food, in this case), the salivation (CR or conditioned response) "died out" in a process called **extinction**.

Why does the removal of an unconditioned stimulus lead to extinction of the conditioned response? One theory is that the presentation of the CS alone leads to new learning. During extinction, the CS–UCS association that was learned is weakened, as the CS no longer predicts the UCS. In the case of Pavlov's dogs, through extinction they learned to not salivate to the metronome's ticking, as it no longer predicted that food was on its way.

Look back at Figure 5.1. Once conditioning is acquired, the conditioned stimulus (CS) and conditioned response (CR) will always come *before* the original unconditioned stimulus (UCS). The UCS, which comes after the CS and CR link, now serves as a strengthener, or reinforcer, of the CS–CR association. Remove that reinforcer, and the CR it strengthens will weaken and disappear—at least for a while.

The term *extinction* is a little unfortunate in that it seems to mean that the original conditioned response is totally gone, dead, never coming back, just like the dinosaurs. Remember that the definition of learning is any relatively *permanent* change in behavior. The fact is that once people learn something, it's almost impossible to "unlearn" it. People can learn new things that replace it or lose their way to it in memory, but it's still there. In the case of classical conditioning, this is easily demonstrated.

After extinguishing the conditioned salivation response in his dogs, Pavlov waited a few weeks, putting the conditioned stimulus (e.g., the metronome) away. There were no more training sessions, and the dogs were not exposed to the metronome's ticking in that time at all. But when Pavlov took the metronome back out and set it ticking, the dogs all began to salivate, although it was a fairly weak response and didn't last very long. This brief recovery of the conditioned response proves that the CR is "still in there" somewhere (remember, learning is *relatively permanent*). It is just suppressed or inhibited by the lack of an association with the unconditioned stimulus of food (which is no longer reinforcing or strengthening the CR). As time passes, this inhibition weakens, especially if the original

*distinctive: separate, having a different quality from something else.

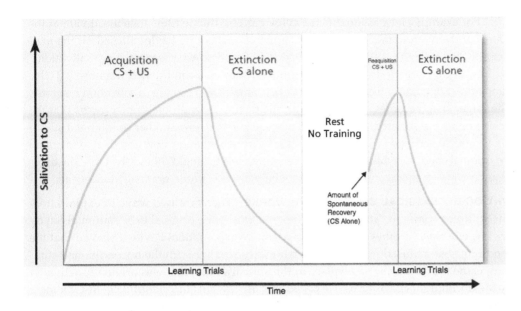

Figure 5.3   Extinction and
Spontaneous Recovery

This graph shows the acquisition, extinction, spontaneous recovery, and reacquisition of a conditioned salivary response. Typically, the measure of conditioning is the number of drops of saliva elicited by the CS on each trial. Note that on the day following extinction, the first presentation of the CS elicits quite a large response. This response is due to spontaneous recovery.

conditioned stimulus has not been present for a while. In **spontaneous recovery** the conditioned response can briefly reappear when the original CS returns, although the response is usually weak and short-lived. See **Figure 5.3** for a graph showing both extinction and spontaneous recovery. People experience classical conditioning in many ways. People who are allergic to cats sometimes sneeze when they see a *picture* of a cat.

HIGHER-ORDER CONDITIONING   Another concept in classical conditioning is **higher-order conditioning** (see **Figure 5.4**). This occurs when a strong conditioned stimulus is paired with a neutral stimulus. The strong CS can actually play the part of a UCS, and the previously neutral stimulus becomes a *second* conditioned stimulus.

Figure 5.4 HIGHER-ORDER CONDITIONING

In Stage 1, a strong salivation response is conditioned to occur to the sound of the metronome (CS_1). In Stage 2, finger snapping (NS) is repeatedly paired with the ticking of the metronome (CS_1) until the dog begins to salivate to the finger snapping alone (now CS_2). This is called higher-order conditioning because one CS is used to create another, "higher" CS.

For example, let's assume that Pavlov has conditioned his dogs to salivate at the sound of the metronome. What would happen if just before Pavlov turned on the metronome, he snapped his fingers? The sequence would now be "snap-ticking-salivation," or "NS-CS-CR" ("neutral stimulus/conditioned stimulus/conditioned response"). If this happens enough times, the finger snap will eventually also produce a salivation response. The finger snap becomes associated with the ticking through the same process that the ticking became associated with the food originally and is now another conditioned stimulus. Of course, the food (UCS) would have to be presented every now and then to maintain the original conditioned response to the metronome's ticking. Without the UCS, the higher-order conditioning would be difficult to maintain and would gradually fade away.

WHY DOES CLASSICAL CONDITIONING WORK?   There are two ways to explain how one stimulus comes to "stand in" for another. One is the original explanation given by Pavlov, whereas the other is based on a cognitive explanation. Pavlov believed that the conditioned stimulus, through its association close in time with the unconditioned stimulus, came to activate the same place in the animal's brain that was originally activated by the unconditioned stimulus. He called this process *stimulus substitution*. But if a mere association in time is all that is needed, why would conditioning *fail to happen* when the CS is presented immediately *after* the UCS?

Robert Rescorla (1988) found that the CS has to provide some kind of information about the coming of the UCS in order to achieve conditioning. In other words, the CS must predict that the UCS is coming. In one study, Rescorla exposed one group of rats to a tone, and just after the tone's onset and while the tone was still audible, an electric shock was administered for some of the tone presentations. Soon the rats became agitated* and reacted in fear by shivering and squealing at the onset of the tone, a kind of conditioned emotional response. With a second group of rats, Rescorla again sounded a tone but administered the electric shock only *after* the tone *stopped*, not while the tone was being heard. That group of rats responded with fear to the *stopping* of the tone (Rescorla, 1968; Rescorla & Wagner, 1972).

The tone for the second group of rats provided a different kind of information than the tone in the first instance. For the first group, the tone meant the shock was coming, whereas for the second group, the tone meant there was no shock while the tone was on. It was the particular *expectancy* created by pairing the tone or its absence with the shock that determined the particular response of the rats. Because this explanation involves the mental activity of consciously expecting something to occur, it is an example of an explanation for classical conditioning called the **cognitive perspective**.

CLASSICAL CONDITIONING APPLIED TO HUMAN BEHAVIOR

5.3 Define conditioned emotional responses, and explain conditioned taste aversions.

Later scientists took Pavlov's concepts and expanded them to explain not only animal behavior but also human behavior. One of the earliest of these studies showed that even an emotional response could be conditioned.

CONDITIONED EMOTIONAL RESPONSES: RATS!   In the first chapter of this text, John B. Watson's classic experiment with "Little Albert" and the white rat was discussed. This study was a demonstration of the classical conditioning of a phobia—an irrational fear response (Watson & Rayner, 1920).

Watson paired the presentation of the white rat to the baby with a loud, scary noise. Although the baby was not initially afraid of the rat, he was naturally afraid of the loud noise and started to cry. Soon, every time the baby saw the rat, he started to cry. In conditioning terms, the loud noise was the UCS, the fear of the noise the UCR, the white rat became the CS, and the fear of the rat (the phobia) was the CR. (It should be pointed out that Watson didn't really "torture" the baby—Albert's fright was temporary. Of course,

After "Little Albert" had been conditioned to fear a white rat, he later demonstrated fear to a rabbit, a dog, a fur coat, and this mask worn by Watson. Can you think of any emotional reactions you experience that might be classically conditioned emotional responses? Do you have any such reactions to similar situations or stimuli?

*agitated: excited, upset.

no ethics committee today would approve an experiment in which an infant experiences such psychological distress.)

Little Albert remains a topic of interest for many researchers and students of psychology alike. Researchers have suggested his true identity was Douglas Merritte, the son of a wet nurse at the hospital where the study took place (Beck & Irons, 2011; Beck et al., 2009). And, if in fact Little Albert was really Douglas Merritte, additional research has revealed that Douglas was neurologically impaired at the time he was tested by Watson and Rayner (due to hydrocephalus, brain infections, and serious allergic reactions) and sadly, later died at six years of age (Fridlund et al., 2012). And while Watson and Rayner's original study still prompts curiosity and controversy, so do the recent investigations, as not everyone believes that Little Albert's identity has been found (Harris, 2011; Powell, 2010; Reese, 2010).

The learning of phobias is a very good example of a certain type of classical conditioning, the **conditioned emotional response (CER)**. Conditioned emotional responses are some of the easiest forms of classical conditioning to accomplish, and our lives are full of them. It's easy to think of fears people might have that are conditioned or learned: a child's fear of the dentist's chair, a puppy's fear of a rolled-up newspaper, or the fear of dogs that is often shown by a person who has been attacked by a dog in the past. But other emotions can be conditioned, too.

The next time you watch television, watch the commercials closely. Advertisers often use certain objects or certain types of people in their ads to generate a specific emotional response in viewers, hoping that the emotional response will become associated with their product. Sexy models, cute little babies, and adorable puppies are some of the examples of stimuli the advertising world uses to tug at our heartstrings, so to speak.

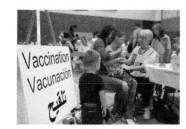

It is even possible to become classically conditioned by simply watching someone else respond to a stimulus in a process called **vicarious conditioning** (Bandura & Rosenthal, 1966; Hygge & Öhman, 1976; Jones & Menzies, 1995). Many years ago, children received vaccination shots in school. The nurse lined the children up, and one by one they had to go forward to get a needle in the arm. When some children received their shots, they cried quite a bit. By the time the nurse got near the end of the line of children, they were all crying—many of them before she ever touched needle to skin. They had learned their fear response from watching the reactions of the other children. The good news is that the same learning principles that can contribute to phobias and anxiety disorders can also be used to treat them, as we'll see in the video *Using Classical Conditioning to Treat Disorders*.

What kind of conditioning could be happening to the children who are waiting to get their vaccination?

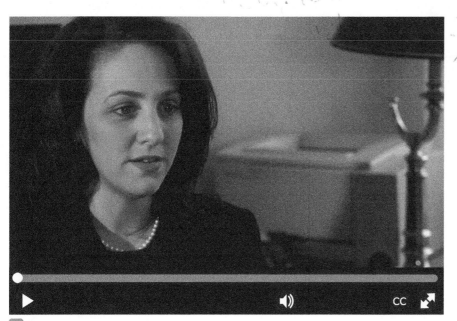

👁 **Watch** the **Video**, *Using Classical Conditioning to Treat Disorders.*

CONDITIONED TASTE AVERSIONS AND BIOLOGICAL PREPAREDNESS   Are there any foods that you just can't eat anymore because of a bad experience with them? Believe it or not, your reaction to that food is a kind of classical conditioning.

Many experiments have shown that laboratory rats will develop a **conditioned taste aversion** for any liquid or food they swallow up to 6 hours before becoming nauseated. Researchers (Garcia et al., 1989; Garcia & Koelling, 1966) found that rats that were given a sweetened liquid and then injected with a drug or exposed to radiation* that caused nausea would not touch the liquid again. In a similar manner, alcoholics who are given a drug to make them violently nauseated when they drink alcohol may learn to avoid drinking any alcoholic beverage. The chemotherapy drugs that cancer patients receive also can create severe nausea, which causes those people to develop a taste aversion for any food they have eaten before going in for the chemotherapy treatment (Berteretche et al., 2004).

💬 But I thought that it took several pairings of these stimuli to bring about conditioning. How can classical conditioning happen so fast?

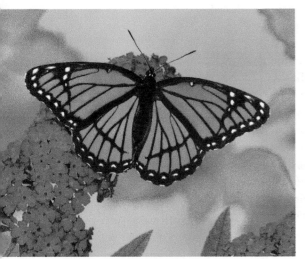

Conditioned taste aversions in nature. This moth is not poisonous to birds, but the monarch butterfly whose coloring the moth imitates is quite poisonous. Birds find their food by vision and will not eat anything that resembles the monarch.

It's interesting to note that birds, which find their food by sight, will avoid any object or insect that simply looks like the one that made them sick. There is a certain species of moth with coloring that mimics the monarch butterfly. That particular butterfly is poisonous to birds, but the moth isn't. The moth's mimicry causes birds to avoid eating it, even though it is quite edible. Whereas mammals are biologically prepared to associate taste with illness, birds are biologically prepared to associate visual characteristics with illness (Shapiro et al., 1980).

As for phobias, fear is a natural emotional response that has ties to survival—we need to remember what the fear-inducing stimuli are so we can safely avoid them in future. Nausea and fear are both examples of involuntary reactions that help organisms survive to reproduce and pass on their genetic material, so the innate tendency to make quick and strong associations between stimuli and these reactions has evolutionary importance.

Biological preparedness for fear of objects that are dangerous makes sense for survival, but when objects are not typically dangerous, it turns out to be very difficult to condition a fear of those objects. In one study, monkeys easily learned to be afraid of a toy snake or crocodile by watching videos of other monkeys reacting fearfully to these stimuli (a good example of vicarious conditioning). But the monkeys never learned to fear flowers or a toy rabbit by the same means (Cook & Mineka, 1989). Snakes and crocodiles are predators; flowers and rabbits are not.

WRITING PROMPT

Do you think that humans are as controlled by their biology as other animals?

▶ | The response entered here will be saved to your notes and may be collected by your instructor if he/she requires it.

[Submit]

---

*radiation: beams of energy.

Concept Map L.O. 5.2, 5.3

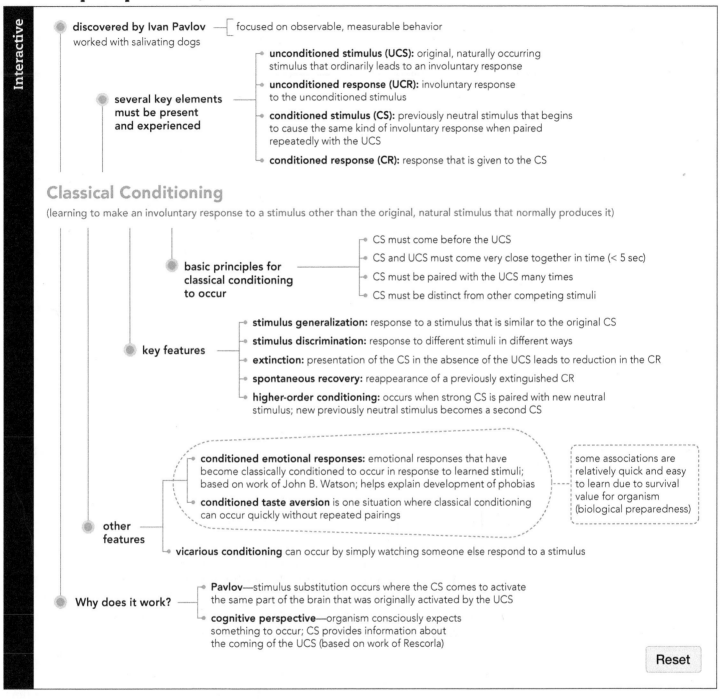

Interactive

● **discovered by Ivan Pavlov** — focused on observable, measurable behavior
worked with salivating dogs

● **several key elements must be present and experienced**
- **unconditioned stimulus (UCS):** original, naturally occurring stimulus that ordinarily leads to an involuntary response
- **unconditioned response (UCR):** involuntary response to the unconditioned stimulus
- **conditioned stimulus (CS):** previously neutral stimulus that begins to cause the same kind of involuntary response when paired repeatedly with the UCS
- **conditioned response (CR):** response that is given to the CS

Classical Conditioning
(learning to make an involuntary response to a stimulus other than the original, natural stimulus that normally produces it)

● **basic principles for classical conditioning to occur**
- CS must come before the UCS
- CS and UCS must come very close together in time (< 5 sec)
- CS must be paired with the UCS many times
- CS must be distinct from other competing stimuli

● **key features**
- **stimulus generalization:** response to a stimulus that is similar to the original CS
- **stimulus discrimination:** response to different stimuli in different ways
- **extinction:** presentation of the CS in the absence of the UCS leads to reduction in the CR
- **spontaneous recovery:** reappearance of a previously extinguished CR
- **higher-order conditioning:** occurs when strong CS is paired with new neutral stimulus; new previously neutral stimulus becomes a second CS

● **other features**
- **conditioned emotional responses:** emotional responses that have become classically conditioned to occur in response to learned stimuli; based on work of John B. Watson; helps explain development of phobias
- **conditioned taste aversion** is one situation where classical conditioning can occur quickly without repeated pairings

  some associations are relatively quick and easy to learn due to survival value for organism (biological preparedness)

- **vicarious conditioning** can occur by simply watching someone else respond to a stimulus

● **Why does it work?**
- **Pavlov**—stimulus substitution occurs where the CS comes to activate the same part of the brain that was originally activated by the UCS
- **cognitive perspective**—organism consciously expects something to occur; CS provides information about the coming of the UCS (based on work of Rescorla)

Reset

Practice Quiz   How much do you remember? ANSWERS ON PAGE AK-1.

Pick the best answer.

1. Michael noticed that whenever he moved his dog's food dish, his dog would come into the kitchen and act hungry and excited. He reasoned that because he feeds the dog using that dish, the sound of the dish had become a(n)
   a. unconditioned stimulus.
   b. conditioned stimulus.
   c. unconditioned response.
   d. conditioned response.

2. Which of the following statements is essential to classical conditioning?
   a. The CS and UCS must come close together in time.
   b. The CS must come immediately after the CR.
   c. The neutral stimulus and UCR must be paired several times before conditioning takes place.
   d. The CS should be something highly unusual.

(continued)

3. Ever since she was scared by a dog as a young child, Angelica has been afraid of all dogs. The fact that she is not only afraid of the original dog but all types of dogs is an example of

   a. extinction.

   b. spontaneous recovery.

   c. stimulus discrimination.

   d. stimulus generalization.

4. Helen has overcome her fear of toy snakes. However, on one occasion her fear returned when she found a toy snake in the cushions of her couch. Such a reaction is called

   a. spontaneous recovery.

   b. higher-order conditioning.

   c. extinction.

   d. stimulus generalization.

5. In Watson's experiment with "Little Albert," the conditioned stimulus was

   a. the white rat.

   b. the loud noise.

   c. the fear of the rat.

   d. the fear of the noise.

6. Cindy had cheesy tacos at a local Mexican restaurant. Later she became terribly ill and suffered bouts of nausea and vomiting. What might we predict based on conditioned taste aversion research?

   a. Cindy will probably develop a strong liking for cheesy tacos.

   b. Cindy will probably be able to eat cheesy tacos with no nausea at all.

   c. Cindy will probably get nauseated the next time she tries to eat cheesy tacos.

   d. Cindy will probably continue to eat cheesy tacos except when she feels nauseous.

7. Rescorla found that the CS must _____ the UCS for conditioning to take place.

   a. replace

   b. come after

   c. come at the same time as

   d. predict

What's in It for Me? Operant Conditioning

 So far, all learning seems to involve involuntary behavior, but I know that I am more than just automatic responses. People do things on purpose, so is that kind of behavior also learned?

All organisms are capable of two kinds of behavior: involuntary and voluntary. If Inez blinks her eyes because a gnat flies close to them, that's a reflex and totally involuntary. But if she then swats at the gnat to frighten it, that's a voluntary choice. She *had* to blink, but she *chose* to swat.

Classical conditioning is the kind of learning that occurs with automatic, involuntary behavior. The kind of learning that applies to voluntary behavior is called *operant conditioning*, which is both different from and similar to classical conditioning.

THE CONTRIBUTIONS OF THORNDIKE AND SKINNER

5.4 **Describe the theory of operant conditioning and how it differs from classical conditioning, and explain the contributions of Thorndike and Skinner.**

While classical conditioning involves the learning of involuntary, automatic responses, operant conditioning is about how organisms learn voluntary responses. **Operant conditioning** is based on the research of Edward L. Thorndike and B. F. Skinner.

FRUSTRATING CATS: THORNDIKE'S PUZZLE BOX AND THE LAW OF EFFECT   Edward L. Thorndike (1874–1949) was one of the first researchers to explore and attempt to outline the laws of learning voluntary responses, although the field was not yet called operant conditioning. Thorndike placed a hungry cat inside a "puzzle box" from which the only escape was to press a lever located on the floor of the box. Thorndike placed a dish of food *outside* the box, so that the hungry cat would be highly motivated to get out. Thorndike observed that the cat would move around the box, pushing and rubbing up against the walls in an effort to escape. Eventually, the cat would accidentally push the lever, opening the door. Upon escaping, the cat was fed from a dish placed just outside the box. The lever is the stimulus, the pushing of the lever is the response, and the consequence is both escape (good) and food (even better).

The cat did not learn to push the lever and escape right away. After a number of trials (and many errors) in a box like this one, the cat took less and less time to push the lever that would open the door (see **Figure 5.5**). It's important not to assume that the cat had "figured out" the connection between the lever and freedom—Thorndike kept moving the lever to a different position, and the cat had to learn the whole process over again. The cat would simply continue to rub and push in the same general area that led to food and freedom the last time, each time getting out and fed a little more quickly.

Based on this research, Thorndike developed the **law of effect**: If an action is followed by a pleasurable consequence, it will tend to be repeated. If an action is followed by an unpleasant consequence, it will tend not to be repeated (Thorndike, 1911). This is the basic principle behind learning voluntary behavior. In the case of the cat in the box, pushing the lever was followed by a pleasurable consequence (getting out and getting fed), so pushing the lever became a repeated response.

💬 So did Thorndike call this operant conditioning?

No, but Thorndike's important and groundbreaking work began the study of what would eventually become *operant conditioning*.

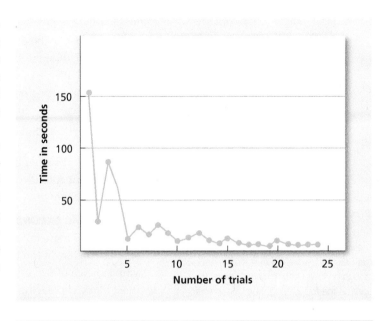

Figure 5.5   Graph of the Time to Learn in Thorndike's Experiment

This is one of the earliest "learning curves" in the history of the experimental study of conditioning. The time required by one of Thorndike's cats to escape from the puzzle box gradually decreased with trials but with obvious reversals.

B. F. SKINNER: THE BEHAVIORIST'S BEHAVIORIST   B. F. Skinner (1904–1990) was the behaviorist who assumed leadership of the field after John Watson. He was even more determined than Watson that psychologists should study only measurable, observable behavior. In addition to his knowledge of Pavlovian classical conditioning, Skinner found in the work of Thorndike a way to explain all behavior as the product of learning. He even gave the learning of voluntary behavior a special name: operant conditioning (Skinner, 1938). Voluntary behavior is what people and animals do to *operate* in the world. When people perform a voluntary action, it is to get something they want or avoid something they don't want, right? So voluntary behavior, for Skinner, is **operant** behavior, and the learning of such behavior is operant conditioning.

The heart of operant conditioning is the effect of consequences on behavior. Thinking back to the section on classical conditioning, learning an involuntary behavior really depends on what comes *before* the response—the unconditioned stimulus and what will become the conditioned stimulus. These two stimuli are the *antecedent* stimuli (antecedent means something that comes before another thing). But in operant conditioning, learning depends on what happens *after* the response—the consequence. In a way, operant conditioning could be summed up as this: "If I do this, what's in it for me?"

THE CONCEPT OF REINFORCEMENT

5.5 **Differentiate between primary and secondary reinforcers and the processes of positive and negative reinforcement.**

"What's in it for me?" represents the concept of **reinforcement**, one of Skinner's major contributions to behaviorism. The word itself means "to strengthen," and Skinner defined reinforcement as anything that, when following a response, causes that response to be more likely to happen again. Typically, this means that reinforcement is a consequence that is in some way pleasurable to the organism, which relates back to Thorndike's law of effect. The "pleasurable consequence" is what's in it for the organism. (Keep in mind that a "pleasurable consequence" might be something like getting food or money when you need it, but it might also mean *avoiding* a tiresome chore,

Dr. Wayne Mitchell

Missouri State Psychology Department

Operant Psychology: Research with Infants

Figure 5.6 A Typical Skinner Box

This rat is learning to press the bar in the wall of the cage in order to get food (delivered a few pellets at a time in the food trough on lower left). In some cases, the light on the top left might be turned on to indicate that pressing the bar will lead to food or to warn of an impending shock delivered by the grate on the floor of the cage.

like doing the dishes or taking out the garbage. I'll do almost anything to get out of doing the dishes, myself!)

Going back to Thorndike's puzzle box research, what was "in it" for the cat? We can see that the escape from the box and the food that the cat received after getting out are both *reinforcement* of the lever-pushing response. Every time the cat got out of the box, it got reinforced for doing so. In Skinner's view, this reinforcement is the reason that the cat learned anything at all. In operant conditioning, reinforcement is the key to learning.

Skinner had his own version of a puzzle box called a "Skinner box" or "operant conditioning chamber" (see **Figure 5.6**). His early research often involved placing a rat into one of these chambers and training it to push down on a bar to get food.

PRIMARY AND SECONDARY REINFORCERS   The events or items that can be used to reinforce behavior are not all alike. Let's say that a friend of yours asks you to help her move some books from the trunk of her car to her apartment on the second floor. She offers you a choice of $25 or a candy bar. Unless you've suffered recent brain damage, you'll most likely choose the money, right? With $25, you could buy more than one candy bar. (At today's prices, you might even be able to afford three.)

Now pretend that your friend offers the same deal to a 3-year-old child who lives downstairs for carrying up some of the paperback books: $25 or a candy bar. Which reward will the child more likely choose? Most children at that age have no real idea of the value of money, so the child will probably choose the candy bar. The money and the candy bar represent two basic kinds of **reinforcers**, items or events that when following a response will strengthen it. The reinforcing properties of money must be learned, but candy gives immediate reward in the form of taste and satisfying hunger.

A reinforcer such as a candy bar that satisfies a basic need like hunger is called a **primary reinforcer**. Examples would be any kind of food (hunger drive), liquid (thirst drive), or touch (pleasure drive). Infants, toddlers, preschool-age children, and animals can be easily reinforced by using primary reinforcers. (It's not a good idea, however, to start thinking of reinforcers as rewards—freedom from pain is also a basic need, so pain itself can be a primary reinforcer when it is *removed*. Removal of a painful stimulus fills a basic need just as eating food when hungry fills the hunger need.)

A **secondary reinforcer** such as money, however, gets its reinforcing properties from being associated with primary reinforcers in the past. A child who is given money to spend soon realizes that the ugly green paper can be traded for candy and treats—primary reinforcers—and so money becomes reinforcing in and of itself. If a person praises a puppy while petting him (touch, a primary reinforcer), the praise alone will eventually make the puppy squirm with delight.

 That sounds very familiar. Isn't this related to classical conditioning?

Secondary reinforcers do indeed get their reinforcing power from the process of classical conditioning. After all, the pleasure people feel when they eat, drink, or get a back rub is an automatic response, and any automatic response can be classically conditioned to occur to a new stimulus. In the case of money, the candy is a UCS for pleasure (the UCR), and the money is present just before the candy is obtained. The money becomes a CS for pleasure, and people certainly do feel pleasure when they have a lot of that green stuff, don't they?

In the case of the puppy, the petting is the UCS, the pleasure at being touched and petted is the UCR. The praise, or more specifically the tone of voice, becomes the CS for pleasure. Although classical and operant conditioning often "work together," as in the

Table 5.1 Comparing Two Kinds of Conditioning

Operant Conditioning	Classical Conditioning
End result is an increase in the rate of an already occurring response.	End result is the creation of a new response to a stimulus that did not normally produce that response.
Responses are voluntary, emitted by the organism.	Responses are involuntary and automatic, elicited by a stimulus.
Consequences are important in forming an association.	Antecedent stimuli are important in forming an association.
Reinforcement should be immediate.	CS must occur immediately before the UCS.
An expectancy develops for reinforcement to follow a correct response.	An expectancy develops for UCS to follow CS.

creation of secondary reinforcers, they are two different processes. **Table 5.1** presents a brief look at how the two types of conditioning differ from each other.

POSITIVE AND NEGATIVE REINFORCEMENT   Reinforcers can also differ in the way they are used. Most people have no trouble at all understanding that following a response with some kind of pleasurable consequence (like a reward) will lead to an increase in the likelihood of that response being repeated. This is called **positive reinforcement**, the reinforcement of a response by the *addition* or experience of a pleasurable consequence, such as a reward or a pat on the back. But many people have trouble understanding that the opposite is also true: Following a response with *the removal or escape* from something *unpleasant* will also increase the likelihood of that response being repeated—a process called **negative reinforcement**. Remember the idea that pain can be a reinforcer if it is removed? If a person's behavior gets pain to stop, the person is much more likely to do that same thing again—which is part of the reason people can get addicted to painkilling medication. (We'll discuss the concepts of positive and negative reinforcement in more detail later on.)

We've discussed what reinforcement is and how it affects the behavior that follows the reinforcement. In the next section we'll discuss the different ways in which reinforcement can be administered as well as the difference between reinforcement and punishment. We'll also look at the role of the stimuli that come *before* the behavior that is to be reinforced and a few other operant conditioning concepts.

SCHEDULES OF REINFORCEMENT: WHY THE ONE-ARMED BANDIT IS SO SEDUCTIVE

5.6 Distinguish among the schedules of reinforcement.

The timing of reinforcement can make a tremendous difference in the speed at which learning occurs and the strength of the learned response. However, Skinner (1956) found that reinforcing every response was not necessarily the best schedule of reinforcement for long-lasting learning as we'll see in the video, *Schedules of Reinforcement.*

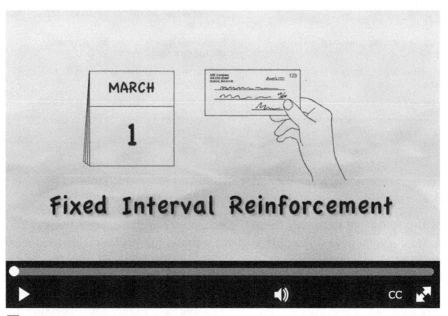

👁 **Watch** the **Video**, *Schedules of Reinforcement.*

THE PARTIAL REINFORCEMENT EFFECT Alicia's mother gives her a quarter every night she remembers to put her dirty clothes in the clothes hamper. Bianca's mother gives her a dollar at the end of the week, but only if Bianca has put her clothes in the hamper every night. Alicia learns more quickly than does Bianca because responses that are reinforced each time they occur are more easily and quickly learned. After a time, the mothers stop giving the girls the money. Which child will stop putting her clothes in the hamper more quickly?

The answer might be surprising. It will more likely be Alicia, who has expected to get a reinforcer (the quarter) after *every single response.* As soon as the reinforcers stop, the behavior extinguishes. Bianca has expected to get a reinforcer only after *seven correct responses.* When the reinforcers stop, Bianca might continue to put the clothes in the hamper for several more days or even another whole week, hoping that the reinforcer will eventually come anyway. Bianca may have learned more slowly than Alicia, but once she learned the connection between putting her clothes in the hamper and getting that dollar, she was less likely to stop doing it—even when her mother failed to give the dollar as expected.

Bianca's behavior illustrates the **partial reinforcement effect** (Skinner, 1956): A response that is reinforced after some, but not all, correct responses will be more resistant to extinction than a response that receives **continuous reinforcement** (a reinforcer for each and every correct response). Although it may be easier to teach a new behavior using continuous reinforcement, partially reinforced behavior is not only more difficult to suppress but also more like real life. Imagine being paid for every hamburger you make or every report you turn in. In the real world, people tend to receive partial reinforcement rather than continuous reinforcement for their work.

Partial reinforcement can be accomplished according to different patterns or schedules. For example, it might be a certain interval of time that's important, such as an office safe that can only be opened at a certain time of day. It wouldn't matter how many times one tried to open the safe if the effort didn't come at the right *time.* On the other hand, it may be the number of responses that is important, as it would be if one had to sell

"Remember, every time he gives you a pellet, reinforce that behavior by pulling the lever."

a certain number of raffle tickets in order to get a prize. When the timing of the response is more important, it is called an *interval schedule*. When it is the number of responses that is important, the schedule is called a *ratio schedule* because a certain number of responses is required for each reinforcer (e.g., 50 raffle tickets for each prize). The other way in which schedules of reinforcement can differ is in whether the number of responses or interval of time is *fixed* (the same in each case) or *variable* (a different number or interval is required in each case). So it is possible to have a fixed interval schedule, a variable interval schedule, a fixed ratio schedule, and a variable ratio schedule (Skinner, 1961).

FIXED INTERVAL SCHEDULE OF REINFORCEMENT The kind of reinforcement schedule most people are more familiar with is called a **fixed interval schedule of reinforcement**, in which a reinforcer is received after a certain, fixed interval of time has passed. If Professor Conner were teaching a rat to press a lever to get food pellets, she might require it to push the lever for 2 minutes to get a pellet. It wouldn't matter how many times the rat pushed the bar press, it would only get the pellet after 2 minutes had passed. If people receive a paycheck once every two weeks (provided that they show up to work in those two weeks), they are being reinforced on this kind of schedule.

As shown in **Figure 5.7**, a fixed interval schedule of reinforcement does not produce a fast rate of responding (notice that the line doesn't go "up" as fast as in the blue fixed ratio line). Since it only matters that at least *one* response is made *during* the specific interval of time, speed is not that important. Eventually, the rat will start pushing the lever only as the interval of time nears its end, causing the *scalloping* effect you see in

Figure 5.7 SCHEDULES OF REINFORCEMENT

There are four schedules of reinforcement, each with its own typical pattern of responding. The responses are cumulative, which means new responses are added to those that come before, and all graphs begin after the learned pattern is well established. Slash marks mean that a reinforcement has been given.

Click on the colored legend boxes to see the pattern of responding with each schedule of reinforcement.

Fixed Interval

Variable Interval

Fixed Ratio

Variable Ratio

The four colored lines show the typical pattern of responding for both fixed and variable interval and ratio schedules of reinforcement. In both the fixed interval and fixed ratio schedules, there is a pause after each reinforcement as the learner briefly "rests." The "scalloped" shape of the fixed interval curve is a typical indicator of this pause, as is the stair-step shape of the fixed ratio curve. In the variable interval and ratio schedules, no such pause occurs, because the reinforcements are unpredictable. Notice that both fixed and variable interval schedules are slower (less steep) than the two ratio schedules because of the need to respond as quickly as possible in the ratio schedules.

the graph. The response rate goes up just before the reinforcer and then drops off immediately after, until it is almost time for the next food pellet. This is similar to the way in which factory workers speed up production just before payday and slow down just after payday (Critchfield et al., 2003).

Paychecks aren't the only kind of fixed schedule that people experience. When do you study the hardest? Isn't it right before a test? If you know when the test is to be given, that's like having a fixed interval of time that is predictable, and you can save your greatest studying efforts until closer to the exam. (Some students save *all* of their studying for the night before the exam, which is not exactly the best strategy.) Another example of a fixed interval schedule would be the way that most people floss and brush their teeth most rigorously* the few days before their next dental exam. In this case, they are probably hoping for negative reinforcement. The cleaner they get their teeth before the appointment, the less time they might have to spend in that chair.

 So if a scheduled test is a fixed interval, then would a pop quiz be a variable interval schedule?

VARIABLE INTERVAL SCHEDULE OF REINFORCEMENT   Pop quizzes are unpredictable. Students don't know exactly what day they might be given a pop quiz, so the best strategy is to study a little every night just in case there is a quiz the next day. Pop quizzes are good examples of a **variable interval schedule of reinforcement**. The interval of time after which the organism must respond in order to receive a reinforcer changes from one time to the next. In a more basic example, a rat might receive a food pellet when it pushes a lever, every 5 minutes on average. Sometimes the interval might be 2 minutes, sometimes 10, but the rat must push the lever at least once *during* that interval to get the pellet. Because the rat can't predict how long the interval is going to be, it pushes the bar more or less continuously, producing the smooth graph in Figure 5.7. Once again, speed is not important, so the rate of responding is slow but steady.

Another example of a variable interval schedule might be the kind of fishing in which people put the pole in the water and wait—and wait, and wait, until a fish takes the bait—if they are lucky. They only have to put the pole in once, but they might refrain from taking it out for fear that just when they do, the biggest fish in the world would swim by. Dialing a busy phone number is also this kind of schedule, as people don't know *when* the call will go through, so they keep dialing and dialing.

FIXED RATIO SCHEDULE OF REINFORCEMENT   In ratio schedules, it is the number of responses that counts. In a **fixed ratio schedule of reinforcement**, the number of responses required to receive each reinforcer will always be the same number.

Notice two things about the fixed ratio graph in Figure 5.7. The rate of responding is very fast, especially when compared to the fixed interval schedule, and there are little "breaks" in the response pattern immediately after a reinforcer is given. The rapid response rate occurs because the rat wants to get to the next reinforcer just as fast as possible, and the number of lever pushes counts. The pauses or breaks come right after a reinforcer, because the rat knows "about how many" lever pushes will be needed to get to the next reinforcer because it's always the same. Fixed schedules—both ratio and interval—are predictable, which allows rest breaks.

In human terms, anyone who does piecework, in which a certain number of items have to be completed before payment is given, is reinforced on a fixed ratio schedule. Some sandwich shops give out punch cards that get punched one time for each sandwich purchased. When the card has 10 punches, for example, the person might get a free sandwich.

When people go fishing, they never know how long they may have to dangle the bait in the water before snagging a fish. This is an example of a variable interval schedule of reinforcement and explains why some people, such as this father and son, are reluctant to pack up and go home.

---

*rigorously: strictly, consistently.

VARIABLE RATIO SCHEDULE OF REINFORCEMENT

💬 The purple line in Figure 5.7 is also very fast, but it's much smoother, like the variable interval graph. Why are they similar?

A **variable ratio schedule of reinforcement** is one in which the number of responses changes from one trial to the next. In the rat example, the rat might be expected to push the bar an average of 20 times to get reinforcement. That means that sometimes the rat would push the lever only 10 times before a reinforcer comes, but at other times it might take 30 lever pushes or more.

Figure 5.7 shows a purple line that is just as rapid a response rate as the fixed ratio schedule because the *number* of responses still matters. But the graph is much smoother because the rat is taking no rest breaks. It can't afford to do so because it *doesn't know* how many times it may have to push that lever to get the next food pellet. It pushes as fast as it can and eats while pushing. It is the *unpredictability* of the variable schedule that makes the responses more or less continuous—just as in a variable interval schedule.

In human terms, people who shove money into the one-armed bandit, or slot machine, are being reinforced on a variable ratio schedule of reinforcement (they hope). They put their coins in (response), but they don't know how many times they will have to do this before reinforcement (the jackpot) comes. People who do this tend to sit there until they either win or run out of money. They don't dare stop because the "next one" might hit that jackpot. Buying lottery tickets is much the same thing, as is any kind of gambling. People don't know how many tickets they will have to buy, and they're afraid that if they don't buy the next one, that will be the ticket that would have won, so they keep buying and buying.

Regardless of the schedule of reinforcement one uses, there are some things that can be done to make using reinforcement of a behavior as effective as possible. One thing also concerns timing: A reinforcer should be given as immediately as possible after the desired behavior. Delaying reinforcement tends not to work well, especially when dealing with animals and small children. (Older children and adults can think about future reinforcements, such as saving up one's money to buy a highly desired item, so delayed reinforcement can work with them.) Care should also be taken to reinforce *only* the desired behavior—for example, many parents make the mistake of giving a child who has not done some chore the promised treat anyway, which completely undermines the child's learning of that chore or task.

THE ROLE OF PUNISHMENT IN OPERANT CONDITIONING

5.7 **Compare and contrast punishment with reinforcement, and list some of the problems associated with using punishment.**

💬 So I think I get reinforcement now, but what about punishment? How does punishment fit into the big picture?

Let's go back to the discussion of positive and negative reinforcement. These strategies are important for *increasing* the likelihood that the targeted behavior will occur again. But what about behavior that we do not want to reoccur?

DEFINING PUNISHMENT **Punishment** is actually the opposite of reinforcement. It is any event or stimulus that, when following a response, causes that response to be less likely to happen again. Punishment *weakens* responses, whereas reinforcement (no matter whether it is positive or negative) *strengthens* responses. Let's look at these two concepts in more detail.

Table 5.2 Four Ways to Modify Behavior	Reinforcement	Punishment
Positive (Adding)	Something valued or desirable	Something unpleasant
	Positive Reinforcement	Punishment by Application
	Example: getting a gold star for good behavior in school	Example: getting a spanking for disobeying
Negative (Removing/Avoiding)	Something unpleasant	Something valued or desirable
	Negative Reinforcement	Punishment by Removal
	Example: fastening a seat belt to stop the alarm from sounding	Example: losing a privilege such as going out with friends

People experience two kinds of things as consequences in the world: things they like (food, money, candy, sex, praise, and so on) and things they don't like (spankings, being yelled at, and experiencing any kind of pain, to name a few). In addition, people experience these two kinds of consequences in one of two ways: Either people experience them directly (such as getting money for working or getting yelled at for misbehaving) or they don't experience them, such as losing an allowance for misbehaving or avoiding a scolding by lying about misbehavior. These four consequences are named and described in **Table 5.2**.

First, take a look at the left column of Table 5.2, the one labeled "Reinforcement." Getting money for working is an example of *positive reinforcement*, the reinforcement of a response by the *addition* or experience of a *pleasurable* consequence, as mentioned earlier. That one everyone understands. But what about avoiding a penalty by turning one's income tax return in on time? That is an example of *negative reinforcement*, the reinforcement of a response by the *removal or escape* from an *unpleasant* consequence. Because the behavior (submitting the return before the deadline) results in *avoiding* an unpleasant stimulus (a penalty), the likelihood that the person will behave that way again (turn it in on time in the future) is *increased*—just as positive reinforcement will increase a behavior's likelihood. Examples are the best way to figure out the difference between these two types of reinforcement, so try to figure out which of the following examples would be positive reinforcement and which would be negative reinforcement:

1. Arnie's father nags him to wash his car. Arnie hates being nagged, so he washes the car so his father will stop nagging.

2. Trey learns that talking in a funny voice gets him lots of attention from his classmates, so now he talks that way often.

3. Allen is a server at a restaurant and always tries to smile and be pleasant because that seems to lead to bigger tips.

4. An Li turns her report in to her teacher on the day it is due because papers get marked down a letter grade for every day they are late.

Here are the answers:

1. Arnie is being negatively reinforced for washing his car because the nagging (unpleasant stimulus) stops when he does so.

2. Trey is getting positive reinforcement in the form of his classmates' attention.

3. Allen's smiling and pleasantness are positively reinforced by the customers' tips.

4. An Li is avoiding an unpleasant stimulus (the marked-down grade) by turning in her paper on time, which is an example of negative reinforcement.

TWO KINDS OF PUNISHMENT

💬 I'm confused—I thought taking something away was a kind of punishment?

People get confused because "negative" sounds like it ought to be something bad, like a kind of punishment. But negative reinforcement strengthens a response, while punishment weakens a response. There are two ways in which punishment can happen, just as there are two ways in which reinforcement can happen.

Now take a look at the right column of Table 5.2, labeled "Punishment." **Punishment by application** occurs when something unpleasant (such as a spanking, scolding, or other unpleasant stimulus) is added to the situation or *applied*. This is the kind of punishment that most people think of when they hear the word *punishment*. This is also the kind of punishment that many child development specialists strongly recommend parents avoid using with their children because it can easily escalate into abuse (Dubowitz & Bennett, 2007; Straus, 2000; Trocmé et al., 2001). A spanking might be *physically* harmless if it is only two or three swats with a hand, but if done in anger or with a belt or other instrument, it becomes abuse, both physical and emotional.

Punishment by removal, on the other hand, is the kind of punishment most often confused with negative reinforcement. In this type of punishment, behavior is punished by the removal of something pleasurable or desired after the behavior occurs. "Grounding" a teenager is removing the freedom to do what the teenager wants to do and is an example of this kind of punishment. Other examples would be placing a child in time-out (removing the attention of the others in the room), fining someone for disobeying the law (removing money), and punishing aggressive behavior by taking away television privileges. This type of punishment is far more acceptable to child development specialists because it involves no physical aggression and avoids many of the problems caused by more aggressive punishments.

The confusion over the difference between negative reinforcement and punishment by removal makes it worth examining the difference just a bit more. Negative reinforcement occurs when a response is followed by the *removal* of an *unpleasant* stimulus. If something unpleasant has just gone away as a consequence of that response, wouldn't that response tend to happen again and again? If the response increases, the consequence has to be a kind of *reinforcement*. The problem is that the name sounds like it should be some kind of punishment because of the word *negative*, and that's exactly the problem that many people experience when they are trying to understand negative reinforcement. They get negative reinforcement mixed up with punishment by removal, in which a *pleasant* thing is removed (like having your driver's license taken away because you caused a bad accident). Because something is removed (taken away) in both cases, people think that they will both have the effect of punishment, or weakening a response. The difference between them lies in *what* is taken away: In the case of negative reinforcement, it is an *unpleasant* thing; in the case of this particular form of punishment, it is a *pleasant* or desirable thing. For a head-to-head comparison of negative reinforcement and this particular type of punishment by removal, see **Table 5.3**.

This young girl's father is applying punishment by removal by forcing her to cut up her credit card.

Table 5.3 Negative Reinforcement Versus Punishment by Removal	
Example of Negative Reinforcement	**Example of Punishment by Removal**
Stopping at a red light to avoid getting in an accident.	Losing the privilege of driving because you got into too many accidents.
Mailing an income tax return by April 15 to avoid paying a penalty.	Having to lose some of your money to pay the penalty for late tax filing.
Obeying a parent before the parent reaches the count of "three" to avoid getting a scolding.	Being "grounded" (losing your freedom) because of disobedience.

PROBLEMS WITH PUNISHMENT   Although punishment can be effective in reducing or weakening a behavior, it has several drawbacks as explained in the video *Problems with Using Punishment.*

👁 **Watch** the **Video**, *Problems with Using Punishment.*

The job of punishment is much harder than that of reinforcement. In using reinforcement, all one has to do is strengthen a response that is already there. But punishment is used to weaken a response, and getting rid of a response that is already well established is not that easy. (Ask any parent or pet owner.) Many times punishment only serves to temporarily suppress or inhibit a behavior until enough time has passed. For example, punishing a child's bad behavior doesn't always eliminate the behavior completely. As time goes on, the punishment is forgotten, and the "bad" behavior may occur again in a kind of spontaneous recovery of the old (and probably pleasurable for the child) behavior.

Look back at Table 5.2 under the "Punishment" column. Punishment by application can be quite severe, and severe punishment does do one thing well: It stops the behavior immediately (Bucher & Lovaas, 1967; Carr & Lovass, 1983). It may not stop it permanently, but it does stop it. In a situation in which a child might be doing something dangerous or self-injurious, this kind of punishment is sometimes more acceptable (Duker & Seys, 1996). For example, if a child starts to run into a busy street, the parent might scream at the child to stop and then administer several rather severe swats to the child's rear. If this is not usual behavior on the part of the parent, the child will most likely never run into the street again.

Other than situations of immediately stopping dangerous behavior, severe punishment has too many drawbacks to be really useful. It should also be discouraged because of its potential for leading to abuse (Dubowitz & Bennett, 2007; Gershoff, 2000; Trocmé et al., 2001):

• Severe punishment may cause the child (or animal) to avoid the punisher instead of the behavior being punished, so the child (or animal) learns the wrong response.

• Severe punishment may encourage lying to avoid the punishment (a kind of negative reinforcement)—again, not the response that is desired.

- Severe punishment creates fear and anxiety, emotional responses that do not promote learning (Baumrind, 1997; Gershoff, 2000, 2002). If the point is to teach something, this kind of consequence isn't going to help.

- Hitting provides a successful model for aggression (Gershoff, 2000; Milner, 1992).

That last point is worth a bit more discussion. In using an aggressive type of punishment, such as spanking, the adult is actually modeling (presenting a behavior to be imitated by the child). After all, the adult is using aggression to get what the adult wants from the child. Children sometimes become more likely to use aggression to get what they want when they receive this kind of punishment (Bryan & Freed, 1982; Larzelere, 1986), and the adult has lost an opportunity to model a more appropriate way to deal with parent–child disagreements. Since aggressive punishment does tend to stop the undesirable behavior, at least for a while, the parent who is punishing actually experiences a kind of negative reinforcement: "When I spank, the unpleasant behavior goes away." This may increase the tendency to use aggressive punishment over other forms of discipline and could even lead to child abuse (Dubowitz & Bennett, 2007). Finally, some children are so desperate for attention from their parents that they will actually misbehave on purpose. The punishment is a form of attention, and these children will take whatever attention they can get, even negative attention.

Punishment by removal is less objectionable to many parents and educators and is the only kind of punishment that is permitted in many public schools. But this kind of punishment also has its drawbacks—it teaches the child what *not* to do but not what the child should do. Both punishment by removal and punishment by application are usually only temporary in their effect on behavior. After some time has passed, the behavior will most likely return as the memory of the punishment gets weaker, allowing spontaneous recovery.

🗨 If punishment doesn't work very well, what can a parent do to keep a child from behaving badly?

The way to make punishment more effective involves remembering a few simple rules:

1. **Punishment should immediately follow the behavior it is meant to punish.** If the punishment comes long after the behavior, it will not be associated with that behavior. (This is also true of reinforcement.)

2. **Punishment should be consistent.** This actually means two things. First, if the parent says that a certain punishment will follow a certain behavior, then the parent must make sure to follow through and do what he or she promised to do. Second, punishment for a particular behavior should stay at the same intensity or increase slightly but never decrease. For example, if a child is scolded for jumping on the bed the first time, the second time this behavior happens the child should also be punished by scolding or by a stronger penalty, such as removal of a favorite toy. But if the first misbehavior is punished by spanking and the second by only a scolding, the child learns to "gamble" with the possible punishment.

3. **Punishment of the wrong behavior should be paired, whenever possible, with reinforcement of the right behavior.** Instead of yelling at a 2-year-old for eating with her fingers, the parent should pull her hand gently out of her plate while saying something such as, "No, we do not eat with our fingers. We eat with our fork," and then placing the fork in the child's hand and praising her for using it. "See, you are doing such a good job with your fork. I'm so proud of you." Pairing punishment (the mild correction of pulling her hand away while saying "No, we do not eat with our fingers") with reinforcement allows parents (and others) to use a much milder punishment and still be effective. It also teaches the desired behavior rather than just suppressing the undesired one.

The following section discusses some very recent research on the problems that can be generated by a particular form of punishment by application: spanking.

Issues in Psychology

The Link between Spanking and Aggression in Young Children

To spank or not to spank has been a controversial issue for many years now. Child development experts have typically advised parents to use other methods of disciplining their children, citing the possibility of encouraging child abuse as well as the role spanking plays in the modeling of aggression. Now the results of a new study suggest that there is a significantly increased risk of higher levels of aggression at age 5 when spanking is used at age 3 (Taylor et al., 2010).

While older studies have found similar results, the study by Dr. Catherine Taylor and her colleagues, Drs. Jennifer Manganello, Shawna Lee, and Janet Rice, differs from those earlier studies in that possible maternal risk factors such as neglect, the mother's use of drugs, and maternal psychological problems were measured and controlled.

In this study, 2,461 mothers participated in reporting their use of spanking at age 3 as well as their children's aggressive behavior at age 3 and then 2 years later at age 5. Factors such as child maltreatment by the mothers, psychological maltreatment, neglect, aggression from the mother's intimate partner, victimization, stress, depression, substance abuse, and the mother's consideration of abortion were also assessed. The Taylor study found that when mothers stated that they spanked their 3-year-olds more than twice in the previous month, those same children at 5 years of age were much more likely to be more aggressive (bullying, for example) when compared to children of mothers who spanked less than twice or not at all when their children were 3. This result held even when the individual differences between the natural aggression levels of the 3-year-olds and the other possible confounding factors were taken into account.

The conclusion seems to be that sparing the rod may spare the child (and those around the child) from an unpleasant personality trait.

Questions for Further Discussion

1. How did your own parents discipline you, and do you think that it affected you in a positive or negative way?
2. Why might spanking at age 3 lead to higher aggression in that same child at age 5?

OTHER ASPECTS OF OPERANT CONDITIONING

5.8 **Describe the role of operant stimuli in controlling behavior as well as other concepts that can enhance or limit operant conditioning.**

We've discussed the role of the antecedent stimulus in classical conditioning, as well as the concepts of extinction, generalization, and spontaneous recovery. These concepts are also important in operant conditioning, but in slightly different ways.

DISCRIMINATIVE STIMULUS: SLOW DOWN, IT'S THE COPS   You see a police car in your rearview mirror and automatically slow down, even if you weren't speeding. The traffic light turns red, so you stop. When you want to get into a store, you head for the door and push or pull on the handle. All of these things—slowing down, stopping, using the door handle—are learned. But how do you know what learned response to make, and when? The police car, the stoplight, and the door handle are all cues, stimuli that tell you what behavior will get you what you want.

A **discriminative stimulus** is any stimulus that provides an organism with a cue for making a certain response in order to obtain reinforcement. For example, a police car is a discriminative stimulus for slowing down, and a stop sign is a cue for stopping because both of these actions are usually followed by negative reinforcement—people don't get a ticket or don't get hit by another vehicle. A doorknob is a cue for where to grab the door in order to successfully open it. In fact, if a door has a knob, people always turn it, but if it has a handle, people usually pull it, right? The two kinds of opening devices each bring forth a different response from people, and their reward is opening the door.

EXTINCTION, GENERALIZATION, AND SPONTANEOUS RECOVERY IN OPERANT CONDITIONING *Extinction* in classical conditioning involves the removal of the UCS, the unconditioned stimulus that eventually acts as a reinforcer of the CS–CR bond. It should come as no surprise, then, that extinction in operant conditioning involves the removal of the reinforcement. Have you ever seen a child throw a temper tantrum in the checkout line because the little one wanted some candy or toy? Many exasperated* parents will cave in and give the child the treat, positively reinforcing the tantrum. The parent is also being negatively reinforced for giving in, because the obnoxious* behavior stops. The only way to get the tantrum behavior to stop is to remove the reinforcement, which means no candy, no treat, and if possible, no attention from the parent. (Not only is this hard enough to do while enduring the tantrum, but also the tantrum behavior may actually get worse before it extinguishes!)

Just as in classical conditioning, operantly conditioned responses also can be generalized to stimuli that are only similar to the original stimulus. For example, what parent has not experienced that wonderful moment when Baby, who is just learning to label objects and people, refers to every man she sees as "Dada"? The name "Dada" is a response to the presence of her own father and is reinforced by his delight and attention to her. But in the beginning, she will generalize her "Dada" response to any man. As other men fail to reinforce her for this response, she'll learn to discriminate between them and her father and only call her father "Dada." In this way, the man who is actually her father becomes a discriminative stimulus just like the stoplight or the doorknob mentioned earlier.

Spontaneous recovery (the recurrence of a conditioned response after extinction) will also happen with operant responses. Anyone who has ever trained animals to do several different tricks will say that when first learning a new trick, most animals will try to get reinforcers by performing their *old* tricks.

APPLICATIONS OF OPERANT CONDITIONING: SHAPING AND BEHAVIOR MODIFICATION

5.9 **Describe how operant conditioning is used to change animal and human behavior, and identify some limitations to its use.**

Operant conditioning is more than just the reinforcement of simple responses. It can be used to modify the behavior of both animals and humans.

 💬 How do the circus trainers get their animals to do all those complicated tricks?

SHAPING When you see an animal in a circus or in a show at a zoo perform tricks, you are seeing the result of applying the rules of conditioning—both classical and operant—to animals. But the more complex tricks are a process in operant conditioning called **shaping**, in which small steps toward some ultimate goal are reinforced until the goal itself is reached.

For example, if Jody wanted to train his dog Rover to jump through a hoop, he would have to start with some behavior that the dog is already capable of doing on its own. Then he would gradually "mold" that starting behavior into the jump—something the dog is capable of doing but not likely to do on its own. Jody would have to start with the hoop on the ground in front of Rover's face and then call the dog through the hoop, using the treat as bait. After Rover steps through the hoop (as the shortest way to the

One way to deal with a child's temper tantrum is to ignore it. The lack of reinforcement for the tantrum behavior will eventually result in extinction.

This dog has been trained to help its physically challenged owner. Operant conditioning principles can be used to train animals to do many useful tasks, including opening the refrigerator.

---

*exasperated: irritated or annoyed.
*obnoxious: highly offensive or undesirable.

treat), Jody should give Rover the treat (positive reinforcement). Then he could raise the hoop just a little, reward him for walking through it again, raise the hoop, reward him, and so on until Rover is jumping through the hoop to get the treat. The goal is achieved by reinforcing each **successive approximation** (small steps one after the other that get closer and closer to the goal). This process is shaping (Skinner, 1974). Through pairing of a sound such as a whistle or clicker with the primary reinforcer of food, animal trainers can use the sound as a secondary reinforcer and avoid having an overfed learner.

While animals can learn many types of behavior through the use of operant conditioning, it seems that not every animal can be taught *anything*. For more on this topic, see the following section on biological constraints.

Raccoons commonly dunk their food in and out of water before eating. This "washing" behavior is controlled by instinct and is difficult to change even using operant techniques.

Classic Studies in Psychology
Biological Constraints on Operant Conditioning

Raccoons are fairly intelligent animals and are sometimes used in learning experiments. In a typical experiment, a behaviorist would use shaping and reinforcement to teach a raccoon a trick. The goal might be to get the raccoon to pick up several coins and drop them into a metal container, for which the raccoon would be rewarded with food. The behaviorist starts by reinforcing the raccoon for picking up a single coin. Then the metal container is introduced, and the raccoon is now required to drop the coin into the slot on the container in order to get reinforcement.

It is at this point that operant conditioning seems to fail. Instead of dropping the coin in the slot, the raccoon puts the coin in and out of the slot and rubs it against the inside of the container, then holds it firmly for a few seconds before finally letting it go. When the requirement is upped to two coins, the raccoon spends several minutes rubbing them against each other and dipping them into the container, without actually dropping them in. In spite of the fact that this dipping and rubbing behavior is not reinforced, it gets worse and worse until conditioning becomes impossible.

Keller and Marian Breland, in their attempt to train a raccoon, found that this problem was not limited to the raccoon (Breland & Breland, 1961). They ran into a similar difficulty with a pig that was being trained to pick up a total of five large wooden coins and put them into a "piggy bank." Although at first successful, the pig became slower and slower at the task over a period of weeks, dropping the coin, rooting (pushing) it around with its nose, picking it up, dropping it again, and rooting some more. This behavior became so persistent that the pig actually did not get enough to eat for the day.

The Brelands concluded that the raccoon and the pig were reverting* to behavior that was instinctual for them. Instinctual behavior is genetically determined and not under the influence of learning. Apparently, even though the animals were at first able to learn the tricks, as the coins became more and more associated with food, the animals began to drift back into the instinctual patterns of behavior that they used with real food. Raccoons rub their food between their paws and dip it in and out of water. Pigs root and throw their food around before eating it. The Brelands called this tendency to revert to genetically controlled patterns **instinctive drift**.

In their 1961 paper describing these and other examples of instinctive drift, the Brelands (both trained by Skinner himself) determined that, contrary to Skinner's original ideas:

1. The animal does NOT come to the laboratory a *tabula rasa*, or "blank slate," and cannot be taught just any behavior.

---

*reverting: to go back in action, thought, speech, and so on.

2. Differences between species of animals matter in determining what behavior can or cannot be conditioned.

3. Not all responses are equally able to be conditioned to any stimulus.

As became quickly obvious in their studies with these animals, each animal comes into the world (and the laboratory) with certain genetically determined instinctive patterns of behavior already in place. These instincts differ from species to species, with the result that there are some responses that simply cannot be trained into an animal regardless of conditioning.

Questions for Further Discussion

1. What other kinds of limitations do animals have in learning?

2. What kinds of behavior might people do that would be resistant to conditioning?

3. How can these research findings about animal behavior be generalized to human behavior?

BEHAVIOR MODIFICATION   Operant conditioning principles such as reinforcement and the process of shaping have been used for many years to change undesirable behavior and create desirable responses in animals and humans—particularly in schoolchildren. The term **behavior modification** refers to the application of operant conditioning (and sometimes classical conditioning) to bring about such changes. The video *Behavior Modification Plan for Improving Heath* describes a sample behavior modification plan for someone who wants to watch less television and exercise more.

◉ **Watch** the **Video**, *Behavior Modification Plan for Improving Health.*

As another example, if a teacher wants to use behavior modification to help a child learn to be more attentive during the teacher's lectures, the teacher may do the following:

1. Select a target behavior, such as making eye contact with the teacher.

2. Choose a reinforcer. This may be a gold star applied to the child's chart on the wall, for example.

3. Put the plan in action. Every time the child makes eye contact, the teacher gives the child a gold star. Inappropriate behavior (such as looking out of the window) is not reinforced with gold stars.

4. At the end of the day, the teacher gives the child a special treat or reward for having a certain number of gold stars. This special reward is decided on ahead of time and discussed with the child.

Both gold stars and wooden sticks can be considered *tokens*, secondary reinforcers that can be traded in for other kinds of reinforcers. The use of tokens to modify behavior is called a **token economy**. (L)(I)(N) K to Learning Objective 13.4. In the example, the child is collecting gold stars to "buy" the special treat at the end of the day. When one thinks about it, the system of money is very much a token economy. People are rewarded for working for money, which they then trade for food, shelter, and so on.

Another tool that behaviorists can use to modify behavior is the process of *time-out*. Time-out is a form of mild punishment by removal in which a misbehaving animal, child, or adult is placed in a special area away from the attention of others. Essentially, the organism is being "removed" from any possibility of positive reinforcement in the form of attention. When used with children, time-out should be limited to 1 minute for each year of age with a maximum time-out of 10 minutes (longer than that and the child can forget why the time-out occurred).

Applied behavior analysis (ABA) is the modern term for a form of behavior modification that uses both analysis of current behavior and behavioral techniques to mold a desired behavior or response.

In ABA, skills are broken down to their simplest steps and then taught to the child through a system of reinforcement. Prompts (such as moving a child's face back to look at the teacher or the task) are given as needed when the child is learning a skill or refuses to cooperate. As the child begins to master a skill and receives reinforcement in the form of treats or praise, the prompts are gradually withdrawn until the child can do the skill independently. Applied behavior analysis is a growing field, with many colleges and universities offering excellent degrees at both the undergraduate and graduate levels. Typical uses for ABA are treating children with disorders, training animals, and developing effective teaching methods for children and adults of all levels of mental abilities (Baer et al., 1968).

An example of how ABA can be used is found in the use of shaping to mold desirable, socially acceptable behavior in individuals with *autism*. Autism is a disorder in which the person has great difficulty in communicating with others, often refusing to look at another person. (L)(I)(N) K to Learning Objective 8.8. This specific application of ABA can be said to have begun with the work of Dr. O. Ivar Lovaas (1964) and his associates, although the basic techniques are those first outlined by Skinner. Lovaas used small pieces of candy as reinforcers to teach social skills and language to children with autism.

Other techniques for modifying behavior have been developed so that even behavior that is normally considered involuntary such as blood pressure and muscle tension can be brought under conscious control. For nearly 60 years, scientists have known how to use feedback of a person's biological information (such as heart rate) to create a state of relaxation (Margolin & Kubic, 1944). **Biofeedback** is the traditional term used to describe this kind of biological feedback of information, and through its use many problems can be relieved or controlled.

A relatively newer biofeedback technique called **neurofeedback** involves trying to change brain-wave activity. (L)(I)(N) K to Learning Objective 2.9. Although this technique uses the latest in technology, the basic principles behind it are much older. Traditionally, this technique was based on recording the electrical activity of the brain, or EEG. To record the EEG, a person would have to be connected to a stand-alone *electroencephalograph*, a machine that amplifies and records the brain's electrical activity. Modern biofeedback and neurofeedback amplifiers are often connected to a computer that records and analyzes the physiological activity of the brain. Neurofeedback can be integrated with video-game-like programs that individuals can use to learn how to produce brain waves or specific types of brain activity associated with specific cognitive or behavioral states (e.g., increased attention, staying focused, relaxed awareness). Individuals learn to make these changes through the principles of operant conditioning (Sherlin et al., 2011). Neurofeedback using the EEG continues to be investigated in specific disorders such as attention-deficit/hyper-activity disorder (ADHD) and in new areas such as the control of chronic pain (Arns et al., 2009; Jensen et al., 2013). Other recent neurofeedback studies have incorporated MRI or fMRI to examine the effects of EEG-based neurofeedback on the brain (Ghaziri et al., 2013; Ros et al., 2013). And in some studies, fMRI is being used as a neurofeedback method in and of itself (Ruiz et al., 2013; Scharnowski et al., 2012; Sulzer et al., 2013).

Concept Map L.O. 5.4, 5.5, 5.6, 5.7, 5.8, 5.9

Interactive

focused on observable, measurable behavior

Thorndike was among the first to study learning of voluntary responses — developed law of effect—action followed by pleasurable consequence will tend to be repeated; action followed by unpleasant consequence will tend not to be repeated

Skinner led field of behaviorism after Watson — coined term *operant conditioning*—voluntary behavior that people and animals do to operate in the world

Operant Conditioning
(learning to make voluntary responses through the effects of positive or negative consequences)

reinforcement any event or stimulus, that when following a response increases the probability that the response will occur again
- **primary reinforcers:** satisfy basic biological needs (e.g., hunger, thirst, touch)
- **secondary reinforcers:** gain reinforcing properties through previous association with primary reinforcers
- **positive reinforcement:** addition, or experiencing of, a pleasurable stimulus
- **negative reinforcement:** removal, escape, or avoidance of unpleasant stimulus

schedules of reinforcement
- **timing of reinforcement** influences speed of learning, strength of learned response, and subsequent behavior pattern
- **continuous reinforcement:** provision of reinforcer for each and every correct response — easier to establish new responses but more sensitive to extinction
- **partial reinforcement:** reinforcing behavior after some but not all correct responses —
  - leads to a response that is resistant to extinction
  - schedule can be specified by the pattern/ratio of responses or by time/interval
  - both ratio and interval schedules can be either fixed or variable

punishment is any event or stimulus that, when following a response, decreases the probability that the response will occur again
- opposite of reinforcement, which increases the probability that the response will occur again
- punishment by application—something unpleasant is added to the situation
- punishment by removal—something pleasurable is removed
- to work—must be immediate, consistent, and paired with reinforcement of actual behavior desired

other features
- stimuli must be discriminative; specific cues lead to specific responses
- some behaviors can be established through shaping, reinforcing small steps, or each successive approximation, toward the ultimate goal
- as in classical conditioning, extinction, generalization, and spontaneous recovery can occur
- instinctive drift, or the tendency to revert to genetically controlled patterns of behavior, can serve as a biological constraint on operant conditioning

behavior modification
- application of operant conditioning principles (sometimes classical conditioning) to change undesirable behaviors and create desirable behaviors in both humans and animals
- token economies, time-out, applied behavior analysis, biofeedback, and neurofeedback use these principles

Reset

Practice Quiz How much do you remember? ANSWERS ON PAGE AK–1.

Pick the best answer.

1. Which of the following is an example of Thorndike's law of effect?
   a. John, a teenager, gets compliments from Carla for wearing a nice shirt. Subsequently, John wears the shirt whenever he thinks he will be seeing Carla.
   b. James always cleans his room or he knows he will be punished.
   c. Josh tries to complete his homework even though he hates having to do it.
   d. Jeremy often sits around inside hoping that someone will call him to go do something.

2. With operant conditioning, _____ are important in forming an association, whereas with classical conditioning, _____ are important in forming an association.
   a. consequences; antecedent stimuli
   b. reflexes; rewards
   c. conditioned stimuli; reflexive stimuli
   d. positive reinforcement; negative reinforcement

3. Joe owned a small repair shop. Each day, he would check the mail to see if any of his customers mailed in a payment for the work he had done for them. Some days, he would receive a check or two. At other times, he would have to wait days before getting another payment. What schedule of reinforcement is evident here?
   a. fixed interval
   b. fixed ratio
   c. variable interval
   d. variable ratio

4. Little Jimmie's mother was upset to find that Jimmie had not picked up his building blocks after repeated requests to do so. The next morning, Jimmie found all his blocks had been picked up and put into a bag on the top of the refrigerator. Jimmie's mother told him that he couldn't play with his blocks for the next two days. Which type of discipline did she use?
   a. negative reinforcement
   b. punishment by application
   c. punishment by removal
   d. positive reinforcement

5. The study by Keller and Marian Breland found that instinctive drift in animal behavior is
   a. caused by confusion between punishment types.
   b. caused by overuse of positive reinforcement.
   c. the result of conscious decisions on the part of animals not to take part in further testing.
   d. genetically determined and not under the influence of learning.

6. Which of the following is the best example of applied behavior analysis?
   a. Tiffany works with children by asking them what they want to accomplish and then helping them attain that goal through different forms of classical conditioning.
   b. Bethany has children watch her repeatedly so as to understand how a task is to be done. Once they have finished the observation, they are then asked to imitate the behavior.
   c. Agatha observes a child to see what purpose a disruptive classroom behavior serves, and identifies a new replacement behavior. She then implements a training program for the new behavior, reinforcing often at the simplest levels and gradually removing reinforcers as the child demonstrates the behavior independently.
   d. Camille wants children to learn a new behavior and uses punishment as the basis for the behavior change.

7. Neurofeedback is a form of_____ and works to change a person's _____ through a series of reinforcements.
   a. classical conditioning; thoughts
   b. operant conditioning; anxieties
   c. observation learning; behaviors
   d. biofeedback; brain activity

"Bathroom? Sure, it's just down that hall to the left, jog right, left, another left, straight past two more lefts, then right, and it's at the end of the third corridor on your right." ©The New Yorker Collection 2000 Pat Byrnes from cartoonbank.com. All Rights Reserved.

Cognitive Learning Theory

In the early days of behaviorism, the original focus of Watson, Skinner, and many of their followers was on observable, measurable behavior. Anything that might be occurring inside a person or animal's head during learning was considered to be of no interest to the behaviorist because it could not be seen or directly measured. Other psychologists, however, were still interested in the mind's influence over behavior. Gestalt psychologists, for instance, were studying the way that the human mind tried to force a pattern on stimuli in the world around the person. **L I N K** to Learning Objectives 1.3. This continued interest in the mind was followed, in the 1950s and 1960s, by the comparison of the human mind to the workings of those fascinating "thinking machines," computers. Soon after, interest in *cognition*, the mental events that take place inside a person's mind while behaving, began to dominate experimental psychology. Many behavioral psychologists could no longer ignore the thoughts, feelings, and expectations that clearly existed in the mind and that seemed to influence observable behavior and eventually began to develop a cognitive learning theory to supplement the more traditional theories of learning (Kendler, 1985). Three important figures often cited as key theorists in the early days of the development of cognitive learning theory were the Gestalt psychologists Edward Tolman and Wolfgang Köhler and modern psychologist Martin Seligman.

TOLMAN'S MAZE-RUNNING RATS: LATENT LEARNING

5.10 **Define and explain the concept of latent learning.**

One of Gestalt psychologist Edward Tolman's best-known experiments in learning involved teaching three groups of rats the same maze, one at a time (Tolman & Honzik, 1930). In the first group, each rat was placed in the maze and reinforced with food for making its way out the other side. The rat was then placed back in the maze, reinforced, and so on until the rat could successfully solve the maze with no errors—the typical maze-learning experiment (see **Figure 5.8**).

The second group of rats was treated exactly like the first, except that they never received any reinforcement upon exiting the maze. They were simply put back in again and again, until the tenth day of the experiment. On that day, the rats in the second group began to receive reinforcement for getting out of the maze. The third group of rats, serving as a control group, was also not reinforced and was not given reinforcement for the entire duration of the experiment.

A strict Skinnerian behaviorist would predict that only the first group of rats would learn the maze successfully because learning depends on reinforcing consequences. At first, this seemed to be the case. The first group of rats did indeed solve the maze after a certain number of trials, whereas the second and third groups seemed to wander aimlessly around the maze until accidentally finding their way out.

On the 10th day, however, something happened that would be difficult to explain using only Skinner's basic principles. The second group of rats, upon receiving the

Figure 5.8 A TYPICAL MAZE

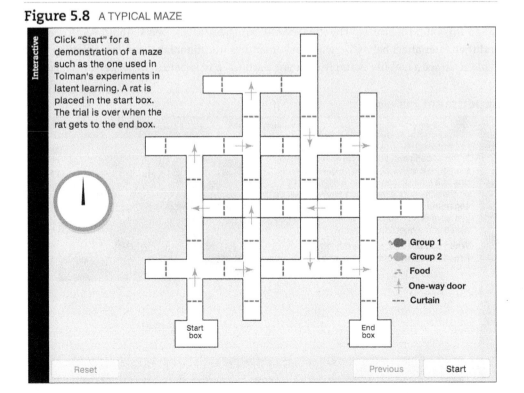

Click "Start" for a demonstration of a maze such as the one used in Tolman's experiments in latent learning. A rat is placed in the start box. The trial is over when the rat gets to the end box.

Group 1
Group 2
Food
One-way door
Curtain

Start box
End box

Reset   Previous   Start

Figure 5.9 Learning Curves for Three Groups of Rats

In the results of the classic study of latent learning, Group 1 was rewarded on each day, while Group 2 was rewarded for the first time on Day 10. Group 3 was never rewarded. Note the immediate change in the behavior of Group 2 on Day 12 (Tolman & Honzik, 1930).

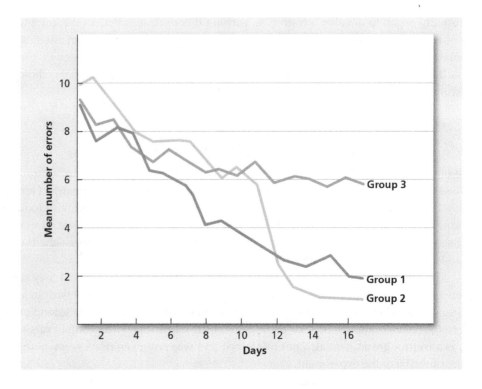

reinforcement for the first time, *should* have then taken as long as the first group to solve the maze. Instead, they began to solve the maze almost immediately (see **Figure 5.9**).

Tolman concluded that the rats in the second group, while wandering around in the first nine days of the experiment, had indeed learned where all the blind alleys, wrong turns, and correct paths were and stored this knowledge away as a kind of "mental map," or *cognitive map*, of the physical layout of the maze. The rats in the second group had learned and stored that learning away mentally but had not *demonstrated* this learning because there was no reason to do so. The cognitive map had remained hidden, or latent, until the rats had a reason to demonstrate their knowledge by getting to the food. Tolman called this **latent learning**. The idea that learning could happen without reinforcement, and then later affect behavior, was not something traditional operant conditioning could explain. To see a real-life example of latent learning, participate in the experiment *Learning*.

Experiment   LEARNING

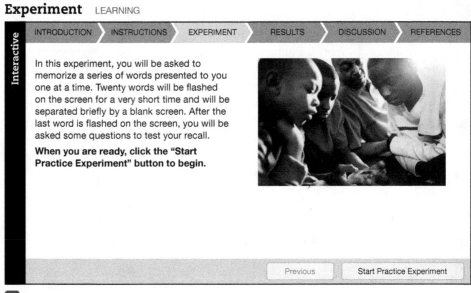

INTRODUCTION   INSTRUCTIONS   EXPERIMENT   RESULTS   DISCUSSION   REFERENCES

In this experiment, you will be asked to memorize a series of words presented to you one at a time. Twenty words will be flashed on the screen for a very short time and will be separated briefly by a blank screen. After the last word is flashed on the screen, you will be asked some questions to test your recall.

When you are ready, click the "Start Practice Experiment" button to begin.

Previous   Start Practice Experiment

Simulate the **Experiment**, *Learning*.

KÖHLER'S SMART CHIMP: INSIGHT LEARNING

5.11 Explain the concept of insight learning.

Another exploration of the cognitive elements of learning came about almost by accident. Wolfgang Köhler (1887–1967) was a Gestalt psychologist who became marooned* on an island in the Canaries (a series of islands off the coast of North Africa) when World War I broke out. Stuck at the primate research lab that had first drawn him to the island, he turned to studies of animal learning.

Another of Köhler's chimpanzees, Grande, has just solved the problem of how to get to the banana by stacking boxes. Does this meet the criteria for insight, or was it simple trial-and-error learning?

In one of his more famous studies (Köhler, 1925), he set up a problem for one of the chimpanzees. Sultan the chimp was faced with the problem of how to get to a banana that was placed just out of his reach outside his cage. Sultan solved this problem relatively easily, first trying to reach through the bars with his arm, then using a stick that was lying in the cage to rake the banana into the cage. As chimpanzees are natural tool users, this behavior is not surprising and is still nothing more than simple trial-and-error learning.

But then the problem was made more difficult. The banana was placed just out of reach of Sultan's extended arm with the stick in his hand. At this point there were two sticks lying around in the cage, which could be fitted together to make a single pole that would be long enough to reach the banana. Sultan first tried one stick, then the other (simple trial and error). After about an hour of trying, Sultan seemed to have a sudden flash of inspiration. He pushed one stick out of the cage as far as it would go toward the banana and then pushed the other stick behind the first one. Of course, when he tried to draw the sticks back, only the one in his hand came. He jumped up and down and was very excited, and when Köhler gave him the second stick, he sat on the floor of the cage and looked at them carefully. He then fitted one stick into the other and retrieved his banana. Köhler called Sultan's rapid "perception of relationships" **insight** and determined that insight could not be gained through trial-and-error learning alone (Köhler, 1925). Although Thorndike and other early learning theorists believed that animals could not demonstrate insight, Köhler's work seems to demonstrate that insight requires a sudden "coming together" of all the elements of a problem in a kind of "aha!" moment that is not predicted by traditional animal learning studies. Ⓛ Ⓘ Ⓝ Ⓚ to Learning Objective 7.2. More recent research has also found support for the concept of animal insight (Heinrich, 2000; Heyes, 1998; Zentall, 2000), but there is still controversy over how to interpret the results of those studies (Wynne, 1999).

SELIGMAN'S DEPRESSED DOGS: LEARNED HELPLESSNESS

5.12 Explain the concept of learned helplessness.

Martin Seligman is now famous for founding the field of *positive psychology*, a new way of looking at the entire concept of mental health and therapy that focuses on the adaptive, creative, and psychologically more fulfilling aspects of human experience rather than on mental disorders. But in the mid to late 1960s Seligman, a learning theorist, and his colleagues accidentally discovered an unexpected phenomenon while doing experiments on dogs using classical conditioning (Seligman, 1975). Their original intention was to study escape and avoidance learning. Seligman and colleagues presented a tone followed by a harmless but painful electric shock to one group of dogs (Overmier & Seligman, 1967; Seligman & Maier, 1967). (See **Figure 5.10** on the next page.) The dogs in this group were harnessed so that they could not escape the shock. The researchers assumed that the dogs would learn to fear the sound of the tone and later try to escape from the tone before being shocked.

These dogs, along with another group of dogs that had not been conditioned to fear the tone, were placed into a special box consisting of a low fence that divided the box into two compartments. The dogs, which were now unharnessed, could easily see over the fence and jump over if they wished—which is precisely what the dogs that

*marooned: in this sense, being placed on an island from which escape is impossible.

Figure 5.10 Seligman's Apparatus

In Seligman's studies of learned helplessness, dogs were placed in a two-sided box. Dogs that had no prior experience with being unable to escape a shock would quickly jump over the hurdle in the center of the box to land on the "safe" side. Dogs that had previously learned that escape was impossible would stay on the side of the box in which the shock occurred, not even trying to go over the hurdle.

Speaker

Dog

Speaker

Hurdle

Shock grid floor

had not been conditioned did as soon as the shock occurred. Imagine the researchers' surprise when, instead of jumping over the fence when the tone sounded, the previously conditioned dogs just sat there. In fact, these dogs showed distress but didn't try to jump over the fence *even when the shock itself began.*

Why would the conditioned dogs refuse to move when shocked? The dogs that had been harnessed while being conditioned had apparently learned in the original tone/shock situation that there was nothing they could do to escape the shock. So when placed in a situation in which escape was possible, the dogs still did nothing because they had learned to be "helpless." They believed they could not escape, so they did not try.

More recently, Seligman's colleague and co-researcher in those early studies, Steven F. Maier, has revisited the phenomenon of learned helplessness from a neuroscientific approach, and this work has provided some new insights. Maier and others have focused on an area of the brain stem that releases serotonin and can play a role in activating the amygdala (which plays an important role in fear and anxiety) but also participates in decreasing activity in brain areas responsible for the "fight-or-flight" response. **LINK** to Learning Objective 2.5.

This combination of increased fear/anxiety with non-escape or freezing is the very behavior associated with learned helplessness. This part of the brain stem (the dorsal raphe nucleus) is a much older part of the brain and not able to determine what type of stressors are controllable. Their research suggests that a higher-level area, a part of the frontal lobe called the *ventromedial prefrontal cortex* (vmPFC), is able to help determine what is controllable. In turn, the vmPFC inhibits the brain stem area and calms the amygdala's response, allowing an animal to effectively respond to a stressor and exhibit control (Amat et al., 2005; Maier et al., 2006; Maier & Watkins, 2005). In other words, it is possible that the dogs in the early studies, rather than learning to be helpless, were *not* learning how to relax and take control of the situation. Maier and colleagues suggest that both training and input from the vmPFC are necessary for animals to learn how to take control (Maier et al., 2006).

🗨 I know some people who seem to act just like those dogs—they live in a horrible situation but won't leave. Is this the same thing?

Seligman extended this theory of **learned helplessness**, the tendency to fail to act to escape from a situation because of a history of repeated failures in the past, to explain *depression.* Depressed people seem to lack normal emotions and become somewhat apathetic, often staying in unpleasant work environments or bad marriages or relationships rather than trying to escape or better their situation. Seligman proposed that this depressive behavior is a form of learned helplessness. Depressed people may have learned in the past that they seem to have no control over what happens to them (Alloy & Clements, 1998). A sense of powerlessness and hopelessness is common to depressed people, and certainly this would seem to apply to Seligman's dogs as well. Maier's recent work also has implications here, especially the focus on the components necessary for learning how to relax and exhibit control: input from the vmPFC, and training (repeated exposures to stressors). This combination provides a mechanism for not only understanding resilience,*

*resilience: the ability to recover quickly from change and/or stress.

but also for possibly helping people foster resilience and avoid anxiety or mood disorders such as posttraumatic stress disorder (PTSD) or depression (Maier et al., 2006). (L)(I)(N)(K) to Learning Objectives 12.6 and 12.9. Maier and colleagues are continuing to study the brain foundations of learned helplessness and examining how factors related to control and controllability not only impact immediate events, but future stressful events as well (Amat et al., 2010; Rozeske et al., 2011; Varela et al., 2012).

Think about how this might apply to other situations. There are many students who feel that they are bad at math because they have had problems with it in the past. Is it possible that this belief could make them not try as hard or study as much as they should? Isn't this kind of thinking also an example of learned helplessness?

Cognitive learning is also an important part of a fairly well-known form of learning, often simplified as "monkey see, monkey do." Let's take a look at learning through watching the actions of others.

Concept Map L.O. 5.10, 5.11, 5.12

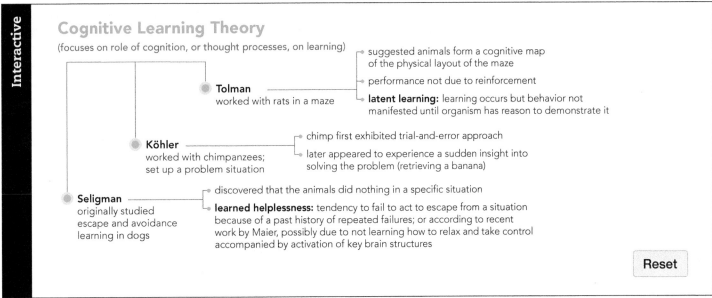

Practice Quiz How much do you remember? ANSWERS ON PAGE AK-1.

Pick the best answer.

1. In Tolman's maze study, the fact that the group of rats receiving reinforcement only after day 10 of the study solved the maze far more quickly than did the rats who had been reinforced from the first day can be interpreted to mean that these particular rats

    a. were much smarter than the other rats.

    b. had already learned the maze in the first 9 days.

    c. had the opportunity to cheat by watching the other rats.

    d. were very hungry and, therefore, learned much more quickly.

2. Lisa's parents have decided to take a 3-week trip to Europe. Consequently, Lisa's mother will not be able to make her famous pies for the upcoming bake sale. When her mother encourages Lisa to bake the pies herself, Lisa panics at first but then finds that she knows how to put the recipe together. Her ability to prepare the recipe is an example of

    a. latent learning.

    b. learned helplessness.

    c. insight learning.

    d. discovery learning.

3. Which theory is commonly represented by the "aha!" phenomenon?

    a. Tolman's latent learning theory

    b. Köhler's insight theory

    c. Seligman's learned helplessness theory

    d. Bandura's observational learning

4. Research by Steven Maier suggests that learned helplessness involves a higher-level region of the brain known as the _____, which helps subjects determine what is controllable.

    a. amygdala

    b. hippocampus

    c. dorsal raphe nucleus

    d. ventromedial prefrontal cortex (vmPFC)

Observational Learning

Observational learning is the learning of new behavior through watching the actions of a model (someone else who is doing that behavior). Sometimes that behavior is desirable, and sometimes it is not, as the next section describes.

BANDURA AND THE BOBO DOLL

5.13 Describe the process of observational learning.

Bandura's classic study in observational learning involved having a preschool child in a room in which the experimenter and a model interacted with toys in the room in front of the child (Bandura et al., 1961). In one condition, the model interacted with the toys in a nonaggressive manner, completely ignoring the presence of a "Bobo" doll (a punch-bag doll in the shape of a clown). In another condition, the model became very aggressive with the doll, kicking it and yelling at it, throwing it in the air and hitting it with a hammer.

When each child was left alone in the room and had the opportunity to play with the toys, a camera filming through a one-way mirror caught the children who were exposed to the aggressive model beating up the Bobo doll in exact imitation of the model (see **Figure 5.11**). The children who saw the model ignore the doll did not act aggressively toward the toy. Obviously, the aggressive children had learned their aggressive actions from merely watching the model—with no reinforcement necessary. The fact that learning can take place without actual performance (a kind of latent learning) is called the **learning/performance distinction**.

> 💬 Ah, but would that child have imitated the model if the model had been punished? Wouldn't the *consequences* of the model's behavior make a difference?

In later studies, Bandura showed a film of a model beating up the Bobo doll. In one condition, the children saw the model rewarded afterward. In another, the model was punished. When placed in the room with toys, the children in the first group beat up the doll, but the children in the second group did not. But when Bandura told the children in the second group that he would give them a reward if they could show him what the model in the film did, each child duplicated the model's actions. Both groups had learned from watching the model, but only the children watching the successful (rewarded) model imitated the aggression with no prompting (Bandura, 1965). Apparently, consequences do matter in motivating a child (or an adult) to imitate a particular model. The tendency for some movies and television programs to make "heroes" out of violent, aggressive "bad guys" is particularly disturbing in light of these findings. In fact,

Figure 5.11 Bandura's Bobo Doll Experiment

In Albert Bandura's famous Bobo doll experiment, the doll was used to demonstrate the impact of observing an adult model performing aggressive behavior on the later aggressive behavior of children. The children in these photos are imitating the adult model's behavior even though they believe they are alone and are not being watched.

Bandura began this research to investigate possible links between children's exposure to violence on television and aggressive behavior toward others.

In one nationwide study of youth in the United States, it was found that young people ages 8 to 18 spend on average almost 7.5 hours per day involved in media consumption (television, computers, video games, music, cell phones, print, and movies), 7 days a week. Furthermore, given the prevalence of media multitasking (using more than one media device at a time), they are packing in approximately 10 hours and 45 minutes of media during those 7.5 hours! (Rideout et al., 2010). While not all media consumption is of violent media, it is quite easy to imagine that some of that media is of a violent nature.

Correlational research stretching over nearly two decades suggests that a link exists between viewing violent television and an increased level of aggression in children (Bushman & Huesmann, 2001; Engelhardt et al., 2013; Huesmann & Eron, 1986; Sacks et al., 2011). ⓛ ⓘ ⓝ ⓚ to Learning Objective 1.8. While correlations do not prove that viewing violence on TV is the *cause* of increased violence, one cannot help but be curious as to the effects, especially given the continuing rise of media consumption in young people, coupled with the multiple ways young people interact with media. As such, there has been an ongoing debate as to the validity of the links between aggression and exposure to media violence (primarily focusing on television, movies, video games, and music). Although still a topic of debate (Ferguson, 2010, 2013), there appears to be a strong body of evidence that exposure to some forms of media violence does have immediate and long-term effects, increasing the likelihood of aggressive verbal and physical behavior and aggressive thoughts and emotions—and the effects appear to impact children, adolescents, and adults (Anderson et al., 2003; Anderson et al., 2010).

THE FOUR ELEMENTS OF OBSERVATIONAL LEARNING

5.14 **List the four elements of observational learning.**

Bandura (1986) concluded, from these studies and others, that observational learning required the presence of four elements.

ATTENTION   To learn anything through observation, the learner must first pay *attention* to the model. For example, a person at a fancy dinner party who wants to know which utensil to use has to watch the person who seems to know what is correct. Certain characteristics of models can make attention more likely. For example, people pay more attention to those people they perceive as similar to them and to people whom they perceive as attractive.

MEMORY   The learner must also be able to retain the *memory* of what was done, such as remembering the steps in preparing a dish that was first seen on a cooking show.

IMITATION   The learner must be capable of reproducing, or *imitating*, the actions of the model. A 2-year-old might be able to watch someone tie shoelaces and might even remember most of the steps, but the 2-year-old's chubby little fingers will not have the dexterity* necessary for actually tying the laces. A person with extremely weak ankles might be able to watch and remember how some ballet move was accomplished but will not be able to reproduce it. The mirror neurons discussed in Chapter Two may be willing, but the flesh is weak. ⓛ ⓘ ⓝ ⓚ to Learning Objective 2.12.

DESIRE   Finally, the learner must have the motivation or *desire* to perform the action. That person at the fancy dinner, for example, might not care which fork or which knife is the "proper" one to use. Also, if a person expects a reward because one has been given in the past, or has been promised a future reward (like the children in the second group of

---

*dexterity: skill and ease in using the hands.

Bandura's study), or has witnessed a model getting a reward (like the children in the first group), that person will be much more likely to imitate the observed behavior. Successful models are powerful figures for imitation, but rarely would we be motivated to imitate someone who fails or is punished.

(An easy way to remember the four elements of modeling is to remember the letters AMID, which stand for the first letters of each of the four elements. This is a good example of using a strategy to improve memory. **LINK** to Learning Objectives PIA.7).

Concept Map L.O. 5.13, 5.14

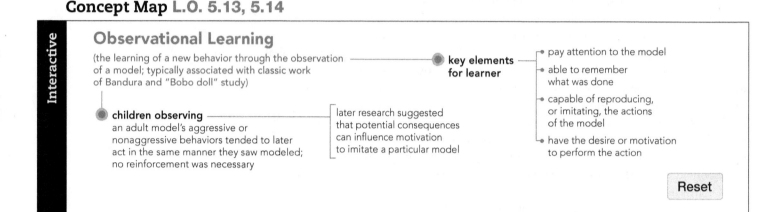

Interactive

Observational Learning

(the learning of a new behavior through the observation of a model; typically associated with classic work of Bandura and "Bobo doll" study)

children observing — an adult model's aggressive or nonaggressive behaviors tended to later act in the same manner they saw modeled; no reinforcement was necessary

later research suggested that potential consequences can influence motivation to imitate a particular model

key elements for learner
- pay attention to the model
- able to remember what was done
- capable of reproducing, or imitating, the actions of the model
- have the desire or motivation to perform the action

Reset

Practice Quiz   How much do you remember?   ANSWERS ON PAGE AK-1.

Pick the best answer.

1. Bandura's studies found that learning can take place without actual performance. What is this referred to as?
   a. learning/performance distinction
   b. insight-based learning
   c. ARID
   d. cognitive learning

2. A famous study conducted by Albert Bandura involved watching children interact with:
   a. jigsaw puzzles
   b. a toy kitchen
   c. a kiddie pool filled with water
   d. a Bobo doll

3. In one nationwide study of kids in the United States, it was discovered that young people between the ages of 8 and 18 years spend approximately _____ hours a day interacting with media, including television, computers, cell phones, and other forms.
   a. 3.5   **c.** 7.5
   b. 5.75   **d.** 9.25

4. What is the correct sequence of the four elements of observational learning?
   a. Attention, Imitation, Desire, Memory
   b. Attention, Memory, Imitation, Desire
   c. Desire, Attention, Memory, Imitation
   d. Memory, Attention, Desire, Imitation

Applying Psychology to Everyday Life

Can You Really Toilet Train Your Cat?

5.15 Provide and describe an example of conditioning in the real world.

(This article has been excerpted with permission of the author and cat-trainer extraordinaire Karawynn Long. Karawynn Long is a published writer and Web designer who lives in Seattle with her family. Sadly, since this article was written, her cat, Misha, has passed away. Ms. Long can be reached at her Web site **www.karawynn.name/mishacat/toilet .html**. The italicized words in brackets are the author's "editorial" comments.)

There have been more books and articles about toilet-training cats than you'd think. In the summer of 1989, when Misha was a small kitten with big ears and enough meow for five cats, I searched out and read a half-dozen of them. And then tried it myself, and discovered there were a couple of things they all failed to mention . . . here's what worked for me and Misha.

The central idea is that the transition from litter box to toilet should be accomplished in a series of stages. [*This is shaping.*] You make a small change and then give your cat time to adjust before you make another small change. If at any time Felix gives the whole thing up and goes on the rug instead, you're pushing him too far too fast; back up a stage or two and try again, more slowly.

The very most important thing to remember is: Lid Up, Seat Down. Post a note on the back of the door or the lid of the toilet if you think you (or your housemates or guests) might forget. And if you are accustomed to closing the bathroom door when it's empty, you'll have to break that habit too. [*In operant conditioning, this is part of "preparing the training arena."*]

Begin by moving the cat's current litter box from wherever it is to one side of the toilet. Make sure he knows where it is and uses it. Rest (this means doing nothing for a period of between a day and a week, depending on how flappable your cat is). Next put something—a stack of newspapers, a phone book, a cardboard box—under the litter box to raise it, say, about an inch. (Magazines are too slick; you don't want the litter box sliding around and making your cat feel insecure. Tape the litter box down if you need to.) Rest. Get another box or phone book and raise it a little higher. Rest. Continue this process until the bottom of the litter box is level with the top of the toilet seat. (For Misha I raised it about two inches per day.) [*Notice that this is the step-by-step process typically used in shaping.*]

At the beginning of this process, your cat could just step into the litter box; later he began jumping up into it, until at some point he probably started jumping up onto the toilet seat first and stepping into the box from there. Lift the seat on your toilet and measure the inside diameter of the top of the bowl at its widest point. Venture forth and buy a metal mixing bowl of that diameter. Do not (I discovered this the hard way) substitute a plastic bowl. A plastic bowl will not support the cat's weight and will bend, dropping into the toilet bowl and spilling litter everywhere, not to mention startling the cat.

Now you move the litter box over so that it's sitting directly over the toilet seat. (If your cat has shown reluctance over previous changes, you might want to split this into two stages, moving it halfway onto the seat and then fully over.) Take away the stack of phone books or whatever you used. Rest. [*Again, notice that everything has to be done in small steps. This is the heart of the shaping process—requiring too large a step will stop the process.*]

Here's the cool part. Take away the litter box entirely. (Ta da!) Nestle the metal mixing bowl inside the toilet bowl and lower the seat. Fill the bowl with about two inches of litter (all of this is much easier if you have the tiny granules of litter that can be scooped out and flushed).

Naturally, any humans using the toilet at this point will want to remove the metal bowl prior to their own use and replace it afterward. The next week or two the whole process is likely to be something of an annoyance; if you begin to think it's not worth it, just remember that you will never have to clean a litter box again.

Watch your cat using the bathroom in the metal bowl. Count the number of feet he gets up on the toilet seat (as opposed to down in the bowl of litter). The higher the number, the luckier you are and the easier your job is going to be . . .

. . . because next you have to teach him proper squatting posture. Catch him beginning to use the toilet as much of the time as possible and show him where his feet are supposed to go. Just lift them right out of the bowl and place them on the seat (front legs

This cat is being trained to use the toilet employing the learning techniques discussed in this section.

in the middle, hind legs on the outside). If he starts out with three or, heaven forbid, all four feet in the bowl, just get the front two feet out first. Praise him all over the place every time he completes the activity in this position. [*The praise is the positive reinforcement and should be done with each successful step.*]

(Misha is very doglike in that he craves approval and praise. If your cat is indifferent to this sort of thing, you can also reward him with small food treats and wean him from them later when the toilet behavior has "set." Just keep the treats as small and infrequent as possible—half a Pounce™ or similar treat per occasion should be plenty.) [*If treats are too frequent, it will make it difficult to phase out the reinforcer after the behavior is well learned.*]

When he is regularly using the toilet with his front feet out (and some cats naturally start from this position), begin lifting a hind foot out and placing it on the seat outside the front paws. Your cat will probably find this awkward at first and try to replace the foot in the litter. Be persistent. Move that foot four times in a row if you have to, until it stays there. Praise and/or treat.

Repeat with the other hind foot, until your cat learns to balance in that squat. Once he's getting all four feet regularly on the seat, it's all easy from here.

Which is fortunate, because the last bit is also the most unpleasant. I suggest that you postpone this stage until you have at least a weekend, and preferably several days, when you (or another responsible party) will be at home most of the time. I skipped through this part in about two days; I only hope that your cat allows you to move along that fast.

Begin reducing the litter in the bowl. Go as fast as he'll feel comfortable with, because as the litter decreases, the odor increases. You'll want to be home at this point so that you can praise him and dump out the contents of the bowl immediately after he's finished, to minimize both the smell and the possibility that your cat, in a confused attempt to minimize the smell on his own, tries to cover it up with litter that no longer exists and ends up tracking unpleasantness into the rest of the house.

By the time you're down to a token teaspoonful of litter in the bottom of the bowl, your next-door neighbors will probably be aware of the precise instant your cat has used the toilet. This is as bad as it gets. The next time you rinse out the metal bowl, put a little bit of water in the bottom. Increase the water level each time, just as you decreased the litter level. Remember—if at any point Felix looks nervous enough about the change to give the whole thing up and take his business to the corner behind the door, back up a step or two and try the thing again more slowly. [*Shaping takes a lot of patience, depending on the behavior being shaped and the learning ability of the animal—or person.*]

Once the water in the mixing bowl is a couple of inches deep and your cat is comfortable with the whole thing, you get to perform the last bit of magic. Take the mixing bowl away, leaving the bare toilet. (Lid Up, Seat Down.)

Voila! Your cat is now toilet trained.

Questions for Further Discussion

1. Why would this technique probably not work with a dog?
2. Are there any safety concerns with teaching a cat in this way?
3. Are there any other difficulties that might arise when doing this training?

Part of the training may include learning to press the flush handle.

Chapter Summary

Definition of Learning

5.1 Discuss the meaning of the term *learning*.

• Learning is any relatively permanent change in behavior brought about by experience or practice and is different from maturation that is genetically controlled.

It Makes Your Mouth Water: Classical Conditioning

5.2 Describe and explain the origins of classical conditioning and its important elements.

• In classical conditioning, one stimulus can, through pairing with another stimulus, come to produce a similar response.

• The unconditioned stimulus (UCS) is a naturally occurring stimulus that produces the innate, or involuntary, unconditioned response (UCR).

• When paired with the UCR, a neutral stimulus eventually begins to elicit an involuntary, and automatic behavior called the conditioned response (CR).

• The neutral stimulus (NS) and UCS must be paired several times and the CS must precede the UCS by only a few seconds.

• Other important aspects of classical conditioning include stimulus generalization, stimulus discrimination, extinction, spontaneous recovery, and higher-order conditioning.

• Pavlov believed that the NS became a substitute for the UCS through association in time.

• The cognitive perspective asserts that the CS has to provide some kind of information or expectancy about the coming of the UCS in order for conditioning to occur.

5.3 Define conditioned emotional responses, and explain conditioned taste aversions.

• Watson demonstrated that a phobia could be learned through classical conditioning by exposing a baby to a white rat and a loud noise, producing conditioned fear of the rat in the baby.

• Conditioned taste aversions occur when an organism becomes nauseated some time after eating a certain food, which then becomes aversive to the organism.

• Some kinds of conditioned responses are more easily learned than others because of biological preparedness.

What's in It for Me? Operant Conditioning

5.4 Describe the theory of operant conditioning and how it differs from classical conditioning, and explain the contributions of Thorndike and Skinner.

• Thorndike developed the law of effect: A response followed by a pleasurable consequence will be repeated, but a response followed by an unpleasant consequence will not be repeated.

• B. F. Skinner named the learning of voluntary responses operant conditioning because voluntary responses are what we use to operate in the world around us.

5.5 Differentiate between primary and secondary reinforcers and the processes of positive and negative reinforcement.

• Reinforcement is the process of strengthening a response by following it with a pleasurable, rewarding consequence.

• A primary reinforcer is a stimulus that satisfies a basic, natural drive, whereas a secondary reinforcer is a stimulus that becomes reinforcing only after being paired with a primary reinforcer.

• In positive reinforcement, a response is followed by the presentation of a pleasurable stimulus, whereas in negative reinforcement, a response is followed by the removal or avoidance of an unpleasant stimulus.

5.6 Distinguish among the schedules of reinforcement.

• Continuous reinforcement occurs when each and every correct response is followed by a reinforcer.

• Partial reinforcement, in which only some correct responses are followed by reinforcement, is much more resistant to extinction. This is called the partial reinforcement effect.

• In a fixed interval schedule of reinforcement, at least one correct response must be made within a set interval of time to obtain reinforcement.

• In a variable interval schedule of reinforcement, reinforcement follows the first correct response made after an interval of time that changes for each reinforcement opportunity.

• In a fixed ratio schedule of reinforcement, a certain number of responses are required before reinforcement is given.

• In a variable ratio schedule of reinforcement, a varying number of responses are required to obtain reinforcement.

5.7 Compare and contrast punishment with reinforcement, and list some of the problems associated with using punishment.

• Punishment is any event or stimulus that, when following a response, makes that response less likely to happen again.

• In punishment by application, a response is followed by the application or experiencing of an unpleasant stimulus, such as a spanking.

• In punishment by removal, a response is followed by the removal of some pleasurable stimulus, such as taking away a child's toy for misbehavior.

• A person who uses aggressive punishment, such as spanking, can act as a model for aggressive behavior.

• Punishment of both kinds normally has only a temporary effect on behavior.

• Punishment can be made more effective by making it immediate and consistent and by pairing punishment of the undesirable behavior with reinforcement of the desirable one.

5.8   Describe the role of operant stimuli in controlling behavior as well as other concepts that can enhance or limit operant conditioning.

- Discriminative stimuli are cues that provide information about what response to make in order to obtain reinforcement.
- Shaping, extinction, generalization and discrimination, and spontaneous recovery are other concepts in operant conditioning.
- Instinctive behavior in animals is resistant to conditioning or modification, a phenomenon called instinctive drift.

5.9   Describe how operant conditioning is used to change animal and human behavior, and identify some limitations to its use.

- Operant conditioning can be used in many settings on both animals and people to change, or modify, behavior. This use is termed *behavior modification* and includes the use of reinforcement and shaping to alter behavior.
- Token economies are a type of behavior modification in which secondary reinforcers, or tokens, are used.
- Applied behavior analysis (ABA) is the modern version of behavior modification and makes use of functional analysis and behavioral techniques to change human behavior.
- Neurofeedback is a type of biofeedback in which the person is typically connected to an electroencephalograph, a machine that records the brain's electrical activity.

Cognitive Learning Theory

5.10   Define and explain the concept of latent learning.

- Tolman found that rats that were allowed to wander in a maze but were not reinforced still showed evidence of having learned the maze once reinforcement became possible. He termed this hidden learning *latent learning*, a form of cognitive learning.

5.11   Explain the concept of insight learning.

- Köhler found evidence of insight, the sudden perception of the relationships among elements of a problem, in chimpanzees.

5.12   Explain the concept of learned helplessness.

- Seligman found that dogs that had been placed in an inescapable situation failed to try to escape when it became possible to do so, remaining in the painful situation as if helpless to leave. Seligman called this phenomenon learned helplessness and found parallels between learned helplessness and depression.

Observational Learning

5.13   Describe the process of observational learning.

- Observational learning is learning through watching others perform, or model, certain actions.
- Bandura's famous Bobo doll experiment demonstrated that young children will imitate the aggressive actions of a model even when there is no reinforcement for doing so.

5.14   List the four elements of observational learning.

- Bandura determined that four elements needed to be present for observational learning to occur: attention, memory, imitation, and desire.

Applying Psychology to Everyday Life: Can You Really Toilet Train Your Cat?

5.15   Provide and describe an example of conditioning in the real world.

- Writer Karawynn Long used shaping, reinforcement, and classical conditioning to train her cat to use the toilet in her bathroom instead of a litter box.

Test Yourself   ANSWERS ON PAGE AK–1.

Pick the best answer.

1. Sheila almost got hit by a car at a street corner because she was too busy texting on her phone. From that day on, Sheila looks before she reaches the street corner. Her change in behavior is a result of
  a. learning.
  b. memory.
  c. motivation.
  d. both sensation and perception.

2. At home, you rattle the chain on your dog's leash every time you prepare to take him for a walk. After several episodes like this, you find that your dog comes running to the front door even when you pick up the leash to put it back in the closet. In this example, what is the conditioned stimulus?
  a. going for a walk
  b. the sound of the leash
  c. the front door
  d. the dog runs to the door

3. A child has been classically conditioned to fear a white rat. If the child does not show fear when shown a black rat, this is called
  a. stimulus generalization.
  b. stimulus discrimination.
  c. spontaneous recovery.
  d. extinction.

4. During the cold winter, you have stopped taking your dog for walks. What's more, your dog has gotten used to the fact that when you accidentally rattle his leash, he isn't going for a walk, and subsequently he doesn't come running to the front door. What has occurred?
  a. stimulus generalization   **c.** spontaneous recovery
  b. stimulus discrimination   **d.** extinction

5. Rhonda had tartar sauce with her fish one night. The next morning she was nauseated and sick for much of the day. The next time she was offered the chance to go out for fish, she felt queasy and declined. Her queasiness at the thought of fish with tartar sauce was probably due to

a. higher-order conditioning.

b. a conditioned taste aversion.

c. stimulus substitution.

d. stimulus generalization.

6. Caitlin works in the psychology department's rat lab. In her studies, she found that many of her lab rats would develop a conditioned taste aversion to certain foods after as little as one trial. Caitlin's psychology professor refers to this as a classic example of

a. biological preparedness.

b. psychological preparedness.

c. instinctive drift.

d. stimulus substitution.

7. Blake finds that if he washes his car prior to going out on the town, more of his friends want to ride along with him. What theory would best explain his willingness to always wash and clean his car before going out?

a. Thorndike's law of effect

b. Skinner's theory of operant conditioning

c. Pavlov's theory of classical conditioning

d. Köhler's insight learning theory

8. In classical conditioning, behavior typically is _____, whereas with operant conditioning, behavior is _____.

a. rewarded; punished

b. biological; internal

c. voluntary; involuntary

d. involuntary; voluntary

9. Where do secondary reinforcers get their power from?

a. Pavlov's classical conditioning

b. Thorndike's law of effect

c. Bandura's observational theory

d. Köhler's insight theory

10. Positive reinforcement results in a(n) _____ in the target behavior and negative reinforcement results in a(n) _____ in the target behavior.

a. increase; decrease

b. increase; increase

c. decrease; decrease

d. decrease; increase

11. Belinda has a terrible headache. If she takes some aspirin and her headache goes away, and as a result Belinda is more likely to take aspirin in the future when she has a headache, this would be an example of

a. positive reinforcement.

b. negative reinforcement.

c. punishment.

d. generalization.

12. Ben gets paid every 2 weeks. In one 2-week period, he worked a total of 20 hours. During another 2-week period, he worked a total of 50 hours. Regardless of the total number of hours he works each week, he is paid every 2 weeks. What schedule of reinforcement is being used?

a. fixed ratio

b. variable ratio

c. fixed interval

d. variable interval

13. Denise is grounded for coming home after curfew. Additionally, her parents have taken away her cell phone for a month. Losing her cell phone privileges is an example of

a. negative reinforcement.

b. punishment by application.

c. punishment by removal.

d. learned helplessness

14. What is the relationship between negative reinforcement and punishment?

a. Both tend to strengthen a response.

b. Both tend to weaken a response.

c. Negative reinforcement strengthens a response while punishment weakens a response.

d. Negative reinforcement weakens a response while punishment strengthens a response.

15. Which of the following is an example of the use of extinction with operant conditioning?

a. A mother ignores her child's temper tantrum so that the behavior ultimately goes away.

b. A mother gives in to her child's demands for candy by buying the child some chocolate so as to quiet him or her.

c. A mother spanks a child when he or she starts throwing a tantrum.

d. A mother gives a child chocolate prior to him or her asking for it so as to keep a tantrum from occurring in the first place.

16. Studies by Keller and Marian Breland found that many animals exhibit instinctive drift. What does this mean?

a. The animals studied could not learn any skills even with the use of reinforcement.

b. The animals studied would learn skills through reinforcement but eventually revert to their genetically controlled patterns of behavior.

c. The animals studied would learn skills through reinforcement and they remained that way no matter how much reinforcement they were given.

d. The animals studied could learn only skills similar to those found in the wild.

17. Jose was lying in bed when he suddenly realized how he might deal with a fast approaching deadline at work. When his coworkers asked how he came up with his idea, he said, "It just came to me out of nowhere." Psychologists would refer to this as

a. latent learning.

b. learned helplessness.

c. insight learning.

d. observational learning.

18. Jody failed repeatedly in college algebra. Finally, she gave up and was seriously considering dropping out of college. One day, her best friend offered to personally help her if she signed up for college algebra again, but she refused. What concept might explain her reluctance?

a. latent learning

b. learned helplessness

c. insight learning

d. observational learning

19. What does AMID stand for?

a. Attention, Memory, Intention, Detention

b. Attention, Memory, Imitation, Desire

c. Ask, Memory, Imitate, Develop

d. Association, Memory, Imitation, Desires

20. Darla has noticed how some of her friends have lost weight and gotten trim by exercising 1–2 hours each day. However, she has no plans to imitate their behavior. What component of Bandura's model of observational learning will explain why Darla has not started a similar weight loss program?

a. Darla's unconscious does not believe she can achieve the goal.

b. Darla is not motivated nor does she have the desire to begin the program.

c. Darla's self-esteem must first be addressed.

d. Darla's unwillingness may be a sign of mental disorder.

Chapter 6
Memory

Most of us, at some point in our busy lives, have trouble remembering things, especially events from the distant past. What if you could remember nearly every day of your life? This rare ability is possessed by Brad Williams, who is known as the "Human Google." Brad is one of a small group of individuals with a syndrome called *hyperthymesia* (hī-pər-thī-mē-sē-uh). A person with hyperthymesia not only has an astonishing and rare ability to recall specific events from his or her personal past but also spends an unusually large amount of time thinking about that personal past. Brad can recall almost any news event or personal event he himself has experienced, particularly specific dates—and even the weather on those dates.

How is your memory of events? Do you find that you remember events from your past differently than others who were also present at that time?

Why study memory?

Without memory, how would we be able to learn anything? The ability to learn is the key to our very survival, and we cannot learn unless we can remember what happened the last time a particular situation arose. Why study forgetting? If we can learn about the ways in which we forget information, we can apply that learning so that forgetting occurs less frequently.

 ## Learning Objectives

6.1   Compare and contrast the three processes of memory.

6.2   Explain how the different models of memory work.

6.3   Explain the process of sensory memory.

6.4   Describe short-term memory and distinguish it from working memory.

6.5   Describe the mechanisms of long-term memory and differentiate among the various types of long-term memory.

6.6   Explain the effects of cues on memory retrieval.

6.7   Describe and distinguish between the processes of recall and recognition and identify problems with eyewitness recognition.

6.8   Describe how some memories are automatically encoded into long-term memory.

6.9   Explain how memories are reconstructed and identify some retrieval problems associated with this.

6.10   Describe the "curve of forgetting" and explain the importance of distributed practice to memory retrieval.

6.11   Identify some common reasons why people forget things.

6.12   Explain the biological bases of memory in the brain.

6.13   Define amnesia and discuss its causes.

6.14   Define Alzheimer's disease and discuss its possible causes and treatments.

What Is Memory?

Is memory a place or a process? The answer to that question is not simple. In reading through this chapter, it becomes clear that memory is a process but that it also has a "place" in the brain. Perhaps the best definition of **memory** is an active system that receives information from the senses, puts that information into a usable form, organizes it as it stores it away, and then retrieves the information from storage (Baddeley, 1996, 2003).

THREE PROCESSES OF MEMORY

6.1 Compare and contrast the three processes of memory.

Although there are several different models of how memory works, all of them involve the same three processes: getting the information into the memory system, storing it there, and getting it back out.

PUTTING IT IN: ENCODING   The first stage in the memory system is to get sensory information (sight, sound, etc.) into a form that the brain can use in a process called **encoding**. Encoding is the set of mental operations that people perform on sensory information to convert that information into a form that is usable in the brain's storage systems. For example, when people hear a sound, their ears turn the vibrations in the air into neural messages from the auditory nerve (*transduction*), which makes it possible for the brain to interpret that sound. **L I N K** to Learning Objective 3.1. Encoding is accomplished differently in each of the three memory storage systems. In one storage system, encoding may involve rehearsing information over and over to keep it in memory, whereas in another system encoding involves elaborating on the meaning of the information—but let's elaborate on that later.

KEEPING IT IN: STORAGE   The next step in memory is to hold on to the information for some period of time in a process called **storage**. This period of time will vary depending on the storage system being used. For example, in one system people hold on to information just long enough to work with it, about 20 seconds or so. In another system, people hold on to information more or less permanently.

GETTING IT OUT: RETRIEVAL   The biggest problem many people have is **retrieval**, getting the information they know they have out of storage. Have you ever handed in an essay test and *then* remembered several other things you could have said? Retrieval problems are discussed in a major section of this chapter.

MODELS OF MEMORY

6.2 Explain how the different models of memory work.

Exactly how does memory work? When the storage process occurs, where does that information go and why? Memory experts have proposed several different ways of looking at memory. The model that many researchers feel is the most comprehensive* and has perhaps been the most influential over the last several decades is the **information-processing model**. This approach focuses on the way information is handled, or processed, through three different systems of memory. The processes of encoding, storage, and retrieval are seen as part of this model.

While it is common to refer to the three systems of the information-processing model as *stages* of memory, that term seems to imply a sequence of events. While many aspects of memory formation may follow a series of steps or stages, there are those who

---

*comprehensive: all inclusive, covering everything.

see memory as a simultaneous* process, with the creation and storage of memories taking place across a series of mental networks "stretched" across the brain (McClelland & Rumelhart, 1988; Plaut & McClelland, 2010; Rumelhart et al., 1986). This simultaneous processing allows people to retrieve many different aspects of a memory all at once, facilitating much faster reactions and decisions—something Brad Williams in our opening story seems to be very good at. This model of memory, derived from work in the development of artificial intelligence (AI), is called the **parallel distributed processing (PDP) model**. In the AI world, PDP is related to *connectionism*, the use of artificial neural networks to explain the mental abilities of humans (Bechtel & Abrahamsen, 2002; Clark, 1991; Marcus, 2001; Schapiro & McClelland, 2009).

Like Brad Williams, the man with the amazing memory described in the opening pages of this chapter, Aurelian Hayman has been diagnosed with hyperthymesia.

The information-processing model assumes that the length of time that a memory will be remembered depends on the stage of memory in which it is stored. Other researchers have proposed that a memory's duration depends on the depth (i.e., the effort made to understand the meaning) to which the information is processed or encoded (Cermak & Craik, 1979; Craik & Lockhart, 1972). If the word *BALL* is flashed on a screen, for example, and people are asked to report whether the word was in capital letters or lowercase, the word itself does not have to be processed very much at all—only its visual characteristics need enter into conscious attention. But if those people were to be asked to use that word in a sentence, they would have to think about what a ball is and how it can be used. They would have to process its meaning, which requires more mental effort than processing just its "looks." This model of memory is called the **levels-of-processing model**. Numerous experiments have shown that thinking about the meaning of something is a deeper level of processing and results in longer retention of the word (Cermak & Craik, 1979; Craik & Tulving, 1975; Paul et al., 2005; Watson et al., 1999).

Each of these models can be used to explain some, if not all, research findings about memory. Whether one of these models will one day become the preferred model of memory has yet to be determined. In science, newer theories may often be combined, sometimes with one another and sometimes with older theories. They may be reworked into a new theory with more power to explain existing data. So although in this textbook the information-processing model of memory may take "center stage" for now, it is important to remember the concepts of the levels at which information is processed and the way in which those processes may take place while reading the rest of this chapter.

Concept Map L.O. 6.1, 6.2

Interactive

What Is Memory?

- an active system that receives, organizes, stores, and retrieves information
- three processes of memory
  - encoding
  - storage
  - retrieval
- models of memory
  - **information-processing model** — focuses on the way information is processed through different stages of memory
  - **levels-of-processing model**
    - focuses on the depth of processing associated with specific information
    - deeper processing associated with longer retention
  - **parallel distributed processing (PDP) model** — focuses on simultaneous processing of information across multiple neural networks

Reset

---

*simultaneous: all at the same time.

Practice Quiz   How much do you remember?   ANSWERS ON PAGE AK-1.

Pick the best answer.

1. Human memory consists of multiple systems that have the ability to store information for periods of time that range from _____ to _____.
   a. seconds; hours.
   b. seconds; our lifetime.
   c. minutes; decades.
   d. hours; our lifetime.

2. Ruth has just finished her research paper and handed it in. As she walks out of the classroom, she realizes that there were a few more things she should have included in the paper. Ruth's problem is in the memory process of
   a. encoding.
   b. storage.
   c. retrieval.
   d. retention.

3. Which model of memory suggests that memory processes occur throughout a neural network simultaneously?
   a. levels-of-processing model
   b. parallel distributed processing model
   c. information-processing model
   d. three-stage model

4. Research has demonstrated you can enhance your memory for specific words if you think about its meaning, how it can be used, and by giving a personal example of its use. This is best accounted for by which model of memory?
   a. levels-of-processing model
   b. parallel distributed processing model
   c. information-processing model
   d. three-stage model

The Information-Processing Model: Three Stages of Memory

Information-processing theory looks at how thought processes such as memory work and uses as its model for human thought the way that a computer functions (Massaro & Cowan, 1993). It was information-processing theorists who first proposed that there are three stages or types of memory systems (see **Figure 6.1**): sensory memory, short-term memory, and long-term memory (Atkinson & Shiffrin, 1968).

SENSORY MEMORY: WHY DO PEOPLE DO DOUBLE TAKES?

6.3 Explain the process of sensory memory.

Sensory memory is the first stage of memory, the point at which information enters the nervous system through the sensory systems—eyes, ears, and so on. Information is encoded into sensory memory as neural messages in the nervous system. As long as those neural messages are traveling through the system, it can be said that people have a "memory" for that information that can be accessed if needed. For example, say Elaina is driving down the street, looking at the people and cars on either side of her vehicle. All of a sudden she thinks, "What? Was that man wearing any pants?" and she looks back to check. How did she know to look back? Her eyes had already moved past the possibly pants-less person, but some part of her brain must have just processed what she saw (most likely the reticular formation, which notices new and important information). This is called a double take and can only be explained by the presence, however brief, of a memory for what she saw. **LINK** to Learning Objective 2.10.

Two kinds of sensory memory that have been studied extensively are iconic (visual) and echoic (auditory) sensory memories. In the sections that follow, these and other types of memories as well as several of the experiments that have added a great deal of information to the understanding of memory will be discussed.

ICONIC SENSORY MEMORY   The example of seeing the possibly pants-less person is an example of how visual sensory memory, or **iconic memory**, works. *Icon* is the Greek word for "image." Iconic memory was studied in several classic experiments by George Sperling (1960).

Figure 6.1 THREE-STAGE PROCESS OF MEMORY

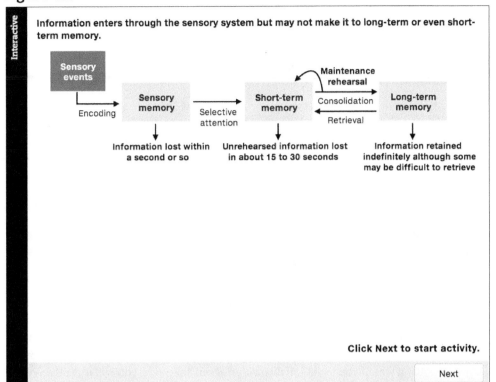

Information enters through the sensory system but may not make it to long-term or even short-term memory.

Information enters through the sensory system, briefly registering in sensory memory. Selective attention moves the information into short-term memory, where it is held while attention (rehearsal) continues. If the information receives enough rehearsal, it will enter and be stored in long-term memory.

Pablo Picasso was one of the most creative artists of his time. Here he is seen drawing an abstract of a woman in the air with a flashlight, using multiple exposures of the camera. What does his ability to "hold" the light image in his head long enough to complete the abstract tell us about his visual memory?

Sperling had found in his early studies that if he presented a row of letters using a machine that allowed very fast presentation, his subjects could only remember about four or five of the letters, no matter how many had been presented.

Sperling became convinced that this method was an inaccurate measure of the capacity of iconic memory because the human tendency to read from top to bottom took long enough that the letters at the top of the grid may have faded from memory by the time the person had "read" the letters on the bottom. He developed a method called the *partial report method*, in which he showed a grid of letters similar to those in **Figure 6.2** but immediately sounded a high, medium, or low tone just after the grid was briefly displayed. Subjects were told to report the top row of letters if they heard the high tone, the middle row for the medium tone, or the lowest row for the low tone. As they didn't hear the tone until after the grid went away, they couldn't look at just one row in advance.

Using this method, Sperling found that subjects could accurately report any of the three rows. This meant that the entire grid was in iconic memory and available to the subjects. The capacity of iconic memory is everything that can be seen at one time.

Sperling also found that if he delayed the tone for a brief period of time, after about half a second, subjects could no longer recall any of the letters from the grid. The icon had completely faded out of sensory memory in that brief time.

In real life, information that has just entered iconic memory will be pushed out very quickly by new information, a process called *masking* (Cowan, 1988, 1995). Research suggests that after only a quarter of a second, old information is replaced by new information.

Some people may have what is properly called **eidetic imagery**, or the ability to access a visual memory over a long period of time. While similar to iconic memory, eidetic imagery is not quite the same thing (Gummerman et al., 1972; Haber, 1979). People with eidetic imagery ability might be able to look quickly at a page in a book, and then by focusing on a blank wall or piece of paper, "read" the words from the image that still lingers in their

Rows of Letters	Tone Signaling Which Row to Report
LHTY	High tone
EPNR	Medium tone
SBAX	Low tone

Figure 6.2 Iconic Memory Test

Sample grid of letters for Sperling's test of iconic memory. To determine if the entire grid existed in iconic memory, Sperling sounded a tone associated with each row after the grid's presentation. Participants were able to recall the letters in the row for which they heard the tone. The graph shows the decrease in the number of letters recalled as the delay in presenting the tone increased.

memory. There is controversy surrounding the existence of this ability, but it is generally believed to be more common in children and diminishes by adolescence or young adulthood (Haber, 1979; Leask et al., 1969; Stromeyer & Psotka, 1971).

  If iconic memory lasts such a brief time, what use is it to us?

Iconic memory actually serves a very important function in the visual system. Chapter Three discussed the way the eyes make tiny little movements called *saccades* that keep vision from adapting to a constant visual stimulus, so that what is stared at steadily doesn't slowly disappear. Iconic memory helps the visual system to view surroundings as continuous and stable in spite of these saccadic movements. It also allows enough time for the brain stem to decide if the information is important enough to be brought into consciousness—like the possibly pants-less person.

ECHOIC SENSORY MEMORY The other type of sensory memory is **echoic memory**, or the brief memory of something a person has heard. A good example of echoic memory is the "What?" phenomenon. You might be reading or concentrating on the television, and your parent, roommate, or friend walks up and says something to you. You sit there for a second or two and then say "What? Oh—yes, I'm ready to eat now," or whatever comment is appropriate. You didn't really process the statement from the other person as he or she said it. You heard it, but your brain didn't interpret it immediately. Instead, it took several seconds for you to realize that (1) something was said, (2) it may have been important, and (3) you'd better try to remember what it was. If you realize all this within about 4 seconds, you will more than likely be able to "hear" an echo of the statement in your head, a kind of "instant replay." Echoic memory's capacity is limited to what can be heard at any one moment and is smaller than the capacity of iconic memory, although it lasts longer—about 2 to 4 seconds (Schweickert, 1993).

Echoic memory is very useful when a person wants to have meaningful conversations with others. It allows the person to remember what someone said just long enough to recognize the meaning of a phrase. As with iconic memory, it also allows people to hold on to incoming auditory information long enough for the lower brain centers to decide if the information is important enough to become conscious. It is echoic memory that allows a musician to tune a musical instrument, for example. The memory of the tuning fork's tone lingers in echoic memory long enough for the person doing the tuning to match that tone on the instrument.

Once these piano strings have been attached to the tuning pins, the piano can be tuned. Tuning a piano requires the use of echoic sensory memory. What other occupations might find a good echoic memory to be an asset?

SHORT-TERM MEMORY

6.4 Describe short-term memory and distinguish it from working memory.

What happens if the lower brain centers send the information on to the higher centers?

If an incoming sensory message is important enough to enter consciousness, that message will move from sensory memory to the next stage of memory, called **short-term memory (STM)**. Unlike sensory memory, short-term memories are held for up to 30 seconds or more.

SELECTIVE ATTENTION: HOW INFORMATION ENTERS **Selective attention** is the ability to focus on only one stimulus from among all sensory input (Broadbent, 1958). It is through selective attention that information enters our STM system. In Dr. Donald E. Broadbent's original filter theory, a kind of "bottleneck" occurs between sensory memory and short-term memory. Only a stimulus that is "important" enough (determined by a kind of "pre-analysis" accomplished by the attention centers in the brain stem) will be selected from all of the information in sensory memory to be consciously analyzed for meaning in STM. When a person is thinking actively about information, that information is said to be conscious and is also in STM. **LINK** to Learning Objective 4.1.

It is somewhat difficult to use Broadbent's selective-attention filter to explain the "cocktail party effect" that has been long established in studies of perception and attention (Bronkhorst, 2000; Cherry, 1953; Handel, 1989). If you've ever been at a party where there's a lot of noise and conversations going on in the background but you are able to notice when someone says your name, you have experienced this effect. The areas of the brain that are involved in selective attention were working even though you were not consciously aware of it, and when that important bit of information (your name) appeared, those areas somehow filtered the information to your conscious awareness—in spite of the fact that you were not paying conscious attention to the other background noise (Hopfinger et al., 2000; Mesgarani & Chang, 2012; Stuss et al., 2002).

Dr. Anne M. Treisman (Treisman, 2006; Triesman & Gelade, 1980) proposed that selective attention operates in a two-stage filtering process: In the first stage, incoming stimuli in sensory memory are filtered on the basis of simple physical characteristics, similar to Broadbent's original idea. Instead of moving to STM or being lost, however, there is only a lessening (attenuation) of the "signal strength" of unselected sensory stimuli in comparison to the selected stimuli. In the second stage only the stimuli that meet a certain threshold of importance are processed. Since the attenuated stimuli are still present at this second stage, something as subjectively important as one's own name may be able to be "plucked" out of the attenuated incoming stimuli. Even when deeply asleep, when the selective attention filter is not working at its peak level, it still functions: a sleeping mother will awake to her infant's cries while sleeping through louder, less important sounds such as a passing train (LaBerge, 1980).

What happens when information does pass through the selective attention filter and into short-term memory? Short-term memory tends to be encoded primarily in auditory (sound) form. That simply means that people tend to "talk" inside their own heads. Although some images are certainly stored in STM in a kind of visual "sketchpad" (Baddeley, 1986), auditory storage accounts for much of short-term encoding. Research in which participants were asked to recall numbers and letters showed that errors were nearly always made with numbers or letters that sounded like the target but not with those that looked like the target word or number (Acheson et al., 2010; Conrad & Hull, 1964).

WORKING MEMORY   Some memory theorists use the term *working memory* as another way of referring to short-term memory. This is not entirely correct: Short-term memory has traditionally been thought of as a thing or a place into which information is put. **Working memory** is more correctly thought of as an active system that processes the information present in short-term memory. Working memory is thought to consist of three interrelated systems: a central executive (a kind of "CEO" or "Big Boss") that controls and coordinates the other two systems, a visual "sketchpad" of sorts, and a kind of auditory "recorder" (Baddeley, 1986; Baddeley & Hitch, 1974; Baddeley & Larsen, 2007; Engle & Kane, 2004). The central executive acts as interpreter for both the visual and auditory information, and the visual and auditory information are themselves contained in short-term memory. For example, when a person is reading a book, the sketchpad will contain images of the people and events of the particular passage being read, while the recorder "plays" the dialogue in the person's head. The central executive helps interpret the information from both systems and pulls it all together. In a sense, then, short-term memory can be seen as being a part of the working memory system (Acheson et al., 2010; Bayliss et al., 2005; Colom et al., 2006; Kail & Hall, 2001).

Another way to think about short-term memory is as if it were a kind of desk where you do your work. You might pull some files out of storage (permanent memory) or someone might hand you some files (sensory input). While the files are on your desk, you can see them, read them, and work with them (working memory). The "files" are now conscious material and will stay that way as long as they are on the desk. If they are not that important or only necessary for a little while, they get "thrown out" (forgotten

Each person at this gathering is involved in a conversation with others, with dozens of such conversations going on at the same time all around. Yet if a person in another conversation says the name of one of the people in the crowd, that person in the crowd will be able to selectively attend to his or her name. This is known as the "cocktail party effect."

as you fail to pay attention to them). If they are important, they might get stored away in the filing system (permanent memory), where they are not conscious until they are once again retrieved—brought out onto the desk.

CAPACITY: THE MAGICAL NUMBER SEVEN   George Miller (1956) wanted to know how much information humans can hold in short-term memory at any one time (or how many "files" will fit on the "desk"). He reviewed several memory studies, including some using a memory test called the digit-span test, in which a series of numbers is read to subjects in the study who are then asked to recall the numbers in order. Each series gets longer and longer, until the subjects cannot recall any of the numbers in order.

Miller reported that the capacity of STM is about seven items or pieces of information, plus or minus two items, or from five to nine bits of information. Miller called this the "magical number seven, plus or minus two." So the "desk" isn't really very big and can hold only so many "files." Current research suggests that younger adults can only hold three to five items at a time without using a memory strategy, and if the information consists of long, confusing, or unfamiliar words the capacity is further reduced (Cowan, 2001; Cowan et al., 2005; Palva et al., 2010).

There is a way to "fool" STM into holding more information than is usual. (Think of it as "stacking" related files on the desk.) If the bits of information are combined into meaningful units, or chunks, more information can be held in STM. For instance, if someone were to recode the sequence of numbers "6547893217" as "654-789-3217," instead of 10 bits of information, there would only be three "chunks" that read like a phone number. This process of recoding, or reorganizing, the information is called chunking. To see how well you do at remembering numbers, participate in the *Digit Span* experiment.

Experiment   DIGIT SPAN

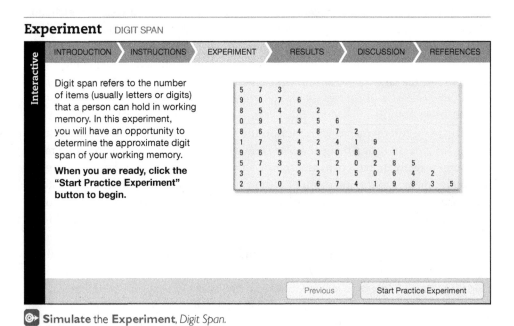

🎬 **Simulate** the **Experiment**, *Digit Span.*

WHY DO YOU THINK THEY CALL IT SHORT TERM?   How long is the "short" of short-term memory? Research has shown that short-term memory lasts from about 12 to 30 seconds without rehearsal (Atkinson & Shiffrin, 1968; Brown, 1958; Peterson & Peterson, 1959). After that, the memory seems to rapidly "decay" or disappear. The findings of a study with mice suggest that in order to form new memories, old memories must be "erased" by the formation of newly formed neurons (Kitamura et al., 2009). Some memories formed in the hippocampus will, without rehearsal, decay as new neurons (and newer memories) are added to the already existing neural circuits.

💬 What do you mean by rehearsal? How long can short-term memories last if rehearsal is a factor?

Most people learn that saying something they want to remember over and over again in their heads, such as repeating a phone number they need just long enough to dial it, can help them remember longer, a process called **maintenance rehearsal**. With maintenance rehearsal, a person is simply continuing to pay attention to the information to be held in memory, and since attention is how that information got into STM in the first place, it works quite well (Atkinson & Shiffrin, 1968; Rundus, 1971). With this type of rehearsal, information will stay in short-term memory until rehearsal stops. When rehearsal stops, the memory rapidly decays and is forgotten. If anything interferes with maintenance rehearsal (such as someone asking you the time of day while you are trying to count money), memories are also likely to be lost.

Interference in STM can also happen if the amount of information to be held in STM exceeds its capacity, "pushing out" what is already in STM to make room for newer information. This is why it might be possible to remember the first few names of people you meet at a party, but as more names are added, they displace the older names. A better way to remember a person's name is to associate the name with something about the person's appearance, a process that helps move the name from STM into more permanent storage. This more permanent storage is long-term memory, which is the topic of the next section.

Working memory is an important area of research and has implications for understanding not only intelligence but also learning and attention disorders such as attention deficit/hyperactivity disorder and various dementia-related memory problems (Alloway et al., 2009; Kensinger et al., 2003; Martinussen et al., 2005). Researchers have trained mice to improve their working memory and found that the mice become more intelligent with improved working memory (e.g., Light et al., 2010). Other researchers have found that working memory is helpful in solving mathematical problems but may actually hurt the ability to solve creative problems (Wiley & Jarosz, 2012). Creative problem solving seems to benefit from a less focused approach than the focused attention taking place in working memory.

It is very important for this pharmacist to count out the number of pills in the prescription accurately. Short-term memory allows her to remember the last number she counted, but if she is interrupted, she will have to start all over again. Short-term memory is very susceptible to interference.

LONG-TERM MEMORY

6.5 Describe the mechanisms of long-term memory and differentiate among the various types of long-term memory.

Long-term memory (LTM) is the system into which all the information is placed to be kept more or less permanently. In terms of capacity, LTM is unlimited (Bahrick, 1984; Barnyard & Grayson, 1996). Think about it: Would there ever really come a time when you could not fit one more piece of information into your head? When you could learn nothing more? There is always room for more information (in spite of what some students may believe).

DURATION As for duration,* the name *long term* says it all. There is a relatively permanent physical change in the brain itself when a long-term memory is formed. That means that many of the memories people have stored away for a long, long time—even since childhood—may still be there. That does not mean that people can always retrieve those memories. The memories may be *available* but not *accessible*. That is, they are still there, but for various reasons (discussed later under the topic of forgetting) people cannot get to them.

💬 I once memorized a poem by repeating it over and over—that's maintenance rehearsal, right? Since I still remember most of the poem, it must be in long-term memory. Is maintenance rehearsal a good way to get information into long-term memory?

Information that is rehearsed long enough may actually find its way into long-term memory. After all, it's how most people learned their Social Security number and the letters

---

*duration: how long something lasts.

These students are rehearsing for a concert. They will use maintenance rehearsal (repeating the musical passages over and over) until they can play their parts perfectly. The movements of their fingers upon their instruments will be stored in long-term memory. How is this kind of long-term memory different from something like the memorized lines of one's part in a play?

of the alphabet (although people cheated a little on the latter by putting the alphabet to music, which makes it easier to retrieve). Most people tend to learn poems and the multiplication tables by maintenance rehearsal, otherwise known as rote learning. *Rote* is like "rotating" the information in one's head, saying it over and over again. But maintenance rehearsal is not the most efficient way of putting information into long-term storage, because to get the information back out, one has to remember it almost exactly as it went in. Try this: What is the 15th letter of the alphabet? Did you have to recite or sing through the alphabet song to get to that letter?

Although many long-term memories are encoded as images (think of the *Mona Lisa*), sounds, smells, and tastes (Cowan, 1988), in general LTM is encoded in meaningful form, a kind of mental storehouse of the meanings of words, concepts, and all the events that people want to keep in mind. Even the images, sounds, smells, and tastes involved in these events have some sort of meaning attached to them that gives them enough importance to be stored long term. If STM can be thought of as a working "surface" or desk, then LTM can be thought of as a huge series of filing cabinets behind the desk, in which files are stored in an organized fashion according to meaning. Files have to be placed into the cabinets in a certain organized fashion to be useful. How else could anyone ever remember any kind of information quickly if the files were not in some order? The best way to encode information into LTM in an organized fashion is to make it meaningful through *elaborative rehearsal.*

ELABORATIVE REHEARSAL **Elaborative rehearsal** is a way of transferring information from STM into LTM by making that information meaningful in some way (Postman, 1975). The easiest way to do this is to connect new information with something that is already well known (Craik & Lockhart, 1972; Harris & Qualls, 2000; Postman, 1975). For example, the French word *maison* means "house." A person could try to memorize that (using maintenance rehearsal) by saying over and over, "*Maison* means house, *maison* means house." But it would be much easier and more efficient if that person simply thought, "*Maison* sounds like masons, and masons build houses." That makes the meaning of the word tie in with something the person already knows (masons, who lay stone or bricks to build houses) and helps in remembering the French term.

As discussed in the beginning of this chapter, Craik and Lockhart (1972) theorized that information that is more "deeply processed," or processed according to its meaning rather than just the sound or physical characteristics of the word or words, will be remembered more efficiently and for a longer period of time. As the levels-of-processing approach predicts, elaborative rehearsal is a deeper kind of processing than maintenance rehearsal and so leads to better long-term storage (Craik & Tulving, 1975).

💬 I can remember a lot of stuff from my childhood. Some of it I learned in school and some of it is more personal, like the first day of school. Are these two different kinds of long-term memories?

Nondeclarative knowledge, such as tying one's shoes, often must be learned by doing, as it is difficult to put into words. Once this child learns how to tie shoes, the knowledge will always be there to retrieve.

TYPES OF LONG-TERM INFORMATION Long-term memories include general facts and knowledge, personal facts, and even skills that can be performed. Memory for skills is called *nondeclarative (implicit) memory* because it usually involves a series of steps or procedures; memory for facts is called *declarative (explicit) memory* because facts are things that are known and can be declared (stated outright). These two types of long-term memory are quite different, as the following sections will explain.

NONDECLARATIVE (IMPLICIT) LTM Memories for skills that people know how to do, like tying shoes and riding a bicycle, are a kind of LTM called **nondeclarative (implicit) memory**. Nondeclarative memories also include emotional associations, habits, and simple conditioned reflexes that may or may not be in conscious awareness, which are often very strong memories. **LINK** to Learning Objectives 5.2 and 5.3. Referring back to Chapter Two, we will recall that the amygdala is the most probable location for emotional associations, such as fear, and the cerebellum in the hindbrain is responsible for storage of memories of conditioned responses, skills, and habits (Debiec et al., 2010; Squire et al., 1993).

Evidence that separate areas of the brain control nondeclarative memory comes from studies of people with damage to the hippocampus area of the brain. This damage causes them to have **anterograde amnesia**, in which new long-term declarative memories cannot be formed. (This disorder is fairly accurately represented by the character of Lenny in the 2000 motion picture *Memento*.) One of the more famous anterograde amnesia patients, H. M., is discussed in detail later in this chapter.

In one study (Cohen et al., 1985), patients with this disorder were taught how to solve a particular puzzle called the Tower of Hanoi (see **Figure 6.3**). Although the patients were able to learn the sequence of moves necessary to solve the puzzle, when brought back into the testing room at a later time they could not remember ever having seen the puzzle before—or, for that matter, the examiner. Yet they were able to solve the puzzle even while claiming that they had never seen it before. Their nondeclarative memories for how to solve the puzzle were evidently formed and stored in a part of the brain separate from the part controlling the memories they could no longer form. Even people with Alzheimer's disease, who also suffer from anterograde amnesia, do not forget how to walk, talk, fasten clothing, or even tie shoes (although they do lose motor ability because the brain eventually fails to send the proper signals). These are all implicit, nondeclarative memories. In fact, it would be rare to find someone who has lost nondeclarative memory. Literally, these are the kind of memories people "never forget."

Nondeclarative memories are not easily retrieved into conscious awareness. Have you ever tried to tell someone how to tie shoes without using your hands to show them? The subjects in the Tower of Hanoi study also provide a good example of implicit memory, as they could solve the puzzle but had no conscious knowledge of how to do so. Such knowledge is in people's memories because they use this information, but they are often not consciously aware of this knowledge (Roediger, 1990). A memory from one's early childhood of being frightened by a dog, for example, may not be a conscious memory in later childhood but may still be the cause of that older child's fear of dogs. Conscious memories for events in childhood, on the other hand, are usually considered to be a different kind of long-term memory called declarative memory.

Figure 6.3   Tower of Hanoi

The Tower of Hanoi is a puzzle that is solved in a series of steps by moving one disk at a time. The goal is to move all of the disks from peg A to peg C; the rules are that a larger disk cannot be moved on top of a smaller one and a disk cannot be moved if there are other disks on top of it. Amnesia patients were able to learn the procedure for solving the puzzle but could not remember that they knew how to solve it.

DECLARATIVE (EXPLICIT) LTM   Nondeclarative memory is about the things that people can *do*, but **declarative (explicit) memory** is about all the things that people can *know*—the facts and information that make up knowledge. People know things such as the names of the planets in the solar system, that adding two and two makes four, and that a noun is the name of a person, place, or thing—all facts that are readily available to anyone who wants to learn them. People can also know more personal facts—what they had for breakfast, their birthdates, and other facts that are not readily available to others. Therefore, there are two types of declarative long-term memories, *semantic* and *episodic* (Nyberg & Tulving, 1996).

General knowledge that anyone has the ability to know and that is often learned in school or by reading is called **semantic memory**. The word *semantic* refers to meaning, so this kind of knowledge is the awareness of the meanings of words, concepts, and terms as well as names of objects, math skills, and so on. This is also the type of knowledge that is used on game shows such as *Jeopardy!*. Semantic memories, like nondeclarative memories, are relatively permanent. But it is possible to "lose the way to" this kind of memory, as discussed in the section on forgetting.

The other kind of factual memory is the personal knowledge that each person has of his or her daily life and personal history, a kind of autobiographical* memory (LePort et al., 2012). Memories of what has happened to people each day, certain birthdays,

Dr. Bogdan Kostic

Missouri State Psychology Department

Repetition and Memory

---

*autobiographical: the story of a person's life as told by that person.

anniversaries that were particularly special, childhood events, and so on are called **episodic memory** because they represent episodes from their lives. Unlike nondeclarative and semantic long-term memories, episodic memories tend to be updated and revised more or less constantly. You can probably remember what you had for breakfast today, but what you had for breakfast two years ago on this date is most likely a mystery. Episodic memories that are especially *meaningful,* such as the memory of the first day of school or your first date, are more likely to be kept in LTM (although they may not be as exact as people sometimes assume they are). The updating process is a kind of survival mechanism, because although semantic and nondeclarative memories are useful and necessary on an ongoing basis, no one really needs to remember every little detail of every day. As becomes obvious later, the ability to forget some kinds of information is very necessary.

Episodic and semantic memories are explicit memories because they are easily made conscious and brought from long-term storage into short-term memory. The knowledge of semantic memories such as word meanings, science concepts, and so on can be brought out of the "filing cabinet" and placed on the "desk" where that knowledge becomes *explicit*, or obvious. The same is often true of personal, episodic memories.

 But sometimes I can't remember all the names of the planets or what I had for breakfast yesterday. Doesn't that make these memories implicit instead of explicit?

The difference between implicit memories, such as how to balance on a bicycle, and explicit memories, such as naming all the planets, is that it is impossible or extremely difficult to bring implicit memories into consciousness. Explicit memories can be forgotten but always have the potential to be made conscious. When someone reminds you of what you had for breakfast the day before, for example, you will remember that you had that knowledge all along—it was just temporarily "mislaid." For a look at the connections among all these types of LTM, see **Figure 6.4**.

LONG-TERM MEMORY ORGANIZATION   As stated before, LTM has to be fairly well organized for retrieval to be so quick. Can you remember the name of your first-grade teacher? If you can, how long did it take you to pull that name out of LTM and "put it on the desk" of STM? It probably took hardly any time at all.

Research suggests that long-term memory is organized in terms of related meanings and concepts (Collins & Loftus, 1975; Collins & Quillian, 1969). In their original study, Allan Collins and M. Ross Quillian (1969) had subjects respond "true" or "false" as quickly as possible to sentences such as "a canary is a bird" and "a canary is an animal." Looking at **Figure 6.5**, we clearly see that information exists in a network with nodes (focal points) of related information linked to each other in a hierarchy.* To verify the

Figure 6.4   Types of Long-Term Memories

Long-term memory can be divided into declarative memories, which are factual and typically conscious (explicit) memories, and nondeclarative memories, which are skills, habits, and conditioned responses that are typically unconscious (implicit). Declarative memories are further divided into episodic memories (personal experiences) and semantic memories (general knowledge).

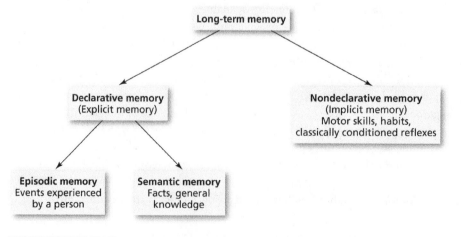

*hierarchy: an ordered list or series.

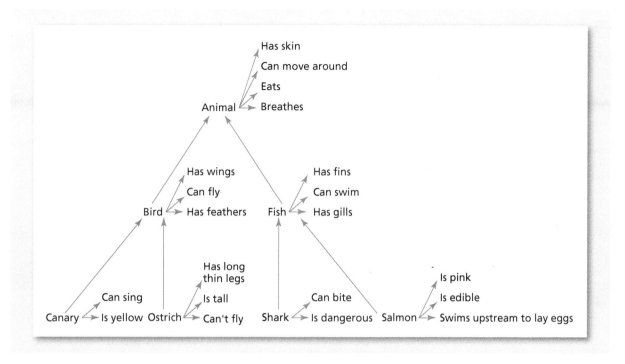

Figure 6.5   An Example of a Semantic Network

In the semantic network model of memory, concepts that are related in meaning are thought to be stored physically near each other in the brain. In this example, canary and ostrich are stored near the concept node for "bird," whereas shark and salmon are stored near "fish." But the fact that a canary is yellow is stored directly with that concept.

statement "a canary is a bird" requires moving to only one node, but "a canary is an animal" would require moving through two nodes and should take longer. This was exactly the result of the 1969 study, leading the researchers to develop the **semantic network model**, which assumes that information is stored in the brain in a connected fashion with concepts that are related to each other stored physically closer to each other than concepts that are not highly related (Collins & Quillian, 1969).

The parallel distributed processing model (Rumelhart et al., 1986) discussed earlier in this chapter can be used to explain how rapidly the different points on the networks can be accessed. Although the access of nodes within a particular category (for example, *birds*) may take place in a serial fashion, explaining the different response times in the Collins and Quillian (1969) study, access across the entire network may take place in a parallel fashion, allowing several different concepts to be targeted at the same time (for example, one might be able to think about *birds*, *cats*, and *trees* simultaneously).

Perhaps the best way to think of how information is organized in LTM is to think about the Internet. A person might go to one Web site and from that site link to many other related sites. Each related site has its own specific information but is also linked to many other related sites, and a person can have more than one site open at the same time. This may be very similar to the way in which the mind organizes the information stored in LTM.

WRITING PROMPT

In thinking about a typical day, how do you use each type of memory: nondeclarative, episodic, and semantic?

▶ The response entered here will be saved to your notes and may be collected by your instructor if he/she requires it.

Submit

Concept Map L.O. 6.3, 6.4, 6.5

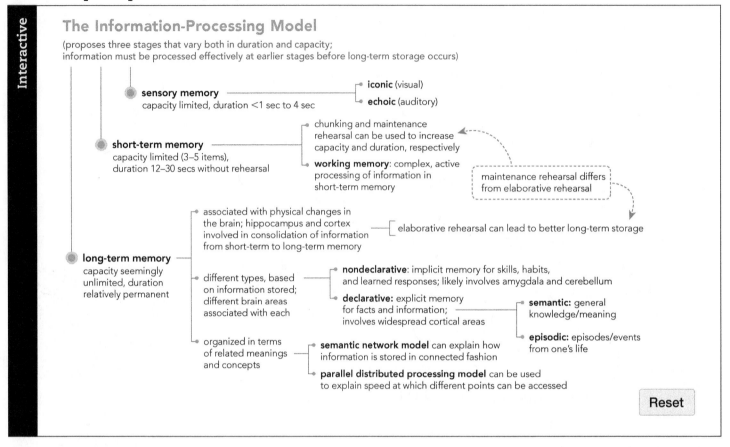

Interactive

The Information-Processing Model

(proposes three stages that vary both in duration and capacity; information must be processed effectively at earlier stages before long-term storage occurs)

sensory memory
capacity limited, duration <1 sec to 4 sec
— **iconic** (visual)
— **echoic** (auditory)

short-term memory
capacity limited (3–5 items),
duration 12–30 secs without rehearsal
— chunking and maintenance rehearsal can be used to increase capacity and duration, respectively
— **working memory**: complex, active processing of information in short-term memory

maintenance rehearsal differs from elaborative rehearsal

long-term memory
capacity seemingly unlimited, duration relatively permanent
— associated with physical changes in the brain; hippocampus and cortex involved in consolidation of information from short-term to long-term memory
— elaborative rehearsal can lead to better long-term storage
— different types, based on information stored; different brain areas associated with each
  — **nondeclarative**: implicit memory for skills, habits, and learned responses; likely involves amygdala and cerebellum
  — **declarative**: explicit memory for facts and information; involves widespread cortical areas
    — **semantic**: general knowledge/meaning
    — **episodic**: episodes/events from one's life
— organized in terms of related meanings and concepts
  — **semantic network model** can explain how information is stored in connected fashion
  — **parallel distributed processing model** can be used to explain speed at which different points can be accessed

Reset

Practice Quiz   How much do you remember?   ANSWERS ON PAGE AK-1.

Pick the best answer.

1. _____ memories are said to linger in the mind for a few seconds, allowing people the chance to keep with the flow of conversations and remember what was just said.
- **a.** Iconic
- **b.** Echoic
- **c.** Short-term
- **d.** Long-term

2. Information enters into short-term memory through a process known as _____.
- **a.** recency effect
- **b.** primacy effect
- **c.** selective attention
- **d.** repetition

3. Of the following, which is the most similar to the concept of long-term memory?
- **a.** a computer hard drive
- **b.** a computer monitor
- **c.** a computer mouse
- **d.** a computer keyboard

4. Amber meets a cute guy named Carson at a party. She wants to make sure she remembers his name so she reminds herself that he has the same name as the capital of Nevada (Carson City). This transferring of information from short-term memory to long-term memory is an example of what type of rehearsal?
- **a.** repetitive
- **b.** imagery
- **c.** elaborative
- **d.** maintenance

5. Brenda has been able to tie her shoes since she was 4 but now finds it difficult to explain to her baby brother how to tie his shoes, although she can easily demonstrate it for him. Brenda's memory for shoe-tying is best characterized as a _____ memory.
- **a.** declarative (explicit)
- **b.** semantic
- **c.** episodic
- **d.** nondeclarative (implicit)

6. When you take your final exam in your psychology class, what type of memory will you most certainly need to access to answer each question?
- **a.** nondeclarative
- **b.** semantic
- **c.** episodic
- **d.** working

Getting It Out: Retrieval of Long-Term Memories

💬 My problem isn't so much getting information *into* my head as finding it later.

Oddly enough, most people's problems with getting information stored in LTM back out again has to do with *how* they put that information *into* LTM.

RETRIEVAL CUES

6.6 Explain the effects of cues on memory retrieval.

Remember the previous discussion about maintenance rehearsal versus elaborative rehearsal? One of the main reasons that maintenance rehearsal is not a very good way to get information into LTM is that saying something over and over only gives one kind of **retrieval cue** (a stimulus for remembering), the sound of the word or phrase. When people try to remember a piece of information by thinking of what it means and how it fits in with what they already know, they are giving themselves cues for meaning in addition to sound. The more cues stored with a piece of information, the easier the retrieval of that information will be (Roediger, 2000; Roediger & Guynn, 1996). ⓁⒾⓃⓀ to Learning Objective PIA.7.

Although most people would assume that cues for retrieval would have to be directly related to the concepts being studied, the fact is that almost anything in one's surroundings is capable of becoming a cue. Have you ever had to take a test in a different classroom than the one in which you learned the material being tested? Do you think that your performance on that test was hurt by being in a different physical context? Researchers have found strong evidence for the concept of **encoding specificity**, the tendency for memory of any kind of information to be improved if retrieval conditions are similar to the conditions under which the information was encoded (Tulving & Thomson, 1973). These conditions, or cues, can be internal or external. *Context-dependent learning* may refer to the physical surroundings a person is in when they are learning specific information. For example, encoding specificity would predict that the best place to take one's chemistry test is in the same room in which you learned the material. Also, it's very common to walk into a room and know that there was something you wanted, but in order to remember it, you have to go back to the room you started in to use your surroundings as a cue for remembering.

In one study, researchers had students who were learning to scuba dive in a pool also learn lists of words while they were either out of the pool or in the pool under the water (Godden & Baddeley, 1975). Subjects were then asked to remember the two lists in each of the two conditions. Words that were learned while out of the pool were remembered significantly better when the subjects were out of the pool, and words that were learned underwater were more easily retrieved if the subjects were underwater while trying to remember.

Physical surroundings at the time of encoding a memory are not the only kinds of cues that can help in retrieval. In another form of encoding specificity called *state-dependent learning*, memories formed during a particular physiological or psychological state will be easier to remember while in a similar state. For example, when you are arguing with someone, it's much easier to remember all of the bad things that person has done than to remember the good times. In one study (Eich & Metcalfe, 1989), researchers had subjects try to remember words that they had read while listening to music. Subjects read one list of words while listening to sad music (influencing their mood to be sad) and another list of words while listening to happy music. When it

When this bride and groom dance together later on in their marriage, they will be able to recall this moment at their wedding and the happiness they felt at that time. State-dependent learning makes it easier for people to recall information stored while in a particular emotional state (such as the happiness of this couple) if the recall occurs in a similar emotional state.

The results of the Godden and Baddeley (1975) study indicated the retrieval of words learned while underwater was higher when the retrieval also took place underwater. Similarly, words learned while out of the water (on land) were retrieved at a higher rate out of the water.

came time to recall the lists, the researchers again manipulated the mood of the subjects. The words that were read while subjects were in a happy mood were remembered better if the manipulated mood was also happy but far less well if the mood was sad. The reverse was also true.

RECALL AND RECOGNITION

6.7 **Describe and distinguish between the processes of recall and recognition and identify problems with eyewitness recognition.**

 💬 Why do multiple-choice tests seem so much easier than essay tests?

There are two kinds of retrieval of memories, *recall* and *recognition*. It is the difference between these two retrieval methods that makes some kinds of exams seem harder than others. In **recall**, memories are retrieved with few or no external cues, such as filling in the blanks on an application form. **Recognition**, on the other hand, involves looking at or hearing information and matching it to what is already in memory. A word-search puzzle, in which the words are already written down in the grid and simply need to be circled, is an example of recognition. The following section takes a closer look at these two important processes.

RECALL: HMM . . . LET ME THINK When someone is asked a question such as "Where were you born?" the question acts as the cue for retrieval of the answer. This is an example of recall, as are essay question, short-answer, and fill-in-the-blank tests that are used to measure a person's memory for information (Borges et al., 1977; Gillund & Shiffrin, 1984; Raaijmakers & Shiffrin, 1992).

Whenever people find themselves struggling for an answer, recall has failed (at least temporarily). Sometimes the answer seems so very close to the surface of conscious thought that it feels like it's "on the tip of the tongue." (If people could just get their tongues out there far enough, they could read it.) This is sometimes called the *tip of the tongue (TOT)* phenomenon (Brown & McNeill, 1966; Burke et al., 1991). Although people may be able to say how long the word is or name letters that start or even end the word, they cannot retrieve the sound or actual spelling of the word to allow it to be pulled into the auditory "recorder" of STM so that it can be fully retrieved. This particular memory problem gets more common as we get older, although it should not be taken as a sign of oncoming dementia unless the increase is sudden (Osshera et al., 2012).

Another interesting feature of recall is that it is often subject to a kind of "prejudice" of memory retrieval, in which information at the beginning and the end of a list, such as a poem or song, tends to be remembered more easily and accurately. This is called the **serial position effect** (Murdock, 1962).

A good demonstration of this phenomenon involves instructing people to listen to and try to remember words that are read to them that are spaced about 4 or 5 seconds apart. People typically use maintenance rehearsal by repeating each word in their heads. They are then asked to write as many of the words down as they can remember. If the frequency of recall for each word in the list is graphed, it will nearly always look like the graph in **Figure 6.6**. To try this demonstration for yourself, participate in the *Serial Position Effect* experiment.

Figure 6.6 Serial Position Effect

In the serial position effect, information at the beginning of a list will be recalled at a higher rate than information in the middle of the list (primacy effect), because the beginning information receives more rehearsal and may enter LTM. Information at the end of a list is also retrieved at a higher rate (recency effect) because the end of the list is still in STM, with no information coming after it to interfere with retrieval.

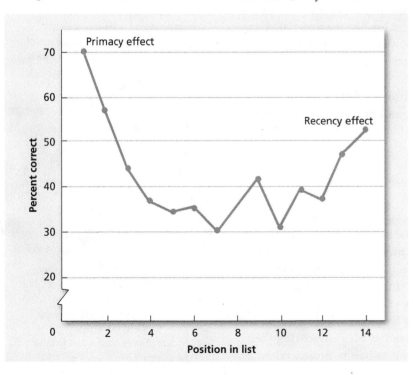

Experiment SERIAL POSITION EFFECT

| Interactive | INTRODUCTION | INSTRUCTIONS | EXPERIMENT | RESULTS | DISCUSSION | REFERENCES |

In this experiment, you will view 5 lists of words. Each list will consist of 12 words and each word will appear for 1 second. After all words have been presented for each list, you will be asked to recall as many of the words as possible.

When you are ready, click the "Start Practice Experiment" button to begin.

GRAPE

Previous   Start Practice Experiment

Simulate the **Experiment**, *Serial Position Effect.*

Words at the very beginning of the list tend to be remembered better than those in the middle of the list. This effect is called the **primacy effect** and is due to the fact that the first few words, when the listener has nothing already in STM to interfere with their rehearsal, will receive far more rehearsal time than the words in the middle, which are constantly being replaced by the next word on the list (Craik, 1970; Murdock, 1962). In fact, the first words may actually move into LTM if they are rehearsed long enough, because rote memorization, although not the best way to remember something, can lead to long-term storage.

At the end of the graph there is another increase in recall. This is the **recency effect**; it is usually attributed to the fact that the last word or two was *just heard* and is still in short-term memory for easy retrieval, with no new words entering to "push" the most recent word or words out of memory (Bjork & Whitten, 1974; Murdock, 1962). The serial position effect works with many different kinds of information. Business schools, for example, often teach their students that they should try not to be "in the middle" for job interviews. Going first or last in the interview process is much more likely to make a person's interview more memorable.

These people are waiting to audition for a play. The person who auditioned first and the one who auditioned last have the greatest chance of being remembered when the time comes for the director to choose. The serial position effect will cause the impression made by the actors who come in the "middle" to be less memorable.

Can knowledge of the serial position effect be of help to students trying to remember the information they need for their classes? Yes—students can take advantage of the recency effect by skimming back over their notes just before an exam. Knowing that the middle of a list of information is more likely to be forgotten means that students should pay more attention to the middle items, and breaking the study sessions up into smaller segments helps reduce the amount of "middle to muddle." (Students can also use *mnemonic strategies* to help offset this memory problem, as well as others. (L)(I)(N)(K) to Learning Objective PIA.7.)

RECOGNITION: HEY, DON'T I KNOW YOU FROM SOMEWHERE?
The other form of memory retrieval is *recognition*, the ability to match a piece of information or a stimulus to a stored image or fact (Borges et al., 1977; Gillund & Shiffrin, 1984; Raaijmakers & Shiffrin, 1992). Recognition is usually much easier than recall because the cue is the actual object, word, sound, and so on that one is simply trying to detect as familiar and known. Examples of tests that use recognition are multiple-choice, matching,

"Hey, good buddy! How you doin'?"   "Can't kick, big fella. What's shakin'?"

and true–false tests. The answer is right there and simply has to be matched to the information already in memory.

Recognition tends to be very accurate for images, especially human faces. In one study, over 2,500 photographs were shown to participants at the rate of one every 10 seconds. Participants were then shown pairs of photographs in which one member of each pair was one of the previously seen photographs. Accuracy for identifying the previous photos was between 85 and 95 percent (Standing et al., 1970).

Recognition isn't foolproof, however. Sometimes there is just enough similarity between a stimulus that is not already in memory and one that is in memory so that a *false positive* occurs (Muter, 1978). A false positive occurs when a person thinks that he or she has recognized something or someone but in fact does not have that something or someone in memory. Eyewitness recognition can be especially prone to false positives, although most people seem to think that "seeing is believing." For more about the problems with eyewitnesses, see the following *Classic Studies in Psychology* feature.

Rachel Happel, M.S.

Missouri State Psychology Department

Accurate Is Memory?

Dr. Elizabeth Loftus is an internationally known expert on the accuracy of eyewitness testimony. She is often called on to testify in court cases.

Classic Studies in Psychology
Elizabeth Loftus and Eyewitnesses

Elizabeth Loftus is a Distinguished Professor of Social Ecology, a Professor of Law, and a Professor of Cognitive Science at the University of California in Irvine. One of the world's leading memory researchers, her focus has been on the accuracy of recall of memories—or rather, the inaccuracies of memory retrieval. She has been an expert witness at more than 200 trials, including that of Ted Bundy, the serial killer who was finally executed in Florida (Neimark, 1996).

Loftus and many others have demonstrated time and again that memory is not an unchanging, stable process but rather is a constantly changing one. People continually update and revise their memories of events without being aware that they are doing so, and they incorporate information gained after the actual event, whether correct or incorrect.

In one classic experiment, Loftus (1975) showed subjects a 3-minute video clip taken from the movie *Diary of a Student Revolution*. In this clip, eight demonstrators run into a classroom and eventually leave after interrupting the professor's lecture in a noisy confrontation. At the end of the video, two questionnaires were distributed containing one key question and 90 "filler" questions. The key question for half of the subjects was, "Was the leader of the four demonstrators who entered the classroom a male?" The other half was asked, "Was the leader of the twelve demonstrators who entered the classroom a male?" One week later, a new set of questions was given to all subjects in which the key question was, "How many demonstrators did you see entering the classroom?" Subjects who were previously asked the question incorrectly giving the number as "four" stated an average recall of 6.4 people, whereas those who read the question incorrectly giving the number as "twelve" recalled an average of 8.9 people. Loftus concluded that subjects were trying to compromise the memory of what they had actually seen—eight demonstrators—with later information. This study, along with many others, clearly demonstrates the heart of Loftus's research: What people see and hear about an event after the fact can easily affect the accuracy of their memories of that event.

Questions for Further Discussion

1. How might police officers taking statements about a crime avoid getting inaccurate information from eyewitnesses?
2. The Innocence Project (**www.innocenceproject.org**) helps prisoners prove their innocence through DNA testing. More than 300 people in the United States have been freed by this testing, and the average time they served in prison before release is 13 years. Is eyewitness testimony enough, or should DNA evidence be required for sending someone to prison?

AUTOMATIC ENCODING: FLASHBULB MEMORIES

6.8 **Describe how some memories are automatically encoded into long-term memory.**

Although some long-term memories need extensive maintenance rehearsal or effortful encoding in the form of elaborative rehearsal to enter from STM into LTM, many other kinds of long-term memories seem to enter permanent storage with little or no effort at all, in a kind of **automatic encoding** (Kvavilashvili et al., 2009; Mandler, 1967; Schneider et al., 1984). People unconsciously notice and seem able to remember a lot of things, such as the passage of time, knowledge of physical space, and frequency of events. For example, a person might make no effort to remember how many times cars have passed down the street but when asked can give an answer of "often," "more than usual," or "hardly any."

A special kind of automatic encoding takes place when an unexpected event or episode in a person's life has strong emotional associations, such as fear, horror, or joy. Memories of highly emotional events can often seem vivid and detailed, as if the person's mind took a "flash picture" of the moment in time. These kinds of memories are called **flashbulb memories** (Neisser, 1982; Neisser & Harsch, 1992; Winningham et al., 2000).

Many people share certain flashbulb memories. People of the "baby boomer" generation remember exactly where they were when the news came that President John F. Kennedy had been shot. Younger generations may remember the horrific events of September 11, 2001, and the disastrous Hurricane Katrina. But personal flashbulb memories also exist. These memories tend to be major emotional events, such as a first date, an embarrassing event, or a particularly memorable birthday party.

Why do flashbulb memories seem so vivid and exact? The answer lies in the emotions felt at the time of the event. Emotional reactions stimulate the release of hormones that have been shown to enhance the formation of long-term memories (Dolcos et al., 2005; McEwen, 2000; McGaugh, 2004; Sharot et al., 2004). While there is evidence for a high degree of accuracy in flashbulb memories of *major events*, the election of President Barack Obama in November 2008 or the death of pop legend Michael Jackson in June 2009, other research reveals that flashbulb memories are just as subject to decay and alterations over time as other kinds of memories (Neisser & Harsch, 1992). In fact, memory of highly stressful events such as experiencing a crime have been shown to be less accurate than other memories, as the video *How Stress Affects Memory* explains. Apparently, no memories are completely accurate after the passage of time. The next section will discuss some of the reasons for faulty memories.

Fans of entertainer Michael Jackson may remember the moment they heard of his death on June 25, 2009. Events like this are so emotional for many people that the memories for the event are stored automatically, as if the mind had taken a "flash" picture of that moment in time. Such "flashbulb" memories seem to be very accurate but are actually no more accurate than any other memory.

👁 **Watch** the **Video**, *How Stress Affects Memory.*

HOW RELIABLE ARE OUR MEMORIES?

6.9 **Explain how memories are reconstructed and identify some retrieval problems associated with this.**

> 💬 I think my memory is pretty good, but my brother and I often have arguments about things that happened when we were kids. Why don't we have the same exact memories? We were both there!

People tend to assume that their memories are accurate when actually memories are revised, edited, and altered on an almost continuous basis. The reason for the changes that occur in memory has to do with the way in which memories are formed as well as how they are retrieved.

CONSTRUCTIVE PROCESSING OF MEMORIES Many people have the idea that when they recall a memory, they are recalling it as if it were an "instant replay." As new memories are created in LTM, old memories can get "lost," but they are more likely to be changed or altered in some way (Baddeley, 1988). In reality, memories (including those very vivid flashbulb memories) are never quite accurate, and the more time that passes, the more inaccuracies creep in.

The early twentieth-century memory schema theorist Sir Frederic Bartlett (1932) saw the process of memory as more similar to creating a story than reading one already written. He viewed memory as a problem-solving activity in which the person tries to retrieve the particulars of some past event—the problem—by using current knowledge and inferring from evidence to create the memory—the solution (Kihlstrom, 2002).

Loftus, along with other researchers (Hyman, 1993; Hyman & Loftus, 1998, 2002), has provided ample evidence for the **constructive processing** view of memory retrieval. In this view, memories are literally "built" from the pieces stored away at encoding. Each time a memory is retrieved, it may be altered or revised in some way to include new information, or details that were there at encoding may be left out of the new retrieval.

An example of how memories are reconstructed occurs when people, upon learning the details of a particular event, revise their memories to reflect their feeling that they "knew it all along." They will discard any incorrect information they actually had and replace it with more accurate information gained after the fact. This tendency of people to falsely believe that they would have accurately predicted an outcome without having been told about it in advance is called **hindsight bias** (Bahrick et al., 1996; Hoffrage et al., 2000). People who have ever done some "Monday morning quarterbacking" by saying that they knew all along who would win the game have fallen victim to hindsight bias.

These men may engage in "Monday morning quarterbacking" as they apply hindsight to their memories of this game. Their memories of the game may be altered by information they get afterward from the television, newspapers, or their friends.

WRITING PROMPT

Think about the last time you argued with a family member about something that happened when you were younger. How might hindsight bias have played a part in your differing memories of the event?

▶ The response entered here will be saved to your notes and may be collected by your instructor if he/she requires it.

Submit

MEMORY RETRIEVAL PROBLEMS Some people may say that they have "total recall." What they usually mean is that they feel that their memories are more accurate than those of other people. As should be obvious by now, true total recall is not a very likely ability for anyone to have. Here are some reasons why people have trouble recalling information accurately.

THE MISINFORMATION EFFECT Police investigators sometimes try to keep eyewitnesses to crimes or accidents from talking with each other. The reason is that if one person tells the other about something she has seen, the other person may later "remember" that same detail, even though he did not actually see it at the time. Such false memories are created by a person being exposed to information after the event. That misleading information can become part of the actual memory, affecting its accuracy (Loftus et al., 1978). This is called the **misinformation effect**. Elizabeth Loftus, in addition to her studies concerning eyewitness testimony, has also done several similar studies that demonstrate the misinformation effect. In one study, subjects viewed a slide presentation of a traffic accident. The actual slide presentation contained a stop sign, but in a written summary of the presentation, the sign was referred to as a yield sign. Subjects who were given this misleading information after viewing the slides were far less accurate in their memories for the kind of sign present than were subjects given no such information. One of the interesting points to be made by this study is that information that comes not only after the original event but also in an entirely different format (i.e., written instead of visual) can cause memories of the event to be incorrectly reconstructed.

FALSE MEMORY SYNDROME   If memory is edited and changed when people are in a state of waking consciousness, alert and making an effort to retrieve information, how much more might memory be changed when people are in an altered state of conscious, such as hypnosis? *False memory syndrome* refers to the creation of inaccurate or false memories through the suggestion of others, often while the person is under hypnosis (Hochman, 1994).

As this young woman observes the activity outside the window, she is storing some of the things she sees into memory while ignoring others. If she were to witness a crime, how would investigators know if her memories of the events were accurate or not? Would hypnotizing her to help her remember be effective? Why or why not?

Research has shown that although hypnosis may make it easier to recall some real memories, it also makes it easier to create false memories (Bowman, 1996). Hypnosis also has been found to increase the confidence people have in their memories regardless of whether those memories are real or false. False memories have been accidentally created by therapists' suggestions during hypnotic therapy sessions (especially those that involve age regression). ⓛ ⓘ ⓝ ⓚ to Learning Objective 4.7. Another study revealed that false memories are created in the brain in much the same way as real memories are formed and that people who look at real visual images and are also asked to imagine looking at visual images were often unable to later distinguish between the real and imagined images (Gonsalves et al., 2004). For more information on false memory syndrome, visit the Web site at **www.fmsfonline.org.**

Clearly, memories obtained through hypnosis should not be considered accurate without solid evidence from other sources.

 💬 But I've heard about people who under hypnosis remember being abused as children. Aren't those memories sometimes real?

The fact that some people recover false memories under certain conditions does not mean that child molestation* does not really happen; nor does it mean that a person who was molested might not push that unwanted memory away from conscious thought. Molestation is a sad fact, with one conservative estimate stating that nearly 20 percent of all females and 7 percent of all males have experienced molestation during childhood (Abel & Osborn, 1992). There are also many therapists and psychological professionals who are quite skilled at helping clients remember events of the past without suggesting possible false memories, and they find that clients do remember information and events that were true and able to be verified but were previously unavailable to the client (Dalenberg, 1996). False memory syndrome is not only harmful to the persons directly involved but also makes it much more difficult for genuine victims of molestation to be believed when they do recover their memories of the painful traumas of childhood.

So can we trust any of our memories at all? There is evidence to suggest that false memories cannot be created for just any kind of memory. The *memories* must at least be plausible, according to the research of cognitive psychologist and memory expert Kathy

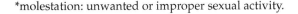

*molestation: unwanted or improper sexual activity.

Pezdek, who with her colleagues has done several studies demonstrating the resistance of children to the creation of implausible false memories (Hyman et al., 1998; Pezdek et al., 1997; Pezdek & Hodge, 1999).

In the 1999 study, Pezdek and Hodge asked children to read five different summaries of childhood events. Two of these events were false, but only one of the two false events was plausible (e.g., getting lost). Although the children were told that all of the events happened to them as small children, the results indicated that the plausible false events were significantly more likely to be remembered as false memories than were the implausible false events (e.g., getting a rectal enema). A second experiment (Pezdek & Hodge, 1999) found similar results: Children were significantly less likely to form a false memory for an implausible false event than for a plausible false event.

The idea that only plausible events can become false memories runs contrary to the earlier work of Loftus and colleagues and to research concerning some very implausible false memories that have been successfully implanted, such as a memory for satanic rituals and alien abductions (Mack, 1994). Loftus and colleagues (Mazzoni et al., 2001) conducted several experiments in which they found that implausible events could be made more plausible by having the experimenters provide false feedback to the participants, who read articles telling of the implausible events as if they had actually happened to other people. The false feedback involved telling the participants that their responses to a questionnaire about fears were typical of people who had been through one of the false events (much as a well-meaning therapist might suggest to a client that certain anxieties and feelings are typical of someone who has been abused). These manipulations were so successful that participants not only developed false memories for the events but also even contradicted their own earlier statements in which they denied having these experiences in childhood. The researchers concluded that two steps must occur before people will be likely to interpret their thoughts and fantasies about false events as true memories:

1. The event must be made to seem as plausible as possible.

2. Individuals are given information that helps them believe that the event could have happened to them personally.

Other variables that are associated with a tendency to recall false events as real (Clancy et al., 2002) may be susceptibility to hypnosis, symptoms of depression, and the tendency to exhibit odd behavior and unusual beliefs (such as alien abduction, past-life regression, or the healing ability of crystals).

Concept Map L.O. 6.6, 6.7, 6.8, 6.9

Interactive

Retrieval of Long-Term Memories

- **getting it out**
  - **retrieval cues** — more cues stored with a piece of information, the easier the retrieval
  - **encoding specificity**
    - **context-dependent learning** — improved memory for information if physical surroundings are similar to those when the memory was first formed
    - **state-dependent learning** — improved memory for information if physiological or psychological state is similar to that when the memory was first formed

- **recall vs. recognition**
  - **recall:** few or no external cues required
    - **retrieval failure:** (e.g., "tip of the tongue")
    - **serial position effect:** memory improved for items at beginning (primacy) and end (recency) of a list
  - **recognition:** match incoming sensory information (e.g., see or hear) to what is already in memory
    - false positives can occur (e.g., eyewitness testimony)

- **automatic encoding** — strong emotional associations can lead to vivid and detailed "flashbulb" memories

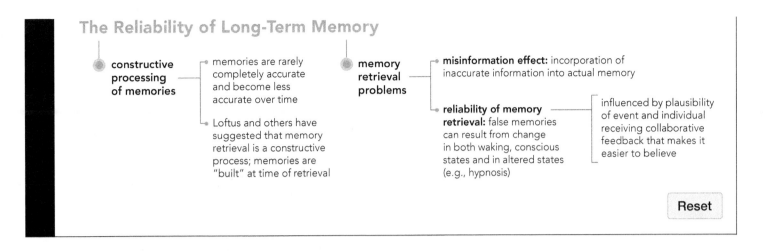

The Reliability of Long-Term Memory

constructive processing of memories
- memories are rarely completely accurate and become less accurate over time
- Loftus and others have suggested that memory retrieval is a constructive process; memories are "built" at time of retrieval

memory retrieval problems
- **misinformation effect:** incorporation of inaccurate information into actual memory
- **reliability of memory retrieval:** false memories can result from change in both waking, conscious states and in altered states (e.g., hypnosis) — influenced by plausibility of event and individual receiving collaborative feedback that makes it easier to believe

Reset

Practice Quiz   How much do you remember?   ANSWERS ON PAGE AK-1.

Pick the best answer.

1. What concept suggests that the best place to study for your psychology final to ensure good retrieval of concepts is your psychology classroom?
   a. serial position effect
   b. encoding specificity
   c. tip of the tongue phenomenon
   d. automatic encoding

2. Jaclynn had written a grocery list but accidentally left it at home. Trying to remember the list, Jaclynn remembers what was at the beginning of the list and what was at the end but not those things in the middle. This is an example of the
   a. encoding specificity effect.
   b. serial position effect.
   c. tip-of-the-tongue effect.
   d. flashbulb memory.

3. Felisha can recall with great detail the day of her wedding and all that occurred. What might psychologists say about these particular flashbulb memories?
   a. The memories were likely enhanced in part by the hormones released during emotional moments.
   b. The memories should last up to 15–20 years.
   c. The memories are unusually accurate.
   d. The memories are stored as nondeclarative memories.

4. In Loftus's 1978 study, subjects viewed a slide presentation of an accident. Later, some of the subjects were asked a question about a yield sign when the actual slides contained pictures of a stop sign.

When presented with this inaccurate information, how did these subjects typically respond?
   a. Most corrected Loftus and recalled seeing a stop sign.
   b. Many began seeing both a stop sign and a yield sign.
   c. Many subjects' overall accuracy dropped when confronted with conflicting information.
   d. Subjects were confused, but only briefly, at which point their accuracy of recalling the event returned.

5. Aaron has no memory of how he got home from a party. He then convinces himself that he must have been abducted by aliens while walking home. Subsequently, he is hypnotized in an attempt to help increase his memories of that evening. Based on the research of memory recall through hypnosis, what might we learn?
   a. Aaron may unknowingly create false memories of what happened that night to justify his belief.
   b. Aaron will be less confident of his memories from the evening.
   c. Hypnosis makes it harder for Aaron to recall memories of the evening in general.
   d. Aaron will not be able to recall the evening but will have memories of being in the womb.

6. A key component for any person to believe that a false event is in fact true is to make sure that the false information is
   a. as plausible as possible.
   b. introduced as soon after the event as possible.
   c. introduced by a source perceived as trustworthy.
   d. introduced no sooner than 24 hours after the event but no later than 15 days.

What Were We Talking About? Forgetting

 💬 Why do we forget things? And why do we forget some things but not others?

Brad Williams, the Human Google of the opening story, seems to have a fairly normal life despite his unusual memory abilities. But the same has not been true of other people with not only the ability to remember nearly everything but also the inability to *forget*.

EBBINGHAUS AND THE FORGETTING CURVE

6.10 Describe the "curve of forgetting" and explain the importance of distributed practice to memory retrieval.

The video *Jill Price: The Woman Who Cannot Forget* describes the case of a woman who remembers every detail of her life, both the good and the bad.

👁 **Watch** the **Video**, *Jill Price: The Woman Who Cannot Forget.*

That is exactly the problem experienced in the case of A. R. Luria's (1968) famous *mnemonist*, Mr. S. (A mnemonist is a memory expert or someone with exceptional memory ability.) He could not easily separate important memories from trivial ones and eventually invented a way to "forget" things—by writing them on a piece of paper and then burning the paper (Luria, 1968).

The ability to forget seems necessary to one's sanity if the experience of Mr. S. is any indicator. But how fast do people forget things? Are there some things that are harder or easier to forget?

Hermann Ebbinghaus (1913) was one of the first researchers to study forgetting. Because he did not want any verbal associations to aid him in remembering, he created several lists of "nonsense syllables," pronounceable but meaningless (such as GEX and WOL). He memorized a list, waited a specific amount of time, and then tried to retrieve the list, graphing his results each time. The result has become a familiar graph: the **curve of forgetting**. This graph clearly shows that forgetting happens quickly within the first hour after learning the lists and then tapers off gradually. (See **Figure 6.7**.) In other words, forgetting is greatest just after learning. This curve can be applied to other types of information as well. Although meaningful material is forgotten much more slowly and much less completely, the pattern obtained when testing for forgetting is similar (Conway et al., 1992).

In his early studies, Ebbinghaus (1885) found that it is also important not to try to "cram" information you want to remember into your brain. Research has found that spacing out one's study sessions, or **distributed practice**, will produce far better retrieval of information studied in this way than does *massed*

Figure 6.7 Curve of Forgetting

Ebbinghaus found that his recall of words from his memorized word lists was greatest immediately after learning the list but rapidly decreased within the first hour. After the first hour, forgetting leveled off.

practice, or the attempt to study a body of material all at once. For example, studying your psychology material for 3 hours may make you feel that you've done some really hard work, and you have. Unfortunately, you won't remember as much of what you studied as you would if you had shorter study times of 30 minutes to an hour followed by short breaks (Cepeda et al., 2006; Dempster & Farris, 1990; Donovan & Radosevich, 1999; Simon & Bjork, 2001). ⓁⒾⓃⓀ to Learning Objective PIA.5.

REASONS WHY WE FORGET

6.11 **Identify some common reasons why people forget things.**

There are several reasons why people forget things. We'll examine three theories here.

ENCODING FAILURE   One of the simplest reasons that people forget is that some things never get encoded in the first place. Your friend, for example, may have said something to you as he walked out the door, and you may have heard him, but if you weren't paying attention to what he said, it would not get past sensory memory. This isn't forgetting so much as it is **encoding failure**, the failure to process information into memory. Researchers (Nickerson & Adams, 1979) developed a test of long-term memory using images of a common object for many people, a penny. Look at **Figure 6.8**. Which view of a stop sign is the correct one? People see stop signs every day, but how many people actually look at them that closely so the information is encoded into long-term memory?

MEMORY TRACE DECAY THEORY   One of the older theories of forgetting involves the concept of a **memory trace**. A memory trace is some physical change in the brain, perhaps in a neuron or in the activity between neurons, which occurs when a memory is formed (Brown, 1958; Peterson & Peterson, 1959). Over time, if these traces are not used, they may **decay**, fading into nothing. It would be similar to what happens when a number of people walk across a particular patch of grass, causing a path to appear in which the grass is trampled down and perhaps turning brown. But if people stop using the path, the grass grows back and the path disappears.

Forgetting in sensory memory and short-term memory seems easy to explain as decay: Information that is not brought to attention in sensory memory or continuously rehearsed in STM will fade away. But is decay a good explanation for forgetting from long-term memory? When referring to LTM, decay theory is usually called **disuse**, and the phrase "use it or lose it" takes on great meaning (Bjork & Bjork, 1992). Although the fading of information from LTM through disuse sounds logical, often people can recall memories they had assumed were long forgotten. There must be other factors involved in the forgetting of long-term memories.

INTERFERENCE THEORY   A possible explanation of LTM forgetting is that although most long-term memories may be stored more or less permanently in the brain, those memories may not always be accessible to attempted retrieval because other information interferes (Anderson & Neely, 1995). (And even memories that are accessible are subject to constructive processing, which can lead to inaccurate recall.) An analogy might be this: The can of paint that Phillip wants may very well be on some shelf in his storeroom, but there's so much other junk in its way that he can't see it and can't get to it. In the case of LTM, interference can come from two different "directions."

PROACTIVE INTERFERENCE   Have you ever switched from driving a car with the gearshift on the steering wheel to one with the gearshift on the floor of the car? If the answer is yes, you probably found that you had some trouble when you first got into the new car. You may have grabbed at the wheel instead of reaching to the gearshift on the floor. The reason you reached for the gearshift in the "old" place is called **proactive interference**: the tendency for older or previously learned material to interfere with the learning (and subsequent retrieval) of new material (See **Figure 6.9** on the next page.)

Another example of proactive interference often occurs when someone gets a new cell phone. People in this situation often find themselves remembering their old cell phone

The fact that this woman can remember the things shown in the pictures even after many years makes it unlikely that the memory trace decay theory can explain all forgetting in long-term memory.

Figure 6.8   Stop!

Many people look at stop signs multiple times a day. Which of these stop signs is closest to an actual stop sign? The answer can be found on the next page.

Figure 6.9 Proactive and Retroactive Interference

If a student were to study for a French exam and then a Spanish exam, interference could occur in two directions. When taking the Spanish exam, the French information studied first may proactively interfere with learning of the Spanish information. But when taking the French exam, the more recently studied Spanish information may retroactively interfere with the retrieval of the French information.

The answer to **Figure 6.8** is the middle right image.

number or some of its digits instead of the new cell phone number when they are trying to give the new number to friends.

RETROACTIVE INTERFERENCE   When newer information interferes with the retrieval of older information, this is called **retroactive interference**. (See Figure 6.9.) What happens when you change back from the car with the gearshift on the floor to the older car with the gearshift on the wheel? You'll probably reach down to the floor at least once or twice because the newer skill retroactively interferes with remembering the old way of doing it.

How might interference work in each of the following cases?

1. Moving from the United States to England, where people drive on the left instead of the right side of the road.

2. Trying to program your old VCR after having the new one for a year.

3. Moving from one computer operating system to a different one, such as from Windows to Mac OS.

The different ways that forgetting occurs are summarized in **Table 6.1**.

Table 6.1 REASONS FOR FORGETTING

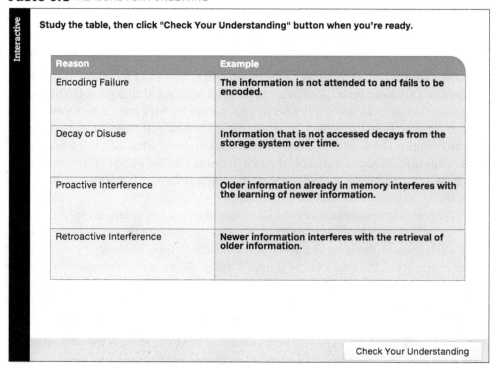

Study the table, then click "Check Your Understanding" button when you're ready.

Reason	Example
Encoding Failure	The information is not attended to and fails to be encoded.
Decay or Disuse	Information that is not accessed decays from the storage system over time.
Proactive Interference	Older information already in memory interferes with the learning of newer information.
Retroactive Interference	Newer information interferes with the retrieval of older information.

Check Your Understanding

Concept Map L.O. 6.10, 6.11

Forgetting
(originally studied by Ebbinghaus in 1913, research produced forgetting curve)

- **distributed practice** produces far better retrieval than massed practice (cramming)
- **encoding failure** nonattended information is not encoded into memory
- **memory trace decay** over time, if not used, neuronal connections can weaken or decay
- **interference** other information interferes with accurate retrieval
  - **proactive:** previously learned
  - **retroactive:** newly acquired

Reset

Practice Quiz   How much do you remember? ANSWERS ON PAGE AK-1.

Pick the best answer.

1. Raven has just finished learning a list of nonsense words given to her by her psychology instructor as part of a class activity. She had 100 percent recall at the end of class. According to Ebbinghaus's curve of forgetting, how quickly will Raven likely forget about 40 percent of the information she has just learned?

   a. within the first 20 minutes after leaving the class

   b. within the first day after leaving the class

   c. nearly a week after the class

   d. nearly a month after the class

2. Collin is asked to repeat what his mother just told him. He says he "forgot" but in reality Collin wasn't paying attention to his mother at all. This is an example of the _____ explanation of forgetting.

   a. interference   **c.** encoding failure

   b. memory trace   **d.** repression

3. Shantel spent a year living abroad in Spain. During that time, her ability to read and speak Spanish grew tremendously. However, now, two years later, Shantel feels she can no longer travel there because she can barely remember a thing. Her problem is most likely due to

   a. encoding failure.   **c.** proactive interference.

   b. retroactive interference.   **d.** decay theory.

4. Thomas is preparing to study for his final exam tomorrow, which is cumulative. He buys 4 energy bars, 3 energy drinks, and a large cup of coffee at the convenience store so that he can go home and attempt to study the entire book overnight. Cramming is an example of _____ practice.

   a. distributed   **c.** punctuated

   b. massed   **d.** frequented

Neuroscience of Memory

Researchers have evidence that specific areas of the brain are physically altered during memory formation. They also theorize that different areas may be involved for different types of memory.

THE BIOLOGICAL BASES OF MEMORY

6.12 Explain the biological bases of memory in the brain.

For example, nondeclarative memories seem to be stored in the cerebellum (Boyd & Winstein, 2004; Daum & Schugens, 1996). Research involving PET scanning techniques strongly suggests that short-term memories are stored in the prefrontal cortex (the very front of the frontal lobe) and the temporal lobe (Goldman-Rakic, 1998; Rao et al., 1997). Memories of fear seem to be stored in the amygdala (Debiec et al., 2010). Watch the video *Memory Retrieval and the Brain* to learn more about the brain structures involved with memory.

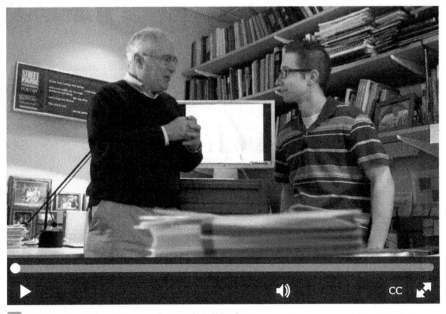

Watch the **Video**, *Memory Retrieval and the Brain.*

As for semantic and episodic long-term memories, evidence suggests that these memories are also stored in the frontal and temporal lobes but not in exactly the same places or in the same location as short-term memories (Weis et al., 2004).

> All that explains is the "where" of memory. Did scientists ever find out the "what" or the exact physical change that happens in the brain when memories are stored?

Several studies have offered evidence that memory formation involves not one physical change but many: changes in the number of receptor sites, changes in the sensitivity of the synapse through repeated stimulation (called *long-term potentiation*), and changes in the dendrites and in the proteins within the neurons (Alkon, 1989; Kandel & Schwartz, 1982; Shomrat et al., 2008; Squire & Kandel, 1999). All of these changes serve to increase the neural connections and make connections that already exist more sensitive to stimulation. These changes that take place as a memory is forming are called **consolidation** (Deger et al., 2012; Griggs et al., 2013; Krüttner et al., 2012). Consolidation may take only a few minutes for some memories, such as learning a new friend's name, but may take years for others, such as learning a new language (Dudai, 2004).

In the discussion of the *hippocampus* (a part of the limbic system) in Chapter Two it was identified as the part of the brain that is responsible for the formation of new long-term declarative memories. A classic case study in psychology provides fairly clear evidence of the role of the hippocampus (Milner et al., 1968). H. M. was a 16-year-old suffering from severe epileptic seizures. H. M.'s hippocampi and adjacent medial temporal lobe structures were removed in an experimental operation that the surgeon hoped would stop his seizures. The hippocampus was not the source of his problem, but it was apparently the source of his ability to store any new information he encountered because without either hippocampus, he was completely unable to remember anything new. H. M., who can now be revealed as Henry Gustav Molaison, died in December 2008, at the age of 82. You can read more about H.M.'s contributions to science at Suzanne Corkin's Web site: **http://newsoffice.mit.edu//2009/3q-corkin** (Carey, 2009). To learn about the H.M. postmortem project being conducted at the University of California, San Diego, go to **http://thebrainobservatory.ucsd.edu** (Carey, 2009).

WHEN MEMORY FAILS: ORGANIC AMNESIA

6.13 Define amnesia and discuss its causes.

Problems in the functioning of the memory areas of the brain cause two forms of severe loss of memory disorders. These problems can result from concussions, brain injuries brought about by trauma, alcoholism (Korsakoff's syndrome), or disorders of the aging brain.

RETROGRADE AMNESIA If the hippocampus is that important to the formation of memories, what would happen if it got temporarily "disconnected"? People who are in accidents in which they received a head injury often are unable to recall the accident itself. Sometimes they cannot remember the last several hours or even days before the accident. This type of amnesia (literally, "without memory") is called **retrograde amnesia**, which is loss of memory from the point of injury backwards (Hodges, 1994). What apparently happens in this kind of memory loss is that the consolidation process, which was busy making the physical changes to allow new memories to be stored, gets disrupted and loses everything that was not already nearly "finished." It's similar to what happens when a computer's power goes out: Whatever you were working on that was not yet saved is gone.

One of the therapies for severe depression is *ECT*, or *electroconvulsive therapy*. **LINK** to Learning Objective 13.11. In one study with depressed patients who were being treated with ECT (Squire et al., 1975), patients were tested for their memory of certain television programs both before and after the treatment. Before treatment, recent programs were recalled in more detail and more often than older ones. But after treatment, these patients seemed to forget the *last three years of programs*, remembering only the older ones. Not only does this indicate that memories are lost when consolidation is interrupted (as it is by the seizure caused by the treatment) but also that consolidation may take not just days or months but sometimes years to be completed.

ANTEROGRADE AMNESIA Concussions can also cause a more temporary version of the kind of amnesia experienced by H. M. This kind of amnesia is called *anterograde amnesia*, or the loss of memories from the point of injury or illness forward (Squire & Slater, 1978). People with this kind of amnesia, like H. M., have difficulty remembering anything new. This is also the kind of amnesia most often seen in people with *senile dementia*, a mental disorder in which severe forgetfulness, mental confusion, and mood swings are the primary symptoms. (Dementia patients also may suffer from retrograde amnesia in addition to anterograde amnesia.) If retrograde amnesia is like losing a document in the computer because of a power loss, anterograde amnesia is like discovering that your hard drive has become defective—you can read data that are already on the hard drive, but you can't store any new information. As long as you are looking at the data in your open computer window (i.e., attending to the data), you can access the data, but as soon as you close that window (stop thinking about it), the information is lost, because it was never transferred to the hard drive (long-term memory).

This is the reason that elderly people with a dementia such as Alzheimer's will sometimes take several doses of medicine because they cannot remember having already taken a dose. It also makes for some very repetitive conversations, such as being told the same story or asked the same question numerous times in the space of a 20-minute conversation. For more about Alzheimer's disease, see *Applying Psychology to Everyday Life* near the end of this chapter.

Major league baseball outfielder Johnny Damon (seen here colliding with player Damian Jackson) suffered a concussion after this injury. Concussions such as this can "wipe out" whatever was in the process of being consolidated into long-term memory. Which type of amnesia would you expect Johnny Damon to have, retrograde or anterograde?

WRITING PROMPT

Why do you think that amnesia (no matter what type it is) seems to affect mainly episodic memories?

▶ | The response entered here will be saved to your notes and may be collected by your instructor if he/she requires it. |

Submit

Concept Map L.O. 6.12, 6.13

Interactive

- different brain areas are associated with different types of memory
  - **procedural memories:** cerebellum
  - **short-term memories:** prefrontal cortex and temporal lobes
  - **semantic and episodic long-term memories:** frontal and temporal lobes (different locations than short-term memories)

- several physical changes in brain are associated with memory formation (consolidation)
  - changes at receptor (long-term potentiation)
  - changes in dendrites

- **hippocampus** plays a vital role in the formation of new declarative long-term memories

Neuroscience of Memory

- **organic amnesia:** caused by problems in brain function associated with brain trauma, disease, or aging
  - retrograde loss of memory from the point of injury backwards
  - anterograde loss of memory from the point of injury forwards — patient H. M. is a classic case study

Reset

Practice Quiz How much do you remember? ANSWERS ON PAGE AK-1.

Pick the best answer.

1. Research strongly suggests that short-term memories are stored in the _____, while memories of fear are stored in the _____.

   a. hippocampus; medial temporal cortex

   b. hypothalamus; superior colliculus

   c. bed nucleus of the stria terminalis; white matter

   d. prefrontal cortex; amygdala

2. Henry Gustav Molaison (H.M.) suffered from profound anterograde amnesia after his _____ were surgically removed in an attempt to control his seizures.

   a. hippocampi   **c.** frontal lobes

   b. amygdalae   **d.** thalami

3. T. J. was in a car accident and suffered a concussion. After he recovered, he found that he could not remember the accident itself or the events of the morning leading up to the accident. T. J. had which kind of amnesia?

   a. retrograde   **c.** Alzheimer's disease

   b. anterograde   **d.** encoding failure

4. The most common type of dementia experienced by adults and the elderly is _____ disease.

   a. multi-infarct   **c.** Hodgkins

   b. Parkinson's   **d.** Alzheimer's

Applying Psychology to Everyday Life
Alzheimer's Disease

6.14 **Define Alzheimer's disease and discuss its possible causes and treatments.**

Nearly 5.3 million Americans of all ages have Alzheimer's disease (Alzheimer's Association, 2010). It is the most common type of dementia found in adults and the elderly, accounting for nearly 60 to 80 percent of all cases of dementia. It is estimated that one out of eight people over the age of 65 has Alzheimer's disease. It has also become the third leading cause of death in late adulthood, with only heart disease and cancer responsible for more deaths (Alzheimer's Association, 2010; Antuono et al., 2001).

With Alzheimer's disease the primary memory problem, at least in the beginning, is anterograde amnesia. Memory loss may be rather mild at first but becomes more severe over time, causing the person to become more and more forgetful about everyday tasks. Eventually more dangerous forgetting occurs, such as taking extra doses of medication or leaving something cooking on the stove unattended. As Alzheimer's disease progresses, memories of the past seem to begin "erasing" as retrograde amnesia also takes hold. It is a costly disease to care for, and caregivers often face severe emotional and financial burdens in caring for a loved one who is slowly becoming a stranger.

What causes Alzheimer's disease is not completely understood. While it is normal for the brain to begin to form beta-amyloid protein deposits (plaques) and for strands of the protein tau to become twisted ("tangles"), people who suffer from Alzheimer's disease are found to have far more of these physical signs of an aging brain (Chen et al., 2012; Lim et al., 2012). One of the neurotransmitters involved in the formation of memories in the hippocampus is acetylcholine, and the neurons that produce this chemical break down in the early stages of the disease (Martyn et al., 2012). While one early-onset form of Alzheimer's appears to be genetic and involves several different genetic variations, this seems to be the case for fewer than 5 percent of the total cases of the disease (Alzheimer's Association, 2010; Bertram & Tanzi, 2005). The sad truth is that there is not one cause, but many, and even those who do not have Alzheimer's disease are not safe from other forms of dementia, such as dementia caused by strokes, dehydration, medications, and so on.

Treatments can slow but not halt or reverse the course of the disease. Five drugs are currently approved for treatment, but as yet only slow down the symptoms for an average of 6 to 12 months. What is known is that the risk factors for Alzheimer's (and many other forms of dementia) are things that can be managed: high cholesterol, high blood pressure, smoking, obesity, Type II diabetes, and lack of exercise all contribute (Alzheimer's Association, 2010;

To track the cell death that occurs in Alzheimer's disease, researchers used MRI technology to scan both patients with Alzheimer's disease and normal elderly subjects. Using supercomputers, the UCLA team created color-coded maps that revealed the degenerative sequence of the disease through novel brain-mapping methods. The wave of gray matter loss was strongly related to the progressive decline in cognitive functioning that is a key feature of the disease. Other researchers have used PET scans, as in the image above, to illustrate differences in brain activity between individuals with and without Alzheimer's disease.

Sweat, 2010). Keeping the brain mentally active is also a way to help prolong good cognitive health. One study's findings indicate that continued everyday learning stimulates brain-derived neurotrophic factors (BDNF) a key protein involved in the formation of memories (Chen et al., 2010). A more recent study suggest that a drug intended for use in treating diabetes, AC253, may be able to restore memory to Alzheimer's affected brain cells (Kimura et al., 2012), while another new drug, ORM-12741, also shows promise (Rouru et al., 2013).

People with dementia or traumatic brain injuries may end up with both types of amnesia. In a study of a recent case of anterograde amnesia a musician suffering brain damage from a bad case of encephalitis (brain inflammation) no longer remembers his past life, friends, or relatives (retrograde amnesia) and can no longer learn new information (anterograde amnesia). Yet he can still play his cello, read music, and can not only play pieces from before his brain injury but can also learn new pieces (Finke et al., 2012). These are nondeclarative skills, and this type of memory is typically unaffected by amnesia, suggesting that a different area of the brain is involved.

Questions for Further Discussion

1. People are now living much longer than their ancestors, and it is no longer unusual to hear of people who are well over 100 years of age. How might this extension of life expectancy be related to an increased rate of Alzheimer's disease?

2. What kinds of social programs or interventions could help people who are taking care of a relative with Alzheimer's?

Chapter Summary

What Is Memory?

6.1 Compare and contrast the three processes of memory.

- Memory can be defined as an active system that receives information from the senses, organizes and alters it as it stores it away, and then retrieves the information from storage.

- The three processes are encoding, storage, and retrieval.

6.2 Explain how the different models of memory work.

- In the levels-of-processing model of memory, information that gets more deeply processed is more likely to be remembered.

- In the parallel distributed processing model of memory, information is simultaneously stored across an interconnected neural network that stretches across the brain.

The Information-Processing Model: Three Memory Systems

6.3 Explain the process of sensory memory.

- Iconic memory is the visual sensory memory in which an after-image or icon will be held in neural form for about one-fourth to one-half second.

- Echoic memory is the auditory form of sensory memory and takes the form of an echo that lasts up to 4 seconds.

6.4 Describe short-term memory and distinguish it from working memory.

- Short-term memory is where information is held while it is conscious and being used. It holds about seven plus or minus two chunks of information and lasts about 30 seconds without rehearsal.

- Working memory is an active system responsible for processing the information in STM.

6.5 Describe the mechanisms of long-term memory and differentiate among the various types of long-term memory.

- Long-term memory is the system in which memories that are to be kept more or less permanently are stored and is unlimited in capacity and relatively permanent in duration.

- Information that is more deeply processed, or processed according to meaning, will be retained and retrieved more efficiently.

- Nondeclarative memories are memories for skills, habits, and conditioned responses.

- Declarative memories are memories for general facts and personal experiences and include both semantic memories and episodic memories.

- LTM is organized in the form of semantic networks, or nodes of related information spreading out from a central piece of knowledge.

Getting It Out: Retrieval of Long-Term Memories

6.6 Explain the effects of cues on memory retrieval.

- Encoding specificity occurs when physical surroundings become encoded as retrieval cues for specific memories.

- State-dependent learning occurs when physiological or psychological states become encoded as retrieval cues for memories formed while in those states.

6.7 Describe and distinguish between the processes of recall and recognition and identify problems with eyewitness recognition.

- Recall is a type of memory retrieval in which the information to be retrieved must be "pulled" out of memory with few or no cues, whereas recognition involves matching information with stored images or facts.
- The serial position effect, or primacy or recency effect, occurs when the first items and the last items in a list of information are recalled more efficiently than items in the middle of the list.
- Loftus and others have found that people constantly update and revise their memories of events.

6.8 Describe how some memories are automatically encoded into long-term memory.

- Automatic encoding of some kinds of information requires very little effort to place information into long-term memory.
- Memory for particularly emotional or traumatic events can lead to the formation of flashbulb memories, memories that seem vivid and detailed but that are no more accurate than any other memories.

6.9 Explain how memories are reconstructed and identify some retrieval problems associated with this.

- Constructive processing is the reconstruction of memories from bits and pieces of information that were stored in different places at the time of encoding.
- Hindsight bias occurs when people falsely believe that they knew the outcome of some event because they have included knowledge of the event's true outcome into their memories of the event itself.
- The misinformation effect is the tendency of people who are given misleading information to incorporate that information into their memories for a particular event.
- Pezdek and colleagues assert that false memories are more likely to be formed for plausible false events than for implausible ones.

What Were We Talking About? Forgetting

6.10 Describe the "curve of forgetting" and explain the importance of distributed practice to memory retrieval.

- Ebbinghaus found that information is mostly lost within 1 hour after learning and then gradually fades away. This is known as the curve of forgetting.

6.11 Identify some common reasons why people forget things.

- Some "forgetting" is actually a failure to encode information.
- Memory trace decay theory assumes the presence of a physical memory trace that decays with disuse over time.
- Forgetting in LTM is most likely due to proactive or retroactive interference.

Neuroscience of Memory

6.12 Explain the biological bases of memory in the brain.

- Evidence suggests that nondeclarative memories are stored in the cerebellum, whereas short-term memories are stored in the prefrontal and temporal lobes of the cortex.
- Semantic and episodic memories may be stored in the frontal and temporal lobes as well but in different locations than short-term memory, whereas memory for fear of objects is most likely stored in the amygdala.
- Consolidation consists of the physical changes in neurons that take place during the formation of a memory.
- The hippocampus appears to be responsible for the storage of new long-term declarative memories.

6.13 Define amnesia and discuss its causes.

- In retrograde amnesia, memory for the past (prior to the injury) is lost, which can be a loss of only minutes or a loss of several years.
- ECT, or electroconvulsive therapy, can disrupt consolidation and cause retrograde amnesia.
- In anterograde amnesia, memory for anything new becomes impossible, although old memories may still be retrievable.

Applying Psychology to Everyday Life: Alzheimer's Disease

6.14 Define Alzheimer's disease and discuss its possible causes and treatments.

- The primary memory difficulty in Alzheimer's is anterograde amnesia, although retrograde amnesia can also occur as the disease progresses.
- Alzheimer's disease has multiple causes, many of which are not yet identified.
- There are various drugs in use or in development for use in slowing or stopping the progression of Alzheimer's disease.
- Exercising and cardiovascular health can help delay or prevent various forms of dementia.

Test Yourself   ANSWERS ON PAGE AK-1.

Pick the best answer.

1. The steps to memory can best be described as follows:
    a. finding it, using it, storing it, using it again.
    b. putting it in, keeping it in, getting it out.
    c. sensing it, perceiving it, remembering it, forgetting it.
    d. a series of passive data files.

2. According to Sperling, what is the capacity of iconic memory?
    a. Everything that can be seen at one time.
    b. Everything that can be heard in one minute.
    c. Everything that can be sensed in one second.
    d. Everything that can be perceived in a lifetime.

3. Which type of memory best explains the "What?" phenomenon?
- **a.** iconic sensory memory
- **b.** echoic sensory memory
- **c.** short-term memory
- **d.** tactile sensory memory

4. For information to travel from sensory memory to short-term memory, it must first be _____ and then encoded primarily into _____ form.
- **a.** unconsciously chosen; auditory
- **b.** selectively attended to; visual
- **c.** biologically chosen; visual
- **d.** selectively attended to; auditory

5. You are introduced to someone at a party. While talking with the person, you realize that you have already forgotten the person's name. Assuming no strategies are used in the attempt to remember their name, how long does it typically take before such information is lost from short-term memory?
- **a.** approximately ¼ of a second
- **b.** usually no more than 4 seconds
- **c.** typically between 12 and 30 seconds
- **d.** Short-term memories typically last a lifetime.

6. Miller's early studies of the capacity of short-term memory suggested that most people could remember approximately _____ bits of information, whereas more recent research suggests it may be _____ to _____ items.
- **a.** two; six; nine
- **b.** three; eight; ten
- **c.** seven; three; five
- **d.** ten; seven; twelve

7. Mary has just met an attractive man named Austin at a party. She wants to make sure she remembers his name. What should she do?
- **a.** Mary should repeat the name continuously so as to commit it to long-term memory.
- **b.** Mary should chunk it by remembering the first three letters as a set and then remembering the remaining letters as a set.
- **c.** Mary should make it more meaningful. For example, she might remind herself that Austin has the same name as the capital of Texas.
- **d.** Mary should create a song to help her remember his name.

8. _____ memory includes what people can do or demonstrate, whereas _____ memory is about what people know and can report.
- **a.** Nondeclarative; declarative
- **b.** Declarative; nondeclarative
- **c.** Semantic; nondeclarative
- **d.** Episodic; semantic

9. The semantic network model of memory suggests that the _____ nodes you must pass through to access information, the longer it will take for you to recall information.
- **a.** fewer
- **b.** more
- **c.** bigger the
- **d.** more complex the

10. Phineas walks out of his office and into the conference room. However, after he leaves his office, he forgets what he was coming into the conference room for. According to the encoding specificity hypothesis, what should Phineas do to regain his lost memory?
- **a.** Phineas should return to his office to help him remember what he had forgotten.
- **b.** Phineas should ask someone else, "What did I come in here for?"
- **c.** Phineas should remain in the conference room and simply relax so that his memory should return.
- **d.** Phineas should consider seeing a doctor, since such memory loss can be a sign of mental illness.

11. Which of the following is an example of a test using recognition?
- **a.** short answer
- **b.** essay
- **c.** fill in the blanks
- **d.** true–false

12. When creating a presentation, many public speaking instructors will tell you to develop a strong opening or attention getter to your presentation as well as a good summary and finish. What aspect of memory best explains these suggestions?
- **a.** parallel distributing processing model of memory
- **b.** chunking
- **c.** elaborative rehearsal theory
- **d.** serial position effect

13. Your mother tells you to dress for success at your interview because it's all about "first impressions." In other words, she is telling you that people often remember what they see first. This belief is in line with what element of memory?
- **a.** the primacy effect
- **b.** the tip-of-the-tongue phenomenon
- **c.** the recency effect
- **d.** the power of false positives

14. Research by Elizabeth Loftus shows that eyewitness recognition is very prone to what psychologists call
- **a.** automatic encoding.
- **b.** a false positive.
- **c.** a flashbulb memory.
- **d.** a recency effect.

15. The tendency of certain elements to enter long-term memory with little or no effort to encode and organize them is what defines
- **a.** encoding specificity.
- **b.** automatic encoding.
- **c.** flashbulb memories.
- **d.** eidetic imagery.

16. The ability to vividly remember where you were and what you were doing when the United States was attacked on September 11, 2001, is an example of
- **a.** eyewitness testimony.
- **b.** encoding specificity hypothesis.
- **c.** false-memory syndrome.
- **d.** flashbulb memory.

17. In Hermann Ebbinghaus's classic study on memory and the forgetting curve, after learning a list of nonsense syllables, forgetting occurred quickly during the first _____ before tapering off.
- **a.** twenty minutes
- **b.** hour
- **c.** five hours
- **d.** nine hours

18. You are surprised by the fact that you cannot remember if Abraham Lincoln's head faces the left or the right on a penny. This is all the more surprising given the fact that you work with money at your job on nearly a daily basis. What would best explain such an inability to recall this information?
- **a.** encoding failure
- **b.** decay theory
- **c.** interference theory
- **d.** distributed practice effect

19. Henry Gustav Molaison, infamously known as H. M., was unable to form new declarative memories. He suffered from what psychologists call
- **a.** psychogenic amnesia.
- **b.** retrograde amnesia.
- **c.** retroactive amnesia.
- **d.** anterograde amnesia.

20. In the case of Henry Gustav Molaison (H.M.), the memory problems that he experienced appeared after brain surgery was performed in the attempt to relieve a severe case of epilepsy. In this surgery, Molaison's _____ and adjacent medial temporal lobe structures were removed, inadvertently leading to an inability to store any new personal or factual information.
- **a.** amygdalae
- **b.** hypothalamus
- **c.** corpus callosum
- **d.** hippocampi

Chapter 7
Cognition: Thinking, Intelligence, and Language

Think about how you interact with the world around you. How often do you simply respond without knowing how or why you do the things you do, say, or think? How much of your conscious experience involves effortful, mindful attention and decision making? These two types of thinking, sometimes referred to as System 1 and System 2, characterize much of how we think and process information (Kahneman, 2011; Stanovich & West, 2000). System 1, which involves making quick decisions and using cognitive shortcuts, is guided by our innate abilities and personal experiences. System 2, which is relatively slow, analytical, and rule-based, is dependent more on our formal educational experiences. Overall, our thinking has to be governed by the interplay between the two.

Do you tend to rely more on instinctual (System 1) or deliberate (System 2) thought processes? How do your thought processes and decision-making strategies vary depending on the situation?

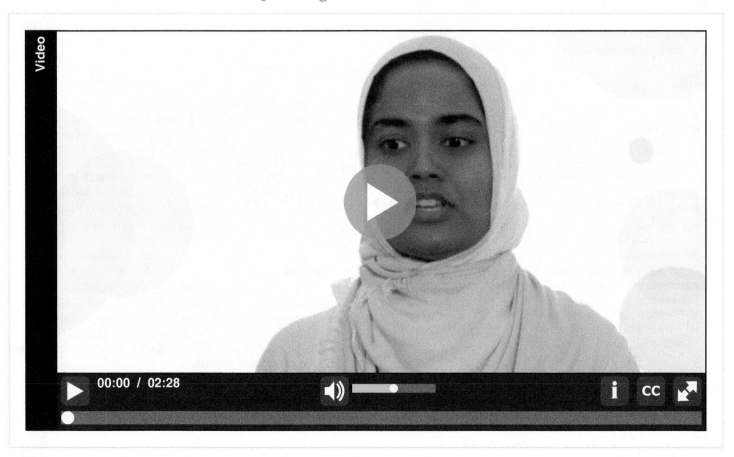

Why study the nature of thought?

To fully understand how we do any of the things we do (such as learning, remembering, and behaving), we need to understand how we think. How do we organize our thoughts? How do we communicate those thoughts to others? What do we mean by intelligence? Why are some people able to learn so much faster than others?

Learning Objectives

7.1   Define cognition and explain how mental images and concepts are involved in the process of thinking.

7.2   Describe some methods people use to solve problems and make decisions.

7.3   Identify three common barriers to successful problem solving.

7.4   Define creativity and identify some characteristics of divergent thinking.

7.5   Compare and contrast different theories on the nature of intelligence.

7.6   Compare and contrast some methods of measuring intelligence and identify ways to evaluate the quality of a test.

7.7   Define intellectual disability, giftedness, and emotional intelligence.

7.8   Evaluate the influence of heredity and environment on the development of intelligence.

7.9   Define language and identify its different elements and structure.

7.10   Evaluate whether or not language influences how people think.

7.11   Summarize the research on the ability of animals to communicate and use language.

7.12   Identify some methods for improving your thinking.

Figure 7.1   Kosslyn's Fictional Island

In Kosslyn's 1978 study, participants were asked to push a button when they had imagined themselves moving from one place on the island to another. As the graph below the picture shows, participants took longer to complete the task when the locations on the image were farther apart.
Source: Kosslyn et al. (1978).

Cognition

What does it mean to think? People are thinking all the time and talking about thinking as well: "What do you think?" "Let me think about that." "I don't think so." So, what does it mean to think?

HOW PEOPLE THINK: MENTAL IMAGERY AND CONCEPTS

7.1 Define cognition and explain how mental images and concepts are involved in the process of thinking.

Thinking, or **cognition** (from a Latin word meaning "to know"), can be defined as mental activity that goes on in the brain when a person is processing information—organizing it, understanding it, and communicating it to others. Thinking includes memory, but it is much more. When people think, they are not only aware of the information in the brain but also are making decisions about it, comparing it to other information, and using it to solve problems.

Thinking also includes more than just a kind of verbal "stream of consciousness." When people think, they often have images as well as words in their minds.

MENTAL IMAGERY   As stated in Chapter Six, short-term memories are encoded in the form of sounds and also as visual images, forming a mental picture of the world. Thus, **mental images** (representations that stand in for objects or events and have a picturelike quality) are one of several tools used in the thought process.

Here's an interesting demonstration of the use of mental images. Get several people together and ask them to tell you *as fast as they can* how many windows are in the place where they live. Usually you'll find that the first people to shout out an answer have fewer windows in their houses than the ones who take longer to respond. You'll also notice that most of them look up, as if looking at some image that only they can see. If asked, they'll say that to determine the number of windows, they pictured where they live and simply counted windows as they "walked through" the image they created in their mind.

💬 So more windows means more time to count them in your head? I guess mentally "walking" through a bigger house in your head would take longer than "walking" through a smaller one.

That's what researchers think, too. They have found that it does take longer to view a mental image that is larger or covers more distance than a smaller, more compact one (Kosslyn et al., 2001; Ochsner & Kosslyn, 1994). In one study (Kosslyn et al., 1978), participants were asked to look at a map of an imaginary island (see **Figure 7.1**). On this map were several landmarks, such as a hut, a lake, and a grassy area. After viewing the map and memorizing it, participants were asked to imagine a specific place on the island, such as the hut, and then to "look" for another place, like the lake. When they mentally "reached" the second place, they pushed a button that recorded reaction time. The greater the physical distance on the map between the two locations, the longer it took participants to scan the image for the second location. The participants were apparently looking at their mental image and scanning it just as if it were a real, physical map.

People are even able to mentally rotate, or turn, images (Shepherd & Metzler, 1971). Kosslyn (1983) asked participants questions such as the following: "Do frogs have lips and a stubby tail?" He found that most participants reported visualizing a frog, starting with the face ("no lips"), then mentally rotating the image so it was facing away from them, and then "zooming in" to look for the stubby tail ("yes, there it is"). A very important aspect of the research on mental rotation is that we tend to engage *mental* images in our mind much like we engage or interact with *physical* objects. When we rotate an object in our minds (or in other ways interact with or manipulate mental images), it is not instantaneous—it takes time, just as it would if we were rotating a physical object with our hands. To see how well you are able to mentally rotate images, try the *Mental Rotation* experiment.

Experiment   MENTAL ROTATION

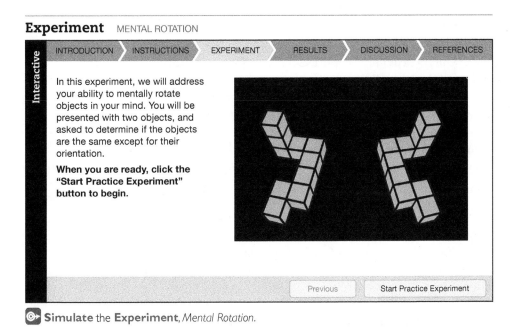

Simulate the **Experiment**, *Mental Rotation.*

In the brain, creating a mental image is almost the opposite of seeing an actual image. With an actual image, the information goes from the eyes to the visual cortex of the occipital lobe and is processed, or interpreted, by other areas of the cortex that compare the new information to information already in memory. **L I N K** to Learning Objective 2.12. In creating a mental image, areas of the cortex associated with stored knowledge send information to the visual cortex, where the image is perceived in the "mind's eye" (Kosslyn et al., 1993; Sparing et al., 2002). PET scans show areas of the visual cortex being activated during the process of forming an image, providing evidence for the role of the visual cortex in mental imagery (Kosslyn et al., 1993, 1999, 2001).

Through the use of functional magnetic resonance imagery (fMRI), researchers have been able to see the overlap that occurs in brain areas activated during visual mental imagery tasks as compared to actual tasks involving visual perception (Ganis et al., 2004). During both types of tasks, activity was present in the frontal cortex (cognitive control), temporal lobes (memory), parietal lobes (attention and spatial memory), and occipital lobes (visual processing). However, the amount of activity in these areas differed between the two types of tasks. For example, activity in the visual cortex was stronger during perception than in imagery, suggesting sensory input activates this area more strongly than memory input. And an important finding overall, those areas activated during visual imagery were a subset of those activated during visual perception, with the greatest similarity in the frontal and parietal regions rather than the temporal and occipital regions. What does this mean? Simply that there is commonality between the processes of visual imagery and visual perception, but it *is not* a complete overlap, and, as the authors point out, the greater overlap *was not* in the temporal and occipital regions (memory and vision functions) that might be assumed to be the most likely areas of overlap given the visual nature of the tasks (Ganis et al., 2004).

CONCEPTS AND PROTOTYPES

  Images are not the only way we think, are they?

Mental images are only one form of mental representation. Another aspect of thought processes is the use of concepts. **Concepts** are ideas that represent a class or category of objects, events, or activities. People use concepts to think about objects or events without having to think about all the specific examples of the category. For example, a person can think about "fruit" without thinking about every kind of fruit there is in the world, which would take far more effort and time. This ability to think in terms of concepts allows us to communicate with each other: If I mention a bird to you, you know what I am referring to, even if we aren't actually thinking of the same *type* of bird.

Concepts not only contain the important features of the objects or events people want to think about, but also they allow the identification of new objects and events that may fit the concept. For example, dogs come in all shapes, sizes, colors, and lengths of fur. Yet most people have no trouble recognizing dogs as dogs, even though they may never before have seen that particular breed of dog. Friends of the author have a dog called a briard, which is a kind of sheepdog. In spite of the fact that this dog is easily the size of a small pony, the author had no trouble recognizing it as a dog, albeit a huge and extremely shaggy one.

Concepts can have very strict definitions, such as the concept of a square as a shape with four equal sides. Concepts defined by specific rules or features are called *formal concepts* and are quite rigid. To be a square, for example, an object must be a two-dimensional figure with four equal sides and four angles adding up to 360 degrees. Mathematics is full of formal concepts. For example, in geometry there are triangles, squares, rectangles, polygons, and lines. In psychology, there are double-blind experiments, sleep stages, and conditioned stimuli, to name a few. Each of these concepts must fit very specific features to be considered true examples.

But what about things that don't easily fit the rules or features? What if a thing has some, but not all, features of a concept?

People are surrounded by objects, events, and activities that are not as clearly defined as formal concepts. What is a vehicle? Cars and trucks leap immediately to mind, but what about a bobsled or a raft? Those last two objects aren't quite as easy to classify as vehicles immediately, but they fit some of the rules for "vehicle." These are examples of *natural concepts*, concepts people form not as a result of a strict set of rules but rather as the result of experiences with these concepts in the real world (Ahn, 1998; Barton & Komatsu, 1989; Rosch, 1973). Formal concepts are well defined, but natural concepts are "fuzzy" (Hampton, 1998). Natural concepts are important in helping people understand their surroundings in a less structured manner than school-taught formal concepts, and they form the basis for interpreting those surroundings and the events that may occur in everyday life.

When someone says "fruit," what's the first image that comes to mind? More than likely, it's a specific kind of fruit like an apple, pear, or orange. It's less likely that someone's first impulse will be to say "guava" or "papaya," or even "banana," unless that person comes from a tropical area. In the United States, apples are a good example of a **prototype**, a concept that closely matches the defining characteristics of the concept

(Mervis & Rosch, 1981; Rosch, 1977). Fruit is sweet, grows on trees, has seeds, and is usually round—all very applelike qualities. Coconuts are sweet and they also grow on trees, but many people in the Northern Hemisphere have never actually seen a coconut tree. They have more likely seen countless apple trees. So people who do have very different experiences with fruit, for instance, will have different prototypes, which are the most basic examples of concepts.

💬 What about people who live in a tropical area? Would their prototype for fruit be different? And would people's prototypes vary in other cultures?

More than likely, prototypes develop according to the exposure a person has to objects in that category. So someone who grew up in an area where there are many coconut trees might think of coconuts as more prototypical than apples, whereas someone growing up in the northwestern United States would more likely see apples as a prototypical fruit (Aitchison, 1992). Culture also matters in the formation of prototypes. Research on concept prototypes across various cultures found greater differences and variations in prototypes between cultures that were dissimilar, such as Taiwan and America, than between cultures that are more similar, such as Hispanic Americans and non–Hispanic Americans living in Florida (Lin et al., 1990; Lin & Schwanenflugel, 1995; Schwanenflugel & Rey, 1986).

How do prototypes affect thinking? People tend to look at potential examples of a concept and compare them to the prototype to see how well they match—which is why it takes most people much longer to think about olives and tomatoes as fruit because they aren't sweet, one of the major characteristics of the prototype of fruit (Rosch & Mervis, 1975). As the video *Mind and Brain* explains, we use a combination of cognitive processes including concepts, prototypes, and mental images to identify objects in our daily lives.

Both of these animals are dogs. They both have fur, four legs, a tail—but the similarities end there. With so many variations in the animals we call "dogs," what is the prototype for "dog"?

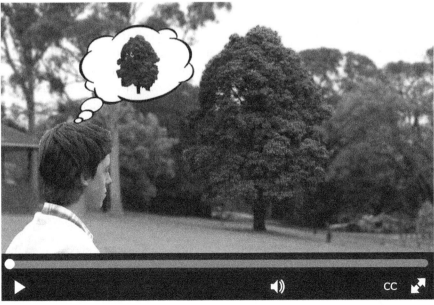

👁 **Watch** the **Video**, *Mind and Brain*.

No matter what type, concepts are one of the ways people deal with all the information that bombards* their senses every day, allowing them to organize their perceptions of the world around them. This organization may take the form of *schemas*, mental generalizations about objects, places, events, and people (for example, one's schema for "library" would no doubt include books and bookshelves), or *scripts*, a kind of schema that involves a familiar sequence of activities (for example, "going to a movie" would include traveling there, getting the ticket, buying snacks, finding the right theater, etc.). Concepts not only help people think, but also they are an important tool in *problem solving*, a type of thinking that people engage in every day and in many different situations.

PROBLEM-SOLVING AND DECISION-MAKING STRATEGIES

7.2 Describe some methods people use to solve problems and make decisions.

 Problem solving is certainly a big part of any college student's life. Is there any one "best" way to go about solving a problem?

Think about it as you read on and solve the following: Put a coin in a bottle and then cork the opening. How can you get the coin out of the bottle without pulling out the cork or breaking the bottle? (For the solution, see the section on Insight.)

As stated earlier, images and concepts are mental tools that can be used to solve problems and make decisions. For the preceding problem, you are probably trying to create an image of the bottle with a coin in it. **Problem solving** occurs when a goal must be reached by thinking and behaving in certain ways. Problems range from figuring out how to cut a recipe in half to understanding complex mathematical proofs to deciding what to major in at college. Problem solving is one aspect of **decision making**, or identifying, evaluating, and choosing among several alternatives. There are several different ways in which people can think in order to solve problems.

TRIAL AND ERROR (MECHANICAL SOLUTIONS) One method is to use **trial and error**, also known as a **mechanical solution**. Trial and error refers to trying one solution after another until finding one that works. For example, if Shelana has forgotten the PIN for her online banking Web site, she can try one combination after another until she finds the one that works, if she has only a few such PINs that she normally uses. Mechanical solutions can also involve solving by *rote*, or a learned set of rules. This is how word problems were solved in grade school, for example. One type of rote solution is to use an algorithm.

ALGORITHMS **Algorithms** are specific, step-by-step procedures for solving certain types of problems. Algorithms will always result in a correct solution, if there is a correct solution to be found and you have enough time to find it. Mathematical formulas are algorithms. When librarians organize books on bookshelves, they also use an algorithm: Place books in alphabetical order within each category, for example. Many puzzles, like a Rubik's Cube®, have a set of steps that, if followed exactly, will always result in solving the puzzle. But algorithms aren't always practical to use. For example, if Shelana didn't have a clue what those four numbers might be, she *might* be able to figure out her forgotten PIN by trying *all possible combinations* of four digits, 0 through 9. She would eventually find the right four-digit combination—but it might take a very long while! Computers, however, can run searches like this one very quickly, so the systematic search algorithm is a useful part of some computer programs.

HEURISTICS Unfortunately, humans aren't as fast as computers and need some other way to narrow down the possible solutions to only a few. One way to do this is to use

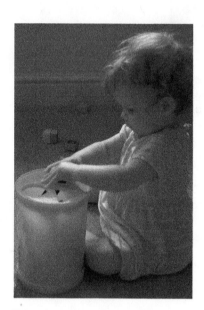

This child may try one piece after another until finding the piece that fits. This is an example of trial-and-error learning.

*bombards: attacks again and again.

a heuristic. A **heuristic**, or "rule of thumb," is a simple rule that is intended to apply to many situations. Whereas an algorithm is very specific and will always lead to a solution, a heuristic is an educated guess based on prior experiences that helps narrow down the possible solutions for a problem. For example, if a student is typing a paper in a word-processing program and wants to know how to format the page, he or she could try to read an entire manual on the word-processing program. That would take a while. Instead, the student could use an Internet search engine or type "format" into the help feature's search program. Doing either action greatly reduces the amount of information the student will have to look at to get an answer. Using the help feature or clicking on the appropriate toolbar word will also work for similar problems.

REPRESENTATIVENESS HEURISTIC   Will using a rule of thumb always work, like algorithms do? Using a heuristic is faster than using an algorithm in many cases, but unlike algorithms, heuristics will *not* always lead to the correct solution. What you gain in speed is sometimes lost in accuracy. For example, a **representativeness heuristic** is used for categorizing objects and simply assumes that any object (or person) that shares characteristics with the members of a particular category is also a member of that category. This is a handy tool when it comes to classifying plants but doesn't work as well when applied to people. The representativeness heuristic can cause errors due to ignoring base rates, the actual probability of a given event. Are all people with dark skin from Africa? Does everyone with red hair also have a bad temper? Are all blue-eyed blondes from Sweden? See the point? The representativeness heuristic can be used—or misused—to create and sustain stereotypes (Kahneman & Tversky, 1973; Kahneman et al., 1982).

AVAILABILITY HEURISTIC   Another heuristic that can have undesired outcomes is the **availability heuristic**, which is based on our estimation of the frequency or likelihood of an event based on how easy it is to recall relevant information from memory or how easy it is for us to think of related examples (Tversky & Kahneman, 1973). Imagine, for example, that after you have already read this entire textbook (it could happen!) you are asked to estimate how many words in the book start with the letter *K* and how many have the letter *K* as the third letter in the word. Which place do you think is more frequent, the first letter or as the third letter? Next, what do you think the ratio of the more frequent placement is to the less frequent placement? What is easier to think of, words that begin with the letter *K* or words that have *K* as the third letter? Tversky & Kahneman (1973) asked this same question of 152 participants for five consonants (*K, N, L, R, V*) that appear more frequently in the third position as compared to the first in a typical text. Sixty-nine percent of the participants indicated that the first position was the more frequent placement and the median estimated ratio was 2:1 for the letter *K*—however, there are typically twice as many words with *K* as the third letter as compared to the first. Can you think of an example where you may have used the availability heuristic and it did not work in your favor?

WORKING BACKWARD   A useful heuristic that *does* work much of the time is to *work backward from the goal*. For example, if you want to know the shortest way to get to the new coffee shop in town, you already know the goal, which is finding the coffee shop. There are probably several ways to get there from your house, and some are shorter than others. Assuming you have the address of the store, for many the best way to determine the shortest route is to look up the location of the store on an Internet map, a GPS, or a smartphone, and compare the different routes by the means of travel (walking versus driving). People actually used to do this with a physical map and compare the routes manually! Think about it, does technology help or hinder some aspects of problem solving? What are, if any, the benefits to using technology for solving some problems as compared to actively engaging in problem solving as a mental challenge?

Smartphones and other portable devices provide tools for easy navigation. How might the use or overuse of these tools affect our ability to navigate when we do not have access to them?

One rule of thumb, or heuristic, involves breaking down a goal into subgoals. This woman is consulting the map to see which of several possible paths she needs to take to get to her goal destination.

 💬 What if my problem is writing a term paper? Starting at the end isn't going to help me much!

SUBGOALS Sometimes it's better to break a goal down into *subgoals*, so that as each subgoal is achieved, the final solution is that much closer. Writing a term paper, for example, can seem overwhelming until it is broken down into steps: Choose a topic, research the topic, organize what has been gathered, write one section at a time, and so on. (L)(I)(N)(K) to Learning Objective PIA.6. Other examples of heuristics include making diagrams to help organize the information concerning the problem or testing possible solutions to the problem one by one and eliminating those that do not work.

💬 Sometimes I have to find answers to problems one step at a time, but in other cases the answer seems to just "pop" into my head all of a sudden. Why do some answers come so easily to mind?

INSIGHT When the solution to a problem seems to come suddenly to mind, it is called insight. Chapter Five contained a discussion of Köhler's (1925) work with Sultan the chimpanzee, which demonstrated that even some animals can solve problems by means of a sudden insight. (L)(I)(N)(K) to Learning Objective 5.11. In humans, insight often takes the form of an "aha!" moment—the solution seems to come in a flash. A person may realize that this problem is similar to another one that he or she already knows how to solve or might see that an object can be used for a different purpose than its original one, like using a dime as a screwdriver.

Remember the problem of the bottle discussed earlier in this chapter? The task was to get the coin out of the bottle without removing the cork or breaking the bottle. The answer is simple: *Push the cork into the bottle and shake out the coin. Aha!*

Insight is not really a magical process, although it can seem like magic. What usually happens is that the mind simply reorganizes a problem, sometimes while the person is thinking about something else (Durso et al., 1994).

Here's a problem that can be solved with insight: Marsha and Marjorie were born on the same day of the same month of the same year to the same mother and the same father, yet they are not twins. How is that possible? Think about it and then look for the answer in the section on Mental Sets. (L)(I)(N)(K) to Learning Objective 7.3.

In summary, thinking is a complex process involving the use of mental imagery and various types of concepts to organize the events of daily life. Problem solving is a special type of thinking that involves the use of many tools, such as trial-and-error thinking, algorithms, and heuristics, to solve different types of problems.

PROBLEMS WITH PROBLEM SOLVING AND DECISION MAKING

7.3 Identify three common barriers to successful problem solving.

Using insight to solve a problem is not always foolproof. Sometimes a solution to a problem remains just "out of reach" because the elements of the problem are not arranged properly or because people get stuck in certain ways of thinking that act as barriers* to solving problems. Such ways of thinking occur more or less automatically, influencing attempts to solve problems without any conscious awareness of that influence. Here's a classic example:

Two strings are hanging from a ceiling but are too far apart to allow a person to hold one and walk to the other. (See **Figure 7.2.**) Nearby is a table with a pair of pliers on it. The goal is to tie the two pieces of string together. How?

Figure 7.2 THE STRING PROBLEM

How do you tie the two strings together if you cannot reach them both at the same time?

———————————

*barrier: something that blocks one's path; an obstacle preventing a solution.

People can become aware of automatic tendencies to try to solve problems in ways that are not going to lead to solutions and in becoming aware can abandon the "old" ways for more appropriate problem-solving methods. Three of the most common barriers to successful problem solving are functional fixedness, mental sets, and confirmation bias.

FUNCTIONAL FIXEDNESS One problem-solving difficulty involves thinking about objects only in terms of their typical uses, which is a phenomenon called **functional fixedness** (literally, "fixed on the function"). Have you ever searched high and low for a screwdriver to fix something around the house? All the while there are several objects close at hand that could be used to tighten a screw: a butter knife, a key, or even a dime in your pocket. Because the tendency is to think of those objects in terms of cooking, unlocking, and spending, we sometimes ignore the less obvious possible uses. The string problem introduced before is an example of functional fixedness. The pair of pliers is often seen as useless until the person realizes it can be used as a weight.

MENTAL SETS Functional fixedness is actually a kind of **mental set**, which is defined as the tendency of people to persist in using problem-solving patterns that have worked for them in the past. Solutions that have worked in the past tend to be the ones people try first, and people are often hesitant or even unable to think of other possibilities. Look at **Figure 7.3** and see if you can solve the dot problem.

People are taught from the earliest grades to stay within the lines, right? That tried-and-true method will not help in solving the dot problem. The solution involves drawing the lines beyond the actual dots.

Answer to insight problem: *Marsha and Marjorie are two of a set of triplets. Gotcha!*

CONFIRMATION BIAS Another barrier to effective decision making or problem solving is **confirmation bias**, the tendency to search for evidence that fits one's beliefs while ignoring any evidence to the contrary. This is similar to a mental set, except that what is "set" is a belief rather than a method of solving problems. Believers in ESP tend to remember the few studies that seem to support their beliefs and psychic predictions that worked out while at the same time "forgetting" the cases in which studies found no proof or psychics made predictions that failed to come true. They remember only that which confirms their bias toward a belief in the existence of ESP. Another example is that people who believe that they are good multitaskers and can safely drive a motor vehicle while talking or texting on their cell phones may tend to remember their own personal experiences, which may not include any vehicle accidents or "near-misses" (that they are aware of). While it might be tempting to think of one's self as a "supertasker," recent research suggests otherwise. When tested on driving simulators while having to perform successfully on two attention-demanding tasks, over 97 percent of individuals are unable to do so without significant impacts on their performance. During the dual-task condition, only 2.5 percent of individuals were able to perform without problems (Watson & Strayer, 2010). This specific example can be quite dangerous, as it is estimated that at least 28 percent of all traffic crashes are caused by drivers using their cell phone and or texting (National Safety Council, 2010).

CREATIVITY

7.4 **Define creativity and identify some characteristics of divergent thinking.**

 💬 So far, we've only talked about logic and pretty straightforward thinking. How do people come up with totally new ideas, things no one has thought of before?

Figure 7.3 THE DOT PROBLEM

Interactive

Can you draw four straight lines so that they pass through all nine dots *without lifting your pencil from the page and without touching any dot more than once?*

The driver of this train was texting from his cell phone immediately before this crash that killed 25 people and injured more than 130 others.

Not every problem can be answered by using information already at hand and the rules of logic in applying that information. Sometimes a problem requires coming up with entirely new ways of looking at the problem or unusual, inventive solutions. This kind of thinking is called **creativity**: solving problems by combining ideas or behavior in new ways (Csikszentmihalyi, 1996; pronounced chĭck-sĕnt-mē-HĪ-ē). Before we learn more, take the survey *What Is Creativity?* to examine your own beliefs about creativity.

Survey   WHAT IS CREATIVITY?

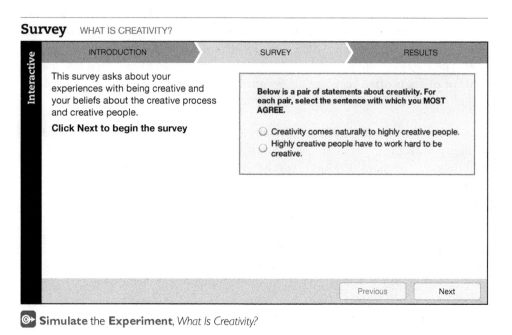

Simulate the **Experiment**, *What Is Creativity?*

Solution to the String Problem The solution to the string problem is to use the pliers as a pendulum to swing the second string closer to you.

The logical method for problem solving that has been discussed so far is based on a type of thinking called **convergent thinking**. In convergent thinking, a problem is seen as having only one answer and all lines of thinking will eventually lead to (converge on) that single answer by using previous knowledge and logic (Ciardiello, 1998). For example, the question "In what ways are a pencil and a pen alike?" can be answered by listing the features that the two items have in common: Both can be used to write, have similar shapes, and so on, in a simple comparison process. Convergent thinking works well for routine problem solving but may be of little use when a more creative solution is needed.

Divergent thinking is the reverse of convergent thinking. Here a person starts at one point and comes up with many different, or divergent, ideas or possibilities based on that point (Finke, 1995). For example, if someone were to ask the question, "What is a pencil used for?" the convergent answer would be "to write." But if the question is put this way: "How many different uses can you think of for a pencil?" the answers multiply: "writing, poking holes, a weight for the tail of a kite, a weapon." Divergent thinking has been attributed not only to creativity but also to intelligence (Guilford, 1967).

What are the characteristics of a creative, divergent thinker? Theorists in the field of creative thinking have found through examining the habits of highly creative people that the most productive periods of divergent thinking for those people tend to occur when they are doing some task or activity that is more or less automatic, such as walking or swimming (Csikszentmihalyi, 1996; Gardner, 1993a; Goleman, 1995). These automatic tasks take up some attention processes, leaving the remainder to devote to creative thinking. The fact that all of one's attention is not focused on the problem is actually a benefit, because divergent thinkers often make links and connections at a level of consciousness just below alert awareness, so that ideas can flow freely without being censored* by the higher mental processes (Goleman, 1995). In other words, having part of one's attention devoted to walking, for example, allows the rest of the mind to "sneak up on" more creative solutions and ideas.

Divergent thinkers will obviously be less prone to some of the barriers to problem solving, such as functional fixedness. For example, what would most people do if it suddenly started to rain while they are stuck in their office with no umbrella? How many people would think of using a see-through vinyl tote bag as a makeshift umbrella?

Creative, divergent thinking is often a neglected topic in the education of young people. Although some people are naturally more creative, it is possible to develop one's creative ability. The ability to be creative is important—coming up with topics for a research paper, for example, is something that many students have trouble doing. Cross-cultural research (Basadur et al., 2002; Colligan, 1983) has found that divergent thinking and problem-solving skills cannot be easily taught in the Japanese or Omaha Native American cultures, for example. In these cultures, creativity in many areas is not normally prized and the preference is to hold to well-established cultural traditions, such as traditional dances that have not varied for centuries. See **Table 7.1** for some ways to become a more divergent thinker.

Many people have the idea that creative people are also a little different from other people. There are artists and musicians, for example, who actually encourage others to see them as eccentric. But the fact is that creative people are actually pretty normal. According to Csikszentmihalyi (1997):

1. Creative people usually have a broad range of knowledge about a lot of subjects and are good at using mental imagery.

2. Creative people aren't afraid to be different—they are more open to new experiences than many people, and they tend to have more vivid dreams and daydreams than others do.

3. Creative people value their independence.

4. Creative people are often unconventional in their work, but not otherwise.

Solution to the Dot Problem When people try to solve this problem, a mental set causes them to think of the dots as representing a box, and they try to draw the line while staying in the box. The only way to connect all nine dots without lifting the pencil from the paper is to draw the lines so they extend out of the box of dots—literally "thinking outside the box."

Table 7.1	Stimulating Divergent Thinking
Brainstorming	Generate as many ideas as possible in a short period of time, without judging each idea's merits until all ideas are recorded.
Keeping a Journal	Carry a journal to write down ideas as they occur or a recorder to capture those same ideas and thoughts.
Freewriting	Write down or record everything that comes to mind about a topic without revising or proofreading until all of the information is written or recorded in some way. Organize it later.
Mind or Subject Mapping	Start with a central idea and draw a "map" with lines from the center to other related ideas, forming a visual representation of the concepts and their connections.

---

*censored: blocked from conscious awareness as unacceptable thoughts.

Concept Map L.O. 7.1, 7.2, 7.3, 7.4

mental imagery
- mental images are representations for objects or events used in mental activities
- mental images are interacted with in similar ways as physical objects (e.g., scanning a map or rotating an object)
- mental images are processed in the brain slightly differently than actual objects — as opposed to seeing actual image (eyes → visual cortex → other cortical areas), cortical areas associated with stored knowledge send info to visual cortex

How People Think

thinking (cognition) refers to mental activities that occur in the brain when processing, organizing, understanding, or communicating information to others

concepts
- are ideas that represent a class or category of objects, events, or activities
- are used to interact and organize information without having to think about or process every specific example of the category
- are represented by prototypes, best examples of the defining characteristics — vary according to personal experience, knowledge, and culture
- are an important tool in problem solving

problem solving and decision making
- thinking and behaving in certain ways to reach a goal
- can involve different strategies, logical methods (convergent thinking)
  - **trial and error** — trying one solution after another until one works
  - **algorithms**
    - specific, step-by-step procedures for solving certain problems
    - always result in correct solution if there is one
  - **heuristics**
    - simple rules intended to apply to many situations
    - educated guesses based on prior experience
    - generally faster than algorithms but will not always lead to correct solution
- **insight**
  - "aha!" moments when solution seems to appear in a flash
  - usually based on reorganization of information

problems with problem solving
- solutions to problems are not always apparent
- problems can be caused by three common barriers
  - **functional fixedness:** only thinking about objects in terms of their typical uses
  - **mental set:** a tendency to persist in using problem-solving patterns that have worked in the past
  - **confirmation bias:** a tendency to search for evidence that fits your beliefs while ignoring evidence to the contrary

Problem Solving and Decision Making Strategies

creativity
- consists of new ways of combining ideas or behavior
- typically the result of divergent thinking
  - less prone to common barriers of problem solving
  - can be stimulated (see Table 7.1)

Reset

Practice Quiz   How much do you remember?   ANSWERS ON PAGE AK-1.

Pick the best answer.

1. What is thinking?
   a. mental activity that involves processing, organizing, understanding, and communicating information
   b. spontaneous, non-directed, and unconscious mental activity
   c. simply and succinctly, it is only our ability to remember
   d. all mental activity except memory

2. People in the United States often think of a sports car when asked to envision a fun, fast form of travel. In this example, a sports car would be considered a
   a. prototype.
   b. natural concept.
   c. formal concept.
   d. mental image.

3. While taking a shower, Miguel suddenly realizes the solution to a problem at work. When later asked how he solved this problem, Miguel said, "The answer just seemed to pop into my head." Miguel's experience is an example of
   a. mechanical solution.
   b. a heuristic.
   c. an algorithm.
   d. insight.

4. Alicia leaves her office building only to find it is raining. She returns to her office and gets a trash bag out of the supply cabinet. Using a pair of scissors, she cuts the bag so that she can put her head and arms through the bag without getting wet. In using the trash bag as a makeshift rain jacket, Alicia has overcome
   a. functional fixedness.
   b. confirmation bias.
   c. creativity bias.
   d. confirmation fixedness.

5. Randall believes that aliens are currently living deep under the ocean. When looking for information about this on the Internet, he ignores any sites that are skeptical of his belief and only visits sites that support his belief. This is an example of
   a. functional fixedness.
   b. confirmation bias.
   c. creativity bias.
   d. confirmation fixedness.

6. If you ask someone to give you as many uses as possible for a piece of paper, what type of thinking is being used?
   a. divergent
   b. functional fixedness
   c. convergent
   d. mental set

7. Which of the following is the best way to encourage divergent, creative thinking?
   a. Go for a walk or engage in some other automatic activity.
   b. Stare at a blank sheet of paper until a new, innovative solution comes to mind.
   c. Engage in many activities simultaneously.
   d. Force yourself to think of something new and creative.

Intelligence

What does it mean to be "smart"? Is this the same as being intelligent? It is likely the answer depends on the immediate task or context. What exactly do we mean by the term *intelligence*?

THEORIES OF INTELLIGENCE

7.5 Compare and contrast different theories on the nature of intelligence.

Is intelligence merely a score on some test, or is it practical knowledge of how to get along in the world? Is it making good grades or being a financial success or a social success? Ask a dozen people and you will probably get a dozen different answers. Before we attempt to answer these questions, take the survey *What Is Intelligence?* to discover more about your own notions of intelligence.

Psychologists have come up with a workable definition that combines many of the ideas just mentioned: They define **intelligence** as the ability to learn from one's experiences, acquire knowledge, and use resources effectively in adapting to new situations or solving problems (Sternberg & Kaufman, 1998; Wechsler, 1975). These are the characteristics that individuals need in order to survive in their culture.

Survey   WHAT IS INTELLIGENCE?

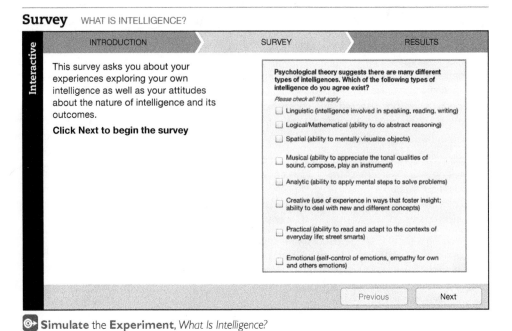

| INTRODUCTION | SURVEY | RESULTS |

This survey asks you about your experiences exploring your own intelligence as well as your attitudes about the nature of intelligence and its outcomes.

Click Next to begin the survey

Psychological theory suggests there are many different types of intelligences. Which of the following types of intelligence do you agree exist?

Please check all that apply

☐ Linguistic (intelligence involved in speaking, reading, writing)

☐ Logical/Mathematical (ability to do abstract reasoning)

☐ Spatial (ability to mentally visualize objects)

☐ Musical (ability to appreciate the tonal qualities of sound, compose, play an instrument)

☐ Analytic (ability to apply mental steps to solve problems)

☐ Creative (use of experience in ways that foster insight; ability to deal with new and different concepts)

☐ Practical (ability to read and adapt to the contexts of everyday life; street smarts)

☐ Emotional (self-control of emotions, empathy for own and others emotions)

Previous   Next

◉ **Simulate** the **Experiment**, *What Is Intelligence?*

Sternberg's practical intelligence is a form of "street smarts" that includes the ability to adapt to one's environment and solve practical problems. These girls are giving their younger brother a drink of water by using a folded leaf as an impromptu cup.

Although we have defined intelligence in a general way, there are differing opinions of the specific knowledge and abilities that make up the concept of intelligence. Charles Spearman (1904) defined intelligence as two primary abilities: the wider ability of *general intelligence*, labeled as **g factor**, and task-specific abilities in certain areas such as music, business, or art, labeled as **s factor** for *specific intelligence*. Some later theorists have suggested that intelligence cannot be defined so simply and have therefore proposed different aspects and abilities. The idea of multiple intelligences was proposed by Howard Gardner (1993b, 1999a), and his theory originally listed seven different kinds of intelligence but later added an eighth and a ninth (Gardner, 1998, 1999b). The nine types of intelligence are described in the video *Gardner's Theory of Intelligence*. Yet another theory suggests that there are three kinds of intelligence. Robert Sternberg's (1988a, 1997b, 2005) triarchic theory of intelligence suggests that intelligence comprises analytical, creative, and practical aspects.

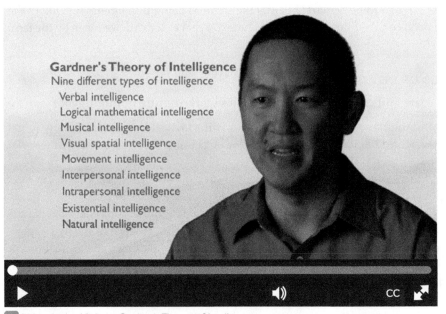

Gardner's Theory of Intelligence
Nine different types of intelligence
  Verbal intelligence
  Logical mathematical intelligence
  Musical intelligence
  Visual spatial intelligence
  Movement intelligence
  Interpersonal intelligence
  Intrapersonal intelligence
  Existential intelligence
  Natural intelligence

CC

◉ **Watch** the **Video**, *Gardner's Theory of Intelligence.*

7.6 Compare and contrast some methods of measuring intelligence and identify ways to evaluate the quality of a test.

The history of intelligence testing spans the twentieth century and has at times been marked by controversies and misuse. A full history of how intelligence testing developed would take at least an entire chapter, so this section will discuss only some of the better known forms of testing and how they came to be. For some additional detail, watch the video *The History of Intelligence Testing: Binet and Terman.*

👁 **Watch** the **Video**, *The History of Intelligence Testing: Binet and Terman.*

💬 It doesn't sound like intelligence would be easy to measure on a test—how do IQ tests work, anyway?

INTELLIGENCE TESTS   The measurement of intelligence by some kind of test is a concept that is less than a century old. It began when educators in France realized that some students needed more help with learning than others did. They thought that if a way could be found to identify these students more in need, they could be given a different kind of education than the more capable students.

BINET'S MENTAL ABILITY TEST   In those early days, a French psychologist named Alfred Binet was asked by the French Ministry of Education to design a formal test of intelligence that would help identify children who were unable to learn as quickly or as well as others, so that they could be given remedial education. Eventually, he and colleague Théodore Simon came up with a test that not only distinguished between fast and slow learners but also between children of different age groups as well (Binet & Simon, 1916). They noticed that the fast learners seemed to give answers to questions that older children might give, whereas the slow learners gave answers that were more typical of a younger child. Binet decided that the key element to be tested was a child's *mental age,* or the average age at which children could successfully answer a particular level of questions.

STANFORD-BINET AND IQ   Lewis Terman (1916), a researcher at Stanford University, adopted German psychologist William Stern's method for comparing mental age and *chronological age* (number of years since birth) for use with the translated and revised

Binet test. Stern's (1912) formula was to divide the mental age (MA) by the chronological age (CA) and multiply the result by 100 to get rid of any decimal points. The resulting score is called an **intelligence quotient**, or **IQ**. (A *quotient* is a number that results from dividing one number by another.)

$$IQ = MA/CA \times 100$$

For example, if a child who is 10 years old takes the test and scores a mental age of 15 (is able to answer the level of questions typical of a 15-year-old), the IQ would look like this:

$$IQ = 15/10 \times 100 = 150$$

The quotient has the advantage of allowing testers to compare the intelligence levels of people of different age groups. While this method works well for children, it produces IQ scores that start to become meaningless as the person's chronological age passes 16 years. (Once a person becomes an adult, the idea of questions that are geared for a particular age group loses its power. For example, what kind of differences would there be between questions designed for a 30-year-old versus a 40-year-old?) Most intelligence tests today, such as the *Stanford-Binet Intelligence Scales, Fifth Edition* (*SB5*) (Roid, 2003) and the Wechsler tests (see the following section), use age-group comparison norms instead. The SB5 is often used by educators to make decisions about the placement of students into special educational programs, both for those with disabilities and for those with exceptionalities. Many children are given this test in the second grade, or age 7 or 8. The SB5 yields an overall estimate of intelligence and verbal and nonverbal domain scores, all comprised of five primary areas of cognitive ability—fluid reasoning, knowledge, quantitative processing, visual–spatial processing, and working memory (Roid, 2003). See **Table 7.2** for descriptions of some items similar to those from the SB5.

THE WECHSLER TESTS   Although the original Stanford-Binet Test is now in its fifth edition and includes different questions for people of different age groups, it is not the only IQ test that is popular today. David Wechsler was the first to devise a series of tests designed for specific age groups. Originally dissatisfied with the fact that the Stanford-Binet was designed for children but being administered to adults, he developed an IQ test specifically for adults. He later designed tests specifically for older school-age children and preschool children, as well as those in the early grades. The Wechsler Adult Intelligence Scale (WAIS-IV; Wechsler, 2008), Wechsler Intelligence Scale for Children (WISC-V; Wechsler, 2014), and the Wechsler Preschool and Primary Scale of Intelligence (WPPSI-IV; Wechsler, 2012) are the three versions of this test, and in the United States these tests are now used more frequently than the Stanford-Binet. In earlier editions,

Table 7.2   Paraphrased Sample Items From the Stanford-Binet Intelligence Test

Age*	Type of Item	Paraphrased Sample Item
2	Board with three differently shaped holes	Child can place correct shape into matching hole on board.
4	Building block bridge	Child can build a simple bridge out of blocks after being shown a model.
7	Similarities	Child can answer such questions as "In what way are a ship and a car alike?"
9	Digit reversal	Child can repeat four digits backward.
Average adult	Vocabulary	Child can define 20 words from a list.

*Age at which item typically is successfully completed.

Source: Roid, G. H. (2003).

Table 7.3 Simulated Sample Items From the Wechsler Adult Intelligence Scale (WAIS-IV)

	Simulated Sample Test Items
Verbal Comprehension Index	
Similarities	In what way are a circle and a triangle alike? In what way are a saw and a hammer alike?
Vocabulary	What is a hippopotamus? What does "resemble" mean?
Information	What is steam made of? What is pepper? Who wrote *Tom Sawyer*?
Perceptual Reasoning Index	
Block Design	After looking at a pattern or design, try to arrange small cubes in the same pattern.
Matrix Reasoning	After looking at an incomplete matrix pattern or series, select an option that completes the matrix or series.
Visual Puzzles	Look at a completed puzzle and select three components from a set of options that would re-create the puzzle, all within a specified time limit.
Working Memory Index	
Digit Span	Recall lists of numbers, some lists forward and some lists in reverse order, and recall a mixed list of numbers in correct ascending order.
Arithmetic	Three women divided 18 golf balls equally among themselves. How many golf balls did each person receive? If two buttons cost $0.15, what will be the cost of a dozen buttons?
Processing Speed Index	
Symbol Search	Visually scan a group of symbols to identify specific target symbols, within a specified time limit.
Coding	Learn a different symbol for specific numbers and then fill in the blank under the number with the correct symbol. (This test is timed.)

Simulated items and descriptions similar to those in the *Wechsler Adult Intelligence Scale—Fourth Edition* (2008).

another way these tests differed from the Stanford-Binet was by having both a verbal and performance (nonverbal) scale, as well as providing an overall score of intelligence (the original Stanford-Binet was composed predominantly of verbal items). While still using both verbal and nonverbal items, the Wechsler tests now organize items into index scales that provide an overall score of intelligence and index scores related to specific cognitive domains. **Table 7.3** has simulated sample items for the WAIS-IV.

TEST CONSTRUCTION: GOOD TEST, BAD TEST?   All tests are not equally good tests. Some tests may fail to give the same results on different occasions for the same person when that person has not changed—making the test useless. These would be considered unreliable tests. **Reliability** of a test refers to the test producing consistent results each time it is given to the same individual or group of people. For example, if Nicholas takes a personality test today and then again in a month or so, the results should be very similar if the personality test is reliable. Other tests might be easy to use and even reliable, but if they don't actually measure what they are supposed to measure, they are also useless. These tests are thought of as "invalid" (untrue) tests. **Validity** is the degree to which a test actually measures what it's supposed to measure. Another aspect of validity is the extent that an obtained score accurately reflects the intended skill or outcome in real-life situations, or *ecological validity*, not just validity for the testing or assessment situation. For example, we hope that someone who passes his or her test for a driver's license will also be able to safely operate a motor vehicle when they are actually on the road. When evaluating a test, consider what a specific test score means and to what, or to whom, it is compared.

Take the hypothetical example of Professor Stumpwater, who—for reasons best known only to him—believes that intelligence is related to a person's golf scores. Let's say that he develops an adult intelligence test based on golf scores. What do we need to look at to determine if his test is a good one?

STANDARDIZATION OF TESTS   First of all, we would want to look at how he tried to standardize his test. *Standardization* refers to the process of giving the test to a large group of people that represents the kind of people for whom the test is designed. One aspect of standardization is in the establishment of consistent and standard methods of test administration. All test subjects would take the test under the same conditions. In the professor's case, this would mean that he would have his sample members play the same number of rounds of golf on the same course under the same weather conditions, and so on. Another aspect addresses the comparison group whose scores will be used to compare individual test results. Standardization groups are chosen randomly from the population for whom the test is intended and, like all samples, must be representative of that population. **L I N K** to Learning Objectives A.1 and 1.7. If a test is designed for children, for example, then a large sample of randomly selected children would be given the test.

NORMS   The scores from the standardization group would be called the *norms*, the standards against which all others who take the test would be compared. Most tests of intelligence follow a *normal curve*, or a distribution in which the scores are the most frequent around the *mean*, or average, and become less and less frequent the further from the mean they occur (see **Figure 7.4**). **L I N K** to Learning Objectives A.2, A.3, and A.4.

On the Wechsler IQ test, the percentages under each section of the normal curve represent the percentage of scores falling within that section for each *standard deviation (SD)* from the mean on the test. The standard deviation is the average variation of scores from the mean. **L I N K** to Learning Objective A.4.

In the case of the professor's golf test, he might find that a certain golf score is the average, which he would interpret as average intelligence. People who scored extremely well on the golf test would be compared to the average, as well as people with unusually poor scores.

The normal curve allows IQ scores to be more accurately estimated than the old IQ scoring method formula devised by Stern. Test designers replaced the old ratio IQ of the earlier versions of IQ tests with **deviation IQ scores**, which are based on the normal

Standard Deviations	-4	-3	-2	-1	0	1	2	3	4
Wechsler IQ	40	55	70	85	100	115	130	145	160
Stanford-Binet 4 IQ	36	52	68	84	100	116	132	148	164
Cumulative %	0.003	0.135	2.275	15.856	50.00	84.134	97.725	99.865	99.997

Figure 7.4   The Normal Curve

The percentages under each section of the normal curve represent the percentage of scores falling within that section for each *standard deviation (SD)* from the mean. Scores on intelligence tests are typically represented by the normal curve. The vertical lines each represent one standard deviation from the mean, which is always set at 100. For example, an IQ of 115 on the Wechsler represents one standard deviation above the mean, and the area under the curve indicates that 34.13 percent of the population falls between 100 and 115 on this test. **L I N K** to Learning Objectives A.2, A.3, A.4 and 1.7. Note: The figure shows the mean and standard deviation for the Stanford-Binet Fourth Edition (Stanford-Binet 4). The Stanford-Binet Fifth Edition was published in 2003 and now has a mean of 100 and a standard deviation of 15 for composite scores.

curve distribution (Eysenck, 1994): IQ is assumed to be normally distributed with a mean IQ of 100 and a typical standard deviation of about 15 (the standard deviation can vary according to the particular test). An IQ of 130, for example, would be two standard deviations above the mean, whereas an IQ of 70 would be two standard deviations below the mean, and in each case the person's score is being compared to the population's average score.

With respect to validity and reliability, the professor's test fares poorly. If the results of the professor's test were compared with other established intelligence tests, there would probably be no relationship at all. Golf scores have nothing to do with intelligence, so the test is not a valid, or true, measure of intelligence.

On the other hand, his test might work well for some people and poorly for others on the question of reliability. Some people who are good and regular golfers tend to score about the same for each game that they play, so for them, the golf score IQ would be fairly reliable. But others, especially those who do not play golf or play infrequently, would have widely varying scores from game to game. For those people, the test would be very unreliable, and if a test is unreliable for some, it's not a good test.

A test can fail in validity but still be reliable. If for some reason Professor Stumpwater chose to use height as a measure of intelligence, an adult's score on Stumpwater's "test" would always be the same, as height does not change by very much after the late teens. But the opposite is not true. If a test is unreliable, how can it accurately measure what it is supposed to measure? For example, adult intelligence remains fairly constant. If a test meant to measure that intelligence gave different scores at different times, it's obviously not a valid measure of intelligence.

> 💬 Just because an IQ test gives the same score every time a person takes it doesn't mean that the score is actually measuring real intelligence, right?

That's right—think about the definition of intelligence for a moment: the ability to learn from one's experiences, acquire knowledge, and use resources effectively in adapting to new situations or solving problems. How can anyone define what "effective use of resources" might be? Does everyone have access to the same resources? Is everyone's "world" necessarily perceived as being the same? Intelligence tests are useful measuring devices but should not necessarily be assumed to be measures of all types of intelligent behavior, or even good measures for all groups of people, as the next section discusses.

IQ TESTS AND CULTURAL BIAS   The problem with trying to measure intelligence with a test that is based on an understanding of the world and its resources is that not everyone comes from the same "world." People raised in a different culture, or even a different economic situation, from the one in which the designer of an IQ test is raised are not likely to perform well on such a test—not to mention the difficulties of taking a test that is written in an unfamiliar language or dialect. In the early days of immigration, people from non-English-speaking countries would score very poorly on intelligence tests, in some cases being denied entry to the United States on the basis of such tests (Allen, 2006).

It is very difficult to design an intelligence test that is completely free of *cultural bias*, a term referring to the tendency of IQ tests to reflect, in language, dialect, and content, the culture of the person or persons who designed the test. A person who comes from the same culture (or even socioeconomic background) as the test designer may have an unfair advantage over a person who is from a different cultural or socioeconomic background (Helms, 1992). If people raised in an Asian culture are given a test designed within a traditional Western culture, many items on the test might make no

How might these two women, apparently from different cultures, come to an agreement on what best defines intelligence?

sense to them. For example, one kind of question might be: Which one of the five is least like the other four?

DOG—CAR—CAT—BIRD—FISH

The answer is supposed to be "car," which is the only one of the five that is not alive. But a Japanese child, living in a culture that relies on the sea for so much of its food and culture, might choose "fish," because none of the others are found in the ocean. That child's test score would be lower but not because the child is not intelligent.

Attempts have been made to create intelligence tests that are as free of cultural influences as is humanly possible. Many test designers have come to the conclusion that it may be impossible to create a test that is completely free of cultural bias (Carpenter et al., 1990). Instead, they are striving to create tests that are at least *culturally fair*. These tests use questions that do not create a disadvantage for people whose culture differs from that of the majority. Many items on a "culture-fair" test require the use of nonverbal abilities, such as rotating objects, rather than items about verbal knowledge that might be culturally specific.

WRITING PROMPT

What kind of questions would you include on an intelligence test to minimize cultural bias?

▶ | The response entered here will be saved to your notes and may be collected by your instructor if he/she requires it.

Submit

 💬 If intelligence tests are so flawed, why do people still use them?

USEFULNESS OF IQ TESTS   IQ tests are generally valid for predicting academic success and job performance (Sackett et al., 2008). This may be truer for those who score at the higher and lower ends of the normal curve, as the predictive value is less clear for those who score in the average range of IQ. The kinds of tests students are given in school are often similar to intelligence tests, and so people who do well on IQ tests typically do well on other kinds of academically oriented tests as well, such as the Scholastic Assessment Test (SAT), the American College Test (ACT), the Graduate Record Examinations (GRE), and actual college examinations. These achievement tests are very similar to IQ tests but are administered to groups of people rather than to individuals. However, recent research suggests skills in self-regulation or levels of motivation may impact IQ measures and raises concerns about situations or circumstances where IQ scores may not be unbiased predictors of academic or job success (Duckworth et al., 2011; Duckworth & Seligman, 2005; Nisbett et al., 2012).

Intelligence testing also plays an important role in neuropsychology, where specially trained psychologists use intelligence tests and other forms of cognitive and behavioral testing to assess neurobehavioral disorders in which cognition and behavior are impaired as the result of brain injury or brain malfunction (National Academy of Neuropsychology, 2001). **LINK** to Learning Objective B.5. As part of their profession, neuropsychologists use intelligence testing in diagnosis (e.g., head injury, learning disabilities, neuropsychological disorders), tracking progress of individuals with such disorders, and in monitoring possible recovery.

INDIVIDUAL DIFFERENCES IN INTELLIGENCE

7.7 Define intellectual disability, giftedness, and emotional intelligence.

Another use of IQ tests is to help identify people who differ from those of average intelligence by a great degree. Although one such group is composed of those who are sometimes called "geniuses" (who fall at the extreme high end of the normal curve for intelligence), the other group is made up of people who, for various reasons, are considered intellectually disabled and whose IQ scores fall well below the mean on the normal curve. In this section we will also discuss another type of proposed intelligence that is not addressed by traditional IQ tests, *emotional intelligence.*

INTELLECTUAL DISABILITY   **Intellectual disability (intellectual developmental disorder)** (formerly *mental retardation* or *developmentally delayed*) is a neurodevelopmental disorder and is defined in several ways. First, the person exhibits deficits in mental abilities, which is typically associated with an IQ score approximately two standard deviations below the mean on the normal curve, such as below 70 on a test with a mean of 100 and standard deviation of 15. Second, the person's *adaptive behavior* (skills that allow people to live independently, such as being able to work at a job, communicate well with others, and grooming skills such as being able to get dressed, eat, and bathe with little or no help) is severely below a level appropriate for the person's age. Finally, these limitations must begin in the developmental period. Intellectual disability occurs in about 1 percent of the population (American Psychiatric Association, 2013).

💬 So how would a professional go about deciding whether or not a child has an intellectual disability? Is the IQ test the primary method?

DIAGNOSIS   Previous editions of the *Diagnostic and Statistical Manual of Mental Disorders (DSM)* relied heavily on IQ tests for determining the diagnosis of *mental retardation* and level of severity. This has changed with the release of the newest edition in 2013, the *Diagnostic and Statistical Manual of Mental Disorders, Fifth Edition (DSM-5)* (American Psychiatric Association, 2013) and is consistent with recommendations from the American Association on Intellectual and Developmental Disabilities (AAIDD) (AAIDD, 2009; Schalock et al., 2010). Recognizing tests of IQ are less valid as one approaches the lower end of the IQ range, and the importance of adaptive living skills in multiple life areas, levels of severity are now based on level of adaptive functioning and level of support the individual requires (American Psychiatric Association, 2013). Thus, a *DSM-5* diagnosis of intellectual disability is based on deficits in intellectual functioning, determined by standardized tests of intelligence and clinical assessment, which impact adaptive functioning across three domains. The domains include conceptual (memory, reasoning, language, reading, writing, math, and other academic skills), social (empathy, social judgment, interpersonal communication, and other skills that impact the ability to make and maintain friendships), and practical (self-management skills that affect personal care, job responsibilities, school, money management, and other areas) (American Psychiatric Association, 2013). Previous editions indicated these deficits must occur prior to 18 years of age, but the *DSM-5* removes the specific age criteria, specifying symptoms must begin during the developmental period.

Intellectual disability can vary from mild to profound. According to the *DSM-5* (American Psychiatric Association, 2013), individuals with mild intellectual disability may not be recognized as having deficits in the conceptual domain until they reach school age where learning difficulties become apparent; as an adult, they are likely to be fairly concrete thinkers. In the social domain, they are at risk of being manipulated as their social judgment and interactions are immature as compared to same-age peers. In the practical domain, they are capable of living independently with proper supports in place but will likely require assistance with more complex life skills such as health care decisions, legal issues, or raising a family (American Psychiatric Association, 2013). This category makes up the vast majority of those with intellectual disabilities. Other classifications in order of severity are moderate, severe, and profound. Conceptually, individuals with profound intellectual disability have a very limited ability to learn beyond simple matching and sorting tasks and socially, have very poor communication skills, although they may recognize and interact nonverbally with well-known family members and other caretakers. In the practical domain, they may be able to participate by watching or assisting but are likely totally dependent upon others for all areas of their care (American Psychiatric Association, 2013). All of these skill deficits are likely compounded by multiple physical or sensory impairments.

CAUSES What causes intellectual disability? Unhealthy living conditions can affect brain development. Examples of such conditions are lead poisoning from eating paint chips (Lanphear et al., 2000), exposure to polychlorinated biphenyls (PCBs) (Darvill et al., 2000), prenatal exposure to mercury (Grandjean et al., 1997), as well as other toxicants (Ericksson et al., 2001; Eskenazi et al., 1999; Schroeder, 2000). Deficits may also be attributed to factors resulting in inadequate brain development or other health risks associated with poverty. Examples include malnutrition, health consequences as the result of not having adequate access to health care, or lack of mental stimulation through typical cultural and educational experiences.

Some of the biological causes of intellectual disability include Down syndrome (Ⓛ Ⓘ Ⓝ Ⓚ to Learning Objective 8.3), fetal alcohol syndrome, and fragile X syndrome. *Fetal alcohol syndrome* is a condition that results from exposing a developing embryo to alcohol, and intelligence levels can range from below average to levels associated with intellectual disability (Olson & Burgess, 1997). In *fragile X syndrome*, an individual (more frequently a male) has a defect in a gene on the X chromosome of the 23rd pair, leading to a deficiency in a protein needed for brain development. Depending on the severity of the damage to this gene, symptoms of fragile X syndrome can range from mild to severe or profound intellectual disability (Dykens et al., 1994; Valverde et al., 2007).

There are many other causes of intellectual disability (Murphy et al., 1998). Lack of oxygen at birth; damage to the fetus in the womb from diseases, infections, or drug use by the mother; and even diseases and accidents during childhood can lead to intellectual disability.

One thing should always be remembered: Intellectual disability affects a person's *intellectual* capabilities and adaptive behaviors. Individuals with an intellectual disability are just as responsive to love and affection as anyone else and need to be loved and to have friends just as all people do. Intelligence is only one characteristic; warmth, friendliness, caring, and compassion also count for a great deal and should not be underrated.

GIFTEDNESS At the other end of the intelligence scale* are those who fall on the upper end of the normal curve (see Figure 7.4), above an IQ of 130 (about 2 percent of the population). The term applied to these individuals is **gifted**, and if their IQ falls above 140 to 145 (less than half of 1 percent of the population), they are often referred to as highly advanced or *geniuses*.

💬 I've heard that geniuses are sometimes a little "nutty" and odd. Are geniuses, especially the really high-IQ ones, "not playing with a full deck," as the saying goes?

People have long held many false beliefs about people who are very, very intelligent. Such beliefs have included that gifted people are weird and socially awkward, physically weak, and more likely to suffer from mental illnesses. From these beliefs come the "mad scientist" of the cinema and the "evil geniuses" of literature.

These beliefs were shattered by a groundbreaking study that was initiated in 1921 by Lewis M. Terman, the same individual responsible for the development of the Stanford-Binet Test. Terman (1925) selected 1,528 children to participate in a longitudinal study. Ⓛ Ⓘ Ⓝ Ⓚ to Learning Objective 8.1. These children, 857 boys and 671 girls, had IQs (as measured by the Stanford-Binet) ranging from 130 to 200. The early findings of

This middle-aged man, named Jack, lives in a small town in Arkansas and serves as a deacon in the local church. He is loved and respected and leads what, for him, is a full and happy life. Jack also has Down syndrome, but he has managed to find his place in the world.

Stanford University psychologist Lewis Terman is pictured at his desk in 1942. Terman spent a good portion of his career researching children with high IQ scores and was the first to use the term gifted to describe these children.

---

*scale: a graded series of tests or performances used in rating individual intelligence or achievement.

this major study (Terman & Oden, 1947) demonstrated that the gifted were socially well adjusted and often skilled leaders. They were also above average in height, weight, and physical attractiveness, putting an end to the myth of the weakling genius. Terman was able to demonstrate not only that his gifted children were *not* more susceptible to mental illness than the general population, but he was also able to show that they were actually more resistant to mental illnesses than those of average intelligence. Only those with the highest IQs (180 and above) were found to have some social and behavioral adjustment problems *as children* (Janos, 1987).

Terman's "Termites," as they came to be called, were also typically successful as adults. They earned more academic degrees and had higher occupational and financial success than their average peers (at least, the men in the study had occupational success—women at this time did not typically have careers outside the home). Researchers Zuo and Cramond (2001) examined some of Terman's gifted people to see if their identity formation as adolescents was related to later occupational success. (L)(I)(N)(K) to Learning Objective 8.13. They found that most of the more successful "Termites" had in fact successfully achieved a consistent sense of self, whereas those who were less successful had not done so.

A book by Joan Freeman called *Gifted Children Grown Up* (Freeman, 2001) describes the results of a similar longitudinal study of 210 gifted and nongifted children in Great Britain. One of the more interesting findings from this study is that gifted children who are "pushed" to achieve at younger and younger ages, sitting for exams long before their peers would do so, often grow up to be disappointed, somewhat unhappy adults. Freeman points to differing life conditions for the gifted as a major factor in their success, adjustment, and well-being: Some lived in poverty and some in wealth, for example. Yet another longitudinal study (Torrance, 1993) found that in both gifted students and gifted adults there is more to success in life than intelligence and high academic achievement. In that study, liking one's work, having a sense of purpose in life, a high energy level, and persistence were also very important factors. If the picture of the genius as mentally unstable is a myth, so, too, is the belief that being gifted will always lead to success, as even Terman found in his original study.

EMOTIONAL INTELLIGENCE   What about people who have a lot of "book smarts" but not much common sense? There are some people like that, who never seem to get ahead in life, in spite of having all that so-called intelligence. It is true that not everyone who is intellectually able is going to be a success in life (Mehrabian, 2000). Sometimes the people who are most successful are those who didn't do all that well in the regular academic setting.

One explanation for why some people who do poorly in school succeed in life and why some who do well in school don't do so well in the "real" world is that success relies on a certain degree of **emotional intelligence**, the accurate awareness of and ability to manage one's own emotions to facilitate thinking and attain specific goals, and the ability to understand what others feel (Mayer & Salovey, 1997; Mayer, Salovey, et al., 2008).

The concept of emotional intelligence was first introduced by Peter Salovey and John Mayer (1990) and later popularized by Dan Goleman (1995). And while Goleman originally suggested emotional intelligence was a more powerful influence on success in life than more traditional views of intelligence, his work and the work of others used the term in a variety of different ways than originally proposed, and claims by some were not backed by scientific evidence. For example, emotional intelligence is not the same as having high self-esteem or being optimistic. One who is emotionally intelligent possesses self-control of emotions such as anger, impulsiveness, and anxiety. Empathy, the ability to understand what others feel, is also a component, as are an awareness of one's own emotions, sensitivity, persistence even in the face of frustrations, and the ability to motivate oneself (Salovey & Mayer, 1990; Mayer & Salovey, 1997).

💬 That all sounds very nice, but how can anything like this be measured?

Is there research to support this idea? In one study, researchers asked 321 participants to read passages written by nonparticipants and try to guess what the nonparticipants were feeling while they were writing (Mayer & Geher, 1996). The assumption was that people who were good at connecting thoughts to feelings would also have a high degree of empathy and emotional intelligence. The participants who more correctly judged the writers' emotional experiences (assessed by both how well each participant's emotional judgments agreed with a group consensus and the nonparticipant's actual report of feelings) also scored higher on the empathy measure and lower on the defensiveness measure. These same participants also had higher SAT scores (self-reported), leading Mayer and colleagues to conclude not only that emotional intelligence is a valid and measurable concept but also that general intelligence and emotional intelligence may be related: Those who are high in emotional intelligence are also smarter in the traditional sense (Mayer et al., 2000). A more recent review found individuals with higher emotional intelligence tended to have better social relationships for both children and adults, better family and intimate relationships, were perceived more positively by others, had better academic achievement, were more successful at work, and experienced greater psychological well-being (Mayer, Roberts, et al., 2008).

Emotional intelligence includes empathy, which is the ability to feel what others are feeling. This doctor is not only able to listen to her patient's problems but also is able to show by her facial expression, body language, and gestures that she understands how the patient feels.

THE NATURE/NURTURE CONTROVERSY REGARDING INTELLIGENCE

7.8 Evaluate the influence of heredity and environment on the development of intelligence.

Are people born with all of the "smarts" they will ever have, or does experience and learning count for something in the development of intellect? The influence of nature (heredity or genes) and nurture (environment) on personality traits has long been debated in the field of human development, and intelligence is one of the traits that has been examined closely. **L I N K** to Learning Objective 8.2.

TWIN AND ADOPTION STUDIES   The problem with trying to separate the role of genes from that of environment is that controlled, perfect experiments are neither practical nor ethical. Instead, researchers find out what they can from *natural experiments,* circumstances existing in nature that can be examined to understand some phenomenon. *Twin studies* are an example of such circumstances.

Identical twins are those who originally came from one fertilized egg and, therefore, share the same genetic inheritance. Any differences between them on a certain trait, then, should be caused by environmental factors. Fraternal twins come from two different eggs, each fertilized by a different sperm, and share only the amount of genetic material that any two siblings would share. Ⓛ Ⓘ Ⓝ Ⓚ to Learning Objective 8.3. By comparing the IQs of these two types of twins reared together (similar environments) and reared apart (different environments), as well as persons of other degrees of relatedness, researchers can get a general, if not exact, idea of how much influence heredity has over the trait of intelligence (see **Figure 7.5**). As can be easily seen from the chart, the greater the degree of genetic relatedness, the stronger the correlation is between the IQ scores of those persons. The fact that genetically identical twins show a correlation of 0.86 means that the environment must play a part in determining some aspects of intelligence as measured by IQ tests. If heredity alone were responsible, the correlation between genetically identical twins should be 1.00. At this time, researchers have determined that the estimated **heritability** (proportion of change in IQ within a population that is caused by hereditary factors) for intelligence is about .50 or 50 percent (Plomin & DeFries, 1998; Plomin & Spinath, 2004). Furthermore, the impact of genetic factors increases with increasing age, but the set of genes or genetic factors remain the same. The effects of the same set of genes becomes larger with increasing age (Posthuma et al., 2009).

 💬 Wait a minute—if identical twins have a correlation of .86, wouldn't that mean that intelligence is 86 percent inherited?

Although the correlation between identical twins is higher than the estimated heritability of .50, that similarity is not entirely due to the twins' genetic similarity. Twins who are raised in the same household obviously share very similar environments as well. Even twins who are reared apart, as seen in adoption studies, are usually placed

Figure 7.5   Correlations Between IQ Scores of Persons with Various Relationships

In the graph on the left, the degree of genetic relatedness seems to determine the agreement (correlation) between IQ scores of the various comparisons. For example, identical twins, who share 100 percent of their genes, are more similar in IQ than fraternal twins, who share only about 50 percent of their genes, even when raised in the same environment. In the graph on the right, identical twins are still more similar to each other in IQ than are other types of comparisons, but being raised in the same environment increases the similarity considerably.

in homes that are similar in socioeconomic and ethnic background—more similar than one might think. So when twins who are genetically similar are raised in similar environments, their IQ scores are also going to be similar. However, similar environmental influences become less important over time (where genetic influences increase over time), accounting for only about 20 percent of the variance in intelligence by age 11 or 12 (Posthuma et al., 2009). In turn, environmental influences tend not to be a factor by adolescence, and with the increasing impact of genetic factors, it has been suggested that the heritability of intelligence might be as high as .91 or 91 percent by the age of 65 (Posthuma et al., 2009).

One of the things that people need to understand about heritability is that estimates of heritability apply only to changes in IQ within a *group* of people, *not to the individual people themselves*. Each individual is far too different in experiences, education, and other nongenetic factors to predict exactly how a particular set of genes will interact with those factors in that one person. Only differences among people *in general* can be investigated for the influence of genes (Dickens & Flynn, 2001). Genes always interact with environmental factors, and in some cases extreme environments can modify even very heritable traits, as would happen in the case of a severely malnourished child's growth pattern. Enrichment, on the other hand, could have improved outcomes. Some observations suggest IQ scores are steadily increasing over time, from generation to generation, in modernized countries, a phenomenon called the *Flynn effect* (Flynn, 2009).

WRITING PROMPT

How might you determine whether flute-playing ability is a highly heritable trait? If you want to improve your flute playing and someone tells you that musical ability is heritable, should you stop practicing?

▶ The response entered here will be saved to your notes and may be collected by your instructor if he/she requires it.

Submit

THE BELL CURVE AND MISINTERPRETATION OF STATISTICS   One of the other factors that has been examined for possible heritable differences in performance on IQ tests is the concept of race. (The term *race* is used in most of these investigations as a way to group people with common skin colors or facial features, and one should always be mindful of how suspect that kind of classification is. Cultural background, educational experiences, and socioeconomic factors typically have far more to do with similarities in group performances than does the color of one's skin.) In 1994, Herrnstein and Murray published the controversial book *The Bell Curve*, in which they cite large numbers of statistical studies (never published in scientific journals prior to the book) that led them to make the claim that IQ is largely inherited. These authors go further by also implying that people from lower economic levels are poor because they are unintelligent.

In their book, Herrnstein and Murray made several statistical errors and ignored the effects of environment and culture. First, they assumed that IQ tests actually do measure intelligence. As discussed earlier, IQ tests are not free of cultural or socioeconomic bias. Furthermore, just being aware of negative stereotypes can result in an individual scoring poorly on intelligence tests or other tasks, a response called **stereotype threat** (Steele & Aronson, 1995; Jameson et al., 2007). So all they really found was a correlation between race and *IQ*, not race and *intelligence*. They also assumed that intelligence itself is very heavily influenced by genetics, with a heritability factor of about .80. The current estimate of the heritability of intelligence is actually about .50 (Plomin & DeFries, 1998).

Concept Map L.O. 7.5, 7.6, 7.7, 7.8

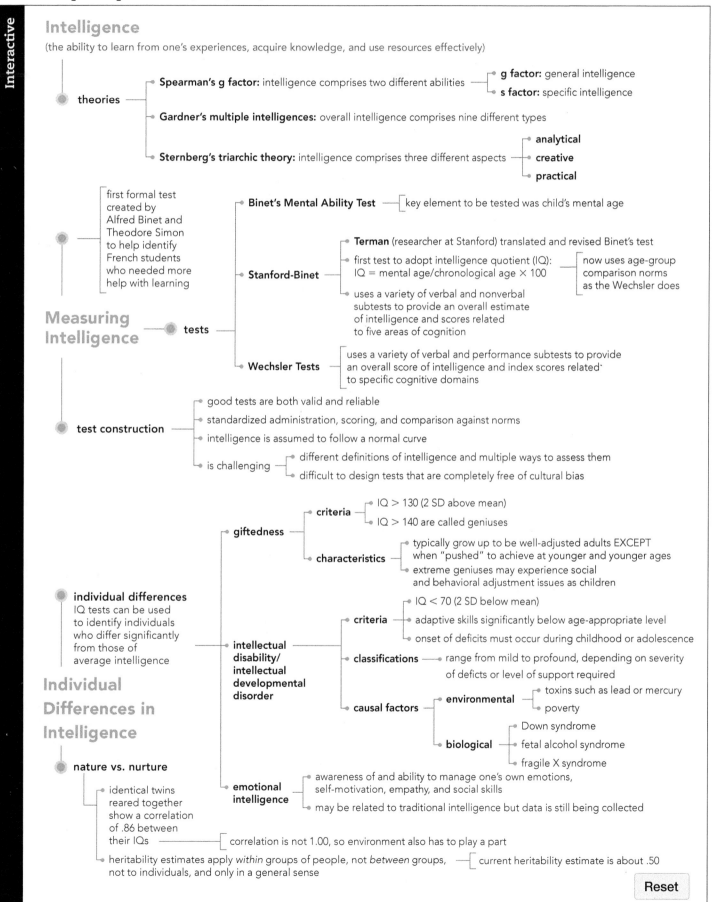

Interactive

Intelligence
(the ability to learn from one's experiences, acquire knowledge, and use resources effectively)

- **theories**
  - **Spearman's g factor:** intelligence comprises two different abilities
    - **g factor:** general intelligence
    - **s factor:** specific intelligence
  - **Gardner's multiple intelligences:** overall intelligence comprises nine different types
  - **Sternberg's triarchic theory:** intelligence comprises three different aspects
    - **analytical**
    - **creative**
    - **practical**

Measuring Intelligence

- first formal test created by Alfred Binet and Theodore Simon to help identify French students who needed more help with learning
- **tests**
  - **Binet's Mental Ability Test** — key element to be tested was child's mental age
  - **Stanford-Binet**
    - **Terman** (researcher at Stanford) translated and revised Binet's test
    - first test to adopt intelligence quotient (IQ): IQ = mental age/chronological age × 100 — now uses age-group comparison norms as the Wechsler does
    - uses a variety of verbal and nonverbal subtests to provide an overall estimate of intelligence and scores related to five areas of cognition
  - **Wechsler Tests** — uses a variety of verbal and performance subtests to provide an overall score of intelligence and index scores related to specific cognitive domains

- **test construction**
  - good tests are both valid and reliable
  - standardized administration, scoring, and comparison against norms
  - intelligence is assumed to follow a normal curve
  - is challenging
    - different definitions of intelligence and multiple ways to assess them
    - difficult to design tests that are completely free of cultural bias

Individual Differences in Intelligence

- **individual differences**
  IQ tests can be used to identify individuals who differ significantly from those of average intelligence
  - **giftedness**
    - **criteria**
      - IQ > 130 (2 SD above mean)
      - IQ > 140 are called geniuses
    - **characteristics**
      - typically grow up to be well-adjusted adults EXCEPT when "pushed" to achieve at younger and younger ages
      - extreme geniuses may experience social and behavioral adjustment issues as children
  - **intellectual disability/ intellectual developmental disorder**
    - **criteria**
      - IQ < 70 (2 SD below mean)
      - adaptive skills significantly below age-appropriate level
      - onset of deficits must occur during childhood or adolescence
    - **classifications** — range from mild to profound, depending on severity of deficts or level of support required
    - **causal factors**
      - **environmental**
        - toxins such as lead or mercury
        - poverty
      - **biological**
        - Down syndrome
        - fetal alcohol syndrome
        - fragile X syndrome
  - **emotional intelligence**
    - awareness of and ability to manage one's own emotions, self-motivation, empathy, and social skills
    - may be related to traditional intelligence but data is still being collected

- **nature vs. nurture**
  - identical twins reared together show a correlation of .86 between their IQs — correlation is not 1.00, so environment also has to play a part
  - heritability estimates apply *within* groups of people, not *between* groups, not to individuals, and only in a general sense — current heritability estimate is about .50

Reset

Practice Quiz How much do you remember? ANSWERS ON PAGE AK-1.

Pick the best answer.

1. Which of the following is NOT one of the intelligences proposed by Gardner's theory?
   a. verbal
   b. visual spatial
   c. sensory
   d. intrapersonal

2. According to Sternberg, intelligence comprises analytical, creative, and _____ aspects.
   a. practical
   b. artistic
   c. scientific
   d. logical

3. Liv is 4 years old. The intelligence test that would most likely be used to determine her IQ is the
   a. WAIS-IV.
   b. WISC-V.
   c. WPPSI-IV.
   d. Dove Test.

4. Professor Becker designed an IQ test. To validate this test, the professor should be careful to do which of the following?
   a. Give the test at least twice to the same group to ensure accuracy.
   b. Select the people in the sample from the population of people for whom the test is designed.
   c. Select only university professors to take the test so that they can critique the questions on the test.
   d. Strive to make sure that the test measures what it is supposed to measure.

5. Lewis Terman's study provided evidence that individuals with high IQs
   a. are generally weaker and lack social skills.
   b. are no better at excelling in their careers than others with average IQs.
   c. show little to no signs of mental illness or adjustment problems.
   d. have more problems with interpersonal relationships except for those with IQs over 180.

6. In recent studies, what do some researchers argue is a more accurate means of gauging success in relationships and careers?
   a. intellectual intelligence
   b. emotional intelligence
   c. heredity studies
   d. stress surveys

7. Which of the following would be an example of a stereotype threat?
   a. Joaquim, who believes IQ tests are unfair to Hispanics, something that his IQ score seems to reflect
   b. Jasmine, who feels she must excel on her IQ test
   c. Tiana, who believes that all testing, no matter the type, is stereotypical and biased
   d. Malik, who believes that tests are equal but must excel so as not to be stereotyped by his friends

---

Language

In Chapter 6 we discussed how language can possibly affect our memory. For example, being asked "Did you see the car bump into the truck?" may prompt a slightly different memory than "Did you see the car smash into the truck?" In this section, we will examine language and how cognition can be affected by language.

THE LEVELS OF LANGUAGE ANALYSIS

7.9 Define language and identify its different elements and structure.

Language is a system for combining symbols (such as words) so that an infinite* number of meaningful statements can be made for the purpose of communicating with others. Language allows people not only to communicate with one another but also to represent their own internal mental activity. In other words, language is a very important part of how people think.

The structures of languages all over the world share common characteristics. They consist of the sounds that exist within a language, word meanings, word order, the rules for making words into other words, the meanings of sentences and phrases, and the rules for practical communication with others.

GRAMMAR **Grammar** is the system of rules governing the structure and use of a language. According to famed linguist Noam Chomsky (Chomsky, 2006; Chomsky et al., 2002), humans have an innate ability to understand and produce language through a device he calls the *language acquisition device*, or *LAD*. He defined the LAD as an innate "program" that contained a *schema* for human language. The children matched the language they heard against this schema and, thus, language developed in a well-researched

---

*infinite: unlimited, without end.

sequence (Chomsky, 1957, 1964, 1981, 1986). While humans may learn the *specific* language (English, Spanish, Mandarin, etc.) through the processes of imitation, reinforcement, and shaping, (L)(I)(N)K to Learning Objectives 5.5, 5.9, and 5.13, the complexities of the grammar of a language are, according to Chomsky, to some degree "wired in" to the developing brain. The LAD "listens" to the language input of the infant's world and then begins to produce language sounds and eventually words and sentences in a pattern found across cultures. This pattern is discussed in greater detail in the next chapter. (L)(I)(N)K to Learning Objective 8.7. Grammar includes phonemes (the basic sounds of language), morphology (the study of the formation of words), rules for the order of words known as syntax, and pragmatics (the practical social expectations and uses of language).

PHONEMES **Phonemes** are the basic units of sound in a language. The *a* in the word *car* is a very different phoneme from the *a* in the word *day*, even though it is the same letter of the alphabet. The difference is in how we say the sound of the *a* in each word. Phonemes are more than just the different ways in which we pronounce single letters, too. *Th, sh,* and *au* are also phonemes. Phonemes for different languages are also different, and one of the biggest problems for people who are trying to learn another language is the inability to both hear and pronounce the phonemes of that other language. Although infants are born with the ability to recognize all phonemes (Werker & Lalonde, 1988), after about 9 months, that ability has deteriorated and the infant recognizes only the phonemes of the language to which the infant is exposed (Boyson-Bardies et al., 1989).

MORPHEMES **Morphemes** are the smallest units of meaning within a language. For example, the word *playing* consists of two morphemes, *play* and *ing*.

SYNTAX **Syntax** is a system of rules for combining words and phrases to form grammatically correct sentences. Syntax is quite important, as just a simple mix-up can cause sentences to be completely misunderstood. For example, "John kidnapped the boy" has a different meaning from "John, the kidnapped boy," although all four words are the same (Lasnik, 1990). Another example of the importance of syntax can be found in the lobby of a Moscow hotel across from a monastery: "You are welcome to visit the cemetery where famous composers, artists, and writers are buried daily except Thursday." So if people want to watch famous composers, artists, and writers being buried, they should not go to this monastery on Thursday.

SEMANTICS **Semantics** are rules for determining the meaning of words and sentences. Sentences, for example, can have the same semantic meaning while having different syntax: "Johnny hit the ball" and "the ball was hit by Johnny."

PRAGMATICS The **pragmatics** of language has to do with the practical aspects of communicating with others, or the social "niceties" of language. Simply put, pragmatics involves knowing things like how to take turns in a conversation, the use of gestures to emphasize a point or indicate a need for more information, and the different ways in which one speaks to different people (Yule, 1996). For example, adults speak to small children differently than they do to other adults by using simpler words. Both adults and children use higher pitched voices and many repeated phrases when talking to infants; such child-directed speech plays an important role in the development of language in children. Part of the pragmatics of language includes knowing just what rhythm and emphasis to use when communicating with others, called *intonation*. When speaking to infants, adults and children are changing the inflection when they use the higher pitch and stress certain words differently than others. Some languages, such as Japanese, are highly sensitive to intonation, meaning that changing the stress or pitch of certain words or syllables of a particular word can change its meaning entirely (Beckman & Pierrehumbert, 1986). For example, the Japanese name "Yoshiko" should be pronounced with the accent or stress on the first syllable: YO-she-koh. This pronunciation of the name means "woman-child." But if the stress is placed on the second syllable (yo-SHE-ko), the name means "woman who urinates."

Pragmatics involves the practical aspects of communicating. This young mother is talking and then pausing for the infant's response. In this way, the infant is learning about taking turns, an important aspect of language development. What kinds of games do adults play with infants that also aid the development of language?

THE RELATIONSHIP BETWEEN LANGUAGE AND THOUGHT

7.10 Evaluate whether or not language influences how people think.

As with the controversy of nature versus nurture, researchers have long debated the relationship between language and thought. Does language actually influence thought, or does thinking influence language?

Two very influential developmental psychologists, Jean Piaget and Lev Vygotsky, often debated the relationship of language and thought (Duncan, 1995). Piaget (1926, 1962) theorized that concepts preceded and aided the development of language. For example, a child would have to have a concept or mental schema for "mother" before being able to learn the word "mama." In a sense, concepts become the "pegs" upon which words are "hung." Piaget also noticed that preschool children seemed to spend a great deal of time talking to themselves—even when playing with another child. Each child would be talking about something totally unrelated to the speech of the other, in a process Piaget called *collective monologue*. Piaget believed that this kind of nonsocial speech was very egocentric (from the child's point of view only, with no regard for the listener) and that as the child became more socially involved and less egocentric, these nonsocial speech patterns would reduce.

Vygotsky, however, believed almost the opposite. He theorized that language actually helped develop concepts and that language could also help the child learn to control behavior—including social behavior (Vygotsky, 1962, 1978, 1987). For Vygotsky, the word helped form the concept: Once a child had learned the word "mama," the various elements of "mama-ness"—*warm, soft, food, safety*, and so on—could come together around that word. Vygotsky also believed that the "egocentric" speech of the preschool child was actually a way for the child to form thoughts and control actions. This "private speech" was a way for children to plan their behavior and organize actions so that their goals could be obtained. Since socializing with other children would demand much more self-control and behavioral regulation on the part of the preschool child, Vygotsky believed that private speech would actually increase as children became more socially active in the preschool years. This was, of course, the opposite of Piaget's assumption, and the evidence seems to bear out Vygotsky's view: Children, especially bright children, do tend to use more private speech when learning how to socialize with other children or when working on a difficult task (Berk, 1992; Berk & Spuhl, 1995; Bivens & Berk, 1990).

The hypothesis that language shapes and influences thoughts was accepted by many theorists, with a few notable exceptions, such as Piaget. One of the best-known versions of this view is the Sapir-Whorf hypothesis (named for the two theorists who developed it, Edward Sapir and his student, Benjamin Lee Whorf). This hypothesis assumes that the thought processes and concepts within any culture are determined by the words of the culture (Sapir, 1921; Whorf, 1956). It has come to be known as the **linguistic relativity hypothesis**, meaning that thought processes and concepts are controlled by (relative to) language. That is, the words people use determine much of the way in which they think about the world around them.

Is there evidence for the linguistic relativity hypothesis? Neither Sapir nor Whorf provided any scientific studies that would support their proposition. There have been numerous studies by other researchers, however. For example, in one study researchers assumed that a language's color names would influence the ability of the people who grew up with that language to distinguish among and perceive colors. The study found that basic color terms did directly influence color recognition memory (Lucy & Shweder, 1979). But an earlier series of studies of the perception of colors by Eleanor Rosch-Heider and others (Rosch-Heider, 1972; Rosch-Heider & Olivier, 1972) had already found just the opposite effect: Members of the Dani tribe, who have only two names for colors, were no different in their ability to perceive all of the colors than were the English speakers in the study. More recent studies (Davies et al., 1998a, 1998b; Laws et al., 1995; Pinker & Bloom, 1990) support Rosch-Heider's findings and the idea of a **cognitive universalism** (concepts are universal and influence the development of language) rather than linguistic relativity.

Other research suggests that although the linguistic relativity hypothesis may not work for fine perceptual discriminations such as those in the Rosch-Heider studies, it may be an appropriate explanation for concepts of a higher level. In one study, researchers showed pictures of two animals to preschool children (Gelman & Markman, 1986). The pictures were of a flamingo and a bat. The children were told that the flamingo feeds its baby mashed-up food but the bat feeds its baby milk. Then they were shown a picture of a blackbird (which looked more like the bat than the flamingo). Half of the children were told that the blackbird was a bird, while the other children were not. When asked how the blackbird fed its baby, the children who had been given the bird label were more likely to say that it fed its baby mashed-up food than were the children who were not given the label, indicating that the preschoolers were making inferences about feeding habits based on category membership rather than perceptual similarity—the word *bird* helped the children who were given that label to place the blackbird in its proper higher level category.

Research continues in the investigation of relationships between language and thought, and it appears to support linguistic relativity and how language can shape our thoughts about space, time, colors, and objects (Boroditsky, 2001,2009). However, researchers do not always agree, and for some studies that offer support, there are others that reinterpret the data, fail to replicate findings, or offer critiques of the original studies, so findings are sometimes still in question (Chen, 2007; January & Kako, 2007).

Psychologists cannot deny the influence of language on problem solving, cognition, and memory. Sometimes a problem can simply be worded differently to have the solution become obvious, and memory (Ⓛ Ⓘ Ⓝ Ⓚ to Learning Objective 6.5) is certainly stored in terms of the semantics of language. Language can definitely influence the perception of others as well—"computer geek" and "software engineer" might be used to describe the same person, but one phrase is obviously less flattering and the image brought to mind is different for the two terms. In the end, trying to determine whether language influences thoughts or thoughts influence language may be like trying to determine which came first, the chicken or the egg.

ANIMAL STUDIES IN LANGUAGE

7.11 **Summarize the research on the ability of animals to communicate and use language.**

💬 I've heard that chimpanzees can be taught to use sign language. Is this for real, or are the chimps just performing tricks like the animals in the circus or the zoo?

There are really two questions about animals and language. The first is "Can animals communicate?" and the second is "Can animals use language?" The answer to the first question is a definite "Yes." Animals communicate in many ways. They use sounds such as the rattle of a rattlesnake or the warning growl of an angry dog. There are also physical behaviors, such as the "dance" of honeybees that tells the other bees where a source of pollen is (Gould & Gould, 1994). But the answer to the second question is more complicated, because language is defined as the use of symbols, and symbols are things that stand for something else. Words are symbols, and gestures can be symbols. But the gestures used by animals are instinctual, meaning they are controlled by the animal's genetic makeup. The honeybee doing the "dance" is controlled completely by instinct, as is the growling dog. In human language, symbols are used quite deliberately and voluntarily, not by instinct, and abstract symbols have no meaning until people assign meaning to them. (Although Chomsky's innate language acquisition device might lead some to think that language for humans is instinctual, it should be noted that the infant's production of speech sounds becomes quite deliberate within a short period of time.)

Can animals be taught to use symbols that are abstract? There have been attempts to teach animals (primates and dolphins) how to use sign language (as animals lack the vocal structure to form spoken words), but many of these attempts were simply not "good

Kanzi looks at the keyboard used in teaching language to chimpanzees. Kanzi's language abilities were learned through watching researchers train his mother rather than directly—much as a human infant learns through listening to the speech of adults.

science." The most successful of these experiments (which is not without its critics as well) has been with Kanzi, a bonobo chimpanzee trained to press abstract symbols on a computer keyboard (Savage-Rumbaugh & Lewin, 1994). Kanzi actually was not the original subject of the study—his mother, Matata, was the chimp being trained. She did not learn many of the symbols, but Kanzi watched his mother use the keyboard and appeared to learn how to use the symbols through that observation. At last count, Kanzi could understand about 150 spoken English words. Trainers who speak to him are not in his view, so he is not responding to physical cues or symbols. He has managed to follow correctly complex instructions up to the level of a 2-year-old child (Savage-Rumbaugh et al., 1998). The most recent studies with Kanzi have him making sounds that seem to have consistent meaning across different situations (Tagliatatela et al., 2003). Nearly 100 videotaped hours of Kanzi engaged in day-to-day activities were analyzed for these sounds. The researchers were able to identify four sounds that seemed to represent banana, grapes, juice, and the word *yes*. (However, remember that four sounds do not come close to making an entire language.)

Other studies, with dolphins (Herman et al., 1993) and with parrots (Pepperberg, 1998, 2007), have also met with some success. Is it real language? The answer seems to be a qualified "yes." The qualification is that none of the animals that have achieved success so far can compare to the level of language development of a 3-year-old human child (Pinker, 1995). However, linguists still debate whether these animals are truly learning language if they are not also learning how to use syntax—combining words into grammatically correct sentences as well as being able to understand the differences between sentences such as "The girl kissed the boy" and "The boy kissed the girl." As yet, there is no conclusive evidence that any of the animals trained in language have been able to master syntax (Demers, 1988; Johnson, 1995; Pinker, 1995).

Concept Map L.O. 7.9, 7.10, 7.11

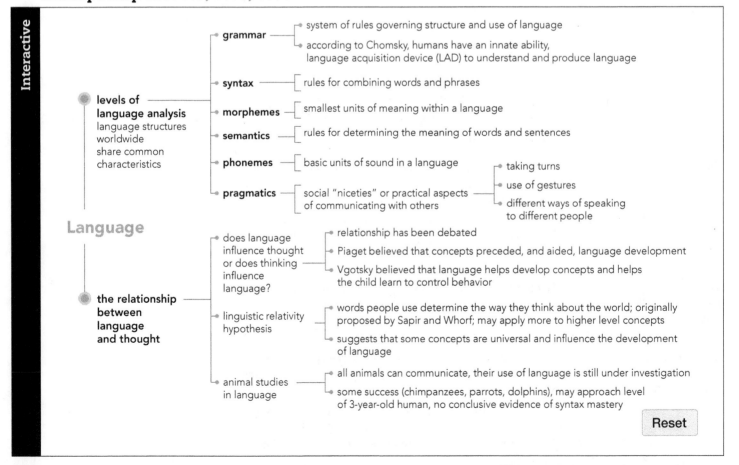

Practice Quiz   How much do you remember?   ANSWERS ON PAGE AK-1.

Pick the best answer.

1. The basic units of sound in a language are known as
   a. grammar.
   c. syntax.
   b. morphemes.
   d. phonemes.

2. According to Noam Chomsky, what is a language acquisition device?
   a. an environmental entity that allows people to learn foreign languages
   b. a biological element of the brain that allows us to learn language
   c. a learning method that many can use to understand the language of infants and small children
   d. a part of the brain that develops during puberty that allows teens and adults to formulate questions and engage others

3. Researchers believe that up to the age of _____, individuals possess the ability to understand phonemes of all languages.
   a. 3 months
   c. 2 years
   b. 9 months
   d. 7 years

4. _____ believed that language helps to develop concepts, whereas _____ believed that concepts must be developed first if language is to follow.
   a. Vygotsky; Piaget
   b. Chomsky; Sapir and Whorf
   c. Piaget; Rosch-Heider
   d. Sapir and Whorf; Vygotsky

Applying Psychology to Everyday Life
Mental and Physical Exercises Combine for Better Cognitive Health

7.12 Identify some methods for improving your thinking.

You may have heard the saying "use it or lose it" and likely think of it in terms of maintaining physical fitness. But it is not limited to that; in many regards, the saying applies as well to our ability to maintain cognitive fitness. However, just as there is a difference between physical activity and physical exercise, there is a difference in mental *activity* and mental *exercise*.

Quite a few computerized brain-training programs and devices have hit the market in the last few years. In addition, a lot of attention in the media has focused on the benefits of specific computer-based brain exercises you can do to improve your cognitive fitness. While some are more scientifically grounded and offer the possibility of real benefits, many more appear to be riding the current wave of interest and may not be useful. For some individuals, practicing certain mental skills through cognitive exercises appears to help with those same skills when tested later. In general, however, research has not identified any benefits that transfer to untrained areas (Owen et al., 2010). Just as being physically active in general will not make you an Olympic athlete, to tune up your cognitive fitness you have to perform proper, focused cognitive exercises.

Wait a minute! You just said most skills don't transfer. That's correct, some do not, but just as in physical training, if you select the proper foundational exercises, you can benefit higher-level cognitive functions. For example, impaired verbal working memory is one of the cognitive dysfunctions in schizophrenia. Deficits in early auditory processing are also present and have negative implications for both verbal learning and memory, and for understanding the semantics and emotional content of speech (Fisher et al., 2009). Imagine the difficulty you would have if you could not follow a conversation with another person because you could not remember what they just said or because you could not comprehend the meaning or the emotions they were expressing in their speech.

In one study, it was found that for a group of individuals with schizophrenia, computerized cognitive exercises that placed increasing demands on auditory perception (a foundational skill) were beneficial (Fisher et al., 2009). Those same individuals later demonstrated significant progress in verbal working memory and global cognition tasks (higher-level skills). Although the cognitive exercise group originally received daily training for 10 weeks, when some participants were studied 6 months later, the researchers found that some of the gains were still evident and that gains overall were positively correlated with improved quality of life at the 6-month assessment point (Fisher et al., 2009). The authors acknowledged that some of the positive effects might have been due to the number of hours of training and the amount of repetition (the authors noted that each exercise was practiced for thousands of trials!). Furthermore, approximately 16 hours were devoted to tasks that had word stimuli or a learning/memory component, while over 30 hours were spent performing tasks that focused on auditory perception, which also engaged working memory.

The noting of the auditory perception tasks involving working memory (**L****I****N** K to Learning Objective 6.4) in the M. Fisher et al. (2009) study is very interesting, especially in light of research suggesting challenging, adaptive training in working memory appears to improve fluid intelligence in young adults (Jaeggi et al., 2008). However, recent research suggests training in working memory may improve working memory capacity on related tasks, but on measures of fluid intelligence, these improvements do not generalize (Harrison et al., 2013). Fluid intelligence is the ability to adapt and deal with new problems or challenges the first time you encounter them, without having to depend on knowledge you already possess.

What else can you do more generally to benefit your cognitive health? Exercise! And this time, we are referring to physical exercise. Physical activity and specifically aerobic fitness has repeatedly been demonstrated to be associated with improved cognitive function across the life span. A physically active lifestyle and greater aerobic fitness has been implicated with better executive control and memory processes in preadolescent children (Chaddock et al., 2010; Hillman et al., 2009), better educational outcomes later in life and improved affect and visuospatial memory in young adults (Åberg et al., 2009; Stroth et al., 2009), increased hippocampal volume (associated with better memory) in elderly adults (Erickson et al., 2009), and as a useful intervention in a group of individuals at high risk of cognitive decline or impairment, especially for females in the group (Baker et al., 2010).

At least one possible benefit of regular aerobic activity is promoting or maintaining functional connectivity among key brain areas of the frontal, temporal, and parietal lobes (Voss et al., 2010). The increases in oxygen and blood flow to the brain play key roles. Other benefits include increased levels of mood-related neurotransmitters including serotonin, norepinephrine, and dopamine, along with neurogenesis in specific brain areas including the hippocampus (Ratey & Hagerman, 2008). In another study, 3 months of aerobic activity and increased fitness were associated with small increases in the size of the hippocampus and improved memory in individuals with schizophrenia. Interestingly, controls without schizophrenia in this research *also* showed increases in their hippocampi associated with increases in aerobic fitness (Pajonk et al., 2010).

So instead of "use it or lose it," perhaps a better saying to keep in mind is "what is good for the heart or body is also good for the mind." If you want to learn more, an interesting overview of research related to exercise and brain health can be found in the book *Spark: The Revolutionary New Science of Exercise and the Brain* by John Ratey and Eric Hagerman (2008).

Questions for Further Discussion

1. Aside from those involving working memory, what other kinds of focused mental exercises might help to keep the brain fit?

2. Should doctors suggest aerobic exercise for their patients interested in maintaining or improving their cognitive functions? What about psychologists working with individuals who have mood or anxiety disorders, or clients with attention problems?

3. Based on this information, what might the implications be for schools that are reducing or eliminating their physical education requirements? What about college students who may experience a decrease in physical activity as compared to when they were in high school?

Chapter Summary

Cognition

7.1 Define cognition and explain how mental images and concepts are involved in the process of thinking

- Thinking (cognition) is mental activity that occurs in the brain when information is being organized, stored, communicated, or processed.
- Mental images represent objects or events and have a picturelike quality.
- Concepts are ideas that represent a class or category of events, objects, or activities.
- Prototypes are examples of a concept that more closely match the defining characteristics of that concept.

7.2 Describe some methods people use to solve problems and make decisions.

- Problem solving consists of thinking and behaving in certain ways to reach a goal.
- Mechanical solutions include trial-and-error learning and rote solutions.
- Algorithms are a type of rote solution in which one follows step-by-step procedures for solving certain types of problems.
- A heuristic or "rule of thumb" is a strategy that narrows down the possible solutions for a problem.
- Insight is the sudden perception of a solution to a problem.

7.3 Identify three common barriers to successful problem solving.

- Functional fixedness is the tendency to perceive objects as having only the use for which they were originally intended.
- Confirmation bias is the tendency to search for evidence that confirms one's beliefs, ignoring any evidence to the contrary.

7.4 Define creativity and identify some characteristics of divergent thinking.

- Divergent thinking involves coming up with as many different answers as possible. This is a kind of creativity (combining ideas or behavior in new ways).
- Creative people are usually good at mental imagery and have knowledge on a wide range of topics, are unafraid to be different, value their independence, and are often unconventional in their work but not in other areas.

Intelligence

7.5 Compare and contrast different theories on the nature of intelligence.

- Intelligence is the ability to understand the world, think rationally or logically, and use resources effectively when faced with challenges or problems.
- Spearman proposed general intelligence, or g factor, as the ability to reason and solve problems, whereas specific intelligence, or s factor, includes task-specific abilities in certain areas such as music, business, or art.
- Gardner proposed nine different types of intelligence, ranging from verbal, linguistic, and mathematical to interpersonal and intrapersonal intelligence.
- Sternberg proposed three types of intelligence: analytical, creative, and practical.

7.6 Compare and contrast some methods of measuring intelligence and identify ways to evaluate the quality of a test.

- The Stanford-Binet Intelligence Test yields an IQ score that was once determined by dividing the mental age of the person by the chronological age and multiplying that quotient by 100, but now involves comparing a person's score to a standardized norm.
- The Wechsler Intelligence Tests yield index scores derived from both verbal and nonverbal subtests and an overall score of intelligence.
- Standardization, validity, and reliability are all important factors in the construction of an intelligence test.
- Deviation IQs are based on the normal curve, defining different levels of intelligence based on the deviation of scores from a common mean.
- IQ tests are often criticized for being culturally biased.

7.7 Define intellectual disability, giftedness, and emotional intelligence.

- Intellectual disability is a neurodevelopmental condition in which IQ falls below 70 and adaptive behavior across conceptual, social, and practical domains of life is severely deficient for a person of a particular chronological age. Symptoms must also first be present during the developmental period.
- The four levels of intellectual disability are mild, moderate, severe, and profound. These are determined by the level of adaptive functioning and level of supports the individual needs in their daily life.
- Causes of intellectual disability include deprived environments as well as chromosome and genetic disorders and dietary deficiencies.
- Gifted persons are defined as those having IQ scores at the upper end of the normal curve (130 or above).
- Terman conducted a longitudinal study that demonstrated that gifted children grow up to be successful adults for the most part.
- Emotional intelligence involves being able to reach goals and engage in productive thinking through accurate awareness and effective management of our own emotions. It also involves our ability to understand what others feel.

7.8 Evaluate the influence of heredity and environment on the development of intelligence.

- Stronger correlations are found between IQ scores as genetic relatedness increases. Heritability of IQ is estimated at .50.

- In 1994, Herrnstein and Murray published *The Bell Curve*, in which they made widely criticized claims about the heritability of intelligence.

Language

7.9 Define language and identify its different elements and structure.

- Language is a system for combining symbols so that an infinite number of meaningful statements can be created and communicated to others.
- Grammar is the system of rules by which language is governed and includes the rules for using phonemes, morphemes, and syntax. Pragmatics refers to practical aspects of language.

7.10 Evaluate whether or not language influences how people think.

- Sapir and Whorf originally proposed that language controls and helps the development of thought processes and concepts, an idea that is known as the linguistic relativity hypothesis.
- Other researchers have found evidence that concepts are universal and directly influence the development of language, called the cognitive universalism viewpoint.

7.11 Summarize the research on the ability of animals to communicate and use language.

- Studies with chimpanzees, parrots, and dolphins have been somewhat successful in demonstrating that animals can develop a basic kind of language, including some abstract ideas.
- Controversy exists over the lack of evidence that animals can learn syntax, which some feel means that animals are not truly learning and using language.

Applying Psychology to Everyday Life: Mental and Physical Exercises Combine for Better Cognitive Health

7.12 Identify some methods for improving your thinking.

- Both specific mental exercises (such as those involving working memory) and physical exercise promoting aerobic fitness are important for optimal cognitive functioning.

Test Yourself   ANSWERS ON PAGE AK-1.

Pick the best answer.

1. Researchers have found that it takes _____ to view a mental image that is larger or covers more distance than a smaller or more compact one.
   a. longer
   b. less time
   c. the same amount of time
   d. half the time

2. Research suggests we engage mental images in our mind _____ the way we engage or interact with physical objects.
   a. a little like
   b. much like
   c. not at all like
   d. randomly and completely different than

3. A psychologist asks people to envision a circle. Next he asks them to draw the circle they envisioned. When comparing the pictures, almost all circles look identical. The fact that a circle typically fits a specific and rigid set of rules is an example of a
   a. formal concept.
   b. natural concept.
   c. fuzzy concept.
   d. prototype.

4. Trial and error is sometimes referred to as a(n)
   a. algorithm.
   b. heuristic.
   c. rule of thumb.
   d. mechanical solution.

5. John and Karen bought a new house with an unfinished basement. To determine how they want to finish it, they lay down tape on the floor showing where walls will go and rooms will be. This process of problem solving is known as
   a. representativeness heuristic.
   b. trial and error.
   c. working backward from the goal.
   d. algorithms.

6. One day at work, Pauline's earring fell on the floor and she was unable to find the back. To keep from losing her earring, Pauline reinserted it and used part of a pencil eraser to keep the earring in place. Using a pencil eraser as a temporary earring back showed that Pauline overcame
   a. a mental set.
   b. functional fixedness.
   c. confirmation bias.
   d. transformation bias.

7. Which of the following questions would be most likely to produce divergent thinking?
   a. "What is a clothes hanger?"
   b. "How do you spell clothes hanger?"
   c. "How many uses can you think of for a clothes hanger?"
   d. "What does a clothes hanger typically look like?"

8. Charles Spearman defined intelligence as being comprised of both general intelligence and _____ intelligence.
   a. specific
   b. global
   c. scientific
   d. contextual

9. According to Sternberg, intelligence is comprised of how many aspects?
   a. one
   b. two
   c. three
   d. four

10. Which of the following tests came first?
    a. The Wechsler tests
    b. The Stanford–Binet
    c. The ACT
    d. Binet's mental ability test

11. Dr. Davenport gives all her classes 45 minutes to complete their psychology test regardless of whether the class meets for 50 minutes, 75 minutes, or even 3 hours. Such a technique ensures test
    a. reliability.
    b. validity.
    c. norms.
    d. standardization.

12. In contrast to comparing mental age to chronological age, most modern tests of intelligence use _____.
   a. Stern's formula.
   b. age-group comparison norms.
   c. creativity assessments.
   d. emotional assessments.

13. The goal of all test developers is to _____ cultural bias in their intelligence tests.
   a. maximize
   b. eliminate
   c. minimize
   d. hide

14. Dr. Miller works with children who have grown up in poor socioeconomic conditions. Many of her clients come from homes that do not emphasize education or social involvement, and opportunities for advancement are practically nonexistent. Many are malnourished, have been exposed to a variety of environmental toxins, and have multiple infections without adequate or timely health care. What might these children be at risk for?
   a. intellectual disability
   b. genetic inhibition
   c. organically induced deprivation
   d. increased emotional intelligence

15. Dr. Thomas has found that William, her patient, has a defect in a gene on the X chromosome of his 23rd pair, which has resulted in a deficiency of a protein needed for William's brain development. William most likely suffers from
   a. Down syndrome.
   b. cretinism.
   c. fragile X syndrome.
   d. fetal alcohol syndrome.

16. In Terman's study of gifted children, mental health issues and relationship problems occurred only in those with IQs of
   a. 150 or higher.
   b. 180 or higher.
   c. 100 or lower.
   d. 45 or lower.

17. What may be the best predictor of why some people do not excel in school but essentially succeed in their life and career choices?
   a. cretinism
   b. phonemes
   c. one's intelligence quotient
   d. emotional intelligence

18. What does the Flynn effect theorize?
   a. Intelligence scores are steadily increasing in modernized countries.
   b. Intelligence scores are decreasing due to an overreliance on technology.
   c. Intelligence scores are relatively stable in contrast to improvement in our educational system.
   d. Intelligence scores are meaningless and should be abandoned.

19. Edward Sapir and Benjamin Whorf theorized that _____, a concept reflected in their linguistic relativity hypothesis.
   a. language shapes thoughts
   b. thoughts shape language
   c. language and thought develop independently
   d. language and thought influence each other

20. Cognitive universalism tends to _____ the linguistic relativity hypothesis.
   a. contradict
   b. support
   c. add further proof to
   d. mildly downplay

Chapter 8
Development Across the Life Span

At a time when many teenagers are hanging out at the mall with friends, 16-year-old Jessica Watson was on a mission to become the youngest individual to sail nonstop and unassisted around the world. She left Sydney, Australia, on October 18, 2009, and returned seven months later, on May 15, 2010, unofficially breaking the previous record (Marks, 2010; Munoz, 2010). Watson's record will remain unrecognized, however. The World Speed Sailing Record Council did away with its "youngest" category to discourage what it considers dangerous and foolhardy attempts by those who are too young. Adolescence is one among many stages of life that we will explore in this chapter. While we will focus on several of the common features of human development in all of those stages, the story of Jessica Watson should be a reminder that each of us is an individual, with different motivations, goals, and desires.

How have you changed since your early teenage years? In what ways are you similar to other individuals of your age and in what ways are you different and unique?

Why study human development?

Beginning to understand how we come to be the people we are is a critical step in understanding ourselves as we are today and who we may become as we grow older. From the moment of conception, each of us is headed down a pathway of change, influenced by our biology, environment, and social interactions, to a final destination that is the same for all of us. The twists and turns of the pathway are what make each of us unique individuals. In this chapter, we'll look at the influences that help determine our developmental pathway through life.

Learning Objectives

8.1 Compare and contrast the special research methods used to study development.

8.2 Explain the relationship between heredity and environmental factors in determining development.

8.3 Summarize the role of chromosomes and genes in determining the transmission of traits and the inheritance of disorders.

8.4 Explain the process of fertilization, including the twinning process.

8.5 Describe the processes and stages of prenatal development and discuss hazards in prenatal development.

8.6 Describe the physical and sensory changes that take place in infancy and childhood.

8.7 Compare and contrast two theories of cognitive development, and discuss the development of language.

8.8 Evaluate claims regarding the causes of autism spectrum disorder.

8.9 Explain the development of personality, social relationships, and self-concept in infancy and childhood, and discuss the first four stages of Erikson's theory.

8.10 Define gender, and discuss the development of gender roles.

8.11 Compare and contrast two theories of gender-role development.

8.12 Describe the physical changes that occur in adolescence, and identify some of the sexually transmitted diseases to which adolescents may be vulnerable.

8.13 Identify the cognitive and personality changes occurring in adolescence.

8.14 Describe the physical and cognitive changes of adulthood, and explain how to improve physical and mental health.

8.15 Summarize some common psychosocial concerns of adulthood and explain how they relate to Erikson's theory.

8.16 Compare and contrast three views of why aging occurs.

8.17 Identify one theory of the stages of death and dying and describe some of the criticisms of this theory.

8.18 Compare and contrast some cross-cultural differences in views of death.

Studying Human Development

What is development? In the context of life, **human development** is the scientific study of the changes that occur in people as they age, from conception until death. This chapter will touch on almost all of the topics covered in the other chapters of this text, such as personality, cognition, biological processes, and social interactions. But in this chapter, all of those topics will be studied in the context of changes that occur as a result of the process of human development.

RESEARCH DESIGNS

8.1 Compare and contrast the special research methods used to study development.

Research in development is affected by the problem of age. In any experiment, the participants who are exposed to the independent variable (the variable in an experiment that is deliberately manipulated by the experimenter) should be randomly assigned to the different experimental conditions. **L I N K** to Learning Objective 1.9. The problem in developmental research is that the age of the people in the study should always be an independent variable, but people cannot be randomly assigned to different age-groups.

Special designs used in researching age-related changes are the **longitudinal design**, in which one group of people is followed and assessed at different times as the group ages; the **cross-sectional design**, in which several different age-groups are studied at one time; and the **cross-sequential design**, which is a combination of the longitudinal and cross-sectional designs (Baltes et al., 1988; Schaie & Willis, 2010).

The longitudinal design has the advantage of looking at real age-related changes as those changes occur in the same individuals. The disadvantages of this method are the lengthy amount of time, money, and effort involved in following participants over the years as well as the loss of participants when they move away, lose interest, or die. The cross-sectional design has the advantages of being quick, relatively inexpensive, and easier to accomplish than the longitudinal design. The main disadvantage is that one is no longer comparing changes in the same individuals as they age; instead, individuals of different ages are being compared to one another. Differences between age-groups are often a problem in developmental research. For example, in comparing the IQ scores of 30-year-olds to 80-year-olds to see how aging affects intelligence, questions arise concerning the differing experiences those two age-groups have had in educational opportunities that might affect IQ scores in addition to any effects of aging. This is known as the **cohort effect**, the particular impact on development that occurs when a group of people share a common time period or common life experience (for example, having been born in the same time period or having gone through a specific historical event together). **Table 8.1** shows a comparison of a longitudinal design, a cross-sectional design, and a cross-sequential design.

In studying human development, developmental psychologists have outlined many theories of how these age-related changes occur. There are some areas of controversy, however, and one of these is the issue of nature versus nurture.

NATURE VERSUS NURTURE

8.2 Explain the relationship between heredity and environmental factors in determining development.

Nature refers to heredity, the influence of inherited characteristics on personality, physical growth, intellectual growth, and social interactions. **Nurture** refers to the influence of the environment on all of those same things and includes parenting styles,

Table 8.1 A Comparison of Three Developmental Research Designs		
Cross-Sectional Design		
Different participants of various ages are compared at one point in time to determine age-related *differences*.	**Group One:** 20-year-old participants **Group Two:** 40-year-old participants **Group Three:** 60-year-old participants	Research done in 2012
Longitudinal Design		
The **same** participants are studied at various ages to determine age-related changes.	**Study One:** 20-year-old participants **Study Two:** Same participants are 40 years old **Study Three:** Same participants are now 60 years old	Research done in 1972 Research done in 1992 Research done in 2012
Cross-Sequential Design		
Different participants of various ages are compared at several points in time, for a period of no more than six years, to determine both age-related differences and age-related changes.	**Study One:** *Group One:* 20-year-old participants *Group Two:* 40-year-old participants **Study Two:** *Group One:* participants will be 25 years old *Group Two:* participants will be 45 years old	Research done in 2012 Research to be done in 2017

physical surroundings, economic factors, and anything that can have an influence on development that does not come from within the person.

 🗨 So, is a person like Hitler born that way, or did something happen to make him the person he was?

How much of a person's personality and behavior is determined by nature, and how much is determined by nurture? This is a key question, and the answer is quite complicated. It is also quite important: Are people like Hitler or Dzhokhar Tsarnaev (the youngest of the two brothers responsible for the bombings at the 2013 Boston Marathon) the result of bad genes? Or was it bad parenting or life-altering experiences in childhood? Or are they the unique combination of both hereditary and environmental influences? After many years of scientific research, most developmental psychologists now agree that the last possibility is the most likely explanation for most of human development: All that people are and all that people become is the product of an interaction between nature and nurture (Davis et al., 2012; Insel & Wang, 2010; Ridley, 1999; Sternberg & Grigorenko, 2006). This does not mean that the controversy no longer exists; for example, intelligence is still a "hot topic" with regard to how much is inherited and how much is learned. There are researchers and theorists who assume a large genetic influence (Bouchard & Segal, 1985; Herrnstein & Murray, 1994; Jensen, 1969; Johnson et al., 2007; Kristensen & Bjerkedal, 2007) and those who believe that culture, economics, nutrition in early childhood, and educational opportunities have a greater impact (Gardner et al., 1996; Gould, 1996; Rose et al., 1984; Wahlsten, 1997).

Behavioral genetics is a relatively new field in the investigation of the origins of behavior in which researchers try to determine how much of behavior is the result of genetic inheritance and how much is due to a person's experiences. As the video *Family and*

Twin Studies explains, behavioral geneticists use a variety of methods to determine this, including family, twin, and adoption studies.

For more on behavioral genetics and links to other sites, go to the Human Genome Project Information site at **obssr.od.nih.gov**.

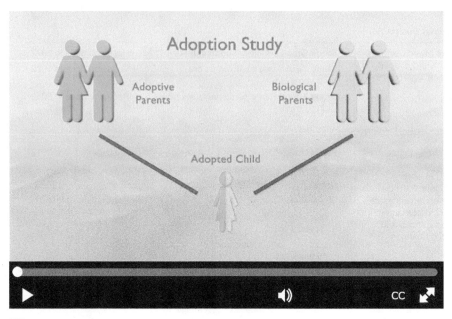

Watch the Video, *Family and Twin Studies.*

THE BASIC BUILDING BLOCKS OF DEVELOPMENT

8.3 Summarize the role of chromosomes and genes in determining the transmission of traits and the inheritance of disorders.

Any study of the human life span must begin with looking at the complex material contained in the cells of the body that carries the instructions for life itself. After discussing the basic building blocks of life, we will discuss how the processes of conception and the development of the infant within the womb take place.

Genetics is the science of heredity. Understanding how genes transmit human characteristics and traits involves defining a few basic terms.

The basic building blocks of life are special DNA molecules that contain the instructions for all of an organism's traits (see **Figure 8.1**). These "instructions" known as genes are sections of the DNA molecules. Genes that are more active in influencing a trait are called **dominant**. A dominant gene will always be expressed in the observable trait. Some disorders, such as Huntington's disease and Marfan's syndrome, are carried by dominant genes. In these disorders, only one parent needs to have the gene for the disorder to be passed on to offspring. More often genetic disorders are carried by recessive genes. **Recessive** genes tend to recede, or fade, into the background when paired with a dominant gene. Diseases carried by recessive genes are only inherited when a child receives two recessive genes, one from each parent. Examples of disorders inherited in this manner are cystic fibrosis (a disease of the respiratory and digestive tracts), sickle-cell anemia (a blood disorder), Tay-Sachs disorder (a fatal neurological disorder), and phenylketonuria or PKU (a problem with digesting the amino acid phenylalanine, which can lead to brain damage). **Figure 8.2** illustrates a typical pattern of inheritance for PKU.

Chromosomes are rod-shaped structures found in the nucleus of each cell and are nothing more than tightly wound strands of genes. Sometimes the chromosome

Figure 8.1 DNA Molecule

In this model of a DNA molecule, the two strands making up the sides of the "twisted ladder" are composed of sugars and phosphates. The "rungs" of the ladder that link the two strands are amines. Amines contain the genetic codes for building the proteins that make up organic life.

itself is the problem. Although each egg and each sperm (the sex cells for females and males, respectively) is only supposed to have 23 chromosomes, in the creation of these cells a chromosome can end up in the wrong cell, leaving one cell with only 22 and the other with 24. If either of these cells survives to "mate," the missing or extra chromosome can cause mild to severe problems in development (American Academy of Pediatrics, 1995; Barnes & Carey, 2002; Centers for Disease Control, 2009; Gardner & Sutherland, 1996).

Figure 8.2 DOMINANT AND RECESSIVE GENES AND PKU

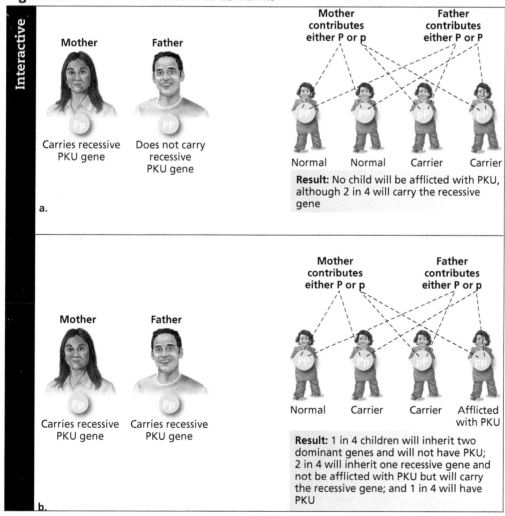

This figure shows the variation of parents carrying zero, one, or two recessive genes and the result of this in their offspring.

(a) If only one parent carries the PKU gene, the children might be carriers but will not have PKU.

(b) Only if both parents are carriers of PKU will a child have the one in four possibility of having PKU.

Down syndrome is a form of developmental delay caused by an extra chromosome 21.

Examples of chromosome disorders include Down syndrome, a disorder in which there is an extra chromosome in what would normally be the twenty-first pair. Symptoms include almond-shaped, wide-set eyes and intellectual disability (Barnes & Carey, 2002; Hernandez & Fisher, 1996). Other chromosome disorders occur when there is an extra sex chromosome in the twenty-third pair, such as Klinefelter's syndrome, in which the twenty-third set of sex chromosomes is XXY, with the extra X producing a male with reduced masculine characteristics, enlarged breasts, obesity, and excessive height (Bock, 1993), and Turner's syndrome, in which the twenty-third pair is actually missing an X, so that the result is a lone X chromosome (Ranke & Saenger, 2001). These females tend to be very short, infertile, and sexually underdeveloped (American Academy of Pediatrics, 1995; Hong et al., 2009; Rovet, 1993).

WRITING PROMPT

The time is coming when choosing the genetic traits of your child is going to be possible. What kinds of ethical and practical problems may arise from this development?

▶ | The response entered here will be saved to your notes and may be collected by your instructor if he/she requires it.

Submit

Concept Map L.O. 8.1, 8.2, 8.3

Interactive

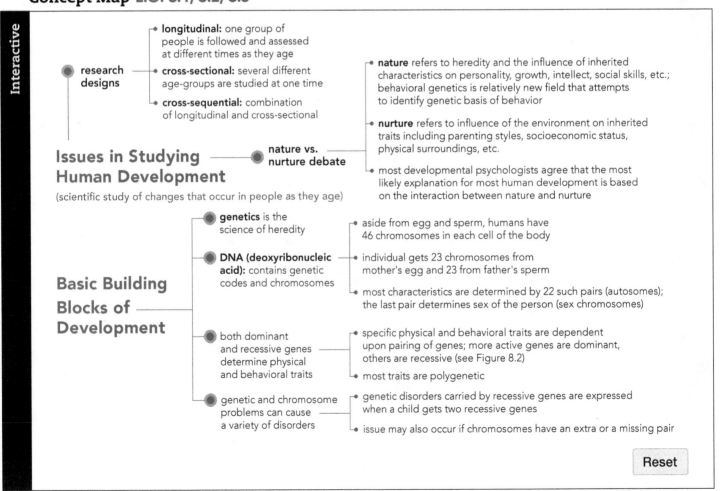

- **research designs**
  - **longitudinal:** one group of people is followed and assessed at different times as they age
  - **cross-sectional:** several different age-groups are studied at one time
  - **cross-sequential:** combination of longitudinal and cross-sectional

Issues in Studying Human Development
(scientific study of changes that occur in people as they age)

- **nature vs. nurture debate**
  - **nature** refers to heredity and the influence of inherited characteristics on personality, growth, intellect, social skills, etc.; behavioral genetics is relatively new field that attempts to identify genetic basis of behavior
  - **nurture** refers to influence of the environment on inherited traits including parenting styles, socioeconomic status, physical surroundings, etc.
  - most developmental psychologists agree that the most likely explanation for most human development is based on the interaction between nature and nurture

Basic Building Blocks of Development

- **genetics** is the science of heredity
- **DNA (deoxyribonucleic acid):** contains genetic codes and chromosomes
  - aside from egg and sperm, humans have 46 chromosomes in each cell of the body
  - individual gets 23 chromosomes from mother's egg and 23 from father's sperm
  - most characteristics are determined by 22 such pairs (autosomes); the last pair determines sex of the person (sex chromosomes)
- both dominant and recessive genes determine physical and behavioral traits
  - specific physical and behavioral traits are dependent upon pairing of genes; more active genes are dominant, others are recessive (see Figure 8.2)
  - most traits are polygenetic
- genetic and chromosome problems can cause a variety of disorders
  - genetic disorders carried by recessive genes are expressed when a child gets two recessive genes
  - issue may also occur if chromosomes have an extra or a missing pair

Reset

Practice Quiz   How much do you remember? ANSWERS ON PAGE AK-1.

Pick the best answer.

1. In a _____ design, one group of people is followed and assessed at different times as the group ages.
- **a.** longitudinal
- **b.** cross-sectional
- **c.** cross-sequential
- **d.** cross-longitudinal

2. The cognitive and social changes students go through because they are born and grow up in an age of smartphones would be referred to as a(n)
- **a.** experimental group.
- **b.** control group.
- **c.** dominance effect.
- **d.** cohort effect.

3. Brandy has naturally blond hair. Based on this information, what do we know about Brandy's parents?
- **a.** At least one of her parents has a recessive gene for blond hair.
- **b.** Each of her parents must have one recessive gene for blond hair.
- **c.** Each of her parents must have one dominant gene for brown hair.
- **d.** Neither of her parents has a recessive gene for blond hair.

4. Which of the following is a disorder resulting from recessive inheritance?
- **a.** Turner's syndrome
- **b.** Klinefelter's syndrome
- **c.** cystic fibrosis
- **d.** Down syndrome

5. Which disorder is characterized by having only one X chromosome in the 23rd pairing?
- **a.** Tay-Sachs disorder
- **b.** Turner's syndrome
- **c.** Klinefelter's syndrome
- **d.** PKU

Prenatal Development

From conception to the actual birth of the baby is a period of approximately 9 months, during which a single cell becomes a complete infant. It is also during this time that many things can have a positive or negative influence on the developing infant.

FERTILIZATION, THE ZYGOTE, AND TWINNING

8.4 Explain the process of fertilization, including the twinning process.

When an egg (also called an **ovum**) and a sperm unite in the process of **fertilization**, the resulting single cell will have a total of 46 chromosomes and is called a **zygote**. Normally, the zygote will begin to divide, first into two cells, then four, then eight, and so on, with each new cell also having 46 chromosomes because the DNA molecules produce duplicates of themselves before each division. (This division process is called mitosis.) Eventually, the mass of cells becomes a baby. When this division process doesn't work exactly this way, twins or multiples are sometimes the result.

There are actually two main types of twins. Twins who are commonly referred to as "identical" are **monozygotic twins**, meaning that the two babies come from one (mono) fertilized egg (zygote). Early in the division process, the mass of cells splits completely—no one knows exactly why—into two separate masses, each of which will develop into a separate infant. The infants will be the same sex and have identical features because they each possess the same set of 46 chromosomes. Nonidentical twins are more an accident of timing and are more common in women who are older and who are from certain ethnic groups (Allen & Parisi, 1990; Bonnelykke, 1990; Imaizumi, 1998). A woman's body may release more than one egg at a time or release an egg after she has already conceived once. If two eggs are fertilized, the woman may give birth to fraternal or **dizygotic twins** (two zygotes) or possibly triplets or some other multiple number of babies (Bryan & Hallett, 2001). This is also more likely to happen to women who are taking fertility drugs to help them get pregnant. (See **Figure 8.3**.)

Identical twins

1 Accounting for about 1 in 250 births, these are created when a single egg is fertilized by one sperm.

2 The egg splits into halves. Each develops into a fetus with the same genetic composition.

Fraternal twins

1 Twice as common as identicals, fraternals arise when two eggs are released at once.

2 If both are fertilized by separate sperm, two fetuses form. Genetically they are just ordinary siblings.

Figure 8.3 Monozygotic and Dizygotic Twins

Because identical twins come from one fertilized egg (zygote), they are called monozygotic. Fraternal twins, who come from two different fertilized eggs, are called dizygotic.

Abby and Brittany Hensel are conjoined twins who share one body from the waist down but are two distinctly different individuals.

Twins are important because they provide developmental psychologists with another way to look at the contribution of nature and nurture to human development. Researchers may seek out genetically identical twins who have been separated at birth, looking at all the ways those twins are alike in spite of being raised in different environments, as well as comparing adopted children to their adoptive parents and to their biological parents. **LINK** to Learning Objective 11.10.

Sometimes in the twinning process, the mass of cells does not completely split apart. When this occurs, the resulting conjoined twins will be joined at the point where the two cell masses remained "stuck." Sometimes this joining may involve only soft tissues. It may also involve the sharing of certain body parts discussed in the next paragraphs. It is estimated that conjoined twins are born only one in 100,000 births, and their survival is also rare (Martínez-Frías et al., 2009).

One set of conjoined twins has become famous over the course of their development. Abigail (Abby) and Brittany Hensel were born in 1992 and are a rare kind of conjoined twin called *diencephalic*—they have two separate heads but share one lower body. Each controls one arm and one leg on one side of the body, yet they somehow manage to move as one (Miller & Doman, 1996).

Abby and Brittany have their own personalities, likes, and dislikes, just as any other siblings do. In 2012, the budding teachers became the stars of their own reality television show, *Abby & Brittany: Joined for Life* (Camacho, 2012). They are healthy and seem to be both happy and well adjusted, surrounded by friends and a loving mother, father, younger brother, and sister.

THREE STAGES OF DEVELOPMENT

8.5 Describe the processes and stages of prenatal development, and discuss hazards in prenatal development.

There are three stages of prenatal development: the germinal period, the embryonic period, and the fetal period.

THE GERMINAL PERIOD   Once fertilization has taken place, the zygote begins dividing and moving down to the uterus, the muscular organ that will contain and protect the developing organism. This process takes about a week, followed by about a week during which the mass of cells, now forming a hollow ball, firmly attaches itself to the wall of the uterus. This two-week period is called the **germinal period** of pregnancy. The placenta also begins to form during this period. The placenta is a specialized organ that provides nourishment and filters away waste products from the developing baby. The umbilical cord also begins to develop at this time, connecting the organism to the placenta.

> How does a mass of cells become a baby with eyes, nose, hands, feet, and so on? How do all those different things come from the same original single cell?

During the germinal period, the cells begin to differentiate, or develop into specialized cells, in preparation for becoming all the various kinds of cells that make up the human body—skin cells, heart cells, and so on. Perhaps the most important of these cells are the stem cells, which stay in a somewhat immature state until needed to produce more cells. Researchers are currently looking into ways to use stem cells found in the umbilical cord to grow new organs and tissues for transplant or to repair neurological damage (Chen & Ende, 2000; Holden & Vogel, 2002; Lu & Ende, 1997; Moreno-Manzanoa et al., 2009). **LINK** to Learning Objective 2.4.

THE EMBRYONIC PERIOD   Once firmly attached to the uterus, the developing organism is called an **embryo**. The **embryonic period** will last from two weeks after conception to eight weeks, and during this time the cells will continue to specialize and become the various organs and structures of a human infant. By the end of eight weeks after conception, the embryo is about 1 inch long and has primitive eyes, nose, lips, teeth, little arms and legs, and a beating heart. Although no organ is fully developed or completely functional at this time, nearly all are "there."

The three periods of pregnancy are the germinal period, lasting about two weeks, the embryonic period, from about two to eight weeks, and the fetal period, which lasts from eight weeks until the end of pregnancy.

CRITICAL PERIODS   As soon as the embryo begins to receive nourishment from the mother through the placenta, it becomes vulnerable to hazards such as diseases of the mother, drugs, and other toxins that can pass from the mother through the placenta to the developing infant. Because of the direct connection between mother and embryo and the fact that all major organs are in the process of forming, we can most clearly see the effects of **critical periods**, times during which some environmental influence can have an impact—often devastating—on the development of the infant. The structural development of the arms and legs, for example, is only affected during the time that they are developing (3½ to 8 weeks), whereas the heart's structure is most affected very early in this period (2½ to 6½ weeks). Other physical and structural problems can occur with the central nervous system (2 to 5 weeks), eyes (3½ to 8½ weeks), and the teeth and roof of the mouth (about 7 to 12 weeks).

PRENATAL HAZARDS: TERATOGENS   Any substance such as a drug, chemical, virus, or other factor that can cause a birth defect is called a **teratogen**. **Table 8.2** shows some common teratogens and their possible negative effects on the developing embryo.

One of the more common teratogens is alcohol. Consumption of alcohol during pregnancy, particularly during the critical embryonic period, can lead to **fetal alcohol syndrome (FAS)**, a series of physical and mental defects including stunted growth, facial deformities, and brain damage (Ethen et al., 2008; Guerri, 2002). Exposure to alcohol in early pregnancy is the leading known cause of intellectual disability (previously called mental retardation) in the Western hemisphere (Abel & Sokol, 1987;

Dr. Melissa Fallone

Missouri State Psychology Department

Effects of Prenatal Drug Exposure

Table 8.2	Common Teratogens
Teratogenic Agent	**Effect on Development**
Measles, Mumps, and Rubella	Blindness, deafness, heart defects, brain damage
Marijuana	Irritability, nervousness, tremors; infant is easily disturbed, startled
Cocaine	Decreased height, low birth weight, respiratory problems, seizures, learning difficulties; infant is difficult to soothe
Alcohol	Fetal alcohol syndrome (intellectual disability, delayed growth, facial malformation), learning difficulties, smaller than normal heads
Nicotine	Miscarriage, low birth weight, stillbirth, short stature, intellectual disability, learning disabilities
Mercury	Intellectual disability, blindness
Vitamin A (high doses)	Facial, ear, central nervous system, and heart defects
Caffeine	Miscarriage, low birth weight
Toxoplasmosis	Brain swelling, spinal abnormalities, deafness, blindness, intellectual disability
High Water Temperatures	Increased chance of neural tube defects

Sources: March of Dimes Foundation (2009); Organization of Teratology Information Specialists (2011); Shepard, T. H. (2001)

Caley et al., 2005). FAS is part of a larger category of permanent birth defects due to maternal alcohol use during pregnancy called *fetal alcohol spectrum disorders (FASD)*. So how much alcohol is safe to drink while pregnant? The answer is clearly "none!"

THE FETAL PERIOD: GROW, BABY, GROW The **fetal period** is a period of tremendous growth lasting from about eight weeks after conception until birth. The length of the developing organism (now referred to as a **fetus**) increases by about 20 times, and its weight increases from about 1 ounce at 2 months to a little over 7 pounds. The organs, while accomplishing most of their differentiation in the embryonic period, continue to develop and become functional. At this time, teratogens will more likely affect the physical functioning (physiology) of the organs rather than their structure. The functioning of the central nervous system, for example, is vulnerable throughout the fetal period, as are the eyes and the external sexual organs.

The last few months continue the development of fat and the growth of the body, until about the end of the 38th week. At 38 weeks, the fetus is considered full term. Babies born before 38 weeks are called *preterm* and may need life support to survive. This is especially true if the baby weighs less than about 5½ pounds at birth. How early can an infant be born and still survive? The age of viability (the point at which it is possible for an infant to survive outside the womb) is between 22 and 26 weeks, with the odds of survival increasing from 10 percent at 22 weeks up to about 85 percent at 26 weeks (National Commission for the Protection of Human Subjects of Biomedical and Behavioral Research, 2006).

The most likely time for a miscarriage, or spontaneous abortion, is in the first three months, as the organs are forming and first becoming functional (Katz, 2007; Speroff et al., 1999). Some 15 to 20 percent of all pregnancies end in miscarriage (Hill, 1998; Medical Economics Staff, 1994). Miscarriages are most likely caused by genetic defects that will not allow the organism to survive and are therefore not preventable.

This pregnant woman is getting a sonogram. Sonograms allow doctors to see any physical deformities and make accurate measurements of gestational age without risk to the mother or the fetus.

Concept Map L.O. 8.4, 8.5

Interactive

Prenatal Development
(from conception to birth of the baby is approximately 9 months in humans)

fertilization, the zygote, and twinning

- egg and sperm unite through process of fertilization, resulting in a single cell (zygote) that has 46 chromosomes

- through mitosis, zygote begins to divide, into two cells, then four, etc., until baby is formed

- alterations in mitosis can result in twins or multiples

germinal period (2-week period following fertilization)

- zygote continues dividing and moving toward the uterus; the placenta and umbilical cord also develop during this time

- cell differentiation is the process that results in specialized cells for all of the various parts of the body

embryonic period (2 weeks after conception to 8 weeks)

- once attached to the uterus, developing organism is called an embryo

- cell specialization continues to occur, resulting in the preliminary versions of various organs

- embryo is vulnerable to hazards such as diseases and substances ingested by the mother as it receives nourishment through the placenta

fetal period (from about 8 weeks to birth)

- developing organism now called a fetus; time of tremendous growth and development

- organs continue to develop and become fully functional

- full-term birth occurs around end of 38th week

- miscarriages (spontaneous abortions) are most likely to occur in the first three months

Reset

Practice Quiz   How much do you remember?   ANSWERS ON PAGE AK-1.

Pick the best answer.

1. Which term best describes Abby and Brittany Hensel?
   a. They are "mono mono" twins.
   b. They are conjoined twins.
   c. They are dizygotic twins.
   d. They are technically not twins at all.

2. Which of the following is a function of the placenta?
   a. It helps the zygote to divide.
   b. It assists the zygote in its movement toward the uterus.
   c. It provides nourishment to the developing baby.
   d. It effectively keeps out all teratogens.

3. The second week through the eighth week of pregnancy is commonly referred to as the _____ stage.
   a. fetal
   b. germinal
   c. placental
   d. embryonic

4. Which of the following is one of the most common teratogens and can result in stunted growth, facial deformities, and brain damage?
   a. alcohol
   b. caffeine
   c. cocaine
   d. mercury

5. When do most miscarriages occur?
   a. In the last three months
   b. In the first week after conception
   c. After the fifth month
   d. In the first three months

Infancy and Childhood Development

  What can babies do? Aren't they pretty much unaware of what's going on around them at first?

Surprisingly, babies can do a lot more than researchers used to believe they could. Since those early days, researchers have developed ways of studying what infants cannot tell us in words.

PHYSICAL DEVELOPMENT

8.6 Describe the physical and sensory changes that take place in infancy and childhood.

Immediately after birth, several things start to happen. The respiratory system begins to function, filling the lungs with air and putting oxygen into the blood. The blood now circulates only within the infant's system because the umbilical cord has been cut. Body temperature is now regulated by the infant's own activity and body fat (which acts as insulation) rather than by the amniotic fluid. The digestive system probably takes the longest to adjust to life outside the womb. This is another reason for the excess body fat. It provides fuel until the infant is able to take in enough nourishment on its own. That is why most babies lose a little weight in the first week after birth.

REFLEXES   Babies come into this world able to interact with it. Infants have a set of innate (existing from birth) involuntary behavior patterns called reflexes. Until an infant is capable of learning more complex means of interaction, reflexes help the infant to survive. **Figure 8.4** on the next page shows five infant reflexes. Pediatricians use these and other reflexes to determine whether or not an infant's nervous system is working properly.

MOTOR DEVELOPMENT: FROM CRAWLING TO A BLUR OF MOTION   Infants manage a tremendous amount of development in motor skills from birth to about 2 years of age. **Figure 8.5** on page 293 shows some of the major physical milestones of infancy. When looking at the age ranges listed, remember that even these ranges are averages based on large samples of infants. An infant may reach these milestones earlier or later than the average and still be considered to be developing normally.

a.

b.

c.

d.

e.

Figure 8.4 Five Infant Reflexes

Shown here are (a) grasping reflex, (b) startle reflex (also known as the Moro reflex), (c) rooting reflex (when you touch a baby's cheek it will turn toward your hand, open its mouth, and search for the nipple), (d) stepping reflex, and (e) sucking reflex. These infant reflexes can be used to check on the health of an infant's nervous system. If a reflex is absent or abnormal, it may indicate brain damage or some other neurological problem.

BRAIN DEVELOPMENT At birth, an infant's brain consists of over 100 billion neurons. Rapid and extensive growth of these neurons occurs as the brain triples in weight from birth to age 3 years, with much of the increase caused by growth of new dendrites, axon terminals, and increasing numbers of synaptic connections (Nelson, 2011). Surprisingly, the development of the infant brain after birth involves a necessary loss of neurons called *synaptic pruning,* as unused synaptic connections and nerve cells are cleared away to make way for functioning connections and cells (Couperus & Nelson, 2006; Graven & Browne, 2008; Kozberg et al., 2013). This process is similar to weeding your garden—you take out the weeds to make room for the plants that you want.

BABY, CAN YOU SEE ME? BABY, CAN YOU HEAR ME? SENSORY DEVELOPMENT

💬 I've heard that babies can't see or hear very much at birth. Is that true?

Researchers have developed a couple of methods to help gauge infant's abilities. Two common methods are the use of *preferential looking* and *habituation.* Preferential looking assumes that the longer an infant spends looking at a stimulus, the more the infant prefers that stimulus over others (Fantz, 1961). Habituation is the tendency for infants (and adults) to stop paying attention to a stimulus that does not change. By exposing the infant to an unchanging sound or picture, for example, researchers can wait for the infant to habituate (look away) and then change the stimulus. If the infant reacts (dishabituates), the infant is capable of detecting that change (Columbo & Mitchell, 2009).

Although most infant sensory abilities are fairly well developed at birth, some require a bit more time to reach "full power." By using techniques such as the habituation method researchers have found that the sense of touch is the most well developed, which makes perfect sense when one realizes how much skin-to-womb contact the baby has had in the last months of pregnancy. The sense of smell is also highly developed. Breast-fed babies can actually tell the difference between their own mother's milk scent and another woman's milk scent within a few days after birth.

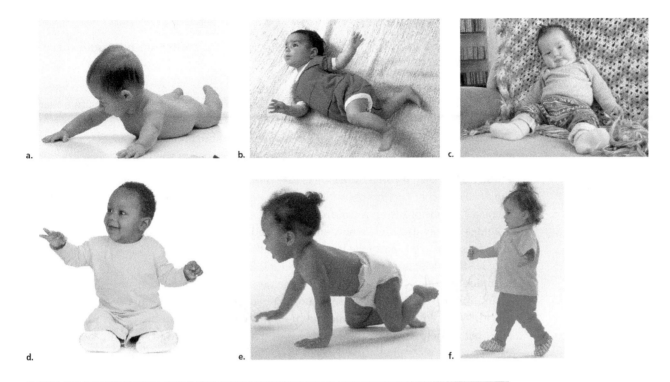

Figure 8.5   Six Motor Milestones

Shown here are (a) raising head and chest—2 to 4 months, (b) rolling over—2 to 5 months, (c) sitting up with support—4 to 6 months, (d) sitting up without support—6 to 7 months, (e) crawling—7 to 8 months, and (f) walking—8 to 18 months. The motor milestones develop as the infant gains greater voluntary control over the muscles in his or her body, typically from the top of the body downward. This pattern is seen in the early control of the neck muscles and the much later development of control of the legs and feet.

Taste is also nearly fully developed. At birth, infants show a preference for sweets (and human breast milk is very sweet) and by four months have developed a preference for salty tastes (which may come from exposure to the salty taste of their mother's skin). Sour and bitter, two other taste sensations, produce spitting up and the making of horrible faces (Ganchrow et al., 1983).

Hearing is functional before birth but may take a little while to reach its full potential after birth. The fluids of the womb must clear out completely. From birth, newborns seem most responsive to high pitches, as in a woman's voice, and low pitches, as in a male's voice.

The least functional sense at birth is vision. The eye is quite a complex organ. **LINK** to Learning Objective 3.3. The rods, which see in black and white and have little visual acuity, are fairly well developed at birth, but the cones, which see color and provide sharpness of vision, will take about another six months to fully develop. So the newborn has relatively poor color perception when compared to sharply contrasting lights and darks until about two months of age (Adams, 1987) and has fairly "fuzzy" vision, much as a nearsighted person would have. The lens of the newborn stays fixed until the muscles that hold it in place mature. Until then the newborn is unable to shift what little focus it has from close to far. Thus, newborns actually have a fixed distance for clear vision of about 7 to 10 inches, which is the distance from the baby's face to the mother's face while nursing (Slater, 2000).

Newborns also have visual preferences at birth, as discovered by researchers using preferential looking, measures of the time that infants spent looking at certain visual stimuli (Fantz, 1961). They found that infants prefer to look at complex patterns rather than simple ones, three dimensions rather than two, and that the most preferred visual stimulus was a human face. The fact that infants prefer human voices and human faces (DeCasper & Fifer, 1980; DeCasper & Spence, 1986; Fantz, 1964; Maurer & Young, 1983) makes it easier for them to form relationships with their caregivers and to develop language later on.

COGNITIVE DEVELOPMENT

8.7 Compare and contrast two theories of cognitive development, and discuss the development of language.

By the time the average infant has reached the age of 1 year, it has tripled its birth weight and added about another foot to its height. The brain triples its weight in the first two years, reaching about 75 percent of its adult weight. By age 5, the brain is at 90 percent of its adult weight. This increase makes possible a tremendous amount of major advances in **cognitive development**, including the development of thinking, problem solving, and memory.

PIAGET'S THEORY: FOUR STAGES OF COGNITIVE DEVELOPMENT   One way of examining the development of cognition is found in the work of Jean Piaget. Piaget believed, based on observations of his own children and others, that children form mental concepts or **schemes** as they experience new situations and events. For example, if Sandy points to a picture of an apple and tells her child, "That's an apple," the child forms a scheme for "apple" that looks something like that picture. Piaget also believed that children first try to understand new things in terms of schemes they already possess in a process called assimilation. The child might see an orange and say "apple" because both objects are round. When corrected, the child might alter the scheme for apple to include "round" and "red." The process of altering or adjusting old schemes to fit new information and experiences is accommodation (Piaget, 1952, 1962, 1983).

Piaget also proposed that there are four distinct stages of cognitive development that occur from infancy to adolescence, as shown in the video *Piaget's Stages* and in **Table 8.3** (Piaget, 1952, 1962, 1983).

⊚ **Watch** the **Video**, *Piaget's Stages.*

THE SENSORIMOTOR STAGE   The **sensorimotor stage** is the first of Piaget's stages. It concerns infants from birth to age 2. In this stage, infants use their senses and motor abilities to learn about the world around them. At first, infants only have the involuntary reflexes present at birth to interact with objects and people. As their sensory and motor development progresses, they begin to interact deliberately with objects by grasping, pushing, tasting, and so on. Infants move from simple repetitive actions,

Table 8.3 PIAGET'S STAGES OF COGNITIVE DEVELOPMENT

Study the table, then click "Check Your Understanding" button when you're ready.

Stage	Age	Cognitive Development
Sensorimotor	Birth to 2 years old	Children explore the world using their senses and ability to move. They develop object permanence and the understanding that concepts and mental images represent objects, people, and events.
Preoperational	2 to 7 years old	Young children can mentally represent and refer to objects and events with words or pictures and they can pretend. However, they can't conserve, logically reason, or simultaneously consider many characteristics of an object.
Concrete Operations	7 to 12 years old	Children at this stage are able to conserve, reverse their thinking, and classify objects in terms of their many characteristics. They can also think logically and understand analogies but only about concrete events.
Formal Operations	12 years old to adulthood	People at this stage can use abstract reasoning about hypothetical events or situations, think about logical possibilities, use abstract analogies, and systematically examine and test hypotheses. Not everyone can eventually reason in all these ways.

Check Your Understanding

such as grabbing their toes, to complex patterns, such as trying to put a shape into a sorting box.

By the end of the sensorimotor stage, infants have fully developed a sense of **object permanence**, the knowledge that an object exists even when it is not in sight. For example, the game of "peek-a-boo" is important in teaching infants that Mommy's smiling face is always going to be behind her hands. This is a critical step in developing language (and eventually abstract thought), as words themselves are symbols of things that may not be present. Symbolic thought, which is the ability to represent objects in one's thoughts with symbols such as words, becomes possible by the end of this stage, with children at 2 years old capable of thinking in simple symbols and planning out actions.

 💬 Why is it so easy for children to believe in Santa Claus and the Tooth Fairy when they're little?

THE PREOPERATIONAL STAGE   The **preoperational stage** (ages 2–7) is a time of developing language and concepts. Children, who can now move freely about in their world, no longer have to rely only on senses and motor skills but now can ask questions and explore their surroundings more fully. Pretending and make-believe play become possible because children at this stage can understand, through symbolic thinking, that a line of wooden blocks can "stand in" for a train. They are limited, however, in several ways. They are not yet capable of logical thought—they can use simple mental concepts but are not able to use those concepts in a more rational, logical sense. They believe that anything that moves is alive, a quality called animism. They tend to believe that what they see is literally true, so when children of this age see Santa Claus in a book, on television, or at the mall, Santa Claus becomes real to them. It doesn't occur to them to think about how Santa might get to every child's house in one night or why those toys are the same ones they saw in the store just last week.

Another limitation is **egocentrism**, the inability to see the world through anyone else's eyes except one's own. For the preoperational child, everyone else must see what the child sees, and what is important to the child must be important to everyone else. For example, 2-year-old Hiba, after climbing out of her crib for the third time, was told by her mother, "I don't want to see you in that living room again tonight!" So Hiba's next appearance was made with her hands over her eyes—if she couldn't see her mother, her mother couldn't see her. Egocentrism is not the same as being egotistical or selfish—it would also be egocentric, but completely unselfish, if 4-year-old Jamal wants to give his grandmother an action figure for her birthday because that's what he would want.

Remember that children in this stage are also overwhelmed by appearances. A child who complains that his piece of pie is smaller than his brother's may be quite happy once his original piece is cut into two pieces—now he thinks he has "more" than his brother. He has focused only on the number of pieces, not the actual amount of the pie. Focusing only on one feature of some object rather than taking all features into consideration is called **centration**. In the pennies example in **Figure 8.6**, children of this stage will focus (or center) on the length of the top line of pennies only and ignore the number of pennies. Centration is one of the reasons that children in this stage often fail to understand that changing the way something looks does not change its substance. The ability to understand that altering the appearance of something does not change its amount (as in the pennies example), its volume, or its mass is called **conservation**.

Preoperational children fail at conservation not only because they centrate (focus on just one feature, such as the number of pieces of pie) but also because they are unable to "mentally reverse" actions. This feature of preoperational thinking is called **irreversibility**. For example, if a preoperational child sees liquid poured from a short, wide glass into a tall, thin glass, the child will assume that the second glass holds more liquid. This failure to "conserve" (save) the volume of liquid as it takes on a different shape in the tall, thin glass is not only caused by the child's centration on the height of the liquid in the second glass but also by the inability of the child to imagine pouring the liquid back into the first glass and having it be the same amount again. Similar "reasoning" causes children of this age to assume that a ball of clay, when rolled out into a "rope" of clay, is now greater in mass.

CONCRETE OPERATIONS   In the **concrete operations stage** (ages 7–12), children finally become capable of conservation and reversible thinking. Centration no longer occurs, as children become capable of considering all the relevant features of any given object. They

Type of conservation	Initial presentation	Transformation	Question	Preoperational child's answer
Number	Two equal lines of pennies	Increase spacing of pennies in one line.	Which line has more pennies?	The longer one.

Figure 8.6   Conservation Experiment

In this conservation task, pennies are laid out in two equal lines. When the pennies in the top line are spaced out, the child who cannot yet conserve will centrate on the top line and assume that there are actually more pennies in that line.

begin to think more logically about beliefs such as Santa Claus, and they ask questions, eventually coming to their own more rational conclusions about the fantasies of early childhood. They are in school, learning all sorts of science and math, and are convinced that they know more than their parents at this point.

The major limitation of this stage is the inability to deal effectively with abstract concepts. Abstract concepts are those that do not have some physical, concrete, touchable reality. For example, "freedom" is an abstract concept. People can define it, they can get a good sense of what it means, but there is no "thing" that they can point to and say, "This is freedom." Concrete concepts, which are the kind of concepts understood by children of this age, are about objects, written rules, and real things. Children need to be able to see it, touch it, or at least see it in their heads to be able to understand it.

These concrete operational children, seen in a science class, have begun to think logically and are able to solve many kinds of problems that were not possible for them to solve while in the preoperational stage.

FORMAL OPERATIONS   In the last of Piaget's stages, **formal operations** (age 12 to adulthood), abstract thinking becomes possible. Teenagers not only understand concepts that have no physical reality, but also they get deeply involved in hypothetical thinking, or thinking about possibilities and even impossibilities. "What if everyone just got along?" "If women were in charge of countries, would there be fewer wars?"

Piaget did not believe that everyone would necessarily reach formal operations. Studies show that only about half of all adults in the United States reach formal operations (Sutherland, 1992). Adults who do not achieve formal operations tend to use a more practical, down-to-earth kind of intelligence that suits their particular lifestyle. Successful college students, however, need formal operational thinking to succeed in their college careers, as most college classes require critical thinking, problem-solving abilities, and abstract thinking based on formal operational skills (Powers, 1984).

Others have proposed another stage beyond formal operations, a relativistic thinking stage found in young adults, particularly those who have found their old ways of thinking in "black and white" terms challenged by the diversity they encounter in the college environment (LaBouvie-vief, 1980, 1992; Perry, 1970). In this kind of thinking, young adults recognize that all problems cannot be solved with pure logic, and there can be multiple points of view for a single problem.

Piaget saw children as active explorers of their surroundings, engaged in the discovery of the properties of objects and organisms within those surroundings. Educators have put Piaget's ideas into practice by allowing children to learn at their own pace, by "hands-on" experience with objects, and by teaching concepts to children that are at an appropriate cognitive level (Brooks & Brooks, 1993). But Piaget's theory has also been criticized on several points. Some researchers believe that the idea of distinct stages of cognitive development is not completely correct and that changes in thought are continuous and gradual rather than reached by jumping from one stage to another (Courage & Howe, 2002; Feldman, 2003; Schwitzgebel, 1999; Siegler, 1996). Others point out that preschoolers are not as egocentric as Piaget seemed to believe (Flavell, 1999) and that object permanence exists much earlier than Piaget thought (Aguiar & Baillargeon, 2003; Baillargeon, 1986).

VYGOTSKY'S THEORY: THE IMPORTANCE OF BEING THERE   Russian psychologist Lev Vygotsky's pioneering work in developmental psychology has had a profound influence on school education in Russia, and interest in his theories continues to grow throughout the world (Bodrova & Leong, 1996; Duncan, 1995). Vygotsky wrote about children's cognitive development but differed from Piaget in his emphasis on the role of others in cognitive development (Vygotsky, 1934/1962, 1978, 1987). Whereas Piaget stressed the importance of the child's interaction with objects as a primary factor in cognitive development, Vygotsky stressed the importance of social and cultural interactions with other people, typically more highly skilled children and adults. Vygotsky

This boy is helping his younger sister learn to read a book. Vygotsky's view of cognitive development states that the help of skilled others aids in making cognitive advances such as this one.

believed that children develop cognitively when someone else helps them by asking leading questions and providing examples of concepts in a process called **scaffolding**. In scaffolding, the more highly skilled person gives the learner more help at the beginning of the learning process and then begins to withdraw help as the learner's skills improve (Rogoff, 1994).

Vygotsky also proposed that each developing child has a **zone of proximal development (ZPD)**, which is the difference between what a child can do alone versus what that child can do with the help of a teacher. For example, if little Jenny can do math problems up to the fourth-grade level on her own but with the help of a teacher can successfully work problems at a sixth-grade level, her ZPD is two years. Suzi might be the same age as Jenny (and might even score the same on a traditional IQ test), but if Suzi can only work math problems at a fifth-grade level with the help of the teacher, Suzi's ZPD is not as great as Jenny's. This might be a better way of thinking about intelligence: It isn't what you know (as measured by traditional tests), it's what you can do.

Other researchers have applied Vygotsky's social focus on learning to the development of a child's memory for personal (autobiographical) events, finding evidence that children learn the culturally determined structures and purposes of personal stories from the early conversations they have with their parents. This process begins with the parent telling the story to the very young child, followed by the child repeating elements of the story as the child's verbal abilities grow. The child reaches the final stage at around age 5 or 6 when the child creates the personal story entirely—an excellent example of scaffolding (Fivush & Nelson, 2004; Fivush et al., 1996; Nelson, 1993). Unlike Piaget, who saw a child's talking to himself or herself as egocentric, Vygotsky thought that private speech was a way for the child to "think out loud" and advance cognitively. As adults, we still do this when we talk to ourselves to help solve a particular problem. Vygotsky's ideas have been put into practice in education through the use of cooperative learning, in which children work together in groups to achieve a common goal, and in reciprocal teaching, in which teachers lead students through the basic strategies of reading until the students themselves become capable of teaching the strategies to others.

STAGES OF LANGUAGE DEVELOPMENT   The development of language is a very important milestone in the cognitive development of a child because language allows children to think in words rather than just images, to ask questions, to communicate their needs and wants to others, and to form concepts (L. Bloom, 1974; P. Bloom, 2000).

Language development in infancy is influenced by the language they hear, a style of speaking known as child-directed speech (the way adults and older children talk to infants and very young children, with higher pitched, repetitious, sing-song speech patterns). Infants and toddlers attend more closely to this kind of speech, which creates a learning opportunity in the dialogue between caregiver and infant (Dominey & Dodane, 2004; Fernald, 1984, 1992; Küntay & Slobin, 2002). Other researchers are looking at the infant's use of gestures and signs (Behne et al., 2005; Lizskowski et al., 2006; Moll & Tomasello, 2007; Tomasello et al., 2007).

Infants also seem to understand far more than they can produce, a phenomenon known as the *receptive–productive lag* (Stevenson et al., 1988). They may be able to produce only one or two words, but they understand much longer sentences from their parents and others.

There are several stages of language development that all children experience, no matter what culture they live in or what language they will learn to speak (Brown, 1973):

1. **Cooing:** At around two months of age, babies begin to make vowel-like sounds.

2. **Babbling:** At about six months, infants add consonant sounds to the vowels to make a babbling sound, which at times can almost sound like real speech. Deaf

This infant has already learned some of the basics of language, including the use of gestures to indicate meaning and enhance communication.

children actually decrease their babbling after six months while increasing their use of primitive hand signs and gestures (Petitto & Marentette, 1991; Petitto et al., 2001).

3. **One-word speech:** Somewhere just before or around age 1, most children begin to say actual words. These words are typically nouns and may seem to represent an entire phrase of meaning. They are called holophrases (whole phrases in one word) for that reason. For example, a child might say "Milk!" and mean "I want some milk!" or "I drank my milk!"

4. **Telegraphic speech:** At around a year and a half, toddlers begin to string words together to form short, simple sentences using nouns, verbs, and adjectives. "Baby eat," "Mommy go," "Doggie go bye-bye" are examples of telegraphic speech. Only the words that carry the meaning of the sentence are used.

5. **Whole sentences:** As children move through the preschool years, they learn to use grammatical terms and increase the number of words in their sentences, until by age 6 or so they are nearly as fluent as an adult, although the number of words they know is still limited when compared to adult vocabulary.

Issues in Psychology
Autism Spectrum Disorder

8.8 **Evaluate claims regarding the causes of autism spectrum disorder.**

Before leaving the topic of cognitive development in infancy, let's briefly discuss a topic that has been making the news for a number of years: the causes underlying autism spectrum disorder. In recent years the rate of diagnosis of autism has increased, from 1 in 110 in 2006 to 1 in 88 at the present time. This increase does not necessarily mean a rise in actual autism cases, however. Methods of diagnosing autism have become far more efficient and the definition of what is labeled as autism has been expanded, accounting for much of the increase (Centers for Disease Control and Prevention, 2013).

Autism spectrum disorder (ASD) is actually a whole range of disorders (with what may be an equally broad range of causes), which cause problems in thinking, feeling, language, and social skills in relating to others (Atladóttir et al., 2009; Johnson & Myers, 2007). Rumors and misinformation about the causes of autism have been circulating on the Internet for many years.

The major source of misinformation began in 1998, when British gastroenterologist Dr. Andrew Wakefield published the results of two studies that seemed to link the MMR (measles, mumps, and rubella) vaccine to autism and bowel disease in children (Wakefield et al., 1998). With a sample size of only 12 children, no control groups, and with neither study being blind—single or double—the studies were quickly denounced as inadequate and dangerous by autism specialists and others (Fitzpatrick, 2004; Judelsohn, 2007; Matthew & Dallery, 2007; Novella, 2007; Stratton et al., 2001a, 2001b). Ⓛ Ⓘ Ⓝ Ⓚ to Learning Objectives 1.9 and 1.10. Nevertheless, Wakefield's publication was followed by measles epidemics due to parents refusing the MMR inoculation for their children. The myth of a link persists, in spite of numerous studies that have consistently failed to show any link between the MMR vaccine and autism (Burns, 2010; Gilberg & Coleman, 2000; Johnson & Myers, 2007; Madsen et al., 2002; Mars et al., 1998; Taylor et al., 1999; Thompson et al., 2007). In 2004, the other authors listed on the study formally retracted the 1998 paper. In 2009, the final blow came to Wakefield's credibility when it was discovered that he had falsified his data.

As a result of the British Medical Council's investigation into Wakefield's actions, Wakefield's medical license was revoked in May of 2010 after the council found him guilty of "serious professional misconduct" (Meikle & Boseley, 2010).

One of the most important things parents can do for the continued health and safety of their infant is to have the baby immunized, following an approved schedule for each type of vaccine. Immunizations today are safe and effective and prevent dangerous and often deadly childhood diseases, such as rubella.

PSYCHOSOCIAL DEVELOPMENT

8.9 **Explain the development of personality, social relationships, and self-concept in infancy and childhood, and discuss the first four stages of Erikson's theory.**

The psychological and social development of infants and children involves the development of personality, relationships, and a sense of being male or female. Although these processes begin in infancy, they will continue in many respects well into adulthood.

 💬 Why are some children negative and whiny while others are sweet and good-natured?

TEMPERAMENT One of the first ways in which infants demonstrate that they have different *personalities* (long-lasting characteristics that make each person different from others) is in their **temperament**, the behavioral and emotional characteristics that are fairly well established at birth. Researchers (Chess & Thomas, 1986; Thomas & Chess, 1977) have been able to identify three basic temperament styles of infants:

1. **Easy:** "Easy" babies are regular in their schedules of waking, sleeping, and eating and are adaptable to change. Easy babies are happy babies and when distressed are easily soothed.

2. **Difficult:** "Difficult" babies are almost the opposite of easy ones. Difficult babies tend to be irregular in their schedules and are very unhappy about change of any kind. They are loud, active, and tend to be crabby rather than happy.

3. **Slow to warm up:** This kind of temperament is associated with infants who are less grumpy, quieter, and more regular than difficult children but who are slow to adapt to change. If change is introduced gradually, these babies will "warm up" to new people and new situations.

Of course, not all babies will fall neatly into one of these three patterns—some children may be a mix of two or even all three patterns of behavior, as Chess and Thomas (1986) discovered. Even so, longitudinal research strongly suggests that these temperament styles last well into adulthood and are strongly influenced by heredity (Kagan, 1998; Kagan et al., 2007; Korn, 1984; Scarpa et al., 1995; Schwartz et al., 2010), although they are somewhat influenced by the environment in which the infant is raised. For example, a "difficult" infant who is raised by parents who are themselves very loud and active may not be perceived as difficult by the parents, whereas a child who is slow to warm up might be perceived as difficult if the parents themselves like lots of change and noise. The first infant is in a situation in which the "goodness of fit" of the infant's temperament to the parents' temperament is very close, but the parents of the second infant are a poor fit in temperament for that less active child (Chess & Thomas, 1986). A poor fit can make it difficult to form an attachment, the important psychosocial–emotional bond we will discuss next.

ATTACHMENT The emotional bond that forms between an infant and a primary caregiver is called **attachment**. Attachment is a very important development in the social and emotional life of the infant, usually forming within the first 6 months of the infant's life and showing up in a number of ways during the second 6 months, such as *stranger anxiety* (wariness of strangers) and *separation anxiety* (fear of being separated from the caregiver). Although attachment to the mother is usually the primary attachment, infants can attach to fathers and to other caregivers as well. Complete the survey *What Has Your Father Done for You?* to reflect back on the relationship you had with your father while you were growing up.

Survey WHAT HAS YOUR FATHER DONE FOR YOU?

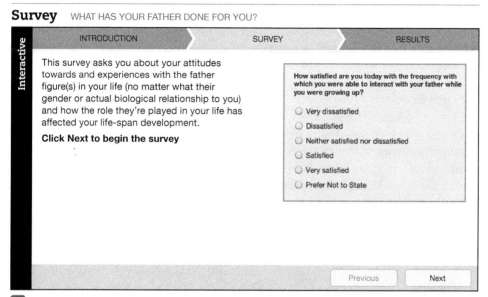

| INTRODUCTION | SURVEY | RESULTS |

This survey asks you about your attitudes towards and experiences with the father figure(s) in your life (no matter what their gender or actual biological relationship to you) and how the role they're played in your life has affected your life-span development.

Click Next to begin the survey

How satisfied are you today with the frequency with which you were able to interact with your father while you were growing up?

○ Very dissatisfied
○ Dissatisfied
○ Neither satisfied nor dissatisfied
○ Satisfied
○ Very satisfied
○ Prefer Not to State

Previous   Next

⊙ **Simulate** the **Experiment**, *What Has Your Father Done for You?*

ATTACHMENT STYLES Mary Ainsworth (Ainsworth, 1985; Ainsworth et al., 1978) came up with a special experimental design to measure the attachment of an infant to the caregiver called the Strange Situation (exposing an infant to a series of leave-takings and returns of the mother and a stranger). Through this measurement technique, Ainsworth and another colleague identified four attachment styles:

1. **Secure:** Infants labeled as secure were willing to get down from their mother's lap when they first entered the room with their mothers. They explored happily, looking back at their mothers and returning to them every now and then (sort of like "touching base"). When the stranger came in, these infants were wary but calm as long as their mother was nearby. When the mother left, the infants got upset. When the mother returned, the infants approached her, were easily soothed, and were glad to have her back.

2. **Avoidant:** In contrast, avoidant babies, though somewhat willing to explore, did not "touch base." They did not look at the stranger or the mother and reacted very little to her absence or her return, seeming to have no interest or concern.

3. **Ambivalent:** The word *ambivalent* means to have mixed feelings about something. Ambivalent babies in Ainsworth's study were clinging and unwilling to explore, very upset by the stranger regardless of the mother's presence, protested mightily when the mother left, and were hard to soothe. When the mother returned, these babies would demand to be picked up but at the same time push the mother away or kick her in a mixed reaction to her return.

4. **Disorganized-disoriented:** In subsequent studies, other researchers (Main & Hesse, 1990; Main & Solomon, 1990) found that some babies seemed unable to decide just how they should react to the mother's return. These disorganized-disoriented infants would approach her but with their eyes turned away from her, as if afraid to make eye contact. In general, these infants seemed fearful and showed a dazed and depressed look on their faces.

It should come as no surprise that the mothers of each of the four types of infants also behaved differently from one another. Mothers of secure infants were loving, warm, sensitive to their infant's needs, and responsive to the infant's attempts at communication. Mothers of avoidant babies were unresponsive, insensitive, and coldly rejecting. Mothers of ambivalent babies tried to be responsive but were inconsistent and insensitive

This toddler shows reluctance to explore his environment, instead clinging to his father's leg. Such clinging behavior, if common, can be a sign of an ambivalent attachment.

to the baby's actions, often talking to the infant about something totally unrelated to what the infant was doing at the time. Mothers of disorganized-disoriented babies were found to be abusive or neglectful in interactions with the infants.

Attachment is not necessarily the result of the behavior of the mother alone, however. The temperament of the infant may play an important part in determining the reactions of the mothers (Goldsmith & Campos, 1982; Skolnick, 1986). For example, an infant with a difficult temperament is hard to soothe. A mother with this kind of infant might come to avoid unnecessary contact with the infant, as did the mothers of the avoidant babies in Ainsworth's studies.

Critics of Ainsworth's Strange Situation research focus on the artificial nature of the design and wonder if infants and mothers would behave differently in the more familiar surroundings of home, even though Ainsworth's experimental observers also observed the infants and mothers in the home prior to the Strange Situation (Ainsworth, 1985). Other research has found results supporting Ainsworth's findings in home-based assessments of attachment (Blanchard & Main, 1979). Other studies have also found support for the concept of attachment styles and stability of attachment over the first six years of life (Lutkenhaus et al., 1985; Main & Cassidy, 1988; Owen et al., 1984; Wartner et al., 1994). Even adult relationships can be seen as influenced by the attachment style of the adult—those who are avoidant tend to have numerous shallow and brief relationships with different partners, whereas those who are ambivalent tend to have repeated breakups and makeups with the same person (Bartholomew, 1990; Hazan & Shaver, 1987).

INFLUENCES ON ATTACHMENT As day care has become more widely acceptable and common, many parents have been concerned about the effect of day care on attachment. Psychologist Jay Belsky and colleagues (Belsky, 2005; Belsky & Johnson, 2005; Belsky et al., 2007) have studied the attachment of infants in day care and concluded that although higher quality of day care (low child-to-caregiver ratio, low turnover in caregivers, and caregivers well educated in child care techniques and theory) is important, especially for cognitive development, positive development including attachment was more clearly related to the quality of parenting the infants and toddlers received at home.

Although there are some cultural differences in attachment, such as the finding that mothers in the United States tend to wait for a child to express a need before trying to fulfill that need, whereas Japanese mothers prefer to anticipate the child's needs (Rothbaum et al., 2000), attachment does not seem to suffer in spite of the differences in sensitivity. Evidence that similar attachment styles are found in other cultures demonstrates the need to consider attachment as an important first step in forming relationships with others. It may set the stage for all relationships that follow (Hu & Meng, 1996; Juffer & Rosenboom, 1997; Keromoian & Leiderman, 1986; Rothbaum et al., 2010).

Before leaving the topic of attachment, let's take a look at one of the first studies that examined the key factors necessary for attachment.

Classic Studies in Psychology
Harlow and Contact Comfort

As psychologists began to study the development of attachment, they at first assumed that attachment to the mother occurred because the mother was associated with satisfaction of primary drives such as hunger and thirst. The mother is always present when the food (a primary reinforcer) is presented, so the mother becomes a secondary reinforcer capable of producing pleasurable feelings. L I N K to Learning Objective 5.5.

Psychologist Harry Harlow felt that attachment had to be influenced by more than just the provision of food. He conducted a number of studies of attachment using infant Rhesus monkeys (Harlow, 1958). Noticing that the monkeys in his lab liked to cling to the soft cloth pad used to line their cages, Harlow designed a study to examine the importance of what he termed *contact comfort*, the seeming attachment of the monkeys to something soft to the touch.

He isolated eight baby Rhesus monkeys shortly after their birth, placing each in a cage with two surrogate (substitute) "mothers." The surrogates were actually a block of wood covered in soft padding and terry cloth and a wire form, both heated from within. For half of the monkeys, the wire "mother" held the bottle from which they fed, while for the other half the soft "mother" held the bottle. Harlow then recorded the time each monkey spent with each "mother." If time spent with the surrogate is taken as an indicator of attachment, then learning theory would predict that the monkeys would spend more time with whichever surrogate was being used to feed them.

The results? Regardless of which surrogate was feeding them, the monkeys all spent significantly more time with the soft, cloth-covered surrogate. In fact, all monkeys spent very little time with the wire surrogate, even if this was the one with the bottle. Harlow and his colleagues concluded that "contact comfort was an important basic affectional or love variable" (Harlow, 1958, p. 574).

Harlow's work represents one of the earliest investigations into the importance of touch in the attachment process and remains an important study in human development.

Questions for Further Discussion

1. Even though the cloth surrogate was warm and soft and seemed to provide contact comfort, do you think that the monkeys raised in this way would behave normally when placed into contact with other monkeys? How might they react?

2. What might be the implications of Harlow's work for human mothers who feed their infants with bottles rather than breast-feeding?

The wire surrogate "mother" provides the food for this infant Rhesus monkey. But the infant spends all its time with the soft, cloth-covered surrogate. According to Harlow, this demonstrates the importance of contact comfort in attachment.

WHO AM I?: THE DEVELOPMENT OF THE SELF-CONCEPT Infants begin life without understanding that they are separate from their surroundings, and also from the other people in their social world. The **self-concept** is the image you have of yourself, and it is based on your interactions with the important people in your life. As infants experience the world around them, they slowly learn to separate "me" from both physical surroundings and the other people in their world.

One way to demonstrate a child's growing awareness of self is known as the *rouge test*. A spot of red rouge or lipstick is put on the end of the child's nose and the child is then placed in front of a mirror. Infants from about six months to a little over a year will reach out to touch the image of the baby in the mirror, reacting as if to another child (Amsterdam, 1972; Courage & Howe, 2002). In fact, some infants crawl or walk to the other side of the mirror to look for the "other." But at about 15 to 18 months of age, the infant begins to touch his or her own nose when seeing the image in the mirror, indicating an awareness that the image in the mirror is the infant's own (Nielsen et al., 2005). As the child grows, the self-concept grows to include gender ("I'm a boy" or "I'm a girl"), physical appearances ("I have brown hair and blue eyes"), and in middle childhood, personality traits and group memberships (Stipek et al., 1990).

> 💬 I've heard that you shouldn't pick a baby up every time it cries—that if you do, it might spoil the baby.

ERIKSON'S THEORY Unfortunately, a lot of people have not only heard this advice but also acted on it by frequently ignoring an infant's crying, which turns out to be a very bad thing for babies. When a baby under six months of age cries, it is an instinctive reaction meant to get the caregiver to tend to the baby's needs—hunger, thirst, pain, and even loneliness. Research has shown that babies whose cries are tended to consistently (that is, the infant is fed when hungry, changed when wet, and so on) in the early months are more securely attached as late as age 1 than those infants whose caregivers frequently allow the infants to cry when there is a need for attention—hunger, pain, or wetness, for example (Brazelton, 1992; Heinicke et al., 2000). Erikson, a psychodynamic theorist who emphasized the importance of social relationships in the development of personality, would certainly disagree with letting a baby "cry it out," although allowing an infant who has been fed, changed, burped, and checked to cry on occasion will not damage attachment.

Erikson trained as a Freudian psychoanalyst but became convinced that social interactions were more important in development than Freud's emphasis on sexual development. Erikson believed that development occurred in a series of eight stages, with the first four of these stages occurring in infancy and childhood (Erikson, 1950; Erikson & Erikson, 1997). (Freud's stages of psychosexual development are covered in detail in a later chapter.) **L I N K** to Learning Objective 11.2. Each stage is an emotional crisis, or a turning point, in personality, and the crisis in each stage must be successfully met for normal, healthy psychological development.

Erikson focused on the relationship of the infant and the child to significant others in the immediate surroundings—parents and then later teachers and even peers. **Table 8.4** summarizes the conflict in each of Erikson's eight stages and some of the implications for future development (Erikson, 1950; Erikson & Erikson, 1997). For now, look at the first four stages in particular.

Table 8.4 Erikson's Psychosocial Stages of Development

Stage	Developmental Crisis	Successful Dealing with Crisis	Unsuccessful Dealing with Crisis
1. Infant Birth to 1 year old	**Trust Versus Mistrust** Infants learn a basic sense of trust dependent upon how their needs are met	If babies' needs for food, comfort, and affection are met, they develop a sense of trust in people and expect those needs to be met in future.	If babies' needs for food, comfort, and affection are not met, they develop a sense of mistrust and do not expect their needs to be met in future.
2. Toddler 1 to 3 years old	**Autonomy Versus Shame and Doubt** Toddlers begin to understand that they can control their own actions.	Toddlers who are successful in controlling their own actions develop indepence.	Toddlers whose attempts at being independent are blocked, they develop a sense of self-doubt and shame for failing.
3. Preschool Age 3 to 5 years old	**Initiative Versus Guilt** Preschool children learn to take responsibility for their own behavior as they develop self control.	If preschoolers succeed in controlling their reactions and behavior, they feel capable and develop a sense of initiative.	If preschoolers fail in controlling their reations and behavior, they feel irresponsible, anxious, and develop a sense of guilt.
4. Elementary School Age 5 to 12 years old	**Industry Versus Inferiority** The school-aged child must learn new skills in both the academic world and the social world. They compare themselves to others to measure their success or failure.	When children feel they have succeeded at learning these skills, they develop a sense of industry, making them feel competent and improving their self-esteem.	When children fail, or feel that they have failed in learning these skills, they feel inferior when compared to others.
5. Adolescence 13 to early 20s	**Identity Versus Role Confusion** Adolescents must decide who they are, what they believe, and what they want to be as an adult.	Adolescents who are able to define their values, goals, and beliefs will develop a stable sense of identity.	Adolescents who are unable to define themselves remain confused and may isolate themselves from others or try to be like everyone else instead of themselves.
6. Early Adulthood 20s and 30s	**Intimacy Versus Isolation** Young adults face the task of finding a person with whom they can share their identity in an ongoing, close personal relationship.	Young adults who successfully find someone and share their identities will have a fulfilling relationship founded on psychological intimacy.	Young adults who are unable to find someone (often because they do not yet have a stable identity to share) will isolate themselves and may experience loneliness, even when involved in shallow relationships with others.
7. Middle Adulthood 40s and 50s	**Generativity Versus Stagnation** The focus of this task is to find a way to be a creative, productive person who is nurturing the next generation.	Adults who are able to focus on the next generation will be productive and creative, leaving a legacy for the future	Adults who are unable to focus outside themselves will remain stagnated, self-centered, and feeling that they have not made a difference.
8. Late Adulthood 60s and beyond	**Ego Integrity Versus Despair** This task involves coming to terms with the end of life, reaching a sense of wholeness and acceptance of life as it has been.	Older adults who are able to come to terms with their lives, things they have done and left undone, and able to "let go" of regrets will have a sense of completion and will see death as simply the last stage of a full life.	Older adults who have not been able to achieve identity or intimacy or generativity, who cannot let go of their regrets, will feel a sense of having left things too late and see death as coming too soon.

Concept Map L.O. 8.6, 8.7, 8.8, 8.9

Interactive

physical development
- immediately after birth, body systems start to function (i.e., respiratory, circulatory, temperature regulation, digestive)
- babies are born with (innate) reflex behaviors (see Fig. 8.4)

sensory development
- touch, taste, and smell are well developed
- hearing is functional but not fully developed
- vision is least developed (rods are functional, cones take about 6 months to fully develop)

motor development
- as with physical and sensory development, normal motor development is related to many factors, such as nutrition, care, and health
- birth to 2 years = period of rapid development (see Fig. 8.5)

Infancy and Childhood Development

Piaget's theory
- suggests children form mental concepts or schemes as they experience new situations and events
  - understand new things in terms of schemes they already possess (assimilation) or through altering or adjusting old schemes to fit new information (accommodation)
- proposes four distinct stages of cognitive development that span infancy to adolescence
  - sensorimotor
  - preoperational
  - concrete operations
  - formal operations

  ⟶ see Table 8.3

Vygotsky's theory
- stresses the importance of social interactions with others, typically more highly skilled children and adults
- children's cognitive development occurs when someone helps them by asking leading questions and providing examples of concepts (scaffolding)
- each child has a zone of proximal development—difference between what they can do alone vs. with aid of a teacher

Infancy and Childhood Development: Cognitive Development

stages of language development
- language allows children to think in words, ask questions, communicate needs and wants, and form concepts
- universal progressive stages
  - cooing, babbling, one-word speech, telegraphic speech, whole sentences

autism spectrum disorder
- neurodevelopmental disorder that involves issues in thinking, feeling, language, and social interactions
- causes are still being investigated but do not appear to be linked to childhood immunizations

psychosocial development
- involves development of personality, relationships, and a sense of being male or female; process begins in infancy and continues into adulthood

important early concepts
- infants demonstrate personality through their temperament (e.g., easy, difficult, slow to warm up), which can also affect, and is affected by, parenting and the environment
- attachment (emotional bond between infant and a primary caregiver) is very important; different attachment styles have been identified by Ainsworth and others (e.g., secure, avoidant, ambivalent, disorganized–disoriented) that appear to be similar, but not identical, across different cultures

Erikson's theory
- suggests development occurs in a series of eight stages (see Table 8.4)
- at each stage an emotional crisis must be successfully met for normal development to occur

Infancy and Childhood Development: Psychosocial Development

Reset

Practice Quiz   How much do you remember?   ANSWERS ON PAGE AK-1.

Pick the best answer.

1. One way researchers study newborn development involves measuring how long infants continue to focus upon a nonchanging stimulus. This technique is referred to as

   a. adaptation.
   b. preferential looking.
   c. longitudinal study.
   d. a cross-sectional design.

2. In which of Piaget's stages is a child who has just developed the ability to conserve?

   a. sensorimotor
   b. preoperational
   c. concrete operations
   d. formal operations

3. Vygotsky defines _____ as the process of helping less as the learner improves at a given task.

   a. scaffolding
   b. habituation
   c. zone of proximal development
   d. metamemory

4. Which of the following tends to occur first in a child's language development?

   a. telegraphic speech
   b. babbling
   c. a holophrase
   d. cooing

5. What kind of attachment, according to Ainsworth, is shown by a baby who clings to his or her mother, gets upset when the mother leaves, and demands to be picked up but at the same time kicks and pushes her away?

   a. secure
   b. avoidant
   c. ambivalent
   d. disorganized-disoriented

6. Studies by Harry Harlow showed that the most important element to developing an attachment is

   a. feeding.
   b. physical contact.
   c. mental challenges.
   d. sleep.

7. According to Erikson, which stage results in a sense of independence because of one's ability to control one's own actions?

   a. trust versus mistrust
   b. autonomy versus shame and doubt
   c. initiative versus guilt
   d. generativity versus stagnation

Gender Development

One important aspect of development that encompasses both physical and psychological changes is gender development, the growing sense of being male or female.

GENDER ROLES

8.10 **Define gender, and discuss the development of gender roles.**

 When do little kids learn the difference between girls and boys?

Whereas sex can be defined as the physical characteristics of being male or female, **gender** is defined as the psychological aspects of being male or female. The expectations of one's culture, the development of one's personality, and one's sense of identity are all affected by the concept of gender.

    Gender roles are the culture's expectations for behavior of a person who is perceived as male or female, including attitudes, actions, and personality traits associated with a particular gender within that culture (Tobach, 2001; Unger, 1979). The process of developing a person's **gender identity** (a sense of being male or female) is influenced by both biological and environmental factors (in the form of parenting and other child-rearing behaviors), although which type of factor has greater influence is still controversial. Most researchers today would agree that biology has an important role in gender identity, at least in certain aspects of gender identity and behavior (Diamond & Sigmundson, 1997; Money, 1994; Reiner, 1999, 2000). In one study, 25 genetically male children who were born with ambiguous genitalia were surgically altered and raised as girls. Now older children and teenagers, they prefer male play activities. Fourteen of these children have openly declared themselves to be boys (Reiner, 2000).

    Environment must also play its part. In most cultures, there are certain roles that males and females are expected to play (gender roles, in other words), and the pressure that can be brought to bear on a person who does not conform to these expectations can be tremendous. In most Western cultures, the pressure to be masculine is even greater for males than the pressure to be feminine is for girls. And although studies of parents' influence on their children's gender typing show that both parents have an impact, they also show that the fathers are almost always more concerned about their sons showing male gender behavior than their daughters showing female gender behavior (Lytton & Romney, 1991). Cultures that are more individualistic (those stressing independence and with loose ties among individuals) and have fairly high standards of living are becoming more nontraditional, especially for women in those cultures, whereas the more traditional views seem to be held by collectivistic cultures (those stressing interdependence and with strong ties among individuals, especially familial ties) that have less wealth, although even in the latter, women were more likely to be less traditional than men (Forbes et al., 2009; Gibbons et al., 1991). Other studies have found that the most nontraditional ideas about gender roles and gender behavior are found in countries such as the Netherlands, Germany, Italy, and England, whereas the most traditional ideas predominate in African and Asian countries such as Nigeria, Pakistan, and Japan (Best & Williams, 2001). The United States, often seen as very nontraditional by researchers, actually was somewhere in the middle in these studies, perhaps due to the large variation in subcultures that exists within this multicultural country.

THEORIES OF GENDER-ROLE DEVELOPMENT

8.11 Compare and contrast two theories of gender-role development.

How do children acquire the knowledge of their society or culture's gender-role expectations? How does that knowledge lead to the development of a gender identity? Although early psychodynamic theorists such as Freud, ⓛⓘⓝⓚ Learning Objective 1.3, believed that children would learn their gender identities as a natural consequence of resolving the sexual conflicts of early childhood, many modern theorists focus on learning and cognitive processes for the development of gender identity and behavior.

SOCIAL LEARNING THEORY Social learning theory, which emphasizes learning through observation and imitation of models, attributes* gender-role development to those processes. Children observe their same-sex parents behaving in certain ways and imitate that behavior. When the children imitate the appropriate gender behavior, they are reinforced with positive attention. Inappropriate gender behavior is either ignored or actively discouraged (Fagot & Hagan, 1991; Mischel, 1966).

GENDER SCHEMA THEORY A theory of gender-role development that combines social learning theory with cognitive development is called **gender schema theory** (Bem, 1987, 1993). In this theory based on the Piagetian concept of schemas, children develop a schema, or mental pattern, for being male or female in much the same way that they develop schemas for other concepts such as "dog," "bird," and "big." As their brains mature, they become capable of distinguishing among various concepts. For example, a "dog" might at first be anything with four legs and a tail, but as children encounter dogs and other kinds of animals and are given instruction, "dog" becomes more specific and the schema for "dog" becomes well defined.

In a similar manner, children develop a concept for "boy" and "girl." Once that schema is in place, children can identify themselves as "boy" or "girl" and will notice other members of that schema. They notice the behavior of other "boys" or "girls" and imitate that behavior. Rather than being simple imitation and reinforcement, as in social learning theory, children acquire their gender role behavior by organizing that behavior around the schema of "boy" or "girl." Evidence for this theory includes the finding

---

*attributes: explains as a cause.

that children can discriminate between male and female faces and voices before age 1 (Martin, 2000), a sign that the world is already being organized into those two concepts. The concept of **androgyny** (Bem, 1975, 1981) describes a gender role characteristic of people whose personalities reflect the characteristics of both males and females, regardless of physical sex. Androgynous people can make decisions based on the situation's demands rather than being masculine or feminine, which allows them to be more flexible in everyday behavior and career choices.

Concept Map L.O. 8.10, 8.11

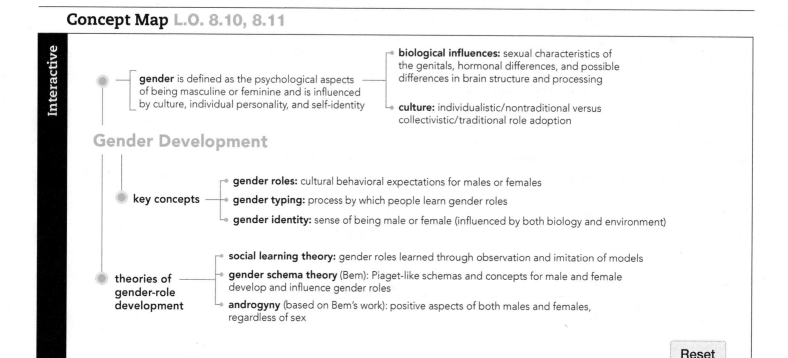

Interactive

gender is defined as the psychological aspects of being masculine or feminine and is influenced by culture, individual personality, and self-identity

- **biological influences:** sexual characteristics of the genitals, hormonal differences, and possible differences in brain structure and processing
- **culture:** individualistic/nontraditional versus collectivistic/traditional role adoption

Gender Development

key concepts
- **gender roles:** cultural behavioral expectations for males or females
- **gender typing:** process by which people learn gender roles
- **gender identity:** sense of being male or female (influenced by both biology and environment)

theories of gender-role development
- **social learning theory:** gender roles learned through observation and imitation of models
- **gender schema theory** (Bem): Piaget-like schemas and concepts for male and female develop and influence gender roles
- **androgyny** (based on Bem's work): positive aspects of both males and females, regardless of sex

Reset

Practice Quiz How much do you remember? ANSWERS ON PAGE AK-1.

Pick the best answer.

1. The development of a person's sense of being male or female is called _____.
   a. gender role.
   b. gender identity.
   c. gender typing.
   d. gender stereotyping.

2. Which of the following is not a biological influence on gender?
   a. hormones secreted during fetal development
   b. the influence of hormones taken by the pregnant mother
   c. exposure to playmates of a particular gender
   d. sex chromosomes

3. In _____ cultures, gender roles are seen as more traditional, whereas in _____ cultures they may be more nontraditional, especially for women.
   a. individualistic; collectivistic
   b. collectivistic; individualistic
   c. European; Asian
   d. affluent; poor

4. Young Thomas watches his father hold the door open while his mother walks in. Subsequently, Thomas tries to hold the door for his mother as well. What theory best explains this behavior?
   a. Androgyny
   b. Sex constancy
   c. Gender schema
   d. Social learning

5. Marcus's personality reflects the characteristics of both males and females, and this combination allows him to be more flexible in everyday behavior and his career choices. The term that describes this combination of male and female personality attributes is:
   a. gender schema
   b. gender-role
   c. androgyny
   d. gender segregation

Adolescence

Adolescence is the period of life from about age 13 to the early 20s during which a young person is no longer physically a child but is not yet an independent, self-supporting adult. Adolescence has been defined as the "teens," from ages 13 to 19, but adolescence also concerns how a person deals with life issues such as work, family, and relationships. So although we can agree there is a clear age of onset, the end of adolescence may come earlier or later for different individuals.

PHYSICAL DEVELOPMENT

8.12 **Describe the physical changes that occur in adolescence, and identify some of the sexually transmitted diseases to which adolescents may be vulnerable.**

💬 Isn't adolescence just the physical changes that happen to your body?

PUBERTY   The clearest sign of the beginning of adolescence is the onset of **puberty**, the physical changes in both primary sex characteristics (growth of the actual sex organs such as the penis or the uterus) and secondary sex characteristics (changes in the body such as the development of breasts and body hair) that occur in the body as sexual development reaches its peak. Puberty occurs as the result of a complex series of glandular activities, stimulated by the "master gland" or the pituitary gland, when the proper genetically determined age is reached. Certain psychosocial and environmental factors such as stress, exercise, and nutrition may also have an impact on the timing of puberty (Ellis et al., 1999; Graber et al., 1995). The thyroid gland increases the rate of growth, and the adrenal glands and sex glands stimulate the growth of characteristics such as body hair, muscle tissue in males, and the menstrual cycle in girls, for example (Grumbach & Kaplan, 1990; Grumbach & Styne, 1998). Puberty often begins about two years after the beginning of the growth spurt, the rapid period of growth that takes place at around age 10 for girls and around age 12 for boys.

In addition to an increase in height, physical characteristics related to being male or female undergo rapid and dramatic change. In fact, the rate of growth and development in puberty approaches that of development in the womb.

BRAIN DEVELOPMENT   After about 4 years, the changes of puberty are relatively complete. The development of the brain, however, continues well into the early 20s. In particular, the prefrontal cortex of the brain, which is responsible in part for impulse control, decision making, and the organization and understanding of information, does not complete its development until about age 25 years (Somerville et al., 2013). It is easy to understand, then, why adolescents may engage in risky behavior even when they know better.

SEXUALLY TRANSMITTED INFECTIONS   The fact that adolescents are often risk-takers makes them very vulnerable to many dangers. One of these dangers is the risk of contracting a sexually transmitted infection (STI), an infection spread primarily through sexual contact. One common STI is *chlamydia,* which if left untreated (and adolescents typically do not seek help) can cause *pelvic inflammatory disorder (PID),* a condition that can damage the lining of the uterus and the fallopian tubes as well as the ovaries and other nearby structures (Miller & Graves, 2000). Other STIs include *syphilis, gonorrhea, genital herpes,* and *genital warts.* AIDS, or acquired immune deficiency syndrome, is caused by a viral infection, specifically the *human immunodeficiency virus,* or *HIV.* A person who has HIV is at risk for developing AIDS in the future. HIV wears down the body's immune system, making the body vulnerable to infections caused by bacteria or viruses that, while harmless in a healthy immune system, will take hold when the immune system is weakened, causing the person to develop AIDS (Folkman & Chesney, 1995). HIV can be transmitted to a person from anyone who has the infection (even if they are not yet sick) in one of three ways. Having unprotected vaginal, oral, or anal sexual contact, which is more likely among impulsive adolescents, is one way. Another is sharing a needle (most often one used to take drugs), and the third is transmitting the virus to a baby while giving birth (Kourtis & Bulterys, 2010).

COGNITIVE AND PSYCHOSOCIAL DEVELOPMENT

8.13 Identify the cognitive and personality changes occurring in adolescence.

The physical development of adolescents has not changed radically in its pattern over the last century, even though aspects of physical development such as puberty do happen earlier than in the past. Cognitive and psychosocial development, however, have changed quite in bit—the adolescent of the early nineteen hundreds was a far different being than the adolescent of the same physical age in the early twenty-first century.

COGNITIVE DEVELOPMENT

💬 If I'm remembering correctly, teenagers should be in Piaget's formal operations stage. So why don't many teenagers think just like adults?

The cognitive development of adolescents is less visible than the physical development but still represents a major change in the way adolescents think about themselves, their peers and relationships, and the world around them.

PIAGET'S FORMAL OPERATIONS REVISITED   Adolescents, especially those who receive a formal high school education, move into Piaget's final stage of formal operations, in which abstract thinking becomes possible. Teenagers begin to think about hypothetical situations, leading to a picture of what an "ideal" world would be like.

Piaget's theory has had a tremendous impact in the education of children and in stimulating research about children's cognitive development (Satterly, 1987). Children in varying cultures usually come to understand the world in the way that Piaget described, although the age at which this understanding comes varies from one child to another.

Although headed into an adult style of thinking, adolescents are not yet completely free of egocentric thought. At this time in life, however, their egocentrism shows up in their preoccupation* with their own thoughts. They do a lot of introspection (turning inward) and may become convinced that their thoughts are as important

---

*preoccupation: extreme or excessive concern with something.

Example of a Moral Dilemma

The ant worked long and hard over the summer to gather food for himself and his family. The grasshopper, who preferred to play and be lazy all summer, laughed at the ant for working so hard. The ant said, "You will be sorry this winter when you have no food." Sure enough, when winter came the very sorry grasshopper, cold and hungry, came to the ant and begged for food and shelter. Should the ant give food and shelter to the grasshopper?

Figure 8.7 Example of a Moral Dilemma

to others as they are to themselves. Two ways in which this adolescent egocentrism emerges are the personal fable and the imaginary audience (Elkind, 1985; Lapsley et al., 1986; Vartanian, 2000).

In the **personal fable**, adolescents have spent so much time thinking about their own thoughts and feelings that they become convinced that they are special, one of a kind, and that no one else has ever had these thoughts and feelings before them. "You just don't understand me, I'm different from you" is a common feeling of teens. The personal fable is not without a dangerous side. Because they feel unique, teenagers may feel that they are somehow protected from the dangers of the world and so do not take the precautions that they should. This may result in an unwanted pregnancy, severe injury or death while racing in a car, drinking and driving, and drug use, to name a few possibilities. "It can't happen to me, I'm special" is a risky but common thought.

The **imaginary audience** shows up as extreme self-consciousness in adolescents. They become convinced that everyone is looking at them and that they are always the center of everyone else's world, just as they are the center of their own. This explains the intense self-consciousness that many adolescents experience concerning what others think about how the adolescent looks or behaves.

MORAL DEVELOPMENT   Another important aspect in the cognitive advances that occur in adolescence concerns the teenager's understanding of "right" and "wrong." Harvard University professor Lawrence Kohlberg was a developmental psychologist who, influenced by Piaget and others, outlined a theory of the development of moral thinking through looking at how people of various ages responded to stories about people caught up in moral dilemmas (see **Figure 8.7** for an example of a dilemma). Kohlberg (1973) proposed three levels of moral development, or the knowledge of right and wrong behavior. These levels are summarized in **Table 8.5**, along with an example of each type of thinking. Although these stages are associated with certain age-groups, adolescents and

Table 8.5   Kohlberg's Three Levels of Morality

Level of Morality	How Rules are Understood	Example
Preconventional morality (typically very young children)	The consequences determine morality; behavior that is rewarded is right; that which is punished is wrong.	A child who steals a toy from another child and does not get caught does not see that action as wrong.
Conventional* morality (older children, adolescents, and most adults)	Conformity to social norms is right; nonconformity is wrong.	A child criticizes his or her parent for speeding because speeding is against the posted laws.
Postconventional morality (about 20 percent of the adult population)	Moral principles determined by the person are used to determine right and wrong and may disagree with societal norms.	A reporter who wrote a controversial story goes to jail rather than reveal the source's identity.

*The term *conventional* refers to general standards or norms of behavior for a particular society, which will differ from one social group or culture to another.

adults can be found at all three levels. For example, a juvenile delinquent tends to be pre-conventional in moral thinking.

Kohlberg's theory has been criticized as being male oriented and biased toward Western cultures, especially since he used only males in his studies (Gilligan, 1982; Snarey, 1985). Carol Gilligan (1982) proposed that men and women have different perspectives on morality: Men tend to judge as moral the actions that lead to a fair or just end, whereas women tend to judge as moral the actions that are nonviolent and hurt the fewest people. Researchers, however, have not found consistent support for gender differences in moral thinking (Walker, 1991). Another criticism is that Kohlberg's assessment of moral development involves asking people what they think should be done in hypothetical moral dilemmas. What people say they will do and what people actually do when faced with a real dilemma are often two different things.

WRITING PROMPT

Have you ever had a decision to make that challenged your moral thinking? In which of Kohlberg's three levels would you classify your decision?

▶ The response entered here will be saved to your notes and may be collected by your instructor if he/she requires it.

Submit

The comedy movie *Mean Girls* portrays the ins and outs of peer pressure and the desire to fit in that many adolescents face.

PSYCHOSOCIAL DEVELOPMENT   The development of personality and social relationships in adolescence primarily concerns the search for a consistent sense of self or personal identity.

ERIKSON'S IDENTITY VERSUS ROLE CONFUSION   The psychosocial crisis that must be faced by the adolescent, according to Erikson, is that of **identity versus role confusion**. (see Table 8.4). In this stage, the teenager must choose from among many options for values in life and beliefs concerning things such as political issues, career options, and marriage (Feldman, 2003). From those options, a consistent sense of self must be found. Erikson believed that teens who have successfully resolved the conflicts of the earlier four stages are much better "equipped" to resist peer pressure to engage in unhealthy or illegal activities and find their own identity during the adolescent years. Those teens who are not as successful come into the adolescent years with a lack of trust in others, feelings of guilt and shame, low self-esteem, and dependency on others. Peer pressure is quite effective on teenagers who desperately want to "fit in" and have an identity of some sort and who feel that others will not want to be with them unless they conform to the expectations and demands of the peer group. They play the part of the model child for the parents, the good student for the teachers, and the "cool" juvenile delinquent to their friends and will be confused about which of the many roles they play are really their own identity.

PARENT/TEEN CONFLICT   Even for the majority of adolescents who end up successfully finding a consistent sense of self, there will be conflicts with parents. Many researchers believe that a certain amount of "rebellion" and conflict is a necessary step in breaking away from childhood dependence on the parents and becoming a self-sufficient* adult (Bengston, 1970; Lynott & Roberts, 1997). Although many people think that these conflicts are intense and concern very serious behavior, the reality is that most parent/teen conflict is over trivial issues—hair, clothing, taste in music, and so on. On the really big moral issues, most parents and teens would be quite surprised to realize that they are in agreement (Giancola, 2006).

*self-sufficient: able to function without outside aid; capable of providing for one's own needs.

Concept Map L.O. 8.12, 8.13

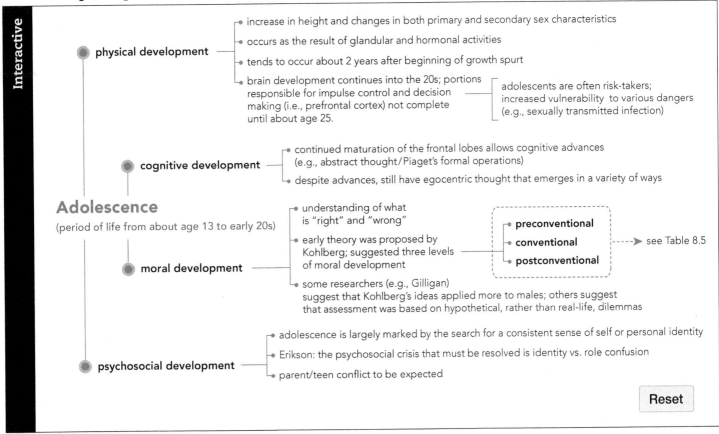

Interactive

physical development
- increase in height and changes in both primary and secondary sex characteristics
- occurs as the result of glandular and hormonal activities
- tends to occur about 2 years after beginning of growth spurt
- brain development continues into the 20s; portions responsible for impulse control and decision making (i.e., prefrontal cortex) not complete until about age 25. — adolescents are often risk-takers; increased vulnerability to various dangers (e.g., sexually transmitted infection)

cognitive development
- continued maturation of the frontal lobes allows cognitive advances (e.g., abstract thought/Piaget's formal operations)
- despite advances, still have egocentric thought that emerges in a variety of ways

Adolescence
(period of life from about age 13 to early 20s)

moral development
- understanding of what is "right" and "wrong"
- early theory was proposed by Kohlberg; suggested three levels of moral development — preconventional / conventional / postconventional ----> see Table 8.5
- some researchers (e.g., Gilligan) suggest that Kohlberg's ideas applied more to males; others suggest that assessment was based on hypothetical, rather than real-life, dilemmas

psychosocial development
- adolescence is largely marked by the search for a consistent sense of self or personal identity
- Erikson: the psychosocial crisis that must be resolved is identity vs. role confusion
- parent/teen conflict to be expected

Reset

Practice Quiz   How much do you remember? ANSWERS ON PAGE AK-1.

Pick the best answer.

1. Changes in the body of young boys such as the appearance and growth of body hair is considered
   a. a primary sex characteristic.
   b. a secondary sex characteristic.
   c. the final stage of puberty.
   d. a sign of postconventional morality.

2. "It can't happen to me. I'm special" is a common component of adolescent ego-centric thinking and characteristic of
   a. a self-concept.   c. a personal fable.
   b. an imaginary audience.   d. a preconventional morality.

3. According to Kohlberg, about one fifth of the adult population is at the _____ level of morality.
   a. preconventional   c. postconventional
   b. conventional   d. preliminary

4. According to Erikson, the task of the adolescent is to
   a. find a consistent sense of self.
   b. develop a sense of initiative.
   c. find intimacy with another.
   d. develop a sense of industry.

5. If Colin is going to argue and disagree with his parents, which of the following topics will he typically be arguing over?
   a. political beliefs
   b. religious beliefs
   c. social values
   d. his taste in clothes

Adulthood and Aging

  When exactly does adulthood begin?

Adulthood can be thought of as the period of life from the early 20s until old age and death. Exactly when adulthood begins is not always easy to determine. In some cultures, adulthood is reached soon after puberty (Bledsoe & Cohen, 1993; Ocholla-Ayayo et al.,

1993), while in other cultures events such as high school graduation or having a job and home separate from one's parents mark entry into adulthood.

PHYSICAL AND COGNITIVE DEVELOPMENT: USE IT OR LOSE IT

8.14 Describe the physical and cognitive changes of adulthood, and explain how to improve physical and mental health.

Adulthood can also be divided into at least three periods: young adulthood, middle age, and late adulthood. Many developmental psychologists now talk about "emerging adulthood" as a time from late adolescence through the 20s and referring to mainly those in developed countries who are childless, do not live in their own home, and are not earning enough money to be independent (Arnett, 2000; Azmitia et al., 2008; Nelson et al., 2008). Decisions about identity, values, and the preparation for a career have begun to take longer, and together with the downturn in the economy, many young people who would have been working and raising families a few decades ago now find that they cannot "leave the nest" so easily.

PHYSICAL DEVELOPMENT Physical changes in young adulthood are relatively minimal. The good news is that the 20s are a time of peak physical health, sharp senses, fewer insecurities, and mature cognitive abilities. The bad news is that even in the early 20s, the signs of aging are already beginning. Oil glands in the neck and around the eyes begin to malfunction, contributing to wrinkles in those areas near the end of the 20s and beginning of the 30s. The 30s may not bring noticeable changes, but vision and hearing are beginning to decline and by around age 40, bifocal lenses may become necessary as the lens of the eye hardens, becoming unable to change its shape to shift focus. Hearing loss may begin in the 40s and 50s but often does not become noticeable until the 60s or 70s, when hearing aids may become necessary.

In the 40s, while most adults are able to experience some security and stability without the worries and concerns of adolescence and young adulthood, physical aging continues: Skin begins to show more wrinkles, hair turns gray (or falls out), vision and hearing decline further, and physical strength may begin to decline (Frontera et al., 1991). In the 50s, these changes continue. Throughout middle age, weight may increase as the rate at which the body functions slows down but eating increases and less time is spent exercising. Height begins to decrease, with about half an inch of height lost for every 10 years past age 40, although people with the bone-loss disease osteoporosis may lose up to 8 inches or more (Cummings & Melton, 2002). Although sexual functioning usually does not decline in middle age, opportunities for sexual activity may be fewer than in the days of young adulthood (Hodson & Skeen, 1994; Williams, 1995). Children, mortgages, and career worries can put a damper on middle-age romance.

In a woman's 40s, the levels of the female hormone estrogen decline as the body's reproductive system prepares to cease that function. Some women begin to experience "hot flashes," a sudden sensation of heat and sweating that may keep them awake at night. Interestingly, in some cultures, particularly those in which the diet contains high amounts of soy products, hot flashes are almost nonexistent (Cassidy et al., 1994; Lock, 1994). However, a recent study suggests that soy intake is not a primary factor (Gold et al., 2013). These changes are called the *climacteric*, and the period of 5 to 10 years over which these changes occur is called *perimenopause*. At an average age of 51, most women will cease ovulation altogether, ending their reproductive years. The cessation of ovulation and the menstrual cycle is called **menopause** (Mishell, 2001). Many women look forward to the freedom from monthly menstruation and fear of unplanned pregnancies (Adler et al., 2000; Hvas, 2001; Leon et al., 2007).

💬 Do men go through anything like menopause?

Men also go through a time of sexual changes, but it is much more gradual and less dramatic than menopause. In males, **andropause** (Carruthers, 2001) usually begins in the

40s with a decline in several hormones, primarily testosterone (the major male hormone). Physical symptoms are also less dramatic but no less troubling: fatigue, irritability, possible problems in sexual functioning, and reduced sperm count. Males, however, rarely lose all reproductive ability.

EFFECTS OF AGING ON HEALTH   It is in middle age that many health problems first occur, although their true cause may have begun in the young adulthood years. Young adults may smoke, drink heavily, stay up late, and get dark tans, and the wear and tear that this lifestyle causes on their bodies will not become obvious until their 40s and 50s.

Some of the common health problems that may show up in middle age are high blood pressure, skin cancer, heart problems, arthritis, and obesity. High blood pressure can be caused by lifestyle factors such as obesity and stress but may also be related to hereditary factors (Rudd & Osterberg, 2002). Sleep problems, such as loud snoring and sleep apnea (in which breathing stops for 10 seconds or more), may also take their toll on physical health. There is some evidence that high blood pressure and apnea are linked, although the link may be as simple as the common cause of obesity (Nieto et al., 2000). The most common causes of death in middle age are heart disease, cancer, and stroke—in that order (McGinnis & Foege, 1993).

COGNITIVE DEVELOPMENT   Intellectual abilities do not decline overall, although speed of processing (or reaction time) does slow down. Compared to a younger adult, a middle-aged person may take a little longer to solve a problem. However, a middle-aged person also has more life experience and knowledge to bring to bear on a problem, which counters the lack of speed. In one study (Salthouse, 1984), for example, older typists were found to outperform younger typists, even though they typed more slowly than the younger subjects. The older typists, because of years of practice, had developed a skill of looking farther ahead in the document they were typing, so that they could type more continuously without looking back at the document. This allowed them to complete their typing more quickly than the younger typists.

Changes in memory ability are probably the most noticeable changes in middle-aged cognition. People find themselves having a hard time recalling a particular word or someone's name. This difficulty in retrieval is probably not evidence of a cognitive decline but is more likely caused by the stresses a middle-aged person experiences and the sheer amount of information that a person of middle years must try to keep straight (Craik, 1994; Launer et al., 1995; Sands & Meredith, 1992). One study suggests that thinking about the positive events of the past activates areas of the brain connected to the brain areas that form newer memories, improving new memory formation (Addis et al., 2010). Think positive!

HOW TO KEEP YOUR BRAIN YOUNG   People who exercise their mental abilities have been found to be far less likely to develop memory problems and even senile dementias such as Alzheimer's in old age (Ball et al., 2002; Colcombe et al., 2003; Fiatarone, 1996). ⓛ ⓘ ⓝ ⓚ to Learning Objective 6.14. "Use it or lose it" is the phrase to remember. Working challenging crossword puzzles, for example, can be a major factor in maintaining a healthy level of cognitive functioning. Reading, having an active social life, going to plays, taking classes, and staying physically active can all have a positive impact on the continued well-being of the brain (Bosworth & Schaie, 1997; Cabeza et al., 2002; Singh-Manoux et al., 2003).

This middle-aged woman works on a crossword puzzle. Mental exercises such as this are one way to keep the brain healthy and fit. What might be some other ways to exercise one's brain?

PSYCHOSOCIAL DEVELOPMENT

8.15 **Summarize some common psychosocial concerns of adulthood and explain how they relate to Erikson's theory.**

In adulthood, concerns involve career, relationships, family, and approaching old age. The late teens and early 20s may be college years for many, although other young people go to work directly from high school. Choosing and entering a career is a very serious task that many young adults have difficulty accomplishing. College students may change majors more than once during the first few years of college, and even after obtaining a bachelor's degree many may either get a job in an unrelated field or go on to a different type of career choice in graduate school. Those who are working may also change careers several times (perhaps as many as five to seven times) and may experience periods of unemployment while between jobs.

ERIKSON'S INTIMACY VERSUS ISOLATION: FORMING RELATIONSHIPS In young adulthood, Erikson saw the primary task to be finding a mate. True **intimacy** is an emotional and psychological closeness that is based on the ability to trust, share, and care (an ability developed during the earlier stages such as trust versus mistrust), while still maintaining one's sense of self. Ⓛ Ⓘ Ⓝ Ⓚ to Learning Objective 10.11. Young adults who have difficulty trusting others and who are unsure of their own identities may find isolation instead of intimacy—loneliness, shallow relationships with others, and even a fear of real intimacy. For example, many marriages end in divorce within a few years, with one partner leaving the relationship—and even the responsibilities of parenting— to explore personal concerns and those unfinished issues of identity. (See Table 8.4.)

ERIKSON'S GENERATIVITY VERSUS STAGNATION: PARENTING In middle adulthood, persons who have found intimacy can now focus outward on others. (Table 8.4). Erikson saw this as parenting the next generation and helping them through their crises, a process he called **generativity**. Educators, supervisors, health care professionals, doctors, and community volunteers might be examples of positions that allow a person to be generative. Other ways of being generative include engaging in careers or some major life work that can become one's legacy to the generations to come. Those who are unable to focus outward and are still dealing with issues of intimacy or even identity are said to be stagnated. People who frequently hand the care of their children over to grandparents or other relatives so that they can go out and "have fun" may be unable to focus on anyone else's needs but their own.

💬 What kind of parent is the best parent—one who's really strict or one who's pretty easygoing?

PARENTING STYLES Parenting children is a very important part of most people's middle adulthood. Diana Baumrind (1967) outlined three basic styles of parenting, each of which may be related to certain personality traits in the child raised by that style of parenting. The video *Impact of Parenting Styles* explains why goodness-of-fit, or matching the parenting style to the child's needs, may be most important.

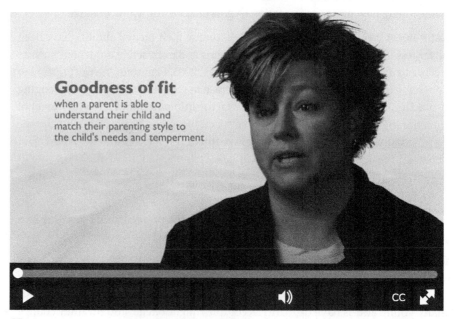

Goodness of fit
when a parent is able to understand their child and match their parenting style to the child's needs and temperment

👁 **Watch** the **Video**, *Impact of Parenting Styles.*

Authoritarian parenting tends to be overly concerned with rules. This type of parent is stern, rigid, demanding perfection, controlling, uncompromising,* and has a tendency to use physical punishment. Children raised in this way are often insecure, timid, withdrawn, and resentful. As teenagers, they will very often rebel against parental authority in very negative and self-destructive ways, such as delinquency (criminal acts committed by minor children), drug use, or premarital sex (Baumrind, 1991, 2005; Sleddens et al, 2011).

Permissive parenting occurs when parents put very few demands on their children for behavior. **Permissive neglectful** parents simply aren't involved with their children, ignoring them and allowing them to do whatever they want until it interferes with what the parent wants. At that point, this relationship may become an abusive one. **Permissive indulgent** parents seem to be too involved with their children, allowing their "little angels" to behave in any way they wish, refusing to set limits on the child's behavior or to require any kind of obedience. Children from both kinds of permissive parenting tend to be selfish, immature, dependent, lacking in social skills, and unpopular with peers (Baumrind, 1991, 2005; Dwairy, 2004; Sledden et al., 2011).

Authoritative parenting involves combining firm limits on behavior with love, warmth, affection, respect, and a willingness to listen to the child's point of view. Authoritative parents are more democratic, allowing the child to have some input into the formation of rules but still maintaining the role of final decision maker. Punishment tends to be nonphysical, such as restrictions, time-out, or loss of privileges. Authoritative parents set limits that are clear and understandable, and when a child crosses the limits, they allow an explanation and then agree on the right way to handle the situation. Children raised in this style of parenting tend to be self-reliant and independent (Baumrind, 1991, 2005; Dwairy, 2004; Sledden et al., 2011; Sorkhabi, 2005; Underwood et al., 2009).

ERIKSON'S EGO INTEGRITY VERSUS DESPAIR: DEALING WITH MORTALITY   As people enter the stage known as late adulthood, life becomes more urgent as the realities of physical aging and the approaching end of life become harder and harder to ignore. (See Table 8.4.) Erikson (1980) believed that at this time people look back on the life they have lived in a process called a life review. In the life review people must deal with mistakes, regrets, and unfinished business. If people can look back and feel that their lives were relatively full and come to terms with regrets and losses, then a feeling of **integrity** or wholeness results. Integrity is the final completion of the identity, or ego. If people have many regrets and lots of unfinished business, they feel despair, a sense of deep regret over things that will never be accomplished because time has run out.

THEORIES OF PHYSICAL AND PSYCHOLOGICAL AGING

8.16 Compare and contrast three views of why aging occurs.

  Why do people age? What makes us go through so many physical changes?

There are a number of theories of why people physically age. Some theories of physical aging point to biological changes in cellular structure, whereas others focus on the influence of external stresses on body tissues and functioning.

CELLULAR CLOCK THEORY   One of the biologically based theories is the cellular clock theory (Hayflick, 1977). In this theory, cells are limited in the number of times they can reproduce to repair damage. Evidence for this theory is the existence of telomeres, structures on the ends of chromosomes that shorten each time a cell reproduces (Martin & Buckwalter, 2001). When telomeres are too short, cells cannot reproduce; damage

---

*uncompromising: not making or accepting any viewpoint other than one's own, allowing no other viewpoints.

One way to age successfully and maintain psychological health is to remain active and involved in life. This woman is volunteering in a grade school classroom as a teacher's aide. This not only allows her to feel useful but also helps her to stay mentally alert and socially involved.

accumulates, resulting in the effects of aging. (Sounds almost like what happens when the warranty is up on a car, doesn't it?)

FREE RADICAL THEORY   One older theory points to outside influences such as stress, physical exertion, and bodily damage and is known as the wear-and-tear theory of aging. In this theory, the body's organs and cell tissues simply wear out with repeated use and abuse. The free radical theory is actually the latest version of the wear-and-tear theory in that it gives a biological explanation for the damage done to cells over time. Free radicals are oxygen molecules that have an unstable electron (negative particle). They bounce around the cell, stealing electrons from other molecules and increasing the damage to structures inside the cell. As people get older, more and more free radicals do more and more damage, producing the effects of aging (Hauck & Bartke, 2001; Knight, 1998).

🗨 I've heard that most older people just want to be left alone and have some peace and quiet. Is that true?

ACTIVITY THEORY   Activity theory (Havighurst et al., 1968) proposes that an elderly person adjusts more positively to aging when remaining active in some way. Elderly people who volunteer at hospitals or schools, those who take up new hobbies or throw themselves full time into old ones, and those who maintain their friendships with others and continue to have social activities have been shown to be happier and live longer than those who withdraw themselves from activity.

DEATH AND DYING

8.17 **Identify one theory of the stages of death and dying, and describe some of the criticisms of this theory.**

There are several ways of looking at the process of dying. One of the more well-known theories is that of Elisabeth Kübler-Ross (Kübler-Ross, 1997), who conducted extensive interviews with dying persons and their caregivers.

Elisabeth Kübler-Ross theorized that people go through five stages of reaction when faced with death (Backer et al., 1994; Kübler-Ross, 1997). These stages are denial, in which people refuse to believe that the diagnosis of death is real; anger, which is really anger at death itself and the feelings of helplessness to change things; bargaining, in which the dying person tries to make a deal with doctors or even with God; depression, which is sadness from losses already experienced (e.g., loss of a job or one's dignity) and those yet to come (e.g., not being able to see a child grow up); and finally acceptance, when the person has accepted the inevitable* and quietly awaits death.

Obviously, some people do not have time to go through all of these stages or even go through them in the listed order (Schneidman, 1983, 1994). Some theorists do not agree with the stage idea, seeing the process of dying as a series of ups and downs, with hope on the rise at times and then falling, to be replaced by a rise in despair or disbelief (Corr, 1993; Maciejewski et al., 2007; Schneidman, 1983, 1994; Weisman, 1972). Still others question the idea of common reactions among dying people, stating that the particular disease or condition and its treatment, the person's personality before the terminal diagnosis, and other life history factors make the process of dying unique and unpredictable (Kastenbaum & Costa, 1977; Zlatin, 1995). The danger in holding too strictly to a stage theory is that people may feel there is a "right" way to face death and a "wrong" way when in fact each person's dying process is unique. Kübler-Ross's theory is also strongly tied to Western cultural values and norms. For a look at how other cultures view death, see the *Applying Psychology to Everyday Life* feature that follows.

*inevitable: something that cannot be avoided or escaped.

Concept Map L.O. 8.14, 8.15, 8.16, 8.17

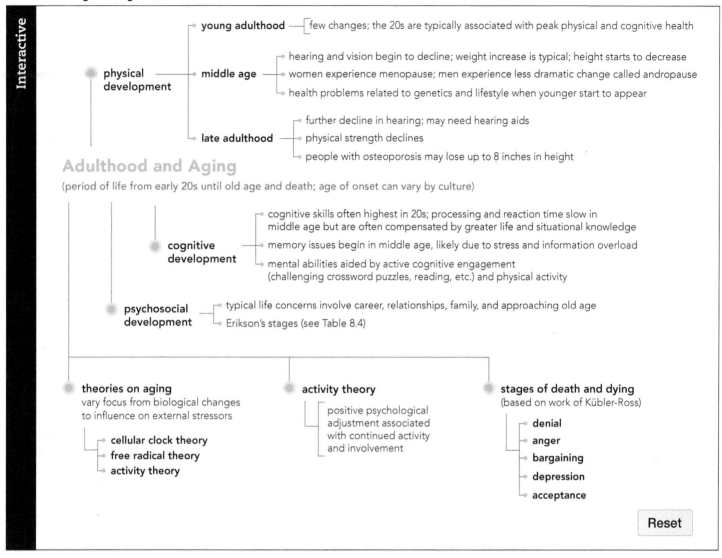

Adulthood and Aging

(period of life from early 20s until old age and death; age of onset can vary by culture)

- **physical development**
  - **young adulthood** — few changes; the 20s are typically associated with peak physical and cognitive health
  - **middle age**
    - hearing and vision begin to decline; weight increase is typical; height starts to decrease
    - women experience menopause; men experience less dramatic change called andropause
    - health problems related to genetics and lifestyle when younger start to appear
  - **late adulthood**
    - further decline in hearing; may need hearing aids
    - physical strength declines
    - people with osteoporosis may lose up to 8 inches in height

- **cognitive development**
  - cognitive skills often highest in 20s; processing and reaction time slow in middle age but are often compensated by greater life and situational knowledge
  - memory issues begin in middle age, likely due to stress and information overload
  - mental abilities aided by active cognitive engagement (challenging crossword puzzles, reading, etc.) and physical activity

- **psychosocial development**
  - typical life concerns involve career, relationships, family, and approaching old age
  - Erikson's stages (see Table 8.4)

- **theories on aging**
  vary focus from biological changes to influence on external stressors
  - cellular clock theory
  - free radical theory
  - activity theory

- **activity theory**
  - positive psychological adjustment associated with continued activity and involvement

- **stages of death and dying**
  (based on work of Kübler-Ross)
  - denial
  - anger
  - bargaining
  - depression
  - acceptance

Reset

Practice Quiz   How much do you remember?   ANSWERS ON PAGE AK-1.

Pick the best answer.

1. What is the most frequent cause of death in middle age?
  a. accidents
  b. gunshot injuries
  c. excessive risk taking
  d. heart disease

2. According to Erikson, the primary task of early adulthood is
  a. completing your education.
  b. finding a mate.
  c. starting a career.
  d. taking care of aging parents.

3. According to Baumrind, which type of parent would most likely say, "Because I said so" or "It's my way or the highway!"
  a. authoritarian
  b. authoritative
  c. permissive neglectful
  d. permissive indulgent

4. As William celebrates his 70th birthday, he finds that he is happy with how things have turned out with his life. According to Erikson, William's life review will cause him
  a. to develop a sense of ego integrity.
  b. a sense of despair, since such reviews often result in depression.
  c. to develop an urgency to begin new projects
  d. to put to writing many of his accomplishments.

5. The structures on the ends of chromosomes that shorten each time a cell reproduces are called
  a. free radicals.
  b. collagen.
  c. telomeres.
  d. DNA.

6. Which theory of aging is compared to the limited number of repairs you can have before your car's warranty runs out?
  a. wear-and-tear theory
  b. cellular clock theory
  c. free radical theory
  d. activity theory

7. What stage might terminally ill patients be in if they refuse to write a last will and testament because they believe that in doing so, they are admitting they will die?
  a. bargaining
  b. anger
  c. depression
  d. denial

Applying Psychology to Everyday Life
Cross-Cultural Views on Death

8.18 **Compare and contrast some cross-cultural differences in views of death.**

In the 1987 movie *The Princess Bride*, a character called Miracle Max (wonderfully played by comedian and actor Billy Crystal) says, "It just so happens that your friend here is only MOSTLY dead. There's a big difference between mostly dead and all dead. Mostly dead is slightly alive." As it turns out, that far-fetched idea of "mostly dead" is not unheard of in other cultures. While Westerners see a person as either dead or alive, in some cultures a person who by Western standards is clearly alive is mourned as already dead—as is the case in many Native American cultures. Let's take a look at two diverse cultures and their views on death and dying, remembering to contrast them with what you know of death and funeral rites common in your own culture.

- In a wealthy Hindu family in India, the dying person is surrounded by family members, even while in the hospital. In addition, many visitors will attend to the dying person, creating a nearly constant flow of visitors in and out of the room. Once the person has passed away, preparations for the funeral period—which can take nearly two weeks—are begun. The body is not sent to a funeral home but rather is taken into the family home until the actual day of the funeral, where a cremation will take place. During the funeral preparation period, visitors and family stream in and out of the deceased's home and an abundance of food—all vegetarian at this time—is prepared and eaten. Until the day of the funeral, mattresses are placed on the floor, and all but the very old and infirm are expected to sleep there; the body of the deceased is also placed on the floor. The family members themselves will eventually wash the body in preparation for wrapping and the trip to the crematorium (Laungani, 1997). In Hinduism, it is believed that the dead person's soul will be reincarnated at either a higher level or a lower level of status, depending upon how the person lived his or her life.

The washed and wrapped body of a Hindu man is being carried to the crematorium by his family members.

- In the culture of the Northern Cheyenne Native American tribe, death is considered only the end of the physical body, while the self and one's Cheyenne nature will persist. The very old and the very young are said to be "close to the spirit," meaning that the infant has just come from the nonphysical world and the aged person is close to returning to it. The Cheyenne, like the Hindu, also believe in reincarnation, so many infants are seen to be the living embodiment of ancestors. Death itself is a long process, with various aspects of one's spirit leaving at different times. The first such "leaving" results in changes in the behavior and the mental activity of the dying person, but the person may still be able to walk and communicate. The second leads to loss of the senses, then consciousness, and finally, breathing. The very last essence to leave is the life principle, the first life given into an infant but the last to leave. This life principle stays in the skeleton until the bones begin to crumble into dust. Thus some Cheyenne believe that bones can become alive again (Strauss, 2004).

Questions for Further Discussion

1. How has your own experience with death, if any, affected you and your outlook on life? What were the cultural trappings of the days leading up to the death and/or the funeral arrangements?

2. How do the customs of the wealthy Hindu family differ from those of the Cheyenne, and how are they alike?

Chapter Summary

Studying Human Development

8.1 Compare and contrast the special research methods used to study development.

- Three special research methods used in developmental research are the longitudinal design, the cross-sectional design, and the cross-sequential design.

8.2 Explain the relationship between heredity and environmental factors in determining development.

- Behavioral genetics is a field investigating the relative contributions to development of heredity (nature) and environment (nurture). Most developmental psychologists agree that development is a product of the interaction between nature and nurture.

8.3 Summarize the role of chromosomes and genes in determining the transmission of traits and the inheritance of disorders.

- Dominant genes control the expression of a trait, whereas recessive gene traits are only expressed when paired with another recessive gene for the same trait. Almost all traits are the result of combinations of genes working together in a process called polygenic inheritance.
- Chromosome disorders include Down syndrome, Klinefelter's syndrome, and Turner's syndrome, whereas genetic disorders include PKU, cystic fibrosis, sickle-cell anemia, and Tay-Sachs disease.

Prenatal Development

8.4 Explain the process of fertilization, including the twinning process.

- The fertilized egg cell is called a zygote and divides into many cells, eventually forming the baby.
- Monozygotic twins are formed when the zygote splits into two separate masses of cells, each of which will develop into a baby identical to the other. When the two masses do not fully separate, conjoined twins occur.
- Dizygotic twins are formed when the mother's body releases multiple eggs and at least two are fertilized or when another ovulation occurs even though the mother has already become pregnant.

8.5 Describe the processes and stages of prenatal development, and discuss hazards in prenatal development.

- The germinal period is the first two weeks of pregnancy in which the dividing mass of cells (blastocyst) moves down the fallopian tube into the uterus.
- The embryonic period begins at two weeks after conception and ends at eight weeks. The vital organs and structures of the baby form during this period, making it a critical one for teratogens to adversely affect the development of those organs and structures.
- The fetal period is from the beginning of the ninth week until the birth of the baby. During the fetal period, tremendous growth occurs, length and weight increase, and organs continue to become fully functional.

Infancy and Childhood Development

8.6 Describe the physical and sensory changes that take place in infancy and childhood.

- Four critical areas of adjustment for the newborn are respiration, digestion, circulation, and temperature regulation.
- Infants are born with reflexes that help the infant survive until more complex learning is possible. These reflexes include sucking, rooting, Moro (startle), grasping, and stepping.
- The senses, except for vision, are fairly well developed at birth. Vision is blurry and lacking in full color perception until about 6 months of age. Gross and fine motor skills develop at a fast pace during infancy and early childhood.

8.7 Compare and contrast two theories of cognitive development, and discuss the development of language.

- Piaget's stages include the sensorimotor stage of sensory and physical interaction with the world, preoperational thought in which language becomes a tool of exploration, concrete operations in which logical thought becomes possible, and formal operations in which abstract concepts are understood and hypothetical thinking develops.
- Vygotsky believed that children learn best when being helped by a more highly skilled peer or adult in a process called scaffolding. The zone of proximal development is the difference between the mental age of tasks the child performs without help and those the child can perform with help.
- The stages of language development are cooing, babbling, one-word speech (holophrases), and telegraphic speech.

8.8 Evaluate claims regarding the causes of autism spectrum disorder.

- Autism spectrum disorder (ASD) is a range of disorders which cause problems in thinking, feeling, language, and social skills in relating to others.
- Dr. Andrew Wakefield falsified data that led to parents refusing to have their children immunized against measles, mumps, and rubella, leading to epidemic outbreaks of these diseases.

8.9 Explain the development of personality, social relationships, and self-concept in infancy and childhood, and discuss the first four stages of Erikson's theory.

- The three basic infant temperaments are easy (regular, adaptable, and happy), difficult (irregular, nonadaptable, and irritable), and slow to warm up (need to adjust gradually to change).
- The four types of attachment are secure, avoidant (unattached), ambivalent (insecurely attached), and disorganized-disoriented (insecurely attached and sometimes abused or neglected).
- Harlow's classic research with infant Rhesus monkeys demonstrated the importance of contact comfort in the attachment process, contradicting the earlier view that attachment was merely a function of associating the mother with the delivery of food.
- In trust versus mistrust, the infant must gain a sense of predictability and trust in caregivers or risk developing a mistrustful nature; in autonomy versus shame and doubt, the toddler needs to become physically independent.

- In initiative versus guilt, the preschool child is developing emotional and psychological independence; in industry versus inferiority, school-age children are gaining competence and developing self-esteem.

Gender Development

8.10 Define gender, and discuss the development of gender roles.

- Gender is the psychological aspects of being male or female.
- Gender roles are the culture's expectations for male and female behavior and personality.
- Gender identity is a person's sense of being male or female.
- There are both biological influences, in the form of hormones and chromosomes, and environmental influences, in the form of parenting, surroundings, and culture, on the formation of gender identity.

8.11 Compare and contrast two theories of gender-role development.

- Social learning theorists believe that gender identity is formed through reinforcement of appropriate gender behavior as well as imitation of gender models.
- Gender schema theorists believe that gender identity is a mental schema that develops gradually, influenced by the growth of the brain and organization of observed male or female behavior around the schema.

Adolescence

8.12 Describe the physical changes that occur in adolescence, and identify some of the sexually transmitted diseases to which adolescents may be vulnerable.

- Adolescence is the period of life from about age 13 to the early 20s during which physical development reaches completion.
- Puberty is a period of about four years during which the sexual organs and systems fully mature and during which secondary sex characteristics such as body hair, breasts, menstruation, deepening voices, and the growth spurt occur.

8.13 Identify the cognitive and personality changes occurring in adolescence.

- Adolescents engage in two kinds of egocentric thinking called the imaginary audience and the personal fable.
- Kohlberg proposed three levels of moral development: preconventional morality, conventional morality, and postconventional morality.
- In Erikson's identity versus role confusion crisis the job of the adolescent is to achieve a consistent sense of self from among all the roles, values, and futures open to him or her.

Adulthood and Aging

8.14 Describe the physical and cognitive changes of adulthood, and explain how to improve physical and mental health.

- Adulthood begins in the early 20s and ends with death in old age. It can be divided into young adulthood, middle adulthood, and late adulthood.

- The 20s are the peak of physical health; in the 30s the signs of aging become more visible, and in the 40s visual problems may occur, weight may increase, strength may decrease, and height begins to decrease.
- Women experience a physical decline in the reproductive system called the climacteric, ending at about age 50 with menopause, when a woman's estrogen levels are at zero and her reproductive capabilities are at an end. Men go through andropause, a less dramatic change in testosterone and other male hormones, beginning in the 40s.
- Many health problems such as high blood pressure, skin cancers, and arthritis begin in middle age, with the most common causes of death in middle age being heart disease, cancer, and stroke.
- Reaction times slow down, but intelligence and memory remain relatively stable.

8.15 Summarize some common psychosocial concerns of adulthood, and explain how they relate to Erikson's theory.

- Erikson's crisis of young adulthood is intimacy versus isolation, in which the young adult must establish an intimate relationship, usually with a mate.
- The crisis of middle adulthood is generativity versus stagnation, in which the task of the middle-aged adult is to help the next generation through its crises, either by parenting, mentoring, or a career that leaves some legacy to the next generation.
- Baumrind proposed three parenting styles: authoritarian (rigid and uncompromising), authoritative (consistent and strict but warm and flexible), and permissive (either indifferent and unconcerned with the daily activities of the child or indulgent and unwilling to set limits on the child).
- Erikson's final crisis is integrity versus despair, in which an older adult must come to terms with mortality.

8.16 Compare and contrast three views of why aging occurs.

- Research strongly indicates that remaining active and involved results in the most positive adjustment to aging; this is a component of activity theory.
- The cellular clock theory is based on the idea that cells only have so many times that they can reproduce; once that limit is reached, damaged cells begin to accumulate.
- The free radical theory states that oxygen molecules with an unstable electron move around the cell, damaging cell structures as they go.

8.17 Identify one theory of the stages of death and dying, and describe some of the criticisms of this theory.

- The five stages of reaction to death and dying are denial, anger, bargaining, depression, and acceptance.

Applying Psychology to Everyday Life: Cross-Cultural Views on Death

8.18 Compare and contrast some cross-cultural differences in views of death.

- In wealthy Hindu families, a dying person is surrounded by family and friends and then honored with a funeral process of nearly two weeks.
- In Northern Cheyenne culture, death is seen as part of the process of the life cycle and takes place in three stages.

Test Yourself
ANSWERS ON PAGE AK-1.

Pick the best answer.

1. The thinking and attitudes of many who survived the Depression of the 1930s changed them for the rest of their lives. This would be an example of a
  a. cohort effect.
  b. cultural group.
  c. longitudinal group.
  d. cross-sequential group.

2. If a person has one gene for blue eyes but actually has brown eyes, blue eyes must be a _____ trait.
  a. dominant
  b. recessive
  c. sex-linked
  d. polygenic

3. In _____ syndrome, the 23rd pair of chromosomes consists of an XXY pairing, resulting in reduced masculine characteristics and excessive height.
  a. PKU
  b. Down
  c. Klinefelter's
  d. Turner's

4. Which of the following represents the fertilization process for monozygotic twins?
  a. One egg is fertilized by two different sperm.
  b. One egg splits and is then fertilized by two different sperm.
  c. One egg is fertilized by one sperm and then splits.
  d. Two eggs are fertilized by the same sperm.

5. What part of an infant's body is said to stay in an immature state until needed to produce more cells?
  a. uterus
  b. stem cells
  c. umbilical cord
  d. placenta

6. Based on today's science and medicine, when does the age of viability begin?
  a. between 8 and 12 weeks
  b. between 12 and 18 weeks
  c. between 22 and 26 weeks
  d. between 28 and 36 weeks

7. Dr. Kahn measures how long baby Lydia looks at a particular stimulus. The technique is known as
  a. preferential looking.
  b. dishabituation.
  c. habituation.
  d. stimulus discrimination.

8. At what age can the typical infant roll over?
  a. 2 months
  b. 5 weeks
  c. 8 months
  d. 12 months

9. Studies of the infant brain show signs of what scientists call synaptic pruning. What occurs during this process?
  a. The brain creates additional neural connections by removing parts of the surrounding bone.
  b. Unused synaptic connections and nerve cells are cleared out to make way for new cells.
  c. New cells work to "rewrite" old cells and ultimately change their functioning.
  d. New cells will not develop until the body makes sufficient physical space within the brain.

10. In which of Piaget's stages does the child become capable of understanding conservation?
  a. sensorimotor
  b. preoperational
  c. formal operations
  d. concrete operations

11. Monique says "milk" when she wants her milk from the kitchen counter. Subsequently, she says "milk" after she has had a drink. Using a single phrase to mean different things is an example of
  a. telephrase.
  b. private speech.
  c. holophrase.
  d. public speech.

12. In the Strange Situation, _____ babies would cry when their mother left the room but were happy upon her return.
  a. secure
  b. avoidant
  c. ambivalent
  d. disorganized-disoriented

13. The expectation of one's culture, the development of one's personality, and sense of identity are all affected by one's _____, which refers to the psychological aspects of being male or female
  a. sex
  b. androgyny
  c. gender
  d. gender role

14. What is a new explanation as to why teenagers and young adults may engage in risky and dangerous behavior?
  a. Such behavior is due to the tremendous pressure applied by peers.
  b. Such behavior is actually hereditary.
  c. Such behavior may be due to unbalanced levels of hormones in the body.
  d. Such behavior may be due to incomplete development of the prefrontal cortex.

15. Samantha enters a classroom where two students are talking. When they stop their discussion, Samantha is certain they must have been talking about her. Such a belief is an example of
  a. the imaginary audience.
  b. the personal fable.
  c. abstract egocentrism.
  d. formal operations.

16. What cognitive changes occurring during middle adulthood are the most noticeable?
  a. Changes in memory begin to occur.
  b. Problem-solving skills diminish.
  c. Hearing begins to decline.
  d. Hair begins to turn gray.

17. Independence and self-reliance in the teenage years is the most likely due to _____ parenting.
  a. authoritarian
  b. authoritative
  c. permissive neglectful
  d. permissive indulgent

18. The crisis of late adulthood, according to Erikson, is
  a. identity versus role confusion.
  b. generativity versus stagnation.
  c. intimacy versus isolation.
  d. integrity versus despair.

19. Which theory of aging states that unstable oxygen molecules tend to steal electrons as they bounce around, thus causing damage to surrounding cells?
  a. cellular clock theory
  b. wear-and-tear theory
  c. free radical theory
  d. activity theory

20. Kip is worried that he is losing his mind because he finds himself angry at a friend who died in an automobile accident. Based on Kübler-Ross's research, what might you tell him?
  a. Anger of this type is self-destructive and unhealthy.
  b. Anger is usually a mask to your true feelings of sadness.
  c. Anger toward a deceased individual is simply not normal and may require psychological counseling.
  d. Anger is a normal reaction to death and not a sign of mental illness.

Chapter 9

Motivation, Stress, and Emotion

Jennifer got excellent grades in high school. She was involved in a variety of activities, but her classes always came first, and she earned an academic scholarship to college. The scholarship required her to maintain a 3.0 GPA—something that she didn't think would be too difficult. Jennifer really enjoyed her college courses as well as the newfound freedoms of college life. With the abundance of social opportunities, she found several new activities to pursue and devoted less time to studying. She was shocked when she got a D on her first exam. She vowed to do better but finished the semester with only a 2.0 GPA and lost her scholarship.

With the help of her academic advisor, Jennifer was able to identify time-management and study strategies and learn to balance her academic and social lives. Her renewed focus enabled her to raise her GPA, later regain and maintain her scholarship, and ultimately graduate.

As a busy college student, how do you stay motivated to succeed?

Video

00:00 / 02:28

Why study motivation, stress, and emotion?

The study of motivation not only helps us understand why some people are more driven to achieve than others but also why we experience certain drives such as hunger. How do we deal with the stresses that come with such drives or that appear when our basic drives are not met? Sexual behavior is another motivated activity, one that many struggle to understand—why are there different sexual orientations, for example? Emotions are a part of everything we do, affecting our relationships with others and our own health, as well as influencing important decisions. In this chapter, we will explore the motives behind our actions and the origins and influences of emotions.

Learning Objectives

9.1 Define motivation, and discuss the key elements of the early instinct and drive-reduction approaches to motivation.

9.2 Explain the characteristics of the three types of needs.

9.3 Identify and explain the key elements of the arousal and incentive approaches to motivation.

9.4 Compare and contrast Maslow's humanistic approach and the self-determination theory.

9.5 Define stress and stressors, and describe two methods for coping with stress.

9.6 Identify the physical and social factors that influence hunger.

9.7 Identify factors that contribute to obesity.

9.8 Explain the motivation for sexual behavior.

9.9 Distinguish among the various sexual orientations, and identify some potential influences on sexual orientation.

9.10 Describe and discuss the three elements of emotion.

9.11 Compare and contrast the common-sense, James–Lange, and Cannon–Bard theories of emotion.

9.12 Identify the key elements in cognitive arousal theory, the facial feedback hypothesis, and the cognitive-mediational theory of emotion.

9.13 Summarize the five steps of the GTD method.

Understanding Motivation

Some people are content to sit and watch life pass them by, while others seem to need far more out of life. Some people want to do great things, while others are happy with more ordinary lives. What motivates people to do the things they do? What exactly is motivation?

EARLY APPROACHES TO UNDERSTANDING MOTIVATION

9.1 **Define motivation, and discuss the key elements of the early instinct and drive-reduction approaches to motivation.**

Motivation is the process by which activities are started, directed, and continued so that physical or psychological needs or wants are met (Petri, 1996). The word itself comes from the Latin word *movere*, which means "to move." Motivation is what "moves" people to do the things they do. For example, when a person is relaxing in front of the television and begins to feel hungry, the physical need for food might cause the person to get up, go into the kitchen, and search for something to eat. The physical need of hunger caused the action (getting up), directed it (going to the kitchen), and sustained the search (finding or preparing something to eat). Hunger is only one example, of course. Loneliness may lead to calling a friend or going to a place where there are people. The desire to get ahead in life motivates many people to go to college. Sexual arousal may motivate a person to look for a sexual partner. Just getting out of bed in the morning is motivated by the need to keep a roof over one's head and food on the table by going to work.

EXTRINSIC AND INTRINSIC MOTIVATION There are different types of motivation. Sometimes people are driven to do something because of an external reward (or the avoidance of an unpleasant consequence), as when someone goes to work at a job to make money and avoid losing possessions such as a house or a car. **L I N K** to Learning Objective 5.5. In **extrinsic motivation**, a person performs an action because it leads to an outcome that is separate from the person (Ryan & Deci, 2000). Other examples would be giving a child money for every "A" on a report card, offering a bonus to an employee for increased performance, or tipping a server in a restaurant for good service. The child, employee, and server are motivated to work for the external or extrinsic rewards. In contrast, **intrinsic motivation** is the type of motivation in which a person performs an action because the act itself is rewarding or satisfying in some internal manner. Psychologist Teresa Amabile (Amabile et al., 1976) found that children's creativity was affected by the kind of motivation for which they worked: Extrinsic motivation decreased the degree of creativity shown in the experimental group's artwork when compared to the creativity levels of the children in the intrinsically motivated control group. To learn more about the factors motivating your behavior, complete the survey *What Motivates You?*

INSTINCTS AND THE EVOLUTIONARY APPROACH Early attempts to understand motivation focused on the biologically determined and innate patterns of behavior called **instincts** that exist in both people and animals. Just as animals are governed by their instincts to migrate, build a nest, mate, and protect their territory, evolutionary theorists proposed that human beings may also be governed by similar instincts (James, 1890; McDougall, 1908). For instance, according to these theorists, the human instinct to reproduce is responsible for sexual behavior, and the human instinct for territorial protection may be related to aggressive behavior.

"How much would you pay for all the secrets of the universe? Wait, don't answer yet. You also get this six-quart covered combination spaghetti pot and clam steamer. Now, how much would you pay?"

Survey   WHAT MOTIVATES YOU?

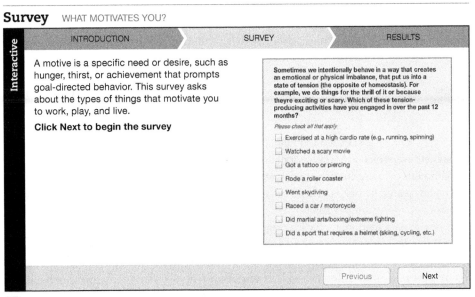

| INTRODUCTION | SURVEY | RESULTS |

A motive is a specific need or desire, such as hunger, thirst, or achievement that prompts goal-directed behavior. This survey asks about the types of things that motivate you to work, play, and live.

Click Next to begin the survey

Sometimes we intentionally behave in a way that creates an emotional or physical imbalance, that put us into a state of tension (the opposite of homeostasis). For example, we do things for the thrill of it or because they're exciting or scary. Which of these tension-producing activities have you engaged in over the past 12 months?

Please check all that apply

☐ Exercised at a high cardio rate (e.g., running, spinning)
☐ Watched a scary movie
☐ Got a tattoo or piercing
☐ Rode a roller coaster
☐ Went skydiving
☐ Raced a car / motorcycle
☐ Did martial arts/boxing/extreme fighting
☐ Did a sport that requires a helmet (skiing, cycling, etc.)

Previous   Next

◉ **Simulate** the **Experiment,** *What Motivates You?*

Dr. Tom Kane

Missouri State Psychology Department

Self-Challenge and Motivation

William McDougall (1908) proposed a total of 18 instincts for humans, including curiosity, flight (running away), pugnacity (aggressiveness), and acquisition (gathering possessions). As the years progressed, psychologists added more and more instincts to the list until there were thousands of proposed instincts. However, none of these early theorists did much more than give names to these instincts. Although there were plenty of descriptions, such as "submissive people possess the instinct of submission," there was no attempt to explain why these instincts exist in humans, if they exist at all (Petri, 1996).

Instinct approaches have faded away because, although they could describe human behavior, they could not explain it. But these approaches did force psychologists to realize that some human behavior is controlled by hereditary factors. This idea remains central in the study of human behavior today. For example, research on the genetics of both cognitive and behavioral traits suggests that hereditary factors can account for more than 50 percent of the variance in some aspects of human cognition, temperament, and personality; and much of this variance is due to the influence of multiple genes or hereditary factors, not just one (Kempf & Weinberger, 2009; Plomin et al., 1994; Plomin & Spinath, 2004).

DRIVE-REDUCTION THEORY   The next approach to gain support involved the concepts of needs and drives. A **need** is a requirement for some material (such as food or water) that is essential for survival of the organism. When an organism has a need, it leads to a psychological tension as well as a physical arousal that motivates the organism to act in order to fulfill the need and reduce the tension. This tension is called a **drive** (Hull, 1943).

Drive-reduction theory proposes just this connection between internal physiological states and outward behavior. In this theory, there are two kinds of drives. **Primary drives** involve the survival needs of the body such as hunger, thirst, and sexual intercourse, whereas **acquired (secondary) drives** are learned through experience or conditioning, such as the need for money or social approval, or the need of recent former smokers to have something to put in their mouths. If this sounds familiar, it should. The concepts of primary and secondary reinforcers from Chapter Four are related to these drives. Primary reinforcers satisfy primary drives, and secondary reinforcers satisfy acquired, or secondary, drives. ⓁⒾⓃⓀ to Learning Objective 5.5.

(left) The human body needs water, especially when a person is working hard or under stress, as this man appears to be. Thirst is a survival need of the body, making it a primary drive, according to drive-reduction theory. What other kinds of needs might be primary drives?

(right) Some people are driven to do strenuous, challenging activities even when there is no physical need to do so. When a drive is acquired through learning, it is called an acquired or secondary drive. Fulfilling an acquired drive provides secondary reinforcement. What might this rock climber find reinforcing about scaling this steep cliff?

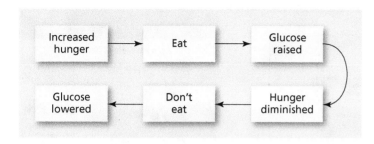

Figure 9.1 Homeostasis

In homeostasis, the body maintains balance in the body's physical states. For example, this diagram shows how increased hunger (a state of imbalance) prompts a person to eat. Eating increases the level of glucose (blood sugar), causing the feelings of hunger to decrease. After a period without eating, the glucose levels become low enough to stimulate the hunger drive once again, and the entire cycle is repeated.

Sean Combs at the Cannes International Film Festival. Many people who are as wealthy as him continue to buy new houses, businesses, clothing, and cars (among other things) even though they do not need them. Such actions are examples of the need for power. How might this need for power be expressed in a person's relationships with others, such as a spouse, employee, or friend?

This theory also includes the concept of **homeostasis**, or the tendency of the body to maintain a steady state. One could think of homeostasis as the body's version of a thermostat—thermostats keep the temperature of a house at a constant level, and homeostasis does the same for the body's functions. When there is a primary drive need, the body is in a state of imbalance. This stimulates behavior that brings the body back into balance, or homeostasis. For example, if Jarrod's body needs food, he feels hunger and the state of tension/arousal associated with that need. He will then seek to restore his homeostasis by eating something, which is the behavior stimulated to reduce the hunger drive (see **Figure 9.1**).

Although drive-reduction theory works well to explain the actions people take to reduce tension created by needs, it does not explain all human motivation. People don't always seek to reduce their inner arousal—sometimes they seek to increase it. Bungee-jumping, parachuting as a recreation, rock climbing, and watching horror movies are all activities that increase the inner state of tension and arousal, and many people love doing these activities. Why? The answer is complex: There are different types of needs, different effects of arousal, different incentives, and different levels of importance attached to many forms of behavior. The following theories explore some of these factors in motivation.

APPROACHES BASED ON PSYCHOLOGICAL NEEDS

9.2 Explain the characteristics of the three types of needs.

Obviously, motivation is about needs. Drive-reduction theory talks about needs, and other theories of motivation include the concept of needs. In many of these theories, most needs are the result of some inner physical drive (such as hunger or sex) that demands to be satisfied, but other theories examine our psychological needs.

MCCLELLAND'S THEORY: AFFILIATION, POWER, AND ACHIEVEMENT NEEDS Harvard University psychologist David C. McClelland (1961, 1987) proposed a theory of motivation that highlights the importance of three psychological needs not typically considered by the other theories: affiliation, power, and achievement.

According to McClelland, human beings have a psychological need for friendly social interactions and relationships with others. Called the **need for affiliation** (abbreviated as nAff in McClelland's writings), people high in this need seek to be liked by others and to be held in high regard by those around them. This makes high-affiliation people good team players, whereas a person high in achievement just might run over a few team members on the way to the top.

A second psychological need proposed by McClelland is the **need for power (nPow)**. Power is not about reaching a goal but about having control over other people. People high in this need would want to have influence over others and make an impact on them. They want their ideas to be the ones that are used, regardless of whether or not their ideas will lead to success. Status and prestige are important, so these people wear expensive clothes, live in expensive houses, drive fancy cars, and dine in the best restaurants. Whereas someone who is a high achiever may not need a lot of money to validate the achievement, someone who is high in the need for power typically sees the money (and cars, houses, jewelry, and other "toys") as the achievement.

The **need for achievement (nAch)** involves a strong desire to succeed in attaining goals, not only realistic ones but also challenging ones. People who are high in nAch look for careers and hobbies that allow others to evaluate them because these high achievers also need to have feedback about their performance in addition to the achievement of reaching the goal. Although many of these people do become wealthy, famous, and publicly successful, others fulfill their need to achieve in ways that lead only to their own personal success, not material riches—they just want the challenge. Achievement motivation appears to be strongly related to success in school, occupational success, and the quality and amount of what a person produces (Collins et al., 2004; Gillespie et al., 2002; Spangler, 1992).

How might the three types of needs discussed in this section relate to the goals of many politicians? Would some needs be more important than others?

▶ The response entered here will be saved to your notes and may be collected by your instructor if he/she requires it.

Submit

PERSONALITY AND nAch: CAROL DWECK'S SELF-THEORY OF MOTIVATION

💬 How do people get to be high achievers?

According to motivation and personality psychologist Carol Dweck (1999), the need for achievement is closely linked to personality factors, including a person's view of how *self* (the beliefs a person holds about his or her own abilities and relationships with others) can affect the individual's perception of the success or failure of his or her actions. This concept is related to the much older notion of locus of control, in which people who assume that they have control over what happens in their lives are considered to be internal in locus of control, and those who feel that their lives are controlled by powerful others, luck, or fate are considered to be external in locus of control (MacDonald, 1970; Rotter, 1966).

Dweck has amassed a large body of empirical research, particularly in the field of education, to support the idea that people's "theories" about their own selves can affect their level of achievement motivation and their willingness to keep trying to achieve success in the face of failure (Dweck, 1986; Dweck & Elliott, 1983; Dweck & Leggett, 1988; Elliott & Dweck, 1988). According to this research, people can form one of two belief systems about intelligence, which in turn affects their motivation to achieve. Those who believe intelligence is fixed and unchangeable often demonstrate an external locus of control, leading them to give up easily or avoid situations in which they might fail—often ensuring their own failure in the process (Dweck & Molden, 2008). They are prone to developing learned helplessness, the tendency to stop trying to achieve a goal because past failure has led them to believe that they cannot succeed. **L I N K** to Learning Objective 5.12.

Their goals involve trying to "look smart" and outperform others ("See, at least I did better than she did"). For example, a student faced with a big exam may avoid coming to class that day, even though that might mean getting an even lower score on a makeup exam.

This does not mean that students with this view of intelligence are always unsuccessful. In fact, Dweck's research (1999) suggests that students who have had a long history of successes may be most at risk for developing a learned helplessness after a big failure precisely because their previous successes have led them to believe in their own fixed intelligence. For example, a child who had never earned anything less than an A in school who then receives his first C might become depressed and refuse to do any more homework, ensuring future failure.

The other type of person believes that intelligence is changeable and can be shaped by experiences and effort in small increases, or increments. These people tend to show an internal locus of control, believing that their own actions and efforts will improve their intelligence (Dweck & Molden, 2008). They work at developing new strategies and get involved in new tasks with the goal of increasing their "smarts." They are motivated to master tasks, and they don't allow failure to destroy their confidence in themselves or prevent them from trying again and again, using new strategies each time.

Based on this and other research, Dweck recommends that parents and teachers praise efforts and the methods that children use to make those efforts, not just successes or ability. Instead of saying, "You're right, how smart you are," the parent or teacher should say something such as, "You are really thinking hard," or "That was a very clever way to think about this problem." In the past, teachers and parents have been told that praise is good

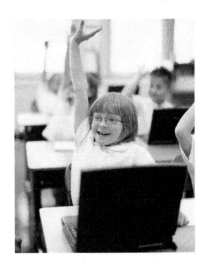

Many people are driven by a need to attain both realistic and challenging goals. This young girl seems eager to provide an answer to the teacher's question, and the teacher's positive feedback will help foster the girl's need for achievement.

and criticism is bad because it might damage a child's self-esteem. Dweck believes that constructive criticism, when linked with praise of effort and the use of strategies, will be a better influence on the child's self-esteem and willingness to challenge themselves than endless praise that can become meaningless when given indiscriminately (Gunderson et al., 2013).

AROUSAL AND INCENTIVE APPROACHES

9.3 Identify and explain the key elements of the arousal and incentive approaches to motivation.

Another explanation for human motivation involves the recognition of yet another type of need, the need for stimulation. A **stimulus motive** is one that appears to be unlearned but causes an increase in stimulation. Examples would be curiosity, playing, and exploration. On the other hand, sometimes our motives for doing things involve the rewards or *incentives* we get when we act, such as eating food even when we are not hungry just because it tastes so good—an example of learned behavior.

AROUSAL THEORY In **arousal theory**, people are said to have an optimal (best or ideal) level of tension. Task performances, for example, may suffer if the level of arousal is too high (such as severe test anxiety) or even if the level of arousal is too low (such as boredom). For many kinds of tasks, a moderate level of arousal seems to be best. This relationship between task performance and arousal has been explained by the **Yerkes–Dodson law** (Teigen, 1994; Yerkes & Dodson, 1908), although Yerkes and Dodson formulated the law referring to stimulus intensity, not arousal level (Winton, 1987).

Of special interest to both sports psychologists and social psychologists, this effect is modified by the difficulty level of the task: Easy tasks demand a somewhat "high-moderate" level for optimal performance, whereas difficult tasks require a "low-moderate" level. **Figure 9.2** shows this relationship in graphic form.

Maintaining an optimal level of arousal, then, may involve reducing tension or creating it (Hebb, 1955). For example, husbands or wives who are underaroused may pick a fight with their spouse. Students who experience test anxiety (a high level of arousal) may seek out ways to reduce that anxiety in order to improve test performance. Students who are not anxious at all may not be motivated to study well, lowering their test performance. Many arousal theorists believe that the optimal level of arousal for most people under normal circumstances is somewhere in the middle, neither too high nor too low.

 If people are supposed to be seeking a level of arousal somewhere around the middle, why do some people love to do things like bungee-jumping?

Even though the average person might require a moderate level of arousal to feel content, some people need less arousal and some need more. The person who needs more arousal is called a **sensation seeker** (Zuckerman, 1979, 1994). Sensation seekers seem to need more complex and varied sensory experiences than do other people. The need does not always have to involve danger. For example, students who travel to other countries to study tend to score higher on scales of sensation seeking than do students who stay at home (Schroth & McCormack, 2000). Sensation seeking may be related to temperament. ⓛ ⓘ ⓝ ⓚ to Learning Objective 8.9. **Table 9.1** has some sample items from a typical sensation-seeking scale.

In one study (Putnam & Stifter, 2002), researchers found evidence of sensation-seeking behavior in children as young as age 2. In this study, 90 children were studied at the ages of 6, 12, 24, and 25 months. In a test of the youngest participants, the babies were shown two sets of toys: (1) a block, a plate, and a cup; and (2) a flashing light, a toy beeper, and a wind-up dragon. The first set was considered a low-intensity stimulus, whereas the second set was labeled a high-intensity stimulus. The infants who reached out for the toys more quickly, particularly the high-intensity toys, were high sensation seekers.

Figure 9.2 Arousal and Performance

The optimal level of arousal for task performance depends on the difficulty of the task. We generally perform easy tasks well if we are at a high-moderate level of arousal (green) and accomplish difficult tasks well if we are at a low-moderate level (red).

Table 9.1 Sample Items from the Zuckerman–Kuhlman Personality Questionnaire

Scale Item	Sensation Seeking
I sometimes do "crazy" things just for fun.	High
I prefer friends who are excitingly unpredictable.	High
I am an impulsive person.	High
Before I begin a complicated job, I make careful plans.	Low
I usually think about what I am going to do before doing it.	Low

Source: Adapted from Zuckerman (2002).

Is a sensation-seeking personality something people have when they are born? Although it is tempting to think of 6-month-old children as having little in the way of experiences that could shape their personalities, the fact is that the first six months of life are full of experiences that might affect children's choices in the future. For example, a very young infant might, while being carried, stick a hand into some place that ends up causing pain. This experience might affect that infant's willingness in the future to put his or her hand in something else through the simple learning process of operant conditioning. ⓁⒾⓃⓀ to Learning Objective 5.5. In a longitudinal study taking place over about four years, researchers found that adolescents who played video games in which high risk-taking is positively presented became more likely to engage in risky behavior and had increased scores on levels of sensation-seeking (Hull et al., 2012).

INCENTIVE APPROACHES

💬 Last Thanksgiving, I had eaten about all I could. Then my aunt brought out a piece of her wonderful pumpkin pie and I couldn't resist—I ate it, even though I was not at all hungry. What makes us do things even when we don't have the drive or need to do them?

It's true that sometimes there is no physical need present, yet people still eat, drink, or react as if they did have a need. Even though that piece of pie was not necessary to reduce a hunger drive, it was very rewarding, wasn't it? And on past occasions, that pie was also delicious and rewarding, so there is anticipation of that reward now. The pie, in all its glorious promise of flavor and sweetness, becomes an incentive to eat. **Incentives** are things that attract or lure people into action.

In **incentive approaches**, behavior is explained in terms of the external stimulus and its rewarding properties. These rewarding properties exist independently of any need or level of arousal and can cause people to act only upon the incentive. Thus, incentive theory is actually based, at least in part, on the principles of learning that were discussed in Chapter Five. ⓁⒾⓃⓀ to Learning Objective 5.5.

By itself, the incentive approach does not explain the motivation behind all behavior. Many theorists today see motivation as a result of both the "push" of internal needs or drives and the "pull" of a rewarding external stimulus. For example, sometimes a person may actually be hungry (the push) but choose to satisfy that drive by selecting a candy bar instead of a celery stick. The candy bar has more appeal to most people, and it therefore has more "pull" than the celery. (Frankly, to most people, just about anything has more pull than celery.)

HUMANISTIC APPROACHES

9.4 Compare and contrast Maslow's humanistic approach and the self-determination theory.

Some final approaches to the study of motivation are humanistic in nature. One of the classic humanistic approaches is that of Maslow, while a more modern approach is represented by self-determination theory.

Does this look fun? If so, you may score relatively higher in sensation seeking.

Figure 9.3 MASLOW'S HIERARCHY OF NEEDS

Study the pyramid, then click "Check Your Understanding" when you're ready.

Maslow proposed that human beings must fulfill the more basic needs, such as physical and security needs, before being able to fulfill the higher needs of self-actualization and transcendence.

Transcendence needs
to find spiritual meaning beyond one's immediate self

Self-actualization needs
to find self-fulfillment and realize one's potential

Aesthetic needs
to appreciate symmetry, order, and beauty

Cognitive needs
to know, understand, and explore

Esteem needs
to achieve, be competent, gain approval and recognition

Belongingness and love needs
to be with others, be accepted, and belong

Safety needs
to feel secure and safe, out of danger

Physiological needs
to satisfy hunger, thirst, fatigue, etc.

Check Your Understanding

In the movie *Castaway*, Tom Hanks's character is stranded on a deserted island. Once he has his needs for food, water, and shelter met, he gets lonely. He finds a volleyball, paints a handprint and then a crude face on it, and names it "Wilson." He talks to the volleyball as if it were a person, at first as a kind of way to talk out the things he needs to do and later as a way of staying relatively sane. The need for companionship is that strong.

MASLOW'S HIERARCHY OF NEEDS The first humanistic theory is based on the work of Abraham Maslow (1943, 1987). Maslow proposed that there are several levels of needs that a person must strive to meet before achieving the highest level of personality fulfillment. According to Maslow, **self-actualization** is the point that is seldom reached at which people have satisfied the lower needs and achieved their full human potential.

These needs include both fundamental deficiency needs, such as the need for food or water, and growth needs, such as the desire for having friends or feeling good about oneself (Maslow, 1971; Maslow & Lowery, 1998). For a person to achieve self-actualization, which is one of the highest levels of growth needs, the primary, fundamental needs must first be fulfilled. The only need higher than self-actualization is transcendence, a search for spiritual meaning beyond one's immediate self, which Maslow added many years after his original hierarchy was formulated. **Figure 9.3** shows the typical way to represent Maslow's series of needs as a pyramid, with the most basic needs for survival at the bottom and the highest needs at the top. This type of ranking is called a hierarchy.*

People move up the pyramid as they go through life, gaining wisdom and the knowledge of how to handle many different situations. But a shift in life's circumstances can result in a shift down to a lower need. Moving up and down and then back up can occur frequently—even from one hour to the next. The times in a person's life in which self-actualization is achieved, at least temporarily, are called **peak experiences**. For Maslow, the process of growth and self-actualization is the striving to make peak experiences happen again and again.

Maslow's theory has had a powerful influence on the field of management (Heil et al., 1998) and has spawned new ideas and concepts of what might be an appropriate revised hierarchy. **LINK** to Learning Objective B.7. In spite of this influence, Maslow's theory is not without its critics. There are several problems with his theory, and the most serious is that there is little scientific support (Drenth et al., 1984). Like Sigmund Freud, Maslow developed his theory based on his own observations of people rather than any

---

*hierarchy: a graded or ranked series.

empirically gathered observations or research. Although many people report that while they were starving, they could think of nothing but food, there is anecdotal evidence in the lives of many people, some of them quite well known, that the lower needs do not have to be satisfied before moving on to a higher need (Drenth et al., 1984). For example, artists and scientists throughout history have been known to deny their own physical needs while producing great works (a self-actualization need).

  💬 Does this theory apply universally?

Maslow's work was based on his studies of Americans. Cross-cultural research suggests that the order of needs on the hierarchy does not always hold true for other cultures, particularly those cultures with a stronger tendency than U.S. culture to avoid uncertainty, such as Greece and Japan. In those countries security needs are much stronger than self-actualization needs in determining motivation (Hofstede, 1980; Hofstede et al., 2002). This means that people in those cultures value job security more than they do job satisfaction (holding an interesting or challenging job). In countries such as Sweden and Norway that stress quality of life over what a person produces, social needs may be more important than self-actualization needs (Hofstede et al., 2002). Ⓛ Ⓘ Ⓝ Ⓚ Learning Objective 11.11.

Other theorists (Alderfer, 1972; Kenrick et al., 2010) have developed and refined Maslow's hierarchy. Douglas Kenrick and colleagues have suggested a modification to Maslow's original hierarchy that encompasses aspects of evolutionary biology, anthropology, and psychology. Their modification incorporates dynamics between internal motives and environmental threats and opportunities (Kenrick et al., 2010). This revision has not been without critique and has spawned further contemplation. Some elements of Kenrick's theory have been challenged, including a questioning of its focus on evolutionary aspects instead of human cultural influences (Kesebir et al., 2010) and its removal of self-actualization from both the pinnacle of the pyramid and from the hierarchy altogether as a stand-alone motive (Peterson & Park, 2010). Just as there are many aspects to motivation, any revision or discussion of an appropriate hierarchy of needs will need to take into account a wide variety of opinions and viewpoints.

SELF-DETERMINATION THEORY (SDT) Another theory of motivation that is similar to Maslow's hierarchy of needs is the **self-determination theory (SDT)** of Richard Ryan and Edward Deci (2000). In this theory, there are three inborn and universal needs that help people gain a complete sense of self and whole, healthy relationships with others. The three needs are autonomy, or the need to be in control of one's own behavior and goals (i.e., self-determination); competence, or the need to be able to master the challenging tasks of one's life; and relatedness, or the need to feel a sense of belonging, intimacy, and security in relationships with others. These needs are common in several theories of personality; the relatedness need is, of course, similar to Maslow's belongingness and love needs, and both autonomy and competence are important aspects of Erikson's theory of psychosocial personality development (Erikson, 1950, 1980). Ⓛ Ⓘ Ⓝ Ⓚ to Learning Objective 8.9.

Ryan, Deci, and their colleagues (Deci et al., 1994; Ryan & Deci, 2000) believe that satisfying these needs can best be accomplished if the person has a supportive environment in which to develop goals and relationships with others. Such satisfaction will not only foster healthy psychological growth but also increase the individual's intrinsic motivation (actions are performed because the act is internally rewarding or satisfying). Evidence suggests that intrinsic motivation is increased or enhanced when a person not only feels competence (through experiencing positive feedback from others and succeeding at what are perceived to be challenging tasks) but also a sense of autonomy or the knowledge that his or her actions are self-determined rather than controlled by others (deCharms, 1968; Deci & Ryan, 1985).

Previous research has found a negative impact on intrinsic motivation when an external reward is given for the performance (Deci et al., 1999), while other studies find

"That is the correct answer, Bill, but I'm afraid you don't win anything for it."
©The New Yorker Collection 1986 Lee Lorenz from cartoonbank.com All Rights Reserved.

negative effects only for tasks that are not interesting in and of themselves (Cameron et al., 2001). When the task itself is interesting to the person (as might be an assignment that an instructor or manager has explained in terms of its importance and future value), external rewards may increase intrinsic motivation, at least in the short term. Although this finding is intriguing, further research is needed to determine if the long-term effects of extrinsic rewards on intrinsic motivation are consistently negative, as the bulk of the research has shown up to now.

💬 But don't we sometimes do things for both kinds of motives?

There are usually elements of both intrinsic and extrinsic motives in many of the things people do. Most teachers, for example, work for money to pay bills (the extrinsic motive) but may also feel that they are helping young children to become better adults in the future, which makes the teachers feel good about themselves (the intrinsic motive).

How universal are these three needs? Some cultures, such as the United States and Great Britain, are *individualistic*, stressing the needs of the individual over the group, independence, and self-reliance. Other cultures are collectivistic, such as those in Japan and China, and stress strong social ties, interdependence, and cooperation. Cross-cultural research indicates that even across such different cultures, the needs for autonomy, mastery, and belongingness are of similar importance (Chirkov, 2009; Chirkov et al., 2011; Ryan et al., 1999; Sheldon, 2012).

MOTIVATION AND STRESS

9.5 Define stress and stressors, and describe two methods for coping with stress.

Earlier, we discussed the concepts of drive reduction and arousal theory and their role in motivational behavior. These concepts are all related to the concept of **stress**, the physical, emotional, cognitive, and behavioral responses to events seen as threatening or challenging. When basic drives are unmet, stress is often the result. For example, when you are hungry, you may experience hunger pains, anxiety, an inability to concentrate, and a physical restlessness until that hunger drive is sated—all signs of stress. In arousal theory, a certain level of arousal in each of those areas is needed for optimum performance, and too much or too little can result in poor outcomes. A certain amount of stress seems to be good for you, in other words.

Taking a test is just one of many possible stressors in a college student's life. What aspects of college life have you found to be stressful? Do other students experience the same degree of stress in response to the same stressors?

Most people experience some degree of stress on a daily basis, and college students are even more likely to face situations and events that require them to make changes and adapt their behavior: Assigned readings, papers, studying for tests, juggling jobs, car problems, relationships, and dealing with deadlines are all examples of things that can cause a person to experience stress.

STRESSORS Stress-causing events are called stressors; they can come from within a person or from an external source and range from relatively mild to severe. Events that can become stressors range from being stuck behind a person in the 10-items-or-less lane of the grocery store who has twice that amount, to dealing with the rubble left after a tornado or a hurricane destroys one's home. Stressors can range from the deadly serious (hurricanes, fires, crashes, combat) to the merely irritating and annoying (delays, rude people, losing one's car keys).

When most of us think of stressors, we think of **distress**, which occurs when people experience unpleasant stressors. One example of distress is a **catastrophe**, an unpredictable event that happens on a large scale and creates tremendous amounts of stress and feelings of threat. Wars, hurricanes, floods, fires, airplane crashes, and other disasters are catastrophes. Although it's easy to think about big disasters and major changes in life as sources of stress, the bulk of the stresses we experience daily actually come from little frustrations, delays, irritations, minor disagreements, and similar small aggravations. These daily annoyances are called **hassles** (Lazarus, 1993; Lazarus & Folkman, 1984).

There's actually a second kind of stressor: an event that causes *eustress*, which results from positive events that still make demands on a person to adapt or change. Marriage, a job promotion, and having a baby may all be positive events for most people, but they all require a great deal of change in people's habits, duties, and often lifestyle, thereby creating stress. Hans Selye (1936) originally coined the term eustress to describe the stress experienced when positive events require the body to adapt. In an update of Selye's original definition, researchers now define **eustress** as the optimal amount of stress that people need to promote health and well-being.

Thomas Holmes and Richard Rahe (1967) believed that any life event that required people to change, adapt, or adjust their lifestyles would result in stress. Like Selye, they assumed that both negative events (such as getting fired) and positive events (such as getting a promotion) demand that a person adjust in some way, and so both kinds of events are associated with stress.

In addition to external stressors, there are also internal, psychological reasons why people find certain events stressful. When there are urgent demands or expectations for a person's behavior coming from an outside source, that person is experiencing **pressure**. Pressure occurs when people feel that they must work harder, faster, or do more, as when meeting a deadline or studying for final exams.

Another factor that increases a person's experience of stress is the degree of control that the person has over a particular event or situation. The less control a person has, the greater the degree of stress. Researchers in both clinical interviews and experimental studies have found that lack of control in a situation actually increases stress disorder symptoms (Breier et al., 1987; Henderson et al., 2012).

Frustration occurs when people are blocked or prevented from achieving a desired goal or fulfilling a perceived need. As a stressor, frustration can be *external*, such as when a car breaks down, a desired job offer doesn't come through after all, or a theft results in the loss of one's belongings. *Internal frustrations*, also known as *personal frustrations*, occur when the goal or need cannot be attained because of internal or personal characteristics. For example, someone who wants to be an astronaut might find that severe motion sickness prevents him or her from such a goal.

Conflict is the psychological distress that occurs when a person has to choose between different and incompatible or opposing goals. These goals can be physical needs, psychological drives, wishes, or even external demands. There are several forms of conflict.

In an **approach–approach conflict**, a person experiences a desire for two goals, each of which is attractive. An example of this conflict might be the need to choose between the chocolate cake or the key lime pie for dessert.

Avoidance–avoidance conflicts are much more stressful than approach–approach. In this conflict, the choice is between two or more goals or events that are unpleasant. Because neither alternative is pleasant, many people avoid making a choice by delaying decisions (Tversky & Shafir, 1992). For example, people who are fearful of dental procedures might face the conflict of suffering the pain of a toothache or going to the dentist.

Approach–avoidance conflicts are a little different in that they only involve one goal or event. That goal or event may have both positive and negative aspects that make the goal appealing and unappealing at the same time. For example, marriage is a big decision to make for anyone and usually has both its attractive features, such as togetherness, sharing good times, and companionship, and also its negative aspects, such as disagreements, money issues, and mortgages.

COPING STRATEGIES **Coping strategies** are actions that people can take to master, tolerate, reduce, or minimize the effects of stressors, and they can include both behavioral strategies and psychological strategies.

One type of coping strategy is to work on eliminating or changing the stressor itself. When people try to eliminate the source of a stress or reduce its impact through their own actions, it is called **problem-focused coping** (Folkman & Lazarus, 1980; Lazarus, 1993). For example, a student might have a problem understanding a particular professor. The professor is knowledgeable but has trouble explaining the concepts of the course in a way that this student can understand. Problem-focused coping might include talking to the professor after class, asking fellow students to clarify the concepts, getting a tutor, or forming a study group with other students who are also having difficulty to pool the group's resources.

Problem-focused coping can work quite well but is not the only method people can use. Most people use both problem-focused coping and **emotion-focused coping** to successfully deal with controllable stressful events (Eschenbeck et al., 2008; Folkman & Lazarus, 1980; Lazarus, 1993; Stowell et al., 2001). Emotion-focused coping is a strategy that involves changing the way a person feels or emotionally reacts to a stressor. This reduces the emotional impact of the stressor and makes it possible to deal with the problem more effectively. For example, the student who is faced with a professor who isn't easy to understand might share his concerns with a friend, talking it through until calm enough to tackle the problem in a more direct manner. Emotion-focused coping also works for stressors that are uncontrollable and for which problem-focused coping is not possible. Someone using emotion-focused coping may decide to view the stressor as a challenge rather than a threat, decide that the problem is a minor one, write down concerns in a journal, or even ignore the problem altogether.

💬 Ignore it? But won't that just make matters worse?

True, ignoring a problem is not a good strategy when there is something a person can actively do about solving the problem. But when it is not possible to change or eliminate the stressor, or when worrying about the stressor can be a problem itself, ignoring the problem is not a bad idea. Researchers working with people who had suffered heart attacks found that those people who worried about a future attack were more likely to suffer from symptoms of severe stress, such as nightmares and poor sleep (both factors that increase the risk of a future heart attack), than were the people who tried to ignore their worries (Ginzburg et al., 2003). **LINK** to Learning Objective 12.4.

One stressor that cannot be ignored for long is hunger, the topic of the next section.

Concept Map L.O. 9.1, 9.2, 9.3, 9.4, 9.5

Interactive

- **types**
  - **intrinsic:** actions are rewarding or satisfying in and of themselves
  - **extrinsic:** actions are performed because they lead to some sort of external outcome
- **instinct**
  - biologically determined/innate patterns of behavior
  - old approach: instincts are mainly descriptions, not explanations; idea that some behavior is hereditary remains an important focus
- **drive reduction**
  - **need:** requirement for something essential for survival; existence of need leads to psychological tension (drive) and physical arousal; satisfying need reduces drive/tension
  - **primary drives** involve survival needs (e.g., hunger, thirst) and maintaining homeostasis
  - **acquired (secondary) drives** are learned through experience or conditioning (e.g., money, social approval)
- **psychological needs**
  - psychological needs have been highlighted in some theories (e.g., McClelland)
    - need for **achievement (nAch)**
    - need for **affiliation (nAff)**
    - need for **power (nPow)**
  - Dweck suggests that the need for achievement is linked to a person's view of self (fixed or changeable) and locus of control

Approaches to Understanding Motivation

(process by which activities are started, directed, and continued so that physical or psychological needs or wants are met)

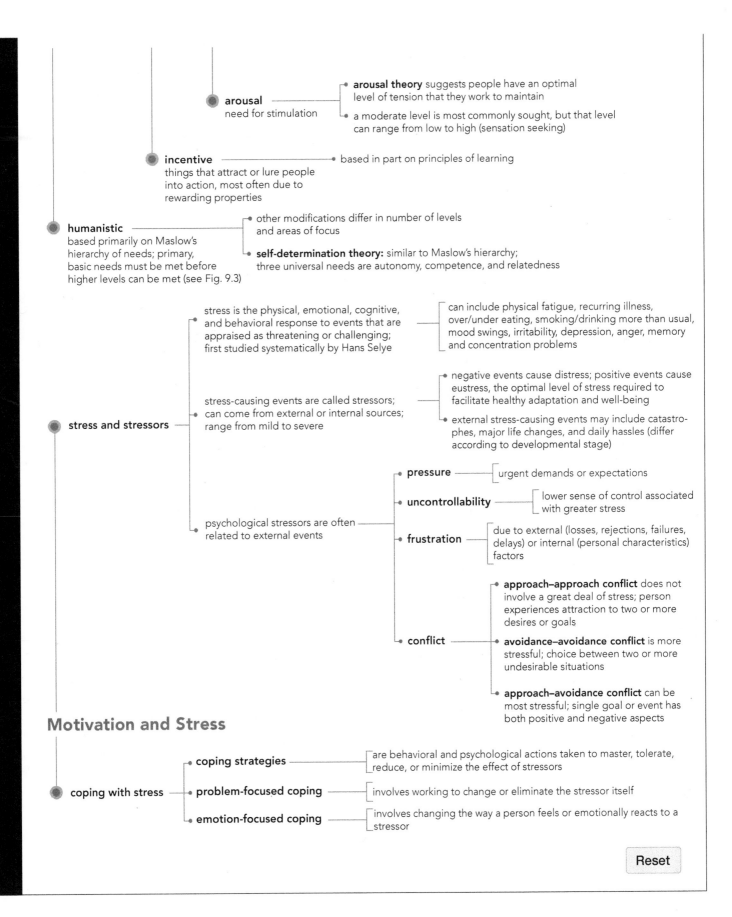

arousal
need for stimulation

arousal theory suggests people have an optimal level of tension that they work to maintain

a moderate level is most commonly sought, but that level can range from low to high (sensation seeking)

incentive
things that attract or lure people into action, most often due to rewarding properties

based in part on principles of learning

humanistic
based primarily on Maslow's hierarchy of needs; primary, basic needs must be met before higher levels can be met (see Fig. 9.3)

other modifications differ in number of levels and areas of focus

self-determination theory: similar to Maslow's hierarchy; three universal needs are autonomy, competence, and relatedness

stress and stressors

stress is the physical, emotional, cognitive, and behavioral response to events that are appraised as threatening or challenging; first studied systematically by Hans Selye

can include physical fatigue, recurring illness, over/under eating, smoking/drinking more than usual, mood swings, irritability, depression, anger, memory and concentration problems

stress-causing events are called stressors; can come from external or internal sources; range from mild to severe

negative events cause distress; positive events cause eustress, the optimal level of stress required to facilitate healthy adaptation and well-being

external stress-causing events may include catastrophes, major life changes, and daily hassles (differ according to developmental stage)

psychological stressors are often related to external events

pressure — urgent demands or expectations

uncontrollability — lower sense of control associated with greater stress

frustration — due to external (losses, rejections, failures, delays) or internal (personal characteristics) factors

conflict

approach–approach conflict does not involve a great deal of stress; person experiences attraction to two or more desires or goals

avoidance–avoidance conflict is more stressful; choice between two or more undesirable situations

approach–avoidance conflict can be most stressful; single goal or event has both positive and negative aspects

Motivation and Stress

coping with stress

coping strategies — are behavioral and psychological actions taken to master, tolerate, reduce, or minimize the effect of stressors

problem-focused coping — involves working to change or eliminate the stressor itself

emotion-focused coping — involves changing the way a person feels or emotionally reacts to a stressor

Reset

Practice Quiz   How much do you remember? ANSWERS ON PAGE AK-1.

Pick the best answer.

1. If a person carries out a behavior to receive an outcome that is separate from the person, this is known as

  a. intrinsic motivation.

  b. extrinsic motivation.

  c. drive-reduction motivation.

  d. instinctual motivation.

2. William McDougall's original research on instinctual motivation proposed a total of _____ instincts for humans, whereas later researchers believed there were _____.

  a. 5; 25

  b. 18; 50

  c. 18; thousands

  d. 100; millions

3. What motivational theory relies heavily on the concept of homeostasis?

  a. instinctual theory

  b. need for affiliation theory

  c. drive-reduction theory

  d. need for achievement theory

4. According to research by Carol Dweck, which of the following would be the best phrase to reinforce a child's behavior?

  a. I'm proud of the way you tried to solve that problem.

  b. Good job. You got the right answer.

  c. Well done. But you must try even harder next time.

  d. Excellent. Now go out and do it again.

5. According to arousal theory, people are motivated toward _____ level of arousal.

  a. their highest

  b. their lowest

  c. their optimum

  d. their minimal

6. In Ryan and Deci's self-determination theory, what is the key to achieving one's needs for autonomy, competence, and relatedness?

  a. an instinctual motivation

  b. support from others around you

  c. a motivation often driven by heredity

  d. a driving desire not to be a failure

7. Studies show that _____ is the optimal amount of stress that people need to positively promote their health and sense of well-being, which coincides with _____ theory.

  a. intensity; cognitive consistency

  b. distress; biological instinct

  c. eustress; arousal

  d. eustress; Maslow's

What, Hungry Again? Why People Eat

Eating is not only a basic survival behavior that reduces a primary drive; it is also a form of entertainment for many and the attractive presentations and social environment of many eating experiences are a powerful incentive.

THE PHYSIOLOGICAL AND SOCIAL COMPONENTS OF HUNGER

9.6 Identify the physical and social factors that influence hunger.

The physical hunger drive involves several factors. If the stomach is empty and contracted, hunger usually occurs. Another factor is the insulin response. **Insulin** and **glucagon** are hormones that are secreted by the pancreas to control the levels of fats, proteins, and carbohydrates in the whole body, including glucose (blood sugar). Insulin, normally released in greater amounts after eating has begun, causes a feeling of more hunger because of a drop in blood sugar levels. ⓛⓘⓝⓚ to Learning Objective 2.6. High blood sugar (which is more likely when one eats sugary foods and white breads, rice, and pasta) leads to more insulin released, which leads to a low blood sugar level, increased appetite, and the tendency to overeat.

When released into the bloodstream, the hormone **leptin** signals the hypothalamus that the body has had enough food, reducing appetite. Also, part of the hypothalamus stops the eating response as blood sugar increases, while another part controls the beginning of eating as insulin levels go up (Neary et al., 2004). ⓛⓘⓝⓚ to Learning Objective 2.11.

The physical controls of hunger are not enough to explain all eating behavior. People often eat when they are not really hungry or just because the food looks so good or smells so good. Social cues also tell people to eat, such as the convention of eating breakfast, lunch, and dinner at certain times. A large part of that convention is actually the result of classical conditioning. Ⓛ Ⓘ Ⓝ Ⓚ to Learning Objective 5.2. The body becomes conditioned to respond with the hunger reflex at certain times of the day; through association with the act of eating, those times of the day have become conditioned stimuli for hunger. Classical conditioning may cause insulin levels to increase even before food is eaten, just as Pavlov's dogs salivated before getting food (Rodin, 1981, 1985).

Cultural factors and gender also play a part in determining hunger and eating habits. In one study, a questionnaire about eating habits was given to both men and women from the United States and Japan. Although no significant differences in what initiates eating existed for men in either culture, women in the United States were found to be much more likely to start eating for emotional reasons, such as depression. Japanese women were more likely to eat because of hunger signals or social demands (Hawks et al., 2003). In this same study, both men and women from the United States were more likely to eat while watching television or movies than were Japanese men and women. Both culture and gender must be taken into account when studying why and under what circumstances people eat.

To see whether you have any implicit preferences toward either healthy food or junk food, participate in the experiment *Implicit Association Test: Food*.

(top) Cultural factors play an important part in why people eat. Women in Japan have been found to be motivated to eat by hunger and social demands, illustrated by the interaction during a meal at this family gathering.

(bottom) Women in the United States may eat because they are depressed or for other emotional reasons, rather than just to appease hunger or as part of a social situation. Obviously, this woman does not need the social trappings of a bowl, dining table, and the company of others to motivate her eating habits—unless you count the cat.

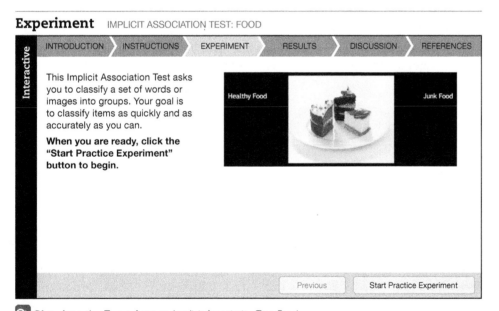

Experiment   IMPLICIT ASSOCIATION TEST: FOOD

| INTRODUCTION | INSTRUCTIONS | EXPERIMENT | RESULTS | DISCUSSION | REFERENCES |

This Implicit Association Test asks you to classify a set of words or images into groups. Your goal is to classify items as quickly and as accurately as you can.

When you are ready, click the "Start Practice Experiment" button to begin.

Healthy Food   Junk Food

Previous   Start Practice Experiment

◉ **Simulate** the **Experiment**, *Implicit Association Test: Food.*

OBESITY

9.7 Identify factors that contribute to obesity.

Several maladaptive eating problems, including anorexia nervosa, bulimia nervosa, and binge-eating disorder, are classified as clinical (mental) disorders in the *Diagnostic and Statistical Manual of Mental Disorders, Fifth Edition*, or *DSM-5* (American Psychiatric Association, 2013), which is a listing of disorders and their symptoms used by psychological professionals to make a diagnosis. These disorders are discussed in a later chapter. Ⓛ Ⓘ Ⓝ Ⓚ to Learning Objective 12.11.

In this chapter, we look at the problem of obesity. Why do some people get fat? Is it just overeating?

Several factors contribute to obesity, a condition in which the body weight of a person is 20 percent or more over the ideal body weight for that person's height. A significant factor in obesity is heredity. There appear to be several sets of genes, some on different chromosomes, which influence a person's likelihood of becoming obese (Barsh et al., 2000). If there is a history of obesity in a particular family, each family member has a risk of becoming obese that is double or triple the risk of people who do not have a family history of obesity (Bouchard, 1997). Hormones also play a part, particularly leptin. Problems with leptin production or detection can lead to overeating (Friedman & Halaas, 1998).

Another factor is certainly overeating. Around the world, as developing countries get stronger economies and their food supplies become stable, the rates of obesity increase dramatically and quickly (Barsh et al., 2000). Foods become more varied and enticing* as well, and an increase in variety is associated with an increase in eating beyond the physiological need to eat (Raynor & Epstein, 2001). In industrialized societies when workers spend more hours in the workplace, there is less time available for preparing meals at home and more incentive to dine out (Chou et al., 2004). When the "dining out" choices include fast food and soft drinks, as is so often the case, obesity rates increase. At about 31 percent (nearly a third of its population), the United States has the highest rate of obesity in the world (Flegal et al., 2010, Friedman, 2000, 2003; Marik, 2000; Mokdad et al., 2001). Over the last 20 years, rates of obesity in developing countries have tripled. Of children from developing countries such as China, the Middle East, Southeast Asia, and the Pacific Islands, 10 to 25 percent are overweight and another 2 to 10 percent are obese (Hossain et al., 2007).

Metabolism slows down as people age. Aside from not changing the eating habits of their youth and lowering their intake, as they earn more income people also often increase the amount of food they consume, thereby assuring a weight gain that may lead to obesity.

---

*enticing: attractive; desirable.

Concept Map L.O. 9.6, 9.7

Interactive

- **hunger**
  - impacted by insulin response; insulin (normally released more after onset of eating) reduces level of glucose in bloodstream (resulting in lower blood sugar and increased hunger); glucagon increases level of glucose
  - ventromedial area of the hypothalamus may be involved in stopping eating when glucose level goes up; lateral hypothalamus appears to influence onset of eating when insulin level goes up
  - person's weight set point and basal metabolic rate are tied to hypothalamus, and the hormone leptin appears to affect appetite
  - hunger and eating behaviors are influenced by social cues and convention (e.g., eating at certain times), culture, and gender

Why People Eat

- **maladaptive eating**
  - **obesity:** body weight 20% or more over ideal (based on height); significantly impacted by genetics, overeating, exercise, and changes in metabolism
  - anorexia nervosa
  - bulimia nervosa
  - binge-eating disorder

  (L)(I)(N)K to Chapter Twelve, Psychological Disorders

Reset

Practice Quiz   How much do you remember? ANSWERS ON PAGE AK-1.

Pick the best answer.

1. Which of the following is *not* a hormone that influences eating behaviors in human beings?

   a. leptin

   b. insulin

   c. serotonin

   d. glucagon

2. Jermaine eats a late breakfast at 10:00 a.m. but finds he is hungry at 11:30 a.m. when he typically eats lunch. What best explains his hunger pains only 90 minutes after eating breakfast?

   a. heredity

   b. social pressure

   c. classical conditioning

   d. self-actualization

3. In a study examining the influence of culture on individual eating habits, researchers found that women from the United States were more likely to eat in response to _____, whereas women from Japan were more likely to eat in response to _____.

   a. stress; depression

   b. being instructed that it was "mealtime"; being told "you will not have another chance to eat today."

   c. the smell of fresh food; the sight of fresh food

   d. emotional cues; hunger signals or social demands

4. In order for a person to be categorized as obese, their body weight would be at least _____ percent higher than would be considered ideal for their height.

   a. 10   **c.** 30

   b. 20   **d.** 40

Sexual Motivation

Yet another motivating factor that is hard to ignore and often causes stress is our sexual behavior. The study of sexual behavior is not the study of the sex act but rather when, with whom, and under what circumstances sexual acts take place.

SEXUAL BEHAVIOR

9.8 Explain the motivation for sexual behavior.

Although other attempts were made to study human sexual behavior before the mid-twentieth-century studies of Alfred Kinsey (Kinsey et al., 1948; Kinsey et al., 1953), his original work remains an important source of information concerning the different ways in which people engage in the sex act. A well-received movie based on Kinsey's life and work was released in the United States in 2004. Remarkably, even more than half a century later and well into the sexual revolution, Kinsey's work is still so controversial that many movie theaters in the United States refused to show the film.

 What were the findings of the report?

THE KINSEY STUDY   In 1948, Alfred Kinsey published a controversial report on the results of a massive survey of sexual behavior he had collected over 10 years (Kinsey et al., 1948). His findings concerning the frequency of behavior such as masturbation, anal sex, and premarital sex rocked many people, who were apparently not ready to believe that so many people had tried alternative sexual behaviors. Kinsey believed that sexual orientation was not an either/or situation in which one is either completely heterosexual or completely homosexual but instead that sexual orientation is on a continuum* with some people falling at either extreme and some falling closer to the middle. The idea that there were many people who fit into that middle range of sexual orientation was shocking and, for many, unbelievable.

Kinsey used highly trained interviewers who conducted face-to-face interviews with the participants, who were all male in the original study. A later survey was published in 1953 that dealt exclusively with females (Kinsey et al., 1953). The participants

Alfred Kinsey conducted many of his interviews face-to-face, as seen here. How might having to answer questions about one's sexual behavior be affected by Kinsey's presence?

---

*continuum: a sequence of values, elements, or behavior that varies by small degrees.

were volunteers supposedly from both rural and urban areas and from different socioeconomic, religious, and educational backgrounds. In reality, a large portion of the participants were well-educated, urban, young Protestants. In Kinsey's survey results, nearly half of the men but less than 20 percent of the women reported having bisexual experiences. More than three times as many men as women had intercourse by age 16 (21 percent versus 6 percent). Men were also more likely to report engaging in premarital sex, extramarital sex, and masturbation than were women. Ten percent of the men and 2 to 6 percent of the women answering the survey identified themselves as predominantly homosexual (Gebhard & Johnson, 1979/1998).

Although Kinsey's data are still quoted in many discussions of sexual behavior, his original surveys were far from perfect. As stated earlier, the participants were almost exclusively white, middle class, and college educated. Older people, those who lived in rural regions, and less educated people were not well represented. Some critics claimed that Kinsey gave far more attention to sexual behavior that was considered unusual or abnormal than he did to "normal" sexual behavior (Geddes, 1954). Also, Kinsey's surveys were no less susceptible to the exaggerations, falsifications, and errors of any method using self-report techniques. Finally, a face-to-face interview might cause some people being interviewed to be inhibited about admitting to certain kinds of sexual behavior, or others might exaggerate wildly, increasing the likelihood of inaccurate data.

THE JANUS REPORT   In 1993, Dr. Samuel S. Janus and Dr. Cynthia L. Janus published the results of the first large-scale study of human sexual behavior since those of Kinsey and colleagues (1948) and Masters and Johnson (1966). This national survey, begun in 1983, sampled 3,000 people from all 48 mainland states. Professors in the fields of sociology, psychology, psychiatry, history, biology, and political science received special training in the survey method and supervised experienced graduate student researchers who also collected survey data. Data were collected through interviews and mass questionnaires. Survey respondents ranged in age from 18 to over 65 and represented all levels of marital status, educational backgrounds, and geographical regions in the United States.

One finding of this massive survey was that nearly 80 percent of men and 70 percent of women had masturbated (although about a fourth to a third stated that this occurred rarely). Other responses indicated that 19 percent of men and nearly 8 percent of women had been involved in full sexual intercourse by age 14. Premarital sex was more commonly reported in men than in women (67 percent for males, 46 percent for females), and men were nearly twice as likely as women to report having had at least one extramarital affair. Whereas more than a fifth of the male respondents and only slightly fewer female respondents reported having at least one homosexual experience, only 9 percent of males and 5 percent of females identified themselves as predominantly homosexual.

EXPLAINING THE SURVEY FINDINGS   Why are men so much more sexually active than women, both before and during marriage? It may be in their genes. Evolutionary theory emphasizes that organisms will do what they must to maximize their chances of passing on their genetic material in their offspring, and that process is different for men and women. Robert Trivers proposed a theory of parental investment to explain the different sexual behavior of men and women (Trivers, 1972). Males of many species, including humans, do not have to invest a lot of time or effort into impregnating a female, so they are better off—genetically speaking—when they seek many sexual encounters with many sexual partners. Females, on the other hand, invest much more time and effort in reproducing: the pregnancy, feeding the infants, and so on. So females are better off being more selective about the males they choose for sex.

In real life terms, this translates into men preferring women who are younger, prettier (immediate sexual attraction being the big draw), and therefore are likely to produce healthy, attractive offspring. Women are more likely to prefer men who are older (which means they will likely have more income and resources), hard workers, and loyal (Buss, 1989, 2007; Buss & Schmitt, 1993, 2011). Men are much more likely than women to have multiple sexual partners, even well into middle age, while women are more likely to have fewer partners over their lifetime (McBurnery et al., 2005; Schutzwohl et al., 2009). This is true for both heterosexual and homosexual men and women (Peplau & Fingerhut, 2007). Men even think about sex differently, having more sexual fantasies than women and of a greater variety (Okami & Shackelford, 2001) as well as simply thinking about sex more often than women (Laumann et al., 1994).

One survey highlights the fact that age is not necessarily a barrier to being sexually active. The survey of over 3,000 people aged 57 to 85 found that many people are sexually active well into their eighties (Lindau et al., 2007). The most common barriers to sexual activity are health problems or lack of a partner rather than lack of desire.

SEXUAL ORIENTATION

9.9 **Distinguish among the various sexual orientations, and identify some potential influences on sexual orientation.**

💬 What makes some people attracted to the same sex?

The term **sexual orientation** refers to a person's sexual attraction and affection for members of either the opposite or the same sex. One of the more important questions that researchers are trying to answer is whether sexual orientation is the product of learning and experience or whether it is biological in origin. As the video *Categories of Sexual Orientation* shows, there are a variety of sexual orientation categories that individuals may identify with, and getting reliable data can be challenging.

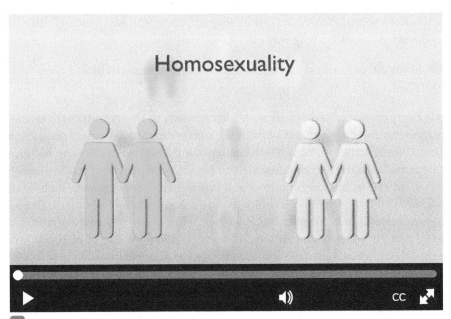

👁 **Watch** the **Video**, *Categories of Sexual Orientation.*

HETEROSEXUAL   The most common sexual orientation is **heterosexual**, in which people are sexually attracted to members of the opposite physical sex, as in a man being attracted to a woman or vice versa. (The Greek word *hetero* means "other," so heterosexual means "other sexual" or attraction for the other sex.) Heterosexuality is a socially acceptable form of sexual behavior in all cultures.

HOMOSEXUAL   It is difficult to get an accurate percentage for **homosexual** orientation, or sexual attraction to members of one's own sex. (The Greek word *homo* means "same.") The problem concerns the discrimination, prejudice, and mistreatment that homosexual people face in most cultures, making it more likely that a homosexual person will lie about his or her sexual orientation to avoid such negative treatment. A national survey

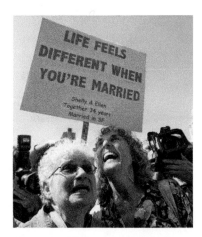

Homosexuality is a sexual orientation that has faced discrimination and prejudice in many cultures. Shelly Bailes and Ellen Pontac, partners for 34 years, highlight the fact that their "coupleness" and a sense of commitment are not limited to heterosexual pairs alone.

estimates that about 2.3 percent of men and 1.3 percent of women aged 15 to 44 years consider themselves to be homosexuals, meaning that their sexual orientations are exclusively or predominantly homosexual (Mosher et al., 2005).

 ● If people have had homosexual as well as heterosexual experiences, does that make them bisexuals?

BISEXUAL   A person who is **bisexual** may be either male or female and is attracted to both sexes. In the same national survey, only 1.8 percent of the men and 2.8 percent of the women considered themselves to be bisexual (Mosher et al., 2005). (It should be noted that many people experiment with alternative sexual behavior before deciding upon their true sexual identity; one bisexual experience does not make a person bisexual any more than one homosexual experience makes a person homosexual.)

Bisexual people do not necessarily have relationships with both men and women at the same time and may vary in the degree of attraction to one sex or the other over time. Many bisexuals may not act on their desires but instead have a long-term monogamous relationship with only one partner.

The survey also found that a nearly equal percentage of men and women—just fewer than 4 percent—considered themselves to be "something else." Obviously, sexual orientation is not as clearly defined as many people have assumed.

DEVELOPMENT OF SEXUAL ORIENTATION   Although heterosexuality may be socially acceptable across cultures, in various cultures homosexuality and bisexuality are not considered acceptable and so people of those orientations have faced prejudice, discrimination, harassment, and much worse. Although attitudes in these cultures are becoming more positive (Loftus, 2001; Tucker & Potocky-Tripodi, 2006), full acceptance of alternatives to heterosexuality is still a long way off.

 ● Is sexual orientation a product of the environment, biology, or both?

This is a very controversial issue for both heterosexuals and homosexuals (Diamond, 1995). If homosexuality is a product of upbringing and environmental experiences, it can be assumed to be a behavior that can be changed, placing a burden of choice to be "normal" or "abnormal" squarely on the shoulders of homosexual people. If it is biological, either through genetic influences or hormonal influences during pregnancy, then it can be seen as a behavior that is no more a choice than whether the infant is born a male or a female. The implications of homosexuality as biological lead to some volatile* issues: If it is not a choice or a learned behavior pattern, then society will no longer be able to expect or demand that homosexuals change their sexual behavior or orientation. Homosexuality then becomes an issue of diversity rather than one of socially unacceptable behavior. In a survey of college students (Elliott & Brantley, 1997), the majority of women reported knowing they were gay or bisexual by their high school/college years, while the majority of men reported knowing they were gay or bisexual by junior high/high school.

In the past several decades, a large body of research in the areas of biological differences in the brains of heterosexual and homosexual males, genetic influences on sexual orientation, and even prenatal influences on sexual orientation has been amassed. One of the earliest studies, for example, found that severe stress experienced by pregnant women during the second trimester of pregnancy (the time during which the sexual differences in genitalia are formed) results in a significantly higher chance of any male children becoming homosexual in orientation (Ellis et al., 1988). Another study found that homosexual men and heterosexual women respond similarly (and quite differently

---

*volatile: explosive.

than heterosexual men) to a testosterone-based pheromone (glandular chemical) that is secreted in perspiration (Savic et al., 2005).

In a recent study, researchers have found that while there has yet to be any actual gene found for the transmission of homosexuality, there are genetic "switches" that can be passed on and which may be the reason that homosexuality tends to run in families (Rice et al., 2012). These switches, called *epi-marks*, control when, where, and how much of the information contained in our genes is expressed. There are sex-specific epi-marks that control the sexual characteristics of the fetus during prenatal development. These sexual characteristics include not only physical sex organ development but also sexual identity and sexual partner preference. Normally epi-marks are created anew with each generation, but occasionally remain to be passed on to the next generation. When that happens, they may cause the reverse of their intended effect, including a reversal of sexual orientation.

Birth order has also been the subject of research in this area, with studies suggesting that the more older brothers a man has, the more likely the younger man is to be homosexual in orientation (Blanchard, 2001; McConaghy et al., 2006). The hypothesis is that with each male birth, the mother of these males develops a kind of "antibody" effect against the Y chromosome and these antibodies pass through the placenta and affect the sexual orientation of the later born males.

Finally, a study used neuroimaging techniques on heterosexual men and women and homosexual men and women. It found that the heterosexual men and homosexual women (both attracted to women, remember) seemed neurologically similar; while homosexual men and heterosexual women (both attracted to males) were neurologically similar (Savic & Lindström, 2008).

The evidence for genetic influences on sexual orientation is increasingly convincing. In studies of male and female homosexuals who have identical twins, fraternal twins, or adopted siblings, researchers found that 52 percent of the identical twin siblings were also gay, compared to 22 percent of the fraternal twins and only 11 percent of the adopted brothers and sisters (Bailey & Pillard, 1991). In a similar study with lesbian women only, 48 percent of identical twins were also gay compared to 16 percent of the fraternal twins and 6 percent of the adopted siblings (Bailey et al., 1993). Other research along similar lines has supported these findings (Bailey et al., 2000; Dawood et al., 2000). However, these findings, too, should be interpreted with caution. Twin studies are difficult to conduct without the influence of environment on behavior. Even twins who are raised apart tend to be reared in similar environments, so that the influence of learning and experience on sexual orientation cannot be entirely ruled out.

Some research suggests that homosexuality may be transmitted by genes carried on the X chromosome, which is passed from mother to son but not from father to son. In 33 out of 40 homosexual brothers, Dean Hamer and colleagues (Hamer et al., 1993) found an area on the X chromosome (in a location called Xq28) that contains several hundred genes that the homosexual brothers had in common in every case, even though other genes on that chromosome were different. This was taken as evidence that the brothers had both inherited a set of genes, donated on the mother's X chromosome, which might be responsible for their sexual orientation. These findings have since been supported in other research (Hu et al., 1994; Turner, 1995).

One of the most common behavioral findings about male homosexuals is that they are consistently "feminine" as children, according to developmental psychologist J. Michael Bailey (Bailey & Zucker, 1995). Bailey has determined that about three-fourths of homosexual male adults were "feminine" boys (defined as boys who were uninterested in sports or rough play, desired to be girls, or had a reputation as a "sissy"), a far greater rate than in the general population of males. Bailey and colleague Ken Zucker interpret these findings as further support for the biological foundations of sexual orientation. Of course, those differences in childhood behavior could also have been the result of attention and other forms of reinforcement from the social environment. It is simply very difficult to separate environmental from biological influences on any aspect of behavior.

One thing is certain: The issue of what causes sexual orientation will continue to generate research and controversy for a long time to come.

Some scientists have wondered why homosexuality still exists, because from an evolutionary point of view—if it is genetic—the genes for homosexuality should have been removed from the gene pool long ago. The following special section takes a look at this issue.

Issues in Psychology
What Is the Evolutionary Purpose of Homosexuality?

Homosexuals do not often reproduce, so why hasn't the trait gone away? One recent theory has to do with something called the "kin selection hypothesis." Even though a homosexual member of a family may not reproduce himself or herself, by nurturing other family members such as nieces and nephews, they would be helping to continue many of their own genes through those kin (Iemmola & Camperio Ciani, 2008; Rahman & Hull, 2005). In Samoa, researchers Paul Vasey and Doug VanderLaan (Vasey & VanderLaan, 2010) studied the *fa'afafine*, men who prefer men as sexual partners and are accepted within that culture as neither man nor woman, much as the *winkte* in Lakota culture. Seeking to determine whether the kin selection hypothesis was a valid hypothesis in this society, the researchers gave fa'afafine, women, and heterosexual men in this culture a survey to measure their willingness to help nieces and nephews in various ways, as well as their willingness to do these same things for unrelated children. The survey results strongly support the kin selection hypothesis, with the fa'afafine far more likely than the women or heterosexual men to help their own kin rather than children in general.

Questions for Further Discussion

1. Samoan culture is not like Western culture. Would the kin selection hypothesis work in the United States to explain homosexuality's continued existence?

2. How do Western homosexual men and women transmit or protect their own genetic material?

Concept Map L.O. 9.8, 9.9

Interactive

differences in sexual behavior
— Kinsey pioneered the study of different types of sexual behavior through face-to-face surveys; study was highly controversial; sampling/representativeness questioned
— suggested sexual orientation occurred on a continuum, not an either/or basis
— the Janus Report (first large-scale survey since Kinsey) examined both normal and deviant sexual behavior

Sexual Motivation

sexual orientation
person's sexual attraction and affection for members of the opposite or same sex

— key concepts
— sexual orientation is likely the product of both biology (i.e., brain structure, genetics) and environment; presence of biological foundations has implications for societal definitions of diversity versus deviance

heterosexuality: attraction to members of the opposite sex; most common and socially acceptable

homosexuality: attraction to members of one's own sex

bisexuality: attraction to members of both sexes

Reset

Practice Quiz   How much do you remember? ANSWERS ON PAGE AK-1.

Pick the best answer.

1. Which of the following was a criticism of Kinsey's research?
  a. The study was incomplete.
  b. The study asked poorly worded questions.
  c. The study was rushed.
  d. The study had a restricted sample.

2. The largest study of human sexual behavior conducted since the work of Alfred Kinsey was begun in 1983, and was spearheaded by:
  a. Alfred Kinsey, Jr.
  c. Sharf and Titus
  b. Janus and Janus
  d. Maron and Butcher

3. Robert Trivers's theory of _____ states one must consider the extent to which pregnancy will require them to make an investment of time and effort when deciding whether to have sex with a potential partner.
  a. parental investment
  c. sexual fluidity
  b. gender schemata
  d. sexual orientation

4. The Savic et al. 2005 study found that homosexual men responded to a pheromone in the same way as
  a. heterosexual men.
  c. heterosexual women.
  b. transsexual men.
  d. homosexual women.

Understanding Emotion

This chapter began with an overview of the motives that drive human behavior. But people do more than just behave—they experience feelings during every human action. Human beings are full of feelings, or emotions, and although emotions may be internal processes, there are outward physical signs of what people are feeling. This section of the chapter explores the world of human emotions and how those emotions are connected to both thinking and actions.

 💬 What part does the way we feel about things play in all of our daily activities—what exactly causes feelings?

Human beings are full of feelings, or emotions, and although emotions may be internal processes, there are outward physical signs of what people are feeling.

THE THREE ELEMENTS OF EMOTION

9.10 Describe and discuss the three elements of emotion.

The Latin word meaning "to move" is the source of both words used in this chapter over and over again—motive and emotion. **Emotion** can be defined as the "feeling" aspect of consciousness, characterized by three elements: a certain physical arousal, a certain behavior that reveals the feeling to the outside world, and an inner awareness of feelings. Before we examine the three elements of emotion, take a moment to complete the survey *How Do You Deal With Your Emotions?* to learn more about how you identify, express, and manage your emotions.

Survey   HOW DO YOU DEAL WITH YOUR EMOTIONS?

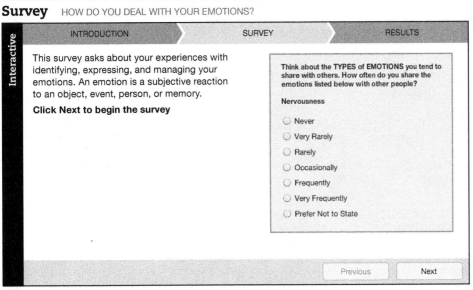

🔵 **Simulate** the **Experiment**, *How Do You Deal With Your Emotions?*

THE PHYSIOLOGY OF EMOTION   Physically, when a person experiences an emotion, an arousal is created by the sympathetic nervous system. Ⓛ Ⓘ Ⓝ Ⓚ to Learning Objective 2.5. The heart rate increases, breathing becomes more rapid, the pupils dilate, and the mouth may become dry. Think about the last time you were angry and then about the last time you were frightened. Weren't the physical symptoms pretty similar? Although facial expressions do differ among various emotional responses (Ekman, 1980; Ekman & Friesen, 1978; Ekman et al., 1969), emotions are difficult to distinguish from one another on the basis of outward bodily reactions alone. For example, it is quite easy to mistake a person who is actually afraid or angry as being aroused if the person's face is not clearly visible, which can lead to much miscommunication and misunderstanding. However, in the laboratory using devices to measure the heart rate, blood pressure, and skin temperature, researchers have found that different emotions may be associated with different physiological reactions: Fear is associated with a decrease in skin temperature, whereas anger is associated with an increase in skin temperature and a greater increase in blood pressure (Larsen et al., 2008; Levenson, 1992; Levenson et al., 1992).

Which parts of the brain are involved in various aspects of emotion? As discussed in Chapter Two, the amygdala, a small area located within the limbic system on each side of the brain, is associated with emotions such as fear and pleasure in both humans and animals (Breiter et al., 1997; Davis & Whalen, 2001; Fanselow & Gale, 2003; Hurlemann et al., 2010; Ritchey et al., 2011) and is also involved in the facial expressions of human emotions (Morris et al., 1998). When the amygdala is damaged in rats, they cannot be classically conditioned to fear new objects—they apparently cannot remember to be afraid (Davidson et al., 2000; Fanselow & Gale, 2003). In humans, damage to the amygdala has been associated with similar effects (LaBar et al., 1995) and with impairment of the ability to determine emotions from looking at the facial expressions of others (Adolphs & Tranel, 2003).

Research now suggests that emotional stimuli travel to the amygdala by both a fast, crude "low road" (subcortical) and a slower but more involved cortical "high road" (LeDoux, 1996, 2007; LeDoux & Phelps, 2008). (See **Figure 9.4**.) The direct route

Figure 9.4 THE "LOW ROAD" AND "HIGH ROAD"

When we are exposed to an emotion-provoking stimulus (such as a shark), the neural signals travel by two pathways to the amygdala. The "low road" is the pathway underneath the cortex and is a faster, simpler path, allowing for quick responses to the stimulus, sometimes before we are consciously aware of the nature of the stimulus. The "high road" uses cortical pathways and is slower and more complex, but it allows us to recognize the threat and, when needed, take more conscious control of our emotional responses. In this particular example, the low road shouts, "Danger!" and we react before the high road says, "It's a shark!"

allows for quick responses to stimuli that are possibly dangerous, sometimes before we actually know what the stimuli are. However, with the awareness provided by the indirect cortical route (specifically, processing by the prefrontal cortex), we can override the direct route and take control of our emotional responses (LeDoux, 1996; LeDoux & Phelps, 2008; Öhman, 2008). It is possible that the direct route may be the primary processing pathway for individuals with emotional disorders (LINK to Learning Objective 12.4) and the indirect, cortical pathway is not able to override the processing initiated by the direct route. This would result in difficulty or inability to control our emotions, or inability to extinguish fears we've already acquired (LeDoux, 1996; LeDoux & Phelps, 2008).

💬 Emotions even work differently depending on which side of the brain is involved.

One area of investigation has been the frontal lobes. Researchers have found that positive emotions are associated with the left frontal lobe of the brain, whereas negative feelings such as sadness, anxiety, and depression seem to be a function of the right frontal lobe (Davidson, 2003; Geschwind & Iacoboni, 2007; Heilman, 2002). In studies where the electrical activity of the brain has been tracked using an electroencephalograph, LINK to Learning Objective 2.8, left frontal lobe activation has been associated with pleasant emotions while right frontal lobe activity has been associated with negative emotional states (Davidson, 2003). Furthermore, increased left frontal lobe activity has been found in individuals trained in meditation, and for the participants in this study, greater left frontal lobe activity was accompanied by a reduction in their anxiety as well as a boost in their immune system (Davidson et al., 2003).

The ability to interpret the facial expressions of others as a particular emotion also seems to be a function of one side of the brain more than the other. Researchers have found that when people are asked to identify the emotion on another person's face, the right hemisphere is more active than the left, particularly in women (Voyer & Rodgers, 2002). This difference begins weakly in childhood but increases in adulthood, with children being less able to identify negative emotions as well as positive emotions when compared to adults (Barth & Boles, 1999; Lane et al., 1995). This finding is consistent with early research that assigns the recognition of faces to the right hemisphere (Berent, 1977; Ellis, 1983).

Other types of emotional processing involve a variety of other brain areas. Different brain areas take primary roles based on the different ways you use to control your emotions, but there is a degree of overlap across several of the strategies. For example, some common strategies for regulating one's emotions include distraction, reappraisal, and controlling the influence of emotions on decision making. All three of these strategies take advantage of the lateral prefrontal cortex and anterior cingulate cortex and, as you might expect from the earlier discussion, the amygdala also comes into play (Beer, 2009). However, distraction appears to be supported by activity in the anterior cingulate cortex, and reappraisal is supported by activity in the lateral orbitofrontal cortex; both are accompanied by lower activity in the amygdala (Beer, 2009).

THE BEHAVIOR OF EMOTION: EMOTIONAL EXPRESSION   How do people behave when they are in the grip of an emotion? Facial expressions, body movements, and actions indicate to others how a person feels. Frowns, smiles, and sad expressions combine with hand gestures, the turning of one's body, and spoken words to produce an understanding of emotion. People fight, run, kiss, and yell along with countless other actions stemming from the emotions they feel.

Facial expressions can vary across different cultures, although some aspects of facial expression seem to be universal. (See **Figure 9.5** on the next page for some examples of universal facial expressions.) Charles Darwin (1898) was one of the first to theorize that emotions were a product of evolution and, therefore, universal: all human

Figure 9.5 Facial Expressions of Emotion

Facial expressions appear to be universal. For example, these faces are interpreted as showing (a) anger, (b) fear, (c) disgust, (d) happiness, (e) surprise, and (f) sadness by people of cultures all over the world. Although the situations that cause these emotions may differ from culture to culture, the expression of particular emotions remains strikingly the same.

beings, no matter what their culture, would show the same facial expression because the facial muscles evolved to communicate specific information to onlookers. For example, an angry face would signal to onlookers that they should act submissively or expect a fight. Darwin's ideas were not in line with the behaviorist movement of the early and middle twentieth century, which promoted environment rather than heredity as the cause of behavior. Nonetheless, other researchers have since found evidence of a universal nature in at least seven basic emotions, giving more support to the evolutionary perspective within psychology (Ekman, 1973; Ekman & Friesen, 1969, 1971). **LINK** to Learning Objective 1.4. Even children who are blind from birth can produce the appropriate facial expressions for any given situation without ever having witnessed those expressions on others. This finding strongly supports the idea that emotional expressions have their basis in biology rather than in learning (Charlesworth & Kreutzer, 1973; Fulcher, 1942).

In their research, Ekman and Friesen found that people of many different cultures (Japanese, Europeans, Americans, and even the Fore tribe of New Guinea) can consistently recognize at least seven facial expressions: anger, fear, disgust, happiness, surprise, sadness, and contempt (Ekman & Friesen, 1969, 1971). Although the emotions and the related facial expressions appear to be universal, exactly when, where, and how an emotion is expressed may be determined by the culture. **Display rules** that can vary from culture to culture (Ekman, 1973; Ekman & Friesen, 1969) are learned ways of controlling displays of emotion in social settings. For example, Japanese people have strict social rules about showing emotion in public situations—they simply do not show emotion, remaining cool, calm, and collected, at least on the outside. But in a more private situation, such as a parent scolding a child within the home, the adult's facial expression would easily be recognized as "angry" by people of any culture. The emotion is universal, and the way it is expressed on the face is universal; whether it is expressed or displayed, however, depends on the learned cultural rules for displaying emotion.

Display rules are different between cultures that are individualistic (placing the importance of the individual above the social group) and those that are collectivistic (placing the importance of the social group above that of the individual). Whereas the culture of the United States is individualistic, for example, the culture of Japan is collectivistic. At least part of the difference between the two types of display rules may be due to these cultural differences (Edelmann & Iwawaki, 1987; Hofstede, 1980; Hofstede et al., 2002). ⓁⒾ Ⓝ Ⓚ to Learning Objective 11.11.

Display rules are also different for males and females. Researchers looking at the display rules of boys and girls found that boys are reluctant to talk about feelings in a social setting, whereas girls are expected and encouraged to do so (Polce-Lynch et al., 1998). With adults, researchers looking at the expression of anger in the workplace found that women are generally less willing than men to express negative emotions, although factors such as status complicate the findings somewhat (Domagalski & Steelman, 2007).

SUBJECTIVE EXPERIENCE: LABELING EMOTION   The third element of emotion is interpreting the subjective feeling by giving it a label: anger, fear, disgust, happiness, sadness, shame, interest, and so on. Another way of labeling this element is to call it the "cognitive element" because the labeling process is a matter of retrieving memories of previous similar experiences, perceiving the context of the emotion, and coming up with a solution—a label.

The label a person applies to a subjective feeling is at least in part a learned response influenced by that person's language and culture. Such labels may differ among people of different cultural backgrounds. For example, researchers in one study (Tsai et al., 2004) found that Chinese Americans who were still firmly rooted in their original Chinese culture were far more likely to use labels to describe their emotions that referred to bodily sensations (such as "dizzy") or social relationships (such as "friendship") than were more "Americanized" Chinese Americans and European Americans, who tended to use more directly emotional words (such as "liking" or "love").

In another study, even the subjective feeling of happiness showed cultural differences (Kitayama & Markus, 1994). In this study, Japanese and U.S. students were found to associate a general positive emotional state with entirely different circumstances. In the case of the Japanese students, the positive state was more associated with friendly or socially engaged feelings. The students from the United States associated their positive emotional state more with feelings that were socially disengaged, such as pride. This finding is a further reflection of the differences between collectivistic and individualistic cultures.

EARLY THEORIES OF EMOTION

9.11 **Compare and contrast the common-sense, James–Lange, and Cannon–Bard theories of emotion.**

   So which of the three elements is the most important?

In the early days of psychology, it was assumed that feeling a particular emotion led first to a physical reaction and then to a behavioral one. This is known as the *common-sense theory of emotion*. Seeing a snarling dog in one's path causes the feeling of fear, which stimulates the body to arousal, followed by the behavioral act of running. People are aroused because they are afraid. (See **Figure 9.6** on the next page.)

Figure 9.6   Common-Sense Theory of Emotion

In the common-sense theory of emotion, a stimulus (snarling dog) leads to an emotion of fear, which then leads to bodily arousal (in this case, indicated by shaking) through the autonomic nervous system (ANS).

	Stimulus	First response	Second response
Common-Sense theory "I'm shaking because I'm afraid."	Snarling dog	*FEAR* Conscious fear	ANS arousal

JAMES–LANGE THEORY OF EMOTION   William James (1884, 1890, 1894), who was also the founder of the functionalist perspective in the early history of psychology, **LINK** to Learning Objective 1.2, disagreed with the idea that emotion led to bodily arousal which then led to action. He believed that the order of the components of emotions was quite different. At nearly the same time, a physiologist and psychologist in Denmark, Carl Lange (1885), came up with an explanation of emotion so similar to James's that the two names are used together to refer to the theory—the **James–Lange theory of emotion**. (See **Figure 9.7**.)

In this theory, a stimulus of some sort (for example, the large snarling dog) produces a physiological reaction. This reaction, which is the arousal of the "fight-or-flight" sympathetic nervous system (wanting to run), produces bodily sensations such as increased heart rate, dry mouth, and rapid breathing. James and Lange believed that the physical arousal led to the labeling of the emotion (fear). Simply put, "I am afraid because I am aroused," "I am embarrassed because my face is red," "I am nervous because my stomach is fluttering," and "I am in love because my heart rate increases when I look at her or him."

What about people who have spinal cord injuries that prevent the sympathetic nervous system from functioning? Although James-Lange would predict that these people should show decreased emotion because the arousal that causes emotion is no longer there, this does not in fact happen. Several studies of people with spinal cord injuries report that these people are capable of experiencing the same emotions after their injury as before, and sometimes even more intensely (Bermond et al., 1991; Chwalisz et al., 1988).

CANNON–BARD THEORY OF EMOTION   Physiologists Walter Cannon (1927) and Philip Bard (1934) theorized that the emotion and the physiological arousal occur more or less at the same time. Cannon, an expert in sympathetic arousal mechanisms, did not feel that the physical changes caused by different emotions were distinct enough to allow them to be perceived as different emotions. Bard expanded on this idea by stating that the sensory information that comes into the brain is sent simultaneously (by the thalamus) to both the cortex and the organs of the sympathetic nervous system. The fear and the bodily reactions are, therefore, experienced at the same time—not one after the other. "I'm afraid and running and aroused!" (See **Figure 9.8**.)

Figure 9.7   James–Lange Theory of Emotion

In the James–Lange theory of emotion, a stimulus leads to bodily arousal first, which is then interpreted as an emotion.

	Stimulus	First response	Second response
James–Lange theory "I'm afraid because I'm shaking."	Snarling dog	ANS arousal, changes in body	*FEAR* Conscious fear

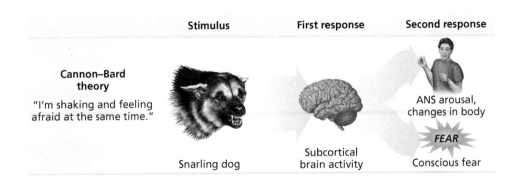

Cannon–Bard theory

"I'm shaking and feeling afraid at the same time."

Snarling dog

Stimulus First response Second response

Subcortical brain activity

ANS arousal, changes in body

FEAR

Conscious fear

Figure 9.8 Cannon–Bard Theory of Emotion

In the Cannon–Bard theory of emotion, a stimulus leads to activity in the brain, which then sends signals to arouse the body and interpret the emotion at the same time.

This theory, known as the **Cannon–Bard theory of emotion**, also had its critics. K. S. Lashley (1938) stated that the thalamus would have to be very sophisticated to make sense of all the possible human emotions and relay them to the proper areas of the cortex and body. It would seem that other areas of the brain must be involved in processing emotional reactions. Studies of people with spinal cord injuries appear to suggest that emotions can be experienced without feedback from the sympathetic organs to the cortex; these studies were cited as a criticism of the James–Lange theory. At first these investigations seem to support the Cannon–Bard version of emotions: People do not need feedback from those organs to experience emotion. However, there is an alternate pathway that does provide feedback from these organs to the cortex; this is the vagus nerve, one of the cranial nerves (LeDoux, 1994). The existence of this feedback pathway makes the case for Cannon–Bard a little less convincing.

MODERN THEORIES OF EMOTION

9.12 **Identify the key elements in cognitive arousal theory, the facial feedback hypothesis, and the cognitive-mediational theory of emotion.**

There are several more modern theories of emotion focusing on cognitive components of emotions in addition to physical and behavioral reactions—the mental interpretation of emotion and behavior.

SCHACHTER-SINGER AND COGNITIVE AROUSAL THEORY OF EMOTION In their **cognitive arousal theory (two-factor theory)**, Schachter and Singer (1962) proposed that two things have to happen before emotion occurs: the physical arousal and a labeling of the arousal based on cues from the surrounding environment. These two events happen at the same time, resulting in the labeling of the emotion. (See **Figure 9.9.**)

For example, if a person comes across a snarling dog while taking a walk, the physical arousal (heart racing, eyes opening wide) is accompanied by the thought (cognition) that this must be fear. Then and only then will the person experience the fear emotion. In other words, "I am aroused in the presence of a scary dog; therefore, I must be afraid."

Schachter-Singer cognitive arousal theory

"This snarling dog is dangerous and that makes me feel afraid."

Snarling dog

Stimulus First response Second response

Cognitive appraisal

ANS arousal, changes in body

FEAR

Conscious fear

Figure 9.9 Schachter–Singer Cognitive Arousal Theory of Emotion

Schachter and Singer's cognitive arousal theory is similar to the James–Lange theory but adds the element of cognitive labeling of the arousal. In this theory, a stimulus leads to both bodily arousal and the labeling of that arousal (based on the surrounding context), which leads to the experience and labeling of the emotional reaction.

The video *Three Theories of Emotion* compares how the James–Lange, Cannon–Bard, and cognitive arousal theory would each explain the emotion of fear.

👁 **Watch** the **Video**, *Three Theories of Emotion.*

Evidence for the cognitive arousal theory was found in what is now a classic experiment, described in the accompanying *Classic Studies in Psychology* feature.

Classic Studies in Psychology
The Angry/Happy Man

In 1962, Stanley Schachter and Jerome Singer designed an experiment to test their theory that emotions are determined by an interaction between the physiological state of arousal and the label, or cognitive interpretation, that a person places on the arousal. Male student volunteers were told that they were going to answer a questionnaire about their reactions to a new vitamin called Suproxin. In reality, they were all injected with a drug called epinephrine, which causes physical arousal in the form of increased heart rate, rapid breathing, and a reddened face—all responses that happen during a strong emotional reaction.

Each student then participated in one of two conditions. In one condition, a confederate* posing as one of the participants started complaining about the experimenter, tearing up his questionnaire and storming out. In the other condition, there was one man who acted more like he was very happy, almost giddy and playing with some of the objects in the room. The "angry" man and the "happy" man in both conditions deliberately behaved in the two different ways as part of the experiment.

After both conditions had played out, participants in each of the two conditions were asked to describe their own emotions. The participants who had been exposed to the "angry" man interpreted their arousal symptoms as anger, whereas those exposed to the "happy" man interpreted their arousal as happiness. In all cases, the actual cause of arousal was the epinephrine, and the physical symptoms of arousal were identical. The only difference between the two groups of participants was their exposure to the two

*confederate: someone who is cooperating with another person on some task.

different contexts. Schachter and Singer's theory would have predicted exactly these results: Physiological arousal has to be interpreted cognitively before it is experienced as a specific emotion.

Although this classic experiment stimulated a lot of research, much of that research has failed to find much support for the cognitive arousal theory of emotion (Reisenzein, 1983, 1994). But this theory did serve to draw attention to the important role that cognition plays in determining emotions. The role of cognition in emotion has been revisited in more modern theories of emotion, as you will see in the following discussions.

Questions for Further Discussion

1. How might observing the emotions of others under more normal circumstances (i.e., not in a drugged state) affect a person's own emotional state?

2. According to Schachter and Singer's theory, for your first date with a person, should you choose a happy movie or a sad one?

3. In this experiment, what was the independent variable manipulated by the experimenters? What was the dependent variable?

4. This experiment used deception, as the participants were not told the true nature of the injection they received. What kind of ethical problems might have arisen from this deception? What problems would the experimenters have had in getting this study approved by an ethics committee today?

THE FACIAL FEEDBACK HYPOTHESIS: SMILE, YOU'LL FEEL BETTER In his (1898) book *The Expression of the Emotions in Man and Animals*, Charles Darwin stated that facial expressions evolved as a way of communicating intentions, such as threat or fear, and that these expressions are universal within a species rather than specific to a culture. He also believed (as in the James–Lange theory) that when such emotions are expressed freely on the face, the emotion itself intensifies—meaning that the more one smiles, the happier one feels.

Modern psychologists have proposed a theory of emotion that is consistent with much of Darwin's original thinking. Called the **facial feedback hypothesis**, this explanation assumes that facial expressions provide feedback to the brain concerning the emotion being expressed, which in turn not only intensifies the emotion but also actually causes the emotion (Buck, 1980; Ekman, 1980; Ekman & Friesen, 1978; Keillor et al., 2002). (See **Figure 9.10**.)

 💬 Does that mean that I don't smile because I'm happy—I'm happy because I smile?

As the old song goes, "put on a happy face" and yes, you'll feel happier, according to the facial feedback hypothesis. One fairly recent study does cast some doubt on the validity of this hypothesis, however. If the facial feedback hypothesis

The facial feedback hypothesis assumes that changing your own facial expression can change the way you feel. Smiling makes people feel happy, and frowning makes people feel sad. This effect seems to have an impact on the people around us as well. Is it hard for you to stay in a bad mood when the people around you are smiling and laughing?

Figure 9.10 Facial Feedback Theory of Emotion

In the facial feedback theory of emotion, a stimulus such as this snarling dog causes arousal and a facial expression. The facial expression then provides feedback to the brain about the emotion. The brain then interprets the emotion and may also intensify it.

	Stimulus	First response			Second response	
Facial feedback theory		ANS arousal in face	Facial expression	Cognitive interpretation of face motions		*FEAR*

Figure 9.11 Lazarus's Cognitive-Mediational Theory of Emotion

In Lazarus's cognitive-mediational theory of emotion, a stimulus causes an immediate appraisal (e.g., "The dog is snarling and not behind a fence, so this is dangerous"). The cognitive appraisal results in an emotional response, which is then followed by the appropriate bodily response.

is correct, then people who have facial paralysis on both sides of the face should be unable to experience emotions in a normal way. But a case study conducted on just such a person revealed that although she was unable to express emotions on her paralyzed face, she could respond emotionally to slides meant to stimulate emotional reactions, just as anyone else would (Keillor et al., 2002). Clearly, the question of how much the actual facial expression determines the emotional experience has yet to be fully answered.

LAZARUS AND THE COGNITIVE-MEDIATIONAL THEORY OF EMOTION As mentioned in the *Classic Studies in Psychology* feature, Schachter and Singer's (1962) study stressed the importance of cognition, or thinking, in the determination of emotions. One of the more modern versions of cognitive emotion theories is Lazarus's **cognitive-mediational theory** (1991). In this theory, the most important aspect of any emotional experience is how the person interprets, or appraises, the stimulus that causes the emotional reaction. To mediate means to "come between," and in this theory, the cognitive appraisal mediates by coming between the stimulus and the emotional response to that stimulus.

For example, remember the person who encountered a snarling dog while walking through the neighborhood? According to Lazarus, the appraisal of the situation would come before both the physical arousal and the experience of emotion. If the dog is behind a sturdy fence, the appraisal would be something like "no threat." The most likely emotion would be annoyance, and the physical arousal would be minimal. But if the dog is not confined, the appraisal would more likely be "danger—threatening animal!" and would be followed by an increase in arousal and the emotional experience of fear. In other words, it's the interpretation of the arousal that results in the emotion of fear, not the labeling as in the Schachter–Singer model, and the interpretation comes first. (See **Figure 9.11**.)

Not everyone agrees with this theory, of course. Some researchers believe that emotional reactions to situations are so fast that they are almost instantaneous, which would leave little time for a cognitive appraisal to occur first (Zajonc, 1998). Others (Kilhstrom et al., 2000) have found that the human brain can respond to a physical threat before conscious thought enters the picture. The simple spinal cord reflex of pain withdrawal discussed in Chapter Two is an example of this—the reflex occurs so quickly that the brain itself is not involved, and the experience of pain is consciously felt after the injured body part is jerked away from the painful stimulus. Ⓛ Ⓘ Ⓝ Ⓚ to Learning Objective 2.4.

💬 Which theory is right?

Human emotions are so incredibly complex that it might not be out of place to say that all of the theories are correct to at least some degree. In certain situations, the cognitive appraisal might have time to mediate the emotion that is experienced (such as falling in love), whereas in other situations, the need to act first and think and feel later is more important. (See **Figure 9.12**.)

Figure 9.12 COMPARISON OF THEORIES OF EMOTION

	Stimulus	**First response**	**Second response**

Common sense theory

"I'm shaking because I'm afraid."

Snarling dog · Conscious fear · ANS arousal

James-Lange theory

"I'm afraid because I'm shaking."

Snarling dog · ANS arousal, changes in body · Conscious fear

Cannon-Bard theory

"I'm shaking and feeling afraid at the same time."

Snarling dog · Subcortical brain activity · ANS arousal, changes in body / FEAR / Conscious fear

Schachter-Singer cognitive arousal theory

"This snarling dog is dangerous and that makes me feel afraid."

Snarling dog · Cognitive appraisal / ANS arousal, changes in body · FEAR Conscious fear

Facial feedback theory

Snarling dog · ANS arousal in face · Facial expression · Cognitive interpretation of face motions · FEAR

Lazarus's cognitive-mediational theory

Snarling dog · Appraisal of threat · FEAR · Bodily response

These figures represent the six different theories of emotion as discussed in the text.

Which of these theories of emotion do you feel is most correct? Why?

▶ | The response entered here will be saved to your notes and may be collected by your instructor if he/she requires it. |

Submit

Concept Map L.O. 9.10, 9.11, 9.12

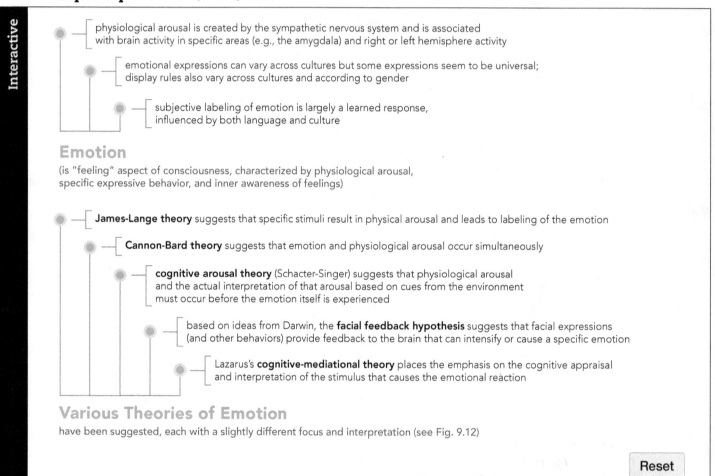

Interactive

- physiological arousal is created by the sympathetic nervous system and is associated with brain activity in specific areas (e.g., the amygdala) and right or left hemisphere activity
- emotional expressions can vary across cultures but some expressions seem to be universal; display rules also vary across cultures and according to gender
- subjective labeling of emotion is largely a learned response, influenced by both language and culture

Emotion

(is "feeling" aspect of consciousness, characterized by physiological arousal, specific expressive behavior, and inner awareness of feelings)

- **James-Lange theory** suggests that specific stimuli result in physical arousal and leads to labeling of the emotion
- **Cannon-Bard theory** suggests that emotion and physiological arousal occur simultaneously
- **cognitive arousal theory** (Schacter-Singer) suggests that physiological arousal and the actual interpretation of that arousal based on cues from the environment must occur before the emotion itself is experienced
- based on ideas from Darwin, the **facial feedback hypothesis** suggests that facial expressions (and other behaviors) provide feedback to the brain that can intensify or cause a specific emotion
- Lazarus's **cognitive-mediational theory** places the emphasis on the cognitive appraisal and interpretation of the stimulus that causes the emotional reaction

Various Theories of Emotion

have been suggested, each with a slightly different focus and interpretation (see Fig. 9.12)

Reset

Practice Quiz How much do you remember? ANSWERS ON PAGE AK-1.

Pick the best answer.

1. The phrase, "I'm embarrassed because my face is red" is best explained by which theory of emotion?

a. Cannon–Bard

b. James–Lange

c. Schachter–Singer

d. traditional theory of emotion

2. "I believe that emotions and physiological arousal tend to happen simultaneously." Which theorist would be responsible for making such a statement?

a. Walter Cannon or Philip Bard

b. William James or Carl Lange

c. Stanley Schachter or Jerome Singer

d. Sigmund Freud or Erik Erikson

3. One day at school, someone collides with you in the hall and knocks you down, causing you to be angry. However, when playing football with friends, if you get knocked down, you do not express anger. What theory best explains how we label each situation and choose the appropriate emotion to show?

a. James–Lange

b. Cannon–Bard

c. Schachter–Singer

d. facial feedback

4. In Schachter and Singer's classic study, participants who received epinephrine and were in the company of the "angry" research confederate interpreted their physiological arousal as _____, whereas those who were exposed to the "happy" confederate interpreted their arousal as _____.

a. anger; happiness.

b. happiness; anger.

c. happiness; happiness.

d. anger; anger.

5. Eileen smiles wherever she goes. She smiles a lot in the classroom, which in turn prompts her fellow students to smile, making them feel happier too. This effect is best explained by which of the following theories of emotion?

a. James–Lange

b. cognitive-mediational

c. Schachter–Singer

d. facial feedback

Applying Psychology to Everyday Life
When Motivation Is Not Enough

9.13 **Summarize the five steps of the GTD method.**

Now that we have discussed a variety of ways in which behavior gets initiated or maintained, what can you do to make sure you complete the tasks you need to finish or address the commitments you've made? Many college students find it difficult to keep track of all of their class assignments and projects, and to remember all of the things they are supposed to do—and when to do them. Keeping on task can be especially challenging when you might not be exactly thrilled about doing some of them in the first place. As such, if motivation is not enough to help you get things accomplished, what else can you do to ensure that you do what needs to be done?

A variety of time- and task-management systems have been developed over the years, each with a slightly different focus on various aspects of motivation. One system suggests you should first identify key principles or important areas in your life (such as family, education, career, etc.). The next step is to sort your to-do list using those key categories, ranking your tasks by priority or in the order you need to do them. Finally, keep track of each item by plotting it on your calendar. This works for some people, but for others it may sound like more steps than you want to do, or feel you need to do.

The book *Getting Things Done: The Art of Stress-Free Productivity* by David Allen and his "Getting Things Done" (or "GTD") methodology can provide a useful structure for a wide range of people who need help, well, in getting things done (Allen, 2001, 2008). Think back to Jennifer, the college student who ran into difficulties after starting college. With a system like GTD, she may have improved her chances of being more successful her first year.

The GTD method consists of five stages of processing your "stuff" into actual outcomes, identifying "next actions" you can actually take to gain and maintain control of your tasks and commitments. The five stages of the GTD method are:

1. Capture anything and everything that has your attention, getting it out of your head and physically collected in one place. This place can be a folder, notebook, computer program, spreadsheet, set of index cards, or the like.

2. Process and define what you can take action on and identify the next steps. For example, instead of "do my research paper," identify actionable next steps such as "pinpoint topic, collect articles, schedule meeting to discuss ideas with classmates," for example.

How do you keep track of all of your class assignments, appointments, and deadlines?

3. Organize information and reminders into categories or contexts, based on how and when you need them. For example, if you need to send an e-mail or text message to your group partners, you probably need to have your phone or computer to do so; "phone" or "computer" might be a context that you use.

4. Complete weekly reviews of your projects, next actions, and new items. To get things done, you need to review what you need to do.

5. Do your next actions, in the appropriate context or time frame for doing so.

Adapted from David Allen's *Getting Things Done: The Art of Stress-Free Productivity* (2001) and *Making It All Work* (2008).

In this discussion we've only highlighted aspects of one specific approach for organizing and keeping on top of all those things you need to get done. A variety of time- and task-management systems and tools are available, many more than we can cover in this textbook. **(L)(I)(N)K** to Learning Objective PIA.2. Finding an approach or strategy that works best for you will likely pay off, not only now while you are in school but also in areas of your personal and future professional lives as well. Take some time now and investigate available strategies that will help you get organized and stay on track to meet your obligations in a timely manner. If you do, the next time you find that motivation and emotion are not enough to prompt you to get what you need done taken care of, you'll be glad you did.

Questions for Further Discussion

1. Aside having a bunch of "lists" and possibly getting things done, what might be some specific personal benefits to keeping track of tasks and projects you have committed to?

2. What sort of personal barriers or roadblocks might you have to not using a time- or task-management system?

Chapter Summary

Understanding Motivation

9.1 Define motivation, and discuss the key elements of the early instinct and drive-reduction approaches to motivation.

- Motivation is the process by which activities are started, directed, and sustained so that physical and psychological needs are fulfilled.

- Instinct approaches proposed that some human actions may be motivated by instincts, which are innate patterns of behavior found in both people and animals.

- Drive-reduction approaches state that when an organism has a need (such as hunger), the need leads to psychological tension that motivates the organism to act, fulfilling the need and reducing the tension.

- Primary drives involve the needs of the body, whereas acquired (secondary) drives are those learned through experience. Homeostasis is the tendency of the body to maintain a steady state.

9.2 Explain the characteristics of the three types of needs.

- The need for achievement is a strong desire to succeed in achieving one's goals, both realistic and challenging.

- The self-theory of emotion links the need for achievement to the concept of locus of control. A belief in control over one's life leads to more attempts to achieve, even in the face of failure. Those who believe that they have little control over what happens to them are more likely to develop learned helplessness.

- The need for affiliation is the desire to have friendly social interactions and relationships with others as well as the desire to be held in high regard by others.

- The need for power concerns having control over others, influencing them, and having an impact on them. Status and prestige are important to people high in this need.

9.3 Identify and explain the key elements of the arousal and incentive approaches to motivation.

- In arousal theory, a person has to maintain an optimal level of arousal. People who need more arousal than others are called sensation seekers.

- In the incentive approach, an external stimulus may be so rewarding that it motivates a person to act toward that stimulus even in the absence of a drive.

9.4 Compare and contrast Maslow's humanistic approach and the self-determination theory.

- Maslow proposed a hierarchy of needs, beginning with basic physiological needs and ending with transcendence needs. The more basic needs must be met before the higher needs can be fulfilled.
- Self-determination theory (SDT) is a model of motivation in which three basic needs are seen as necessary to an individual's successful development: autonomy, competence, and relatedness.
- Intrinsic motivation occurs when people act because the act itself is satisfying or rewarding, whereas extrinsic motivation occurs when people receive an external reward (such as money) for the act.

9.5 Define stress and stressors, and describe two methods for coping with stress.

- Stress is the physical, emotional, and behavioral responses that occur when events (stressors) are identified as threatening or challenging.
- Stress that has a negative impact is called distress. Eustress is the optimal amount of stress that people need to function well.
- Catastrophes are events such as floods or crashes.
- Hassles are the daily frustrations and irritations experienced by people that have an impact on day-to-day health.
- Four sources of stress are pressure, uncontrollability, frustration, and conflict.
- Problem-focused coping is used when the problem can be eliminated or changed so that it is no longer stressful or so that the impact of the stressor is reduced.
- Emotion-focused coping is often used with problem-focused coping and involves changing one's emotional reactions to a stressor.

What, Hungry Again? Why People Eat

9.6 Identify the physical and social factors that influence hunger.

- The physiological components of hunger include signals from the stomach and the hypothalamus, and the increased secretion of insulin.
- The social components of hunger include social cues for when meals are to be eaten, cultural customs and food preferences, and the use of food as a comfort device or as an escape from unpleasantness.

9.7 Identify factors that contribute to obesity.

- Maladaptive eating may lead to obesity.
- A third of the population of the U.S. is obese.

Sexual Motivation

9.8 Explain the motivation for sexual behavior.

- Alfred Kinsey conducted a series of sexual behavior surveys revealing some highly controversial findings about the kinds of sexual behavior common among people in the United States.
- Janus and Janus published the results of a large-scale survey of sexual behavior in the United States. Their survey results did not differ widely from those of Kinsey but looked at many more types of sexual behavior and factors related to sexual behavior than did Kinsey's surveys.

9.9 Distinguish among the various sexual orientations, and identify some potential influences on sexual orientation.

- Research suggests that there are biological differences between heterosexuals and homosexuals and that there may be genetic influences as well.
- The kin selection hypothesis states that homosexual men may ensure the continuation of their genes by nurturing family members such as nieces and nephews.

Understanding Emotion

9.10 Describe and discuss the three elements of emotion.

- Emotion is the "feeling" aspect of consciousness and includes physical, behavioral, and subjective (cognitive) elements.

9.11 Compare and contrast the common-sense, James–Lange, and Cannon–Bard theories of emotion.

- The James–Lange theory states that a stimulus creates a physiological response, which then leads to the labeling of the emotion.
- The Cannon–Bard theory asserts that the physiological reaction and the emotion are simultaneous, as the thalamus sends sensory information to both the cortex of the brain and the organs of the sympathetic nervous system.

9.12 Identify the key elements in cognitive arousal theory, the facial feedback hypothesis, and the cognitive-mediational theory of emotion.

- In Schachter and Singer's cognitive arousal theory, both the physiological arousal and the actual interpretation of that arousal must occur before the emotion itself is experienced. This interpretation is based on cues from the environment.
- In the facial feedback hypothesis, facial expressions provide feedback to the brain about the emotion being expressed on the face, intensifying the emotion.
- In the cognitive-mediational theory of emotion, the cognitive component of emotion (the interpretation) precedes both the physiological reaction and the emotion itself.

Applying Psychology to Everyday Life: When Motivation Is Not Enough

9.13 Summarize the five steps of the GTD method.

- Motivation and emotion are sometimes not enough to prompt human behavior.
- Time- or task-management systems can help you keep track of commitments and accomplish specific tasks and general goals.

Test Yourself ANSWERS ON PAGE AK-1.

Pick the best answer.

1. Jasmine often requires her friends' approval when she buys new outfits. Her need is an example of a(n) _____ drive.
   a. primary
   b. acquired (secondary)
   c. innate
   d. instinctive

2. Eli enjoys woodcarving. Although none of his teenage friends are interested, he often spends hours creating several different pieces. His enjoyment of the task is all his own, and he rarely shows others his work. Many would call his motivation _____ in nature.
   a. instinctual
   b. arousal
   c. extrinsic
   d. intrinsic

3. The approach to motivation that forced psychologists to consider the value of homeostasis in motivation was the _____ approach.
   a. arousal
   b. drive-reduction
   c. instinct
   d. incentive

4. Motivational theories such as _____ are physical in terms of their needs whereas _____ is based on psychological motives.
   a. drive theory; instinctual theory
   b. biological theory; drive theory
   c. drive theory; McClelland's need theory
   d. need for power; drive theory

5. Dodi is always looking for new hobbies. He prefers exciting hobbies that will get him noticed. In his company, Dodi constantly asks for feedback from customers so he can know what he needs to do to be the best. Dodi is high in the need for _____.
   a. achievement.
   b. affiliation.
   c. power.
   d. attention.

6. An important component to Carol Dweck's theory of motivation is
   a. one's view of self.
   b. an understanding of classical conditioning and its impact on motivation.
   c. the importance of heredity on biological motivations.
   d. an understanding of emotions.

7. According to the arousal theory, people are typically motivated toward _____ point of arousal.
   a. the highest
   b. the optimal
   c. the easiest
   d. the quickest

8. According to Maslow, what is meant by a peak experience?
   a. that point, even for a moment, when someone reaches a state of self-actualization
   b. the point at which someone reaches transcendence
   c. the point at which someone begins to work through the hierarchy
   d. the point at which someone must descend back down the hierarchy to address a previous need that is no longer secure

9. Jacob believes he is in control of his own destiny. He feels he is secure in the friendships he has with others. However, he still feels the need to master many of the challenges in his own life and career. According to self-determination theory, which stage is Jacob still working to complete?
   a. autonomy
   b. competence
   c. relatedness
   d. affiliation

10. Gary is having trouble with psychology and statistics. He goes to the school's academic help center for tutoring and spends extra time working on problems at home. Gary's method of coping is
    a. problem focused.
    b. emotion focused.
    c. defensive focused.
    d. internal.

11. Unpredictable, large-scale events that create a great deal of stress and feelings of threat are called _____.
    a. major life events.
    b. catastrophes.
    c. hassles.
    d. major hassles.

12. Leptin is a hormone involved in
    a. appetite reduction.
    b. metabolism control.
    c. digestion of fatty foods.
    d. neurotransmissions.

13. Studies indicate that women from _____ are more likely to eat because their body tells them they are hungry.
    a. Hungary
    b. the United States
    c. Italy
    d. Japan

14. The Kinsey report indicates that more than _____ as many men had intercourse by age 16 than did women.
    a. ten times
    b. four times
    c. three times
    d. twice

15. LeDoux's work on the physiology involving emotions has focused on what part of the brain?
    a. thalamus
    b. hippocampus
    c. prefrontal cortex
    d. amygdala

16. Research on facial expressions has taught us that facial expressions appear to be
    a. inherent to a region and therefore mean different things in different countries.
    b. inherent to a culture and therefore mean different things to different cultures.
    c. learned.
    d. universal.

17. What is meant by a display rule?

    a. an understanding of when and under what conditions emotions and feelings may be displayed within a culture

    b. an understanding of what behaviors can be expressed when someone is new to a situation

    c. an understanding of how children are to act in the presence of adults

    d. an understanding of how to hide emotions from others

18. What theory of emotion states that the emotion typically occurs before arousal and behavior?

    a. James and Lange's theory

    b. Schachter and Singer's theory

    c. Cannon and Bard's theory

    d. the original, or common-sense, theory

19. Which theory of emotion relies heavily on cognition and labeling?

    a. the original, or common-sense, theory

    b. Schachter and Singer's theory

    c. Cannon and Bard's theory

    d. James and Lange's theory

20. The first stage of David Allen's Getting Things Done (GTD) method is _____ anything and everything that has your attention

    a. reviewing.

    b. doing.

    c. capturing.

    d. organizing

Chapter 10
Social Psychology

Early in May of 2013, a man helped three young woman escape from a decade of captivity. Amanda Berry, Gina DeJesus, and Michelle Knight had been kidnapped as young girls and held captive in a house in Cleveland, Ohio. Charles Ramsey, who lived next door, had been eating dinner one night when he heard Amanda's cries for help. Instead of turning back to his dinner, he went to the aid of the young woman, helping her and the other victims escape. Ramsey's actions may not seem heroic at first—it's what anyone should, and would, do, right? But psychologists have long known that just the opposite is often true. A well-known principle in social psychology is the *bystander effect*: The likelihood of someone who is in trouble being helped decreases as the number of witnesses or bystanders increases. As we'll learn, there are many aspects of how people influence the actions and even the thinking of others.

How are your actions influenced by others, including your friends, family, and coworkers? Are there certain actions or personal beliefs that you feel are consistent regardless of your social surroundings?

Why study social psychology?

If people lived in total isolation from other people, there would be no reason to study the effect that other people have on the behavior of individuals and groups. But human beings are social creatures—we live with others, work with others, and play with others. The people who surround us all of our lives have an impact on our beliefs and values, decisions and assumptions, and the way we think about other people in general. Why are some people prejudiced toward certain other people? Why do we obey some people but not others? What causes us to like, to love, or to hate others? The answers to all these questions and many more can be found in the study of social psychology.

Learning Objectives

10.1 Explain the factors influencing people or groups to conform to the actions of others.

10.2 Define compliance, and compare three common ways to gain the compliance of others.

10.3 Explain the factors making obedience more likely.

10.4 Distinguish among the three components of an attitude, and describe the processes behind attitude formation and change.

10.5 Explain how people react when attitudes and behavior are not the same.

10.6 Explain the process of social categorization, including impression formation and implicit personality theories.

10.7 Define attribution, and describe the processes involved in attribution.

10.8 Define and distinguish between prejudice and discrimination, and explain how people become prejudiced.

10.9 Summarize some methods for reducing prejudice.

10.10 Explain and discuss the influence of social factors on stress reactions and coping with stress.

10.11 Describe and compare the factors governing attraction and love.

10.12 Describe and explain the different kinds of love according to the triangular theory of love.

10.13 Define aggression, and explain the influences of biology and learning on aggressive behavior.

10.14 Define altruism, and explain the bystander effect.

10.15 Define and describe the field of social neuroscience.

Social Influence

Chapter One defined psychology as the scientific study of behavior and mental processes, including how people think and feel. The field of **social psychology** also looks at behavior and mental processes but includes as well the social world in which we exist, as we are surrounded by others to whom we are connected and by whom we are influenced in so many ways. It is the scientific study of how a person's behavior, thoughts, and feelings influence and are influenced by social groups.

People live in a world filled with other people. An infant is born into a world with adults who have an impact on the infant's actions, personality, and growth. Adults must interact with others on a daily basis. Such interactions provide ample opportunity for the presence of other people to directly or indirectly influence the behavior, feelings, and thoughts of each individual in a process called **social influence**. (This influence exists even if the presence of others is merely implied.) There are many forms of social influence. People can influence others to follow along with their own actions or thoughts, to agree to do things even when the person might prefer to do otherwise, and to be obedient to authorities.

CONFORMITY

10.1 **Explain the factors influencing people or groups to conform to the actions of others.**

Have you ever noticed someone looking up at something? Did the urge to look up to see what that person was looking at become so strong that you actually found yourself looking up? This common practical joke always works, even when people suspect that it's a joke. It clearly demonstrates the power of **conformity**: changing one's own behavior to more closely match the actions of others.

In 1936, social psychologist Muzafer Sherif conducted a study in which participants were shown into a darkened room and exposed to a single point of light. Under those conditions, a point of light will seem to move because of tiny, involuntary movements of the eye. ⓁⒾⓃⓀ to Learning Objective 3.14. The participants were not told of this effect and reported the light moved anywhere from a few inches to several feet. When a confederate (a person chosen by the experimenter to deliberately manipulate the situation) also gave estimates, the original participants began to make estimates of motion that were more and more similar to those of the confederate (Sherif, 1936). This early experiment on conformity has been criticized because the judgments being made were ambiguous* (i.e., the light wasn't really moving, so any estimate within reason would sound good). Would participants be so easily swayed if the judgments were more specifically measurable and certain?

ASCH'S CLASSIC STUDY ON CONFORMITY Solomon Asch (1951) conducted the first of his classic studies on conformity by having seven participants gather in a room. They were told that they were participating in an experiment on visual judgment. They were then shown a white card with only one line on it followed by another white card with three lines of varying lengths. The task was to determine which line on the second card was most similar to the line on the first card (see **Figure 10.1**).

In reality, only the next-to-the-last person in the group was a real participant. The others were all confederates (people following special directions from the experimenter) who were instructed to pick the same incorrect line from the comparison lines. Would the real participant, having heard the others pick what seemed to be the wrong answer, change to conform to the group's opinion? Surprisingly, the participants conformed to the group answer a little over one-third of the time. Asch also found that the number of confederates

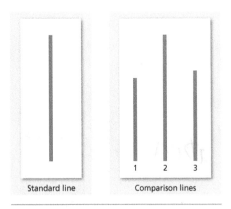

Standard line   Comparison lines

Figure 10.1 Stimuli Used in Asch's Study

Participants in Asch's famous study on conformity were first shown the standard line. They were then shown the three comparison lines and asked to determine to which of the three was the standard line most similar. Which line would you pick? What if you were one of several people, and everyone who answered ahead of you chose line 3? How would that affect your answer?

Source: Adapted from Asch (1956).

*ambiguous: having no clear interpretation or able to be interpreted in many ways rather than just one way.

mattered: Conformity increased with each new confederate until there were four confederates; more than that did not increase the participants' tendency to conform (Asch, 1951). In a later experiment, Asch (1956) found that conformity decreased if there was just one confederate who gave the correct answer—apparently, if participants knew that there was at least one other person whose answer agreed with their own, the evidence of their own eyes won out over the pressure to conform to the group. Subsequent research in the United States has found less conformity among participants, perhaps suggesting that the Asch conformity effect was due to the more conforming nature of people in the era and culture of the United States in the 1950s (Lalancette & Standing, 1990; Nicholson et al., 1985; Perrin & Spencer, 1980, 1981). In other cultures, however, studies have found conformity effects similar to those in Asch's study (Neto, 1995). Still others have found even greater effects of conformity in collectivist cultures such as Hong Kong, Japan, and Zimbabwe (Bond & Smith, 1996; Kim & Markus, 1999). This cultural difference may exist only when face-to-face contact is a part of the task, however. One study found that when the Asch judgment task is presented in an online format (participants were in communication but not able to see each other), the cultural difference disappears (Cinnirella & Green, 2007).

"Sure, I follow the herd—not out of brainless obedience, mind you, but out of a deep and abiding respect for the concept of community."

©The New Yorker Collection 2003 Alex Gregory from cartoonbank.com. All Rights Reserved.

 What about gender—are men or women more conforming?

Research shows that gender differences are practically nonexistent unless the situation involves behavior that is not private. If it is possible to give responses in private, conformity is no greater for women than for men, but if a public response is required, women do tend to show more conformity than men (Eagly, 1987; Eagly et al., 2000; Eagly & Carly, 2007). This effect may be due to the socialization that women receive in being agreeable and supportive; however, the difference in conformity is quite small.

Why do people feel the need to conform at all? One factor at work is normative social influence, the need to act in ways that we feel will let us be liked and accepted by others (Hewlin, 2009; Kaplan & Miller, 1987). We use the behavior and attitudes of other people as our "measuring stick" of what is "normal." We then judge how we are doing against that "norm." Have you ever laughed at a joke you really didn't get because everyone else was laughing? That's an example of normative social influence. Another factor at work is informational social influence, in which we take our cues for how to behave from other people when we are in a situation that is not clear or ambiguous (Isenberg, 1986). In this case, the behavior of the people around us provides us with information about how we should act, and so we conform to their actions.

THE HAZARDS OF GROUPTHINK Shortly after the terrorist attack on the World Trade Center in New York, President George W. Bush and his administration made the decision to invade Iraq, find Saddam Hussein, and stop him before he could use his "weapons of mass destruction" that the administration and its advisers believed were hidden in Iraq. This decision to invade a country that had not committed an open act of war against the United States was made and executed without building any broad-based support from allies. Although there were advisers who thought the action to be a mistake, no one person was willing to stand up to the rest of the group and challenge the group's decision and assumptions. Many now see this decision (a costly decision in terms of lost lives and casualties, huge amounts of monetary expenditures, and—according to many—the tarnishing of the diplomatic status of the United States in the eyes of the rest of the world) as a prime example of **groupthink**. Groupthink occurs when people within a group feel it is more important to maintain the group's cohesiveness than to consider the facts realistically (Hogg & Hains, 1998; Janis, 1972, 1982; Schafer & Crichlow, 1996). Other examples include the sinking of the Titanic in 1912 (the group responsible for designing and building the ship assumed it was unsinkable and did not even bother to include enough lifeboats on board for all the passengers), the *Challenger* disaster of 1986

On April 20, 2010, an explosion occurred on the *Deepwater Horizon* oil drilling rig in the Gulf of Mexico. Oil flowed into the Gulf for three months, but the environmental impact will no doubt be felt for years. How might groupthink apply in this situation?

Table 10.1 Characteristics of Groupthink

Characteristic	Description
Invulnerability*	Members feel they cannot fail.
Rationalization	Members explain away warning signs and help each other rationalize their decision.
Lack of introspection	Members do not examine the ethical implications of their decision because they believe that they cannot make immoral choices.
Stereotyping	Members stereotype their enemies as weak, stupid, or unreasonable.
Pressure	Members pressure each other not to question the prevailing opinion.
Lack of disagreement	Members do not express opinions that differ from the group consensus.
Self-deception	Members share in the illusion that they all agree with the decision.
Insularity	Members prevent the group from hearing disruptive but potentially useful information from people who are outside the group.

*Invulnerability: quality of being unable to be attacked or harmed.

Source: Janis (1972, 1982).

in which a part on the shuttle was known by a few to be unacceptable (but no one spoke up to delay the launch), and the Bay of Pigs disaster during the Kennedy administration. **Table 10.1** summarizes several "symptoms" of groupthink devised by social psychologist and groupthink expert Irving Janis (1972, 1982).

Several things can be done to minimize the possibility of groupthink (Hart, 1998; McCauley, 1998; Moorhead et al., 1998). For example, leaders should remain impartial, and the entire group should seek the opinions of people outside the group. Any voting should be done on secret ballots rather than by a show of hands, and it should be made clear that group members will be held responsible for decisions made by the group.

WRITING PROMPT

Can you think of a time when you conformed with the actions of a group of friends, even though you disagreed with their actions? Based on Asch's studies and studies on groupthink, why do you think you conformed?

▶ | The response entered here will be saved to your notes and may be collected by your instructor if he/she requires it. |

Submit

COMPLIANCE

10.2 **Define compliance, and compare three common ways to gain the compliance of others.**

💬 I have a friend who watches infomercials on the shopping channels and buys stuff that isn't worth the money or that doesn't work like it's supposed to work. Why do people fall for pitches like that?

Marketing products is really very much a psychological process. In fact, the whole area of **consumer psychology** is devoted to figuring out how to get people to buy things that someone is selling. ⓛ ⓘ ⓝ ⓚ to Learning Objective B.7. But infomercials are not the only means by which people try to get others to do what they want them to do. **Compliance** occurs when people change their behavior as a result of another person or group asking or directing them to change. The person or group asking for the change in behavior typically doesn't have any real authority or power to command a change; when that authority does exist and behavior is changed as a result, it is called obedience, which is the topic of the next major section of this chapter.

A number of techniques that people use to get the compliance of others clearly show the relationship of compliance to the world of marketing, as they refer to techniques that door-to-door salespersons would commonly use. A common example of these techniques will also occur to anyone who has ever bought a car, as the video *Compliance Techniques* explains.

👁 **Watch** the **Video**, *Compliance Techniques.*

A neighbor asks you to keep an eye on his house while he is on vacation. You agree, thinking that it's a rather small request. Later that day, the neighbor asks if you would kindly water his plants while he's gone. This is a little bit more involved and requires more of your time and energy—will you do it? If you are like most people, you probably will comply with this second larger request. In the **foot-in-the-door technique**, the first small request acts as an opener. When compliance with a smaller request is followed by a larger request, people are quite likely to comply because they have already agreed to the smaller one and they want to behave consistently with their previous response (Cialdini et al., 1995; Dillard, 1990, 1991; Freedman & Fraser, 1966; Meineri & Guéguen, 2008).

Closely related to the foot-in-the-door technique is its opposite: the **door-in-the-face technique** (Cialdini et al., 1975). In this method, the larger request comes first, which is usually refused. This is followed by a second smaller and more reasonable request that often gets compliance. An example of this would be if the neighbor first asked you to take care of his dog and cat in your home. After you refused to do so, the neighbor might ask if you would at least water his plants, which you would probably do.

Another compliance technique, also common in the world of sales, is called the **lowball technique** (Bator & Cialdini, 2006; Burger & Petty, 1981; Weyant, 1996). In this technique, once a commitment is made, the cost of that commitment is increased. (In the sense used here, cost does not necessarily mean money; cost can also mean time, effort, or other kinds of sacrifices.) For example, let's say that a professor agrees to write a textbook for a publishing company. Once committed to that process, the professor discovers that the task involves not only writing but also traveling to meet with editors, working nights and weekends to meet deadlines, and making the commitment to take time off from her teaching job to finish the text on time for publication. (This example is purely hypothetical, of course.)

Cultural differences exist in people's susceptibility to these techniques. For the foot-in-the-door technique in particular, research has shown that people in individualist cultures (such as the United States) are more likely to comply with the second request than are people in collectivist cultures (such as Japan). The research suggests that people in collectivist cultures are not as concerned with being consistent with previous behavior because they are less focused on their inner motivation than are people in individualist cultures, who are more concerned with their inner motives and consistency (Cialdini et al., 1999; Petrova et al., 2007). (L)(I)(N)(K) to Learning Objective 11.11.

The concept of compliance, along with conformity, also figures heavily in cult behavior, as the following *Psychology in the News* section explains.

Psychology in the News
Anatomy of a Cult

On September 3rd, 2012, the Reverend Sun Myung Moon, leader of the Unification Church and self-proclaimed messiah, died at the age of 92 (Brown, 2012). The Unification Church, founded by Moon in 1954, has expanded throughout the world and is a prime example of a cult. The term *cult* literally refers to any group of people with a particular religious or philosophical set of beliefs and identity. In the strictest sense of the word, the Roman Catholic Church and Protestantism are cults within the larger religion of Christianity. But most people associate the term *cult* with a negative connotation:* A group of people whose religious or philosophical beliefs and behavior are so different from that of mainstream organizations that they are viewed with suspicion and seen as existing on the fringes of socially acceptable behavior. Although many cults exist without much notice from more mainstream groups, at times members of cults have horrified the public with their actions, as was the case with the Reverend Jim Jones and the People's Temple.

In 1997, the followers of the Heaven's Gate cult, who believed that aliens in a spaceship were coming in the tail of the Hale-Bopp comet, committed suicide under the leadership of Marshall Applewhite. They believed that their souls would be taken up by the comet aliens.

Why would any person get so caught up in cult beliefs that suicide, and in some cases, murder becomes a desired behavior? It seems that people who are under a lot of stress, dissatisfied with their lives, unassertive, gullible, dependent, feel a desire to belong to a group, and who are unrealistically idealistic ("we can solve all the world's problems if everyone will just love each other") are the most likely targets of cult recruitment (Langone, 1996). Young people rebelling against parental authority or trying to become independent of families are prime targets.

Cult leaders have certain techniques of persuasion that are common to most cult organizations. The first step is usually something called "love-bombing" by current cult members, who shower the recruits with affection and attention, and claim to understand just how the potential cult members feel. Then efforts are made to isolate the recruits from family and friends who might talk them out of joining. This is accomplished in part by keeping the recruits so busy with rigid rituals, ways of dress, meditations, and other activities that they do not allow the recruits time to think about what is happening. Cults also teach their members how to stop questioning thoughts or criticisms, which are typically seen as sins or extremely undesirable behavior. In other words, cults promote a high degree of conformity and compliance (Singer & Lalich, 1995; Zimbardo & Hartley, 1985).

Commitments to the cult are small at first, such as attending a music concert or some other cult function. Eventually, a major step is requested by the cult, such as quitting one's job, turning over money or property to the cult, or similar commitments. Leaving a cult is quite difficult, as members of the cult in good standing will often track down a "deserter."

*connotation: the meaning of a word or concept that is more suggestive than directly stated.

In 1978, the Reverend Jim Jones, leader of the People's Temple in Jonestown, Guyana, ordered his followers to drink poisoned drinks or shoot each other. Of the cult members, 640 adults died and 274 children were either killed by their own hands or those of their parents. (Chidester, 2003)

Parents, friends, and other family members have been known to hire special "deprogrammers" to help their loved one recover from cult membership, willingly or unwillingly. Sometimes people actually have to "kidnap" their loved one out of the cult environment. Nevertheless, as difficult as it is to leave, 90 percent or more of cult members do eventually get out (Barker, 1983, 2007; Galanter, 1983).

Cults have existed all through recorded history and will probably continue to exist in the future. Most cults do not pose a physical threat to their members or others, but the examples of the followers of Jim Jones, Marshall Applewhite, and David Koresh (the Waco, Texas, disaster in 1993) clearly demonstrate that cults, like any group of people, can become deadly.

Questions for Further Discussion

1. In what ways are the methods used by cults on new recruits similar to the methods used by the military when training new soldiers?

2. Is it ethical for the family members of an adult to "kidnap" and deprogram a cult vmember?

3. Which methods of compliance do cults seem to use to recruit new members?

4. Do you think that the followers of the late Osama bin Laden constitute a cult? Why or why not?

OBEDIENCE

10.3 Explain the factors making obedience more likely.

There is a difference between the concepts of compliance, which is agreeing to change one's behavior because someone else asks for the change, and **obedience**, which is changing one's behavior at the direct order of an authority figure. A salesperson who wants a person to buy a car has no real power to force that person to buy, but an authority figure is a person with social power—such as a police officer, a teacher, or a work supervisor—who has the right to demand certain behavior from the people under the authority figure's command or supervision.

How far will people go in obeying the commands of an authority figure? What factors make obedience more or less likely? These are some of the questions that researchers have been investigating for many years. The answers to these questions became very important not only to researchers but also to people everywhere after the atrocities committed by the soldiers in Nazi Germany—soldiers who were "just following orders."

MILGRAM'S SHOCKING RESEARCH Social psychologist Stanley Milgram set out to find answers to these questions. He was aware of Asch's studies of conformity and wondered how much impact social influence could have on a behavior that was more meaningful than judging the length of lines on cards. He designed what has become one of the most famous (even notorious*) experiments in the history of psychology.

Through ads placed in the local newspaper, Milgram recruited people who were told that they would be participating in an experiment to test the effects of punishment on learning behavior (Milgram, 1963, 1974). The participants believed that they had randomly been assigned to either the "teacher" role or the "learner" role, when in fact the "learner" was a confederate already aware of the situation. The task for the learner was a simple memory test for paired words.

The "teacher" was seated in front of a machine through which the shocks would be administered and the level of the shocks changed. (See **Figure 10.2**.) For each mistake made by the "learner," the "teacher" was instructed to increase the level of shock by 15 volts. The learner (who was not actually shocked) followed a carefully arranged script by pounding on the wall and playing a series of pre-recorded audio responses (sounds of

Figure 10.2 Control Panel in Milgram's Experiment

In Stanley Milgram's classic study on obedience, the participants were presented with a control panel like this one. Each participant ("teacher") was instructed to give electric shocks to another person (the "learner," who only pretended to be shocked by pounding on the wall and playing a pre-recorded audio tape of grunts, protests, and screams). At what point do you think you would have refused to continue the experiment?

*notorious: widely and unfavorably known.

discomfort, asking for the experiment to end, screaming) or remained silent as if unconscious—or dead. As the "teachers" became reluctant to continue administering the shocks, the experimenter in his white lab coat, which signified authority said, for example, "The experiment requires you to continue" or "You must continue," and reminded the "teacher" that the experimenter would take full responsibility for the safety of the "learner."

How many of the participants continued to administer what they believed were real shocks? Milgram surveyed psychiatrists, college students, and other adults prior to the experiments for their opinions on how far the participants would go in administering shocks. Everyone predicted that the participants would all refuse to go on at some point, with most believing that the majority of the participants would start refusing as soon as the "learner" protested—150 volts. None of those he surveyed believed that any participant would go all the way to the highest voltage.

So were they right? Far from it—in the first set of experiments, 65 percent of the "teachers" went all the way through the experiment's final 450 volt shock level, although many were obviously uncomfortable and begged to be allowed to stop. Of those "teachers" who did protest and finally stop, not one of them stopped before reaching 300 volts!

 So what happened? Were those people sadists? Why would they keep shocking someone like that?

No one was more stunned than Milgram himself. He had not believed that his experiments would show such a huge effect of obedience to authority. These results do not appear to be some random "fluke" resulting from a large population of cruel people residing in the area. These experiments have been repeated at various times, in the United States and in other countries, and the percentage of participants who went all the way consistently remained between 61 and 66 percent (Blass, 1999; Slater et al., 2006).

 That's incredible—I just don't believe that I could do something like that to someone else.

EVALUATION OF MILGRAM'S RESEARCH Researchers have looked for particular personality traits that might be associated with high levels of obedience but have not found any one trait or group of traits that consistently predicts who will obey and who will not in experiments similar to Milgram's original studies (Blass, 1991). The people who "went all the way" were not necessarily more dependent or susceptible to being controlled by others; they were simply people like most other people, caught in a situation of "obey or disobey" the authority. Although some have suggested that Milgram's results may have been due to the same kind of foot-in-the-door technique of persuasion as discussed earlier, with participants more likely to go on with each next demanding step of the experiment because they had already agreed to the smaller increments of shock, as yet no research supports this idea (Gilbert, 1981).

Milgram's research also raised a serious ethical question: How far should researchers be willing to go to answer a question of interest? Some have argued that the participants in Milgram's studies may have suffered damaged self-esteem and serious psychological stress from the realization that they were willing to administer shocks great enough to kill another person, just on the say-so of an experimenter (Baumrind, 1964). Milgram (1964b) responded to the criticism by citing his follow-up study of the participants, in which he found that 84 percent of the participants were glad to have been a part of the experiment and only 1.3 percent said that they were sorry they had been in the experiment. A follow-up psychiatric exam one year later also found no signs of harm or trauma to the participants. Even so, most psychologists do agree that under the current ethical rules that exist for such research, this study would never be allowed to happen today. **L I N K** to Learning Objective 1.11.

There has been at least one attempt to replicate Milgram's study in recent years, although the shock was limited to only 150 volts (Burger, 2009). In that study, the confederates asked to end the study at 150 volts and the participants were asked whether they should continue or not. Regardless of their answer, the study was ended at that point. The results showed that the participants were only slightly less likely to obey than those in Milgram's study.

Concept Map L.O. 10.1, 10.2, 10.3

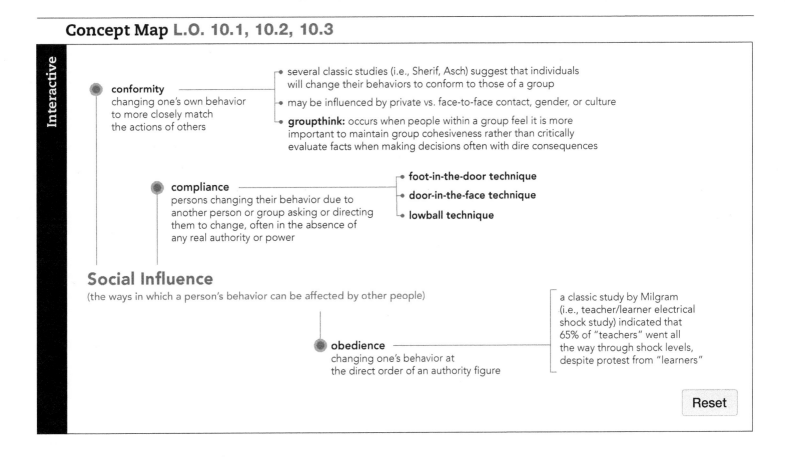

Practice Quiz   How much do you remember? ANSWERS ON PAGE AK-1.

Pick the best answer.

1. In Asch's study, conformity decreased when
 a. at least four confederates were present.
 b. at least one confederate agreed with the participant.
 c. the participant was a male.
 d. the participant had high self-esteem.

2. Which of the following would not be effective in minimizing groupthink?
 a. Caroline wants her team to openly vote by a show of hands either for or against her business plan.
 b. Karen openly invites input from all team members and even those outside her team.
 c. Annina reminds her team that everyone will be held responsible for the ultimate decision of her group.
 d. Juanita works hard to remain impartial to all ideas no matter what they are.

3. Conner needs just $20 more to go out with his friends. He asks his mother for $50 but she tells him he can have $30 instead.

In the end, Conner ended up with $10 more than he originally planned. What technique did Connor use?
 a. foot-in-the-door technique   **c.** lowball technique
 b. door-in-the-face technique   **d.** planned obedience

4. Who among the following might be the least likely target for a cult?
 a. Sharona, who is fairly gullible and very idealistic
 b. Benji, who is very stressed about his job and his life in general
 c. Dan, who is curious about other forms of religion and independent
 d. Geneva, who tends to be unassertive and wants to belong

5. In Burger's follow-up study to Milgram's obedience experiment, participants
 a. refused to obey the experimenter after the shock reached 200 volts.
 b. were only slightly less likely to obey than those in Milgram's study.
 c. suffered severe psychological problems after the study was concluded.
 d. asked to leave the study after shock levels reached 300 volts.

Social Cognition

Social cognition focuses on the ways in which people think about other people and how those cognitions influence behavior toward those other people. In this section, we'll concentrate on how we perceive others and form our first impressions of them, as well as how we explain the behavior of others and ourselves.

ATTITUDES

10.4 **Distinguish among the three components of an attitude, and describe the processes behind attitude formation and change.**

One area of social cognition concerns the formation and influence of attitudes on the behavior and perceptions of others. An **attitude** can be defined as a tendency to respond positively or negatively to a certain idea, person, object, or situation (Triandis, 1971). This tendency, developed through people's experiences as they live and work with others, can affect the way they behave toward those ideas, people, objects, and situations and can include opinions, beliefs, and biases. In fact, attitudes influence the way people view these things before they've actually been exposed to them (Petty et al., 2003).

> 💬 What do you mean—how can an attitude have an effect on something that hasn't happened yet?

Attitudes are not something people have when they are born. They are learned through experiences and contact with others and even through direct instruction from parents, teachers, and other important people in a person's life. Because attitudes involve a positive or negative evaluation of things, it's possible to go into a new situation, meet a new person, or be exposed to a new idea with one's "mind already made up" to like or dislike, agree or disagree, and so on (Eagly & Chaiken, 1993; Petty et al., 2003). For example, children are known for making up their minds about certain foods before ever tasting them, simply because the foods are "green." Those children may have tried a green food in the past and disliked it and now are predisposed* to dislike any green food whether they've tasted it or not.

THE ABC MODEL OF ATTITUDES   Attitudes are actually made of up to three different parts, or components, as shown in **Figure 10.3**. These components should not come as a surprise to anyone who has been reading the other chapters in this text because, throughout the text, references have been made to personality and traits being composed of the ways people think, feel, and act. By using certain terms to describe these three things, psychologists have come up with a handy way to describe the three components of attitudes (Eagly & Chaiken, 1993, 1998; Fazio & Olsen, 2003).

AFFECTIVE COMPONENT   The affective component of an attitude is the way a person feels toward the object, person, or situation. Affect is used in psychology to mean "emotions" or "feelings," so the affective component is the emotional component. For example, some people might feel that country music is fun and uplifting.

BEHAVIOR COMPONENT   The behavior component of an attitude is the action that a person takes in regard to the person, object, or situation. For example, a person who feels that country music is fun is likely to listen to country music, buy country music MP3s, or go to a country music concert.

COGNITIVE COMPONENT   Finally, the cognitive component of an attitude is the way a person thinks about the person, object, or situation. These thoughts, or cognitions,

---

*predisposed: referring to a tendency to respond in a particular way based on previous experience.

Figure 10.3 THREE COMPONENTS OF AN ATTITUDE

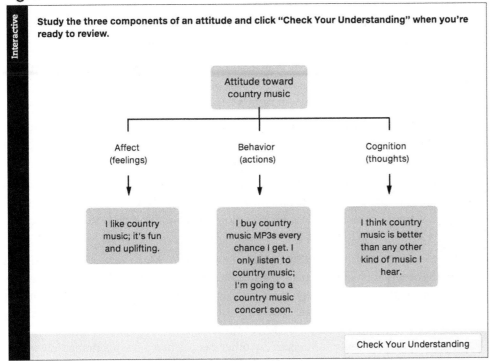

Attitudes consist of the way a person feels and thinks about something, as well as the way the person chooses to behave. If you like country music, you are also likely to think that country music is good music. You are also more likely to listen to this style of music, buy this type of music, and even go to a performance. Each of the three components influences the other two.

include beliefs and ideas about the focus of the attitude. For example, the country music lover might believe that country music is superior to other forms of music.

> 💬 So if you know what someone thinks or feels about something, you can predict what that person will do, right?

Oddly enough, attitudes turn out to be pretty poor predictors of actual behavior in a number of controlled research studies. One survey of such research conducted in the 1960s found that what people say and what people do are often two very different things (Wicker, 1971). One factor in matching attitudes and behavior concerns how specific the attitude itself is. People may hold a general attitude about something without reflecting that attitude in their actual behavior. For example, doctors generally hold the attitude that people should do everything they can to protect their health and promote wellness, yet many doctors still smoke tobacco, fail to exercise, and often get too little sleep. But a very specific attitude, such as "Exercise is important to my immediate health," will more likely be associated with the behavior of exercising (Ajzen, 2001; Ajzen & Fishbein, 2000).

Some attitudes are stronger than others, and strong attitudes are more likely to predict behavior than weak ones. A person who quit smoking because of failing health might have a stronger attitude toward secondhand smoke than someone who quit smoking on a dare, for example. The importance or salience* of a particular attitude in a given situation also has an impact on behavior—the more important the attitude appears, the more likely the behavior will match the attitude. Someone who is antismoking might

*salience: importance or having the quality of being obvious or easily seen.

be more likely to confront a smoker breaking the rules in a hospital, for example, than a smoker outside the building (Eagly & Chaiken, 1998).

ATTITUDE FORMATION   Attitude formation is the result of a number of different influences with only one thing in common: They are all forms of learning.

DIRECT CONTACT   One way in which attitudes are formed is by direct contact with the person, idea, situation, or object that is the focus of the attitude. For example, a child who tries and dislikes brussels sprouts will form a negative attitude about brussels sprouts.

DIRECT INSTRUCTION   Another way attitudes are formed is through direct instruction, either by parents or some other individual. Parents may tell their children that smoking cigarettes is dangerous and unhealthy, for example.

INTERACTION WITH OTHERS   Sometimes attitudes are formed because the person is around other people with that attitude. If a person's friends, for example, all hold the attitude that smoking is cool, that person is more likely to think that smoking is cool as well (Eddy et al., 2000; Hill, 1990; Shean et al., 1994).

VICARIOUS CONDITIONING (OBSERVATIONAL LEARNING)   Many attitudes are learned through the observation of other people's actions and reactions to various objects, people, or situations. Just as a child whose mother shows a fear of dogs may develop a similar fear, a child whose mother or father shows a positive attitude toward classical music may grow into an adult with a similarly positive attitude.

Attitudes are not only influenced by other people in a person's immediate world but also by the larger world of the educational system (many attitudes may be learned in school or through reading books) and the mass media of magazines, television, and the movies—a fact of which advertisers and marketing experts are well aware (Gresham & Shimp, 1985; MacKenzie et al., 1986).

ATTITUDE CHANGE: THE ART OF PERSUASION

 Sometimes people learn attitudes that aren't necessarily good ones, right? So can attitudes change?

Because attitudes are learned, they are also subject to change with new learning. The world is full of people, companies, and other organizations that want to change people's attitudes. It's all about the art of **persuasion**, the process by which one person tries to change the belief, opinion, position, or course of action of another person through argument, pleading, or explanation.

Persuasion is not a simple matter. Several factors become important in predicting how successful any persuasive effort at attitude change might be. These factors include the following:

- **Source:** The communicator is the person delivering the message. There is a strong tendency to give more weight to people who are perceived as experts, as well as those who seem trustworthy, attractive, and similar to the person receiving the message (Eagly & Chaiken, 1975; Petty & Cacioppo, 1986, 1996; Priester & Petty, 1995).
- **Message:** The actual message should be clear and well organized (Booth-Butterfield, 1996). It is usually more effective to present both sides of an argument to an audience that has not yet committed to one side or the other (Crowley & Hoyer, 1994; Petty & Cacioppo, 1996; Petty et al., 2003). Messages that are directed at producing fear are more effective if they produce only a moderate amount of fear and also provide information about how to avoid the fear-provoking consequences (Kleinot & Rogers, 1982; Meyrick, 2001; Petty, 1995; Rogers & Mewborn, 1976).
- **Target Audience:** The characteristics of the people who are the intended target of the message of persuasion are also important in determining the effectiveness of the message. The age of the audience members can be a factor, for example.

Researchers have found that people who are in the young adult stage of the late teens to the mid-20s are more susceptible to persuasion than are older people (Visser & Krosnick, 1998).

- **Medium:** The form through which a person receives a message is also important. For example, seeing and hearing a politician's speech on television may have a very different effect than simply reading about it in the newspaper or online. The visual impact of the television coverage is particularly important because it provides an opportunity for the source of the message to be seen as attractive, for example.

How easily influenced a person is will also be related to the way people tend to process information. In the **elaboration likelihood model** of persuasion (Petty & Cacioppo, 1986), it is assumed that people either elaborate (add details and information) based on what they hear (the facts of the message), or they do not elaborate at all, preferring to pay attention to the surface characteristics of the message (length, who delivers it, how attractive the message deliverer is, etc.). Two types of processing are hypothesized in this model: **central-route processing**, in which people attend to the content of the message, and **peripheral-route processing**, a style of information processing that relies on peripheral cues (cues outside of the message content itself) such as the expertise of the message source, the length of the message, and other factors that have nothing to do with the message content. This style of processing causes people not to pay attention to the message itself but instead to base their decisions on those peripheral factors (Petty & Cacioppo, 1986; Stiff & Mongeau, 2002). For example, the author once participated on a jury panel in which one woman voted "guilty" because the defendant had "shifty eyes" and not because of any of the evidence presented.

How the jurors in this courtroom interpret and process the information they are given will determine the outcome of the trial. Those who listen carefully to what is said by persons involved in the trial are using central-route processing. There may be some jurors, however, who are more affected by the appearance, dress, attractiveness, or tone of voice of the lawyers, defendant, and witnesses. When people are persuaded by factors other than the message itself, it is called peripheral-route processing.

WRITING PROMPT

Imagine that you are asked to create a television commercial to sell a new product. Given what you know of the factors that effectively influence persuasion, how might you persuade a customer?

▶ | The response entered here will be saved to your notes and may be collected by your instructor if he/she requires it. |

[Submit]

COGNITIVE DISSONANCE: WHEN ATTITUDES AND BEHAVIOR CLASH

10.5 Explain how people react when attitudes and behavior are not the same.

💬 As stated earlier, sometimes what people say and what they do are very different. I once pointed this out to a friend of mine who was behaving this way, and he got really upset over it. Why did he get so upset?

When people find themselves doing things or saying things that don't match their idea of themselves as smart, nice, or moral, for example, they experience an emotional discomfort (and physiological arousal) known as **cognitive dissonance** (Aronson, 1997; Festinger, 1957; Kelly et al., 1997). (*Dissonance* is a term referring to an inconsistency or lack of agreement.)

When people experience cognitive dissonance, the resulting tension and arousal are unpleasant, and their motivation is to change something so that the unpleasant feelings and tension are reduced or eliminated. There are three basic things that people can do to reduce cognitive dissonance:

1. Change their conflicting behavior to make it match their attitude.

2. Change their current conflicting cognition to justify their behavior.

3. Form new cognitions to justify their behavior.

The video *Cognitive Dissonance* explains this using the example of a cigarette smoker.

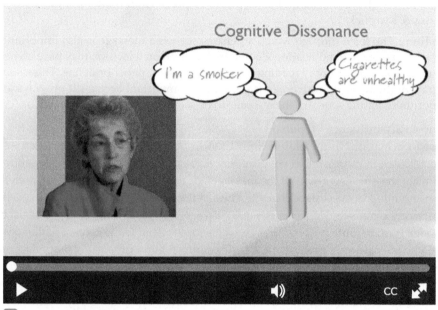

◉ **Watch** the **Video**, *Cognitive Dissonance.*

In a classic experiment conducted at Stanford University by psychologist Leon Festinger and colleague James Carlsmith (Festinger & Carlsmith, 1959), each male student volunteer was given an hour-long, very boring task of sorting wooden spools and turning wooden pegs. After the hour, the experimenters asked the participant to tell the female volunteer in the waiting room that the task was enjoyable. While half of the participants were paid only $1 to try to convince the waiting woman, the other participants were paid $20. (In the late 1950s, $20 was a considerable sum of money—the average income was $5,000, the average car cost $3,000, and gas was only 25 cents a gallon.)

At the time of this study, many researchers would have predicted that the more the participants were paid to lie, the more they would come to like the task, because they were getting more reinforcement ($20) for doing so. But what actually happened was that those participants who were paid only $1 for lying actually convinced themselves that the task was interesting and fun. The reason is cognitive dissonance: Participants who were paid only $1 experienced discomfort at thinking that they would lie to someone for only a dollar. Therefore, they must not be lying—the task really was pretty interesting, after all, and fun, too! Those who were paid more experienced no dissonance because they knew exactly why they were lying—for lots of money—and the money was a sufficient amount to explain their behavior to their satisfaction. Although most people don't want to be thought of as liars, back then, getting paid enough money to fill the gas tank of one's car three or four times over was incentive enough to tell what probably seemed to be a harmless fib. Those who were paid only $1 had to change their attitude toward the task so that they would not really be lying and could maintain their self-image of honesty. (See **Figure 10.4**.)

SOCIAL CATEGORIZATION

10.6 **Explain the process of social categorization, including impression formation and implicit personality theories.**

One of the processes that occurs when people meet someone new is the assignment of that person to some kind of category or group. This assignment is usually based on characteristics the new person has in common with other people or groups with whom the perceiver has had prior experience. This **social categorization** is mostly automatic and occurs without conscious awareness of the process (Macrae & Bodenhausen, 2000). Although this is a natural process (human beings are just born categorizers ⒧ⓘⓝ k to Learning Objective 7.1), sometimes it can cause problems. When the characteristics used

Inducement	Attitude
$1	+1.35
$20	− 0.5
Control	− .45

*Based on a –5 to +5 scale, where –5 means "extremely boring" and +5 means "extremely interesting"

Figure 10.4   Cognitive Dissonance: Attitude Toward a Task

After completing a boring task, some participants were paid $1 and some $20 to convince others waiting to do the same task that the task was interesting and fun. Surprisingly, the participants who were paid only $1 seemed to change their own attitude toward the task, rating it as interesting, whereas those who were paid $20 rated the task no differently than a control group did.

Source: Adapted from Festinger and Carlsmith (1959).

to categorize the person are superficial* ones that have become improperly attached to certain ideas, such as "red hair equals a bad temper," social categorization can result in a **stereotype**, a set of characteristics that people believe is shared by all members of a particular social category (Fiske, 1998). Stereotypes (though not always negative) are very limiting, causing people to misjudge what others are like and often to treat them differently as a result. Add the process of stereotyping to the primacy effect and it becomes easy to see how important first impressions really are. That first impression not only has more importance than any other information gathered about a person later on but may include a stereotype that is resistant to change as well (Hilton & von Hipple, 1996; Hugenberg & Bodenhausen, 2003).

 💬 It sounds as though we'd be better off if people didn't use social categorization.

Social categorization does have an important place in the perception of others. It allows people to access a great deal of information that can be useful about others, as well as helping people to remember and organize information about the characteristics of others (Macrae & Bodenhausen, 2000). The way to avoid falling into the trap of negatively stereotyping someone is to be aware of existing stereotypes and apply a little critical thinking: "Okay, so he's a guy with a tattoo on his arm. That doesn't mean that he's overly aggressive—it just means he has a tattoo."

IMPRESSION FORMATION   When one person meets another for the first time, it is the first opportunity either person will have to make initial evaluations and judgments about the other. That first opportunity is a very important one in **impression formation**, the forming of the first knowledge a person has about another person. Impression formation, part of the social categorization process, includes assigning the other person to a number of categories and drawing conclusions about what that person is likely to do—it's really all about prediction. Impression formation is another kind of social cognition.

There is a primacy effect in impression formation: The first time people meet someone, they form an impression of that person that persists even though they may later have other contradictory information about that person (DeCoster & Claypool, 2004; Luchins, 1957). So the old saying is pretty much on target: First impressions do count.

IMPLICIT PERSONALITY THEORIES   In the process of social categorization, the categories into which people place others are often based on something called an **implicit personality theory**. Implicit personality theories are sets of assumptions that people have about how different types of people, personality traits, and actions are all related and form in childhood (Dweck et al., 1995; Erdley & Dweck, 1993). For example, many people have an implicit personality theory that includes the idea that happy people are also friendly people and people who are quiet are shy. Although these assumptions or beliefs are not necessarily true, they do serve the function of helping to organize schemas, or mental patterns that represent (in this case) what a person believes about certain "types" of people. (The concept of schema here is similar to the complex schemes proposed by Piaget. (L)(I)(N)(K) to Learning Objective 8.7.) Of course, schemas formed in this way can easily become stereotypes when people have limited experience with others who are different from themselves, especially in superficial ways such as skin color or other physical characteristics (Levy et al., 1998).

There is a test designed to measure the implicit attitudes that make up one's implicit personality theory, called the Implicit Association Test, or IAT (Greenwald & Banaji, 1995; Greenwald et al., 1998). The test, taken by computer, measures the degree of association between certain pairs of concepts. For example, you might see the word "pleasant" on one side of the computer screen and the word "unpleasant" on the other side. In the middle would be

At this job fair in Shanghai, China, thousands of applicants wait hopefully in line for an opportunity to get a job interview. Making a good first impression is important in any job interview situation, but when the competition numbers in the thousands, the people who will most likely get interviews are those who are neatly dressed and well-groomed.

*superficial: on the surface.

another word that may be associated with one or the other of the two categories. You would be asked to sort the word into the appropriate category by pressing certain keys as quickly as you can. The computer measures reaction times, and it is the difference in reaction times over a series of similar comparisons that reveals implicit attitudes (Nosek et al., 2007). To try it out for yourself, participate in the experiment *Implicit Association Test: Prejudice.*

There is evidence to suggest that implicit personality theories may differ from culture to culture as well as from individual to individual. For example, one study found that Americans and Hong Kong Chinese people have different implicit personality theories about how much the personality of an individual is able to change. Whereas Americans assume that personality is relatively fixed and unchanging, Chinese people native to Hong Kong assume that personalities are far more changeable (Chiu et al., 1997).

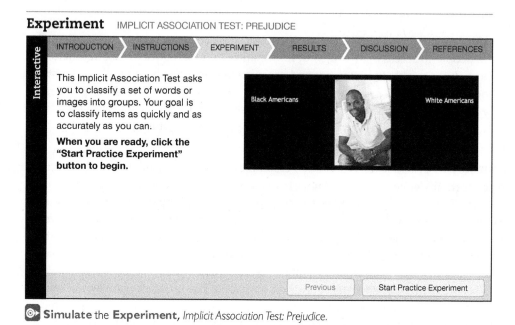

Experiment IMPLICIT ASSOCIATION TEST: PREJUDICE

Simulate the **Experiment**, *Implicit Association Test: Prejudice.*

ATTRIBUTION

10.7 Define attribution, and describe the processes involved in attribution.

Another aspect of social cognition is the need people seem to have to explain the behavior of other people. Have you ever watched someone who was doing something you didn't understand? Chances are you were going through a number of possible explanations in your head: "Maybe he's sick, or maybe he sees something I can't see," and so on. It seems to be human nature to want to know why people do the things they do so that we know how to behave toward them and decide whom we might want to use as role models. If no obvious answer is available, people tend to come up with their own reasons. People also need an explanation for their own behavior. This need is so great that if an explanation isn't obvious, it causes the distress known as cognitive dissonance. The process of explaining both one's own behavior and the behavior of other people is called **attribution**.

CAUSES OF BEHAVIOR   **Attribution theory** was originally developed by social psychologist Fritz Heider (1958) as a way of explaining not only why things happen but also why people choose the particular explanations of behavior that they do. There are basically two kinds of explanations—those that involve an external cause and those that assume that causes are internal.

When the cause of behavior is assumed to be from external sources, such as the weather, traffic, educational opportunities, and so on, it is said to be a **situational cause**. The observed behavior is assumed to be caused by whatever situation exists for the person at that time. For example, if John is late, his lateness might be explained by heavy traffic or car problems.

On the other hand, if the cause of behavior is assumed to come from within the individual, it is called a **dispositional cause**. In this case, it is the person's internal personality characteristics that are seen as the cause of the observed behavior. Someone attributing John's behavior to a dispositional cause, for example, might assume that John was late because his personality includes being careless of his and other people's time.

These kinds of attributions also have an emotional component. When people are happy in a marriage, for example, researchers have found that when a spouse's behavior has a positive effect, the tendency is to attribute it to an internal cause ("he did it because he wanted me to feel good"). When the effect is negative, the behavior is attributed to an external cause ("she must have had a difficult day"). But if the marriage is an unhappy one, the opposite attributions occur: "He is only being nice because he wants something from me" or "She's being mean because it's her nature to be crabby" (Fincham et al., 2000; Karney & Bradbury, 2000).

FUNDAMENTAL ATTRIBUTION ERROR

💬 But what else determines which type of cause a person will use? For example, what determines how people explain the behavior of someone they don't already know or like?

Dr. Leslie Echols

Missouri State Psychology Department

Attribution Theory and Academic Motivation

The most well-known attributional bias is the **fundamental attribution error**, which is the tendency for people observing someone else's actions to overestimate the influence of that person's internal characteristics on behavior and underestimate the influence of the situation (whereas in explaining our own behavior, the tendency to use situational attributions instead of personal is called the *actor–observer bias* because we are the actor, not the observer). In other words, people tend to explain the actions of others based on what "kind" of person they are rather than looking for outside causes such as social influences or situations (Blanchard-Fields et al., 2007; Harman, 1999; Jones & Harris, 1967; Leclerc & Hess, 2007; Weiner, 1985). (For example, people hearing about Milgram's "shock" study tend to assume that something is wrong with the "teachers" in the study rather than explaining their behavior within the circumstances of the situation.)

 💬 But why do we do that? Why not assume an external cause for everyone?

When people are the actors, they are very aware of the situational influences on their own behavior. For example, tardy John was actually the one driving to work, and he knows that heavy traffic and a small accident made him late to work—he was there, after all. But an outside observer of John's behavior doesn't have the opportunity to see all of the possible situational influences and has only John himself in focus and, thus, assumes that John's tardiness is caused by some internal personality flaw.

Other research has shown that when students are given an opportunity to make attributions about cheating, they make the fundamental attribution error and demonstrate actor–observer bias: If others are cheating, it's because they are not honest people, but if the students themselves are cheating it is because of the situation (Bogle, 2000).

Although the fundamental attribution error has been found in American culture (Jones & Harris, 1967), would the same error occur in a culture that is very different from American culture, such as in Japan? This is the question asked by researchers Masuda and Kitayama (2004), who had both American and Japanese participants ask a target person to read a prewritten attitudinal statement. The participants were then asked to give their opinion on the target's real attitude. American participants made the classic error, assuming that the target's attitude matched the reading. The Japanese participants, however, assumed that the person's attitude might be different from the statement—the person might have been under social obligation to write the piece. Japanese society is a collectivistic culture, and a Japanese person might expect to write a paper to please a teacher or employer, even though the paper's contents do not necessarily express the writer's attitudes. A summary of the research in cross-cultural differences in attribution provides further support for the idea that the fundamental attribution error is not a universal one (Peng et al., 2000). The work of Miller (1984) and many other researchers (Blanchard-Fields et al., 2007; Cha & Nam, 1985; Choi & Nisbett, 1998; Choi et al., 1999; Lee et al., 1996; Morris & Peng, 1994; Morris et al., 1995; Norenzayan et al., 1999) strongly suggests that in more interdependent, collectivist cultures found in China, Hong Kong, Japan, and Korea people tend to assume that external situational factors are more responsible for the behavior of other people than are internal dispositional factors. This finding is exactly the reverse of the fundamental attribution error so common in individualist Western cultures such as the United States.

Even age is a factor in how likely someone is to fall prey to the fundamental attribution error. Several studies (Blanchard-Fields & Horhota, 2005; Follett & Hess, 2002; Leclerc & Hess, 2007) have found that older adults show a stronger bias toward attributing the actions of another to internal causes than do younger people.

Concept Map L.O. 10.4, 10.5, 10.6, 10.7

Interactive

Social Cognition

focuses on the ways in which people think about other people and how those cognitions affect behavior

attitudes
tendency to respond positively or negatively toward a certain idea, person, object, or situation; learned through experience

- comprise affective, behavioral, and cognitive components
- are not great predictors of behavior although tend to have more influence as they become more specific and salient
- attitude formation can be the result of several processes
  - **direct contact**
  - **direct instruction**
  - **interaction with others**
  - **vicarious conditioning (observational learning)**
- can change through persuasion and are contingent upon both the message and the target audience; elaboration likelihood model suggests that the route/level of information processing (central vs. peripheral) influences ease of persuasion

cognitive dissonance
emotional discomfort as the result of engaging in behavior that is inconsistent with personal cognitions

- can be reduced by (1) changing behavior, (2) changing cognition, or (3) forming new cognitions to justify behavior

Impression Formation and Attribution

impression formation
forming of first knowledge about another person; influenced by primacy effect

social categorization
automatic and unconscious assignment of a new acquaintance to some category or group

- **stereotypes:** set of characteristics believed to be shared by all members of a particular category; can be useful (by limiting information processing)
- categories assigned are based on implicit personality theory, the set of assumptions formed in childhood about different types of people

attribution is a process by which we explain both our own behavior and the behavior of others; based on attribution theory (Heider)

- **situational:** cause of behavior is assumed to come from external sources
- **dispositional:** cause of behavior is assumed to come from within the individual
- **fundamental attribution error** is the tendency to overestimate the influence of another person's internal characteristics on behavior and underestimate the external/situational factors; influenced by age and culture

Reset

Practice Quiz   How much do you remember?   ANSWERS ON PAGE AK-1.

Pick the best answer.

1. Which of the following represents the affective component of an attitude?

   a. "I love to go to the clubs—it makes me so happy!"

   b. "Tonight, we're going to that new club downtown."

   c. "It is interesting to watch people when I'm out at a club."

   d. "I'm going to wear a new outfit to the club tonight."

2. As an attorney, you always recommend to your clients that they dress up in professional clothes for their day in court. What aspect of persuasion are you focusing upon?

   a. the source   **c.** the audience

   b. the message   **d.** the media

3. One of your friends tells you, "I didn't like the environmental-awareness presentation today. First of all it was too long, not to mention the person who gave it was drinking out of a polystyrene cup and drove away in a huge SUV." What kind of processing might your friend be using?

   a. central-route processing

   b. peripheral-route processing

   c. cognitive-route processing

   d. visual-route processing

4. According to the phenomenon known as social categorization, what is most influential in helping us form an attitude about someone or something?

   a. That which is repeated several times.

   b. Those things that happen last, also known as the recency effect.

   c. Those things that happen in the middle.

   d. Those things that happen first, also known as the primacy effect.

5. Kohanna thinks that everyone who smiles must always be happy and those people who are quiet must be naturally shy. Such assumptions are the bases for

   a. stereotypes.

   b. attribution theory.

   c. implicit personality theory.

   d. attitudes.

6. Caleb almost always shows up late for work. His friends attribute this to Caleb's laziness. This is an example of a _____ cause.

   a. situational

   b. dispositional

   c. dispensational

   d. superficial

7. How might someone who unknowingly is committing the fundamental attribution error explain Stanley Milgram's obedience study?

   a. Subjects in that study were highly influenced by the power of Milgram and his team.

   b. Subjects in that study desired a high degree of positive reinforcement.

   c. Subjects in that study wanted to be part of Milgram's group.

   d. Subjects in that study must have been the kind of people who like to hurt others.

Social Interaction

Social influence and social cognition are two of three main areas included in the field of social psychology. The third major area has to do with social interactions with others, or the relationships between people, both casual and intimate. Social interactions include prejudice and discrimination, liking and loving, and aggression and prosocial behavior.

EXPLAINING PREJUDICE AND DISCRIMINATION

10.8 Define and distinguish between prejudice and discrimination, and explain how people become prejudiced.

In the section about attitudes, we discussed the idea that some attitudes—stereotypes—can be formed by using only superficial information about a person or group of people. When a person holds an unsupported and often negative stereotyped attitude about the members of a particular social group, it is called **prejudice**.

    When prejudicial attitudes cause members of a particular social group to be treated differently than others in situations that call for equal treatment, it is called **discrimination**. Prejudice is the attitude and discrimination is the behavior that can result from that attitude. Although laws can be made to minimize discriminatory behavior, it is not

On September 6, 1957, this high school in Little Rock, Arkansas, became integrated, allowing African American students to attend school with White students. The desegregation laws were aimed at stopping discrimination but attitudes of prejudice persisted then, and to some degree still exist today. The courts can make laws against discrimination, but changing prejudicial attitudes is much more difficult.

These Korean demonstrators were protesting the riots that followed the 1992 not guilty verdict in the beating of Rodney King. The riots lasted six days, killing 42 people and damaging 700 buildings in mainly Korean and other Asian American neighborhoods. The Asian American population of Los Angeles, California, became scapegoats for aggression.

possible to have laws against holding certain attitudes. In other words, discrimination can be controlled and in some cases eliminated, but the prejudicial attitude that is responsible for the discrimination cannot be so easily controlled or eliminated.

TYPES OF PREJUDICE AND DISCRIMINATION There are many kinds of prejudice. There are also many kinds of discrimination that occur as a result of prejudice, notably: ageism, or prejudicial attitudes toward the elderly or teenagers (among others); sexism; racism, or prejudice toward those from different ethnic groups; prejudice toward those from different religions, those from different economic levels, those who are overweight, those who are too thin, or those who have a different sexual orientation. Prejudice can also vary in terms of what type of people or groups make the most likely targets. In any society, there will always be **in-groups** and **out-groups**, or "us" versus "them." The in-group is all the people with whom a particular person identifies, and the out-groups are everyone else (Brewer, 2001; Hewstone et al., 2002; Tajfel & Turner, 1986). The formation of in-groups and out-groups begins in childhood (Ruble et al., 2004) and continues as children become adults.

Once an in-group is established, prejudice toward and discriminatory treatment of the out-group or groups soon follow (Brewer, 2001). Members of the out-groups are usually going to become stereotyped according to some superficial characteristic, such as skin color or hair color, and getting rid of a stereotype once formed is difficult at best (Cameron et al., 2001; Hamilton & Gifford, 1976).

Conflicts between groups are usually greater when there are other pressures or stresses going on, such as war, economic difficulties, or other misfortunes. When such pressures exist, the need to find a scapegoat becomes stronger. A scapegoat is a person or a group, typically a member or members of an out-group, who serves as the target for the frustrations and negative emotions of members of the in-group. (The term comes from the ancient Jewish tradition of sending a goat out into the wilderness with the symbolic sins of all the people on its head.)

Scapegoats are going to be the group of people with the least power, and the newest immigrants to any area are typically those who have the least power at that time. That is why many social psychologists believe that the rioting that took place in Los Angeles, California, in the spring of 1992 occurred in the areas it did. This was the time of the infamous Rodney King beating. Rodney King was an African American man who was dragged out of his car onto the street and severely beaten by four police officers. The beating was caught on tape by a bystander. At the trial, the officers were found not guilty of assault with a deadly weapon. This decision was followed by a series of violent riots (Knight, 1996).

The puzzling thing about these riots is that the greatest amount of rioting and violence did not take place in the neighborhoods of the mostly white police officers or in the African American neighborhoods. The rioting was greatest in the neighborhoods of the Asian Americans and Asians who were the most recent immigrants to the area. When a group has only recently moved into an area, as the Asians had, that group has the least social power and influence in that new area. So the rioters took out their frustrations not on the people seen as directly responsible for those frustrations but on the group of people with the least power to resist.

HOW PEOPLE LEARN PREJUDICE

As we will see in the *Classic Studies in Psychology* section, even children are, under the right circumstances, prone to developing prejudiced attitudes. Is all prejudice simply a matter of learning, or are there other factors at work? Several theories have been proposed to explain the origins and the persistence of prejudice. In **social cognitive** theory, prejudice is seen as an attitude that is formed as other attitudes are formed, through direct instruction, modeling, and other social influences on learning.

REALISTIC CONFLICT THEORY   The **realistic conflict theory** of prejudice states that increasing prejudice and discrimination are closely tied to an increasing degree of conflict between the in-group and the out-group when those groups are seeking a common resource, such as land or available jobs (Horowitz, 1985; Taylor & Moghaddam, 1994). Because the examples of this from history and modern times are so numerous, it is possible to list only a few: the conflict between the early Crusaders and the Muslims, between the Jewish people and the Germans, the hatred between the Irish Catholics and the Irish Protestants, and the conflict between the native population of you-name-the-country and the colonists who want that land. The section that follows is a classic study that illustrates how easily in-groups and out-groups can be formed and how quickly prejudice and discrimination follow.

Classic Studies in Psychology
Brown Eyes, Blue Eyes

Dr. Bob Jones
Missouri State Psychology Department
Accent Prejudice

In a small town in Iowa in 1968, a few days after the assassination of Dr. Martin Luther King, Jr., a second-grade teacher named Jane Elliot tried to teach her students a lesson in prejudice and discrimination. She divided her students into two groups, those with blue eyes and those with brown eyes.

On the first day of the lesson, the blue-eyed children were given special privileges, such as extra time at recess and getting to leave first for lunch. She also told the blue-eyed children that they were superior to the brown-eyed children, telling the brown-eyed children not to bother taking seconds at lunch because it would be wasted. She kept the blue-eyed children and the brown-eyed children apart (Peters, 1971).

When Elliot became critical of the brown-eyed out-group, she soon found that the blue-eyed children also began to criticize, belittle, and viciously attack the brown-eyed children. By the end of the day, the blue-eyed children felt and acted superior, and the brown-eyed children were miserable. The lowered test scores of the brown-eyed children reflected their misery. Two days later, the brown-eyed children became the favored group and the effects from the first two days appeared again but in reverse this time: The blue-eyed children began to feel inferior and their test scores dropped.

The fact that test scores reflected the treatment received by the out-group is a stunning one, raising questions about the effects of prejudice and discrimination on the education of children who are members of stereotyped out-groups. That the children were so willing to discriminate against their own classmates, some of whom were their close friends before the experiment, is also telling. In his book about this classroom experiment, *A Class Divided*, Peters (1971) reported that the students who were part of the original experiment, when reunited 15 years later to talk about the experience, said that they believed that this early experience with prejudice and discrimination helped them to become less prejudiced as young adults.

Questions for Further Discussion

1. Is there anything about this experiment that you find disturbing?
2. How do you think adults might react in a similar experiment?
3. Are there any ethical concerns with what Elliot did in her classroom?
4. What kinds of changes might have occurred in the personalities and performances of the children if the experiment had continued for more than two days with each group?

Social comparison involves comparing yourself to others so that your self-esteem is protected. What do you think each of these young girls might be thinking?

SOCIAL IDENTITY THEORY In **social identity theory**, three processes are responsible for the formation of a person's identity within a particular social group and the attitudes, concepts, and behavior that go along with identification with that group (Tajfel & Turner, 1986). The first process is social categorization, as discussed earlier in this chapter. Just as people assign categories to others (such as black, white, student, teacher, and so on) to help organize information about those others, people also assign themselves to social categories to help determine how they should behave. The second element of social identity theory is identification, or the formation of one's **social identity**. A social identity is the part of one's self-concept that includes the view of oneself as a member of a particular social group within the social category—typically, the in-group. The third aspect of social identity theory is **social comparison**, Festinger's (1954) concept in which people compare themselves favorably to others to improve their own self-esteem: "Well, at least I'm better off than that person." (Members of the out-group make handy comparisons.)

With respect to prejudice, social identity theory helps to explain why people feel the need to categorize or stereotype others, producing the in-group sense of "us versus them" that people adopt toward out-groups. Prejudice may result, at least in part, from the need to increase one's own self-esteem by looking down on others.

STEREOTYPE VULNERABILITY As discussed previously, stereotypes are the widespread beliefs a person has about members of another group. Not only do stereotypes affect the way people perceive other people, but also stereotypes can affect the way people see themselves and their performance (Snyder et al., 1977). **Stereotype vulnerability** refers to the effect that a person's knowledge of another's stereotyped opinions can have on that person's behavior (Steele, 1992, 1997). Research has shown that when people are aware of stereotypes that are normally applied to their own group by others, they feel anxious about behaving in ways that might support that stereotype. This fear results in anxiety and self-consciousness that have negative effects on their performance in a kind of **self-fulfilling prophecy**, or the effect that expectations can have on outcomes.

Stereotype vulnerability is highly related to *stereotype threat*, in which members of a stereotyped group are made anxious and wary of any situation in which their behavior might confirm a stereotype (Hyde & Kling, 2001; Steele, 1999). **L I N K** to Learning Objective 7.8. In one study, researchers administered a difficult verbal test to both Caucasian and African American participants (Steele & Aronson, 1995). Half of the African American participants were asked to record their race on a demographic* question before the test, making them very aware of their minority status. Those participants showed a significant decrease in scores on the test when compared to the other participants, both African American and Caucasian, who did not answer such a demographic question. They had more incorrect answers, had slower response times, answered fewer questions, and demonstrated more anxiety when compared to the other participants (Steele & Aronson, 1995). Similar effects of stereotype threat on performance also have been found in women (Gonzales et al., 2002; Steele, 1997; Steele et al., 2002) and for athletes in academic settings (Yopyk & Prentice, 2005).

OVERCOMING PREJUDICE

10.9 Summarize some methods for reducing prejudice.

The best weapon against prejudice is education: learning about people who are different from you in many ways. The best way to learn about others is to have direct contact with them and learn to see them as people rather than as outsiders or strangers. Intergroup

---

*demographic: having to do with the statistical characteristics of a population.

contact is very common in college settings, for example, where students and faculty from many different backgrounds live, work, and study together. Because they go through many of the same experiences (midterms, finals, and so on), people from these diverse* backgrounds find common ground to start building friendships and knowledge of each other's cultural, ethnic, or religious differences.

EQUAL STATUS CONTACT   Contact between social groups can backfire under certain circumstances, however, as seen in a famous study (Sherif et al., 1961) called the "Robber's Cave." In this experiment conducted at a summer camp called Robber's Cave, 22 white, well-adjusted 11- and 12-year-old boys were divided into two groups. The groups each lived in separate housing and were kept apart from each other for daily activities. During the second week, after in-group relationships had formed, the researchers scheduled highly competitive events pitting one group against the other. Intergroup conflict quickly occurred, with name-calling, fights, and hostility emerging between the two groups.

The third week involved making the two groups come together for pleasant, non-competitive activities, in the hopes that cooperation would be the result. Instead, the groups used the activities of the third week as opportunities for more hostility. It was only after several weeks of being forced to work together to resolve a series of crises (created deliberately by the experimenters) that the boys lost the hostility and formed friendships between the groups. When dealing with the crises, the boys were forced into a situation of **equal status contact**, in which they were all in the same situation with neither group holding power over the other. Equal status contact has been shown to reduce prejudice and discrimination, along with stimulating ongoing, positive cooperation. It appears that personal involvement with people from another group must be cooperative and occur when all groups are equal in terms of power or status to have a positive effect on reducing prejudice (Pettigrew & Tropp, 2000; Robinson & Preston, 1976).

THE "JIGSAW CLASSROOM"   One possible way to help promote contact between people from different backgrounds to occur in a cooperative fashion is to make success at a task depend on the cooperation of each person in a group of people of mixed abilities or statuses. If each member of the group has information that is needed to solve the problem at hand, a situation is created in which people must depend on one another to meet their shared goals (Aronson et al., 1978). Ordinarily, school classrooms are not organized along these lines but are instead more competitive and, therefore, more likely to create conflict between people of different abilities and backgrounds.

In a "**jigsaw classroom**," students have to work together to reach a specific goal. Each student is given a "piece of the puzzle," or information that is necessary for solving the problem and reaching the goal (Aronson et al., 1978; Clarke, 1994). Students then share their information with other members of the group. Interaction between diverse students is increased, making it more likely that those students will come to see each other as partners and form friendly relationships rather than labeling others as members of an out-group and treating them differently. This technique works at the college level as well as in the lower school grades (Johnson et al., 1991; Lord, 2001).

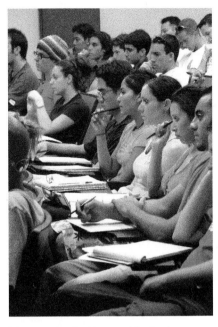

Intergroup contact is one of the best ways to combat prejudice. When people have an opportunity to work together, as the students in this diverse classroom do, they get to know each other on common ground. Can you think of the first time you had direct contact with someone who was different from you? How did that contact change your viewpoint?

SOCIAL FACTORS IN STRESS: PEOPLE WHO NEED PEOPLE

10.10 Explain and discuss the influence of social factors on stress reactions and coping with stress.

Dealing with other people and the rules of social interactions can be a major source of stress. Two prominent social factors in creating stressful living conditions that are both economically based are poverty and job stress.

---

*diverse: different, varied.

POVERTY   Living in poverty is stressful for many reasons. Lack of sufficient money to provide the basic necessities of life can lead to many stressors for both adults and children: overcrowding, lack of medical care, increased rates of disabilities due to poor prenatal care, noisy environments, increased rates of illness (such as asthma in childhood) and violence, social stigma, and substance abuse (Aligne et al., 2000; Bracey, 1997; Leroy & Symes, 2001; Park et al., 2002; Renchler, 1993; Rouse, 1998; Schmitz et al., 2001).

JOB STRESS   Even if a person has a job and is making an adequate salary, stresses associated with the workplace add to daily stressors. Some of the typical sources of stress in the workplace include the workload, lack of variety or meaningfulness in work, lack of control over decisions, long hours, poor physical work conditions, and lack of job security (Murphy, 1995).

Stress at work can result in the same symptoms as stress from any other source: headaches, high blood pressure, indigestion, and other physical symptoms; anxiety, irritability, anger, depression, and other psychological symptoms; and behavioral symptoms such as overeating, drug use, poor job performance, or changes in family relationships (Anschuetz, 1999).

HOW CULTURE AFFECTS STRESS   When a person from one culture must live in another culture, that person may experience a great deal of stress. Acculturation means the process of adapting to a new or different culture, often the dominant culture (Sodowsky et al., 1991). The stress resulting from the need to change and adapt to the dominant or majority culture is called **acculturative stress** (Berry & Kim, 1998; Berry & Sam, 1997).

The method by which a minority person enters into the majority culture can also have an impact on the degree of stress that person will experience (Berry & Kim, 1988). *Integration* involves maintaining one's original cultural identity while still forming positive relationships with dominant culture members. For example, a person may observe cultural traditions in the home but interact with members of the dominant culture according to local customs, dress, and expectations. For people who choose integration, acculturative stress is usually low (Ward & Rana-Deuba, 1999).

In *assimilation*, the minority person gives up the old cultural identity and completely adopts the ways of the majority culture. Assimilation leads to moderate levels of stress, most likely owing to the loss of cultural patterns and rejection by other members of the minority culture who have not chosen assimilation (LaFromboise et al., 1993; Lay & Nguyen, 1998).

Separation is a pattern in which the minority person rejects the majority culture's ways and tries to maintain the original cultural identity. Members of the minority culture refuse to learn the language of the dominant culture, and they live where others from their culture live, socializing only with others from their original culture. Separation results in a fairly high degree of stress, and that stress will be even higher if the separation is forced (by discrimination from the majority group) rather than voluntary (self-imposed withdrawal from the majority culture).

The greatest acculturative stress will most likely be experienced by people who have chosen to be *marginalized*; that is, they neither maintain contact with the original culture nor join the majority culture. They essentially live on the margins of both cultures without feeling or becoming part of either culture and without a social support system. Marginalized individuals do not have the security of the familiar culture of origin or the acceptance of the majority culture and may suffer a loss of identity and feel alienated from others (Roysircai-Sodowsky & Maestas, 2000).

💬 I hear the term *social support system* all the time now. Exactly what is it?

THE POSITIVE BENEFITS OF SOCIAL SUPPORT   A **social support system** is the network of friends, family members, neighbors, coworkers, and others who can offer help to a person in need. That help can take the form of advice, physical or monetary support, information, emotional support, love and affection, or companionship. Research has consistently shown that having a good social support system is of critical importance in a person's ability to cope with stressors: People with good social support systems tend to live longer and are less likely to die from illnesses or injuries than those without such support (Gardner & Oswald, 2004; Kulik & Mahler, 1989, 1993; Pynnönen et al., 2013; Vaillant, 2002). Social support has been found to have a positive effect on the immune system (Holt-Lunstad et al., 2003) and improves the mental health and physical functioning of people who have lupus, a chronic inflammatory disease that can affect nearly any part of the body (Sutcliffe et al., 1999; Ward et al., 1999) as well as those with cancer and HIV (Carver & Antoni, 2004; Gonzalez et al., 2004).

Social support can make a stressor seem less threatening because people with such support know that help is available. Having people to talk to about one's problems reduces the physical symptoms of stress—talking about frightening or frustrating events with others can help people think more realistically about the threat, for example, and talking with people who have had similar experiences can help put the event into perspective. **Ⓛ Ⓘ Ⓝ Ⓚ** to Learning Objective 13.6.

HOW CULTURE AND RELIGION AFFECT COPING WITH STRESS   Imagine this scene: You are driving out in the country when you come upon an elderly man working on a large wooden box, polishing it with great care. You stop to talk to the man and find out that the box is his own coffin, and he spends his days getting it ready, tending to it with great care. He isn't frightened of dying and doesn't feel strange about polishing his own coffin. How would you react?

If you were from the same rural area of Vietnam as the elderly man, you would probably think nothing strange is going on. For elderly people in the Vietnamese culture, thoughts of death and the things that go along with dying, such as a coffin, are not as stressful as they are to people from Western cultures. In fact, stress isn't all that common a term in Vietnamese society compared to Western societies (Phan & Silove, 1999).

In the case of people living in Vietnam and even Vietnamese immigrants to other countries, mental illness is explained by an imbalance between the male and female elements of a person, or by a loss of soul, evil spirits, or a weakening of the nerves. Coping with stress in Vietnamese culture may include performing rituals, consulting a fortune-teller, or eating certain foods (Phan & Silove, 1999). In many Asian cultures, meditation is a common stress-relief tool, including the art of tai chi, a form of meditational exercise (Yip, 2002). Cultures also vary in how much they engage their social network to help them cope.

Obviously, culture is an important factor in the kinds of coping strategies an individual may adopt and even in determining the degree of stress that is experienced. Mental health professionals should make an effort to include an assessment of a person's cultural background as well as immediate circumstances when dealing with adjustment problems due to stress.

A belief in a higher power can also be a source of great comfort in times of stress. There are several ways that religious beliefs can affect the degree of stress people experience and the ability to cope with that stress (Hill & Butter, 1995; Pargament, 1997).

First, most people who hold strong religious beliefs belong to a religious organization and attend regular religious functions, such as services at a synagogue, mosque, temple, or church. This membership can be a vital part of a person's social support system (Koenig et al., 1999).

Another way that religion helps people cope involves the rituals and rites that help people feel better about personal weaknesses, failures, or feelings of inadequacy (Koenig et al., 2001). These include rituals such as confession of sins or prayer services during times of stress. Finally, religious beliefs can give meaning to things that otherwise seem

Coping with illness is always made easier when one has social support. Here, a man recovering in the hospital is visited by a volunteer and her dog. Animals are also a good source of social support, and people who have animals have been shown to recover from illnesses and stressors more quickly (Allen et al., 2002).

These Peruvian villagers in a cemetery are honoring their loved ones who have passed away. The Day of the Dead is not only a celebration of the lives of those who have passed on but also a celebration for the living, who use this holiday to gain a sense of control over one of life's most uncontrollable events—death itself. What rituals or ceremonies do people of other cultures use to cope with death?

to have no meaning or purpose, such as viewing death as a pathway to a paradise, or the destruction of one's home in a natural disaster as a reminder to place less attachment on material things.

Many religions also encourage healthy behavior and eating habits through their prohibitions on such activities as overeating, drinking alcohol, smoking, drug use, and sexual activity outside marriage. Some research even suggests that people with religious commitments live longer than those who have no such beliefs, although this is correlational research and should not be interpreted as concluding that religious belief causes longer life expectancies (Hummer et al., 1999; Koenig et al., 1999; Strawbridge et al., 1997; Thoresen & Harris, 2002). (L)(I)(N)K to Learning Objective 1.8.

LIKING AND LOVING: INTERPERSONAL ATTRACTION

10.11 **Describe and compare the factors governing attraction and love.**

Prejudice pretty much explains why people don't like each other. What does psychology say about why people like someone else? There are some "rules" for those whom people like and find attractive. Liking or having the desire for a relationship with someone else is called **interpersonal attraction**, and there's a great deal of research on the subject. (Who wouldn't want to know the rules?)

Several factors are involved in the attraction of one person to another, including both superficial physical characteristics, such as physical beauty and proximity, as well as elements of personality.

PHYSICAL ATTRACTIVENESS   When people think about what attracts them to other people, one of the topics that usually arises is the physical attractiveness of the other person. Some research suggests that physical beauty is one of the main factors that influence people's choices for selecting people they want to know better, although other factors may become more important in the later stages of relationships (Eagly et al., 1991; Feingold, 1992; White, 1980).

PROXIMITY—CLOSE TO YOU   The closer together people are physically, such as working in the same office building or living in the same dorm, the more likely they are to form a relationship. **Proximity** refers to being physically near someone else. People choose friends and lovers from the pool of people available to them, and availability depends heavily on proximity.

One theory about why proximity is so important involves the idea of repeated exposure to new stimuli, sometimes called the *mere exposure effect*. The more people experience something, whether it is a song, a picture, or a person, the more they tend to like it. The phrase "it grew on me" refers to this reaction. When people are in physical proximity to each other, repeated exposure may increase their attraction to each other.

BIRDS OF A FEATHER—SIMILARITY   Proximity does not guarantee attraction, just as physical attractiveness does not guarantee a long-term relationship. People tend to like being around others who are similar to them in some way. The more people find they have in common with others—such as attitudes, beliefs, and interests—the more they tend to be attracted to those others (Hartfield & Rapson, 1992; Moreland & Zajonc, 1982; Neimeyer & Mitchell, 1998). Similarity as a factor in relationships makes sense when seen in terms of validation of a person's beliefs and attitudes. When other people hold the same attitudes and beliefs and do the same kinds of actions, it makes a person's own concepts seem more correct or valid.

 Isn't there a saying that "opposites attract"? Aren't people sometimes attracted to people who are different instead of similar?

There is often a grain of truth in many old sayings, and "opposites attract" is no exception. Some people find that forming a relationship with another person who has complementary qualities (characteristics in the one person that fill a need in the other) can be very rewarding (Carson, 1969; Schmitt, 2002). Research does not support this view of attraction, however. It is similarity, not complementarity, that draws people together and helps them stay together (Berscheid & Reis, 1998; McPherson et al., 2001).

RECIPROCITY OF LIKING   Finally, people have a very strong tendency to like people who like them, a simple but powerful concept referred to as **reciprocity of liking**. In one experiment, researchers paired college students with other students (Curtis & Miller, 1986). Neither student in any of the pairs knew the other member. One member of each pair was randomly chosen to receive some information from the experimenters about how the other student in the pair felt about the first member. In some cases, target students were led to believe that the other students liked them and, in other cases, that the targets disliked them.

When the pairs of students were allowed to meet and talk with each other again, they were friendlier, disclosed more information about themselves, agreed with the other person more, and behaved in a warmer manner if they had been told that the other student liked them. The other students came to like these students better as well, so liking produced more liking.

The only time that liking someone does not seem to make that person like the other in return is if a person suffers from feelings of low self-worth. In that case, finding out that someone likes you when you don't even like yourself makes you question his or her motives. This mistrust can cause you to act unfriendly to that person, which makes the person more likely to become unfriendly to you in a kind of self-fulfilling prophecy (Murray et al., 1998).

Psychology in the News
Facing Facebook—The Social Nature of Online Networking

There are some interesting research findings concerning the online networking phenomenon. For example, people using particular sites seem to have certain things in common. The findings of one study suggest that the student's choice of social network sites is related to racial identity, ethnic identity, and the education level of the student's parents (Hargittai, 2007). White students prefer Facebook, and Hispanic students prefer MySpace; and while Asian and Asian American students use Facebook more than MySpace, they use less popular sites like Xanga and Friendster more than any other ethnic group does. The more education the parents have, the more likely the student is to use Facebook and Xanga, and the less likely to use MySpace.

In China, the popular social networking site is Ozone, but Chinese users of this site spend less time on it, have fewer contacts, and seem to consider its use as less important when compared to users of Facebook in the United States (Jackson & Wang, 2013). When you consider the self-promotion focus of such social networking sites, it doesn't seem surprising that Chinese users, coming from a collectivistic cultural background that promotes connections with others over individual independence, would be less likely to use such a resource.

In another study, researchers found that young people who already experience positive social relationships use the online sites to enhance those same relationships, contrary to the stereotyped view that it would be the socially inept who would gravitate toward the anonymous nature of online networking (Mikami et al., 2010). Those who are less well adjusted either did not use social networking sites or used them in more negative ways: using excessive bad language, making hostile remarks, showing aggressive gestures, or posting unflattering or suggestive photographs.

There may also be gender differences in how people organize their social networking. In a recent study, researchers found that females have more "friends," do more buying and selling, and are more likely to "friend" people who make the request than are males (Szell & Thurner, 2013). The study also found that females take fewer risks online than do males. Males talk to larger groups of contacts and are less likely to "friend" other males than females. They respond very quickly to females requesting a friendship.

Finally, one study's findings suggest that users of social networking sites spend a lot more time on "social searching," which is defined as searching a site for specific information about a certain person, group, or event, than they do on "social browsing," defined as surveying the site without any specific target in mind (Wise et al., 2010). Users were also found to be more emotionally and positively engaged when searching rather than browsing. Again, this runs counter to the complaints of some who feel that such sites encourage time-wasting browsing. Instead, people are actively searching for information they desire.

Questions for Further Discussion

1. Why might certain networking sites be more attractive to one ethnicity over another?

2. How do you find yourself using networking sites, and how does that relate to the findings of these studies?

LOVE IS A TRIANGLE—ROBERT STERNBERG'S TRIANGULAR THEORY OF LOVE

10.12 Describe and explain the different kinds of love according to the triangular theory of love.

Dictionary definitions of love refer to a strong affection for another person due to kinship, personal ties, sexual attraction, admiration, or common interests.

💬 But those aren't all the same kind of relationships. I love my family and I love my friends, but in different ways.

Psychologists generally agree that there are different kinds of love. One psychologist, Robert Sternberg, outlined a theory of what he determined were the three main components of love and the different types of love that combinations of these three components can produce (Sternberg, 1986, 1988b, 1997a).

THE THREE COMPONENTS OF LOVE According to Sternberg, love consists of three basic components: intimacy, passion, and commitment.

Intimacy, in Sternberg's view, refers to the feelings of closeness that one has for another person or the sense of having close emotional ties to another. Intimacy in this sense is not physical but psychological. Friends have an intimate relationship because they disclose things to each other that most people might not know, they feel strong emotional ties to each other, and they enjoy the presence of the other person.

Passion is the physical aspect of love. Passion refers to the emotional and sexual arousal a person feels toward the other person. Passion is not simply sex; holding hands, loving looks, and hugs can all be forms of passion.

Commitment involves the decisions one makes about a relationship. A short-term decision might be, "I think I'm in love." An example of a more long-term decision is, "I want to be with this person for the rest of my life."

THE LOVE TRIANGLES   A love relationship between two people can involve one, two, or all three of these components in various combinations. The combinations can produce seven different forms of love, as can be seen in the video *Sternberg's Triangular Theory of Love.*

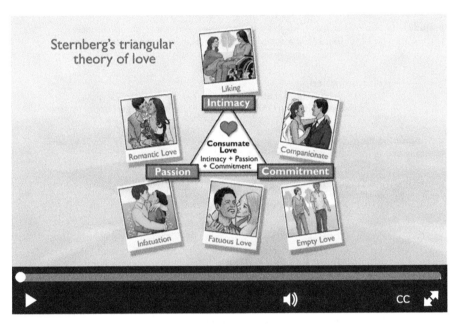

👁 **Watch** the **Video,** *Sternberg's Triangular Theory of Love.*

Two of the more familiar and more heavily researched forms of love from Sternberg's theory are romantic love and companionate love. When intimacy and passion are combined, the result is the more familiar **romantic love**, which is sometimes called passionate love by other researchers (Bartels & Zeki, 2000; Diamond, 2003; Hartfield, 1987). Romantic love is often the basis for a more lasting relationship. In many Western cultures, the ideal relationship begins with liking, then becomes romantic love as passion is added to the mix, and finally becomes a more enduring form of love as a commitment is made.

When intimacy and commitment are the main components of a relationship, it is called **companionate love**. In companionate love, people who like each other, feel emotionally close to each other, and understand one another's motives have made a commitment to live together, usually in a marriage relationship. Companionate love is often the binding tie that holds a marriage together through the years of parenting, paying bills, and lessening physical passion (Gottman & Krokoff, 1989; Steinberg & Silverberg, 1987). In many non-Western cultures, companionate love is seen as more sensible. Choices for a mate on the basis of compatibility are often made by parents or matchmakers rather than the couple themselves (Duben & Behar, 1991; Hortaçsu, 1999; Jones, 1997; Thornton & Hui-Sheng, 1994).

Finally, when all three components of love are present, the couple has achieved consummate love, the ideal form of love that many people see as the ultimate goal. This is also the kind of love that may evolve into companionate love when the passion lessens during the middle years of a relationship's commitment.

Concept Map L.O. 10.8, 10.9, 10.10, 10.11, 10.12

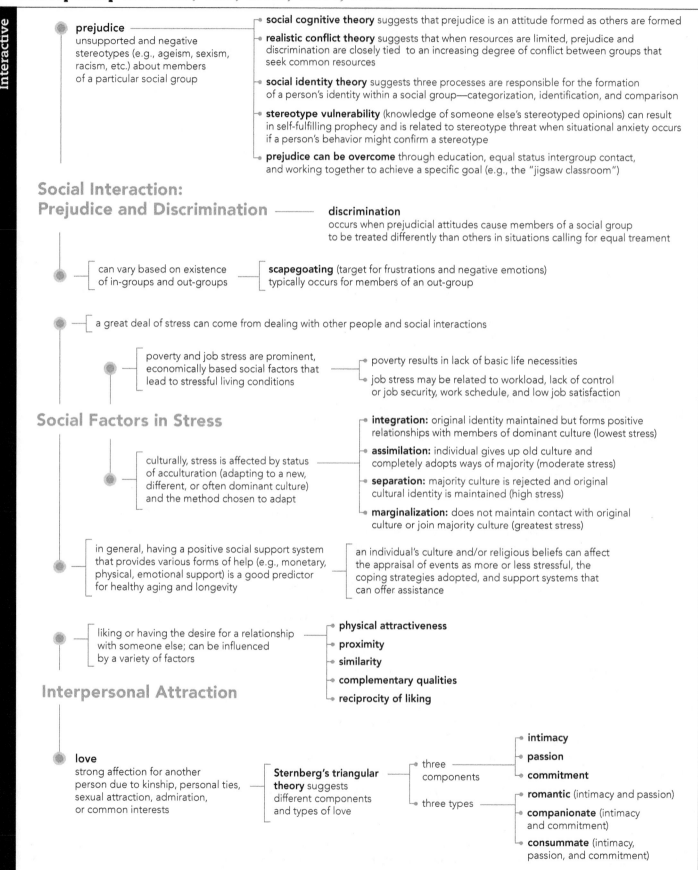

Interactive

prejudice
unsupported and negative stereotypes (e.g., ageism, sexism, racism, etc.) about members of a particular social group

- **social cognitive theory** suggests that prejudice is an attitude formed as others are formed
- **realistic conflict theory** suggests that when resources are limited, prejudice and discrimination are closely tied to an increasing degree of conflict between groups that seek common resources
- **social identity theory** suggests three processes are responsible for the formation of a person's identity within a social group—categorization, identification, and comparison
- **stereotype vulnerability** (knowledge of someone else's stereotyped opinions) can result in self-fulfilling prophecy and is related to stereotype threat when situational anxiety occurs if a person's behavior might confirm a stereotype
- **prejudice can be overcome** through education, equal status intergroup contact, and working together to achieve a specific goal (e.g., the "jigsaw classroom")

Social Interaction: Prejudice and Discrimination

discrimination
occurs when prejudicial attitudes cause members of a social group to be treated differently than others in situations calling for equal treament

can vary based on existence of in-groups and out-groups

scapegoating (target for frustrations and negative emotions) typically occurs for members of an out-group

a great deal of stress can come from dealing with other people and social interactions

poverty and job stress are prominent, economically based social factors that lead to stressful living conditions

- poverty results in lack of basic life necessities
- job stress may be related to workload, lack of control or job security, work schedule, and low job satisfaction

Social Factors in Stress

culturally, stress is affected by status of acculturation (adapting to a new, different, or often dominant culture) and the method chosen to adapt

- **integration:** original identity maintained but forms positive relationships with members of dominant culture (lowest stress)
- **assimilation:** individual gives up old culture and completely adopts ways of majority (moderate stress)
- **separation:** majority culture is rejected and original cultural identity is maintained (high stress)
- **marginalization:** does not maintain contact with original culture or join majority culture (greatest stress)

in general, having a positive social support system that provides various forms of help (e.g., monetary, physical, emotional support) is a good predictor for healthy aging and longevity

an individual's culture and/or religious beliefs can affect the appraisal of events as more or less stressful, the coping strategies adopted, and support systems that can offer assistance

liking or having the desire for a relationship with someone else; can be influenced by a variety of factors

- **physical attractiveness**
- **proximity**
- **similarity**
- **complementary qualities**
- **reciprocity of liking**

Interpersonal Attraction

love
strong affection for another person due to kinship, personal ties, sexual attraction, admiration, or common interests

Sternberg's triangular theory suggests different components and types of love

three components
- **intimacy**
- **passion**
- **commitment**

three types
- **romantic** (intimacy and passion)
- **companionate** (intimacy and commitment)
- **consummate** (intimacy, passion, and commitment)

Reset

Practice Quiz   How much do you remember? ANSWERS ON PAGE AK-2.

Pick the best answer.

1. Prejudice is about _____ whereas discrimination is about _____.

    a. beliefs; perceptions   **c.** behavior; attitudes

    b. perceptions; beliefs   **d.** attitudes; behavior

2. What are two of the most prominent social factors in creating stressful living conditions?

    a. poverty and job stress

    b. income level and marital status

    c. overall health and personality

    d. motivation level and heredity

3. Joaquin moved from Nicaragua to the United States. He learned to speak and write English, changed his last name so that it would sound more "American," and no longer maintains any of his old culture's styles of dress or customs. Joaquin has used which method of entering the majority culture?

    a. integration   **c.** separation

    b. assimilation   **d.** marginalization

4. What effect, if any, does religion have on one's stress?

    a. Religion has not been shown to affect one's stress.

    b. Religion can actually increase one's stress.

    c. Religion can help to alleviate stress in young people, but not in senior citizens.

    d. Religion can help people effectively cope with stress in multiple ways.

5. What does the research say about the concept of opposites attract?

    a. While it goes against the concept of similarity, it is real and research can prove it.

    b. Opposites attract is really more an example of proximity although studies show that opposites can and often are attracted to one another.

    c. Research notes that opposites attract but is unable to explain why this happens.

    d. Studies do not support this idea and instead note that similarity is what tends to draw people together.

6. In grade school, 12-year-old Chase does not know 12-year-old Corrine well, but starts to like her when he hears from her friends that she has a crush on him. This is an example of

    a. reciprocity of liking.

    b. similarity.

    c. mere exposure.

    d. proximity.

7. According to Sternberg, when all three components of love are present, a couple possesses _____ love.

    a. romantic

    b. passionate

    c. companionate

    d. consummate

Aggression and Prosocial Behavior

People have a tendency to either behave negatively or positively toward other people. When behavior is negative, it can become violent. But sometimes the choice is to act to help others rather than hurt them, and the next section discusses the differences between those two extremes.

AGGRESSION

10.13 Define aggression, and explain the influences of biology and learning on aggressive behavior.

Unfortunately, violence toward others is another form of social interaction. When one person hurts or tries to destroy another person deliberately, either with words or with physical behavior, psychologists call it **aggression**. One common cause of aggressive behavior is frustration, which occurs when a person is prevented from reaching some desired goal. The concept of aggression as a reaction to frustration is known as the frustration–aggression hypothesis (Berkowitz, 1993; Miller et al., 1941). Many sources of frustration can lead to aggressive behavior. Pain, for example, produces negative sensations that are often intense and uncontrollable, leading to frustration and often aggressive acts against the nearest available target (Berkowitz, 1993). Loud noises, excessive heat, the irritation of someone else's cigarette smoke, and even awful smells can lead people to act out in an aggressive manner (Anderson, 1987; Rotton & Frey, 1985; Rotton et al., 1979; Zillmann et al., 1981).

Frustration is not the only source of aggressive behavior. Many early researchers, including Sigmund Freud (1930), believed that aggression was a basic human instinct, part of our death instinct. Famed sociobiologist Konrad Lorenz (1966) saw aggression as an instinct for fighting to promote the survival of our species. In evolutionary terms, those early humans who were most successful in protecting their territory, resources, and offspring were probably more aggressive, and so survived to pass on their genetic material (Buss, 2009; Cosmides & Tooby, 2013). But if aggression is an instinct present in all humans, it should occur in far more similar patterns across cultures than it does. Instinctual behavior, as often seen in animals, is not modifiable by environmental influences. Modern approaches include explanations of aggression as a biological phenomenon or a learned behavior.

AGGRESSION AND BIOLOGY   There is some evidence that human aggression has at least partially a genetic basis. Studies of twins have shown that if one identical twin has a violent temper, the identical sibling will most likely also have a violent temper. This agreement between twins' personalities happens more often with identical twins than with fraternal twins (Miles & Carey, 1997; Rowe et al., 1999). It may be that some gene or complex of genes makes certain people more susceptible to aggressive responses under the right environmental conditions.

As discussed in Chapter Two, certain areas of the brain seem to control aggressive responses. The frontal lobes, amygdala and other structures of the limbic system have been shown to trigger aggressive responses when stimulated in both animals and humans (Adams, 1968; Albert & Richmond, 1977; LaBar et al., 1995; Scott et al., 1997; Yang et al., 2010). Charles Whitman, the Tower of Texas sniper, who in 1966 killed his mother, his wife, and then shot and killed 12 more people before finally being killed by law enforcement officers, left a note asking for an examination of his brain. An autopsy did reveal a tumor that was pressing into his amygdala (Lavergne, 1997).

There are also chemical influences on aggression. Testosterone, a male sex hormone, has been linked to higher levels of aggression in humans (Archer, 1991). This may help to explain why violent criminals tend to be young, male, and muscular. They typically have high levels of testosterone and low levels of serotonin, another important chemical found in the brain (Alexander et al., 1986; Brown & Linnoila, 1990; Coccaro & Kavoussi, 1996; Dabbs et al., 2001; Robins, 1996).

 💬 Don't some people get pretty violent after drinking too much? Does alcohol do something to those brain chemicals?

Alcohol does have an impact on aggressive behavior. Psychologically, alcohol acts to release inhibitions, making people less likely to control their behavior even if they are not yet intoxicated. Biologically, alcohol affects the functioning of many neurotransmitters and in particular is associated with a decrease in serotonin (Virkkunen & Linnoila, 1996). **L I N K** to Learning Objective 2.3. In one study, volunteers were asked to administer electric shocks to an unseen "opponent" in a study reminiscent of Milgram's shock experiment. The actual responses to the shock were simulated by a computer, although the volunteers believed that the responses were coming from a real person. The volunteers were told it was a test of reaction time and learning (Bushman, 1997). Volunteers participated both before consuming alcohol and after consuming alcohol. Participants were much more aggressive in administering stronger shocks after drinking.

THE POWER OF SOCIAL ROLES   Although frustration, genetics, body chemicals, and even the effects of drugs can be blamed for aggressive behavior to some degree, much of human aggression is also influenced by learning. The social learning theory explanation for aggression states that aggressive behavior is learned (in a process called observational learning) by watching aggressive models get reinforced for their aggressive behavior (Bandura, 1980; Bandura et al., 1961). **L I N K** to Learning Objective 5.13. Aggressive models can be parents, siblings, friends, or people on television.

There is some evidence to suggest that even taking on a particular social role, such as that of a soldier, can lead to an increase in aggressive behavior. A **social role** is the pattern of behavior that is expected of a person who is in a particular social position. For example, "doctor" is a social role that implies wearing a white coat, asking certain types of questions, and writing prescriptions, among other things.

A deeply disturbing experiment was conducted by famed social psychologist Philip Zimbardo at Stanford University in 1971. The experiment was recorded on film from the beginning to a rather abrupt end: About 70 young men, most of whom were college students, volunteered to participate for two weeks. They were told that they would be randomly assigned the social role of either a guard or a prisoner in the experiment. The "guards" were given uniforms and instructions not to use violence but to maintain control of the "prison." The "prisoners" were booked at a real jail, blindfolded, and transported to the campus "prison," actually the basement of one of the campus buildings. On day 2, the prisoners staged a revolt (not planned as part of the experiment), which was quickly crushed by the guards. The guards then became increasingly more aggressive, using humiliation to control and punish the prisoners. For example, prisoners were forced to clean out toilet bowls with their bare hands. The staff observing the experiment had to release five of the prisoners who became so upset that they were physically ill. The entire experiment was canceled on the fifth day, after one of the prisoners reported to Zimbardo that what the experimenters were doing to the young men was terrible (Zimbardo, 1971).

This photograph shows a "guard" searching a "prisoner" in Zimbardo's famous Stanford prison experiment. The students in the experiment became so deeply involved in their assigned roles that Zimbardo had to cancel the experiment after only five days—less than half the time originally scheduled for the study.

The conclusions of Zimbardo and his colleagues highlighted the influence that a social role, such as that of "guard," can have on perfectly ordinary people. Although history is full of examples of people behaving horribly to others while filling a particular role, one need not travel very far into the past to find an example.

During the war in Iraq in 2003, an army reserve general was suspended from duty while an investigation into reported prisoner abuses was conducted. Between October and December 2003, investigators found numerous cases of cruel, humiliating, and other startling abuses of the Iraqi prisoners by the army military police stationed at the prison of Abu Ghraib (Hersh, 2004). Among the cruelties reported were pouring cold water on naked detainees, beating them with a broom handle or chair, threatening them with rape, and one case of actually carrying out the threat. How could any normal person have done such things? The "guards" in the Stanford prison study were normal people, but the effect of putting on the uniform and taking on the social role of guard changed their behavior radically. Is it possible that a similar factor was at work at Abu Ghraib? The behavior of the guards at Abu Ghraib was not part of a formal, controlled study, so further research will be needed to determine to what degree the social roles at work in situations like this influence the kind of behavior seen in this real-life example.

A U.S. soldier mistreats an Iraqi prisoner at the Abu Ghraib prison in Iraq. Investigators into alleged abuses at this prison found numerous sadistic and brutal acts committed by U.S. military personnel on the prisoners.

No one can deny that abused children are exposed to powerful models of aggression. Their abusing parents get reinforced for their aggressive behavior when they get what they want from the child. No one can deny that there are people who were abused who go on to become abusers. Contrary to popular belief, however, most children who suffer abuse do not grow up to become abusers themselves—only one-third of abused children do so (Kaufman & Zigler, 1993; Oliver, 1993). Some abused children receive help and overcome the damage from their childhood, whereas others withdraw, isolating themselves rather than becoming abusive (Dodge et al., 1990).

VIOLENCE IN THE MEDIA AND AGGRESSION

💬 I've heard that violent television programs can cause children to become more aggressive. How true is that?

Bandura's early study in which small children viewed a video of an aggressive model was one of the first attempts to investigate the effect of violence in the media on children's aggressive behavior (Bandura et al., 1963). Ⓛ Ⓘ Ⓝ K to Learning Objective 5.13. Since then, many researchers have examined the impact of television and other media violence on the aggressive behavior of children of various ages. The earliest conclusions were similar: Children who are exposed to high levels of violent media are more aggressive than children who are not (Baron & Reiss, 1985; Bushman & Huesmann, 2001; Centerwall, 1989; Geen & Thomas, 1986; Huesmann & Miller, 1994; Huesmann et al., 1997; Huesmann et al., 2003; Villani, 2001). Other research has suggested that these earlier studies have been seriously flawed in several ways, and often subject to a bias held by the general population: Violent video games are bad for you.

Some research suggests that linking video games to school shooters may be a mistake. There are many other factors left out or otherwise skipped over when conducting this type of research. One meta-analysis (a careful statistical analysis of a large number of studies on a particular topic, able to more accurately measure the sizes of research effects than any one smaller study can measure) of 26 studies examining the relationship between exposure to media violence and violent aggressive behavior concluded that size effects were too small to provide evidence for a correlational relationship between the two variables (Savage & Yancey, 2008). The authors of the study stress that variables such as socioeconomic status, parents' education level, parental violence, conditions of neglect, and intelligence levels of the participants would need to be methodically controlled in any study of aggression and media effects.

Another meta-analysis (Ferguson & Kilburn, 2009) came to similar conclusions. These researchers found evidence of poor measures of aggressive behavior (remember the importance of operational definitions from Chapter One?) as well as a tendency for publication bias: the willingness of journal editors to publish studies with relatively small effect sizes (i.e., small correlations between the variables) as long as the conclusions of the study were in line with the popular consensus of the times. In a later study Ferguson (2010) found that the presence of depression and depressive symptoms was a much more relevant predictor of violent aggression than the playing of violent video games. Remember, many of the school shooters in years past showed or left evidence of depressive symptoms prior to their aggressive acts. Adachi and Willoughby (2011), in an examination of previous correlational studies, point out that many of these studies have two major limitations. First, these earlier studies failed to consider the video games used in the research in terms of their difficulty levels, the pace of the action, and the competitive level—they looked only at violent content, ignoring these other factors. Second, the particular measures of aggression used could also be seen as measuring competitiveness, a major flaw in the operational definition of a key variable. Are those studies measuring aggressive behavior, or are they measuring competitive behavior? Finally, it is important to realize that despite some very strong support for exposure to violent media being related to aggression (Anderson et al., 2003; Anderson et al., 2010), the bulk of the research has been correlational, not experimental. Remember, correlation does not prove causation! Ⓛ Ⓘ Ⓝ K to Learning Objective 1.8.

PROSOCIAL BEHAVIOR

10.14 Define altruism, and explain the bystander effect.

Another and far more pleasant form of human social interaction is **prosocial behavior**, or socially desirable behavior that benefits others rather than brings them harm.

ALTRUISM   One form of prosocial behavior that almost always makes people feel good about other people is **altruism**, or helping someone in trouble with no expectation of reward and often without fear for one's own safety. Although no one is surprised by the behavior of a mother who enters a burning house to save her child, some people are often surprised when total strangers step in to help, risking their own lives for people they do not know.

Sociobiologists—scientists who study the evolutionary and genetic bases of social organizations in both animals and humans—see altruistic behavior as a way of preserving one's genetic material, even at the cost of one's own life. This is why the males of certain species of spiders, for example, seem to willingly become "dinner" for the female mates they have just fertilized, ensuring the continuation of their genes through the offspring she will produce (Koh, 1996). It also explains the mother or father who risks life and limb to save a child.

But why do people risk their own lives to help total strangers? One answer may lie in the structure of the brain. Using brain imaging techniques, researchers have found evidence that a brain region known as the temporoparietal junction (TPJ) is larger in individuals who make altruistic choices, particularly in the right hemisphere (Marishima et al., 2012). This area was also more active during decision making that involved a greater cost of helping to the individual.

More importantly, why do people sometimes refuse to help when their own lives are not at risk?

WHY PEOPLE WON'T HELP   On March 13, 1964, at about 3:15 in the morning, Winston Mosely saw Catherine "Kitty" Genovese in the parking lot of her apartment complex, stabbed her, left, and then came back nearly half an hour later to rape and stab her to death in the entryway of the complex. Upon learning of the crime, a reporter for *The New York Times* wrote a story in which he claimed that at least 38 people heard or watched some part of the fatal attack from their apartment windows, and that not one of these people called the police until after the attack was over (Delfiner, 2001; Gado, 2004; Rosenthal, 1964). This story outraged the public and has since become a symbol of bystander apathy.

In recent years, the truth of that fateful event has come to light, and the details may be more complex than originally reported. According to trial records, the two attacks occurred much closer in time than originally believed. At the first attack, a man shouted out his window "Leave that girl alone!" and Moseley fled. Another man supposedly called the police after that first attack, although there is no record of the call. The second attack took place in the entryway to the apartment complex—a far more sheltered area in which there could have been only a few witnesses. At this point, another witness, Sophia Farrar, told a friend to call the police while she went to Kitty Genovese's aid and held her until an ambulance arrived (Cook, 2014; Manning et al., 2007). Even though some did call for help and at least one came to Kitty's aid, there were several witnesses who still stood by and did nothing. One man, whose apartment door opened onto the entryway where the second attack occurred, cracked open his apartment door, saw the attack—and closed the door (Cook, 2014).

People were outraged by the apparent indifference and lack of sympathy for the poor woman's plight. Why did those people simply stand by and watch or listen? Social psychologists would explain that the lack of response to Kitty Genovese's screams for help was not due to indifference or a lack of sympathy but instead to the presence of other people.

Forty-three years later on June 23, 2007, 27-year-old LaShanda Calloway was stabbed to death during an argument in a convenience store. It took two minutes for someone to call 911. Surveillance video captured the attack, including the five shoppers who stepped over her bleeding form and continued shopping. One customer did stop—to take a picture of Ms. Calloway as she lay dying on the floor (Hegeman, 2007). When other people are present at the scene or are assumed to be present, individuals are affected by two basic principles of social psychology: the bystander effect and diffusion of responsibility.

The **bystander effect** refers to the finding that the likelihood of a bystander (someone observing an event and close enough to offer help) to help someone in trouble decreases as the number of bystanders increases. If only one person is standing by, that person is far more likely to help than if there is another person, and the addition of each new bystander decreases the possibility of helping behavior even more (Darley & Latané, 1968; Eagly & Crowley, 1986; Latané & Darley, 1969). In the case of Kitty Genovese, there

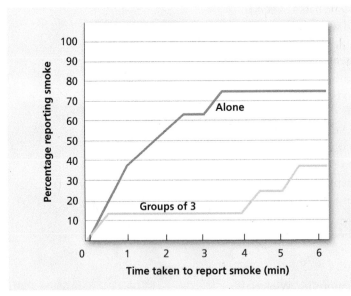

Figure 10.5 Elements Involved in Bystander Response

As you can see in the accompanying graph, the time taken to report smoke and the percentage of people reporting smoke both depended on how many people were in the room at the time the smoke was observed. If alone, a person was far more likely to report the smoke and report it more quickly than when there were three people in the room.

Source: Latané and Darley (1969).

were 38 "bystanders" at the windows of the apartment buildings, and none of them helped. Five shoppers stepped over the bleeding body of LaShanda Calloway, and none of them helped.

💬 But why does the number of bystanders matter?

Diffusion of responsibility is the phenomenon in which a person fails to take responsibility for either action or inaction because of the presence of other people who are seen to share the responsibility (**Figure 10.5**) (Leary & Forsyth, 1987). Diffusion of responsibility is a form of attribution in which people explain why they acted (or failed to act) as they did because of others. "I was just following orders," "Other people were doing it," and "There were a lot of people there, and I thought one of them would do something" are all examples of statements made in such situations. Kitty Genovese received no help because there were too many potential "helpers," and not one of the people listening to her cries for help took the responsibility to intervene—they thought surely someone else was doing something about it.

FIVE DECISION POINTS IN HELPING BEHAVIOR   In all of the experiments reported in the preceding section, there were people who did try to help in every condition. What kind of decision-making process might they have gone through before deciding to help? What are the requirements for deciding when help is needed? Darley and Latané (1968) identified several decision points that a bystander must face before helping someone in trouble: noticing the situation, defining it as an emergency, taking responsibility for acting, planning a course of action, and finally taking that action. These decision points, which are discussed in the video *The Bystander Effect*, are still considered valid over 40 years later.

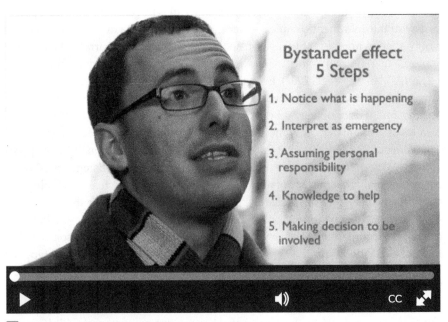

👁 **Watch** the **Video**, *The Bystander Effect.*

Aside from these five factors, there are other influences on the decision to help. For example, the more ambiguity* there is in a situation, the less likely it becomes that

---

*ambiguity: having the quality of being difficult to identify specific elements of the situation.

the situation will be defined as an emergency. If there are other people nearby, especially if the situation is ambiguous, bystanders may rely on the actions of the others to help determine whether or not the situation is an emergency. Since all the bystanders are doing this, the situation will very likely be seen as a nonemergency because no one is moving to help.

Another factor is the mood of the bystanders. People in a good mood are generally more likely to help than people in a bad mood, but oddly enough, they are not as likely to help if helping would destroy the good mood. Gender of the victim is also a factor, with women more likely to receive help than men if the bystander is male but not if the bystander is female. Physically attractive people are more likely to be helped. Victims who look like "they deserve what is happening" are also less likely to be helped. For example, a man lying on the side of the street who is dressed in shabby clothing and appears to be drunk will be passed by, but if he is dressed in a business suit, people are more likely to stop and help. Racial and ethnicity differences between victim and bystander also decrease the probability of helping (Richards & Lowe, 2003; Tukuitonga & Bindman, 2002).

Concept Map L.O. 10.13, 10.14

Aggression and Prosocial Behavior

aggression occurs when one person verbally or physically hurts or tries to destroy another person; often the result of frustration

- aggression may be partly attributed to genetics and can be triggered by variations in brain function (i.e., amygdala activation) and internal or external chemical influences (e.g., testosterone, alcohol)

much of aggression is influenced by learning but not totally deterministic
- partially explained by social learning theory—social roles (expected behavior in particular social situation) determine much of behavior (e.g., Zimbardo's Stanford Prison study)
- childhood exposure to abuse does not necessarily mean that one will grow up to be an abuser
- short-term exposure to violent media (video games, television, movies) has been correlated with increases in both physical and verbal aggression and aggressive thoughts and emotions

prosocial, or socially desirable, behavior benefits others
- **altruism:** helping someone with no expectation of reward and often at personal risk
- can be influenced by helper's mood and victim's gender, attractiveness, or "just rewards"; racial and ethnic differences can decrease probability of helping
- refusal to help another can be negatively affected by the presence of others (bystander effect/diffusion of responsibility) rather than indifference or a lack of sympathy; also influenced by individual's appraisal of situation

Reset

Practice Quiz How much do you remember? ANSWERS ON PAGE AK-1.

Pick the best answer.

1. When people are unable to reach a goal, frustration may result, which can ultimately turn into

    a. aggression.   **c.** confusion.

    b. pain.   **d.** depression.

2. Increased levels of aggression in those who drink alcohol may be due to a decrease in what neurotransmitter?

    a. dopamine   **c.** endorphins

    b. serotonin   **d.** GABA

3. Studies of the brain have found that the _____ is influential in the presence of _____ behavior.

    a. occipital lobe; aggressive

    b. medulla; shy

    c. suprachiasmatic nucleus; passive

    d. temporoparietal junction; altruistic

4. Which of the following scenarios probably will not result in the bystander effect?

 a. You come across someone lying on a busy sidewalk in a large city.

 b. You see someone pass out at a concert.

 c. You drive past an automobile accident where a crowd has gathered.

 d. You come across someone lying on a walking path while you are walking alone at your local nature center.

5. Once a situation has been defined as an emergency, the next step in the decision-making process is

 a. noticing.

 b. taking action.

 c. taking responsibility.

 d. planning a course of action.

Applying Psychology to Everyday Life
Peeking Inside the Social Brain

10.15 Define and describe the field of social neuroscience.

As scientists develop better techniques for studying the workings of the brain, researchers in many fields of psychology are able to find the neural bases for human behavior. Social psychology is no exception, and the study of how our bodies and brains work during social behaveor is called **social neuroscience** (Cacioppo & Berntson, 1992). In the discussion of altruism, the temporoparietal junction, or TPJ, was named as one of the areas of the brain involved in prosocial behavior (Marishima et al., 2012). That research was accomplished with an fMRI, a brain-scanning technique that allows not only the structure but also the functioning of the living brain to be examined during various tasks and activities. **LINK** to Learning Objective 2.9.

The TPJ, located where the temporal and parietal lobes meet, is also a key neural structure involved in competitive behavior. Researchers pitted people against either a computer or another person, and found that the TPJ is active when the person is trying to predict the actions of the human opponent, but not the computer opponent (Carter et al., 2012). Research with non-human primates highlights the importance of the prefrontal cortex, the area of the brain at the very front of the large frontal lobes. The findings of that study suggest that primates make decisions about sharing behavior in three different parts of the prefrontal lobe (Chang et al., 2013). One can only guess that human sharing decisions are at least as complex, if not more so.

What all of these studies (and many, many more) mean is that there are specific structures and places in our brains for social interactions and decisions. It is important that we try to understand as much as we can about the "social brain" for many reasons, but chief among them is gaining and understanding of diseases and disorders which may be linked to the social areas of the brain (Adolphs, 2010). Consider autism, a developmental disorder than includes impaired social functioning, or Alzheimer's, Parkinson's, or Huntington's disease, all of which also have impaired social functioning. Many psychological disorders also involve abnormal social behavior; depression, the various personality disorders, and anxiety disorders, to name a few. Understanding how these malfunctions occur within the brain is a huge step on the road to changing that behavior. Where social psychologists once studied human interactions through observing outward behavior, social neuroscientists now study the most intimate workings of the social brain.

Questions for Further Discussion

1. Can you think of other diseases or disorders which include disrupted social behavior?

2. What are the drawbacks of drawing parallels between non-human primate behavior and human behavior?

Chapter Summary

Social Influence

- Social psychology is the scientific study of how a person's thoughts, feelings, and behavior are influenced by the real, imagined, or implied presence of other people.

10.1 Explain the factors influencing people or groups to conform to the actions of others.

- In Asch's experiment, subjects conformed to group opinion about one-third of the time, and conformity decreased if just one confederate gave the correct answer.
- Cross-cultural research has found that collectivistic cultures show more conformity than individualistic cultures.
- Gender differences do not exist in conformity unless the response is not private, in which case women are more conforming than men.
- Groupthink occurs when a decision-making group feels that it is more important to maintain group unanimity and cohesiveness than to consider the facts realistically.

10.2 Define compliance, and compare three common ways to gain the compliance of others.

- Compliance occurs when a person changes behavior as a result of another person asking or directing that person to change.
- Three common ways of getting compliance from others are the foot-in-the-door technique, the door-in-the-face technique, and the lowball technique.
- Cults use love-bombing, isolation, rituals, and activities to keep new recruits from questioning and critical thinking. Cults also use the foot-in-the-door technique.

10.3 Explain the factors making obedience more likely.

- Milgram found that 65 percent of people obeyed the authority figure of an experimenter in his classic shock study.

Social Cognition

10.4 Distinguish among the three components of an attitude, and describe the processes behind attitude formation and change.

- Attitudes are tendencies to respond positively or negatively to ideas, persons, objects, or situations.
- The three components of an attitude are the affective (emotional) component, the behavioral component, and the cognitive component.
- Attitudes are often poor predictors of behavior unless the attitude is very specific or very strong.
- Attitudes can be formed through direct contact, direct instruction, interaction with others, and observation of others.
- Persuasion is the process by which one person tries to change the attitudes of others through argument, pleading, or explanation.
- The key elements in persuasion are the source of the message, the message itself, the target audience, and the medium of the message.

- In the elaboration likelihood model, central-route processing involves attending to the content of the message itself, whereas peripheral-route processing involves attending to factors not involved in the message.

10.5 Explain how people react when attitudes and behavior are not the same.

- Cognitive dissonance is discomfort or distress that occurs when a person's actions do not match the person's attitudes.

10.6 Explain the process of social categorization, including impression formation and implicit personality theories.

- Social categorization occurs when a person, upon meeting someone new, assigns that person to a category or group on the basis of characteristics the person has in common with other people or groups with whom the perceiver has prior experience.
- Impression formation is the forming of the first knowledge a person has about another person.
- An implicit personality theory is a form of social cognition in which a person has sets of assumptions about different types of people, personality traits, and actions that are assumed to be related to each other.

10.7 Define attribution, and describe the processes involved in attribution.

- Attribution is the process of explaining the behavior of others as well as one's own behavior.
- A situational cause is an explanation of behavior based on factors in the surrounding environment or situation.
- A dispositional cause is an explanation of behavior based on the internal personality characteristics of the person being observed.
- The fundamental attribution error is the tendency to overestimate the influence of internal factors on behavior while underestimating the influence of the situation.

Social Interaction

10.8 Define and distinguish between prejudice and discrimination, and explain how people become prejudiced.

- Prejudice is a negative attitude that a person holds about the members of a particular social group. Discrimination occurs when members of a social group are treated differently because of prejudice toward that group.
- In-groups are the people with whom a person identifies, whereas out-groups are everyone else at whom prejudice tends to be directed.
- Scapegoating refers to the tendency to direct prejudice and discrimination at out-group members who have little social power or influence. New immigrants are often the scapegoats for the frustration and anger of the in-group.
- Conflict between groups increases prejudice and discrimination according to realistic conflict theory.
- Social cognitive theory views prejudice as an attitude acquired through direct instruction, modeling, and other social influences.

- In the blue-eyed brown-eyed experiment, children quickly began to discriminate against whichever group was the out-group during a certain time period.
- Social identity theory sees a person's formation of a social sense of self within a particular group as being due to three things: social categorization, social identity, and social comparison.
- Stereotype vulnerability refers to the effect that a person's knowledge of the stereotypes that exist against his or her social group can have on that person's behavior.
- People who are aware of stereotypes may unintentionally come to behave in a way that makes the stereotype real in a self-fulfilling prophecy.

10.9 Summarize some methods for reducing prejudice.

- Intergroup contact is more effective in reducing prejudice if the groups have equal status.
- Prejudice and discrimination can also be reduced when a superordinate goal that is large enough to override all other goals needs to be achieved by all groups.
- Prejudice and discrimination are reduced when people must work together to solve a problem because each person has an important key to solving the problem, creating a mutual interdependence. This technique used in education is called the "jigsaw classroom."

10.10 Explain and discuss the influence of social factors on stress reactions and coping with stress.

- Different cultures perceive stressors differently, and coping strategies will also vary from culture to culture.
- People with religious beliefs also have been found to cope better with stressful events.

10.11 Describe and compare the factors governing attraction and love.

- Interpersonal attraction refers to liking or having the desire for a relationship with another person.
- People tend to form relationships with people who are in physical proximity to them, similar to them, or who complement them in areas they themselves may be lacking.

10.12 Describe and explain the different kinds of love according to the triangular theory of love.

- Love is a strong affection for another person due to kinship, personal ties, sexual attraction, admiration, or common interests.
- Sternberg states that the three components of love are intimacy, passion, and commitment.

- Romantic love is intimacy with passion, companionate love is intimacy with commitment, and consummate love contains all three components.

Aggression and Prosocial Behavior

10.13 Define aggression, and explain the influences of biology and learning on aggressive behavior.

- Aggression is behavior intended to hurt or destroy another person and may be physical or verbal. Frustration is a major source of aggression.
- Biological influences on aggression may include genetics, the amygdala and limbic system, and testosterone and serotonin levels.
- Social roles are powerful influences on the expression of aggression. Social learning theory states that aggression can be learned through direct reinforcement and through the imitation of successful aggression by a model.
- Studies of the connection between violent media exposure and increased levels of aggression are supportive of a connection, but are primarily correlational in nature.

10.14 Define altruism, and explain the bystander effect.

- Prosocial behavior is behavior that is socially desirable and benefits others.
- Altruism is prosocial behavior in which a person helps someone else without expectation of reward or recognition, often without fear for his or her own safety.
- The bystander effect means that people are more likely to get help from others if there are one or only a few people nearby rather than a larger number because of diffusion of responsibility.
- The five steps in making a decision to help are noticing, defining an emergency, taking responsibility, planning a course of action, and taking action.

Applying Psychology to Everyday Life: Peeking inside the Social Brain

10.15 Define and describe the field of social neuroscience.

- Social neuroscience is the study of how biological processes influence social behavior. Studies use fMRI and other imaging techniques to discover areas of the brain involved in social actions.

Test Yourself   ANSWERS ON PAGE AK-2.

Pick the best answer.

1. Saul admits that he conforms so as to be liked by others. This is known as
   a. compliance.
   b. obedience.
   c. informational social influence.
   d. normative social influence.

2. According to the text, in which of the following has groupthink been known to occur?
   a. presidential elections
   b. the fall of communism
   c. mass suicides by cults
   d. the sinking of the *Titanic*

3. Maria was approached by her neighbor, asking her to adopt two to three kittens that were abandoned by their mother. Although Maria refused to take in three kittens, she did agree to adopt just one. What compliance technique did her neighbor use on Maria?

a. foot-in-the-door
b. door-in-the-face
c. lowball
d. double foot-in-the-door

4. When examining Stanley Milgram's research, some have suggested that a teacher's willingness to deliver potentially lethal shocks may be more a product of _____ than of obedience, but as of yet no research supports this specific conclusion.

a. the foot-in-the-door technique
b. the door-in-the-face technique
c. lowballing
d. the "that's not all" technique

5. The public service messages that encourage parents to sit down with their children and talk frankly about drugs are promoting which method of attitude formation?

a. direct contact
b. direct instruction
c. vicarious conditioning
d. observational learning

6. Researchers have found that a _____ degree of fear in a message makes it more effective, particularly when it is combined with _____.

a. maximum; information about how to prevent the fearful consequences
b. minimum; threats
c. moderate; threats
d. moderate; information about how to prevent the fearful consequences

7. Sandy was a juror in the trial for a man accused of stealing guns from a sporting goods store. The defendant was not very well-spoken and came from a very poor background, but Sandy listened carefully to the evidence presented and made her decision based on that. Sandy was using _____ processing.

a. central-route
b. peripheral-route
c. cognitive-route
d. visual-route

8. If LaShonda experiences a sense of cognitive dissonance between her attitude and behavior, which of the following would help her reduce that uncomfortable sensation?

a. thinking constantly about the mismatch
b. maintaining her existing attitude
c. discussing the inconsistency with others
d. changing her behavior

9. Gerard goes to a job interview dressed in patched blue jeans, a torn T-shirt, and sandals. His hair is uncombed and he hasn't shaved in a few days. Obviously, Gerard knows nothing about

a. cognitive dissonance.
b. attitude formation.
c. impression formation.
d. groupthink.

10. If behavior is assumed to be caused by external characteristics, this is known as

a. a situational cause.
b. a dispositional cause.
c. a fundamental attribution error.
d. actor–observer bias.

11. Thomas likes to "hang with the guys." These people with whom Thomas identifies most strongly with are called a(n)

a. referent group.
b. in-group.
c. out-group.
d. "them" group.

12. The "Robber's Cave" experiment showed the value of _____ in combating prejudice.

a. "jigsaw classrooms"
b. an equal status contact
c. subordinate goals
d. stereotyping vulnerability

13. Huong has moved from China to the United States. While she dresses and acts like her American friends, she still has retained much of her cultural heritage and attends traditional Chinese dance classes on the weekends. This is an example of

a. assimilation.
b. integration.
c. separation.
d. marginalization.

14. Which of the following people may have the greatest ability to cope with stress?

a. Mary, a very religious person who is involved in her community
b. Carrie, who works hard but doesn't have any apparent hobbies or other interests
c. Jeri, who has few friends and whose family lives far away from her
d. Larry, who is highly driven to succeed

15. Vivian and Steve met at work. At first they were just friends, but over time, they found themselves falling in love—or as Vivian tells her friends, "Steve just grew on me!" According to research in interpersonal attraction, the most likely explanation for their attraction is

a. mere exposure.
b. personal attractiveness.
c. fate.
d. reciprocity of liking

16. According to Sternberg, a couple whose love is based on intimacy and passion but who are not yet committed to a long-term relationship are in the form of love called _____ love.

a. companionate
b. consummate
c. affectionate
d. romantic

17. The concept that aggression results from a social role is based on what psychological theory?

a. humanistic
b. social learning
c. psychoanalytical
d. cognitive

18. To which two processes do most social psychologists attribute the failure of those around LaShanda Calloway to help her?

a. bystander effect and altruism
b. aggression and diffusion of responsibility
c. altruism and diffusion of responsibility
d. bystander effect and diffusion of responsibility

19. While serving as a chaperone for her son's class trip to the museum, Cara witnessed someone fall down a flight of stairs. She was able to request emergency assistance by simply dialing 9-1-1 on her cell phone. Which step in the decision process for helping was Cara?

a. noticing
b. taking action
c. taking responsibility
d. planning a course of action

20. Which of the following would the field of social neuroscience be most likely to study?

a. what parts of the brain influence social behavior
b. how influential heredity is on social behavior
c. what impact head trauma has on developing relationships
d. what impact friends have in resolving conflicts

Chapter 11
Theories of Personality

Many people have heard the story of the "Jim" twins, James Arthur Springer and James Edward Lewis, identical twins separated just after birth. At age 39 Springer and Lewis were the first set of twins studied by University of Minnesota psychologist Thomas Bouchard, who examined the differences and similarities between identical and fraternal twins raised apart from each other (Bouchard et al., 1990).

The two "Jims" were remarkably similar. They shared interests in mechanical drawing and carpentry, they smoked and drank the same amount, and they even both divorced women named Linda before marrying women named Betty. It is easy to attribute these similarities to their shared genetics. But Springer and Lewis were both raised in Ohio by parents from relatively similar socioeconomic backgrounds—how much of their similarity to each other might be due to those conditions?

In what ways are you similar to and different from your siblings? How has your personality been shaped by your environment?

Why study personality?

Personality is the sum total of who you are—your attitudes and reactions, both physical and emotional. It's what makes each person different from every other person in the world. How can any study of human behavior not include the study of who we are and how we got to be that way?

Learning Objectives

11.1 Define personality, and explain how the various perspectives in psychology view personality.

11.2 Describe how Freud's view of the mind and personality formed a basis for psychodynamic theory.

11.3 Explain how the neo-Freudians modified Freud's theory and how modern psychodynamic theory differs from that of Freud.

11.4 Compare different learning theories of personality, including the theories of Bandura and Rotter.

11.5 Evaluate the strengths and limitations of the social cognitive view of personality.

11.6 Describe how humanists such as Carl Rogers explain personality.

11.7 Evaluate the strengths and limitations of the humanistic view of personality.

11.8 Define the trait perspective, and describe early attempts to use traits to conceptualize personality.

11.9 Describe and evaluate the five-factor model and other recent trait theories of personality.

11.10 Explain how behavioral geneticists use twin and adoption studies to study personality

11.11 Define heritability, and explain how environmental influences, such as culture, can also impact personality.

11.12 Describe Lazarus's two-step process of how people think about and appraise a stressor.

11.13 Explain how personality factors can influence our ability to cope with stressors.

11.14 Identify the advantages and disadvantages of using interviews, behavioral assessments, and personality inventories.

11.15 Identify the advantages and disadvantages of using projective personality tests.

11.16 Outline ways to become a more optimistic thinker.

Perspectives on Personality

11.1 **Define personality, and explain how the various perspectives in psychology view personality.**

Personality is the unique way in which each individual thinks, acts, and feels throughout life. Personality should not be confused with **character**, which refers to value judgments made about a person's morals or ethical behavior; nor should it be confused with **temperament**, the enduring characteristics with which each person is born, such as irritability or adaptability. Temperament is based in one's biology, either through genetic influences, prenatal influences, or a combination of those influences, and forms the basis upon which one's larger personality is built. Both character and temperament are vital parts of personality, however. Every adult personality is a combination of temperaments and personal history of family, culture, and the time during which they grew up (Kagan, 2010).

Personality is an area of the still relatively young field of psychology in which there are several ways in which the characteristic behavior of human beings can be explained. However, the investigation of personality goes back quite some time. For example, physiological roots of personality were suggested as early as the fourth century B.C.E. by Empedocles and later by Hippocrates, with Hippocrates's work later influencing Galen in the second century C.E. (Dumont, 2010). Hippocrates and Galen believed that temperament or personality was related to the relative balance of the four physical humors of the body: blood, black bile, yellow bile, and phlegm.

One reason no single explanation of personality exists is because personality is still difficult to measure precisely and scientifically, and different perspectives of personality have arisen. Overall, these tend to examine the source of personality, such as individual behavioral dispositions or situational processes, mediating factors that may be conscious or unconscious (Mischel & Shoda, 1995). Sources likely overlap and influence each other, such as the interaction of biological, developmental, social, and cultural factors. Perspectives also examine sources from different ways. In addition to those highlighted below, some are influenced by early schools of thought in psychology such as structuralism, functionalism, Gestalt learning, or the cognitive perspective. And among others, theories or perspectives may also use a "lens" stemming from such areas as motivated-cognition, cognitive-affective processing, self-narrative, evolution, or social adaption (Buss, 2009, 2011; Higgins & Scholer, 2010; McAdams & Olson, 2010; Mischel & Shoda, 1995). From a foundational aspect, we will focus on several traditional perspectives in personality theory:

- The *psychodynamic perspective* had its beginnings in the work of Sigmund Freud and still exists today. It focuses on the role of the unconscious mind in the development of personality. This perspective is also heavily focused on biological causes of personality differences.

- The *behaviorist perspective* is based on the theories of learning as discussed in Chapter Five. This approach focuses on the effect of the environment on behavior and as addressed here, includes aspects of social cognitive theory in that interactions with others and personal thought processes also influence learning and personality.

- The *humanistic perspective* first arose as a reaction against the psychoanalytic and behaviorist perspectives and focuses on the role of each person's conscious life experiences and choices in personality development.

- The *trait perspective* differs from the other three in its basic goals: The psychodynamic, behaviorist, and humanistic perspectives all seek to explain the process that causes personality to form into its unique characteristics, whereas trait theorists are more concerned with the end result—the characteristics themselves. Although some trait theorists assume that traits are biologically determined, others make no such assumption.

Before we begin our study of the various personality perspectives, take a moment to complete the survey, *What Has Shaped Your Personality?*, to learn more about what factors may have influenced your own personality.

Survey   WHAT HAS SHAPED YOUR PERSONALITY?

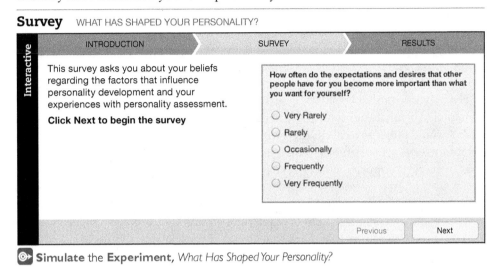

Simulate the **Experiment,** *What Has Shaped Your Personality?*

Concept Map L.O. 11.1

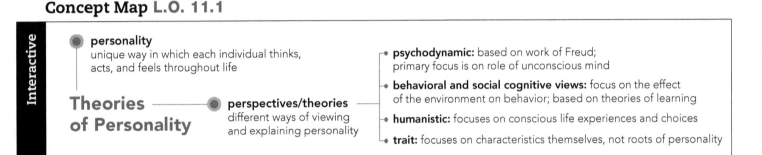

Practice Quiz   How much do you remember?   ANSWERS ON PAGE AK-1.

Pick the best answer.

1. If you are asked to describe your best friends by explaining how they act, typically feel, and what they think about, you would be describing their
  a. temperament.
  b. character.
  c. personality.
  d. mood.

2. Laila does not approve of her sister's boyfriend. She tells their mother, "He just doesn't strike me as a very nice guy. He doesn't seem to be decent, and I think he would be very dishonorable!" The girls' mother tells her daughter, "Why are you always being so judgmental of other people? Seriously, how can you be so sure that you are right about this guy's _____?"
  a. character
  b. personality
  c. temperament
  d. upbringing

3. According to early theorists like Hippocrates and Galen, temperament or personality was believed to be related to the relative balance of the four physical humors (liquids) in the body. Which of the following was not one of them?
  a. blood   **c.** phlegm
  b. water   **d.** yellow bile

4. Why is it that no single explanation of personality exists within the field of psychology today?
  a. Because it has been determined that men and women have fundamental personality differences that make a single explanation across all human beings impossible.
  b. Because it has been determined that people of different racial backgrounds have fundamental personality differences that make a single explanation across all human beings impossible.
  c. Because although Freud's theories were scientifically shown to be accurate and superior to all other models, they have been resisted because of their politically incorrect nature.
  d. Because it is very difficult to precisely and scientifically describe and measure what personality truly is.

The Psychodynamic Perspective of Personality

Sigmund Freud (1856–1939) was the founder of the psychodynamic movement in psychology. Many of his patients sat or reclined on the couch above while he sat in a chair, listening to them and developing his psychoanalytic theory of personality.

It's hard to understand how Freud developed his ideas about personality unless we have some knowledge of the world in which he and his patients lived. He was born and raised in Europe during the Victorian Age, a time of sexual repression. People growing up in this period were told by their church that sex should take place only in the context of marriage and then only to make babies. To enjoy sexual intercourse was considered a sin. Men were understood to be unable to control their "animal" desires at times, and a good Victorian husband would father several children with his wife and then turn to a mistress for sexual comfort, leaving his virtuous* wife untouched. Women, especially those of the upper classes, were not supposed to have sexual urges. It is no wonder that many of Freud's patients were wealthy women with problems stemming from unfulfilled sexual desires or sexual repression. Freud's "obsession" with sexual explanations for abnormal behavior seems more understandable in light of his cultural background and that of his patients.

Freud came to believe that there were layers of consciousness in the mind. His belief in the influence of the unconscious mind on conscious behavior, published in *The Psychopathology of Everyday Life* (Freud, 1901), shocked the Victorian world.

THE MAN AND THE COUCH: SIGMUND FREUD AND THE ORIGINS OF THE PSYCHODYNAMIC PERSPECTIVE

11.2 Describe how Freud's view of the mind and personality formed a basis for psychodynamic theory.

Freud believed that the mind was divided into three parts: the preconscious, conscious, and unconscious (Freud, 1900). (See **Figure 11.1**.) While no one really disagreed with the idea of a conscious mind in which one's current awareness exists, or even of

Figure 11.1 Freud's Conception of the Personality

This iceberg represents the three levels of the mind. The part of the iceberg visible above the surface is the conscious mind. Just below the surface is the preconscious mind, everything that is not yet part of the conscious mind. Hidden deep below the surface is the unconscious mind, feelings, memories, thoughts, and urges that cannot be easily brought into consciousness. While two of the three parts of the personality (ego and superego) exist at all three levels of awareness, the id is completely in the unconscious mind.

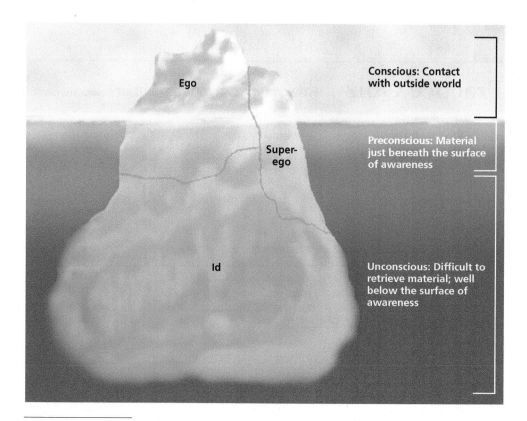

Ego

Super-ego

Id

Conscious: Contact with outside world

Preconscious: Material just beneath the surface of awareness

Unconscious: Difficult to retrieve material; well below the surface of awareness

*virtuous: morally excellent.

a preconscious mind containing memories, information, and events of which one can easily become aware, the **unconscious mind** (also called "the unconscious") was the real departure for the professionals of Freud's day. Freud theorized that there is a part of the mind that remains hidden at all times, surfacing only in symbolic form in dreams and in some of the behavior people engage in without knowing why they have done so. Even when a person makes a determined effort to bring a memory out of the unconscious mind, it will not appear directly, according to Freud. Freud believed that the unconscious mind was the most important determining factor in human behavior and personality.

FREUD'S DIVISIONS OF THE PERSONALITY   Freud believed, based on observations of his patients, that personality itself could be divided into three parts, each existing at one or more levels of conscious awareness (see Figure 11.1). The way these three parts of the personality develop and interact with one another became the heart of his theory (Freud, 1923, 1933, 1940).

ID: IF IT FEELS GOOD, DO IT   The first and most primitive part of the personality, present in the infant, is the **id**. *Id* is a Latin word that means "it." The id is a completely unconscious, pleasure-seeking, amoral part of the personality that exists at birth, containing all of the basic biological drives: hunger, thirst, self-preservation, and sex, for example.

 Wait a minute—Freud thought babies have sex drives?

Yes, Freud thought babies have sex drives, which shocked and outraged his colleagues and fellow Victorians. By "sex drive" he really meant "pleasure drive," the need to seek out pleasurable sensations. People do seem to be pleasure-seeking creatures, and even infants seek pleasure from sucking and chewing on anything they can get into their mouths. In fact, thinking about what infants are like when they are just born provides a good picture of the id. Infants are demanding, irrational, illogical, and impulsive. They want their needs satisfied immediately, and they don't care about anyone else's needs or desires. (A word of caution: The fact that infant behavior seems to fit Freud's concept of the id is not proof that the id exists. It simply means that Freud came up with the concept of the id to fit what he already knew about infants.)

Freud called this need for satisfaction the **pleasure principle**, which can be defined as the desire for immediate gratification of needs with no regard for the consequences. The pleasure principle can be summed up simply as "if it feels good, do it."

EGO: THE EXECUTIVE DIRECTOR   People normally try to satisfy an infant's needs as quickly as possible. Infants are fed when hungry, changed when wet, and tended to whenever they cry. But as infants begin to grow, adults start denying them their every wish. There will be things they cannot touch or hold, and they must learn to wait for certain things, such as food. Freud would say that reality has reared its ugly head, and the id simply cannot deal with the reality of having to wait or not getting what it wants. Worse still would be the possibility of punishment as a result of the id's unrestrained actions.

According to Freud, to deal with reality, a second part of the personality develops called the **ego**. The ego, from the Latin word for "I," is mostly conscious and is far more rational, logical, and cunning than the id. The ego works on the **reality principle**, which is the need to satisfy the demands of the id only in ways that will not lead to negative consequences. This means that sometimes the ego decides to deny the id its desires because the consequences would be painful or too unpleasant.

For example, while an infant might reach out and take an object despite a parent's protests, a toddler with the developing ego will avoid taking the object when the parent says, "No!" to avoid punishment—but may go back for the object when the parent is not looking. A simpler way of stating the reality principle, then, is "if it feels good, do it, but only if you can get away with it."

If everyone acted on the pleasure principle, the world would be pretty scary. How does knowing right from wrong come into Freud's theory?

SUPEREGO: THE MORAL WATCHDOG   Freud called the third and final part of the personality, the moral center of personality, the **superego**. The superego (also Latin, meaning "over the self") develops as a preschool-aged child learns the rules, customs, and expectations of society. The superego contains the **conscience**, the part of the personality that makes people feel guilt, or *moral anxiety*, when they do the wrong thing. It is not until the conscience develops that children have a sense of right and wrong. (Note that the term *conscience* is a different word from *conscious*. They may look and sound similar, but they represent totally different concepts.)

THE ANGEL, THE DEVIL, AND ME: HOW THE THREE PARTS OF THE PERSONALITY WORK TO-GETHER   Anyone who has ever watched cartoons while growing up has probably seen these three parts of the personality shown in animated form—the id is usually a little devil, the superego an angel, and the ego is the person or animal caught in the middle, trying to decide what action to take. So, the id makes demands, the superego puts restrictions on how those demands can be met, and the ego has to come up with a plan that will quiet the id but satisfy the superego. Sometimes the id or the superego does not get its way, resulting in a great deal of anxiety for the ego itself. This constant state of conflict is Freud's view of how personality works; it is only when the anxiety created by this conflict gets out of hand that disordered behavior arises. Note that despite the id being portrayed as the devil in the example, the id is not "evil," it is concerned with survival and immediate gratification.

The **psychological defense mechanisms** are ways of dealing with anxiety through unconsciously distorting one's perception of reality. These defense mechanisms were mainly outlined and studied by Freud's daughter, Anna Freud, who was a psychoanalyst (Benjafield, 1996; A. Freud, 1946). In order for the three parts of the personality to function, the constant conflict among them must be managed, and Freud assumed that the defense mechanisms were one of the most important tools for dealing with the anxiety caused by this conflict. A list of the defense mechanisms, their definitions, and examples of each appears in **Table 11.1**.

STAGES OF PERSONALITY DEVELOPMENT

 So the id exists at birth, but the other two parts of the personality develop later—how much later? When is personality finished?

Freud believed that personality development occurs in a series of **psychosexual stages** that are determined by the developing sexuality of the child. At each stage, a different *erogenous zone*, or area of the body that produces pleasurable feelings, becomes important and can become the source of conflicts. Conflicts that are not fully resolved can result in **fixation**, or getting "stuck" to some degree in a stage of development. The child may grow into an adult but will still carry emotional and psychological "baggage" from that earlier fixated stage.

ORAL STAGE (FIRST 18 MONTHS)   The first stage is called the **oral stage** because the erogenous zone is the mouth. The conflict that can arise here, according to Freud, will be over weaning (taking the mother's breast away from the child, who will now drink from a cup). Weaning that occurs too soon or too late can result in too little or too much satisfaction of the child's oral needs, resulting in the activities and personality traits associated with an orally fixated adult personality: overeating, drinking too much, chain smoking, talking too much, nail biting, gum chewing, and a tendency to be either too dependent

Table 11.1 THE PSYCHOLOGICAL DEFENSE MECHANISMS

Study the table, then click "Check Your Understanding" button when you're ready.

Defense Mechanism and Definition	Example
Denial: refusal to recognize or acknowledge a threatening situation.	Pat is an alcoholic who denies being an alcoholic.
Repression: "pushing" threatening or conflicting events or situations out of conscious memory.	Regan, who was sexually abused as a child, cannot remember the abuse at all.
Rationalization: making up acceptable excuses for unacceptable behavior.	"If I don't have breakfast, I can have that piece of cake later on without hurting my diet."
Projection: placing one's own unacceptable thoughts onto others, as if the thoughts belonged to them and not to oneself.	Britni is attracted to her sister's husband but denies this and believes the husband is attracted to her.
Reaction formation: forming an emotional reaction or attitude that is the opposite of one's threatening or unacceptable actual thoughts.	Charley is unconsciously attracted to Sean but outwardly voices an extreme hatred of homosexuals.
Displacement: expressing feelings that would be threatening if directed at the real target onto a less threatening substitute target.	Sandra gets reprimanded by her boss and goes home to angrily pick a fight with her husband.
Regression: falling back on childlike patterns as a way of coping with stressful situations.	Four-year-old Blaine starts wetting his bed after his parents bring home a new baby.
Identification: trying to become like someone else to deal with one's anxiety.	Samantha really admires Emily, the most popular girl in school, and tries to copy her behavior and dress.
Compensation (substitution): trying to make up for areas in which a lack is perceived by becoming superior in some other area.	Ethan is not good at athletics, so he puts all of his energies into becoming an academic scholar.
Sublimation: turning socially unacceptable urges into socially acceptable behavior.	Ryder, who is very aggressive, becomes a mixed martial arts fighter.

Check Your Understanding

and optimistic (when the oral needs are overindulged) or too aggressive and pessimistic (when the oral needs are denied).

ANAL STAGE (18 TO 36 MONTHS)   As the child becomes a toddler, Freud believed that the erogenous zone moves from the mouth to the anus, because he also believed that children got a great deal of pleasure from both withholding and releasing their feces at will. This stage is, therefore, called the **anal stage**.

Obviously, Freud thought that the main area of conflict here is toilet training, the demand that the child use the toilet at a particular time and in a particular way. This invasion of reality is part of the process that stimulates the development of the ego during this stage. Fixation in the anal stage, from toilet training that is too harsh, can take one of two forms. The child who rebels openly will refuse to go in the toilet and, according to Freud, translate in the adult as an *anal expulsive personality*, someone who sees messiness as a statement of personal control and who is somewhat destructive and hostile. Some children, however, are terrified of making a mess and rebel passively—refusing to go at all or retaining the feces. No mess, no punishment. As adults, they are stingy, stubborn, and excessively neat. This type is called the *anal retentive personality*.

PHALLIC STAGE (3 TO 6 YEARS)   As the child grows older, the erogenous zone shifts to the genitals. Children have discovered the differences between the sexes by now, and most have also engaged in perfectly normal self-stimulation of the genitals, or masturbation. One can only imagine the horror of the Victorian parent who discovered a child engaged in masturbation. People of that era believed that masturbation led to all manner of evils, including mental illness.

This awakening of sexual curiosity and interest in the genitals is the beginning of what Freud termed the **phallic stage**. (The word *phallic* comes from the Greek word *phallos* and means "penis.") Freud believed that when boys realized that the little girl down the street had no penis they developed a fear of losing the penis called *castration anxiety*, while girls developed *penis envy* because they were missing a penis. If this seems an odd focus on male anatomy, remember the era—the Western world at that time was very

For females, chastity belts like this were occasionally used to prevent intercourse or masturbation. The openings allowed for urination and defecation but their size and design, such as metal teeth in this one, did not allow for intercourse or masturbation to easily take place.

male-oriented and male-dominated. Fortunately, nearly all psychoanalysts have long since abandoned the concept of penis envy (Horney, 1939, 1973; Slipp, 1993). The conflict in the phallic stage centers on the awakening sexual feelings of the child. Freud essentially believed that boys develop both sexual attraction to their mothers and jealousy of their fathers during this stage, a phenomenon called the **Oedipus complex**. (Oedipus was a king in a Greek tragedy who unknowingly killed his father and married his mother.)

The sexual attraction is not that of an adult male for a female but more of a sexual curiosity that becomes mixed up with the boy's feelings of love and affection for his mother. Of course, his jealousy of his father leads to feelings of anxiety and fears that his father, a powerful authority figure, might get angry and do something terrible—remember that castration anxiety? To deal with this anxiety, two things must occur by the time the phallic stage ends. The boy will *repress* his sexual feelings for his mother and *identify* with his father. (*Identification* is one of the defense mechanisms used to combat anxiety.) The boy tries to be just like his father in every way, taking on the father's behavior, mannerisms, values, and moral beliefs as his own, so that Daddy won't be able to get angry with the boy. Girls go through a similar process called the **Electra complex** with their father as the target of their affections and their mother as the rival. The result of identification is the development of the superego, the internalized moral values of the same-sex parent.

What happens when things go wrong? If a child does not have a same-sex parent with whom to identify, or if the opposite-sex parent encourages the sexual attraction, fixation can occur. Fixation in the phallic stage usually involves immature sexual attitudes as an adult. People who are fixated in this stage, according to Freud, will often exhibit promiscuous* sexual behavior and be very vain. The vanity is seen as a cover-up for feelings of low self-worth arising from the failure to resolve the complex, and the lack of moral sexual behavior stems from the failure of identification and the inadequate formation of the superego. Additionally, men with this fixation may be "mama's boys" who never quite grow up, and women with this fixation may look for much older father figures to marry.

LATENCY STAGE (6 YEARS TO PUBERTY) Remember that by the end of the phallic stage, children have pushed their sexual feelings for the opposite sex into the unconscious in another defensive reaction, repression. From age 6 to the onset of puberty, children will remain in this stage of hidden, or *latent*, sexual feelings, so this stage is called **latency**. In this stage, children grow and develop intellectually, physically, and socially but not sexually. This is the age at which boys play only with boys, girls play only with girls, and each thinks the opposite sex is pretty awful.

GENITAL STAGE (PUBERTY ON) When puberty does begin, the sexual feelings that were once repressed can no longer be ignored. Bodies are changing and sexual urges are once more allowed into consciousness, but these urges will no longer have the parents as their targets. Instead, the focus of sexual curiosity and attraction will become other adolescents, celebrities, and other objects of adoration. Since Freud tied personality development into sexual development, the genital stage represented the final process in Freud's personality theory, as well as the entry into adult social and sexual behavior.

THE NEO-FREUDIANS AND THE PSYCHODYNAMIC PERSPECTIVE

11.3 **Explain how the neo-Freudians modified Freud's theory and how modern psychodynamic theory differs from that of Freud.**

At first Freud's ideas were met with resistance and ridicule by the growing community of doctors and psychologists. Eventually, a number of early psychoanalysts, objecting

---

*promiscuous: having sexual relations with more than one partner.

to Freud's emphasis on biology and particularly on sexuality, broke away from a strict interpretation of psychoanalytic theory, instead altering the focus of **psychoanalysis** (the term Freud applied to both his explanation of the workings of the unconscious mind and the development of personality and the therapy he based on that theory) to the impact of the social environment. Ⓛ Ⓘ Ⓝ Ⓚ to Learning Objective 1.3. At the same time they retained many of Freud's original concepts such as the id, ego, superego, and defense mechanisms.

THE NEO-FREUDIANS   These early psychoanalysts became the **neo-Freudians**, or "new" Freudian psychoanalysts. This section briefly covers some of the more famous neo-Freudians.

JUNG   Carl Gustav Jung ("YOONG") disagreed with Freud about the nature of the unconscious mind. Jung believed that the unconscious held much more than personal fears, urges, and memories. He believed that there was not only a **personal unconscious**, as described by Freud, but a **collective unconscious** as well (Jung, 1933).

According to Jung, the collective unconscious contains a kind of "species" memory, memories of ancient fears and themes that seem to occur in many folktales and cultures. These collective, universal human memories were called **archetypes** by Jung. There are many archetypes, but two of the more well known are the *anima/animus* (the feminine side of a man/the masculine side of a woman) and the *shadow* (the dark side of personality, called the "devil" in Western cultures). The side of one's personality that is shown to the world is termed the *persona*.

ADLER   Alfred Adler was also in disagreement with Freud over the importance of sexuality in personality development. Adler (1954) developed the theory that as young, helpless children, people all develop feelings of inferiority when comparing themselves to the more powerful, superior adults in their world. The driving force behind all human endeavors, emotions, and thoughts for Adler was not the seeking of pleasure but the seeking of superiority. The defense mechanism of *compensation*, in which people try to overcome feelings of inferiority in one area of life by striving to be superior in another area, figured prominently in Adler's theory (see Table 11.1).

HORNEY   Karen Horney (horn-EYE) disagreed with Freudian views about the differences between males and females and most notably with the concept of penis envy. She countered with her own concept of "womb envy," stating that men felt the need to compensate for their lack of child-bearing ability by striving for success in other areas (Burger, 1997).

Rather than focusing on sexuality, Horney focused on the **basic anxiety** created in a child born into a world that is so much bigger and more powerful than the child. While people whose parents gave them love, affection, and security would overcome this anxiety, others with less secure upbringings would develop **neurotic personalities** and maladaptive ways of dealing with relationships. Some children, according to Horney, try to deal with their anxiety by moving toward people, becoming dependent and clingy. Others move against people, becoming aggressive, demanding, and cruel. A third way of coping would be to move away from people by withdrawing from personal relationships.

ERIKSON   Erik Erikson (1950, 1959, 1982) was an art teacher who became a psychoanalyst by studying with Anna Freud. He also broke away from Freud's emphasis on sex, preferring instead to emphasize the social relationships that are important at every stage of life. Erikson's eight psychosocial stages are discussed in detail in Chapter Eight. Ⓛ Ⓘ Ⓝ Ⓚ to Learning Objective 8.9.

Of the three ways children deal with anxiety according to Horney, which way do you think this child might be using?

It sounds as if all of these theorists became famous by ditching some of Freud's original ideas. Is Freud even worth studying anymore?

CURRENT THOUGHTS ON FREUD AND THE PSYCHODYNAMIC PERSPECTIVE Although Freud's original psychoanalytic theory seems less relevant in today's sexually saturated world, many of his concepts have remained useful and still form a basis for many modern personality theories, and the psychodynamic perspective. The idea of the defense mechanisms has had some research support and has remained useful in clinical psychology as a way of describing people's defensive behavior and irrational thinking. The concept of an unconscious mind also has some research support.

As strange as the idea of an unconscious mind that guides behavior must have seemed to Freud's contemporaries, modern researchers have had to admit that there are influences on human behavior that exist outside of normal conscious awareness. Although much of this research has taken place in the area of hypnosis and subliminal perception (Borgeat & Goulet, 1983; Bryant & McConkey, 1989; Kihlstrom, 1987, 1999, 2001), other researchers have looked at the concept of implicit memory and implicit learning (Frensch & Runger, 2003). **L I N K** to Learning Objective 6.5.

This might be a good time to point out a very important fact about Freud's theory: He did no experiments to arrive at his conclusions about personality. His theory is based on his own observations (case studies) of numerous patients. Basing his suppositions on his patients' detailed memories of their childhoods and life experiences, he interpreted their behavior and reminiscences to develop his theory of psychoanalysis. He felt free to interpret what his patients told him of their childhoods as fantasy or fact, depending on how well those memories fit in with his developing theory. For example, many of Freud's patients told him that they were sexually abused by fathers, brothers, and other close family members. Freud was apparently unable to accept these memories as real and decided that they were fantasies, making them the basis of the Oedipal conflict. He actually revised his original perceptions of his patients' memories of abuse as real in the face of both public and professional criticism from his German colleagues (Masson, 1984).

Freud based much of his diagnoses of patients' problems on the interpretations of dreams (**L I N K** to Learning Objective 4.6) and the results of the patient's free association (talking about anything without fear of negative feedback). These "sources" of information are often criticized as being too ambiguous and without scientific support for the validity of his interpretations. The very ambiguity of these sources of information allowed Freud to fit the patient's words and recollections to his own preferred interpretation, as well as increasing the possibility that his own suggestions and interpretations, if conveyed to the patient, might alter the actual memories of the patient, who would no doubt be in a very suggestible state of mind during therapy (Grünbaum, 1984).

Another criticism of Freud's theory concerns the people upon whose dreams, recollections, and comments the theory of psychoanalysis was based. Freud's clients were almost all wealthy Austrian women living in the Victorian era of sexual repression. Critics state that basing his theory on observations made with such a demographically limited group of clients promoted his emphasis on sexuality as the root of all problems in personality, as women of that social class and era were often sexually frustrated. Freud rarely had clients who did not fit this description, and so his theory is biased in terms of sexual frustrations (Robinson, 1993).

Although most professionals today view Freud's theory with a great deal of skepticism, his influence on the modern world cannot be ignored. Freudian concepts have had an impact on literature, movies, and even children's cartoons. People who have never taken a course in psychology are familiar with some of Freud's most basic concepts, such as the defense mechanisms. He was also one of the first theorists to emphasize the importance of childhood experiences on personality development—in spite of the fact that he did not work extensively with children.

It has only been in the last several decades that people have had the necessary tools to examine the concepts of the unconscious mind. One can only wonder how Freud might have changed his theory in light of what is known about the workings of the human brain and the changes in society that exist today.

WRITING PROMPT

What aspects of psychodynamic theory do you think still have relevance in today's world? Was there one neo-Freudian whose theory appealed to you, and if so, why?

▶ | The response entered here will be saved to your notes and may be collected by your instructor if he/she requires it. |

Submit

Concept Map L.O. 11.2, 11.3

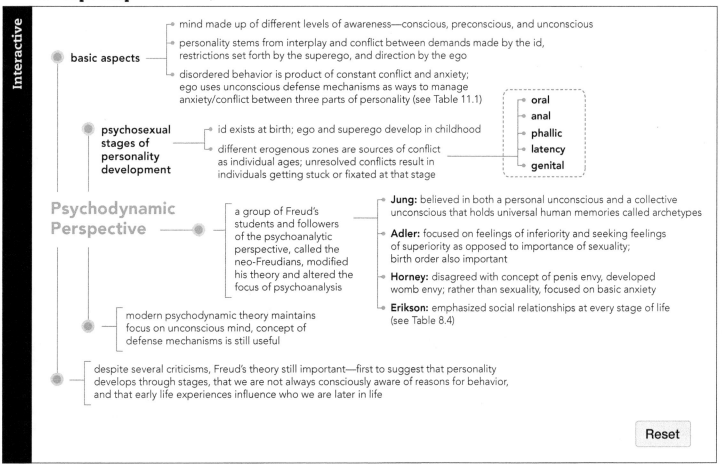

Practice Quiz   How much do you remember? ANSWERS ON PAGE AK-1.

Pick the best answer.

1. According to Freud, the _____ mind was the most important determining factor in human behavior and personality.
  a. preconscious   **c.** conscience
  b. conscious   **d.** unconscious

2. According to Freud, which part of the personality is totally buried within each individual?
  a. ego   **c.** id
  b. superego   **d.** conscience

3. The awakening of sexual curiosity and interest in the genitals is the beginning of what Freud termed the
   a. oral stage.
   c. phallic stage.
   b. anal stage.
   d. latency stage.

4. Many of Kyle's friends like to dress up on Halloween as devils, vampires, and zombies. According to Carl Jung's theory, what archetype is being expressed?
   a. anima
   c. persona
   b. animus
   d. shadow

5. Which neo-Freudian believed personality was mostly a product of dealing with anxieties during childhood?
   a. Karen Horney
   b. Erik Erikson
   c. Carl Jung
   d. Alfred Adler

The Behaviorist and Social Cognitive View of Personality

At the time that Freud's theory was shocking the Western world, another psychological perspective was also making its influence known. In Chapter Five the theories of classical and operant conditioning were discussed in some detail. *Behaviorists* (researchers who use the principles of conditioning to explain the actions and reactions of both animals and humans) and *social cognitive theorists* (researchers who emphasize the influence of social and cognitive factors on learning) have a very different view of personality.

LEARNING THEORIES

11.4 Compare different learning theories of personality, including the theories of Bandura and Rotter.

For the behaviorist, personality is nothing more than a set of learned responses or **habits** (DeGrandpre, 2000; Dollard & Miller, 1950). In the strictest traditional view of Watson and Skinner, everything a person or animal does is a response to some environmental stimulus that has been reinforced or strengthened by a reward in some way.

 So how does a pattern of rewarding certain behavior end up becoming part of some kind of personality pattern?

Think about how a traditional behaviorist might explain a shy personality. Beginning in childhood, a person might be exposed to a parent with a rather harsh discipline style (stimulus). Avoiding the attention of that parent would result in fewer punishments and scoldings, so that avoidance response is negatively reinforced—the "bad thing" or punishment is avoided by keeping out of sight and quiet. Later, that child might generalize that avoidance response to other authority figures and adults, such as teachers. In this way, a pattern (habit) of shyness would develop.

Of course, many learning theorists today do not use only classical and operant conditioning to explain the development of the behavior patterns referred to as personality. **Social cognitive learning theorists**, who emphasize the importance of both the influences of other people's behavior and of a person's own expectancies on learning, hold that observational learning, modeling, and other cognitive learning techniques can lead to the formation of patterns of personality. **L I N K** to Learning Objective 5.13.

One of the more well-researched learning theories that includes the concept of cognitive processes as influences on behavior is the social cognitive theory of Albert Bandura. In the **social cognitive view**, behavior is governed not just by the influence of external stimuli and response patterns but also by cognitive processes such as anticipating, judging, and memory, as well as learning through the imitation of models. In fact, you might remember Bandura's work with observation learning and imitation of models from his Bobo doll study. (L)(I)(N)(K) to Learning Objective 5.13.

BANDURA'S RECIPROCAL DETERMINISM AND SELF-EFFICACY Bandura (1989) believes that three factors influence one another in determining the patterns of behavior that make up personality: the environment, the behavior itself, and personal or cognitive factors that the person brings into the situation from earlier experiences (see **Figure 11.2**). These three factors each affect the other two in a reciprocal, or give-and-take, relationship. Bandura calls this relationship **reciprocal determinism**.

Take a look at Figure 11.2. The environment includes the actual physical surroundings, the other people who may or may not be present, and the potential for reinforcement in those surroundings. The intensity and frequency of the behavior will not only be influenced by the environment but will also have an impact on that environment. The person brings into the situation previously reinforced responses (personality, in other words) and mental processes such as thinking and anticipating.

Here's how this might work: Richard walks into a classroom filled with other students, but no teacher is present at this time. (This is the *environment*.) Part of Richard's *personal* characteristics includes the desire to have attention from other people by talking loudly and telling jokes, which has been very rewarding to him in the past (past reinforcements are part of his cognitive processes, or expectancies of future rewards for his behavior). Also in the past, he has found that he gets more attention when an authority figure is not present. His *behavior* will most likely be to start talking and telling jokes, which will continue if he gets the reaction he expects from his fellow students. If the teacher walks in (the *environment* changes), his behavior will change. If the other students don't laugh, his behavior will change. In the future Richard might be less likely to behave in the same way because his expectations for reward (a cognitive element of his *personal* variables) are different.

One of the more important personal variables that Bandura talks about is **self-efficacy**, a person's expectancy of how effective his or her efforts to accomplish a goal will be in any particular circumstance (Bandura, 1998). (Self-efficacy is not the same concept as *self-esteem*, which is the positive values a person places on his or her sense of worth.)

People's sense of self-efficacy can be high or low, depending on what has happened in similar circumstances in the past (success or failure), what other people tell them about their competence, and their own assessment of their abilities. For example, if Fiona has an opportunity to write an extra-credit paper to improve her grade in psychology, she will be more likely to do so if her self-efficacy is high: She has gotten good grades on such papers in the past, her teachers have told her that she writes well, and she knows she can write a good paper. According to Bandura, people high in self-efficacy are more persistent and expect to succeed, whereas people low in self-efficacy expect to fail and tend to avoid challenges (Bandura, 1998).

ROTTER'S SOCIAL LEARNING THEORY: EXPECTANCIES Julian Rotter (1966, 1978, 1981, 1990) devised a theory based on a basic principle of motivation derived from Thorndike's law of effect: People are motivated to seek reinforcement and avoid punishment. He viewed personality as a relatively stable set of *potential* responses to various situations. If in the past, a certain way of responding led to a reinforcing or pleasurable consequence, that way of responding would become a pattern of responding, or part of the "personality" as learning theorists see it.

One very important pattern of responding in Rotter's view became his concept of **locus of control**, the tendency for people to assume that they either have control or do not have control over events and consequences in their lives. (L)(I)(N)(K) to Learning

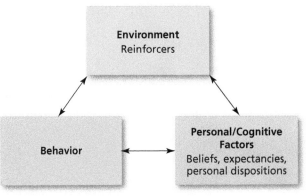

Figure 11.2   Reciprocal Determinism

In Bandura's model of reciprocal determinism, three factors influence behavior: the environment, which consists of the physical surroundings and the potential for reinforcement; the person (personal/cognitive characteristics that have been rewarded in the past); and the behavior itself, which may or may not be reinforced at this particular time and place.

According to Rotter, what would be the most likely form of locus of control experienced by this young woman?

Objective 9.2. People who assume that their own actions and decisions directly affect the consequences they experience are said to be *internal* in locus of control, whereas people who assume that their lives are more controlled by powerful others, luck, or fate are *external* in locus of control (MacDonald, 1970; Rotter, 1966). Rotter associated people high in internal locus of control with the personality characteristics of high achievement motivation (the will to succeed in any attempted task). Those who give up too quickly or who attribute events in their lives to external causes can fall into patterns of learned helplessness and depression (Abramson et al., 1978, 1980; Gong-Guy & Hammen, 1980).

Like Bandura, Rotter (1978, 1981) also believed that an interaction of factors would determine the behavioral patterns that become personality for an individual. For Rotter, there are two key factors influencing a person's decision to act in a certain way given a particular situation: expectancy, and reinforcement value. **Expectancy** is fairly similar to Bandura's concept of self-efficacy in that it refers to the person's subjective feeling that a particular behavior will lead to a reinforcing consequence. A high expectancy for success is similar to a high sense of self-efficacy and is also based on past experiences with successes and failures. *Reinforcement value* refers to an individual's preference for a particular reinforcer over all other possible reinforcing consequences. Things or circumstances that are particularly appealing to us have a higher reinforcement value than other possible reinforcers.

CURRENT THOUGHTS ON THE SOCIAL COGNITIVE VIEW OF PERSONALITY

11.5 Evaluate the strengths and limitations of the social cognitive view of personality.

Behaviorism as an explanation of the formation of personality has its limitations. The classic theory does not take mental processes into account when explaining behavior, nor does it give weight to social influences on learning. The social cognitive view of personality, unlike traditional behaviorism, does include social and mental processes and their influence on behavior. Unlike psychoanalysis, the concepts in this theory can and have been tested under scientific conditions (Backenstrass et al., 2008; Bandura, 1965; Catanzaro et al., 2000; DeGrandpre, 2000; Domjan et al., 2000; Skinner, 1989). Some of this research has investigated how people's expectancies can influence their control of their own negative moods. Although some critics think that human personality and behavior are too complex to explain as the result of cognitions and external stimuli interacting, others point out that this viewpoint has enabled the development of therapies based on learning theory that have become effective in changing undesirable behavior. ⓁⓘⓃⓚ to Learning Objective 13.4.

Concept Map L.O. 11.4, 11.5

Interactive

- for behaviorists, personality is a set of learned responses and habits, gained through classical and operant conditioning
- in social cognitive view, both learning (individual and through imitation of models) and cognitive processes (such as anticipation, judgment, and memory) are important

- **Bandura:** concept of self-efficacy; believed three factors were important: the environment, the behavior itself, and personal or cognitive experiences from earlier experiences; each affect the other two in a reciprocal way—reciprocal determinism (see Figure 11.2)
- **Rotter:** theory based on principles of motivation derived from Thorndike's law of effect; personality is set of potential responses to various situations, including one's locus of control (internal vs. external), sense of expectancy, and preference for particular reinforcers.

Behaviorist and Social Cognitive Perspective

Reset

Practice Quiz   How much do you remember? ANSWERS ON PAGE AK-1.

Pick the best answer.

1. According to the behavioral theory, personality primarily consists of
   a. unconscious forces.
   b. learned responses.
   c. biologically driven traits.
   d. personal choices.

2. Albert Bandura considers _____ as a person's expectancy of how effective his or her efforts to accomplish a goal will be in any particular circumstance.
   a. self-image
   b. self-esteem
   c. self-awareness
   d. self-efficacy

3. You have walked in late to class and your psychology professor is explaining how one personality theorist sees personality as a relatively stable set of potential responses to various situations. You know immediately that your professor is talking about the theories of
   a. Julian Rotter.   **c.** Albert Bandura.
   b. B. F. Skinner.   **d.** John Watson.

4. Nina appreciates compliments about her new photography business but really values constructive criticism, because she knows that she is capable of addressing any concerns that are raised by a customer. According to Julian Rotter, Nina has a(n)
   a. strong self-concept.   **c.** internal locus of control.
   b. real self.   **d.** external locus of control.

The Third Force: Humanism and Personality

As first discussed in Chapter One, in the middle of the twentieth century the pessimism of Freudian psychodynamic theory with its emphasis on conflict and animalistic needs, together with the emphasis of behaviorism on external control of behavior, gave rise to a third force in psychology: the *humanistic perspective*.

CARL ROGERS AND THE HUMANISTIC PERSPECTIVE

11.6 **Describe how humanists such as Carl Rogers explain personality.**

The **humanistic perspective**, led by psychologists such as Carl Rogers and Abraham Maslow, wanted psychology to focus on the things that make people uniquely human, such as subjective emotions and the freedom to choose one's own destiny. As Maslow's theory was discussed more fully in Chapter Nine, in this chapter the discussion of the humanistic view of personality will focus on the theory of Carl Rogers. A brief overview of the humanistic perspective is also offered in the video, *Humanistic Perspective on Personality*.

"It's always 'Sit,' 'Stay,' 'Heel'—never 'Think,' 'Innovate,' 'Be yourself.'"

Watch the **Video**, *Humanistic Perspective on Personality.*

Both Maslow and Rogers (1961) believed that human beings are always striving to fulfill their innate capacities and capabilities and to become everything that their genetic potential will allow them to become. This striving for fulfillment is called the **self-actualizing tendency**. An important tool in human self-actualization is the development of an image of oneself, or the **self-concept**. The self-concept is based on what people are told by others and how the sense of **self** is reflected in the words and actions of important people in one's life, such as parents, siblings, coworkers, friends, and teachers.

REAL AND IDEAL SELF   Two important components of the self-concept are the *real self* (one's actual perception of characteristics, traits, and abilities that form the basis of the striving for self-actualization) and the *ideal self* (the perception of what one should be or would like to be). The ideal self primarily comes from important, significant others in a person's life, especially our parents when we are children. Rogers believed that when the real self and the ideal self are very close or similar to each other, people feel competent and capable, but when there is a mismatch between the real self and ideal self, anxiety and neurotic behavior can be the result. (See **Figure 11.3**.)

The two halves of the self are more likely to match if they aren't that far apart at the start. When a person has a realistic view of the real self, and the ideal self is something that is actually attainable, there usually isn't a problem of a mismatch. It is when a person's view of self is distorted or the ideal self is impossible to attain that problems arise. Once again, how the important people (who can be either good or bad influences) in a person's life react to the person can greatly impact the degree of agreement, or congruence, between real and ideal selves. However, as an individual develops, they look less to others for approval and disapproval, and more within themselves to decide if they are living in a way that is satisfying to them (Rogers, 1951, 1961).

Figure 11.3 REAL AND IDEAL SELVES

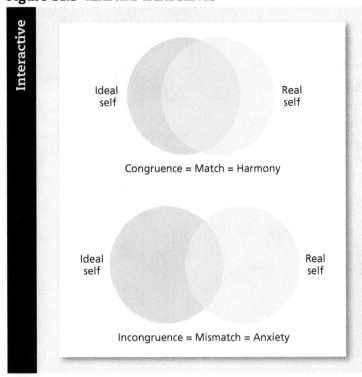

Congruence = Match = Harmony

Incongruence = Mismatch = Anxiety

According to Rogers, the self-concept includes the real self and the ideal self. The real self is a person's actual perception of traits and abilities, whereas the ideal self is the perception of what a person would like to be or thinks he or she should be. When the ideal self and the real self are very similar (matching), the person experiences harmony and contentment. When there is a mismatch between the two selves, the person experiences anxiety and may engage in neurotic behavior.

CONDITIONAL AND UNCONDITIONAL POSITIVE REGARD   Rogers defined **positive regard** as warmth, affection, love, and respect that come from the significant others (parents, admired adults, friends, and teachers) in people's experience. Positive regard is vital to people's ability to cope with stress and to strive to achieve self-actualization. Rogers believed that **unconditional positive regard**, or love, affection, and respect with no strings attached, is necessary for people to be able to explore fully all that they can achieve and become. Unfortunately, some parents, spouses, and friends give **conditional positive regard**, which is love, affection, respect, and warmth that depend, or seem to depend, on doing what those people want.

Here is an example: As a freshman, Sasha was thinking about becoming a math teacher, a computer programmer, or an elementary school teacher. Karen, also a freshman, already knew that she was going to be a doctor. Whereas Sasha's parents had told her that what she wanted to become was up to her and that they would love her no matter what, Karen's parents had made it very clear to her as a small child that they expected her to become a doctor. She was under the very strong impression that if she tried to choose any other career, she would lose her parents' love and respect. Sasha's parents were giving her unconditional positive regard, but Karen's parents (whether they intended to do so or not) were giving her conditional positive regard. Karen was obviously not as free as Sasha to explore her potential and abilities.

For Rogers, a person who is in the process of self-actualizing, actively exploring potentials and abilities and experiencing a match between the real self and ideal self, is a **fully functioning person**. Fully functioning people are in touch with their own feelings and abilities and are able to trust their innermost urges and intuitions (Rogers, 1961). To become fully functioning, a person needs unconditional positive regard. In Rogers's view, Karen would not have been a fully functioning person.

 💬 What kind of people are considered to be fully functioning? Is it the same thing as being self-actualized?

Although the two concepts are highly related, there are some subtle differences. Self-actualization is a goal that people are always striving to reach, according to Maslow (1987). Ⓛ Ⓘ Ⓝ Ⓚ to Learning Objective 9.4. In Rogers's view, only a person who is fully functioning is capable of reaching the goal of self-actualization. To be fully functioning is a necessary step in the process of self-actualization. Maslow (1987) listed several people who he considered to be self-actualized people: Albert Einstein, Mahatma Gandhi, and Eleanor Roosevelt, for example. These were people who Maslow found to have the self-actualized qualities of being creative, autonomous, and unprejudiced. In Rogers's view, these same people would be seen as having trusted their true feelings and innermost needs rather than just going along with the crowd.

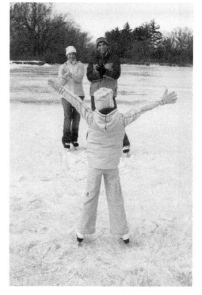

These proud parents are giving their daughter unconditional positive regard.

CURRENT THOUGHTS ON THE HUMANISTIC VIEW OF PERSONALITY

11.7 **Evaluate the strengths and limitations of the humanistic view of personality.**

Humanistic views of personality paint a very rosy picture. Some critics believe that the picture is a little too rosy, ignoring the more negative aspects of human nature. For example, would humanistic theory easily explain the development of sociopathic personalities who have no conscience or moral nature? Or could a humanist explain the motivation behind terrorism?

Humanistic theory is also very difficult to test scientifically. Little research support exists for this viewpoint, which could be considered more a philosophical view of human behavior than it is a psychological explanation. Its greatest impact has been in the development of therapies designed to promote self-growth and help people better understand themselves and others. Ⓛ Ⓘ Ⓝ Ⓚ to Learning Objective 13.3.

Despite these apparent flaws, some of the premises of positive psychology have their roots in humanistic psychology. The term "positive psychology" was first used by Maslow in 1954 when he stressed the need for psychology to focus on human potential, rather than problems (Maslow, 1954). However, the field of positive psychology itself has emerged more recently and strives to understand how human beings prosper during difficult times and focuses on the science of subjective, individual, and group factors that foster positive experiences (Seligman & Csikszentmihalyi, 2000). Both positive psychology and humanism share a focus on human potential, identification of strengths, and the positive aspects of what it means to be a human (Mahoney, 2005; Seligman, 2005; Snyder & Lopez, 2005; Waterman, 2013).

Concept Map L.O. 11.6, 11.7

Interactive

Humanistic Perspective

(referred to as the third force in psychology; based largely on work of Rogers and Maslow)

Rogers: believed that humans are always striving to fulfill their innate capacities and capabilities (self-actualizing tendency)

self-concept is based on an individual's view of his or her real self and ideal self; when close/similar, people feel capable and competent; when there is mismatch, anxiety and neurotic behavior can occur

self-actualization is facilitated through positive regard, especially unconditional positive regard

when there is congruence between real and ideal selves, one is considered to be fully functioning and capable of reaching the goal of self-actualization

Reset

Practice Quiz How much do you remember? ANSWERS ON PAGE AK-1.

Pick the best answer.

1. What did Carl Rogers mean by the term "fully functioning person"?
   a. Someone who is working to discover his or her real self.
   b. Someone who is working to discover his or her ideal self.
   c. Someone who is experiencing a match between his or her real and ideal self, and who is also trusting of their innermost intuitions and urges.
   d. Someone who has discovered his or her self-efficacy.

2. Which psychologist is credited along with Carl Rogers as being one of the early pioneers of the humanistic perspective?
   a. B.F. Skinner
   b. Abraham Maslow
   c. William James
   d. Fritz Perls

3. Which of the following are two important aspects of Carl Rogers's theory?
   a. the real self and the ideal self
   b. the tangible self and the abstract self
   c. the conscious self and the unconscious self
   d. the shadow self and the light self

4. Jeff is having a conversation with his daughter about a fight that occurred at school in which his daughter received detention. What would Jeff probably say to his daughter if he were to use unconditional positive regard?
   a. "I love you very much, but I'm not happy about what you did."
   b. "I have taught you better than that, and I expect you to shape up."
   c. "I might not think this is such a big deal, but your father is going to be furious."
   d. "I'm very disappointed in you, and I won't tolerate any trouble-makers in my house."

Trait Theories: Who Are You?

The theories discussed so far attempt to explain how personality develops or how factors within or external to the individual influence personality. These theories may also provide psychologists and other professionals with hints as to how personality may be changed. However, not all personality theories have the same goals.

ALLPORT AND CATTELL: EARLY ATTEMPTS TO LIST AND DESCRIBE TRAITS

11.8 Define the trait perspective and describe early attempts to use traits to conceptualize personality.

Trait theories are less concerned with the explanation for personality development and changing personality than they are with describing personality and predicting behavior based on that description. A **trait** is a consistent, enduring way of thinking, feeling, or behaving, and trait theories attempt to describe personality in terms of a person's traits. The video *Trait Theories of Personality* describes this perspective in more detail.

Trait Theories

Reserved		Outgoing
Concrete thinker		Abstract thinker
Easily upset		Emotionally stable
Submissive		Dominant
Serious		Happy-go-lucky
Rule defying		Conscientious
Shy		Bold
Tough-minded		Sensitive
Trusting		Suspicious
Practical		Imaginative
Forthright		Shrewd
Self-assured		Apprehensive
Conservative		Experimenting
Group-dependent		Self-sufficient
Undisciplined		Controlled
Relaxed		Tense

▶ ◀)) CC

👁 **Watch** the **Video**, *Trait Theories of Personality.*

ALLPORT One of the earliest attempts to list and describe the traits that make up personality can be found in the work of Gordon Allport (Allport & Odbert, 1936). Allport and his colleague H. S. Odbert literally scanned the dictionary for words that could be traits, finding about 18,000, then paring that down to 200 traits after eliminating synonyms. Allport believed (with no scientific evidence, however) that these traits were literally wired into the nervous system to guide one's behavior across many different situations and that each person's "constellation" of traits was unique. (In spite of Allport's lack of evidence, behavioral geneticists have found support for the heritability of personality traits, and these findings are discussed in the next section of this chapter.)

CATTELL AND THE 16PF Two hundred traits is still a very large number of descriptors. How might an employer be able to judge the personality of a potential employee by looking at a list of 200 traits? A more compact way of describing personality was needed. Raymond Cattell (1990) defined two types of traits as *surface traits* and *source traits*. **Surface traits** are like those found by Allport, representing the personality characteristics easily seen by other people. **Source traits** are those more basic traits that underlie the surface traits. For example, shyness, being quiet, and disliking crowds might all be surface traits related to the more basic source trait of **introversion**, a tendency to withdraw from excessive stimulation.

Using a statistical technique that looks for groupings and commonalities in numerical data called *factor analysis*, Cattell identified 16 source traits (Cattell, 1950, 1966), and although he later determined that there might be another 7 source traits to make a total of 23 (Cattell & Kline, 1977), he developed his assessment questionnaire, *The Sixteen Personality Factor (16PF) Questionnaire* (Cattell, 1995), based on just 16 source traits. These 16 source traits are seen as trait dimensions, or continuums, in which there are two opposite traits at each end with a range of possible degrees for each trait measurable along the dimension. For example, someone scoring near the "reserved" end of the "reserved/outgoing" dimension would be more introverted than someone scoring in the middle or at the opposite end.

MODERN TRAIT THEORIES

11.9 **Describe and evaluate the five-factor model and other recent trait theories of personality.**

Sixteen factors are still quite a lot to discuss when talking about someone's personality. Later researchers attempted to reduce the number of trait dimensions to a more manageable number, with several groups of researchers arriving at more or less the same five trait dimensions (Botwin & Buss, 1989; Jang et al., 1998; McCrae & Costa, 1996).

THE BIG FIVE: OCEAN, OR THE FIVE-FACTOR MODEL OF PERSONALITY The five trait dimensions have become known as the **five-factor model**, or the **Big Five** (see **Table 11.2**), and represent the core description of human personality—that is, the only dimensions necessary to understand what makes us tick.

As shown in the table, these five trait dimensions can be remembered by using the acronym OCEAN, in which each of the letters is the first letter of one of the five dimensions of personality.

- **Openness** can best be described as a person's willingness to try new things and be open to new experiences. People who try to maintain the status quo and who don't like to change things would score low on openness.

- **Conscientiousness** refers to a person's organization and motivation, with people who score high in this dimension being those who are careful about being places on time and careful with belongings as well. Someone scoring low on this dimension, for example, might always be late to important social events or borrow belongings and fail to return them or return them in poor condition.

- **Extraversion** is a term first used by Carl Jung (1933), who believed that all people could be divided into two personality types: **extraverts** and **introverts**. Extraverts are outgoing and sociable, whereas introverts are more solitary and dislike being the center of attention.

- **Agreeableness** refers to the basic emotional style of a person, who may be easygoing, friendly, and pleasant (at the high end of the scale) or grumpy, crabby, and hard to get along with (at the low end).

Table 11.2 THE BIG FIVE

Study the table, then click "Check Your Understanding" button when you're ready.

High Scorer Characteristics	Factor	Low Scorer Characteristics
Creative, artistic, curious, imaginative	Openness (O)	Conventional, down-to-earth, uncreative nonconforming
Organized, reliable, neat, ambitious	Conscientiousness (C)	Unreliable, lazy, careless, negligent, spontaneous
Talkative, optimistic, sociable, affectionate	Extraversion (E)	Reserved, comfortable being alone, stays in the background
Good-natured, trusting, helpful	Agreeableness (A)	Rude, uncooperative, irritable, aggressive, competitive
Worrying, insecure, anxious, temperamental	Neuroticism (N)	Calm, secure, relaxed, stable

Check Your Understanding

Source: Adapted from McCrae & Costa (1990).

- **Neuroticism** refers to emotional instability or stability. People who are excessive worriers, overanxious, and moody would score high on this dimension, whereas those who are more even-tempered and calm would score low.

Robert McCrae and Paul Costa proposed that these five traits are not interdependent. In other words, knowing someone's score on extraversion would not give any information about scores on the other four dimensions, allowing for a tremendous amount of variety in personality descriptions.

CURRENT THOUGHTS ON THE TRAIT PERSPECTIVE Some theorists have cautioned that personality traits will not always be expressed in the same way across different situations. Walter Mischel, a social cognitive theorist, has emphasized that there is a **trait–situation interaction** in which the particular circumstances of any given situation are assumed to influence the way in which a trait is expressed (Mischel & Shoda, 1995). An outgoing extravert, for example, might laugh, talk to strangers, and tell jokes at a party. That same person, if at a funeral, would still talk and be open, but the jokes and laughter would be less likely to occur. However, the five-factor model provides a dimensional approach to classifying personality structure (as opposed to a categorical approach), which is consistent with possible alternative approaches to diagnosing personality disorders discussed in the most recent edition of the *Diagnostic and Statistical Manual of Mental Disorders* (*DSM-5*; American Psychiatric Association, 2013). Ⓛ Ⓘ Ⓝ Ⓚ to Learning Objective 12.3.

The five-factor model has been studied and tested by numerous researchers and through various methods, including neuroimaging. A study by Dr. Colin DeYoung and colleagues (DeYoung et al., 2010) seems to suggest that there are indeed certain areas of the brain associated with certain personality traits. By using a questionnaire about the Big Five personality traits and structural magnetic resonance imaging techniques, DeYoung and colleagues found that the trait of *extraversion* was associated with a higher brain volume in the medial orbitofrontal cortex (underside of frontal lobe, directly above the eyes). This area of the brain is associated with recognizing the value of rewarding information. *Neuroticism* was associated with lower brain volume in several areas responding to threat, punishment, and negative emotions. Reduced volumes were found in the dorsomedial prefrontal cortex (toward the top and middle of the prefrontal cortex) and in the left posterior hippocampus. Neuroticism was also associated with higher brain volume in the middle cingulate cortex (cortical component of limbic system), associated with error detection and response to pain.

Areas of the brain associated with the intentions of actions and mental states of others were correlated to *agreeableness*, with the area of the posterior cingulate cortex showing a greater volume in individuals high in that trait and a lesser volume in the left superior temporal sulcus. *Conscientiousness* seemed associated with the left lateral prefrontal cortex, an area located on the side of the frontal lobes involved in planning, working memory, and voluntary control of behavior. (The researchers did look at areas that might be associated with the fifth of the Big Five traits, *openness*, but failed to find any significant differences.) This study, and the others like it that are sure to follow, is part of the growing area of personality neuroscience and an important step in linking personality to the physical structure and functioning of the brain.

But what about people from different cultures? Although regional variations exist, cross-cultural research from 56 countries has found evidence of these five trait dimensions in all primary cultural regions of the world (Schmitt et al., 2007). Furthermore, it appears these dimensions are evident or recognizable not only in most languages and cultures; they are also consistent when assessed by either self-ratings or observers (Allik et al., 2013; McCrae & Terracciano, 2005). This cultural commonality raises the question of the origins of the Big Five trait dimensions: Are child-rearing practices across all those cultures similar enough to result in these five aspects of personality, or could these five dimensions have a genetic component that transcends cultural differences? The next section will discuss the evidence for a genetic basis of the Big Five.

Concept Map L.O. 11.8, 11.9

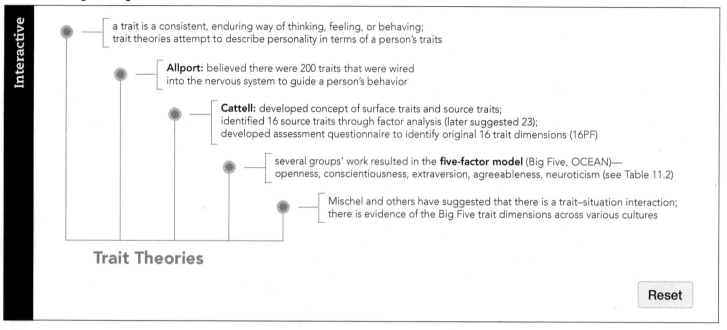

Interactive

a trait is a consistent, enduring way of thinking, feeling, or behaving; trait theories attempt to describe personality in terms of a person's traits

Allport: believed there were 200 traits that were wired into the nervous system to guide a person's behavior

Cattell: developed concept of surface traits and source traits; identified 16 source traits through factor analysis (later suggested 23); developed assessment questionnaire to identify original 16 trait dimensions (16PF)

several groups' work resulted in the **five-factor model** (Big Five, OCEAN)— openness, conscientiousness, extraversion, agreeableness, neuroticism (see Table 11.2)

Mischel and others have suggested that there is a trait–situation interaction; there is evidence of the Big Five trait dimensions across various cultures

Trait Theories

Reset

Practice Quiz   How much do you remember?   ANSWERS ON PAGE AK-1.

Pick the best answer.

1. Trait theories are less concerned with _____ and more concerned with _____.
   a. changing personality; predicting behaviors
   b. describing personality; explaining personality development
   c. predicting personality; changing personality
   d. predicting behavior; changing personality

2. A colleague at work is asked to describe you to the new manager. Most likely, the traits they will use in their description are examples of
   a. common traits.   c. source traits.
   b. cardinal traits.   d. surface traits.

3. Cattell's initial research and use of factor analysis essentially scaled down many, many different ways of describing aspects of personality into _____ source traits.
   a. 10   c. 5
   b. 16   d. 2

4. In the Big Five theory of personality, "E" stands for
   a. empathy.
   b. energy.
   c. external.
   d. extraversion.

Personality: Genetics and Culture

  What about genetics? How much of our personality is inherited?

When was the last time you were around a lot of family members other than your own? Was it a reunion? Or maybe when meeting your significant other's family for the first time? Did you notice any commonalities in the way different family members interacted, spoke, or behaved? This section will explore the "nature" side of personality, or the degree that some of our personality is linked to our parents and close relations.

BEHAVIORAL GENETICS

11.10 **Explain how behavioral geneticists use twin and adoption studies to study personality.**

The field of **behavioral genetics** is devoted to the study of just how much of an individual's personality is due to inherited traits. Animal breeders have known for a long time that selective breeding of certain animals with specific desirable traits can produce changes not only in size, fur color, and other physical characteristics but also in the temperament of the animals (Isabel, 2003; Trut, 1999). As stated earlier in this chapter, temperament consists of the characteristics with which each person is born and is, therefore, determined by biology to a great degree. If the temperaments of animals can be influenced by manipulating patterns of genetic inheritance, then it is only one small step to assume that at least those personality characteristics related to temperament in human beings may also be influenced by heredity.

Animal breeders have an advantage over those who are studying the influence of genes in human behavior. Those who breed animals can control the mating of certain animals and the conditions under which those animals are raised. Human research cannot ethically or practically develop that degree of control and so must fall back on the accidental "experiments" of nature and opportunity, studies of twins and adopted persons.

TWIN STUDIES   The difference between monozygotic (identical) and dizygotic (fraternal) twins was discussed in Chapter Eight. (L) (I) (N) K to Learning Objective 8.4. As discussed previously, identical twins share 100 percent of their genetic material, having come from one fertilized egg originally, whereas fraternal twins share only about 50 percent of their genetic material, as any other pair of siblings would. By comparing identical twins to fraternal twins, especially when twins can be found who were not raised in the same environment, researchers can begin to find evidence of possible genetic influences on various traits, including personality. (See **Figure 11.4**.)

The results of the Minnesota twin study have revealed that identical twins are more similar than fraternal twins or unrelated people in intelligence, leadership abilities, the tendency to follow rules, and the tendency to uphold traditional cultural expectations (Bouchard, 1997; Finkel & McGue, 1997). They are also more alike with regard to

James Arthur Springer and James Edward Lewis, otherwise known as the "Jim" twins. Although separated shortly after birth and reunited at age 39, they exhibited many similarities in personality and personal habits. Although genetics may explain some of these similarities, what other factors might also be at work?

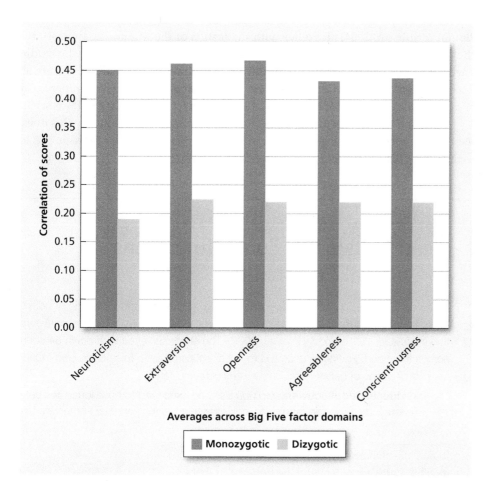

Averages across Big Five factor domains

Monozygotic   **Dizygotic**

Figure 11.4   Personalities of Identical and Fraternal Twins

Identical and fraternal twins differ in the way they express the Big Five personality factors. In a recent study, data from 696 twin pairs suggest identical twins have a correlation of about 45 percent for self-ratings across each of the Big Five factor domains, whereas fraternal twins have a correlation of about 22 percent. These findings support the idea that some aspects of personality are genetically based.
Based on: Kandler et al. (2010)

nurturance,* empathy,* and assertiveness (Neale et al., 1986), and aggressiveness (Miles & Carey, 1997). This similarity holds even if the twins are raised in separate environments.

ADOPTION STUDIES   Another tool of behavioral geneticists is to study adopted children and their adoptive and birth families. If studying genetically identical twins raised in different environments can help investigators understand the genetic influences on personality, then studying *unrelated* people who are raised in the *same* environment should help investigators discover the influence of environment. By comparing adopted children to their adoptive parents and siblings and, if possible, to their biological parents who have not raised them, researchers can uncover some of the shared and nonshared environmental and genetic influences on personality.

Adoption studies have confirmed what twin studies have shown: Genetic influences account for a great deal of personality development, regardless of shared or non-shared environments (Hershberger et al., 1995; Loehlin et al., 1985; Loehlin et al., 1998). Through this kind of study, for example, a genetic basis has been suggested for shyness (Plomin et al., 1988) and aggressiveness (Brennan et al., 1997).

CURRENT FINDINGS ON THE HERITABILITY OF PERSONALITY

11.11 Define heritability, and explain how environmental influences, such as culture, can also impact personality.

One important aspect of genetic studies is the concept of heritability, or how much some trait within a population can be attributed to genetic influences, and the extent individual genetic variation impacts differences in observed behavior (**L I N K** to Learning Objective 7.8). Several studies have found that the five personality factors of the five-factor model have nearly a 50 percent rate of heritability across several cultures (Bouchard, 1994; Herbst et al., 2000; Jang et al., 1996; Loehlin, 1992; Loehlin et al., 1998). Personality's relationship to psychopathology is also being investigated via genetic techniques (Plomin & Spinath, 2004). Together with the results of the Minnesota twin study and other research (Lubinski, 2000; Lykken & Tellegen, 1996; Plomin, 1994), the studies of genetics and personality seem to indicate that variations in personality traits are about 25 to 50 percent inherited (Jang et al., 1998). This also means that environmental influences apparently account for about half of the variation in personality traits as well.

Although the five factors have been found across several cultures, this does not mean that different cultures do not have an impact on personality. For more on this topic, see the *Classic Studies in Psychology* section that follows.

Classic Studies in Psychology
Geert Hofstede's Four Dimensions of Cultural Personality

In the early 1980s, organizational management specialist Geert Hofstede conducted a massive study into the work-related values of employees of IBM, a multinational corporation (Hofstede, 1980; Hofstede et al., 2002). The study surveyed workers in 64 countries across the world. Hofstede analyzed the data collected from this survey and found four basic dimensions of personality along which cultures differed.

1. **Individualism/collectivism:** *Individualistic cultures* tend to have loose ties between individuals, with people tending to look after themselves and their immediate families

---

*nurturance: affectionate care and attention.

*empathy: the ability to understand the feelings of others.

only. Members of such cultures have friends based on shared activities and interests, and may belong to many different loosely organized social groups. Autonomy,* change, youth, security of the individual, and equality are all highly valued. In contrast, in a *collectivistic culture*, people are from birth deeply tied into very strong in-groups, typically extended families that include grandparents, aunts and uncles, and cousins. Loyalty to the family is highly stressed, and the care of the family is placed before the care of the individual. Group membership is limited to only a few permanent groups that have tremendous influence over the individual. The values of this kind of culture are duty, order, tradition, respect for the elderly, group security, and respect for the group status and hierarchy.* Whereas the United States and Great Britain are examples of individualistic cultures, Japan, China, Korea, Mexico, and Central America are much more collectivistic.

2. **Power distance:** This dimension refers to the degree to which the less powerful members of a culture accept and even expect that the power within the culture is held in the hands of a select few rather than being more evenly distributed. Countries such as the Philippines, Mexico, many Arab countries, and India were found to be high in such expectations, whereas countries such as Austria, Sweden, Australia, Great Britain, and the United States were low in power distance.

3. **Masculinity/femininity:** Referring to how a culture distributes the roles played by men and women within the culture, this dimension varies more for the men within a culture than for the women. "Masculine" cultures are assertive and competitive, although more so for men than for women, and "feminine" cultures are more modest and caring. Both men and women in "feminine" countries have similar, caring values, but in "masculine" countries, the women are not quite as assertive and competitive as the men, leading to a greater difference between the sexes in masculine countries. Japan, Austria, Venezuela, Italy, Switzerland, Mexico, Ireland, Jamaica, the United States, Great Britain, and Germany were found to be masculine countries, whereas Sweden, Norway, the Netherlands, Denmark, Costa Rica, Yugoslavia, Finland, Chile, Portugal, Thailand, and Guatemala were ranked as more feminine.

4. **Uncertainty avoidance:** Some cultures are more tolerant of uncertainty, ambiguity,* and unstructured situations. Cultures that do not tolerate such uncertainty and lack of structure tend to have strict rules and laws with lots of security and safety measures and tend toward a philosophical/religious belief of One Truth (and "we have it!"). Cultures that are more accepting of uncertainty are more tolerant of different opinions and have fewer rules. They tend to allow many different religious beliefs to exist side by side and are less anxious and emotional than people in uncertainty-avoiding countries. Uncertainty-avoiding countries include Greece, Portugal, Guatemala, Uruguay, Belgium, El Salvador, Japan, Yugoslavia, and Peru, whereas those that are more tolerant of uncertainty include Singapore, Jamaica, Denmark, Sweden, Hong Kong, Ireland, Great Britain, Malaysia, India, Philippines, the United States, Canada, and Indonesia.

Dr. Christie Cathey

Missouri State Psychology Department

Cultural Psychology

Note that the Big Five personality dimensions of Costa and McCrae (2000) are not necessarily in competition with Hofstede's dimensions. Hofstede's dimensions are cultural personality traits, whereas those of the Big Five refer to individuals.

Questions for Further Discussion

1. Was your own culture listed for any of these dimensions? If so, do you agree with the personality dimension assigned to your culture?

2. If your culture was not listed for a personality dimension, where do you think your culture would fall on that dimension?

---

*autonomy: the quality of being self-directed or self-controlled.
*hierarchy: in this sense, a body of persons in authority over others.
*ambiguity: the quality of being uncertain and indistinct.

Concept Map L.O. 11.10, 11.11

- **biology of personality**
  - behavioral genetics studies how much of an individual's personality is due to inherited traits
  - identical twins are more similar than fraternal twins or unrelated people in many facets of personality
  - adoption studies of twins have confirmed that genetic influences account for a great deal of personality development, regardless of shared or nonshared environments
  - personality factors of the five-factor model have nearly a 50% rate of heritability across cultures; variations in personality are about 25–50% inherited

Personality: Genetics and Culture

Reset

Practice Quiz   How much do you remember? ANSWERS ON PAGE AK-1.

Pick the best answer.

1. What is a major shortcoming in the field of behavioral genetics in terms of their studies on human personality traits?
   a. Behavioral geneticists are unable to conduct controlled research studies on human subjects.
   b. Behavioral geneticists are unable to scientifically validate anything.
   c. Behavioral geneticists are unable to conduct studies on animals, only on humans.
   d. Behavioral geneticists conduct their studies by looking at single individuals over a long period of time, thus slowing the rate by which they can gather data.

2. Because _____ twins share 100% of their genes, the study of these types of twins allows researchers to draw stronger conclusions about one's genetic contribution to one's personality.
   a. encapsulated
   b. dizygotic
   c. monozygotic
   d. germinal

3. What, if anything, have adoption studies taught us regarding the relationship between heredity and personality?
   a. Adoption studies are a new area of study and have yet to offer any information on the effects of heredity on personality.
   b. Adoption studies have confirmed that personality can be strongly influenced by genetics.
   c. Adoption studies have not supported many behavioral genetics studies, thus questioning the idea that personality can be influenced by genetics.
   d. Adoption studies have resulted in conflicting findings, with some strongly supporting the influence of heredity on personality while others suggest that heredity has no influence whatsoever.

4. A large study conducted by _____ in the early 1980s identified four different personality dimensions along which cultures differed.
   a. Geert Hofstede
   b. Stanley Schachter
   c. Walter Mischel
   d. Thomas Bouchard

The Influence of Personality: Dealing with Stress and Life Challenges

It should be no surprise that personality influences all aspects of our day-to-day lives. From the clothes we wear, the people we hang out with, and even the food we eat, personality can play a role. But what about everyday challenges such as finding a parking place during key class times, finding out you have to work a second shift the night before having a research paper due, or perhaps more serious life issues such as finding out you just lost your job, or that a loved one has fallen ill? The way an individual interprets a given situation or stressful event, the methods they choose to address the stressor, and the actual impact of the event, vary through differences in individual cognitive factors and other aspects of our personality. In this section we will discuss some of the ways personality and associated factors can influence the way we face such challenges and the way we cope or manage stress. **LINK** to Learning Objective 9.5.

11.12 Describe Lazarus's two-step process of how people think about and appraise a stressor.

Cognitive psychologist Richard Lazarus developed a cognitive view of stress called the *cognitive–mediational* theory of emotions, in which the way people think about and appraise a stressor is a major factor in how stressful that particular stressor becomes (Lazarus, 1991, 1999; Lazarus & Folkman, 1984). **L I N K** to Learning Objective 9.12. According to Lazarus, there is a two-step process in assessing the degree of threat or harm of a stressor and how one should react to that stressor.

PRIMARY APPRAISAL The first step in appraising a stressor is called **primary appraisal**, which involves estimating the severity of the stressor and classifying it as a threat (something that could be harmful in the future), a challenge (something to be met and defeated), or a harm or loss that has already occurred. If the stressor is appraised as a threat, negative emotions may arise that inhibit the person's ability to cope with the threat. For example, a student who has not read the text or taken good notes will certainly appraise an upcoming exam as threatening. If the stressor is seen as a challenge, however, it is possible to plan to meet that challenge, which is a more positive and less stressful approach. For example, the student who has read, studied, and feels prepared is much more likely to appraise the upcoming exam as an opportunity to do well.

Perceiving a stressor as a challenge instead of a threat makes coping with the stressor (or the harm it may already have caused) more likely to be successful. Whereas perceiving the stressor as an embarrassment, or imagining future failure or rejection, is more likely to lead to increased stress reactions, negative emotions, and an inability to cope well (Folkman, 1997; Lazarus, 1993). Think positive!

SECONDARY APPRAISAL In **secondary appraisal**, people who have identified a threat or harmful effect must estimate the resources that they have available for coping with the stressor. Resources might include social support, money, time, energy, ability, or any number of potential resources, depending on the threat. If resources are perceived as adequate or abundant, the degree of stress will be considerably less than if resources are missing or lacking. Using the example of the student and the upcoming exam, a student who feels that she has the time to study and the ability to understand the material in that time will feel much less distress than the student who has little time to study and doesn't feel that she understood all the content of the lectures covered on the exam.

11.13 Explain how personality factors can influence our ability to cope with stressors.

Of course, how one cognitively assesses a stressor has a lot to do with one's personality. People with certain kinds of personality traits—such as aggressiveness or a naturally high level of anxiety, for example—seem to create more stress for themselves than may exist in the actual stressor. Even as long ago as the early 1930s, psychologists have had evidence that personality characteristics are a major factor in predicting health. A longitudinal study begun in 1932 (Lehr & Thomae, 1987) found that personality was almost as important to longevity* as were genetic, physical, or lifestyle factors. Other researchers have found that people who live to be very old—into their 90s and even over 100 years—tend to be relaxed, easygoing, cheerful, and active. People who have the opposite

---

*longevity: how long people live

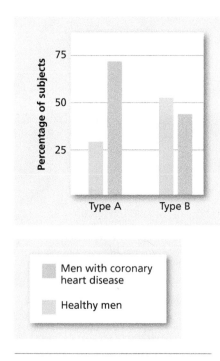

Figure 11.5 Personality and Coronary Heart Disease

The two bars on the left represent men with Type A personalities. Notice that within the Type A men, there are more than twice as many who suffer from coronary heart disease as those who are healthy. The two bars on the right represent men with Type B personalities. Far more Type B personalities are healthier than are Type A personalities, and there are far fewer Type B personalities with coronary heart disease when compared to Type A personalities.

Source: Miller et al. (1991, 1996).

Type Z behavior

personality traits, such as aggressiveness, stubbornness, inflexibility, and tenseness, typically do not live as long as the *average* life expectancy (Levy et al., 2002).

Those positive and negative personality traits are some of the factors associated with two personality types that have been related to how people deal with stress and the influence of certain personality characteristics on coronary heart disease.

TYPE A AND TYPE B In 1974, medical doctors Meyer Freidman and Ray Rosenman published a book titled *Type A Behavior and Your Heart.* The book was the result of studies spanning three decades of research into the influence of certain personality characteristics on coronary heart disease (Friedman & Kasanin, 1943; Friedman & Rosenman, 1959; Rosenman et al., 1975). Since then, numerous researchers have explored the link between what Friedman called Type A and Type B personalities.

Type A people are workaholics—they are very competitive, ambitious, hate to waste time, and are easily annoyed. They feel a constant sense of pressure and have a strong tendency to try to do several things at once. Often successful but frequently unsatisfied, they always seem to want to go faster and do more, and they get easily upset over small things. A typical Type A finds it difficult to relax and do nothing—Type A people take work with them on vacation, a laptop to the beach, and do business over the phone in the car.

In contrast, **Type B** people are not that competitive or driven, tend to be easygoing and slow to anger, and seem relaxed and at peace. Type B people are more likely to take a book to the beach to cover up their face than to actually read the book.

In 1961, the Western Collaborative Group Study (Rosenman et al., 1975) assessed 3,500 men and followed them for 8 years. For example, participants were asked to agree or disagree with statements such as "I can relax without guilt," in which strong agreement indicates a Type B personality. The results were that Type A men were 3 times more likely to develop heart disease than were Type B men. (See **Figure 11.5**.)

The Framingham Heart Study found that the risk of coronary heart disease for women who work and are also Type A is four times that of Type B working women (Eaker & Castelli, 1988). Other research has narrowed the key factors in Type A personality and heart disease to one characteristic: hostility* (Fredrickson et al., 1999; Matthews et al., 2004; Williams, 1999; Williams et al., 1980). In a study of 424 patients who had undergone exploratory surgery for coronary heart disease, the presence of heart disease was related both to being Type A and to being hostile, with hostility being the more significant factor in the hardening of the arteries to the heart (Williams, 2001; Williams et al., 1980).

Numerous studies support the link between hostility and increased risk of coronary heart disease. A study of hostility levels and risk factors for heart disease in over 4,000 young adults found that increases in hostility over a 5-year follow-up study were associated with a rise in high blood pressure, one of the major risk factors of heart disease (Markovitz et al., 1997). Another study of anger in young men and their risk for premature heart disease found that over a period of slightly more than three decades, the young men who had exhibited high levels of hostility in their youth were far more likely to develop premature cardiovascular disease, particularly heart attacks, than were those men who had lower levels of anger and hostility (Chang et al., 2002). Similar studies found that hostility in college-aged males and females was significantly related to increased risk of heart disease, particularly if levels of hostility rose in middle age (Brondolo et al., 2003; Siegler et al., 2003).

Even children may not escape the hostility–heart disease link. One study found that children and adolescents who scored high on assessments of hostility were more likely to show physical changes such as obesity, resistance to insulin, high blood pressure, and elevated levels of triglycerides 3 years after the initial measurements of hostility had been made (Raikkonen et al., 2003).

---

*hostility: feelings of conflict, anger, and ill will that are long lasting.

💬 What about people who don't blow their top but try to keep everything "in" instead? Wouldn't that be bad for a person's health?

TYPE C   A third personality type was identified by researchers Temoshok and Dreher (1992) as being associated with a higher incidence of cancer. **Type C** people tend to be very pleasant and try to keep the peace but find it difficult to express emotions, especially negative ones. They tend to internalize their anger and often experience a sense of despair over the loss of a loved one or a loss of hope. They are often lonely. These personality characteristics are strongly associated with cancer, and people who have cancer and this personality type often have thicker cancerous tumors as well (Eysenck, 1994; Temoshok & Dreher, 1992). Just as the stress of hostility puts the cardiovascular systems of Type A people at greater risk, the internalized negative emotions of the Type C personality may increase the levels of harmful stress hormones, weaken the immune system, and slow recovery.

A word of caution here: "personality type" theories have come under criticism in recent years. Many consider them to be too simplistic—many people would not fall easily into one type or another. Nevertheless, many of the personality traits associated with these types do seem to be associated with stress and longevity. Many of the characteristics of the Type A personality, for example, fit the description of neuroticism. Ⓛ Ⓘ Ⓝ Ⓚ to Learning Objective 11.8. One longitudinal study's findings indicate that these characteristics are associated with an increased risk of an earlier death because people with these traits engage in poor health habits—poor diet, excessive drinking, smoking, and lack of exercise, to name a few (Mroczek et al., 2009).

THE HARDY PERSONALITY   Not all Type A people are prone to heart disease. Some people actually seem to thrive on stress instead of letting stress wear them down. These people have what is called the **hardy personality**, a term first coined by psychologist Suzanne Kobasa (1979). Hardy people (call them "Type H") differ from ordinary, hostile Type A people and others who suffer more ill effects due to stress in three ways:

- Hardy people have a deep sense of *commitment* to their values, beliefs, sense of identity, work, and family life.

- Hardy people also feel that they are in *control* of their lives and what happens to them.

- Hardy people tend to interpret events in primary appraisal differently than people who are not hardy. When things go wrong, they do not see a frightening problem to be avoided but instead a *challenge* to be met and answered.

Why would those three characteristics (often known as the three "Cs" of hardiness) lessen the negative impact of stress? Commitment makes a person more willing to make sacrifices and to deal with hardships than if commitment were lacking. Think about it: Have you ever had a job that you hated? Every little frustration and every snag was very stressful, right? Now think about doing something you love to do. The frustrations and snags that inevitably come with any endeavor just don't seem quite as bad when you are doing something you really want to do, do they?

As for control, uncontrollability is one of the major factors cited as increasing stress, as was discussed in Chapter 9. Seeing events as challenges rather than problems also changes the level of stress experienced, a difference similar to that felt when riding a roller coaster: If riding the coaster is your own idea, it's fun; if someone makes you ride it, it's not fun.

The tendency for hardiness may even have genetic roots. Researchers have recently found that there seems to be a biochemical link between feeling miserable and an increased risk of death, and that there may be a genetic variation in some individuals that actually severs that link, making that individual more biologically resilient or hardy (Cole et al., 2010).

The four personality types discussed so far could be summed up this way: If life gives you lemons,

- Type A people get enraged and throw the lemons back, having a minor heart attack while doing so.

- Type B people gather all the lemons and make lemonade.

- Type C people don't say anything but fume inside where no one can see.

- Type H people gather the lemons, make lemonade, sell it, turn it into a franchise business, and make millions. (Remember, laughing is good for you!)

EXPLANATORY STYLE: OPTIMISTS AND PESSIMISTS   In addition to personality type, there are other personal factors that have an influence on people's reactions to stressors. One of these factors is the attitude that people have toward the things that happen to them in life.

Optimists are people who always tend to look for positive outcomes. *Pessimists* seem to expect the worst to happen. For an optimist, a glass is half full, whereas for a pessimist, the glass is half empty. Researchers have found that optimism is associated with longer life and increased immune-system functioning (Maruta et al., 2002; Mosing et al., 2012; Segerstrom & Sephton, 2010). The results for pessimists were not good: They had a much higher death rate than did the optimists, more problems with physical and emotional health, more pain, less ability to take part in social activities, and less energy than optimists. Other studies link being optimistic to higher levels of helper T cells (immune system cells that direct and increase the functioning of the immune system) and higher levels of natural killer cells, the body's antivirus, and anticancer cells (Segerstrom et al., 1998; Segerstrom & Sephton, 2010). For some advice on how to become more optimistic, see the *Applying Psychology* feature at the end of the chapter.

Concept Map L.O. 11.12, 11.13

Practice Quiz   How much do you remember?   ANSWERS ON PAGE AK-1.

Pick the best answer.

1. Which of the following questions would be most immediately addressed by conducting what Richard Lazarus refers to as a primary appraisal?

    a. "Will school be canceled tomorrow?"

    b. "Do I need to go grocery shopping?"

    c. "Do I know where to go in the library to research the paper that I have to write?"

    d. "How big of a deal is this problem?"

2. According to Richard Lazarus, when someone asks themselves, "How can I deal with this potentially harmful stressor?" the individual is focused on a _____ appraisal.

    a. primary

    b. secondary

    c. tertiary

    d. minimal

3. Greg rushes to an appointment, arriving 20 minutes early, whereas Aaron arrives with only minutes to spare. Slightly annoyed when Greg points this out, Aaron replies very casually, "Hey, I'm here." We might assume Greg has more of a _____ personality while Aaron is more _____.

    a. Type A; Type B   **c.** Type B; Type C

    b. Type A; Type C   **d.** Type C; Type A

4. Soleil has been very upset with her boss for the past few days, because she was reprimanded for something that was not her fault. Soleil's boyfriend keeps encouraging her to talk to her boss about the problem, but Soleil always has difficulty expressing negative emotions, and thus keeps them stuffed inside. Soleil appears to have a _____ personality

    a. Type A   **c.** Type C

    b. Type B   **d.** Hardy

Assessment of Personality

💬 With all the different theories of personality, how do people find out what kind of personality they have?

The methods for measuring or assessing personality vary according to the theory of personality used to develop those methods, as one might expect. However, most psychological professionals doing a personality assessment on a client do not necessarily tie themselves down to one theoretical viewpoint only, preferring to take a more *eclectic* view of personality. The eclectic view is a way of choosing the parts of different theories that seem to best fit a particular situation, rather than using only one theory to explain a phenomenon. In fact, looking at behavior from multiple perspectives can often bring insights into a person's behavior that would not easily come from taking only one perspective. Many professionals will not only use several different perspectives but also several of the assessment techniques that follow. Even so, certain methods are more commonly used by certain kinds of theorists, as can be seen in **Table 11.3** on the next page.

Personality assessments may also differ in the purposes for which they are conducted. For example, sometimes a researcher may administer a personality test of some sort to participants in a research study so that the participants may be classified according to certain personality traits. There are tests available to people who simply want to learn more about their own personalities. Finally, clinical and counseling psychologists, psychiatrists, and other psychological professionals use these personality assessment tools in the diagnosis of disorders of personality. ⓁⒾⓃⓀ to Learning Objective 12.16.

INTERVIEWS, BEHAVIORAL ASSESSMENTS, AND PERSONALITY INVENTORIES

11.14 Identify the advantages and disadvantages of using interviews, behavioral assessments, and personality inventories.

As covered in the last section, the methods for measuring or assessing personality vary according to the theory of personality used to develop those methods. They also vary according to the type of data that is desired. We will first examine a variety of methods aimed at providing more objective data.

Table 11.3 Who Uses What Method?	
Type of Assessment	**Most Likely Used By . . .**
Interviews	Psychoanalysts, humanistic therapists
Projective Tests	Psychoanalysts
Rorschach	
Thematic Apperception Test	
Behavioral Assessments	Behavioral and social cognitive therapists
Direct observation	
Rating scales	
Frequency counts	
Personality Inventories	Trait theorists
Sixteen Personality Factor Questionnaire (16PF)	
Revised Neuroticism/Extraversion/Openness Personality Inventory (NEO-PI-R)	
Myers-Briggs Type Indicator (MBTI)	
Eysenck Personality Questionnaire (EPQ)	
Keirsey Temperament Sorter II	
California Psychological Inventory (CPI)	
Minnesota Multiphasic Personality Inventory, Version II (MMPI-2)	

INTERVIEWS   Some therapists ask questions and note down the answers in a survey process called an **interview**. LINK to Learning Objective 1.7. This type of interview, unlike a job interview, is likely to be *unstructured* and flow naturally from the beginning dialogue between the client and the psychologist.

  So an interview is a kind of self-report process?

Yes, when psychologists interview clients, clients must report on their innermost feelings, urges, and concerns—all things that only they can directly know.

BEHAVIORAL ASSESSMENTS   Behaviorists do not typically want to "look into the mind." Because behaviorists assume that personality is merely habitually learned responses to stimuli in the environment, the preferred method for a behaviorist would be to watch that behavior unfold in the real world.

In **direct observation**, the psychologist observes the client engaging in ordinary, everyday behavior, preferably in the natural setting of home, school, or workplace, for example. A therapist who goes to the classroom and observes that tantrum behavior only happens when a child is asked to do something involving fine motor abilities (like drawing or writing) might be able to conclude that the child has difficulty with those skills and throws a tantrum to avoid the task.

Other methods often used by behavioral therapists and other assessors are rating scales and frequency counts. In a **rating scale**, a numerical rating is assigned, either by the assessor or the client, for specific behaviors (Nadeau et al., 2001). In a **frequency count**, the assessor literally counts the frequency of certain behaviors within a specified time limit. Educators make use of both rating scales and frequency counts to diagnose behavioral problems such as attention-deficit/hyperactivity disorder (ADHD) and aspects of personality such as social-skill level through the various grade levels.

PERSONALITY INVENTORIES   Trait theorists are typically more interested in personality descriptions. They tend to use an assessment known as a **personality inventory**, a questionnaire that has a standard list of questions and only requires certain specific answers, such as "yes," "no," and "can't decide." The standard nature of the questions (everyone gets the same list) and the lack of open-ended answers make these assessments far more objective and reliable than projective tests (Garb et al., 1998), although they are still a form of self-report. One such personality inventory is Cattell's 16PF, described earlier in this chapter. Costa and McCrae have recently revised their *Revised Neuroticism/Extraversion/Openness Personality Inventory (NEO-PI-R)*, which is based on the five-factor model of personality traits and is still being published. The newer version is the NEO-PI-3, which has been made easier to read for use with adolescents and has new norms (McCrae et al., 2005; McCrae, Martin, et al., 2005). You can answer select questions from the NEO-PI for yourself by completing the experiment, *IPIP Neo Personality Inventory*.

Experiment   IPIP NEO PERSONALITY INVENTORY

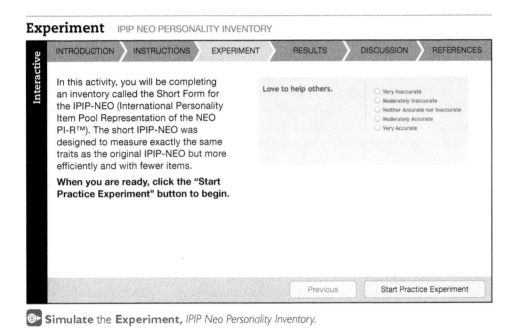

INTRODUCTION   INSTRUCTIONS   EXPERIMENT   RESULTS   DISCUSSION   REFERENCES

In this activity, you will be completing an inventory called the Short Form for the IPIP-NEO (International Personality Item Pool Representation of the NEO PI-R™). The short IPIP-NEO was designed to measure exactly the same traits as the original IPIP-NEO but more efficiently and with fewer items.

When you are ready, click the "Start Practice Experiment" button to begin.

Love to help others.

○ Very Inaccurate
○ Moderately Inaccurate
○ Neither Accurate nor Inaccurate
○ Moderately Accurate
○ Very Accurate

Previous   Start Practice Experiment

Simulate the **Experiment,** *IPIP Neo Personality Inventory.*

Other common personality tests include the Eysenck Personality Questionnaire (Eysenck & Eysenck, 1993), the Keirsey Temperament Sorter II (Keirsey, 1998), the California Psychological Inventory (Gough, 1995), and the Sixteen Personality Factor Questionnaire (Cattell, 1994).

THE MBTI   Another inventory in common use is the *Myers-Briggs Type Indicator (MBTI)*. This inventory is based on the ideas of Carl Jung and looks at four personality dimensions. The *sensing/intuition* (S/N) dimension includes people who prefer to rely on what they can see, hear, and so on through their own physical senses (sensing) and, on its opposite end, those who look for patterns and trust their hunches (intuition). Sensing people are very detail oriented, preferring to work only with the known facts, whereas intuitive people are more willing to use metaphors, analogies, and look for possibilities. The *thinking/feeling* (T/F) dimension runs from those who prefer to use logic, analysis, and experiences that can be verified as facts (thinkers) to those who tend to make decisions based on their personal values and emotional reactions (feeling). *Introversion/extraversion* (I/E) is the same classic dimension that began with Jung and is represented in nearly every personality theory, including the Big Five. *Perceiving/judging* (P/J) describes those who are willing to adapt and modify decisions, be spontaneous, and who are naturally curious and tend to put off making a final decision so that all possibilities are covered (perceiving) as well as those who are the opposite: the action-oriented, decisive, get-the-task-done-and-don't-look-back type (judging). These four dimensions can differ for each individual, resulting in 16 (4 × 4) possible personality types: ISTJ, ISTP, ISFP, ISFJ, and so on (Briggs & Myers, 1998).

The Myers-Briggs is often used to assess personality to help people know the kinds of careers for which they may best be suited. For example, a person who scored high on the extravert, sensing, thinking, and judging dimensions would be an ESTJ. A typical description of this personality type would be a person who needs to analyze information and bring order to the outer world. Such people are organizers, energetic in completing tasks, and practical. They also take their responsibilities seriously and expect others to do so as well. School administrators, for example, are often ESTJs.

Dr. Paul Deal

Missouri State Psychology Department

Assessing Abnormal Behavior: The MMPI-2

THE MMPI-2   By far the most common personality inventory is the *Minnesota Multiphasic Personality Inventory, Version II*, or *MMPI-2*, which specifically tests for abnormal behavior and thinking patterns in personality (Butcher & Rouse, 1996; Butcher et al., 2000, 2001). This questionnaire consists of 567 statements such as "I am often very tense" or "I believe I am being plotted against." The person taking the test must answer "true," "false," or "cannot say." The MMPI has 10 clinical scales and 8 validity scales in addition to numerous subscales. Each scale tests for a particular kind of behavior. The thinking and behavior patterns assessed include those associated with relatively mild personality problems such as excessive worrying and shyness as well as patterns representative of disorders such as schizophrenia and depression. (L I N K) to Learning Objectives 12.9 and 12.14.

 🗩 How can you tell if a person is telling the truth on a personality inventory?

Validity scales, which are built into any well-designed psychological inventory, are intended to indicate whether or not a person taking the inventory is responding honestly. Responses to certain items on the test will indicate if people are trying to make themselves look better or worse than they are, for example, and certain items are repeated throughout the test in a slightly different form, so that anyone trying to "fake" the test will have difficultly responding to those items consistently (Butcher et al., 2001). For example, if one of the statements is "I am always happy" and a person responds "true" to that statement, the suspicion would be that this person is trying to look better than he or she really is. If several of the validity scale questions are answered in this way, the conclusion is that the person is not being honest.

EVALUATING INTERVIEWS, BEHAVIORAL ASSESSMENTS, AND PERSONALITY INVENTORIES   In this section we have discussed a variety of assessment techniques aimed at providing objective data. Each of these has advantages and disadvantages. For example, the same problems that exist with self-report data (such as surveys) exist with interviews. Clients can lie, distort the truth, misremember, or give what they think is a socially acceptable answer instead of true information. Interviewers themselves can be biased, interpreting what the client says in light of their own belief systems or prejudices. Freud certainly did this when he refused to believe that his patients had actually been sexually molested as children, preferring to interpret that information as a fantasy instead of reality (Russell, 1986).

Another problem with interviews is something called the **halo effect**, which is a tendency to form a favorable or unfavorable impression of someone at the first meeting, so that all of a person's comments and behavior after that first impression will be interpreted to agree with the impression—positively or negatively. The halo effect can happen in any social situation, including interviews between a psychological professional and a client. First impressions really do count, and people who make a good first impression because of clothing, personal appearance, or some other irrelevant* characteristic will seem to have a "halo" hanging over their heads—they can do no wrong after that (Lance et al., 1994; Thorndike, 1920). And of course, as we discussed in Chapter 10, negative first impressions are hard to change.

Problems with behavioral assessments can include the observer effect (when a person's behavior is affected by being watched) and observer bias, which can be controlled by having multiple observers and correlating their observations with each other. **LINK** to Learning Objective 1.7. As with any kind of observational method, there is no control over the external environment. A person observing a client for a particular behavior may not see that behavior occur within the observation time—much as some car problems never seem to show up when the mechanic is examining the car.

The advantage of personality inventories over projective tests (which we will cover shortly) and interviews is that inventories are standardized (i.e., everyone gets exactly the same questions and the answers are scored in exactly the same way). In fact, responses to inventories are often scored on a computer. Observer bias and bias of interpretation are simply not possible, because this kind of assessment is objective rather than subjective. The validity and reliability of personality inventories are generally recognized as being greatly superior to those of projective tests (Anastasi & Urbina, 1997).

There are some problems, however. The validity scales, for example, are a good check against cheating, but they are not perfect. Some people are still able to fake their answers and respond in what they feel are the socially appropriate ways (Anastasi & Urbina, 1997; Hicklin & Widiger, 2000). Despite the best intentions of the test creators, individual responses to specific questions may also vary as they may be interpreted in different ways by different individuals, and are very likely to be subject to cultural influences (Kagan, 2010). Other problems have to do with human nature itself: Some people may develop a habit of picking a particular answer rather than carefully considering the statement, whereas others may simply grow tired of responding to all those statements and start picking answers at random.

PROJECTIVE TESTS

11.15 Identify the advantages and disadvantages of using projective personality tests.

Have you ever tried to see "shapes" in the clouds? You might see a house where another person might see the same cloud as a horse. The cloud isn't really either of those things but can be *interpreted* as one or the other, depending on the person doing the interpretation. That makes a cloud an ambiguous stimulus—one that is capable of being interpreted in more than one way.

In just this way, psychoanalysts (and a few other psychologists) show their clients ambiguous visual stimuli and ask the clients to tell them what they see. The hope is that the client will project unconscious concerns onto the visual stimulus, revealing them to the examiner. Tests using this method are called **projective tests**. Such tests can be used to explore a client's personality or used as a diagnostic tool to uncover problems in personality.

THE RORSCHACH INKBLOTS One of the more well-known projective tests is the **Rorschach inkblot test**, developed in 1921 by Swiss psychiatrist Hermann Rorschach (ROR-shok). There are 10 inkblots, 5 in black ink on a white background and 5 in colored inks on a white background. (See **Figure 11.6** for an image similar to a Rorschach-type inkblot.)

Figure 11.6 Rorschach Inkblot Example

A facsimile of a Rorschach inkblot. A person being tested is asked to tell the interviewer what he or she sees in an inkblot similar to the one shown. Answers are neither right nor wrong but may reveal unconscious concerns. What do you see in this inkblot?

---

*irrelevant: not applying to the case or example at hand.

Figure 11.7 Thematic Apperception Test Example

A sample from the Thematic Apperception Test (TAT). When you look at this picture, what story does it suggest to you? Who is the person? Why is he climbing a rope?

People being tested are asked to look at each inkblot and simply say whatever it might look like to them. Using predetermined categories and responses commonly given by people to each picture (Exner, 1980), psychologists score responses on key factors, such as reference to color, shape, figures seen in the blot, and response to the whole or to details.

Rorschach tested thousands of inkblots until he narrowed them down to the 10 in use today. They are still used to describe personality, diagnose mental disorders, and predict behavior (Watkins et al., 1995; Weiner, 1997). However, along with the use of other projective techniques in general, their use is controversial given questions about some scoring methods and overall validity (Lilienfeld et al., 2000).

THE TAT First developed in 1935 by psychologist Henry Murray and his colleagues (Morgan & Murray, 1935), the **Thematic Apperception Test (TAT)** consists of 20 pictures, all black and white, that are shown to a client. The client is asked to tell a story about the person or people in the picture, who are all deliberately drawn in ambiguous situations (see **Figure 11.7**). Again, the story developed by the client is interpreted by the psychoanalyst, who looks for revealing statements and projection of the client's own problems onto the people in the pictures.

These are only two of the more well-known projective tests. Other types of projective tests include the Sentence Completion test, Draw-A-Person, and House-Tree-Person. In the Sentence Completion test, the client is given a series of sentence beginnings, such as "I wish my mother . . ." or "Almost every day I feel . . . ," and asked to finish the sentence, whereas in the Draw-A-Person and House-Tree-Person, the client is asked to draw the named items.

💬 But how can anyone know if the interpretation is correct? Isn't there a lot of room for error?

EVALUATING PROJECTIVE TESTS Projective tests are by their nature very **subjective** (valid only within the person's own perception), and interpreting the answers of clients is almost an art. It is certainly not a science and is not known for its accuracy. Problems lie in the areas of reliability and validity. In Chapter Seven, *reliability* was defined as the tendency of a test to give the same score every time it is administered to the same person or group of people, and *validity* was defined as the ability of the test to measure what it is intended to measure. ⓛⓘⓝⓚ to Learning Objective 7.6. Projective tests, with no standard grading scales, have both low reliability and low validity (Gittelman-Klein, 1978; Lilienfeld, 1999; Lilienfeld et al., 2000; Wood et al., 1996). A person's answers to the Rorschach, for example, might be quite different from one day to the next, depending on the person's mood and what scary movie might have been on television the previous night.

Projective tests may sound somewhat outdated, but many psychologists and psychiatrists still use this type of testing (McGrath & Carroll, 2012). Some psychologists believe that the latest versions of these tests and others like them still have practical use and some validity (Choca, 2013; Meyer & Kurtz, 2006; Weiner, 2013), especially when a client's answers on these tests are used as a starting point for digging deeper into the client's recollections, concerns, and anxieties.

WRITING PROMPT

Should employers require prospective employees to take a personality test? Why or why not? Would such a requirement make more sense in certain professions, and, if so, what professions might those be?

▶ The response entered here will be saved to your notes and may be collected by your instructor if he/she requires it.

Submit

Concept Map L.O. 11.14, 11.15

Interactive

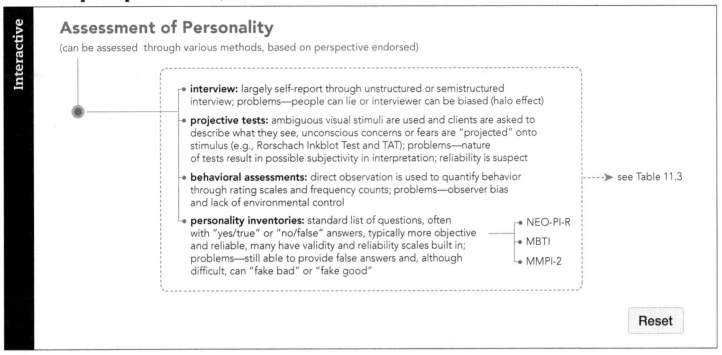

Assessment of Personality
(can be assessed through various methods, based on perspective endorsed)

- **interview:** largely self-report through unstructured or semistructured interview; problems—people can lie or interviewer can be biased (halo effect)

- **projective tests:** ambiguous visual stimuli are used and clients are asked to describe what they see, unconscious concerns or fears are "projected" onto stimulus (e.g., Rorschach Inkblot Test and TAT); problems—nature of tests result in possible subjectivity in interpretation; reliability is suspect

- **behavioral assessments:** direct observation is used to quantify behavior through rating scales and frequency counts; problems—observer bias and lack of environmental control ----→ see Table 11.3

- **personality inventories:** standard list of questions, often with "yes/true" or "no/false" answers, typically more objective and reliable, many have validity and reliability scales built in; problems—still able to provide false answers and, although difficult, can "fake bad" or "fake good"
  - NEO-PI-R
  - MBTI
  - MMPI-2

Reset

Practice Quiz   How much do you remember?   ANSWERS ON PAGE AK-1.

Pick the best answer.

1. Which of the following personality assessments might be best suited for objectively identifying abnormal patterns of behavior or thinking?
   a. Personal interview
   b. MBTI
   c. MMPI-2
   d. TAT

2. What is the function of a validity scale?
   a. to determine if a person is giving an accurate response
   b. to determine how a subject really feels
   c. to help better explain the results of a personality test
   d. to offer both a diagnosis of abnormal behavior plus a positive therapeutic treatment

3. A person taking the Minnesota Multiphasic Personality Inventory (MMPI-2) would have their answers scored over a series of _____ clinical scales and _____ validity scales.
   a. 4; 8
   b. 8; 4
   c. 8; 10
   d. 10; 8

4. Of the following, which would not be an example of a projective personality test?
   a. the Sentence Completion test
   b. The Draw-A-Person
   c. The Myers-Briggs Type Indicator (MBTI)
   d. the Thematic Apperception Test (TAT)

Applying Psychology to Everyday Life
Becoming More Optimistic

11.16 Outline ways to become a more optimistic thinker.

Martin Seligman is a social learning psychologist who developed the concept of *learned helplessness*, **LINK** to Learning Objective 5.12, and began the positive psychology movement. He has outlined four ways in which optimism may affect how long a person lives (Seligman, 2002):

- Optimists are less likely to develop learned helplessness, the tendency to stop trying to achieve a goal that has been blocked in the past.

- Optimists are more likely than pessimists to take care of their health by preventive measures (such as going to the doctor regularly, eating right, and exercising) because they believe that their actions make a difference in what happens to them. (Remember, this is a characteristic of hardy people as well.)
- Optimists are far less likely than pessimists to become depressed, and depression is associated with mortality because of the effect of depression on the immune system.
- Optimists have more effectively functioning immune systems than pessimists do, perhaps because they experience less psychological stress.

Seligman (1998) has also found that optimists are more successful in their life endeavors than pessimists are. Optimistic politicians win more elections, optimistic students get better grades, and optimistic athletes win more contests.

As the work of Martin Seligman and others has shown, optimistic thinking is a good thing. (L I N K) to Learning Objective 11.13. How can you become more optimistic? Optimism is mostly a matter of controlling mood or emotional reactions to situations. The way to become an optimist is to monitor one's own thinking. Recognition of negative thoughts is the first step, followed by disputing those same negative thoughts (Seligman, 2002). The problem is that most people don't really think about their thoughts or characterize them as negative or pessimistic, which means that the damaging effects of such thinking are left uncontrolled. Here's a plan to follow to become an optimistic thinker:

1. When a bad mood strikes, stop and think about what just went through your head.
2. When you've recognized the negative statements, treat them as if they came from someone else—someone who is trying to make your life miserable. Think about the damage the statement is doing to you.
3. Argue with those thoughts. Challenge each negative statement and replace it with a more positive statement.

Example: "I'll never get this term paper finished, it's too hard and there's so much going on that it's impossible!"

1. What words in this statement make it pessimistic? "Never" is a long time. Why is it too hard? Is it really impossible, or just difficult? Is it just one part of the paper that seems so hard, or is it the whole thing?
2. That statement isn't going to help me at all; it just makes me feel worse and that makes me unmotivated to work on the paper.
3. I can finish the term paper. I'm just going to have to devote more time to working on it. I can make a timetable for finishing the different parts of the paper and stop spending so much time watching television and escaping into other activities that can wait until the paper is finished. I've been in situations like this before and managed, so I can manage now, too.

Notice that the third way of thinking is much more positive and hopeful. It includes ways to get around what seemed too hard or impossible in the negative statement. Essentially, the last step in becoming a more optimistic thinker is to learn to argue with yourself and correct distorted or faulty thinking. Recognizing faulty thinking can be difficult at first. The following questions may help people to home in on* negative thinking:

1. In thinking about the thoughts you have had in the last few hours, how many of them were negative thoughts? How could you change those thoughts to be more positive?
2. When thinking about people you know who make a lot of negative self-statements or who are always minimizing their efforts or putting themselves down, how does their behavior make you feel? How do you think their behavior makes them feel?

Questions for Further Discussion

1. Do you think you are an optimist, a pessimist, or somewhere in between?
2. What are some things you can do in your own life to become more optimistic?

*home in on: in this instance, to move toward a target or goal.

Chapter Summary

Perspectives on Personality

11.1 Define personality, and explain how the various perspectives in psychology view personality

- Personality is the unique way individuals think, feel, and act. It is different from character and temperament but includes those aspects.
- The four traditional perspectives in the study of personality are the psychodynamic, behavioristic (including social cognitive theory), humanistic, and trait perspectives.

The Psychodynamic Perspective on Personality

11.2 Describe how Freud's view of the mind and personality formed a basis for psychodynamic theory.

- The three divisions of the mind are the conscious, preconscious, and unconscious. The unconscious can be revealed in dreams.
- The three parts of the personality are the id, ego, and superego.
- The id works on the pleasure principle and the ego works on the reality principle; the superego is the moral center of personality, containing the conscience, and is the source of moral anxiety.
- The conflicts between the demands of the id and the rules and restrictions of the superego lead to anxiety for the ego, which uses defense mechanisms to deal with that anxiety.
- The personality develops in a series of psychosexual stages: oral (id dominates), anal (ego develops), phallic (superego develops), latency (period of sexual repression), and genital (sexual feelings reawaken with appropriate targets).
- The Oedipus and Electra complexes (sexual "crushes" on the opposite-sex parent) create anxiety in the phallic stage, which is resolved through identification with the same-sex parent.
- Fixation occurs when conflicts are not fully resolved during a stage, resulting in adult personality characteristics reflecting childhood inadequacies.

11.3 Explain how the neo-Freudians modified Freud's theory and how modern psychodynamic theory differs from that of Freud.

- The neo-Freudians changed the focus of psychoanalysis to fit their own interpretation of the personality, leading to the more modern version known as the psychodynamic perspective.
- Jung developed a theory of a collective unconscious.
- Adler proposed feelings of inferiority as the driving force behind personality.
- Horney developed a theory based on basic anxiety and rejected the concept of penis envy.
- Erikson developed a theory based on social rather than sexual relationships, covering the entire life span.
- Current research has found support for the defense mechanisms and the concept of an unconscious mind that can influence conscious behavior, but other concepts cannot be scientifically researched.

The Behaviorist and Social Cognitive View of Personality

11.4 Compare different learning theories of personality, including the theories of Bandura and Rotter.

- Behaviorists define personality as a set of learned responses or habits.
- The social cognitive view of personality includes the concept of reciprocal determinism, in which the environment, characteristics of the person, and the behavior itself all interact.
- Self-efficacy is a characteristic in which a person perceives a behavior as more or less effective based on previous experiences, the opinions of others, and perceived personal competencies.
- Locus of control is a determinant of personality in which one either assumes that one's actions directly affect events and reinforcements one experiences or that such events and reinforcements are the result of luck, fate, or powerful others.
- Personality, in the form of potential behavior patterns, is also determined by an interaction between one's expectancies for success and the perceived value of the potential reinforcement.

11.5 Evaluate the strengths and limitations of the social cognitive view of personality.

- Behaviorist personality theory has scientific support but is criticized as being too simplistic.

The Third Force: Humanism and Personality

11.6 Describe how humanists such as Carl Rogers explain personality.

- Humanism developed as a reaction against the negativity of psychoanalysis and the deterministic nature of behaviorism.
- Carl Rogers proposed that self-actualization depends on proper development of the self-concept.
- The self-concept includes the real self and the ideal self. When these two components do not match or agree, anxiety and disordered behavior result.
- Unconditional positive regard from important others in a person's life helps the formation of the self-concept and the congruity of the real and ideal selves, leading to a fully functioning person.

11.7 Evaluate the strengths and limitations of the humanistic view of personality.

- Humanistic theory is not easy to test scientifically, but its principles have been beneficial in therapy situations.

Trait Theories: Who Are You?

11.8 Define the trait perspective, and describe early attempts to use traits to conceptualize personality.

- Trait theorists describe personality traits in order to predict behavior.
- Allport first developed a list of about 200 traits and believed that these traits were part of the nervous system.

- Cattell reduced the number of traits to between 16 and 23 with a computer method called factor analysis.

11.9 Describe and evaluate the five-factor model and other recent trait theories of personality.

- Several researchers have arrived at five trait dimensions that have research support across cultures, called the Big Five or five-factor model. The five factors are openness, conscientiousness, extraversion, agreeableness, and neuroticism.
- Personality neuroscience is a growing area of research, and brain structure differences associated with some aspects of the Big Five dimensions of personality have been identified using structural MRI.
- Cross-cultural research has found support for the five-factor model of personality traits in a number of different cultures; future research will explore the degree to which child-rearing practices and heredity may influence the five personality factors.

Personality: Genetics and Culture

11.10 Explain how behavioral geneticists use twin and adoption studies to study personality

- Behavioral genetics is a field of study of the relationship between heredity and personality.
- Studies of twins and adopted children have found support for a genetic influence on many personality traits, including intelligence, leadership abilities, traditionalism, nurturance, empathy, assertiveness, neuroticism, and extraversion.

11.11 Define heritability, and explain how environmental influences, such as culture, can also impact personality.

- Heritability of personality, or how much some trait within a population can be attributed to genetic influences, ranges from about 25 to 50 percent.
- Geert Hofstede's research has suggested there may be four dimensions of cultural personality, including individualism/collectivism, power distance, masculinity/femininity, and uncertainty avoidance.
- Hofstede's dimensions are cultural personality traits, whereas those of the Big Five refer to individuals.

The Influence of Personality: Dealing with Stress and Life Challenges

11.12 Describe Lazarus's two-step process of how people think about and appraise a stressor.

- The cognitive appraisal approach states that how people think about a stressor determines, at least in part, how stressful that stressor will become.
- The first step in appraising a stressor is called primary appraisal, in which the person determines whether an event is threatening, challenging, or a harm or loss that has already occurred. Threatening events are more stressful than those seen as challenging.
- The second step is secondary appraisal, in which the person assesses the resources available to deal with the stressor, such as time, money, and social support.

11.13 Explain how personality factors can influence our ability to cope with stressors.

- Type A personalities are ambitious, time conscious, hostile, and angry workaholics who are at increased risk of coronary heart disease, primarily due to their anger and hostility.
- Type B personalities are relaxed and easygoing and have one-third the risk of coronary heart disease as do Type A personalities if male, and one-fourth the risk if female and working outside the home.
- Type C personalities are pleasant but repressed, internalizing their negative emotions.
- Hardy people are hard workers who lack the anger and hostility of the Type A personality, instead seeming to thrive on stress.
- Optimists look for positive outcomes and experience far less stress than pessimists, who take a more negative view.

Assessment of Personality

11.14 Identify the advantages and disadvantages of using interviews, behavioral assessments, and personality inventories.

- Interviews are used primarily by psychoanalysts and humanists and can include structured or unstructured interviews; disadvantages of interviews can include the halo effect and bias of the interpretation on the part of the interviewer.
- Behavioral assessments are primarily used by behaviorists and include direct observation of behavior, rating scales of specific behavior, and frequency counts of behavior. Behavioral assessments have the disadvantage of the observer effect, which causes an observed person's behavior to change, and observer bias on the part of the person doing the assessment.
- Personality inventories are typically developed by trait theorists and provide a detailed description of certain personality traits. They are objective tests rather than subjective.
- The NEO-PI-R is based on the five-factor model, whereas the Myers-Briggs Type Indicator is based on Jung's theory of personality types. The MMPI-2 is designed to detect abnormal personality.
- Personality inventories include validity scales to prevent cheating, but such measures are not perfect and cheating is sometimes possible.

11.15 Identify the advantages and disadvantages of using projective personality tests.

- Projective tests are based on the defense mechanism of projection and are used by psychoanalysts. Projective tests include the Rorschach inkblot test and the Thematic Apperception Test.
- Projective tests can be useful in finding starting points to open a dialogue between therapist and client but have been criticized for being low in reliability and validity.

Applying Psychology to Everyday Life: Becoming More Optimistic

11.16 Outline ways to become a more optimistic thinker.

- The best way to become more optimistic is to recognize negative thoughts and change them to more helpful positive thoughts.

Test Yourself   ANSWERS ON PAGE AK-1.

Pick the best answer.

1. If you are describing characteristics of your child such as irritability or adaptability, psychologists would say you are not describing their personality but rather their

   a. character.
   c. mood.
   b. consciousness.
   d. temperament.

2. According to Freud, the _____ works off of the pleasure principle whereas the _____ is often perceived as the executive director of your personality.

   a. id; ego
   c. superego; id
   b. ego; superego
   d. superego; ego

3. You are shocked to hear that two of your coworkers who seemingly hated one another are now getting married. According to Freud, what defense mechanism best explains their prior behavior?

   a. projection
   c. repression
   b. reaction formation
   d. regression

4. Four-year-old Brandon has watched his father as he has mowed the lawn. This year, Brandon has asked for a lawn mower of his own for his birthday. Freud would say that Brandon is beginning the process of _____ as a way of resolving his Oedipal conflict.

   a. compensation
   c. sublimation
   b. denial
   d. identification

5. Your professor explains how all females have an inner masculine side that adds to their personality. According to Jung, this concept is known as a(n)

   a. anima.
   c. animus.
   b. shadow.
   d. source trait.

6. According to Adler, the defense mechanism of _____ is important in our personality development, as we attempt to overcome feelings of inferiority.

   a. compensation
   c. sublimation
   b. denial
   d. identification

7. Karen Horney's study of one's personality focused on

   a. environmental influences through adulthood.
   b. biological changes during adolescence.
   c. trait-based characteristics that were present in infancy.
   d. anxiety during childhood.

8. Candice believes that fate will help her find the right man with whom to live her life. According to Rotter, she has a(n)

   a. external locus of control.
   c. strong self-efficacy.
   b. internal locus of control.
   d. perceived sense of control.

9. Keisha works hard at her job because she believes it will increase her chances for a promotion. According to Julian Rotter's theory, her effort is an example of what he calls

   a. reinforcement value.
   c. archetypes.
   b. expectancy.
   d. latency stage.

10. What is a primary advantage of the social cognitive view of personality over the psychodynamic view?

   a. The social cognitive view tries to explain how people become the people they are.
   b. The social cognitive view stresses the importance of early childhood in personality development.
   c. The social cognitive view is fully able to explain all the complexities of human behavior.
   d. The social cognitive view has concepts that can be tested scientifically.

11. Which perspective of psychology focuses on the role of each person's conscious life experiences and choices in personality development?

   a. trait
   c. humanistic
   b. behavior
   d. psychodynamic

12. An old motto of the U.S. Army was, "Be all you can be." This concept fits well with Carl Rogers's theory of

   a. unconditional positive regard.
   b. empathy.
   c. self-actualizing tendency.
   d. real versus the ideal self.

13. According to Rogers, a mismatch between the real and ideal self

   a. typically motivates individuals to close the gap.
   b. can result in anxiety and neurotic behavior.
   c. causes one to better understand their unconscious motives.
   d. causes an increase in unconditional positive regard.

14. To explain an individual's personality, trait theorists would look to

   a. early childhood emotional traumas.
   b. the kind of love, warmth, and affection given to the person by his or her parents.
   c. the early experiences of rewards and punishments for certain behavior.
   d. the constellation of personality characteristics possessed by the person.

15. Studies of the heritability of personality traits have found

   a. little evidence to support the belief that personality can be passed by genetics.
   b. evidence to support the belief that personality can be passed by genetics but only in highly developed countries.
   c. strong evidence to support some personality traits can be passed by genetics.
   d. strong evidence that personality is passed exclusively by genetics.

16. Jolene rarely takes any work home, preferring to leave her work worries at the office. She is a bit carefree and not as ambitious as some of the other women in her office. Instead, Jolene likes to have a lot of leisure time whenever possible. She is also easygoing and doesn't lose her temper often, preferring to avoid conflict. Which of the following statements about Jolene is most likely TRUE?

   a. She has a Type A personality.
   b. She has a Type B personality.
   c. She has a Type C personality.
   d. Jolene's risk of coronary heart disease is high.

17. Azriel seems to thrive on stress and feels very much in control of his life. He would probably be labeled with a _____ personality.

   a. Type A
   c. Type C
   b. Type B
   d. hardy

18. Which type of assessment would be the most reliable?

   a. subjective test
   c. personality inventory
   b. projective test
   d. observational study

19. The _____ is based on the five-factor model whereas _____ is based on the work of Raymond Cattell.

   a. NEO-PI-R; 16PF
   c. MMPI-2; MBTI
   b. MBTI; NEO-PI-R
   d. 16PF; MMPI-2

20. Which of the following is not one of the pairs of personality attributes claimed to be assessed by the Myers-Briggs Type Indicator (MBTI)?

   a. sensing/intuition (S/N)
   c. introversion/extraversion (I/E)
   b. thinking/feeling (T/F)
   d. positivity/negativity (P/N)

Chapter 12
Psychological Disorders

Do you or someone you know have any quirky beliefs or behaviors? Have you ever been sad for more than a day? What about being very energetic or extremely happy for the better part of a week? Maybe you are a "checker." Have you ever double- or triple-checked a door to see if you locked it? Today it may not be that uncommon to observe someone walking down the street and apparently talking to herself or himself, only then to observe they are actually wearing a Bluetooth headset. It also may mean one thing to see someone lying down on the sidewalk outside a local restaurant, and something slightly different if you see someone lying on the sidewalk outside a campus dorm or classroom building, and yet still different meanings if it is a student versus a faculty member.

Have you ever questioned if someone's way of thinking or acting was normal? How do you know if a behavior is normal or abnormal?

Why study abnormal behavior and mental processes?

Because it is all around us, which raises many questions: How should one react? What should be done to help? What kind of person develops a mental illness? Could this happen to someone close to you? The key to answering these questions is to develop an understanding of just what is meant by abnormal behavior and thinking, and the different ways in which thinking and behavior can depart from the "normal" path.

Learning Objectives

12.1 Describe how mental illness has been explained in the past and how abnormal behavior and thinking are defined today.

12.2 Identify some of the models used to explain psychological disorders.

12.3 Describe the different types of psychological disorders and their prevalence, and evaluate the advantages and disadvantages of using diagnostic labels.

12.4 Identify the different types of anxiety disorders and their symptoms.

12.5 Describe obsessive-compulsive disorder and stress-related disorders.

12.6 Explain some potential causes of anxiety, trauma, and stress disorders.

12.7 Describe various dissociative disorders, and explain how they develop.

12.8 Summarize the various explanations for dissociative disorders.

12.9 Describe different disorders of mood, including major depressive disorder and bipolar disorders.

12.10 Compare and contrast behavioral, social cognitive, and biological explanations for depression and other disorders of mood.

12.11 Identify three different types of eating disorders and the treatment options associated with each.

12.12 Summarize some of the risk factors associated with eating disorders, including cultural factors.

12.13 Describe types of sexual dysfunction, and explain how they may develop.

12.14 Describe the main symptoms of schizophrenia, distinguishing between positive and negative symptoms.

12.15 Evaluate the genetic and environmental influences on schizophrenia.

12.16 Classify the different types of personality disorders.

12.17 Summarize some of the potential causes of personality disorders.

12.18 Identify some methods to overcome test anxiety.

These human skull casts show signs of trephining, a process in which holes were cut into the skulls of a living person, perhaps to release "demons" that were making the person's behavior or thinking odd or disturbed. Some who were treated in this way must have survived, as some of the holes show evidence of healing.

Source: New York Public Library / Science Source.

What Is Abnormality?

Exactly what is meant by the term *abnormal behavior*? When is thinking, or a mental process *maladaptive*? Abnormal or maladaptive as compared to what? Who gets to decide what is normal and what is not? Has the term always meant what it means now? We'll explore these questions and others in this section.

CHANGING VIEWS OF ABNORMALITY

12.1 **Describe how mental illness has been explained in the past and how abnormal behavior and thinking are defined today.**

The study of abnormal behavior and psychological dysfunction is called **psychopathology**. Defining abnormality is a complicated process, and our view of what is abnormal has changed significantly over time.

A VERY BRIEF HISTORY OF PSYCHOLOGICAL DISORDERS   Dating from as early as 3000 B.C.E., archaeologists have found human skulls with small holes cut into them, and close examination indicates that the holes were made while the person was still alive. Many of the holes show evidence of healing, meaning that the person survived the process. Although *trephining,* or cutting holes into the skull of a living person, is still done today to relieve pressure of fluids on the brain, in ancient times the reason may have had more to do with releasing the "demons" possessing the poor victim (Gross, 1999).

Hippocrates (460–377 B.C.E.), a Greek physician during the time in which the rest of the world and even many Greeks believed in the demonic possession explanation of mental illness, challenged that belief with his assertion that illnesses of both the body and the mind were the result of imbalances in the body's vital fluids, or *humors*. Although Hippocrates was not correct in his assumptions about the humors of the body (phlegm, black bile, blood, and yellow bile), his was the first recorded attempt to explain abnormal thinking or behavior as due to some biological process.

Moving forward in time, people of the Middle Ages believed in spirit possession (a belief influenced by the teachings of the Roman Catholic Church and the remnants of other religious/cultural systems) as one cause of abnormality. The treatment of choice for such maladies was a religious one: *exorcism*, or the formal casting out of the demon through a religious ritual (Lewis, 1995). During the Renaissance, belief in demonic possession (in which the possessed person was seen as a victim) gave way to a belief in witchcraft, and mentally ill persons were most likely called witches and put to death.

Fast forward to the present day, psychological disorders are often viewed from a *medical model* in that they can be diagnosed according to various symptoms and have an *etiology,** course*, and *prognosis* (Kihlstrom, 2002). In turn, psychological disorders can be treated, and like many physical ailments, some may be "cured" whereas other psychological disorders will require lifelong attention. And while numerous perspectives in psychology are not medical in nature, the idea of diagnosis and treatment of symptoms bridges many of them. This chapter will focus on the types of psychological disorders and some of their possible causes. We will focus more on psychological treatment and therapies in the next chapter. Ⓛ Ⓘ Ⓝ Ⓚ to Chapter Thirteen: Psychological Therapies.

HOW CAN WE DEFINE WHAT IS ABNORMAL?   Defining abnormal behavior, abnormal thinking, or abnormality is not as simple as it might seem at first. The easy way out is to say that abnormal behavior is behavior that is not normal, abnormal thinking is thinking that is not normal, but what does that mean? It's complicated, as you'll see by

---

*etiology—the origin, cause, or set of causes for a disorder.

considering different criteria for determining abnormality. Before we explore different criteria for identifying abnormality and mental illness, take a moment to reflect on your own beliefs in the survey *Are You Normal?*

Survey   ARE YOU NORMAL?

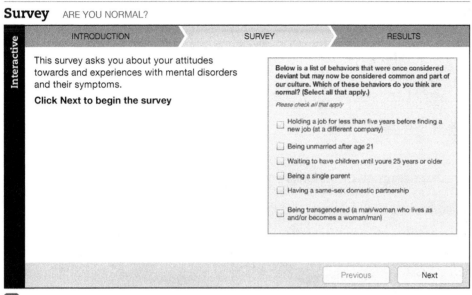

INTRODUCTION   SURVEY   RESULTS

This survey asks you about your attitudes towards and experiences with mental disorders and their symptoms.

Click Next to begin the survey

Below is a list of behaviors that were once considered deviant but may now be considered common and part of our culture. Which of these behaviors do you think are normal? (Select all that apply.)

Please check all that apply

☐ Holding a job for less than five years before finding a new job (at a different company)

☐ Being unmarried after age 21

☐ Waiting to have children until youre 25 years or older

☐ Being a single parent

☐ Having a same-sex domestic partnership

☐ Being transgendered (a man/woman who lives as and/or becomes a woman/man)

Previous   Next

◉ **Simulate** the **Experiment,** *Are You Normal?*

STATISTICAL OR SOCIAL NORM DEVIANCE   One way to define *normal* and *abnormal* is to use a statistical definition. Frequently occurring behavior would be considered normal, and behavior that is rare would be abnormal. Or how much behavior or thinking deviates from the norms of a society. For example, refusing to wear clothing in a society that does not permit nudity would likely be rare and be seen as abnormal. But deviance (variation) from social norms is not always labeled as negative or abnormal. For instance, a person who decides to become a monk and live in a monastery in the United States would be exhibiting unusual behavior, and certainly not what the society considers a standard behavior, but it wouldn't be a sign of abnormality.

The **situational context** (the social or environmental setting of a person's behavior) can also make a difference in how behavior or thinking is labeled. For example, if a man comes to a therapist complaining of people listening in on his phone conversations and spying on all his activities, the therapist's first thought might be that the man is suffering from thoughts of persecution. But if the man then explains that he is in a witness protection program, the complaints take on an entirely different and quite understandable tone.

SUBJECTIVE DISCOMFORT   One sign of abnormality is when the person experiences a great deal of **subjective discomfort**, or emotional distress while engaging in a particular behavior or thought process. A woman who suffers from a fear of going outside her house, for example, would experience a great deal of anxiety when trying to leave home and distress over being unable to leave. However, all thoughts or behavior that might be considered abnormal do not necessarily create subjective discomfort in the person having them or committing the act—a serial killer, for example, does not experience emotional distress after taking someone's life, and some forms of disordered behavior involve showing no emotions at all.

INABILITY TO FUNCTION NORMALLY   Thinking or behavior that does not allow a person to fit into society or function normally can also be labeled abnormal. These may be termed **maladaptive**, meaning that the person finds it hard to adapt to the demands of day-to-day living. Maladaptive thinking or behavior may initially help a person cope but has

By what criterion (or criteria) of abnormality might this person be considered abnormal? Would your perception of him change if the context were a Fourth of July celebration? What if he was in a park and not in front of a tax office?

harmful or damaging effects. For example, a woman who cuts herself to relieve anxiety does experience initial relief but is harmed by the action. Maladaptive thinking or behavior are key elements in the definition of abnormality.

A WORKING DEFINITION OF ABNORMALITY

💬 I've heard people call the different things other people do "crazy" or "weird." How do psychologists decide when people are really mentally ill and not just a little odd?

To get a clear picture of abnormality, it is often necessary to take all of the factors just discussed into account. Psychologists and other psychological professionals must consider several different criteria when determining whether or not psychological functioning or behavior is abnormal (at least two of these criteria must be met to form a diagnosis of abnormality):

1. Is the thinking or behavior unusual, such as experiencing severe panic when faced with a stranger or being severely depressed in the absence of any stressful life situations?

2. Does the thinking or behavior go against social norms? (And keep in mind that social norms change over time—e.g., homosexuality was once considered a psychological disorder rather than a variation in sexual orientation.)

3. Does the behavior or psychological function cause the person significant subjective discomfort?

4. Is the thought process or behavior maladaptive, or does it result in an inability to function?

5. Does the thought process or behavior cause the person to be dangerous to self or others, as in the case of someone who tries to commit suicide or who attacks other people without reason?

Abnormal thinking or behavior that includes at least two of these five criteria are perhaps best classified by the term **psychological disorder**, which is defined as any pattern of behavior or psychological functioning that causes people significant distress, causes them to harm themselves or others, or harms their ability to function in daily life.

Before moving on, it is important to clarify how the term *abnormality* is different from the term *insanity*. Only psychological professionals can diagnose disorders and determine the best course of treatment for someone who suffers from mental illness. Lawyers and judges are sometimes charged with determining how the law should address crimes committed under the influence of mental illness. Psychologists and psychiatrists determine whether or not certain thinking or behavior is abnormal, but they do not decide whether a certain person is insane. In the United States, *insanity* is not a psychological term; it is a legal term used to argue that a mentally ill person who has committed a crime should not be held responsible for his or her actions because that person was unable to understand the difference between right and wrong at the time of the offense. This argument is called the *insanity defense*.

MODELS OF ABNORMALITY

12.2 Identify some of the models used to explain psychological disorders.

  What causes psychological disorders?

Recognition of abnormal behavior and thinking depends on the "lens," or perspective, from which it is viewed. Different perspectives determine how the disordered behavior or thinking is explained. And as we will see in Chapter Thirteen, those same perspectives influence how psychological disorders are treated.

THE BIOLOGICAL MODEL: MEDICAL CAUSES FOR PSYCHOLOGICAL DISORDERS The **biological model** proposes that psychological disorders have a biological or medical cause (Gamwell & Tomes, 1995). This model explains disorders such as anxiety, depression, and schizophrenia as caused by faulty neurotransmitter systems, genetic problems, brain damage and dysfunction, or some combination of those causes. For example, as you may recall from the discussion of trait theory and the five-factor theory of personality traits, **LINK** to Learning Objectives 11.8 and 11.9, a growing body of evidence suggests that basic personality traits are as much influenced by genetic inheritance as they are by experience and upbringing, even across cultures (Bouchard, 1994; Herbst et al., 2000; Jang et al., 1996; Loehlin, 1992; Loehlin et al., 1998). One of the Big Five factors was neuroticism, for example, and it is easy to see how someone who scores high in neuroticism would be at greater risk for anxiety-based disorders.

As discussed earlier in the chapter, the biological or medical model has had a great deal of influence, especially in the language used to describe disorders: *mental illness, symptoms of disorder*, and terms such as *diagnosis, mental patient, mental hospital, therapy,* and *remission* all come from medical terminology. The use of such terms, although still widespread, may tend to bias the assumptions of professionals who are not psychiatrists or medical doctors toward a biological cause for disordered psychological functioning or behavior, or the idea that disorders might be diseases that can be "cured." Many disorders can effectively be controlled but may not be fully resolved.

THE PSYCHOLOGICAL MODELS Although biological explanations of psychological disorders are influential, they are not the only ways or even the first ways in which disorders are explained. Several different theories of personality were discussed in Chapter Eleven. These theories of personality can be used to describe and explain the formation of not only personality but disordered thinking, behavior, and abnormal personality as well.

PSYCHODYNAMIC VIEW: HIDING PROBLEMS The psychodynamic model, based on the work of Freud and his followers, **LINK** to Learning Objectives 11.2, 11.3, explains disordered thinking and behavior as the result of repressing one's threatening thoughts, memories, and concerns in the unconscious mind (Carducci, 1998). These repressed thoughts and urges try to resurface, and disordered functioning develops as a way of keeping the thoughts repressed. According to this view, a woman who has unacceptable thoughts of sleeping with her brother-in-law might feel "dirty" and be compelled to wash her hands every time those thoughts threaten to become conscious, ridding herself symbolically of the "dirty" thoughts.

BEHAVIORISM: LEARNING PROBLEMS Behaviorists, who define personality as a set of learned responses, have no trouble explaining disordered behavior as being learned just like normal behavior (Skinner, 1971; Watson, 1913). For example, when Emma was a small child, a spider dropped onto her leg, causing her to scream and react with fear. Her mother made a big fuss over her, giving her lots of attention. Each time Emma saw a spider after this, she screamed again, drawing attention to herself. Behaviorists would say that Emma's fear of the spider was classically conditioned, and her screaming reaction was positively reinforced by all the attention. (L)(I)(N)K to Learning Objectives 5.2 and 5.5.

COGNITIVE PERSPECTIVE: THINKING PROBLEMS **Cognitive psychologists** study the way people think, remember, and mentally organize information; they see maladaptive functioning as resulting from illogical thinking patterns (Mora, 1985). A cognitive psychologist might explain Emma's fear of spiders as distorted thinking: "All spiders are vicious and will bite me, and I will die!" Emma's particular thinking patterns put her at a higher risk of depression and anxiety than those of a person who thinks more logically.

THE SOCIOCULTURAL PERSPECTIVE In the **sociocultural perspective** of abnormality, abnormal thinking or behavior (as well as normal) is seen as the product of behavioral shaping within the context of family influences, the social group to which one belongs, and the culture within which the family and social group exist. In particular, cultural differences in abnormal thoughts or actions must be addressed when psychological professionals are attempting to assess and treat members of a culture different from that of the professional. **Cultural relativity** is a term that refers to the need to consider the unique characteristics of the culture in which the person with a disorder was nurtured to be able to correctly diagnose and treat the disorder (Castillo, 1997). For example, in most traditional Asian cultures, mental illness is often seen as a shameful thing that brings disgrace to one's family. This leads many Asian people suffering from disorders that would be labeled as depression or even schizophrenia to report bodily symptoms rather than emotional or mental ones, because bodily ailments are more socially acceptable (Fedoroff & McFarlane, 1998; Lee, 1995; Ritts, 1999). Disorders unique to specific cultures have previously been referred to as *culture-bound syndromes*. For example, anorexia nervosa and bulimia nervosa have traditionally been most often found in Western societies.

The conceptualization of culture and its influences on psychological function and disorders has been expanded in the most recent publication of the *Diagnostic and Statistical Manual of Mental Disorders*, the *DSM-5*. The idea of "culture-bound" has been replaced by three concepts: **cultural syndromes**, *cultural idioms of distress*, and *cultural explanations or perceived cause* (American Psychiatric Association, 2013). Cultural syndromes may or may not be recognized as an illness within the culture but are nonetheless recognizable as a distinct set of symptoms or characteristics of distress. Cultural idioms of distress refer to terms or phrases used to describe suffering or distress within a given cultural context. And cultural explanations or perceived cause are culturally defined ways of explaining the source or cause of symptoms or illness (American Psychiatric Association, 2013).

It is important to take into account other background and influential factors such as socioeconomic status and education level. Another area of awareness should be primary language and, if applicable, degree of acculturation (adapting to or merging with another culture). Psychosocial functioning has been part of the diagnostic process for some time now, but traditionally, greater attention has been paid to specifically identifying symptoms of pathology rather than focusing on the environmental factors that influence an individual's overall level of functioning (Ro & Clark, 2009). For example, in one study, college students of Mexican heritage with migrant farming backgrounds reported more symptoms of anxiety and depression as compared to nonmigrant college students of Mexican heritage (Mejía & McCarthy, 2010). The nature of migrant farming poses different stressors than those faced by nonmigrant families.

BIOPSYCHOSOCIAL PERSPECTIVE: ALL OF THE ABOVE The biological, psychological, and sociocultural influences on abnormality are no longer seen as independent causes. Instead, these influences interact with one another to cause the various forms of disorders. For example, a person may have a genetically inherited tendency for a type of disorder, such as anxiety, but may not develop a full-blown disorder unless the family and social

A migrant farming background has been found to be related to increased symptoms of anxiety and depression among college students of Mexican heritage when compared to those without a migrant background.

environments produce the right stressors at the right time in development. We will see later how this idea specifically applies to a theory of schizophrenia. How accepting a particular culture is of a specific disorder will also play a part in determining the exact degree and form that disorder might take. This is known as the **biopsychosocial model** of disorder, which has become a very influential way to view the connection between mind and body.

DIAGNOSING AND CLASSIFYING DISORDERS

12.3 Describe the different types of psychological disorders and their prevalence, and evaluate the advantages and disadvantages of using diagnostic labels.

Have you ever asked a young child, or remember from being one yourself, "What's wrong?" when they reported not feeling well? If so, you likely received a variety of answers describing their tummy ache, ouchie, or boo boo. And in turn, you may have not known exactly what was wrong due to differences in their descriptive language and yours, especially when you could not see where or why they were hurting. The same applies to understanding and treating psychological disorders. Having a common set of terms and systematic way of describing psychological and behavioral symptoms is vital not only to correct identification and diagnosis but also in communication among and between psychological professionals and other health-care providers.

THE *DSM-5* One international resource is the World Health Organization's (WHO's) *International Classification of Diseases* (*ICD*), currently in its tenth edition (*ICD-10*). In the United States, the prevalent resource to help psychological professionals diagnose psychological disorders has been the *Diagnostic and Statistical Manual of Mental Disorders* (*DSM*), first published in 1952. The *DSM* has been revised multiple times as our knowledge and ways of thinking about psychological disorders has changed. The most recent version, which was released in 2013, is the *Diagnostic and Statistical Manual of Mental Disorders, Fifth Edition* (*DSM-5*) (American Psychiatric Association, 2013). It also includes changes in organization of disorders, modifications in terminology used to describe disorders and their symptoms, and discusses the possibility of dimensional assessments for some disorders in future versions of the manual. The *DSM* has been useful in providing clinicians with descriptions and criteria for diagnosing mental disorders but it has not been without its share of controversy as the video *The DSM* explains.

👁 Watch the Video, *The DSM*.

The *DSM-5* describes about 250 different psychological disorders. Each disorder is described in terms of its symptoms, the typical path the disorder takes as it progresses, and a checklist of specific criteria that must be met in order for the diagnosis of that disorder to be made. Whereas previous editions of the manual divided disorders and relevant facts about the person being diagnosed along five different categories, or axes, the *DSM-5* uses a single axis for all disorders, with provisions for also noting significant and relevant facts about the individual. For example, whereas the *DSM-IV* used Axis I for mental disorders, Axis II for personality disorders and mental retardation (now called *intellectual disability*), and Axis III for medical diagnoses, the *DSM-5* combines all of these disorders and diagnoses into a single list (American Psychiatric Association, 2013).

A few of the 20 categories of disorders that can be diagnosed include depressive disorders, anxiety disorders, schizophrenia spectrum and other psychotic disorders, feeding and eating disorders, and neurodevelopmental disorders such as ADHD (American Psychiatric Association, 2013). Other categories include personality disorders, intellectual disability, trauma- and stressor-related disorders, and obsessive-compulsive and related disorders.

HOW COMMON ARE PSYCHOLOGICAL DISORDERS?

 ● That sounds like a lot of possible disorders, but most people don't get these problems, right?

Actually, psychological disorders are more common than most people might think. In any given year, about 26.2 percent of American adults over age 18 suffer from a mental disorder (National Institute of Mental Health, 2010); that comes to about 61.5 million people in the United States using 2010 census data. Fortunately, only about 5.8 percent of the U.S. population, or 1 in 17 adults, suffers from a severe mental disorder. Statistically, mental disorders are the leading cause of disability in the United States and Canada (National Institute of Mental Health, 2010). It is quite common for people to suffer from more than one mental disorder at a time, such as a person with depression who also has a substance-abuse disorder, or a person with an anxiety disorder who also suffers from sleep disorders. Approximately 45 percent of individuals with a mental disorder meet criteria for two or more disorders (National Institute of Mental Health, 2010). **Table 12.1** has percentages of selected psychological disorders in the United States. (Note that this table does not include all of the disorders that occur in the 61.5 million adults in the United States mentioned earlier in this paragraph.)

THE PROS AND CONS OF LABELS   With its lists of disorders and their corresponding symptoms, the *DSM-5* helps psychological professionals diagnose patients and provide those patients with labels that explain their conditions. In the world of psychological diagnosis and treatment, labels like *depression, anxiety,* and *schizophrenia* can be very helpful: They make up a common language in the mental health community, allowing psychological professionals to communicate with each other clearly and efficiently. Labels establish distinct diagnostic categories that all professionals recognize and understand, and they help patients receive effective treatment.

However, labels can also be dangerous—or, at the very least, overly prejudicial. In 1972, researcher David Rosenhan asked healthy participants to enter psychiatric hospitals and complain that they were hearing voices. All of the participants, whom Rosenhan called "pseudopatients," were admitted into the hospitals and diagnosed with either schizophrenia or manic depression (now called bipolar disorder). Once the pseudopatients were admitted, they stopped pretending to be ill and acted as they normally would, but

Table 12.1 YEARLY OCCURRENCE OF PSYCHOLOGICAL DISORDERS IN THE UNITED STATES

Click on terms to see more detail about the yearly occurrence of psychological disorders in the United States*.

Bipolar and Depressive Disorders	9.5% of the U.S. population 22.3 million people
Major depressive disorder	6.7% of the U.S. population 15.7 million people
Persistent depressive disorder (dysthymia)	1.5% of the U.S. population 3.5 million people
Bipolar disorder	2.6% of the U.S. population 6.1 million people
Anxiety, Obsessive-Compulsive, and Trauma-Related Disorders	18.1% of the U.S. population 42.5 million people
Specific phobia	8.7% of the U.S. population 20.4 million people
Social anxiety disorder (social phobia)	6.8% of the U.S. population 16 million people
Panic disorder	2.7% of the U.S. population 6.3 million people
Agoraphobia	0.8% of the U.S. population 1.9 million people
Generalized anxiety disorder	3.1% of the U.S. population 7.3 million people
Obsessive-compulsive disorder	1.0% of the U.S. population 2.3 million people
Posttraumatic stress disorder	3.5% of the U.S. population 8.2 million people
Schizophrenia	1.1% of the U.S. population 2.6 million people

*Percentage of adults over age 18 affected annually and approximate number within the population based on 2010 United States Census data.
Adapted from National Institute of Mental Health (2013). Terminology in tables is from both the *DSM-IV* and *DSM-5* (American Psychiatric Association, 2000, 2013).

the hospital staff's interpretation of the pseudopatients' normal behavior was skewed by the label of mental illness. For example, hospital workers described one pseudopatient's relatively normal relationships with family and friends as evidence of a psychological disorder, and another pseudopatient's note-taking habits were considered to be a pathological behavior. The pseudopatients had been diagnosed and labeled, and those labels stuck, even when actual symptoms of mental illness disappeared. Rosenhan concluded that psychological labels are long-lasting and powerful, affecting not only how other people see mental patients but how patients see themselves (Rosenhan, 1973).

Labels can be time-saving and even life-saving tools, but they can also bias us, affect our judgment, and give us preconceived notions that may very well turn out to be false. Just to be clear, the diagnostic labels listed in the *DSM-5* are intended to help both psychologists and patients, and they *do* help. As you read on, remember the power that labels have to shape our perceptions of reality.

Before describing the various categories and types of disorders, here is a word of caution: It's very easy to see oneself in these disorders. Medical students often become convinced that they have every one of the symptoms for some rare, exotic disease they have been studying. Psychology students studying abnormal behavior can also become convinced that they have some mental disorder, a problem that can be called "psychology student's syndrome." The problem is that so many psychological disorders are really ordinary variations in human behavior taken to an extreme. For example, some people are natural-born worriers. They look for things that can go wrong around every corner. That doesn't make them disordered—it makes them pessimistic worriers. Remember, it doesn't become a disorder until the worrying causes them significant distress, causes them to harm themselves or others, or harms their ability to function in everyday life. So if you start "seeing" yourself or even your friends and family in any of the following discussions, don't panic—all of you are *probably* okay.

Concept Map L.O. 12.1, 12.2, 12.3

what is abnormality?

- **psychopathology** is the study of abnormal behavior and psychological dysfunction; mental illness has been defined in various ways throughout history (e.g., possession, evil spirits, bodily imbalances)
- current definitions of abnormality are based on several factors
  - **statistical or social norm deviance**
  - **subjective discomfort**
  - **inability to function normally**
- disorders vary according to culture; cultural sensitivity and relativity are necessary in diagnosing and treating psychological disorders
- overall, psychological disorders are any pattern of behavior or thinking that causes significant distress, causes people to harm themselves or others, or harms their ability to function in daily life

Psychological Disorders

models of abnormality
explanations for disordered thinking or behavior depend on theoretical model used to explain personality in general

- **biological model:** proposes that psychological disorders have a biological or medical cause; the medical model also influences approaches to diagnosis, treatment, and possible outcomes for a given disorder
- **psychological models:** propose that disorders are the result of various forms of emotional, behavioral, or thought-related malfunctioning
  - **psychodynamic**
  - **behavioral**
  - **cognitive**
- **sociocultural perspective:** thinking and behavior are the products of family, social, and cultural influences; what is normal in one culture may be abnormal in another
- **biopsychosocial perspective:** incorporates biological, psychological, and sociocultural factors

Diagnosing and Classifying Disorders

- the *Diagnostic and Statistical Manual of Mental Disorders (DSM)* was first published in 1952, current version *(DSM-5)* published in 2013
- describes and provides diagnostic criteria for approximately 250 different psychological disorders
- in general, approximately 26% of adults over age 18 in the United States suffer from a mental disorder (see Table 12.1)

[Reset]

Practice Quiz   How much do you remember?   ANSWERS ON PAGE AK-1.

Pick the best answer.

1. How would the Greek physician Hippocrates have typically dealt with someone suffering from mental illness?
   a. He would have made a hole in the patient's skull to release the pressure, a process known today as trephining.
   b. He would focus on correcting the imbalance of bodily fluids, or humors.
   c. He would have someone conduct the religious ritual known as an exorcism.
   d. He would have tried to understand the person's unconscious and the forces at work there.

2. Lisa has just been fired from her new job for consistently arriving 2 hours late for work. Lisa tries to explain that she must often drive back home to ensure that all the doors are locked and that no appliances have been left on. Lisa's condition is abnormal from the _____ definition.
   a. maladaptive
   b. situational context
   c. social deviance
   d. subjective discomfort

3. In the United States, insanity is a term typically used by
   a. psychologists.
   b. psychiatrists.
   c. the social work system.
   d. the legal system.

4. Elliot became widowed after nearly 40 years of marriage. He has convinced himself that no one will ever love him again. His irrational thinking has caused him to suffer from depression, and he rarely leaves his house. What perspective might best explain his behavior?
   a. psychodynamic
   b. cognitive
   c. behavioral
   d. biological

5. Which of the following concepts is not specifically associated with the *DSM-5* examination of culture-related disorders?
   a. cultural syndrome
   b. cultural idioms of distress
   c. cultural explanations or perceived cause
   d. cultural binding

Disorders of Anxiety, Trauma, and Stress: What, Me Worry?

In this section we will examine disorders in which the most dominant symptom is excessive or unrealistic anxiety. In addition to anxiety disorders, we will also address disorders that many people associate with anxiety symptoms, including *obsessive-compulsive disorder*, *posttraumatic stress disorder*, and *acute stress disorders*. These were classified as anxiety disorders in previous editions of the *DSM*. However, they now fall under different categories in the *DSM-5*. *Obsessive-compulsive disorder* now falls in the category of "Obsessive-Compulsive and Related Disorders" while *posttraumatic stress disorder* and *acute stress disorder* are found under "Trauma- and Stressor-Related Disorders" (American Psychiatric Association, 2013).

ANXIETY DISORDERS

12.4 Identify the different types of anxiety disorders and their symptoms.

The *DSM-5* category of **anxiety disorders** includes disorders in which the most dominant symptom is excessive or unrealistic anxiety. Anxiety can take very specific forms, such as a fear of a specific object, or it can be a very general emotion, such as that experienced by someone who is worried and doesn't know why.

 💬 But doesn't everybody have anxiety sometimes? What makes it a disorder?

Everyone does have anxiety, and some people have a great deal of anxiety at times. When talking about anxiety disorders, the anxiety is either excessive—greater than it should be given the circumstances—or unrealistic. If final exams are coming up and a student hasn't studied enough, that student's anxiety is understandable and realistic. But a student who has studied, has done well in all the exams, and is very prepared and still worries *excessively* about passing is showing an unrealistic amount of anxiety. For more about test anxiety, see the *Applying Psychology to Everyday Life* section in this chapter. People who are in danger of losing their job might experience quite a bit of anxiety, but its source is obvious and understandable. But someone whose life is going well and for whom nothing bad is looming in the future, and who still feels extremely anxious may be experiencing an anxiety disorder. **Free-floating anxiety** is the term given to anxiety that seems to be unrelated to any realistic and specific, known factor, and it is often a symptom of an anxiety disorder (Freud, 1977).

PHOBIC DISORDERS: WHEN FEARS GET OUT OF HAND One of the more specific anxiety disorders is a **phobia**, an irrational, persistent fear of something. The "something" might be an object or a situation or may involve social interactions. For example, many people would feel fear if they suddenly came upon a live snake as they were walking and would take steps to avoid the snake. Although those same people would not necessarily avoid a *picture* of a snake in a book, a person with a phobia of snakes would. Avoiding a live snake is rational; avoiding a picture of a snake is not.

SOCIAL ANXIETY DISORDER (SOCIAL PHOBIA) **Social anxiety disorder** (also called *social phobia*) involves a fear of interacting with others or being in a social situation and is one of the most common phobias people experience (Kessler et al., 2012). People with social anxiety disorder are afraid of being evaluated in some negative way by others, so they tend to avoid situations that could lead to something embarrassing or humiliating. They are very self-conscious as a result. Common types of social phobia are stage fright, fear of public speaking, and fear of urinating in a public restroom. Not

Many people get nervous when they have to speak in front of an audience. Fear of public speaking is a common social phobia. Can you remember a time when you experienced a fear like this?

surprisingly, people with social phobias often have a history of being shy as children (Sternberger et al., 1995).

SPECIFIC PHOBIAS A **specific phobia** is an irrational fear of some object or specific situation, such as a fear of dogs, or a fear of being in small, enclosed spaces (**claustrophobia**). Some examples of other specific phobias include a fear of spiders (*arachnophobia*), darkness (*nyctophobia*), injections (*trypanophobia*), fear of dental work (*odontophobia*), fear of blood (*hematophobia*), and fear of heights (**acrophobia**).

AGORAPHOBIA A third type of phobia is **agoraphobia**, a Greek name that literally means "fear of the marketplace." It is the fear of being in a place or situation from which escape is difficult or impossible if something should go wrong (American Psychiatric Association, 2013). Furthermore, the anxiety is present in more than one situation. Someone is diagnosed with agoraphobia if they feel anxiety in at least two of five possible situations such as using public transportation like a bus or plane, being out in an open space such as on a bridge or in a parking lot, being in an enclosed space such as a grocery store or movie theatre, standing in line or being in a crowd like at a concert, or being out of the home alone (American Psychiatric Association, 2013).

Agoraphobia may include a fear of crossing bridges, although this bridge is enough to test anyone's courage.

💬 If a person has agoraphobia, it might be difficult to even go to work or to the store, right?

Exactly. People with specific phobias can usually avoid the object or situation without too much difficulty and people with social phobias may simply avoid jobs and situations that involve meeting people face to face. But people with agoraphobia cannot avoid their phobia's source because it is simply being outside in the real world. A severe case of agoraphobia can make a person's home a prison, leaving the person trapped inside unable to go to work, shop, or engage in any kind of activity that requires going out of the home.

PANIC DISORDER Fourteen-year-old Dariya was sitting in science class watching a film. All of a sudden, she started feeling really strange. Her ears seemed to be stuffed with cotton and her vision was very dim. She was cold, had broken out in a sweat, and felt extremely afraid for no good reason. Her heart was racing, and she immediately became convinced that she was dying. A friend sitting behind her saw how pale she had become and tried to ask her what was wrong, but Dariya couldn't speak. She was in a state of panic and couldn't move.

Dariya's symptoms are the classic symptoms of a **panic attack**, a sudden onset of extreme panic with various physical symptoms: racing heart, rapid breathing, a sensation of being "out of one's body," dulled hearing and vision, sweating, and dry mouth (Kumar & Oakley-Browne, 2002). Many people who have a panic attack think that they are having a heart attack and can experience pain as well as panic, but the symptoms are caused by the panic, not by any actual physical disorder. Psychologically, the person having a panic attack is in a state of terror, thinking that this is it, death is happening, and many people may feel a need to escape. The attack happens without warning and quite suddenly. Although some panic attacks can last as long as half an hour, some last only a few minutes, with most attacks peaking within 10 to 15 minutes.

Having a panic attack is not that unusual, especially for adolescent girls and young adult women (Eaton et al., 1994; Hayward et al., 1989, 2000). Researchers have also found evidence that cigarette smoking greatly increases the risk of panic attacks in adolescents and young adults (Johnson, 2000; Zvolensky et al., 2003). Regardless, it is only when panic attacks occur more than once or repeatedly, and cause persistent worry or changes in behavior, that they become a **panic disorder**. Many people try to figure out what triggers a panic attack and then do their best to avoid the situation if possible. If driving a car sets off an attack, they don't drive. If being in a crowd sets off an attack, they don't go where crowds are.

GENERALIZED ANXIETY DISORDER

 🗩 What about people who are just worriers? Can that become a disorder?

Remember free-floating anxiety? That's the kind of anxiety that has no known specific source and may be experienced by people with **generalized anxiety disorder**, in which excessive anxiety and worries (apprehensive expectations) occur more days than not for at least 6 months. People with this disorder may also experience anxiety about a number of events or activities (such as work or school performance). These feelings of anxiety have no particular source that can be pinpointed, nor can the person control the feelings even if an effort is made to do so.

People with this disorder are just plain worriers (Ruscio et al., 2001). They worry *excessively* about money, their children, their lives, their friends, the dog, as well as things no one else would see as a reason to worry. They feel tense, edgy, get tired easily, and may have trouble concentrating. They have muscle aches, they experience sleeping problems, and are often irritable—all signs of stress. Generalized anxiety disorder is often found occurring with other anxiety disorders and depression.

OTHER DISORDERS RELATED TO ANXIETY

12.5 **Describe obsessive-compulsive disorder and stress-related disorders.**

As discussed earlier, despite anxiety being a common symptom, the following disorders are not classified as anxiety disorders in the *DSM-5*. *Obsessive-compulsive disorder* now falls in the category of "Obsessive-Compulsive and Related Disorders" while *posttraumatic stress disorder* and *acute stress disorder* are found under "Trauma- and Stressor-Related Disorders" (American Psychiatric Association, 2013).

OBSESSIVE-COMPULSIVE DISORDER Sometimes people get a thought running through their head that just won't go away, like when a song gets stuck in one's mind. If that particular thought causes a lot of anxiety, it can become the basis for an **obsessive-compulsive disorder**, or OCD. OCD is a disorder in which intruding* thoughts that occur repeatedly (obsessions, such as a fear that germs are on one's hands) are followed by some repetitive, ritualistic behavior or mental acts (compulsions, such as repeated hand washing, counting, etc.). The compulsions are meant to lower the anxiety caused by the thought (Soomro, 2001).

🗩 I knew someone who had just had a baby, and she spent the first few nights home with the baby checking it to see if it was breathing—is that an obsessive-compulsive disorder?

No, many parents check their baby's breathing often at first. Everyone has a little obsessive thinking on occasion or some small ritual that makes them feel better. The difference is whether a person *likes* to perform the ritual (but doesn't *have* to) or feels *compelled* to perform the ritual and feels extreme anxiety if unable to do so. You may wash your hands a time or two after picking up garbage but it is entirely different if you *must* wash them a *thousand times* to prevent getting sick. The distress caused by a failure or an inability to successfully complete the compulsion is a defining feature of OCD.

ACUTE STRESS DISORDER (ASD) AND POSTTRAUMATIC STRESS DISORDER (PTSD) Both general and specific stressors were discussed in Chapter Nine: Motivation, Stress, and Emotion. Two trauma- and stressor-related disorders—*acute stress disorder* and *posttraumatic stress disorder*—are related to exposure to significant and traumatic stressors. The

"RONALD IS EXTREMELY COMPULSIVE."

www.cartoonstock.com

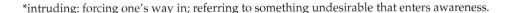

*intruding: forcing one's way in; referring to something undesirable that enters awareness.

After the BP oil spill in April of 2010, anywhere from 35 to 45 percent of people living around or near the Gulf of Mexico reported suffering symptoms of stress (Abramson et al., 2010).

trauma, severe stress, and anxiety experienced by people after 9/11, Hurricane Katrina, the East Japan Earthquake, and the April 2013 Boston Marathon bombings can lead to **acute stress disorder (ASD)**. The symptoms of ASD often occur immediately after the traumatic event and include anxiety, dissociative symptoms (such as emotional numbness/lack of responsiveness, not being aware of surroundings, dissociative amnesia), recurring nightmares, sleep disturbances, problems in concentration, and moments in which people seem to "relive" the event in dreams and flashbacks for as long as one month following the event. One study gathered survey information from Katrina evacuees at a major emergency shelter and found that 62 percent of those sampled met the criteria for having acute stress disorder (Mills et al., 2007).

When the symptoms associated with ASD last for more than one month, the disorder is then called **posttraumatic stress disorder (PTSD)**. In the same study (Mills et al., 2007), researchers concluded that it was likely that anywhere from 38 to 49 percent of all the evacuees sampled were at risk of developing PTSD that would still be present 2 years after the disaster. Furthermore, whereas the onset of ASD often occurs immediately after the traumatic event, the symptoms of PTSD may not occur until 6 months or later after the event (American Psychiatric Association, 2013). Treatment of these stress disorders may involve psychotherapy and the use of drugs to control anxiety. (L I N K) to Learning Objective 13.10. The video *PTSD* describes PTSD in more detail.

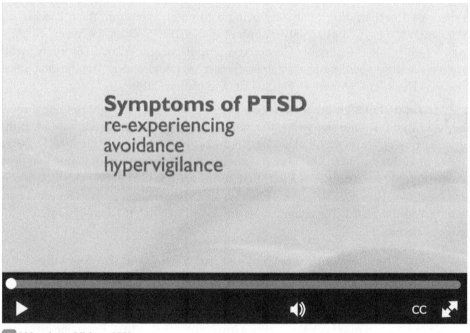

Symptoms of PTSD
re-experiencing
avoidance
hypervigilance

👁 **Watch** the Video, *PTSD.*

Researchers have found that women have almost twice the risk of developing PTSD than do men and that the likelihood increases if the traumatic experience took place before the woman was 15 years old (Breslau et al., 1997, 1999). However, female and male veterans tend to have similar symptoms of PTSD, at least for military-related stressors (King et al., 2013). Furthermore, exposure to multiple traumatic events increases the risk of developing PTSD. Data from the World Health Organization World Mental Health Survey Initiative surveys revealed individuals with four or more traumatic events not only had more complex cases of PTSD, but also greater impairment in their functional abilities (Karam et al., 2014). Children may also suffer different effects from stress than do adults. Severe PTSD has been linked to a decrease in the size of the hippocampus in children with the disorder

Psychological Disorders 463

(Carrion et al., 2007). The hippocampus is important in the formation of new long-term declarative memories (**L I N K** to Learning Objectives 2.11, 6.5, 6.12), and this may have a detrimental effect on learning and the effectiveness of treatments for these children. One study of older veterans over a 7-year period (Yaffe et al., 2010) found that those with PTSD were more likely to develop dementia (10.6 percent risk) when compared to those without PTSD (only 6.6 percent risk).

Some life experiences lend themselves to people experiencing traumatic events. For example, the rate of PTSD (self-reported) among combat-exposed military personnel has tripled since 2001 (Smith et al., 2008). Lastly, individuals with ASD and PTSD likely perceive the world around them differently. A study of assault and motor vehicle accident survivors treated in a South London, UK, emergency room suggested individuals with ASD or PTSD were more likely to identify trauma-related pictures than neutral pictures, as compared to trauma survivors not diagnosed with ASD or PTSD. Furthermore, such preferential processing of trauma-related information may be more strongly primed in individuals with PTSD (Kleim et al., 2012) and is supported by fMRI studies demonstrating heightened brain processing in areas associated with associative learning and priming in individuals with PTSD (Sartory et al., 2013). **L I N K** to Learning Objective 6.5.

CAUSES OF ANXIETY, TRAUMA, AND STRESS DISORDERS

12.6 **Explain some potential causes of anxiety, trauma, and stress disorders.**

Different perspectives on how personality develops offer different explanations for these disorders. For example, the psychodynamic model sees anxiety as a kind of danger signal that repressed urges or conflicts are threatening to surface (Freud, 1977). A phobia is seen as a kind of displacement, in which the phobic object is actually only a symbol of whatever the person has buried deep in his or her unconscious mind—the true source of the fear. A fear of knives might mean a fear of one's own aggressive tendencies, or a fear of heights may hide a suicidal desire to jump.

BEHAVIORAL AND COGNITIVE FACTORS   Behaviorists believe that anxious behavioral reactions are learned. They see phobias, for example, as nothing more than classically conditioned fear responses, as was the case with "Little Albert" (Rachman, 1990; Watson & Rayner, 1920). **L I N K** to Learning Objective 5.3. Cognitive psychologists see anxiety disorders as the result of illogical, irrational thought processes. One way in which people with anxiety disorders show irrational thinking (Beck, 1976, 1984) is through **magnification**, or the tendency to "make mountains out of molehills" by interpreting situations as being far more harmful, dangerous, or embarrassing than they actually are. In panic disorder, for example, a person might interpret a racing heartbeat as a sign of a heart attack instead of just a momentary arousal.

Cognitive-behavioral psychologists may see anxiety as related to another distorted thought process called **all-or-nothing thinking**, in which a person believes that his or her performance must be perfect or the result will be a total failure. **Overgeneralization** (a single negative event interpreted as a never-ending pattern of defeat), jumping to conclusions without facts to support that conclusion, and **minimization** (giving little or no emphasis to one's successes or positive events and traits) are other examples of irrational thinking.

BIOLOGICAL FACTORS   Growing evidence exists that biological factors contribute to anxiety disorders. Several disorders, including generalized anxiety disorder, panic disorders, phobias, and OCD, tend to run in families, pointing to a genetic basis for these disorders. Furthermore, genetic factors in PTSD seem to influence both the risk of developing the disorder and the likelihood individuals may be involved in potentially dangerous situations (Hyman & Cohen, 2013). Functional neuroimaging studies, **L I N K** to

Anxiety disorders affect children as well as adults.

Learning Objective 2.9, have revealed that the amygdala, an area of the limbic system, is more active in phobic people responding to pictures of spiders than in nonphobic people (LeDoux, 2003; Rauch et al., 2003) and also more active in individuals with PTSD and social anxiety disorder, suggesting excessive conditioning and exaggerated responses to stimuli that would typically elicit minimal fear-related responses (Hyman & Cohen, 2013). (L)(I)(N)(K) to Learning Objectives 2.11, 6.12 and 9.10.

CULTURAL VARIATIONS   Anxiety disorders are found around the world, although the particular form the disorder takes might be different in various cultures. For example, in some Latin American cultures anxiety can take the form of *ataque de nervios*, or "attack of nerves," in which the person may have fits of crying, shout uncontrollably, experience sensations of heat, and become very aggressive, either verbally or physically. These attacks usually come after some stressful event such as the death of a loved one (American Psychiatric Association, 2013). Several syndromes that are essentially types of phobias are specific to certain cultures. For example, *koro*, found primarily in China and a few other South Asian and East Asian countries, involves a fear that one's genitals are shrinking (Pfeiffer, 1982), and *taijin kyofusho* (TKS), found primarily in Japan, involves excessive fear and anxiety, but in this case it is the fear that one will do something in public that is socially inappropriate or embarrassing, such as blushing, staring, or having an offensive body odor (Kirmayer, 1991). Panic disorder occurs at similar rates in adolescents and adults in the United States and parts of Europe, but is found less often in Asian, African, and Latin American countries. Within the United States, American Indians have significantly higher rates whereas Latinos, African Americans, Caribbean blacks, and Asian Americans have significantly lower rates as compared to non-Latino whites (American Psychiatric Association, 2013).

Concept Map L.O. 12.4, 12.5, 12.6

Interactive

Disorders of Anxiety, Trauma, and Stress
(most dominant symptom is excessive or unrealistic anxiety, or related to traumatic stress)

- anxiety can be free-floating (nonspecific, anxious in general) or more specific, as in the case of phobias
  - social anxiety disorder (social phobia)
  - specific phobias (e.g., **claustrophobia, acrophobia**)
  - **agoraphobia**

- **panic disorder** consists of an individual having recurrent panic attacks that cause ongoing worry and concern

- **generalized anxiety disorder** involves excessive worry about lots of things and occurs more days than not

- **obsessive-compulsive disorder (OCD)** consists of recurring anxiety-provoking thoughts or obsessions that are only relieved through ritualistic or repetitive behaviors or mental events

- **acute stress disorder (ASD)**
  posttraumatic stress disorder (PTSD) → caused by significant and traumatic stressors; diagnosis differs according to duration and onset of symptoms, including dissociation, nightmares, and reliving the event.

- causes
  - **behavioral:** anxious behavioral reactions are learned
  - **cognitive:** anxiety is result of illogical, irrational thought processes
    - **magnification**
    - **all-or-none thinking**
    - **overgeneralization**
    - **minimization**
  - **biological:** anxiety is due to dysfunction in several neurotransmitter systems (e.g., serotonin, GABA) and/or difference in brain activation; panic disorder is also hereditary
  - **cultural:** anxiety disorders found around the world but particular forms vary across cultures

Reset

Practice Quiz   How much do you remember? ANSWERS ON PAGE AK-1.

Pick the best answer.

1. Who is most likely to be diagnosed with a phobic disorder?
  a. Brianne, who is afraid of snakes after nearly being bitten while running
  b. Calista, who is afraid of snakes after watching a documentary on poisonous snakes found in her region
  c. Jennifer, who is morbidly afraid of snakes and refuses to even look at a picture of a snake
  d. Both Calista and Jennifer's behavior would qualify as a phobic disorder.

2. Amelia has recently given birth to her first child. She mentions that she often goes into her baby's bedroom to check if he is still breathing. Would this qualify as an obsessive-compulsive disorder (OCD)?
  a. If Amelia continues to carry out this behavior for more than one or two days, this would qualify as an OCD.
  b. If Amelia and her husband both carry out this behavior, then it would qualify as an OCD.
  c. If Amelia enjoys frequently checking to see that her baby is breathing, then this would qualify as an OCD.
  d. As long as Amelia is not compelled to check on her baby and does not suffer from severe anxiety if she is unable to do so, then this is not an OCD.

3. Sandy took part in the April 2013 Boston Marathon, where two bombs were detonated near the finish line killing three spectators. For approximately two weeks after the marathon, Sandy was unable to sleep or concentrate and often found herself reliving the moment she heard the bombs explode. What disorder might Sandy be diagnosed with?
  a. acute stress disorder
  b. posttraumatic stress disorder
  c. phobic disorder
  d. panic disorder

4. Melanie has just received an exam grade in her psychology class. She earned a grade of 89%, which is a "B." All of her work during the semester thus far has earned "A" grades, and she is very upset about the exam score. "This is the worst thing that could possibly have happened," she laments to her best friend, Keesha, who just rolls her eyes. A cognitive psychologist would suggest that Melanie is employing the cognitive distortion called _____
  a. all-or-nothing thinking
  b. overgeneralization
  c. magnification
  d. minimization

Dissociative Disorders: Altered Identities

Just as there is sometimes overlap of symptoms between different diagnoses, various disorders can be related to similar circumstances or phenomena. As already discussed, exposure to trauma is a key component to ASD and PTSD, and both may include symptoms of dissociation. Dissociation plays a more prominent role in the dissociative disorders, where the dissociative symptoms encompass many aspects of everyday life, and not just memories of the traumatic events themselves or the time around them (American Psychiatric Association, 2013).

TYPES OF DISSOCIATIVE DISORDERS

12.7 **Describe various dissociative disorders and explain how they develop.**

Dissociative disorders involve a break, or dissociation, in consciousness, memory, or a person's sense of identity. They are found in individuals that have experienced trauma and may include feelings of detachment, or alterations in emotion, perception, or behavior.

DISSOCIATIVE AMNESIA AND FUGUE: WHO AM I AND HOW DID I GET HERE? In *dissociative amnesia*, the individual cannot remember personal information such as one's own name or specific personal events—the kind of information contained in episodic long-term memory. **LINK** to Learning Objective 6.5. Dissociative amnesia may sound like retrograde amnesia, but it differs in its cause. In retrograde amnesia, the memory loss is typically caused by a physical injury, such as a blow to the head. In dissociative amnesia, the cause is psychological rather than physical. The "blow" is a mental one, not a physical one. The reported memory loss is usually associated with a stressful or emotionally traumatic experience, and may be a loss of memory for only one small segment of time, or it may involve a total loss of one's personal memories. For example, a soldier might remember being in combat but be unable to recall the death of a friend he witnessed, or a person might forget his or her entire life. These memories usually resurface, sometimes quickly, and sometimes after a long delay. Dissociative amnesia can occur with or without *fugue*. The Latin word *fugere* means "flight" and is the word from which the term *fugue* is taken. A *dissociative fugue* occurs when a person suddenly travels away from home (the flight) and afterwards cannot remember the trip or even personal information such as identity. The individual may become confused about identity, sometimes even taking on a whole new identity in the new place (Nijenhuis, 2000). Such flights usually take place after an emotional trauma and are more common in times of disasters or war.

DISSOCIATIVE IDENTITY DISORDER: HOW MANY AM I? Perhaps the most controversial dissociative disorder is **dissociative identity disorder (DID)**, formerly known as multiple personality disorder. In this disorder, a person seems to experience at least two or more distinct personalities existing in one body. There may be a "core" personality, who usually knows nothing about the other personalities and is the one who experiences "blackouts" or losses of memory and time. Fugues are common in DID, with the core personality experiencing unsettling moments of "awakening" in an unfamiliar place or with people who call the person by another name (Kluft, 1984).

With the publication of several famous books and movies made from those books, DID became well known to the public. Throughout the 1980s, psychological professionals began to diagnose this condition at an alarming rate—"multiple personality," as it was then known, had become the "fad" disorder of the late twentieth century, according to some researchers (Aldridge-Morris, 1989; Boor, 1982; Cormier & Thelen, 1998; Showalter, 1997). In the last decade, the diagnosis of DID has come under scrutiny, with many (but not all) professionals now doubting the validity of previous diagnoses.

CAUSES OF DISSOCIATIVE DISORDERS

12.8 Summarize the various explanations for dissociative disorders.

Psychodynamic theory sees the repression of threatening or unacceptable thoughts and behavior as a defense mechanism at the heart of all disorders, and the dissociative disorders in particular seem to have a large element of repression—motivated forgetting—in them. In the psychodynamic view, loss of memory or disconnecting one's awareness from a stressful or traumatic event is adaptive in that it reduces the emotional pain (Dorahy, 2001).

Cognitive and behavioral explanations for dissociative disorders are connected: The person may feel guilt, shame, or anxiety when thinking about disturbing experiences or thoughts and start to avoid thinking about them. This "thought avoidance" is negatively reinforced by the reduction of the anxiety and unpleasant feelings and eventually will become a habit of "not thinking about" these things. This is similar to what many people do when faced with something unpleasant, such as an injection or a painful procedure such as having a root canal. They "think about something else." In doing that, they are deliberately not thinking about what is happening to them at the moment and the experience of pain is decreased. People with dissociative disorders may simply be better at doing this sort of "not thinking" than other people are.

Also, consider the positive reinforcement possibilities for a person with a dissociative disorder: attention from others and help from professionals. Shaping may play a role in some cases, with a therapist unintentionally paying more attention to the client who talks about "feeling like someone else."

There are possible biological sources for dissociations, as well. Researchers have found that people with *depersonalization/derealization disorder* (a dissociative disorder in which people feel detached and disconnected from themselves, their bodies, and their surroundings) have lower brain activity in the areas responsible for their sense of body awareness than do people without the disorder (Simeon et al., 2000). Other research has provided evidence that people with DID show significant differences in PET scan activity taken when different "personalities" are present (Reinders et al., 2001; Tsai et al., 1999). It is also possible individuals with DID may be more elaborative when forming memories and are better at memory recall as a result (García-Campayo et al., 2009).

Dissociative symptoms and features can also be found in other cultures. The trance-like state known as *amok* in which a person suddenly becomes highly agitated and violent (found in Southeast Asia and Pacific Island cultures) is usually associated with no memory for the period during which the "trance" lasts (Suryani & Jensen, 1993). But a study that reviewed historical literature throughout the centuries found no mention or tales of what would be labeled as dissociative amnesia in the stories or nonfiction writings of any culture prior to the 1800s (Pope et al., 2007). The authors concluded that dissociative amnesia may be more of a nineteenth-century cultural phenomenon than a neuropsychological one.

Concept Map L.O. 12.7, 12.8

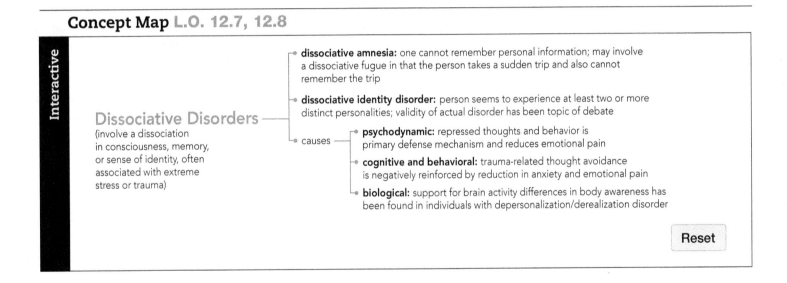

Interactive

Dissociative Disorders
(involve a dissociation in consciousness, memory, or sense of identity, often associated with extreme stress or trauma)

- **dissociative amnesia:** one cannot remember personal information; may involve a dissociative fugue in that the person takes a sudden trip and also cannot remember the trip
- **dissociative identity disorder:** person seems to experience at least two or more distinct personalities; validity of actual disorder has been topic of debate
- causes
  - **psychodynamic:** repressed thoughts and behavior is primary defense mechanism and reduces emotional pain
  - **cognitive and behavioral:** trauma-related thought avoidance is negatively reinforced by reduction in anxiety and emotional pain
  - **biological:** support for brain activity differences in body awareness has been found in individuals with depersonalization/derealization disorder

Reset

Practice Quiz   How much do you remember?   ANSWERS ON PAGE AK-1.

Pick the best answer.

1. What is the major difference between dissociative amnesia and retrograde amnesia?
  a. Retrograde amnesia patients often suffer from some form of physical brain trauma.
  b. Individuals suffering from dissociative amnesia often have a history of memory loss that seems to be hereditary.
  c. Those suffering from dissociative amnesia have prior damage to the brain, which in turn causes memory loss.
  d. Retrograde amnesia patients often have suffered from painful psychological trauma.

2. Increased media coverage surrounding this disorder in the 1980s likely led to it becoming the "fad" disorder of the late 20th century.
  a. Autistic disorder
  b. Dissociative identity disorder
  c. Somatic symptom disorder
  d. Attention-deficit/hyperactivity disorder

3. Which of the following two perspectives in psychology would be most connected in terms of explaining the origins of dissociative disorders?
  a. Humanistic and neuropsychological explanations
  b. Gestalt and social-cognitive explanations
  c. Psychodynamic and biopsychology explanations.
  d. Cognitive and behavioral explanations.

4. Dissociative symptoms and features can be found in many different cultures. For example, in Southeast Asian and Pacific Islander cultures, people sometimes experience a trancelike state called _____ that is associated with increased agitation and violent tendencies.
  a. "TKS"
  b. koro
  c. amok
  d. susto

Disorders of Mood: The Effect of Affect

When was the last time you felt down and sad? Or maybe a period of excitement or jubilation? Did these come about as the result of normal, day-to-day events or circumstances and change accordingly? Imagine how the experience of such feelings would impact your life if they lasted for much longer periods of time, were much more persistent across life events, and if you were unable to identify the source or cause for such emotions. That is often the case when someone experiences a disordered mood.

MAJOR DEPRESSIVE DISORDER AND BIPOLAR DISORDERS

12.9 **Describe different disorders of mood, including major depressive disorder and bipolar disorders.**

In psychological terms, the word **affect** is used to mean "emotion" or "mood." **Mood disorders** are disturbances in emotion and are also referred to as affective disorders. Although the range of human emotions runs from deep, intense sadness, and despair to extreme happiness and elation, under normal circumstances people stay in between those extremes—neither too sad nor too happy, but content (see **Figure 12.1**). It is when stress or some other factor pushes a person to one extreme or the other that mood disorders can result. Mood disorders can be relatively mild or moderate (straying only a short distance from the "average") or they can be extreme (existing at either end of the full range). Another major change in the *DSM-5* was to separate disorders previously and collectively classified as "mood disorders" into different categories. As such, in the *DSM-5*, disorders of mood can be found under "Bipolar and Related Disorders" or "Depressive Disorders." Given disordered mood is still a common feature, these disorders will be examined together here.

MAJOR DEPRESSIVE DISORDER When a deeply depressed mood comes on fairly suddenly and either seems to be too severe for the circumstances or exists without any external cause for sadness, it is called **major depressive disorder**. Major depression would fall at the far extreme of sadness on **Figure 12.1**. People suffering from major depressive disorder are depressed for most of every day, take little or no pleasure in any activities, feel tired, have trouble sleeping or sleep too much, experience changes in appetite and significant weight changes, experience excessive guilt or feelings of worthlessness, and have trouble concentrating. Some people with this disorder also suffer from delusional thinking and may experience hallucinations. Most of these symptoms occur on a daily basis, lasting for the better part of the day (American Psychiatric Association, 2013).

Some people with depression may have thoughts of death or suicide, including suicide attempts. Death by suicide is the most serious negative outcome for the person with depression. It is the third leading cause of death among young people from 15 to 24 years of age, and more than 90 percent of suicides are associated with a psychological disorder, with depression being the most likely cause (Hyman & Cohen, 2013; National Institute of Mental Health, 2008). If you or someone you know is thinking about suicide, confidential assistance is available from the National Suicide Prevention Lifeline, 1-800-273-TALK (8255).

Major depressive disorder is the most common of the diagnosed disorders of mood and is 1.5 to 3 times more likely to be diagnosed in women as it is in men (American Psychiatric Association, 2013). This is true even across various cultures (Kessler et al.,

Figure 12.1 The Range of Emotions

Most people experience a range of emotions over the course of a day or several days, such as mild sadness, calm contentment, or mild elation and happiness. A person with a disorder of mood experiences emotions that are extreme and, therefore, abnormal.

| Extreme sadness | Mild sadness | Normal emotions | Mild elation | Extreme elation |

2012; Seedat et al., 2009). Many possible explanations have been proposed for this gender difference, including the different hormonal structure of the female system (menstruation, hormonal changes during and after pregnancy, menopause, etc.) and different social roles played by women in the culture (Blehar & Oren, 1997). Research has found little support for hormonal influences in general, instead finding that the role of hormones and other biological factors in depression is unclear. Furthermore, studies have found that the degree of differences between male and female rates of depression is decreasing and is nonexistent in college students and single adults, leading some to conclude that gender roles and social factors such as marital status, career type, and number of children may have more importance in creating the gender difference than biological differences (McGrath et al., 1992; Nolen-Hoeksema, 1990; Seedat et al., 2009; Weissman & Klerman, 1977). Women also tend to ruminate, or repeatedly focus more on negative emotions, more than men, and this may also be a contributing factor for reported gender differences in prevalence rates for both depression and anxiety (Nolen-Hoeksema, 2012).

BIPOLAR DISORDERS Major depressive disorder is sometimes referred to as a *unipolar disorder* because the emotional problem exists at only one end, or "pole," of the emotional range. When a person experiences periods of mood that can range from severe depression to **manic** episodes (excessive excitement, energy, and elation), that person is said to suffer from a type of **bipolar disorder** (American Psychiatric Association, 2013). However, while an individual may experience periods of mood at the two extremes, in some instances the individual may only experience mood that spans from normal to manic, and may or may not experience episodes of depression, called *bipolar I disorder*. In the manic episodes, the person is extremely happy or euphoric* without any real cause to be so happy. Restlessness, irritability, an inability to sit still or remain inactive, and seemingly unlimited energy are also common. The person may seem silly to others and can become aggressive when not allowed to carry out the grand (and sometimes delusional) plans that may occur in mania. Speech may be rapid and jump from one topic to another. Oddly, people in the manic state are often very creative until their lack of organization renders their attempts at being creative useless (Blumer, 2002; McDermott, 2001; Rothenberg, 2001). In *bipolar II disorder*, spans of normal mood are interspersed with episodes of major depression and episodes of *hypomania*, a level of mood that is elevated but at a level below or less severe than full mania (American Psychiatric Association, 2013).

Dr. Dave Lutz

Missouri State Psychology Department

Research on Diagnosing Pediatric Bipolar Disorder

 💬 That sounds almost like a description of an overactive child— can't sit still, can't concentrate—are the two disorders related?

The answer to that question is actually part of an ongoing controversy. There does seem to be a connection between attention-deficit/hyperactivity disorder (ADHD) and the onset of bipolar disorder in adolescence (Carlson et al., 1998), but only a small percentage of children with ADHD go on to develop bipolar disorder. Recent evidence has found significantly higher rates of ADHD among relatives of individuals with bipolar disorder, and a higher prevalence of bipolar disorder among relatives of individuals with ADHD (Faraone et al., 2012). The symptoms of bipolar disorder include irrational thinking and other manic symptoms that are not present in ADHD (Geller et al., 1998). Confusion between the two disorders arises because hyperactivity (excessive movement and an inability to concentrate) is a symptom of both disorders. In one study, researchers compared children diagnosed with both bipolar disorder and ADHD to children diagnosed with ADHD only on measures of academic performance and a series of neurological tests (Henin et al., 2007). They found that the two groups responded in very similar ways, showing the same deficits in information-processing abilities, with only one exception:

---

*euphoric: having a feeling of vigor, well-being, or high spirits.

The children with both disorders performed more poorly on one measure of processing speed when compared to children with only ADHD. The researchers concluded that the neurological deficits often observed in children with bipolar disorder are more likely to be due to the ADHD rather than the bipolar disorder itself. Children with bipolar disorder also seem to suffer from far more severe emotional and behavioral problems than those with ADHD (Ferguson-Noyes, 2005; McDougall, 2009).

CAUSES OF DISORDERED MOOD

12.10 **Compare and contrast behavioral, social cognitive, and biological explanations for depression and other disorders of mood.**

Explanations of depression and other disorders of mood today come from the perspectives of behavioral, social cognitive, and biological theories as well as genetics.

Behavioral theorists link depression to learned helplessness (Seligman, 1975, 1989), whereas social cognitive theorists point to distortions of thinking such as blowing negative events out of proportion and minimizing positive, good events (Beck, 1976, 1984). In the social cognitive view, depressed people continually have negative, self-defeating thoughts about themselves, which depress them further in a downward spiral of despair. Learned helplessness has been linked to an increase in such self-defeating thinking and depression in studies with people who have experienced uncontrollable, painful events (Abramson et al., 1978, 1980). This link does not necessarily mean that negative thoughts *cause* depression; it may be that depression increases the likelihood of negative thoughts (Gotlib et al., 2001). One study found that when comparing adolescents who were depressed to those who were not, the depressed group faced risk factors specifically associated with the social cognitive environment, such as being female or a member of an ethnic minority, living in poverty, regular use of drugs (including tobacco and alcohol), and engaging in delinquent behavior (Costello et al., 2008). In contrast, those in the non-depressed group of adolescents were more likely to come from two-parent households; had higher self-esteem; and felt connected to parents, peers, and school. Clearly, learned helplessness in the face of discrimination, prejudice, and poverty may be associated with depression in these adolescents. A recent study has also found that when therapists focus on helping clients to change their way of thinking, depression improves significantly when compared to therapy that focuses only on changing behavior; these results lend support to the cognitive explanation of distorted thinking as the source of depression (Strunk et al., 2010).

Biological explanations of disordered mood focus on the effects of brain chemicals such as serotonin, norepinephrine, and dopamine; drugs used to treat depression and mania typically affect the levels of these three neurotransmitters, either alone or in combination (Cohen, 1997; Cummings & Coffey, 1994; Ruhe et al., 2007).

Genes also play a part in these disorders. The fact that the more severe mood disorders are not a reaction to some outside source of stress or anxiety but rather seem to come from within the person's own body, together with the tendency of mood disorders to appear in genetically related individuals at a higher rate, suggests rather strongly that inheritance may play a significant part in these disorders (Barondes, 1998; Farmer, 1996). It is possible that some mood disorders share a common gene, but actual rates vary. For example, genetic risks are higher in bipolar disorder as compared to unipolar depression (Hyman & Cohen, 2013; McMahon et al., 2010). More than 65 percent of people with bipolar disorder have at least one close relative with either bipolar disorder or major depression (Craddock et al., 2005; National Institute of Mental Health Genetics Workgroup, 1998; Sullivan et al., 2000). Twin studies have shown that if one identical twin has either major depression or bipolar disorder, the chances that the other twin will also develop a mood disorder are about 40 to 70 percent (Muller-Oerlinghausen et al., 2002).

Depression may be caused by conflicts with others, learned reactions, illogical thought patterns, or brain dysfunction—or some combination of all of these factors.

Concept Map L.O. 12.9, 12.10

Interactive

Disorders of Mood
(involve a disturbance
in mood or emotion;
can be mild or severe)

- **major depressive disorder:** deeply depressed mood; most commonly diagnosed mood disorder, twice as common in women
- **bipolar disorders:** experience of mood from normal to manic, possibly with episodes of depression, or the experience of normal mood interrupted by episodes of depression and hypomania
- causes
  - **psychodynamic:** depression is repressed anger originally aimed at parents or other authority figures
  - **behavioral:** depression is linked to learned helplessness
  - **social cognitive:** distorted thinking and negative, self-defeating thoughts
  - **biological:** variation in neurotransmitter systems (e.g., serotonin, norepinephrine, dopamine) or specific brain activity; genes and heritability also play a part

Reset

Practice Quiz How much do you remember? ANSWERS ON PAGE AK-1.

Pick the best answer.

1. Jorge finds himself feeling depressed most of the day. He is constantly tired yet he sleeps very little. He has feelings of worthlessness that have come on suddenly and seemingly have no basis in reality. What might Jorge be diagnosed with?
  a. seasonal affective disorder
  b. acute depressive disorder
  c. major depressive disorder
  d. bipolar disorder

2. Studies have suggested the increased rates of major depressive disorder in women may have a basis in _____
  a. gender roles, social factors, and emotional processing.
  b. hormonal differences.
  c. biological differences.
  d. heredity.

3. Cleo suffers from a psychological disorder that involves swings between major depressive periods and hypomanic states. Given this information, which of the following would be the most appropriate diagnosis?
  a. bipolar I disorder
  b. bipolar II disorder
  c. cyclothymia
  d. schizoaffective disorder

4. Biological explanations of disordered mood have focused on the effects of several different brain chemicals, and medications used to treat these disorders are designed to work on these various neurotransmitter systems. Which of the following is not one of the chemicals that has been implicated in mood disorders?
  a. serotonin
  b. dopamine
  c. norepinephrine
  d. melatonin

Eating Disorders and Sexual Dysfunction

Thus far we have talked about disorders that have primarily focused on mood, anxiety, stress, and trauma. We will now shift to disorders of a slightly different type and will first examine eating disorders and then sexual dysfunction.

EATING DISORDERS

12.11 Identify three different types of eating disorders and the treatment options associated with each.

There are a variety of disorders that relate to the intake of food, or in some cases non-nutritive substances, or in the elimination of bodily waste. These are found in the *DSM-5* under "Feeding and Eating Disorders." We will specifically examine three eating disorders: *anorexia nervosa, bulimia nervosa,* and *binge-eating disorder.*

ANOREXIA NERVOSA **Anorexia nervosa**, often called **anorexia**, is a condition in which a person (typically young and female) reduces eating to the point that their body weight is significantly low, or less than minimally expected. For adults, this is likely a body mass

This young model is not merely thin; by medical standards she is probably at a weight that would allow her to be labeled as having anorexia. The "thin is in" mentality that dominates the field of fashion design models is a major contributor to the Western cultural concept of very thin women as beautiful and desirable. The model pictured here is a far cry from the days of sex symbol Marilyn Monroe, who was rumored to be a size 12.

index (BMI; weight in kilograms/height in meters^2) less than 18.5 (American Psychiatric Association, 2013). Hormone secretion becomes abnormal, especially in the thyroid and adrenal glands. The heart muscles become weak and heart rhythms may alter. Other physical effects of anorexia may include diarrhea, loss of muscle tissue, loss of sleep, low blood pressure, and lack of menstruation in females.

Some individuals with anorexia will eat in front of others (whereas individuals with bulimia tend to binge eat as secretly as possible) but then force themselves to throw up or take large doses of laxatives. They are often obsessed with exercising and with food—cooking elaborate meals for others while eating nothing themselves. They have extremely distorted body images, seeing fat where others see only skin and bones.

What can be done to treat anorexia? If the weight loss is severe (40 percent or more below expected normal weight), dehydration, severe chemical imbalances, and possibly organ damage may result. Hospitalization should occur before this dangerous point is reached. Psychological counseling will also be part of the hospital treatment, which may last from 2 to 4 months. Those individuals with anorexia who are not so severely malnourished as to be in immediate danger can be treated outside of the hospital setting. Psychological treatment strategies might include supportive clinical management, interpersonal therapy, cognitive-behavioral therapy, group therapy, or family-based therapy (Hay, 2013). **L I N K** to Learning Objective 13.6. The prognosis for full recovery is not as hopeful as it should be; only 40 to 60 percent of all individuals with anorexia who receive treatment will make a recovery. For some individuals with anorexia who do gain weight, the damage already done to the heart and other body systems may still be so great that an early death is a possibility (Neumarker, 1997). Overall, the estimated mortality rate in anorexia is highest among all of the eating disorders, and much higher than any other psychological disorder (Arcelus et al., 2011).

BULIMIA NERVOSA **Bulimia nervosa**, often called **bulimia**, is a condition in which a person develops a cycle of "binging," or overeating enormous amounts of food at one sitting, and then using inappropriate methods for avoiding weight gain (American Psychiatric Association, 2013). Most individuals with bulimia engage in "purging" behaviors, such as deliberately vomiting after the binge or misuse of laxatives, but some may not, using other inappropriate methods to avoid weight gain such as fasting the day or two after the binge or engaging in excessive exercise (American Psychiatric Association, 2013). There are some similarities to anorexia: The victims are usually female, are obsessed with their appearance, diet excessively, and believe themselves to be fat even when they are quite obviously not fat. But individuals with bulimia are typically a little older than individuals with anorexia at the onset of the disorder—early 20s rather than early puberty. Individuals with bulimia often maintain a normal weight, making the disorder difficult to detect. The most obvious difference between the two conditions is that the individual with bulimia will eat, and eat to excess, binging on huge amounts of food—an average of 3,500 calories in a single binge and as much as 50,000 calories in one day (Humphries, 1987; Mitchell et al., 1981; Oster, 1987). A typical binge may include a gallon of ice cream, a package of cookies, and a gallon of milk—all consumed as quickly as possible.

 But wait a minute—if individuals with bulimia are so concerned about gaining weight, why do they binge at all?

The binge itself may be prompted by an anxious or depressed mood, social stressors, feelings about body weight or image, or intense hunger after attempts to diet. The binge continues due to a lack of, or impairment in, self-control once the binge begins. The individual is unable to control when to stop eating or how much to eat. Eating one cookie while trying to control weight can lead to a binge—after all, since the diet is completely blown, why not go all out? This kind of thought process is another example of the cognitive distortion of all-or-nothing thinking.

Like anorexia, bulimia comes with many serious health consequences: severe tooth decay and erosion of the lining of the esophagus from the acidity of the vomiting; enlarged salivary glands; potassium, calcium, and sodium imbalances that can be very dangerous; damage to the intestinal tract from overuse of laxatives, heart problems, fatigue, and seizures (Berg, 1999).

Treatment of bulimia can involve many of the same measures taken to treat anorexia. In addition, the use of antidepressant medication can be helpful, especially those that affect serotonin levels such as the SSRIs (Mitchell et al., 2013). The prognosis for recovery of the individual with bulimia is somewhat more hopeful than that of anorexia. Therapist-led cognitive-behavioral therapy is the best empirically supported therapy and there is developing evidence for some guided self-help approaches (Hay, 2013). A cognitive therapist is very direct, forcing clients to see how their beliefs do not stand up when considered in "the light of day" and helping them form new, more constructive ways of thinking about themselves and their behavior. Ⓛ Ⓘ Ⓝ Ⓚ to Learning Objective 13.5.

BINGE-EATING DISORDER   **Binge-eating disorder** also involves uncontrolled binge eating but differs from bulimia primarily in that individuals with binge-eating disorder do not purge or use other inappropriate methods for avoiding weight gain (American Psychiatric Association, 2013). Treatment of binge-eating disorder may use some of the same strategies used for anorexia and bulimia, with the added issue of weight loss management in those with obesity.

CAUSES OF EATING DISORDERS

12.12 Summarize some of the risk factors associated with eating disorders, including cultural factors.

Dr. Brooke Whisenhunt

Missouri State Psychology Department

Body Image Research

The causes of anorexia, bulimia, and binge-eating disorder are not yet fully understood, but the greatest risk factor appears to be someone being an adolescent or young adult female (Keel & Forney, 2013). Increased sensitivity to food and its reward value may play a role in bulimia and binge-eating disorder while fear and anxiety may become associated with food in anorexia nervosa, with altered activity or functioning of associated brain structures in each (Friedrich et al., 2013; Kaye et al., 2009; Kaye et al., 2013). Research continues to investigate genetic components for eating disorders, as they account for 40 to 60 percent of the risk for anorexia, bulimia, and binge-eating disorder, and although several genes have been implicated, the exact ones to focus on have not yet been identified (Trace et al., 2013; Wade et al., 2013).

Although many researchers have believed eating disorders, especially anorexia, are cultural syndromes that only show up in cultures obsessed with being thin (as many Western cultures are), eating disorders are also found in non-Western cultures (Miller & Pumariega, 1999). What differs between Western and non-Western cultures is the rate at which such disorders appear. For example, Chinese and Chinese American women are far less likely to suffer from eating disorders than are non-Hispanic White women (Pan, 2000). Why wouldn't Chinese American women be more likely to have eating disorders after being exposed to the Western cultural obsession with thinness? Pan (2000) assumes that whatever Chinese cultural factors "protect" Chinese women from developing eating disorders may also still have a powerful influence on Chinese American women.

One problem with studying anorexia and bulimia in other cultures is that the behavior of starving oneself may be seen in other cultures as having an entirely different purpose than in Western cultures. One key component of anorexia, for example, is a fear of being fat, a fear that is missing in many other cultures. Yet women in those cultures have starved themselves for other socially recognized reasons: religious fasting or unusual ideas about nutrition (Castillo, 1997).

Anorexia and bulimia have also been thought to occur only rarely in African American women, but that characterization seems to be changing. Researchers are seeing an increase in anorexia and bulimia among young African American women of all socioeconomic levels (Crago et al., 1996; Mintz & Betz, 1998; Pumariega & Gustavson, 1994). If clinicians and doctors are not aware that these disorders can affect more than the typical White, young, middle-class to upper-middle-class woman, important signs and symptoms of eating disorders in non-White or non-Western people may allow these disorders to go untreated until it is too late.

WRITING PROMPT

How might the proliferation of various media and the Internet affect the development of eating disorders in cultures not previously impacted by them?

▶ The response entered here will be saved to your notes and may be collected by your instructor if he/she requires it.

Submit

SEXUAL DYSFUNCTIONS AND PROBLEMS

12.13 Describe types of sexual dysfunction and explain how they may develop.

A **sexual dysfunction** is a problem with sexual functioning, or with the actual physical workings of the sex act. Sexual dysfunctions involve problems in three possible areas of sexual activity: sexual interest, arousal, and response. Broadly speaking, sexual dysfunctions may be *organic*, stemming from physical sources or disorders, or *psychogenic*, related to psychological factors such as worry and anxiety. However, body and mind influence each other's functioning and these categories are not mutually exclusive (Lewis et al., 2010).

💬 How common are problems like these—aren't they pretty rare?

Results of surveys from around the globe suggest that about 40 to 45 percent of women and 20 to 30 percent of men have at least one sexual dysfunction, and the rate increases as we age (Lewis et al., 2010). In the stress-filled world that many people live in today, it isn't all that surprising to find such a high degree of dysfunction. In fact, the figures may actually be higher than those reported in the survey. As stated in Chapter One, one of the hazards of doing survey research is that people don't always tell the truth (to Learning Objective 1.7). If a person is going to lie about sexual problems, the most likely lie (or distorted truth) would probably be to deny or minimize such problems.

For all of the sexual dysfunctions, treatment can include medication, psychotherapy, hormone therapy, stress reduction, sex therapy, and behavioral training. For example, Masters and Johnson (1970) recommended a technique called *sensate focus* for treatment of premature ejaculation, in which each member of a couple engages in a series of exercises meant to focus attention on his or her own sensual experiences during various stages of sexual arousal and activity. Male erectile disorder is now commonly treated with drug therapy.

There are a variety of physical sexual dysfunctions included in the *DSM-5* that may be caused by psychological stressors. Although not directly related to the sequence or timing of the sexual response cycle, some are related to desire and arousal, others to the mechanics or physical aspects of sexual intercourse, and some to the timing or inability to reach orgasm. Sexual desire or arousal disorders include *female sexual interest/arousal disorder* and *male hypoactive sexual desire disorder*. Disorders related to the physical act of intercourse include *erectile disorder* and *genito-pelvic pain/penetration disorder*. And lastly, disorders related to the timing or inability to reach orgasm include *premature (early) ejaculation, female orgasmic disorder*, and *delayed ejaculation* (American Psychiatric Association, 2013).

Sexual dysfunctions and problems can be caused by purely *organic factors* (e.g., illness or side effects from drugs), *sociocultural factors* (such as negative attitudes toward sexual behavior), or *psychological factors* stemming from either personality problems, traumatic events, or relationship problems. More commonly, such problems can stem from a combination of these influences.

Organic factors include physical problems such as illnesses, side effects from medication, the effects of surgeries, physical disabilities, and even the use of illegal and legal drugs, such as cocaine, alcohol, and nicotine. Chronic illnesses such as diabetes, cancer, or strokes also belong in this category of factors.

Sociocultural influences on sexual attitudes and behavior also exist and may be a source of psychological stress leading to sexual dysfunction. In the United States and some other Western cultures, people may have experienced instruction from their parents (both direct and indirect teaching) that actually influenced them to form negative attitudes toward sex and sexual activities, such as masturbation.

Psychological stressors also include individual psychological problems, such as low self-esteem, anxiety over performance of the sex act, depression, self-consciousness about one's body image, anxiety disorders, or a history of previous sexual abuse or assault. Another source of psychological stress leading to sexual dysfunctions is the relationship between the two sexual partners. The sexual dysfunction may be only an outward symptom of an underlying problem with the relationship.

Concept Map L.O. 12.11, 12.12, 12.13

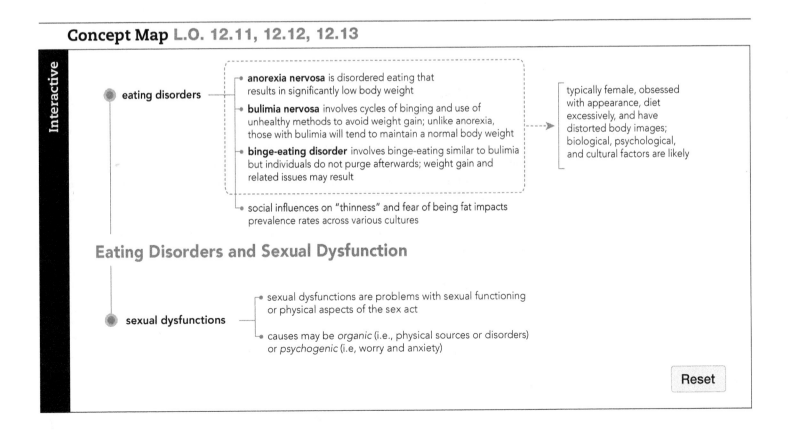

Interactive

eating disorders

- **anorexia nervosa** is disordered eating that results in significantly low body weight
- **bulimia nervosa** involves cycles of binging and use of unhealthy methods to avoid weight gain; unlike anorexia, those with bulimia will tend to maintain a normal body weight
- **binge-eating disorder** involves binge-eating similar to bulimia but individuals do not purge afterwards; weight gain and related issues may result

typically female, obsessed with appearance, diet excessively, and have distorted body images; biological, psychological, and cultural factors are likely

- social influences on "thinness" and fear of being fat impacts prevalence rates across various cultures

Eating Disorders and Sexual Dysfunction

sexual dysfunctions

- sexual dysfunctions are problems with sexual functioning or physical aspects of the sex act
- causes may be *organic* (i.e., physical sources or disorders) or *psychogenic* (i.e, worry and anxiety)

Reset

Practice Quiz   How much do you remember? ANSWERS ON PAGE AK-1.

Pick the best answer.

1. Olivia is a teenager who has been diagnosed with anorexia nervosa. What percentage of individuals with anorexia that receive treatment make a recovery?
- **a.** 40 to 60 percent
- **b.** 70 to 80 percent
- **c.** 80 to 90 percent
- **d.** approximately 95 percent

2. Which of the following characteristics best describes differences between bulimia nervosa and anorexia nervosa?
- **a.** Individuals with anorexia nervosa have less severe health risks than individuals with bulimia nervosa.
- **b.** Individuals with bulimia nervosa may have a normal body weight whereas those with anorexia nervosa tend to be severely under their expected body weight.
- **c.** Individuals with anorexia nervosa have been known to binge like those with bulimia nervosa on occasion.
- **d.** Anorexia nervosa tends to occur in early adulthood whereas bulimia nervosa often starts in early adolescence.

3. Researchers believe that 40 to 60 percent of the risk for anorexia, bulimia, and binge-eating disorder are due to
- **a.** genetic factors.
- **b.** hormonal factors.
- **c.** environmental factors.
- **d.** psychological factors.

4. What is the major cause of organic sexual dysfunction?
- **a.** stress
- **b.** paraphilias
- **c.** physical causes
- **d.** economic status

5. Surveys suggest that about _____ percent of women and _____ percent of men have at least one sexual dysfunction.
- **a.** 10; 25
- **b.** 40–45; 20–30
- **c.** 80; 50
- **d.** 10–20; 30–40

Schizophrenia: Altered Reality

Once known as *dementia praecox*, a Latin-based term meaning "out of one's mind before one's time," *schizophrenia* was renamed by Eugen Bleuler, a Swiss psychiatrist, to better illustrate the division (*schizo-*) within the brain (*phren*) among thoughts, feelings, and behavior that seems to take place in people with this disorder (Bleuler, 1911; Möller & Hell, 2002). Because the term literally means "split mind," it has often been confused with dissociative identity disorder, which was at one time called "split personality."

SYMPTOMS OF SCHIZOPHRENIA

12.14 **Describe the main symptoms of schizophrenia, distinguishing between positive and negative symptoms.**

Today, **schizophrenia** is described as a long-lasting **psychotic** disorder (involving a severe break with reality), in which there is an inability to distinguish what is real from fantasy as well as disturbances in thinking, emotions, behavior, and perception. The disorder typically arises in the late teens or early 20s, affects both males and females, and is consistent across cultures.

Schizophrenia includes several different kinds of symptoms. Disorders in thinking are a common symptom and are called **delusions**. Although delusions are not prominent in everyone with schizophrenia, they are the symptom that most people associate with this disorder. Delusions are false beliefs about the world that the person holds and that tend to remain fixed and unshakable even in the face of evidence that disproves the delusions. Common schizophrenic delusions include *delusions of persecution*, in which people believe that others are trying to hurt them in some way; *delusions of reference*, in which people believe that other people, television characters, and even books are specifically talking to them; *delusions of influence*, in which people believe that they are being controlled by external forces, such as the devil, aliens, or cosmic forces; and *delusions of grandeur* (or *grandiose delusions*), in which people are convinced that they are powerful people who can save the world or have a special mission (American Psychiatric Association, 2013).

Delusional thinking alone is not enough to merit a diagnosis of schizophrenia, as other symptoms must be present (American Psychiatric Association, 2013). Speech disturbances are common: People with schizophrenia will make up words, repeat words or sentences persistently, string words together on the basis of sounds (called *clanging*, such as "come into house, louse, mouse, mouse and cheese, please, sneeze"), and experience sudden interruptions in speech or thought. Thoughts are significantly disturbed as well, with individuals with schizophrenia having a hard time linking their thoughts together in a logical fashion and, in advanced schizophrenia, possibly expressing themselves in a meaningless and jumbled mixture of words and phrases sometimes referred to as a *word salad*. Attention is also a problem for many people with schizophrenia. They seem to have trouble "screening out" information and stimulation that they don't really need, causing them to be unable to focus on information that is relevant (Asarnow et al., 1991; Luck & Gold, 2008).

People with schizophrenia may also have **hallucinations**, in which they hear voices or see things or people that are not really there. Hearing voices is actually more common and one of the key symptoms in making a diagnosis of schizophrenia (Kuhn & Nasar, 2001; Nasar, 1998). Hallucinations involving touch, smell, and taste are less common but also possible. Emotional disturbances are also a key feature of schizophrenia. **Flat affect** is a condition in which the person shows little or no emotion. Emotions can also be excessive and/or inappropriate—a person might laugh when it would be more appropriate to cry or show sorrow, for example. The person's behavior may also become disorganized and extremely odd. The person may not respond to the outside world and either doesn't move at all, maintaining often odd-looking postures for hours on end, or moves about wildly in great agitation. Both extremes, either wildly excessive movement or total lack thereof are referred to as **catatonia**.

Another way of describing symptoms in schizophrenia is to group them by the way they relate to normal functioning. **Positive symptoms** appear to reflect an excess or distortion of normal functions, such as hallucinations and delusions. **Negative symptoms** appear to reflect a decrease of normal functions, such as poor attention or lack of affect (American Psychiatric Association, 2013). According to the American Psychiatric Association (2013), at least two or more of the following symptoms must be present frequently for at least one month to diagnose schizophrenia: delusions, hallucinations, disorganized speech, negative symptoms, and grossly disorganized or catatonic behavior, and at least one of the two symptoms has to be delusions, hallucinations, or disorganized speech. The video *Schizophrenia* summarizes the key biological, psychological, and social components of the disorder.

Dr. John Nash is a famous mathematician who won the Nobel Prize for mathematics in 1994. His fame, however, is more due to the fact that Nash once suffered from a form of schizophrenia in which he experienced delusions of persecution. He at one time believed that aliens were trying to contact him through the newspaper (delusions of reference). His life story and remarkable recovery from schizophrenia are portrayed in the 2001 movie *A Beautiful Mind*, which starred Russell Crowe as Nash.

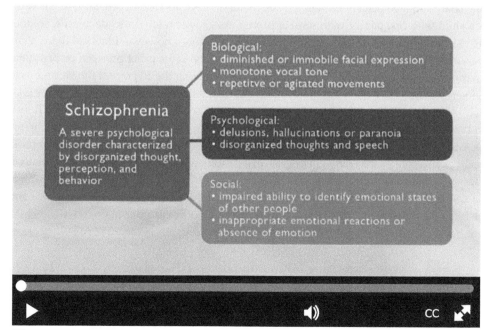

👁 **Watch** the **Video**, *Schizophrenia.*

Nathaniel Ayers, a homeless musician, is pictured in 2003 in front of the Midnight Mission shelter in Los Angeles, California. Mr. Ayers's life is the subject of the 2009 movie *The Soloist* starring Jamie Foxx. Mr. Ayers was a Julliard-trained musician who developed schizophrenia.

CAUSES OF SCHIZOPHRENIA

12.15 Evaluate the genetic and environmental influences on schizophrenia.

When trying to explain the cause or causes of schizophrenia, biological models and theories prevail, as it appears to be most likely caused by a combination of genetic and environmental factors. This is captured by the neurodevelopmental model, or neurodevelopmental hypothesis, of schizophrenia (Rapoport et al., 2005; Rapoport et al., 2012). Biological explanations of schizophrenia have generated a significant amount of research pointing to genetic origins, prenatal influences such as the mother experiencing viral infections during pregnancy, inflammation in the brain, chemical influences (dopamine, GABA, glutamate, and other neurotransmitters), and brain structural defects (frontal lobe defects, deterioration of neurons, and reduction in white matter integrity) as the causes of schizophrenia (Brown & Derkits, 2010; Cardno & Gottesman, 2000; Gottesman & Shields, 1982; Harrison, 1999; Kety et al., 1994; Nestor et al., 2008; Rijsdijk et al., 2011; Söderlund et al., 2009). Dopamine was first suspected when amphetamine users began to show schizophrenia-like psychotic symptoms. One of the side effects of amphetamine usage is to increase the release of dopamine in the brain. Drugs used to treat schizophrenia decrease the activity of dopamine in areas of the brain responsible for some of the positive symptoms. However, it is not that simple, the prefrontal cortex (an area of the brain involved in planning and organization of information) of people with schizophrenia has been shown to produce lower levels of dopamine than normal (Harrison, 1999), resulting in attention deficits (Luck & Gold, 2008) and poor organization of thought, negative symptoms of the disorder.

Further support for a biological explanation of schizophrenia comes from studies of the incidence of the disorder across different cultures. If schizophrenia were caused mainly by environmental factors, the expectation would be that rates of schizophrenia would vary widely from culture to culture. There is some variation for immigrants and children of immigrants, but about 7 to 8 individuals out of 1,000 will develop schizophrenia in their lifetime, regardless of the culture (Saha et al., 2005).

Family, twin, and adoption studies have provided strong evidence that genes are a major means of transmitting schizophrenia. The highest risk for developing schizophrenia if one has a blood relative with the disorder is faced by monozygotic (identical) twins, who share 100 percent of their genetic material, with a risk factor of about 50 percent (Cardno & Gottesman, 2000; Gottesman & Shields, 1976, 1982; Gottesman et al., 1987). Dizygotic twins, who share about 50 percent of their genetic material, have about a 17 percent risk, the same as a child with one parent with schizophrenia. As genetic relatedness decreases, so does the risk (see **Figure 12.2**). Twin studies are not perfect tools, however; identical twins share the same womb but are not necessarily exposed to the same exact prenatal or postnatal environments, causing some to urge caution in interpreting the 50 percent figure; and even twins reared apart are often raised in similar childhood environments (Davis et. al., 1995).

Adoption studies also support the genetic basis of schizophrenia (Sullivan, 2005; Tienari et al., 2004). In one study, the biological and adoptive relatives of adoptees with schizophrenia were compared to a control group of adoptees without schizophrenia but from similar backgrounds and conditions (Kety et al., 1994). The adoptees with schizophrenia had relatives with schizophrenia but *only among their biological relatives*. When the prevalence of schizophrenia was compared between the biological relatives of the adoptees with schizophrenia and the biological relatives of the control group, the rate of the disorder in the relatives of the group with schizophrenia was 10 times higher than in the control group (Kety et al., 1994).

💬 There's something I don't understand. If one identical twin has the gene and the disorder, shouldn't the other one always have it, too? Why is the rate only 50 percent?

If schizophrenia were entirely controlled by genes, identical twins would indeed both have the disorder at a risk of 100 percent, not merely 50 percent. Obviously, there

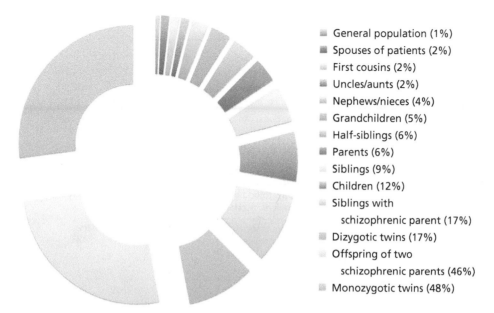

- General population (1%)
- Spouses of patients (2%)
- First cousins (2%)
- Uncles/aunts (2%)
- Nephews/nieces (4%)
- Grandchildren (5%)
- Half-siblings (6%)
- Parents (6%)
- Siblings (9%)
- Children (12%)
- Siblings with schizophrenic parent (17%)
- Dizygotic twins (17%)
- Offspring of two schizophrenic parents (46%)
- Monozygotic twins (48%)

Figure 12.2 Genetics and Schizophrenia

This chart shows a definite pattern: The greater the degree of genetic relatedness, the higher the risk of schizophrenia in individuals related to each other. The only individual to carry a risk even close to that of identical twins (who share 100 percent of their genes) is a person who is the child of two parents with schizophrenia. Based on Gottesman (1991).

is some influence of environment on the development of schizophrenia. One model that has been proposed is the **stress-vulnerability model**, which assumes that persons with the genetic "markers" for schizophrenia have a physical vulnerability to the disorder but will not develop schizophrenia unless they are exposed to environmental or emotional stress at critical times in development, such as puberty (Harrison, 1999; Weinberger, 1987). That would explain why only one twin out of a pair might develop the disorder when both carry the genetic markers for schizophrenia—the life stresses for the affected twin were different from those of the one who remained healthy. The immune system is activated during stress, and one study has found that in recent-onset schizophrenia (the early stages of the disorder) the brain's immune system secretes high levels of an inflammation-fighting substance, indicating a possible infection (Söderlund et al., 2009). This leads to the possibility that schizophrenia might one day be treatable with anti-inflammatory medications.

The development of brain-scanning techniques such as magnetic resonance imaging (MRI) and functional MRI (fMRI) has made studies of the structure as well as the functioning of the brains of those with schizophrenia possible. In one study, researchers using *diffusion tensor imaging* (DTI), Ⓛ Ⓘ Ⓝ Ⓚ to Learning Objective 2.9, in addition to other neurological testing found that, when compared to healthy control participants, participants with schizophrenia showed structural differences in two particular areas of the brain (Nestor et al., 2008). Specifically, a white matter tract called the cingulum bundle (CB) that lies under the cingulate gyrus and links part of the limbic system, and another that links the frontal lobe to the temporal lobe, were found to have significantly less myelin coating on the axons of the neurons within the bundle. This makes these areas of the brain less efficient in sending neural messages to other cells, resulting in decreased memory and decision-making ability. The CB has been implicated in other studies of schizophrenia using DTI, which suggests that the less myelin and lower neural efficiency is partly responsible for attention problems in schizophrenia (Kubicki et al., 2009) and lower white matter integrity in areas of the frontal lobe might be associated with genetic predisposition to schizophrenia (Camchong et al., 2009). Measuring cortical thickness and tracking changes in the volume of gray matter and white matter is also providing valuable information about the abnormal patterns of brain development in schizophrenia and other disorders (Gogtay et al., 2008; Gogtay & Thompson, 2010; Goldman et al., 2009).

Nestor et al. (2008) used diffusion tensor imaging to investigate schizophrenia. Two of the brain areas examined were the cingulum bundle (CB, consisting of fibers underlying the cingulate gyrus linking parts of the limbic system) and the uncinate fasciculus (UF, neural fibers linking the frontal lobe to the temporal lobe). The cingulum bundle is depicted in the image above. For individuals with schizophrenia, both the CB and UF fiber pathways were found to have neurons with significantly less myelin, making them less efficient in information transfer, and resulting in decreased memory and decision-making ability. Image courtesy of Dr. Paul Nestor.

Concept Map L.O. 12.14, 12.15

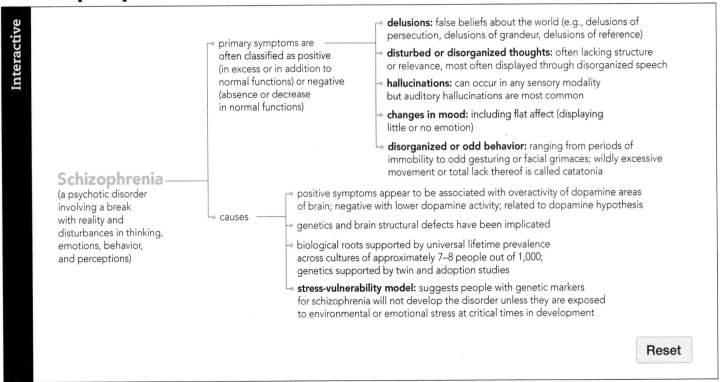

Schizophrenia (a psychotic disorder involving a break with reality and disturbances in thinking, emotions, behavior, and perceptions)

primary symptoms are often classified as positive (in excess or in addition to normal functions) or negative (absence or decrease in normal functions)

- **delusions:** false beliefs about the world (e.g., delusions of persecution, delusions of grandeur, delusions of reference)
- **disturbed or disorganized thoughts:** often lacking structure or relevance, most often displayed through disorganized speech
- **hallucinations:** can occur in any sensory modality but auditory hallucinations are most common
- **changes in mood:** including flat affect (displaying little or no emotion)
- **disorganized or odd behavior:** ranging from periods of immobility to odd gesturing or facial grimaces; wildly excessive movement or total lack thereof is called catatonia

causes

- positive symptoms appear to be associated with overactivity of dopamine areas of brain; negative with lower dopamine activity; related to dopamine hypothesis
- genetics and brain structural defects have been implicated
- biological roots supported by universal lifetime prevalence across cultures of approximately 7–8 people out of 1,000; genetics supported by twin and adoption studies
- **stress-vulnerability model:** suggests people with genetic markers for schizophrenia will not develop the disorder unless they are exposed to environmental or emotional stress at critical times in development

Reset

Interactive

Practice Quiz   How much do you remember?. ANSWERS ON PAGE AK-1.

Pick the best answer.

1. David believes that characters in a popular science fiction show are secretly sending him messages. This would be an example of a delusion of
a. persecution.
b. grandeur.
c. influence.
d. reference.

2. Dr. Haldol has several patients with schizophrenia who appear to exhibit excessive or distorted characteristics in relation to what one might consider normal functioning. Specific symptoms include varied hallucinations and multiple delusions. According to the *DSM-5*, these are referred to as
a. flat affect.
b. positive symptoms.
c. negative symptoms.
d. catatonia.

3. Charles has suffered from schizophrenia for many years, and now resides in a group treatment facility. One day a nurse approaches him and quietly tells him that his sister, who has been fighting cancer for many months, died that morning. Charles has no appreciable facial reaction, and in a very monotone voice says, "okay." The nurse is not surprised by Charles's lack of response to the awful news, because she knows that _____ is one symptom often seen in those suffering from schizophrenia.
a. clang associations
b. echolalia
c. flat affect
d. perseveration

4. Neuroimaging studies examining potential causes of schizophrenia have discovered that an area of the brain called the _____ appears to have significantly less myelin coating on the axons of its neurons in people with schizophrenia compared to those without the condition.
a. cingulum bundle
b. striate nuclei
c. putamen
d. lateral geniculate nucleus of the thalamus

Personality Disorders: I'm Okay, It's Everyone Else Who's Weird

Personality disorders are a little different from other psychological disorders in that the disorder does not affect merely one aspect of the person's life, such as a higher than normal level of anxiety or a set of distorted beliefs, but instead affects the entire life adjustment of the person. The disorder is the personality itself, not one aspect of it. However, despite personality disorders affecting the entire person, current research suggests they are not always life-long in nature as once believed.

CATEGORIES OF PERSONALITY DISORDERS

12.16 **Classify the different types of personality disorders.**

In **personality disorder**, a person has an excessively rigid, maladaptive pattern of behavior and ways of relating to others (American Psychiatric Association, 2013). This rigidity and the inability to adapt to social demands and life changes make it very difficult for the individual with a personality disorder to fit in with others or have relatively normal social relationships. The *DSM-5* lists 10 primary types of personality disorder across three basic categories (American Psychiatric Association, 2013): those in which the people are seen as odd or eccentric by others (Paranoid, Schizoid, Schizotypal); those in which the behavior of the person is very dramatic, emotional, or erratic (Antisocial, Borderline, Histrionic, Narcissistic); and those in which the main emotion is anxiety or fearfulness (Avoidant, Dependent, Obsessive-Compulsive). These categories are labeled Cluster A, Cluster B, and Cluster C, respectively.

ANTISOCIAL PERSONALITY DISORDER One of the most well researched of the personality disorders is **antisocial personality disorder (ASPD)**. People with ASPD are literally "against society." The antisocial person may habitually break the law, disobey rules, tell lies, and use other people without worrying about their rights or feelings. The person with ASPD may be irritable or aggressive. These individuals may not keep promises or other obligations and are consistently irresponsible. They may also seem indifferent, or able to rationalize taking advantage of or hurting others. Typically they borrow money or belongings and don't bother to repay the debt or return the items, they are impulsive, they don't keep their commitments either socially or in their jobs, and they tend to be very selfish, self-centered, and manipulative. There is a definite gender difference in ASPD with many more males diagnosed with this disorder than females (American Psychiatric Association, 2013). The habitual disregard for both the law and rights of others may be confused with the terms *sociopath* or *psychopath*. Although some people with psychopathic personality may be diagnosed with ASPD, the majority of individuals with ASPD are not psychopathic.

BORDERLINE PERSONALITY DISORDER People with **borderline personality disorder (BLPD)** have relationships with other people that are intense and relatively unstable. They are impulsive, have an unstable sense of self, and are intensely fearful of abandonment. Life goals, career choices, friendships, and even sexual behavior may change quickly and dramatically. Close personal and romantic relationships are marked by extreme swings from idealization to demonization. Periods of depression are not unusual, and some may engage in excessive spending, drug abuse, or suicidal behavior (suicide attempts may be part of the manipulation used against others in a relationship). Emotions are often inappropriate and excessive, leading to confusion with *histrionic personality disorder*. What makes the individual with BLPD different is the pattern of self-destructiveness, chronic loneliness, and disruptive anger in close relationships (American Psychiatric Association, 2013). The frequency of this disorder being diagnosed in women is nearly three times greater than in men (American Psychiatric Association, 2013).

CAUSES OF PERSONALITY DISORDERS

12.17 **Summarize some of the potential causes of personality disorders.**

Cognitive-behavioral theorists talk about how specific behavior can be learned over time through the processes of reinforcement, shaping, and modeling. More cognitive explanations involve the belief systems formed by the personality-disordered persons, such as the paranoia, extreme self-importance, and fear of being unable to cope by oneself of the paranoid, narcissistic, and dependent personalities, for example.

There is some evidence of genetic factors in personality disorders (Reichborn-Kjennerud, 2008). Close biological relatives of people with disorders such as antisocial, schizotypal, and borderline are more likely to have these disorders than those who are not related (American Psychiatric Association, 2013; Kendler et al., 2006; Reichborn-Kjennerud et al., 2007; Torgersen et al., 2008). Adoption studies of children whose biological parents had antisocial personality disorder show an increased risk for that disorder in those children, even though raised in a different environment by different people (American Psychiatric Association, 2013). A longitudinal study has linked the temperaments of children at age 3 to antisocial tendencies in adulthood, finding that those children with lower fearfulness and inhibitions were more likely to show antisocial personality characteristics in a follow-up study at age 28 (Glenn et al., 2007).

Other causes of personality disorders have been suggested. Antisocial personalities are emotionally unresponsive to stressful or threatening situations when compared to others, which may be one reason that they are not afraid of getting caught (Arnett et al., 1997; Blair et al., 1995; Lykken, 1995). This unresponsiveness seems to be linked to lower than normal levels of stress hormones in antisocial persons (Fairchild et al., 2008; Lykken, 1995).

Disturbances in family relationships and communication have also been linked to personality disorders and, in particular, to antisocial personality disorder (Benjamin, 1996; Livesley, 1995). Childhood abuse, neglect, overly strict parenting, overprotective parenting, and parental rejection have all been put forth as possible causes, making the picture of the development of personality disorders a complicated one. It is safe to say that many of the same factors (genetics, social relationships, and parenting) that help to create ordinary personalities also create disordered personalities.

Concept Map L.O. 12.16, 12.17

Interactive

Personality Disorders
(involve excessively rigid and maladaptive patternsof behavior and ways ofrelating to others)

- **antisocial personality disorder:** minimal to no regard for value of others' rights or feelings; more common in men
- **borderline personality disorder:** relationships with others that are intense and unstable; often moody, manipulative, and untrusting of others; more common in women
- causes
  - **cognitive-behavioral:** specific behaviors learned over time, associated with maladaptive belief systems
  - genetic factors play a role, with many showing increased rates of heritability
  - variances in stress tolerance and disturbances in family relationships and communication have also been linked to personality disorders

Reset

Practice Quiz   How much do you remember?. ANSWERS ON PAGE AK-1.

Pick the best answer.

1. Which of the following is not an accurate portrayal of antisocial personality disorder?
   a. Most people with this disorder are female.
   b. Most people with this disorder are male.
   c. People with this disorder experience little or no guilt for their criminal acts.
   d. People with this disorder are consistently irresponsible and don't keep commitments.

2. Studies show that _____ personality disorders occur more frequently in women whereas _____ personality disorders happen more often in men.
   a. antisocial; borderline
   b. borderline; schizotypal
   c. schizotypal; antisocial
   d. borderline; antisocial

3. One physiological cause of antisocial personality disorder that has been suggested is that people with this condition have:
 a. lack of appropriate short-term memory related to ethical and moral rules, caused by deficient function in the hippocampus.
 b. lower than normal levels of stress hormones.
 c. increased synaptic pruning in the prefrontal cortex.
 d. heightened sensitivity to external stimuli in the amygdala

4. Due to the inappropriate and excessive emotions often experienced by people with borderline personality disorder, they are often confused with those who suffer from _____ personality disorder.
 a. schizoid
 b. narcissistic
 c. dependent
 d. histrionic

Applying Psychology to Everyday Life
Taking the Worry Out of Exams

12.18 Identify some methods to overcome test anxiety.

Imagine this scenario: You sit down to take your midterm exam, feeling that you are prepared and ready. Once you get the test in front of you, well, maybe you start to feel just a bit more nervous, your hands get sweaty, your stomach may ache; and when you look at the first question—your mind becomes a complete blank!

These are a few of the common symptoms of *test anxiety*, the personal experience of possible negative consequences or poor outcomes on an exam or evaluation, accompanied by a cluster of cognitive, affective, and behavioral symptoms (Zeidner & Matthews, 2005). Cognitive symptoms may consist of worrying excessively about an exam, expecting to do poorly no matter how hard you study, or even finding it hard to start studying in the first place. Then, while taking the test, you might find you do not understand certain directions or questions, "go blank" when looking at the items, or feel like you cannot concentrate on the exam in front of you because your mind keeps wandering. *Affective* or emotional symptoms may include body tension and heightened physiological arousal including sweaty palms, upset stomach, difficulty breathing, and the like, prior to and/or during the exam. *Behavioral* aspects may include procrastination, deficient study skills, or avoiding studying altogether.

While not yet recognized as a clinical disorder in the *DSM-5*, test anxiety has caused countless students considerable stress and agony over the years. Remember "psychology student's syndrome"? You may not really have any of the psychological disorders we've discussed in this chapter, but chances are good that you *have* experienced test anxiety a time or two. One way to make the development of a true anxiety disorder less likely is to deal realistically with milder forms of anxiety *before* they escalate, and the main intent of this section is to help you achieve that.

So, what can you do if you experience test anxiety and want to get your worrying under control? First, determine why you want to do well on the test in the first place. Do you really want to demonstrate your understanding of the material or are you hoping just to pass? Try to find an internal motivation to do well on the exam rather than simply relying on extrinsic reasons. Even if you are taking a test in a subject you don't necessarily enjoy, try to identify something you want to accomplish, and get your focus off the goal of simply earning a passing grade.

Second, develop some type of strategy for controlling both your cognitive state and behavior, before and during the exam. Review the study tips we presented in the Psychology in Action section of this book. (L I N K) to Learning Objective PIA.5. As mentioned there, if you are well prepared, you are less likely to worry. Avoid cramming and take advantage of the additive effects of distributed practice. Refer back to that information and review suggestions that will help you manage your tasks and your time. Schedule regular study sessions and avoid or limit distractions (email, phone, text messages, television, noisy roommates, and the like may seem to provide welcome escapes from studying, but they will only keep you from your intended goal). You've read the chapter on memory (or at least you should have!) and now know that spacing out your study and using meaningful, elaborative rehearsal over multiple study periods is going to yield much better results than an all-out cramming marathon the night before an exam. (L I N K) to Learning Objectives 6.5 and 6.10.

The way you approach an exam can have a significant impact on the testing experience and how you manage yourself during that exam (Davis et al., 2008). Instead of focusing on how nervous you are and how sure you are that you aren't going to be able to remember anything, turn that thinking around and recognize how much energy you have going into the exam (Dundas et al., 2009). Positive self-talk can be very valuable in this kind of situation (and is a good example of cognitive therapy at work). A recent study demonstrated that competence-priming (imagining a person who is successful at a related task) lowered the relationship between test anxiety and test performance (Lang & Lang, 2010). Additionally, instead of focusing on the whole exam, take control and address one question at a time, first answering the questions you know—that will build your confidence and help you progress through the test. Also control your body; try to stay relaxed, and breathe normally. If you get distracted, consciously redirect yourself back to the next question. Before you know it, you will have completed the entire exam—whew!

Questions for Further Discussion

1. Have you ever experienced test anxiety? What methods did you use to get your worrying under control?

2. What factors, other than the ones listed here, might influence the anxiety one feels when taking an exam?

Chapter Summary

What Is Abnormality?

12.1 Describe how mental illness has been explained in the past and how abnormal behavior and thinking are defined today.

• Psychopathology is the study of abnormal behavior and psychological dysfunction.

• In ancient times holes were cut in an ill person's head to let out evil spirits in a process called trephining. Hippocrates believed that mental illness came from an imbalance in the body's four humors, whereas in the early Renaissance period the mentally ill were labeled as witches.

• Abnormality can be characterized as thinking or behavior that is statistically rare, deviant from social norms, causes subjective discomfort, does not allow day-to-day functioning, or causes a person to be dangerous to self or others.

• In the United States, *insanity* is a legal term, not a psychological term.

12.2 Identify some of the models used to explain psychological disorders.

• In biological models of abnormality, the assumption is that mental illnesses are caused by chemical or structural malfunctions in the nervous system.

• Psychodynamic theorists assume that abnormal thinking and behavior stems from repressed conflicts and urges that are fighting to become conscious.

• Behaviorists see abnormal behavior or thinking as learned.

• Cognitive theorists see abnormal behavior as coming from irrational beliefs and illogical patterns of thought.

• The sociocultural perspective conceptualizes all thinking and behavior as the product of learning and shaping of behavior within the context of family, social group, and culture.

• Cultural relativity refers to the need to consider the norms and customs of another culture when diagnosing a person from that culture with a disorder.

• The biopsychosocial model views abnormal thinking and behavior as the sum result of biological, psychological, social, and cultural influences

Diagnosing and Classifying Disorders

12.3 Describe the different types of psychological disorders and their prevalence, and evaluate the advantages and disadvantages of using diagnostic labels.

• *The Diagnostic and Statistical Manual of Mental Disorders, Fifth Edition (DSM-5)* is a manual of psychological disorders and their symptoms.

- Approximately 26.2 percent of American adults over age 18 suffer from some type of mental disorder in any given year.

Disorders of Anxiety, Trauma, and Stress: What, Me Worry?

12.4 Identify the different types of anxiety disorders and their symptoms.

- Anxiety disorders are all disorders in which the most dominant symptom is excessive and unrealistic anxiety.
- Phobias are irrational, persistent fears. Three types of phobias are social anxiety disorder (social phobia), specific phobias, and agoraphobia.
- Panic disorder is the sudden and recurrent onset of intense panic for no reason, with all the physical symptoms that can occur in sympathetic nervous system arousal.
- Generalized anxiety disorder is a condition of intense and unrealistic anxiety that lasts 6 months or more.

12.5 Describe obsessive-compulsive disorder and stress-related disorders.

- Obsessive-compulsive disorder consists of an obsessive, recurring thought that creates anxiety and a compulsive, ritualistic, and repetitive behavior or mental action that reduces that anxiety.
- Significant and traumatic stressors can lead to acute stress disorder or posttraumatic stress disorder. The diagnosis differs according to duration and onset but includes symptoms of anxiety, dissociation, nightmares, and reliving the event.

12.6 Explain some potential causes of anxiety, trauma, and stress disorders

- Psychodynamic explanations of anxiety and related disorders point to repressed urges and desires that are trying to come into consciousness, creating anxiety that is controlled by the abnormal behavior.
- Behaviorists state that disordered behavior is learned through both operant conditioning and classical conditioning techniques.
- Cognitive psychologists believe that excessive anxiety comes from illogical, irrational thought processes.
- Biological explanations of anxiety-related disorders include neurotransmitter dysfunction, in particular the serotonin and GABA systems.
- Genetic transmission may be responsible for anxiety-related disorders among related persons.

Dissociative Disorders: Altered Identities

12.7 Describe the various dissociative disorders and explain how they develop.

- Dissociative disorders involve a break in consciousness, memory, or both. These disorders include dissociative amnesia, with or without fugue, and dissociative identity disorder.

12.8 Summarize the various explanations for dissociative disorders.

- Psychodynamic explanations point to repression of memories, seeing dissociation as a defense mechanism against anxiety.

- Cognitive and behavioral explanations see dissociative disorders as a kind of avoidance learning.
- Biological explanations point to lower than normal activity levels in the areas responsible for body awareness in people with dissociative disorders.

Disorders of Mood: The Effect of Affect

12.9 Describe different disorders of mood, including major depressive disorder and bipolar disorders.

- Mood disorders, also called affective disorders, are severe disturbances in emotion.
- Major depressive disorder has a fairly sudden onset and is extreme sadness and despair, typically with no obvious external cause. It is the most common of the mood disorders and is more common in women than in men.
- Bipolar disorders are characterized by shifts in mood that may range from normal to manic, with or without episodes of depression (bipolar I disorder), or spans of normal mood interspersed with episodes of major depression and hypomania (bipolar II disorder).

12.10 Compare and contrast behavioral, social cognitive, and biological explanations for depression and other disorders of mood

- Learning theories link depression to learned helplessness.
- Cognitive theories see depression as the result of distorted, illogical thinking.
- Biological explanations of mood disorders look at the function of serotonin, norepinephrine, and dopamine systems in the brain.
- Mood disorders are more likely to appear in genetically related people, with higher rates of risk for closer genetic relatives.

Eating Disorders and Sexual Dysfunctions

12.11 Identify three different types of eating disorders and the treatment options associated with each.

- Maladaptive eating problems include anorexia nervosa, bulimia nervosa, and binge-eating disorder.
- Effective treatment of anorexia nervosa may require hospitalization for stabilization of physical needs.
- Psychological treatment of eating disorders may include interpersonal therapy, cognitive-behavioral therapy, group therapy, or family-based therapy; weight loss strategies may be required in binge eating disorder and only 40 to 60 percent of individuals with anorexia who receive treatment will make a recovery.

12.12 Summarize some of the risk factors associated with eating disorders, including cultural factors.

- Genetics, increased sensitivity to the rewarding value of food or food-related anxiety, altered brain function, and being female contribute to risk of being diagnosed with an eating disorder.

12.13 Describe types of sexual dysfunction, and explain how they may develop.

- Sexual dysfunctions are problems with sexual functioning. They may be caused by physical problems, interpersonal or sociocultural issues, or psychological problems, and can affect sexual interest, arousal, and response.

- These dysfunctions include female sexual interest/arousal disorder, male hypoactive sexual desire disorder, erectile disorder, genito-pelvic pain/penetration disorder, premature (early) ejaculation, female orgasmic disorder, and delayed ejaculation.

Schizophrenia: Altered Reality

12.14 **Describe the main symptoms of schizophrenia, distinguishing between positive and negative symptoms.**

- Schizophrenia is a split between thoughts, emotions, and behavior. It is a long-lasting psychotic disorder in which reality and fantasy become confused.
- Symptoms of schizophrenia include delusions (false beliefs about the world), hallucinations, emotional disturbances, attentional difficulties, disturbed speech, and disordered thinking.
- Positive symptoms are excesses of behavior associated with increased dopamine activity in some parts of the brain, whereas negative symptoms are deficits in behavior associated with decreased dopamine activity in other parts of the brain.

12.15 **Evaluate the genetic and environmental influences on schizophrenia.**

- Biological explanations for schizophrenia focus on dopamine, structural defects in the brain, and genetic influences. Rates of risk of developing schizophrenia increase drastically as genetic relatedness increases, with the highest risk faced by an identical twin whose twin sibling has schizophrenia.

Personality Disorders: I'm Okay, It's Everyone Else Who's Weird

12.16 **Classify the different types of personality disorders.**

- Personality disorders are extremely rigid, maladaptive patterns of behavior that prevent a person from normal social interactions and relationships.

- In antisocial personality disorder a person consistently violates the rights of others.
- In borderline personality disorder a person is clingy, moody, unstable in relationships, and suffers from problems with identity.

12.17 **Summarize some of the potential causes of personality disorders.**

- Cognitive-learning theorists see personality disorders as a set of learned behavior that has become maladaptive—bad habits learned early on in life. Belief systems of the personality disordered person are seen as illogical.
- Biological relatives of people with personality disorders are more likely to develop similar disorders, supporting a genetic basis for such disorders.
- Biological explanations look at the lower than normal stress hormones in antisocial personality disordered persons as responsible for their low responsiveness to threatening stimuli.
- Other possible causes of personality disorders may include disturbances in family communications and relationships, childhood abuse, neglect, overly strict parenting, overprotective parenting, and parental rejection.

Applying Psychology to Everyday Life: Taking the Worry Out of Exams

12.18 **Identify some methods to overcome test anxiety.**

- Test anxiety is the personal experience of possible negative consequences or poor outcomes on an exam or evaluation.
- Some ways to deal with test anxiety are to find an internal motivation, develop strategies for studying and controlling your emotional reactions, and focusing on the positive rather than the negative.

Test Yourself   ANSWERS ON PAGE AK-1.

Pick the best answer.

1. What is the most likely reason that someone would perform an exorcism?
   a. to relieve fluid pressure on the brain
   b. to look into the brain to see what is wrong
   c. to release evil spirits
   d. to restore balance to the body's humors

2. In 1972, a jet carrying a rugby team from Peru crashed high in the snow-covered Andes Mountains. Many of the players survived for over two months by eating the remains of those who died. Psychologists justified their cannibalism because that was the only way they could have survived so long without food. By what definition might their behavior best be classified?
   a. statistical   c. maladaptive
   b. subjective discomfort d. situational context

3. Which of the following is an example of cultural relativity?
   a. Dr. Han believes that the voices his patient is hearing stem from a biological instead of a psychological cause.
   b. While Dr. Howard believes that hypnosis is the best way to understand all disorders, his approach is not shared by his colleagues.
   c. While Dr. Akido knows that his patient, Aki, believes her anxiety has a biological explanation, in learning more about her family of origin, he suspects it has a psychological cause.
   d. Dr. Roland uses a behavioral approach to treat all his clients who are younger than age 10.

4. How many axes does the *DSM-5* use to aid mental health professionals in making a diagnosis?
   a. one   c. four
   b. two   d. five

5. *Trypanophobia*, also known as a fear of receiving an injection, is an example of
- **a.** obsession.
- **b.** social phobia.
- **c.** anxiety attack.
- **d.** specific phobia.

6. Aaron hates to go to restaurants for fear that he will be seated in the far back of the restaurant and be unable to get out in case of an emergency. This may be a symptom of
- **a.** social phobia.
- **b.** specific phobia.
- **c.** agoraphobia.
- **d.** claustrophobia.

7. Ria experienced a sudden attack of intense fear when she was boarding a plane with her friends to fly to Mexico for spring break. Ria's heart raced, she became dizzy, and she was certain she would die in a plane crash if she boarded the plane. Subsequently she did not go on her trip, and the plane arrived safely in Mexico 3 hours later. Ria experienced
- **a.** a depressive episode.
- **b.** a panic attack.
- **c.** panic disorder.
- **d.** agoraphobia.

8. Dr. Kirby has been meeting with 9-year-old Loren, whose family lost everything in a tornado. In her initial visit, Loren was diagnosed with acute stress disorder. During a 2-month follow-up with Dr. Kirby, Loren is still exhibiting many of the same symptoms. What should Dr. Kirby do?
- **a.** Dr. Kirby will revise Loren's diagnosis from ASD to posttraumatic stress disorder.
- **b.** Dr. Kirby will revise Loren's diagnosis from ASD to generalized anxiety disorder.
- **c.** Dr. Kirby will continue treatment for acute stress disorder for at least 6 months.
- **d.** Dr. Kirby should tell Loren she is cured so as to speed her recovery.

9. Survivors of natural disasters like Hurricane Sandy in 2012 may experience higher incidences of
- **a.** personality disorders
- **b.** posttraumatic stress disorder.
- **c.** eating disorders.
- **d.** schizophrenia.

10. Lizette notices an unusual lump in her right breast while taking a shower. For a moment, she grows concerned especially because breast cancer runs in her family. However, she convinces herself that it will probably go away in a few weeks. What cognitive process is Lizette applying?
- **a.** magnification
- **b.** overgeneralization
- **c.** all-or-nothing thinking
- **d.** minimization

11. Dissociative amnesia is different from retrograde amnesia because
- **a.** dissociative amnesia is typically psychological in origin.
- **b.** retrograde amnesia has been shown to not actually exist.
- **c.** dissociative amnesia is caused by a physical blow to the head.
- **d.** retrograde amnesia is caused by psychological trauma.

12. Depersonalization/derealization disorder is a type of dissociative disorder that has been found to have possible _____ foundations for the experience of detachment.
- **a.** biological
- **b.** psychodynamic
- **c.** behavioral
- **d.** cognitive

13. Which type of depression is the most common type of mood disorder?
- **a.** bipolar disorder
- **b.** mania
- **c.** seasonal affective disorder
- **d.** major depressive disorder

14. A behavioral theorist would be most likely to link depression to _____, whereas a social cognitive theorist would probably point to _____.
- **a.** distortions in thinking; learned helplessness
- **b.** biological abnormalities; distortions in thinking
- **c.** unconscious forces; learned helplessness
- **d.** learned helplessness; distortions in thinking

15. Individuals with bulimia nervosa often rationalize that since they have had a single treat, their diet is ruined and therefore they might as well go ahead and eat excessively. Such irrational thinking is an example of the cognitive distortion known as
- **a.** overgeneralization.
- **b.** all or nothing thinking.
- **c.** magnification.
- **d.** minimization.

16. Binge-eating disorder is different from bulimia nervosa in that individuals with binge-eating disorder
- **a.** typically eat much smaller portions before purging the food.
- **b.** do not typically purge the food they eat.
- **c.** only purge their food after several binge sessions.
- **d.** often resort to anorexic methods to rid themselves of the food they have eaten.

17. Sexual dysfunctions and problems can be caused by
- **a.** organic factors.
- **b.** organic and sociocultural factors.
- **c.** organic, psychological, and sociocultural factors.
- **d.** hereditary factors primarily.

18. Rodney has been diagnosed with schizophrenia. He rarely smiles and often shows little emotion to any situation. Psychologists refer to this characteristic as
- **a.** catatonia.
- **b.** flat affect.
- **c.** positive symptoms.
- **d.** negative symptoms.

19. What neurotransmitter was first believed to be the cause of schizophrenia?
- **a.** GABA
- **b.** serotonin
- **c.** epinephrine
- **d.** dopamine

20. Colleen found herself attracted to her psychology instructor. She would frequently go by his office just to be near him. When he didn't respond to her advances, Colleen eventually told him that she had thoughts of killing herself so that he would spend time trying to counsel her. What personality disorder best describes Colleen's thinking and behavior?
- **a.** borderline personality disorder
- **b.** schizoid personality disorder
- **c.** schizotypal personality disorder
- **d.** antisocial personality disorder

Chapter 13
Psychological Therapies

A set of films were made in the mid-1960s, "Three Approaches to Psychotherapy," that focused on three pioneering therapists working with a single client, "Gloria." Often referred to as the "Gloria tapes" or "Gloria films," this collection provided many students of psychology and professionals in training their first look into what actually may occur during a therapy session.

Each of the therapists worked with Gloria to address concerns she was experiencing as a recently divorced mother. In doing so, each demonstrated aspects of their respective techniques and theories. The therapists were none other than Carl Rogers demonstrating his *person-centered therapy*, Fritz Perls demonstrating his *Gestalt therapy*, and Albert Ellis demonstrating his *rational therapy* or *rational emotive therapy* (later developed into *rational emotive behavior therapy*).

The field of psychology has grown a great deal since the Gloria films were made, and potential clients now have many more sources of information available to them regarding therapy options.

What information might be most useful for someone interested in pursuing a particular therapy or treatment for a psychological disorder?

00:00 / 02:28

Why study therapies for psychological disorders?

There are almost as many therapy methods as there are disorders. Correctly matching the type of therapy to the disorder can mean the difference between a cure or a crisis. It is important to know the choices available for treatment and how they relate to the different kinds of disorders so that an informed decision can be made and the best possible outcome can be achieved for mental health and wellness.

Learning Objectives

13.1 Describe how psychological disorders were treated historically, and identify the two broad categories of therapy used today.

13.2 Describe the basic elements of Freud's psychoanalysis, and explain how psychodynamic approaches differ today.

13.3 Identify the basic elements of the humanistic therapies known as person-centered therapy and Gestalt therapy, and evaluate each.

13.4 Explain how behavior therapists use classical and operant conditioning to treat disordered behavior, and evaluate the effectiveness of these techniques.

13.5 Summarize the goals and basic elements of cognitive therapies, and evaluate their effectiveness.

13.6 Compare and contrast different forms of group therapy.

13.7 Evaluate the advantages and disadvantages of group therapy.

13.8 Summarize the research on the effectiveness of psychotherapy, including cybertherapy.

13.9 Describe some of the factors that influence the effectiveness of therapy.

13.10 Categorize and describe the various types of drugs used to treat psychological disorders.

13.11 Explain how electroconvulsive therapy, psychosurgery, and other emerging biomedical techniques are used to treat psychological disorders today.

13.12 Identify some practical applications of virtual reality for treating psychological disorders.

In this famous painting by French artist Robert Fleury, French psychiatrist Dr. Philippe Pinel orders the chains removed from patients at a Paris asylum for insane women. Pinel was one of the first psychiatrists to recommend humane treatment of the mentally ill.

Treatment of Psychological Disorders: Past to Present

13.1 Describe how psychological disorders were treated historically, and identify the two broad categories of therapy used today.

As discussed in Chapter Twelve, although psychological or social causes might have been identified for some disorders, until the late 1700s, people suffering severe mental illnesses were sometimes thought to be possessed by demons or evil spirits, and the "treatments" to rid the person of these spirits were severe and deadly. Even within the last 200 years, a period of supposedly more "enlightened" awareness, the mentally ill did not always receive humane* treatment.

> 💬 I've seen movies about mental hospitals, and they didn't look like great places to be in even now—how bad was it back then? What did people do with relatives who were ill that way?

The first truly organized effort to do something with mentally ill persons began in England in the middle of the sixteenth century. Bethlehem Hospital in London (later known as "Bedlam") was converted into an asylum (a word meaning "place of safety") for the mentally ill. In reality, the first asylums were little more than prisons where the mentally ill were chained to their beds. "Treatments" consisted of bloodletting (which more often than not led to death or the need for lifelong care for the patient), beatings, ice baths in which the person was submerged until passing out or suffering a seizure, and induced vomiting in a kind of spiritual cleansing (Hunt, 1993). This cleansing or purging was meant to rid the body of physical impurities so that the person's mind and soul could function more perfectly.

It was not until 1793 that efforts were made to treat the mentally ill with kindness and guidance—known as "moral treatment"—rather than beating them or subjecting them to the harsh physical purging that had been commonplace. It was at this time that Philippe Pinel personally unchained the inmates at La Bicêtre Asylum in Paris, France, beginning the movement of humane treatment of the mentally ill (Brigham, 1844; Curtis, 1993).

Today, we can group the primary approaches to **therapy** (treatment methods aimed at making people feel better and function more effectively) into two broad categories. One category is based primarily in psychological theory and techniques; people tell the therapist about their problems, and the therapist listens and tries to help them understand those problems or assists them in changing the behaviors related to the problem. The other category uses medical interventions to bring the symptoms under control. Although we can separate treatments into these two larger categories, in actual practice, many effective treatment strategies or treatment plans combine facets of both. Just as there is no one single "cause" of a disorder (Maxmen et al., 2009), different psychological treatments are often used in tandem or combined with biomedical interventions. Furthermore, many psychology professionals do not limit themselves to a single technique and are **eclectic**, using more than one treatment approach or technique to best meet the needs of the people they are working with. The fields of clinical psychology and counseling psychology are diverse, and professionals have a wide variety of educational and training experiences. ⓛⓘⓝⓚ to Learning Objective B.5. Before we

---

*humane: marked by compassion, sympathy, or consideration for humans (and animals).

discuss the various types of therapy in more detail, take a moment to evaluate your own views on, and experiences with, therapy in the survey, *How Do You Take Care of Your Mental Health?*

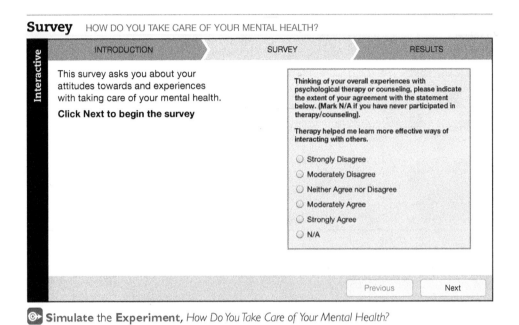

Survey HOW DO YOU TAKE CARE OF YOUR MENTAL HEALTH?

Simulate the **Experiment,** *How Do You Take Care of Your Mental Health?*

Psychotherapy typically involves an individual, couple, or small group of individuals working directly with a therapist and discussing their concerns or problems. The goal of most psychotherapy is to help both mentally healthy and psychologically disordered persons understand themselves better (Goin, 2005; Wolberg, 1977). Because understanding of one's motives and actions is called *insight*, therapies aimed mainly at this goal are called **insight therapies**. A therapy that is directed more at changing behavior than providing insights into the reasons for that behavior is called **action therapy**. Many psychological professionals use a combination of insight and action therapeutic* methods.

The other main type of therapy uses some biological treatment in the form of a medical procedure to bring about changes in the person's disordered behavior. **Biomedical therapies** include the use of drugs, surgical methods, electric shock treatments, and noninvasive stimulation techniques. It is important to understand that biomedical therapy often eliminates or alleviates the symptoms of a disorder, while psychotherapy addresses issues associated with the disorder, and when used together, these two types of therapy facilitate* each other (Maxmen et al., 2009). For example, when medications are needed, individuals taking the proper medications are going to benefit more from psychotherapy, as their symptoms will be better controlled. Furthermore, psychotherapy, not medication, is going to help them better understand what the symptoms of their disorder are and facilitate adjustment, other coping strategies, and proactive ways of addressing the disorder or its related outcomes (Maxmen et al., 2009).

---

*therapeutic: providing or assisting in a cure.

*facilitate: to assist, make possible, or make easier.

Concept Map L.O. 13.1

Interactive

- **modern treatments**
  - **psychotherapy:** based on psychological techniques, individuals talk about their problems and the therapist assists them in understanding and changing behavior
    - **insight therapies**
    - **action therapies**
  - **biomedical therapy:** uses medical interventions to bring symptoms under control
- **early interventions**
  - historically, psychological or social causes identified for some disorders; for others, individuals with mental illness were believed to be possessed by demons or evil spirits
  - organized treatment began in England around the middle 1500s
  - Pinel started the "moral treatment" movement in France

Treatment of Psychological Disorders

Reset

Practice Quiz   How much do you remember?   ANSWERS ON PAGE AK-1.

Pick the best answer.

1. One of the first therapists to begin a movement toward the humane treatment of patients was
  a. Robert Fleury.
  b. Philippe Pinel.
  c. Sigmund Freud.
  d. Josef Breuer.

2. The Bethlehem Hospital in London, later known as "_____" was converted into an asylum for the mentally ill. While it may have been intended as a place of safety, it and many other such early facilities were little more than prisons.
  a. Mayhem
  b. Chronos
  c. Chaos
  d. Bedlam

3. Raul has decided to seek psychotherapy for some personal difficulties he has been having. While on the telephone with one possible clinician, he asks her to describe the kind of treatment approach that she uses with clients. "I don't limit myself to a single theory or approach," the therapist answers. "Instead I operate in a(n) _____ fashion, integrating various treatment approaches based on the specific needs of each client."
  a. eclectic
  b. Gestalt
  c. supratheoretical
  d. atheoretical

4. Which of the following is *not* one of the main types of therapy noted by your textbook that helps people improve their overall functioning?
  a. Insight therapy
  b. Action therapy
  c. Biomedical therapy
  d. Regressive therapy

"*Why do you think you cross the road?*"

"Why do you think you cross the road?"

Insight Therapies: Psychodynamic and Humanistic Approaches

We'll begin our discussion of psychotherapy with two types of insight therapies: psychodynamic therapy and humanistic therapy. While these approaches use different methods, they both strive to gain an understanding of one's motives and actions.

PSYCHOTHERAPY BEGINS: FREUD'S PSYCHOANALYSIS

13.2   **Describe the basic elements of Freud's psychoanalysis, and explain how psychodynamic approaches differ today.**

💬 So what exactly happens in psychoanalysis? I've heard lots of stories about it, but what's it really like?

In a sense, Freud took the sixteenth-century method of physical cleansing to a different level. Instead of a physical purge, cleansing for Freud meant removing all the "impurities" of the unconscious mind that he believed were responsible for his patients' psychological and nervous disorders. (Freud was a medical doctor and referred to the people who came to him for help as "patients.") The impurities of the unconscious mind were considered to be disturbing thoughts, socially unacceptable desires, and immoral urges that originated in the id, the part of the personality that is itself unconscious and driven by basic needs for survival and pleasure. **(L) (I) (N) (K)** to Learning Objective 11.2.

PSYCHOANALYSIS Freud believed that his patients used these unconscious thoughts to prevent anxiety, and as such, the thoughts would not be easily brought into conscious awareness. Freud designed a therapy technique to help his patients feel more relaxed, open, and able to explore their innermost feelings without fear of embarrassment or rejection. This method was called **psychoanalysis**, and it is an insight therapy that emphasizes revealing the unconscious conflicts, urges, and desires that are assumed to cause disordered emotions and behavior (Freud, 1904; Mitchell & Black, 1996). This is the original reason for the couch in Freud's version of psychoanalysis; people lying on the couch were more relaxed and would, Freud thought, feel more dependent and childlike, making it easier for them to "get at" those early childhood memories. An additional plus was that he could sit behind the patients at the head of the couch and take notes. Without the patients being able to see his reactions to what they said, they remained unaffected by his reactions.

Freud also made use of two techniques to try to reveal the repressed information in his patients' unconscious minds. These techniques were the interpretation of dreams and allowing patients to talk freely about anything that came to mind.

DREAM INTERPRETATION *Dream interpretation*, or the analysis of the elements within a patient's reported dream, formed a large part of Freud's psychoanalytic method. **(L) (I) (N) (K)** to Learning Objective 4.6. Freud believed that repressed material often surfaced in dreams, although in symbolic form. The *manifest content* of the dream was the actual dream and its events, but the **latent content** was the hidden, symbolic meaning of those events that would, if correctly interpreted, reveal the unconscious conflicts that were creating the nervous disorder (Freud, 1900).

FREE ASSOCIATION The other technique for revealing the unconscious mind was a method originally devised by Freud's coworker, Josef Breuer (Breuer & Freud, 1895). Breuer encouraged his patients to say freely whatever came into their minds without fear of being negatively evaluated or condemned. As the patients talked, they began to reveal things that were loosely associated with their flow of ideas, often revealing what Breuer felt were hidden, unconscious concerns. Freud adopted this method of **free association**, believing that repressed impulses and other material were trying to "break free" into consciousness and would eventually surface using this technique.

RESISTANCE AND TRANSFERENCE Other components of Freud's original psychoanalytic method were **resistance** (the point at which the patient becomes unwilling to talk about certain topics) and **transference** (when the therapist becomes a symbol of a parental authority figure from the past). Therapists can also experience *countertransference*, in which the therapist has a transference reaction to the patient. This reaction might not always be to the benefit of the patient. As in all of the therapeutic approaches, peer and professional supervision helps therapists recognize potential issues in providing effective therapy.

EVALUATION OF PSYCHOANALYSIS AND PSYCHODYNAMIC APPROACHES Freud's original theory, on which he based his interpretations of his patients' revelations, has been criticized as having several flaws, which were discussed in Chapter Eleven. These included the lack of scientific research to support his claims, his unwillingness to believe some of the things revealed by his patients when those revelations did not fit into his view of the world, and his almost obsessive need to assume that problems with sex and sexuality were at the heart of nearly every nervous disorder.

Psychotherapy often takes place one-on-one, with a client and therapist exploring various issues together to achieve deeper insights or to change undesirable behavior.

Few psychoanalysts today still use Freud's original methods, which could take years to produce results. The couch is gone, and the *client* (a term used to support the active role of the person seeking help and to avoid implying "sickness," as might result when using the term *patient*) may sit face to face with the therapist. The client may also stand or walk about. Rather than remaining quiet until the client says something revealing, the modern psychoanalyst is far more **directive**, asking questions, suggesting helpful behavior, and giving opinions and interpretations earlier in the relationship, which helps speed up the therapeutic process. Today's psychoanalysts also focus less on the id as the motivator of behavior, instead looking more at the ego or sense of self as the motivating force behind all actions (Prochaska & Norcross, 2003). Some psychoanalysts also focus on the process of transference more than on other typical aspects of traditional psychoanalysis, leading to the more general method called **psychodynamic therapy**. Psychodynamic therapy is typically shorter in duration than traditional psychoanalysis.

Even so, all of the psychodynamic techniques require the client to be fairly intelligent and verbally able to express his or her ideas, feelings, and thoughts effectively. People who are extremely withdrawn or who suffer from the more severe psychotic disorders are not good candidates for this form of psychotherapy. People who have nonpsychotic adjustment disorders, such as anxiety or dissociative disorders, are more likely to benefit from psychodynamic therapy.

INTERPERSONAL PSYCHOTHERAPY Interpersonal psychotherapy (IPT) is a psychotherapy developed to address depression. It is an insight therapy focusing on relationships of the individual with others and the interplay between mood and the events of everyday life (Bleiberg & Markowitcz, 2014). It is based on the interpersonal theories of Adolph Meyer and Harry Stack Sullivan along with the attachment theory of John Bowlby, and it focuses on interpersonal relationships and functioning (Bleiberg & Markowitcz, 2014). It is one of the few theories derived from psychodynamic thinking that does have some research support for its effectiveness in treating depression, particularly when combined with medication (Mufson et al., 2004; Reynolds et al., 1999). Despite its origins, IPT is not considered to be a psychodynamic therapy as it combines aspects of humanistic and cognitive–behavioral therapies, making it truly eclectic.

HUMANISTIC THERAPY: TO ERR IS HUMAN

13.3 Identify the basic elements of the humanistic therapies known as person-centered therapy and Gestalt therapy, and evaluate each.

Unlike psychodynamic therapists, humanistic theorists do not focus on unconscious, hidden conflicts. Instead, humanists focus on conscious, subjective experiences of emotion and people's sense of self, as well as the more immediate experiences in their daily lives rather than early childhood experiences of the distant past (Cain & Seeman, 2001; Rowan, 2001; Schneider et al., 2001). **LINK** to Learning Objective 1.4. Humanistic therapy emphasizes the importance of the choices made by individuals and the potential to change one's behavior. The two most common therapy styles based on humanistic theory are Carl Rogers's person-centered therapy and Fritz Perls's Gestalt therapy; both are primarily insight therapies.

TELL ME MORE: ROGERS'S PERSON-CENTERED THERAPY Chapter Eleven discussed the basic elements of Rogers's theory of personality, which emphasizes the sense of self (Rogers, 1961). To sum it up quickly, Rogers proposed that everyone has a *real self* (how people see their actual traits and abilities) and an *ideal self* (how people think they should be). The closer the real and ideal selves match up, the happier and more well adjusted the person. To have these two self-concepts match, people need to receive *unconditional positive regard*, which is love, warmth, respect, and affection without any conditions attached. If people think that there are conditions put on the love and affection they receive, their ideal selves will be determined by those conditions and become more difficult to achieve, resulting in a mismatch of selves and unhappiness.

 💬 So the key to getting over unhappiness would be to get the real and ideal selves closer together? How does a therapist do that?

Rogers believed that the goal of the therapist should be to provide the unconditional positive regard that has been absent from the troubled person's life and to help the person recognize the discrepancies between the real and ideal selves. He also believed that the person would actually have to do most of the work, talking out problems and concerns in an atmosphere of warmth and acceptance from the therapist, so he originally called the people in this therapy relationship "clients" instead of "patients," to put the therapeutic relationship on a more equal footing. As a result, Rogers's therapy is very **nondirective** because the person actually does all the real work, with the therapist merely acting as a sounding board. However, therapists may help individuals redirect or reallocate their attention to focus on feelings not fully processed previously (Prochaska & Norcross, 2009). Later, the term *client* was changed to the even more neutral term *person*. His therapy is now called **person-centered therapy** because the person is truly the center of the process.

BASIC ELEMENTS Rogers (1961) saw three key elements as being necessary in any successful person–therapist relationship:

- **Authenticity** The therapist must show **authenticity** in a genuine, open, and honest response to the individual. It is easier for some professionals to "hide" behind the role of the therapist, as was often the case in psychoanalysis. In person-centered therapy, the therapist has to be able to tolerate a person's differences without being judgmental.

- **Unconditional Positive Regard** Another key element of person-centered therapy is the warm, accepting, completely uncritical atmosphere that the therapist must create for the people they work with. Having respect for an individual and their feelings, values, and goals, even if they are different from those of the therapist, is called **unconditional positive regard**.

- **Empathy** Lastly, the therapist needs to be able to see the world through the eyes of the person they are working with. The therapist has to be able to acknowledge what people are feeling and experiencing by using a kind of understanding called **empathy**. This involves listening carefully and closely to what individuals are saying and trying to feel what they feel. Therapists must also avoid getting their own feelings mixed up with their clients' feelings (e.g., countertransference).

A person-centered therapist typically responds in a way that seeks clarification and demonstrates attempts to understand the experience of the individual. **Reflection** refers to a technique therapists use to allow clients to continue to talk and have insights without the interference of the therapist's interpretations and possible biases. Reflection is literally a kind of mirroring of clients' statements. Here's an example from one of Rogers's own therapy sessions with a client (Meador & Rogers, 1984, p. 143):

CLIENT: I just ain't no good to nobody, never was, and never will be.

ROGERS: Feeling that now, hm? That you're just no good to yourself, no good to anybody. Never will be any good to anybody. Just that you're completely worthless, huh?—Those really are lousy feelings. Just feel that you're no good at all, hm?

CLIENT: Yeah.

MOTIVATIONAL INTERVIEWING A variation of person-centered therapy is *motivational interviewing*, or MI (Miller & Rollnick, 2002), which has been described by Hal Arkowitz and William R. Miller as "client-centered therapy with a twist" (p. 4). In contrast to person-centered therapy, MI has specific goals, to reduce ambivalence about

A Rogerian person-centered therapist listens with calm acceptance to anything the client says. A sense of empathy with the client's feelings is also important.

In Gestalt therapy, it is not unusual to find a client talking to an empty chair. The chair represents some person from the past with whom the client has unresolved issues, and this is the opportunity to deal with those issues.

change and to increase intrinsic motivation to bring that change about (Arkowitcz & Miller, 2008). For a therapist, the four principles of MI are to express empathy, develop discrepancy between the client's present behaviors and values, roll with resistance, and support the client's self-efficacy (Miller & Rollnick, 2002). Although it was originally developed and validated as effective for addictive disorders, it has also been useful in the treatment of anxiety and mood disorders (Arkowitcz & Miller, 2008; Barlow et al., 2013).

GESTALT THERAPY Another therapy based on humanistic ideas is called **Gestalt therapy**. The founder of this therapeutic method is Fritz Perls, who believed that people's problems often stemmed from hiding important parts of their feelings from themselves. If some part of a person's personality, for example, is in conflict with what society says is acceptable, the person might hide that aspect behind a false "mask" of socially acceptable behavior. As happens in Rogers's theory when the real and ideal selves do not match, in Gestalt theory the person experiences unhappiness and maladjustment when the inner self does not match the mask (Perls, 1951, 1969).

💬 That sounds pretty much like the same thing, only with slightly different words. How is Gestalt therapy different from person-centered therapy?

The two therapy types are similar because they are both based in humanism. But whereas person-centered therapy is nondirective, allowing the client to talk out concerns and eventually come to insights with only minimal guidance from the therapist, Gestalt therapists are very directive, often confronting clients about the statements they have made. This means that a Gestalt therapist does more than simply reflect back clients' statements; instead, a Gestalt therapist actually leads clients through a number of planned experiences, with the goal of helping clients to become more aware of their own feelings and take responsibility for their own choices in life, both now and in the past. These experiences might include a dialogue that clients have with their own conflicting feelings in which clients actually argue both sides of those feelings. Clients may talk with an empty chair to reveal their true feelings toward the person represented by the chair or take on the role of a parent or other person with whom they have a conflict so that the clients can see things from the other person's point of view. The Gestalt therapist pays attention to body language as well as to the events going on in the client's life at the time of therapy. Unlike psychoanalysis, which focuses on the *hidden past*, Gestalt therapy focuses on the *denied past*. Gestalt therapists do not talk about the unconscious mind. They believe everything is conscious but that it is possible for some people to simply refuse to "own up" to having certain feelings or to deal with past issues. By looking at the body language, feelings both stated and unstated, and the events in the life of the client, the therapist gets a *gestalt*—a whole picture—of the client.

EVALUATION OF THE HUMANISTIC THERAPIES Humanistic therapies have been used to treat psychological disorders, help people make career choices, deal with workplace problems, and counsel married couples. Person-centered therapy in particular can be a very "hands-off" form of therapy because it is so nondirective: Most often, there's nothing that the therapist says that the client has not already said, so the therapist runs a lower risk of misinterpretation. However, omission or not reflecting some things back might be a source of error.

Unfortunately, humanistic therapies have several of the same drawbacks as Freudian psychoanalysis and other forms of modern psychodynamic therapy. There is little experimental research to support the basic ideas on which this type of therapy is founded, but humanists have always preferred to use case studies to build their theories. People must be intelligent, verbal, and able to express their thoughts, feelings, and experiences in a logical manner, which makes humanistic therapies a somewhat less practical choice for treating the more serious mental disorders such as schizophrenia.

Concept Map L.O. 13.2, 13.3

Insight Therapies

Interactive

- **Freud's psychoanalysis and related techniques**
  - Freud developed the technique of **psychoanalysis**, an insight therapy aimed at revealing unconscious conflicts, urges, and desires
  - **dream interpretation:** involved deciphering the hidden, latent content from the manifest content, the actual dream itself
  - **free association:** originally developed by Breuer, involved patients freely talking about whatever came to mind; believed to reveal hidden, unconscious concerns
  - **modern psychodynamic approach:** more directive than it was historically and typically focuses more on the ego or sense of self rather than the id, when looking at reasons behind behavior
  - **evaluation:** although techniques have been modified, still lacks scientific support for basic premises and requires client to be fairly intelligent and verbally expressive

- **interpersonal therapy (IPT)**
  - eclectic therapy with some theoretical roots in the psychodynamic approach but combines aspects from humanistic and cognitive–behavioral therapies

- **humanistic therapy** — focuses on the conscious, subjective experience of emotion and people's sense of self; promotes insight and emphasizes the importance of individual choice and the potential to change one's behavior
  - **person-centered therapy**
    - developed by Carl Rogers; focuses on match between real self and ideal self; maladjustment is result of not matching; unconditional positive regard is important for congruence between real and ideal selves
    - therapist uses a nondirective approach and four basic elements to develop the person–therapist relationship
      - reflection
      - unconditional positive regard
      - empathy
      - authenticity
  - **evaluation:** little scientific support for basic premises and requires client to be fairly intelligent and verbally expressive
  - **Gestalt therapy**
    - developed by Fritz Perls; focuses on match between actual and ideal self; focuses on the gestalt, or "whole picture"
    - therapist uses a very directive approach to lead the client through a number of planned experiences (e.g., self-dialogue, "empty chair" technique), with the goal of increasing self-awareness
    - although aspects of the individual's past are examined, the focus is on denied past, not hidden past; everything is conscious but possibly not in the "here and now"

- **motivational interviewing** — "client-centered with a twist"; has specific goals to reduce ambivalence about change and increase intrinsic motivation

Reset

Practice Quiz How much do you remember? ANSWERS ON PAGE AK-1.

Pick the best answer.

1. Although the term may apply to many therapies, transference is typically associated with _____ therapies.
   a. behavioral
   b. humanistic
   c. biomedical
   d. psychodynamic

2. Motivational interviewing is an alternative therapy to what therapeutic approach?
   a. psychodynamic therapy
   b. Gestalt therapy
   c. humanistic therapy
   d. group therapy

3. Dr. Ellington is directive in his approach with clients. He pays close attention to body language and often focuses on a client's denied past. What type of therapeutic approach is Dr. Ellington using?
   a. humanistic approach
   b. Gestalt approach
   c. group approach
   d. behavioral approach

4. Which of the following cases would a humanistic approach probably be least effective in treating?
   a. Leilani, a university professor who has feelings of inadequacy
   b. Kayla, a professional musician who feels worthless and suffers from depression
   c. Miranda, a corporate executive who suffers from marked delusions and active auditory hallucinations
   d. Felicia, a homemaker who suffers from the traumatic memories of her abusive childhood

Action Therapies: Behavior Therapies and Cognitive Therapies

While insight therapies strive to understand the motives behind one's behavior, action therapies are focused on changing the behavior itself. In behavior therapies, the goal is to change behavior through the use of learning techniques, while cognitive therapies strive to change maladaptive thoughts.

BEHAVIOR THERAPIES: LEARNING ONE'S WAY TO BETTER BEHAVIOR

13.4 **Explain how behavior therapists use classical and operant conditioning to treat disordered behavior, and evaluate the effectiveness of these techniques.**

💬 The last chapter talked about how behaviorists have a very different way of looking at abnormality—it's all learned. So do behaviorists do any kind of therapy?

That's right—the basic concept behind behaviorism is that all behavior, whether "normal" or "abnormal," is learned through the same processes of classical and operant conditioning. **Behavior therapies** aim to change behavior through the use of the same kinds of learning techniques that people (and animals) use to learn any new responses. The abnormal or undesirable behavior is not seen as a symptom of anything else but rather is the problem itself. Learning created the problem, and new learning can correct it (Onken et al., 1997; Skinner, 1974; Sloan & Mizes, 1999). The video *Behavior Therapies* provides an overview of these therapies.

"Freudian—What's the nature of the trouble, and when did it begin? Behavior Therapist—Let's drive it around and see what happens"
Sidney Harris/Sciencecartoonsplus.com

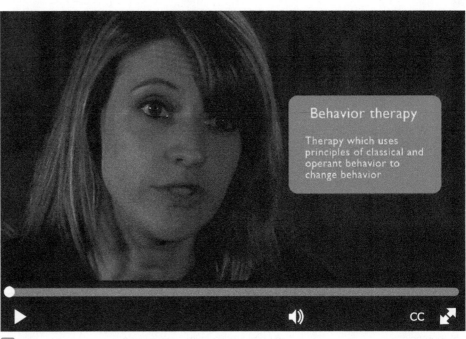

Behavior therapy

Therapy which uses principles of classical and operant behavior to change behavior

👁 **Watch** the **Video**, *Behavior Therapies.*

THERAPIES BASED ON CLASSICAL CONDITIONING Classical conditioning is the learning of involuntary responses by pairing a stimulus that normally causes a particular response with a new, neutral stimulus. After enough pairings, the new stimulus will also cause the response to occur. 🔗 to Learning Objectives 5.2 and 5.3. Through classical conditioning, old and undesirable automatic responses can be replaced by desirable ones. There are several techniques that have been developed using this type of learning to treat disorders such as phobias, anxiety disorders, and obsessive-compulsive disorder.

Using learning techniques to change undesirable behavior and increase desirable behavior has a long history (Hughes, 1993; Lovaas, 1987; Lovaas et al., 1966). Originally called **behavior modification**, the more recent adaptation of these techniques is **applied behavior analysis**. The newer term better highlights the need for a functional analysis of the behavior to be modified, which is then followed by the use of conditioning techniques to modify the behavior.

SYSTEMATIC DESENSITIZATION   **Systematic desensitization**, in which a therapist guides the client through a series of steps meant to reduce fear and anxiety, is normally used to treat phobic disorders and consists of a three-step process. First, the client must learn to relax through deep muscle relaxation training. Next, the client and the therapist construct a list, beginning with the object or situation that causes the least fear to the client, eventually working up to the object or situation that produces the greatest degree of fear. Finally, under the guidance of the therapist the client begins at the first item on the list that causes minimal fear and looks at it, thinks about it, or actually confronts it, all while remaining in a relaxed state. By pairing the old conditioned stimulus (the fear object) with a new relaxation response that is incompatible* with the emotions and physical arousal associated with fear, the person's fear is reduced and relieved. The person then proceeds to the next item on the list of fears (called a *hierarchy of fears*) until the phobia is gone (see **Table 13.1**).

AVERSION THERAPY   Another way to use classical conditioning is to reduce the frequency of undesirable behaviors, such as smoking or overeating, by teaching the client to pair an aversive (unpleasant) stimulus with the stimulus that results in the undesirable response, in a process called **aversion therapy**. For example, someone who wants to stop smoking might go to a therapist who uses a *rapid-smoking* technique, in which

Dr. Danae Hudson

Missouri State Psychology Department

Treating Phobias: Systematic Desensitization

Table 13.1 FEAR HIERARCHY

Study the table, then click "Check Your Understanding" button when you're ready.

Fear Level	Situation
100	Being bitten by a rabbit
90	Petting a rabbit on the head
80	Petting a rabbit on the back
70	Holding a rabbit
60	Touching a rabbit held by someone else
50	Seeing someone I trust hold a rabbit
40	Being in a room with a rabbit
30	Thinking about petting a rabbit
20	Looking at pictures of rabbits
10	Watching the movie "Hop"

Items are ranked by level of fear from most fearful, Fear = 100, to least fearful, Fear = 0.

Check Your Understanding

---

*incompatible: referring to two or more things that cannot exist together or at the same time.

the client is allowed to smoke but must take a puff on the cigarette every 5 or 6 seconds. As nicotine is a poison, such rapid smoking produces nausea and dizziness, both unpleasant effects.

  Could you use aversion therapy to help someone with a phobia?

Because phobias are already very unpleasant, aversive conditioning is not the most useful method of therapy. But although desensitization remains one of the more common therapies for phobias, it does not always bring quick results.

EXPOSURE THERAPIES Behavioral techniques that introduce the client to situations, under carefully controlled conditions, which are related to their anxieties or fears are called **exposure therapies**. Exposure can be accomplished through a variety of routes and is intended to promote new learning. It can be *in vivo* ("in life"), where the client is exposed to the actual anxiety-related stimulus; *imaginal*, where the client visualizes or imagines the stimulus; and even *virtual*, where virtual reality (VR) technology is used (Najavits, 2007). (For more on virtual reality in psychology, see the *Applying Psychology to Everyday Life* section at the end of this chapter.)

For example, if Chang-sun has social anxiety disorder (fairly rare for Korean males, at a lifetime prevalence of only about 0.1 percent) (Sadock et al., 2007), for in vivo exposure he might have to attend a social event; for imaginal exposure he might be asked to visualize himself attending a social event; and for virtual exposure, Chang-sun might experience a social event, such as attending a dinner party, through VR technology.

Exposure methods can introduce the feared stimulus gradually, or quite suddenly. A gradual, or *graded*, exposure involves the client and therapist developing a fear hierarchy as in systematic desensitization: Exposure begins at the least feared event and progresses through to the most feared, similar to desensitization. If the exposure is rapid and intense, it begins with the most feared event and is called **flooding** (Gelder, 1976; Olsen, 1975). Flooding is used under very controlled conditions and, like graded exposure, produces extinction of the conditioned fear response by preventing an escape or avoidance response (e.g., Chang-sun would not be allowed to leave the party). Exposure therapy is sometimes called "exposure and response prevention" for that reason.

Eye-movement desensitization and reprocessing, or EMDR, is an exposure-based therapy, sometimes used in the treatment of posttraumatic stress disorder (PTSD). As originally formulated, it involves very brief and repeated imaginal flooding, cognitive reprocessing and desensitization of the fearful event, and rapid eye movements or other bilateral stimulation (Shapiro, 2001, 2012). It is also used with phobias and other anxiety-related disorders, although PTSD remains a primary disorder for which this therapy is most commonly used. It is a somewhat controversial therapy as it evolved from the founder's personal observation, not psychological theory or modification of techniques for other disorders, and past research has suggested the eye movements serve little to no purpose (Monson et al., 2014).

THERAPIES BASED ON OPERANT CONDITIONING Operant conditioning techniques include reinforcement, extinction, shaping, and modeling to change the frequency of voluntary behavior. Ⓛ Ⓘ Ⓝ Ⓚ to Learning Objectives 5.8, 5.9, and 5.14. In the treatment of psychological disorders, the goal is to reduce the frequency of undesirable behavior and increase the frequency of desirable responses.

One of the advantages of using operant conditioning to treat a problem behavior is that results are usually quickly obtained rather than having to wait through years of more insight-oriented forms of therapy. When bringing the behavior under control (rather than finding out why it occurs in the first place) is the goal, operant and other behavioral techniques are very practical. There's an old joke about a man whose fear of things hiding under his bed is cured by a behavioral therapist in one night. The therapist simply cut the legs off the bed.

MODELING   **Modeling**, or learning through the observation and imitation of a model, is discussed in Chapter Five. The use of modeling as a therapy is based on the work of Albert Bandura, which states that a person with specific fears or someone who needs to develop social skills can learn to do so by watching someone else (the model) confront those fears or demonstrate the needed social skills (Bandura et al., 1969). In **participant modeling**, a model demonstrates the desired behavior in a step-by-step, gradual process. The client is encouraged by the therapist to imitate the model in the same gradual, step-by-step manner (Bandura, 1986; Bandura et al., 1974). The model can be a person actually present in the same room with the client or someone viewed on video. For example, a model might first approach a dog, then touch the dog, then pet the dog, and finally hug the dog. A child (or adult) who fears dogs would watch this process and then be encouraged to repeat the steps that the model demonstrated.

Behavioral therapists can give parents or others advice and demonstrations on how to carry out behavioral techniques. Once a person knows what to do, modeling is a fairly easy technique. Modeling has been effective in helping children with dental fears (Klorman et al., 1980; Ollendick & King, 1998), social withdrawal (O'Connor, 1972), obsessive-compulsive disorder (Roper et al., 1975), and phobias (Hintze, 2002).

USING REINFORCEMENT   *Reinforcement* is the strengthening of a response by following it with some pleasurable consequence (positive reinforcement) or the removal of an unpleasant stimulus (negative reinforcement). Reinforcement of both types can form the basis for treatment of people with behavioral problems.

In a **token economy**, objects known as *tokens* can be traded for food, candy, treats, or special privileges. Clients earn tokens for behaving correctly or accomplishing behavioral goals or may also lose tokens for inappropriate behavior. (L)(I)(N)(K) to Learning Objective 5.9. Token economies have also been used successfully in modifying the behavior of relatively disturbed persons in mental institutions, such as people with schizophrenia or depressed persons (Dickerson et al., 1994; Glynn, 1990; McMonagle & Sultana, 2002).

Another method based on the use of reinforcement involves making a **contingency contract** with the client (Salend, 1987). This contract is a formal agreement between therapist and client (or teacher and student, or parent and child) in which both parties' responsibilities and goals are clearly stated. Such contracts are useful in treating specific problems such as drug addiction (Talbott & Crosby, 2001), educational problems (Evans & Meyer, 1985; Evans et al., 1989), and eating disorders (Brubaker & Leddy, 2003). Because the stated tasks, penalties, and reinforcements are clearly stated and consistent, both parties are always aware of the consequences of acting or failing to act within the specifications of the contract, making this form of behavioral treatment fairly effective. Consistency is one of the most effective tools in using both rewards and punishments to mold behavior. (L)(I)(N)(K) to Learning Objective 5.7.

USING EXTINCTION   *Extinction* involves the removal of a reinforcer to reduce the frequency of a particular response. In modifying behavior, operant extinction often involves removing one's attention from the person when that person is engaging in an inappropriate or undesirable behavior. With children, this removal of attention may be a form of **time-out**, in which the child is removed from the situation that provides reinforcement (Kazdin, 1980). In adults, a simple refusal by the other persons in the room to acknowledge the behavior is often successful in reducing the frequency of that behavior.

EVALUATION OF BEHAVIOR THERAPIES   Behavior therapies may be more effective than other forms of therapy in treating specific behavioral problems, such as bed-wetting, overeating, drug addictions, and phobic reactions (Burgio, 1998; Wetherell, 2002).

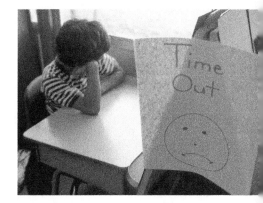

This boy is sitting in the "time-out" corner at his school. By removing the attention that he found rewarding, the teacher is attempting to extinguish the behavior that earned the boy a time-out. Do you see anything in this time-out corner that might make it less effective?

More serious psychological disorders, such as severe depression or schizophrenia, do not respond as well overall to behavioral treatments, although improvement of specific symptoms can be achieved (Glynn, 1990; McMonagle & Sultana, 2002). Bringing symptoms under control is an important step in allowing a person to function normally in the social world, and behavior therapies are a relatively quick and efficient way to eliminate or greatly reduce such symptoms. However, some behavioral paradigms are not simple to establish or continually implement, and steps have to be taken so adaptive behaviors can be generalized to other situations and maintained in the future (Prochaska & Norcross, 2009).

COGNITIVE THERAPIES: THINKING IS BELIEVING

13.5 **Summarize the goals and basic elements of cognitive therapies, and evaluate their effectiveness.**

Cognitive therapy (Beck, 1979; Freeman et al., 1989) was developed by Aaron T. Beck and is focused on helping people change their ways of thinking. Rather than focusing on the behavior itself, the cognitive therapist focuses on the distorted thinking and unrealistic beliefs that lead to maladaptive behavior (Hollon & Beck, 1994), especially those distortions relating to depression (Abela & D'Allesandro, 2002; McGinn, 2000). The goal is to help clients test, in a more objective, scientific way, the truth of their beliefs and assumptions, as well as their attributions concerning both their own behavior and the behavior of others in their lives. **(L I N K)** to Learning Objective 10.7. Then they can recognize thoughts that are distorted and negative and replace them with more positive, helpful thoughts. Because the focus is on changing thoughts rather than gaining deep insights into their causes, this kind of therapy is primarily an action therapy.

BECK'S COGNITIVE THERAPY

  What are these unrealistic beliefs?

Cognitive therapy focuses on the distortions of thinking. **(L I N K)** to Learning Objective 11.4. Here are some of the more common distortions in thought that can create negative feelings and unrealistic beliefs in people:

- **Arbitrary inference**: This refers to "jumping to conclusions" without any evidence. Arbitrary means to decide something based on nothing more than personal whims. Example: "Suzy canceled our lunch date—I'll bet she's seeing someone else!"

- **Selective thinking**: In selective thinking, the person focuses only on one aspect of a situation, leaving out other relevant facts that might make things seem less negative. Example: Peter's teacher praised his paper but made one comment about needing to check his punctuation. Peter assumes that his paper is lousy and that the teacher really didn't like it, ignoring the other praise and positive comments.

- **Overgeneralization**: Here a person draws a sweeping conclusion from one incident and then assumes that the conclusion applies to areas of life that have nothing to do with the original event. Example: "I got yelled at by my boss. My boyfriend is going to break up with me and kick me out of the apartment—I'll end up living in a van down by the river."

- **Magnification and minimization**: Here a person blows bad things out of proportion while not emphasizing good things. Example: A student who has received good grades on every other exam believes that the C she got on the last quiz means she's not going to succeed in college.

- **Personalization**: In personalization, an individual takes responsibility or blame for events that are not really connected to the individual. Example: When Sandy's husband comes home in a bad mood because of something that happened at work, she immediately assumes that he is angry with her.

A cognitive therapist tries to get clients to look at their beliefs and test them to see how accurate they really are. The first step is to identify an illogical or unrealistic belief, which the therapist and client do in their initial talks. Then the client is guided by the therapist through a process of asking questions about that belief, such as "When did this belief of mine begin?" or "What is the evidence for this belief?"

💬 Don't those questions sound like critical thinking, which was discussed in Chapter One?

COGNITIVE–BEHAVIORAL THERAPY Cognitive therapy really is critical thinking applied to one's own thoughts and beliefs. Just as cognitive psychology grew out of behaviorism, Ⓛ Ⓘ Ⓝ Ⓚ to Learning Objectives 1.3 and 1.4, therapies using cognitive methods have behavioral elements within them as well, leading to the term **cognitive–behavioral therapy (CBT)**.

Cognitive–behavioral therapy, or CBT, focuses on the present rather than the past (like behaviorism) but also assumes that people interact with the world with more than simple, automatic reactions to external stimuli. People observe the world and the people in the world around them, make assumptions and inferences* based on those observations or cognitions, and then decide how to respond (Rachman & Hodgson, 1980). As a form of cognitive therapy, CBT also assumes that disorders come from illogical, irrational cognitions and that changing the thinking patterns to more rational, logical ones will relieve the symptoms of the disorder, making it an action therapy. CBT has three basic elements: cognitions affect behavior, cognitions can be changed, and behavior change can result from cognitive change (Dobson & Block, 1988). Cognitive–behavioral therapists may also use any of the tools that behavioral therapists use to help clients alter their actions. The three basic goals of any cognitive–behavioral therapy follow.

1. Relieve the symptoms and help clients resolve the problems.
2. Help clients develop strategies that can be used to cope with future problems.
3. Help clients change the way they think from irrational, self-defeating thoughts to more rational, self-helping, positive thoughts.

ELLIS AND RATIONAL EMOTIVE BEHAVIOR THERAPY (REBT) Albert Ellis proposed a version of CBT called **rational emotive behavior therapy (REBT)**, in which clients are taught a way to challenge their own irrational beliefs with more rational, helpful statements (Ellis, 1997, 1998). Here are some examples of irrational beliefs:

• Everyone should love and approve of me (if they don't, I am awful and unlovable).

• When things do not go the way I wanted and planned, it is terrible and I am, of course, going to get very disturbed. I can't stand it!

 💬 But I've felt that way at times. Why are these statements so irrational?

Notice that these statements have one thing in common: It's either all or nothing. Can a person really expect the love and affection of every single person? Is it realistic to expect things to work as planned every time? Rational emotive behavioral therapy is about challenging these types of "my way or nothing" statements, helping people to realize that life can be good without being "perfect." In REBT,

---

*inferences: conclusions drawn from observations and facts.

therapists take a very directive role, challenging the client when the client makes statements like those listed earlier, assigning homework, using behavioral techniques to modify behavior, and arguing with clients about the rationality of their statements.

EVALUATION OF COGNITIVE AND COGNITIVE–BEHAVIORAL THERAPIES Cognitive and cognitive–behavioral therapies are less expensive than the typical insight therapy because they are comparatively short-term therapies. As in behavior therapy, clients do not have to dig too deep for the hidden sources of their problems. Instead, cognitive-based therapies get right to the problems themselves, helping clients deal with their symptoms more directly. In fact, one of the criticisms of these therapies as well as behavior therapies is that they treat the symptom, not the cause. However, it should be noted that in the cognitive viewpoint, the maladaptive thoughts are seen as the cause of the problems, not merely the symptoms. There is also an element of potential bias because of the therapist's opinions as to which thoughts are rational and which are not (Westen, 2005).

Nevertheless, cognitive and cognitive–behavioral therapies have considerable success in treating many types of disorders, including depression, stress disorders, eating disorders, anxiety disorders, personality disorders, and even—in addition to other forms of therapy—some symptoms of schizophrenia (Barlow et al., 2007; Beck, 2007; Craske & Barlow, 2014; Heimberg & Magee, 2014; Monson et al., 2014; Tarrier & Taylor, 2014; Young et al., 2014). As an offshoot of behaviorism, the learning principles that are the basis of cognitive–behavioral therapies are considered empirically* sound (Barlow et al., 2007; Masters et al., 1987). For a summary of the various types of psychotherapies discussed up to this point, see **Table 13.2**.

Table 13.2 CHARACTERISTICS OF PSYCHOTHERAPIES

Study the table, then click "Check Your Understanding" button when you're ready.

Type of Therapy (Key People)	Goal	Methods
Psychodynamic therapy (Freud)	Insight	Aims to reveal unconscious conflicts through dream interpretation, free association, resistance and transference
Humanistic therapy • Person-centered therapy (Rogers) • Gestalt therapy (Perls)	Insight	Nondirective therapy; client does most of the talking; key elements are authenticity, unconditional positive regard, and empathy. Directive therapy; therapist uses leading questions and role-playing to help client accept all parts of their feelings and experiences
Behavior therapy (Watson, Jones, Skinner, Bandura)	Action	Based on principles of classical and operant conditioning; aimed at changing behavior without concern for causes of behavior
Cognitive therapy (Beck) • CBT (various professionals) • REBT (Ellis)	Action	Aims to help clients overcome problems by learning to think more rationally and logically Clients are challenged in their irrational beliefs and helped to restructure their thinking

Check Your Understanding

---

*empirical: capable of being verified or disproved by observation or experiment.

Concept Map L.O. 13.4, 13.5

behavior therapies
action-based therapies operating on the premise that all behaviors, both normal and abnormal, are learned; applied behavior analysis involves functional analysis and learning techniques to increase desirable behaviors and decrease undesirable behaviors

techniques based on classical conditioning—pairing of stimuli

- systematic desensitization
- aversion therapy
- **exposure therapies:** expose individual to anxiety-provoking stimulus in real or imagined form, in a gradual or sudden (**flooding**) manner

techniques based on operant conditioning—reinforcement, extinction, shaping, and modeling

- **participant modeling**
- **token economies (reinforcement)**
- **contingency contracting (reinforcement)**
- **time-out (extinction)**

evaluation: more effective than others for specific behavioral problems (e.g., bed-wetting, overeating, drug addictions, phobic reactions)

Action Therapies

cognitive therapies
action-based therapies that focus on helping people change their ways of thinking; emphasis on identifying distorted and unrealistic beliefs that lead to maladaptive behavior and problem emotions and then replacing them with more-positive, helpful thoughts

Beck's cognitive therapy identifies several common distortions

- **arbitrary inference (jumping to conclusions)**
- **selective thinking**
- **overgeneralization**
- **magnification and minimization**
- **personalization**

cognitive–behavioral therapy (CBT) uses cognitive methods that have behavioral elements within them as well

rational emotive behavior therapy (REBT) was developed by Albert Ellis; teaches clients to challenge their own irrational beliefs with more rational, helpful statements

evaluation: typically shorter and less expensive than insight therapies; treating the symptom, not the cause, is both a feature and a criticism; especially effective for many disorders, including depression, anxiety disorders, and personality disorders

Reset

Practice Quiz   How much do you remember? ANSWERS ON PAGE AK-1.

Pick the best answer.

1. Behavior-based therapies are _____ based whereas psychodynamic and humanistic therapies are _____ based.
 a. insight; action
 b. action; insight
 c. rationale; medically
 d. medically; action

2. Dr. Kali works with clients to help them learn deep relaxation. He has them list their fears from least to most anxiety provoking. Dr. Kali then slowly exposes his clients to each of their fears and assists them in gaining control of their anxiety. His approach is best known as
 a. aversion therapy.
 b. fear therapy.
 c. flooding.
 d. systematic desensitization.

3. Dr. Williams uses exposure-based therapies to treat many of her patients. Client A is actually confronted with the situation that causes her anxiety while Client B is asked to think about and visualize the frightening situation. Client A's treatment method would be described as _____, whereas client B's treatment method is _____.
 a. virtual; in vivo
 b. imaginal; virtual
 c. in vivo; imaginal
 d. virtual; in vivo

4. Which of the following therapies has been successful in the establishment of desirable behaviors and modification of problem behaviors by allowing an individual to earn special privileges or treats, such as food and candy?
 a. token economies
 b. aversion therapy
 c. systematic desensitization
 d. flooding

5. Nicole's therapist tells her that she is applying arbitrary inference to her thinking, which ultimately is causing her to be depressed. Which of the following is an example of Nicole's arbitrary inference?
 a. Nicole maximizes the bad things she experiences while minimizing the good aspects of life.
 b. Nicole focuses strictly on a single negative event while ignoring less negative aspects.
 c. Nicole tends to jump to conclusions with little or no evidence to support her beliefs.
 d. Nicole tends to overgeneralize a single bad event and assume all things about her life are failing.

Group Therapies: Not Just for the Shy

Not everyone that receives psychological treatment does so individually with a therapist. There are conditions and situations where psychological professionals work with more than one client at a time, and circumstances when individuals benefit by seeing how others address concerns and challenges. People can work with other individuals in group therapy, family therapy, and in self-help groups.

TYPES OF GROUP THERAPIES

13.6 Compare and contrast different forms of group therapy.

An alternative to individual therapy, in which the client and the therapist have a private, one-on-one session, is **group therapy**, in which a group of clients with similar problems gather together to discuss their problems under the guidance of a single therapist (Yalom, 1995).

Group therapy can be accomplished in several ways. The therapist may use either an insight or cognitive–behavioral style, although person-centered, Gestalt, and behavior therapies seem to work better in group settings than psychodynamic and cognitive–behavioral therapies (Andrews, 1989).

In addition to the variations in the style of therapy, the group structure can also vary. There may be small groups formed of related persons or other groups of unrelated persons that meet without the benefit of a therapist. Their goal is to share their problems and provide social and emotional support for each other.

FAMILY COUNSELING   One form of group therapy is **family counseling** or **family therapy**, in which all of the members of a family who are experiencing some type of problem—marital problems, problems in child discipline, or sibling rivalry, for example—are seen by the therapist as a group. The therapist may also meet with one or more family members individually at times, but the real work in opening the lines of communication among family members is accomplished in the group setting (Frankel & Piercy, 1990; Pinsoff & Wynne, 1995). The family members may include grandparents, aunts and uncles, and in-laws as well as the core family. This is because family therapy focuses on the family as a whole unit or system of interacting "parts." No one person is seen as "the problem" because all members of the family system are part of the problem: They are experiencing it, rewarding it, or by their actions or inactions causing it to occur in the first place.

The goal in family therapy, then, is to discover the unhealthy ways in which family members interact and communicate with one another and change those ways to healthier, more productive means of interaction. Family therapists work not only with families but also with couples who are in a committed relationship, with the goal of improving communication, helping the couple to learn better ways of solving their problems and disagreements, and increasing feelings of intimacy and emotional closeness (Christensen et al., 1995; Heavey et al., 1993).

SELF-HELP GROUPS   Many people may feel that a therapist who has never had, for example, a drug problem would be unable to truly understand their situation; and they may also feel that someone who has experienced addiction and beaten it is more capable of providing real help. Therapists are also often in short supply, and they charge a fee for leading group-therapy sessions. These are reasons some people choose to meet with others who have problems similar to their own, with no therapist in charge. Called **self-help groups** or **support groups**, these groups are usually formed around

In group therapy, several people who share similar problems gather with a therapist to discuss their feelings and concerns. The presence of others who are going through the same kind of emotional difficulties can be comforting as well as provide the opportunity for insights into one's own problems by hearing about the problems of others.

a particular problem. Some examples of self-help groups are Alcoholics Anonymous, Overeaters Anonymous, and Narcotics Anonymous, all of which have groups meeting all over the country at almost any time of the day or night. There are countless smaller support groups for nearly every condition imaginable, including anxiety, phobias, having a parent with dementia, having difficult children, depression, and dealing with stress—to name just a few. The advantages of self-help groups are that they are free and provide the social and emotional support that a group session can provide (Bussa & Kaufman, 2000). Self-help groups do not have leaders but instead have people who volunteer monthly or weekly to lead individual meetings. So the person who is in charge of organizing the meetings is also a member of the group, with the same problem as all the other members.

EVALUATION OF GROUP THERAPY

13.7 Evaluate the advantages and disadvantages of group therapy.

There are many advantages to using group therapy over other forms of therapy. Group therapy can provide help to people who might be unable to afford individual psychotherapy. Because the therapist can see several clients at one time, this type of therapy is usually less expensive than individual therapy. It also offers social and emotional support from people who have problems that are similar or nearly identical to one's own. This advantage is an important one; studies have shown that breast cancer patients who were part of a group-therapy process had much higher survival and recovery rates than those who received only individual therapy or no psychotherapy (Fawzy et al., 1993; Spiegel et al., 1989).

Group therapy is not appropriate for all situations, and there can be disadvantages. Clients must share the therapist's time during the session. People who are not comfortable in social situations or who have trouble speaking in front of others may not find group therapy as helpful as those who are more verbal and social by nature. However, while an extremely shy person may initially have great difficulty speaking up in a group setting, cognitive–behavioral group therapy can be effective for social anxiety disorder (Heimberg & Becker, 2002; Turk et al., 2008).

Concept Map L.O. 13.6, 13.7

Interactive

Group Therapies

- alternative to individual therapy; group of clients meet together to discuss similar problems with a single therapist or pair of therapists
- may use a variety of styles, but person-centered, Gestalt, and behavioral seem to work best; may also take several different forms
  - family therapy
  - problem-based groups
- **self-help groups** may also be effective; do not have a therapist directly involved
- **evaluation:** advantages include lower cost, exposure to ways other people view and handle same type of problems, social and emotional support; disadvantages include greater exposure, less one-on-one contact with therapist, and some problems hard to treat in group setting

Reset

Practice Quiz How much do you remember? ANSWERS ON PAGE AK-1.

Pick the best answer.

1. Which of the following may be an effective option for some concerns if a therapist isn't available in your local community?
 a. family therapy
 b. group therapy
 c. self-help group
 d. psychodynamic therapy

2. Erika and William, along with their children Maximillian and Stella, are all seeing a psychologist to help work through some difficulties that have been occurring in their home. From time to time, their therapist opts to work with one of them instead of all four at once. This group of individuals is receiving _____ therapy.
 a. family therapy
 b. group therapy
 c. self-help group
 d. psychodynamic therapy

3. Catherine runs a weekly meeting of Alcoholics Anonymous, and several dozen members come every week. In addition, each week some new members show up to see what the group is all about, and some members who were there the previous week do not return. Which of the following is most likely true about Catherine?
 a. Catherine has probably never experienced a substance-related problem herself.
 b. Catherine is probably a licensed psychologist.
 c. Catherine is probably a licensed psychiatrist.
 d. Catherine has likely experienced some problems with alcohol in her past, and is probably not a professional therapist

4. Which of the following is *not* a noted advantage of group psychotherapy?
 a. Group therapy is less expensive than individual psychotherapy.
 b. Group therapy offers social support from people facing similar challenges.
 c. Group therapy is appropriate for anyone, so it is more "available" to those with personal struggles.
 d. Group therapy offers emotional support from people facing similar challenges.

Does Psychotherapy Really Work?

🗨 There sure are a lot of psychotherapies, but do any of them really work?

In the 1950s, Hans Eysenck did one of the earliest studies of the effectiveness of therapy. His conclusion was that the people receiving psychotherapy did not recover at any higher rate than those who had no psychotherapy and that the passage of time alone could account for all recovery.

STUDIES OF EFFECTIVENESS

13.8 **Summarize the research on the effectiveness of psychotherapy, including cybertherapy.**

Eysenck's classic survey created a major controversy within the world of clinical and counseling psychology. Other researchers began their own studies to find evidence that would contradict Eysenck's findings. One such effort reviewed studies that the researchers considered to be well controlled and concluded that the psychotherapies did not differ from one another in effectiveness (Luborsky et al., 1975). Of course, that can mean either that the psychotherapies were all equally effective or that they were all equally ineffective. (Reminder—many psychological professionals take an eclectic approach, using more than one psychotherapy technique.)

There are numerous problems with studying the effectiveness of psychotherapy. Controlled studies can be done using an experimental group of people who receive a particular psychotherapy and a control group of people who are put on a waiting list, but this is less than ideal. The control group is not getting the attention from the therapist, for one thing, and so there would be no placebo-effect expectations about getting better because of therapy (Shapiro & Shapiro, 1997). Also, not all therapies take the same

THE SEVEN DWARFS AFTER THERAPY

"William, Chris, Ben, Richard, Neal, Jason, Roger"

amount of time to be effective. For example, psychoanalysis, even in its short form, takes longer than a behavioral therapy. In a short-term study, behavioral therapy would obviously look more effective. Action therapies such as behavior therapy measure the success of the therapy differently than do insight therapies; in a behavioral therapy, the reduction of the undesired behavior is easy to objectively measure, but gaining insights and feelings of control, self-worth, self-esteem, and so on are not as easily evaluated (Shadish et al., 2002).

Studies that do not use empirical procedures but instead try to determine if the clients who have been helped by the therapy in general are plagued by problems such as experimenter bias (the therapist expects the therapy to work and is also the one assessing the progress of the client), the inaccuracies of self-report information, and the same placebo-effect expectations cited by Shapiro and Shapiro (Seligman, 1995; Wampold, 1997). Ⓛ Ⓘ Ⓝ Ⓚ to Learning Objective 1.10.

Nevertheless, more recent surveys have shown that people who have received psychotherapy believe that they have been helped more often than not (*Consumer Reports*, 1995; Kotkin et al., 1996). The *Consumer Reports* research was a survey of the magazine's readers in which those who had been or were currently clients in psychotherapy rated the effectiveness of the therapy they received. Here are the findings from a summary of this and several other similar surveys (Lambert & Ogles, 2004; Seligman, 1995; Thase, 1999):

- An estimated 75–90 percent of people feel that psychotherapy has helped them.
- The longer a person stays in therapy, the greater the improvement.

Other studies have found that some psychotherapies are more effective for certain types of disorders (Clarkin et al., 2007; Hollon et al., 2002) but that no one psychotherapy is the most effective or works for every type of problem.

Although psychotherapy usually occurs face-to-face with a therapist, a new type of therapy known as **cybertherapy** is offered via the Internet. This method of delivery may have the advantages of lower or no cost, availability of therapy opportunities for those unable to get to a therapist easily, access to support groups online, and relative anonymity. However, there is no guarantee that the cybertherapist has any credentials or training in psychotherapy. Although some cybertherapists use voice or video conferencing, some only use text-based chat. When there is no face-to-face or voice-to-voice contact, the therapist has no access to body language or vocal tones in trying to assess a client's emotional and psychological state.

What have studies shown regarding the effectiveness of cybertherapy? A group of researchers in Germany found that people who were treated as inpatients and then allowed to "meet" with a group therapist in an Internet chat room showed a significantly lower risk of negative changes in their mental status than a control group (Golkaramnay et al., 2007). The dropout rate from the Internet group was very low, and most patients "attended" the chat room sessions, which suggests that the ease of using a computer to connect to a group-therapy session may make it a viable option for some people needing continued therapy opportunities.

CHARACTERISTICS OF EFFECTIVE THERAPY

13.9 Describe some of the factors that influence the effectiveness of therapy.

💬 So how does a person with a problem know what kind of therapist to go to? How do you pick a good one?

As the *Psychology in the News* feature that follows describes, an increasing number of college students are seeking help for psychological disorders. It can sometimes be hard to know where to turn for professional help, and how to determine which type of therapy is a good fit for you. The video *Finding the Right Therapist* offers some advice.

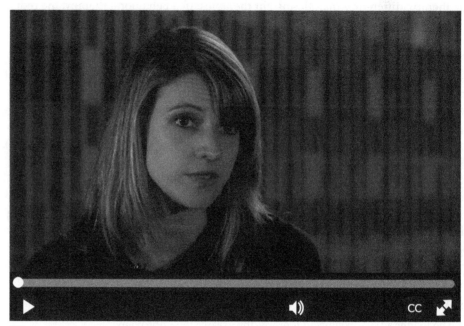

👁 **Watch** the **Video**, *Finding the Right Therapist.*

As discussed before, many psychological professionals today take an eclectic view of psychotherapy, using a combination of methods or switching methods to fit the particular client's needs or specific problems.

COMMON FACTORS APPROACH   The *common factors approach* in psychotherapy is a modern approach to eclecticism and focuses on those factors common to successful outcomes from different forms of therapy (Norcross, 2005). These factors are seen as the source of the success rather than specific differences among therapies. The most important common factor of a successful psychotherapy may be the relationship between the client and the therapist, known as the **therapeutic alliance**. This relationship should be caring, warm, and accepting, and be characterized by empathy, mutual respect, and understanding. Therapy should also offer clients a *protected setting* in which to release emotions and reveal private thoughts and concerns and should help clients understand why they feel the way they do and provide them with ways to feel better. Other common factors in therapy effectiveness are *opportunity for catharsis* (relieving pent-up emotions), *learning and practice of new behaviors*, and *positive experiences* for the client (Norcross, 2005).

EVIDENCE-BASED TREATMENT   An ongoing area of research in psychology is related to identifying those treatments and other aspects of treatment that work best for specific disorders. Some treatments may not only be ineffective for certain disorders, some treatments or alternative therapies may even prove to be dangerous or harmful. Especially in light of managed health care and tight budgets, clients benefit through *evidence-based practice*. Empirically supported or **evidence-based treatment** (EBT) refers to techniques or interventions that have produced desired outcomes, or therapeutic change in controlled studies (Barlow et al., 2013; Kazdin, 2008). Evidence-based practice includes systematic reviews of relevant and valid information that ranges from assessment to intervention (American Psychological Association, 2005; Hunsley & Mash, 2008; Kazdin, 2008; Nathan & Gorman, 2007). Some examples of evidence-based, or empirically supported, treatments are exposure therapies, cognitive–behavioral, and cognitive processing for PTSD (Ehlers et al., 2010; Najavits, 2007; Monson et al., 2014), cognitive–behavioral treatment for panic disorder with agoraphobia (Barlow et al., 2007; Craske & Barlow, 2014), cognitive–behavioral individual and group therapy for social anxiety disorder (Heimberg & Magee, 2014), cognitive therapy for depression (Young et al., 2014), antipsychotic drugs for schizophrenia (Sharif et al., 2007), and interpersonal psychotherapy for depression (Bleiberg & Markowitcz, 2014).

Psychology in the News
Mental Health on Campus

The college experience is supposed to be one of intellectual and social development, but it is also a time of strife and stress for many. From exams to living conditions (commuting, new roommates, living in a dorm), relationship issues (immediate family, significant others), and adjustment in general, college life can be quite stressful. The shootings and other campus crises over the past few years are just one indicator of the level of psychological dysfunction that can occur in extreme circumstances.

These circumstances can make preexisting conditions worse or prompt the development of new psychological disorders. According to the American College Counseling Association's *2009 National Survey of Counseling Center Directors*, of the 2.6 million students represented in the survey, approximately 270,000 sought counseling (Gallagher, 2009). Of those students receiving services in college counseling centers, 16 percent are referred for psychiatric evaluation and 25 percent are on psychiatric medication. The majority of counseling center directors believe there is an increase in the number of students coming to campus already on psychiatric medication, and there is a trend toward a greater number of students on campus recognized with severe psychological problems. Increases are being noted in medication management, crisis intervention, learning disabilities, self-injury (e.g., self-cutting), illicit drug use, alcohol abuse, eating disorders, and sexual assault concerns or problems related to earlier sexual abuse (Gallagher, 2009).

As revealed by the *2009–2010 Community College Counselors Survey*, these increases are especially troublesome given the added stress of the ongoing economic situation in the United States. Consequences of economic stressors include increases in enrollment, more signs of anxiety and depression in both students and college employees, and an increased need for mental health services (American College Counseling Association's Community College Task Force, 2010). The top four presenting problems were stress, depression, anxiety disorders, and academic problems.

So what can you do with this information? First, if you are not familiar with your college's counseling resources, learn more about what is offered. Even if you do not have a serious psychological disorder, counselors can assist you in identifying and developing effective coping strategies. Second, take care of yourself, get enough sleep, eat healthy foods (not just instant noodles or macaroni and cheese), exercise, and take time for yourself to relax. Finally, know that you are not alone if you do experience difficulties and that a variety of resources are likely available to help you along the path to your college degree.

Questions for Further Discussion

1. Do you know any of your fellow students who have used your college's counseling center? If so, what was their experience like?

2. What do you believe to be the greatest stressor in college life today?

CULTURAL, ETHNIC, AND GENDER CONCERNS IN PSYCHOTHERAPY Consider the following situation (adapted from Wedding, 2004).

> *K. is a 24-year-old Korean American. She lived with her parents, who were both born and reared in Korea before moving to the United States as adults. She came to a therapist because she was depressed and unhappy with her lack of independence. Her father was angry about her plans to marry a non-Korean. Her therapist immediately began assertiveness training and role-playing to prepare K. to deal with her father. The therapist was disappointed when K. failed to keep her second appointment.*

This example of an actual case demonstrates a problem that exists in the therapist–client relationship for many clients when the ethnicity or culture of the client is different from that of the therapist. This cultural difference makes it difficult for therapists to understand the exact nature of their clients' problems and for clients to benefit from therapies that do not match their needs (Matsumoto, 1994; Moffic, 2003; Wedding, 2004). The values of different cultures and ethnic groups are not universally the same. How, for example, could a well-educated, White female therapist from an upper-middle-class family understand the problems of a Hispanic adolescent boy from a poor family living in substandard housing if she did not acknowledge the differences between them? In this case, the gender, ethnicity, and economic background of the client and therapist are all vastly different.

In the case of K., for example, the therapist mistakenly assumed that the key to improving K.'s situation was to make her more assertive and independent from her family, particularly her father. This Western idea runs counter to Korean cultural values. Korean culture stresses interdependence, not independence. K.'s real problem may have been her feelings of guilt about her situation and her father's anger. She may have wanted help in dealing with her family situation and her feelings about that situation, not help in becoming more independent.

For therapy to be effective, the client must continue in treatment until a successful outcome is reached. K. never came back after the first session. One of the problems that can occur when the culture or ethnic backgrounds of the client and therapist are mismatched, as in K.'s case, is that the therapist may project his or her values onto the client, failing to achieve true empathy with the client's feelings or even to realize what the client's true feelings are, thus causing the client to drop out of therapy. Studies of such situations have found that members of minority racial or ethnic groups drop out of therapy at a significantly higher rate than the majority group clients (Brown et al., 2003; Cooper et al., 2003; Flaherty & Adams, 1998; Fortuna et al., 2010; Sue, 1977, 1992; Sue et al., 1994; Vail, 1976; Vernon & Roberts, 1982).

 Are differences in gender that important? For example, do women prefer female therapists, but men would rather talk to another man?

Research on gender and therapist–client relationships varies. When talking about White, middle-class clients, it seems that both men and women prefer a female therapist (Jones et al., 1987). But African American clients were more likely to drop out of therapy if the therapist was the *same* sex as the client (Vail, 1976); male Asian clients seemed to prefer a male therapist; and female Asian clients stayed in therapy equally long with either male or female therapists (Flaherty & Adams, 1998; Flaskerud, 1991).

Four barriers to effective psychotherapy exist when the culture or ethnic backgrounds of client and therapist are different (Sue & Sue, 2008):

1. **Culture-bound values.** Including individual centered versus other (or others) centered, verbal/emotional/behavioral expressiveness, communication patterns from client to counselor, nuclear family, and so forth (Sue & Sue, 2008). Differing

cultural values can cause therapists to fail at forming an empathetic relationship (Sattler, 1977; Wedding, 2004).

2. **Class-bound values.**   Adherence to time schedules, ambiguous approach to problems, looking for long-range goals (Sue & Sue, 2008). Clients from impoverished backgrounds may have values and experiences that the therapist cannot understand (Wedding, 2004).

3. **Language.**   Use of standard English, emphasis on verbal communication (Sue & Sue, 2008). Speaking different languages becomes a problem in understanding what both client and therapist are saying and in psychological testing (Betancourt & Jacobs, 2000; Lewis, 1996).

4. **Nonverbal communication.**   Body language, or nonverbal communication, can also differ between cultures and ethnicities. The physical distance between the client and therapist, the use of gestures, and eye contact, for example, can cause misunderstandings during the session and in interpretation of the client's moods and intentions (Galanti, 1997; Like et al., 1996). People in some cultures are content with long periods of silence whereas others are not, direct eye contact is desirable in some cultures and offensive in others, and even facial expressions of emotion vary from very expressive (as with many Hispanic people) to nonexpressive (as with many Asian people).

The American Psychiatric Association (2013) has included information for psychology professionals concerning cultural issues and culture syndromes. ⓛ ⓘ ⓝ ⓚ to Learning Objective 12.2. All therapists need to make an effort to become aware of cultural differences, syndromes, and possible gender issues. Sociopolitical issues should also be examined (Sue & Sue, 2008).

WRITING PROMPT

Which of the forms of psychotherapy discussed so far would probably work best for a client who has commitment issues in relationships? Why?

▶ | The response entered here will be saved to your notes and may be collected by your instructor if he/she requires it.

Submit

Concept Map **L.O. 13.8, 13.9**

Interactive

- effectiveness is not easy to study due to different theories, techniques, time frames for success, etc.; tendency of some therapists to be eclectic (using variety of techniques) is also a challenge
  - common factors approach: focuses on those factors common to successful outcomes from different forms of therapy
  - clients benefit through evidence-based practice, or empirically validated treatment—identification of treatments and other aspects of treatment that work best for specific disorders

- where effective, greater success is often tied to the relationship between the therapist and client (therapeutic alliance), a sense of safety, and longer time in therapy

- cultural, ethnic, and gender concerns should also be examined; these factors can affect not only the therapeutic alliance but also identification of actual problem(s) and treatment options

Does Psychotherapy Work?

Reset

Practice Quiz   How much do you remember?   ANSWERS ON PAGE AK-1.

Pick the best answer.

1. Dr. Cavendish is trying to establish what is known as a therapeutic alliance with her clients. What specifically should she do to accomplish this goal?
   a. She should work to better understand the disorder that she is treating.
   b. She should be more confrontational in her approach so as to make clients aware of their difficulties.
   c. She should be more empathetic and caring when working with her clients.
   d. She should openly consult with others on all cases to ensure quality therapeutic treatment.

2. Research shows that African American clients prefer a therapist _____ whereas Asian men prefer a _____ therapist.
   a. of the opposite sex; male
   b. of the same sex; female
   c. of the same culture; Hispanic
   d. who is female; White

3. What do studies show about the overall effectiveness of cybertherapy?
   a. It is a fad, and studies indicate that cybertherapy is relatively ineffective.
   b. Cybertherapy can be effective for people who otherwise might be unable to get to a therapist.
   c. Studies indicate that many clients who use chat rooms as part of their cybertherapy often stop showing up after one to two sessions.
   d. There currently are not enough studies to indicate whether cybertherapy is or is not effective.

4. _____ refers to techniques or interventions that have produced desired outcomes, or therapeutic change in controlled studies.
   a. Client-friendly
   b. Insurance-approved
   c. Clinically valid
   d. Evidence-based treatment

Biomedical Therapies

Just as a therapist trained in psychoanalysis is more likely to use that technique, a therapist whose perspective on personality and behavior is biological will most likely turn to medical techniques to manage disordered behavior. Even psychotherapists who are not primarily biological in orientation may combine psychotherapy with medical treatments that are supervised by a medical doctor working with the psychologist. As medical doctors, psychiatrists are almost inevitably biological in perspective and, thus, use **biomedical therapies** (directly affecting the biological functioning of the body and brain) in addition to any psychotherapy technique they may favor. The biomedical therapies fall into several approaches and may consist of drug therapy, shock therapy, surgical treatments, or noninvasive stimulation techniques.

PSYCHOPHARMACOLOGY

13.10 **Categorize and describe the various types of drugs used to treat psychological disorders.**

The use of drugs to control or relieve the symptoms of a psychological disorder is called **psychopharmacology**. Although these drugs are sometimes used alone, they are more often combined with some form of psychotherapy and are more effective as a result (Kearney & Silverman, 1998; Keller et al., 2000). There are four basic categories of drugs used to treat psychotic disorders, anxiety disorders, the manic phase of mood disorders, and depression.

ANTIPSYCHOTIC DRUGS   Drugs used to treat psychotic symptoms, such as hallucinations, delusions, and bizarre behavior, are called **antipsychotic drugs**. These drugs can be classified into two categories, the classical, or *typical antipsychotics*, and newer *atypical antipsychotics*. The first of the typical antipsychotics to be developed was *chlorpromazine*. The first-generation antipsychotics caused "neurolepsis," or psychomotor slowing and reduced emotionality, and thus were referred to as *neuroleptics*, due to the neurological side effects they produced (Julien et al., 2011; Preston et al., 2008; Stahl, 2013). **Table 13.3** lists several typical and atypical antipsychotic drugs and their side effects.

Table 13.3 TYPES OF DRUGS USED IN PSYCHOPHARMACOLOGY

Study the table, then click "Check Your Understanding" button when you're ready.

Classification	Treatment Areas	Side Effects	Examples
Antipsychotic: Typical antipsychotic	Positive (excessive) symptoms such as delusions or hallucinations	Motor problems, tardive dyskinesia	chlorpromazine, droperidol, haloperidol
Antipsychotic: Atypical antipsychotic	Positive and some negative symptoms of psychoses	Fewer than typical antipsychotic; clozapine may cause serious blood disorder	risperidone, clozapine, aripiprazole
Antianxiety: Minor Tranquilizers	Symptoms of anxiety and phobic reactions	Slight sedative effect; potential for physical dependence	alprazolam, lorazepam, diazepam
Antimanic	Manic behavior	Potential for toxic buildup	lithium, anticonvulsant drugs
Antidepressants: MAOIs	Depression	Weight gain, constipation, dry mouth, dizziness, headache, drowsiness, insomnia, some sexual arousal disorders	iproniazid, isocarboxazid, phenelzine sulfite, tranylcypromine
Antidepressants: Tricyclics	Depression	Skin rashes, blurred vision, lowered blood pressure, weight loss	imipramine, desipramine, amitriptyline, doxepin
Antidepressants: SSRIs	Depression	Nausea, nervousness, insomnia, diarrhea, rash, agitation, some sexual arousal problems	fluoxetine, sertraline, paroxetine

Check Your Understanding

Typical antipsychotic drugs work by blocking certain dopamine receptors in the brain, namely the D2 receptor, thereby reducing the effect of dopamine in synaptic transmission (Julien et al., 2011; Preston et al., 2008; Stahl, 2013). However, because they block more pathways in the dopamine system than are involved in psychosis, with prolonged use they tend to cause problems. Such problems include movement disorders similar to those in Parkinson's disease, sometimes called *extrapyramidal symptoms*, and others such as *tardive dyskinesia*. Tardive dyskinesia is a syndrome caused by long-term treatment and can even persist when typical antipsychotic medications are no longer being used. The syndrome is characterized by the person making facial and tongue movements such as repeatedly sticking their tongue out, grimacing, or constant chewing, or causing repetitive involuntary jerks or dance-like movements of the arms and legs (Julien et al., 2011; Preston et al., 2008; Stahl, 2013).

The atypical antipsychotics may also suppress dopamine but to a much greater degree in the one dopamine pathway that seems to cause psychotic problems. These drugs also block or partially block certain serotonin receptors, resulting in fewer negative side effects and occasionally some improvement in the negative symptoms of schizophrenia (Julien et al., 2011; Preston et al., 2008; Stahl, 2013). Despite their effectiveness, the atypical antipsychotics may also have unwanted side effects, such as weight gain, diabetes, blood lipid level changes, or changes in the electrical rhythms of the heart (Julien et al., 2011). One of these, clozapine, can cause a potentially fatal reduction in the white blood cells of the body's immune system in a very small percentage of people. For this reason, the blood of patients on clozapine is closely monitored, and it is not considered to be a first choice when selecting treatment options but used more often when other antipsychotic drugs are ineffective (Stahl, 2013).

Newer classes of atypical antipsychotics include *partial dopamine agonists* that affect the release of dopamine rather than blocking its receptors in the brain, and other agents that have agonistic or antagonistic properties for dopamine and serotonin (Stahl, 2013). (An *agonist* facilitates whereas an *antagonist* blocks or reduces effects.) Drugs are also being investigated that are linked to the actions of *glutamate*. Ⓛ Ⓘ Ⓝ Ⓚ to Learning Objective 2.3.

 💬 How long do people generally have to take these antipsychotic medications?

In some cases, a person might have a psychotic episode that lasts only a few months or a few years and may need drug treatment only for that time. But in most cases, especially in schizophrenia that starts in adolescence or young adulthood, medication must be taken for the rest of the person's life. Long-term use of antipsychotics, particularly the older typical drugs, has been associated with a decrease in cognitive functioning such as impaired memory and sedation, possibly due to the chemical actions of the drugs themselves. The hope for newer atypical antipsychotics is that they will not only produce fewer negative side effects but also have less impact on the cognitive processes of those persons taking these drugs (Julien et al., 2011; Stahl, 2013).

ANTIANXIETY DRUGS   The traditional **antianxiety drugs** are the minor tranquilizers or *benzodiazepines* such as Xanax, Ativan, and Valium. All of these drugs have a sedative effect and in the right dose can start to relieve symptoms of anxiety within 20 to 30 minutes of taking the drug by mouth (Preston et al., 2008). Although many side effects are possible, the main concern in using these drugs is their potential for addiction as well as abuse in the form of taking larger doses to "escape" (National Institute on Drug Abuse [NIDA]).

MOOD-STABILIZING DRUGS   For many years, the treatment of choice for bipolar disorder and episodes of mania has been *lithium*, a metallic chemical element that in its salt form (lithium carbonate) evens out both the highs and the lows of bipolar disorder. It is generally recommended that treatment with lithium continue at maintenance levels in people with recurring bipolar disorder. Lithium affects the way sodium ions in neuron and muscle cells are transported, although it is not clear exactly how this affects mood. Side effects typically disappear quickly, although the use of lithium has been associated with weight gain. Diet needs to be controlled when taking lithium because lowered levels of sodium in the diet can cause lithium to build up to toxic levels, as can any substance that removes water from the body such as the caffeine in sodas, tea, and coffee.

Anticonvulsant drugs, normally used to treat seizure disorders, have also been used to treat mania. Examples are carbamazepine, valproic acid (Depakote), and lamotrigine. These drugs can be as effective in controlling mood swings as lithium and can also be used in combination with lithium treatments (Bowden et al., 2000; Thase & Sachs, 2000). Some atypical antipsychotics work as mood stabilizers and may be used alone or in conjunction with anticonvulsant medications (Julien et al., 2011; Preston et al., 2008; Stahl, 2013).

ANTIDEPRESSANT DRUGS   As is so often the case in scientific discoveries, the first types of drugs used in the treatment of depression were originally developed to treat other disorders. Iproniazid, for example, was used to treat tuberculosis symptoms in the early 1950s and was found to have a positive effect on mood, becoming the first modern **antidepressant** (Trujillo & Chinn, 1996). This drug became the first of the *monoamine oxidase inhibitors* (MAOIs), a class of antidepressants that blocks the activity of an enzyme called monoamine oxidase. Monoamine oxidase is the brain's "cleanup worker" because its primary function is to break down the neurotransmitters norepinephrine, serotonin, and dopamine—the three neurotransmitters most involved in control of mood. Under normal circumstances, the excess neurotransmitters are broken down *after* they have done their "job" in mood control. In depression, these neurotransmitters need more time to do their job, and the MAOIs allow them that time by inhibiting the enzyme's action.

Some common MAOIs in use today are isocarboxazid (Marplan), phenelzine sulfate (Nardil), and tranylcypromine sulfate (Parnate). These drugs can produce some unwanted side effects, although in most cases the side effects decrease or disappear with continued treatment: weight gain, constipation, dry mouth, dizziness, headache, drowsiness or insomnia, and sexual arousal disorders are possible. People taking MAOIs in general should also be careful about eating certain smoked, fermented, or pickled foods, drinking certain beverages, or taking some other medications due to a risk of severe high blood pressure in combination with consumption of these items, although there are a couple of MAOIs that do not require any dietary restrictions (Stahl, 2013). And while these precautions are very important, certain drug–drug interactions may be more common and sometimes even lethal, so individuals taking MAOIs should work closely with their health-care professionals to monitor adverse drug interactions (Julien et al., 2011; Preston et al., 2008; Stahl, 2013).

The second category of antidepressant drug to be developed is called the *tricyclic antidepressants*. These drugs were discovered in the course of developing treatments for schizophrenia (Trujillo & Chinn, 1996). Tricyclics, so called because of their molecular structure consisting of three rings (cycles), increase the activity of serotonin and norepinephrine in the nervous system by inhibiting their reuptake into the synaptic vesicles of the neurons. (L)(I)(N)K to Learning Objective 2.3. Some common tricyclics are imipramine (Tofranil), desipramine (Norpramin, Pertofrane), amitriptyline (Elavil), and doxepin (Sinequan, Adapin). Side effects of these drugs, which may also decrease over the course of treatment, are very similar to those of the MAOIs but can also include skin rashes, blurred vision, lowered blood pressure, and weight gain (Julien et al., 2011; Preston et al., 2008; Stahl, 2013).

The effect of the MAOIs and the tricyclics on the action of the three critical neurotransmitters led researchers to try to develop drugs that would more specifically target the critical neural activity involved in depression with fewer negative side effects. This led to the development of the *selective serotonin reuptake inhibitors* (SSRIs), drugs that inhibit the reuptake process of only serotonin. This causes fewer side effects while still providing effective antidepressant action, making these drugs relatively safe when compared to the older antidepressants. But like the other two classes of antidepressants, the SSRIs may take from 2 to 6 weeks to produce effects. Some of the better-known SSRIs are fluoxetine (Prozac), sertraline (Zoloft), and paroxetine (Paxil). Other classes of antidepressants have been or are being investigated, including *serotonin-norepinephrine reuptake inhibitors* (SNRIs), *serotonin partial agonist/ reuptake inhibitors* (SPARIs), *norepinephrine-dopamine reuptake inhibitors* (NDRIs), *selective norepinephrine reuptake inhibitors* (NRIs), and *serotonin antagonist/reuptake inhibitors* (SARIs).

There is also research examining the potential use of subanesthetic doses of *ketamine* as an antidepressant due to its apparent ability to have immediate antidepressant effects and reduction of suicidal thoughts (Stahl, 2013). The effects are not permanent, but its effects can come on within a few hours and last for several days, and up to a week in some individuals (DiazGranados, Ibrahim, Brutsche, Newberg, et al., 2010; DiazGranados, Ibrahim, Brutsche, Ameli, et al., 2010; Zarate et al., 2012; Zarate et al., 2006).

Concerns have arisen that children and teenagers taking newer antidepressant medications may have an increased risk of suicide versus those not receiving treatment. Recent meta-analyses have provided conflicting information, with some data suggesting an increased risk for suicide while other data does not support an increased risk (Gibbons et al., 2012; Hetrick et al., 2012). Where there is an increased risk, it is possible depressive symptoms are being addressed while suicidal thoughts and behavior are not reduced. Regardless, caution is urged, especially in children and teens being treated with newer antidepressant medications.

At what age do you think children and/or teenagers should be able to decide if they will take medications to treat abnormal psychological functioning or behavior?

▶ | The response entered here will be saved to your notes and may be collected by your instructor if he/she requires it. |

Submit

Overall, many psychological professionals today believe that combining psychotherapy with medical therapies—particularly drug therapy—is a more effective approach to treating many disorders. Cognitive–behavioral therapy in combination with drug therapy has been shown to be particularly effective in treating depression (Dew et al., 2007; Frank et al., 2007; Rohde et al., 2008). Even individuals with such disorders as schizophrenia benefit from psychotherapy, with strategies ranging from family and community support-based programs to individual or group-based cognitive–behavioral therapy proving to be valuable conjunctive therapies to psychopharmacological treatment (Stahl, 2013). Across all forms of treatment options for mental health issues, it is important to identify strategies that work for the individual. Data from the World Health Organization World Mental Health surveys found that across the countries surveyed, 31.7 percent of individuals receiving treatment for mental health issues had dropped out of treatment in the previous 12 months, with ranges from 26.3 to 45.1 percent, varying by the country's economic status (Wells et al., 2013). Furthermore, drop out was most likely after only one or two visits to their treatment provider (Wells et al., 2013).

OTHER BIOMEDICAL TREATMENTS: ECT, PSYCHOSURGERY, AND EMERGING TECHNIQUES

13.11 **Explain how electroconvulsive therapy, psychosurgery, and other emerging biomedical techniques are used to treat psychological disorders today.**

As addressed at the beginning of the chapter, psychological disorders have been treated in a variety of ways, via a variety of medical means, and some treatments have been better options than others. Unfortunately, some methods were used indiscriminately, were ineffective, or caused more harm than good. That has changed and current alternative biomedical options are effective options when other strategies have not been successful, and are sometimes the best option.

ELECTROCONVULSIVE THERAPY

💬 How are electroconvulsive therapy and psychosurgery used to treat psychological disorders today?

Many people are—well—*shocked* to discover that **electroconvulsive therapy (ECT)** is still in use to treat cases of severe depression. ECT involves the delivery of an electric shock to either one side or both sides of a person's head, resulting in a seizure or convulsion of the body and the release of a flood of neurotransmitters in the brain (American Psychiatric Association [APA] Committee on Electroconvulsive Therapy, 2001). The result is an almost immediate improvement in mood, and ECT is used not only in severe cases of depression that have not responded to drug treatments or psychotherapy, or where the side effects of medication are not acceptable, but also in the treatment of several other severe disorders, such as schizophrenia and severe mania, that are not responding to alternate treatments (APA Committee on Electroconvulsive Therapy, 2001; Pompili et al., 2013).

In the 1930s, doctors actually were researching the possible uses of inducing seizures in treating schizophrenia, although the seizures were induced through means of a drug (camphor) in those early experiments. It was Italian researchers Cerletti and Bini who first used electricity to induce a seizure in a man with schizophrenia, who fully recovered after only 11 such treatments (Endler, 1988; Fink, 1984; Shorter, 1997). Soon doctors were using ECT on every kind of severe mental disorder. In those early days, no anesthesia was used because the shock was severe enough to result in a loss of consciousness (most of the time). Broken bones, bitten tongues, and fractured teeth were not untypical "side effects."

Today's ECT is far more controlled and humane. It is only used to treat severe disorders, and written and informed consent is required in most states. ECT has been found to be most useful for severe depression that has not responded to medications or psychotherapy and in cases where suicide is a real possibility or has already been attempted. ECT works more quickly than antidepressant medications, so it can play an important role in helping to prevent suicide attempts (APA Committee on Electroconvulsive Therapy, 2001). However, ECT should not be considered a "cure." It is a way to get a person suffering from severe depression into a state of mind that is more receptive to other forms of therapy or psychotherapy. Relapse is very possible in individuals receiving ECT, and maintenance or continuation therapies are an important treatment strategy to pursue (Nordenskjold et al., 2011; Petrides et al., 2011).

Electroconvulsive therapy consists of applying an electric shock to one or both sides of the head. The result is rapid improvement in mood. It has been shown to be most effective in treating severe depression that has not responded to medication or where medication side effects cannot be tolerated.

💬 What are some of the side effects? Wasn't there something from an earlier chapter about this therapy affecting memory?

ECT does have several negative side effects, some of which last longer than others. Memory is definitely affected, as ECT disrupts the consolidation process and prevents the formation of long-term memories. (L I N K) to Learning Objective 6.13. This causes both retrograde amnesia, the loss of memories for events that happen close to the time of the treatment, and anterograde amnesia, the rapid forgetting of new material (APA Committee on Electroconvulsive Therapy, 2001; Lisanby et al., 2000; Weiner, 2000). The retrograde effects can extend to several months before and a few weeks after treatment and the older memories may return with time, whereas the anterograde amnesia is more temporary, clearing up in a few weeks after treatment. Only a very few patients suffer more severe and long-lasting cognitive difficulties, and it is not easy to determine whether these difficulties originate with the treatment or the disorder the person exhibits (Smith, 2001). When ECT is used today, an effort is made to reduce as many side effects as possible. The modern patient is given muscle relaxants to reduce the effects of the convulsion as well as a very short-term anesthetic. Despite its efficacy, the utilization of ECT in general is not uniform. In the United States, racial differences in the use of ECT appear to be present, with Black Americans with depression less likely to pursue or receive ECT treatment as compared to White Americans, and the overall use of ECT in general appears to be declining (Case et al., 2013; Case et al., 2012).

PSYCHOSURGERY Just as surgery involves cutting into the body, **psychosurgery** involves cutting into the brain to remove or destroy brain tissue for the purpose of relieving symptoms of mental disorders. One of the earliest and best-known psychosurgical techniques is the **prefrontal lobotomy**, in which the connections of the prefrontal cortex to other areas of the brain are severed. The lobotomy was developed in 1935 by Portuguese neurologist Dr. Antonio Egas Moniz, who was awarded the Nobel Prize in medicine for his contribution to psychosurgery (Cosgrove & Rauch, 1995; Freeman & Watts, 1937). Walter Freeman and James W. Watts modified Moniz's technique and developed a procedure called the *transorbital lobotomy*, during which an instrument resembling an ice pick, called a leucotome, was inserted through the back of the eye socket and into the brain to sever the brain fibers. It was this technique that became widely used, and unfortunately sometimes overused, in the pursuit of relief for so many people suffering from mental illness.

💬 But I thought lobotomies left most people worse off than before—didn't it take away their emotions or something?

Although it is true that some of the early lobotomy patients did seem less agitated, anxious, and delusional, it is also true that some early patients did not survive the surgery (about 6 percent died, in fact) and others were left with negative changes in personality: apathy, lack of emotional response, intellectual dullness, and childishness, to name a few. Fortunately, the development of antipsychotic drugs, beginning with chlorpromazine, together with the results of long-term studies that highlighted serious side effects of lobotomies, led to the discontinuation of lobotomies as a psychosurgical technique (Cosgrove & Rauch, 1995; Swayze, 1995). Some famous recipients of the last decades of lobotomies (and the disorders for which the procedure was performed) were Rosemary Kennedy, sister of John F. Kennedy (mild intellectual disability), and Rose Williams, sister of playwright Tennessee Williams (schizophrenia).

💬 Are there any psychosurgical techniques in use today since the lobotomy is no longer used?

The woman on the left is Rosemary Kennedy, sister of President John F. Kennedy. The man on the right is her father, U.S. Ambassador to Great Britain Joseph Kennedy. About 6 years after this photograph was taken, Rosemary, who had mild intellectual disability and whose behavior had become difficult to control, was subjected to a transorbital lobotomy. The results were disastrous, and she remained institutionalized until her death on January 7, 2005.

The lobotomy is gone, but there is a different and more modern technique called **bilateral anterior cingulotomy**, in which magnetic resonance imaging, ⓛⓘⓝⓚ to Learning Objective 2.9, is used to guide an electrode to a specific area of the brain called the cingulate gyrus. This area connects the frontal lobes to the limbic system, which controls emotional reactions. By running a current through the electrode, a very small and specific area of brain cells can be destroyed. This process is called *lesioning*. ⓛⓘⓝⓚ to Learning Objective 2.8. Cingulotomies have been shown to be effective in about one-third to one-half of cases of major depression, bipolar disorder, and certain forms of obsessive-compulsive disorder that have not responded to any other therapy techniques (Dougherty et al., 2002; Kuhn et al., 2010; Spangler et al., 1996). Because this is deliberate brain damage and quite permanent, all other possible treatments must be exhausted before a bilateral cingulotomy will be performed and, unlike the early days of lobotomies, it can be performed only with the patient's full and informed consent (Rodgers, 1992; Spangler et al., 1996). In fact, because of the ethical, social, and legal implications of psychosurgery in general, today only a very small number of such surgeries are carried out in a few medical centers across the world (Cosgrove & Rauch, 1995).

EMERGING TECHNIQUES Some new noninvasive techniques for effecting changes in the brain were discussed in Chapter Two including repetitive transcranial magnetic stimulation (rTMS), where magnetic pulses are applied to the cortex, and transcranial direct current stimulation (tDCS), which uses scalp electrodes to pass very low amplitude direct currents to the brain. These new and exciting strategies are being evaluated as possible treatment options for a variety of psychological disorders or in assisting researchers to better understand the brain mechanisms underlying them, including PTSD, depression, stroke, spinal cord injuries, and ADHD, along with many others (Adeyemo et al., 2012; Benito et al., 2012; Boggio et al., 2009; Cristancho et al., 2013; Helfrich et al., 2012; Nitsche et al., 2009). Another technique highlighted in Chapter Two is deep brain stimulation (DBS), and it is being evaluated as a treatment modality for both depression and OCD (Harvard Mental Health Letter, 2010; Huff et al., 2010). Exciting research is also investigating the use of DBS for individuals with chronic anorexia nervosa who have not responded well to other treatments, with initial results suggesting some individuals have improved body mass index (BMI), mood, and anxiety symptoms after DBS treatment (Lipsman et al., 2013).

Repetitive transcranial magnetic stimulation (rTMS) uses a pulsating magnetic field to activate specific parts of the brain's surface. As seen above, by placing an electromagnet on the scalp, rTMS can be used to stimulate small areas of the cortex and is being evaluated as a way to control some psychological symptoms, such as those related to depression and PTSD.

Concept Map L.O. 13.10, 13.11

Interactive

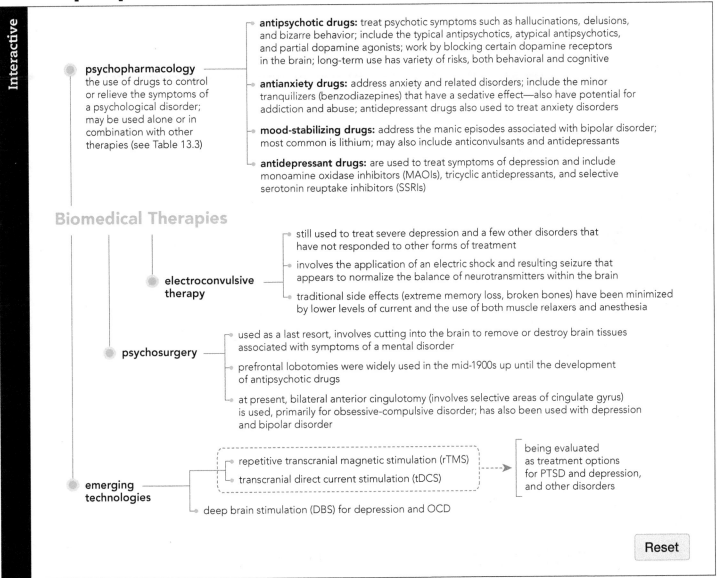

psychopharmacology the use of drugs to control or relieve the symptoms of a psychological disorder; may be used alone or in combination with other therapies (see Table 13.3)

antipsychotic drugs: treat psychotic symptoms such as hallucinations, delusions, and bizarre behavior; include the typical antipsychotics, atypical antipsychotics, and partial dopamine agonists; work by blocking certain dopamine receptors in the brain; long-term use has variety of risks, both behavioral and cognitive

antianxiety drugs: address anxiety and related disorders; include the minor tranquilizers (benzodiazepines) that have a sedative effect—also have potential for addiction and abuse; antidepressant drugs also used to treat anxiety disorders

mood-stabilizing drugs: address the manic episodes associated with bipolar disorder; most common is lithium; may also include anticonvulsants and antidepressants

antidepressant drugs: are used to treat symptoms of depression and include monoamine oxidase inhibitors (MAOIs), tricyclic antidepressants, and selective serotonin reuptake inhibitors (SSRIs)

Biomedical Therapies

electroconvulsive therapy
- still used to treat severe depression and a few other disorders that have not responded to other forms of treatment
- involves the application of an electric shock and resulting seizure that appears to normalize the balance of neurotransmitters within the brain
- traditional side effects (extreme memory loss, broken bones) have been minimized by lower levels of current and the use of both muscle relaxers and anesthesia

psychosurgery
- used as a last resort, involves cutting into the brain to remove or destroy brain tissues associated with symptoms of a mental disorder
- prefrontal lobotomies were widely used in the mid-1900s up until the development of antipsychotic drugs
- at present, bilateral anterior cingulotomy (involves selective areas of cingulate gyrus) is used, primarily for obsessive-compulsive disorder; has also been used with depression and bipolar disorder

emerging technologies
- repetitive transcranial magnetic stimulation (rTMS)
- transcranial direct current stimulation (tDCS)
  → being evaluated as treatment options for PTSD and depression, and other disorders
- deep brain stimulation (DBS) for depression and OCD

Reset

Practice Quiz   How much do you remember?   ANSWERS ON PAGE AK-1.

Pick the best answer.

1. Which of the following is the main concern in using the traditional antianxiety drugs to relieve symptoms of anxiety?
 a. The potential for these drugs to cause addiction and to be abused.
 b. The frequency with which these drugs have negative interactions with other medications.
 c. The fact that these drugs are all major tranquilizers that will render the user unproductive.
 d. The likelihood of extrapyramidal neurological side effects.

2. Today's electroconvulsive shock therapy is often quite useful in the treatment of
 a. dissociative identity disorder.
 b. schizophrenia.
 c. mild anxiety.
 d. severe depression.

3. A new therapeutic technique known as deep brain stimulation (DBS) is showing promise in the treatment of
 a. anorexia nervosa.
 b. phobias.
 c. personality disorders.
 d. mania.

4. Prolonged use of antipsychotic medication can lead to a side effect called _____, which is characterized by involuntary facial and tongue movements (e.g., grimacing, constant chewing), or repetitive involuntary jerks or dance-like movements of the arms and legs.
 a. agranulocytosis
 b. tardive dyskinesia
 c. synesthesia
 d. neuromalignant disorder

Virtual reality can be used to expose patients to phobic objects and situations. Dr. JoAnn Difede, director of the Anxiety and Traumatic Stress Studies Program at Weill Cornell Medical College, left, has adapted virtual reality therapy to treat World Trade Center survivors.

A soldier injured in the Lebanon war undergoes therapy with an Israeli-developed virtual reality "Computer Assisted Rehabilitation Environment" (CAREN) system.

Applying Psychology to Everyday Life
Virtual Reality Therapies

13.12 Identify some practical applications of virtual reality for treating psychological disorders.

Virtual reality is a software-generated three-dimensional simulated environment. Imagine yourself playing a video game, but instead of viewing your character on the screen in front of you, you are immersed in the visual and auditory world created by the game designers, seeing and hearing through the eyes and ears of your character. While playing a video game in this manner might be a lot of fun, there are some very practical uses of virtual reality (VR) for treating psychological disorders.

One of the main uses of VR as a therapy incorporates exposure therapy of some form. Exposure therapy involves preventing a person with a phobia, for example, from avoiding the presentation of the phobic object—preventing the typical avoidance response and eventually resulting in extinction of the conditioned fear. Using VR ensures that the person being treated cannot avoid exposure, as the sight and sound of the animal, open spaces, or whatever the phobia involves is always right in front of him or her. A study that was conducted at the University of Manchester, England, and led by Professor Nick Tarrier focused on helping people with phobias about driving cars by having them wear sophisticated goggles that allowed them to experience a virtual driving environment (University of Manchester, 2009). Special sensors on chest and fingers measured anxiety levels. The real advantage of VR psychotherapy was that there was no physical risk to the phobic driver, therapist, or other drivers on a real road.

Posttraumatic stress disorder (PTSD) is another mental health issue benefiting from the use of VR psychotherapy. Cases of this disorder are rising (and with the BP oil spill disaster discussed in Chapter Fourteen and other such stressors, psychologists expect the number of PTSD cases to continue to rise), and traditional treatments are not always effective. Although still a relatively new area of research, evidence suggests virtual reality psychotherapy may be as effective as traditional exposure methods in the treatment of PTSD and may especially be appealing for clients that do not want to pursue traditional exposure methods or techniques (Goncalves et al., 2012; Motraghi et al., 2013). Another advantage is the more vivid and realistic imagery possible with VR, especially for patients who are asked to "imagine" the scenarios that disturb them who may not be highly skilled in visualization. Think also of the portability of VR: There are currently handheld VR devices that eventually could be used to deliver therapy for PTSD, for example, to survivors of earthquakes, tsunamis, hurricanes, and other massive disasters around the world.

Questions for Further Discussion

1. What other disorders can you think of that might benefit from virtual reality psychotherapy?

2. Can you think of any disadvantages to this method of therapy?

Chapter Summary

Treatment of Psychological Disorders: Past to Present

13.1 Describe how psychological disorders were treated historically, and identify the two broad categories of therapy used today.

- Mentally ill people began to be confined to institutions called asylums in the mid-1500s. Treatments were harsh and often damaging.

- Philippe Pinel became famous for demanding that the mentally ill be treated with kindness, personally unlocking the chains of inmates at Bicêtre Asylum in Paris, France.

- Psychotherapy involves a person talking to a psychological professional about the person's problems.

- Psychotherapy for the purpose of gaining understanding into one's motives and actions is called insight therapy, whereas psychotherapy aimed at changing disordered behavior directly is called action therapy.

- Biomedical therapy uses a medical procedure to bring about changes in behavior.

Insight Therapies: Psychodynamic and Humanistic Approaches

13.2 Describe the basic elements of Freud's psychoanalysis, and explain how psychodynamic approaches differ today.

- Sigmund Freud developed a treatment called psychoanalysis that focused on releasing a person's hidden, repressed urges and concerns from the unconscious mind.
- Psychoanalysis uses interpretation of dreams, free association, positive and negative transference, and resistance to help patients reveal their unconscious concerns.
- Freud's original therapy technique is criticized for its lack of scientific research and his own personal biases that caused him to misinterpret much of what his patients revealed.
- Modern psychodynamic therapists have modified the technique so that it takes less time and is much more direct, and they do not focus on the id and sexuality as Freud did.

13.3 Identify the basic elements of the humanistic therapies known as person-centered therapy and Gestalt therapy, and evaluate each.

- Humanistic therapies focus on the conscious mind and subjective experiences to help clients gain insights.
- Person-centered therapy is very nondirective, allowing the client to talk through problems and concerns while the therapist provides a supportive background.
- The three basic elements of person-centered therapy are authenticity of the therapist in the client's perception, unconditional positive regard given to the client by the therapist, and the empathy of the therapist for the client.
- Gestalt therapy is more directive, helping clients to become aware of their feelings and to take responsibility for their choices in life.
- Gestalt therapists try to help clients deal with things in their past that they have denied and will use body language and other nonverbal cues to understand what clients are really saying.
- Humanistic therapies are also not based in experimental research and work best with intelligent, highly verbal persons.

Action Therapies: Behavior Therapies and Cognitive Therapies

13.4 Explain how behavior therapists use classical and operant conditioning to treat disordered behavior, and evaluate the effectiveness of these techniques.

- Behavior therapies are action therapies that do not look at thought processes but instead focus on changing the abnormal or disordered behavior itself through classical or operant conditioning.
- Classical conditioning techniques for changing behavior include systematic desensitization, aversion therapy, and exposure therapy.
- Therapies based on operant conditioning include modeling, reinforcement and the use of token economies, and extinction.

- Behavior therapies can be effective in treating specific problems, such as bed-wetting, drug addictions, and phobias, and can help improve some of the more troubling behavioral symptoms associated with more severe disorders.

13.5 Summarize the goals and basic elements of cognitive therapies, and evaluate their effectiveness.

- Cognitive therapy is oriented toward teaching clients how their thinking may be distorted and helping clients to see how inaccurate some of their beliefs may be.
- Some of the cognitive distortions in thinking include arbitrary inference, selective thinking, overgeneralization, magnification and minimization, and personalization.
- Cognitive–behavioral therapies are action therapies that work at changing a person's illogical or distorted thinking.
- The three goals of cognitive–behavioral therapies are to relieve the symptoms and solve the problems, to develop strategies for solving future problems, and to help change irrational, distorted thinking.
- Rational emotive behavior therapy is a directive therapy in which the therapist challenges clients' irrational beliefs, often arguing with clients and even assigning them homework.
- Although CBT has seemed successful in treating depression, stress disorders, and anxiety, it is criticized for focusing on the symptoms and not the causes of disordered behavior.

Group Therapies: Not Just for the Shy

13.6 Compare and contrast different forms of group therapy.

- Group therapy can be accomplished using many styles of psychotherapy and may involve treating people who are all part of the same family, as in family counseling.
- Group therapy can also be accomplished without the aid of a trained therapist in the form of self-help or support groups composed of other people who have the same or similar problems.
- Group therapy is most useful to persons who cannot afford individual therapy and who may obtain a great deal of social and emotional support from other group members.

13.7 Evaluate the advantages and disadvantages of group therapy.

- Group therapy has the advantages of low cost, exposure to other people with similar problems, social interaction with others, and social and emotional support from people with similar disorders or problems. It has also been demonstrated to be very effective for people with social anxiety.
- Disadvantages of group therapy can include the need to share the therapist's time with others in the group, the lack of a private setting in which to reveal concerns, and the inability of people with severe disorders to tolerate being in a group.

Does Psychotherapy Really Work?

13.8 Summarize the research on the effectiveness of psychotherapy, including cybertherapy.

- Eysenck's early survey of client improvement seemed to suggest that clients would improve as time passed, with or without therapy.

- Surveys of people who have received therapy suggest that psychotherapy is more effective than no treatment at all.
- Surveys reveal that 75 to 90 percent of people who receive therapy report improvement, the longer a person stays in therapy the better the improvement, and psychotherapy works as well alone as with drugs.
- Some types of psychotherapy are more effective for certain types of problems, and no one psychotherapy method is effective for all problems.
- Cybertherapy is therapy that is offered on the Internet. Cybertherapists may or may not be trained in psychotherapy, but cybertherapy offers the advantages of anonymity and therapy for people who cannot otherwise get to a therapist.

13.9 Describe some of the factors that influence the effectiveness of therapy.

- Effective therapy should be matched to the particular client and the particular problem, there should exist a therapeutic alliance between therapist and client, and a protected setting in which clients can release emotions and reveal private thoughts is essential.
- When the culture, ethnic group, or gender of the therapist and the client differs, misunderstandings and misinterpretations can occur due to differences in cultural/ethnic values, socioeconomic differences, gender roles, and beliefs.
- The four barriers to effective psychotherapy that exist when the backgrounds of client and therapist differ are language, cultural values, social class, and nonverbal communication.

Biomedical Therapies

13.10 Categorize and describe the various types of drugs used to treat psychological disorders.

- Biomedical therapies include the use of drugs, induced convulsions, and surgery to relieve or control the symptoms of mental disorders.
- Antipsychotic drugs are used to control delusions, hallucinations, and bizarre behavior and include the typical antipsychotics, atypical antipsychotics, and partial dopamine agonists.
- Antianxiety drugs are used to treat anxiety and related disorders and include the benzodiazepines and certain antidepressant drugs.

- Mood-stabilizing drugs are used to treat bipolar disorder and include lithium and certain anticonvulsant drugs.
- Antidepressant drugs are used in the treatment of depression and include monoamine oxidase inhibitors (MAOIs), tricyclic antidepressants, and selective serotonin reuptake inhibitors (SSRIs).

13.11 Explain how electroconvulsive therapy, psychosurgery, and other emerging biomedical techniques are used to treat psychological disorders today.

- Electroconvulsive therapy, or ECT, is used to treat severe depression, bipolar disorder, and schizophrenia and involves the use of a muscle relaxant, a short-term anesthetic, and induction of a seizure under controlled conditions.
- One of the earliest psychosurgeries was the prefrontal lobotomy, in which the front part of the frontal lobe was cut away from the back part of the brain, producing effects ranging from a disappearance of symptoms to a lack of emotional response and dulling of mental functions.
- Modern psychosurgery includes the bilateral cingulotomy, used to treat major depression, bipolar disorders, and certain forms of obsessive-compulsive disorder that have not responded to other forms of treatment.
- Emerging technologies for treatment of psychological disorders include repetitive transcranial magnetic stimulation (rTMS), transcranial direct current stimulation (tDCS), and deep brain stimulation (DBS).

Applying Psychology to Everyday Life: Virtual Realities

13.12 Identify some practical applications of virtual reality for treating psychological disorders.

- Virtual reality therapy is a computer-based simulation of environments that can be used to treat disorders such as phobias and PTSD with less risk than that of actual exposure to anxiety-provoking stimuli.
- Virtual reality therapy is particularly useful as a delivery system for exposure therapy.

Test Yourself   ANSWERS ON PAGE AK–2

Pick the best answer.

1. Clara is going to a therapist to gain a better understanding of why she has self-destructive relationships with all her friends. This type of therapy is known as _____ therapy.
   a. insight
   b. action
   c. behavioral
   d. biomedical

2. The hidden meaning of a dream is the _____ content, according to Freud.
   a. repressed
   b. latent
   c. manifest
   d. sexual

3. Through the technique of _____, a person-centered therapist conveys they are trying to comprehend the experience of the person with whom they are working.
   a. reflection
   b. unconditional positive regard
   c. empathy
   d. authenticity

4. What differentiates motivational interviewing from person-centered therapy?

   a. Motivational interviewing has specific goals of reducing ambivalence about change and increasing intrinsic motivation to bring changes about whereas traditional person-centered therapy does not.

   b. Motivational interviewing focuses on unconscious motives whereas traditional person-centered therapy focuses on the self.

   c. Motivational interviewing allows the client to talk about anything they wish whereas traditional person-centered therapy is more direct.

   d. Motivational interviewing is a behavioral therapeutic technique whereas person-centered therapy is a biomedical therapy.

5. Which of the following clients would probably get the least benefit from a humanistic therapy?

   a. Colin, who is bright but confused about self-image

   b. Cole, who is very talkative and open in discussing feelings

   c. Colleen, who enjoys exploring the inner workings of the mind

   d. Cody, who has a hard time putting thoughts and feelings into words in a logical manner

6. To overcome her fear of balloons, because of the loud sound they might suddenly make should they pop, Bella must sit in a room filled with balloons while the therapist continuously pops each one. After a while, Bella realizes that her fear is unjustified and even begins to pop balloons herself. This technique is known as

   a. systematic desensitization.   **c.** flooding.

   b. aversion therapy.   **d.** extinction.

7. Megan's daughter Kayla was afraid of dogs. Megan took Kayla to a therapist to help her overcome her fear but was surprised when the therapist brought a dog into the room. At first Kayla was asked to watch from across the room as the therapist showed her how to approach and pet the dog and not grab its tail. Eventually, Kayla was asked to come over and mimic the behavior she had observed. After just a few sessions, Kayla was no longer fearful of dogs. What technique did the therapist use with Kayla?

   a. virtual exposure   **c.** flooding

   b. aversion therapy   **d.** participant modeling

8. Maria sat down with her daughter, Zoe, and together wrote out a list of things that Zoe was expected to do each day and the rewards she would get if she accomplished them, as well as the penalties she would face if she did not do them. This is most like which technique?

   a. token economy   **c.** extinction

   b. time-out   **d.** contingency contracting

9. For both children and adults, and for many undesirable behaviors, the use of _____ or some form of "time-out" can be quite effective.

   a. arbitrary inference   **c.** positive reinforcement

   b. extinction   **d.** negative reinforcement

10. Stephan gets a text message from his girlfriend saying that she will have to work overtime tonight. Stephan immediately assumes his girlfriend is seeing someone else at work. Beck would say that Stephan has engaged in what type of distorted thinking?

   a. arbitrary inference   **c.** overgeneralization

   b. selective thinking   **d.** personalization

11. Devin's wife comes home angry from her job, and he immediately assumes that he has done something wrong. Such irrational thinking is an example of

   a. overgeneralization.   **c.** arbitrary inference.

   b. personalization.   **d.** selective thinking.

12. Latanya tends to blow negative events out of proportion to their importance (magnification) while ignoring relevant positive events (minimization). What therapeutic technique may work best to help Latanya?

   a. group therapy

   b. virtual therapy

   c. bilateral anterior cingulotomy

   d. rational emotive behavior therapy (REBT)

13. Which therapy style requires the therapist to actively challenge a client's irrational beliefs?

   a. person-centered

   b. frontal lobotomy

   c. rational emotive behavior therapy (REBT)

   d. cognitive restructuring

14. Family therapy is a form of group therapy in which

   a. non-professionals lead a selected group of family members with similar concerns.

   b. the entire family participates as no one person is seen as the problem.

   c. family members meet to single out the individual who is causing problems in the family dynamic.

   d. psychology professionals treat their own family members.

15. If Dr. Phelps uses an eclectic approach to her work as a therapist, what specifically is she doing?

   a. Dr. Phelps tends to rely on the unconscious as the source for all therapeutic treatments.

   b. Dr. Phelps tends to rely on a behavioral approach in the treatment of her clients.

   c. Dr. Phelps uses only the newest and most innovative approaches to treating her clients.

   d. Dr. Phelps uses one, or a combination, of any number of therapeutic treatments depending on the situation.

16. With regard to treatment of psychological disorders, many psychological professionals believe medications work best in combination with

   a. electroconvulsive therapy.   **c.** psychosurgery.

   b. psychotherapy.   **d.** deep brain stimulation.

17. Typical antipsychotic drugs work by blocking what neurotransmitter?

   a. norepinephrine   **c.** dopamine

   b. serotonin   **d.** epinephrine

18. Bradley has been on an antipsychotic drug for many years to control his schizophrenia. He has developed repetitive, involuntary jerks and movements of the face, lips, legs, and body. These side effects make up a syndrome known as

   a. the "Thorazine shuffle."   **c.** tardive dyskinesia.

   b. neurolepsis.   **d.** psychotic syndrome.

19. As part of the medical treatment trial she is participating in for severe and suicidal depression, Kierra was given subanesthetic doses of _____, which is being investigated due to its seemingly immediate, although short-term, effects

   a. ketamine   **c.** valproic acid

   b. lithium   **d.** paroxetine

20. In bilateral anterior cingulotomy,

   a. the front of the brain is cut away from the back.

   b. a thin wire electrode is used to destroy a small area of brain tissue.

   c. an electric shock is used to stimulate certain areas of the brain.

   d. a drug is injected into the brain to destroy a large area of brain tissue.

Appendix A
Statistics in Psychology

Why study statistics?

Psychology is a science, and scientists must have ways of describing, summarizing, and analyzing the numerical data gathered through systematic observation and experimentation. Statistics allow researchers to do all of these things in a meaningful, logical fashion.

Learning Objectives

A.1 Define statistics, and explain why they are important to psychologists and psychology majors.

A.2 Describe the types of tables and graphs that represent patterns in data.

A.3 Identify the three measures of central tendency and explain how they are impacted by the shape of the distribution.

A.4 Identify the types of statistics used to examine variations in data.

A.5 Describe how inferential statistics can be used to determine if differences in sets of data are large enough to be due to something other than chance variation.

A.6 Explain how statistics are used to predict one score from another.

What Are Statistics?

A.1 Define statistics, and explain why they are important to psychologists and psychology majors.

Many students in psychology wonder why the field uses such seemingly complicated mathematics. The answer is easy. Psychologists base their field on research findings. Data are collected and they have to be analyzed. *Statistics* is the field that gives us the tools to do that.

Psychologists have to be able to do two things with the data they collect. The first is to summarize the information from a study or experiment. The second is to make judgments and decisions about the data. We are interested if groups differ from each other. We are also interested in how one group of variables is related to another.

Statistics is the branch of mathematics that is concerned with the collection and interpretation of data from samples (Agresti & Finlay, 1997; Aron et al., 2005). A sample is a group of people selected, usually randomly, from a larger population of people. If you asked what the average height of teenage males was, and you calculated the average from just your high school, that average would be a statistic.

Statistical analysis is a way of trying to account for the error that exists in almost any body of data. Psychology is only one of many fields that use the following types of statistics.

In this appendix we will take a look at describing data—seeing if groups differ from each other and seeing if two variables are related to each other. Those are the basic ideas of psychological statistics. The more advanced techniques are just bigger and better versions of these ideas. Many psychology students sometimes panic at the thought of taking statistics. However, it is crucial to the field and not really that hard if you put your mind to it and don't freeze yourself up. Why is it so important? Even if you are not the kind of psychologist who uses statistics on a daily basis, all psychologists have to be able to read and understand the research others are doing, and understanding what the statistical analyses of that research is really saying is crucial. Here's a practical hint: Students with good research and statistical skills are much more employable and make more money than those who don't try to master research skills. It's nice to care about people, but you need all the skills you can get in today's world. Statistics and research design is one really profitable set of skills.

Practice Quiz   How much do you remember?   ANSWERS AVAILABLE IN ANSWER KEY.

Pick the best answer.

1. _____ is the branch of mathematics that is concerned with the collection and interpretation of data from samples.
   a. Statistics
   b. Psychometrics
   c. Probabilities
   d. Coefficients

2. What is the primary advantage of using statistical analysis in a research study?
   a. It allows you to confirm the hypotheses that were set forth when you started the research.
   b. It allows you to attempt to account for any of the error that exists in virtually any body of data.
   c. It allows you to demonstrate that you, as the researcher, are competent to examine and interpret the results of your research.
   d. It allows you to get your research proposal approved by an institutional review board and, later, allows your research to be published.

3. Which of the following is the underlying question of any psychological research statistics?
   a. Is behavior determined by "nature" or "nurture?"
   b. Do people want to be "good" or "bad" in their general behaviors?
   c. Is there a singular commonality that underlies all behaviors?
   d. Are groups different from each other and are two variables related to each other?

Descriptive Statistics

Descriptive statistics are a way of organizing numbers and summarizing them so that they can be understood. There are two main types of descriptive statistics:

- **Measures of Central Tendency.** Measures of central tendency are used to summarize the data and give you one score that seems typical of your sample.

- **Measures of Variability.** Measures of variability are used to indicate how spread out the data are. Are they tightly packed or are they widely dispersed?

The actual descriptive statistics are best understood after we explain the concept of a frequency distribution.

One way psychologists get started in a research project is to look at their data, but just looking at a list of numbers wouldn't do much good, so we make a graph or chart. Then we can look for patterns.

FREQUENCY DISTRIBUTIONS

A.2 Describe the types of tables and graphs that represent patterns in data.

A **frequency distribution** is a table or graph that shows how often different numbers, or scores, appear in a particular set of scores. For example, let's say that you have a sample of 30 people, the size of some psychology classes. You ask them how many glasses of water they drink each day. You could represent the answers as shown in **Table A.1**. Just by looking at this table, it is clear that typical people drink between 4 and 8 glasses of water a day.

Tables can be useful, especially when dealing with small sets of data. Sometimes a more visual presentation gives a better "picture" of the patterns in a data set, and that is when researchers use graphs to plot the data from a frequency distribution. One common graph is a **histogram**, or a bar graph. **Figure A.1** shows how the same data from Table A.1 would look in a bar graph.

Another type of graph used in frequency distributions is the **polygon**, a line graph. **Figure A.2** shows the same data in a polygon graph.

THE NORMAL CURVE Frequency polygons allow researchers to see the shape of a set of data easily. For example, the number of people drinking glasses of water in Figure A.2 is easily seen to be centered about 6 glasses (central tendency) but drops off below 4 glasses and above 8 glasses a day (variability). Our frequency polygon has a high point and the frequency decreases on both sides.

A common frequency distribution of this type is called the **normal curve**. It has a very specific shape and is sometimes called the *bell curve*. Look at **Figure A.3** on the next page. This curve is almost a perfect normal curve, and many things in life are not that perfect. The normal curve is used as a model for many things that are measured, such as intelligence, height, or weight, but even those measures only come close to a perfect distribution (provided large numbers of people are measured). One of the reasons that the normal curve is so useful is that it has very specific relationships to measures of central tendency and a measurement of variability, known as the standard deviation.

OTHER DISTRIBUTION TYPES: SKEWED AND BIMODAL Distributions aren't always normal in shape. Some distributions are described as *skewed*. This occurs when the distribution is not even on both sides of a central score with the highest frequency (like in our example).

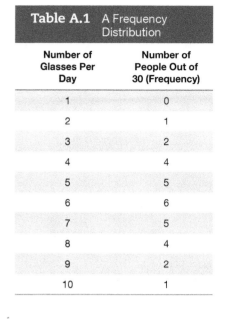

Table A.1	A Frequency Distribution
Number of Glasses Per Day	**Number of People Out of 30 (Frequency)**
1	0
2	1
3	2
4	4
5	5
6	6
7	5
8	4
9	2
10	1

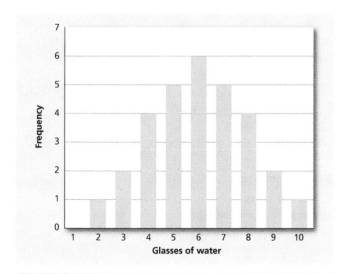

Figure A.1 A Histogram

Histograms, or bar graphs, provide a visual way to look at data from frequency distributions. In this graph, for example, the height of the bars indicates that most people drink between 4 and 8 glasses of water (represented by the five highest bars in the middle of the graph).

Figure A.2 A Polygon

A polygon is a line graph that can represent the data in a frequency distribution in much the same way as a bar graph but allows the shape of the data set to be easily viewed.

Figure A.3   The Normal Curve

The normal curve, also known as the bell curve because of its unique shape, is often the way in which certain characteristics such as intelligence or weight are represented in the population. The highest point on the curve typically represents the average score in any distribution.

Instead, the scores are concentrated toward one side of the distribution. For example, what if a study of people's water-drinking habits in a different class revealed that most people drank around 7 to 8 glasses of water daily, with no one drinking more than 8? The frequency polygon shown in **Figure A.4** reflects this very different distribution.

In this case, scores are piled up in the high end with most people drinking 7 or 8 glasses of water a day. The graphs in **Figure A.5** show a **skewed distribution**. Skewed distributions are called positively or negatively skewed, depending on where the scores are concentrated. A concentration in the high end would be called **negatively skewed**. A concentration in the low end would be called **positively skewed**. The direction of the extended tail determines whether it is positively (tail to right) or negatively (tail to left) skewed. Here's an example. What do you think about the distribution of heights of hobbits (the little guys from *The Lord of the Rings*) and NBA basketball players (who are usually tall)? Might not these frequency distributions of height in Figure A.5 be appropriate?

Some frequency polygons show two high points rather than just one (see **Figure A.6**) and are called **bimodal distributions**. In this example, we have a distribution of scores from a 10-point pop quiz and we see that one group of students seemed to do well and one group didn't. Bimodal distributions usually indicate that you have two separate groups being graphed in one polygon. What would the distribution of height for men and women look like?

MEASURES OF CENTRAL TENDENCY

A.3 **Identify the three measures of central tendency and explain how they are impacted by the shape of the distribution.**

A frequency distribution is a good way to look at a set of numbers, but there's still a lot to look at—isn't there some way to sum it all up? One way to sum up numerical data is to find out what a "typical" score might be, or some central number around which all the others seem to fall. This kind of summation is called a **measure of central tendency**, or the number that best represents the central part of a frequency distribution. There are three different measures of central tendency: the mean, the median, and the mode.

MEAN The most commonly used measure of central tendency is the **mean**, the arithmetic average of a distribution of numbers. That simply indicates that you add up all the numbers in a particular set and then divide them by how many numbers there are. This is usually the way teachers get the grade point average for a particular student, for example. If Rochelle's grades on the tests she has taken so far are 86, 92, 87, and 90, then the teacher would add 86 + 92 + 87 + 90 = 355, and then divide 355 by 4 (the number of scores) to get the mean, or grade point average, of 88.75. Here is the formula for the mean:

$$\text{Mean} = \Sigma X/N$$

What does this mean?

- Σ is a symbol called sigma. It is a Greek letter and it is also called the summation sign.

- X represents a score. Rochelle's grades are represented by X.

- ΣX means add up or sum all the X scores or
$\Sigma X = 86 + 92 + 37 + 90 = 355$.

- N means the number of scores. In this case, there are four grades.
We then divide the sum of the scores (ΣX) by N to get the mean or

$$\text{Mean} = \Sigma X/N = \frac{355}{4} = 88.75$$

Figure A.4   A Frequency Polygon

Skewed distributions are those in which the most frequent scores occur at one end or the other of the distribution, as represented by this frequency polygon in which most people are seen to drink at least 7 to 8 glasses of water each day.

The mean is a good way to find a central tendency if the set of scores clusters around the mean with no extremely different scores that are either far higher or far lower than the mean.

MEDIAN

💬 I remember that sometimes my teacher would "curve" the grades for a test, and it was always bad when just one person did really well and everyone else did lousy—is that what you mean about extremely different scores?

Yes, the mean doesn't work as well when there are extreme scores, as you would have if only two students out of an entire class had a perfect score of 100 and everyone else scored in the 70s or lower. If you want a truer measure of central tendency in such a case, you need one that isn't affected by extreme scores. The **median** is just such a measure. A median is the score that falls in the middle of an *ordered* distribution of scores. Half of the scores will fall above the median, and half of the scores will fall below it. If the distribution contains an odd number of scores, it's just the middle number, but if the number of scores is even, it's the average of the two middle scores. The median is also the 50th percentile. Look at **Table A.2** for an example of the median.

The mean IQ of this group would be 114.6, but the median would be 101 (the average between Evan with 102 and Fethia with 100, the average of the two middle numbers). This may not look like much of a difference, but it's really a change of about 13.6 IQ points—a big difference. Also, think about measures of income in a particular area. If most people earn around $35,000 per year in a particular area but there are just a few extremely wealthy people in the same area who earn $1,000,000 a year, a mean of all the annual incomes would no doubt make the area look like it was doing much better than it really is economically. The median would be a more accurate measure of the central tendency of such data.

MODE The **mode** is another measure of central tendency, in which the most frequent score is taken as the central measure. In the numbers given in Table A.2, the mode would be 100 because that number appears more times in the distribution than any other. Three people have that score. This is the simplest measure of central tendency and is also more useful than the mean in some cases, especially when there are two sets of frequently appearing scores. For example, suppose a teacher notices that on the last exam the scores fall into two groups, with about 15 students making a 95 and another 14 students making a 67. The mean *and* the median would probably give a number somewhere between those two scores—such as 80. That number tells the teacher a lot less about the distribution of scores than the mode would because, in this case, the distribution is **bimodal**—there are two very different yet very frequent scores. (Refer back to Figure A.6 for another example.)

MEASURES OF CENTRAL TENDENCY AND THE SHAPE OF THE DISTRIBUTION When the distribution is normal or close to it, the mean, median, and mode are the same or very similar. There is no problem. When the distribution is not normal, then the situation requires a little more explanation.

SKEWED DISTRIBUTIONS If the distribution is skewed, then the mean is pulled in the direction of the tail of the distribution. The mode is still the highest point and the median

Figure A.5 Skewed Distribution

These frequency polygons show how distributions can be skewed in two different directions. The graph on the left represents the frequency of heights among hobbits (the little people from the fantasy *The Lord of the Rings*) and is positively skewed because the long "tail" goes to the right, or positive direction. The graph on the right shows the frequency of heights among NBA basketball players and is negatively skewed—the tail points to the left.

Figure A.6 A Bimodal Distribution

When a distribution is bimodal, it means that there are two high points instead of just one. For example, in the pop-quiz scores represented on this graph there are two "most frequent" scores—6 and 8. This most likely represents two groups of students, with one group being less successful than the other.

Table A.2	Intelligence Test Scores For 10 People								
Name	Allison	Ben	Carol	Denise	Evan	Fethia	George	Hal	Inga	Jay
IQ	160	150	139	102	102	100	100	100	98	95

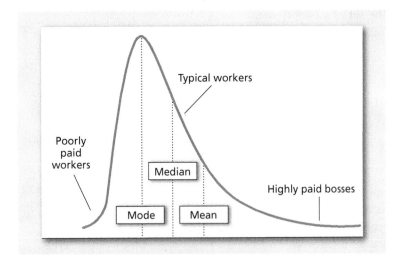

Figure A.7 Positively Skewed Distribution

In a skewed distribution, the high scores on one end will cause the mean to be pulled toward the tail of the distribution, making it a poor measure of central tendency for this kind of distribution. For example, in this graph many workers make very little money (represented by the mode) while only a few workers make a lot of money (the tail). The mean in this case would be much higher than the mode because of those few high scores distorting the average. In this case, the median is a much better measure of central tendency because it tends to be unaffected by extremely high or extremely low scores such as those in this distribution.

is between the two. Let's look at an example. In **Figure A.7** we have a distribution of salaries at a company. A few people make a low wage, most make a mid-level wage, and the bosses make a lot of money. This gives us a positively skewed distribution with the measures of central tendency placed as in the figure. As mentioned earlier, with such a distribution, the median would be the best measure of central tendency to report. If the distribution were negatively skewed (tail to the left), the order of the measures of central tendency would be reversed.

BIMODAL DISTRIBUTIONS If you have a bimodal distribution, then none of the measures of central tendency will do you much good. You need to discover why you appear to have two groups in your one distribution.

MEASURES OF VARIABILITY

A.4 Identify the types of statistics used to examine variations in data.

Descriptive statistics can also determine how much the scores in a distribution differ, or vary, from the central tendency of the data. These **measures of variability** are used to discover how "spread out" the scores are from each other. The more the scores cluster around the central scores, the smaller the measure of variability will be, and the more widely the scores differ from the central scores, the larger this measurement will be.

There are two ways that variability is measured. The simpler method is by calculating the **range** of the set of scores, or the difference between the highest score and the lowest score in the set of scores. The range is somewhat limited as a measure of variability when there are extreme scores in the distribution. For example, if you look at Table A.2, the range of those IQ scores would be 160–95, or 65. But if you just look at the numbers, you can see that there really isn't that much variation except for the three highest scores of 139, 150, and 160.

The other measure of variability that is commonly used is the one that is related to the normal curve, the **standard deviation**. This measurement is simply the square root of the average squared difference, or deviation, of the scores from the mean of the distribution. The mathematical formula for finding the standard deviation looks complicated, but it is really nothing more than taking each individual score, subtracting the mean from it, squaring that number (because some numbers will be negative and squaring them gets rid of the negative value), and adding up all of those squares. Then this total is divided by the number of scores and the square root of that number is the standard deviation. In the IQ example, it would go like this:

$$\text{Standard Deviation Formula } SD = \sqrt{[\Sigma(X - M)^2/N]}$$

The mean (M) of the 10 IQ scores is 114.6. To calculate the standard deviation we

1. Subtract each score from the mean to get a deviation score $\rightarrow (X - M)$
2. We square each deviation score $\rightarrow (X - M)^2$
3. We add them up. Remember that's what the sigma (Σ) indicates $\rightarrow \Sigma(X - M)^2$
4. We divide the sum of the squared deviation by N (the number of scores) $\rightarrow \Sigma(X - M)^2/N$
5. We take the square root ($\sqrt{\ }$) of the sum for our final step. $\sqrt{[\Sigma(X - M)^2/N]}$

The process is laid out in **Table A.3**.

The standard deviation is equal to 23.5. What that tells you is that this particular group of data deviates, or varies, from the central tendencies quite a bit—there are some very different scores in the data set, or in this particular instance, three noticeably different scores.

Table A.3   Finding the Standard Deviation

Score	Deviation from the Mean ($X \pm M$)	Squared Deviation
160.00	45.40	2,061.16
	(ex. 160 − 114.60 = 45.40)	($45.40^2 = 2,061.16$)
150.00	35.40	1,253.16
139.00	24.40	595.36
102.00	−12.60	158.76
102.00	−12.60	158.76
100.00	−14.60	213.16
100.00	−14.60	213.16
100.00	−14.60	213.16
98.00	−16.60	275.56
95.00	−19.60	384.16
Sum of Scores (ΣX) = 1,146.00 $\overline{\text{Mean} = (\Sigma X)/N}$ = 1,146/10 = 114.60	$\Sigma(X - M) = 0.00$	$\Sigma(X - M)^2 = 5,526.40$ $\overline{\text{Standard Deviation}}$ $= \sqrt{[\Sigma(X - M)^2/N]}$ $= \sqrt{5,526.40/10} = 23.5$

This procedure may look very complicated. Let us assure you that computers and inexpensive calculators can figure out the standard deviation simply by entering the numbers and pressing a button. No one does a standard deviation by hand anymore.

How does the standard deviation relate to the normal curve? Let's look at the classic distribution of IQ scores. It has a mean of 100 and a standard deviation of 15 as set up by the test designers. It is a bell curve. With a true normal curve, researchers know exactly what percent of the population lies under the curve between each standard deviation from the mean. For example, notice that in the percentages in **Figure A.8**, one standard deviation above the mean has 34.13 percent of the population represented by the graph under that section. These are the scores between the IQs of 100 and 115. One standard deviation below the mean (−1) has exactly the same percent, 34.13, under that section—the scores between 85 to 100. This means that 68.26 percent of the population falls within one standard deviation from the mean, or one average "spread" from the center of the distribution. For example, "giftedness" is normally defined as having an IQ score that is two standard deviations *above* the mean. On the Wechsler Intelligence Scales, this means having an IQ of 130 or greater because the Wechsler's standard deviation is 15. But if the test a person took to determine giftedness was the Stanford-Binet Fourth Edition (the previous version of the

Standard Deviations	−4	−3	−2	−1	0	1	2	3	4
Wechsler IQ	40	55	70	85	100	115	130	145	160
Stanford-Binet 4 IQ	36	52	68	84	100	116	132	148	164
Cumulative %	0.003	0.135	2.275	15.856	50.00	84.134	97.725	99.865	99.997

Figure A.8   IQ Normal Curve

Scores on intelligence tests are typically represented by the normal curve. The dotted vertical lines each represent one standard deviation from the mean, which is always set at 100. For example, an IQ of 116 on the Stanford-Binet Fourth Edition (Stanford-Binet 4) represents one standard deviation above the mean, and the area under the curve indicates that 34.13 percent of the population falls between 100 and 116 on that test. The Stanford-Binet Fifth Edition was published in 2003 and it now has a mean of 100 and a standard deviation of 15 for composite scores.

test), the IQ score must have been 132 or greater because the standard deviation of that test was 16, not 15. The current version, the Stanford-Binet Fifth Edition, was published in 2003 and it now has a mean of 100 and a standard deviation of 15 for composite scores.

Although the "tails" of this normal curve seem to touch the bottom of the graph, in theory they go on indefinitely, never touching the base of the graph. In reality, though, any statistical measurement that forms a normal curve will have 99.72 percent of the population it measures falling within three standard deviations either above or below the mean. Because this relationship between the standard deviation and the normal curve does not change, it is always possible to compare different test scores or sets of data that come close to a normal curve distribution. This is done by computing a **z score**, which indicates how many standard deviations you are away from the mean. It is calculated by subtracting the mean from your score and dividing by the standard deviation. For example, if you had an IQ of 115, your z score would be 1.0. If you had an IQ of 70, your z score would be −2.0 So on any exam, if you had a positive z score you did relatively well. A negative z score means you didn't do as well. The formula for a z score is:

$$Z = (X - M)/SD$$

Practice Quiz How much do you remember? ANSWERS AVAILABLE IN ANSWER KEY.

Pick the best answer.

1. Dr. Kopelowoski has just given an examination to his Introduction to Psychology class. Because this is a class of over 500 students, it would be difficult for him to assess the results looking at each score one at a time. If he wants to know how many students earned an A, a B, and so on, which of the following might be the best for him to program his computer to provide?

   a. A measure of central tendency
   b. A mean
   c. A frequency distribution
   d. A correlation coefficient

2. Because of its very specific shape, a "normal" distribution is also often described as a _____ curve.

   a. bell
   b. positively skewed
   c. negatively skewed
   d. multimodal

3. Aaron has just received his grade on the third exam of his chemistry class. He earned a 90 on this test. He is happy because his grades have been steadily increasing since the start of the term. On the first exam he earned an 80, and on the second exam he earned an 86. Which of the following represents the approximate mean of the three exam scores?

   a. 80
   b. 85
   c. 88
   d. 255

4. Which of the following would be most useful if you want to know how many standard deviations from the mean a single score in a data set falls?

   a. A *t*-score
   b. A *z*-score
   c. A deviation coefficient
   d. A variance determination

Inferential Statistics

Descriptive methods of statistics are useful for organizing and summarizing numbers or scores. But what method is useful when it comes to comparing sets of numbers or scores to see if there are differences between them that are great enough to be caused by something other than chance variation?

LOOKING AT DIFFERENCES: STATISTICAL SIGNIFICANCE

A.5 **Describe how inferential statistics can be used to determine if differences in sets of data are large enough to be due to something other than chance variation.**

Inferential statistics consist of statistical techniques that allow researchers to determine the difference between results of a study that are meaningful and those that are merely due to chance variations. Inferential statistics also allow researchers to draw conclusions, or make *inferences*, about the results of research and about whether those results are only true for the specific group of animals or people involved in the study or whether the results can be applied to, or *generalized* to, the larger population from which the study participants were selected.

For example, in the Cheryan (Cheryan et al., 2009) study of the difference in male and female students' attitudes toward computer science when exposed to environments that were either stereotypically masculine or non-stereotypical, there were a lot of variables that simply could not be controlled completely, even with random assignment of participants to the two conditions. Ⓛ Ⓘ Ⓝ Ⓚ to Learning Objective 1.9. For example, there was no guarantee that random assignment would account for the interfering effects of female participants who might have really liked the science fiction toys, posters, and pizza they saw in one of the test conditions. Maybe any difference found between the males and females was due to pure luck or chance and not to the variables under study.

In any analysis that compares two or more sets of data, there's always the possibility of error in the data that comes from either within the group (all participants in one group, for example, will not be exactly like each other) or differences between groups (the experimental group and the control group are formed with different people, so there are differences between the two groups that have nothing to do with the manipulations of the experimenter). When researchers want to know if the differences they find in the data that come from studies like the Cheryan experiment are large enough to be caused by the experimental manipulation and *not* just by the chance differences that exist within and between groups, they have to use a kind of statistical technique that can take those chance variations into account. These kinds of statistical analysis use inferential statistics.

Inferential statistical analysis also allows researchers to determine how much confidence they should have in the results of a particular experiment. As you might remember, results from other kinds of studies that look for relationships—observations, surveys, and case studies—are often analyzed with descriptive statistics, especially correlations. But experiments look for *causes* of relationships, and researchers want to have some evidence that the results of their experiments really mean what they think they mean.

There are many different kinds of inferential statistical methods. The method that is used depends on the design of the experiment, such as the number of independent and dependent variables or the number of experimental groups. All inferential statistics have one thing in common—they look for differences in group measurements that are **statistically significant**. Statistical significance is a way to test differences to see how likely those differences are to be real and not just caused by the random variations in behavior that exist in everything animals and people do.

For example, in a classic study investigating the effects of intrinsic versus extrinsic motivation on children's creativity, Dr. Teresa Amabile's 1982 study showed that the collages of the children who were promised prizes (an extrinsic reward) were judged to be less creative than those of the children who created collages just for fun. Ⓛ Ⓘ Ⓝ Ⓚ to Learning Objective 9.1. But was that difference between the creativity scores of the two groups a real difference, or was it merely due to chance variations in the children's artistic creations? Dr. Amabile used an inferential test on her results that told her that the difference was too big to be just chance variations, which means her results were *significant*—they were most likely to be real differences. How likely? Tests of significance give researchers the probability that the results of their experiment were caused by chance and not by their experimental manipulation. For example, in one test called a *t*-test, the scores of the children's artwork would have been placed into a formula that would result in a single number (t) that evaluates the probability that the difference between the two group means is due to pure chance or luck. That number would be compared to a value that exists in a table of possible t values, which tells researchers the probability that the result is due to chance or luck. If the number obtained by the calculation is bigger than the value in the table, there will be a probability associated with that number in the table. The probability, symbolized by the letter p, will tell researchers the probability that the difference was due to chance. In Dr. Amabile's case, the probability was $p < .05$ which means the probability that the results were due to chance alone was less than 5 out of 100. Another way of stating the same result is that Dr. Amabile could be 95 percent certain that her results were real and not due to chance. Dr. Amabile would, thus, report that the study found a **significant difference**, which means a difference thought not to be due to chance.

There are several statistical techniques to test if groups are different from each other. Here are some common ones you might encounter if you read journal articles.

- ***t*-test**—determines if two means are different from each other.
- ***F*-test or analysis of variance**—determines if three or more means are different from each other. Can also evaluate more than one independent variable at a time.
- **chi-square**—compares frequencies of proportions between groups to see if they are different. For example, the proportion of women hired at a company is too low and might indicate discrimination. *Chi* is pronounced like the beginning of the word *kite*. Don't say "chee." It will be ugly.

If you do take a statistics course, you will find out that most analyses are done by computers and you don't have to manually go through the long formulas.

We've already talked about the correlation coefficient. Let's see how psychologists can predict one variable from another by using it. Ⓛ Ⓘ Ⓝ Ⓚ to Learning Objective 1.8.

THE CORRELATION COEFFICIENT

A.6 Explain how statistics are used to predict one score from another.

A *correlation* is a measure of the relationship between two or more variables. For example, if you wanted to know if scores on the SAT are related to grade point average, you could get SAT scores and GPAs from a group of people and enter those numbers into a mathematical formula, which will produce a number called the **correlation coefficient**. The correlation coefficient represents the direction of the relationship and its strength. Chapter One discusses correlation in more detail and also emphasizes that correlation does not allow the assumption that one variable causes the other.

💬 Is the formula for the correlation coefficient really complicated?

Actually, the definitional formula for finding a correlation coefficient is not very complicated. Here it is:

$$r = \frac{\Sigma Z_x Z_y}{n}$$

The *r* is the correlation coefficient, the number representing the strength and direction of the relationship between the two variables. Z_x and Z_y are the z scores for each score. If you remember, the z score tells you how many standard deviations a score is away from the mean. You would calculate the Z_x and Z_y for each subject, multiply, and add them up. Then divide by the number of subjects. There is a very complicated-looking formula based on the raw scores.

$$r = \frac{\Sigma XY - \dfrac{\Sigma X \, \Sigma Y}{N}}{\sqrt{\left(\Sigma X^2 - \dfrac{(\Sigma X)^2}{N}\right)\left(\Sigma Y^2 - \dfrac{(\Sigma Y)^2}{N}\right)}}$$

Don't worry. You can do all this work on inexpensive calculators or on computers using common statistical programs or spreadsheets. Let's take the following example of two sets of scores, one on a test of drawing ability with scores from 1 (poor) to 5 (excellent) and the other on a test of writing ability using the same scale (see **Table A.4**).

If we plugged our data set into our calculator or spreadsheet, we would find that r (the correlation coefficient) equals 0.86. That would indicate a fairly strong correlation. If you continue studies in statistics, you will find out how to see if the correlation coefficient we calculated is statistically significant or, if you recall, not due to just dumb luck when we picked our subjects. In our case, the r is very significant and would happen by chance only 1 in 100 times!

Remember that the correlation coefficient has values that range between $+1.0$ and -1.0. The closer the r is to these values, the stronger the relationship. A positive r means a positive relationship, whereas a negative r means a negative relationship. Ⓛⓘⓝⓚ to Learning Objective 1.8; see Figure 1.3.

Our example had us trying to see if two scores were related. It is also possible to see if three or more scores are related with various techniques. The most common one is called multiple regression.

Table A.4		
	Drawing (X)	Writing (Y)
Student 1	3	5
Student 2	1	2
Student 3	2	3
Student 4	4	4
Student 5	1	3
Student 6	4	6
Student 7	2	3
Student 8	3	4
Student 9	5	5
Student 10	1	2

Practice Quiz   How much do you remember?   ANSWERS AVAILABLE IN ANSWER KEY.

Pick the best answer.

1. _____ statistics consist of techniques that allow researchers to determine the difference between results of a study that are meaningful and those that are merely due to chance variations.

   a. Inferential   **c.** Predictive

   b. Parametric   **d.** Descriptive

2. Andrew is conducting a test where he has three different participant groups and he wants to analyze the variance between the three groups. In other words, he wants to know whether the means of each group are significantly different from each other. Which of the following would he want to calculate?

   a. An z-test   **c.** A F-test

   b. A t-test   **d.** A chi-square test

3. Bailey is conducting a correlational study that examines the frequency with which it rains in her town and the atmospheric pressure at noon on each day. When she is done, she calculates a correlation coefficient that will summarize the relationship between these two variables. This coefficient is going to be summarized by the lower-case letter _____.

   a. c **c.** p

   b. r **d.** e

4. If a researcher wants to demonstrate that their findings depict a significant difference between participant groups, which of the following statistical statements would need to be made?

   a. $p \le .05$ **c.** $t \ge 2.50$

   b. $r = \pm 1.00$ **d.** $z \le 100$

Chapter Summary

What Are Statistics?

A.1 Define statistics, and explain why they are important to psychologists and psychology majors.

- Statistics is a branch of mathematics that involves the collection, description, and interpretation of numerical data.
- Students who understand the process of research and the statistical methods used in research are more desirable to many university and business institutions than those who lack such skills.

Descriptive Statistics

A.2 Describe the types of tables and graphs that represent patterns in data.

- Descriptive statistics are ways of organizing numbers and summarizing them so that they can be understood.

- Frequency distributions are tables or graphs that show the patterns in a set of scores and can be a table, a bar graph or histogram, or a line graph or polygon.
- The normal curve is a special frequency polygon that is symmetrical and has the mean, median, and mode as the highest point on the curve.

A.3 Identify the three measures of central tendency and explain how they are impacted by the shape of the distribution.

- Measures of central tendency are ways of finding numbers that best represent the center of a distribution of numbers and include the mean, median, and mode.

A.4 Identify the types of statistics used to examine variations in data.

- Measures of variability provide information about the differences within a set of numbers and include the range and the standard deviation.

Inferential Statistics

A.5 Describe how inferential statistics can be used to determine if differences in sets of data are large enough to be due to something other than chance variation.

- Inferential statistics involves statistical analysis of two or more sets of numerical data to reduce the possibility of error in measurement and determine statistical significance of the results of research.

A.6 Explain how statistics are used to predict one score from another.

- The correlation coefficient is a number that represents the strength and direction of a relationship existing between two variables.

Test Yourself   ANSWERS AVAILABLE IN ANSWER KEY.

Pick the best answer.

1. Polygons and histograms are examples of
   a. frequency distributions.
   b. correlations.
   c. inferential statistics.
   d. mode.

2. If a chart shows that more than 80 percent of the students received scores above 80 in the class, one would describe the chart as
   a. normal distribution.
   b. positively skewed.
   c. negatively skewed.
   d. bell-shaped.

3. Your psychology instructor posts the results of the midterm exam on a histogram chart. On the chart, you see a high frequency of Bs and a high frequency of Ds. How else might you describe the results?
   a. This is a normal curve.
   b. This chart is skewed and bimodal.
   c. This chart is a typical bell-shaped chart.
   d. This chart is incapable of expressing an accurate picture of the results.

4. The mean, median, and mode are all measures of
   a. correlations.
   b. inferential statistics.
   c. variability.
   d. central tendency.

5. Imagine that the following is a set of grades from your class's first psychology exam: 71, 71, 71, 73, 75, 76, 81, 86, 97. What is the median score?
   a. 71   **c.** 9
   b. 75   **d.** 700

6. Imagine that the following is a set of grades from your first psychology exam: 71, 71, 71, 73, 75, 76, 81, 86, 97. What is the mode?
   a. 71   **c.** 9
   b. 75   **d.** 700

7. In the normal curve,
   a. the mean, median, and mode are all on the highest point of the curve.
   b. the mean is on the highest point whereas the median and mode are on either side of the mean.
   c. the median is on the highest point whereas the mean and mode are on either side of the median.
   d. the standard deviation is located at the highest point of the curve.

8. _____ is a way of organizing numbers and summarizing them so that they can be understood whereas _____ allows researchers to draw conclusions about the results of research.
   a. Correlational research; mean statistics
   b. Inferential statistics; descriptive statistics
   c. Descriptive statistics; inferential statistics
   d. Inferential statistics; mean, medium, and mode

9. Dr. White finds that the results of his *t*-test are significant at $p < .05$. That means that he can be
   a. reasonably assured that the results are not due to chance.
   b. reasonably assured that the results are due to chance.
   c. 5 percent certain that the results are not due to chance.
   d. 95 percent certain that the results are not due to chance.

10. Your best friend tells you he got a correlational score of 14.6 from the research he conducted. What can you infer from his finding?
   a. Your friend's research shows only a small correlation since 14.6 is close to zero.
   b. Your friend's research shows a positive score in 14.6 and therefore a positive relationship exists.
   c. Your friend's research is inconclusive. You need more than a correlational score of 14.6 to know if there is any statistical significance.
   d. Your friend's analysis is flawed. Correlational scores range only from −1.00 to +1.00.

Appendix B
Applied Psychology and Psychology Careers

Why study applied psychology?

Many different kinds of psychologists study or work in many different fields. Whereas early psychologists were still discovering the processes that govern the human mind, today's psychologists are more often applying information and principles gained from research to people in the real world. Why study careers in psychology? With so many different areas of focus, a career in psychology can be varied and exciting. There is much more to psychology than helping people who have mental health problems.

Professor John Gambon of Ozarks Technical and Community College in Springfield, Missouri, begins his class like any other. After a few minutes two students rush in and each throw two water balloons at the professor. As they run out, they yell something about fried eggs. Professor Gambon, soaked from the balloons, asks his students to write down everything they just saw, including what was said. After a few minutes, he gathers up the paperwork and invites his two balloon-throwing accomplices back into the room.

As he reads the papers of his students, many realize that they made mistakes in identifying the perpetrators. Quite often, students mismatch hair color, height, facial features, and even the clothes that each was wearing. What's more, nearly 90 percent claim that they heard the two men yell, "That was for last Friday!" When students are shown the truth, many are shocked at their overall inaccuracy at identifying the two men.

Work such as this is not new to Professor Gambon. He has worked as a consultant in several trials where the issue of accurately identifying someone has been brought into question. His cases include several homicides, assault, breaking and entering, and armed robbery.

His demonstrations show the overall unreliability of eyewitness identification, as outlined by psychologist Elizabeth Loftus. LINK to Learning Objective 6.7. The kind of issues that influence an eyewitness's accuracy include the presence of a weapon (people tend to look at a weapon more than the physical attributes of the assailant), time of day, fatigue, and the amount of time between the crime and when they are required to recall it. Clearly, there are flaws inherent in eyewitness identification.

Forensic psychology is just one of many areas in which psychological principles can be applied to issues and concerns of everyday life. This appendix will look at several areas of applied psychology as well as the types of careers that are open to someone who studies psychology today.

Learning Objectives

B.1   Define applied psychology.

B.2   Describe the different types of psychological professionals and identify their educational background and training.

B.3   List the kinds of careers that are available to someone with a master's degree in psychology.

B.4   List the kinds of careers that are available to someone with a bachelor's degree in psychology.

B.5   Describe some of the areas of specialization in psychology.

B.6   Describe how psychology interacts with other career fields.

B.7   Explain the fields of industrial/organizational psychology and human factors psychology.

B.8   Summarize the history of the I/O field and describe some of the research being done by I/O psychologists today.

B.9   Describe some of the techniques used by sports psychologists.

What Is Applied Psychology?

B.1 Define applied psychology.

The term **applied psychology** refers to using findings from psychological research to solve real-world problems. The psychological professional, who might be a psychiatrist, a psychologist, or even a psychiatric social worker (as described later in this appendix), may do testing or use some other type of assessment and then describe a plan of action intended to solve whatever problem is of concern. As is evident in the opening comments about John Gambon, you can see that his training in psychology and his specialized knowledge enabled him to testify in court as an expert witness. This is a practical application of psychological tools to a real problem—the professional literally "applies" psychology.

 It seems to me that psychology could be useful in a lot of different areas, not just education. In fact, wasn't that what all those "Applying Psychology" sections at the end of each chapter were about?

Every chapter in this text (and even this appendix) does end with some application of psychology to the real world. The field of applied psychology isn't just one field but rather a lot of different areas that all share the common goal of using psychology in a practical way. A large number of areas can be considered applied psychology, including one of the broadest areas of psychology: clinical and counseling psychology. For example, health psychologists examine the effects of stress on physical as well as mental health; educational and school psychologists look for ways to improve student learning and apply the findings to the classroom; sports psychologists help athletes prepare themselves mentally for competition; human-factors psychologists deal with the way people and machines interact; forensic psychologists deal with psychological issues within the legal system; and industrial/organizational (I/O) psychologists deal with the work environment. In addition, environmental psychologists examine the interaction of people with their surroundings at work, in social settings, and in schools, homes, and other buildings. Those surroundings include not just the physical structures but also the particular population of people who live, work, and play in those surroundings. Other psychologists look at the factors that influence people to buy certain products, analyze the best ways to market a product, and examine the buying habits of the typical consumer.

This appendix includes information on the different roles of psychological professionals and the type of education required for many professions, along with a brief overview of many of the specialized areas in psychology. The remainder of this appendix briefly explores how psychology can be used in practical ways in several different areas of life: the environment, law, education, the military, sports, and the world of work.

Practice Quiz How much do you remember? ANSWERS ON PAGE AK-1.

Pick the best answer.

1. The term _____ psychology refers to using findings from psychological research to solve real-world problems.

    a. applied   **c.** pragmatic

    b. practical   **d.** academic

2. Which of the following types of psychologists might be most interested in dealing with the work environment?

    a. A vocational psychologist

    b. A health psychologist

    c. A psychiatric social worker

    d. An industrial/organizational psychologist

3. Charlotte has designed a new type of gear shift to be used in automobiles with an automatic transmission. Before she proposes it to the major car manufacturers, she wants to make sure that it will be more advantageous for people who drive such cars. With which of the following types of psychologist would Charlotte most want to consult about her design?

    a. An environmental psychologist

    b. An industrial/organizational psychologist

    c. A human-factors psychologist

    d. A machinery psychologist

Psychology as a Career

When most people think of psychology as a potential career, they assume certain things about the profession: For example, to help people with their problems one has to be a psychologist, all psychologists are doctors, and all psychologists counsel mentally ill people. None of these assumptions are completely true.

TYPES OF PSYCHOLOGICAL PROFESSIONALS

B.2 **Describe the different types of psychological professionals and identify their educational background and training.**

There are several types of professionals who work in psychology. These professionals have different training with different focuses and may have different goals.

PSYCHIATRIC SOCIAL WORKERS A **psychiatric social worker** is trained in the area of social work and usually possesses a master of social work (M.S.W.) degree and may be licensed in the state he or she works as a licensed clinical social worker (LCSW). These professionals focus more on the social conditions that can have an impact on mental disorders, such as poverty, overcrowding, stress, and drug abuse. They may administer psychotherapy (talking with clients about their problems) and often work in a clinical setting where other types of psychological professionals are available.

PSYCHIATRISTS A **psychiatrist** has a medical doctorate (M.D. or D.O.) degree and is a physician who specializes in the diagnosis and treatment of psychological disorders. Like any other medical doctor who may specialize in emergency medicine, treating the diseases of the elderly, treating infants and children, or any other special area of medicine, psychiatrists are able to write prescriptions and perform medical procedures on their patients. They simply have special training in the diagnosis and treatment of disorders that are considered to be mental disorders, such as schizophrenia, depression, or extreme anxiety. Because they are medical doctors, they tend to have a biopsychological perspective on the causes of and treatments for such disorders.

Psychologists specialize in many different areas and work in many different settings. This child psychologist is evaluating the young boy by using puppets and dolls to encourage the boy to talk about his feelings.

PSYCHOLOGISTS   A **psychologist** doesn't have a medical degree but instead undergoes intense academic training, learning about many different areas of psychology before choosing an area in which to specialize. Psychologists typically have either a doctor of philosophy (Ph.D.) or doctor of psychology (Psy.D.) degree. (People who hold a master of science or M.S. degree are not usually called psychologists except in a few states. They can be called therapists or counselors, or they may be teachers or researchers.)

💬 What's the difference between a Ph.D. and a Psy.D.?

The Ph.D. is a type of degree that usually indicates the highest degree of learning available in almost any subject area—psychology, the study of languages, education, philosophy, the sciences, and many others. It is typically very research oriented, and earning the degree usually requires a previous master's degree in addition to course work for the doctorate itself, as well as a dissertation—a scholarly work of research in the area of focus that is as long as a book and may even be published as a book.

The Psy.D. is a type of degree developed in the late 1970s that is focused less on research and more on the practical application of psychological principles (Peterson, 1976, 1982). In addition to academic course work such as that required for the Ph.D., this degree may require a major paper instead of a dissertation, with the difference being that the paper is not a report of research designed and conducted by the student but is rather a large-scale term paper. Each year of a Psy.D. program will also require the student to participate in a *practicum*, an actual experience with observing and eventually conducting therapy and treatments under supervision.

Unlike psychiatrists, psychologists typically cannot prescribe medicines or perform medical procedures. Some states are seeking legislative changes to allow psychologists to prescribe psychotropic medications if they receive special education in the use of prescription drugs. Such privileges were first pursued by the U.S. military. The reasoning behind this move, for which the American Psychological Association has been lobbying since 1984, involves both cost and the delay in receiving mental health services. If a person sees a psychologist and then has to go to a psychiatrist for medical prescriptions, the cost can be prohibitive. There are also fewer psychiatrists in some states than in others, causing long waits for mental health services from those doctors—delays that can sometimes lead to an increase in suicide rates for patients who are not getting the help they need. Although some psychologists in the military or Indian Health Service can already prescribe, as of May 2013, only two states and one territory (New Mexico, Louisiana, and Guam) have successfully afforded prescription privileges to psychologists.

Some psychologists provide counseling or therapy and use a variety of techniques and approaches. ⓛⓘⓝⓚ to Learning Objectives 13.2–13.7. However, many psychologists do no counseling at all. There are psychologists who only engage in assessment, those who teach at colleges or universities, those who do only research in those same institutions or for industries, and those who do a combination of teaching and research (and some that do a combination of teaching, research, and counseling or clinical practice). Other psychologists are involved in designing equipment and workplaces, developing educational methods, or working as consultants to businesses and the court system.

Although becoming a psychologist requires a doctorate degree of some kind, many career fields can benefit from a four-year college degree in psychology as the basis of that career or going on to obtain a master's degree in psychology.

CAREERS WITH A MASTER'S DEGREE IN PSYCHOLOGY

B.3 List the kinds of careers that are available to someone with a master's degree in psychology.

While individuals earning a master's degree in psychology are not typically able to engage in the same level of independent research or practice of psychology as someone with a doctoral degree, they can still work in a variety of areas, both within and beyond the field of psychology. They may work directly under the supervision of a doctoral psychologist if engaged in clinical, counseling, or school psychology, or engaged in assessment. Others work outside of the field in jobs requiring research or analysis skills and work in health, industry, or government areas.

For those interested in counseling or providing therapy, many states allow individuals with master's degrees and prerequisite training and supervision experiences to become licensed to provide unsupervised counseling and therapy. Titles may vary by state, but some of the areas and titles associated with licensed master's level work include licensed marriage and family therapist (LMFT), licensed professional counselor (LPC), licensed mental health counselor (LMHC), or licensed clinical social worker (LCSW). These individuals may work in a larger organization or work independently in private practice. Beyond these areas, some individuals with a master's degree in psychology become certified or licensed to serve as school counselors at various levels and may work in an elementary, middle, or high school.

CAREERS WITH A BACHELOR'S DEGREE IN PSYCHOLOGY

B.4 List the kinds of careers that are available to someone with a bachelor's degree in psychology.

Although people earning only the baccalaureate (bachelor's) degree in psychology cannot be called psychologists or provide therapy in a private practice, there are many career fields open to such a person. More than 1 million bachelor's degrees in psychology have been awarded since 1970, and since 2000 the number has increased each year (Landrum, 2009; Snyder & Dillow, 2010). A bachelor's degree in psychology can be highly flexible and adaptable to many different kinds of careers (Landrum, 2009; Landrum & Davis, 2007; Schwartz, 2000). While surveys, both by the American Psychological Association and others, reveal many may work in health-related or social fields, individuals with a bachelor's degree in psychology may be employed in research development or research management, administration, business, education and teaching, professional services, sales, or management (Grocer & Kohout, 1997; Landrum, 2009).

Other possible careers include marketing researcher, social worker, and communications specialist (Landrum & Davis, 2007; Schwartz, 2000). With its emphasis on critical thinking and empirical observation, psychology trains people for a variety of potential workplace environments and requirements. Psychology is an excellent major even if you intend to do graduate work in some other career: Business, law, childcare, teaching, and management are only a few of the areas that relate to psychology.

Many people with a bachelor's degree in psychology work in health-related or social fields, such as this social worker who is working with a mother and child.

AREAS OF SPECIALIZATION

B.5 Describe some of the areas of specialization in psychology.

💬 You said that some psychologists teach or do research. What kind of research do they do?

There are many different areas in which psychologists may focus their energies. They conduct experiments, surveys, observations, and so on to gather more information for their particular field of interest, to find support for current theories, or to develop new ones. Let's look at some of the areas in which psychologists may specialize.

CLINICAL PSYCHOLOGY Even though not all psychologists do counseling or therapy, many psychologists do. **Clinical psychology** is the most similar of the areas to psychiatry in that professionals with this focus traditionally work with individuals with more serious forms of mental illness. It is also the area of specialization with the largest number of psychologists. Clinical psychologists, like psychiatrists, diagnose and treat psychological disorders in people. However, the clinical psychologist cannot prescribe drugs or medical therapies (with the exceptions discussed earlier, of course) but instead relies on listening or observing the client's problems, possibly administering psychological tests, and then providing explanations for the client's behavior and feelings or directing the client in specific actions to make positive changes in his or her life.

COUNSELING PSYCHOLOGY **Counseling psychology** is similar to clinical psychology in that this type of psychologist diagnoses and treats problems. The difference is that a counseling psychologist usually works with relatively healthy people who have less severe forms of mental illness or problems, such as adjustment to college, marriage, family life, work problems, and so on. As of 2008, nearly 73 percent of surveyed psychologists currently providing health services identified themselves as clinical psychologists or counseling psychologists (Michalski et al., 2010). (L I N K) to Learning Objective 1.5.

DEVELOPMENTAL PSYCHOLOGY **Developmental psychology** is an area that focuses on the study of change, or development. Developmental psychologists are interested in changes in the way people think, in how people relate to others, and in the ways people feel over the entire span of life. These psychologists work in academic settings such as colleges and universities and may do research in various areas of development. They do not provide therapy. (L I N K) to Learning Objective 8.1.

EXPERIMENTAL PSYCHOLOGY **Experimental psychology** encompasses several different areas such as learning, memory, thinking, perception, motivation, and language. The focus of these psychologists, however, is on doing research and conducting studies and experiments with both people and animals in various areas. They tend to work in academic settings, especially in large universities. (L I N K) to Learning Objective 1.5.

SOCIAL PSYCHOLOGY **Social psychology** is an area that focuses on how human behavior is affected by the presence of other people. For example, social psychologists explore areas such as prejudice, attitude change, aggressive behavior, and interpersonal attraction. Although most social psychologists work in academic settings teaching and doing research, some work in federal agencies and big business doing practical (applied) research. In fact, many social psychologists are experimental psychologists who perform their experiments in real-world settings rather than the laboratory to preserve the natural reactions of people. When people are in an artificial setting, they often behave in self-conscious ways, which is not the behavior the researcher wishes to study. (L I N K) to Learning Objective 10.1.

PERSONALITY PSYCHOLOGY **Personality psychology** focuses on the differences in personality among people. These psychologists may look at the influence of heredity on personality. They study the ways in which people are both alike and different. They look at the development of personality and do personality assessment. They may be involved in forming new theories of how personality works or develops. Personality psychologists work in academic settings, doing research and teaching. (L I N K) to Learning Objective 11.1.

PHYSIOLOGICAL PSYCHOLOGY **Physiological psychology** is an area that focuses on the study of the biological bases of behavior. Many professionals now refer to this area as *behavioral neuroscience* or *biopsychology*. Physiological psychologists study the brain, nervous system, and the influence of the body's chemicals, such as hormones and the chemicals in the brain, on human behavior. They study the effects of drug use and possible genetic influences on some kinds of abnormal and normal human behavior, such as schizophrenia or aspects of intelligence. Most physiological psychologists, like experimental psychologists, work in an academic setting. (L I N K) to Learning Objective 2.1.

NEUROPSYCHOLOGY   **Neuropsychology** is an area within the field of psychology in which professionals explore the relationships between the brain systems and behavior. Neuropsychologists may be engaged in research or more focused on the assessment, diagnosis, treatment, and/or rehabilitation of individuals with various neurological, medical, neurodevelopmental, or psychiatric conditions (National Academy of Neuropsychology, 2001). (L I N K) to Learning Objective 7.6.

COMPARATIVE PSYCHOLOGY   **Comparative psychology** is an area that focuses exclusively on animals and animal behavior. By comparing and contrasting animal behavior with what is already known about human behavior, comparative psychologists can contribute to the understanding of human behavior by studying animals. Research in animal behavior also helps people to learn how to treat animals more humanely and to coexist with the animals in a common environment. Comparative psychologists might work in animal laboratories in a university or may do observation and studies of animals in the animals' natural habitats.

Psychologists in these areas may do research that is directed at discovering basic principles of human behavior (basic research) or they may engage in research designed to find solutions to practical problems of the here and now (applied research). (L I N K) to Learning Objective 1.5. There are many other areas in which psychologists may specialize that focus almost exclusively on applied research. These areas are those most often associated with applied psychology.

PSYCHOLOGY BEYOND THE CLASSROOM

B.6 Describe how psychology interacts with other career fields.

Individuals working in psychology can serve an important role in many different fields. Some are extensions of the areas of specialization just covered. Other fields are well suited due to the general, and sometimes specific, skills psychology professionals can provide.

PSYCHOLOGY AND HEALTH   **Health psychology** focuses on the relationship of human behavior patterns and stress reactions to physical health with the goal of improving and helping to maintain good health while preventing and treating illness. For example, a health psychologist might design a program to help people lose weight or stop smoking. Stress management techniques are also a major focus of this area. Health psychologists may work in hospitals, clinics, medical schools, health agencies, academic settings, or private practice.

In one study (Kerwin et al., 2010), researchers found an association between obesity in older women and a decline in memory functioning in those women. This finding was particularly true for women carrying the excess weight around their hips (pear shapes) and less so for women carrying the excess weight around their waists (apple shapes). The study controlled for other health variables, such as diabetes, heart disease, and stroke. This is a good example of the kind of research that health psychologists conduct. Other areas studied by health psychologists include the influence of optimistic attitudes on the progress of disease, the link between mental distress and health, and the promotion of wellness and hope in an effort to prevent illness.

PSYCHOLOGY AND EDUCATION   **Educational psychology** is concerned with the study of human learning. As educational psychologists come to understand some of the basic aspects of learning, they develop methods and materials for aiding the process of learning. For example, educational psychologists helped to design the phonics method of teaching children to read. This type of psychologist may have a doctorate of education (Ed.D.) rather than a Ph.D. and typically works in academic settings.

What types of research might an educational psychologist conduct? The August 2013 issue of *Journal of Educational Psychology* included articles on teacher self-efficacy and instructional quality, stereotype threat in girls' math performance (L I N K) to Learning

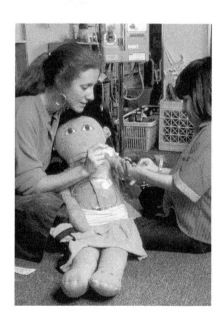

This woman is a health psychologist. She is helping this girl to control her fear of receiving an injection by letting her act out giving an injection to a special doll.

School psychologists often administer tests to assess a child's level of achievement, intelligence, or psychological well-being.

Objective 7.8), student motivation, and effects of teacher's professional competence on both instruction and student development—just to name a few.

School psychology is related to, but not at all the same as, educational psychology. Whereas educational psychologists may do research and develop new learning techniques, school psychologists may take the results of that research or those methods and apply them in the actual school system. School psychologists work directly with children in the school setting. They do testing and other forms of assessment to place children in special programs or to diagnose educational problems such as dyslexia or attention-deficit/hyperactivity disorder. They may act as consultants to teachers, parents, and educational administrators. Counseling students is actually a relatively small part of the job of a school psychologist, although counseling takes a much bigger role when tragedies strike a school. When traumatic events such as the unexpected and tragic death of a classmate or even larger-scale tragedies such as the numerous school shootings of the past decade take place, school psychologists are often called on to offer help and counseling to students.

PSYCHOLOGY AND SPORTS Sports psychology is a relatively new and fast-growing field in which the main focus is on helping athletes and others involved in sports activities prepare mentally, rather than just physically, for participation in sports. The idea behind this field is that a superior physical performance is not enough to guarantee success; rather, the mind must be prepared for the activity by setting clear short-term goals, holding positive thoughts, using visualization of the goal, stopping negative thoughts, and other techniques based primarily in the cognitive perspective. For example, a sports psychologist might have a golfer, who has been having trouble with the accuracy of his drives, perform visualization exercises, mentally seeing himself hit the ball down the fairway again and again. Sports psychologists work in athletic organizations and may have a private practice or do consulting work. (For more on the techniques used in sports psychology, see the *Applying Psychology to Everyday Life* section at the end of this appendix.)

PSYCHOLOGY AND THE MILITARY Within the military, psychologists work in a variety of areas ranging from assessment, teaching, management, research, and the provision of mental health services. The variety of psychologists in this field may include clinical, counseling, experimental, I/O, or human factors, among others, and may reflect any specialty area in the field of psychology. In short, they apply psychological skills to human issues in military environments, working with both military personnel and their families (American Psychological Association, Division 19, 2010). One poignant example, the rise of suicides in the armed forces associated with the conflicts in Iraq and Afghanistan have placed demands on both the military and military families at a level not seen before (Berman et al., 2010).

A Fort Lewis Army psychologist demonstrates a headset from the "Virtual Reality Iraq" therapy program on April 18, 2007, in Spanaway, Washington. The virtual reality program, which simulates the sights, sounds, and smells of combat, will be used in working with soldiers suffering from posttraumatic stress disorder.

PSYCHOLOGY AND THE LAW Psychologists have often been involved in the world of legal matters in various ways. Social psychologists often do research in the areas of criminal behavior and may consult with attorneys or other agents of the court system on such topics as witness credibility, jury selection, and the kind of influences that exist for decision-making processes. Developmental psychologists may become involved in determining the accuracy of and influences on the testimony of children and adolescents, as well as the needs of children caught up in a custody battle between divorced or divorcing parents. Cognitive psychologists may become expert witnesses on the accuracy of memory and eyewitness testimony or ways to determine the truth or falsehood of statements made by witnesses or defendants. Clinical psychologists may deliver their services directly to incarcerated prisoners or may conduct assessments of intelligence and/or mental status to determine whether or not a person charged with a crime should stand trial.

All of the forms of psychological involvement in legal matters mentioned here can be considered as part of the growing field of **forensic psychology**. Forensic psychology is the practice of psychology related to the legal system and it involves examining criminal evidence and aiding law enforcement investigations into criminal activities. Some forensic psychologists provide information and advice to officials in the legal system, such as lawyers or judges; some act as expert witnesses (like Professor John Gambon in the opening story); some actually diagnose and treat criminals within the prison system; and others may administer psychological tests to criminal defendants. Forensic psychologists may aid either the prosecution or the defense in a trial by helping determine which potential jurors would be the best or worst choices. This type of professional may do consulting work in addition to maintaining a regular private practice in clinical or counseling psychology, or may work entirely within the justice system as a police psychologist or a full-time jury expert, for example.

PSYCHOLOGY AND THE COMMUNITY   **Community psychology** is an area that focuses on both individuals and their community. This field is often concerned with issues at various levels, including individual, group, neighborhood, and organizational. It is an area that focuses on promoting health and preventing common societal issues across all levels. Community psychology aims to understand human behavior in context, and recognizes the role of human diversity in promoting change. Advocacy is a key role for individuals in this area as they work to promote social justice, or practices and policies that directly impact aspects of life such as equal opportunity for all people, prevention of violence, and active citizenship. Community psychologists are involved in a variety of life activities and may be engaged in promoting mental health, physical health, educational interventions, or work policies.

PSYCHOLOGY AND THE ENVIRONMENT   Another broad area in which psychological principles can be applied to solve practical problems is the area of managing the environment. **Environmental psychology** is an area that focuses on the relationship between human behavior and the environment in which the behavior takes place, such as an office, store, school, dormitory, or hospital. Because the concern of researchers in this field deals directly with behavior in a particular setting, research is always conducted in that setting rather than in a laboratory. Environmental psychologists may work with other professionals such as urban or city planners, economists, engineers, and architects, helping those professionals to plan the most efficient buildings, parks, housing developments, or plants.

Practice Quiz   How much do you remember? ANSWERS ON PAGE AK-1.

Pick the best answer.

1. Dr. Saschi works at a hospital and is regularly called to the emergency room to assist with patients who are having acute mental health crises. She often prescribes psychotropic medications to help these patients get stabilized. Which of the following degrees has Dr. Saschi most likely earned?

   a. An Ed.D.   **c.** An M.D.

   b. A Ph.D.   **d.** A Psy.D.

2. Rochelle has earned a Master's degree but decided not to pursue her doctorate. She does, however, want to provide counseling and therapy to clients, but does not want to be supervised for her entire career. After several years of training and appropriate supervision, she has achieved a degree that, in her state, will allow her to have this career. Which of the following would *not likely* be a title that Rochelle may now hold?

   a. LCP (Licensed Children's Psychologist)

   b. LPC (Licensed Professional Counselor)

   c. LMHC (Licensed Mental Health Counselor)

   d. LMFT (Licensed Marriage and Family Therapist)

3. _____ psychologists are primarily interested in changes in the way people think, in how people relate to others, and in the ways people feel over the entire span of life. They often work in academic settings, such as colleges and universities, and may do research in various areas. They do not generally provide therapy.

   a. Counseling

   b. Developmental

   c. Sociocultural

   d. Environmental

4. Dr. Kandlend has spent his entire career working with chimpanzees, studying the ways that their behavioral profiles are both similar to and different from human beings. Dr. Kandlend is probably a(n) _____ psychologist.

   a. physiological

   b. zoological

   c. forensic

   d. comparative

Psychology and Work

Work is a tremendous part of many people's lives. People often spend more time at work than they do with their families or in social activities. One of the largest branches of applied psychology focuses on how psychology can help people in management, productivity, morale,* and many other areas of the world of work.

WHAT ARE INDUSTRIAL/ORGANIZATIONAL PSYCHOLOGY AND HUMAN FACTORS PSYCHOLOGY?

B.7 **Explain the fields of industrial/organizational psychology and human factors psychology.**

Industrial/organizational (I/O) psychology is concerned with the relationships between people and their work environments. I/O psychologists may help in personnel selection, administer job performance assessments, design work schedules that help workers adjust to new work hours with less difficulty, or design new work areas to increase morale and productivity. Psychologists in this field may study the behavior of entire organizations. They are often hired by corporations and businesses to deal with the hiring and assessment of employees. They may research and develop ways for workers to be more efficient and productive. They may work in business, government agencies, and academic settings. **Table B.1** briefly lists some of the areas of specialization.

Human factors psychologists design machines that are more practical and comfortable for people to use. For example, this keyboard is designed to reduce the risk of pain in the wrists and increase accuracy in typing.

A specific kind of I/O specialist, called a *human factors engineer*, focuses on ergonomics, or designing machines, furniture, and other devices that people have to use so that those devices are the most practical, comfortable, and logical for human use. **Human factors psychology** consists of these researchers and designers who study the way humans and machines interact with each other. They may work directly in the companies involved in the design of appliances, airplane controls, and the operation of computers or other mechanical devices. For example, recall a recent iPhone® commercial about how your thumb can reach all parts of the screen. Or have you ever seen an ergonomic chair? Most likely a human factors engineer was involved in the design or testing of these products.

Psychologists working in I/O settings apply psychological principles and theories to the workplace. For example, Maslow's humanistic theory and hierarchy of needs (L I N K to Learning Objective 9.4) has had a powerful influence on the field of management

Table B.1 Areas in I/O Psychology	
Areas in Industry	**Areas in Organizations**
Job analysis	Social behavior of work teams
Job evaluation and compensation	Job satisfaction
Characteristics critical to effective management	Personality characteristics critical to job performance
Personnel recruiting, selection, and placement	Relationships between management and workers
Occupational training	Leadership characteristics and training
Examination of working conditions	Consumer psychology
Interviewing and testing	Motivational concerns
Performance appraisal and feedback	Conflict management

*morale: a sense of common purpose, enthusiasm, confidence, and loyalty.

(Heil et al., 1998). Douglas McGregor, in his explanations of two different styles of management (McGregor, 1960), relates the older and less productive "Theory X" (workers are unmotivated and need to be managed and directed) to Maslow's lower needs and the newer, more productive style of management called "Theory Y" (workers want to work and want that work to be meaningful) to the higher needs.

THE HISTORY OF INDUSTRIAL/ORGANIZATIONAL PSYCHOLOGY AND THE FIELD TODAY

B.8 Summarize the history of the I/O field and describe some of the research being done by I/O psychologists today.

Industrial/organizational psychology got its start near the beginning of the twentieth century with the work of Walter D. Scott, a former student of famed physiologist and founder of the first psychological laboratory, Wilhelm Wundt. Scott applied psychological principles to hiring, management, and advertising techniques (Schultz & Schultz, 2004). He also wrote one of the first books about the application of psychology to industry and advertising, called *The Theory and Practice of Advertising* (Scott, 1908). Another early figure in the newly developing field of I/O psychology was Hugo Munsterberg, a psychologist also trained by Wundt, who conducted research on such varied topics as the power of prayer and eyewitness testimony (Hothersall, 1995). Munsterberg wrote a book about eyewitness testimony called *On the Witness Stand* (1907) and later wrote *Psychology and Industrial Efficiency* (1913).

The I/O field became important during World War I when the army needed a way to test the intelligence of potential recruits. Psychologist Robert Yerkes, who would later become known for his groundbreaking research in comparative psychology while working with the great apes, developed the Army Alpha and Army Beta tests. The Army Alpha test was used with applicants who were able to read, whereas the Army Beta test was administered to applicants who were illiterate (McGuire, 1994; Yerkes, 1921).

In the mid-1920s a series of studies conducted by Elton Mayo for the Western Electric Company (Franke & Kaul, 1978; Parsons, 1992; Roethlisberger & Dickson, 1939) broadened the field. These were the first studies to view the workplace as a social system rather than as just a production line. Instead of treating workers as simply other pieces of equipment, these studies suggested that allowing workers some input into the decision-making process not only improved worker morale but also reduced workers' resistance to changes in the workplace. These studies led the way for others to examine how management of employees and production could be improved. For example, Google® is one of the leaders in creating a rewarding work environment and providing various perks to its employees. It was selected as *Fortune* magazine's top company to work for in both 2012 and 2013 ("Best Companies to Work For 2013–Fortune"). From free gourmet food to an on-site laundry and dry cleaner, and both indoor and outdoor recreation facilities, Google works to create an intimate environment for its employees (Mangalindan, 2012). Management theories and strategies may also be applied to other kinds of settings such as schools, colleges, and universities. Yet another setting I/O psychologists are currently involved in is working with NASA for the planned 2030 trip to Mars (Novotney, 2013, March). I/O psychologists are researching ways to improve team selection and training for the astronauts who will have to endure a longer and farther space voyage than anyone ever has, a trip that will take close to three years. Promotion of resiliency, adaptability, and group cohesion are some of the areas being investigated, especially in light of the lack of privacy and cramped quarters they will be living in.

These women were participants in one of the early industrial/organizational psychology experiments conducted by Elton Mayo for the Western Electric Company.

Issues in Psychology
Workplace Violence

Acts of violence in the workplace have increased dramatically in the past few decades—nearly tripling in the 1980s alone (Baron, 1993). Psychologists are devoting time and energy to studying the reasons for this violence and are looking for ways to recognize and prevent future incidents. Some highlights from research in workplace violence show that people in some types of jobs face a higher probability of becoming a victim of a crime because of the characteristics of the job. For example, three of the most likely occupations are police officers, corrections officers, and taxi drivers (Centers for Disease Control and Prevention, 2009). For taxi drivers (along with convenience-store clerks), it is the availability of cash and the solitary nature of the job that entices many criminals to attempt robbery. In the case of police and correctional officers, violence is part of the very nature of their job. Consider the following statistics:

- Between 1992 and 2006, there were 11,613 workplace homicide victims reported.
- Of those homicides, 11.6 police officers out of every 100,000 were killed on the job compared to the national average for all occupations of 4.0 out of every 100,000.
- From 2004 to 2008 there was an average of 564 work-related homicides each year—10 percent of all fatal work injuries.
- Four out of every 5 homicide victims in 2008 were male.
- Men were more likely to be killed by a stranger, while women were more likely to be killed by a relative or personal acquaintance.
- In 2008, there were 30 multiple-fatality workplace homicide incidents, with an average of two people dying in each incident. Most were shot, and in 12 percent of the shootings the assailants were coworkers or former coworkers (Bureau of Labor Statistics, 2010).

Industrial/organizational psychologists have developed a term for the employee who becomes highly violent and commits violent crimes resulting in serious injury or death to other employees: the berserker. What are the characteristics of persons who "go berserk" in the workplace? Typically, they have at least a high school diploma or some college. Their self-esteem, or sense of worth as a person, is intimately tied to their job. They tend to like watching violent television or movies. Prevention of violence in the workplace can include some simple, commonsense steps as well as more complicated training and preparation (Arbury, 2005; Harvey & Keashly, 2003; Security Director's Report, 2008; VandenBos & Bulatao, 1996):

- entrances and exits that are well lighted
- presence of video cameras or security guards, especially at night
- criminal background checks performed on all potential new employees
- training managers and supervisors to identify signs of potential workplace violence, including such things as employees (1) who have a tendency to use verbal threats or who use low-grade acts of violence, such as pushing or shoving; (2) who are fascinated with and have access to firearms; or (3) who appear desensitized to television and movie violence and show a preference for watching such media.

Questions for Further Discussion

1. Refer back to the Learning and Social Psychology chapters. **LINK** to Chapter Five: Learning and Chapter Ten: Social Psychology. What might be some other reasons for workplace violence?

2. In what ways might a psychologist serve as a resource for individuals working in an occupation with higher risks of violence?

The aftermath of workplace violence: A somber crowd gathers at a candlelight vigil Sunday, August 8, 2010, in honor of the victims of a workplace shooting at a Connecticut beer distribution company, which took place on August 3, 2010. Less than one week prior to this vigil, Omar Thornton killed eight coworkers and wounded two others before killing himself at the Hartford Distributors building.

Practice Quiz   How much do you remember?   ANSWERS ON PAGE AK-1.

Pick the best answer.

1. Dr. Irish is an industrial/organizational psychologist who has just been hired by a major electronics production company. His job there will include many different responsibilities. Which of the following is not likely to be high on his list of responsibilities?

   a. Studying the way the human workers interact with the various machines on the production floor

   b. Helping to select personnel

   c. Administering job performance assessments

   d. Designing new work areas to increase morale and productivity

2. Which of the following would a human factors psychologist have the most input in designing?

   a. A new ergonomic chair that reduces muscle fatigue in the legs and back

   b. A new smartphone application that allows you to track your spending

   c. A book of recipes for single parents who do not have a lot of time to cook

   d. A list of maps that will show college students the closest stores that offer various products

3. One of the earliest industrial/organization psychologists, _____, was a student of famed researcher Wilhelm Wundt, and wrote a book entitled *The Theory and Practice of Advertising*.

   a. Keith Engelhorn

   b. William James

   c. Walter D. Scott

   d. Robert Yerkes

4. Approximately 10 percent of all fatal work injuries are due to:

   a. chemical spills.

   b. work-related homicides.

   c. toxic inhalations.

   d. slip-and-fall incidents.

Applying Psychology to Everyday Life
Techniques Used by Sports Psychologists

B.9   Describe some of the techniques used by sports psychologists.

Many athletes become frustrated when their performance seems to be less than it could be or when they reach some "roadblock" on their way to achieving new goals. The techniques that follow are designed to help athletes get around the roadblocks and get the most out of their performance. The same techniques are also helpful in the careers of acting, musical performance, professional speaking, teaching, or any career in which there is an element of performance in front of others.

1. *Visualization.*   In this technique, athletes try to "see" their performance in their minds as if watching from the sidelines before actually doing it.

2. *Imagery/mental rehearsal.*   Similar to visualization, imagery can be used to mentally rehearse the desired performance. Instead of visualizing oneself as if from the sidelines, however, imagery/mental rehearsal involves actually "seeing" and "feeling" the performance in one's mind from one's own viewpoint. This helps prepare the muscles that will be used for action.

3. *Distraction desensitization.*   Athletes can be trained to ignore distractions, such as the shouts of spectators.

4. *Thought stopping.*   People often have negative thoughts about things that might happen: "I'm going to miss it, I just know it!" is a good example of a negative, self-defeating thought. Sports psychologists train athletes to stop such thoughts in the making, replacing them with more positive thoughts: "I can do this. I've done it before and it was easy."

5. *Confidence training.*   Another thing that sports psychologists do is try to build confidence and self-esteem in the athletes who come to them for help. Lack of confidence in one's own abilities is a major roadblock.

6. *Focus training.*   Athletes can also be trained to focus attention, often through the use of hypnosis, concentrative meditation, or similar psychological techniques.

The sports psychologist on the right is helping Red Sox player David Ortiz work through his frustration at being injured during the game.

7. *Relaxation training.*   Athletes can be trained to use special breathing methods, tension and relaxation of muscles, and other strategies for relaxation to reduce anxiety and tension before a performance.

8. *Autogenic training.*   Autogenic essentially means "from within the self." In the sense used here, autogenic training involves helping athletes learn about their physiological responses to stress. Once learned, athletes can gain control over these responses, such as learning to slow one's heart rate or to lower anxiety.

9. *Fostering realistic goals and expectations.*   Sports psychologists try to teach athletes that although setting goals is important, setting unrealistic goals can lead to burnout, frustration, and feelings of failure. Sports psychologists try to help athletes modify their expectations and goals to be more realistic.

10. *Fostering team unity.*   Sports psychologists may also work with entire teams of athletes, helping them to become a unit that works as one single "organism" while still providing support for each individual athlete.

Questions for Further Discussion

1. What are some other occupations in which people might benefit from using some of these techniques?

2. Are there factors outside of the game itself that might interfere with fostering team unity?

Chapter Summary

What Is Applied Psychology?

B.1 Define applied psychology.

- Applied psychology refers to using psychological principles and research to solve problems in the real world.

Psychology as a Career

B.2 Describe the different types of psychological professionals and identify their educational background and training.

- Different types of psychological professionals vary by level of education and training. Examples include psychiatrists, psychiatric social workers, and psychologists.
- Psychologists hold either a Ph.D. or Psy.D. degree.

B.3 List the kinds of careers that are available to someone with a master's degree in psychology.

- Individuals with a master's degree may work under the supervision of a doctoral-level psychology professional, practice independently if licensed, or work in private or educational settings.

B.4 List the kinds of careers that are available to someone with a bachelor's degree in psychology.

- Education, statistical consulting, administration and other business occupations, as well as health services are examples of careers that a person with a bachelor's degree in psychology might enter.

B.5 Describe some of the areas of specialization in psychology.

- Areas of specialization include clinical and counseling psychology, developmental, experimental, social, personality, and physiological psychology, neuropsychology, and comparative psychology.

B.6 Describe how psychology interacts with other career fields

- Health psychology is an area in which the goal is to discover relationships between human behavior, including stress factors, and physical health, with the intention of preventing and treating ill health.
- Educational psychologists study the processes of human learning to develop new techniques and methods, whereas school psychologists apply those methods in the school, administer assessments, recommend placement, and provide counseling and diagnosis of educational problems.
- Sports psychologists help athletes prepare themselves mentally for participation in sports.
- Psychologists working in the military represent almost all subfields of psychology and work with both military personnel and their families in military environments.
- Psychologists may act as expert witnesses for legal matters, help in jury selection, provide clinical services to defendants or prisoners, or produce personality profiles of various types of criminals in the field of forensic psychology.

- Community psychologists help solve social issues and work to promote health for individuals and for the larger community in which people live.
- Environmental psychology looks at the relationship between human behavior and the physical environment in which that behavior takes place.

Psychology and Work

B.7 **Explain the fields of industrial/organizational psychology and human factors psychology.**

- Industrial/organizational psychology is concerned with how people function in and are affected by their work environments.
- Human factors is a type of I/O psychology in which the focus is on the way humans and machines interact with each other, designing or helping to design the machines used by people in various science and industrial settings.

B.8 **Summarize the history of the I/O field and describe some of the research being done by I/O psychologists today.**

- The I/O field began in the twentieth century with the application of psychological principles to hiring, management, and advertising.

Applying Psychology to Everyday Life: Techniques Used by Sports Psychologists

B.9 **Describe some of the techniques used by sports psychologists.**

- Sports psychologists use many techniques to help athletes better their performances, including visualization, imagery, thought stopping, confidence training, relaxation training, and fostering team unity.

Test Yourself
ANSWERS AVAILABLE IN ANSWER KEY.

Pick the best answer.

1. Which of the following professionals has a medical degree?
   a. clinical psychologist
   b. psychiatrist
   c. psychiatric social worker
   d. counseling psychologist

2. Elaine has always wanted to be a psychologist. She dreams of helping people with their problems and wants to become "Dr. Elaine." However, she is not interested in conducting scientific research or in becoming a medical doctor. What type of degree would be best for Elaine to pursue?
   a. a master's degree in psychology
   b. a Ph.D.
   c. a Psy.D.
   d. a master's degree in social work

3. Dr. Troxell conducts scientific studies on topics such as the power of prejudice, attitude change, aggressive behavior, and interpersonal attraction in teenagers. Dr. Troxell's area of specialization is most likely in _____ psychology.
   a. social
   b. personality
   c. comparative
   d. developmental

4. Dr. Cavendish is a _____ psychologist who conducts experiments using only animals as her subjects. She hopes to use her findings to better understand human behavior.
   a. experimental
   b. comparative
   c. developmental
   d. social

5. What type of psychologist would be most likely to put together an anti-bullying program for middle school students?
   a. experimental
   b. clinical
   c. forensic
   d. educational

6. In working with a professional athlete, what aspects of performance might a sports psychologist likely focus on?
   a. strength and agility training
   b. focus and relaxation
   c. memory and motivation
   d. perceptual and problem solving

7. Dr. Lewis studies the topic of crowding. She often wonders why people can feel crowded in an elevator that has 8–10 people in it but not at a large sporting event where over 2,000 people are present. What is Dr. Lewis's specialty?
   a. developmental
   b. physiological
   c. social
   d. environmental

8. Which type of psychologist is most concerned with maximizing job satisfaction in night-shift employees?
   a. industrial/organizational
   b. clinical
   c. forensic
   d. environmental

9. Suzanne is working to redesign the controls for a new type of plane so that pilots can tell the difference between instruments in the dark just by the way each control feels. Suzanne is probably a(n) _____ psychologist.
   a. industrial/organizational
   b. human factors
   c. experimental
   d. military

10. Thought stopping, mental rehearsal, and focus training are some of the tools of the _____ psychologist.
    a. experimental
    b. clinical
    c. sports
    d. military

Answer Key

Psychology in Action

Practice Quiz page PIA-7
1. a; 2. d; 3. c; 4. b;

Practice Quiz page PIA-11
1. a; 2. a; 3. c; 4. d;

Practice Quiz page PIA-16
1. a; 2. c; 3. d; 4. a; 5. a; 6. c

Test Yourself page PIA-18
1. a; 2. d; 3. c; 4. c; 5. a; 6. c; 7. d; 8. b; 9. a; 10. a

Chapter 1

Practice Quiz page 6
1. a; 2. b; 3. c; 4. d

Practice Quiz page 13
1. b; 2. a; 3. a; 4. a

Practice Quiz page 20
1. d; 2. c; 3. a; 4. d; 5. a

Practice Quiz page 36
1. a; 2. c; 3. b; 4. c; 5. a; 6. b; 7. c

Test Yourself pages 40–41
1. c; 2. b; 3. c; 4. d; 5. b; 6. d; 7. d; 8. d; 9. b; 10. a; 11. b;
12. a; 13. c; 14. b; 15. b; 16. a; 17. c; 18. a; 19. d; 20. c

Chapter 2

Practice Quiz page 52
1. a; 2. b; 3. b; 4. a; 5. a; 6. d

Practice Quiz page 60
1. a; 2. d; 3. b; 4. b; 5. a;

Practice Quiz page 66
1. c; 2. a; 3. c; 4. c

Practice Quiz page 71
1. d; 2. c; 3. a; 4. b

Practice Quiz page 82
1. d; 2. d; 3. d; 4. b; 5. a; 6. b

Test Yourself pages 86–87
1. b; 2. c; 3. c; 4. a; 5. a; 6. c; 7. b; 8. b; 9. d; 10. b; 11. d;
12. b; 13. c; 14. d; 15. a; 16. a; 17. d; 18. b; 19. d; 20. b

Chapter 3

Practice Quiz page 93
1. d; 2. a; 3. d; 4. a

Practice Quiz page 101
1. a; 2. b; 3. c; 4. a; 5. b; 6. b

Practice Quiz page 107
1. a; 2. c; 3. b; 4. a; 5. d

Practice Quiz page 111
1. c; 2. d; 3. d; 4. b

Practice Quiz page 115
1. d; 2. b; 3. a; 4. b; 5. a

Practice Quiz page 125
1. b; 2. c; 3. b; 4. a; 5. c; 6. a; 7. b

Test Yourself pages 128–129
1. b; 2. d; 3. a; 4. b; 5. a; 6. c; 7. b; 8. b; 9. a; 10. a; 11. b;
12. b; 13. c; 14. a; 15. a; 16. c; 17. a; 18. d; 19. b; 20. c

Chapter 4

Practice Quiz page 134
1. d; 2. a; 3. c; 4. b

Practice Quiz page 145
1. d; 2. c; 3. a; 4. c; 5. d; 6. c; 7. c

Practice Quiz page 150
1. a; 2. c; 3. c; 4. d; 5. c

Practice Quiz page 159
1. a; 2. d; 3. a; 4. c; 5. b; 6. a

Test Yourself pages 162–163
1. a; 2. b; 3. d; 4. c; 5. a; 6. a; 7. c; 8. b; 9. d; 10. b; 11. a;
12. d; 13. c; 14. b; 15. a; 16. b; 17. a; 18. c; 19. c; 20. a

Chapter 5

Practice Quiz page 167
1. a; 2. b; 3. c; 4. d

Practice Quiz page 175
1. b; 2. a; 3. d; 4. a; 5. a; 6. c; 7. d

Practice Quiz page 194
1. a; 2. a; 3. c; 4. c; 5. d; 6. c; 7. d

Practice Quiz page 199
1. b; 2. a; 3. b; 4. d

Practice Quiz page 202
1. a; 2. d; 3. c; 4. b

Test Yourself pages 206–207
1. a; 2. b; 3. b; 4. d; 5. b; 6. a; 7. a; 8. d; 9. a; 10. b; 11. b;
12. c; 13. c; 14. c; 15. a; 16. b; 17. c; 18. b; 19. b; 20. b

Chapter 6

Practice Quiz page 212
1. b; 2. c; 3. b; 4. a

Practice Quiz page 222
1. b; 2. c; 3. a; 4. c; 5. d; 6. b

Practice Quiz page 231
1. b; 2. b; 3. a; 4. c; 5. a; 6. a

Practice Quiz page 235
1. a; 2. c; 3. d; 4. b

Practice Quiz page 238
1. d; 2. a; 3. b; 4. d

Test Yourself pages 257–259
1. b; 2. a; 3. b; 4. d; 5. c; 6. c; 7. c; 8. a; 9. b; 10. a; 11. d;
12. d; 13. a; 14. b; 15. b; 16. d; 17. b; 18. a; 19. d; 20. d

Chapter 7

Practice Quiz page 255
1. a; 2. a; 3. d; 4. a; 5. b; 6. a; 7. a

Practice Quiz page 270
1. c; 2. a; 3. c; 4. d; 5. c; 6. b; 7. a

Practice Quiz page 275
1. d; 2. b; 3. b; 4. a

Test Yourself pages 278–279
1. a; 2. b; 3. a; 4. d; 5. c; 6. b; 7. c; 8. a; 9. c; 10. d; 11. a;
12. b; 13. c; 14. a; 15. c; 16. b; 17. d; 18. a; 19. a; 20. a

Chapter 8

Practice Quiz page 287
1. a; 2. d; 3. b; 4. c; 5. b

Practice Quiz page 291
1. b; 2. c; 3. d; 4. a; 5. d

Practice Quiz page 306
1. b; 2. c; 3. a; 4. d; 5. c; 6. b; 7. b

Practice Quiz page 308
1. b; 2. c; 3. b; 4. d; 5. c

Practice Quiz page 313
1. b; 2. c; 3. c; 4. a; 5. d

Practice Quiz page 319
1. d; 2. b; 3. a; 4. a; 5. c; 6. b; 7. d

Test Yourself page 323
1. a; 2. b; 3. c; 4. c; 5. b; 6. c; 7. a; 8. a; 9. b; 10. d; 11. c;
12. a; 13. c; 14. d; 15. a; 16. a; 17. b; 18. d; 19. c; 20. d

Chapter 9

Practice Quiz page 338
1. b; 2. c; 3. c; 4. a; 5. c; 6. b; 7. c

Practice Quiz page 341
1. c; 2. c; 3. d; 4. b

Practice Quiz page 347
1. d; 2. b; 3. a; 4. c

Practice Quiz page 358
1. b; 2. a; 3. c; 4. a; 5. d

Test Yourself pages 362–363
1. b; 2. d; 3. b; 4. c; 5. a; 6. a; 7. b; 8. a; 9. b; 10. a; 11. b;
12. a; 13. d; 14. c; 15. d; 16. d; 17. a; 18. d; 19. b; 20. c

Chapter 10

Practice Quiz page 373
1. b; 2. a; 3. b; 4. c; 5. b

Practice Quiz page 383
1. a; 2. a; 3. b; 4. d; 5. c; 6. b; 7. d

Practice Quiz page 395
1. d; 2. a; 3. b; 4. d; 5. d; 6. a; 7. d

Practice Quiz page 401
1. a; 2. b; 3. d; 4. d; 5. c

Test Yourself pages 404–405
1. d; 2. a; 3. b; 4. a; 5. b; 6. d; 7. a; 8. d; 9. c; 10. a; 11. b;
12. b; 13. b; 14. a; 15. a; 16. d; 17. b; 18. d; 19. b; 20. a

Chapter 11

Practice Quiz page 409
1. c; 2. a; 3. b; 4. d

Practice Quiz page 417
1. d; 2. c; 3. c; 4. d; 5. a

Practice Quiz page 421
1. b; 2. d; 3. a; 4. c

Practice Quiz page 424
1. c; 2. b; 3. a; 4. a

Practice Quiz page 428
1. a; 2. d; 3. b; 4. d

Practice Quiz page 432
1. a; 2. c; 3. b; 4. a

Practice Quiz page 437
1. d; 2. b; 3. a; 4. c

Practice Quiz page 443
1. c; 2. a; 3. d; 4. c

Test Yourself pages 447
1. d; 2. a; 3. b; 4. d; 5. c; 6. a; 7. d; 8. a; 9. b; 10. d; 11. c;
12. c; 13. b; 14. d; 15. c; 16. b; 17. d; 18. c; 19. a; 20. d

Chapter 12

Practice Quiz page 458
1. b; 2. a; 3. d; 4. b; 5. d

Practice Quiz page 465
1. c; 2. d; 3. a; 4. c

Practice Quiz page 467
1. a; 2. b; 3. d; 4. c

Practice Quiz page 471
1. c; 2. a; 3. b; 4. d

Practice Quiz page 476
1. a; 2. b; 3. a; 4. c; 5. b

Practice Quiz page 480
1. d; 2. b; 3. c; 4. a

Test Yourself pages 486–487
1. c; 2. d; 3. c; 4. a; 5. d; 6. c; 7. b; 8. a; 9. b; 10. d; 11. a;
12. a; 13. d; 14. d; 15. b; 16. b; 17. c; 18. b; 19. d; 20. a

Chapter 13

Practice Quiz page 492
1. b; 2. d; 3. a; 4. d

Practice Quiz page 497
1. d; 2. c; 3. b; 4. c

Practice Quiz page 505
1. b; 2. d; 3. c; 4. a; 5. c

Practice Quiz page 508
1. c; 2. a; 3. d; 4. c

Practice Quiz page 514
1. c. 2. a; 3. b; 4. d

Practice Quiz page 521
1. a; 2. d; 3. a; 4. b

Test Yourself pages 524–525
1. a; 2. b; 3. a; 4. a; 5. d; 6. c; 7. d; 8. d; 9. b; 10. a; 11. b;
12. d; 13. c; 14. b; 15. d; 16. b; 17. c; 18. c; 19. a; 20. b

Appendix A

Practice Quiz page A-2
1. a; 2. b; 3. d

Practice Quiz page A-8
1. c; 2. a; 3. b; 4. b

Practice Quiz page A-11
1. a; 2. c; 3. b; 4. a

Test Yourself pages A-12
1. a; 2. c; 3. b; 4. d; 5. b; 6. a; 7. a; 8. c; 9. d; 10. d

Appendix B

Practice Quiz page B-3
1. a; 2. d; 3. c

Practice Quiz page B-9
1. c; 2. a; 3. b; 4. d

Practice Quiz page B-13
1. a; 2. a; 3. c; 4. b

Test Yourself pages B-15
1. b; 2. c; 3. a; 4. b; 5. d; 6. b; 7. d; 8. a; 9. b; 10. c

Glossary

absolute threshold the lowest level of stimulation that a person can consciously detect 50 percent of the time the stimulation is present.

accommodation as a monocular cue, the brain's use of information about the changing thickness of the lens of the eye in response to looking at objects that are close or far away.

acculturative stress stress resulting from the need to change and adapt a person's ways to the majority culture.

acquired (secondary) drives those drives that are learned through experience or conditioning, such as the need for money or social approval.

acrophobia fear of heights.

action potential the release of the neural impulse consisting of a reversal of the electrical charge within the axon.

action therapy therapy in which the main goal is to change disordered or inappropriate behavior directly.

activation-information-mode model (AIM) revised version of the activation-synthesis explanation of dreams in which information that is accessed during waking hours can have an influence on the synthesis of dreams.

activation-synthesis hypothesis premise that states that dreams are created by the higher centers of the cortex to explain the activation by the brain stem of cortical cells during REM sleep periods.

activity theory theory of adjustment to aging that assumes older people are happier if they remain active in some way, such as volunteering or developing a hobby.

acute stress disorder (ASD) a disorder resulting from exposure to a major stressor, with symptoms of anxiety, dissociation, recurring nightmares, sleep disturbances, problems in concentration, and moments in which people seem to "relive" the event in dreams and flashbacks for as long as 1 month following the event.

adolescence the period of life from about age 13 to the early 20s, during which a young person is no longer physically a child but is not yet an independent, self-supporting adult.

adrenal glands endocrine glands located on top of each kidney that secrete over 30 different hormones to deal with stress, regulate salt intake, and provide a secondary source of sex hormones affecting the sexual changes that occur during adolescence.

aerial (atmospheric) perspective the haziness that surrounds objects that are farther away from the viewer, causing the distance to be perceived as greater.

affect in psychology, a term indicating "emotion" or "mood."

afferent (sensory) neuron a neuron that carries information from the senses to the central nervous system.

afterimages images that occur when a visual sensation persists for a brief time even after the original stimulus is removed.

aggression behavior intended to hurt or destroy another person.

agonists chemical substances that mimic or enhance the effects of a neurotransmitter on the receptor sites of the next cell, increasing or decreasing the activity of that cell.

agoraphobia fear of being in a place or situation from which escape is difficult or impossible.

alcohol the chemical resulting from fermentation or distillation of various kinds of vegetable matter.

algorithms very specific, step-by-step procedures for solving certain types of problems.

all-or-none referring to the fact that a neuron either fires completely or does not fire at all.

all-or-nothing thinking the tendency to believe that one's performance must be perfect or the result will be a total failure.

alpha waves brain waves that indicate a state of relaxation or light sleep.

altered state of consciousness state in which there is a shift in the quality or pattern of mental activity as compared to waking consciousness.

altruism prosocial behavior that is done with no expectation of reward and may involve the risk of harm to oneself.

amphetamines stimulants that are synthesized (made) in laboratories rather than being found in nature.

amygdala brain structure located near the hippocampus, responsible for fear responses and memory of fear.

anal stage second stage occurring from about 1 to 3 years of age, in which the anus is the erogenous zone and toilet training is the source of conflict.

androgyny describes a gender role characteristic of people whose personalities reflect the characteristics of both males and females, regardless of gender.

andropause gradual changes in the sexual hormones and reproductive system of middle-aged males.

anorexia nervosa (anorexia) a condition in which a person reduces eating to the point that a weight loss of 15 percent below the ideal body weight or more occurs.

antagonists chemical substances that block or reduce a cell's response to the action of other chemicals or neurotransmitters.

anterograde amnesia loss of memory from the point of injury or trauma forward, or the inability to form new long-term memories.

antianxiety drugs drugs used to treat and calm anxiety reactions, typically minor tranquilizers.

antidepressant drugs drugs used to treat depression and anxiety.

antipsychotic drugs drugs used to treat psychotic symptoms such as delusions, hallucinations, and other bizarre behavior.

antisocial personality disorder (ASPD) disorder in which a person has no morals or conscience and often behaves in an impulsive manner without regard for the consequences of that behavior.

anxiety disorders disorders in which the main symptom is excessive or unrealistic anxiety and fearfulness.

applied behavior analysis (ABA) modern term for a form of functional analysis and behavior modification that uses a variety of behavioral techniques to mold a desired behavior or response.

applied psychology the use of psychological concepts in solving real-world problems.

applied research research aimed at answering real-world, practical problems.

approach–approach conflict conflict occurring when a person must choose between two desirable goals.

approach–avoidance conflict conflict occurring when a person must choose or not choose a goal that has both positive and negative aspects.

archetypes Jung's collective, universal human memories.

arousal theory theory of motivation in which people are said to have an optimal (best or ideal) level of tension that they seek to maintain by increasing or decreasing stimulation.

association areas areas within each lobe of the cortex responsible for the coordination and interpretation of information, as well as higher mental processing.

attachment the emotional bond between an infant and the primary caregiver.

attitude a tendency to respond positively or negatively toward a certain person, object, idea, or situation.

attribution theory the theory of how people make attributions.

attribution the process of explaining one's own behavior and the behavior of others.

auditory canal short tunnel that runs from the pinna to the eardrum.

auditory nerve bundle of axons from the hair cells in the inner ear.

authenticity the genuine, open, and honest response of the therapist to the client.

authoritarian parenting style of parenting in which parent is rigid and overly strict, showing little warmth to the child.

authoritative parenting style of parenting in which parents combine warmth and affection with firm limits on a child's behavior.

automatic encoding tendency of certain kinds of information to enter long-term memory with little or no effortful encoding.

autonomic nervous system (ANS) division of the PNS consisting of nerves that control all of the involuntary muscles, organs, and glands.

availability heuristic estimating the frequency or likelihood of an event based on how easy it is to recall relevant information from memory or how easy it is for us to think of related examples.

aversion therapy form of behavioral therapy in which an undesirable behavior is paired with an aversive stimulus to reduce the frequency of the behavior.

avoidance–avoidance conflict conflict occurring when a person must choose between two undesirable goals.

axon terminals branches at the end of the axon.

axon tubelike structure that carries the neural message to other cells.

barbiturates depressant drugs that have a sedative effect.

basic anxiety anxiety created when a child is born into the bigger and more powerful world of older children and adults.

basic research research for the sake of gaining scientific knowledge.

behavior modification the use of operant conditioning techniques to bring about desired changes in behavior.

behavior modification the use of operant conditioning techniques to bring about desired changes in behavior; the use of learning techniques to modify or change undesirable behavior and increase desirable behavior (may also be referred to as applied behavior analysis).

behavior therapies action therapies based on the principles of classical and operant conditioning and aimed at changing disordered behavior without concern for the original causes of such behavior.

behavioral genetics field of study devoted to discovering the genetic bases for personality characteristics.

behaviorism the science of behavior that focuses on observable behavior only.

benzodiazepines drugs that lower anxiety and reduce stress.

beta waves brain waves which are very small and very fast.

bilateral anterior cingulotomy psychosurgical technique in which an electrode wire is inserted into the anterior cingulate gyrus, with guidance from magnetic resonance imaging, to destroy a very small portion of that brain area with electric current.

bimodal distributions frequency distribution in which there are two high points rather than one.

bimodal condition in which a distribution has two modes.

binge-eating disorder a condition in which a person overeats, or binges, on enormous amounts of food at one sitting, but unlike bulimia nervosa, the individual does not then purge or use other unhealthy methods to avoid weight gain.

binocular cues cues for perceiving depth based on both eyes.

binocular disparity the difference in images between the two eyes, which is greater for objects that are close and smaller for distant objects.

biofeedback use of feedback about biological conditions to bring involuntary responses, such as blood pressure and relaxation, under voluntary control.

biological model model of explaining behavior as caused by biological changes in the chemical, structural, or genetic systems of the body.

biological psychology or behavioral neuroscience branch of neuroscience that focuses on the biological bases of psychological processes, behavior, and learning.

biomedical therapies therapies that directly affect the biological functioning of the body and brain.

biopsychological perspective perspective that attributes human and animal behavior to biological events occurring in the body, such as genetic influences, hormones, and the activity of the nervous system.

biopsychosocial model perspective in which abnormal behavior is seen as the result of the combined and interacting forces of biological, psychological, social, and cultural influences.

bipolar disorder severe mood swings between major depressive episodes and manic episodes.

bisexual person attracted to both men and women.

blind spot area in the retina where the axons of the three layers of retinal cells exit the eye to form the optic nerve, insensitive to light.

borderline personality disorder (BLPD) maladaptive personality pattern in which the person is moody, unstable, lacks a clear sense of identity, and often clings to others.

bottom-up processing the analysis of the smaller features to build up to a complete perception.

brightness constancy the tendency to perceive the apparent brightness of an object as the same even when the light conditions change.

Broca's aphasia condition resulting from damage to Broca's area, causing the affected person to be unable to speak fluently, to mispronounce words, and to speak haltingly.

bulimia nervosa a condition in which a person develops a cycle of "bingeing," or overeating enormous amounts of food at one sitting, and then using unhealthy methods to avoid weight gain.

bystander effect referring to the effect that the presence of other people has on the decision to help or not help, with help becoming less likely as the number of bystanders increases.

caffeine a mild stimulant found in coffee, tea, and several other plant-based substances.

Cannon–Bard theory of emotion theory in which the physiological reaction and the emotion are assumed to occur at the same time.

case study study of one individual in great detail.

catastrophe an unpredictable, large-scale event that creates a tremendous need to adapt and adjust as well as overwhelming feelings of threat.

catatonia disturbed behavior ranging from statue-like immobility to bursts of energetic, frantic movement, and talking.

central nervous system (CNS) part of the nervous system consisting of the brain and spinal cord.

central-route processing type of information processing that involves attending to the content of the message itself.

centration in Piaget's theory, the tendency of a young child to focus only on one feature of an object while ignoring other relevant features.

cerebellum part of the lower brain located behind the pons that controls and coordinates involuntary, rapid, fine motor movement.

cerebral hemispheres the two sections of the cortex on the left and right sides of the brain.

cerebrum the upper part of the brain consisting of the two hemispheres and the structures that connect them.

character value judgments of a person's moral and ethical behavior.

circadian rhythm a cycle of bodily rhythm that occurs over a 24-hour period.

classical conditioning learning to elicit an involuntary response to a stimulus other than the original, natural stimulus that normally produces the response.

claustrophobia fear of being in a small, enclosed space.

clinical psychology area of psychology in which the psychologists diagnose and treat people with psychological disorders that may range from mild to severe.

closure the tendency to complete figures that are incomplete.

cocaine a natural drug derived from the leaves of the coca plant.

cochlea snail-shaped structure of the inner ear that is filled with fluid.

cognitive arousal theory (two-factor theory) theory of emotion in which both the physical arousal and the labeling of that arousal based on cues from the environment must occur before the emotion is experienced.

cognitive development the development of thinking, problem solving, and memory.

cognitive dissonance sense of discomfort or distress that occurs when a person's behavior does not correspond to that person's attitudes.

cognitive neuroscience study of the physical changes in the brain and nervous system during thinking.

cognitive perspective modern theory in which classical conditioning is seen to occur because the conditioned stimulus provides information or an expectancy about the coming of the unconditioned stimulus.

cognitive psychologists psychologists who study the way people think, remember, and mentally organize information.

cognitive therapy therapy in which the focus is on helping clients recognize distortions in their thinking and replace distorted, unrealistic beliefs with more realistic, helpful thoughts.

cognitive universalism theory that concepts are universal and influence the development of language.

cognitive–behavioral therapy (CBT) action therapy in which the goal is to help clients overcome problems by learning to think more rationally and logically.

cognitive–mediational theory theory of emotion in which a stimulus must be interpreted (appraised) by a person in order to result in a physical response and an emotional reaction.

cohort effect the impact on development occurring when a group of people share a common time period or common life experience.

collective unconscious Jung's name for the memories shared by all members of the human species.

community psychology area of psychology in which psychologists serve at various levels including individual, group, and community, focusing on promoting social welfare and preventing social problems.

companionate love type of love consisting of intimacy and commitment.

comparative psychology area of psychology in which the psychologists study animals and their behavior for the purpose of comparing and contrasting it to human behavior.

compliance changing one's behavior as a result of other people directing or asking for the change.

computed tomography (CT) brain-imaging method using computer-controlled X-rays of the brain.

concept map a visual organization of the key concepts, terms, and definitions that are found in each section and is an excellent way to "see" how various concepts are linked together.

concepts ideas that represent a class or category of objects, events, or activities.

concrete operations stage Piaget's third stage of cognitive development in which the school-age child becomes capable of logical thought processes but is not yet capable of abstract thinking.

conditional positive regard positive regard that is given only when the person is doing what the providers of positive regard wish.

conditioned emotional response (CER) emotional response that has become classically conditioned to occur to learned stimuli, such as a fear of dogs or the emotional reaction that occurs when seeing an attractive person.

conditioned response (CR) learned response to a conditioned stimulus.

conditioned stimulus (CS) stimulus that becomes able to produce a learned response by being paired with the original unconditioned stimulus.

conditioned taste aversion development of a nausea or aversive response to a particular taste because that taste was followed by a nausea reaction, occurring after only one association.

cones visual sensory receptors found at the back of the retina, responsible for color vision and sharpness of vision.

confirmation bias the tendency to search for evidence that fits one's beliefs while ignoring any evidence that does not fit those beliefs.

conflict the psychological distress occurring when a person has to choose between different and incompatible or opposing goals.

conformity changing one's own behavior to match that of other people.

conscience part of the superego that produces guilt, depending on how acceptable behavior is.

consciousness a person's awareness of everything that is going on around him or her at any given moment, which is used to organize behavior.

conservation in Piaget's theory, the ability to understand that simply changing the appearance of an object does not change the object's nature.

consolidation the changes that take place in the structure and functioning of neurons when a memory is formed.

constructive processing referring to the retrieval of memories in which those memories are altered, revised, or influenced by newer information.

consumer psychology branch of psychology that studies the habits of consumers in the marketplace.

contiguity the tendency to perceive two things that happen close together in time as being related.

contingency contract a formal, written agreement between the therapist and client (or teacher and student) in which goals for behavioral change, reinforcements, and penalties are clearly stated.

continuity the tendency to perceive things as simply as possible with a continuous pattern rather than with a complex, broken-up pattern.

continuous reinforcement the reinforcement of each and every correct response.

control group subjects in an experiment who are not subjected to the independent variable and who may receive a placebo treatment.

convergence the rotation of the two eyes in their sockets to focus on a single object, resulting in greater convergence for closer objects and lesser convergence if objects are distant.

convergent thinking type of thinking in which a problem is seen as having only one answer, and all lines of thinking will eventually lead to that single answer, using previous knowledge and logic.

coping strategies   actions that people can take to master, tolerate, reduce, or minimize the effects of stressors.

coronary heart disease (CHD)   the buildup of a waxy substance called plaque in the arteries of the heart.

corpus callosum   thick band of neurons that connects the right and left cerebral hemispheres.

correlation   a measure of the relationship between two variables.

correlation coefficient   a number derived from the formula for measuring a correlation and indicating the strength and direction of a correlation.

cortex   outermost covering of the brain consisting of densely packed neurons, responsible for higher thought processes and interpretation of sensory input.

counseling psychology   area of psychology in which the psychologists help people with problems of adjustment.

creativity   the process of solving problems by combining ideas or behavior in new ways.

critical periods   times during which certain environmental influences can have an impact on the development of the infant.

critical thinking   making reasoned judgments about claims.

cross-sectional design   research design in which several different age-groups of participants are studied at one particular point in time.

cross-sequential design   research design in which participants are first studied by means of a cross-sectional design but are also followed and assessed longitudinally.

cultural relativity   the need to consider the unique characteristics of the culture in which behavior takes place.

cultural syndromes   sets of particular symptoms of distress found in particular cultures, which may or may not be recognized as an illness within the culture.

curve of forgetting   a graph showing a distinct pattern in which forgetting is very fast within the first hour after learning a list and then tapers off gradually.

cybertherapy   psychotherapy that is offered on the Internet. Also called online, Internet, or Web therapy or counseling.

dark adaptation   the recovery of the eye's sensitivity to visual stimuli in darkness after exposure to bright lights.

decay   loss of memory due to the passage of time, during which the memory trace is not used.

decision making   process of cognition that involves identifying, evaluating, and choosing among several alternatives.

declarative (explicit) memory   type of long-term memory containing information that is conscious and known.

delta waves   long, slow waves that indicate the deepest stage of sleep.

delusions   false beliefs held by a person who refuses to accept evidence of their falseness.

dendrites   branchlike structures that receive messages from other neurons.

dependent variable   variable in an experiment that represents the measurable response or behavior of the subjects in the experiment.

depressants   drugs that decrease the functioning of the nervous system.

depth perception   the ability to perceive the world in three dimensions.

descriptive statistics   a way of organizing numbers and summarizing them so that patterns can be determined.

developmental psychology   area of psychology in which the psychologists study the changes in the way people think, relate to others, and feel as they age.

deviation IQ scores   a type of intelligence measure that assumes that IQ is normally distributed around a mean of 100 with a standard deviation of about.

diffusion of responsibility   occurring when a person fails to take responsibility for actions or for inaction because of the presence of other people who are seen to share the responsibility.

diffusion   process of molecules moving from areas of high concentration to areas of low concentration.

direct observation   assessment in which the professional observes the client engaged in ordinary, day-to-day behavior in either a clinical or natural setting.

directive   therapy in which the therapist actively gives interpretations of a client's statements and may suggest certain behavior or actions.

discrimination   treating people differently because of prejudice toward the social group to which they belong.

discriminative stimulus   any stimulus, such as a stop sign or a doorknob, that provides the organism with a cue for making a certain response in order to obtain reinforcement.

display rules   learned ways of controlling displays of emotion in social settings.

dispositional cause   cause of behavior attributed to internal factors such as personality or character.

dissociation   divided state of conscious awareness.

dissociative identity disorder (DID)   disorder occurring when a person seems to have two or more distinct personalities within one body.

distress   the effect of unpleasant and undesirable stressors.

distributed practice   spacing the study of material to be remembered by including breaks between study periods.

disuse   another name for decay, assuming that memories that are not used will eventually decay and disappear.

divergent thinking   type of thinking in which a person starts from one point and comes up with many different ideas or possibilities based on that point.

dizygotic twins   often called fraternal twins, occurring when two eggs each get fertilized by two different sperm, resulting in two zygotes in the uterus at the same time.

dominant   referring to a gene that actively controls the expression of a trait.

door-in-the-face technique   asking for a large commitment and being refused and then asking for a smaller commitment.

double-blind study   study in which neither the experimenter nor the subjects know if the subjects are in the experimental or control group.

drive   a psychological tension and physical arousal arising when there is a need that motivates the organism to act in order to fulfill the need and reduce the tension.

drive-reduction theory   approach to motivation that assumes behavior arises from physiological needs that cause internal drives to push the organism to satisfy the need and reduce tension and arousal.

drug tolerance   as the person continues to use the drug, larger and larger doses of the drug are needed to achieve the same initial effects of the drug.

echoic memory   the brief memory of something a person has just heard.

eclectic   approach to therapy that results from combining elements of several different approaches or techniques.

educational psychology   area of psychology in which the psychologists are concerned with the study of human learning and development of new learning techniques.

efferent (motor) neuron   a neuron that carries messages from the central nervous system to the muscles of the body.

ego part of the personality that develops out of a need to deal with reality, mostly conscious, rational, and logical.

egocentrism the inability to see the world through anyone else's eyes.

eidetic imagery the ability to access a visual memory for 30 seconds or more.

elaboration likelihood model model of persuasion stating that people will either elaborate on the persuasive message or fail to elaborate on it and that the future actions of those who do elaborate are more predictable than those who do not.

elaborative rehearsal a method of transferring information from STM into LTM by making that information meaningful in some way.

electroconvulsive therapy (ECT) form of biomedical therapy to treat severe depression in which electrodes are placed on either one or both sides of a person's head and an electric current is passed through the electrodes that is strong enough to cause a seizure or convulsion.

electroencephalograph machine designed to record the electroencephalogram.

embryo name for the developing organism from two weeks to eight weeks after fertilization.

embryonic period the period from two to eight weeks after fertilization, during which the major organs and structures of the organism develop.

emotion the "feeling" aspect of consciousness, characterized by a certain physical arousal, a certain behavior that reveals the emotion to the outside world, and an inner awareness of feelings.

emotional intelligence the awareness of and ability to manage one's own emotions as well as the ability to be self-motivated, able to feel what others feel, and socially skilled.

emotion-focused coping coping strategies that change the impact of a stressor by changing the emotional reaction to the stressor.

empathy the ability of the therapist to understand the feelings of the client.

encoding failure failure to process information into memory.

encoding specificity the tendency for memory of information to be improved if related information (such as surroundings or physiological state) available when the memory is first formed is also available when the memory is being retrieved.

encoding the set of mental operations that people perform on sensory information to convert that information into a form that is usable in the brain's storage systems.

endocrine glands glands that secrete chemicals called hormones directly into the bloodstream.

environmental psychology area of psychology in which the focus is on how people interact with and are affected by their physical environments.

enzymatic degradation process by which structure of neurotransmitter is altered so it can no longer act on a receptor.

episodic memory type of declarative memory containing personal information not readily available to others, such as daily activities and events.

equal status contact contact between groups in which the groups have equal status with neither group having power over the other.

eustress the effect of positive events, or the optimal amount of stress that people need to promote health and well-being.

evidence-based treatment (EBT) also called empirically supported treatment, refers to interventions, strategies, or techniques that have been found to produce therapeutic and desired changes during controlled research studies.

evolutionary perspective perspective that focuses on the biological bases of universal mental characteristics that all humans share.

excitatory synapse synapse at which a neurotransmitter causes the receiving cell to fire.

expectancy a person's subjective feeling that a particular behavior will lead to a reinforcing consequence.

experiment a deliberate manipulation of a variable to see if corresponding changes in behavior result, allowing the determination of cause-and-effect relationships.

experimental group subjects in an experiment who are subjected to the independent variable.

experimental psychology area of psychology in which the psychologists primarily do research and experiments in the areas of learning, memory, thinking, perception, motivation, and language.

experimenter effect tendency of the experimenter's expectations for a study to unintentionally influence the results of the study.

explicit memory memory that is consciously known, such as declarative memory.

exposure therapies behavioral techniques that expose individuals to anxiety- or fear-related stimuli, under carefully controlled conditions, to promote new learning.

extinction the disappearance or weakening of a learned response following the removal or absence of the unconditioned stimulus (in classical conditioning) or the removal of a reinforcer (in operant conditioning).

extraverts people who are outgoing and sociable.

extrinsic motivation type of motivation in which a person performs an action because it leads to an outcome that is separate from or external to the person.

facial feedback hypothesis theory of emotion that assumes that facial expressions provide feedback to the brain concerning the emotion being expressed, which in turn causes and intensifies the emotion.

family counseling (family theraphy) a form of group therapy in which family members meet together with a counselor or therapist to resolve problems that affect the entire family.

fertilization the union of the ovum and sperm.

fetal alcohol syndrome (FAS) the physical and mental defects caused by consumption of alcohol during pregnancy.

fetal period the time from about eight weeks after conception until the birth of the child.

fetus name for the developing organism from eight weeks after fertilization to the birth of the baby.

figure–ground the tendency to perceive objects, or figures, as existing on a background.

five-factor model model of personality traits that describes five basic trait dimensions.

fixation disorder in which the person does not fully resolve the conflict in a particular psychosexual stage, resulting in personality traits and behavior associated with that earlier stage.

fixed interval schedule of reinforcement schedule of reinforcement in which the interval of time that must pass before reinforcement becomes possible is always the same.

fixed ratio schedule of reinforcement schedule of reinforcement in which the number of responses required for reinforcement is always the same.

flashbulb memories type of automatic encoding that occurs because an unexpected event has strong emotional associations for the person remembering it.

flat affect a lack of emotional responsiveness.

flooding technique for treating phobias and other stress disorders in which the person is rapidly and intensely exposed to the fear-provoking situation or object and prevented from making the usual avoidance or escape response.

foot-in-the-door technique asking for a small commitment and, after gaining compliance, asking for a bigger commitment.

forensic psychology area of psychology concerned with people in the legal system, including psychological assessment of criminals, jury selection, and expert witnessing.

formal operations stage Piaget's last stage of cognitive development, in which the adolescent becomes capable of abstract thinking.

free association psychoanalytic technique in which a patient was encouraged to talk about anything that came to mind without fear of negative evaluations.

free-floating anxiety anxiety that is unrelated to any realistic, known source.

frequency count assessment in which the frequency of a particular behavior is counted.

frequency distribution a table or graph that shows how often different numbers or scores appear in a particular set of scores.

frequency theory theory of pitch that states that pitch is related to the speed of vibrations in the basilar membrane.

frontal lobes areas of the brain located in the front and top, responsible for higher mental processes and decision making as well as the production of fluent speech.

frustration the psychological experience produced by the blocking of a desired goal or fulfillment of a perceived need.

fully functioning person a person who is in touch with and trusting of the deepest, innermost urges and feelings.

functional fixedness a block to problem solving that comes from thinking about objects in terms of only their typical functions.

functional magnetic resonance imaging (fMRI) MRI-based brain-imaging method that allows for functional examination of brain areas through changes in brain oxygenation.

functionalism early perspective in psychology associated with William James, in which the focus of study is how the mind allows people to adapt, live, work, and play.

fundamental attribution error the tendency to overestimate the influence of internal factors in determining behavior while underestimating situational factors.

g factor the ability to reason and solve problems, or general intelligence.

gender identity the individual's sense of being male or female.

gender roles the culture's expectations for masculine or feminine behavior, including attitudes, actions, and personality traits associated with being male or female in that culture.

gender schema theory theory of gender identity acquisition in which a child develops a mental pattern, or schema, for being male or female and then organizes observed and learned behavior around that schema.

gender the behavior associated with being male or female.

general adaptation syndrome (GAS) the three stages of the body's physiological reaction to stress, including alarm, resistance, and exhaustion.

generalized anxiety disorder disorder in which a person has feelings of dread and impending doom along with physical symptoms of stress, which lasts 6 months or more.

generativity providing guidance to one's children or the next generation, or contributing to the well-being of the next generation through career or volunteer work.

genetics the science of heredity. Understanding how genes transmit human characteristics and traits involves defining a few basic terms.

germinal period first two weeks after fertilization, during which the zygote moves down to the uterus and begins to implant in the lining.

gestalt psychology early perspective in psychology focusing on perception and sensation, particularly the perception of patterns and whole figures.

gestalt therapy form of directive insight therapy in which the therapist helps clients to accept all parts of their feelings and subjective experiences, using leading questions and planned experiences such as role-playing.

gifted the 2 percent of the population falling on the upper end of the normal curve and typically possessing an IQ of 130 or above.

glial cells cells that provide support for the neurons to grow on and around, deliver nutrients to neurons, produce myelin to coat axons, clean up waste products and dead neurons, influence information processing, and, during prenatal development, influence the generation of new neurons.

glucagon hormone that is secreted by the pancreas to control the levels of fats, proteins, and carbohydrates in the body by increasing the level of glucose in the bloodstream.

gonads sex glands; secrete hormones that regulate sexual development and behavior as well as reproduction.

grammar the system of rules governing the structure and use of a language.

group therapy form of therapy or treatment during which a small group of clients with similar concerns meet together with a therapist to address their issues.

groupthink kind of thinking that occurs when people place more importance on maintaining group cohesiveness than on assessing the facts of the problem with which the group is concerned.

gustation the sensation of a taste.

habits in behaviorism, sets of well-learned responses that have become automatic.

habituation tendency of the brain to stop attending to constant, unchanging information.

hallucinations false sensory perceptions, such as hearing voices that do not really exist.

hallucinogenics drugs including hallucinogens and marijuana that produce hallucinations or increased feelings of relaxation and intoxication.

hallucinogens drugs that cause false sensory messages, altering the perception of reality.

halo effect tendency of an interviewer to allow positive characteristics of a client to influence the assessments of the client's behavior and statements.

hardy personality a person who seems to thrive on stress but lacks the anger and hostility of the Type A personality.

hassles the daily annoyances of everyday life.

health psychology area of psychology focusing on how physical activities, psychological traits, and social relationships affect overall health and rate of illnesses; area of psychology in which the psychologists focus on the relationship of human behavior patterns and stress reactions to physical health.

heritability proportion of change in IQ within a population that is caused by hereditary factors.

heroin narcotic drug derived from opium that is extremely addictive.

hertz (Hz) cycles or waves per second, a measurement of frequency.

heterosexual person attracted to the opposite sex.

heuristic an educated guess based on prior experiences that helps narrow down the possible solutions for a problem. Also known as a "rule of thumb."

higher-order conditioning occurs when a strong conditioned stimulus is paired with a neutral stimulus, causing the neutral stimulus to become a second conditioned stimulus.

hindsight bias the tendency to falsely believe, through revision of older memories to include newer information, that one could have correctly predicted the outcome of an event.

hippocampus curved structure located within each temporal lobe, responsible for the formation of long-term memories and the storage of memory for location of objects.

histogram   a bar graph showing a frequency distribution.

homeostasis   the tendency of the body to maintain a steady state.

homosexual   person attracted to the same sex.

hormones   chemicals released into the bloodstream by endocrine glands.

human development   the scientific study of the changes that occur in people as they age from conception until death.

human factors psychology   area of industrial/organizational psychology concerned with the study of the way humans and machines interact with each other.

humanistic perspective   the "third force" in psychology that focuses on those aspects of personality that make people uniquely human, such as subjective feelings and freedom of choice.

hypnosis   state of consciousness in which the person is especially susceptible to suggestion.

hypothalamus   small structure in the brain located below the thalamus and directly above the pituitary gland, responsible for motivational behavior such as sleep, hunger, thirst, and sex.

hypothesis   tentative explanation of a phenomenon based on observations.

iconic memory   visual sensory memory, lasting only a fraction of a second.

id   part of the personality present at birth and completely unconscious.

identity versus role confusion   fifth stage of personality development in which the adolescent must find a consistent sense of self.

imaginary audience   type of thought common to adolescents in which young people believe that other people are just as concerned about the adolescent's thoughts and characteristics as they themselves are.

immune system   the system of cells, organs, and chemicals of the body that responds to attacks from diseases, infections, and injuries.

implicit personality theory   sets of assumptions about how different types of people, personality traits, and actions are related to each other.

impression formation   the forming of the first knowledge that a person has concerning another person.

incentive approaches   theories of motivation in which behavior is explained as a response to the external stimulus and its rewarding properties.

incentives   things that attract or lure people into action.

independent variable   variable in an experiment that is manipulated by the experimenter.

industrial/organizational (I/O) psychology   area of psychology concerned with the relationships between people and their work environment.

Inferential statistics   statistical analysis of two or more sets of numerical data to reduce the possibility of error in measurement and to determine if the differences between the data sets are greater than chance variation would predict.

information-processing model   model of memory that assumes the processing of information for memory storage is similar to the way a computer processes memory in a series of three stages.

in-groups   social groups with whom a person identifies; "us."

inhibitory synapse   synapse at which a neurotransmitter causes the receiving cell to stop firing.

insight therapies   therapies in which the main goal is helping people to gain insight with respect to their behavior, thoughts, and feelings.

insight   the sudden perception of relationships among various parts of a problem, allowing the solution to the problem to come quickly.

insomnia   the inability to get to sleep, stay asleep, or get a good quality of sleep.

instinct approach   approach to motivation that assumes people are governed by instincts similar to those of animals.

instinctive drift   tendency for an animal's behavior to revert to genetically controlled patterns.

instincts   the biologically determined and innate patterns of behavior that exist in both people and animals.

insulin   a hormone secreted by the pancreas to control the levels of fats, proteins, and carbohydrates in the body by reducing the level of glucose in the bloodstream.

integrity   sense of wholeness that comes from having lived a full life and the ability to let go of regrets; the final completion of the ego.

intellectual disability (intellectual developmental disorder)   condition in which a person's behavioral and cognitive skills exist at an earlier developmental stage than the skills of others who are the same chronological age; may also be referred to as developmentally delayed. This condition was formerly known as mental retardation.

intelligence quotient (IQ)   a number representing a measure of intelligence, resulting from the division of one's mental age by one's chronological age and then multiplying that quotient by 100.

intelligence   the ability to learn from one's experiences, acquire knowledge, and use resources effectively in adapting to new situations or solving problems.

interneuron   a neuron found in the center of the spinal cord that receives information from the afferent neurons and sends commands to the muscles through the efferent neurons. Interneurons also make up the bulk of the neurons in the brain.

interpersonal attraction   liking or having the desire for a relationship with another person.

interpersonal psychotherapy (IPT)   form of therapy for depression which incorporates multiple approaches and focuses on interpersonal problems.

interview   method of personality assessment in which the professional asks questions of the client and allows the client to answer, either in a structured or unstructured fashion.

intimacy   an emotional and psychological closeness that is based on the ability to trust, share, and care, while still maintaining a sense of self.

intrinsic motivation   type of motivation in which a person performs an action because the act itself is rewarding or satisfying in some internal manner.

introversion   dimension of personality in which people tend to withdraw from excessive stimulation.

introverts   people who prefer solitude and dislike being the center of attention.

irreversibility   in Piaget's theory, the inability of the young child to mentally reverse an action.

James–Lange theory of emotion   theory in which a physiological reaction leads to the labeling of an emotion.

jigsaw classroom   educational technique in which each individual is given only part of the information needed to solve a problem, causing the separate individuals to be forced to work together to find the solution.

just noticeable difference (jnd or the difference threshold)   the smallest difference between two stimuli that is detectable 50 percent of the time.

kinesthetic sense   sense of the location of body parts in relation to the ground and each other.

language   a system for combining symbols (such as words) so that an unlimited number of meaningful statements can be made for the purpose of communicating with others.

latency   fourth stage occurring during the school years, in which the sexual feelings of the child are repressed while the child develops in other ways.

latent content   the symbolic or hidden meaning of dreams.

latent learning   learning that remains hidden until its application becomes useful.

law of effect   law stating that if an action is followed by a pleasurable consequence, it will tend to be repeated, and if followed by an unpleasant consequence, it will tend not to be repeated.

learned helplessness the tendency to fail to act to escape from a situation because of a history of repeated failures in the past.

learning/performance distinction referring to the observation that learning can take place without actual performance of the learned behavior.

learning a relatively permanent change in behavior brought about by experience or practice.

leptin the hormone signals the hypothalamus that the body has had enough food, reducing appetite. Also, part of the hypothalamus stops the eating response as blood sugar increases, while another part controls the beginning of eating as insulin levels go up.

lesioning an electrical current strong enough to kill off the target neurons is sent through the tip of the wire.

levels-of-processing model model of memory that assumes information that is more "deeply processed," or processed according to its meaning rather than just the sound or physical characteristics of the word or words, will be remembered more efficiently and for a longer period of time.

limbic System a group of several brain structures located primarily under the cortex and involved in learning, emotion, memory, and motivation.

light adaptation the recovery of the eye's sensitivity to visual stimuli in light after exposure to darkness.

linear perspective the tendency for parallel lines to appear to converge on each other.

linguistic relativity hypothesis the theory that thought processes and concepts are controlled by language.

locus of control the tendency for people to assume that they either have control or do not have control over events and consequences in their lives.

longitudinal design research design in which one participant or group of participants is studied over a long period of time.

long-term memory (LTM) the system of memory into which all the information is placed to be kept more or less permanently.

lowball technique getting a commitment from a person and then raising the cost of that commitment.

LSD (lysergic acid diethylamide) powerful synthetic hallucinogen.

magnetic resonance imaging (MRI) brain-imaging method using radio waves and magnetic fields of the body to produce detailed images of the brain.

magnification the tendency to interpret situations as far more dangerous, harmful, or important than they actually are.

maintenance rehearsal practice of saying information to be remembered over and over in one's head in order to maintain it in short-term memory.

major depressive disorder severe depression that comes on suddenly and seems to have no external cause, or is too severe for current circumstances.

maladaptive anything that does not allow a person to function within or adapt to the stresses and everyday demands of life.

manic having the quality of excessive excitement, energy, and elation or irritability.

marijuana mild hallucinogen (also known as *pot or weed*) derived from the leaves and flowers of a particular type of hemp plant.

MDMA (Ecstasy or X) designer drug that can have both stimulant and hallucinatory effects.

mean the arithmetic average of a distribution of numbers.

measure of central tendency numbers that best represent the most typical score of a frequency distribution.

measures of variability measurement of the degree of differences within a distribution or how the scores are spread out.

median the middle score in an ordered distribution of scores, or the mean of the two middle numbers; the 50th percentile.

meditation mental series of exercises meant to refocus attention and achieve a trancelike state of consciousness.

medulla the first large swelling at the top of the spinal cord, forming the lowest part of the brain, which is responsible for life-sustaining functions such as breathing, swallowing, and heart rate.

memory trace physical change in the brain that occurs when a memory is formed.

memory an active system that receives information from the senses, puts that information into a usable form, organizes it as it stores it away, and then retrieves the information from storage.

menopause the cessation of ovulation and menstrual cycles and the end of a woman's reproductive capability.

mental images mental representations that stand for objects or events and have a picture-like quality.

mental set the tendency for people to persist in using problem-solving patterns that have worked for them in the past.

minimization the tendency to give little or no importance to one's successes or positive events and traits.

mirror neurons neurons that fire when an animal or person performs an action and also when an animal or person observes that same action being performed by another.

misinformation effect the tendency of misleading information presented after an event to alter the memories of the event itself.

mnemonic a memory trick or strategy to help people remember.

mode the most frequent score in a distribution of scores.

modeling learning through the observation and imitation of others.

monocular cues (pictorial depth cues) cues for perceiving depth based on one eye only.

monozygotic twins identical twins formed when one zygote splits into two separate masses of cells, each of which develops into a separate embryo.

mood disorders disorders in which mood is severely disturbed

morphemes the smallest units of meaning within a language.

morphine narcotic drug derived from opium, used to treat severe pain.

motion parallax the perception of motion of objects in which close objects appear to move more quickly than objects that are farther away.

motivation the process by which activities are started, directed, and continued so that physical or psychological needs or wants are met.

motor cortex ear section of the frontal lobe, responsible for sending motor commands to the muscles of the somatic nervous system.

motor pathway nerves coming from the CNS to the voluntary muscles, consisting of efferent neurons.

Müller–Lyer illusion illusion of line length that is distorted by inward-turning or outward-turning corners on the ends of the lines, causing lines of equal length to appear to be different.

myelin fatty substances produced by certain glial cells that coat the axons of neurons to insulate, protect, and speed up the neural impulse.

narcolepsy sleep disorder in which a person falls immediately into REM sleep during the day without warning.

narcotics a class of opium-related drugs that suppress the sensation of pain by binding to and stimulating the nervous system's natural receptor sites for endorphins.

natural killer cell immune system cell responsible for suppressing viruses and destroying tumor cells.

nature the influence of our inherited characteristics on our personality, physical growth, intellectual growth, and social interactions.

need for achievement (nAch) a need that involves a strong desire to succeed in attaining goals, not only realistic ones but also challenging ones.

need for affiliation (nAff) the need for friendly social interactions and relationships with others.

need for power (nPow) the need to have control or influence over others.

need a requirement of some material (such as food or water) that is essential for survival of the organism.

negative reinforcement the reinforcement of a response by the removal, escape from, or avoidance of an unpleasant stimulus.

negative symptoms symptoms of schizophrenia that are less than normal behavior or an absence of normal behavior; poor attention, flat affect, and poor speech production.

negatively skewed a distribution of scores in which scores are concentrated in the high end of the distribution.

neo-Freudians followers of Freud who developed their own competing psychodynamic theories.

nerves bundles of axons coated in myelin that travel together through the body.

nervous system an extensive network of specialized cells that carries information to and from all parts of the body.

neurofeedback form of biofeedback using brain-scanning devices to provide feedback about brain activity in an effort to modify behavior.

neuron the basic cell that makes up the nervous system and that receives and sends messages within that system.

neuroplasticity the ability within the brain to constantly change both the structure and function of many cells in response to experience or trauma.

neuropsychology area of psychology in which the psychologists specialize in the research or clinical implications of brain–behavior relationships.

neuroscience a branch of the life sciences that deals with the structure and function of neurons, nerves, and nervous tissue.

neurotic personalities personalities typified by maladaptive ways of dealing with relationships in Horney's theory.

neurotransmitter chemical found in the synaptic vesicles that, when released, has an effect on the next cell.

neutral stimulus (NS) stimulus that has no effect on the desired response.

nicotine the active ingredient in tobacco.

night terrors relatively rare disorder in which the person experiences extreme fear and screams or runs around during deep sleep without waking fully.

nightmares bad dreams occurring during REM sleep.

nondeclarative (implicit) memory type of long-term memory including memory for skills, procedures, habits, and conditioned responses. These memories are not conscious but are implied to exist because they affect conscious behavior.

nondirective therapy style in which the therapist remains relatively neutral and does not interpret or take direct actions with regard to the client, instead remaining a calm, nonjudgmental listener while the client talks.

non-REM (NREM) sleep any of the stages of sleep that do not include REM.

normal curve a special frequency polygon in which the scores are symmetrically distributed around the mean, and the mean, median, and mode are all located on the same point on the curve, with scores decreasing as the curve extends from the mean.

nurture the influence of the environment on personality, physical growth, intellectual growth, and social interactions.

obedience changing one's behavior at the command of an authority figure.

object permanence the knowledge that an object exists even when it is not in sight.

objective introspection the process of examining and measuring one's own thoughts and mental activities.

observational learning learning new behavior by watching a model perform that behavior.

observer bias tendency of observers to see what they expect to see.

observer effect tendency of people or animals to behave differently from normal when they know they are being observed.

obsessive-compulsive disorder disorder in which intruding, recurring thoughts or obsessions create anxiety that is relieved by performing a repetitive, ritualistic behavior or mental act (compulsion).

occipital lobe section of the brain located at the rear and bottom of each cerebral hemisphere containing the visual centers of the brain.

Oedipus complex/Electra complex situation occurring in the phallic stage in which a child develops a sexual attraction to the opposite-sex parent and jealousy of the same-sex parent.

olfaction (olfactory sense) the sensation of smell.

olfactory bulbs areas of the brain located just above the sinus cavity and just below the frontal lobes that receive information from the olfactory receptor cells.

operant conditioning the learning of voluntary behavior through the effects of pleasant and unpleasant consequences to responses.

operant any behavior that is voluntary.

operational definition definition of a variable of interest that allows it to be directly measured.

opponent-process theory theory of color vision that proposes visual neurons (or groups of neurons) are stimulated by light of one color and inhibited by light of another color.

optimists people who expect positive outcomes.

oral stage first stage occurring in the first year of life in which the mouth is the erogenous zone and weaning is the primary conflict.

out-groups social groups with whom a person does not identify; "them."

ovaries the female gonads.

overgeneralization the tendency to interpret a single negative event as a never-ending pattern of defeat and failure; distortion of thinking in which a person draws sweeping conclusions based on only one incident or event and applies those conclusions to events that are unrelated to the original.

overlap (interposition) the assumption that an object that appears to be blocking part of another object is in front of the second object and closer to the viewer.

ovum the female sex cell, or egg.

oxytocin One part of the pituitary controls things associated with pregnancy, through the hormone **oxytocin**, such as production of milk for nursing infants and the onset of labor, as well as the levels of salt and water in the body, through the hormone *vasopressin*.

pancreas endocrine gland; controls the levels of sugar in the blood.

panic attack sudden onset of intense panic in which multiple physical symptoms of stress occur, often with feelings that one is dying.

panic disorder disorder in which panic attacks occur frequently enough to cause the person difficulty in adjusting to daily life.

parallel distributed processing (PDP) model a model of memory in which memory processes are proposed to take place at the same time over a large network of neural connections.

parasympathetic division part of the ANS that restores the body to normal functioning after arousal and is responsible for the day-to-day functioning of the organs and glands.

parietal lobes sections of the brain located at the top and back of each cerebral hemisphere containing the centers for touch, taste, and temperature sensations.

partial reinforcement effect the tendency for a response that is reinforced after some, but not all, correct responses to be very resistant to extinction.

participant modeling   technique in which a model demonstrates the desired behavior in a step-by-step, gradual process while the client is encouraged to imitate the model.

participant observation   a naturalistic observation in which the observer becomes a participant in the group being observed.

PCP   synthesized drug now used as an animal tranquilizer that can cause stimulant, depressant, narcotic, or hallucinogenic effects.

peak experiences   according to Maslow, times in a person's life during which self-actualization is temporarily achieved.

perception   the method by which the sensations experienced at any given moment are interpreted and organized in some meaningful fashion.

perceptual set (perceptual expectancy)   the tendency to perceive things a certain way because previous experiences or expectations influence those perceptions.

peripheral nervous system (PNS)   all nerves and neurons that are not contained in the brain and spinal cord but that run through the body itself.

peripheral-route processing   type of information processing that involves attending to factors not involved in the message, such as the appearance of the source of the message, the length of the message, and other noncontent factors.

permissive indulgent   permissive parenting in which parents are so involved that children are allowed to behave without set limits.

permissive neglectful   permissive parenting in which parents are uninvolved with a child or child's behavior.

permissive parenting   style of parenting in which parent makes few, if any, demands on a child's behavior.

personal fable   type of thought common to adolescents in which young people believe themselves to be unique and protected from harm.

personal unconscious   Jung's name for the unconscious mind as described by Freud.

personality disorder   disorders in which a person adopts a persistent, rigid, and maladaptive pattern of behavior that interferes with normal social interactions.

personality inventory   a table or graph that shows how often different numbers or scores appear in a particular set of scores.

personality psychology   area of psychology in which the psychologists study the differences in personality among people.

personality   the unique and relatively stable ways in which people think, feel, and behave.

person-centered therapy   a nondirective insight therapy based on the work of Carl Rogers in which the client does all the talking and the therapist listens.

persuasion   the process by which one person tries to change the belief, opinion, position, or course of action of another person through argument, pleading, or explanation.

phallic stage   third stage occurring from about 3 to 6 years of age, in which the child discovers sexual feelings.

phobia   an irrational, persistent fear of an object, situation, or social activity.

phonemes   the basic units of sound in language.

physical dependence   condition occurring when a person's body becomes unable to function normally without a particular drug.

physiological psychology   area of psychology in which the psychologists study the biological bases of behavior.

pineal gland   endocrine gland located near the base of the cerebrum; secretes melatonin.

pinna   the visible part of the ear.

pitch   psychological experience of sound that corresponds to the frequency of the sound waves; higher frequencies are perceived as higher pitches.

pituitary gland   gland located in the brain that secretes human growth hormone and influences all other hormone-secreting glands (also known as the master gland).

place theory   theory of pitch that states that different pitches are experienced by the stimulation of hair cells in different locations on the organ of Corti.

placebo effect   the phenomenon in which the expectations of the participants in a study can influence their behavior.

plagiarism   the copying of someone else's exact words (or a close imitation of the words) and presenting them as your own.

pleasure principle   principle by which the id functions; the immediate satisfaction of needs without regard for the consequences.

polygon   line graph showing a frequency distribution.

pons   the larger swelling above the medulla that connects the top of the brain to the bottom and that plays a part in sleep, dreaming, left–right body coordination, and arousal.

population   the entire group of people or animals in which the researcher is interested.

positive regard   warmth, affection, love, and respect that come from significant others in one's life.

positive reinforcement   the reinforcement of a response by the addition or experience of a pleasurable stimulus.

positive symptoms   symptoms of schizophrenia that are excesses of behaviour or occur in addition to normal behavior; hallucinations, delusions, and distorted thinking.

positively skewed   a distribution of scores in which scores are concentrated in the low end of the distribution.

positron emission tomography (PET)   brain-imaging method in which a radioactive sugar is injected into a person and a computer compiles a color-coded image of the activity of the brain.

posttraumatic stress disorder (PTSD)   a disorder resulting from exposure to a major stressor, with symptoms of anxiety, dissociation, nightmares, poor sleep, reliving the event, and concentration problems, lasting for more than 1 month.

pragmatics   aspects of language involving the practical ways of communicating with others, or the social "niceties" of language.

prefrontal lobotomy   psychosurgery in which the connections of the prefrontal cortex to other areas of the brain are severed.

prejudice   negative attitude held by a person about the members of a particular social group.

preoperational stage   Piaget's second stage of cognitive development in which the preschool child learns to use language as a means of exploring the world.

pressure   the psychological experience produced by urgent demands or expectations for a person's behavior that come from an outside source.

primacy effect   tendency to remember information at the beginning of a body of information better than the information that follows.

primary appraisal   the first step in assessing stress, which involves estimating the severity of a stressor and classifying it as either a threat or a challenge.

primary drives   those drives that involve needs of the body such as hunger and thirst.

primary reinforcer   any reinforcer that is naturally reinforcing by meeting a basic biological need, such as hunger, thirst, or touch.

proactive interference   memory problem that occurs when older information prevents or interferes with the learning or retrieval of newer information.

problem solving   process of cognition that occurs when a goal must be reached by thinking and behaving in certain ways.

problem-focused coping coping strategies that try to eliminate the source of a stressor or reduce its impact through direct actions.

projective tests personality assessments that present ambiguous visual stimuli to the client and ask the client to respond with whatever comes to mind.

prosocial behavior socially desirable behavior that benefits others.

prototype an example of a concept that closely matches the defining characteristics of a concept.

proximity the tendency to perceive objects that are close to each other as part of the same grouping.

psychiatric social worker a social worker with some training in therapy methods who focuses on the environmental conditions that can have an impact on mental disorders, such as poverty, overcrowding, stress, and drug abuse.

psychiatrist a medical doctor who has specialized in the diagnosis and treatment of psychological disorders.

psychoactive drugs drugs that alter thinking, perception, and memory.

psychoanalysis Freud's term for both the theory of personality and the therapy based on it; an insight therapy based on the theory of Freud, emphasizing the revealing of unconscious conflicts.

psychodynamic perspective modern version of psychoanalysis that is more focused on the development of a sense of self and the discovery of other motivations behind a person's behavior than sexual motivations.

psychodynamic therapy a newer and more general term for therapies based on psychoanalysis, with an emphasis on transference, shorter treatment times, and a more direct therapeutic approach.

psychological defense mechanisms unconscious distortions of a person's perception of reality that reduce stress and anxiety.

psychological dependence the feeling that a drug is needed to continue a feeling of emotional or psychological well-being.

psychological disorder any pattern of behavior that causes people significant distress, causes them to harm others, or harms their ability to function in daily life.

psychologist a professional with an academic degree and specialized training in one or more areas of psychology.

psychology the scientific study of behavior and mental processes.

psychoneuroimmunology the study of the effects of psychological factors such as stress, emotions, thoughts, and behavior on the immune system.

psychopathology the study of abnormal behavior.

psychopharmacology the use of drugs to control or relieve the symptoms of psychological disorders.

psychosexual stages five stages of personality development proposed by Freud and tied to the sexual development of the child.

psychosurgery surgery performed on brain tissue to relieve or control severe psychological disorders.

psychotic term applied to a person who is no longer able to perceive what is real and what is fantasy.

puberty the physical changes that occur in the body as sexual development reaches its peak.

punishment by application the punishment of a response by the addition or experience of an unpleasant stimulus.

punishment by removal the punishment of a response by the removal of a pleasurable stimulus.

punishment any event or object that, when following a response, makes that response less likely to happen again.

random assignment process of assigning subjects to the experimental or control group randomly, so that each subject has an equal chance of being in either group.

range the difference between the highest and lowest scores in a distribution.

rapid eye movement (REM) stage of sleep in which the eyes move rapidly under the eyelids and the person is typically experiencing a dream.

rating scale assessment in which a numerical value is assigned to specific behavior that is listed in the scale.

rational emotive behavior therapy (REBT) cognitive–behavioral therapy in which clients are directly challenged in their irrational beliefs and helped to restructure their thinking into more rational belief statements.

realistic conflict theory theory stating that prejudice and discrimination will be increased between groups that are in conflict over a limited resource.

reality principle principle by which the ego functions; the satisfaction of the demands of the id only when negative consequences will not result.

recall type of memory retrieval in which the information to be retrieved must be "pulled" from memory with very few external cues.

recency effect tendency to remember information at the end of a body of information better than the information at the beginning of it.

receptor sites three-dimensional proteins on the surface of the dendrites or certain cells of the muscles and glands, which are shaped to fit only certain neurotransmitters.

recessive referring to a gene that influences the expression of a trait only when paired with an identical gene.

reciprocal determinism Bandura's explanation of how the factors of environment, personal characteristics, and behavior can interact to determine future behavior.

reciprocity of liking tendency of people to like other people who like them in return.

recognition the ability to match a piece of information or a stimulus to a stored image or fact.

reflection therapy technique in which the therapist restates what the client says rather than interpreting those statements.

reflex arc the connection of the afferent neurons to the interneurons to the efferent neurons, resulting in a reflex action.

reflex an unlearned, involuntary response that is not under personal control or choice.

reinforcement any event or stimulus that, when following a response, increases the probability that the response will occur again.

reinforcers any events or objects that, when following a response, increase the likelihood of that response occurring again.

relative size perception that occurs when objects that a person expects to be of a certain size appear to be small and are, therefore, assumed to be much farther away.

reliability the tendency of a test to produce the same scores again and again each time it is given to the same people.

REM behavior disorder a rare disorder in which the mechanism that blocks the movement of the voluntary muscles fails, allowing the person to thrash around and even get up and act out nightmares.

REM rebound increased amounts of REM sleep after being deprived of REM sleep on earlier nights.

replicate in research, repeating a study or experiment to see if the same results will be obtained in an effort to demonstrate reliability of results.

replication in research repetition of a study or experiment to see if the same results will be obtained in an effort to demonstrate reliability of results.

representative heuristic assumption that any object (or person) sharing characteristics with the members of a particular category is also a member of that category.

representative sample   randomly selected sample of subjects from a larger population of subjects.

resistance   occurring when a patient becomes reluctant to talk about a certain topic, by either changing the subject or becoming silent.

resting potential   the state of the neuron when not firing a neural impulse.

reticular formation (RF)   an area of neurons running through the middle of the medulla and the pons and slightly beyond that is responsible for general attention, alertness, and arousal.

retrieval cue   a stimulus for remembering.

retrieval   getting information that is in storage into a form that can be used.

retroactive interference   memory retrieval problem that occurs when newer information prevents or interferes with the retrieval of older information.

retrograde amnesia   loss of memory from the point of some injury or trauma backwards, or loss of memory for the past.

reuptake   process by which neurotransmitters are taken back into the synaptic vesicles.

reversible figures   visual illusions in which the figure and ground can be reversed.

rods   visual sensory receptors found at the back of the retina, responsible for noncolor sensitivity to low levels of light.

romantic love   type of love consisting of intimacy and passion.

Rorschach inkblot test   projective test that uses 10 inkblots as the ambiguous stimuli.

s factor   the ability to excel in certain areas, or specific intelligence.

scaffolding   process in which a more skilled learner gives help to a less skilled learner, reducing the amount of help as the less skilled learner becomes more capable.

scheme   in this case, a mental concept formed through experiences with objects and events.

schizophrenia   severe disorder in which the person suffers from disordered thinking, bizarre behavior, hallucinations, and inability to distinguish between fantasy and reality.

school psychology   area of psychology in which the psychologists work directly in the schools, doing assessments, educational placement, and diagnosing educational problems.

scientific method   system of gathering data so that bias and error in measurement are reduced.

secondary appraisal   the second step in assessing a threat, which involves estimating the resources available to the person for coping with the stressor.

secondary reinforcer   any reinforcer that becomes reinforcing after being paired with a primary reinforcer, such as praise, tokens, or gold stars.

selective attention   the ability to focus on only one stimulus from among all sensory input.

self-concept   the image of oneself that develops from interactions with important significant people in one's life.

self   an individual's awareness of his or her own personal characteristics and level of functioning.

self-actualization   according to Maslow, the point that is seldom reached at which people have sufficiently satisfied the lower needs and achieved their full human potential.

self-actualizing tendency   the striving to fulfill one's innate capacities and capabilities.

self-determination theory (SDT)   theory of human motivation in which the social context of an action has an effect on the type of motivation existing for the action.

self-efficacy   individual's expectancy of how effective his or her efforts to accomplish a goal will be in any particular circumstance.

self-fulfilling prophecy   the tendency of one's expectations to affect one's behavior in such a way as to make the expectations more likely to occur.

self-help groups (support group)   a group composed of people who have similar problems and who meet together without a therapist or counselor for the purpose of discussion, problem solving, and social and emotional support.

semantic memory   type of declarative memory containing general knowledge, such as knowledge of language and information learned in formal education.

semantic network model   model of memory organization that assumes information is stored in the brain in a connected fashion, with concepts that are related stored physically closer to each other than concepts that are not highly related.

semantics   the rules for determining the meaning of words and sentences.

sensation seeker   someone who needs more arousal than the average person.

sensation   the process that occurs when special receptors in the sense organs are activated, allowing various forms of outside stimuli to become neural signals in the brain.

sensorimotor stage   Piaget's first stage of cognitive development in which the infant uses its senses and motor abilities to interact with objects in the environment.

sensory adaptation   tendency of sensory receptor cells to become less responsive to a stimulus that is unchanging.

sensory conflict theory   an explanation of motion sickness in which the information from the eyes conflicts with the information from the vestibular senses, resulting in dizziness, nausea, and other physical discomfort.

sensory memory   the very first stage of memory; the point at which information enters the nervous system through the sensory systems.

sensory pathway   nerves coming from the sensory organs to the CNS consisting of afferent neurons.

serial position effect   tendency of information at the beginning and end of a body of information to be remembered more accurately than information in the middle of the body of information.

sexual dysfunction   a problem in sexual functioning.

sexual orientation   a person's sexual attraction and affection for members of either the opposite or the same sex.

shape constancy   the tendency to interpret the shape of an object as being constant, even when its shape changes on the retina.

shaping   the reinforcement of simple steps in behavior that lead to a desired, more complex behavior.

short-term memory (STM)   the memory system in which information is held for brief periods of time while being used.

significant difference   a difference between groups of numerical data that is considered large enough to be due to factors other than chance variation.

similarity   the tendency to perceive things that look similar to each other as being part of the same group.

single photon emission computed tomography (SPECT)   neuroimaging method that is similar to PET but uses a different radioactive tracer and can be used to examine brain blood flow.

single-blind study   study in which the subjects do not know if they are in the experimental or the control group.

situational cause   cause of behavior attributed to external factors, such as delays, the action of others, or some other aspect of the situation.

situational context   the social or environmental setting of a person's behavior.

size constancy   the tendency to interpret an object as always being the same actual size, regardless of its distance.

skewed distribution frequency distribution in which most of the scores fall to one side or the other of the distribution.

skin senses the sensations of touch, pressure, temperature, and pain.

sleep apnea disorder in which the person stops breathing for 10 seconds or more.

sleep deprivation any significant loss of sleep, resulting in problems in concentration and irritability.

sleep paralysis the inability of the voluntary muscles to move during REM sleep.

sleepwalking (somnambulism) occurring during deep sleep, an episode of moving around or walking around in one's sleep.

social anxiety disorder (social phobia) fear of interacting with others or being in social situations that might lead to a negative evaluation.

social categorization the assignment of a person one has just met to a category based on characteristics the new person has in common with other people with whom one has had experience in the past.

social cognition the mental processes that people use to make sense of the social world around them.

social cognitive learning theorists theorists who emphasize the importance of both the influences of other people's behavior and the influences of a person's own expectancies of learning.

social cognitive view learning theory that includes cognitive processes such as anticipating, judging, memory, and imitation of models.

social cognitive referring to the use of cognitive processes in relation to understanding the social world.

social comparison the comparison of oneself to others in ways that raise one's self-esteem.

social identity theory theory in which the formation of a person's identity within a particular social group is explained by social categorization, social identity, and social comparison.

social identity the part of the self-concept including one's view of self as a member of a particular social category.

social influence the scientific study of how a person's thoughts, feelings, and behavior influence and are influenced by social groups.

social neuroscience the study of the relationship between biological systems and social processes and behavior.

social psychology the scientific study of how a person's thoughts, feelings, and behavior are influenced by the real, imagined, or implied presence of others.

social role the pattern of behavior that is expected of a person who is in a particular social position.

social support system the network of family, friends, neighbors, coworkers, and others who can offer support, comfort, or aid to a person in need.

social-cognitive theory of hypnosis theory that assumes that people who are hypnotized are not in an altered state but are merely playing the role expected of them in the situation.

sociocultural perspective perspective that focuses on the relationship between social behavior and culture.

soma the cell body of the neuron responsible for maintaining the life of the cell.

somatic nervous system division of the PNS consisting of nerves that carry information from the senses to the CNS and from the CNS to the voluntary muscles of the body.

somatosensory cortex area of neurons running down the front of the parietal lobes responsible for processing information from the skin and internal body receptors for touch, temperature, body position, and possibly taste.

somesthetic senses the body senses consisting of the skin senses, the kinesthetic sense, and the vestibular senses.

source traits the more basic traits that underlie the surface traits, forming the core of personality.

spatial or unilateral neglect condition produced most often by damage to the parietal lobe association areas of the right hemisphere resulting in an inability to recognize objects or body parts in the left visual field.

specific phobia fear of objects or specific situations or events.

spinal cord a long bundle of neurons that carries messages between the body and the brain and is responsible for very fast, lifesaving reflexes.

spontaneous recovery the reappearance of a learned response after extinction has occurred.

sports psychology area of psychology in which the psychologists help athletes and others to prepare themselves mentally for participation in sports activities.

standard deviation the square root of the average squared deviations from the mean of scores in a distribution; a measure of variability.

statistically significant referring to differences in data sets that are larger than chance variation would predict.

statistics branch of mathematics concerned with the collection and interpretation of numerical data.

stem cells special cells found in tissues of the body that are capable of manufacturing other cell types when those cells need to be replaced due to damage or wear and tear.

stereotype threat a set of characteristics that people believe is shared by all members of a particular social category.

stereotype vulnerability the effect that people's awareness of the stereotypes associated with their social group has on their behavior.

stereotype a set of characteristics that people believe is shared by all members of a particular social category.

stimulants drugs that increase the functioning of the nervous system.

stimulatory hallucinogenics drugs that produce a mixture of psychomotor stimulant and hallucinogenic effects.

stimulus discrimination the tendency to stop making a generalized response to a stimulus that is similar to the original conditioned stimulus because the similar stimulus is never paired with the unconditioned stimulus.

stimulus generalization the tendency to respond to a stimulus that is only similar to the original conditioned stimulus with the conditioned response.

stimulus motive a motive that appears to be unlearned but causes an increase in stimulation, such as curiosity.

storage holding onto information for some period of time.

stress the term used to describe the physical, emotional, cognitive, and behavioral responses to events that are appraised as threatening or challenging.

stress-vulnerability model explanation of disorder that assumes a biological sensitivity, or vulnerability, to a certain disorder will result in the development of that disorder under the right conditions of environmental or emotional stress.

structuralism early perspective in psychology associated with Wilhelm Wundt and Edward Titchener, in which the focus of study is the structure or basic elements of the mind.

subjective discomfort emotional distress or emotional pain.

subjective referring to concepts and impressions that are only valid within a particular person's perception and may be influenced by biases, prejudice, and personal experiences.

successive approximations small steps in behavior, one after the other, that lead to a particular goal behavior.

superego part of the personality that acts as a moral center.

surface traits aspects of personality that can easily be seen by other people in the outward actions of a person.

sympathetic division (fight-or-flight system)   part of the ANS that is responsible for reacting to stressful events and bodily arousal.

synapse (synaptic gap)   microscopic fluid-filled space between the synaptic knob of one cell and the dendrites or surface of the next cell.

synesthesia   disorder in which the signals from the various sensory organs are processed in the wrong cortical areas, resulting in the sense information being interpreted as more than one sensation.

syntax   the system of rules for combining words and phrases to form grammatically correct sentences.

systematic desensitization   behavior technique used to treat phobias, in which a client is asked to make a list of ordered fears and taught to relax while concentrating on those fears.

temperament   the behavioral characteristics that are fairly well established at birth, such as easy, difficult, and slow to warm up.

temporal lobes   areas of the brain located along the side, starting just behind the temples, containing the neurons responsible for the sense of hearing and meaningful speech.

teratogen   any factor that can cause a birth defect.

testes   the male gonads.

texture gradient   the tendency for textured surfaces to appear to become smaller and finer as distance from the viewer increases.

thalamus   part of the limbic system located in the center of the brain, this structure relays sensory information from the lower part of the brain to the proper areas of the cortex and processes some sensory information before sending it to its proper area.

Thematic Apperception Test (TAT)   projective test that uses 20 pictures of people in ambiguous situations as the visual stimuli.

therapeutic alliance   the relationship between therapist and client that develops as a warm, caring, accepting relationship characterized by empathy, mutual respect, and understanding.

therapy   treatment methods aimed at making people feel better and function more effectively.

theta waves   brain waves indicating the early stages of sleep.

thinking, or cognition   mental activity that goes on in the brain when a person is organizing and attempting to understand information and communicating information to others.

thyroid gland   endocrine gland found in the neck; regulates metabolism.

time-out   an extinction process in which a person is removed from the situation that provides reinforcement for undesirable behavior, usually by being placed in a quiet corner or room away from possible attention and reinforcement opportunities.

token economy   type of behavior modification in which desired behavior is rewarded with tokens.

top-down processing   the use of preexisting knowledge to organize individual features into a unified whole.

trait theories   theories that endeavor to describe the characteristics that make up human personality in an effort to predict future behavior.

trait   a consistent, enduring way of thinking, feeling, or behaving.

trait–situation interaction   the assumption that the particular circumstances of any given situation will influence the way in which a trait is expressed.

transduction   the process of converting outside stimuli, such as light, into neural activity.

transference   in psychoanalysis, the tendency for a patient or client to project positive or negative feelings for important people from the past onto the therapist.

trial and error (mechanical solution)   problem-solving method in which one possible solution after another is tried until a successful one is found.

trichromatic theory   theory of color vision that proposes three types of cones: red, blue, and green.

t-test   type of inferential statistical analysis typically used when two means are compared to see if they are significantly different.

Type 2 diabetes   disease involving failure of the pancreas to secrete enough insulin, necessitating medication, usually diagnosed before the age of 40 and can be associated with obesity.

Type A personality   person who is ambitious, time conscious, extremely hardworking, and tends to have high levels of hostility and anger as well as being easily annoyed.

Type B personality   person who is relaxed and laid-back, less driven and less competitive than Type A, and slow to anger.

Type C personality   pleasant but repressed person, who tends to internalize his or her anger and anxiety and who finds expressing emotions difficult.

unconditional positive regard   positive regard that is given without conditions or strings attached; referring to the warmth, respect, and accepting atmosphere created by the therapist for the client in personcentered therapy.

unconditioned response (UCR)   an involuntary response to a naturally occurring or unconditioned stimulus.

unconditioned stimulus (UCS)   a naturally occurring stimulus that leads to an involuntary response.

unconscious mind   level of the mind in which thoughts, feelings, memories, and other information are kept that are not easily or voluntarily brought into consciousness.

validity   the degree to which a test actually measures what it's supposed to measure.

variable interval schedule of reinforcement   schedule of reinforcement in which the interval of time that must pass before reinforcement becomes possible is different for each trial or event.

variable ratio schedule of reinforcement   schedule of reinforcement in which the number of responses required for reinforcement is different for each trial or event.

vestibular senses   the sensations of movement, balance, and body position.

vicarious conditioning   classical conditioning of an involuntary response or emotion by watching the reaction of another person.

visual accommodation   the change in the thickness of the lens as the eye focuses on objects that are far away or close.

volley principle   theory of pitch that states that frequencies from about 400 Hz to 4000 Hz cause the hair cells (auditory neurons) to fire in a volley pattern, or take turns in firing.

waking consciousness   state in which thoughts, feelings, and sensations are clear and organized, and the person feels alert.

Wernicke's aphasia   condition resulting from damage to Wernicke's area, causing the affected person to be unable to understand or produce meaningful language.

withdrawal   physical symptoms that can include nausea, pain, tremors, crankiness, and high blood pressure, resulting from a lack of an addictive drug in the body systems.

working memory   an active system that processes the information in short-term memory.

Yerkes–Dodson law   law stating performance is related to arousal; moderate levels of arousal lead to better performance than do levels of arousal that are too low or too high. This effect varies with the difficulty of the task: Easy tasks require a high-moderate level, whereas more difficult tasks require a low-moderate level.

z score   a statistical measure that indicates how far away from the mean a particular score is in terms of the number of standard deviations that exist between the mean and that score.

zone of proximal development (ZPD)   Vygotsky's concept of the difference between what a child can do alone versus what that child can do with the help of a teacher.

zygote   cell resulting from the uniting of the ovum and sperm.

References

Abadinsky, H. (1989). *Drug abuse: An introduction*. Chicago: Nelson-Hall Series in Law, Crime, and Justice.

Abel, E. L., & Sokol, R. J. (1987). Incidence of fetal alcohol syndrome and economic impact of FAS-related anomalies: Drug alcohol syndrome and economic impact of FAS-related anomalies. *Drug and Alcohol Dependency, 19*(1), 51–70.

Abel, G. G., & Osborn, C. A. (1992). The paraphilias: The extent and nature of sexually deviant and criminal behavior. In J. M. W. Bradford (Ed.), *Psychiatric clinics of North America* (Vol. 15, pp. 675–687). Philadelphia: W. B. Saunders.

Abela, J. R. Z., & D'Allesandro, D. U. (2002). Beck's cognitive theory of depression: The diathesis-stress and causal mediation components. *British Journal of Clinical Psychology, 41*, 111–128.

Åberg, M. A., Pedersen, N. L., Torén, K., Svartengren, M., Bäckstrand, B., Johnsson, T., et al. (2009). Cardiovascular fitness is associated with cognition in young adulthood. *Proceedings of the National Academy of Sciences, 106*(49), 20906–20911.

Abramson, D., Redlener, I., Stehling–Ariza, T., Sury, J., Banister, A., & Soo Park, Y. (2010). Impact on children and families of the Deepwater Horizon Oil Spill: Preliminary findings of the Coastal Population Impact Study. National Center for Disaster Preparedness Mailman School of Public Health at Columbia University August 3rd, 2010. Retrieved December 15, 2013, from www.eoearth.org/article/Impact_on_children_and_families_of_the_Deepwater_Horizon_oil_spill?topic=50364

Abramson, L. Y., Garber, J., & Seligman, M. E. P. (1980). Learned helplessness in humans: An attributional analysis. In J. Garber & M. E. P. Seligman (Eds.), *Human helplessness* (pp. 3–34). New York: Academic Press.

Abramson, L. Y., Seligman, M. E. P., & Teasdale, J. D. (1978). Learned helplessness in humans: Critique and reformulation. *Journal of Abnormal Psychology, 87*, 49–74.

Acheson, D. J., MacDonald, M. C., & Postle, B. R. (2010). The interaction of concreteness and phonological similarity in verbal working memory. *Journal of Experimental Psychology: Learning, Memory and Cognition, 36*(1), 17–36.

Adachi, P. J. C., & Willoughby, T. (2011a). The effect of violent video games on aggression: Is it more than just the violence? *Aggression and Violent Behavior, 16*, 55–62. doi:10.1016/j.avb.2010.12.002

Adachi, P. J. C., & Willoughby, T. (2011b). The effect of video game competition and violence on aggressive behavior: Which characteristic has the greatest influence? *Psychology of Violence, 1*(4), 259–274. doi:10.1037/a0024908

Adams, D. B. (1968). The activity of single cells in the midbrain and hypothalamus of the cat during affective defense behavior. *Archives Italiennes de Biologie, 106*, 243–269.

Adams, R. J. (1987). An evaluation of colour preferences in early infancy. *Infant Behaviour and Development, 10*, 143–150.

Addis, D. R., Leclerc, C. M., Muscatell, K., & Kensinger, E. A. (2010). There are age related changes in neural connectivity during the encoding of positive, but not negative, information. *Cortex, 46*, 9.

Ader, R. (2003). Conditioned immunomodulation: Research needs and directions. *Brain, Behavior, and Immunity, 17*(1), 51–57.

Adeyemo, B. O., Simis, M., Macea, D. D., & Fregni, F. (2012). Systematic review of parameters of stimulation, clinical trial design characteristics, and motor outcomes in non-invasive brain stimulation in stroke. *Frontiers in Psychiatry, 3*, 88. doi:10.3389/fpsyt.2012.00088

Adler, A. (1954). *Understanding human nature*. New York: Greenburg Publisher.

Adler, S. R., Fosket, J. R., Kagawa-Singer, M., McGraw, S. A., Wong-Kim, E., Gold, E., et al. (2000). Conceptualizing menopause and midlife: Chinese American and Chinese women in the U.S. *Maturitas, 35*(1), 11–23.

Adolphs, R. (2010). Conceptual challenges and directions for social neuroscience. *Neuron, 65*(6), 752–767.

Adolphs, R., Gosselin, F., Buchanan, T. W., Tranel, D., Schyns, P., & Damasio, A. R. (2005). A mechanism for impaired fear recognition after amygdala damage. *Nature, 433*, 68–72.

Adolphs, R., & Tranel, D. (2003). Amygdal a damage impairs emotion recognition from scenes only when they contain facial expressions. *Neuropsychologia, 41*, 1281–1289.

Agresti, A., & Finlay, B. (1997). *Statistical methods for the social sciences*. Upper Saddle River, NJ: Prentice Hall.

Aguiar, A., & Baillargeon, R. (2003). Perseverative responding in a violation-of-expectation task in 6.5-month-old infants. *Cognition, 88*(3), 277–316.

Ahn, W. (1998). Why are different features central for natural kinds and artifacts? The role of causal status in determining feature centrality. *Cognition, 69*, 135–178.

Ainsworth, M. D. S. (1985). Attachments across the life span. *Bulletin of the New York Academy of Medicine, 61*, 792–812.

Ainsworth, M. D. S., Blehar, M. C., Waters, E., & Wall, S. (1978). *Patterns of attachment: A study of the strange situation*. Hillsdale, NJ: Erlbaum.

Aitchison, J. (1992). Good birds, better birds, and amazing birds: The development of prototypes. In P. J. Arnaud & H. Béjoint (Eds.), *Vocabulary and applied linguistics* (pp. 71–84). London: Macmillan.

Ajzen, I. (2001). Nature and operation of attitudes. *Annual Review of Psychology, 52*, 27–58.

Ajzen, I., & Fishbein, M. (2000). Attitudes and the attitude-behavior relation: Reasoned and automatic processes. In W. Stroebe & M. Hewstone (Eds.), *European review of social psychology* (pp. 1–33). New York: Wiley.

Albert, D. J., & Richmond, S. E. (1977). Reactivity and aggression in the rat: Induction by alpha-adrenergic blocking agents injected ventral to anterior septum but not into lateral septum. *Journal of Comparative and Physiological Psychology, 91*, 886–896. [DBA] *Physiology and Behavior, 20*, 755–761.

Alderfer, C. P. (1972). *Existence, relatedness and growth: Human needs in organisational settings*. New York: Free Press.

Aldridge-Morris, R. (1989). *Multiple personality: An exercise in deception*. Hillsdale, NJ: Erlbaum.

Alexander, G., DeLong, M. R., & Strick, P. L. (1986). Parallel organization of functionally segregated circuits linking basal ganglia and cortex. *Annual Review of Neuroscience, 9*, 357–381.

Aligne, C. A., Auinger, P., Byrd, R. S., & Weitzman, M. (2000). Risk factors for pediatric asthma contributions of poverty, race, and urban residence. *American Journal of Respiratory Critical Care Medicine, 162*(3), 873–877.

Alkon, D. (1989). Memory storage and neural systems. *Scientific American, 261*(1), 42–50.

Allen, D. (2001). *Getting things done: The art of stress-free productivity*. New York: Viking Adult.

Allen, D. (2008). *Making it all work*. New York: Viking Adult.

Allen, F. (1994). *Secret formula*. New York: HarperCollins.

Allen, G. E. (2006). *Intelligence tests and immigration to the United States, 1900–1940*. Hoboken, NJ: Wiley.

Allen, G., & Parisi, P. (1990). Trends in monozygotic and dizygotic twinning rates by maternal age and parity. Further analysis of Italian data, 1949–1985, and rediscussion of U.S. Data, 1964–1985. *Acta Genetic Medicine and Gemellology, 39*, 317–328.

Allen, K., Blascovich, J., & Mendes, W. (2002). Cardiovascular reactivity and the presence of pets, friends, and spouses: The truth about cats and dogs. *Psychosomatic Medicine, 64*, 727–739.

Allik, J., Realo, A., & McCrae, R. R. (2013). Universality of the five-factor model of personality. In T. A. Widiger & P. T. Costa (Eds.), *Personality disorders and the five-factor model of personality* (3rd ed., pp. 61–74). Washington, DC: American Psychological Association.

Alloway, T. P., Rajendran, G., & Archibald, L. (2009). Working memory in children with developmental disorders. *Journal of Learning Disabilities, 42*(4), 372–382.

Alloy, L. B., & Clements, C. M. (1998). Hopelessness theory of depression: Tests of the symptom component. *Cognitive Therapy and Research, 22*, 303–335.

Allport, G. W., & Odbert, H. S. (1936). Trait names: A psycho-lexical study. *Psychological Monographs, 47*(211).

Alm, H., & Nilsson, L. (1995). The effects of a mobile telephone conversation on driver behaviour in a car following situation. *Accident Analysis and Prevention, 27*(5), 707–715.

Alzheimer's Association. (2010). Alzheimer's disease facts and figures. *Alzheimer's and Dementia, 6*, 4–54.

Amabile, T. M., DeJong, W., & Lepper, M. R. (1976). Effects of externally imposed deadlines on subsequent intrinsic motivation. *Journal of Personality and Social Psychology, 34*, 92–98.

Amaral, D. G., & Strick, P. L. (2013). The organization of the central nervous system. In E. R. Kandel, J. H. Schwartz, T. M. Jessell, S. A. Siegelbaum, & A. J. Hudspeth (Eds.), *Principles of neural science* (5th ed., pp. 337–355). USA: McGraw-Hill.

Amat, J., Aleksejev, R. M., Paul, E., Watkins, L. R., & Maier, S. F. (2010). Behavioral control over shock blocks behavioral and neurochemical effects of later social defeat. *Neuroscience, 165*(4), 1031–1038.

Amat, J., Baratta, M. V., Paul, E., Bland, S. T., Watkins, L. R., & Maier, S. F. (2005). Medial prefrontal cortex determines how stressor controllability affects behavior and dorsal raphe nucleus. *Nature Neuroscience, 8*(3), 365–371.

American Academy of Pediatrics. (1995). Health supervision for children with turner syndrome. *Pediatrics, 96*(6), 1166–1173.

American Association on Intellectual and Developmental Disabilities [AAIDD]. (2009). *FAQ on intellectual disability*. Retrieved June 8, 2010, from www.aamr.org/content_104.cfm

American College Counseling Association's (ACCA) Community College Task Force. (2010). *2009–2010 Community college counselors survey*. Retrieved August 12, 2010, from www.collegecounseling.org/pdf/2009-2010_Community_College_Counselors_Survey_Results.pdf

American Psychiatric Association. (2010). *APA modifies DSM naming convention to reflect publication changes.* Retrieved from American Psychiatric Association Web site: http://www.dsm5.org/Newsroom/Documents/DSM-Name-Change.pdf

American Psychiatric Association. (2013). *Diagnostic and statistical manual of mental disorders* (5th ed.). Washington, DC: Author.

American Psychiatric Association Committee on Electroconvulsive Therapy. (2001). *The practice of electroconvulsive therapy: Recommendations for treatment, training, and privileging* (2nd ed.). Washington, DC: American Psychiatric Association.

American Psychological Association. (2002). Ethical principles of psychologists and code of conduct. *American Psychologist, 57,* 1060–1073.

American Psychological Association. (2005). *Policy statement on evidence-based practice in psychology.* Retrieved from http://www.apa.org/practice/guidelines/evidence-based.pdf

American Psychological Association Division 19. (2010). *Society for military psychology.* Retrieved from http://www.apadivision19.org/about.htm

Amsterdam, B. (1972). Mirror self-image reactions before age two. *Developmental Psychobiology, 5*(4), 297–305. doi:10.1002/dev.420050403

Anastasi, A., & Urbina, S. (1997). *Psychological testing* (7th ed.). Upper Saddle River, NJ: Prentice-Hall.

Anderson, C. A. (1987). Temperature and aggression: Effects on quarterly, yearly, and city rates of violent and nonviolent crime. *Journal of Personality and Social Psychology, 52*(6), 1161–1173.

Anderson, C. A., Berkowitz, L., Donnerstein, E., Huesmann, L. R., Johnson, J. D., Linz, D., et al. (2003). The influence of media violence on youth. *Psychological Science in the Public Interest, 4*(3), 81–110.

Anderson, L. W., Krathwohl, D. R., Airasian, P. W., Cruikshank, K. A., Mayer, R. E., Pintrich, P. R., et al. (Eds.). (2001). *A taxonomy for learning, teaching, and assessing—a revision of Bloom's taxonomy of educational objectives.* New York: Addison Wesley Longman.

Anderson, M. C., & Neely, J. H. (1995). Interference and inhibition in memory retrieval. In E. L. Bjork & R. A. Bjork (Eds.), *Handbook of perception and cognition, vol. 10. Memory.* San Diego, CA: Academic Press.

Anderson, C. A., Shibuya, A., Ihori, N., Swing, E. L., Bushman, B. J., Sakamoto, A., . . . Saleem, M. (2010). Violent video game effects on aggression, empathy, and prosocial behavior in eastern and western countries: A meta-analytic review. Psychological Bulletin, 136(2), 151-173. doi: 10.1037/a0018251.

Andrews, J. D. W. (1989). Integrating visions of reality: Interpersonal diagnosis and the existential vision. *American Psychologist, 44,* 803–817.

Anschuetz, B. L. (1999). The high cost of caring: Coping with workplace stress. *The Journal, the Newsletter of the Ontario Association of Children's Aid Societies, 43*(3), 1–63.

Antuono, P. G., Jones, J. L., Wang, Y., & Li, S. (2001). Decreased glutamate [plus] glutamine in Alzheimer's disease detected in vivo with (1)H-MRS at 0.5 T. *Neurology, 56*(6), 737–742.

Arbury, S. (2005, March 4). *Workplace violence: Training young workers in preventative strategies.* Washington, DC: NFIB Business Toolbox.

Arcelus, J., Mitchell, A. J., Wales, J., & Nielsen, S. (2011). Mortality rates in patients with anorexia nervosa and other eating disorders: A meta-analysis of 36 studies. *Archives of General Psychiatry, 68*(7), 724–731. doi:10.1001/archgenpsychiatry.2011.74

Archer, J. (1991). The influence of testosterone on human aggression. *British Journal of Psychology, 82,* 1–28.

Arkowitz, H., & Miller, W. R. (2008). Learning, applying, and extending motivational interviewing. In H. Arkowitz, H. A. Westra, W. R. Miller, & S. Rollnick (Eds.), *Motivational interviewing in the treatment of psychological disorders* (pp. 1–25). New York: Guilford Press.

Armstrong, R. (1997). When drugs are used for rape. *Journal of Emergency Nursing, 23*(4), 378–381.

Arnett, J. J. (2000). Emerging adulthood: A theory of development from the late teens through the twenties. *American Psychologist, 55*(5), 469–480.

Arnett, P. A., Smith, S. S., & Newman, J. P. (1997). Approach and avoidance motivation in psychopathic criminal offenders during passive avoidance. *Journal of Personality and Social Psychology, 72*(6), 1413–1428.

Arns, M., de Ridder, S., Strehl, U., Breteler, M., & Coenen, A. (2009). Efficacy of neurofeedback treatment in ADHD: The effects on inattention, impulsivity and hyperactivity: A meta-analysis. *Clinical EEG and Neuroscience, 40*(3), 180–189.

Arns, M., van der Heijden, K. B., Arnold, L. E., & Kenemans, J. L. (2013). Geographic variation in the prevalence of attention-deficit/hyperactivity disorder: The sunny perspective. *Biological Psychiatry.* doi:10.1016/j.biopsych.2013.02.010

Aron, A., Aron, E., & Coups, E. (2005). *Statistics for the behavioral and social sciences: Brief course* (4th ed.). Upper Saddle River, NJ: Prentice-Hall.

Aronson, E. (1997). Back to the future. Retrospective review of Leon Festinger's—a theory of cognitive dissonance. *American Journal of Psychology, 110,* 127–137.

Aronson, E., Blaney, N., Stephan, C., Sikes, J., & Snapp, M. (1978). *The jigsaw classroom.* Beverly Hills, CA: Sage.

Asarnow, R. F., Granholm, E., & Sherman, T. (1991). Span of apprehension in schizophrenia. In H. A. Nasrallah, S. R. Steinhauer, J. H. Gruzelie, & J. Zubin (Eds.), *Handbook of Schizophrenia, Vol. 5: Neuropsychology, psychophysiology and information processing* (pp. 335–370). Amsterdam: Elsevier.

Asch, S. E. (1951). Effects of group pressure upon the modification and distortion of judgement. In H. Guetzkow (Ed.), *Groups, leadership and men.* Pittsburgh: Carnegie Press.

Asch, S. E. (1956). Studies of independence and conformity: A minority of one against a unanimous majority. *Psychological Monographs, 70*(Whole no. 416).

Aserinsky, E., & Kleitman, N. (1953). Regularly occurring periods of eye motility, and concomitant phenomena, during sleep. *Science, 118,* 273–274.

Ash, M. G. (1998). *Gestalt psychology in German culture, 1890–1967: Holism and the quest for objectivity.* Cambridge: Cambridge University Press.

Asp, E., & Tranel, D. (2013). False tagging theory. In D. T. Stuss & R. T. Knight (Eds.), *Principles of frontal lobe function* (pp. 383–416). New York: Oxford University Press.

Assaf, Y., & Pasternak, O. (2008). Diffusion tensor imaging (DTI)-based white matter mapping in brain research: A review. *Journal of Molecular Neuroscience, 34*(1), 51–61.

Atkinson, R. C., & Shiffrin, R. M. (1968). Human memory: A proposed system and its control processes. In K. W. Spence & J. T. Spence (Eds.), *The psychology of learning and motivation* (Vol. 2, pp. 89–105). New York: Academic Press.

Atladóttir, H. O., Pedersen, M. G., Thorsen, C., Mortensen, P. B., Deleuran, B., Eaton, W. W., et al. (2009). Association of family history of autoimmune diseases and autism spectrum disorders. *Pediatrics, 124*(2), 687–694.

Azmitia, M., Syed, M., & Radmacher, K. (2008). On the intersection of personal and social identities: Introduction and evidence from a longitudinal study of emerging adults. In M. Azmitia, M. Syed, & K. Radmacher (Eds.), *The intersections of personal and social identities: New Directions for Child and Adolescent Development* (Vol. 120, pp. 1–16). San Francisco: Jossey-Bass.

Babiloni, C., Vecchio, F., Buffo, P., Buttiglione, M., Cibelli, G., & Rossini, P. M. (2010). Cortical responses to consciousness of schematic emotional facial expressions: A high resolution EEG study. *Human Brain Mapping, 8,* 8.

Backenstraß, M., Pfeiffer, N., Schwarz, T., Catanzaro, S. J., & Mearns, J. (2008). Reliability and validity of the German version of the generalized expectancies for Negative Mood Regulation (NMR) scale. *Diagnostica, 54,* 43–51.

Backer, B., Hannon, R., & Russell, N. (1994). *Death and dying: Understanding and care* (2nd ed.). Albany, NY: Delmar.

Baddeley, A. D. (1986). *Working memory.* London: Oxford University Press.

Baddeley, A. D. (1988). Cognitive psychology and human memory. *Trends in Neurosciences, 11,* 176–181.

Baddeley, A. D. (1996). Exploring the central executive. *Quarterly Journal of Experimental Psychology, 49A,*5–28.

Baddeley, A. D. (2003). Working memory: Looking back and looking visual forward. *Nature Reviews Neuroscience, 4*(10), 829–839.

Baddeley, A. D., & Hitch, G. (1974). Working memory. In G. A. Bower (Ed.), *The psychology of learning and motivation* (Vol. 8, pp. 47–89). New York: Academic Press.

Baddeley, A. D., & Larsen, J. D. (2007). The phonological loop unmasked? A comment on the evidence for a "perceptual-gestural" alternative. *Quarterly Journal of Experimental Psychology, 60*(4), 497–504.

Baehr, E. K., Revelle, W., & Eastman, C. I. (2000). Individual difference in the phase amplitude of the human circadian temperature rhythm: With an emphasis on morningness-eveningness. *Journal of Sleep Research, 9,* 117–127.

Baer, D. M., Wolf, M. M., & Risley, T. R. (1968). Some current dimensions of applied behavior analysis. *Journal of Applied Behavior Analysis, 1,* 91–97.

Bahrick, H. (1984). Fifty years of second language attrition: Implications for programmatic research. *Modern Language Journal, 68,* 105–118.

Bahrick, H. P., Hall, L. K., & Berger, S. A. (1996, September). Accuracy and distortion in memory for high school grades. *Psychological Science, 7,* 265–271.

Bailey, J. M., Dunne, M. P., & Martin, N. G. (2000). Genetic and environmental influences on sexual orientation and its correlates in an Australian twin sample. *Journal of Personality and Social Psychology, 78*(3), 524–536.

Bailey, J. M., & Pillard, R. C. (1991). A genetic study of male sexual orientation. *Archives of General Psychiatry, 48,* 1089–1096.

Bailey, J. M., Pillard, R. C., Neale, M. C., & Agyei, Y. (1993). Heritable factors influence sexual orientation in women. *Archives of General Psychiatry, 50,* 217–223.

Bailey, J. M., & Zucker, K. J. (1995). Childhood sex-typed behavior and sexual orientation: A conceptual analysis and quantitative review. *Developmental Psychology, 31,* 43–55.

Baillargeon, R. (1986). Representing the existence and the location of hidden objects: Object permanence in 6- and 8-month-old infants. *Cognition, 23,* 21–41.

Baker, L. D., Frank, L. L., Foster-Schubert, K., Green, P. S., Wilkinson, C. W., McTiernan, A., et al. (2010). Effects of aerobic exercise on mild cognitive impairment: A controlled trial. *Archives of Neurology, 67*(1), 71–79.

Ball, K., Berch, D. B., Helmers, K. F., Jobe, J. B., Leveck, M. D., Marsiske, M., et al. (2002). Advanced cognitive training for independent and vital elderly study group. Effects of cognitive training interventions with older adults: A randomized controlled trial. *Journal of the American Medical Association, 288,* 2271–2281.

Baltes, P. B., Reese, H. W., & Nesselroade, J. R. (1988). *Introduction to research methods, life-span developmental psychology.* Hillsdale, NJ: Erlbaum.

Bandura, A. (1965). Influence of models' reinforcement contingencies on the acquisition of imitative responses. *Journal of Social Psychology, 1,* 589–595.

Bandura, A. (1980). The social learning theory of aggression. In R. A. Falk & S. S. Kim (Eds.), *The war system: An interdisciplinary approach* (p. 146). Boulder, CO: Westview Press.

Bandura, A. (1986). *Social foundations of thought and action: A social cognitive theory*. Englewood Cliffs, NJ: Prentice Hall.

Bandura, A. (1989). Human agency in social cognitive theory. *American Psychologist, 44,* 1175–1184.

Bandura, A. (1998). Exploration of fortuitous determinants of life paths. *Psychological Inquiry, 9,* 95–99.

Bandura, A., Blanchard, E. B., & Ritter, B. (1969). Relative efficacy of desensitization and modeling approaches for inducing behavioral, affective, and attitudinal changes. *Journal of Personality and Social Psychology, 13,* 173–199.

Bandura, A., Jeffrey, R. W., & Wright, C. L. (1974). Efficacy of participant modeling as a function of response induction aids. *Journal of Abnormal Psychology, 83,* 56–64.

Bandura, A., & Rosenthal, T. L. (1966). Vicarious classical conditioning as a functioning of arousal level. *Journal of Personality and Social Psychology, 3,* 54–62.

Bandura, A., Ross, D., & Ross, S. A. (1961). Transmission of aggression through imitation of aggressive models. *Journal of Abnormal and Social Psychology, 63,* 575–582.

Bandura, A., Ross, D., & Ross, S. A. (1963). Imitation of film- mediated aggressive models. *Journal of Abnormal and Social Psychology, 66,* 3–11.

Bard, P. (1934). On emotional expression after decortication with some remark on certain theoretical views. *Psychological Review, 41,* 309–329, 424–449.

Bargh, J. A., Chen, M., & Burrows, C. (1996). Automaticity of social behavior: Direct effects of trait construct and stereotype activation on action. *Journal of Personality and Social Psychology, 71*(2), 230–244.

Barker, E. (1983). The ones who got away: People who attend unification church workshops and do not become Moonies. In E. Barker (Ed.), *Of gods and men: New religious movements in the West.* Macon, GA: Mercer University Press.

Barker, E. (2007). Religious movements: Cult and anticult since Jonestown. In M. Hamilton (Ed.), *Sociology of religion. Critical concepts in sociology* (Vol. 5, pp. 157–177)., Abingdon, UK: Routledge.

Barkley, R. A., Murphy, K. R., & Fischer, M. (2008). *ADHD in adults: What the science says.* New York: Guilford Press.

Barlow, D. H., Allen, L. B., & Basden, S. L. (2007). Psychological treatments for panic disorders, phobias, and generalized anxiety disorder. In P. E. Nathan & J. M. Gorman (Eds.), *A guide to treatments that work* (3rd ed., pp. 351–394). New York, NY: Oxford University Press.

Barlow, D. H., Bullis, J. R., Comer, J. S., & Ametaj, A. A. (2013). Evidence-based psychological treatments: An update and a way forward. *Annual Review of Clinical Psychology, 9,* 1–27. doi:10.1146/annurev-clinpsy-050212-185629

Barnes, A. M., & Carey, J. C. (2002, January 11). *Common problems of babies with trisomy 18 or 13.* Rochester, NY: Support Organization for Trisomy 18, 13, and Related Disorders.

Barnes, V., Schneider, R., Alexander, C., & Staggers, F. (1997). Stress, stress reduction, and hypertension in African Americans: An updated review. *Journal of the National Medical Association, 89*(7), 464–476.

Barnyard, P., & Grayson, A. (1996). *Introducing psychological research.* London: Macmillan Press.

Baron, J. N., & Reiss, P. C. (1985). Same time, next year: Aggregate analyses of the mass media and violent behavior. *American Sociological Review, 50,* 347–363.

Baron, S. A. (1993). *Violence in the workplace.* Ventura, CA: Pathfinder Publishing of California.

Barsalou, L. W. (1992). *Cognitive psychology: An overview for cognitive scientists.* Hillsdale, NJ: Lawrence Erlbaum.

Barsch, J. (1996). *Barsch learning style inventory* (Rev. ed.). Novato, CA: Academic Therapy Publications.

Barsh, G. S., Farooqi, I. S., & O'Rahilly, S. (2000). Genetics of body-weight regulation. *Nature, 404,* 644–651.

Bartels, A., & Zeki, S. (2000). The neural basis of romantic love. *NeuroReport, 11,* 3829–3834.

Barth, J. M., & Boles, D. B. (1999, September). *Positive relations between emotion recognition skills and right hemisphere processing.* Paper presented at the 11th Annual Convention of the American Psychological Society, Denver, CO.

Bartholomew, K. (1990). Avoidance of intimacy: An attachment perspective. *Journal of Social and Personal Relationships, 7,* 147–178.

Bartlett, N. R. (1965). Dark and light adaptation. In C. H. Graham (Ed.), *Vision and visual perception.* New York: Wiley.

Barton, M. E., & Komatsu, L. K. (1989). Defining features of natural kinds and artifacts. *Journal of Psycholinguistic Research, 18,* 433–447.

Bartoshuk, L. M. (1993). The biological basis for food perception and acceptance. *Food Quality and Preference, 4*(1–2), 21–32.

Bartoshuk, L. M., Duffy, V. B., Hayes, J. E., Moskowitz, H. R., & Snyder, D. J. (2006). Psychophysics of sweet and fat perception in obesity: Problems, solutions and new perspectives. *Philosophical Transactions of the Royal Society of London. Series B, Biological Sciences, 361*(1471), 1137–1148.

Bartoshuk, L. M., Fast, K., & Snyder, D. J. (2005). Differences in our sensory worlds. *Current Directions in Psychological Science, 14*(3), 122–125.

Basadur, M., Pringle, P., & Kirkland, D. (2002). Crossing cultures: Training effects on the divergent thinking attitudes of Spanish- speaking South American managers. *Creativity Research Journal, 14*(3, 4), 395–408.

Bator, R. J., & Cialdini, R. B. (2006). The nature of consistency motivation: Consistency, aconsistency, and anticonsistency in a dissonance paradigm. *Social Influence, 1,* 208–233.

Baumrind, D. (1964). Some thoughts on ethics of research: After reading milgram's "behavioral study of obedience." *American Psychologist, 19,* 421–423.

Baumrind, D. (1967). Child care practices anteceding three patterns of preschool behavior. *Genetic Psychology Monograph, 75,* 43–88.

Baumrind, D. (1991). The influence of parenting style on adolescent competence and substance abuse. *Journal of Early Adolescence, 11*(1), 56–95.

Baumrind, D. (1997). Necessary distinctions. *Psychological Inquiry, 8,* 176–182.

Baumrind, D. (2005). Patterns of parental authority and adolescent autonomy. In J. Smetana (Ed.), *New directions for child development: Changes in parental authority during adolescence* (pp. 61–69). San Francisco: Jossey-Bass.

Bayliss, D. M., Baddeley, J. C., & Gunn, D. M. (2005). The relationship between short-term memory and working memory: Complex span made simple? *Memory, 13*(3–4), 414–421.

Beauchamp, G. K., & Mennella, J. A. (2011). Flavor perception in human infants: Development and functional significance. *Digestion, 83*(Suppl. 1), 1–6. doi:10.1159/000323397

Bechtel, W., & Abrahamsen, A. (2002). *Connectionism and the mind: Parallel processing, dynamics, and evolution in networks* (2nd ed.). Oxford, UK: Basil Blackwell.

Beck, A. T. (1976). *Cognitive therapy and the emotional disorders.* New York: International Universities Press.

Beck, A. T. (1979). *Cognitive therapy and the emotional disorders.* New York: Penguin Books.

Beck, A. T. (1984). Cognitive approaches to stress. In C. Lehrer & R. L. Woolfolk (Eds.), *Clinical guide to stress management.* New York: Guilford Press.

Beck, H. P., & Irons, G. (2011). Finding Little Albert: A seven-year search for psychology's lost boy. *The Psychologist, 25,* 180–181.

Beck, H. P., Levinson, S., & Irons, G. (2009). Finding Little Albert: A journey to John B. Watson's infant laboratory. *American Psychologist, 64*(7), 605–614. doi:10.1037/a0017234

Beck, J. S. (2007). *Cognitive therapy for personality disorders.* Retrieved November 17, 2010, from http://www.academyofct.org/Library/InfoManage/Guide.asp?FolderID=196

Beckman, M., & Pierrehumbert, J. (1986). Intonational structure in English and Japanese. *Phonology Year Book III,* 15–70.

Beer, J. S. (2009). The neural basis of emotion regulation: Making emotion work for you and not against you. In M. S. Gazzaniga (Ed.), *The cognitive neurosciences* (pp. 961–972). Cambridge, MA: MIT Press.

Behne, T., Carpenter, M., & Tomasello, M. (2005). One-year-olds comprehend the communicative intentions behind gestures in a hiding game. *Developmental Science, 8,* 492–499.

Békésy, G. V. (1960). *Experiments in hearing* (E. G. Wever, Trans.). New York: McGraw-Hill.

Belsky, J. (2005). Differential susceptibility to rearing influence: An evolutionary hypothesis and some evidence. In B. Ellis & D. Bjorklund (Eds.), *Origins of the social mind: Evolutionary psychology and child development* (pp. 139–163). New York: Guilford Press.

Belsky, J., & Johnson, C. D. (2005). Developmental outcome of children in day care. In J. Murph, S. D. Palmer, & D. Glassy (Eds.), *Health in child care: A manual for health professionals* (4th ed., pp. 81–95). Elks Grove Village, IL: American Academy of Pediatrics.

Belsky, J., Vandell, D., Burchinal, M., Clarke-Stewart, K. A., McCartney, K., Owen, M., et al. (2007). Are there long-term effects of early child care? *Child Development, 78,* 681–701.

Bem, S. L. (1975). Sex role adaptability: The consequence of psychological androgyny. *Journal of Personality and Social Psychology, 31,* 634–643.

Bem, S. L. (1981). Gender schema theory: A cognitive account of sex typing. *Psychological Review, 88,* 354–364.

Bem, S. L. (1987). Gender schema theory and the romantic tradition. In P. Shaver & C. Hendrick (Eds.), *Review of personality and social psychology* (Vol. 7, pp. 251–271). Newbury Park, CA: Sage.

Bem, S. L. (1993). Is there a place in psychology for a feminist analysis of the social context? *Feminism and Psychology, 3,* 247–251.

Bengston, V. L. (1970). The generation gap. *Youth and Society, 2,* 7–32.

Benito, J. M., Kumru, H. P., Murillo, N. P., Costa, U. P., Medina, J. P., Tormos, J. M. P., et al. (2012). Motor and gait improvement in patients with incomplete spinal cord injury induced by high- frequency repetitive transcranial magnetic stimulation. *Topics in Spinal Cord Injury Rehabilitation, 18*(2), 106–112. doi:10.1310/sci1802-106

Benjafield, J. J. G. (1996). *A history of psychology.* Boston: Allyn & Bacon.

Benjamin, S. L. (1996). An interpersonal theory of personality disorders. In J. F. Clarkin & M. F. Lenzenweger (Eds.), *Major theories of personality disorder.* New York: Guilford Press.

Benowitz, N. L. (1988). Pharmacologic aspects of cigarette smoking and nicotine addiction. *New England Journal of Medicine, 319,* 1318–1330.

Ben-Shakhar, G., Bar-Hillel, M., Bliu, Y., Ben-Abba, E., & Flug, A. (1986). Can graphology predict occupational success? Two empirical studies and some methodological ruminations. *Journal of Applied Psychology, 71,* 645–653.

Benson, H. (1975). *The relaxation response.* New York: Morrow.

Benson, H., Beary, J., & Carol, M. (1974). The relaxation response. *Psychiatry, 37,* 37–46.

Benson, H., Rosner, B. A., Marzetta, B. R., & Klemchuk, H. M. (1974). Decreased blood pressure in pharmacologically treated hypertensive patients who regularly elicited the relaxation response. *Lancet, 1*(7852), 289–291.

Benton, D., & Parker, P. Y. (1998). Breakfast, blood glucose, and cognition. *American Journal of Clinical Nutrition, 67*(4), 772S–778S.

Berent, S. (1977). Functional asymmetry of the human brain in the recognition of faces. *Neuropsychologia, 15,* 829–831.

Berg, F. (1999). Health risks associated with weight loss and obesity treatment programs. *Journal of Social Issues, 55*(2), 277–297.

Berk, L. E. (1992). Children's private speech: An overview of theory and the status of research. In R. M. Diaz & L. E. Berk (Eds.), *Private speech: From social interaction to self-regulation* (pp. 17–53). Hillsdale, NJ: Erlbaum.

Berk, L. E., & Spuhl, S. T. (1995). Maternal interaction, private speech, and task performance in preschool children. *Early Childhood Research Quarterly, 10,* 145–169.

Berkowitz, L. (1993). *Aggression: Its causes, consequences and control.* New York: McGraw-Hill.

Berman, A., Bradley, J. C., Carroll, B., Certain, R. D., Gabrelcik, J. C., Green, R., et al. (2010). *The challenge and the promise: Strengthening the force, preventing suicide and saving lives. Final report of the Department of Defense task force on the prevention of suicide by members of the armed forces.* Washington, DC: U.S. Government.

Bermond, B., Nieuwenhuyse, B., Fasotti, L., & Schuerman, J. (1991). Spinal cord lesions, peripheral feedback, and intensities of emotional feelings. *Cognition and Emotion, 5,* 201–220.

Bernat, E., Shevrin, H., & Snodgrass, M. (2001). Subliminal visual oddball stimuli evoke a P300 component. *Clinical Neurophysiology, 112,* 159–171.

Berry, J. W., & Kim, U. (1998). Acculturation and mental health. In P. R. Dasen, J. W. Berry, & N. Sartorius (Eds.), *Health and cross-cultural psychology: Toward applications* (pp. 207–236). Newbury Park, CA: Sage.

Berry, J. W., & Sam, D. L. (1997). Acculturation and adaptation. In J. W. Berry, M. H. Segall, & C. Kagitcibasi (Eds.), *Handbook of cross-cultural psychology, Vol. 3: Social behaviour and applications* (2nd ed., pp. 291–326). Boston: Allyn & Bacon.

Berscheid, E., & Reis, H. T. (1998). Attraction and close relationships. In D. T. Gilbert, S. T. Fiske, & G. Lindzey (Eds.), *The handbook of social psychology, Vol. 2* (4th ed., pp. 193–281). New York: McGraw-Hill.

Berteretche, M. V., Dalix, A. M., Cesar d'Ornano, A. M., Bellisle, F., Khayat, D., & Faurion, A. (2004). Decreased taste sensitivity in cancer patients under chemotherapy. *Supportive Care in Cancer, 12*(8), 571–576.

Bertram, L., & Tanzi, R. E. (2005). The genetic epidemiology of neurodegenerative disease. *The Journal of Clinical Investigation, 115*(6), 1449–1457.

Best, D. L., & Williams, J. E. (2001). Gender and culture. In D. Matsumoto (Ed.), *The handbook of culture and psychology* (pp. 195–212). New York: Oxford University Press.

Betancourt, J. R., & Jacobs, E. A. (2000). Language barriers to informed consent and confidentiality: The impact on women's health. *Journal of American Medical Women's Association, 55,* 294–295.

Beyer, B. K. (1995). *Critical thinking.* Bloomington, IN: Phi Delta Kappa Educational Foundation.

Beyreuther, K., Biesalski, H. K., Fernstrom, J. D., Grimm, P., Hammes, W. P., Heinemann, U., et al. (2007). Consensus meeting: Monosodium glutamate, an update. *European Journal of Clinical Nutrition, 61,* 304–313.

Binet, A., & Simon, T. (1916). *The development of intelligence in children.* Baltimore: Williams & Wilkins.

Bivens, J. A., & Berk, L. E. (1990). A longitudinal study of the development of elementary school children's private speech. *Merrill-Palmer Quarterly, 36,* 443–463.

Bjork, R. A., & Bjork, E. L. (1992). A new theory of disuse and an old theory of stimulus fluctuation. In A. Healy, S. Kosslyn, & R. Shiffrin (Eds.), *From learning processes to cognitive processes: Essays in honor of William K. Estes* (Vol. 2, pp. 35–67). Hillsdale, NJ: Erlbaum.

Bjork, R. A., & Whitten, W. B. (1974). Recency-sensitive retrieval processes in long-term free recall. *Cognitive Psychology, 6,* 173–189.

Blackmon, L. R., Batton, D. G., Bell, E. F., Engle, W. A., Kanto, W. P., Martin, G. I., et al. (2003). Apnea, sudden infant death syndrome, and home monitoring. *Pediatrics, 111*(4), 914–917.

Blair, R. J. R., Sellars, C., Strickland, I., Clark, F., Williams, A. O., Smith, M., et al. (1995). Emotion attributions in the psychopath. *Personality and Individual Differences, 19*(4), 431–437.

Blanchard, M., & Main, M. (1979). Avoidance of the attachment figure and social-emotional adjustment in day-care infants. *Developmental Psychology, 15,* 445–446.

Blanchard, R. (2001). Fraternal birth order and the maternal immune hypothesis of male homosexuality. *Hormones and Behavior, 40*(2), 105–114.

Blanchard-Fields, F., Chen, Y., Horhota, M., & Wang, M. (2007). Cultural differences in the relationship between aging and the correspondence bias. *Journals of Gerontology Series B: Psychological Sciences and Social Sciences, 62*(6), 362–365.

Blanchard-Fields, F., & Horhota, M. (2005). Age differences in the correspondence bias: When a plausible explanation matters. *Journals of Gerontology Series B: Psychological Sciences and Social Sciences, 60*(5), 259–267.

Blank, T., & Prinz, M. (2013). Microglia as modulators of cognition and neuropsychiatric disorders. *Glia, 61*(1), 62–70. doi: 10.1002/glia.22372

Blass, T. (1991). Understanding behavior in the Milgram obedience experiment: The role of personality, situations, and their interactions. *Journal of Personality and Social Psychology, 60,* 398–413.

Blass, T. (1999). The Milgram paradigm after 35 years: Some things we now know about obedience to authority. *Journal of Applied Social Psychology, 25,* 955–978.

Bledsoe, C. H., & Cohen, B. (1993). *Social dynamics of adolescent fertility in sub-Saharan Africa.* Washington, DC: National Academy Press.

Blehar, M. C., & Oren, D. A. (1997, June 27). Gender differences in depression. *Medscape General Medicine, 1*(2). Retrieved June 27, 2004, from http://www.medscape.com/viewarticle/719236

Bleiberg, K. L., & Markowitz, J. C. (2008). Interpersonal psychotherapy for depression. In D. H. Barlow (Ed.), *Clinical handbook of psychological disorders* (pp. 306–327). New York, NY: The Guilford Press.

Bleuler, E. (1911, reissued 1950). *Dementia praecox or the group of schizophrenias.* New York: International Universities Press.

Block, N. (2005). Two neural correlates of consciousness. *Trends in Cognitive Sciences, 9,* 41–89.

Bloom, B. S. (Ed.). (1956). *Taxonomy of educational objectives, the classification of educational goals—Handbook I: Cognitive domain.* New York: McKay.

Bloom, L. (1974). Talking, understanding and thinking. In R. Schiefelbusch & L. L. Lloyd (Eds.), *Language perspectives: Acquisition, retardation and intervention.* New York: Macmillan.

Bloom, P. (2000). *How children learn the meaning of words.* Cambridge, MA: MIT Press.

Blumer, D. (2002). The illness of Vincent van Gogh. *American Journal of Psychiatry, 159*(4), 519–526.

Bock, R. (1993, August). *Understanding Klinefelter syndrome: A guide for XXY males and their families* (NIH Publication No. 93-3202). Washington, DC: National Institutes of Health, Office of Research Reporting. Retrieved August 10, 2010, from http://www.nichd.nih.gov/publications/pubs/klinefelter.cfm

Bodrova, E., & Leong, D. J. (1996). *Tools of the mind: The Vygotskian approach to early childhood education.* Englewood Cliffs, NJ: Prentice Hall.

Boggio, P. S., Campanha, C., Valasek, C. A., Fecteau, S., Pascual- Leone, A., & Fregni, F. (2010). Modulation of decision-making in a gambling task in older adults with transcranial direct current stimulation. *The European Journal of Neuroscience, 31*(3), 593–597.

Boggio, P. S., Fregni, F., Valasek, C., Ellwood, S., Chi, R., Gallate, J., et al. (2009). Temporal lobe cortical electrical stimulation during the encoding and retrieval phase reduces false memories. *PLoS One, 4*(3), e4959.

Boggio, P. S., Rocha, M., Oliveira, M. O., Fecteau, S., Cohen, R. B., Campanha, C., et al. (2009). Noninvasive brain stimulation with high-frequency and low-intensity repetitive transcranial magnetic stimulation treatment for posttraumatic stress disorder. *The Journal of Clinical Psychiatry, 29,* 29.

Bogle, K. D. (2000). Effect of perspective, type of student, and gender on the attribution of cheating. *Proceedings of the Oklahoma Academy of Science, 80,* 91–97.

Bond, R. A., & Smith, P. B. (1996). Culture and conformity: A meta- analysis of studies using Asch's (1952, 1956) line judgment task. *Psychological Bulletin, 119,* 111–137.

Bondarenko, L. A. (2004). Role of methionine in nocturnal melatonin peak in the pineal gland. *Bulletin of Experimental Biological Medicine, 137*(5), 431–432.

Bonnelykke, B. (1990). Maternal age and parity as predictors of human twinning. *Acta Genetic Medicine and Gemellology, 39,* 329–334.

Boor, M. (1982). The multiple personality epidemic: Additional cases and inferences regarding diagnosis, etiology, dynamics, and treatment. *Journal of Nervous and Mental Disease, 170,* 302–304.

Booth-Butterfield, S. (1996). Message characteristics. *Steve's Primer of Practical Persuasion and Influence.* Retrieved August 2, 2004, from http://www.austincc.edu/colangelo/1311/persuasivecharacteristics.htm

Borgeat, F., & Goulet, J. (1983, June). Psychophysiological changes following auditory subliminal suggestions for activation and deactivation. *Perceptual and Motor Skills, 56*(3), 759–766.

Borges, M. A., Stepnowsky, M. A., & Holt, L. H. (1977). Recall and recognition of words and pictures by adults and children. *Bulletin of the Psychonomic Society, 9,* 113–114.

Boroditsky, L. (2001). Does language shape thought? Mandarin and English speakers' conceptions of time. *Cognitive Psychology, 43*(1), 1–22.

Boroditsky, L. (2009). How does our language shape the way we think? In M. Brockman (Ed.), *What's next? Dispatches on the future of science* (pp. 116–129). New York: Vintage.

Bosworth, H. B., & Schaie, K. W. (1997). The relationship of social environment, social networks, and health outcomes in the Seattle Longitudinal Study: Two analytical approaches. *Journals of Gerontology Series B: Psychological Sciences and Social Sciences, 52*(5), 197–205.

Botwin, M. D., & Buss, D. M. (1989). The structure of act data: Is the Five-Factor Model of personality recaptured? *Journal of Personality and Social Psychology, 56,* 988–1001.

Bouchard, C., Tremblay, A., Nadeau, A., Dussault, J., Despres, J. P., Theriault, G., et al. (1990). Long-term exercise training with constant energy intake. 1: Effect on body composition and selected metabolic variables. *International Journal on Obesity*, 14(1), 57–73.

Bouchard, T. J., Jr. (1997). Whenever the twain shall meet. *The Science*, 37(5), 52–57.

Bouchard, T. (1994). Genes, environment, and personality. *Science*, 264, 1700–1701.

Bouchard, T. J., Jr., & Segal, N. L. (1985). Environment and IQ. In B. B. Wolman (Ed.), *Handbook of intelligence: Theories, measurements, and applications* (pp. 391–464). New York: Wiley.

Bowden, C. L., Calabrese, J. R., McElroy, S. L., Gyulai, L., Wassef, A., Petty, F., et al. (2000). For the Divalproex Maintenance Study Group. A randomized, placebo-controlled 12-month trial of divalproex and lithium in treatment of outpatients with bipolar I disorder. *Archives of General Psychiatry*, 57(5), 481–489.

Bowman, E. S. (1996). Delayed memories of child abuse: Part II: An overview of research findings relevant to understanding their reliability and suggestibility. *Dissociation: Progress in the Dissociative Disorders*, 9, 232–243.

Boyd, C. H., & Peeler, C. M. (2004, May). *Highlighting vs note taking: A comparison of students' performance on tests.* Poster presented at 16th Annual Convention of the American Psychological Society, Chicago, IL.

Boyd, L. A., & Winstein, C. J. (2004). Cerebellar stroke impairs temporal but not spatial accuracy during implicit motor learning. *Neurorehabilitation and Neural Repair*, 18(3), 134–143.

Boyson-Bardies, B., deHalle, P., Sagart, L., & Durand, C. (1989). A cross-linguistic investigation of vowel formats in babbling. *Journal of Child Language*, 16, 1–17.

Bracey, G. (1997). A few facts about poverty. *Phi Delta Kappan*, 79, 163–164.

Brazelton, T. B. (1992). *Touchpoints: Your child's emotional and behavioral development.* Reading, MA: Addison-Wesley.

Brecher, M., Wang, B. W., Wong, H., & Morgan, J. P. (1988). Phencyclidine and violence: Clinical and legal issues. *Journal of Clinical Psychopharmacology*, 8, 397–401.

Breier, A., Albus, M., Pickar, D., Zahn, T. P., Wolkowitz, O. M., & Paul, S. M. (1987). Controllable and uncontrollable stress in humans: Alterations in mood, neuroendocrine and psychophysiological function. *American Journal of Psychiatry*, 144, 1419–1425.

Breiter, H. C., Gollub, R. L., Weisskoff, R. M., Kennedy, D. N., Makris, N., Berke, J. D., et al. (1997). Acute effects of cocaine on human brain activity and emotion. *Neuron*, 19(3), 591–611.

Breland, K., & Breland, M. (1961). The misbehavior of organisms. *American Psychologist*, 16, 681–684.

Bremmer, J. D. (2005). *Brain imaging handbook.* New York: W. W. Norton.

Brennan, J. F. (2002). *History and systems of psychology* (6th ed.). Upper Saddle River, NJ: Prentice Hall.

Brennan, P. A., Raine, A., Schulsinger, F., Kirkegaard-Sorensen, L., Knop, J., Hutchings, B., et al. (1997). Psychophysiological protective factors for male subjects at high risk for criminal behavior. *American Journal of Psychiatry*, 154, 853–855.

Breslau, N., Chilcoat, H. D., Kessler, R. C., Peterson, E. L., & Lucia, V. C. (1999). Vulnerability to assaultive violence: Further specification of the sex difference in posttraumatic stress disorder. *Psychological Medicine*, 29, 813–821.

Breslau, N., Davis, G. C., Andreski, P., & Peterson, E. L. (1997). Sex differences in posttraumatic stress disorder. *Archives of General Psychiatry*, 54(11), 1044–1048.

Brewer, M. B. (2001). Ingroup identification and intergroup conflict: When does in-group love become outgroup hate? In R. D. Ashmore, L. Jussim, & D. Wilder (Eds.), *Social identity, intergroup conflict, and conflict reduction*. New York: Oxford University Press.

Brick, J. (2003). The characteristics of alcohol: Chemistry, use and abuse. In J. Brick (Ed.), *Handbook of the medical consequences of alcohol and drug abuse* (pp. 1–11). New York: Haworth Medical Press.

Briem, V., & Hedman, L. R. (1995). Behavioural effects of mobile telephone use during simulated driving. *Ergonomics*, 38, 2536–2562.

Briggs, K. C., & Myers, I. B. (1998). *The Myers-Briggs Type Indicator-Form M.* Palo Alto, CA: Consulting Psychologists Press.

Brigham, A. (1844). Asylums exclusively for the incurably insane. *Classic article in the American Journal of Psychiatry*, 151, 50–70.

Broadbent, D. (1958). *Perception and communication.* Elmsford, NY: Pergamon.

Brondolo, E., Rieppi, R., Erickson, S. A., Bagiella, E., Shapiro, P. A., McKinley, P., et al. (2003). Hostility, interpersonal interactions, and ambulatory blood pressure. *Psychosomatic Medicine*, 65, 1003–1011.

Bronkhorst, A. W. (2000). The cocktail party phenomenon: A review on speech intelligibility in multiple-talker conditions. *Acta Acustica United with Acustica*, 86, 117–128. Retrieved from http://eaa-fenestra.org/products/acta-acustica/most-cited/acta_86_2000_Bronkhorst.pdf

Brooks, J. G., & Brooks, M. G. (1993). *In search of understanding: The case for constructivist classrooms.* Alexandria, VA: The Association for Supervision and Curriculum Development.

Brown, A. S., & Derkits, E. J. (2010). Prenatal infection and schizophrenia: A review of epidemiologic and translational studies. *The American Journal of Psychiatry*, 167(3), 261–280. doi:10.1176/appi.ajp.2009.09030361

Brown, C., Taylor, J., Green, A., Lee, B. E., Thomas, S. B., & Ford, A. (2003). *Managing depression in African Americans: Consumer and provider perspectives* [Final Report to Funders]. Pittsburgh: Mental Health Association of Allegheny County.

Brown, C. A., & Jones, A. K. P. (2010). Meditation experience predicts less negative appraisal of pain: Electrophysiological evidence for the involvement of anticipatory neural responses. *Pain*. doi:10.1016/j.pain.2010.04.017

Brown, E. (2012, September 2). Sun Myung Moon dies at 92; Washington Times owner led the Unification Church. *The Washington Post*. Retrieved May 24, 2013, from http://www.washingtonpost.com/world/asia_pacific/sun-myungmoon-dies-at-92-washington-times-owner-led-the-unification-church/2012/09/02/001b747a-f531-11e1-aab7-f199a16396cf_story.html

Brown, G., Lawrence, T. B., & Robinson, S. L. (2005). Territoriality in management organizations. *Academy of Management Review*, 30(3), 577–594.

Brown, G. L., & Linnoila, M. I. (1990). CSF serotonin metabolite (5-HIAA) studies in depression, impulsivity, and violence. *Journal of Clinical Psychiatry*, 51(4), 31–43.

Brown, J. (1958). Some tests of the decay theory of immediate memory. *Quarterly Journal of Experimental Psychology*, 10, 12–21.

Brown, R. (1973). *A first language: The early stages.* Cambridge, MA: Harvard University Press.

Brown, R., & McNeill, D. (1966). The "tip of the tongue" phenomenon. *Journal of Verbal Learning and Verbal Behavior*, 5(4), 325–337.

Brown, W. M., Finn, C. J., Cooke, B. M., & Breedlove, S. M. (2002). Differences in finger length ratios between self-identified "butch" and "femme" lesbians. *Archives of Sexual Behavior*, 31(1), 123-127. doi: 10.1023/A:1014091420590

Browne, D. (2004). Do dolphins know their own minds? *Biology and Philosophy*, 19, 633–653.

Browne, M. N., & Keeley, S. M. (2009). *Asking the right questions: A guide to critical thinking* (9th ed., pp. 37–129). Upper Saddle River, NJ: Pearson Prentice-Hall.

Broyles, S. (2006). Subliminal advertising and the perpetual popularity of playing to people's paranoia. *Journal of Consumer Affairs*, 40(2), 392–406.

Brubaker, D. A., & Leddy, J. J. (2003). Behavioral contracting in the treatment of eating disorders. *The Physician and Sportsmedicine*, 31(9).

Brunner, E. J., Hemingway, H., Walker, B., Page, M., Clarke, P., Juneja, M., et al. (2002). Adrenocortical, autonomic and inflammatory causes of the metabolic syndrome: Nested case-control study. *Circulation*, 106, 2659–2665.

Bryan, E. B., & Hallett, F. (2001). *Guidelines for professionals. Twins and triplets: The first five years and beyond.* London: Multiple Births Foundation.

Bryan, J., & Freed, F. (1982). Corporal punishment: Normative data and sociological and psychological correlates in a community college population. *Journal of Youth and Adolescence*, 11(2), 77–87.

Bryant, R. A., & McConkey, K. M. (1989). Hypnotic blindness: A behavioral and experimental analysis. *Journal of Abnormal Psychology*, 98, 71–77.

Brzustowicz, L. M., Simone, J., Mohseni, P., Hayter, J. E., Hodgkinson, K. A., Chow, E. W., et al. (2004). Linkage disequilibrium mapping of schizophrenia susceptibility to the CAPON region of chromosome 1q22. *American Journal of Human Genetics*, 74(5), 1057–1063.

Buccino, G., Binkofski, F., Fink, G. R., Fadiga, L., Fogassi, L., Gallese, V., et al. (2001). Action observation activates premotor and parietal areas in a somatotopic manner: An fMRI study. *European Journal of Neuroscience*, 13(2), 400–404.

Bucher, B. D., & Lovaas, O. I. (1967). Use of aversive stimulation in behavior modification. In M. R. Jones (Ed.), *Miami symposium on the prediction of behavior 1967: Aversive stimulation* (pp. 77–145). Coral Gables: University of Miami Press.

Buck, L. B., & Bargmann, C. I. (2013). Smell and taste: The chemical senses. In E. R. Kandel, J. H. Schwartz, T. M. Jessell, S. A. Siegelbaum, & A. J. Hudspeth (Eds.), *Principles of neural science* (5th ed., pp. 712–735). USA: McGraw Hill.

Buck, R. (1980). Nonverbal behavior and the theory of emotion: The facial feedback hypothesis. *Journal of Personality and Social Psychology*, 38, 811–824.

Bullock, T. H., Bennett, M. V., Johnston, D., Josephson, R., Marder, E., & Fields, R. D. (2005). Neuroscience. The neuron doctrine, redux. *Science*, 310(5749), 791–793.

Bunge, M. (1984). What is pseudoscience? *The Skeptical Inquirer*, 9(1), 36–46.

Bureau of Labor Statistics. (2010). *Census of fatal occupational injuries.* Retrieved August 9, 2010, from http://www.bls.gov/iif/ oshcfoi1.htm

Burger, J. M. (1997). The psychoanalytic approach: Neo-Freudian theory, application, and assessment. In *Personality* (4th ed.). Pacific Grove, CA: Brooks/Cole.

Burger, J. M. (2009). Replicating Milgram: Would people still obey today? *American Psychologist*, 64, 1–11.

Burger, J. M., & Petty, R. E. (1981). The low-ball compliance technique: Task or person commitment? *Journal of Personality and Social Psychology*, 40, 492–500.

Burgio, K. L. (1998). Behavioral vs. drug treatment for urge urinary incontinence in older women: A randomized controlled trial. *Journal of the American Medical Association*, 280, 1995–2000.

Burke, D. M., MacKay, D. G., Worthley, J. S., & Wade, E. (1991). On the tip of the tongue: What causes word finding failures in young and older adults. *Journal of Memory and Language*, 30, 542–579.

Burns, J. F. (2010, May 24). British medical council bars doctor who linked vaccine with autism. *New York Times*. Retrieved from http://www.nytimes.com

Bush, G., Frazier, J. A., Rauch, S. L., Seidman, L. J., Whalen, P. J., Jenike, M. A., et al. (1999). Anterior cingulate cortex dysfunction in Attention-Deficit/Hyperactivity Disorder revealed by fMRI and the Counting Stroop. *Biological Psychiatry*, 45(12), 1542–1552.

Bush, G., Spencer, T. J., Holmes, J., Shin, L. M., Valera, E. M., Seidman, L. J., et al. (2008). Functional magnetic resonance imaging of methylphenidate and placebo in Attention-Deficit/Hyperactivity Disorder during the Multi-Source Interference Task. *Archives of General Psychiatry*, 65(1), 102–114.

Bushman, B. J. (1997). Effects of alcohol on human aggression: Validity of proposed explanations. In M. Galanter (Ed.), *Recent developments in alcoholism. Vol. 1: Alcohol and violence—Epidemiology, neurobiology, psychology, family issues* (pp. 227–243). New York: Plenum Press.

Bushman, B. J., & Huesmann, L. R. (2001). Effects of televised violence on aggression. In D. G. Singer & J. L. Singer (Eds.), *Handbook of children and the media* (Chapter 11, pp. 223–254). Thousand Oaks, CA: Sage.

Buss, D. M. (1989). Sex differences in human mate preferences: Evolutionary hypotheses testing in 37 cultures. *Behavioral and Brain Sciences*, 12, 1–49.

Buss, D. M. (2007). The evolution of human mating. *Acta Psychologica Sinica*, 39(3), 502–512.

Buss, D. M. (2009). The multiple adaptive problems solved by human aggression. *Behavioral and Brain Sciences*, 32, 271–272.

Buss, D. M. (2011). Personality and the adaptive landscape: The role of individual differences in creating and solving social adaptive problems. In D. M. Buss & P. H. Hawley (Eds.), *The evolution of personality and individual differences(pp. 29-60)*. New York: Oxford University Press.

Buss, D. M., Larsen, R. J., Westen, D., & Semmelroth, J. (1992). Sex differences in jealousy: Evolution, physiology, and psychology. *Psychological Science*, 3, 251–255.

Buss, D. M., & Schmitt, D. (1993). Sexual strategies theory: An evolutionary perspective on human mating. *Psychological Review*, 100(2), 204–232. doi:10.1037/0033-295X.100.2.204

Buss, D. M., & Schmitt, D. (2011). Evolutionary psychology and feminism. *Sex Roles*, 64(9–10), 768–787. doi:10.1007/s11199-011-9987-3

Bussa, B., & Kaufman, C. (2000). What can self-help do? *The Journal of the California Alliance of the Mentally Ill*, 2(2), 34–45.

Butcher, J. N., Graham, J. R., Ben-Poarth, Y. S., Tellegen, A., Dahlstrom, W. G., & Kaemmer, B. (2001). *Minnesota Multiphasic Personality Inventory-2. Manual for administration, scoring, and interpretation* (Rev. ed.). Minneapolis: University of Minnesota Press.

Butcher, J. N., & Rouse, S. V. (1996). Personality: Individual differences and clinical assessment. *Annual Review of Psychology*, 47, 87–111.

Butcher, J. N., Rouse, S. V., & Perry, J. N. (2000). Empirical description of psychopathology in therapy clients: Correlates of MMPI-2 scales. In J. N. Butcher (Ed.), *Basic sources on the MMPI-2* (pp. 487–500). Minneapolis: University of Minnesota Press.

Cabeza, R., Anderson, N. D., Locantore, J. K., & McIntosh, A. R. (2002). Aging gracefully: Compensatory brain activity in high-performing older adults. *NeuroImage*, 17(3), 1394–1402.

Cabeza, R., & Nyberg, L. (2000). Imaging cognition II: An empirical review of 275 PET and fMRI studies. *Journal of Cognitive Neuroscience*, 12(1), 1–47.

Cacioppo, J. T., Berntson, G. G. (1992). Social psychological contributions to the decade of the brain: Doctrine of multilevel analysis. *American Psychologist*, 47, 1019–1028.

Cain, D., & Seeman, J. (Eds.). (2001). *Humanistic psychotherapies: Handbook of research and practice*. Washington, DC: APA Publications.

Caley, L. M., Kramer, C., & Robinson, L. K. (2005). Fetal alcohol spectrum disorder. *The Journal of School Nursing*, 21(3), 139–146.

Camacho, M. (2012). Abby and Brittany. *Common Sense Media*. Retrieved April 26, 2013, from http://www.commonsensemedia.org/tv-reviews/abby-andbrittany

Camchong, J., Lim, K. O., Sponheim, S. R., & Macdonald, A. W. (2009). Frontal white matter integrity as an endophenotype for schizophrenia: Diffusion tensor imaging in monozygotic twins and patients' nonpsychotic relatives. *Frontiers in Human Neuroscience*, 3, 35.

Cameron, J., Banko, K. M., & Pierce, W. D. (2001). Pervasive negative effects of rewards on intrinsic motivation: The myth continues. *The Behavior Analyst*, 24, 1–44.

Cami, J., Farre, M., Mas, M., Roset, P. N., Poudevida, S., Mas, A., et al. (2000). Human pharmacology of 3, 4-methylenedioxymethamphetamine ("ecstasy"): Psychomotor performance and subjective effects. *Journal of Clinical Psychopharmacology*, 20, 455–466.

Cannon, W. B. (1927). The James-Lange theory of emotion: A critical examination and an alternative theory. *American Journal of Psychology*, 39, 10–124.

Cardno, A. G., & Gottesman, I. I. (2000). Twin studies of schizophrenia: From bow-and-arrow concordances to star wars Mx and functional genomics. *American Journal of Medical Genetics*, 97(1), 12–17.

Carducci, B. (1998). *The psychology of personality*. Pacific Grove, CA: Brooks/Cole Publishing Co.

Carey, B. (2009, December 21). Building a search engine of the brain, slice by slice. *New York Times*. Retrieved June 10, 2010, from http://www.nytimes.com/2009/12/22/health/22brain.html?ref=henry_gustav_molaison

Carlsen, A. (2013, March 18). *Some people really can taste the rainbow* [web log post]. Retrieved from http://www.npr.org/blogs/thesalt/2013/03/12/174132392/synesthetes-really- can-taste-the-rainbow

Carlson, G. A., Jensen, P. S., & Nottelmann, E. D. (Eds.). (1998). Current issues in childhood bipolarity [Special issue]. *Journal of Affective Disorders*, 51.

Carnot, M. J., Dunn, B., Cañas, A. J., Gram, P., & Mudloon, J. (2001). *Concept maps vs. Web pages for information searching and browsing*. Retrieved May 28, 2008, from http://www.ihmc.us/users/acanas/publications/CMapsVSWebPagesExp1/CMapsVSWebPagesExp1.htm

Carpenter, P. A., Just, M. A., & Shell, P. (1990). What one intelligence test measures: A theoretical account of the processing in the Raven Progressive Matrices test. *Psychological Review*, 97(3), 404–431.

Carr, E. G., & Lovaas, O. I. (1983). Contingent electric shock as a treatment for severe behavior problems. In S. Axelrod & J. Apsche (Eds.), *The effects of punishment on human behavior* (pp. 221–245). New York: Academic Press.

Carrion, V. G., Weems, C. F., & Reiss, A. L. (2007). Stress predicts brain changes in children: A pilot longitudinal study on youth stress, posttraumatic stress disorder, and the hippocampus. *Pediatrics*, 119(3), 509–516.

Carruthers, M. (2001). A multifactorial approach to understanding andropause. *Journal of Sexual and Reproductive Medicine*, 1, 69–74.

Carskadon, M. A., & Dement, W. C. (2005). Normal human sleep overview. In M. H. Kryger, T. Roth, & W. C. Dement (Eds.), *Principles and practice of sleep medicine* (4th ed., pp. 13–23). Philadelphia: Elsevier/Saunders.

Carskadon, M. A., & Dement, W. C. (2011). Normal human sleep: An overview. In M. H. Kryger, T. Roth, & W. C. Dement (Eds.), *Principles and practice of sleep medicine*. St. Louis, MO: Elsevier Saunders.

Carson, R. C. (1969). *Interaction concepts of personality*. Chicago: Aldine.

Carter, R. M., Bowling, D. L., Reeck, C., & Huettel, S. (2012). A distinct role of the temporal-parietal junction in predicting socially guided decisions. *Science*, 337(6090), 109–111.

Carter, C., Bishop, J., Kravits, S. L., D'Agostino, J. V. (Ed. consultant). (2002). *Keys to college studying: Becoming a lifelong learner*. Upper Saddle River, NJ: Prentice Hall.

Carver, C. S., & Antoni, M. H. (2004). Finding benefit in breast cancer during the year after diagnosis predicts better adjustment 5 to 8 years after diagnosis. *Health Psychology*, 26, 595–598.

Case, B. G., Bertollo, D. N., Laska, E. M., Price, L. H., Siegel, C. E., Olfson, M., et al. (2013). Declining use of electroconvulsive therapy in United States general hospitals. *Biological Psychiatry*, 73(2), 119–126. doi:10.1016/j.biopsych.2012.09.005

Case, B. G., Bertollo, D. N., Laska, E. M., Siegel, C. E., Wanderling, J. A., & Olfson, M. (2012). Racial differences in the availability and use of electroconvulsive therapy for recurrent major depression. *Journal of Affective Disorders*, 136(3), 359–365.

Cassidy, A., Bingham, S., & Setchell, K. D. R. (1994). Biological effects of a diet of soy protein rich in isoflavones on the menstrual cycle of premenopausal women. *American Journal of Clinical Nutrition*, 60, 333–340.

Castillo, R. J. (1997). Eating disorders. In R. J. Castillo (Ed.), *Culture and mental illness: A client-centered approach* (p. 152). Pacific Grove, CA: Brooks/Cole.

Catani, M., & Thiebaut de Schotten, M. (2012). *Atlas of human brain connections*. New York, NY: Oxford University Press.

Catanzaro, S. J., Wasch, H. H., Kirsch, I., & Mearns, J. (2000). Coping-related expectancies and dispositions as prospective predictors of coping responses and symptoms: Distinguishing mood regulation expectancies, dispositional coping, and optimism. *Journal of Personality*, 68, 757–788.

Cattell, R. B. (1950). *Personality: A systematic, theoretical, and factual study*. New York: McGraw-Hill.

Cattell, R. B. (Ed.). (1966). *Handbook of multivariate experimental psychology*. Chicago: Rand McNally.

Cattell, R. B. (1990). Advances in Cattellian personality theory. In L. A. Pervin (Ed.), *Handbook of personality: Theory and research* (pp. 101–110). New York: Guilford Press.

Cattell, R. B. (1994). *Sixteen Personality Factor Questionnaire* (5th ed.). Champaign, IL: Institute for Personality and Ability Testing.

Cattell, R. B. (1995). Personality structure and the new fifth edition of the 16PF. *Educational and Psychological Measurement*, 55(6), 926–937.

Cattell, R. B., & Kline, P. (1977). *The scientific analysis of personality and motivation*. New York: Academic Press.

Cave, K. R., & Kim, M. (1999). Top-down and bottom-up attentional control: On the nature of interference from a salient distractor. *Perception and Psychophysics*, 61, 1009–1023.

Centers for Disease Control and Prevention (CDC). (1992). *Smoking and health in the Americas: The Surgeon General's report*. Atlanta, GA: National Center for Chronic Disease Prevention and Health Promotion.

Centers for Disease Control and Prevention (CDC). (2008a). Annual smoking-attributable mortality, years of potential life lost, and economic costs—United States, 2000-2004. *Morbidity and Mortality Weekly Report*, 57(45), 1226–1228.

Centers for Disease Control and Prevention (CDC), 2008b Centers for Disease Control and Prevention (CDC). (2008b, October 3). HIV Prevalence Estimates—United States, 2006 Centers for Disease Control and Prevention. *Morbidity and Mortality Weekly Report*, 57(39), 1073–1076.

Centers for Disease Control and Prevention (CDC). (2009a). *HIV/AIDS surveillance report 2007* (Vol. 19). Atlanta, GA: National Center for Chronic Disease Prevention and Health Promotion.

Centers for Disease Control and Prevention (CDC). (2009b). *Health effects of cigarette smoking*. Retrieved January 13, 2010, from http://www.cdc.gov/tobacco/data_statistics/fact_sheets/health_effects/effects_cig_smoking/index.htm

Centers for Disease Control and Prevention (CDC). (2010). *How tobacco smoke causes disease: The biology and behavioral basis for smoking-attributable disease: A report of the Surgeon General*. Retrieved March 27, 2013, from http://www.cdc.gov/tobacco/data_statistics/sgr/2010/index.htm

Centers for Disease Control and Prevention (CDC). (2011a). *FastStats: Alcohol use*. Retrieved March 27, 2013, from http://www.cdc.gov/nchs/fastats/alcohol.htm

Centers for Disease Control and Prevention (CDC). (2011b). *Vaccines & immunizations: Some common misconceptions*. Retrieved April 26, 2013, from http://www.cdc.gov/vaccines/vac-gen/6mishome.htm

Centers for Disease Control and Prevention (CDC). (2013). *Vaccine safety: Addressing common concerns*. Retrieved April 26, 2013, from http://www.cdc.gov/vaccine-safety/Concerns/Index.html

Centers for Disease Control and Prevention. (2014). *HIV transmission*. Divisions of HIV/AIDS Prevention, Retrieved June 10, 2014 from http://www.cdc.gov/hiv/basics/transmission.html

Centerwall, B. S. (1989). Exposure to television as a risk factor for violence. *American Journal of Epidemiology, 129*, 643–652.

Cepeda, N. J., Pashler, H., Vul, E., Wixted, J. T., & Rohrer, D. (2006). Distributed practice in verbal recall tasks: A review and quantitative synthesis. *Psychological Bulletin, 132*, 354–380.

Cermak, L., & Craik, F. (1979). *Levels of processing in human memory*. Hillsdale, NJ: Erlbaum.

Cha, J. H., & Nam, K. D. (1985). A test of Kelley's cube theory of attribution: A cross-cultural replication of McArthur's study. *Korean Social Science Journal, 12*, 151–180.

Chaddock, L., Hillman, C. H., Buck, S. M., & Cohen, N. J. (2010). Aerobic fitness and executive control of relational memory in preadolescent children. *Medicine and Science in Sports and Exercise*. doi:10.1249/MSS.0b013e3181e9af48

Chandola, T., Britton, A., Brunner, E., Hemingway, H., Malik, M., Kumari, M., et al. (2008). Work stress and coronary heart disease: What are the mechanisms? *European Heart Journal*. doi:10.1093/eurheartj/ehm584

Chang, P. P., Ford, D. E., Meoni, L. A., Wang, N., & Klag, M. J. (2002). Anger in young men and subsequent premature cardiovascular disease: The precursors study. *Archives of Internal Medicine, 162*, 901–906.

Chang, S. W., Gariepy, J. F., & Platt, M. L. (2013). Neuronal reference frames for social decisions in primate frontal cortex. *Nature Neuroscience, 16*, 243–250.

Charlesworth, W. R., & Kreutzer, M. A. (1973). Facial expression of infants and children. In P. Ekman (Ed.), *Darwin and facial expression: A century of research in review*. New York: Academic.

Chen, J. Y. (2007). Do Chinese and English speakers think about time differently? Failure of replicating Boroditsky (2001). *Cognition, 104*(2), 427–436.

Chen, L. Y., Rex, C. S., Sanaiha, Y., Lynch, G., & Gall, C. M. (2010). Learning induces neurotrophin signaling at hippocampal synapses. *Proceedings of the National Academy of Sciences, 107*(15), 7030–7035.

Chen, R., & Ende, N. (2000). The potential for the use of mononuclear cells from human umbilical cord blood in the treatment of amyotrophic lateral sclerosis in SOD1 mice. *Journal of Medicine, 31*, 21–31.

Chen, Y., Huang, X., Zhang, Y.-W., Rockenstein, E., Bu, G., Golde, T. E., Masliah, E., & Xu, H. (2012). Alzheimer's β-Secretase (BACE1) regulates the cAMP/PKA/CREB pathway independently of β-Amyloid. *Journal of Neuroscience, 32*(33), 11390. doi: 10.1523/JNEUROSCI.0757-12.2012

Cherry, E. C. (1953). Some experiments on the recognition of speech, with one and with two ears. *Journal of the Acoustical Society of America, 25*(5), 975–979.

Cheryan, S., Plaut, V., Davis, P., & Steele, C. (2009). Ambient belonging: How stereotypical cues impact gender participation in computer science. *Journal of Personality and Social Psychology, 97*(6), 1045–1060.

Chess, S., & Thomas, A. (1986). *Temperament in clinical practice*. New York: Guilford Press.

Chesterton, L. S., Barlas, P., Foster, N. E., Baxter, G. D., & Wright, C. C. (2003). Gender differences in pressure pain threshold in healthy humans. *Pain, 101*, 259–266.

Cheyne, J. A. (2003). Sleep paralysis and the structure of waking-nightmare hallucinations. *Dreaming, 13*(3), 163–179.

Chidester, D. (2003). *Salvation and suicide: Jim Jones, the peoples temple, and Jonestown* (Rev. ed., pp. 1–51). Bloomington: Indiana University Press.

Chirkov, V. I. (2009). A cross-cultural analysis of autonomy in education: A self-determination theory perspective. *Theory and Research in Education, 7*(2), 253–262.

Chirkov, V. I., Lebedeva, N. M., Molodtsova, I., & Tatarko, A. (2011). Social capital, motivational autonomy, and health behavior: A comparative study of Canadian and Russian youth. In D. Chadee & A. Kosti (Eds.), *Social psychological dynamics* (pp. 211–241). Trinidad: University of West Indies Press.

Chiu, C., Hong, Y., & Dweck, C. S. (1997). Lay dispositionism and implicit theories of personality. *Journal of Personality and Social Psychology, 73*, 19–30.

Choca, J. P. (2013). *The Rorschach inkblot test: An interpretive guide for clinicians*. Washington, DC: American Psychological Association.

Chomsky, N. (1986). *Knowledge of language: Its nature, origin and use*. New York: Praeger.

Chomsky, N. (2006). *Language and mind* (3rd ed.). New York: Cambridge University Press.

Chomsky, N., Belletti, A., & Rizzi, L. (2002). *On nature and language*. New York: Cambridge University Press.

Chou, S. Y., Grossman, M., & Saffer, H. (2004). An economic analysis of adult obesity: Results from the behavioral risk factor surveillance system. *Journal of Health Economics, 23*, 565–587.

Christensen, A., Jacobson, N. S., & Babcock, J. C. (1995). Integrative behavioral couple therapy. In N. S. Jacobson & A. S. Gurman (Eds.), *Clinical handbook of couple therapy* (pp. 31–64). New York: Norton.

Chwalisz, K., Diener, E., & Gallagher, D. (1988). Autonomic arousal feedback and emotional experience: Evidence from the spinal cord injured. *Journal of Personality and Social Psychology, 54*, 820–828.

Cialdini, R. B., Trost, M. R., & Newsom, J. T. (1995). Preference for consistency: The development of a valid measure and the discovery of surprising behavioral implications. *Journal of Personality and Social Psychology, 69*, 318–328.

Cialdini, R. B., Vincent, J., Lewis, S., Catalan, J., Wheeler, D., & Darby, B. (1975). Reciprocal concessions procedure for inducing compliance: The door-in-the-face technique. *Journal of Personality and Social Psychology, 31*, 206–215.

Cialdini, R. B., Wosinska, W., Barrett, D., Butner, J., & Gornik-Durose, M. (1999). Compliance with a request in two cultures: The differential influence of social proof and commitment/consistency on collectivists and individualists. *Personality and Social Psychology Bulletin, 25*, 1242–1253.

Ciardiello, A. (1998). Did you ask a good question today? Alternative cognitive and metacognitive strategies. *Journal of Adolescent and Adult Literacy, 42*, 210–219.

Cinnirella, M., & Green, B. (2007). Does "cyber-conformity" vary cross-culturally? Exploring the effect of culture and communication medium on social conformity. *Computers in Human Behavior, 23*(4), 2011–2025.

Clancy, S. A., McNally, R. J., Schacter, D. L., Lenzenweger, M. F., & Pitman, R. K. (2002). Memory distortion in people reporting abduction by aliens. *Journal of Abnormal Psychology, 111*(3), 455–461.

Clark, A. (1991). *Microcognition: Philosophy, cognitive science, and parallel distributed processing*. Cambridge, MA: MIT Press, Reprint edition (1989).

Clarke, A. R., Barry, R. J., McCarthy, R., Selikowitz, M., Johnstone, S. J., Hsu, C. I., et al. (2007). Coherence in children with Attention-Deficit/Hyperactivity Disorder and excess beta activity in their EEG. *Clinical Neurophysiology, 118*(7), 1472–1479.

Clarke, J. (1994). Pieces of the puzzle: The jigsaw method. In S. Sharan (Ed.), *Handbook of cooperative learning methods* (pp. 34–50). Westport, CT: Greenwood Press.

Clarkin, J. F., Levy, K. N., Lenzenweger, M. F., & Kernberg, O. F. (2007). Evaluating three treatments for borderline personality disorder: A multiwave study. *American Journal of Psychiatry, 164*(6), 922–928.

Coccaro, E. F., & Kavoussi, R. J. (1996). Neurotransmitter correlates of impulsive aggression. In D. M. Stoff & R. B. Cairns (Eds.), *Aggression and violence* (pp. 67–86). Mahwah, NJ: Erlbaum.

Cohen, L. J. (1997). Rational drug use in the treatment of depression. *Pharmacotherapy, 17*, 45–61.

Cohen, N. J., Eichenbaum, R., Decedo, J. C., & Corkin, S. (1985). Preserved learning capacity in amnesia: Evidence for multiple memory systems. In L. S. Squire & N. Butters (Eds.), *Neuropsychology of memory*. New York: Guilford Press.

Cohen, S., & Herbert, T. B. (1996). Health psychology: Psychological factors and physical disease from the perspective of human psychoneuroimmunology. *Annual Review of Psychology, 47*, 113–142.

Cohen, S., Janicki-Deverts, D., & Miller, G. E. (2007). Psychological stress and disease. *Journal of the American Medical Association, 298*(14), 1685–1687.

Colcombe, S. J., Erickson, K. I., Raz, N., Webb, A. G., Cohen, N. J., McAuley, E., et al. (2003). Aerobic fitness reduces brain tissue loss in aging humans. *Journal of Gerontology Series A: Biological Sciences and Medical Sciences, 58*, 176–180.

Cole, S. W., Arevalo, J. M. G., Takahashi, R., Sloan, E. K., Lutgendorf, S. K., Sood, A. K., et al. (2010). Computational identification of genesocial environment interaction oat the human IL6 locus. *Proceedings of the National Academy of Sciences of the United States of America*. Retrieved September 27, 2010, from http://www.pnas.org/content/107/12/5681.full

The College Board. (2011). *Time management tips for students*. Retrieved May 31, 2013, from http://www.collegeboard.com/ student/plan/college-success/116.html

Colligan, J. (1983). Musical creativity and social rules in four cultures. *Creative Child and Adult Quarterly, 8*, 39–44.

Collins, A. M., & Loftus, E. F. (1975). A spreading activation theory of semantic processing. *Psychological Review, 82*, 407–428.

Collins, A. M., & Quillian, M. R. (1969). Retrieval time from semantic memory. *Journal of Verbal Learning and Verbal Behaviour, 8*, 240–247.

Collins, C. J., Hanges, P. J., & Locke, E. A. (2004). The relationship of achievement motivation to entrepreneurial behavior: A meta-analysis. *Human Performance, 17*(1), 95–117.

Colom, R., Shih, P. C., Flores-Mendoza, C., & Quiroga, M. A. (2006). The real relationship between short-term memory and working memory. *Memory, 14*(7), 804–813.

Columbo, J., & Mitchell, D. W. (2009). Infant visual habituation. *Neurobiology of Learning and Memory, 92*(2), 225–234.

Committee on Animal Research and Ethics. (2004). *Research with animals in psychology.* Retrieved October 12, 2004, from www.apa.org/science/animal2.html

Cone-Wesson, B. (2005). Prenatal alcohol and cocaine exposure: Influences on cognition, speech, language, and hearing. *Journal of Communication Disorders, 38*(4), 279–302.

Conrad, R., & Hull, A. J. (1964). Information, acoustic confusion, and memory span. *British Journal of Psychology, 55,* 429–432.

Conway, M. A., Cohen, G., & Stanhope, N. (1992). Very long-term memory for knowledge acquired at school and university. *Applied Cognitive Psychology, 6,* 467–482.

Cook, K. (2014). *Kitty Genovese: The Murder, the Bystander, the Crime, the Crime that Changed America.* New York, W.W. Norton & Company, Inc.

Cook, M., & Mineka, S. (1989). Observational conditioning of fear to fear-relevant versus fear-irrelevant stimuli in rhesus monkeys. *Journal of Abnormal Psychology, 98*(4), 448–459.

Coolidge, F. L. (2006). *Dream interpretation as a psychotherapeutic technique.* London: Radcliffe.

Cooper, L. A., Gonzales, J. J., Gallo, J. J., Rost, K. M., Meredith, L. S., Rubenstein, L. V., et al. (2003). The acceptability of treatment for depression among African-American, Hispanic, and White primary care patients. *Medical Care, 41*(4), 479–489.

Corbetta, M., Kincade, M. J., Lewis, C., Snyder, A. Z., & Sapir, A. (2005). Neural basis and recovery of spatial attention deficits in spatial neglect. *Nature Neuroscience, 8,* 1603–1610.

Cormier, J. F., & Thelen, M. H. (1998). Professional skepticism of multiple personality disorder. *Professional Psychology: Research and Practice, 29,* 163–167.

Corr, C. A. (1993). Coping with dying: Lessons that we should and should not learn from the work of Elisabeth Kubler-Ross. *Death Studies, 17,* 69–83.

Cosgrove, G. R., & Rauch, S. L. (1995). Psychosurgery. *Neurosurgery Clinics of North America, 6,* 167–176.

Cosmides, L., & Tooby, J. (2013). Evolutionary psychology: New perspectives on cognition and motivation. *Annual Review of Psychology, 64,* 201–229.

Costa, P. T., Jr., & McCrae, R. R. (2000). The Revised NEO Personality Inventory (NEO PI-R). In J. Cheek & E. M. Donahue (Eds.), *Handbook of personality inventories.* New York: Plenum.

Costello, D. M., Swendsen, J., Rose, J. S., & Dierker, L. C. (2008). Risk and protective factors associated with trajectories of depressed mood from adolescence to early adulthood. *Journal of Consulting and Clinical Psychology, 76*(2), 173–183.

Couperus, J. W., & Nelson, C. A. (2006). Early brain development and plasticity. In K. McCartney & D. Phillips (Eds.), *The Blackwell handbook of early childhood development* (pp. 85–105). Oxford, UK: Blackwell Press.

Courage, M. L., & Howe, M. L. (2002). From infant to child: The dynamics of cognitive change in the second year of life. *Psychological Bulletin, 128,* 250–277.

Cowan, N. (1988). Evolving conceptions of memory storage, selective attention, and their mutual constraints within the human information processing system. *Psychological Bulletin, 104,* 163–191.

Cowan, N. (1995). *Attention and memory: An integrated framework* (Oxford Psychology Series, No. 26). Oxford, NY: Oxford University Press.

Cowan, N. (2001). The magical number 4 in short-term memory: A reconsideration of mental storage capacity. *Behavioral and Brain Sciences, 24,* 97–185.

Craddock, N., O'Donovan, M. C., & Owen, M. J. (2005). The genetics of schizophrenia and bipolar disorder: Dissecting psychosis. *Journal of Medical Genetics, 42,* 288–299.

Crago, M. B., Shisslak, C. M., & Estes, L. S. (1996). Eating disturbances among American minority groups: A review. *International Journal of Eating Disorders, 19,* 239–248.

Craik, F. I. M. (1970). The fate of primary memory items in free recall. *Journal of Verbal Learning and Verbal Behavior, 9,* 143–148.

Craik, F. I. M. (1994). Memory changes in normal aging. *Current Directions in Psychological Science, 3*(5), 155–158.

Craik, F. I. M., & Lockhart, R. S. (1972). Levels of processing. A framework for memory research. *Journal of Verbal Learning and Verbal Behaviour, 11,* 671–684.

Craik, F. I. M., & Tulving, E. (1975). Depth of processing and the retention of words in episodic memory. *Journal of Experimental Psychology: General, 104,* 268–294.

Craske, M. G., & Barlow, D. H. (2014). Panic disorder and agoraphobia. In D. H. Barlow (Ed.), *Clinical handbook of psychological disorders: A step-by-step treatment manual* (5th ed., pp. 1–61). New York: Guilford Press.

Crick, F., & Koch, C. (1990). Towards a neurobiological theory of consciousness. *Seminars in the Neurosciences, 2,* 263–275.

Crick, F., & Koch, C. (2003). A framework for consciousness. *Nature Neuroscience, 6,* 119–127.

Cristancho, M. A., Helmer, A., Connolly, R., Cristancho, P., & O'Reardon, J. P. (2013). Transcranial magnetic stimulation maintenance as a substitute for maintenance electroconvulsive therapy: A case series. *J ECT, 29*(2), 106–108. doi:10.1097/ YCT.0b013e31827a70ba

Critchfield, T. S., Haley, R., Sabo, B., Colbert, J., & Macropoulis, G. (2003). A half century of scalloping in the work habits of the United States congress. *Journal of Applied Behavior Analysis, 36*(4), 465–486.

Crowley, A. E., & Hoyer, W. D. (1994). An integrative framework for understanding two-sided persuasion. *Journal of Consumer Research, 20,* 561–574.

Csikszentmihalyi, M. (1996). *Creativity: Flow and the psychology of discovery and invention.* New York: Harper Perennial.

Cummings, J. L., & Coffey, C. E. (1994). Neurobiological basis of behavior. In C. E. Coffey & J. L. Cummings (Eds.), *Textbook of geriatric neuropsychiatry* (pp. 72–96). Washington, DC: American Psychiatric Press.

Cummings, S. R., & Melton, L. J., III. (2002). Epidemiology and outcomes of osteo-porotic fractures. *Lancet, 359*(9319), 1761–1767.

Curtis, R. C., & Miller, K. (1986). Believing another likes or dislikes you: Behaviors making the beliefs come true. *Journal of Personality and Social Psychology, 51,* 284–290.

Curtis, R. H. (1993). *Great lives: Medicine.* New York: Charles Scribner's Sons Books for Young Readers.

Dabbs, J. M., Jr., Bernieri, F. J., Strong, R. K., Campo, R., & Milun, R. (2001). Going on stage: Testosterone in greetings and meetings. *Journal of Research in Personality, 35,* 27–40.

Dalenberg, C. J. (1996). Accuracy, timing and circumstances of disclosure in therapy of recovered and continuous memories of abuse. *The Journal of Psychiatry and Law, 24*(2), 229–275.

Daly, M., Wilson, M., & Weghorst, S. J. (1982). Male sexual jealousy. *Ethology and Sociobiology, 3,* 11–27.

Damasio, H., Grabowski, T., Frank, R., Galaburda, A. M., & Damasion, A. R. (1994). The return of Phineas Gage: Clues about the brain from the skull of a famous patient. *Science, 264,* 1102–1105.

Dani, J., Burrill, C., & Demmig-Adams, B. (2005). The remarkable role of nutrition in learning and behavior. *Nutrition and Food Science, 35*(4), 258–263.

Darley, J. M., & Latané, B. (1968). Bystander intervention in emergencies: Diffusion of responsibility. *Journal of Personality and Social Psychology, 8,* 377–383.

Darvill, T., Lonky, E., Reihman, J., Stewart, P., & Pagano, J. (2000). Prenatal exposure to PCBs and infant performance on the Fagan test of infant intelligence. *Neurotoxicology, 21*(6), 1029–1038.

Darwin, C. (1859). *The origin of species by means of natural selection.* London: John Murray.

Darwin, C. (1898). *The expression of the emotions in man and animals.* New York: D. Appleton.

Daum, I., & Schugens, M. M. (1996). On the cerebellum and classical conditioning. *Current Directions in Psychological Science, 5,* 58–61.

Davidson, R. J. (2003). Affective neuroscience and psychophysiology: Toward a synthesis. *Psychophysiology, 40*(5), 655–665.

Davidson, R. J., Kabat-Zinn, J., Schumacher, J., Rosenkranz, M., Muller, D., Santorelli, S., et al. (2003). Alterations in brain and immune function produced by mindfulness meditation. *Psychosomatic Medicine, 65,* 564–570.

Davidson, R. J., Putman, K. M., & Larson, C. L. (2000). Dysfunction in the neural circuitry of emotion regulation—a possible prelude to violence. *Science, 289,* 591–594.

Davies, I. R. L., Laws, G., Corbett, G. G., & Jerrett, D. J. (1998). Cross-cultural differences in colour vision: Acquired "colour blindness" in Africa. *Personality and Individual Differences, 25,* 1153–1162.

Davies, I. R. L., Sowden, P., Jerrett, D. T., Jerrett, T., & Corbett, G. G. (1998). A crosscultural study of English and Setswana speakers on a colour triads task: A test of the Sapir-Whorf hypothesis. *British Journal of Psychology, 89,* 1–15.

Davis, C. J., Harding, J. W., & Wright, J. W. (2003). REM sleep deprivation induced deficits in the latency-to-peak induction and maintenance of long-term potentiation within the CA1 region of hippocampus. *Brain Research, 973,* 293–297.

Davis, H. A., DiStefano, C., & Schutz, P. A. (2008). Identifying patterns of appraising tests in first-year college students: Implications for anxiety and emotion regulation during test taking. *Journal of Educational Psychology, 100*(4), 942–960. doi:10.1037/ a0013096

Davis, K. F., Parker, K. P., & Montgomery, G. (2004). Sleep in infants and young children: Part 1: Normal sleep. *Journal of Pediatric Healthcare, 18*(2), 65–71.

Davis, M., & Whalen, P. J. (2001). The amygdala: Vigilance and emotion. *Molecular Psychiatry, 6,* 13–34.

Davis, O. S. P., Haworth, C. M. A., Lewis, C. M., & Plomin, R. (2012). Visual analysis of geocoded twin data puts nature and nurture on the map. *Molecular Psychiatry, 17,* 867–874. doi:10.1038/mp.2012.68

Dean, G., & Kelly, I. W. (2000). Does astrology work? Astrology and skepticism 1975–2000. In P. Kurtz (Ed.), *Skepticism: A 25 year retrospective* (pp. 191–207). Amherst, NY: Prometheus Books.

Dean, G., Kelly, I. W., Sakolfske, D. H., & Furnham, A. (1992). Graphology and human judgment. In B. L. Beyerstein & D. F. Beyerstein (Eds.), *The write stuff: Evaluations of graphology—The study of handwriting analysis* (pp. 342–396). Amherst, NY: Prometheus Books.

Dębiec, J., Díaz-Mataix, L., Bush, D. E. A., Doyère, V., & LeDoux, J. E. (2010). The amygdala encodes specific sensory features of an aversive reinforcer. *Nature Neuroscience, 13,* 536–537.

DeCasper, A. J., & Fifer, W. P. (1980). Of human bonding: Newborns prefer their mothers' voices. *Science, 208,* 1174–1176.

DeCasper, A. J., & Spence, M. J. (1986). Prenatal maternal speech influence on newborns' perception of sounds. *Infant Behaviour and Development, 9,* 133–150.

deCharms, R. (1968). *Personal causation.* New York: Academic Press.

Deci, E. L., Eghrari, H., Patrick, B. C., & Leone, D. R. (1994). Facilitating internalization: The self-determination theory perspective. *Journal of Personality, 62,* 119–142.

Deci, E. L., Koestner, R., & Ryan, R. M. (1999). A meta-analytic review of experiments examining the effects of extrinsic rewards on intrinsic motivation. *Psychological Bulletin, 125,* 627–668.

DeCoster, J., & Claypool, H. M. (2004). A meta-analysis of priming effects on impression formation supporting a general model of informational biases. *Personality and Social Psychology Review, 8*(1), 2–27.

Deger, M., Helias, M., Rotter, S., & Diesmann, M. (2012). Spike- timing dependence of structural plasticity explains cooperative synapse formation in the neocortex. *PLoS Computational Biology, 8*(9), e1002689. doi:10.1371/journal.pcbi.1002689

DeGrandpre, R. J. (2000). A science of meaning: Can behaviorism bring meaning to psychological science? *American Psychologist, 55*, 721–739.

Deinzer, R., Kleineidam, C. H., Winkler, R., Idel, H., & Bachg, D. (2000). Prolonged reduction of salivary immunoglobulin A (slgA) after a major academic exam. *International Journal of Psychophysiology, 37*, 219–232.

Delagrange, P., & Guardiola-Lemaitre, B. (1997). Melatonin, its receptors, and relationships with biological rhythm disorders. *Clinincal Neuropharmacology, 20*, 482–510.

Delaney, A. J., Crane, J. W., & Sah, P. (2007). Noradrenaline modulates transmission at a central synapse by a presynaptic mechanism. *Neuron, 56*(6), 880–892.

Delfiner, R. (2001, November 16). Kitty left at death's door. *New York Post*. Retrieved from http://www.nypost.com.

Dement, W. C. (1960). The effect of dream deprivation. *Science, 131*, 1705–1707.

Dement, W. C., Henry, P., Cohen, H., & Ferguson, J. (1969). Studies on the effect of REM deprivation in humans and animals. In K. H. Pribram (Ed.), *Mood, states, and mind*. Baltimore: Penguin.

Demers, R. A. (1988). Linguistics and animal communication. In F. J. Newmeyer (Ed.), *Language form and language function* (pp. 314–335). Cambridge, MA: MIT Press.

Dempster, F. N., & Farris, R. (1990). The spacing effect: Research and practice. *Journal of Research and Development in Education, 23*(2), 97–101.

Deng, L. X., Deng, P., Ruan, Y., Xu, Z. C., Liu, N. K., Wen, X., et al. (2013). A novel growth-promoting pathway formed by gdnf-overexpressing schwann cells promotes propriospinal axonal regeneration, synapse formation, and partial recovery of function after spinal cord injury. *The Journal of Neuroscience, 33*(13), 5655–5667. doi:10.1523/jneurosci.2973-12.2013

Deregowski, J. B. (1969). Perception of the two-pronged trident by two- and three-dimensional perceivers. *Journal of Experimental Psychology, 82*, 9–13.

De Valois, R. L., & De Valois, K. K. (1993). A multi-stage color model. *Vision Research, 33*(8), 1053–1065.

De Valois, R. L., & Jacobs, G. H. (1968). Primate color vision. *Science, 162*, 553–540.

Dew, M. A., Whyte, E. M., Lenze, E. J., Houck, P. R., Mulsant, B. H., Pollock, B. G., et al. (2007). Recovery from major depression in older adults receiving augmentation of antidepressant pharmacotherapy. *American Journal of Psychiatry, 164*(6), 892–899.

DeYoung, C. G., Hirsh, J. B., Shane, M. S., Papademetris, X., Rajeevan, N., & Gray, J. R. (2010). Testing predictions from personality neuroscience: Brain structure and the Big Five. *Psychological Science, 21*(6), 820–828.

Diamond, L. M. (2003). What does sexual orientation orient? A biobehavioral model distinguishing romantic love and sexual desire. *Psychological Review, 110*, 173–192.

Diamond, M., & Sigmundson, H. K. (1997). Sex reassignment at birth. Long-term review and clinical implications. *Archives of Pediatric Adolescent Medicine, 151*(3), 298–304.

DiazGranados, N., Ibrahim, L. A., Brutsche, N. E., Ameli, R., Henter, I. D., Luckenbaugh, D. A., et al. (2010). Rapid resolution of suicidal ideation after a single infusion of an N-methyl-D-aspartate antagonist in patients with treatment-resistant major depressive disorder. *The Journal of Clinical Psychiatry, 71*(12), 1605–1611. doi:10.4088/JCP.09m05327blu

DiazGranados, N., Ibrahim, L., Brutsche, N. E., Newberg, A., Kronstein, P., Khalife, S., et al. (2010). A randomized add-on trial of an N-methyl-Daspartate antagonist in treatment-resistant bipolar depression. *Archives of General Psychiatry, 67*(8), 793–802. doi:10.1001/archgenpsychiatry.2010.90

Dickens, W. T., & Flynn, J. R. (2001, April). Heritability estimates vs. large environmental effects: The IQ paradox resolved. *Psychological Review, 108*(2), 346–369.

Dickerson, F., Ringel, N., Parente, F., & Boronow, J. (1994). Seclusion and restraint, assaultiveness, and patient performance in a token economy. *Hospital and Community Psychiatry, 45*, 168–170.

Digman, J. M. (1990). Personality structure: Emergence of the five-factor model. *Annual Review of Psychology, 41*, 417–440.

Dillard, J. (1990). Self-inference and the foot-in-the-door technique: Quantity of behavior and attitudinal mediation. *Human Communication Research, 16*, 422–447.

Dillard, J. (1991). The current status of research on sequential- request compliance techniques. *Personality and Social Psychology Bulletin, 17*, 282–288.

Dobson, K. S., & Block, L. (1988). Historical and philosophical bases of the cognitive behavioral therapies. In K. S. Dobson (Ed.), *Handbook of cognitive-behavioral therapies* (pp. 3–38). New York: Guilford Press.

Dodge, K. A., Bates, J. E., & Pettit, G. S. (1990). Mechanisms in the cycle of violence. *Science, 250*, 1678–1683.

Dolcos, F., LaBar, K. S., Cabeza, R., & Purves, D. (2005). Remembering one year later: Role of the amygdala and the medial temporal lobe memory system in retrieving emotional memories. *Proceedings of the National Academy of Sciences, USA*. doi:10.1073/ pnas.0409848102

Dollard, J., & Miller, N. F. (1950). *Personality and psychotherapy*. New York: McGraw-Hill.

Domhoff, G. W. (1996). *Finding meaning in dreams: A quantitative approach*. New York: Plenum Publishing.

Domhoff, G. W. (2005). The content of dreams: Methodologic and theoretical implications. In M. Kryger, T. Roth, & W. Dement (Eds.), *Principles and practices of sleep medicine* (4th ed., pp. 522–534). Philadelphia: Saunders.

Domhoff, G. W., & Schneider, A. (2008). Similarities and differences in dream content at the cross-cultural, gender, and individual levels. *Consciousness and Cognition, 17*, 1257–1265.

Dominey, P. F., & Dodane, C. (2004). Indeterminacy in language acquisition: The role of child-directed speech and joint attention. *Journal of Neurolinguistics, 17*(2–3), 121–145.

Donohue, S. E., James, B., Eslick, A. N., & Mitroff, S. R. (2012). Cognitive pitfall! Videogame players are not immune to dual-task costs. *Attention, Perception, & Psychophysics*. doi: 10.3758/s13414-012-0323-y

Donovan, J. J., & Radosevich, D. R. (1999). A meta-analytic review of the distribution of practice effect: Now you see it, now you don't. *Journal of Applied Psychology, 84*, 795–805.

Dorahy, M. J. (2001). Dissociative identity disorder and memory dysfunction: The current state of experimental research and its future directions. *Clinical Psychology Review, 21*(5), 771–795.

Dougherty, D. D., Baer, L., Cosgrove, G. R., Cassem, E. H., Price, B. H., Nierenberg, A. A., et al. (2002). Prospective long-term follow-up of 44 patients who received cingulotomy for treatment-refractory obsessive-compulsive disorder. *The American Journal of Psychiatry, 159*(2), 269–275.

Drenth, P. J., Thierry, H., Willems, P. J., & de Wolff, C. J. (1984). *Handbook of work and organizational psychology*. Chichester, UK: Wiley.

Druckman, D., & Bjork, R. A. (Eds.). (1994). *Learning, remembering, believing: Enhancing human performance* (Study conducted by the National Research Council). Washington, DC: National Academy Press.

Duben, A., & Behar, C. (1991). *Istanbul households: Marriage, family and fertility 1880–1940*. Cambridge, NY: Cambridge University Press.

Dubowitz, H., & Bennett, S. (2007). Physical abuse and neglect of children. *Lancet, 369*(9576), 1891–1899.

Duckworth, A. L., Quinn, P. D., Lynam, D. R., Loeber, R., & Stouthamer-Loeber, M. (2011). Role of test motivation in intelligence testing. *Proceedings of the National Academy of Sciences, 108*(19), 7716–7720. doi:10.1073/pnas.1018601108

Duckworth, A. L., & Seligman, M. E. P. (2005). Self-discipline outdoes IQ in predicting academic performance of adolescents. *Psychological Science, 16*(12), 939–944. doi:10.1111/j.1467-9280.2005.01641.x

Dudai, Y. (2004). The neurobiology of consolidations, or, how stable is the engram? *Annual Review of Psychology, 55*, 51–86.

Duker, P. C., & Seys, D. M. (1996). Long-term use of electrical aversion treatment with self-injurious behaviors. *Research in Developmental Disabilities, 17*, 293–301.

Dumont, F. (2010). *A history of personality psychology*. New York, NY: Cambridge University Press.

Duncan, R. M. (1995). Piaget and Vygotsky revisited: Dialogue or assimilation? *Developmental Review, 15*, 458–472.

Dundas, I., Wormnes, B. R., & Hauge, H. (2009). Making exams a manageable task. *Nordic Psychology, 61*(1), 26–41.

Dunn, R., Beaudry, J. S., & Klavas, A. (1989). Survey of research on learning styles. *Educational Leadership, 46*(6), 50–57.

Dunn, R., Denig, S., & Lovelace, M. K. (2001, February 1). Multiple intelligences and learning styles: Two sides of the same coin or different strokes for different folks? *Teacher Librarian, 28*, 9–15.

Durrant, M. (Ed.). (1993). *Aristotle's De anima in focus*. London: Routledge.

Durso, F., Rea, C., & Dayton, T. (1994). Graph-theoretic confirmation of restructuring during insight. *Psychological Science, 5*, 94–98.

Dwairy, M. (2004). Parenting styles and mental health of Palestinian-Arab adolescents in Israel. *Transcultural Psychiatry, 41*(2), 233–252.

Dweck, C. S. (1986). Motivational processes affecting learning. *American Psychologist, 41*(10), 1040–1048.

Dweck, C. S. (1999). *Self-theories: Their role in motivation, personality and development*. Philadelphia: Psychology Press.

Dweck, C. S., & Leggett, E. L. (1988). A social-cognitive approach to motivation and personality. *Psychological Review, 95*, 256–273.

Dweck, C. S., & Molden, D. C. (2008). Self-theories: The construction of free will. In J. Baer, J. C. Kaufman, & R. F. Baumeister (Eds.), *Are we free? Psychology and free will* (pp. 44–64). New York: Oxford University Press.

Dweck, C. S., Chiu, C., & Hong, Y. (1995). Implicit theories and their role in judgments and reactions: A world from two perspectives. *Psychological Inquiry, 6*, 267–285.

Dweck, C. S., & Elliott, E. (1983). Achievement motivation. In P. Mussen (Ed.), *Handbook of child psychology: Vol. 4. Socialization, personality, and social development* (pp. 643–691). New York: Wiley.

Dykens, E. M., Hodapp, R. M., & Leckman, J. F. (1994). *Behavior and development in fragile X syndrome*. Thousand Oaks, CA: Sage.

Eagleman, D. M. (2001). Visual illusions and neurobiology. *Nature Reviews: Neuroscience, 2*(12), 920–926.

Eagly, A. H. (1987). *Sex difference in social behavior: A social-role interpretation*. Hillsdale, NJ: Erlbaum.

Eagly, A. H., Ashmore, R. D., Makhijani, M. G., & Longo, L. C. (1991). What is beautiful is good, but . . . : A meta-analytic review of the physical attractiveness stereotype. *Psychological Bulletin, 110*, 109–128.

Eagly, A. H., & Carli, L. L. (2007). *Through the labyrinth: The truth about how women become leaders* (pp. 119–136). Boston: Harvard Business School Press.

Eagly, A. H., & Chaiken, S. (1975). An attribution analysis of the effect of communicator characteristics on opinion change: The case of communicator attractiveness. *Journal of Personality and Social Psychology, 37*, 136–144.

Eagly, A. H., & Chaiken, S. (1993). *The psychology of attitudes.* Fort Worth, TX: Harcourt Brace.

Eagly, A. H., & Chaiken, S. (1998). Attitude structure and function. In D. T. Gilbert, S. T. Fiske, & G. Lindzey (Eds.), *The handbook of social psychology* (4th ed., pp. 269–322). New York: McGraw-Hill.

Eagly, A. H., & Crowley, M. (1986). Gender and helping behavior: A meta-analytic review of the social psychological literature. *Psychological Bulletin, 100*, 283–308.

Eagly, A. H., Wood, W., & Diekman, A. B. (2000). Social role theory of sex differences and similarities: A current appraisal. In T. Eckes & H. M. Trautner (Eds.), *The developmental social psychology of gender* (pp. 123–174). Mahwah, NJ: Erlbaum.

Eaker, E. D., & Castelli, W. P. (1988). Type A behavior and mortality from coronary disease in the Framingham Study. *New England Journal of Medicine, 319*, 1480–1481.

Eaton, W. W., Kessler, R. C., Wittchen, H. U., & Magee, W. J. (1994). Panic and panic disorder in the United States. *American Journal of Psychiatry, 151*(3), 413–420.

Eddy, J., Fitzhugh, E., & Wang, M. (2000). Smoking acquisition: Peer influence and self-selection. *Psychological Reports, 86*, 1241–1246.

Edelmann, R. J., & Iwawaki, S. (1987). Self-reported expression of embarrassment in five European cultures. *Psychologia: An International Journal of Psychology, 30*, 205–216.

Edlund, J. E., Heider, J. D., Scherer, C. R., Farc, M.-M., & Sagarin, B. J. (2006). Sex differences in jealousy in response to actual infidelity. *Evolutionary Psychology, 4*, 462–470.

Ehlers, A., Bisson, J., Clark, D. M., Creamer, M., Pilling, S., Richards, D., et al. (2010). Do all psychological treatments really work the same in posttraumatic stress disorder? *Clinical Psychology Review, 30*(2), 269–276.

Eich, E., & Metcalfe, J. (1989). Mood dependent memory for internal vs. external events. *Journal of Experimental Psychology: Learning, Memory and Cognition, 15*, 443–455.

Eiden, R. D., McAuliffe, S., Kachadourian, L., Coles, C., Colder, C., & Schuetze, P. (2009). Effects of prenatal cocaine exposure on infant reactivity and regulation. *Neurotoxicology and Teratology, 31*, 60–68.

Ekman, P. (1973). Darwin and cross-cultural studies of facial expression. In P. Ekman (Ed.), *Darwin and facial expression: A century of research in review.* New York: Academic Press.

Ekman, P. (1980). Asymmetry in facial expression. *Science, 209*, 833–834.

Ekman, P., & Friesen, W. (1969). The repertoire of nonverbal behavior: Categories, origins, usage, and coding. *Semiotica, 1*, 49–98.

Ekman, P., & Friesen, W. V. (1971). Constants across cultures in the face and emotion. *Journal of Personality and Social Psychology, 17*(2), 124–129.

Ekman, P., & Friesen, W. V. (1978). *The facial action coding system.* Palo Alto, CA: Consulting Psychologists Press.

Ekman, P., Sorensen, E. R., & Friesen, W. V. (1969). Pan-cultural elements in facial displays of emotion. *Science, 164*, 86–88.

Elkind, D. (1985). Egocentrism redux. *Developmental Review, 5*, 218–226.

Elliott, E., & Dweck, C. (1988). Goals: An approach to motivation and achievement. *Journal of Personality and Social Psychology, 54*, 5–12.

Elliott, L., & Brantley, C. (1997). *Sex on campus: The naked truth about the real sex lives of college students.* New York: Random House.

Ellis, A. (1998). *The Albert Ellis reader: A guide to well-being using rational emotive behavior therapy.* Secaucus, NJ: Carol Publishing Group.

Ellis, B. J., McFayden-Ketchum, S. A., Dodge, K. A., Pettit, G. S., & Bates, J. E. (1999). Quality of early family relationships and individual differences in the timing of pubertal maturation in girls: A longitudinal test on an evolutionary model. *Journal of Personality and Social Psychology, 77*, 387–401.

Ellis, H. D. (1983). The role of the right hemisphere in face perception. In A. W. Young (Ed.), *Functions of the right cerebral hemisphere* (pp. 33–64). London: Academic Press.

Ellis, L., Ames, M. A., Peckham, W., & Burke, D. (1988). Sexual orientation of human offspring may be altered by severe maternal stress during pregnancy. *The Journal of Sex Research, 25*, 152–157.

Emeny, R. T., Lacruz, M.-E., Baumert, J., Zierer, A., von Eisenhart Rothe, A., Autenrieth, C., et al. (2012). Job strain associated CRP is mediated by leisure time physical activity: Results from the MONICA/ KORA study. *Brain, Behaviour and Immunity, 26*, 1077–1084.

Emeny, R. T., Zierer, A., Lacruz, M.-E., Baumert, J., Herder, C., Gornitzka, G., et al. (2013). Job strain–associated inflammatory burden and long-term risk of coronary events: Findings from the MONICA/KORA Augsburg case-cohort study. *Psychosomatic Medicine, 75*(3), 317–325.

Endler, N. S. (1988). The origins of electroconvulsive therapy (ECT). *Convulsive Therapy, 4*, 5–23.

Engle, R. W., & Kane, M. J. (2004). Executive attention, working memory capacity, and a two-factor theory of cognitive control. *The Psychology of Learning and Motivation, 44*, 145–199.

Engelhardt, C. R., & Bartholow, B. D. (2013). Aggression, risk factors of (pp. 14–17). In Matthew S. Eastin (Ed.), *Encyclopedia of media violence.* Sage Publications.

Engelhardt, C. R., Bartholow, B. D., Kerr, G. T. & Bushman, B. J. (2011). This is your brain on violent video games: Neural desensitization to violence predicts increased aggression following violent video game exposure. Journal of Experimental Social Psychology, 47, 1033–1036.

Enns, J. T., & Coren, S. (1995). The box alignment illusion: An orientation illusion induced by pictorial depth. *Perception and Psychophysics, 57*, 1163–1174.

Ephraim, P. L., Wegener, S. T., MacKenzie, E. J., Dillingham, T. R., & Pezzin, L. E. (2005). Phantom pain, residual limb pain and back pain in persons with limb loss: Results of a national survey. *Archives of Physical Medicine and Rehabilitation, 86*, 1910–1919.

Epping-Jordan, M., Waltkins, S. S., Koob, G. F., & Markou, A. (1998). Dramatic decreases in brain reward function during nicotine withdrawal. *Nature, 393*, 76–79.

Erdley, C. A., & Dweck, C. S. (1993). Children's implicit personality theories as predictors of their social judgments. *Child Development, 64*, 863–878.

Erickson, K. I., Prakash, R. S., Voss, M. W., Chaddock, L., Hu, L., Morris, K. S., et al. (2009). Aerobic fitness is associated with hippocampal volume in elderly humans. *Hippocampus, 19*(10), 1030–1039.

Erikson, E. H. (1950). *Childhood and society.* New York: Norton.

Erikson, E. H. (1959). Growth and crises of the healthy personality. *Psychological Issues, 1*, 50–100.

Erikson, E. H. (1980). Elements of a psychoanalytic theory of psychosocial development. In S. Greenspan & G. Pollock (Eds.), *The course of life, Vol. 1* (pp. 11–61). Washington, DC: U.S. Department of Health and Human Services.

Erikson, E. H. (1982). *The life cycle completed.* New York: Norton.

Erikson, E. H., & Erikson, J. M. (1997). *The life cycle completed.* New York: Norton.

Eriksson, P., Ankarberg, E., Viberg, H., & Fredriksson, A. (2001). The developing cholinergic system as target for environmental toxicants, nicotine and polychlorinated biphenyls (PCBs): Implications for neurotoxicological processes in mice. *Neurotoxicity Research, 3*(1), 37–51.

Escandon, A., Al-Hammadi, N., & Galvin, J. E. (2010). Effect of cognitive fluctuation on neuropsychological performance in aging and dementia. *Neurology, 74*, 210–217.

Eschenbeck, H., Kohlmann, C. W., & Lohaus, A. (2008). Gender differences in coping strategies in children and adolescents. *Journal of Individual Differences, 28*(1), 18–26.

Ethen, M. K., Ramadhani, T. A., Scheuerle, A. E., Canfield, M. A., Wyszynski, D. F., Druschel, C. M., et al. (2008). Alcohol consumption by women before and during pregnancy. *Maternal and Child Health Journal, 13*(2), 274–285. doi:10.1007/s10995-008-0328-2

Evans, I. M., & Meyer, L. H. (1985). *An educative approach to behavior problems: A practical decision model for interventions with severely handicapped learners.* Baltimore: Paul H. Brookes.

Evans, W. H., Evans, S. S., & Schmid, R. E. (1989). *Behavior and instructional management: An ecological approach.* Boston: Allyn & Bacon.

Everson, S. (1995). Psychology. In J. Barnes (Ed.), *The Cambridge companion to Aristotle* (pp. 168–194). Cambridge, UK: Cambridge University Press.

Exner, J. E. (1980). But it's only an inkblot. *Journal of Personality Assessment, 44*, 562–577.

Experts urge caution in using deep brain stimulation. (2010). *Harvard Mental Health Letter, 26*(8), 6–7.

Eysenck, H. J. (1994a). *Test your IQ.* Toronto: Penguin Books.

Eysenck, H. J. (1994b). Synergistic interaction between psychosocial and physical factors in the causation of lung cancer. In C. Lewis, C. O'Sullivan, & J. Barraclough (Eds.), *The psychoimmunology of human cancer* (pp. 163–178). London: Oxford University Press.

Eysenck, H. J., & Eysenck, S. B. G. (1993). *Eysenck Personality Questionnaire* [Revised]. London: Hodder & Stoughton Educational.

Fagot, B. I., & Hagan, R. (1991). Observations of parent reactions to sex-stereotyped behaviours: Age and sex effects. *Child Development, 62*, 617–628.

Fairchild, G., Van Goozen, S. H., Stollery, S. J., & Goodyer, I. M. (2008). Fear conditioning and affective modulation of the startle reflex in male adolescents with early-onset or adolescence-onset conduct disorder and healthy control subjects. *Biological Psychiatry, 63*(3), 279–285.

Fanselow, M. S., & Gale, G. D. (2003). The amygdala, fear, and memory. *Annals of the New York Academy of Sciences, 985*, 125–134.

Fantz, R. L. (1961). The origin of form perception. *Scientific American, 204*, 66–72.

Fantz, R. L. (1964). Visual experience in infants: Decreased attention to familiar patterns relative to novel ones. *Science, 146*, 668–670.

Faraone, S. V., Biederman, J., & Wozniak, J. (2012). Examining the comorbidity between attention deficit hyperactivity disorder and bipolar I disorder: A metaanalysis of family genetic studies. *The American Journal of Psychiatry, 169*(12), 1256–1266. doi:10.1176/appi.ajp.2012.12010087

Farthing, W. (1992). *The psychology of consciousness.* Upper Saddle River, NJ: Prentice-Hall.

Fawzy, F. I., Fawzy, N. W., Hyun, C. S., Elashoff, R., Guthrie, D., Fahey, J. L., et al. (1993). Malignant melanoma effects of an early structured psychiatric intervention, coping, and affective state on recurrence and survival 6 years later. *Archives of General Psychiatry, 50*(9), 681–689.

Fazel-Rezai, R., & Peters, J. F. (2005). P300 wave feature extraction: Preliminary results, in *Proceedings of the 18th Annual Canadian Conference on Electrical and Computer Engineering (CCECE '05)* (pp. 390–393). Saskatoon, Saskatchewan, Canada.

Fazio, R. H., & Olson, M. A. (2003). Attitudes: Foundations, functions, and consequences. In M. A. Hogg & J. Cooper (Eds.), *The Handbook of Social Psychology* (pp. 139–160). London: Sage.

Fechner, G. T. (1860). *Elemente der Psykophysik*. Leipzig: Breitkopf und Härtel.

Fedoroff, I. C., & McFarlane, T. (1998). Cultural aspects of eating disorders. In S. S. Kazarian & D. R. Evans (Eds.), *Cultural clinical psychology: Theory, research and practice* (pp. 152–176). New York: Oxford University Press.

Feingold, A. (1992). Good-looking people are not what we think. *Psychological Bulletin, 111*, 304–341.

Felder, R. M., & Spurlin, J. E. (2005). Applications, reliability and validity of the index of learning styles. *International Journal of Engineering Education, 21*(1), 103–112.

Feldman, D. H. (2003). Cognitive development in childhood. In I. B. Weiner, R. M. Lerner, M. A. Easterbrooks, & J. Mistry (Eds.), *Handbook of psychology: Developmental psychology: Vol. 6* (pp. 195–201). New York: Wiley.

Ferguson, C. J. (2010). Video games and youth violence: A prospective analysis in adolescents. *Journal of Youth and Adolescence.* doi:10.1007/s10964-010-9610-x

Ferguson, C. J. (2013). Violent video games and the supreme court: Lessons for the scientific community in the wake of brown v. Entertainment merchants association. *American Psychologist, 68*(2), 57–74. doi: 10.1037/a0030597

Ferguson, C. J., & Kilburn, J. (2009). The public health risks of media violence: A meta-analytic review. *Journal of Pediatrics, 154*, 759–763.

Ferguson-Noyes, N. (2005). Bipolar disorder in children. *Advanced Nurse Practitioner, 13*, 35.

Fernald, A. (1984). The perceptual and affective salience of mothers' speech to infants. In L. Feagans, C. Garvey, & R. Golinkoff (Eds.), *The origins and growth of communication*. Norwood, NJ: Ablex.

Fernald, A. (1992). Human maternal vocalizations to infants as biologically relevant signals: An evolutionary perspective. In J. H. Barkow, L. Cosmides, & J. Tooby (Eds.), *The adapted mind: Evolutionary psychology and the generation of culture*. New York: Oxford University Press.

Feroah, T. R., Sleeper, T., Brozoski, D., Forder, J., Rice, T. B., & Forster, H. V. (2004, April 17–21). *Circadian slow wave sleep and movement behavior are under genetic control in inbred strains of rat*. Paper presented at the American Physiological Society Annual Conference, Washington, DC.

Festinger, L. (1954). A theory of social comparison processes. *Human Relations, 7*, 117–140.

Festinger, L. (1957). *A theory of cognitive dissonance*. Stanford, CA: Stanford University Press.

Festinger, L., & Carlsmith, J. (1959). $1/$20 experiment: Cognitive consequences of forced compliance. *Journal of Abnormal and Social Psychology, 58*(2), 203–210.

Fiatarone, M. A. (1996). Physical activity and functional independence in aging. *Research Quarterly for Exercise and Sport, 67*, 70–75.

Fincham, F. D., Harold, G. T., & Gano-Phillips, S. (2000). The longitudinal association between attributions and marital satisfaction: Direction of effects and role of efficacy expectations. *Journal of Family Psychology, 14*, 267–285.

Finger, S. (1994). *Origins of neuroscience: A history of explorations into brain function*. New York: Oxford University Press.

Fink, M. (1984). Meduna and the origins of convulsive therapy. *American Journal of Psychiatry, 141*, 1034–1041.

Finke, C., Esfahani, N. E., & Ploner, C. J. (2012). Preservation of musical memory in an amnesic professional cellist. *Current Biology, 22*(15), R59.

Finke, R. (1995). Creative realism. In S. Smith, T. Ward, & R. Finke (Eds.), *The creative cognition approach* (pp. 301–326). Cambridge, MA: Cambridge University Press.

Fischl, B., Liu, A., & Dale, A. M. (2001). Automated manifold surgery: Constructing geometrically accurate and topologically correct models of the human cerebral cortex. *IEEE Transactions on Medical Imaging, 20*, 70–80.

Fisher, M., Holland, C., Merzenich, M. M., & Vinogradov, S. (2009). Using neuroplasticity-based auditory training to improve verbal memory in schizophrenia. *The American Journal of Psychiatry, 166*(7), 805–811.

Fisher, R., Salanova, V., Witt, T., Worth, R., Henry, T., Gross, R., et al. (2010). Electrical stimulation of the anterior nucleus of thalamus for treatment of refractory epilepsy. *Epilepsia, 17*, 17.

Fiske, S. T. (1998). Stereotyping, prejudice, and discrimination. In D. T. Gilbert & S. T. Fiske (Eds.), *The handbook of social psychology* (4th ed., Vol. 2, pp. 357–411). New York: McGraw-Hill.

Fitzpatrick, M. (2004). *MMR and autism* (pp. 133–149). New York: Routledge.

Fivush, R., Haden, C., & Reese, E. (1996). Remembering, recounting, and reminiscing: The development of autobiographical memory in social context. In D. C. Rubin (Ed.), *Remembering our past: Studies in autobiographical memory* (pp. 341–359). New York: Cambridge University Press.

Fivush, R., & Nelson, K. (2004). Culture and language in the emergence of autobiographical memory. *Psychological Science, 15*(9), 573.

Flaherty, J. A., & Adams, S. A. (1998). Therapist-patient race and sex matching: Predictors of treatment duration. *Psychiatric Times, 15*(1).

Flaskerud, J. H. (1991). Effects of an Asian client-therapist language, ethnicity and gender match on utilization and outcome of therapy. *Community Mental Health Journal, 27*, 31–42.

Flavell, J. H. (1999). Cognitive development: Children's knowledge about the mind. *Annual Review of Psychology, 50*, 21–45.

Flegal, K. M., Carroll, M. D. & Ogden, C. L. (2012). Prevalence of obesity and trends in the distribution of body mass index among US adults, 1999-2010. *Journal of the American Medical Association, 307*(5): 491-497.

Fleming, M. F., & Barry, K. L. (1992). Clinical overview of alcohol and drug disorders. In M. F. Fleming & K. L. Barry (Eds.), *Addictive disorders*. St. Louis: Mosby Year Book.

Flemons, W. W. (2002). Obstructive sleep apnea. *New England Journal of Medicine, 347*, 498–504.

Flynn, J. R. (2009). *What is intelligence? Beyond the Flynn effect*. New York: Cambridge University Press.

Folkard, S., Arendt, J., & Clark, M. (1993). Can melatonin improve shift workers' tolerance of the night shift? Some preliminary findings. *Chronobiology International: The Journal of Biological and Medical Rhythm Research, 10*(5), 315–320.

Folkman, S. (1997). Positive psychological states and coping with severe stress. *Social Science and Medicine, 45*, 1207–1221.

Folkman, S., & Chesney, M. A. (1995). Coping with HIV infection. In M. Stein & A. Baum (Eds.), *Perspectives in behavioral medicine* (pp. 115–133). Hillsdale, NJ: Lawrence Erlbaum.

Folkman, S., & Lazarus, R. S. (1980). An analysis of coping in a middle-aged community sample. *Journal of Health and Social Behavior, 21*(3), 219–239.

Follett, K. J., & Hess, T. M. (2002). Aging, cognitive complexity, and the fundamental attribution error. *Journals of Gerontology Series B: Psychological Sciences and Social Sciences, 57*, 312–323.

Forbes, G., Zhang, X., Doroszewicz, K., & Haas, K. (2009). Relationships between individualism-collectivism, gender, and direct or indirect aggression: A study in China, Poland, and the U.S. *Aggressive Behavior, 35*(1), 24–30.

Fornito, A., Yucel, M., & Pantelis, C. (2009). Reconciling neuroimaging and neuropathological findings in schizophrenia and bipolar disorder. *Current Opinion in Psychiatry, 22*(3), 312–319.

Fortuna, L. R., Alegria, M., & Gao, S. (2010). Retention in depression treatment among ethnic and racial minority groups in the United States. *Depression and Anxiety, 27*(5), 485–494. doi:10.1002/da.20685

Foulkes, D. (1982). *Children's dreams*. New York: Wiley.

Foulkes, D., & Schmidt, M. (1983). Temporal sequence and unit comparison composition in dream reports from different stages of sleep. *Sleep, 6*, 265–280.

Frank, E., Kupfer, D. J., Buysse, D. J., Swartz, H. A., Pilkonis, P. A., Houck, P. R., et al. (2007). Randomized trial of weekly, twice-monthly, and monthly interpersonal psychotherapy as maintenance treatment for women with recurrent depression. *American Journal of Psychiatry, 164*(5), 761–767.

Franke, R. H., & Kaul, J. D. (1978). The Hawthorne experiments: First statistical interpretation. *American Sociological Review, 43*, 623–643.

Frankel, B. R., & Piercy, F. P. (1990). The relationship among selected supervisor, therapist, and client behaviors. *Journal of Marital and Family Therapy, 16*, 407–421.

Franklin, D. (1990). Hooked: Why isn't everyone an addict? *In Health, 4*(6), 38–52.

Fredrickson, B. L., Maynard, K. E., Helms, M. J., Haney, T. L., Siegler, I. C., & Barefoot, J. C. (2000). Hostility predicts magnitude and duration of blood pressure response to anger. *Journal of Behavioral Medicine, 23*, 229–243.

Freeman, A., Simon, K. M., Beutler, L. E., & Arkowitz, H. (Eds.). (1989). *Comprehensive handbook of cognitive therapy*. New York: Plenum Press.

Freedman, J., & Fraser, S. (1966). Compliance without pressure: The foot-in-the-door technique. *Journal of Personality and Social Psychology, 4*, 195–202.

Freeman, J. (2001). *Gifted children grown up*. London: David Fulton.

Freeman, W., & Watts, J. W. (1937). Prefrontal lobotomy in the treatment of mental disorders. *Southern Medical Journal, 30*, 23–31.

Frensch, P. A., & Runger, D. (2003). Implicit learning. *Current Directions in Psychological Science, 12*, 13–18.

Freud, A. (1946). *The ego and the mechanisms of defense* (American ed.). New York: I.U.P.

Freud, S. (1900). The interpretation of dreams. *S. E., 4–5*. (cf. J. Crick, Trans., 1999). London: Oxford University Press.

Freud, S. (1901). The psychopathology of everyday life. *S. E., 6*, 1–290.

Freud, S. (1904). *Psychopathology of everyday life*. New York: Macmillan; London: Fisher Unwin.

Freud, S. (1923). The ego and the id. *S. E., 19*, 12–66.

Freud, S. (1930). *Civilization and its discontents*. New York: Jonathon Cape and Co.

Freud, S. (1931). Female sexuality. *Pelican Freud Library, 7*, 367.

Freud, S. (1933). *New introductory lectures on psycho-analysis*. London: Hogarth Press.

Freud, S. (1940). Splitting of the ego in the process of defence. *International Journal of Psychoanalysis, 22*, 65. (1938, *S. E., 23*, 275–278).

Freud, S. (1977). *Inhibitions, symptoms and anxiety. Standard edition of the complete works of Sigmund Freud*. New York: W. W. Norton.

Freud, S., Strachey, J., & Riviere, J. (1990). *The ego and the id (The standard edition of the complete psychological works of Sigmund Freud)*. New York: W. W. Norton and Company.

Fridlund, A. J., Beck, H. P., Goldie, W. D., & Irons, G. (2012). Little Albert: A neurologically impaired child. *History of Psychology, 15*(4), 302–327.

Friederich, H.-C., Wu, M., Simon, J. J., & Herzog, W. (2013). Neurocircuit function in eating disorders. *International Journal of Eating Disorders, 46*(5), 425–432. doi:10.1002/eat.22099

Friedman, J. M. (2000). Obesity in the new millennium. *Nature, 404,* 632–634.

Friedman, J. M. (2003). A war on obesity, not the obese. *Science, 299*(5608), 856–858.

Friedman, J. M., & Halaas, J. L. (1998). Leptin and the regulation of body weight in mammals. *Nature, 395,* 763.

Friedman, M., & Kasanin, J. D. (1943). Hypertension in only one of identical twins. *Archives of Internal Medicine, 72,* 767–774.

Friedman, M., & Rosenman, R. H. (1959). Association of specific behavior pattern with blood and cardiovascular findings. *Journal of the American Medical Association, 169,* 1286–1296.

Frontera, W. R., Hughes, V. A., Lutz, K. J., & Evans, W. J. (1991). A cross-sectional study of muscle strength and mass in 45- to 78-year-old men and women. *Journal of Applied Physiology, 71,* 644–650.

Fulcher, J. S. (1942). "Voluntary" facial expression in blind and seeing children. *Archives of Psychology, 38,* 1–49.

Furumoto, L. (1979). Mary Whiton Calkins (1863–1930): Fourteenth president of the American psychological association. *Journal of the History of Behavioral Sciences, 15,* 346–356.

Furumoto, L. (1991). Portraits of pioneers in psychology. In G. A. Kimble, M. Wertheimer, & C. White (Eds.), *From "Paired associates" to a psychology of self: The intellectual odyssey of Mary Whiton Calkins* (pp. 57–72). Washington, DC: American Psychological Association.

Gable, R. S. (2004). Acute toxic effects of club drugs. *Journal of Psychoactive Drugs, 36*(1), 303–313.

Gado, M. (2004). A cry in the night: The Kitty Genovese murder. *Court TV's Crime Library: Criminal Minds and Methods.* Retrieved August 2, 2004, from www.crimelibrary.com/serial_killers/predators/kitty_genovese/1.html?sect=2

Galanter, M. (1983). Unification church ("Moonie") dropouts: Psychological readjustment after leaving a charismatic religious group. *American Journal of Psychiatry, 140*(8), 984–989.

Galanti, G. A. (1997). *Caring for patients from different cultures* (2nd ed.). Philadelphia: University of Pennsylvania Press.

Gallagher, R. P. (2009). *National Survey of Counseling Center Directors, 2009.* The American College Counseling Association (ACCA). Retrieved from http://www.iacsinc.org/2009%20National%20Survey.pdf

Gamwell, L., & Tomes, N. (1995). *Madness in America: Cultural and medical perspectives of mental illness before 1914.* Ithaca, NY: Cornell University Press.

Ganchrow, J. R., Steiner, J. E., & Munif, D. (1983). Neonatal facial expressions in response to different qualities and intensities of gustatory stimuli. *Infant Behavior Development, 6,* 473–478.

Ganis, G., Thompson, W. L., & Kosslyn, S. M. (2004). Brain areas underlying visual mental imagery and visual perception: An fMRI study. Brain research. *Cognitive Brain Research, 20*(2), 226–241.

Garb, H. N., Florio, C. M., & Grove, W. M. (1998). The validity of the Rorschach and the Minnesota Multiphasic Personality Inventory: Results from metaanalyses. *Psychological Science, 9,* 402–404.

Garcia, J., Brett, L. P., & Rusiniak, K. W. (1989). Limits of Darwinian conditioning. In S. B. Klein & R. R. Mowrer (Eds.), *Contemporary learning theories: Instrumental conditioning theory and the impact of biological constraints on learning* (pp. 237–275). Hillsdale, NJ: Erlbaum.

Garcia, J., & Koelling, R. A. (1966). Relation of cue to consequence in avoidance learning. *Psychonomic Science, 4,* 123.

Garcia-Campayo, J., Fayed, N., Serrano-Blanco, A., & Roca, M. (2009). Brain dysfunction behind functional symptoms: Neuroimaging and somatoform, conversive, and dissociative disorders. *Current Opinion in Psychiatry, 22*(2), 224–231.

Gardner, E. P., & Johnson, K. O. (2013). Sensory coding. In E. R. Kandel, J. H. Schwartz, T. M. Jessell, S. A. Siegelbaum, & A. J. Hudspeth (Eds.), *Principles of neural science* (5th ed., pp. 449–474). USA: McGraw-Hill.

Gardner, H. (1993a). *Creating minds: An anatomy of creativity seen through the lives of Freud, Einstein, Picasso, Stravinsky, Eliot, Graham, and Ghandi.* New York: Basic Books.

Gardner, H. (1993b). *Multiple intelligences: The theory in practice.* New York: Basic Books.

Gardner, H. (1998). Are there additional intelligences? The case for naturalist, spiritual, and existential intelligences. In J. Kane (Ed.), *Education, information, and transformation* (pp. 111–131). Upper Saddle River, NJ: Merrill-Prentice Hall.

Gardner, H. (1999a). *Intelligence reframed: Multiple intelligences for the 21st century.* New York: Basic Books.

Gardner, H. (1999b, February). Who owns intelligence? *Atlantic Monthly,* 67–76.

Gardner, H., Kornhaber, M. L., & Wake, W. K. (1996). *Intelligence: Multiple perspectives.* Orlando, FL: Harcourt Brace.

Gardner, J., & Oswald, A. J. (2004). How is mortality affected by money, marriage, and stress? *Journal of Health Economics, 23*(6), 1181–1207.

Gardner, R. J. M., & Sutherland, G. R. (1996). *Chromosome abnormalities and genetic counseling* (Oxford Monographics on Medical Genetics No. 29). New York: Oxford University Press.

Garland, E. J., & Smith, D. H. (1991). Simultaneous prepubertal onset of panic disorder, night terrors, and somnambulism. *Journal of American Academic Child and Adolescent Psychiatry, 30*(4), 553–555.

Garnier-Dykstra, L. M., Caldeira, K. M., Vincent, K. B., O'Grady, K. E., & Arria, A. M. (2012). Nonmedical use of prescription stimulants during college: Four-year trends in exposure opportunity, use, motives, and sources. *Journal of American College Health, 60*(3), 226–234.

Gazzaniga, M. S. (2006). *The ethical brain: The science of our moral dilemmas.* New York: HarperCollins.

Gazzaniga, M. S. (2009). *Human: The science behind what makes us unique.* New York: Harper Perennial.

Geary, D. C. (2000). Evolution and proximate expression of human paternal investment. *Psychological Bulletin, 126,* 55–77.

Geary, D. C. (2012). Sex differences. In V. S. Ramachandran (Editor-in-chief), *Encyclopedia of human behavior* (2nd ed.). San Diego, CA: Elsevier.

Gebhard, P. H., & Johnson, A. B. (1998, 1979). *The Kinsey data: Marginal tabulations of 1938–1963 interviews conducted by the institute for sex research.* Philadelphia: W. B. Saunders.

Geddes, D. P. (Ed.). (1954). *An analysis of the Kinsey reports.* New York: New American Library.

Geen, R. G., & Thomas, S. L. (1986). The immediate effects of media violence on behavior. *Journal of Social Issues, 42,* 7–27.

Geier, J., Bernáth, L., Hudák, M., & Sára, L. (2008). Straightness as the main factor of the Hermann grid illusion. *Perception, 37*(5), 651–665.

Gelder, M. (1976). Flooding. In T. Thompson & W. Dockens (Eds.), *Applications of behavior modification* (pp. 250–298). New York: Academic Press.

Geller, B., Williams, M., Zimerman, B., Frazier, J., Beringer, L., & Warner, K. L. (1998). Prepubertal and early adolescent bipolarity differentiate from ADHD by manic symptoms, grandiose delusions, ultra-rapid or ultradian cycling. *Journal of Affective Disorders, 51*(2), 81–91.

Gelman, S. A., & Markman, E. M. (1986). Categories and induction in young children. *Cognition, 23,* 183–209.

Gershoff, E. T. (2002). Corporal punishment by parents and associated child behaviors and experiences: A meta-analytic and theoretical review. *Psychological Bulletin, 128*(4), 539-579. doi: 10.1037//0033-2909.128.4.539

Gershoff, E. T. (2000). The short- and long-term effects of corporal punishment on children: A meta-analytical review. In D. Elliman & M. A. Lynch, *The physical punishment of children* (pp. 196–198).

Geschwind, D. H., & Iacoboni, M. (2007). Structural and functional asymmetries of the frontal lobes. In B. L. Miller & J. K. Cummings (Eds.), *The human frontal lobes* (2nd ed., pp. 68–91). New York: Guilford Press.

Ghaziri, J., Tucholka, A., Larue, V., Blanchette-Sylvestre, M., Reyburn, G., Gilbert, G., et al. (2013). Neurofeedback training induces changes in white and gray matter. *Clinical EEG and Neuroscience.* doi:10.1177/1550059413476031

Giancola, F. (2006). The generation gap: More myth than reality. *Human Resource Planning, 29*(4), 32–37.

Gibbons, J. L., Stiles, D. A., & Shkodriani, G. M. (1991). Adolescents' attitudes toward family and gender roles: An international comparison. *Sex Roles, 25,* 625–643.

Gibbons, R. D., Brown, C. H., Hur, K., Davis, J., & Mann, J. J. (2012). Suicidal thoughts and behavior with antidepressant treatment: Reanalysis of the randomized placebo-controlled studies of fluoxetine and venlafaxine. *Archives of General Psychiatry, 69*(6), 580–587.

Gilberg, C., & Coleman, M. (2000). *The biology of the autistic syndromes* (3rd ed.). London: MacKeith Press.

Gilbert, S. J. (1981). Another look at the Milgram obedience studies: The role of the graduated series of shocks. *Personality and Social Psychology Bulletin, 7*(4), 690–695.

Gill, S. T. (1991). Carrying the war into the never-never land of psi. *Skeptical Inquirer, 15*(1), 269–273.

Gillespie, M. A., Kim, B. H., Manheim, L. J., Yoo, T., Oswald, F. L., & Schmitt, N. (2002, June). The development and validation of biographical data and situational judgment tests in the prediction of college student success. Presented in A. M. Ryan (Chair), *Beyond g: Expanding thinking on predictors of college success.* Symposium conducted at the 14th Annual Convention of the American Psychological Society, New Orleans, LA.

Gilligan, C. (1982). *In a different voice: Psychological theory and women's development.* Cambridge, MA: Harvard University Press.

Gillund, G., & Shiffrin, R. M. (1984). A retrieval model for both recognition and recall. *Psychological Review, 91,* 1–67.

Ginzburg, K., Solomon, Z., Koifman, B., Keren, G., Roth, A., Kriwisky, M., et al. (2003). Trajectories of post-traumatic stress disorder following myocardial infarction: A prospective study. *Journal of Clinical Psychiatry, 64*(10), 1217–1223.

Gittelman-Klein, R. (1978). Validity in projective tests for psychodiagnosis in children. In R. L. Spitzer & D. F. Klein (Eds.), *Critical issues in psychiatric diagnosis* (pp. 141–166). New York: Raven Press.

Glenn, A. L., Raine, A., Mednick, S. A., & Venables, P. (2007). Early temperamental and psychophysiological precursors of adult psychopathic personality. *Journal of Abnormal Psychology, 116*(3), 508–518.

Glucksman, M. .L. (2006). Psychoanalytic and psychodynamic education in the 21st century. *Journal of American Academy of Psychoanalysis, 34,* 215–222.

Glynn, S. M. (1990). Token economy approaches for psychiatric patients: Progress and pitfalls over 25 years. *Behavior Modification, 14,* 383–407.

Godden, D. R., & Baddeley, A. D. (1975). Context-dependent memory in two natural environments: On land and underwater. *British Journal of Psychology, 66,* 325–331.

Goel, V., & Grafman, J. (1995). Are the frontal lobes implicated in "planning" functions? Interpreting data from the Tower of Hanoi. *Neuropsychologia, 33*(5), 623–642.

Gogtay, N., & Thompson, P. M. (2010). Mapping gray matter development: Implications for typical development and vulnerability to psychopathology. *Brain and Cognition, 72*(1), 6–15.

Gogtay, N., Lu, A., Leow, A. D., Klunder, A. D., Lee, A. D., Chavez, A., et al. (2008). Three-dimensional brain growth abnormalities in childhood-onset schizophrenia visualized by using tensor-based morphometry. *Proceedings of the National Academy of Sciences of the United States of America, 105*(41), 15979–15984.

Goin, M. K. (2005). Practical psychotherapy: A current perspective on the psychotherapies. *Psychiatric Services, 56*(3), 255–257.

Gold, E. B., Leung, K., Crawford, S. L., Huang, M. H., Waetjen, L. E., & Greendale, G. A. (2013). Phytoestrogen and fiber intakes in relation to incident vasomotor symptoms: Results from the Study of Women's Health across the Nation. *Menopause, 20*(3), 305–314. doi:10.1097/GME.0b013e31826d2f43

Goldman, A. L., Pezawas, L., Mattay, V. S., Fischl, B., Verchinski, B. A., Chen, Q., et al. (2009). Widespread reductions of cortical thickness in schizophrenia and spectrum disorders and evidence of heritability. *Archives of General Psychiatry, 66*(5), 467–477.

Goldman-Rakic, P. S. (1998). The prefrontal landscape: Implications of functional architecture for understanding human mentation and the central executive. In A. C. Roberts, T. W. Robbins, & L. Weiskrantz (Eds.), *The prefrontal cortex: Executive and cognitive functions* (pp. 87–102). Oxford, UK: Oxford University Press.

Goldsmith, H. H., & Campos, J. (1982). Toward a theory of infant temperament. In R. Emde & R. Harmon (Eds.), *The development of attachment and affiliative systems: Psychobiological aspects* (pp. 161–193). New York: Plenum Press.

Goleman, D. (1995). *Emotional intelligence: Why it can matter more than IQ.* New York: Bantam Books.

Golkaramnay, V., Bauer, S., Haug, S., Wolf, M., & Kordy, H. (2007). The exploration of the effectiveness of group therapy through an Internet chat as aftercare: A controlled naturalistic study. *Pychotherapy and Psychosomatics, 76,* 219–225.

Goncalves, R., Pedrozo, A. L., Coutinho, E. S., Figueira, I., & Ventura, P. (2012). Efficacy of virtual reality exposure therapy in the treatment of PTSD: A systematic review. *PLoS One, 7*(12), e48469. doi:10.1371/journal.pone.0048469

Gong-Guy, E., & Hammen, C. (1980). Causal perceptions of stressful events in depressed and nondepressed outpatients. *Journal of Abnormal Psychology, 89,* 662–669.

Gonsalves, B., Reber, P. J., Gitelman, D. R., Parrish, T. B., Mesulam, M. M., & Paller, K. A. (2004). Neural evidence that vivid imagining can lead to false remembering. *Psychological Science, 15,* 655–660.

Gonzales, P. M., Blanton, H., & Williams, K. J. (2002). The effects of stereotype threat and double-minority status on the test performance of Latino women. *Personality and Social Psychology Bulletin, 28*(5), 659–670.

Gonzalez, J. S., Penedo, F. J., Antoni, M. H., Durán, R. E., Fernandez, M. I., McPherson-Baker, S., et al. (2004). Social support, positive states of mind, and HIV treatment adherence in men and women living with HIV/AIDS. *Health Psychology, 23*(4), 413–418.

Goodglass, H., Kaplan, E., & Barresi, B. (2001). *The assessment of aphasia and related disorders* (3rd ed.). Baltimore: Lippincott, Williams & Wilkins.

Goodman, E. S. (1980). Margaret Floy Washburn (1871–1939) first woman Ph.D. in psychology. *Psychology of Women Quarterly, 5,* 69–80.

Gotlib, I. H., Sivers, H., Canli, T., Kasch, K. L., & Gabrieli, J. D. E. (2001, November). Neural activation in depression in response to emotional stimuli. In I. H. Gotlib (Chair) (Ed.), *New directions in the neurobiology of affective disorders.* Symposium conducted at the annual meeting of the Society for Research in Psychopathology, Madison, WI.

Gottesman, I. I. (1991). *Schizophrenia genesis: The origins of madness.* New York: W. H. Freeman.

Gottesman, I. I., McGuffin, P., & Farmer, A. E. (1987). Clinical genetics as clues to the "Real" genetics of schizophrenia (A decade of modest gains while playing for time). *Schizophrenia Bulletin, 13,* 23–47.

Gottesman, I. I., & Shields, J. (1976). A critical review of recent adoption, twin and family studies of schizophrenia: Behavioural genetics perspectives. *Schizophrenia Bulletin, 2,* 360–401.

Gottesman, I. I., & Shields, J. (1982). *Schizophrenia: The epigenetic puzzle.* New York: Cambridge University Press.

Gottman, J. M., & Krokoff, L. J. (1989). Marital interaction and satisfaction: A longitudinal view. *Journal of Consulting and Clinical Psychology, 57,* 47–52.

Gough, H. G. (1995). *California Psychological Inventory* (3rd ed.). Palo Alto, CA: Consulting Psychologist-Press.

Gould, J. L., & Gould, C. G. (1994). *The animal mind.* New York: Scientific American Library.

Goyal, M., Singh, S., Sibinga, E. M. S., Gould, N. F., Rowland- Seymour, A., Sharma, R., et al. (2014). Meditation programs for psychological stress and well-being: A systematic review and meta-analysis. *Journal of the American Medical Association: Internal Medicine.* doi:10.1001/jamainternmed.2013.13018

Graber, J. A., Brooks-Gunn, J., & Warren, M. P. (1995). The antecedents of menarcheal age: Heredity, family environment, and stressful life events. *Child Development, 66,* 346–359.

Graf, W. D., Nagel, S. K., Epstein, L. G., Miller, G., Nass, R., & Larriviere, D. (2013). Pediatric neuroenhancement: Ethical, legal, social, and neurodevelopmental implications. *Neurology, 80*(13), 1251–1260. doi:10.1212/WNL.0b013e318289703b

Grandjean, P., Weihe, P., White, R. F., Debes, F., Araki, S., Yokoyama, K., et al. (1997). Cognitive deficit in 7-year-old children with prenatal exposure to methylmercury. *Neurotoxicology and Teratology, 19*(6), 417–428.

Graven, S. N., & Browne, J. V. (2008). Sleep and brain development: The critical role of sleep in fetal and early neonatal brain development. *Newborn & Infant Nursing Review, 8,* 173–179.

Greeley, A. (1987). Mysticism goes mainstream. *American Health, 1,* 47–49.

Greenwald, A. G., & Banaji, M. R. (1995). Implicit social cognition: Attitudes, self-esteem, and stereotypes. *Psychological Review, 102,* 4–27.

Greenwald, A. G., McGhee, D. E., & Schwartz, J. K. L. (1998). Measuring individual differences in implicit cognition: The Implicit Association Test. *Journal of Personality and Social Psychology, 74,* 1464–1480.

Gregory, R. L. (1990). *Eye and brain, the psychology of seeing.* Princeton, NJ: Princeton University Press.

Gresham, L. G., & Shimp, T. A. (1985). Attitude toward the advertisement and brand attitudes: A classical conditioning prospective. *Journal of Advertising, 14*(1), 10–17, 49.

Griggs, E. M., Young, E. J., Rumbaugh, G., & Miller, C. A. (2013). MicroRNA-182 regulates amygdala-dependent memory formation. *Journal of Neuroscience, 33*(4), 1734. doi:10.1523/JNEUROSCI.2873-12.2013

Grocer, S., & Kohout, J. (1997). *The 1995 APA survey of 1992 baccalaureate recipients.* Washington, DC: American Psychological Association.

Gross, C. G. (1999). A hole in the head. *The Neuroscientist, 5,* 263–269.

Grumbach, M. M., & Kaplan, S. L. (1990). The neuroendocrinology of human puberty: An ontogenetic perspective. In M. M. Grumbach, P. C. Sizonenko, & M. L. Aubert (Eds.), *Control of the onset of puberty* (pp. 1–6). Baltimore: Williams & Wilkins.

Grumbach, M. M., & Styne, D. M. (1998). Puberty: Ontogeny, neuroendocrinology, physiology, and disorders. In J. D. Wilson, D. W. Foster, H. M. Kronenberg, & P. R. Larsen (Eds.), *Williams textbook of endocrinology* (9th ed., pp. 1509–1625). Philadelphia: W. B. Saunders.

Grünbaum, A. (1984). *The foundations of psychoanalysis: A philosophical critique.* Berkeley: University of California Press.

Guerri, C. (2002). Mechanisms involved in central nervous system dysfunctions induced by prenatal ethanol exposure. *Neurotoxicity Research, 4*(4), 327–335.

Guilford, J. P. (1967). *The nature of human intelligence.* New York: McGraw-Hill.

Gummerman, K., Gray, C. R., & Wilson, J. M. (1972). An attempt to assess eidetic imagery objectively. *Bulletin of the Psychonomic Society, 28,* 115–118.

Gunderson, E. A., Gripshover, S. J., Romero, C., Dweck, C. S., Goldin-Meadow, S., & Levine, S. C. (2013). Parent praise to 1- to 3-year-olds predicts children's motivational frameworks 5 years later. *Child Development,* ePub ahead of print. doi:10.1111/cdev.12064

Gupta, M. (1994). Sexuality in the Indian sub-continent. *Sex and Marital Therapy, 9,* 57–69.

Guthrie, R. V. (2004). *Even the rat was white: A historical view of psychology.* Boston: Allyn & Bacon.

Haber, R. N. (1979). Twenty years of haunting eidetic imagery: Where's the ghost? *The Behavioral and Brain Sciences, 2,* 583–619.

Hall, A. P., & Henry, J. A. (2006). Acute toxic effects of 'Ecstasy' (MDMA) and related compounds: Overview of pathophysiology and clinical management. *British Journal of Anaesthesia, 96*(6), 678–685.

Hall, C. (1966). *Studies of dreams collected in the laboratory and at home.* Institute of Dream Research Monograph Series (No. 1). Santa Cruz, CA: Privately printed.

Hall, W., & Degenhardt, L. (2009). Adverse health effects of non-medical cannabis use. *Lancet, 374,* 1383–1391.

Hamer, D. H., Hu, S., Magnuson, V. L., Hu, N., & Pattatucci, A. M. L. (1993). A linkage between DNA markers on the X chromosome and male sexual orientation. *Science, 261,* 321–327.

Hampton, J. A. (1998). Similarity-based categorization and fuzziness of natural categories. *Cognition, 65,* 137–165.

Han, X., Chen, M., Wang, F., Windrem, M., Wang, S., Shanz, S., et al. (2013). Forebrain engraftment by human glial progenitor cells enhances synaptic plasticity and learning in adult mice. *Cell Stem Cell, 12*(3), 342–353. doi:10.1016/j.stem.2012.12.015

Handel, S. (1989). *Listening: An introduction to the perception of auditory events.* Cambridge, MA: MIT Press.

Hargittai, E. (2007). Whose space? Differences among users and non-users of social network sites. *Journal of Computer-Mediated Communication, 13*(1), article 14. Retrieved from http://jcmc.indiana.edu/vol13/issue1/hargittai.html

Harlow, H. F. (1958). The nature of love. *American Psychologist, 13,* 573–685.

Harman, G. (1999). Moral philosophy meets social psychology: Virtue ethics and the fundamental attribution error. *Proceedings of the Aristotelian Society, 1998–99, 99,* 315–331.

Harris, B. (2011). Letting go of little albert: Disciplinary memory, history, and the uses of myth. *Journal of the History of the Behavioral Sciences, 47*(1), 1–17. doi:10.1002/jhbs.20470

Harris, J. L., & Qualls, C. D. (2000). The association of elaborative or maintenance rehearsal with age, reading comprehension, and verbal working memory performance. *Aphasiology, 14*(5–6), 515–526.

Harrison, P. J. (1999). The neuropathology of schizophrenia: A critical review of the data and their interpretation. *Brain, 122,* 593–624.

Harrison, T. L., Shipstead, Z., Hicks, K. L., Hambrick, D. Z., Redick, T. S., & Engle, R. W. (2013). Working memory training may increase working memory capacity but not fluid intelligence. *Psychological Science.* doi:10.1177/0956797613492984

Hart, P. (1998). Preventing group-think revisited: Evaluating and reforming groups in government. *Organizational Behavior and Human Decision Processes, 73*(2–3), 306–326.

Hartfield, E. (1987). Passionate and companionate love. In R. J. Sternberg & M. L. Barnes (Eds.), *The psychology of love* (pp. 191–217). New Haven, CT: Yale University Press.

Hartfield, E., & Rapson, R. L. (1992). Similarity and attraction in intimate relationships. *Communication Monographs, 59,* 209–212.

Harvey, S., & Keashly, L. (2003). Predicting the risk for aggression in the workplace: Risk factors, self-esteem and time at work. *Social Behaviour and Personality: An International Journal, 31*(8), 807–814.

Hassan, S., Karpova, Y., Baiz, D., Yancey, D., Pullikuth, A., Flores, A., et al. (2013). Behavioral stress accelerates prostate cancer development in mice. *Journal of Clinical Investigation, 123,* 874–886. doi:10.1172/JCI63324

Hauck, S. J., & Bartke, A. (2001). Free radical defenses in the liver and kidney of human growth hormone transgenic mice. *Journal of Gerontology and Biological Science, 56,* 153–162.

Havighurst, R. J., Neugarten, B. L., & Tobin, S. N. S. (1968). Disengagement and patterns of aging. In B. L. Neugarten (Ed.), *Middle age and aging: A reader in social psychology* (pp. 161–172). Chicago: University of Chicago Press.

Hawks, S. R., Madanat, H. N., Merrill, R. M., Goudy, M. B., & Miyagawa, T. (2003). A cross-cultural analysis of "motivation for eating" as a potential factor in the emergence of global obesity: Japan and the United States. *Health Promotion International, 18*(2), 153–162.

Hay, P. (2013). A systematic review of evidence for psychological treatments in eating disorders: 2005–2012. *International Journal of Eating Disorders, 46*(5), 462–469. doi:10.1002/eat.22103

Hayflick, L. (1977). The cellular basis for biological aging. In C. E. Finch & L. Hayflick (Eds.), *Handbook of biology of aging* (p. 159). New York: Van Nostrand Reinhold.

Hayward, C., Killen, J. D., Kraemer, H. C., & Taylor, C. B. (2000). Predictors of panic attacks in adolescents. *Journal of the American Academy of Child and Adolescent Psychiatry, 39*(2), 207–214.

Hayward, C., Killen, J. D., & Taylor, C. B. (1989). Panic attacks in young adolescents. *American Journal of Psychiatry, 146*(8), 1061–1062.

Hazan, C., & Shaver, P. (1987). Romantic love conceptualized as an attachment process. *Journal of Personality and Social Psychology, 52,* 511–524.

Heavey, C. L., Layne, C., & Christensen, A. (1993). Gender and conflict structure in marital interaction: A replication and extension. *Journal of Consulting and Clinical Psychology, 61,* 16–27.

Hebb, D. O. (1955). Drives and the CNS (Conceptual Nervous System). *Psychological Review, 62,* 243–254.

Hegeman, R. (2007, July 4). *Police: Shoppers stepped over victim.* Associated Press. Retrieved from http://abcnews.go.com/US/wireStory?id=3342724.

Heider, F. (1958). *The psychology of interpersonal relations.* New York: Wiley.

Heikkila, K., Nyberg, S. T., Theorell, T., Fransson, E. I., Alfredsson, L., Bjorner, J. B., et al. (2013, February 7). Work stress and risk of cancer: Meta-analysis of 5700 incident cancer events in 116 000 European men and women. *BMJ, 346*(1), f165. doi:10.1136/bmj.f165

Heil, G., Maslow, A., & Stephens, D. (1998). *Maslow on management.* New York: Wiley.

Heilman, K. M. (2002). *Matter of mind: A neurologist's view of brain-behavior relationships.* New York: Oxford University Press.

Heilman, K. M., Watson, R., & Valenstein, E. (1993). Neglect and related disorders. In K. Heilman & E. Valenstein (Eds.), *Clinical neuropsychology.* New York: Oxford University Press.

Heimberg, R. G., & Becker, R. E. (2002). *Cognitive-behavioral group therapy for social phobia: Basic mechanisms and clinical strategies.* New York: Guilford Press.

Heimberg, R. G., & Magee, L. (2014). Social anxiety disorder. In D. H. Barlow (Ed.), *Clinical handbook of psychological disorders: A step-by-step treatment manual* (5th ed., pp. 114–154). New York: Guilford Press.

Heimer, L. (1995). *The human brain and spinal cord: Functional neuroanatomy and dissection guide.* New York: Springer-Verlag.

Heinicke, C. M., Goorsky, M., Moscov, S., Dudley, K., Gordon, J., Schneider, C., et al. (2000). Relationship-based intervention with at-risk mothers: Factors affecting variations in outcome. *Infant Mental Health Journal, 21,* 133–155.

Heinrich, B. (2000). Testing insight in ravens. In C. Heyes & L. Huber (Eds.), *The evolution of cognition.* Cambridge, MA: MIT Press.

Helfrich, C., Pierau, S. S., Freitag, C. M., Roeper, J., Ziemann, U., & Bender, S. (2012). Monitoring cortical excitability during repetitive transcranial magnetic stimulation in children with ADHD: A single-blind, sham-controlled TMS-EEG study. *PLoS One, 7*(11), e50073.

Helms, J. E. (1992). Why is there no study of cultural equivalence in standardized cognitive ability testing? *American Psychologist, 47*(9), 1083–1101.

Henderson, R. K., Snyder, H. R., Gupta, T., & Banich, M. T. (2012). When does stress help or harm? The effects of stress controllability and subjective stress response on Stroop performance. *Frontiers in Psychology, 3,* 179.

Henin, A., Mick, E., Biederman, J., Fried, R., Wozniak, J., Faraone, S. V., et al. (2007). Can bipolar disorder-specific neuropsychological impairments in children be identified? *Journal of Consulting and Clinical Psychology, 75*(2), 210–220.

Henningfield, J. E., Clayton, R., & Pollin, W. (1990). Involvement of tobacco in alcoholism and illicit drug use. *British Journal of Addition, 85,* 279–292.

Henningfield, J. E., Cohen, C., & Slade, J. D. (1991). Is nicotine more addictive than cocaine? *British Journal of Addiction, 86,* 565–569.

Herberman, R. B., & Ortaldo, J. R. (1981). Natural killer cells: Their role in defenses against disease. *Science, 214,* 24–30.

Herbst, J. H., Zonderman, A. B., McCrae, R. R., & Costa, P. T., Jr. (2000). Do the dimensions of the Temperament and Character Inventory map a simple genetic architecture? Evidence from molecular genetics and factor analysis. *American Journal of Psychiatry, 157,* 1285–1290.

Herman, L. M., Pack, A. A., & Morrell-Samuels, P. (1993). Representational and conceptual skills of dolphins. In H. L. Roitblatt, L. M. Herman, & P. E. Nachtigall (Eds.), *Language and communication: Comparative perspectives.* Hillsdale, NJ: Erlbaum.

Hernandez, D., & Fisher, E. M. (1996). Down syndrome genetics: Unravelling a multifactorial disorder. *Human Molecular Genetics, 5,* 1411–1416.

Herrnstein, R. J., & Murray, C. (1994). *The bell curve: The reshaping of American life by differences in intelligence.* New York: Free Press.

Hersh, S. M. (2004, May 10). Annals of national security: Torture at Abu Ghraib. *The New Yorker.* Retrieved from http://www.newyorker.com

Hershberger, S. L., Plomin, R., & Pedersen, N. L. (1995, October). Traits and metatraits: Their reliability, stability, and shared genetic influence. *Journal of Personality and Social Psychology, 69*(4), 673–685.

Hetrick, S. E., McKenzie, J. E., Cox, G. R., Simmons, M. B., & Merry, S. N. (2012). Newer generation antidepressants for depressive disorders in children and adolescents. *Cochrane Database of Systematic Reviews (Online), 11,* CD004851. doi:10.1002/14651858.CD004851.pub3

Herxheimer, A., & Petrie, K. J. (2001). Melatonin for preventing and treating jet lag. *Cocharane Database of Systematic Reviews, 1,* CD 001520.

Hewlin, P. F. (2009). Wearing the cloak: Antecedents and consequences of creating facades of conformity. *Journal of Applied Psychology, 94*(3), 727–741.

Hewstone, M., Rubin, M., & Willis, H. (2002). Intergroup bias. *Annual Review of Psychology, 53,* 575–604.

Heyes, C. M. (1998). Theory of mind in nonhuman primates. *Behavior and Brain Science, 21,* 101–148.

Hicklin, J., & Widiger, T. A. (2000). Convergent validity of alternative MMPI-2 personality disorder scales. *Journal of Personality Assessment, 75*(3), 502–518.

Higgins, E. T., & Scholer, A. A. (2010). When is personality revealed? A motivated cognition approach. In O. P. John, R. W. Robins, & L. A. Pervin (Eds.), *Handbook of personality: Theory and research* (pp. 182–207). New York: Guilford Press.

Hilgard, E. R., & Hilgard, J. R. (1994). *Hypnosis in the relief of pain* (Rev. ed.). New York: Brunner/Mazel.

Hill, J. A. (1998). Miscarriage risk factors and causes: What we know now. *OBG Management, 10,* 58–68.

Hill, P. C., & Butter, E. M. (1995). The role of religion in promoting physical health. *Journal of Psychology and Christianity, 14*(2), 141–155.

Hillman, C. H., Pontifex, M. B., Raine, L. B., Castelli, D. M., Hall, E. E., & Kramer, A. F. (2009). The effect of acute treadmill walking on cognitive control and academic achievement in preadolescent children. *Neuroscience, 159*(3), 1044–1054.

Hilton, J. L., & von Hipple, W. (1996). Stereotypes. *Annual Review of Psychology, 47,* 237–271.

Hilts, P. J. (1998, August 2). Is nicotine addictive? It depends on whose criteria you use. *New York Times,* p. C3.

Hines, T. (2003). *Pseudoscience and the paranormal: A critical examination of the evidence.* Amherst, NY: Prometheus Books.

Hintze, J. M. (2002). Interventions for fears and anxiety problems. In M. R. Shinn, H. R. Walker, & G. Stoner (Eds.), *Interventions for academic and behavior problems II: Preventive and remedial approaches* (pp. 939–954). Bethesda, MD: National Association of School Psychologists.

Hnasko, T. S., Chuhma, N., Zhang, H., Goh, G. Y., Sulzer, D., Palmiter, R. D., et al. (2010). Vesicular glutamate transport promotes dopamine storage and glutamate corelease in vivo. *Neuron, 65,* 643–656.

Hobson, J. (1988). *The dreaming brain.* New York: Basic Books.

Hobson, J. A., & McCarley, R. (1977). The brain as a dream state generator: An activation-synthesis hypothesis of the dream process. *American Journal of Psychiatry, 134,* 1335–1348.

Hobson, J., Pace-Schott, E., & Stickgold, R. (2000). Dreaming and the brain: Towards a cognitive neuroscience of conscious states. *Behavioral and Brain Sciences, 23*(6), 793–1121.

Hochman, J. (1994). Buried memories challenge the law. *National Law Journal, 1,* 17–18.

Hodges, J. R. (1994). Retrograde amnesia. In A. Baddeley, B. A. Wilson, & F. Watts (Eds.), *Handbook of memory disorders* (pp. 81–107). New York: Wiley.

Hodgson, B. (2001). *In the arms of Morpheus: The tragic history of laudanum, morphine, and patent medicines.* New York: Firefly Books.

Hodson, D. S., & Skeen, P. (1994). Sexuality and aging: The hammerlock of myths. *The Journal of Applied Gerontology, 13,* 219–235.

Hoeft, F., Gabrieli, J. D. E., Whitfield-Gabrieli, S., Haas, B. W., Bammer, R., Menon, V., et al. (2012). Functional brain basis of hypnotizability. *Archives of General Psychiatry, 69*(10), 1064.

Hoffrage, U., Hertwig, R., & Gigerenzer, G. (2000). Hindsight bias: A by-product of knowledge updating? *Journal of Experimental Psychology: Learning, Memory, and Cognition, 26,* 566–581.

Hofstede, G. H. (1980). *Culture's consequences, international differences in work-related values.* Beverly Hills, CA: Sage.

Hofstede, G. J., Pedersen, P. B., & Hofstede, G. H. (2002). *Exploring culture: Exercises, stories, and synthetic cultures.* Yarmouth, ME: Intercultural Press.

Hogg, M. A., & Hains, S. C. (1998). Friendship and group identification: A new look at the role of cohesiveness in groupthink. *European Journal of Social Psychology, 28*(1), 323–341.

Holden, C., & Vogel, G. (2002). Plasticity: Time for a reappraisal? *Science, 296,* 2126–2129.

Hollon, S. D., These, M., & Markowitz, J. (2002). Treatment and prevention of depression. *Psychological Science in the Public Interest, 3,* 39–77.

Hollon, S. D., & Beck, A. T. (1994). Cognitive and cognitive- behavioral therapies. In A. E. Bergin & S. L. Garfield (Eds.), *Handbook of psychotherapy and behavior change* (4th ed., p. 428). Chichester, UK: Wiley.

Holman, E. A., Silver, R. C., Poulin, M., Andersen, J., Gil-Rivas, V., & McIntosh, D. N. (2008). Terrorism, acute stress, and cardiovascular health: A 3-year national study following the September 11th attacks. *Archives of General Psychiatry, 65,* 73–80.

Holmes, T. H., & Rahe, R. H. (1967). The Social Readjustment Rating Scale. *Journal of Psychosomatic Research II,*213–218.

Hong, D., Scaletta-Kent, J., & Kesler, S. (2009). Cognitive profile of Turner syndrome. *Developmental Disabilities Research Reviews, 15*(4), 270–278. doi:10.1002/ddrr.79

Hood, D. C. (1998). Lower-level visual processing and models of light adaptation. *Annual Review of Psychology, 49,* 503–535.

Hopfinger, J. B., Buonocore, M. H., & Mangun, G. R. (2000). The neural mechanisms of top-down attentional control. *Nature Neuroscience, 3,* 284–291.

Horne, J. A., & Staff, C. H. (1983). Exercise and sleep: Body heating effects. *Sleep, 6,* 36–46.

Horney, K. (1939). *New ways in psychoanalysis.* New York: Norton.

Horney, K. (1973, 1967). *Feminine psychology.* New York: Norton.

Horowitz, D. L. (1985). *Ethnic groups in conflict.* Berkeley: University of California Press.

Hortaçsu, N. (1999). The first year of family and couple initiated marriages of a Turkish sample: A longitudinal investigation. *International Journal of Psychology, 34*(1), 29–41.

Hossain, P., Kawar, B., & El Nahas, M. (2007). Obesity and diabetes in the developing world—a growing challenge. *New England Journal of Medicine, 356*(9), 973.

Hothersall, D. (1995). *History of psychology* (pp. 162–165). New York: McGraw-Hill.

Hovland, C. I. (1937). The generalization of conditioned responses. I. The sensory generalization of conditioned responses with varying frequencies of tone. *Journal of General Psychology, 17,* 1251–1248.

Hu, P., & Meng, Z. (1996, August). *An examination of infant-mother attachment in China.* Poster session presented at the meeting of the International Society for the Study of Behavioral Development, Quebec City, Quebec, Canada.

Hu, X., Pornpattananangkul, N., & Rosenfeld, J. P. (2013). N200 and p300 as orthogonal and integrable indicators of distinct awareness and recognition processes in memory detection. *Psychophysiology, 50*(5), 454–464. doi:10.1111/psyp.12018

Hu, S., Pattatucci, A. M. L., Patterson, C., Li, L., Fulker, D. W., Cherny, S. S., et al. (1994). Linkage between sexual orientation and chromosome Xq28 in males but not in females. *Nature Genetics, 11,* 248–256.

Hubel, D. H., & Wiesel, T. N. (1959). Receptive fields of single neurons in the cat's striate cortex. *The Journal of Physiology, 148,* 574–591.

Huesmann, L. R., & Eron, L. (1986). *Television and the aggressive child: A cross-national comparison.* Hillsdale, NJ: Erlbaum.

Huesmann, L. R., & Miller, L. S. (1994). Long-term effects of repeated exposure to media violence in childhood. In L. R. Huesmann (Ed.), *Aggressive behavior: Current perspectives* (pp. 153–183). New York: Plenum Press.

Huesmann, L. R., Moise, J. F., & Podolski, C. L. (1997). The effects of media violence on the development of antisocial behavior. In D. M. Stoff, J. Breiling, & J. D. Maser (Eds.), *Handbook of antisocial behavior* (pp. 181–193). New York: Wiley.

Huesmann, L. R., Moise-Titus, J., Podolski, C. L., & Eron, L. D. (2003). Longitudinal relations between children's exposure to TV violence and their aggressive and violent behavior in young adulthood: 1977–1992. *Developmental Psychology, 39*(2), 201–221.

Huff, W., Lenartz, D., Schormann, M., Lee, S. H., Kuhn, J., Koulousakis, A., et al. (2010). Unilateral deep brain stimulation of the nucleus accumbens in patients with treatment-resistant obsessive-compulsive disorder: Outcomes after one year. *Clinical Neurology and Neurosurgery, 112*(2), 137–143.

Hugenberg, K., & Bodenhausen, G. V. (2003). Facing prejudice: Implicit prejudice and the perception of facial threat. *Psychological Science, 14,* 640–643.

Hughes, J. (1993). Behavior therapy. In T. R. Kratochwill & R. J. Morris (Eds.), *Handbook of psychotherapy with children and adolescents* (pp. 185–220). Boston: Allyn & Bacon.

Hughes, S. M., Harrison, M. A., & Gallup, G. G., Jr. (2007). Sex differences in romantic kissing among college students: An evolutionary perspective. *Evolutionary Psychology, 5*(3), 612–631.

Hull, C. L. (1943). *Principles of behavior.* New York: Appleton-Century.

Hull, J. G., Draghici, A. M., & Sargent, J. D. (2012). A longitudinal study of risk glorifying video games and reckless driving. *Psychology of Popular Media Culture, 1*(4), 244–253. doi:10.1037/a0029510

Hummer, R. A., Rogers, R. G., Nam, C. B., & Ellison, C. G. (1999). Religious involvement and U.S. adult mortality. *Demography, 36*(2), 273–285.

Humphries, L. L. (1987). Bulimia: Diagnosis and treatment. *Comprehensive Therapy, 13,* 12–15.

Hunsley, J., & Mash, E. J. (2008). Developing criteria for evidence- based assessment: An introduction to assessments that work. In J. Hunsley & E. J. Mash (Eds.), *A guide to assessments that work* (3rd ed.). New York: Guilford Press.

Hunt, E. (2001). Multiple views of multiple intelligence [Review of Intelligence reframed: Multiple intelligence in the 21st century.] *Contemporary Psychology, 46,* 5–7.

Hunt, M. (1993). *The story of psychology.* New York: Doubleday.

Hurlemann, R., Patin, A., Onur, O. A., Cohen, M. X., Baumgartner, T., Metzler, S., et al. (2010). Oxytocin enhances amygdala-dependent, socially reinforced learning and emotional empathy in humans. *Journal of Neuroscience, 301,* 4999–5007.

Hurley, D. (1989). The search for cocaine's methadone. *Psychology Today, 23*(7–8), 54.

Hurley, S., & Nudds, M. (Eds.). (2006). *Rational animals?* Oxford, UK: Oxford University Press.

Hurvich, L. M., & Jameson, D. (1957). An opponent-process theory of color vision. *Psychological Review, 64,* 384–404.

Hvas, L. (2001). Positive aspects of menopause: A qualitative study. *Maturitas, 39*(1), 11–17.

Hyde, J. S., & Kling, K. C. (2001). Women, motivation, and achievement. *Psychology of Women Quarterly, 25,* 264–378.

Hygge, S. A., & Öhman, A. (1976). The relation of vicarious to direct instigation and conditioning of electrodermal responses. *Scandanavian Journal of Psychology, 17*(1), 217–222.

Hyman, I. E., Gilstrap, L. L., Decker, K., & Wilkinson, C. (1998). Manipulating remember and know judgements of autobiographical memories. *Applied Cognitive Psychology, 12,* 371–386.

Hyman, I. E., Jr. (1993). Imagery, reconstructive memory, and discovery. In B. Roskos-Ewoldsen, M. J. Intons-Peterson, & R. E. Anderson (Eds.), *Imagery, creativity, and discovery: A cognitive perspective* (pp. 99–121). The Netherlands: Elsevier Science.

Hyman, I. E., Jr., & Loftus, E. F. (1998). Errors in autobiographical memories. *Clinical Psychology Review, 18,* 933–947.

Hyman, I. E., Jr., & Loftus, E. F. (2002). False childhood memories and eyewitness memory errors. In M. L. Eisen, J. A. Quas, & G. S. Goodman (Eds.), *Memory and suggestibility in the forensic interview* (pp. 63–84). Mahwah, NJ: Erlbaum.

Hyman, S. E., & Cohen, J. D. (2013). Disorders of mood and anxiety. In E. R. Kandel, J. H. Schwartz, T. M. Jessell, S. A. Siegelbaum, & A. J. Hudspeth (Eds.), *Principles of neural science* (5th ed., pp. 1402–1424). USA: McGraw-Hill.

Iacoboni, M., Woods, R. P., Brass, M., Bekkering, H., Mazziotta, J. C., & Rizzolatti, G. (1999). Cortical mechanisms of human imitation. *Science, 286,* 2526–2528.

Iber, C., Ancoli-Israel, S., Chesson, A. L., Jr., & Quan, S. F. (2007). *The AASM manual for the scoring of sleep and associated events: Rules, terminology and technical specifications.* Westchester, IL: American Academy of Sleep Medicine.

Iemmola, F., & Camperio Ciani, A. (2008). New evidence of genetic factors influencing sexual orientation in men: Female fecundity increase in the maternal line. *Archives of Sexual Behavior, 38*(3), 393–399.

Imaizumi, Y. (1998). A comparative study of twinning and triplet rates in 17 countries, 1972–1996. *Acta Genetic Medicine and Gemellology, 47,* 101–114.

Insel, T. R., & Wang, P. S. (2010). Rethinking mental illness. *The Journal of the American Medical Association, 303*(19), 1970–1971.

Isabel, J. (2003). *Genetics: An introduction for dog breeders.* Loveland, CO: Alpine.

Isenberg, D. J. (1986). Group polarization: A critical review and meta-analysis. *Journal of Personality and Social Psychology, 50*(6), 1141–1151.

Iwamoto, E. T., & Martin, W. (1988). A critique of drug self-administration as a method for predicting abuse potential of drugs. *National Institute on Drug Abuse Research Monograph, 1046,* 81457–81465.

Izard, C. (1988). Emotion-cognition relationships and human development. In C. Izard, J. Kagan, & R. Zajonc (Eds.), *Emotions, cognition, and behavior.* New York: Cambridge University Press.

Jackson, R. (2001). *Plato: A beginner's guide.* London: Hoder & Stroughton.

Jackson, L. A., & Wang, J.-L. (2013). Cultural differences in social networking site use: A comparative study of China and the United States. *Computers in Human Behavior, 29*(3), 910. doi:10.1016/j.chb.2012.11.024

Jackson, M. L., Gunzelmann, G., Whitney, P., Hinson, J. M., Belenky, G., Rabat, A., et al. (2013). Deconstructing and reconstructing cognitive performance in sleep deprivation. *Sleep Medicine Reviews, 17*(3), 215–225. doi:10.1016/j.smrv.2012.06.007

Jackson, T., Iezzi, T., Gunderson, J., Fritch, A., & Nagasaka, T. (2002). Gender differences in pain perception: The mediating role of self-efficacy beliefs. *Sex Roles, 47,* 561–568.

Jaeggi, S. M., Buschkuehl, M., Jonides, J., & Perrig, W. J. (2008). Improving fluid intelligence with training on working memory. *Proceedings of the National Academy of Sciences, USA, 105*(19), 6829–6833.

James, W. (1884). What is an emotion? *Mind, 9,* 188–205.

James, W. (1890). *Principles of psychology.* New York: Henry Holt.

James, W. (1894). The physical basis of emotion. *Psychological Review, 1,* 516–529.

James, W. (2002, 1890). *The principles of psychology* (Vols. 1 and 2). Cambridge, MA: Harvard University Press.

Jameson, M., Diehl, R., & Danso, H. (2007). Stereotype threat impacts college athletes' academic performance. *Current Research in Social Psychology, 12*(5), 68–79.

Jang, K. L., Livesley, W. J., & Vernon, P. A. (1996). Heritability of the Big Five personality dimensions and their facets: A twin study. *Journal of Personality, 64,* 577–591.

Jang, K. L., McCrae, R. R., Angleitner, A., Riemann, R., & Livesley, W. J. (1998). Heritability of facet-level traits in a cross-cultural twin sample: Support for a hierarchical model of personality. *Journal of Personality and Social Psychology, 74,* 1556–1565.

Janis, I. (1972). *Victims of groupthink.* Boston: Houghton-Mifflin.

Janis, I. (1982). *Groupthink* (2nd ed.). Boston: Houghton-Mifflin.

Janos, P. M. (1987). A fifty-year follow-up of Terman's youngest college students and IQ-matched agemates. *Gifted Child Quarterly, 31,* 55–58.

January, D., & Kako, E. (2007). Re-evaluating evidence for linguistic relativity: Reply to Boroditsky (2001). *Cognition, 104*(2), 417–426.

Jehn, K., Northcraft, G., & Neale, M. (1999). Why differences make a difference: A field study of diversity, conflict, and performance in workgroups. *Administrative Science Quarterly, 44,* 741–763.

Jensen, A. R. (1969). How much can we boost IQ and scholastic achievement? *Harvard Educational Review, 39,* 1–123.

Jensen, M. P., Gertz, K. J., Kupper, A. E., Braden, A. L., Howe, J. D., Hakimian, S., et al. (2013). Steps toward developing an EEG biofeedback treatment for chronic pain. *Applied Psychophysiology and Biofeedback.* doi:10.1007/s10484-013-9214-9

Ji, K., Akgul, G., Wollmuth, L. P., & Tsirka, S. E. (2013). Microglia actively regulate the number of functional synapses. *PLoS ONE, 8*(2), e56293. doi:10.1371/journal.pone.0056293

Johnson, J., Cohen, P., Pine, D. S., Klein, D. F., Kasen, S., & Brook, J. S. (2000). Association between cigarette smoking and anxiety disorders during adolescence and early adulthood. *Journal of the American Medical Association, 284*(18), 2348–2351.

Johnson, C. P., & Myers, S. M. (Council on Children with Disabilities). (2007). Identification and evaluation of children with autism spectrum disorders. *Pediatrics, 120*(5), 1183–1215.

Johnson, D., Johnson, R., & Smith, K. (1991). *Active learning: Cooperation in the college classroom.* Edna, MN: Interaction Book Company.

Johnston, L. D., O'Malley, P. M., Bachman, J. G., & Schulenberg, J. E. (2007, September). *Monitoring the future national survey results on drug use, 1975–2006: Vol. 1. Secondary school students 2006.* Bethesda, MD: National Institute on Drug Abuse.

Jones, E. E., & Harris, V. A. (1967). The attribution of attitudes. *Journal of Experimental Social Psychology, 3,* 1–24.

Jones, E. J., Krupnick, J. L., & Kerig, P. K. (1987). Some gender effects in a brief psychotherapy. *Psychotherapy, 24,* 336–352.

Jones, M. C. (1924). A laboratory study of fear: The case of Peter. *Pedagogical Seminary, 31,* 308–315.

Judelsohn, R. G. (2007, November–December). Vaccine safety: Vaccines are one of public health's great accomplishments. *Skeptical Inquirer, 31*(6). Retrieved June 13, 2010, from http://www.csicop.org/si/show/vaccine_safety_vaccines_are_one_of_public_healthrsquos_great_accomplishment/

Juffer, F., & Rosenboom, L. G. (1997). Infant-mother attachment of internationally adopted children in the Netherlands. *International Journal of Behavioral Development, 20*(1), 93–107.

Julien, R. M., Advokat, C. D., & Comaty, J. E. (2011). *A primer of drug action: A comprehensive guide to the actions, uses, and side effects of psychoactive drugs* (12th ed.). New York: Worth Publishers.

Jung, C. (1933). *Modern man in search of a soul.* New York: Harcourt Brace.

Kabat-Zinn, J., Lipworth, L., & Burney, R. (1985). The clinical use of mindfulness meditation for the self-regulation of chronic pain. *Journal of Behavioral Medicine, 8,* 163–190.

Kabat-Zinn, J., Lipworth, L., Burney, R., & Sellers, W. (1986). Four year follow-up of a meditation-based program for the self regulation of chronic pain: Treatment outcomes and compliance. *Clinical Journal of Pain, 2,* 159–173.

Kable, J. A., Coles, C. D., Lynch, M. E., & Platzman, K. (2008). Physiological responses to social and cognitive challenges in 8-year olds with a history of prenatal cocaine exposure. *Developmental Psychobiology, 50*(3), 251–265.

Kagan, J. (1998). *Galen's prophecy: Temperament in human nature* (pp. 237–260, 270–274). New York: Basic Books.

Kagan, J. (2010). *The temperamental thread.* New York: Dana Press.

Kagan, J., Snidman, N., Kahn, V., & Towsley, S. (2007). The preservation of two infant temperaments into adolescence. *SRCD Monographs, 72*(2), 76–80.

Kahan, M., & Sutton, N. (1998). Overview: Methadone treatment for the opioid-dependent patient. In B. Brands & J. Brands (Eds.), *Methadone maintenance: A physician's guide to treatment* (pp. 1–15). Toronto, ON: Addiction Research Foundation.

Kahneman, D. (2011). *Thinking, fast and slow.* New York: Farrar, Straus and Giroux.

Kahneman, D., Slovic, P., & Tversky, A. (1982). *Judgment under uncertainty: Heuristics and biases.* New York: Cambridge University Press.

Kahneman, D., & Tversky, A. (1973). On the psychology of prediction. *Psychological Review, 80,* 237–251.

Kail, R., & Hall, L. K. (2001). Distinguishing short-term memory from working memory. *Memory and Cognition, 29*(1), 1–9.

Kakko, J., Svanborg, K. D., Kreek, M. J., & Heilig, M. (2003). 1-year retention and social function after buprenorphine-associated relapse prevention treatment for heroin dependence in Sweden: A randomised, placebo-controlled trial. *Lancet, 361,* 662–668.

Kales, A., Soldatos, C., Bixler, E., Ladda, R. L., Charney, D. S., Weber, G., et al. (1980). Hereditary factors in sleepwalking and night terrors. *British Journal of Psychiatry, 137,* 111–118.

Kandel, E. R., & Schwartz, J. H. (1982). Molecular biology of learning: Modulation of transmitter release. *Science, 218,* 433–443.

Kaplan, M. F., & Miller, C. E. (1987). Group decision making and normative versus informational influence: Effects of type of issue and assigned decision rule. *Journal of Personality and Social Psychology, 53*(2), 306–313.

Karney, B. R., & Bradbury, T. N. (2000). Attributions in marriage: State or trait? A growth curve analysis. *Journal of Personality and Social Psychology, 78,* 295–309.

Karpicke, J. D. (2012). Retrieval-based learning: Active retrieval promotes meaningful learning. *Current Directions in Psychological Science, 21*(3), 157–163. doi:10.1177/0963721412443552

Karpicke, J. D., & Blunt, J. R. (2011). Retrieval practice produces more learning than elaborative studying with concept mapping. *Science.* doi:10.1126scoemce/1199327

Kastenbaum, R., & Costa, P. T., Jr. (1977). Psychological perspective on death. *Annual Review of Psychology, 28,* 225–249.

Katz, V. L. (2007). Spontaneous and recurrent abortion: Etiology, diagnosis, treatment. In V. L. Katz, G. M. Lentz, R. A. Lobo, & D. M. Gershenson (Eds.), *Comprehensive gynecology* (5th ed.). Philadelphia: Mosby Elsevier.

Kaufman, J., & Zigler, E. (1993). The intergenerational transmission of abuse is overstated. In R. J. Gelles & D. R. Loseke (Eds.), *Current controversies on family violence.* Newbury Park, CA: Sage.

Kaye, W. H., Fudge, J. L., & Paulus, M. (2009). New insights into symptoms and neurocircuit function of anorexia nervosa. *Nature Reviews Neuroscience, 10*(8), 573–584. doi:10.1038/nrn2682

Kaye, W. H., Wierenga, C. E., Bailer, U. F., Simmons, A. N., & Bischoff-Grethe, A. (2013). Nothing tastes as good as skinny feels: The neurobiology of anorexia nervosa. *Trends in Neurosciences, 36*(2), 110–120. doi:10.1016/j.tins.2013.01.003

Kazdin, A. E. (1980). Acceptability of time out from reinforcement procedures for disruptive behavior. *Behavior Therapy, 11*(3), 329–344.

Kazdin, A. E. (2008). Evidence-based treatment and practice: New opportunities to bridge clinical research and practice, enhance the knowledge base, and improve patient care. *American Psychologist, 63*(3), 146–159. doi:10.1037/0003-066x.63.3.146

Kearney, C. A., & Silverman, W. K. (1998). A critical review of pharmacotherapy for youth with anxiety disorders: Things are not as they seem. *Journal of Anxiety Disorders, 12,* 83–102.

Keel, P. K., & Forney, K. J. (2013). Psychosocial risk factors for eating disorders. *The International Journal of Eating Disorders, 46*(5), 433–439. doi:10.1002/eat.22094

Keillor, J., Barrett, A., Crucian, G., Kortenkamp, S., & Heilman, K. (2002). Emotional experience and perception in the absence of facial feedback. *Journal of the International Neuropsychological Society, 8*(1), 130–135.

Keirsey, D. (1998). *Please understand me II: Temperament character intelligence.* Del Mar, CA: Prometheus Nemesis Book Company.

Keller, M. B., McCullough, J. P., Klein, D. N., Arnow, B., Dunner, D., Gelenberg, A., et al. (2000). A comparison of nefazodone, the cognitive behavioral-analysis system of psychotherapy, and their combination for the treatment of chronic depression. *New England Journal of Medicine, 342*(20), 1462–1470.

Kelly, I. (1980). The scientific case against astrology. *Mercury, 10*(13), 135.

Kelly, J. A., McAuliffe, T. L., Sikkema, K. J., Murphy, D. A., Somlai, A. M., Mulry, G., et al. (1997). Reduction in risk behavior among adults with severe mental illness who learned to advocate for HIV prevention. *Psychiatric Services, 48*(10), 1283–1288.

Kempf, L., & Weinberger, D. R. (2009). Molecular genetics and bioinformatics: An outline for neuropsychological genetics. In T. E. Goldberg & D. R. Weinberger (Eds.), *The genetics of cognitive neuroscience* (pp. 3–26). Cambridge, MA: MIT Press.

Kendall, P. (1983). Stressful medical procedures: Cognitive-behavioral strategies for stress management and prevention. In D. Meichenbaum & M. Jaremko (Eds.), *Stress reduction and prevention* (pp. 159–190). New York: Plenum Press.

Kendall, P. C., Hudson, J. L., Gosch, E., Flannery-Schroeder, E., & Suveg, C. (2008). Cognitive-behavioral therapy for anxiety disordered youth: A randomized clinical trial evaluating child and family modalities. *Journal of Consulting and Clinical Psychology, 76*(2), 282–297.

Kendler, K. S. (1985). Diagnostic approaches to schizotypal personality disorders: A historical perspective. *Schizophrenia Bulletin, 11,* 538–553.

Kendler, K. S., Czajkowski, N., Tambs, K., Torgersen, S., Aggen, S. H., Neale, M. C., et al. (2006). Dimensional representations of DSM-IV cluster A personality disorders in a population-based sample of Norwegian twins: A multivariate study. *Psychological Medicine, 36*(11), 1583–1591. doi:10.1017/s0033291706008609

Kenny, A. (1968). Mind and body. In *Descartes: A study of his philosophy* (p. 279). New York: Random House.

Kenny, A. (1994). Descartes to Kant. In A. Kenny (Ed.), *The Oxford history of Western philosophy* (pp. 107–192). Oxford, UK: Oxford University Press.

Kenrick, D. T., Griskevicius, V., Neuberg, S. L., & Schaller, M. (2010). Renovating the pyramid of needs: Contemporary extensions built upon ancient foundations. *Perspectives on Psychological Science, 5*(3), 292–314.

Kensinger, E. A., Shearer, D. K., Locascio, J. J., Growdon, J. H., & Corkin, S. (2003). Working memory in mild Alzheimer's disease and early Parkinson's disease. *Neuropsychology, 17*(2), 230–239.

Keromoian, R., & Leiderman, P. H. (1986). Infant attachment to mother and child caretaker in an East African community. *International Journal of Behavioral Development, 9,* 455–469.

Kerwin, D. R., Zhang, Y., Kotchen, J. M., Espeland, M. A., Van Horn, L., McTigue, K. M., et al. (2010). The cross-sectional relationship between body mass index, waist-hip ratio, and cognitive performance in postmenopausal women enrolled in the women's health initiative. *Journal of the American Geriatric Society, 58,* 1427–1432. [Article first published online July 14, 2010]. doi:10.1111/j.1532-5415.2010.02969.x

Kesebir, S., Graham, J., & Oishi, S. (2010). A theory of human needs should be human-centered, not animal-centered. *Perspectives on Psychological Science, 5*(3), 315–319.

Kessler, R. C., Petukhova, M., Sampson, N. A., Zaslavsky, A. M., & Wittchen, H. U. (2012). Twelve-month and lifetime prevalence and lifetime morbid risk of anxiety and mood disorders in the United States. *International Journal of Methods in Psychiatric Research, 21*(3), 169–184. doi:10.1002/mpr.1359

Kety, S. S., Wender, P. H., Jacobsen, B., Ingaham, L. J., Jansson, L., Faber, B., et al. (1994). Mental illness in the biological and adoptive relatives of schizophrenic adoptees. *Archives of General Psychiatry, 51,* 442–455.

Kiecolt-Glaser, J. K. (2009). Psychoneuroimmunology: Psychology's gateway to the biomedical future. *Perspectives on Psychological Science, 4*(4), 367.

Kiecolt-Glaser, J. K., Fisher, L. D., Ogrocki, P., Stout, J. C., Speicher, C. E., & Glaser, R. (1987). Marital quality, marital disruption, and immune function. *Psychosomatic Medicine, 49,* 13–34.

Kiecolt-Glaser, J. K., Glaser, R., Gravenstein, S., Malarkey, W. B., & Sheridan, J. (1996). Chronic stress alters the immune response to influenza virus vaccine in older adults. *Proceedings of the National Academy of Sciences, USA, 93*(7), 3043–3047.

Kiecolt-Glaser, J. K., Marucha, P. T., Malarkey, W. B., & Marcado, A. M. (1995). Slowing of wound healing by psychological stress. *Lancet, 346,* 1194–1196.

Kiecolt-Glaser, J. K., McGuire, L., Robles, T., & Glaser, R. (2002). Psychoneuroimmunology: Psychological influences on immune function and health. *Journal of Consulting and Clinical Psychology, 70,* 537–547.

Kihlstrom, J. F. (1985). Hypnosis. *Annual Review of Psychology, 36,* 385–418.

Kihlstrom, J. F. (1987). The cognitive unconscious. *Science, 237,* 1445–1452.

Kihlstrom, J. F. (1999). Conscious and unconscious cognition. In R. J. Sternberg (Ed.), *The nature of cognition* (pp. 173–203). Cambridge, MA: MIT Press.

Kihlstrom, J. F. (2001). Hypnosis and the psychological unconscious. In Howard S. Friedman (Ed.), *Assessment and therapy: Specialty articles from the encyclopedia of mental health* (pp. 215–226). San Diego, CA: Academic Press.

Kihlstrom, J. F. (2002). Memory, autobiography, history. *Proteus: A Journal of Ideas, 19*(2), 1–6.

Kihlstrom, J. F., Mulvaney, S., Tobias, B., & Tobis, I. (2000). The emotional unconscious. In E. Eich, J. Kihlstrom, G. Bower, J. Forgas, & P. Niedenthal (Eds.), *Cognition and emotion* (pp. 30–86). New York: Oxford University Press.

Kim, H., & Markus, H. R. (1999). Deviance or uniqueness, harmony or conformity? A cultural analysis. *Journal of Personality and Social Psychology, 77,* 785–800.

Kimura, R., Mactavish, E., Yang, J., Westaway, D., & Jhamandas, J. H. (2012). Beta amyloid-induced depression of hippocampal long-term potentiation is mediated through the amylin receptor. *Journal of Neuroscience, 32*(48), 17401–17406. doi:10.1523/%u200BJNEUROSCI.3028-12.2012

King, M. W., Street, A. E., Gradus, J. L., Vogt, D. S., & Resick, P. A. (2013). Gender differences in posttraumatic stress symptoms among OEF/OIF veterans: An item response theory analysis. *Journal of Traumatic Stress, 26*(2), 175–183. doi:10.1002/jts.21802

Kinsey, A. C., Pomeroy, W. B., & Martin, C. E. (1948). *Sexual behavior in the human male.* Philadelphia: W. B. Saunders.

Kinsey, A. C., Pomeroy, W. B., Martin, C. E., & Gebhard, P. H. (1953). *Sexual behavior in the human female.* New York: W. B. Saunders.

Kirmayer, L. J. (1991). The place of culture in psychiatric nosology: Taijin kyofusho and the DSM-III-TR. *Journal of Nervous and Mental Disease, 179,* 19–28.

Kirsch, I. (2000). The response set theory of hypnosis. *American Journal of Clinical Hypnosis, 42*(3–4), 274–292.

Kirsch, I., & Lynn, S. J. (1995). The altered state of hypnosis: Changes in the theoretical landscape. *American Psychologist, 50,* 846–858.

Kitamura, T., Saitoh, Y., Takashima, N., Murayama, A., Niibori, Y., Ageta, H., et al. (2009). Adult neurogenesis modulates the hippocampus-dependent period of associative fear memory. *Cell, 139*(4), 814–827.

Kitayama, S., & Markus, H. R. (1994). Introduction to cultural psychology and emotion research. In S. Kitayama & H. R. Markus (Eds.), *Emotion and culture: Empirical studies of mutual influence* (pp. 1–22). Washington, DC: American Psychological Association.

Kleim, B., Ehring, T., & Ehlers, A. (2012). Perceptual processing advantages for trauma-related visual cues in post-traumatic stress disorder. *Psychological Medicine, 42*(1), 173–181. doi:10.1017/s0033291711001048

Klein, R. G., Mannuzza, S., Olazagasti, M. A., Roizen, E., Hutchison, J. A., Lashua, E. C., et al. (2012). Clinical and functional outcome of childhood Attention-Deficit/Hyperactivity Disorder 33 years later. *Archives of General Psychiatry, 69*(12), 1295–1303. doi:10.1001/archgenpsychiatry.2012.271

Klein, S. B., & Mowrer, R. R. (1989). *Contemporary learning theories: Pavlovian conditioning and the status of traditional learning theory.* Hillsdale, NJ: Erlbaum.

Kleinot, M. C., & Rogers, R. W. (1982). Identifying effective components of alcohol misuse prevention programs. *Journal of Studies on Alcohol, 43,* 802–811.

Klorman, R., Hilpert, P. L., Michael, R., LaGana, C., & Sveen, O. B. (1980). Effects of coping and mastery modeling on experienced and inexperienced pedodontic patients' disruptiveness. *Behavior Therapy, 11,* 156–168.

Kluft, R. P. (1984). Introduction to multiple personality disorder. *Psychiatric Annals, 14,* 19–24.

Klüver, H., & Bucy, P. C. (1939). Preliminary analysis of functions of the temporal lobes in monkeys. *Archives of Neurological Psychiatry, 42,* 979–1000.

Knight, A. (1996). *The life of the law: The people and cases that have shaped our society, from King Alfred to Rodney King.* New York: Crown Publishing Group.

Knight, J. A. (1998). Free radicals: Their history and current status in aging and disease. *Annals of Clinical and Laboratory Science, 28,* 331–346.

Kobasa, S. (1979). Stressful life events, personality, and health: An inquiry into hardiness. *Journal of Personality and Social Psychology, 37*(1), 1–11.

Koch, C., & Mormann, F. (2010). The neurobiology of consciousness. In G. Mashour (Ed.), *Consciousness, awareness, and anesthesia* (pp. 24–46). New York: Cambridge University Press.

Koenig, H. G., Hays, J. C., Larson, D. B., George, L. K., Cohen, H. J., McCullough, M. E., et al. (1999). Does religious attendance prolong survival? A six-year follow-up study of 3,968 older adults. *Journal of Gerontology, 54A,*M370–M377.

Koenig, H. G., McCullough, M. E., & Larson, D. B. (2001). *Handbook of religion and health.* Oxford, UK: Oxford University Press.

Koester, J., & Siegelbaum, S. A. (2013). Membrane potential and the passive electrical properties of the neuron. In E. R. Kandel, J. H. Schwartz, T. M. Jessell, S. A. Siegelbaum & A. J. Hudspeth (Eds.), *Principles of neural science* (5th ed., pp. 148–171). USA: McGraw Hill

Koh, J. K. (1996). *A guide to common Singapore spiders* (BP Guide to Nature series). Singapore: Singapore Science Center.

Kohlberg, L. (1973). Continuities in childhood and adult moral development revisited. In P. Baltes & K. W. Schaie (Eds.), *Life-span development psychology: Personality and socialization.* San Diego, CA: Academic Press.

Köhler, W. (1925, 1992). *Gestalt psychology: An introduction to new concepts in modern psychology (reissue).* New York: Liveright.

Koob, G. F., & Le Moal, M. (2005). Plasticity of reward neurocircuitry and the 'dark side' of drug addiction. *Nature Neuroscience, 8*(11), 1442–1444.

Korn, S. (1984). Continuities and discontinuities in difficult/easy temperament: Infancy to young adulthood. *Merrill Palmer Quarterly, 30,* 189–199.

Kosslyn, S. M., Alpert, N. M., Thompson, W. L., Maljkovic, V., Weise, S. B., Chabris, C. F., et al. (1993). Visual mental imagery activates topographically organized visual cortex: PET investigations. *Journal of Cognitive Neuroscience, 5,* 263–287.

Kosslyn, S. M., Ball, T. M., & Reiser, B. J. (1978). Visual images preserve metric spatial information: Evidence from studies of image scanning. *Journal of Experimental Psychology: Human Perception and Performance, 4,* 47–60.

Kosslyn, S. M., Ganis, G., & Thompson, W. L. (2001). Neural foundations of imagery. *Nature Reviews Neuroscience, 2,* 635–642.

Kosslyn, S. M., Pascual-Leone, A., Felician, O., Camposano, S., Keenan, J. P., Thompson, W. L., et al. (1999). The role of area 17 in visual imagery: Convergent evidence from PET and rTMS. *Science, 284,* 167–170.

Kotkin, M., Daviet, C., & Gurin, J. (1996). The *Consumer Reports* mental health survey. *American Psychologist, 51*(10), 1080–1082.

Kourtis, A. P., & Bulterys, M. (2010). Mother-to-child transmission of HIV: pathogenesis, mechanisms and pathways. *Clinical Perinatology, 37,* 721–737.

Kratofil, P. H., Baberg, H. T., & Dimsdale, J. E. (1996). Self-mutilation and severe self-injurious behavior associated with amphetamine psychosis. *General Hospital Psychiatry, 18,* 117–120.

Kovacs, K., Lajtha, A., & Sershen, H. (2010). Effect of nicotine and cocaine on neurofilaments and receptors in whole brain tissue and synaptoneurosome preparations. *Brain Research Bulletin, 82*(1–2), 109–117.

Kozberg, M., Chen, B. R., De Leo, S. E., Bouchard, M. B., & Hillman, E. M. C. (2013). Resolving the transition from negative to positive blood oxygen level dependent responses in the developing brain. *Proceedings of the National Academy of Sciences of the United States of America (PNAS).* Published online ahead of print, February 20, 2013. doi:10.1073/pnas.1212785110

Kriegstein, A., & Alvarez-Buylla, A. (2009). The glial nature of embryonic and adult neural stem cells. *Annual Review of Neuroscience, 32*(1), 149–184.

Kristensen, P., & Bjerkedal, T. (2007). Explaining the relation between birth order and intelligence. *Science, 316*(5832), 1717.

Krüttner, S., Stepien, B., Noordermeer, J. N., Mommaas, M. A., Mechtler, K., Dickson, B. J., et al. (2012). Drosophila CPEB Orb2A mediates memory independent of its RNA-binding domain. *Neuron, 76*(2), 383. doi:10.1016/j.neuron.2012.08.028

Kryger, M., Lavie, P., & Rosen, R. (1999). Recognition and diagnosis of insomnia. *Sleep, 22,* S421–S426.

Kubicki, M., Niznikiewicz, M., Connor, E., Nestor, P., Bouix, S., Dreusicke, M., et al. (2009). Relationship between white matter integrity, attention, and memory in schizophrenia: A diffusion tensor imaging study. *Brain Imaging and Behavior, 3*(2), 191–201.

Kübler-Ross, E. (1997). *The wheel of life: A memoir of living and dying.* New York: Touchstone.

Kuhn, H. W., & Nasar, S. (Eds.). (2001). *The essential John Nash.* Princeton, NJ: Princeton University Press.

Kuhn, J., Gründler, T. O. J., Lenartz, D., Sturm, V., Klosterkötter, J., & Huff, W. (2010). Deep brain stimulation for psychiatric disorders. *Deutsches Ärzteblatt International, 107*(7), 105–113.

Kulik, J. A., & Mahler, H. I. M. (1989). Social support and recovery from surgery. *Health Psychology, 8,* 221–238.

Kulik, J. A., & Mahler, H. I. M. (1993). Emotional support as a moderator of adjustment and compliance after coronary bypass surgery: A longitudinal study. *Journal of Behavioral Medicine, 16,* 45–63.

Kulmala, J., von Bonsdorff, M. B., Stenholm, S., Tormakangas, T., von Bonsdorff, M. E., Nygard, C.-H., et al. (2013). Perceived stress symptoms in midlife predict disability in old age: A 28-year prospective cohort study. *The Journals of Gerontology Series A: Biological Sciences and Medical Sciences.* doi: 10.1093/Gerona/gls339

Kumar, S., & Oakley-Browne, M. (2002). Panic disorder. *Clinical Evidence, 7,* 906–912.

Küntay, A., & Slobin, D. I. (2002). Putting interaction back into child language: Examples from Turkish. *Psychology of Language and Communication, 6,* 5–14.

Kupfer, D. J., & Reynolds, C. F., III. (1997). Management of insomnia. *New England Journal of Medicine, 336*(5), 341–346.

Kuriki, I., Ashida, H., Murakami, I., & Kitaoka, A. (2008). Functional brain imaging of the Rotating Snakes illusion by fMRI. *Journal of Vision, 8*(10), 16.1–16.10.

Kvavilashvili, L., Mirani, J., Schlagman, S., Foley, K., & Dornbrot, D. E. (2009). Consistency of flashbulb memories of September 11 over long delays: Implications for consolidation and wrong time slice hypotheses. *Journal of Memory and Language, 61*(4), 556–572.

LaBar, K. S., LeDoux, J. E., Spencer, D. D., & Phelps, E. A. (1995). Impaired fear conditioning following unilateral temporal lobectomy to humans. *Journal of Neuroscience, 15,* 6846–6855.

LaBerge, D. (1980). Unitization and automaticity in perception. In J. H. Flowers (Ed.), *Nebraska symposium on motivation* (pp. 53–71). Lincoln: University of Nebraska Press.

Labouvie-Vief, G. (1980). Beyond formal operations: Uses and limits of pure logic in lifespan development. *Human Development, 23,* 114–146.

Labouvie-Vief, G. (1992). A neo-Piagetian perspective on adult cognitive development. In R. Sternberg & C. Berg (Eds.), *Intellectual development* (pp. 197–228). Cambridge, UK: Cambridge University Press.

Lacayo, A. (1995). Neurologic and psychiatric complications of cocaine abuse. *Neuropsychiatry, Neuropsychology, and Behavioral Neurology, 8*(1), 53–60.

LaFromboise, T., Coleman, H. L. K., & Gerton, J. (1993). Psychological impact of biculturalism: Evidence and theory. *Psychological Bulletin, 114,* 395–412.

Lagopoulos, J., Xu, J., Rasmussen, I., Vik, A., Malhi, G. S., Eliassen, C. F., et al. (2009). Increased theta and alpha EEG activity during nondirective meditation. *The Journal of Alternative and Complementary Medicine, 15*(11), 1187.

Lal, S. (2002). Giving children security: Mamie Phipps Clark and the radicalization of child psychology. *American Psychologist, 57*(1), 20–28.

Lalancette, M.-F., & Standing, L. G. (1990). Asch fails again. *Social Behavior and Personality, 18*(1), 7–12.

Lambert, M. J., & Ogles, B. M. (2004). The efficacy and effectiveness of psychotherapy. In M. J. Lambert (Ed.), *Handbook of psychotherapy and behavior change* (5th ed., pp. 139–193). New York: Wiley.

Lance, C. J., LaPointe, J. A., & Fisicaro, S. (1994). Tests of three causal models of halo rater error. *Organizational Behavior and Human Decision Performance, 57,* 83–96.

Landrum, R. E. (2009). *Finding jobs with a psychology bachelor's degree.* Washington, DC: American Psychological Association.

Landrum, R. E., & Davis, S. F. (2007). *The psychology major: Career options and strategies for success* (3rd ed.). Upper Saddle River, NJ: Prentice Hall.

Lang, J. W. B., & Lang, J. (2010). Priming competence diminishes the link between cognitive test anxiety and test performance. *Psychological Science, 21*(6), 811–819.

Lange, C. (1885). *The emotions.* Reprinted in C. G. Lange & W. James (Eds.), *The emotions.* New York: Harner.

Langone, M. C. (1996). Clinical update on cults. *Psychiatric Times, 13*(7), 1–3.

Lanphear, B. P., Dietrich, K., Auinger, P., & Cox, C. (2000). Cognitive deficits associated with blood lead concentrations <10 micrograms/dL in U.S. children and adolescents. *Public Health Reports, 115*(6), 521–529.

Lapsley, D. K., Milstead, M., Quintana, S. M., Flannery, D., & Buss, R. R. (1986). Adolescent egocentrism and formal operations: Tests of a theoretical assumption. *Developmental Psychology, 22,* 800–807.

Larsen, J. T., Berntson, G. G., Poehlmann, K. M., Ito, T. A., & Cacioppo, J. T. (2008). The psychophysiology of emotion. In M. Lewis, J. M. Haviland-Jones, & L. F. Barrett (Eds.), *Handbook of emotions* (3rd ed., pp. 180–195). New York: Guilford Press.

Larzelere, R. (1986). Moderate spanking: Model or deterrent of children's aggression in the family? *Journal of Family Violence, 1*(1), 27–36.

Lashley, K. S. (1938). The thalamus and emotion. *The Psychological Review, 45,* 21–61.

Lasnik, H. (1990). Metrics and morphophonemics in early English verse. In *University of Connecticut Working Papers in Linguistics: Vol. 3* (pp. 29–40). Storrs: University of Connecticut.

Latané, B., & Darley, J. M. (1969). Bystander "apathy." *American Scientist, 57*(2), 244–268.

Laumann, E. O., Gagnon, J. H., Michael, R. T., & Michaels, S. (1994). *The social organization of sexuality: Sexual practices in the United States* (pp. 77–145). Chicago: University of Chicago Press.

Launer, L., Masaki, K., Petrovitch, H., Foley, D., & Havlik, R. (1995). The association between midlife blood pressure levels and late-life cognitive function. *Journal of the American Medical Association, 272*(23), 1846–1851.

Laungani, P. (1997). Death in a Hindu Family. In C. M. Parkes, P. Laungani, & B. Young (Eds.), *Death and bereavement across cultures* (pp. 52–72). London: Routledge.

Lavergne, G. M. (1997). *A sniper in the tower: The true story of the Texas Tower massacre.* New York: Bantam.

Laviolette, S. R., Lauzon, N. M., Bishop, S. F., Sun, N., & Tan, H. (2008, August 6). Dopamine signaling through D1-like versus D2-like receptors in the nucleus accumbens core versus shell differentially modulates nicotine reward sensitivity. *Journal of Neuroscience, 28*(32), 8025–8033.

Laws, G., Davies, I., & Andrews, C. (1995). Linguistic structure and nonlinguistic cognition: English and Russian blues compared. *Language and Cognitive Processes, 10,* 59–94.

Lay, C., & Nguyen, T. T. I. (1998). The role of acculturation-related and acculturation non-specific daily hassles: Vietnamese- Canadian students and psychological distress. *Canadian Journal of Behavioural Science, 30*(3), 172–181.

Lazarus, R. S. (1991). *Emotion and adaptation.* New York: Oxford University Press.

Lazarus, R. S. (1993). From psychological stress to the emotions: A history of changing outlooks. *Annual Review of Psychology, 44,* 1–22.

Lazarus, R. S. (1999). *Stress and emotion: A new synthesis.* New York: Springer.

Lazarus, R. S., & Folkman, S. (1984). *Stress, appraisal and coping.* New York: Springer.

Leary, M. R., & Forsyth, D. R. (1987). Attributions of responsibility for collective endeavors. *Review of Personality and Social Psychology, 8,* 167–188.

Leask, J., Haber, R. N., & Haber, R. B. (1969). Eidetic imagery in children: II. Longitudinal and experimental results. *Psychonomic Monograph Supplements, 3,* 25–48.

Leccese, A. P., Pennings, E. J. M., & De Wolff, F. A. (2000). *Combined use of alcohol and psychotropic drugs. A review of the literature.* Leiden, The Netherlands: Academisch Ziekenhuis Leiden (AZL).

Leclerc, C. M., & Hess, T. M. (2007). Age differences in the bases for social judgments: Tests of a social expertise perspective. *Experimental Aging Research, 33*(1), 95–120.

LeDoux, J. (1994). Emotion, memory and the brain. *Scientific American, 270,* 32–39.

LeDoux, J. E. (1996). *The emotional brain: The mysterious underpinnings of emotional life.* New York: Simon & Schuster.

LeDoux, J. E. (2003). The emotional brain, fear, and the amygdala. *Cellular and Molecular Neurobiology, 23*(4–5), 727–738.

LeDoux, J. E. (2007). The amygdala. *Current Biology, 17*(20), R868–R874.

LeDoux, J. E., & Damasio, A. R. (2013). Emotions and feelings. In E. R. Kandel, J. H. Schwartz, T. M. Jessell, S. A. Siegelbaum, & A. J. Hudspeth (Eds.), *Principles of neural science* (5th ed., pp. 1079–1094). USA: McGraw-Hill.

LeDoux, J. E., & Phelps, E. A. (2008). Emotional networks in the brain. In M. Lewis, J. M. Haviland-Jones, & L. F. Barrett (Eds.), *Handbook of emotions* (3rd ed., pp. 159–179). New York: Guilford Press.

Lee, F., Hallahan, M., & Herzog, T. (1996). Explaining real life events: How culture and domain shape attributions. *Personality and Social Psychology Bulletin, 22,* 732–741.

Lee, M., & Shlain, B. (1986). *Acid dreams: The complete social history of LSD: The CIA, the sixties, and beyond.* New York: Grove Press.

Lee, P. A. (1995). Physiology of puberty. In K. L. Becker (Ed.), *Principles and practice of endocrinology and metabolism* (pp. 822–830). Philadelphia: J. B. Lippincott.

Lee, S. H., Kim, E. Y., Kim, S., & Bae, S. M. (2010). Event-related potential patterns and gender effects underlying facial affect processing in schizophrenia patients. *Neuroscience Research, 7,* 7.

Lehr, U., & Thomae, H. (1987). *Patterns of psychological aging. Results from the Bonne Aging Longitudinal Study (BOLSA).* Stuttgart, Germany: Enke.

Leon, P., Chedraui, P., Hidalgo, L., & Ortiz, F. (2007). Perceptions and attitudes toward the menopause among middle-aged women from Guayaquil, Ecuador. *Maturitas, 57*(3), 233–238.

LePort, A. K., Mattfeld, A. T., Dickinson-Anson, H., Fallon, J. H., Stark, C. E., Kruggel, F., et al. (2012). Behavioral and neuroanatomical investigation of highly superior autobiographical memory (HSAM). *Neurobiology of Learning and Memory, 98*(1), 78. doi:10.1016/j.nlm.2012.05.002

Leroy, C., & Symes, B. (2001). Teachers' perspectives on the family backgrounds of children at risk. *McGill Journal of Education, 36*(1), 45–60.

Levenson, R. W. (1992). Autonomic nervous system differences among emotions. *Psychological Sciences, 3,* 23–27.

Levenson, R. W., Ekman, P., Heider, K., & Friesen, W. V. (1992). Emotion and autonomic nervous system activity in the Minangkabau of West Sumatra. *Journal of Personality and Social Psychology, 62,* 972–988.

Levy, B. R., Slade, M. D., Kunkel, S. R., & Kasl, S. V. (2002). Longevity increased by positive self-perceptions of aging. *Journal of Personality and Social Psychology, 83,* 261–269.

Levy, S. R., Stroessner, S. J., & Dweck, C. S. (1998). Stereotype formation and endorsement: The role of implicit theories. *Journal of Personality and Social Psychology, 74,* 1421–1436.

Lewis, D. K. (1996, June). A cross-cultural model for psychotherapy: Working with the African-American client. *Perspectives on Multiculturalism and Cultural Diversity,* VI(2).

Lewis, J. R. (1995). *Encyclopedia of afterlife beliefs and phenomenon.* Detroit, MI: Visible Ink Press.

Lewis, R. W., Fugl-Meyer, K. S., Corona, G., Hayes, R. D., Laumann, E. O., Moreira, E. D., Jr., et al. (2010). Definitions/epidemiology/risk factors for sexual dysfunction. *The Journal of Sexual Medicine, 7*(4, pt. 2), 1598–1607. doi:10.1111/j.1743-6109.2010.01778.x

Liechti, M. E., & Vollenweider, F. X. (2001). Which neuroreceptors mediate the subjective effects of MDMA in humans? A summary of mechanistic studies. *Human Psychopharmacology, 16,* 589–598.

Light, K. R., Kolata, S., Wass, C., Denman-Brice, A., Zagalsky, R., & Matzel, L. D. (2010). Working memory training promotes general cognitive abilities in genetically heterogeneous mice. *Current Biology, 20*(8), 777–782.

Like, R., Steiner, P., & Rubel, A. (1996). Recommended core curriculum guidelines on culturally sensitive and competent care. *Family Medicine, 27,* 291–297.

Lilienfeld, S. O. (1999). Projective measures of personality and psychopathology: How well do they work? *Skeptical Inquirer, 23*(5), 32–39.

Lilienfeld, S. O., Wood, J. M., & Garb, H. N. (2000). The scientific status of projective techniques. *Psychological Science in the Public Interest, 1*(2), 27–66. doi:10.1111/1529-1006.002

Lim, Y. Y., Ellis, K. A., Pietrzak, R. H., Ames, D., Darby, D., Harrington, K., et al. (2012). Stronger effect of amyloid load than APOE genotype on cognitive decline in healthy older adults. *Neurology, 79*(16), 1645. doi:10.1212/WNL.0b013e31826e9ae6

Lin, C. S., Lyons, J. L., & Berkowitz, F. (2007). Somatotopic identification of language-SMA in language processing via fMRI. *Journal of Scientific and Practical Computing, 1*(2), 3–8.

Lin, P. J., & Schwanenflugel, P. J. (1995). Cultural familiarity and language factors in the structure of category knowledge. *Journal of Cross-Cultural Psychology, 26,* 153–168.

Lin, P. J., Schwanenflugel, P. J., & Wisenbaker, J. M. (1990). Category typicality, cultural familiarity, and the development of category knowledge. *Developmental Psychology, 26,* 805–813.

Lindau, S. T., Schumm, P., Laumann, E. O., Levinson, W., O'Muircheartaigh, C. A., & Waite, L. J. (2007). A study of sexuality and health among older adults in the United States. *New England Journal of Medicine, 357*(8), 762–764.

Lipsman, N., Woodside, D. B., Giacobbe, P., Hamani, C., Carter, J. C., Norwood, S. J., et al. (2013). Subcallosal cingulate deep brain stimulation for treatment-refractory anorexia nervosa: A phase 1 pilot trial. *Lancet, 381*(9875), 1361–1370. doi:10.1016/s0140-6736(12)62188-6

Lisanby, S. H., Maddox, J. H., Prudic, J., Devanand, D. P., & Sackeim, H. A. (2000). The effects of electroconvulsive therapy on memory of autobiographical and public events. *Archives of General Psychiatry, 57,* 581–590.

Livesley, J. W. (Ed.). (1995). *The DSM-IV personality disorders.* New York: Guilford Press.

Lizskowski, U., Carpenter, M., Striano, T., & Tomasello, M. (2006). 12- and 18-month olds point to provide information for others. *Journal of Cognition and Development, 7,* 173–187.

Lock, M. (1994). Menopause in cultural context. *Experimental Gerontology, 29*(3–4), 307–317.

Loehlin, J. C. (1992). *Genes and environment in personality development.* Newbury Park, CA: Sage.

Loehlin, J. C., McCrae, R. R., Costa, P. T., Jr., & John, O. P. (1998). Heritabilities of common and measure-specific components of the Big Five personality factors. *Journal of Research in Personality, 32,* 431–453.

Loehlin, J. C., Willerman, L., & Horn, J. M. (1985). Personality resemblances in adoptive families when the children are late-adolescent or adult. *Journal of Personality and Social Psychology, 48,* 376–392.

Loftus, E. (1975). Leading questions and the eyewitness report. *Cognitive Psychology, 7,* 560–572.

Loftus, E. F., Miller, D. G., & Burns, H. J. (1978). Semantic integration of verbal information into a visual memory. *Journal of Experimental Psychology: Human Learning, 4,* 19–31.

Loftus, J. (2001). America's liberalization in attitudes toward homosexuality, 1973 to 1998. *American Sociological Review, 66*(5), 762–782.

Loo, S. K., Hale, T. S., Macion, J., Hanada, G., McGough, J. J., McCracken, J. T., et al. (2009). Cortical activity patterns in ADHD during arousal, activation and sustained attention. *Neuropsychologia, 47*(10), 2114–2119.

Lord, T. R. (2001). 101 reasons for using cooperative learning in biology teaching. *The American Biology Teacher, 63*(1), 30–38.

Lorenz, K. (1966). *On Aggression* (p. ix). (M. K. Wilson, Trans.) New York: Harcourt, Brace & World, Inc.

Lovaas, O. I. (1987). Behavioral treatment and normal educational and intellectual functioning in young autistic children. *Journal of Consulting and Clinical Psychology, 55,* 3–9.

Lovaas, O. I., Berberich, J. P., Perloff, B. F., & Schaffer, B. (1966). Acquisition of imitative speech by schizophrenic children. *Science, 151,* 705–707.

Lu, S., & Ende, N. (1997). Potential for clinical use of viable pluripotent progenitor cells in blood bank stored human umbilical cord blood. *Life Sciences, 61,* 1113–1123.

Lubinski, D. (2000). Scientific and social significance of assessing individual differences: "Sinking shafts at a few critical points." *Annual Review of Psychology, 51,* 405–444.

Luborsky, L., Singer, B., & Luborsky, L. (1975). Comparative studies of psychotherapies: Is it true that "everyone has won and all must have prizes"? *Archives of General Psychiatry, 32,* 995–1008.

Luchins, A. S. (1957). Primacy-recency in impression formation. In C. Hovland (Ed.), *The order of presentation in persuasion* (pp. 33–40, 55–61). New Haven, CT: Yale University Press.

Luck, S. J., & Gold, J. M. (2008). The construct of attention in schizophrenia. *Biological Psychiatry, 64*(1), 34–39.

Lucy, J. A., & Shweder, R. A. (1979). Whorf and his critics: Linguistic and nonlinguistic influences on color memory. *American Anthropologist, 81,* 581–615.

Luria, A. R. (1965). Two kinds of motor perseveration in massive injury of the frontal lobes. *Brain, 88,* 1–10.

Luria, A. R. (1968). *The mind of a mnemonist* (pp. 24, 25). New York: Basic Books.

Lutkenhaus, P., Grossmann, K. E., & Grossman, K. (1985). Infant-mother attachment at twelve months and style of interaction with a stranger at the age of three years. *Child Development, 56,* 1538–1542.

Lykken, D. T. (1995). *The antisocial personalities.* Hillsdale, NJ: Erlbaum.

Lykken, D. T., & Tellegen, A. (1996). Happiness is a stochastic phenomenon. *Psychological Science, 7,* 186–189.

Lynott, P. P., & Roberts, R. (1997). The developmental stake hypothesis and changing perceptions of intergenerational relations, 1971–1985. *The Gerontologist, 37,* 394–405.

Lytton, H., & Romney, D. M. (1991). Parents' sex-differentiated socialization of boys and girls: A meta-analysis. *Psychological Bulletin, 109,* 267–296.

MacDonald, A. P. (1970). Internal-external locus of control and the practice of birth control. *Psychological Reports, 27,* 206.

MacDonald, D., Kabani, N., Avis, D., & Evens, A. C. (2000). Automated 3D extraction of inner and outer surfaces of cerebral cortex from MRI. *Neuroimage, 12,* 340–356.

Maciejewski, P. K., Zhang, B., Block, S. D., & Prigerson, H. G. (2007). An empirical examination of the stage theory of grief. *The Journal of the American Medical Association, 297*(7), 716–723. doi:10.1001/jama.297.7.716

Mack, J. E. (1994). *Abduction.* New York: Scribner.

MacKenzie, S. B., Lutz, R. J., & Belch, G. E. (1986, May). The role of attitude toward the ad as a mediator of advertising effectiveness: A test of competing explanations. *Journal of Marketing Research, 23,* 130–143.

Macknik, S. L., King, M., Randi, J., Robbins, A., Teller, Thompson, J., et al. (2008). Attention and awareness in stage magic: Turning tricks into research. *Nature Reviews: Neuroscience, 9*(11), 871–879.

Macknik, S. L., & Martinez-Conde, S. (2009). Real magic: Future studies of magic should be grounded in neuroscience. *Nature Reviews: Neuroscience, 10*(3), 241–241.

Macquet, P., & Franck, G. (1996). Functional neuroanatomy of human rapid eye movement sleep and dreaming. *Nature, 383,* 163–166.

Macrae, C. N., & Bodenhausen, G. V. (2000). Social cognition: Thinking categorically about others. *Annual Review of Psychology, 51,* 93–120.

Madsen, K. M., Hviid, A., Vestergaard, M., Schendel, D., Wohlfahrt, J., Thorsen, P., et al. (2002). A population-based study of measles, mumps, rubella vaccine and autism. *New England Journal of Medicine, 347,* 1477–1482.

Mahoney, M. J. (2005). Constructivism and positive psychology. In C. R. Snyder & S. J. Lopez (Eds.), *Handbook of positive psychology* (pp. 745–750). New York: Oxford University Press.

Mahowald, M. W., & Schenck, C. H. (1996). NREM sleep parasomnias. *Neurologic Clinics, 14,* 675–696.

Maier, S. F., Amat, J., Baratta, M. V., Paul, E., & Watkins, L. R. (2006). Behavioral control, the medial prefrontal cortex, and resilience. *Dialogues in Clinical Neuroscience, 8*(4), 397–406.

Maier, S. F., & Watkins, L. R. (2005). Stressor controllability and learned helplessness: The roles of the dorsal raphe nucleus, serotonin, and corticotropin-releasing factor. *Neuroscience and Biobehavioral Reviews*, 29(4–5), 829–841.

Main, M., & Cassidy, J. (1988). Categories of response to reunion with the parent at age 6: Predictable from infant attachment classifications and stable over a 1 month period. *Developmental Psychology*, 24, 415–426.

Main, M., & Hesse, E. (1990). Parents' unresolved traumatic experiences are related to infant disorganized attachment status; is frightened and/or frightening parental behaviour the linking mechanism? In M. T. Greenberg, D. Cicchetti, & E. M. Cummings (Eds.), *Attachment in the preschool years: Theory, research and intervention* (pp. 161–182). Chicago: University of Chicago Press.

Main, M., & Solomon, J. (1990). Procedures for identifying infants as disorganized/disoriented during the Ainsworth Strange Situation. In M. T. Greenberg, D. Cicchetti, & E. M. Cummings (Eds.), *Attachment in the preschool years: Theory, research and intervention* (pp. 121–160). Chicago: University of Chicago Press.

Maletic, V., Robinson, M., Oakes, T., Iyengar, S., Ball, S. G., & Russell, J. (2007). Neurobiology of depression: An integrated view of key findings. *The International Journal of Clinical Practice*, 61(12), 2030–2040.

Mandler, G. (1967). Organization and memory. In K. W. Spence & J. T. Spence (Eds.), *The psychology of learning and motivation, Vol. 1* (pp. 327–372). New York: Academic Press.

Mangalindan, J. P. (2012). *Google: The king of perks—CNN Money*. Retrieved May 30, 2013, from http://money.cnn.com/galleries/2012/technology/1201/gallery.best-companies-google-perks.fortune/index.html

Manning, R., Levine, M., & Collins, A. (2007). The Kitty Genovese murder and the social psychology of helping: The parable of the 38 witnesses. *American Psychologist*, 62(6), 555-562. doi:10.1037/0003-066X.62.6.555

Manusov, V., & Patterson, M. L. (Eds.). (2006). *The Sage handbook of nonverbal communication* (p. 289). Thousand Oaks, CA: Sage.

Marcus, G. F. (2001). *The algebraic mind: Integrating connectionism and cognitive science (learning, development, and conceptual change)*. Cambridge, MA: MIT Press.

March of Dimes Foundation, 2009. Organization of Teratology Information Specialists, 2011.

Maren, S., & Fanselow, M. S. (1996). The amygdala and fear conditioning: Has the nut been cracked? *Neuron, 16*, 237–240.

Margolin, S., & Kubic, L. S. (1944). An apparatus for the use of breath sounds as a hypnogogic stimulus. *American Journal of Psychiatry, 100*, 610.

Marik, P. E. (2000). Leptin, obesity, and obstructive sleep apnea. *Chest, 118*, 569–571.

Markovitz, J. H., Lewis, C. E., Sanders, P. W., Tucker, D., & Warnock, D. G. (1997). Relationship of diastolic blood pressure with cyclic GMP excretion among young adults (the CARDIA study): Influence of a family history of hypertension. *Journal of Hypertension, 15*(9), 955–962.

Marks, K. (2010, May 16). Round-the-world teenage sailor Jessica Watson gets hero's welcome in Australia. *The Christian Science Monitor*. Retrieved June 27, 2010, from http://www.csmonitor.com/World/Asia-Pacific/2010/0516/Round-the-world-teenage-sailor-Jessica-Watson-gets-hero-s-welcome-in-Australia

Mars, A. E., Mauk, J. E., & Dowrick, P. (1998). Symptoms of pervasive developmental disorders as observed in prediagnostic home videos of infants and toddlers. *Journal of Pediatrics, 132*, 500–504.

Martin, C. L. (2000). Cognitive theories of gender development. In T. Eckes & H. M. Trautner (Eds.), *The developmental social psychology of gender* (pp. 91–121). Mahwah, NJ: Lawrence Erlbaum.

Martin, J. A., & Buckwalter, J. J. (2001). Telomere erosion and senescence in human articular cartilage chondrocytes. *Journal of Gerontology and Biological Science, 56*(4), 172–179.

Martinussen, R., Hayden, J., Hogg-Johnson, S., & Tannock, R. (2005). A metaanalysis of working memory components in children with Attention-Deficit/Hyperactivity Disorder. *Journal of the American Academy of Child & Adolescent Psychiatry, 44*(4), 377–384.

Martyn, A. C., De Jaeger, X., Magalhaes, A. C., Kesarwani, R., Goncalves, D. F., Raulic, S., et al. (2012). Elimination of the vesicular acetylcholine transporter in the forebrain causes hyperactivity and deficits in spatial memory and long-term potentiation. *Proceedings of the National Academy of Sciences, 109*(43), 17651–17656. doi:10.1073/pnas.1215381109

Maruta, T., Colligan, R. C., Malinchoc, M., & Offord, K. P. (2002, August). Optimism-pessimism assessed in the 1960s and self- reported health status 30 years later. *Mayo Clinic Proceedings, 77*, 748–753.

Maslow, A. (1943). A theory of human motivation. *Psychological Review, 50*, 370–396.

Maslow, A. (1954). *Motivation and personality*. New York: Harper & Row.

Maslow, A. (1971). *The farther reaches of human nature*. New York: Viking Press.

Maslow, A. (1987). *Motivation and personality* (3rd ed.). New York: Harper & Row.

Maslow, A., & Lowery, R. (Eds.). (1998). *Toward a psychology of being* (3rd ed.). New York: Wiley.

Massaro, D. W., & Cowan, N. (1993). Information processing models: Microscopes of the mind. *Annual Review of Psychology, 44*, 383–426.

Masson, J. M. (1984). *The assault on truth: Freud's suppression of the seduction theory*. New York: Farrar, Straus & Giroux.

Masters, J. C., Burish, T. G., Holton, S. D., & Rimm, D. C. (1987). *Behavior therapy: Techniques and empirical finding*. San Diego, CA: Harcourt Brace Jovanovich.

Masters, W. H., & Johnson, V. E. (1966). *Human sexual response*. Boston: Little, Brown.

Masuda, T., & Kitayama, S. (2004). Perceiver-induced constraint and attitude attribution in Japan and the U.S.: A case for the cultural dependence of the correspondence bias. *Journal of Experimental Social Psychology, 40*, 409–416.

Matsumoto, D. (1994). *People: Psychology from a cultural perspective* (pp. 144–147). Pacific Grove, CA: Brooks-Cole.

Matthew, N., & Dallery, J. (2007). Mercury rising: Exploring the vaccine-autism myth. *Skeptic, 13*(3). Retrieved May 3, 2010, from http://www.skeptic.com/eskeptic/07-06-20/#feature

Matthews, K. A., Gump, B. B., Harris, K. F., Haney, T. L., & Barefoot, J. C. (2004). Hostile behaviors predict cardiovascular mortality among men enrolled in the Multiple Risk Factor Intervention trial. *Circulation, 109*, 66–70.

Maurer, D., & Young, R. (1983). Newborns' following of natural and distorted arrangements of facial features. *Infant Behaviour and Development, 6*, 127–131.

Mavromatis, A. (1987). *Hypnagogia: The unique state of consciousness between wakefulness and sleep*. London: Routledge & Kegan Paul.

Mavromatis, A., & Richardson, J. T. E. (1984). Hypnagogic imagery. *International Review of Mental Imagery, 1*, 159–189.

Maxmen, J. S., Ward, N. G., & Kilgus, M. D. (2009). *Essential psychopathology and its treatment*. New York: W. W. Norton & Company.

Mayer, J. D., & Geher, G. (1996). Emotional intelligence and the identification of emotion. *Intelligence, 22*, 89–113.

Mayer, J. D., Roberts, R. D., & Barsade, S. G. (2008). Human abilities: Emotional intelligence. *Annual Review of Psychology, 59*(1), 507–536. doi:10.1146/annurev.psych.59.103006.093646

Mayer, J. D., & Salovey, P. (1997). What is emotional intelligence? In P. Salovey & D. Sluyter (Eds.), *Emotional development and emotional intelligence: Educational implications* (pp. 3–31). New York: Basic Books.

Mayer, J. D., Salovey, P., & Caruso, D. R. (2000). Models of emotional intelligence. In R. J. Sternberg (Ed.), *Handbook of human intelligence* (2nd ed., pp. 396–420). New York: Cambridge University Press.

Maziade, M., Bissonnette, L., Rouillard, E., Martinez, M., Turgeon, M., Charron, L., et al. (1997). 6P24-22 region and major psychoses in the Eastern Quebec population. *American Journal of Medical Genetics, 74*, 311–318.

Mazzoni, G. A. L., Loftus, E. F., & Kirsch, I. (2001). Changing beliefs about implausible autobiographical events: A little plausibility goes a long way. *Journal of Experimental Psychology: Applied, 7*(1), 51–59.

McAdams, D. P., & Olson, B. D. (2010). Personality development: Continuity and change over the life course. *Annual Review of Psychology, 61*, 517–542. doi:10.1146/annurev.psych.093008.100507

McBurney, D. H., Zapp, D., & Streeter, S. (2005). Preferred number of sexual partners: Tails of distributions and tales of mating systems. *Evolution and Human Behavior, 26*(3), 271–278.

McCann, S. J. H., & Stewin, L. L. (1988). Worry, anxiety, and preferred length of sleep. *Journal of Genetic Psychology, 149*, 413–418.

McCauley, C. (1998). Group dynamics in Janis's theory of groupthink: Backward and forward. *Organizational Behavior and Human Decision Processes, 73*(2–3), 142–162.

McClelland, D. C. (1961). *The achieving society*. Princeton, NJ: Van Nostrand.

McClelland, D. C. (1987). *Human motivation*. Cambridge, MA: Cambridge University Press.

McClelland, J. L., & Rumelhart, D. E. (1988). *Explorations in parallel distributed processing*. Cambridge, MA: MIT Press.

McConaghy, N., Hadzi-Pavlovic, D., Stevens, C., Manicavasagar, V., Buhrich, N., & Vollmer-Conna, U. (2006). Fraternal birth order and ratio of heterosexual/homosexual feelings in women and men. *Journal of Homosexuality, 51*(4), 161–174.

McCrae, R. R., & Costa, P. T., Jr. (1996). Toward a new generation of personality theories: Theoretical contexts for the five-factor model. In J. S. Wiggins (Ed.), *The five-factor model of personality: Theoretical perspectives* (pp. 51–87). New York: Guilford Press.

McCrae, R. R., Martin, T. A., & Costa, P. T., Jr. (2005). Age trends and age norms for the NEO Personality Inventory-3 in adolescents and adults. *Assessment, 12*(4), 363–373. doi:10.1177/1073191105279724

McCrae, R. R., & Terracciano, A. (2005). Universal features of personality traits from the observer's perspective: Data from 50 cultures. *Journal of Personality and Social Psychology, 88*(3), 547–561. doi:10.1037/0022-3514.88.3.547

McCrae, R. R., Terracciano, A., & 78 Members of the Personality Profiles of Cultures Project. (2005). Universal features of personality traits from the observer's perspective: Data from 50 cultures. *Journal of Personality and Social Psychology, 88*, 547–561.

McDaniel, M. A., Howard, D. C., & Einstein, G. O. (2009). The read-recite-review study strategy: Effective and portable. *Psychological Science, 20*(4), 516–522.

McDermott, J. F. (2001). Emily Dickinson revisited: A study of periodicity in her work. *American Journal of Psychiatry, 158*(5), 686–690.

McDougall, T. (2009). Nursing children and adolescents with bipolar disorder. *Journal of Child and Adolescent Psychiatric Nursing, 22*, 33–39.

McDougall, W. (1908). *An introduction to social psychology*. London: Methuen & Co.

McGaugh, J. L. (2004). The amygdala modulates the consolidation of memories of emotionally arousing experiences. *Annual Review Neuroscience, 27*, 1–28.

McGinn, L. K. (2000). Cognitive behavioral therapy of depression: Theory, treatment, and empirical status. *American Journal of Psychotherapy, 54,* 254–260.

McGinnis, J. M., & Foege, W. H. (1993). Actual causes of death in the United States. *Journal of the American Medical Association, 270*(18), 2207–2212.

McGrath, E., Keita, G. P., Strickland, B. R., & Russo, N. F. (1992). *Women and depression: Risk factors and treatment issues.* Washington, DC: American Psychological Association.

McGrath, R. E., & Carroll, E. J. (2012). The current status of "projective" "tests". In H. Cooper, P. M. Camic, D. L. Long, A. T. Panter, D. Rindskopf, & K. J. Sher (Eds.), *APA handbook of research methods in psychology, Vol 1: Foundations, planning, measures, and psychometrics* (pp. 329–348). Washington, DC: American Psychological Association.

McGregor, D. (1960). *The human side of enterprise.* New York: McGraw-Hill.

McGuire, F. (1994). Army alpha and beta tests of intelligence. In R. J. Sternberg (Ed.), *Encyclopedia of intelligence* (Vol. 1, pp. 125–129). New York: Macmillan.

McLaughlin, S. K., & Margolskee, R. F. (1994). Vertebrate taste transduction. *American Scientist, 82,* 538–545.

McMahon, F. J., Akula, N., Schulze, T. G., Muglia, P., Tozzi, F., Detera-Wadleigh, S. D., et al. (2010). Meta-analysis of genome-wide association data identifies a risk locus for major mood disorders on 3p21.1. *Nature Genetics, 42*(2), 128–131. doi:10.1038/ng.523

McMonagle, T., & Sultana, A. (2002). Token economy for schizophrenia (Cochrane Review). In *The Cochrane library, issue 2.* Oxford: Update Software.

McPherson, J. M., Smith-Lovin, L., & Cook, J. M. (2001). Birds of a feather: Homophily in social networks. *Annual Review of Sociology, 27,* 415–444.

Meador, B. D., & Rogers, C. R. (1984). Person-centered therapy. In R. J. Corsini (Ed.), *Current psychotherapies* (3rd ed., pp. 142–195). Itasca, IL: Peacock.

Medical Economics Staff. (1994). *PDR family guide to women's health & prescription drugs.* Montvale, NJ: Medical Economics Company.

Mehrabian, A. (2000). Beyond IQ: Broad-based measurement of individual success potential or "emotional intelligence." *Genetic, Social, and General Psychology Monographs, 126,* 133–239.

Meikle, J., & Boseley, S. (2010, May 24). MMR row doctor Andrew Wakefield struck off register. *The Guardian* (London). Retrieved April 26, 2013, from http://www.guardian.co.uk/society/2010/may/24/mmr-doctor-andrew-wakefield-struck-off;

Meineri, S., & Guéguen, N. (2008). An application of the foot- in-the-door strategy in the environmental field. *European Journal of Social Sciences, 7,* 71–74.

Mejía, O. L., & McCarthy, C. J. (2010). Acculturative stress, depression, and anxiety in migrant farmwork college students of Mexican heritage. *International Journal of Stress Management, 17*(1), 1–20.

Melzack, R., & Wall, P. D. (1996). *The challenge of pain.* London: Penguin Books.

Mennella, J. A., & Trabulsi, J. C. (2012). Complementary foods and flavor experiences: Setting the foundation. *Annals of nutrition & metabolism, 60*(Suppl. 2), 40–50. doi:10.1159/000335337

Mental health: Does psychotherapy help? (1995, November). *Consumer Reports, 60,* 734–739.

Merikle, M. P. (2000). Subliminal perception. In A. E. Kazdin (Ed.), *Encyclopedia of psychology* (Vol. 7, pp. 497–499). New York: Oxford University Press.

Mervis, C. B., & Rosch, E. (1981). Categorization of natural objects. *Annual Review of Psychology, 32,* 89–115.

Mesgarani, N., & Chang, E. F. (2012). Selective cortical representation of attended speaker in multi-talker speech perception. *Nature, 485,* 233–236. doi:10.1038/nature11020

Meyer, G. J., & Kurtz, J. E. (2006). Advancing personality assessment terminology: Time to retire 'objective' and 'projective' as personality test descriptors. *Journal of Personality Assessment, 87*(3), 223–225.

Meyrick, J. (2001). Forget the blood and gore: An alternative message strategy to help adolescents avoid cigarette smoking. *Health Education, 101*(3), 99–107.

Michalski, D., Mulvey, T., & Kohoout, J. (2010). *2008 American Psychological Association survey of psychology health service providers.* Retrieved April 5, 2010, from http://www.apa.org/workforce/publications/08-hsp/report.pdf

Mikami, A. Y., Szwedo, D. E., Allen, J. P., Evans, M. A., & Hare, A. L. (2010). Adolescent peer relationships and behavior problems predict young adults' communication on social networking websites. *Developmental Psychology, 46,* 46–56.

Miles, D. R., & Carey, G. (1997). Genetic and environmental architecture of human aggression. *Journal of Personality and Social Psychology, 72,* 207–217.

Milgram, S. (1963). Behavioral study of obedience. *Journal of Abnormal and Social Psychology, 67,* 371–378. doi:10.1037/h0040525

Milgram, S. (1964b). Issues in the study of obedience: A reply to Baumrind. *American Psychologist, 19,* 848–852.

Milgram, S. (1974). *Obedience to authority: An experimental view.* New York: Harper & Row.

Miller, J. G. (1984). Culture and the development of everyday social explanation. *Journal of Personality and Social Psychology, 46,* 961–978.

Miller, K., & Doman, J. M. R. (1996, April). Together forever. *Life Magazine,* 46–56.

Miller, K. E., & Graves, J. C. (2000). Update on the prevention and treatment of sexually transmitted diseases. *American Family Physician, 61,* 379–386.

Miller, M. E., & Bowers, K. S. (1993). Hypnotic analgesia: Dissociated experience or dissociated control? *Journal of Abnormal Psychology, 102,* 29–38.

Miller, M. N., & Pumariega, A. (1999). Culture and eating disorders. *Psychiatric Times, 16*(2), 1–4.

Miller, N. E., Sears, R. R., Mowrer, O. H., Doob, L. W., & Dollard, J. (1941). The frustration-aggression hypothesis. *Psychological Review, 48,* 337–342.

Miller, T. Q., Smith, T. W., Turner, C. W., Guijarro, M. L., & Hallet, A. J. (1996). A meta-analytic review of research on hostility and physical health. *Psychological Bulletin, 119,* 322–348.

Miller, T. Q., Turner, C. W., Tindale, R. S., Posavac, E. J., & Dugoni, B. L. (1991). Reasons for the trend toward null findings in research on type A behavior. *Psychological Bulletin, 110,* 469–485.

Miller, W. R., & Rollnick, S. (2002). *Motivational interviewing: Preparing people for change* (2nd ed.). New York: Guilford Press.

Mills, M. A., Edmondson, D., & Park, C. L. (2007). Trauma and stress response among Hurricane Katrina evacuees. *American Journal of Public Health, 97*(1), 116–123.

Milner, B., Corkin, S., & Teuber, H. L. (1968). Further analysis of the hippocampal syndrome: 14-year follow-up study of H. M. *Neuropsychologia, 6,* 215–234.

Milner, J. (1992, January). Risk for physical child abuse: Adult factors. *Violence Update,* 9–11.

Mintz, L. B., & Betz, N. E. (1988). Prevalence and correlates of eating disordered behaviors among undergraduate women. *Journal of Counseling Psychology, 35,* 463–471.

Mischel, W. (1966). A social learning view of sex differences in behaviour. In E. E. Maccoby (Ed.), *The development of sex differences* (pp. 56–81). Stanford, CA: Stanford University Press.

Mischel, W., & Shoda, Y. (1995). A cognitive-affective system theory of personality: Reconceptualizing situations, dispositions, dynamics, and invariances in personality structure. *Psychological Review, 102,* 246–268.

Mishell, D. R. (2001). Menopause. In M. A. Stenchever et al. (Eds.), *Comprehensive gynecology* (4th ed., pp. 1217–1258). St. Louis, MO: Mosby.

Missonnier, P., Hasler, R., Perroud, N., Herrmann, F. R., Millet, P., Richiardi, J., et al. (2013). EEG anomalies in adult ADHD subjects performing a working memory task. *Neuroscience.* doi:10.1016/j.neuroscience.2013.03.011

Mitchell, J. E., Pyle, R. L., & Eckert, E. D. (1981). Frequency and duration of binge-eating episodes in patients with bulimia. *American Journal of Psychiatry, 138,* 835–836.

Mitchell, J. E., Roerig, J., & Steffen, K. (2013). Biological therapies for eating disorders. *International Journal of Eating Disorders, 46*(5), 470–477. doi:10.1002/eat.22104

Mitchell, S. A., & Black, M. J. (1996). *Freud and beyond: A history of modern psychoanalytic thought* [Reprint ed.]. New York: HarperCollins.

Miyatake, A., Morimoto, Y., Oishi, T., Hanasaki, N., Sugita, Y., Iijima, S., et al. (1980). Circadian rhythm of serum testosterone and its relation to sleep: Comparison with the variation in serum luteinizing hormone, prolactin, and cortisol in normal men. *Journal of Clinical Endocrinology and Metabolism, 51*(6), 1365–1371.

Moffic, H. S. (2003). Seven ways to improve "cultural competence." *Current Psychiatry, 2*(5), 78.

Mogil, J. S. (1999). The genetic mediation of individual differences in sensitivity to pain and its inhibition. *Proceedings of the National Academy of Sciences, USA, 96*(14), 7744–7751.

Mokdad, A. H., Bowman, B. A., Ford, E. S., Dietz, W. H., Vinicor, F., Bales, V. S., et al. (2001). Prevalence of obesity, diabetes, and obesity related health risk factors. *Journal of the American Medical Association, 289,* 76–79.

Moll, H., & Tomasello, M. (2007). How 14- and 18-month-olds know what others have experienced. *Developmental Psychology, 43,* 309–317.

Möller, A., & Hell, D. (2002). Eugen Bleuler and forensic psychiatry. *International Journal of Law and Psychiatry, 25,* 351–360.

Money, J. (1994). *Sex errors of the body and related syndromes.* Baltimore: Paul H. Brookes.

Monson, C. M., Resick, P. A., & Rizvi, S. L. (2014). Posttraumatic stress disorder. In D. H. Barlow (Ed.), *Clinical handbook of psychological disorders: A step-by-step treatment manual* (5th ed., pp. 62–113). New York: Guilford Press.

Montgomery, C., & Fisk, J. E. (2008). Ecstasy-related deficits in the updating component of executive processes. *Human Psychopharmacology, 23*(6), 495–511.

Moody, R., & Perry, P. (1993). *Reunions: Visionary encounters with departed loved ones.* London: Little, Brown.

Moore, T. E. (1988). The case against subliminal manipulation. *Psychology and Marketing, 5,* 297–316.

Moore, T. H., Zammit, S., Lingford-Hughes, A., Barnes, T. R., Jones, P. B., Burke, M., et al. (2007). Cannabis use and risk of psychotic or affective mental health outcomes: A systematic review. *Lancet, 370,* 293–294, 319–328.

Moore-Ede, M. C., Sulzman, F. M., & Fuller, C. A. (1982). *The clocks that time us.* Cambridge, MA: Harvard University Press.

Moorhead, G., Neck, C. P., & West, M. S. (1998). The tendency toward defective decision making within self-managing teams: The relevance of groupthink for the 21st century. *Organizational Behavior and Human Decision Processes, 73*(2–3), 327–351.

Mora, G. (1985). History of psychiatry. In H. I. Kaplan & B. J. Sadock (Eds.), *Comprehensive textbook of psychiatry* (pp. 2034–2054). Baltimore: Williams & Wilkins.

Moreland, R. L., & Zajonc, R. B. (1982). Exposure effects in person perceptions: Familiarity, similarity, and attraction. *Journal of Experimental Social Psychology, 18*(5), 395–415.

Moreno-Manzano, V., Rodriguez-Jimenez, F. J., Acena-Bonilla, J. L., Fustero-Lardies, S., Erceg, S., Dopazo, J., et al. (2009). FM19G11, a new HIF modulator, affects stem cell differentiation status. *Journal of Biological Chemistry, 285*(2), 1333–1342.

Morgan, C. A., Rasmusson, A., Pietrzak, R. H., Coric, V., & Southwick, S. M. (2009). Relationships among plasma dehydroepiandrosterone and dehydroepiandrosterone sulfate, cortisol, symptoms of dissociation, and objective performance in humans exposed to underwater navigation stress. *Biological Psychiatry, 66*(4), 334–340.

Morgan, C. D., & Murray, H. A. (1935). A method for investigating fantasies: The Thematic Apperception Test. *Archives of Neurology and Psychiatry, 34,* 298–306.

Morris, J. S., Friston, K. J., Buche, L. C., Frith, C. D., Young, A. W., Calder, A. J., et al. (1998). A neuromodulatory role for the human amygdala in processing emotional facial expressions. *Brain, 121,* 47–57.

Morris, M., Nisbett, R. E., & Peng, K. (1995). Causal understanding across domains and cultures. In D. Sperber, D. Premack, & A. J. Premack (Eds.), *Causal cognition: A multidisciplinary debate* (pp. 577–612). Oxford, UK: Oxford University Press.

Morris, M. W., & Peng, K. (1994). Culture and cause: American and Chinese attributions social and physical events. *Journal of Personality and Social Psychology, 67,* 949–971.

Morishima, Y., Schunk, D., Bruhin, A., Ruff, C. C., & Fehr, E. (2012). Linking brain structure and activation in temporoparietal junction to explain the neurobiology of human altruism. *Neuron, 75*(1), 73–79. doi: 10.1016/j.neuron.2012.05.021

Morrow, C. E., Culbertson, J. L., Accornero, V. H., Xue, L., Anthony, J. C., & Bandstra, E. S. (2006). Learning disabilities and intellectual functioning in school-aged children with prenatal cocaine exposure. *Developmental Neuropsychology, 30*(3), 905–931.

Moruzzi, G., & Magoun, H. W. (1949). Brainstem reticular formation and activation of the EEG. *Electroencephalographs in Clinical Neurophysiology, 1,* 455–473.

Mosher, W. D., Chandra, A., & Jones, J. (2005). *Sexual behavior and selected health measures: Men and women 15–44 years of age, United States, 2002* (Advance data from vital and health statistics; no 362). Hyattsville, MD: National Center for Health Statistics.

Mosing, M. A., Medland, S. E., McRae, A., Landers, J. G., Wright, M. J., & Martin, N. G. (2012). Genetic influences on life span and its relationship to personality: A 16-year follow-up study of a sample of aging twins. *Psychosomatic Medicine, 74*(1), 16–22. doi: 10.1097/PSY.0b013e3182385784

Motraghi, T. E., Seim, R. W., Meyer, E. C., & Morissette, S. B. (2013). Virtual reality exposure therapy for the treatment of posttraumatic stress disorder: A methodological review using consort guidelines. *Journal of Clinical Psychology.* doi:10.1002/jclp.22051

Mowat, F. (1988). *Woman in the mists: The story of Dian Fossey and the mountain gorillas of Africa.* New York: Warner Books.

Mroczek, D. K., Spiro, A., & Turiano, N. A. (2009). Do health behaviors explain the effect of neuroticism on mortality? Longitudinal findings from the VA Normative Aging Study. *Journal of Research in Personality, 43*(4), 653.

Mufson, L. H., Dorta, K. P., Olfson, M., Weissman, M. M., & Hoagwood, K. (2004). Effectiveness research: Transporting interpersonal psychotherapy for depressed adolescents (IPT-A) from the lab to school-based health clinics. *Clinical Child and Family Psychology Review, 7*(4), 251–261.

Mukamel, R., Ekstrom, A. D., Kaplan, J., Iacoboni, M., & Fried, I. (2010). Single-neuron responses in humans during execution and observation of actions. *Current Biology, 20,* 750–756.

Muller-Oerlinghausen, B., Berghofer, A., & Bauer, M. (2002). Bipolar disorder. *Lancet, 359,* 241–247.

Mueller, P. A., & Oppenheimer, D. M. (2014). The pen is mightier than the keyboard: Advantages of longhand over laptop note taking. *Psychological Science.* doi: 10.1177/0956797614524581

Munoz, D. (2010, May 15). Australian teenager finishes round-world solo sail. *Reuters.* Retrieved May 15, 2010, from http://www. reuters.com/article/idUS-TRE64E0D920100515

Münsterberg, H. (1913). *Psychology and industrial efficiency.* Boston: Houghton Mifflin.

Murdock, B. B., Jr. (1962). The serial position effect in free recall. *Journal of Experimental Psychology, 64,* 482–488.

Murphy, C. C., Boyle, C., Schendel, D., Decouflé, P., & Yeargin- Allsopp, M. (1998). Epidemiology of mental retardation in children. *Mental Retardation and Developmental Disabilities Research Reviews, 4,* 6–13.

Murphy, L. R. (1995). Managing job stress: An employee assistance/human resource management partnership. *Personnel Review, 24*(1), 41–50.

Murray, S. L., Holmes, J. G., MacDonald, G., & Ellsworth, P. C. (1998). Through the looking glass darkly? When self-doubts turn into relationship insecurities. *Journal of Personality and Social Psychology, 75,* 1459–1480.

Nadeau, K. G., Quinn, P., & Littman, E. (2001). *AD/HD self-rating scale for girls.* Springfield, MD: Advantage Books.

Najavits, L. M. (2007). Psychosocial treatments for postraumatic stress disorder. In P. E. Nathan & J. M. Gorman (Eds.), *A guide to treatments that work* (3rd ed., pp. 513–530). New York: Oxford University Press.

Nasar, S. (1998). *A beautiful mind: A biography of John Forbes Nash, Jr., winner of the Nobel Prize in economics 1994.* New York: Simon & Schuster.

Nathan, P. E., & Gorman, J. M. (2007). *Psychosocial treatments for posttraumatic stress disorder* (3rd ed.). New York: Oxford University Press.

National Academy of Neuropsychology. (2001, May). *NAN definition of a clinical neuropsychologist* [Electronic version]. Retrieved April 13, 2010, from http://www.nanonline.org/NAN/Files/PAIC/PDFs/NANPositionDefNeuro.pdf

National Commission for the Protection of Human Subjects of Biomedical and Behavioral Research. (2006). *Fetal viability and death: United States.* Retrieved April 26, 2013, from https://scholarworks.iupui.edu/bitstream/handle/1805/583/OS76-127_VII.pdf?sequence=1

National Institute of Mental Health. (2008). *Suicide in the U.S.: Statistics and Prevention* (NIH Publication No. 06-4594). Retrieved from http://www.nimh.nih.gov/health/publications/suicide-in-the-us-statistics-and-prevention/index.shtml

National Institute of Mental Health (NIMH). (2010). *The numbers count: Mental disorders in America.* Retrieved from http://www.nimh.nih.gov/health/publications/the-numbers-count-mental-disorders-in-america/index.shtml

National Institute of Mental Health. (2013). *Statistics.* Retrieved May 14, 2013, from http://www.nimh.nih.gov/statistics/index.shtml

National Institute of Mental Health (NIMH) Genetics Workgroup. (1998). *Genetics and mental disorders* (NIH Publication No. 98-4268). Rockville, MD: National Institute of Mental Health.

National Institute on Alcoholism and Alcohol Abuse (NIAAA). (2007). *Data/statistical tables.* Retrieved July 25, 2007, from http://www.niaaa.nih.gov/Resources/DatabaseResources/QuickFacts/default.htm

National Institute on Drug Abuse (NIDA). (2006, May). *NIDA Infofacts: MDMA (Ecstasy).* Retrieved May 5, 2010, from http://www.nida.nih.gov/Infofacts/ecstasy.html

National Safety Council. (2010). *National safety council estimates that at least 1.6 million crashes are caused each year by drivers using cell phones and texting.* Retrieved June 5, 2011, from http://www.nsc.org/Pages/NSCestimates16millioncrashescausedbydriversusingcellphonesandtexting.aspx

Neale, M. C., Rushton, J. P., & Fulker, D. W. (1986). The heritability of items from the Eysenck Personality Questionnaire. *Personality and Individual Differences, 7,* 771–779.

Neary, N. M., Goldstone, A. P., & Bloom, S. R. (2004). Appetite regulations: From the gut to the hypothalamus. *Clinical Endocrinology, 60*(2), 153–160.

Nielsen, M., Suddendorf, T., & Slaughter, V. (2006). Mirror self-recognition beyond the face. *Child Development, 77,* 176-185

Neimark, J. (1996). The diva of disclosure, memory researcher Elizabeth Loftus. *Psychology Today, 29*(1), 48–80.

Neimeyer, R. A., & Mitchell, K. A. (1998). Similarity and attraction: A longitudinal study. *Journal of Social and Personality Relationships, 5,* 131–148.

Neisser, U. (1982). Snapshots or benchmarks? In U. Neisser (Ed.), *Memory observed: Remembering in natural contexts* (pp. 43–48). San Francisco: W. H. Freeman.

Neisser, U., & Harsch, N. (1992). Phantom flashbulbs: False recollections of hearing the news about challenger. In E. Winograd & U. Neisser (Eds.), *Affect and accuracy in recall: Studies of "flashbulb memories"* (pp. 9–31). New York: Cambridge University Press.

Nelson, C. A. (2011). Brain development and behavior. In A. M. Rudolph, C. Rudolph, L. First, G. Lister, & A. A. Gershon (Eds.), *Rudolph's pediatrics* (22nd ed.). New York: McGraw-Hill.

Nelson, D. B., Sammel, M. D., Freeman, E. W., Lin, H., Gracia, C. R., & Schmitz, K. H. (2008). Effect of physical activity on menopausal symptoms among urban women. *Medicine and Science in Sports & Exercise, 40*(1), 50–58.

Nelson, K. (1993). The psychological and social origins of autobiographical memory. *Psychological Science, 4,* 7–14.

Nestor, P. G., Kubicki, M., Niznikiewicz, M., Gurrera, R. J., McCarley, R. W., & Shenton, M. E. (2008). Neuropsychological disturbance in schizophrenia: A diffusion tensor imaging study. *Neuropsychology, 22*(2), 246–254.

Neto, F. (1995). Conformity and independence revisited. *Social Behavior and Personality, 23*(3), 217–222.

Neumarker, K. (1997). Mortality and sudden death in anorexia nervosa. *International Journal of Eating Disorders, 21,* 205–212.

Neville, H. J., & Bavelier, D. (2000). Specificity and plasticity in neurocognitive development in humans. In M. S. Gazzaniga (Ed.), *The new cognitive neurosciences* (2nd ed., pp. 83–99). Cambridge, MA: MIT Press.

Nicholson, N., Cole, S., & Rocklin, T. (1985). Conformity in the Asch situation: A comparison between contemporary British and U.S. students. *British Journal of Social Psychology, 24,* 59–63.

Nickell, J. (1995). Crop circle mania wanes: An investigative update. *Skeptical Inquirer, 19*(3), 41–43.

Nickerson, R. S., & Adams, J. J. (1979). Long-term memory for a common object. *Cognitive Psychology, 11,* 287–307.

Niedermeyer, E. (2005). Historical aspects. In E. Niedermeyer & F. Lopes da Silva (Eds.), *Electroencephalography: Basic principles, clinical applications, and related fields* (5th ed., pp. 1–15). Philadelphia: Lippincott, Williams & Wilkins.

Nieto, F., Young, T. B., Lind, B. K., Shahar, E., Samet, J. M., Redline, S., et al. (2000). Association of sleep-disordered breathing, sleep apnea, and hypertension in a large, community-based study. *Journal of the American Medical Association, 283*(14), 1829–1836.

Nigg, J. T. (2006). *What causes ADHD? Understanding what goes wrong and why.* New York: Guilford Press.

Nigg, J. T. (2010). Attention-Deficit/Hyperactivity Disorder: Endophenotypes, structure, and etiological pathways. *Current Directions in Psychological Science, 19*(1), 24–29.

Nijenhuis, E. R. (2000). Somatoform dissociation: Major symptoms of dissociative disorders. *Journal of Trauma and Dissociation, 1*(4), 7–29.

Nikolajsen, L., & Jensen, T. S. (2001). Phantom limb pain. *British Journal of Anaesthesia, 87,* 107–116.

Nisbett, R. E., Aronson, J., Blair, C., Dickens, W., Flynn, J., Halpern, D. F., et al. (2012). Intelligence: New findings and theoretical developments. *American Psychologist, 67*(2), 130–159.

Nitsche, M. A., Boggio, P. S., Fregni, F., & Pascual-Leone, A. (2009). Treatment of depression with transcranial direct current stimulation (tDCS): A review. *Experimental Neurology, 219*(1), 14–19.

Nolen-Hoeksema, S. (1990). *Sex differences in depression.* Palo Alto, CA: Stanford University Press.

Nolen-Hoeksema, S. (2012). Emotion regulation and psychopathology: The role of gender. *Annual Review of Clinical Psychology, 8,* 161–187. doi:10.1146/annurevclinpsy-032511-143109

Norcross, J. C. (2005). A primer on psychotherapy integration. In J. C. Norcross & M. R. Goldfried (Eds.), *Handbook of psychotherapy integration* (2nd ed., pp. 3–23). New York: Oxford University Press.

Nordenskjold, A., von Knorring, L., & Engstrom, I. (2011). Predictors of time to relapse/recurrence after electroconvulsive therapy in patients with major depressive disorder: A population-based cohort study. *Depression Research and Treatment,* Article ID 470985. doi:10.1155/2011/470985

Norenzayan, A., Choi, I., & Nisbett, R. E. (1999). Eastern and Western perceptions of causality for social behavior: Lay theories about personalities and situations. In D. A. Prentice & D. T. Miller (Eds.), *Cultural divides* (pp. 239–272). New York: Russell Sage Foundation.

Norrbrink Budh, C., Lund, I., Hultling, C., Levi, R., Werhagen, L., Ertzgaard, P., et al. (2003). Gender-related differences in pain in spinal cord injured individuals. *Spinal Cord, 41,* 122–128.

Nosek, B. A., Greenwald, A. G., & Banaji, M. R. (2007). The Implicit Association Test at age 7: A methodological and conceptual review. In J. A. Bargh (Ed.), *Automatic processes in social thinking and behavior* (pp. 265–292). New York: Psychology Press.

Nosich, G. M. (2008). *Learning to think things through: A guide to critical thinking across the curriculum* (3rd ed., pp. 2–16). Upper Saddle River, NJ: Prentice-Hall.

Novak, J. D. (1995). Concept mapping: A strategy for organizing knowledge. In S. M. Glynn & R. Duit (Eds.), *Learning science in the schools: Research reforming practice* (pp. 229–245). Mahwah, NJ: Lawrence Erlbaum Associates.

Novak, M., Bjorck, L., Giang, K. W., Heden-Stahl, C., Wilhelmsen, L., & Rosengren, A. (2013). Perceived stress and incidence of Type 2 diabetes: A 35-year follow-up study of middle-aged Swedish men. *Diabetic Medicine, 30*(1), e8. doi:10-1111/dme.12037

Novella, S. (2007, November–December). The anti-vaccination movement. *Skeptical Inquirer.* Retrieved May 21, 2010, from http://www.csicop.org/si/show/anti-vaccination_movement/www.guardian.co.uk/science/2007/feb/24/badscience.uknews

Novotney, A. (2013, March). I/O psychology goes to Mars. *Monitor on Psychology, 44*(3), 38.

Nyberg, L., & Tulving, E. (1996). Classifying human long-term memory: Evidence from converging dissociations. *European Journal of Cognitive Psychology, 8*(2), 163–183.

Oberman, L. M., & Ramachandran, V. S. (2007). The simulating social mind: The role of simulation in the social and communicative deficits of autism spectrum disorders. *Psychological Bulletin, 133,* 310–327.

Ocholla-Ayayo, A. B. C., Wekesa, J. M., & Ottieno, J. A. M. (1993). *Adolescent pregnancy and its implications among ethnic groups in Kenya* (Vol. 1, pp. 381–395). In International Population Conference, Montreal, Canada, International Union for the Scientific Study of Population.

Ochsner, K., & Kosslyn, S. M. (1994). Mental imagery. In V. S. Ramaschandran (Ed.), *Encyclopedia of human behavior.* New York: Academic Press.

O'Connor, R. D. (1972). Relative efficacy of modeling, shaping, and the combined procedures for modification of social withdrawal. *Journal of Abnormal Psychology, 79,* 327–334.

Ohayon, M. M., Priest, R. G., Caulet, M., & Guilleminault, C. (1996). Hypnagogic and hypnopompic hallucinations: pathological phenomena? *British Journal of Psychiatry,169,* 459–467.

Öhman, A. (2008). Fear and anxiety. In M. Lewis, J. M. Haviland-Jones, & L. F. Barrett (Eds.), *Handbook of emotion* (3rd ed., pp. 709–729). New York: Guilford Press.

Okami, P., & Shackelford, T. K. (2001). Human sex differences in sexual psychology and behavior. *Annual Review of Sex Research, 12,* 186–241.

Olin, B. R. (Ed.). (1993). Central nervous system drugs, sedatives and hypnotics, barbiturates. In *Facts and comparisons drug information* (pp. 1398–1413). St. Louis, MO: Facts and Comparisons.

Oliver, J. E. (1993). Intergenerational transmission of child abuse: Rates, research, and clinical interpretations. *American Journal of Psychiatry, 150,* 1315–1324.

Ollendick, T. H., & King, N. J. (1998). Empirically supported treatments for children with phobic and anxiety disorders: Current status. *Journal of Clinical Child Psychology, 27*(2), 156–167.

Olsen, P. (1975). *Emotional flooding.* Baltimore: Penguin Books.

Olson, H. C., & Burgess, D. M. (1997). Early intervention for children prenatally exposed to alcohol and other drugs. In M. J. Guralnick (Ed.), *The effectiveness of early intervention* (pp. 109–146). Baltimore: Brookes.

Oman, C. M. (1990). Motion sickness: A synthesis and evaluation of the sensory conflict theory. *Canadian Journal of Physiological Pharmacology, 68,* 294–303.

Onken, L. S., Blaine, J. D., & Battjes, R. J. (1997). Behavioral therapy research: A conceptualization of a process. In S. W. Henggeler & A. B. Santos (Eds.), *Innovative approaches for difficult-to-treat populations* (pp. 477–485). Washington, DC: American Psychiatric Press.

Ophir, E., Nass, C., & Wagner, A. D. (2009). Cognitive control in media multitaskers. *Proceedings of the National Academy of Sciences of the United States of America, 106*(37), 15583–15587.

Osshera, L., Flegala, K. E., & Lustiga, C. (2012). Everyday memory errors in older adults. *Aging, Neuropsychology, and Cognition, 20*(2), 220–242. doi:10.1080/13825585.2012.690365

Oster, J. R. (1987). The binge-purge syndrome: A common albeit unappreciated cause of acid-base and fluid-electrolyte disturbances. *Southern Medical Journal, 80,* 58–67.

Oswald, I. (1959). Sudden bodily jerks on falling asleep. *Brain, 82,* 92–103.

Overeem, S., Mignot, E., Gert van Dijk, J., & Lammers, G. J. (2001). Narcolepsy: Clinical features, new pathophysiological insights, and future perspectives. *Journal of Clinical Neurophysiology, 18*(2), 78–105.

Overmier, J. B., & Seligman, M. E. P. (1967). Effects of inescapable shock on subsequent escape and avoidance behavior. *Journal of Comparative Physiology and Psychology, 63,* 23–33.

Owen, A. M., Hampshire, A., Grahn, J. A., Stenton, R., Dajani, S., & Burns, A. S. (2010). Putting brain training to the test. *Nature, 465*(7299), 775–778.

Owen, M. T., Easterbrooks, M. A., Chase-Lansdale, L., & Goldberg, W. A. (1984). The relation between maternal employment status and the stability of attachments to mother and to father. *Child Development, 55,* 1894–1901.

Pajonk, F. G., Wobrock, T., Gruber, O., Scherk, H., Berner, D., Kaizl, I., et al. (2010). Hippocampal plasticity in response to exercise in schizophrenia. *Archives of General Psychiatry, 67*(2), 133–143.

Palmer, S. E. (1992). Common region: A new principle of perceptual grouping. *Cognitive Psychology, 24*(3), 436–447.

Palva, J. M., Monto, S., Kulashekhar, S., & Palva, S. (2010). Neuronal synchrony reveals working memory networks and predicts individual memory capacity. *Proceedings of the National Academy of Sciences, USA, 107*(16), 7580–7585.

Pan, A. S. (2000). Body image, eating attitudes, and eating behaviors among Chinese, Chinese-American and non-Hispanic White women. *Dissertation Abstracts International, Section B: The Sciences and Engineering, 61*(1–B), 544.

Paparelli, A., Di Forti, M., Morrison, P. D., & Murray, R. M. (2011). Drug-induced psychosis: How to avoid star gazing in schizophrenia research by looking at more obvious sources of light. *Frontiers in Behavioral Neuroscience, 5,* 1. doi:10.3389/fnbeh.2011.00001

Pargament, K. I. (1997). *The psychology of religion and coping: Theory, research, and practice.* New York: Guilford Press.

Park, J., Turnbull, A. P., & Turnbull, H. R. (2002). Impacts of poverty on quality of life in families of children with disabilities. *Exceptional Children, 68,* 151–170.

Pashler, H., McDaniel, M., Rohrer, D., & Bjork, R. (2009). Learning styles: Concepts and evidence. *Psychological Science in the Public Interest, 9*(3), 105–119.

Parsons, H. M. (1992). Hawthorne: An early OBM experiment. *Journal of Organizational Behavior Management, 12*(1), 27–43.

Paul, B. M., ElvevÅg, B., Bokat, C. E., Weinberger, D. R., & Goldberg, T. E. (2005). Levels of processing effects on recognition memory in patients with schizophrenia. *Schizophrenia Research, 74*(1), 101–110.

Pavlov, I. P. (1906). The scientific investigation of the psychical faculties or processes in the higher animals. *Science, 24,* 613–619.

Pavlov, I. P. (1926). *Conditioned reflexes.* London: Oxford University Press.

Pavlov, I. P. (1927). *Conditioned reflexes: An investigation of the physiological activity of the cerebral cortex* (Translated and edited by G. V. Anrep). London: Oxford University Press.

Peng, K., Ames, D. R., & Knowles, E. D. (2000). Culture and human inference: Perspectives from three traditions. In D. Matsumoto (Ed.), *The handbook of culture and psychology* (pp. 245–264). New York: Oxford University Press.

Peplau, L. A., & Fingerhut, A. W. (2007). The close relationships of lesbians and gay men. *Annual Review of Psychology, 58,* 10.1–10.20.

Peplau, L. A., & Taylor, S. E. (1997). *Sociocultural perspectives in social psychology: Current readings.* Upper Saddle River, NJ: Prentice-Hall.

Pepperberg, I. M. (1998). Talking with Alex: Logic and speech in parrots. *Scientific American Presents: Exploring Intelligence, 9*(4), 60–65.

Pepperberg, I. M. (2007). Grey parrots do not always "parrot": The roles of imitation and phonological awareness in the creation of new labels from existing vocalizations. *Language Sciences, 29*(1), 1–13.

Perls, F. (1951). *Gestalt therapy.* New York: Julian Press.

Perls, F. (1969). *Gestalt therapy verbatim*. Moab, UT: Real People Press.

Perrin, S., & Spencer, C. P. (1980). The asch effect—a child of its time. *Bulletin of the British Psychological Society, 33*, 405–406.

Perrin, S., & Spencer, C. P. (1981). Independence or conformity in the Asch experiment as a reflection of cultural and situational factors. *British Journal of Social Psychology, 20*(3), 205–209.

Perrine, D. M. (1997). *The chemistry of mind-altering drugs*. Washington, DC: American Chemical Society.

Peters, W. A. (1971). *A class divided*. Garden City, NY: Doubleday.

Peterson, C., & Park, N. (2010). What happened to self-actualization? *Perspectives on Psychological Science, 5*(3), 320–322.

Peterson, D. R. (1976). Need for the doctor of psychology degree in professional psychology. *American Psychologist, 31*, 792–798.

Peterson, D. R. (1982). Origins and development of the doctor of psychology concept. In G. R. Caddy, D. C. Rimm, N. Watson, & J. H. Johnson (Eds.), *Educating professional psychologists* (pp. 19–38). New Brunswick, NJ: Transaction Books.

Peterson, L. R., & Peterson, M. J. (1959). Short-term retention of individual items. *Journal of Experimental Psychology, 58*, 193–198.

Petitto, L. A., Holowka, S., Sergio, L. E., & Ostry, D. (2001). Language rhythms in baby hand movements. *Nature, 413*, 35.

Petitto, L. A., & Marentette, P. F. (1991). Babbling in the manual mode: Evidence for the ontogeny of language. *Science, 251*, 1493–1496.

Petri, H. (1996). *Motivation: Theory, research and application* (4th ed.). Belmont, CA: Wadsworth.

Petrides, G., Tobias, K. G., Kellner, C. H., & Rudorfer, M. V. (2011). Continuation and maintenance electroconvulsive therapy for mood disorders: A review of the literature. *Neuropsychobiology, 64*(3), 129–140. doi:10.1159/000328943

Petrova, P. K., Cialdini, R. B., & Sills, S., J. (2007). Compliance, consistency, and culture: Personal consistency and compliance across cultures. *Journal of Experimental Social Psychology, 43*, 104–111.

Pettigrew, T. F., & Tropp, L. R. (2000). Does intergroup contact reduce prejudice? Recent meta-analytic findings. In S. Oskamp (Ed.), *Reducing prejudice and discrimination: Social psychological perspectives* (pp. 93–114). Mahwah, NJ: Erlbaum.

Petty, R. E. (1995). Attitude change. In A. Tesser (Ed.), *Advances in social psychology* (pp. 194–255). New York: McGraw-Hill.

Petty, R. E., & Cacioppo, J. (1986). *Communication and persuasion: Central and peripheral routes to attitude change*. New York: Springer- Verlag.

Petty, R. E., & Cacioppo, J. (1996). *Attitudes and persuasion: Classic and contemporary approaches* (reprint). Boulder, CO: Westview Press.

Petty, R. E., Wheeler, S. C., & Tormala, Z. L. (2003). Persuasion and attitude change. In T. Millon & M. J. Lerner (Eds.), *Handbook of psychology: Volume 5: Personality and social psychology* (pp. 353–382). Hoboken, NJ: Wiley.

Pezdek, K., Finger, K., & Hodge, D. (1997). Planting false childhood memories: The role of event plausibility. *Psychological Science, 8*, 437–441.

Pezdek, K., & Hodge, D. (1999). Planting false childhood memories in children: The role of event plausibility. *Child Development, 70*, 887–895.

Pfeiffer, W. M. (1982). Culture-bound syndromes. In I. Al-Issa (Ed.), *Culture and psychopathology* (pp. 201–218). Baltimore: University Park Press.

Phan, T., & Silove, D. (1999). An overview of indigenous descriptions of mental phenomena and the range of traditional healing practices amongst the Vietnamese. *Transcultural Psychiatry, 36*, 79–94.

Piaget, J. (1926). *The language and thought of the child*. New York: Harcourt Brace.

Piaget, J. (1952). *The origins of intelligence in children*. New York: Norton.

Piaget, J. (1962). *Play, dreams and imitation in childhood*. New York: Norton.

Piaget, J. (1983). Piaget's theory. In W. Kessen (Ed.), *Handbook of child psychology: Volume 1. Theoretical models of human development* (pp. 103–128). New York: Wiley.

Pilon, M., Montplaisir, J., & Zadra, A. (2008). Precipitating factors of somnambulism: Impact of sleep deprivation and forced arousals. *Neurology, 70*, 2284–2290.

Pinker, S. (1995). Language acquisition. In L. R. Gleitman & M. Liberman (Eds.), *An invitation to cognitive science* (2nd ed., pp. 135–182). Cambridge: MIT Press.

Pinker, S., & Bloom, P. (1990). Natural language and natural selection. *Behavioral and Brain Sciences, 13*(4), 707–784.

Pinsof, W. M., & Wynne, L. C. (1995). The efficacy of marital and family therapy: An empirical overview, conclusions, and recommendations. *Journal of Marital and Family Therapy, 21*, 585–613.

Plaut, D. C., & McClelland, J. L. (2010). Locating object knowledge in the brain: A critique of Bowers' (2009) attempt to revive the grandmother cell hypothesis. *Psychological Review, 117*, 284–288.

Plomin, R. (1994). The nature of nurture: The environment beyond the family. In R. Plomin (Ed.), *Genetics and experience: The interplay between nature and nurture* (pp. 82–107). Thousand Oaks, CA: Sage.

Plomin, R., & DeFries, J. C. (1998, May). Genetics of cognitive abilities and disabilities. *Scientific American*, 62–69.

Plomin, R., Owen, M. J., & McGuffin, P. (1994). The genetic basis of complex human behaviors. *Science, 264*(5166), 1733–1739.

Plomin, R., & Spinath, F. M. (2004). Intelligence: Genetics, genes, and genomics. *Journal of Personality and Social Psychology, 86*(1), 112–129.

Plomin, R. N. L., Pederson, G. E., McClearn, J. R., Nesselroade, C. S., & Bergman, H. F. (1988). EAS temperaments during the last half year of the life span: Twins reared apart and twins raised together. *Psychology of Aging, 4*, 43–50.

Plug, C., & Ross, H. E. (1994). The natural moon illusion: A multi-factor angular account. *Perception, 23*, 321–333.

Plum, F., & Posner, J. B. (1985). *The diagnosis of stupor and coma*. Philadelphia: F. A. Davis.

Pogue-Geile, M. F., & Yokley, J. L. (2010). Current research on the genetic contributors to schizophrenia. *Current Directions in Psychological Science, 19*, 214–219. doi:10.1177/0963721410378490. Retrieved from http://cdp.sagepub.com/content/19/4/214.abstract

Polce-Lynch, M., Myers, B. J., Kilmartin, C. T., Forssmann-Falck, R., & Kliewer, W. (1998). Gender and age patterns in emotional expression, body image, and self-esteem: A qualitative analysis. *Sex Roles, 38*, 1025–1050.

Polewan, R. J., Vigorito, C. M., Nason, C. D., Block, R. A., & Moore, J. W. (2006). A cartesian reflex assessment of face processing. *Behavioral and Cognitive Neuroscience Reviews, 3*(5), 3–23.

Pollitt, E., & Matthews, R. (1998). Breakfast and cognition: An integrative summary. *American Journal of Clinical Nutrition, 67*(4), 804S–813S.

Pompili, M., Lester, D., Dominici, G., Longo, L., Marconi, G., Forte, A., et al. (2013). Indications for electroconvulsive treatment in schizophrenia: A systematic review. *Schizophrenia Research, 146*(1–3), 1–9. doi:10.1016/j.schres.2013.02.005

Pope, H. G., Poliakoff, M. B., Parker, M. P., Boynes, M., & Hudson, J. I. (2007). Is dissociative amnesia a culture-bound syndrome? Findings from a survey of historical literature. *Psychological Medicine, 37*(2), 225–233.

Pormerleau, C. S., & Pormerleau, O. F. (1994). Euphoriant effects of nicotine. *Tobacco Control, 3*, 374.

Posthuma, D., de Geus, E. J. C., & Deary, I. J. (2009). The genetics of intelligence. In T. E. Goldberg & D. R. Weinberger (Eds.), *The genetics of cognitive neuroscience*. Cambridge, MA: The MIT Press.

Postman, L. (1975). Tests of the generality of the principle of encoding specificity. *Memory and Cognition, 3*, 663–672.

Powell, R. A. (2010). Little Albert still missing. *American Psychologist, 65*(4), 299–300. doi:10.1037/a0019288

Powers, M. H. (1984). A computer-assisted problem-solving method for beginning chemistry students. *The Journal of Computers in Mathematics and Science Teaching, 4*(1), 13–19.

Pratkanis, A. R., & Greenwald, A. G. (1988). Recent perspectives on unconscious processing: Still no marketing applications. *Psychology and Marketing, 5*, 337–353.

Pratt, J. A. (1991). Psychotropic drug tolerance and dependence: Common underlying mechanisms? In E. Pratt (Ed.), *The biological bases of drug tolerance and dependence* (pp. 2–28). London: Academic Press/Harcourt Brace Jovanovich.

Preston, J. D., O'Neal, J. H., & Talaga, M. C. (2008). *Handbook of clinical psychopharmacology for therapists* (5th ed.). Oakland, CA: New Harbinger Publications.

Priester, J. M., & Petty, R. E. (1995). Source attributions and persuasion: Perceived honesty as a determinant of message scrutiny. *Personality and Social Psychology Bulletin, 21*, 637–654.

Prigerson, H. G., Bierhals, A. J., Kasi, S. V., Reynolds, C. F., Shear, M. K., Day, N., et al. (1997). Traumatic grief as a risk factor for mental and physical morbidity. *American Journal of Psychiatry, 154l*,616–623.

Pritchard, T. C. (2012). Gustatory system. In J. K. Mai & G. Paxinos (Eds.), *The human nervous system* (pp. 1187–1218). London, UK: Academic Press.

Prochaska, J. O., & Norcross, J. C. (2003). *Systems of psychotherapy* (5th ed.). Belmont, CA: Wadsworth.

Prochaska, J. O., & Norcross, J. C. (2009). *Systems of psychotherapy: A transtheoretical analysis*. Belmont, CA: Brooks/Cole, Cengage Learning.

Pumariega, A. J., & Gustavson, C. R. (1994). Eating attitudes in African-American women: The essence. *Eating Disorders: Journal of Treatment and Prevention, 2*, 5–16.

Putnam, S. P., & Stifter, C. A. (2002). Development of approach and inhibition in the first year: Parallel findings for motor behavior, temperament ratings and directional cardiac response. *Developmental Science, 5*, 441–451.

Puts, D. A., Jordan, C. L., & Breedlove, S. M. (2006). O brother, where art thou? The fraternal birth-order effect on male sexual orientation. *Proceedings of the National Academy of Sciences, USA, 103*(28), 10531–10532.

Pynnönen, K., Törmäkangas, T., Rantanen, T., & Lyyra, T. (2013). Do mobility, cognitive functioning, and depressive symptoms mediate the association between social activity and mortality risk among older men and women? *European Journal of Ageing.* doi:10.1007/s10433-013-0295-3

Quintero, J. E., Kuhlman, S. J., & McMahon, D. G. (2003). The biological clock nucleus: A multiphasic oscillator network regulated by light. *Journal of Neuroscience, 23*, 8070–8076.

Raaijmakers, J. G. W., & Shiffrin, R. M. (1992). Models for recall and recognition. *Annual Review of Psychology, 43*, 205–234.

Rabins, P., Appleby, B. S., Brandt, J., DeLong, M. R., Dunn, L. B., Gabriels, L., et al. (2009). Scientific and ethical issues related to deep brain stimulation for disorders of mood, behavior, and thought. *Archives of General Psychiatry, 66*(9), 931–937.

Rachman, S. (1990). The determinants and treatments of simple phobias. *Advances in Behavioral Research and Therapy, 12*(1), 1–30.

Rachman, S. J., & Hodgson, R. J. (1980). *Obsessions and compulsions.* Englewood Cliffs, NJ: Prentice Hall.

Rahman, Q., & Hull, M. S. (2005). An empirical test of the kin selection hypothesis for male homosexuality. *Archives of Sexual Behavior, 34,* 461–467.

Raikkonen, K., Matthews, K. A., & Salomon, K. (2003). Hostility predicts metabolic syndrome risk factors in children and adolescents. *Health Psychology, 22,* 279–286.

Rainforth, M. V., Schneider, R. H., Nidich, S. I., Gaylord-King, C., Salerno, J. W., & Anderson, J. W. (2007). Stress reduction programs in patients with elevated blood pressure: A systematic review and meta-analysis. *Current Hypertension Reports, 9,* 520–528.

Ramachandran, V. S., & Blakeslee, S. (1998). *Phantoms in the brain.* New York: Quill William Morrow.

Ramon y Cajal, S. (1995). *Histology of the nervous system of man and vertebrates*(English translation by N. Swanson & L. M. Swanson*).* New York: Oxford University Press.

Ranke, M. B., & Saenger, P. (2001, July 28). Turner's syndrome. *Lancet, 358*(9278), 309–314.

Rao, S. C., Rainer, G., & Miller, E. K. (1997). Integration of what and where in the primate prefrontal cortex. *Science, 276,* 821–824.

Rapoport, J. L., Addington, A. M., Frangou, S., & Psych, M. R. (2005). The neurodevelopmental model of schizophrenia: Update 2005. *Molecular Psychiatry, 10*(5), 434–449. doi:10.1038/sj.mp.4001642

Rapoport, J. L., Giedd, J. N., & Gogtay, N. (2012). Neurodevelopmental model of schizophrenia: Update 2012. *Molecular Psychiatry, 17*(12), 1228–1238. doi:10.1038/mp.2012.23

Ratey, J. J., & Hagerman, E. (2008). *Spark: The revolutionary new science of exercise and the brain.* New York: Little, Brown and Company.

Ratiu, P., Talos, I. F., Haker, S., Lieberman, D., & Everett, P. (2004). The tale of Phineas Gage, digitally remastered. *Journal of Neurotrauma, 21*(5), 637–643. doi: 10.1089/089771504774129964

Rauch, S. L., Shin, L. M., & Wright, C. I. (2003). Neuroimaging studies of amygdala function in anxiety disorders. *Annals of the New York Academy of Sciences, 985,* 389–410.

Raynor, H. A., & Epstein, L. H. (2001). Dietary variety, energy regulation and obesity. *Psychological Bulletin, 127*(3), 325–341.

Reason, J. T., & Brand, J. J. (1975). *Motion sickness.* London: Academic Press.

Rechtschaffen, A., & Kales, A. (1968). *A manual of standardized terminology, techniques, and scoring system for sleep stages of human subjects.* Washington, DC: U.S. Department of Health, Education, and Welfare Public Health Service - NIH/NIND.

Reese, H. W. (2010). Regarding Little Albert. *American Psychologist, 65*(4), 300–301. doi:10.1037/a0019332

Reichborn-Kjennerud, T. (2008). Genetics of personality disorders. *Psychiatric Clinics of North America, 31,* 421.

Reichborn-Kjennerud, T., Czajkowski, N., Neale, M. C., Orstavik, R. E., Torgersen, S., Tambs, K., et al. (2007). Genetic and environmental influences on dimensional representations of DSM-IV cluster C personality disorders: A population-based multivariate twin study. *Psychological Medicine, 37*(5), 645–653. doi:10.1017/s0033291706009548

Reinders, A., Quak, J., Nijenhuis, E. R., Korf, J., Paans, A. M., Willemsen, A. T., & den Boer, J. A. (2001, June). *Identity state-dependent processing of neutral and traumatic scripts in dissociative identity disorder as assessed by PET.* Oral presentation at the 7th Annual Meeting of the Organisation for Human Brain Mapping, Brighton, UK.

Reiner, W. G. (1999). Assignment of sex in neonates with ambiguous genitalia. *Current Opinions in Pediatrics, 11*(4), 363–365.

Reiner, W. G. (2000, September 29). *The genesis of gender identity in the male: Prenatal androgen effects on gender identity and gender role.* Oral presentation at New York University Child Study Center, Grand Rounds Summary, New York.

Reisenzein, R. (1983). The Schachter theory of emotion: Two decades later. *Psychological Bulletin, 94,* 239–264.

Reisenzein, R. (1994). Pleasure-arousal theory and the intensity of emotions. *Journal of Personality and Social Psychology, 7*(6), 1313–1329.

Renchler, R. (1993). *Poverty and learning* (ERIC Digest No. 83). Eugene, OR: ERIC Clearinghouse on Educational Management. (ERIC Document Reproduction Service No. ED 357 433)

Rescorla, R. A. (1968). Probability of shock in the presence and absence of CS in fear conditioning. *Journal of Comparative and Physiological Psychology, 66,* 1–5.

Rescorla, R. A. (1988). Pavlovian conditioning—it's not what you think. *American Psychologist, 43,* 151–160.

Rescorla, R. A., & Wagner, A. R. (1972). A theory of Pavlovian conditioning: Variations in the effectiveness of reinforcement and nonreinforcement. In A. H. Black & W. F. Prokasy (Eds.), *Classical conditioning II: Current theory and research* (pp. 64–99). New York: Appleton-Century-Crofts.

Reynold, C. F., Frank, E., Perel, J. M., Imber, S. D., Cornes, C., Miller, M. D., et al. (1999). Nortriptyline and interpersonal psychotherapy as maintenance therapies for recurrent depression: A randomized controlled trial in patients older than 59 years. *Journal of the American Medical Association, 281*(1), 39–45.

Reynolds, J. (2002). *Succeeding in college: Study skills and strategies.* Upper Saddle River, NJ: Prentice-Hall.

Rezvani, A. H., & Levin, E. D. (2001). Cognitive effects of nicotine. *Biological Psychiatry, 49,* 258–267.

Rice, W. R., Friberg, U., & Gavrilets, S. (2012). Homosexuality as a consequence of epigenetically canalized sexual development. *The Quarterly Review of Biology, 87*(4), 344–368.

Richards, C. F., & Lowe, R. A. (2003). Researching racial and ethnic disparities in emergency medicine. *Academic Emergency Medicine, 10*(11), 1169–1175.

Richardson, J., & Morgan, R. (1997). *Reading to learn in the content areas.* Belmont, CA: Wadsworth Publishing Company.

Rideout, V. J., Foehr, U. G., & Roberts, D. F. (2010). *Generation M2: Media in the lives of 8- to 18-year-olds.* Menlo Park, CA: Henry J. Kaiser Family Foundation.

Ridley, M. (1999). *Genome: The autobiography of a species in 23 chapters.* London: Fourth Estate.

Ridley, M. (2002). Crop circle confession. *Scientific American.* Retrieved February 17, 2010, from http://www.sciam.com/article.cfm?chanID=sa006&articleID=00038B16-ED5F-1D29-97CA809EC588EEDF

Rieber, R. W., & Robinson, D. K. (2001). *Wilhelm Wundt in history: The making of a scientific psychology.* New York: Kluwer Academic.

Rijsdijk, F. V., Gottesman, I. I., McGuffin, P., & Cardno, A. G. (2011). Heritability estimates for psychotic symptom dimensions in twins with psychotic disorders. *American Journal of Medical Genetics Part B, Neuropsychiatric Genetics, 156B*(1), 89–98. doi:10.1002/ajmg.b.31145

Ritts, V. (1999). *Infusing culture into psychopathology: A supplement for psychology instructors.* Retrieved June 19, 2004, from www.stlcc.cc.mo.us/mc/ users/vritts/psypath.htm

Rizzolatti, G., Fabbri-Destro, M., & Cattaneo, L. (2009). Mirror neurons and their clinical relevance. *Nature Clinical Practice Neurology, 5*(1), 24–34.

Ro, E., & Clark, L. A. (2009). Psychosocial functioning in the context of diagnosis: Assessment and theoretical issues. *Psychological Assessment, 21*(3), 313–324.

Robins, L. N. (1996). *Deviant children grown up.* Baltimore: Williams & Wilkins.

Robinson, F. P. (1970). *Effective study* (4th ed.). New York: Harper & Row.

Robinson, J. W., & Preston, J. D. (1976). Equal status contact and modification of racial prejudice: A reexamination of the contact hypothesis. *Social Forces, 54,* 911–924.

Robinson, P. (1993). *Freud and his critics.* Berkeley: University of California Press.

Rodgers, J. E. (1992). *Psychosurgery: Damaging the brain to save the mind.* New York: HarperCollins.

Rodin, J. (1981). Current status of the internal-external hypothesis for obesity. *American Psychologist, 36,* 361–372.

Rodin, J. (1985). Insulin levels, hunger, and food intake: An example of feedback loops in body weight regulation. *Health Psychology, 4,* 1–24.

Roediger, H. L. (1990). Implicit memory: Retention without remembering. *American Psychologist, 45,* 1043–1056.

Roediger, H. L., III. (2000). Why retrieval is the key process to understanding human memory. In E. Tulving (Ed.), *Memory, consciousness and the brain: The Tallinn Conference* (pp. 52–75). Philadelphia: Psychology Press.

Roediger, H. L., III, & Guynn, M. J. (1996). Retrieval processes. In E. L. Bjork & R. A. Bjork (Eds.), *Memory* (pp. 197–236). New York: Academic Press.

Roethlisberger, F. J., & Dickson, W. J. (1939). *Management and the worker.* Cambridge, MA: Harvard University Press.

Roffman, R. A., Stephens, R. S., Simpson, E. E., & Whitaker, D. L. (1988). Treatment of marijuana dependence: Preliminary results. *Journal of Psychoactive Drugs, 20*(1), 129–137.

Roffwarg, H. P., Muzio, J. N., & Dement, W. C. (1966). Ontogenetic development of the human sleep-dream cycle. *Science, 152*(3722), 604–619.

Rogers, C. R. (1951). *Client-centered therapy.* Boston: Houghton Mifflin Co.

Rogers, C. R. (1961). *On becoming a person: A therapist's view of psychotherapy.* Boston: Houghton/Mifflin.

Rogers, R. W., & Mewborn, C. R. (1976). Fear appeals and attitude change: Effects of a threat's noxiousness, probability of occurrence, and the efficacy of the coping responses. *Journal of Personality and Social Psychology, 34,* 54–61.

Rogoff, B. (1994). Developing understanding of the idea of communities of learners. *Mind, Culture, and Activity, 1*(4), 209–229.

Rohde, P., Silva, S. G., Tonev, S. T., Kennard, B. D., Vitiello, B., Kratochvil, C. J., et al. (2008). Achievement and maintenance of sustained improvement during TADS continuation and maintenance therapy. *Archives of General Psychiatry, 65*(4), 447–455.

Roid, G. H. (2003). *Stanford-Binet intelligence scales* (5th ed.). Itasca, IL: Riverside.

Roper, G., Rachman, S., & Marks, I. (1975). Passive and participant modeling in exposure treatment of obsessive-compulsive neurotics. *Behaviour Research and Therapy, 13,* 271–279.

Ros, T., Theberge, J., Frewen, P. A., Kluetsch, R., Densmore, M., Calhoun, V. D., et al. (2013). Mind over chatter: Plastic up-regulation of the Fmri salience network directly after EEG neurofeedback. *Neuroimage, 65,* 324–335. doi:10.1016/j.neuroimage.2012.09.046

Rosch, E. (1973). On the internal structure of perceptual and semantic categories. In T. E. Moore (Ed.), *Cognitive development and the acquisition of language* (pp. 111–144). New York: Academic Press.

Rosch, E. (1977). Human categorization. In N. Warren (Ed.), *Advances in cross-cultural psychology* (Vol. 1, pp. 1–72). London: Academic Press.

Rosch, E., & Mervis, C. B. (1975). Family resemblances: Studies in the internal structures of categories. *Cognitive Psychology, 7*, 573–605.

Rosch-Heider, E. (1972). Universals in color naming and memory. *Journal of Experimental Psychology, 93*, 10–20.

Rosch-Heider, E., & Olivier, D. C. (1972). The structure of the color space in naming and memory for two languages. *Cognitive Psychology, 3*, 337–354.

Rosenfeld, J. P., Labkovsky, E., Winograd, M., Lui, M. A., Vandenboom, C., & Chedid, E. (2008). The Complex Trial Protocol (CTP): A new, countermeasure-resistant, accurate, P300-based method for detection of concealed information. *Psychophysiology, 45*(6), 906–919.

Rosenman, R. H., Brand, R. I., Jenkins, C. D., Friedman, M., Straus, R., & Wurm, M. (1975). Coronary heart disease in the Western Collaborative Group Study, final follow-up experience of 2 years. *Journal of the American Medical Association, 233*, 812–817.

Rosenthal, A. M. (1964). *Thirty-eight witnesses: The Kitty Genovese case.* New York: McGraw-Hill.

Rosenthal, R., & Jacobson, L. (1968). *Pygmalion in the classroom.* New York: Holt, Rinehart & Winston.

Ross, H. E., & Ross, G. M. (1976). Did Ptolemy understand the moon illusion? *Perception, 5*, 377–385.

Rossini, P. M., Altamura, C., Ferreri, F., Melgari, J. M., Tecchio, F., Tombini, M., et al. (2007). Neuroimaging experimental studies on brain plasticity in recovery from stroke. *Eura Medicophys, 43*(2), 241–254.

Rothbaum, B. O., Hodges, L. F., Kooper, R., Opdyke, D., Williford, J. S., & North, M. (1995). Effectiveness of computer-generated (virtual reality) graded exposure in the treatment of acrophobia. *American Journal of Psychiatry, 152*, 626–628.

Rothbaum, F., Morelli, G., & Rusk, N. (2010). Attachment, learning and coping: The interplay of cultural similarities and differences. In C. Y. Chiu, Y. Y. Hong, & M. Gelfand (Eds.), *Advances in culture and psychology* (Vol. 1, pp. 153–215). New York: Oxford University Press.

Rothbaum, R., Weisz, J., Pott, M., Miyake, K., & Morelli, G. (2000). Attachment and culture: Security in Japan and the U.S. *American Psychologist, 55*, 1093–1104.

Rothenberg, A. (2001). Bipolar illness, creativity, and treatment. *Psychiatric Quarterly, 72*(2), 131–147.

Rotter, J. B. (1966). Generalized expectancies for internal versus external control of reinforcements. *Psychological Monographs, 80*(Whole no. 609).

Rotter, J. B. (1978). Generalized expectancies for problem solving and psychotherapy. *Cognitive Therapy and Research, 2*, 1–10.

Rotter, J. B. (1981). The psychological situation in social learning theory. In D. Magnusson (Ed.), *Toward a psychology of situations: An interactional perspective.* Hillsdale, NJ: Erlbaum.

Rotter, J. B. (1990). Internal versus external control of reinforcement: A case history of a variable. *American Psychologist, 45*, 489–493.

Rotton, J., & Frey, J. (1985). Air pollution, weather, and violent crime: Concomitant time-series analysis of archival data. *Journal of Personality and Social Psychology, 49*, 1207–1220.

Rotton, J., Frey, J., Barry, T., Milligan, M., & Fitzpatrick, M. (1979). The air pollution experience and physical aggression. *Journal of Applied Social Psychology, 9*, 397–412.

Rouru, J., Wesnes, K., Hänninen, J., Murphym M., Riordan, H., & Rinne, J. (2013, March 16–23). *Safety and efficacy of ORM-12741 on cognitive and behavioral symptoms in patients with Alzheimer's disease: A randomized, double-blind, placebo-controlled, parallel group, multicenter, proof-of-concept 12 week study.* Paper presented at American Academy of Neurology 65th Annual Meeting, San Diego, CA.

Rouse, B. A. (1998). *Substance and mental health statistics source book.* Rockville, MD: Department of Health and Human Services, Substance Abuse and Mental Health Services Administration (SAMHSA).

Rovet, J. (1993). The psychoeducational characteristics of children with turner's syndrome. *Journal of Learning Disabilities, 26*, 333–341.

Rowan, J. (2001). *Ordinary ecstacsy.* Hove, UK: Brunner-Routledge.

Rowe, D. C., Almeida, D. A., & Jacobson, K. C. (1999). School context and genetic influences on aggression in adolescence. *Psychological Science, 10*, 277–280.

Roysircai-Sodowsky, G. R., & Maestas, M. V. (2000). Acculturation, ethnic identity, and acculturative stress: Evidence and measurement. In R. H. Dana (Ed.), *Handbook of cross-cultural and multicultural assessment* (pp. 131–172). Mahwah, NJ: Erlbaum.

Rozeske, R. R., Evans, A. K., Frank, M. G., Watkins, L. R., Lowry, C. A., & Maier, S. F. (2011). Uncontrollable, but not controllable, stress desensitizes 5-HT1A receptors in the dorsal raphe nucleus. *The Journal of Neuroscience, 31*(40), 14107–14115. doi:10.1523/jneurosci.3095-11.2011

Ruble, D., Alvarez, J., Bachman, M., Cameron, J., Fuligni, A., Garcia Coll, C., et al. (2004). The development of a sense of "we": The emergence and implications of children's collective identity. In M. Bennett & F. Sani (Eds.), *The development of the social self.* New York: Psychology Press.

Rudd, P., & Osterberg, L. G. (2002). Hypertension: Context, pathophysiology, and management. In E. J. Topol (Ed.), *Textbook of cardiovascular medicine* (pp. 91–122). Philadelphia: Lippincott, Williams & Wilkins.

Ruhe, H. G., Mason, N. S., & Schene, A. H. (2007). Mood is indirectly related to serotonin, norepinephrine and dopamine levels in humans: A meta-analysis of monoamine depletion studies. *Molecular Psychiatry, 12*(4), 331–359.

Ruiz, S., Birbaumer, N., & Sitaram, R. (2013). Abnormal neural connectivity in schizophrenia and FMRI-brain-computer interface as a potential therapeutic approach. *Frontiers in Sychiatry, 4*, 17. doi:10.3389/fpsyt.2013.00017

Rumelhart, D. E., Hinton, G. E., & McClelland, J. L. (1986). A general framework for parallel distributed processing. In D. E. Rumelhart, J. L. McClelland, & the PDP Research Group (Eds.), *Parallel distributed processing: Explorations in the microstructure of cognition: Vol. 1. Foundations* (pp. 45–76). Cambridge, MA: MIT Press.

Russell, D. E. (1986). *The secret trauma: Incest in the lives of girls and women.* New York: Basic Books.

Rutherford, A. (2000). Mary Cover Jones (1896–1987). *The Feminist Psychologist, 27*(3), 25.

Ryan, R. M., Chirkov, V. I., Little, T. D., Sheldon, K. M., Timoshina, E. L., & Deci, E. L. (1999). The American dream in Russia: Extrinsic aspirations and well-being in two cultures. *Personality and Social Psychology Bulletin, 25*, 1509–1524.

Ryan, R. M., & Deci, E. L. (2000). Intrinsic and extrinsic motivations: Classic definitions and new directions. *Contemporary Educational Psychology, 25*, 54–67.

Sabatini, E., Della Penna, S., Franciotti, R., Ferretti, A., Zoccolotti, P., Rossini, P. M., et al. (2009). Brain structures activated by overt and covert emotional visual stimuli. *Brain Research Bulletin, 79*(5), 258–264.

Sackett, P. R., Borneman, M. J., & Connelly, B. S. (2008). High stakes testing in higher education and employment: Appraising the evidence for validity and fairness. *American Psychologist, 63*(4), 215–227. doi:10.1037/0003-066X.63.4.215

Sacks, D. P., Bushman, B. J., & Anderson, C. A. (2011). Do violent video games harm children? Comparing the scientific amicus curiae "experts" in *Brown v Entertainment Merchants Association. Northwestern University Law Review Colloquy, 106*, 1–12.

Sacks, O. (1990). *The man who mistook his wife for a hat and other clinical tales.* New York: HarperPerennial.

Sadock, B. J., Kaplan, H. I., & Sadock, V. A. (2007). *Kaplan & Sadock's synopsis of psychiatry: Behavioral sciences/clinical psychiatry* (10th ed.). Philadelphia, PA: Lippincott Williams & Wilkins.

Sagan, C. (1977). *The dragons of Eden: Speculations on the evolution of human intelligence.* New York: Random House.

Saha, S., Chant, D., Welham, J., & McGrath, J. (2005). A systematic review of the prevalence of schizophrenia. *PLoS Medicine, 2*(5), e141.

Salamone, J. D., & Correa, M. (2012). The mysterious motivational functions of mesolimbic dopamine. *Neuron, 76*(3), 470–485.

Salend, S. J. (1987). Contingency management systems. *Academic Therapy, 22*, 245–253.

Salovey, P., & Mayer, J. D. (1990). Emotional intelligence. *Imagination, Cognition, and Personality, 9*, 185–211.

Salthouse, T. A. (1984). The skill of typing. *Scientific American, 250*(2), 128–135.

Sanbonmatsu, D. M., Strayer, D. L., Medeiros-Ward, N., & Watson, J. M. (2013). Who multi-tasks and why? Multi-tasking ability, perceived multi-tasking ability, impulsivity, and sensation seeking. *PLoS ONE 8*(1), e54402. doi:10.1371/journal.pone.0054402

Sanders, L. D., Weber-Fox, C. M., & Neville, H. J. (2008). Varying degrees of plasticity in different subsystems within language. In J. R. Pomerantz (Ed.), *Topics in integrative neuroscience: From cells to cognition* (pp. 125–153). New York: Cambridge University Press.

Sands, L. P., & Meredith, W. (1992). Intellectual functioning in late midlife. *Journal of Gerontological and Psychological Science, 47*, 81–84.

Sanes, J. R., & Jessell, T. M. (2013a). Experience and the refinement of synaptic connections. In E. R. Kandel, J. H. Schwartz, T. M. Jessell, S. A. Siegelbaum, & A. J. Hudspeth (Eds.), *Principles of neural science* (5th ed., pp. 1259–1283). USA: McGraw-Hill.

Sanes, J. R., & Jessell, T. M. (2013b). Repairing the damaged brain. In E. R. Kandel, J. H. Schwartz, T. M. Jessell, S. A. Siegelbaum, & A. J. Hudspeth (Eds.), *Principles of neural science* (5th ed., pp. 1284–1305). USA: McGraw-Hill.

Santhakumar, V., Wallner, M., & Otis, T. S. (2007). Ethanol acts directly on extrasynaptic subtypes of GABAA receptors to increase tonic inhibition. *Alcohol, 41*(3), 211–221.

Sapir, E. S. (1921). *Language: An introduction to the study of speech.* New York: Harcourt, Brace.

Sapolsky, R. M. (2004). *Why Zebras don't get ulcers* (3rd ed., pp. 1, 144–145). New York: Owl Books.

Sarbin, T. R., & Coe, W. C. (1972). *Hypnosis: A social psychological analysis of influence communication.* New York: Holt, Rinehart, & Winston.

Sartory, G., Cwik, J., Knuppertz, H., Schurholt, B., Lebens, M., Seitz, R. J., et al. (2013). In search of the trauma memory: A meta-analysis of functional neuroimaging studies of symptom provocation in posttraumatic stress disorder (PTSD). *PLoS ONE, 8*(3), e58150. doi:10.1371/journal.pone.0058150

Sastry, K. S., Karpova, Y., Prokopovich, S., Smith, A. J., Essau, B., Gersappe, A., et al. (2007). Epinephrine protects cancer cells from apoptosis via activation of cAMP-dependent protein kinase and BAD phosphorylation. *Journal of Biological Chemistry, 282*(19), 14094–14100.

Satterly, D. (1987). Piaget and education. In R. L. Gregory (Ed.), *The Oxford companion to the mind* (pp. 110–143). Oxford: Oxford University Press.

Sattler, J. M. (1977). The effects of therapist-client racial similarity. In A. S. Gurman & A. M. Razin (Eds.), *Effective psychotherapy: A handbook of research* (pp. 252–290). Elmsford, NY: Pergamon.

Savage, J., & Yancey, C. (2008). The effects of media violence exposure on criminal aggression: A meta-analysis. *Criminal Justice and Behavior, 35*(6), 772–791. doi:10.1177/0093854808316487

Savage-Rumbaugh, S., & Lewin, R. (1994). *Kanzi*. New York: Wiley.

Savage-Rumbaugh, S., Shanker, S., & Taylor, T. J. (1998). *Apes, language and the human mind*. Oxford, UK: Oxford University Press.

Savic, I., Berglund, H., & Lindstrom, P. (2005). Brain response to putative pheromones in homosexual men. *Proceedings of the National Academy of Sciences, USA, 102*(20), 7356–7361.

Savic, I., & Lindstrom, P. (2008). PET and MRI show differences in cerebral asymmetry and functional connectivity between homo- and heterosexual subjects. *Proceedings of the National Academy of Sciences, USA, 105*(27), 9403–9408.

Scarpa, A., Raine, A., Venables, P. H., & Mednick, S. A. (1995). The stability of inhibited/uninhibited temperament from ages 3 to 11 years in Mauritian children. *Journal of Abnormal Child Psychology, 23*, 607–618.

Schachter, S., & Singer, J. E. (1962). Cognitive, social and physiological determinants of emotional states. *Psychological Review, 69*, 379–399.

Schafer, M., & Crichlow, S. (1996). Antecedents of groupthink: A quantitative study. *Journal of Conflict Resolution, 40*, 415–435.

Schaie, K. W., & Willis, S. L. (2010). *Handbook of the psychology of aging* (7th ed., pp. 27–29). Maryland Heights, Montana: Academic Press.

Schalock, R. L., Borthwick-Duffy, S. A., Buntinx, W. H. E., Coultier, D. L., & Craig, E. M. P. (2010). *Intellectual disability: Definition, classification, and systems of supports* (11th ed.). Washington, DC: American Association on Intellectual and Developmental Disabilities.

Schapiro, A. C., & McClelland, J. L. (2009). A connectionist model of a continuous developmental transition in the balance scale task. *Cognition, 110*(1), 395–411.

Scharnowski, F., Hutton, C., Josephs, O., Weiskopf, N., & Rees, G. (2012). Improving visual perception through neurofeedback. *The Journal of Neuroscience, 32*(49), 17830–17841. doi:10.1523/jneurosci.6334-11.2012

Schiller, P. H., & Carvey, C. E. (2005). The Hermann grid illusion revisited. *Perception, 34*(11), 1375–1397.

Schmitt, D. P. (2002). Personality, attachment and sexuality related to dating relationship outcomes: Contrasting three perspectives on personal attribute interaction. *British Journal of Social Psychology, 41*(4), 589–610.

Schmitt, D. P., Allik, J., McCrae, R. R., & Benet-Martinez, V. (2007). The geographic distribution of big five personality traits: Patterns and profiles of human self-description across 56 nations. *Journal of Cross-Cultural Psychology, 38*(2), 173–212. doi:10.1177/0022022106297299

Schmitt, K. C., & Reith, M. E. A. (2010). Regulation of the dopamine transporter. *Annals of the New York Academy of Sciences, 1187*, 316.

Schmitz, C., Wagner, J., & Menke, E. (2001). The interconnection of childhood poverty and homelessness: Negative impact/points of access. *Families in Society, 82*(1), 69–77.

Schnabel, J. (1994). *Round in circles* (pp. 267–277). London: Hamish Hamilton.

Schneider, K. J., Bugental, J. F. T., & Fraser, J. F. (Eds.). (2001). *Handbook of humanistic psychology*. Thousand Oaks, CA: Sage.

Schneider, R. H., Grim, C. E., Rainforth, M. V., Kotchen, T., Nidich, S. I., Gaylord-King, C., . . . Alexander, C. N. (2012). Stress reduction in the secondary prevention of cardiovascular disease: Randomized, controlled trial of transcendental meditation and health education in blacks. *Circulation: Cardiovascular Quality and Outcomes, 5*(6), 750-758. doi: 10.1161/circoutcomes.112.967406

Schneider, R. H., Staggers, F., Alexander, C. N., Sheppard, W., Rainforth, M., Kondwani, K., et al. (1995). A randomized controlled trial of stress reduction for hypertension in older African Americans. *Hypertension, 26*(5), 820–827.

Schneider, W., Dumais, S., & Shriffrin, R. (1984). *Automatic and control processing and attention*. London: Academic Press.

Schneidman, E. (1983). *Death of man*. New York: Jason Aronson.

Schneidman, E. (1994). *Death: Current perspectives*. New York: McGraw-Hill.

Schols, L., Haan, J., Riess, O., Amoiridis, G., & Przuntek, H. (1998). Sleep disturbance in spinocerebellar ataxias: Is the SCA3 mutation a cause of restless legs syndrome? *Neurology, 51*, 1603–1607.

Schroeder, S. R. (2000). Mental retardation and developmental disabilities influenced by environmental neurotoxic insults. *Environmental Health Perspectives, 108*(Suppl. 3), 395–399.

Schroth, M. L., & McCormack, W. A. (2000). Sensation seeking and need for achievement among study-abroad students. *The Journal of Social Psychology, 140*, 533–535.

Schultz, D. P., & Schultz, S. E. (2004). *A History of Modern Psychology*, pp. 239–242. Belmont, CA: Wadsworth.

Schutzwohl, A., Fuchs, A., McKibbin, W. F., & Shackelford, T. K. (2009). How willing are you to accept sexual requests from slightly unattractive to exceptionally attractive imagined requestors? *Human Nature, 20*(3), 282–293.

Schwanenflugel, P., & Rey, M. (1986). Interlingual semantic facilitation: Evidence from common representational system in the bilingual lexicon. *Journal of Memory and Language, 25*, 605–618.

Schwartz, C. E., Kunwar, P. S., Greve, D. N., Moran, L. R., Viner, J. C., Covino, J. M., et al. (2010). Structural differences in adult orbital and ventromedial prefrontal cortex predicted by infant temperament at 4 months of age. *Archives of General Psychiatry, 67*(1), 78–84. doi:10.1001/archgenpsychiatry.2009.171

Schwartz, J. H., Barres, B. A., & Goldman, J. E. (2013). The cells of the nervous system. In E. R. Kandel, J. H. Schwartz, T. M. Jessell, S. A. Siegelbaum, & A. J. Hudspeth (Eds.), *Principles of neural science* (5th ed., pp. 71–99). USA: McGraw-Hill.

Schwartz, J. H., & Javitch, J. A. (2013). Neurotransmitters. In E. R. Kandel, J. H. Schwartz, T. M. Jessell, S. A. Siegelbaum, & A. J. Hudspeth (Eds.), *Principles of neural science* (5th ed., pp. 289–306). USA: McGraw-Hill.

Schwartz, S. K. (2000). *Working your degree*. Retrieved March 6, 2010, from http://cnnfn.cnn.com/2000/12/08/career/q_degreepsychology/

Schweickert, R. (1993). A multinomial processing tree model for degradation and redintegration in immediate recall. *Memory and Cognition, 21*, 168–175.

Schwitzgebel, E. (1999). Representation and desire: A philosophical error with consequences for theory-of-mind research. *Philosophical Psychology, 12*, 157–180.

Scott, S. K., Young, A. W., Calder, A. J., Hellawell, D. J., Aggleton, J. P., & Johnson, M. (1997). Impaired auditory recognition of fear and anger following bilateral amygdala lesions. *Nature, 385*(6613), 254–257.

Scott, W. D. (1908). *The theory and practice of advertising*. Boston, MA: Small, Maynard, & Company.

Security Director's Report. (2008). Experts identify four trends in workplace violence. *Institute of Management and Administration, Inc., 8*(6), 1–15.

Seedat, S., Scott, K. M., Angermeyer, M. C., Berglund, P., Bromet, E. J., Brugha, T. S., et al. (2009). Cross-national associations between gender and mental disorders in the world health organization world mental health surveys. *Archives of General Psychiatry, 66*(7), 785-795. doi: 10.1001/archgenpsychiatry.2009.36

Segall, M. H., Campbell, D. T., & Herskovits, M. J. (1966). *The influence of culture on perception*. Indianapolis, IN: Bobbs-Merrill.

Segerstrom, S. C., & Sephton, S. E. (2010). Optimistic expectancies and cell-mediated immunity: The role of positive affect. *Psychological Science, 21*(3), 448–455. doi: 10.1177/0956797610362061

Segerstrom, S. C., Taylor, S. E., Kemeny, M. E., & Fahey, J. L. (1998). Optimism is associated with mood, coping, and immune change in response to stress. *Journal of Personality and Social Psychology, 74*(6), 1646–1655.

Seligman, M. (1975). *Helplessness: Depression, development and death*. New York: W. H. Freeman.

Seligman, M. (1989). *Helplessness*. New York: W. H. Freeman.

Seligman, M. (1995). The effectiveness of psychotherapy: The *Consumer Reports* study. *American Psychologist, 50*, 965–975.

Seligman, M. (1998). *Learned optimism: How to change your mind and your life* (2nd ed.). New York: Pocket Books.

Seligman, M. (2002). *Authentic happiness*. New York: Free Press.

Seligman, M., & Maier, S. F. (1967). Failure to escape traumatic shock. *Journal of Experimental Psychology, 74*, 1–9.

Seligman, M. E. P. (2005). Positive psychology, positive prevention, and positive therapy. In C. R. Snyder & S. J. Lopez (Eds.), *Handbook of positive psychology* (pp. 3–9). New York: Oxford University Press.

Seligman, M. E. P., & Csikszentmihalyi, M. (2000). Positive psychology: An introduction. *American Psychologist, 55*(1), 5–14. doi:10.1037/0003-066x.55.1.5

Selye, H. (1936). Syndrome produced by diverse nocuous agents. *Nature, 138*, 32.

Selye, H. (1956). *The stress of life*. New York: McGraw-Hill.

Selye, H. (1976). *The stress of life* (Rev. ed.). New York: McGraw-Hill.

Shackelford, T. K., Buss, D. M., & Bennett, K. (2002). Forgiveness or breakup: Sex differences in responses to a partner's infidelity. *Cognition and Emotion, 16*(2), 299–307.

Shadish, W., Cook, T. D., & Campbell, D. T. (2002). *Experimental and quasi-experimental designs for generalized causal inferences*. New York: Houghton Mifflin.

Shafton, A. (1995). *Dream reader: Contemporary approaches to the understanding of dreams (SUNY series in dream studies)* (pp. 40–46). New York: State University of New York Press.

Shapiro, A. K., & Shapiro, E. (1997). *The powerful placebo*. Baltimore: Johns Hopkins University Press.

Shapiro, F. (2001). *Eye movement desensitization and reprocessing: Basic principles, protocols, and procedures*. New York: Guilford Press.

Shapiro, F. (2012). *Getting past your past: Take control of your life with self-help techniques from EMDR therapy*. New York: Rodale.

Shapiro, K. L., Jacobs, W. J., & LoLordo, V. M. (1980). Stimulus relevance in Pavlovian conditioning in pigeons. *Animal Learning and Behavior, 8*, 586–594.

Sharif, Z., Bradford, D., Stroup, S., & Lieberman, J. (2007). Pharmacological treatment of schizophrenia. In P. E. Nathan & J. M. Gorman (Eds.), *A guide to treatments that work* (3rd ed., pp. 203–241). New York: Oxford University Press.

Sharot, T., Delgado, M. R., & Phelps, E. A. (2004). How emotion enhances the feeling of remembering. *Nature Neuroscience, 7*(12), 1376–1380.

Shean, R. E., de Klerk, N. H., Armstrong, B. K., & Walker, N. R. (1994). Seven-year follow-up of a smoking-prevention program for children. *Australian Journal of Public Health, 18,* 205–208.

Sheldon, K. M. (2012). The self-determination theory perspective on positive mental health across cultures. *World Psychiatry, 11*(2), 101–102.

Sheldon, S. H. (2002). Sleep in infants and children. In T. L. Lee- Chiong, M. J. Sateia, & M. A. Carskadon (Eds.), *Sleep medicine* (pp. 99–103). Philadelphia: Hanley & Belfus.

Shepherd, G. M. (2012). *Neurogastronomy: How the brain creates flavor and why it matters.* New York: Columbia University Press.

Shepard, R. N., & Metzler, J. (1971). Mental rotation of three- dimensional objects. *Science, 171,* 701–703.

Shepard, T. H. (2001). *Catalog of teratogenic agents* (10th ed.). Baltimore: Johns Hopkins University Press.

Sherif, M. (1936). *The psychology of social norms.* New York: Harper & Row.

Sherif, M., Harvey, O. J., White, B. J., Hood, W. R., & Sherif, C. W. (1961). *Intergroup conflict and cooperation: The Robber's Cave experiment.* Norman: University of Oklahoma Book Exchange.

Sherlin, L. H., Arns, M., Lubar, J., Heinrich, H., Kerson, C., Strehl, U., et al. (2011). Neurofeedback and basic learning theory: Implications for research and practice. *Journal of Neurotherapy: Investigations in Neuromodulation, Neurofeedback and Applied Neuroscience, 15*(4), 292–304.

Shomrat, T., Zarrella, I., Fiorito, G., & Hochner, B. (2008). The octopus vertical lobe modulates short-term learning rate and uses LTP to acquire long-term memory. *Current Biology, 18,* 337–342.

Shore, L. A. (1990). Skepticism in light of scientific literacy. *Skeptical Inquirer, 15*(1), 3–4.

Shorter, E. (1997). *A history of psychiatry: From the era of the asylum to the age of Prozac.* New York: Wiley.

Showalter, E. (1997). *Hystories: Hysterical epidemics and modern culture.* New York: Columbia University Press.

Shuglin, A. (1986). The background chemistry of MDMA. *Journal of Psychoactive Drugs, 18*(4), 291–304.

Siegel, R. K., & West, L. J. (Eds.). (1975). *Hallucinations: Behavior, experience, and theory* (2nd ed.). New York: Wiley.

Siegel, S. (1969). Effects of CS habituation on eyelid conditioning. *Journal of Comparative and Physiological Psychology, 68*(2), 245–248.

Siegler, I. C., Costa, P. T., Brummett, B. H., Helms, M. J., Barefoot, J. C., Williams, R. B., et al. (2003). Patterns of change in hostility from college to midlife in the UNC alumni heart study predict high-risk status. *Psychosomatic Medicine, 65,* 738–745.

Siegler, R. S. (1996). *Emerging minds: The process of change in children's thinking.* New York: Oxford University Press.

Simeon, D., Guralnik, O., Hazlett, E. A., Spiegel-Cohen, J., Hollander, E., & Buchsbaum, M. S. (2000). Feeling unreal: A PET study of depersonalization disorder. *American Journal of Psychiatry, 157,* 1782–1788.

Simon, D. A., & Bjork, R. A. (2001). Metacognition in motor learning. *Journal of Experimental Psychology: Learning, Memory, and Cognition, 27*(4), 907–912.

Singer, M. T., & Lalich, J. (1995). *Cults in our midst.* San Francisco: Jossey-Bass.

Singh-Manoux, A., Richards, M., & Marmot, M. (2003). Leisure activities and cognitive function in middle age: Evidence from the Whitehall II study. *Journal of Epidemiology and Community Health, 57,* 907–913.

Skinner, B. F. (1938). *The behavior of organisms: An experimental analysis.* New York: Appleton-Century-Crofts.

Skinner, B. F. (1956). A case history in scientific method. *American Psychologist, 11,* 221–233.

Skinner, B. F. (1961). *Cumulative record: Definitive edition.* New York: Appelton-Century-Crofts.

Skinner, B. F. (1971). *Beyond freedom and dignity.* New York: Knopf.

Skinner, B. F. (1974). *About behaviorism.* New York: Knopf.

Skinner, B. F. (1989). The origins of cognitive thought. In *Recent issues in the analysis of behavior.* Princeton, NC: Merrill Publishing Company.

Skolnick, A. (1986). Early attachment and personal relationships across the life course. In P. B. Baltes, D. L. Featherman, & R. M. Lerner (Eds.), *Life-span development and behavior* (Vol. 7). Hillsdale, NJ: Erlbaum.

Slater, A. (2000). Visual perception in the young infant: Early organisation and rapid learning. In D. Muir & A. Slater (Eds.), *Infant development: The essential readings.* Oxford, UK: Blackwell.

Slater, M., Antley, A., Davison, A., Swapp, D., Guger, C., Barker, C., et al. (2006). A virtual reprise of the Stanley Milgram obedience experiments. *PLoS ONE, 1*(1), e39. doi:10.1371/journal.pone.0000039

Sleddens, E. F., Gerards, S. M., Thijs, C., de Vries, N. K., & Kremers, S. P. (2011). General parenting, childhood overweight and obesity-inducing behaviors: A review. *International Journal of Pediatric Obesity, 6*(2–2), e12–27.

Slipp, S. (1993). *The Freudian mystique: Freud, women and feminism.* New York: New York University Press.

Sloan, D. M., & Mizes, J. S. (1999). Foundations of behavior therapy in the contemporary healthcare context. *Clinical Psychology Review, 19,* 255–274.

Smith, D. (2001). Shock and disbelief. *Atlantic Monthly, 2,* 79–90.

Smith, M. A., Roediger, H. L., & Karpicke, J. D. (2013). Covert retrieval practice benefits retention as much as overt retrieval practice. *Journal of Experimental Psychology. Learning, Memory, and Cognition.* doi: 10.1037/a0033569

Smith, T. C., Ryan, M. A. K., Wingard, D. L., Sallis, J. F., & Kritz- Silverstein, D. (2008). New onset and persistent symptoms of post-traumatic stress disorder self-reported after deployment and combat exposures: Prospective population based U.S. military cohort study. *British Medical Journal, 336*(7640), 366–371.

Smolen, P., Baxter, D. A., Byrne, J. H., (2006). A model of the roles of essential kinases in the induction and expression of late long-term potentiation. *Biophysical Journal, 90,* 2760–2775.

Snarey, J. R. (1985). Cross-cultural universality of social-moral development: A critical review of Kohlbergian research. *Psychological Bulletin, 97*(2), 202–232.

Snyder, C. R., & Lopez, S. J. (2005). The future of positive psychology. In C. R. Snyder & S. J. Lopez (Eds.), *Handbook of positive psychology* (pp. 751–767). New York: Oxford University Press.

Snyder, D. J., & Bartoshuk, L. M. (2009). Epidemiological studies of taste function: Discussion and perspectives. *Annals of the New York Academy of Sciences, 1170,* 574–580.

Snyder, M., Tanke, E. D., & Berscheid, E. (1977). Social perception and interpersonal behavior: On the self-fulfilling nature of social stereotypes. *Journal of Personality and Social Psychology, 35,*656–666.

Snyder, S. H. (2002). Forty years of neurotransmitters. *Archives of General Psychiatry, 59,* 983–994.

Snyder, T. D., & Dillow, S. A. (2010). *Digest of education statistics 2009* (NCES Publication No. NCES 2010-013). Washington, DC: National Center for Education Statistics, Institute of Education Sciences, U.S. Department of Education.

Söderlund, J., Schröder, J., Nordin, C., Samuelsson, M., Walther- Jallow, L., Karlsson, H., et al. (2009). Activation of brain interleukin-1 in schizophrenia. *Molecular Psychiatry, 14*(12), 1069.

Sodowsky, G. R., Lai, E. W., & Plake, B. S. (1991). Moderating effects of socio-cultural variables on acculturation attitudes of Hispanics and Asian Americans. *Journal of Counseling & Development, 70,* 194–204.

Somerville, L. H., Jones, R. M., Ruberry, E. J., Dyke, J. P., Glover, G., & Casey, B. J. (2013). The medial prefrontal cortex and the emergence of self-conscious emotion in adolescence. *Psychological Science, 24,* 1554–1562.

Soomro, G. M. (2001). Obsessive-compulsive disorder. *Clinical Evidence, 6,* 754–762.

Sorkhabi, N. (2005). Applicability of Baumrind's parent typology to collective cultures: Analysis of cultural explanations of parent socialization effects. *International Journal of Behavioral Development, 29*(6), 552–563.

Spangler, W. D. (1992). Validity of questionnaire and TAT measures of need for achievement: Two meta-analyses. *Psychological Bulletin, 112,* 140–154.

Spangler, W. J., Cosgrove, G. R., Ballantine, H. T., Jr., Cassem, E. H., Rauch, S. L., Nierenberg, A., et al. (1996). Magnetic resonance image-guided stereotactic cingulotomy for intractable psychiatric disease. *Neurosurgery, 38,* 1071–1076.

Sparing, R., Mottaghy, F., Ganis, G., Thompson, W. L., Toepper, R., Kosslyn, S. M., et al. (2002). Visual cortex excitability increases during visual mental imagery—a TMS study in healthy human subjects. *Brain Research, 938,* 92–97.

Speca, M., Carlson, L. E., Goodey, E., & Angen, E. (2000). A randomized wait-list controlled clinical trial: The effects of a mindfulness meditation-based stress reduction program on mood and symptoms of stress in cancer outpatients. *Psychosomatic Medicine, 6,* 2613–2622.

Speroff, L., Glass, R. H., & Kase, N. G. (1999). Recurrent early pregnancy loss. In *Clinical Gynecologic endocrinology and infertility* (pp. 1042–1055). Philadelphia: Lippincott, Williams & Wilkins.

Sperry, R. W. (1968). Mental unity following surgical disconnection of the cerebral hemispheres. In *The Harvey lectures* (pp. 293–323). New York: Academic Press.

Spiegel, D., Bloom, J. R., & Gottheil, E. (1989). Effects of psychosocial treatment on survival of patients with metastatic breast cancer. *Lancet, 2,* 888–891.

Springer, S. P., & Deutsch, G. (1998). *Left brain, right brain: Perspectives from cognitive neuroscience* (5th ed.). New York: W. H. Freeman.

Squire, L. R., & Kandel, E. (1999). *Memory: From mind to molecule.* New York: Scientific American Library.

Squire, L. R., & Kandel, E. R. (2009). *Memory: From mind to molecules* (2nd ed.). Greenwood-village, CO: Roberts and Company Publishers.

Squire, L. R., Knowlton, B., & Musen, G. (1993). The structure and organization of memory. *Annual Review of Psychology, 44,* 453–495.

Squire, L. R., & Slater, P. C. (1978). Anterograde and retrograde memory impairment in chronic amnesia. *Neuropsychologia, 16,* 313–322.

Squire, L. R., Slater, P. C., & Chace, P. M. (1975). Retrograde amnesia: Temporal gradient in very long-term memory following electroconvulsive therapy. *Science, 187,* 77–79.

Standing, L., Conezio, J., & Haber, R. N. (1970). Perception and memory for pictures: Single-trial learning of 2500 visual stimuli. *Psychonomic Science, 19,* 73–74.

Stanovich, K. E., & West, R. F. (2000). Individual differences in reasoning: Implications for the rationality debate? *Behavioral and Brain Sciences*, 23(5), 645–665; discussion 665–726.

Stahl, S. M. (2013). *Stahl's essential psychopharmacology: Neuroscientific basis and practical applications* (4th ed.). New York, NY: Cambridge University Press.

Steele, C. M. (1992). Race and the schooling of Black Americans. *The Atlantic Monthly*, 269(4), 68–78.

Steele, C. M. (1997). A threat in the air: How stereotypes shape intellectual identity and performance. *American Psychologist*, 52, 613–629.

Steele, C. M. (1999, August). Thin ice: "stereotype threat" and Black college students. *The Atlantic Monthly*, 284, 44–54.

Steele, C. M., & Aronson, J. (1995). Stereotype threat and the intellectual test performance of African Americans. *Journal of Personality and Social Psychology*, 69, 797–811.

Steele, J., James, J. B., & Barnett, R. C. (2002). Learning in a man's world: Examining the perceptions of undergraduate women in male-dominated academic areas. *Psychology of Women Quarterly*, 26, 46–50.

Stein-Behrens, B., Mattson, M. P., Chang, I., Yeh, M., & Sapolsky, R. (1994). Stress exacerbates neuron loss and cytoskeletal pathology in the hippocampus. *Journal of Neuroscience*, 14, 5373–5380.

Steinberg, L., & Silverberg, S. B. (1987). Influences on marital satisfaction during the middle stages of the family life cycle. *Journal of Marriage and the Family*, 49, 751–760.

Steriade, M., & McCarley, R. W. (1990). *Brainstem control of wakefulness and sleep*. New York: Plenum.

Sternberg, R. J. (1986). A triangular theory of love. *Psychological Review*, 93, 119–135.

Sternberg, R. J. (1988a). Triangulating love. In R. Sternberg & M. Barnes (Eds.), *The psychology of love* (pp. 119–138). New Haven, CT: Yale University Press.

Sternberg, R. J. (1988b). *The triarchic mind: A new theory of human intelligence*. New York: Viking-Penguin.

Sternberg, R. J. (1996). *Successful intelligence: How practical and creative intelligence determine success in life*. New York: Simon & Schuster.

Sternberg, R. J. (1997). Construct validation of a triangular love scale. *European Journal of Social Psychology*, 27, 313–335.

Sternberg, R. J., & Grigorenko, E. L. (2006). Cultural intelligence and successful intelligence. *Group Organization Management*, 31, 27–39.

Sternberg, R. J., & Kaufman, J. C. (1998). Human abilities. *Annual Review of Psychology*, 49, 479–502.

Sternberger, R. R., Turner, S. M., Beidel, D. C., & Calhoun, K. S. (1995). Social phobia: An analysis of possible developmental factors. *Journal of Abnormal Psychology*, 194, 526–531.

Stevenson, M. B., Roach, M. A., Leavitt, L. A., Miller, J. F., & Chapman, R. S. (1988). Early receptive and productive language skills in preterm and full-term 8-month-old infants. *Journal of Psycholinguistic Research*, 17(2), 169–183.

Stickgold, R., Hobson, J. A., Fosse, R., & Fosse, M. (2001). Sleep, learning and dreams: Off-line memory reprocessing. *Science*, 294, 1052–1057.

Stiff, J. B., & Mongeau, P. A. (2002). *Persuasive communication* (2nd ed.). New York: Guilford Press.

Stipek, D. J., Gralinski, J. H., & Kopp, C. B. (1990). Self-concept development in the toddler years. *Developmental Psychology*, 26(6), 972–977.

Stoodley, C. J., & Schmahmann, J. D. (2009). Functional topography in the human cerebellum: A meta-analysis of neuroimaging studies. *NeuroImage*, 44(2), 489–501. doi:10.1016/j.neuroimage.2008.08.039

Stowell, J. R., Kiecolt-Glaser, J. K., & Glaser, R. (2001). Perceived stress and cellular immunity: When coping counts. *Journal of Behavioral Medicine*, 24(4), 323–339.

Stratton, K., Gable, A., & McCormick, M. C. (Eds.). (2001a). *Immunization safety review: Thimerosal-containing vaccines and neurodevelopmental disorders*. Washington, DC: National Academies Press.

Stratton, K., Wilson, C. B., & McCormick, M. C. (Eds.). (2001b). *Immunization safety review: Measles-mumps-rubella vaccine and autism*. Washington, DC: National Academies Press.

Straus, M. A. (2000). Corporal punishment of children and adult depression and suicidal ideation. In *Beating the devil out of them: Corporal punishment in American families and its effects on children* (pp. 60–77). New York: Lexington Books.

Strauss, A. S. (2004). The meaning of death in Northern Cheyenne culture. In A. C. G. M. Robben (Ed.), *Death, mourning, and burial: A cross-cultural reader* (pp. 71–76). Malden, MA: Blackwell.

Strawbridge, W. J., Cohen, R. D., Shema, S. J., & Kaplan, G. A. (1997). Frequent attendance at religious services and mortality over 28 years. *American Journal of Public Health*, 87, 957–961.

Strayer, D. L., Drews, F. A., & Crouch, D. J. (2006). A comparison of the cell phone driver and the drunk driver. *Human Factors*, 48, 381–391.

Strayer, D. L., & Johnston, W. A. (2001). Driven to distraction: Dual-task studies of simulated driving and conversing on a cellular phone. *Psychological Science*, 12, 462–466.

Stromeyer, C. F., III, & Psotka, J. (1971). The detailed texture of eidetic images. *Nature*, 237, 109–112.

Stroth, S., Hille, K., Spitzer, M., & Reinhardt, R. (2009). Aerobic endurance exercise benefits memory and affect in young adults. *Neuropsychological Rehabilitation*, 19(2), 223–243.

Strunk, D. R., Brotman, M. A., & DeRubeis, R. J. (2010). The process of change in cognitive therapy for depression: Predictors of early inter-session symptom gains. *Behaviour Research and Therapy*, 48(7), 599–606.

Stubbs, R. J., van Wyk, M. C. W., Johnstone, A. M., & Harbron, C. G. (1996). Breakfasts high in protein, fat or carbohydrate: Effect on within-day appetite and energy balance. *European Journal of Clinical Nutrition*, 50, 409–417.

Stuss, D. T., Binns, M. A., Murphy, K. J., & Alexander, M. P. (2002). Dissociations within the anterior attentional system: Effects of task complexity and irrelevant information on reaction time speed and accuracy. *Neuropsychology*, 16, 500–513.

Sue, D. W., & Sue, D. (2008). *Counseling the culturally diverse*. Hoboken, NJ: John Wiley & Sons, Inc.

Sue, S. (1977). Community mental health services to minority groups: Some optimism, some pessimism. *American Psychologist*, 32, 616–624.

Sue, S. (1992). Ethnicity and mental health: Research and policy issues. *Journal of Social Issues*, 48(2), 187–205.

Sue, S., Zane, N., & Young, K. (1994). Research on psychotherapy in culturally diverse populations. In A. Bergin & S. Garfield (Eds.), *Handbook of psychotherapy and behavior change* (pp. 783–817). New York: Wiley.

Sullivan, P. F. (2005). The genetics of schizophrenia. *PLoS Med*, 2(7), e212. doi:05-PLME-RIT-0198R1

Sullivan, P. F., Neale, M. C., & Kendler, K. S. (2000). Genetic epidemiology of major depression: Review and meta-analysis. *American Journal of Psychiatry*, 157, 1552–1562.

Sulzer, J., Sitaram, R., Blefari, M. L., Kollias, S., Birbaumer, N., Stephan, K. E., et al. (2013). Neurofeedback-mediated self-regulation of the dopaminergic midbrain. *Neuroimage*, 75C, 176–184. doi:10.1016/j.neuroimage.2013.02.041

Suryani, L., & Jensen, S. (1993). *Trance and possession in Bali: A window on Western multiple personality, possession disorder, and suicide*. New York: Oxford University Press.

Sutcliffe, N., Clarke, A. E., Levinton, C., Frost, C., Gordon, C., & Isenberg, D. A. (1999). Associates of health status in patients with systemic lupus erythematosus. *Journal of Rheumatology*, 26, 2352–2356.

Sutherland, P. (1992). *Cognitive development today: Piaget and his critics*. London: Paul Chapman.

Swayze, V. W., II. (1995). Frontal leukotomy and related psychosurgical procedures in the era before antipsychotics (1935–1954): A historical overview. *American Journal of Psychiatry*, 152(4), 505–515.

Szell, M., & Thurner, S. (2013). How women organize social networks different from men. *Scientific Reports*, 3, 1214. doi:10.1038/srep01214

Taglialatela, J. P., Savage-Rumbaugh, E. S., & Baker, L. A. (2003). Vocal production by a language-competent bonobo (*Pan paniscus*). *International Journal of Comparative Psychology*, 24, 1–17.

Tajfel, H., & Turner, J. C. (1986). The social identity theory of intergroup behaviour. In S. Worchel & W. G. Austin (Eds.), *The psychology of intergroup relations* (Vol. 2, pp. 7–24). New York: Nelson Hall.

Takeuchi, T., Ogilvie, R. D., Murphy, T. I., & Ferrelli, A. V. (2003). EEG activities during elicited sleep onset. REM and NREM periods reflect difference mechanisms of dream generation. *Clinical Neurophysiology*, 114(2), 210–220.

Talbott, G. D., & Crosby, L. R. (2001). Recovery contracts: Seven key elements. In R. H. Coombs (Ed.), *Addiction recovery tools* (pp. 127–144). Thousand Oaks, CA: Sage.

Tarrier, N., & Taylor, R. (2014). Schizophrenia and other psychotic disorders. In D. H. Barlow (Ed.), *Clinical handbook of psychological disorders: A step-by-step treatment manual* (5th ed., pp. 502–532). New York: Guilford Press.

Taylor, B., Miller, E., Farrington, C. P., Petropoulos, M. C., Favot-Mayaud, I., Li, J., et al. (1999). Autism and measles, mumps, and rubella vaccine: No epidemiological evidence for a causal association. *Lancet*, 353, 2026–2029.

Taylor, C., Manganello, J. A., Lee, S. J., & Rice, J. C. (2010). Mothers' spanking of 3-year-old children and subsequent risk of children's aggressive behavior. *Pediatrics*, 125, 1057–1065.

Taylor, D. M., & Moghaddam, F. M. (1994). *Theories of intergroup relations: International social psychological perspectives* (2nd ed.). Westport, CT: Praeger.

Teigen, K. (1994). Yerkes-Dodson: A law for all seasons. *Theory and Psychology*, 4, 525–547.

Temoshok, L., & Dreher, H. (1992). *The Type C connection: The behavioral links to cancer and your health*. New York: Random House.

Terman, L. M., & Oden, M. H. (1947). *The gifted child grows up: 25 years' follow-up of a superior group: Genetic studies of genius* (Vol. 4). Stanford, CA: Stanford University Press.

Tevis, M. (1994). George I. Sanchez. In L. Glenn Smith & Joan K. Smith (Eds.), *Lives in education: A narrative of people and ideas* (2nd ed., pp. 346–354). New York: St. Martin's Press.

Thase, M. E. (1999). When are psychotherapy and pharmacotherapy combinations the treatment of choice for major depressive disorders? *Psychiatric Quarterly*, 70(4), 333–346.

Thase, M. E., & Sachs, G. S. (2000). Bipolar depression: Pharmacotherapy and related therapeutic strategies. *Biological Psychiatry*, 48(6), 558–572.

The University of Manchester. (2009). Virtual solution to driving phobias [Press release]. Retrieved from http://www.psych-sci.manchester.ac.uk/aboutus/press-releases/virtualdriving

Thiedke, C. C. (2001). Sleep disorders and sleep problems in childhood. *American Family Physician, 63,* 277–284.

Thigpen, C. H., & Cleckley, H. M. (1992, Rev.). *The three faces of Eve.* London: Secker & Warburg.

Thomas, A., & Chess, S. (1977). *Temperament and development.* New York: Brunner/ Mazel.

Thompson, W. W., Price, C., Goodson, B., Shay, D. K., Benson, P., Hinrichsen, V. L., et al. (2007). Early thimerosal exposure and neuropsychological outcomes at 7 to 10 years. *The New England Journal of Medicine, 357*(13), 1281–1292.

Thoresen, C. E., & Harris, H. S. (2002). Spirituality and health: What's the evidence and what's needed? *Annals of Behavioral Medicine, 24,* 3–13.

Thorndike, E. L. (1911). *Animal intelligence: Experimental studies.* New York: Macmillan.

Thorndike, E. L. (1920). A constant error on psychological rating. *Journal of Applied Psychology, 5,* 25–29.

Thornton, A., & Hui-Sheng, L. (1994). Continuity and change. In A. Thornton & Hui-Sheng (Eds.), *Social change and the family in Taiwan* (pp. 396–410). Chicago: University of Chicago Press.

Tienari, P., Wynne, L. C., Sorri, A., Lahti, I., Laksy, K., Moring, J., et al. (2004). Genotype-environment interaction in schizophrenia- spectrum disorder: Long-term follow-up study of Finnish adoptees. *The British Journal of Psychiatry, 184,* 216–222.

Tobach, E. (2001). Development of sex and gender. In J. Worell (Ed.), *Encyclopedia of women and gender* (pp. 315–332). San Diego, CA: Academic Press.

Toga, A. W., & Thompson, P. M. (2003). Mapping brain asymmetry. *Nature Reviews Neuroscience, 4,* 37–48.

Toker, S., Shirom, A., Melamed, S., & Armon, G. (2012). Work characteristics as predictors of diabetes incidence among apparently healthy employees. *Journal of Occupational Health Psychology, 17*(3), 259. doi: 10.1037/a0028401

Tolman, E. C. (1932). *Purposive behavior in animals and man.* New York: Century.

Tolman, E. C., & Honzik, C. H. (1930). Introduction and removal of reward and maze learning in rats. *University of California Publications in Psychology, 4,* 257–275.

Tomasello, M., Carpenter, M., & Lizskowski, U. (2007). A new look at infant pointing. *Child Development, 78,* 705–722.

Torgersen, S., Czajkowski, N., Jacobson, K., Reichborn-Kjennerud, T., Roysamb, E., Neale, M. C., et al. (2008). Dimensional representations of DSMIV cluster B personality disorders in a population-based sample of Norwegian twins: A multivariate study. *Psychological Medicine, 38*(11), 1617–1625. doi:10.1017/s0033291708002924

Torrance, E. P. (1993). The Beyonders in a thirty-year longitudinal study of creative achievement. *Roeper Review, 15*(3), 131–135.

Trace, S. E., Baker, J. H., Penas-Lledo, E., & Bulik, C. M. (2013). The genetics of eating disorders. *Annual Review of Clinical Psychology, 9,* 589–620. doi:10.1146/ annurev-clinpsy-050212-185546

Trappey, C. (1996). A meta-analysis of consumer choice and subliminal advertising. *Psychology and Marketing, 13,* 517–530.

Treisman, A. [M.]. (2006). How the deployment of attention determines what we see. *Visual Cognition, 14,* 411–443.

Treisman, A. M., & Gelade, G. (1980). A feature integration theory of attention. *Cognitive Psychology, 12,* 97–136.

Treisman, M. (1977). Motion sickness: An evolutionary hypothesis. *Science, 197,* 493.

Triandis, H. (1971). *Attitude and attitude change.* New York: Wiley.

Trivers, R. L. (1972). Parental investment and sexual selection. In B. Campbell (Ed.), *Sexual selection and the descent of man, 1871–1971* (pp. 136–179). Chicago: Aldine-Atherton.

Trocmé, N., MacLaurin, B., Fallon, B., Daciuk, J., Billingsley, D., Tourigny, M., et al. (2001). *Canadian incidence study of reported child abuse and neglect: Final report* (pp. 30–31). Ottawa, ON: Minister of Public Works and Government Services Canada.

Troncoso, X. G., Macknik, S. L., Otero-Millan, J., & Martinez-Conde, S. (2008). Microsaccades drive illusory motion in the enigma illusion. *Proceedings of the National Academy of Sciences, USA, 105*(41), 16033–16038.

Trujillo, K. A., & Chinn, A. B. (1996). *Drugs and the Brain: Antidepressants.* California State University. Retrieved July 20, 2004, from www.csusm.edu/DandB/AD.html#history

Tsai, G. E., Condle, D., Wu, M.-T., & Chang, I.-W. (1999). Functional magnetic resonance imaging of personality switches in a woman with dissociative identity disorder. *Harvard Review of Psychiatry, 7,* 119–122.

Tsai, J. L., Simeonova, D. I., & Watanabe, J. T. (2004). Somatic and social: Chinese Americans talk about emotion. *Personality and Social Psychology Bulletin, 30*(9), 1226–1238.

Tsapogas, J. (2006). *Characteristics of Doctoral Scientists and Engineers in the United States: 2003,* NSF, 06-320. Arlington, VA: National Science Foundation, Division of Science Resources Statistics.

Tucker, E. W., & Potocky-Tripodi, M. (2006). Changing heterosexuals' attitudes toward homosexuals: A systematic review of the empirical literature. *Research on Social Work Practice, 16*(2), 176–190.

Tucker, M. A., Hirota, Y., Wamsley, E. J., Lau, H., Chaklader, A., & Fishbein, W. (2006). A daytime nap containing solely non-REM sleep enhances declarative but not procedural memory. *Neurobiology of Learning and Memory, 86*(2), 241–247.

Tukuitonga, C. F., & Bindman, A. B. (2002). Ethnic and gender differences in the use of coronary artery revascularisation procedures in New Zealand. *New Zealand Medical Journal, 115,* 179–182.

Tulving, E., & Thomson, D. M. (1973). Encoding specificity and retrieval processes in episodic memory. *Psychological Review, 80,* 352–373.

Tupak, S. V., Dresler, T., Badewien, M., Hahn, T., Ernst, L. H., Herrmann, M. J., et al. (2013). Inhibitory transcranial magnetic theta burst stimulation attenuates prefrontal cortex oxygenation. *Human Brain Mapping, 34*(1), 150–157. doi:10.1002/ hbm.21421

Turk, C. L., Heimberg, R. G., & Magee, L. (2008). Social anxiety disorder. In D. H. Barlow (Ed.), *Clinical handbook of psychological disorders* (pp. 123–163). New York: Guilford Press.

Turner, W. J. (1995). Homosexuality, Type 1: An Xq28 phenomenon. *Archives of Sexual Behavior, 24*(2), 109–134.

Tversky, A., & Kahneman, D. (1973). Availability: A heuristic for judging frequency and probability. *Cognitive Psychology, 5*(2), 207–232.

Tversky, A., & Shafir, E. (1992). The disjunction effect in choice under uncertainty. *Psychological Science, 3*(5), 305–309.

Ulmer, J. L., Parsons, L., Moseley, M., & Gabrieli, J. (Eds.). (2006). *White matter in cognitive neuroscience: Advances in diffusion tensor imaging and its applications* (Annals of the New York Academy of Sciences, Vol. 1064). New York: The New York Academy of Sciences.

Underwood, M. K., Beron, K. J., & Rosen, L. H. (2009). Continuity and change in social and physical aggression from middle childhood through early adolescence. *Aggressive Behavior, 35*(5), 357–375.

Unger, R. (1979). Toward a redefinition of sex and gender. *American Psychologist, 34,* 1085–1094.

Vail, A. (1976). Factors influencing lower class, black patients' remaining in treatment. *Clinical Psychology, 29,* 12–14.

Vaillant, G. E. (2002). Adaptive mental mechanisms: Their role in a positive psychology. *American Psychologist, 55,* 89–98.

Valverde, R., Pozdnyakova, I., Kajander, T., Venkatraman, J., & Regan, L. (2007). Fragile X mental retardation syndrome: Structure of the KH1-KH2 domains of fragile X mental retardation protein. *Structure, 9,* 1090–1098.

Van de Castle, R. (1994). *Our dreaming mind.* New York: Ballantine Books.

van der Merwe, A., & Garuccio, A. (Eds.). (1994). *Waves and particles in light and matter.* New York: Plenum Press.

van der Stelt, O., van der Molen, M., Boudewijn Gunning, W., & Kok, A. (2010). Neuroelectrical signs of selective attention to color in boys with Attention-Deficit/Hyperactivity disorder. *Cognitive Brain Research, 12*(2), 245–264.

VandenBos, G. R., & Bulatao, E. Q. (Eds.). (1996). *Violence on the job: Identifying risks and developing solutions.* Washington DC: American Psychological Association.

Van Dongen, H. P. A., Maislin, G., Mullington, J. M., & Dinges, D. F. (2003). The cumulative cost of additional wakefulness: Dose- response effects on neurobehavioral functions and sleep physiology from chronic sleep restriction and total sleep deprivation. *Sleep, 26,* 117–126.

Van Horn, J. D., Irimia,, A., Torgerson, C. M., Chambers, M. C., Kikinis, R., & Toga, A. W. (2012). Mapping connectivity damage in the case of Phineas Gage. *PLoS ONE, 7*(5), e37454. doi:10.1371/journal.pone.0037454

Varela, J. A., Wang, J., Christianson, J. P., Maier, S. F., & Cooper, D. C. (2012). Control over stress, but not stress per se increases prefrontal cortical pyramidal neuron excitability. *The Journal of Neuroscience, 32*(37), 12848–12853. doi:10.1523/jneurosci.2669-12.2012

Vartanian, L. R. (2000). Revisiting the imaginary audience and personal fable constructs of adolescent egocentrism: A conceptual review. *Adolescence, 35*(140), 639–661.

Vasey, P. L., & VanderLaan, D. P. (2010). An adaptive cognitive dissociation between willingness to help kin and nonkin in Samoan Fa'afafine. *Psychological Science, 21*(2), 292–297.

Vecsey, C. G., Baillie, G. S., Jaganath, D., Havekes, R., Daniels, A., Wimmer, M., et al. (2009). Sleep deprivation impairs cAMP signaling in the hippocampus. *Nature, 461*(7267), 1122–1125.

Vernon, S. W., & Roberts, R. E. (1982). Use of RDC in a tri-ethnic community survey. *Archives of General Psychiatry, 39,* 47.

Villani, S. (2001). Impact of media on children and adolescents: A 10-year review of the research. *Journal of the American Academy on Child and Adolescent Psychiatry, 40*(4), 392–401.

Virkkunen, M., & Linnoila, M. (1996). Serotonin and glucose metabolism in impulsively violent alcoholic offenders. In D. M. Stoff & R. B. Cairns (Eds.), *Aggression and violence* (pp. 87–100). Mahwah, NJ: Erlbaum.

Visser, P. S., & Krosnick, J. A. (1998). Development of attitude strength over the life cycle: Surge and decline. *Journal of Personality and Social Psychology, 75*(6), 1389–1410.

Vogel, G. W. (1975). A review of REM sleep deprivation. *Archives of General Psychiatry, 32,* 749–761.

Vogel, G. W. (1993). Selective deprivation, REM sleep. In M. A. Carskadon (Ed.), *The encyclopedia of sleep and dreaming.* New York: Macmillan.

Vogt, B. A., & Palomero-Gallagher, N. (2012). Cingulate cortex. In J. K. Mai & G. Paxinos (Eds.), *The human nervous system* (pp. 943–987). London, UK: Academic Press.

Voineskos, A. N., Lobaugh, N. J., Bouix, S., Rajji, T. K., Miranda, D., Kennedy, J. L., et al. (2010). Diffusion tensor tractography findings in schizophrenia across the adult lifespan. *Brain: A Journal of Neurology, 17*, 17.

Vokey, J. R., & Read, J. D. (1985). Subliminal messages: Between the devil and the media. *American Psychologist, 40*, 1231–1239.

Volkow, N. D., Wang, G.-J., Newcorn, J., Telang, F., Solanto, M. V., Fowler, J. S., et al. (2007). Depressed dopamine activity in caudate and preliminary evidence of limbic involvement in adults with Attention-Deficit/Hyperactivity Disorder. *Archives of General Psychiatry, 64*(8), 932–940.

von Helmholtz, H. (1852). On the theory of compound colours. *Philosophical Magazine, 4*, 519–535.

von Helmholtz, H. L. F. (1863, 1954). *Die Lehre von den Tonempfindungen als physiologische Grundlage fur die Theorie der Musik [On the sensations of tone as a physiological basis for the theory of music]* (Alexander J. Ellis, Trans.). . New York: Dover.

Voss, M. W., Erickson, K. I., Prakash, R. S., Chaddock, L., Malkowski, E., Alves, H., et al. (2010). Functional connectivity: A source of variance in the association between cardiorespiratory fitness and cognition? *Neuropsychologia, 48*(5), 1394–1406.

Voyer, D., & Rodgers, M. (2002). Reliability of laterality effects in a dichotic listening task with nonverbal material. *Brain and Cognition, 48*, 602–606.

Vygotsky, L. S. (1962, 1934). *Thought and language.* Cambridge, MA: MIT Press.

Vygotsky, L. S. (1978). *Mind in society: The development of higher psychological processes.* Cambridge, MA: Harvard University Press.

Vygotsky, L. S. (1987). Thought and word. In R. W. Riebe & A. S. Carton (Eds.), *The collected works of L. S. Vygotsky: Vol. 1. Problems of general psychology* (pp. 243–288). New York: Plenum.

Wade, T. D., Gordon, S., Medland, S., Bulik, C. M., Heath, A. C., Montgomery, G. W., et al. (2013). Genetic variants associated with disordered eating. *The International Journal of Eating Disorders.* doi: 10.1002/eat.22133

Wahlsten, D. (1997). The malleability of intelligence is not constrained by heritability. In B. Devlin, S. E. Fienberg, & K. Roeder (Eds.), *Intelligence, genes, and success: Scientists respond to the bell curve* (pp. 71–87). New York: Springer.

Wakefield, A. J., Murch, S. H., Anthony, A., Linnell, J., Casson, D. M., Malik, M., et al. (1998). Ileal-lymphoid-nodular hyperplasia, non-specific colitis, and pervasive developmental disorder in children. *The Lancet, 351*, 9103.

Walker, L. J. (1991). Sex differences in moral reasoning. In W. M. Kurtines & J. L. Gewirtz (Eds.), *Handbook of moral behavior and development: Vol. 2. Research* (pp. 333–364). Hillsdale, NJ: Erlbaum.

Walter, C. (2008). Affairs of the lips. *Scientific American Mind, 19*(6), 24.

Wampold, B. E. (1997). Methodological problems in identifying efficacious psychotherapies. *Psychotherapy Research, 7*, 21–43.

Wang, Z., David, P., Srivastava, J., Powers, S., Brady, C., D'Angelo, J., et al. (2012). Behavioral performance and visual attention in communication multitasking: A comparison between instant messaging and online voice chat. *Computers in Human Behavior, 28*(3), 968.

Ward, A. S., Li, D. H., Luedtke, R. R., & Emmett-Oglesby, M. W. (1996). Variations in cocaine self-administration by inbred rat strains under a progressive-ratio schedule. *Psychopharmacology, 127*(3), 204–212.

Ward, C., & Rana-Deuba, A. (1999). Acculturation and adaptation revisited. *Journal of Cross-Cultural Psychology, 30*, 422–442.

Ward, J., Mattic, K. R. P., & Hall, W. (1999). *Methadone maintenance treatment and other opioid replacement therapies.* Sydney, Australia: Harwood Academic.

Wartner, U. G., Grossmann, K., Fremmer-Bombik, E., & Suess, G. (1994). Attachment patterns at age six in south Germany: Predictability from infancy and implications for preschool behavior. *Child Development, 65*, 1014–1027.

Washburn, M. F. (1908). *The animal mind: A text-book of comparative psychology.* New York: Macmillan.

Wasserman, E. A., & Miller, R. R. (1997). What's elementary about associative learning? *Annual Review of Psychology, 48*, 573–607.

Waterman, A. S. (2013). The humanistic psychology–positive psychology divide: Contrasts in philosophical foundations. *American Psychologist, 68*(3), 124–133. doi:10.1037/a0032168

Watkins, C. E., Campbell, V. L., Nieberding, R., & Hallmark, R. (1995). Contemporary practice of psychological assessment by clinical psychologists. *Professional Psychology: Research and Practice, 26*, 54–60.

Watson, D. L., Hagihara, D. K., & Tenney, A. L. (1999). Skill-building exercises and generalizing psychological concepts to daily life. *Teaching of Psychology, 26*, 193–195.

Watson, J. B. (1913). Psychology as the behaviorist views it. *Psychological Review, 20*, 158–177.

Watson, J. B. (1924). *Behaviorism.* New York: Norton.

Watson, J. B., & Rayner, R. (1920). Conditioned emotional responses. *Journal of Experimental Psychology, 3*, 1–14.

Watson, J. M., & Strayer, D. L. (2010). Supertaskers: Profiles in extraordinary multitasking ability. *Psychonomic Bulletin and Review, 17*(4), 479–485.

Weaver, F. M., Follett, K., Stern, M., Hur, K., Harris, C., Marks, W. J., Jr., et al. (2009). Bilateral deep brain stimulation vs. best medical therapy for patients with advanced Parkinson disease: A randomized controlled trial. *Journal of the American Medical Association, 301*(1), 63–73.

Webb, W. B. (1992). *Sleep: The gentle tyrant* (2nd ed.). Bolton, MA: Ander.

Wechsler, D. (1975). *The collected papers of David Wechsler.* New York: Academic Press.

Wechsler, D. (2008). *Wechsler adult intelligence scale.* (4th ed.). Bloomington, MN: Pearson.

Wechsler, D. (2012). *Wechsler preschool and primary scale of intelligence.* (4th ed.). Bloomington, MN: Pearson.

Wechsler, D. (2014). *Wechsler intelligence scale for children.* (5th ed.) Bloomington, MN: Pearson.

Wedding, D. (2004). Cross-cultural counseling and psychotherapy. In R. J. Corsini & D. Wedding (Eds.), *Current psychotherapies* (7th ed., p. 485). Itasca, IL: Peacock.

Weinberger, D. R. (1987). Implications of normal brain development for the pathogenesis of schizophrenia. *Archives of General Psychiatry, 44*, 660–668.

Weiner, B. (1985). An attributional theory of achievement motivation. *Psychological Review, 92*, 548–573.

Weiner, I. B. (1997). Current status of the Rorschach Inkblot Method. *Journal of Personality Assessment, 68*, 5–19.

Weiner, I. B. (2013). Applying Rorschach assessment. In G. P. Koocher, J. C. Norcross & B. A. Greene (Eds.), *Psychologists' desk reference* (pp. 148–152). New York: Oxford University Press.

Weiner, R. D. (2000). Retrogade amnesia with electroconvulsive therapy: Characteristics and implications. *Archives of General Psychiatry, 57*, 591–592.

Weis, S., Klaver, P., Reul, J., Elger, C. E., & Fernandez, G. (2004). Temporal and cerebellar brain regions that support both declarative memory formation and retrieval. *Cerebral Cortex, 14*, 256–267.

Weisman, A. (1972). *On dying and denying.* New York: Behavioral Publications.

Weissman, M. M., Bland, R. C., Joyce, P. R., Newman, S., Wells, J. E., & Wittchen, H. U. (1993). Sex differences in rates of depression: Cross-national perspectives. *Journal of Affective Disorders, 29*, 77–84.

Wells, J. E., Browne, M. O., Aguilar-Gaxiola, S., Al-Hamzawi, A., Alonso, J., Angermeyer, M. C., et al. (2013). Drop out from out-patient mental healthcare in the world health organization's world mental health survey initiative. *The British Journal of Psychiatry, 202*(1), 42–49. doi:10.1192/bjp.bp.112.113134

Wenneberg, S. R., Schneider, R. H., Walton, K. G., Maclean, C. R., Levitsky, D. K., Mandarino, J. V., et al. (1997). Anger expression correlates with platelet aggregation. *Behavioral Medicine, 22*(4), 174–177.

Werker, J. F., & Lalonde, C. E. (1988). Cross-language speech perceptions: Initial capabilities and developmental change. *Developmental Psychology, 24*, 672–683.

Wertheimer, M. (1982). *Productive thinking.* Chicago: University of Chicago Press.

Westen, D. (2005). Cognitive neuroscience and psychotherapy: Implications for psychotherapy's second century. In G. Gabbard, J. Beck, & J. Holmes (Eds.), *Oxford textbook of psychotherapy.* Oxford, UK: Oxford University Press.

Wetherell, J. L. (2002). Behavior therapy for anxious older adults. *Behavior Therapist, 25*, 16–17.

Wever, E. G. (1949). *Theory of hearing.* New York: John Wiley & Sons.

Wever, E. G., & Bray, C. W. (1930). The nature of acoustic response: The relation between sound frequency and frequency of impulses in the auditory nerve. *Journal of Experimental Psychology, 13*(5), 373–387.

Weyant, J. M. (1996). Application of compliance techniques to direct-mail requests for charitable donations. *Psychology and Marketing, 13*, 157–170.

White, G. L. (1980). Physical attractiveness and courtship progress. *Journal of Personality and Social Psychology, 39*, 660–668.

White, J. N., Hutchens, T., & Lubar, J. (2005). Quantitative EEG assessment during neuropsychological task performance in adults with attention deficit hyperactivity disorder. *Journal of Adult Development, 12*(2), 113–121.

Whorf, B. L. (1956). *Language, thought and reality.* New York: Wiley.

Wicker, A. W. (1971). An examination of the "other variables" explanation of attitude—behavior inconsistency. *Journal of Personality and Social Psychology, 19*, 18–30.

Wierenga, C. E., Stricker, N. H., McCauley, A., Simmons, A., Jak, A. J., Chang, Y. L., et al. (2010). Increased functional brain response during word retrieval in cognitively intact older adults at genetic risk for Alzheimer's disease. *Neuroimage, 15*, 15.

Wiley, J., & Jarosz, A. F. (2012). Working memory capacity, attentional focus, and problem solving. *Current Directions in Psychological Science, 21*(4), 258.

Williams, J. A., Pascual-Leone, A., & Fregni, F. (2010). Interhemispheric modulation induced by cortical stimulation and motor training. *Physical Therapy, 90*(3), 398–410.

Williams, M. E. (1995). *The American Geriatrics Society's complete guide to aging and mental health.* New York: Random House.

Williams, R. B. (2001). Hostility: Effects on health and the potential for successful behavioral approaches to prevention and treatment. In A. Baum, T. A. Revenson, & J. E. Singer (Eds.), *Handbook of health psychology.* Mahwah, NJ: Erlbaum.

Williams, R. B., Haney, T. L., Lee, K. L., Kong, Y. H., Blumenthal, J. A., & Whalen, R. E. (1980). Type A behavior, hostility, and coronary atherosclerosis. *Psychosomatic Medicine, 42*(6), 539–549.

Winningham, R. G., Hyman, I. E., Jr., & Dinnel, D. L. (2000). Flashbulb memories? The effects of when the initial memory report was obtained. *Memory, 8*, 209–216.

Winton, W. M. (1987). Do introductory textbooks present the Yerkes-Dodson law correctly? *American Psychologist, 42*(2), 202–203.

Wise, K., Alhabash, S., & Park, H. (2010). Emotional responses during social information seeking on Facebook. *Cyberpsychology, Behavior, and Social Networking, 13*(5), 555–562.

Wiseman, R. (2007). *Quirkology: How we discover the big truths in small things* (pp. 7–8, 28–29). New York: Basic Books.

Wolberg, L. R. (1977). *The technique of psychotherapy*. New York: Grune & Stratton.

Wood, J. M., Nezworski, M. T., & Stejskal, W. J. (1996). The comprehensive system for the Rorschach: A critical examination. *Psychological Science, 7*(1), 3–10, 14–17.

Woodhouse, A. (2005). Phantom limb sensation. *Clinical and Experimental Pharmacology and Physiology, 32*(1–2), 132–134.

Wu, C.-C., Lee, G. C., & Lai, H.-K. (2004). Using concept maps to aid analysis of concept presentation in high school computer textbooks. *Education and Information Technologies, 9*(20), 185–197.

Wyman, P. A., Moynihan, J., Eberly, S., Cox, C., Cross, W., Jin, X., et al. (2007). Association of family stress with natural killer cell activity and the frequency of illnesses in children. *Archives of Pediatric and Adolescent Medicine, 161*, 228–234.

Wynne, C. (1999). Do animals think? The case against the animal mind. *Psychology Today, 32*(6), 50–53.

Yaffe, K., Vittinghoff, E., Lindquist, K., Barnes, D., Covinsky, K. E., Neylan, T., et al. (2010). Posttraumatic stress disorder and risk of dementia among U.S. veterans. *Archives of General Psychiatry, 67*(6), 608–613.

Yalom, I. (1995). *The theory and practice of group psychotherapy* (4th ed.). New York: Basic Books.

Yamaguchi, S., Isejima, H., Matsuo, T., Okura, R., Yagita, K., Kobayashi, M., et al. (2003). Synchronization of cellular clocks in the suprachiasmatic nucleus. *Science, 302*, 1408–1412.

Yang, Y., Raine, A., & Colletti, P. (2010). Morphological alterations in the prefrontal cortex and the amygdala in unsuccessful psychopaths. *Journal of Abnormal Psychology, 119*, 546–554.

Yerkes, R. M. (Ed.). (1921). Psychological examining in the United States army. *Memoirs of the National Academy of Sciences, 15*, 1–890.

Yerkes, R. M., & Dodson, J. D. (1908). The relation of strength of stimulus to rapidity of habit formation. *Journal of Comparative Neurology and Psychology, 18*, 459–482.

Yip, Y. L., & Clark, L. (2002). Pivot: Taiji's Wu Gong Yee vs White Crane's Chan Hak Fu. *Qi: The Journal of Traditional Eastern Health & Fitness, 12*(3), 20-48.

Yopyk, D., & Prentice, D. A. (2005). Am I an athlete or a student? Identify salience and stereotype threat in student-athletes. *Basic and Applied Social Psychology, 27*(4), 29–336.

Young, J. E., Rygh, J. L., Weinberger, A. D., & Beck, A. T. (2008). Cognitive therapy for depression. In D. H. Barlow (Ed.), *Clinical handbook of psychological disorders* (pp. 250–305). New York: Guilford Press.

Young, J. E., Rygh, J. L., Weinberger, A. D., & Beck, A. T. (2014). Cognitive therapy for depression. In D. H. Barlow (Ed.), *Clinical handbook of psychological disorders: A step-by-step treatment manual* (5th ed., pp. 275–331). New York: Guilford Press.

Young, S. N. (Ed.). (1996). Melatonin, sleep, aging, and the health protection branch. *Journal of Psychiatry Neuroscience, 21*(3), 161–164.

Yule, G. (1996). *Pragmatics*. Oxford, UK: Oxford University Press.

Zadra, A., Desautels, A., Petit, D., & Montplaisir, J. (2013). Somnambulism: Clinical aspects and pathophysiological hypotheses. *The Lancet Neurology, 12*(3), 285.

Zadra, A., Pilon, M., & Montplaisir, J. (2008). Polysomnographic diagnosis of sleepwalking: Effects of sleep deprivation. *Annals of Neurology, 63*(4), 513–519.

Zajonc, R. B. (1980). Feeling and thinking: Preferences need no inferences. *American Psychologist, 35*, 151–175.

Zajonc, R. B. (1984). On the primacy of affect. *American Psychologist, 39*, 117–123.

Zajonc, R. B. (1998). Emotions. In D. T. Gilbert & S. T. Fiske (Eds.), *Handbook of social psychology* (4th ed., Vol. 1, pp. 591–632). New York: McGraw-Hill.

Zarate, C. A., Jr., Brutsche, N. E., Ibrahim, L., Franco-Chaves, J., DiazGranados, N., Cravchik, A., et al. (2012). Replication of Ketamine's antidepressant efficacy in bipolar depression: A randomized controlled add-on trial. *Biological Psychiatry, 71*(11), 939–946. doi:10.1016/j.biopsych.2011.12.010

Zarate, C. A., Jr., Singh, J. B., Carlson, P. J., Brutsche, N. E., Ameli, R., Luckenbaugh, D. A., et al. (2006). A randomized trial of an N-methyl-D-aspartate antagonist in treatment-resistant major depression. *Archives of General Psychiatry, 63*(8), 856–864. doi:10.1001/archpsyc.63.8.856

Zedler, B. (1995). Mary Whiton Calkins. In M. E. Waithe (Ed.), *A history of women philosophers: Vol. 4* (pp. 103–123). Netherlands: Kluwer Academic Publishers.

Zeidner, M., & Matthews, G. (2005). Evaluative anxiety. In A. Elliott & C. Dweck (Eds.), *Handbook of competence and motivation* (pp. 141–146). New York: Guilford Press.

Zeki, S. (2001). Localization and globalization in conscious vision. *Annual Review of Neuroscience, 24*, 57–86.

Zentall, T. R. (2000). Animal intelligence. In R. J. Sternberg (Ed.), *Handbook of intelligence*. Cambridge, MA: Cambridge University Press.

Zilles, K. (1990). Cortex. In G. Paxinos (Ed.), *The human nervous system* (pp. 757–802). San Diego, CA: Academic.

Zilles, K., & Amunts, K. (2012). Architecture of the cerebral cortex. In J. K. Mai & G. Paxinos (Eds.), *The human nervous system* (pp. 836–895). London, UK: Academic Press.

Zillmann, D., Baron, R., & Tamborini, R. (1981). Social costs of smoking: Effects of tobacco smoke on hostile behavior. *Psychology Journal of Applied Social, 11*, 548–561.

Zimbardo, P. G. (1970). The human choice: Individuation, reason, and order versus deindividuation, impulse, and chaos. In N. J. Arnold & D. Levine (Eds.), *Nebraska Symposium on Motivation, 1969*. Lincoln: University of Nebraska Press.

Zimbardo, P. G. (1971). The pathology of imprisonment. *Society, 9*(4–8), 4.

Zimbardo, P. G., & Hartley, C. F. (1985). Cults go to high school: A theoretical and empirical analysis of the initial stage in the recruitment process. *Cultic Studies Journal, 2*, 91–148.

Zimbardo, P., Maslach, C., & Haney, C. (2000). Reflections on the Stanford Prison Experiment: Genesis, transformations, consequences. In T. Blass (Ed.), *Obedience to authority: Current perspectives on the Milgram paradigm* (pp. 193–237). London: Lawrence Erlbaum.

Zisapel, N. (2001). Circadian rhythm sleep disorders: Pathophysiology and potential approaches to management. *CNS Drugs, 15*(4), 311–328.

Zlatin, D. M. (1995). Life themes: A method to understand terminal illness. *Omega: Journal of Death and Dying, 31*(3), 189–206. doi:10.2190/E4BA-ML04-E2BK-7YJE

Zorilla, E. P., Luborsky, L., McKay, J. R., Rosenthal, R., Houldin, A., Tax, A., et al. (2001). The relationship of depression and stressors to immunological assays: A meta-analytic review. *Brain, Behavior, and Immunity, 15*, 199–226.

Zuckerman, M. (1979). *Sensation seeking: Beyond the optimal level of arousal*. Hillsdale, NJ: Erlbaum.

Zuckerman, M. (1994). *Behavioral expression and biosocial bases of sensation seeking*. New York: Cambridge University Press.

Zvolensky, M. J., Schmidt, M. B., & Stewart, S. H. (2003). Panic disorder and smoking. *Clinical Psychology: Science and Practice, 10*, 29–51.

Credits

Photo Credits

Psychology in Action Page PIA-2 Shutterstock; Page PIA-4 Corbis/SuperStock; Page PIA-4 Andrew Holbrooke/Corbis; Page PIA-8 TK; Page PIA-8 TK; Page PIA-9 TK; Page PIA-10 imageBROKER/Alamy; Page PIA-11 Bill Varie/Corbis; Page PIA-12 James Marshall/Corbis; Page PIA-13 keepsake/Corbis; Page PIA-14 Stewart Cohen/Corbis; Page PIA-15 Pulp Photography/Corbis.

Chapter 1 Page 2 TK; Page 5 Fancy/Alamy; Page 6 INTERFOTO/Alamy; Page 7 Nancy R Cohen/Getty Images, Inc.; Page 8 The University of Akron/Archives of the History of American Psychology; Page 8 Clark University Press, Special Collections; Page 11 G. Paul Bishop; Page 13 Nina Leen/Getty Images, Inc.; Page 15 Courtesy, Dr. Arthur W. Toga, Laboratory of Neuro Imaging, UCLA School of Medicine; Page 16 CREATISTA/Shutterstock; Page 19 Bill Aron/PhotoEdit; Page 20 Jeff Greenberg/The Image Works; Page 22 Adam Seward/Alamy; Page 23 Jeff Greenberg/The Image Works; Page 24 BSIP SA/Alamy; Page 25 George Price/The New Yorker Collection/The Cartoon Bank; Page 28 Leo Cullum/The New Yorker Collection/The Cartoon Bank; Page 28 Bill Aron/PhotoEdit; Page 31 John Henley/Corbis; Page 33 Tom Chalkley/The New Yorker Collection/The Cartoon Bank; Page 37 Jack Barker/Alamy.

Chapter 2 Page 42 TK; Page 45 Secchi Lecaque/Photo Researchers, Inc./Science Source; Page 48 Alamy/Alamy RF; Page 49 Peter Arnold/Getty Images, Inc.; Page 53 Image Source/Getty Images, Inc.; Page 57 Peter Hvizdak/The Image Works; Page 61 Paul CC Collis/Alamy; Page 68 Richard T Nowitz/Photo Researchers, Inc./Science Source; Page 69 Noland White, Ph.D; Page 69 Noland White, Ph.D; Page 69 Mark Herreid/Shutterstock; Page 69 Noland White, Ph.D; Page 70 Noland White, Ph.D; Page 70 Medical-on-Line/Alamy; Page 70 Philippe Psaila/Photo Researchers, Inc./Science Source; Page 73 moodboard/Corbis; Page 75 Vladislav Sabanov/Shutterstock; Page 76 Courtesy Walter L. Isaac, Phd.; Page 77 Bettmann/Corbis; Page 78 Paul Burns/Corbis; Page 79 Marcelo Santos/Getty Images, Inc.

Chapter 3 Page 88 TK; Page 92 Beth Dixson/Corbis; Page 94 Noland White, Ph.D; Page 98 Bryan Allen/Corbis; Page 99 Fritz Goro/Getty Images, Inc.; Page 102 Charles Barsotti/The New Yorker Collection/The Cartoon Bank; Page 105 Giry Daniel/Corbis; Page 108 Science Source; Page 108 Noland White, Ph.D; Page 111 Robin Sachs/PhotoEdit; Page 113 Stephen Morton/Associated Press; Page 114 Vince Streano/Corbis; Page 118 Grant Faint/Getty Images, Inc.; Page 118 Shaen Adey/Dorling Kindersley Limited; Page 118 sborisov/Fotolia; Page 118 Creative Eye/Mira.com; Page 122 Larry Landolfi/Photo Researchers, Inc./Science Source; Page 122 Created by and courtesy of Dr. Akiyoshi Kitaoka, Ritsumeikan University.; Page 123 Created by and courtesy of Jorge Otero-Millan, Martinez-Conde Laboratory, Barrow Neurological Institute.; Page 125 Chris Connor/Newscom.

Chapter 4 Page 130 TK; Page 132 Sunny S Unal/Corbis; Page 134 AUGUST/Corbis; Page 135 SW Productions/Photodisc/Getty Images, Inc.; Page 139 Charles Gullung/Corbis; Page 139 Mark Seelen/Corbis; Page 139 Joe Dator/The New Yorker Collection/The Cartoon Bank; Page 141 Bill Abbott/CartoonStock; Page 142 Dana Fradon/The New Yorker Collection/The Cartoon Bank; Page 148 Bettmann/Corbis; Page 152 Monkey Business Images/Shutterstock; Page 152 Bettmann/Corbis; Page 153 Spencer Grant/PhotoEdit; Page 153 68/Ocean/Corbis; Page 154 PN2/ARB WENN Photos/Newscom; Page 154 Ashley Cooper/Corbis; Page 157 Brand X Pictures/Stockbyte/Getty Images, Inc.; Page 157 Lee Powers/Photo Researchers, Inc./Science Source; Page 160 Chris Harvey/Shutterstock.

Chapter 5 Page 164 TK; Page 166 King Features Syndicate; Page 167 Novosti/Science Source; Page 172 Benjamin Harris; Page 173 Jim West/Alamy; Page 174 StevenRussellSmithPhotos/Shutterstock; Page 178 Nina Leen/Getty Images, Inc.; Page 180 Joe Dator/The New Yorker Collection/The Cartoon Bank; Page 182 Deklofenak/Shutterstock; Page 185 Myrleen Pearson/PhotoEdit; Page 189 David Lassman/The Image Works; Page 189 Nancy Richmond/The Image Works; Page 190 Bonnie Kamin/PhotoEdit; Page 194 Pat Byrnes/The New Yorker Collection/The Cartoon Bank; Page 197 SuperStock, Inc.; Page 200 Albert Bandura; Page 203 Mel Evans/Associated Press; Page 204 Mel Evans/Associated Press.

Chapter 6 Page 208 Lightspring/Shutterstock; Page 211 Huw Evans/Associated Press; Page 213 Gjon Mili/Getty Images, Inc.; Page 214 Bob Krist/Corbis; Page 215 Norbert von der Groeben/The Image Works; Page 217 Whisson/Jordan/Corbis RF; Page 218 Tim Pannell/Corbis; Page 218 Dex Image/Corbis; Page 223 Mort Walker/King Features Syndicate; Page 223 Frank Burek/Corbis; Page 225 Rainer Holz/Corbis; Page 225 Lee Lorenz/The New Yorker Collection/The Cartoon Bank; Page 226 Don Shrubshell/Associated Press; Page 227 Newscom; Page 228 Ryan McVay/Getty Images, Inc.; Page 229 zeljkodan/Shutterstock; Page 233 Richard Lord/The Image Works; Page 236 Lacy Atkins/Corbis; Page 238 Dr. Robert Friedland/Photo Researchers, Inc./Science Source.

Chapter 7 Page 242 mtkang/Shutterstock; Page 247 Eric Isselee/Shutterstock; Page 248 Jennie Hart/Alamy; Page 249 Brigette Sullivan/Alamy; Page 250 AVAVA/Shutterstock; Page 251 Hector Mata/Associated Press; Page 261 Ian Cumming/Getty Images, Inc.; Page 264 Randy Olson/Aurora Photos; Page 264 Roy Delgado/CartoonStock; Page 265 Stanford University Libraries; Page 266 Mark Richards/PhotoEdit; Page 271 Carson Ganci/Corbis; Page 274 Frans Lanting Studio/Alamy.

Chapter 8 Page 280 Production Perig/Fotolia; Page 284 Pasieka/Photo Researchers, Inc./Science Source; Page 285 Frank & Ernest reprinted by permission of Tom Thaves; Page 286 CNRI/Science Photo Library/Science Source; Page 288 Abby and Brittany Hensel; Page 289 BSIP SA/Alamy; Page 289 Petit Format/Photo Researchers, Inc./Science Source; Page 289 Petit Format/Photo Researchers, Inc./Science Source; Page 290 Chad Ehlers/Alamy; Page 292 Laura Elliott/Pearson Education; Page 292 Denise Hager, Catchlight Visual Services/Alamy; Page 292 Elizabeth Crews/The Image Works; Page 292 UIG via Getty Images; Page 292 Bloomimage/Corbis; Page 293 Dave King/Dorling Kindersley Limited; Page 293 Elizabeth Crews Photography; Page 293 /Geri Engberg Photography; Page 293 Gelpi JM/Shutterstock; Page 293 Jo Foord/Dorling Kindersley Limited; Page 293 Jo Foord/Dorling Kindersley Limited; Page 297 David Tothill/Alamy; Page 297 Dennis MacDonald/PhotoEdit; Page 298 Mike Good/Dorling Kindersley Limited; Page 299 Saturn Still/Science Photo Library/Science Source; Page 301 Radius Images/

Text Credits

approach to socialization. In D. A. Goslin (Ed.), Handbook of socialization: Theory in research (pp. 347–480). Boston: Houghton-Mifflin.; Page 320 The Princess Bride movie.

Chapter 9 Page 331 Table 9.1 Reproduced with permission. Originally published in Big Five Assessment by BOELE De Raad 8 Macro Penguin, ISBN 0-88937-242-X (c) Hogrefe and Huber Publishers www.Hogrefe.com; Page 332 Figure 9.3 From MOTIVATION AND PERSONALITY 3rd edition by Abraham H. Maslow, edited by Robert D. Frager & James Fadiman. Copyright © 1987. Printed and electronically reproduced by permission of Pearson Education, Inc., Upper Saddle River, NJ 07458.; Page 348 Figure 9.4 from Marin/Hock, 1e The "Low Road" and "High Road. Based on Fig 11.12, p. 428 in Krause/Corts, Introduction to Psychological Science 1e, 2012.

Chapter 10 Page 367 Figure 10.1 Source: Adapted from Asch, S. E. (1956). Studies of independence and conformity: A minority of one against a unanimous majority. Psychological Monographs, 70 (Whole no. 416).; Page 368 Table 10.1 Janis 1972, 1988.; Page 378 Figure 10.4 Source: Adapted from Festinger, L., & Carlsmith, J. (1959). $1/$20 experiment: Cognitive consequences of forced compliance. Journal of Abnormal and Social Psychology, 58(2), 203–210.; Page 400 Figure 10.5 Source: Latané & Darley (1 969). Darley, J. M., & Latané, B. (1968). Bystander intervention in emergencies: Diffusion of responsibility.

Journal of Personality and Social Psychology, 8, 377–383. Copyright © 1968 by the American Psychological Association.

Chapter 11 Page 419 Figure 11.2 Self-Efficacy The Exercise of Control by Albert Bandura. Copyright © 1997 by W. H. Freeman and Company. Used with the permission of Worth Publishers.; Page 426 Table 11.2 Source: Adapted from McCrae & Costa (1990). From PERSONALITY IN ADULTHOOD 2nd edition by Robert R. MacCrae and Paul T. Costa. Copyright © 1990 by Guilford Publications. Reprinted with permission of the Guilford Publications; Page 434 Figure 11.5 Source: Data from Miller et al. (1991, 1996).

Chapter 12 Page 457 Table 12.1 Source: Adapted from National Institute of Mental Health (2013). Table uses terminology from both the DSM-IV and DSM-5 (American Psychiatric Association, 2000, 2013); Page 479 Figure 12.2 Copyrighted by Pearson Education, Upper Saddle River, NJ.

Chapter 13 Page 495 Meador, B. D., & Rogers, C. R. (1984). Person-centered therapy. In R. J. Corsini (Ed.), Current psychotherapies (3rd ed., pp. 142–195). Itasca, IL: Peacock.; Page 512 adapted from Wedding, D. (2004). Cross-cultural counseling and psychotherapy. In R. J. Corsini & D. Wedding (Eds.), Current psychotherapies (7th ed., p. 485). Itasca, IL: Peacock.

Name Index

Subject Index